Object Structures

Addison-Wesley Eiffel in Practice Series

Bertrand Meyer, Consulting Editor

Addison-Wesley Eiffel in Practice Series specifically addresses the practical issues of programming with the Eiffel language and its relationship to object-oriented technology. The series provides serious programmers with pragmatic books that are technically sophisticated. Each book will cover wholly a specific aspect of Eiffel programming and will contain useful source code and/or applications that allow programmers to experiment with the concepts covered in the material. In addition to the corporate marketplace, the series will be of particular interest to academic institutions throughout the world.

Object Structures

Building Object-Oriented Software Components with Eiffel

Jacob Gore

Eastern New Mexico University, Portales, New Mexico, USA

ToolCASE Computing Inc., Englewood, Colorado, USA

ADDISON-WESLEY PUBLISHING COMPANY, INC.

Reading, Massachusetts • Menlo Park, California • New York • Don Mills, Ontario
Wokingham, England • Amsterdam • Bonn • Sydney • Singapore • Tokyo
Madrid • San Juan • Seoul • Milan • Mexico City • Taipei

Many of the designations used by manufacturers and sellers to distinguish their products are claimed as trademarks. Where those designations appear in this book and Addison-Wesley was aware of a trademark claim, the designations have been printed in initial caps or all caps.

The authors and publishers have taken care in the preparation of this book, but make no expressed or implied warranty of any kind and assume no responsibility for errors or omissions. No liability is assumed for incidental or consequential damages in connection with or arising out of the use of the information or programs contained herein.

Extracts from the *Eiffel Library Standard, Vintage '95* have been used by permission of NICE, the Nonprofit International Consortium for Eiffel. NICE controls the name *Eiffel* and manages the evolution of the language.

The publisher offers discounts on this book when ordered in quantity for special sales.

For more information, please contact:

Corporate & Professional Publishing Group
Addison-Wesley Publishing Company
One Jacob Way
Reading, Massachusetts 01867

Library of Congress Cataloging-in-Publication Data

Gore, Jacob, 1963–
Object structures : building object-oriented software components with Eiffel / Jacob Gore.
p. cm. -- (Addison-Wesley Eiffel in practice series)
Includes bibliographical references and index.
ISBN 0-201-63480-5 (pbk. : alk. paper)
1. Object-oriented programming (Computer science) 2. Eiffel (Computer program language) I. Title. II. Series.
QA76.64.G66 1996
005.1—dc20 95-48397
CIP

Copyright © 1996 by Addison-Wesley Publishing Company, Inc.

All rights reserved. No part of this publication may be reproduced, stored in a retrieval system, or transmitted, in any form, or by any means, electronic, mechanical, photocopying, recording, or otherwise, without the prior consent of the publisher.

Printed in the United States of America. Published simultaneously in Canada.

Text printed on recycled and acid-free paper

ISBN 0-201-63480-5
1 2 3 4 5 6 7 8 9-CRW-99989796
First Printing, March 1996.

To my family.

Contents

Preface

This book serves two basic purposes. It is a study of applied object-oriented component design, as well as a treatise of object structures: ways to organize objects for various purposes, with an engineering analysis of the trade-offs involved. It is aimed at students in the undergraduate computer science curriculum, and at practicing professionals interested in learning object-oriented programming.

A few words now to the professional, the student, and the teacher. Then I will explain why Eiffel was chosen as the supporting programming language—a question that is of interest to all three.

To the Professional

I address you first, because I think you require the shortest explanation. You have probably already used data structures in your work; in fact, you have probably studied them in school. I expect that you do not need another book on data structures. *This is not another book on data structures.*

Yes, readers of this text will study the familiar data structures: arrays, lists, queues, stacks, trees, etc. But in the process, they will study good software engineering techniques, gain an understanding of software component design, discover how to create interchangeable implementation of components, and analyze the trade-offs involved in choosing an implementation for a specific job.

Still, if all you want to learn is some object-oriented programming, then why not practice on something you are familiar with, like data structures?

To the Student

You are the reason this book emphasizes what it does. Chances are that you are enrolled in what in computer-science-education terminology is called "the CS-2 course"—the second semester of the computer science curriculum recommended by ACM.[1] It does not have to be taken precisely in the second semester:

[1]ACM stands for "Association for Computing Machinery," though most of its members are human.

Many schools, including the one where I teach now, present this course on a different schedule.

There are two reasons for this course. Its nominal purpose is to teach you the use and analysis of data structures—a very important topic for any computer scientist. Its complementary purpose is to give you a chance to practice good computer programming. See, it makes no sense to have a course in just "programming," you have to have *something* to write programs about! So, CS-2 makes you write programs with data structures, which you need to learn anyway.

If you have eavesdropped on what I said to the practitioner, you know that this text deals with much more than data structures. Yes, they are important, and you will be studying them. But at least as important is the skill set this book presents in designing and writing these structures. The techniques you will learn in this course can be used in development of large software systems, because they work by organizing software solutions into consistent and manageable components.

If your prior programming experience is limited to programs that fit into one component, this course will do wonders for your ability to be successful in large software projects.

Finally, allow me to point out a fact that should be obvious, but somehow always needs to be exposed. Many students at the CS-2 level still believe the theory of "learning by photosynthesis":

> If you spend enough time in the presence of brilliance, you will walk away enlightened.

Sorry, folks, it just does not work that way. You cannot become a decent programmer by attending enough lectures any more than you can become a decent guitar player by attending enough concerts. Do the exercises. Question each line, and understand its purpose. Invest the time to do it right.

To the Teacher

Generally, there are two philosophies for data structure courses:

1. "This is where we subject them to pointers, more programming, pointers, longer programs, pointers, maybe an abstract data type or two, a bunch of sorting algorithms, pointers, trees and more recursion, and pointers."
2. "This is where we play with data structures, spending as little effort on programming as necessary, covering as much variety and beauty as possible."

This blatant straw-man fallacy may lead you to believe that I favor Philosophy 2. No, not for CS-2—but I do appreciate it. For a beautiful example of a book that supports this approach, examine Derick Wood's excellent text [13]. If I were going to use the second approach, I would adopt that book and do all programming in ML (though he uses Pascal): Do binary search trees in 30 minutes and move on!

My students certainly do need additional programming experience at the CS-2 level.

But I do have a problem with Philosophy 1. Grab a few of your data structures course graduates, and ask them "What is a list?"

Did they say something like "It's when you take a bunch of records and add pointers to them to connect them together"?

If so, then they certainly learned their pointers. However,

1. They cannot say what a list *is*. They do not distinguish between a definition of a data structure and its implementation.
2. They do not separate the structure (the container) from the payload.

Not convinced? Ask them what operations make sense for lists.

I rest my case.

Various textbooks attempt to remedy this problem by introducing data abstraction as an "advanced topic," usually in the form of a chapter on stack and queue ADTs. I have found that students tend to treat it as they do any advanced topic: "First, I better learn the basics, then I'll worry about abstraction."

To be fair, abstraction has been working its way toward Chapter 1 in new textbooks, but I have seen none that use it consistently, from cover to cover. This book does.

The other problem with typical ADT presentations is that they only examine one implementation for each ADT. In my experience, that does not get the point across. Students tend to view abstraction walls as something the teacher invented to make their lives more complicated, and then tried to back up with proclamations of vague morality. A typical discussion goes like this:

> "So what if I stuck a pointer into the middle of my data structure; the program *works,* doesn't it?!"
>
> "But if you ever changed the implementation, the program may stop working!"
>
> "Well, when it does, *then* I'll deal with it!"

My solution to this problem is to get them to deal with it immediately, by requiring at least two distinct implementations for each structure. This works remarkably well, even when using a language with weak (or nonexistent) abstraction enforcement, such as Pascal or C.

Putting It All Together

Object-oriented programming allows us to put all of these solutions together into a consistent and straightforward presentation. Abstraction *is* "the basics." The software just begs to be organized into components. Containers and payloads stay apart. And then there is Bertrand Meyer's *Design by Contract,* a natural way to allocate responsibility among the building blocks of the system.

This is what distinguishes a course in *object structures* from one in data structures: the methodical and systematic way in which each structure is defined, analyzed, and executed.

The Choice of Language

This aspect is important for the practitioner, and the student, and the teacher.

This book uses Eiffel, a purely object-oriented programming language designed specifically for software engineering. The job at hand is to teach good software engineering through the study of object structures. As I write this, Eiffel is the best tool for this job.

A common notion is that we should "teach a language" that is most likely to be used by the students when they get jobs in the industry. At the time of this writing, Eiffel is *not* such a language. Shouldn't I use the language that will be in most demand?

Hmmm . . . that would be FORTRAN or COBOL. Oh, sorry . . . wrong year, wrong generation of students.

Oh, yes . . . PL/I or COBOL. No . . . wrong year, wrong generation.

Ah: BASIC or COBOL! Uhm, no, wrong year, wrong generation.

Let's see . . . Pascal or COBOL? No, wrong year, wrong generation.

Well, here's a sure thing: Ada and COBOL! Nope, wrong year, wrong (and short) generation.

Got it. It's C and COBOL. Missed again: wrong year, wrong generation.

No, it's C++ and SQL. Home, sweet home. "Talkin' 'bout my generation!"

Well, folks, that's six wrong generations in 45 years. Planning for a very early retirement?

When it comes to choosing a language, I am a pragmatist. Under the circumstances and for the task at hand, Eiffel is the best choice. There are languages with more theoretically appealing features, but Eiffel combines simplicity and power with pragmatism. There are languages that are more widespread, but none of them is nearly as well suited to designing and implementing object structures. They lack important features or mix in a large number of distractions irrelevant to the topic at hand (this is especially true of hybrid object-oriented languages such as C++).

There are also languages that arguably improve on Eiffel, but Eiffel is the most widespread among the languages most suitable for learning object structures.

After you learn object structures with Eiffel, you can pick up a book about the bandwagon language of the day, and learn it in a couple of weeks. Then, for practice, you may want to go back and reimplement some of the object structures in that language—by then you will understand the material sufficiently not to get lost in language-imposed details. Then you will have the best of both worlds.

Prerequisites

Since this text's primary target audience is the CS-2 student, it does assume a minimal background in programming. In particular, I expect the reader to be familiar with such concepts as step-by-step execution, assignment statements, loops, and parameter passing.

I do *not* expect prior exposure to object-oriented programming; the book is written to be a thorough introduction into that paradigm. Nor do I expect prior experience with Eiffel—but I do expect the reader to use the language reference manual on occasion.

To My Friends and Colleagues

I greatly appreciate your assistance in creating this book. My thanks go to **Bertrand Meyer** for laying the foundation for the utilized methodology and for the numerous discussions on various aspects of Eiffel and their implications. I also thank other folks at Interactive Software Engineering whose help was timely and instrumental in my utilization of the ISE compiler system, especially **David Quarrie**, **Darcy Harrison**, and **Annie Meyer**.

The help of **Steve Tynor** of Tower Technology has been prompt and invaluable. It extended way beyond support of the Tower compiler system—discussions with Steve helped me understand many of the subtleties of Eiffel. I am also grateful to him for communicating with the NICE standards committees on my behalf. My thanks also go to **Rock Howard** of Tower, whose personal attention helped me on many occasions, and made it possible for my class to use a fine Eiffel environment when our budget was lacking.

Frieder Monninger of SIG Computer GmbH provided timely help in making sure that SIG's shareware Eiffel compiler could also be used with the examples in this book.

Doug Jackson helped me hash out and clarify many of the ideas and approaches used in this book, and he double-checked the mathematical claims. I hope our students appreciate his skill in the foundations of computer science as much as I do. **Pavel Dolgonos** also helped me out with some of the algebraic background (it's amazing how rusty it gets if you don't use it).

Many of the improvements in the book were suggested by the reviewers: **Richie Bielak** of CAL FP (US), Inc., **Henry A. Etlinger** of Rochester Institute of Technology, **Jim McKim** of the Hartford Graduate Center, **Jacques LaFrance** of Oklahoma State University, **Jean-Jacques Moreau** of Hewlett-Packard Laboratories, **Kathy Stark** of Sun Microsystems, **Ernesto Surribas** of UNAM (Universidad Nacional Autónoma de México), and **Chris Van Wyk** of Drew University.

All of the folks in the **Department of Mathematical Sciences** at Eastern New Mexico University have been very supportive of my efforts, and provided an excellent working environment. I am especially grateful to **Thurman Elder** and **Doug Jackson** (whom I have already thanked, but not enough). I want to thank **Betty Lyon** for lending me her antique radio to photograph, **Solomon White**, a student in the department, for helping me photograph it (and lending his camera), and **Pavel and Lior Dolgonos** for developing the prints.

Speaking of students—they may not be able to tell by the grades they got, but I *am* grateful to those who went through the course while the lecture notes and then the manuscript were in development. I especially want to thank **Erin Powers**, who read the material carefully and pointed out mistakes and unclear passages.

I am grateful to **Leon Farfel**, my partner in ToolCASE Computing, for fielding some of the projects in which he would much rather have let me partake.

I thank **Mike Hendrickson** at Addison-Wesley for helping to keep the project on track and for subtly coercing me into writing a better book. I wish to express my appreciation to **Katie Duffy** for facilitating the project. Finally, I am grateful in advance to everybody else on the Addison-Wesley team who will be putting this book into print and delivering it to market.

Part I

Introduction

1 Object Structures

This chapter introduces **objects** and **object structures.** It explains what they are and what to look for while studying them.

1.1 The Study of Object Structures

Object structures are mechanisms for keeping track of numerous objects in software. If a problem calls for more objects than can be reasonably identified with individual names, we must have a way to keep them organized so that they can be systematically located. This is the role that object structures play: They are objects that keep track of other objects.

Studying an object structure has two major components: the *what* and the *how.* Our first concern when encountering a new structure is to establish *what* it is and *what* it does. Then we will consider several competing answers to the question "*How* can we set it up and write it so that it behaves that way?" We will compare the various ways to implement each object structure and analyze the trade-offs involved.

As students and authors of object structures, our attitude is that of service providers: Somebody comes to us with a need for a way to keep track of objects for a specific purpose, and our task is to provide them with object structures that fulfill those requirements. To do that, we must be able to state clearly what our data structures expect from the rest of the software, and what they will in turn ensure, "if used as directed," as is often said on product boxes. This methodology is known as "Design by Contract" [3, 4]. It greatly simplifies overall programming of the system by clearly dividing responsibilities among objects, which are often written by different programmers. Design by Contract will permit us to create truly interchangeable implementations of object structures, so that we can not only pick the best implementation for a given utilization, but also replace it with a different one should the circumstances of its use change.

The study of object structures grew out of what is called "data structures." At the time this is written, data structure courses still outnumber courses in object structures, and no other object structure text is available. Readers who have been exposed to data structure studies will find many similarities in the material—after all, the object-oriented programming paradigm is closely related to the data processing paradigm: Both are procedural, but the object-oriented one offers better organized software. Although we study object structures instead of data structures, we still concern ourselves with efficient use of time and space. However, we keep a clear distinction between what makes something a certain type of object, and the various ways of implementing it in software.

1.2 Objects

An object is a software component. It often represents a physical object in "the real world," but it can represent abstract objects equally well. For example, there may be objects in the software system that correspond to specific automobiles, or to telephones, or to springs and pulleys, or to people—all of which are physical. They can also correspond to intangibles: bank accounts, theorems, telephone numbers, coordinates, and ages (Figure 1.1).

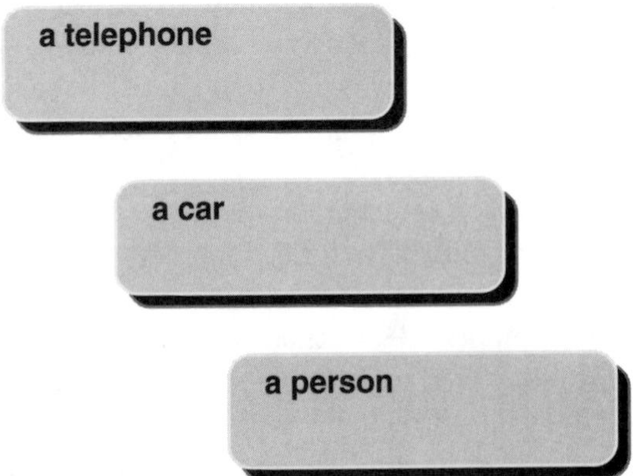

Figure 1.1 Examples of objects. Observe that their covers are opaque: We cannot examine or manipulate their contents at our whim.

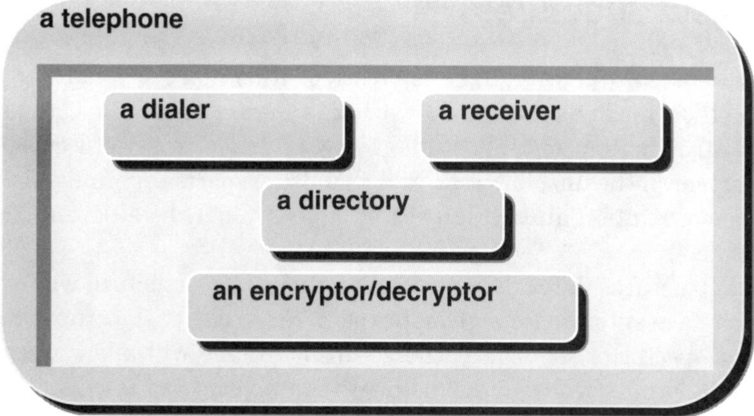

Figure 1.2 A peek inside a phone object. A telephone *contains* its own instances of other objects.

As in the physical world, objects may contain other objects. For example, a line object may contain two endpoint objects; a book may contain chapters; a telephone may contain a dialer, a receiver, and a number directory (which in turn contains associations of labeled buttons and telephone numbers); an automobile may contain an engine, doors, etc. (Figure 1.2).

It is also possible for an object to keep track of other objects without actually containing them. A person may be able to identify his or her father, mother, and house, without (one would certainly hope) containing any of them. A car dealer may have a list of unsold cars, and they are not physically contained in the list (Figure 1.3).

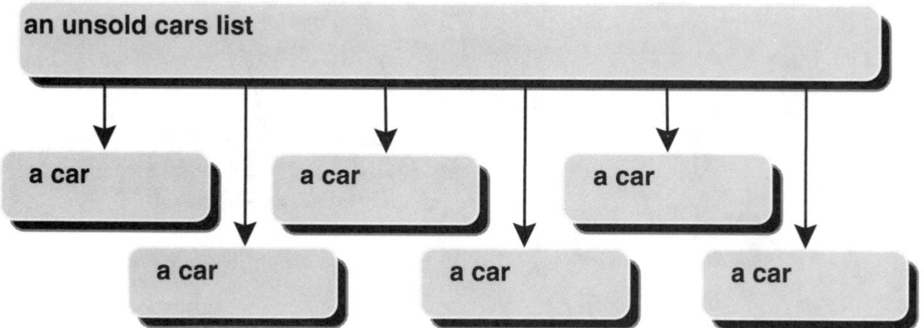

Figure 1.3 A list of unsold cars. This object *keeps track* of other objects without actually containing them.

1.3 Object Structures

Object structures are objects that keep track of other objects, generally without containing them, such as the unsold car list in Figure 1.3. An object may occur in several structures at once: A student may be listed in several class lists; a car may appear in the unsold list as well as a list of sports cars and a list of low-mileage demonstration units (Figure 1.4); a person may be a parent of several other persons.

Object structures differ in behavior. A user picks a structure whose behavior makes it easiest to use for a given purpose. Some object structures will keep objects in a specific order, while others will not. Some will allow access to all objects, while others will only let us deal with objects at the edges. Of those that order their objects, some will do it chronologically (based on when the object got added to the structure), others will use an ordering scheme imposed by the objects themselves.

Once an object structure is selected, trade-offs among its possible implementations need to be considered. Object structures usually utilize internal objects to do "bookkeeping" and to keep track of the objects assigned to them,

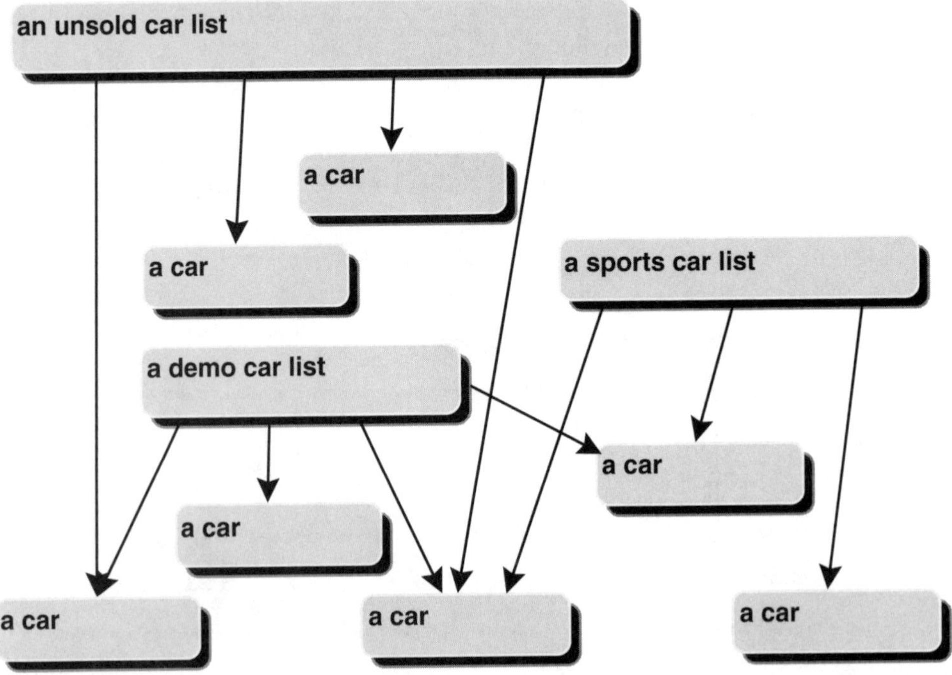

Figure 1.4 Several object structures may keep track of the same object.

and the space they occupy may be a consideration in choosing an implementation. These bookkeeping objects can be chosen to speed up certain aspects of an object structure's behavior—usually at the expense of making other aspects less efficient. Sadly, the "No Free Lunch" law does apply to object structures: *There is always a trade-off.*

For pedagogical reasons, this text groups object structures according to the overall design of their implementations. Part II of this text will concentrate on **linear** object structures: those where the tracked objects are organized along a straight line. Part III will deal with keeping track of objects that are identifiable by some feature: ordering them in the object structure according to that feature, and using that feature (and, if applicable, the ordering) to locate a specific object in a linear structure. Part IV will study how searching can be sped up by using object structures organized in two dimensions rather than one.

We will use the remainder of Part I to learn how to create and interact with objects.

2 Objects and Classes

The language used in this text is Eiffel.[1] We chose Eiffel because, of the widely available languages, it offers by far the best support for the methodology presented. It is also easy to learn, and will not distract the student much from the task at hand. While one is likely to be forced to use a less suitable language in the workplace, once the foundation is laid, adapting to the syntax and limitations or advantages of a different language should be relatively easy—just a matter of reading a good book on that language and working with it.

We will be introducing aspects of Eiffel as they are needed. Readers who are uncomfortable with this approach are referred to Robert Switzer's *Eiffel: An Introduction* [10]. The definitive book on the language Eiffel (meant to be detailed enough for Eiffel compiler writers) is Bertrand Meyer's *Eiffel: The Language* [5].

As an illustration, we will create a class of letters (the kind that make up words, not the kind that get delivered). We will use letter objects in later chapters, where our object structures will need "guinea pigs" to track.

2.1 Objects and Classes in Eiffel

How do we go about defining objects? In Figure 1.4, there were many objects, but they fell into two types of objects: cars and lists. It would be madness to have to define every single car "from scratch," since they are all quite similar. What we do instead is define a whole **class** of cars, by describing their common **features.** Features are the set of questions and actions that can be asked of an object. Cars have many, many features, so before we present a class definition, let us pick a more manageable example. While we are at it, we will create

[1] *Eiffel* is a trademark of NICE, the Nonprofit International Consortium for Eiffel.

an object that we can easily use to test our object structures in the following chapters.

For our purposes, a class of **letters** is very convenient (we can use it later as something to track with our object structures). What can a letter object be asked? As a start, it can be programmed as follows:

- To report the letter it stores as a character (characters are built into Eiffel, so they are off-the-shelf building blocks and do not need to be defined by us);
- To set the letter it stores to another character;
- To report if it is upper case;
- To report if it is lower case;
- To identify its position in the alphabet; and
- To report a string representation of itself (which can later be printed).

The entire Eiffel definition of this class is presented in Listing 2.1. Note the naming and capitalization conventions:

- Class names are all upper case;
- The predefined entity *Result* is capitalized (we will encounter other predefined entities later);
- Everything else is lower case; and
- Underscores are used to separate words within a name.

```
class LETTER inherit
    ANY
        redefine
            out
        end;

creation make

feature

    character: CHARACTER;
            --The character representation of the letter.

    make (initial: CHARACTER) is
            --Create a new letter, load it with initial.
        require
```

Listing 2.1 Full definition of class *LETTER*. (*Note:* The current definition of Eiffel contains an unnecessary restriction that forbids using the name "*character*" for an entity. Few compilers enforce it; if yours does, use a different name, such as "*char*".)

```
        do
            character := initial;
        end; --make

    set_character(new: CHARACTER) is
            --Change the letter to new.
        require
            ('a' <= new and new <= 'z') or ('A' <= new and new <= 'Z')
        do
            character := new;
        end; --set_character

    is_lower_case: BOOLEAN is
            --Is this a lower case letter?
        do
            Result := 'a' <= character and character <= 'z';
        end; --is_lower_case
    is_upper_case: BOOLEAN is
            --Is this an upper case letter?
        do
            Result := 'A' <= character and character <= 'Z';
        end; --is_upper_case
    alphabet_position: INTEGER is
            --Relative position in the English alphabet ('A' is 1).
        do
            --This implementation works on any system on which
            --the character codes for the upper case letters are continuous,
            --and so are character codes for the lower case letters.
            if is_upper_case then
                Result := character.code - ('A').code + 1;
            else
                Result := character.code - ('a').code + 1;
            end;
        end; --alphabet_position

    out: STRING is
            --String representation of this letter.
        do
            Result := character.out;
        end; --out

invariant

    either_upper_or_lower: is_upper_case /= is_lower_case;

end --class LETTER
```

Listing 2.1 (*continued*)

Eiffel is not case sensitive, so an Eiffel compiler will understand you if you write "*Character*" or "*character*" or even "*CHaRaCHTeR*" instead of the conventional "*CHARACTER*"—but other Eiffel programmers may not. Most software is written in multiprogrammer teams, and flaunting team coding conventions is an easy way to get fired.

In the text, **identifiers** (which is compilerese for "names") are italicized (e.g., "*character*") and **keywords** ("words defined for us by the compiler") are shown in boldface (e.g., "**feature**"). When a compiler processes Eiffel code, it is usually all in one font, but some Eiffel code editors may offer this typesetting convention to programmers.

Everything between a "--" and the end of a line is a comment and is skipped by the compiler. Semicolons (";") separate program statements.[2]

Let us now step through the *LETTER* example. As promised, we restrict ourselves to those aspects of Eiffel's syntax and semantics that are relevant to the subject at hand. We will use the notation "<marker>" to indicate a placeholder for programmer-supplied code.

2.1.1 Class Declaration

The format of a class declaration is:

```
class <class name> inherit
   <parent class name>
      <feature adaptations>
creation <names of features that can initialize objects of this class>
feature
   <feature declarations>
invariant
   <what must be true about any object of this class>
end --class <class name>
```

2.1.2 Redefining an Inherited Feature

In an object-oriented software system, classes of objects are related to each other by means of **classification.** Briefly (we will study this in more detail in Chapter 4), one class may be an **heir** of another (the latter is known as the **parent** of the former).

---

[2] Semicolons in Eiffel are optional in most situations. However, the Eiffel style guidelines [5, Appendix A] recommend their use.

An heir inherits all features from its parent class, and may provide its own, additional features. It may also provide a better[3] way of implementing some of the features that it inherited. When that happens, Eiffel insists that we explicitly mention that fact in the **inherit** clause. Otherwise, the compiler will assume that we accidentally used a feature name that we already had, thanks to our generous parent.

But what is this class *ANY* anyway, and why do we need to inherit its features? Well, we do not have much choice in the matter. *ANY* is the ancestor of all programmer-supplied classes in an Eiffel system: all classes we write will inherit, directly or indirectly, from *ANY*. If we omitted the whole "**inherit** . . . **redefine** . . . **end**" part, we would be inheriting everything from *ANY* by default.

ANY provides many useful features, and this automatic inheritance will save us from writing a lot of code. For example, the *print* feature we will use in Listing 2.2 is inherited by *LETTER_TESTER* from *ANY*. One of the features that *ANY* provides is *out,* which reports the preferred character string representation of the object. That representation is used by the inherited feature *print* to display the object. Feature *out* will be redefined in most of the classes we write, because we will want to customize it so that each object's string representation is most obvious to the reader.

2.1.3 Feature Declarations

The section headed with keyword "**feature**" lists features of objects of class *LETTER* that may be requested by other objects. There are two types of features: **entities** and **routines.** Class *LETTER* contains only one entity: *character,* which is a member of the predefined class *CHARACTER*. Entity declarations take the form

<entity name>: <class name>;

After a declaration "*e*: *C*", we say that entity *e* is **of type** *C*. This means that *e* may keep track of objects that are members of class *C*.[4]

Routines themselves generally fall into two categories: the kind that modify the state of the object (commonly referred to as "procedures") and those that compute and return a value without altering the object ("functions"). Routine declarations take the form

---

[3] We know better than our parents, right?

[4] We will see in Chapter 4 how *e* may also keep track of objects whose classes are heirs of *C*.

```
<routine name>(<parameter declarations>): <type of Result> is
        --Brief description.
    require
        <what must be true before this routine is invoked>
    local
        <declarations of entities local to this routine>
    do
        <steps to take to perform this routine>
    ensure
        <what is promised to be true after this routine exits>
    end; --<routine name>
```

If the routine takes no parameters, omit "(<parameter declarations>)". If it does not compute and return a value, omit ": <type of *Result*>".

Parameter declarations look just like entity declarations, but they do not declare new entities: They name values that are passed to the routine by the object that invoked it. The first value passed gets the first name, the second gets named with the second name, and so on (class *LETTER* does not have routines that require more than one parameter). The invoking object is responsible for seeing that the value passed through a parameter is allowable for that parameter's type.

The Boolean expressions (called "**assertions**") listed in the **require** section are known as the **preconditions** of the routine. The object that requests this feature must assure that all the preconditions are true (otherwise the whole program may crash, or produce unpredictable results). If there are no preconditions, then the whole **require** section can be omitted.

The **local** section can be used to introduce temporary entities to use in the **do** section of this routine. It is also omitted when no local entities are needed.

The statements in the **do** section are performed when the routine is invoked. If the routine computes a value, it must assign that value to the predefined local entity *Result,* from where it will be passed by the Eiffel system back to the calling object.

The **ensure** section states what must be true after the routine is executed. We will discuss it in detail in Section 3.1.1.

2.1.4 The Class Invariant

The expressions listed in the **class invariant** must be true about any object of that class. They define what it means for an object of this class to be **valid.** A feature may make these assertions temporarily untrue while it is executing, but it must restore their truthfulness before it is finished.

2.1.5 The if Statement

The form of the **if** statement is

if <condition> **then**
<things to do if the condition is true>
else
<things to do if the condition is false>
end;

The "else" part may be omitted. (Programmers of Pascal, C, and other languages that use the Algol-60 form of **if**, take note: There is no "begin," and the **end** is required.)

It takes only one condition to select one of two choices. In some situations, there are several choices, distinguished by several conditions:

if <Condition 1> **then**
<things to do if Condition 1 is true>
elseif <Condition 2> **then**
<things to do if Condition 1 is false and Condition 2 is true>
.
.
.
elseif <Condition n> **then**
<things to do if Conditions $1-(n-1)$ are false and Condition n is true>
else
<things to do if Conditions $1-n$ are false>
end;

(The short form of the **if** statement is just the long form with zero **elseif** parts.)

2.1.6 Odds and Ends

":=" is the assignment operator (pronounced "gets"). "<=" stands for "≤". The Boolean operators **and** and **or** evaluate both of their sides.[5]

[5] The compiler's optimizer may decide that only one side needs to be evaluated, but a programmer cannot count on it. Eiffel also provides short-circuiting forms ("**or else**" and "**and then**"), which will be discussed in Section 3.1.1.

2.2 Requesting a Feature of an Object

Another object would use our class declaration along the lines shown in Listing 2.2. We already saw how to declare an object's entity. Listing 2.2 does something very similar to declare an entity called *a_letter* of type *LETTER*: it uses a **local** section to declare an entity local to the feature *test.* The name "*a_letter*" refers to that particular entity only within the scope of routine *test.*

2.2.1 Creating an Object

The statement

```
!!a_letter.make('J');
```

instructs the Eiffel system to allocate a new object of class *LETTER* and makes entity *a_letter* refer to that object. Then it asks that object to initialize itself by executing the creation routine *make*(*initial*: *CHARACTER*) with *initial* set to `'J'`.

The purpose of a creation routine is to turn a blank blob of memory into an object that is a valid member of this class (in other words, one for which the class invariant is true).

```
class LETTER_TESTER

creation test

feature

    test is
            --Test an object of class LETTER.
        local
            a_letter: LETTER;
        do
            !!a_letter.make('J');
            print("The letter ");
            print(a_letter);
            print(" is number ");
            print(a_letter.alphabet_position);
            print(" in the alphabet.%N");
        check
            a_letter.is_upper_case;
        end;
```

Listing 2.2 An example of using an object of class *LETTER*.

```
            a_letter.set_character('k');
            print("The letter ");
            print(a_letter);
            print(" is number ");
            print(a_letter.alphabet_position);
            print(" in the alphabet.%N");
            check
                a_letter.is_lower_case;
            end;

            print("%NTest finished.%N");
        end; --test
end --class LETTER_TESTER
```

Listing 2.2 *(continued)*

2.2.2 Requesting a Feature

The form of requesting a feature of an object[6] is

<anything that identifies the object>.<feature name>(<actual parameters>)

If there are no parameters, omit the "(<actual parameters>)".

Usually, an entity name will appear to the left of the dot, but it can be anything that identifies an object. For example, "*a_letter.character*" results in an object of type *CHARACTER,* and we can request features of it without assigning it to an entity. Thus,

a_letter.character.code.out

performs the following three actions:

1. Feature *character* is requested of the *LETTER* object identified by entity *a_letter,* and it results in an object of type *CHARACTER*.
2. Feature *code* is requested of that *CHARACTER* object, and it results in an object of type *INTEGER* (whose value is, on most systems, the ASCII representation of that character).

[6]Other names for asking an object to do something are "sending a message to the object" and "calling a feature of the object."

3. Feature *out* is requested of that *INTEGER* object, and it results in the string of decimal digit characters that a human reader would interpret as that number.

It is important to know what exactly happens when a string of feature requests like this is encountered, but all one needs to remember is that only one feature can be requested of an object at a time. With this in mind, there is only one possible way to interpret the statement in the above example: "((*a_letter.character*).*code*).*out*" (in fact, it could be written with the parentheses, but they are not needed).

When an object requests a feature that happens to be an entity, it may use its value but may not change it. For instance,

print(*a_letter.character*)

is perfectly reasonable, but

Invalid Eiffel! *a_letter.character* := 'Q'

is *illegal*. Thus, features that are entities behave exactly like features that are functions with no parameters. This allows an author of a class to change the implementation of a feature from computing it "on the fly" using a function to storing it in an entity, without bothering the objects that use that feature.

It is also possible to omit the "<anything that identifies the object>." part. In that case, the feature is implicitly requested of the object that is executing the statement. For example,

print(*a_letter*);

requests the feature *print* of the current object (the member of class *LETTER_TESTER* that is executing that line).

There is also a way to refer to the current object explicitly. There is an automatic feature called "*Current*" which always refers to the current object.[7] Thus, another way to write the above *print* request is

Current.print(*a_letter*);

---

[7] It is safe to pretend that *Current* is inherited from *ANY*, though for reasons too technical to discuss here it is not.

2.2.3 Creation Routines vs. Regular Features

In the *LETTER* example, routines *make(initial:CHARACTER)* and *set_character(initial:CHARACTER)* are very similar. Yet, they are requested quite differently in our example:

!!*a_letter.make*('x');

versus

a_letter.set_character('x');

"!!*a_letter*" creates a blank object and "*.make*('x')" initializes it. We could not have just said "*a_letter.make*('x')" (without the "!!"), because *a_letter* was not referring to any object of class *LETTER* yet!

Outside of a creation statement, all features (creation or noncreation) can be requested of valid objects, and *only* of valid objects. (Recall that an object is valid if and only if it has been created and it obeys its class invariant.)

Creation routines, however, are special. They may be used in creation statements, and the invariant is moot until a creation routine is finished initializing the object.

Thus, though *make* and *set_character* happen to perform the same actions in their **do** section, they are intended for fundamentally different purposes: *make* is intended to initialize a newly created object, while *set_character* is meant to modify one that already exists.

But despite the fact that we intend to use them in different circumstances, *make* and *set_character* are identical. As a shortcut, Eiffel provides a way to declare them both at the same time, as shown in Listing 2.3. Note that we are

```
make, set_character(contents: CHARACTER) is
        --Make the letter contain contents.
    require
        ('a' <= contents and contents <= 'z') or
        ('A' <= contents and contents <= 'Z')
    do
        character := contents;
    end; --make, set_character
```

Listing 2.3 When two routines happen to do the same thing, they can be declared simultaneously.

still restricted to using the name "*make*" in creation statements, since it was the only name we listed in the **creation** part of the class *LETTER* declaration.

2.2.4 How *print* Works

The routine *print*(*x*), inherited from class *ANY*, prints out the string that is the result of *x.out*. If the object passed to *print* is a *STRING* that contains a percent sign (`'%'`) (as does the constant string `" in the alphabet.%N"`), then the feature *out* defined in class *STRING* will perform some formatting transformations. For instance, the `"%N"` gets replaced with a "new line" output command (usually a "carriage return, line feed" sequence).

2.3 Inside, Outside

Objects have solid shells. It is not possible for one object to manipulate entities within another object without the latter's cooperation. The **feature** section can specify what types of objects may request the features listed within it by listing those types in curly braces ({ . . . }) after the word **feature** (for example, "**feature** {*LETTER*}"). Features listed in a "**feature** {*X*}" part may be requested by an object only if its class is *X* or an heir of *X*. The predefined type *NONE* is used to protect features that are nobody's business but the object's: "**feature** {*NONE*}". If the type restriction is omitted, then "**feature** {*ANY*}" is assumed. Since all classes are heirs of *ANY*, any object may request those features.

The external view of a letter object, such as the one identified by entity *a_letter* of Listing 2.2, is shown in Figure 2.1: The hard shell hides all internal features, but buttons are provided for requesting the advertised ones (called

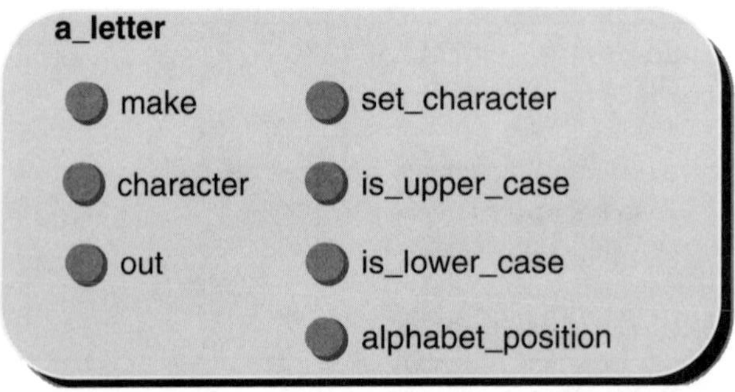

Figure 2.1 The outside view of an object of class *LETTER*.

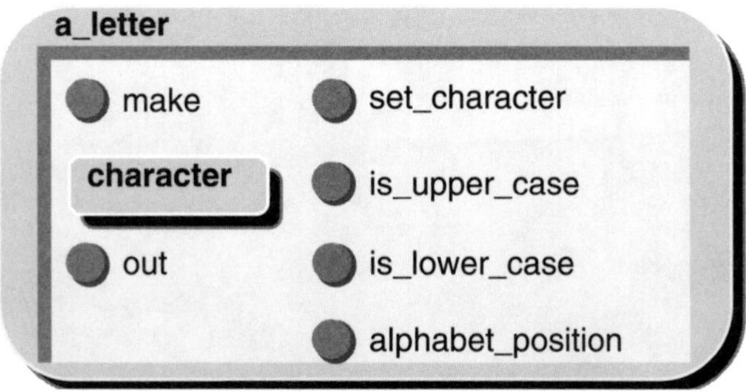

Figure 2.2 The inside view of an object of class *LETTER*.

"*exported features*"). On the other hand, the inside view (visible only to the program segments within the definition of the object's class and of the heirs of its class), shown in Figure 2.2, includes the fact that *character* is an entity, thus allowing assignments of objects to it. It would also include all the "**feature** {*NONE*}" features, if we had any.

Summary

Objects are software components encased in shells. An object's internal representation cannot be accessed directly from the outside; instead, one utilizes the features of an object to communicate with it. When a feature is requested, the object decides how to accommodate the request.

Objects that behave the same way under the same circumstances are members of a class. A class definition in Eiffel specifies what features objects in that class make available to other objects, and how those features are implemented.

The class definition also includes the class invariant, which is a set of Boolean expressions (assertions) that are true about all objects in that class. An object that obeys its invariant is said to be valid. Creation routines take an uninitialized new object and make it valid. All features of the class must maintain the validity of its objects.

Exercise

1. Use your Eiffel system to compile *LETTER* and *LETTER_TESTER* and run *LETTER_TESTER*'s *test* feature.

3 Pairs

The first object structure we consider is a *PAIR*. It is very simple: It keeps track of two things (Figure 3.1). It is hardly résumé material, but it will serve as an example for creating more complicated object structures, and it will give you an opportunity to get accustomed to the particular programming environment you will use for developing object structures.

3.1 What a *PAIR* Is and What It Does

In order for a pair to keep track of two objects, what do we want a *PAIR* object to do once it is created? There is not much that it can do: It can make a given object its first object (we will call that feature "*set_first*"); it can make a given object its second object ("*set_second*"); it can tell us what objects are currently its first and the second objects ("*first*" and "*second*"). We can also ask it to represent itself as a string using the common notation for pairs: "(<first>, <second>)." This gives us the outside view of class *PAIR* shown in Figure 3.2 and also a skeleton of the class definition in Listing 3.1.

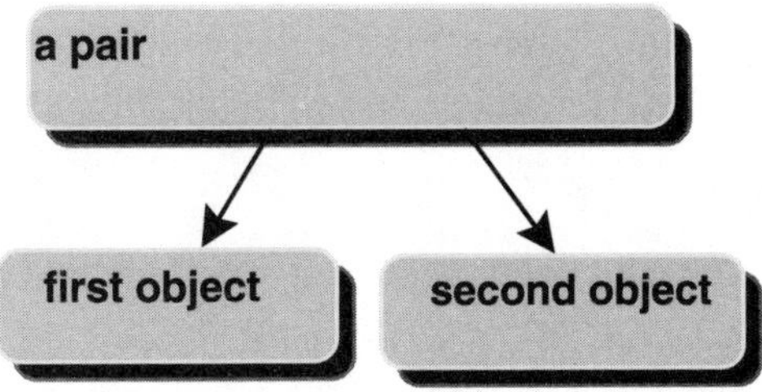

Figure 3.1 A *PAIR* object. Its job is to keep track of two objects.

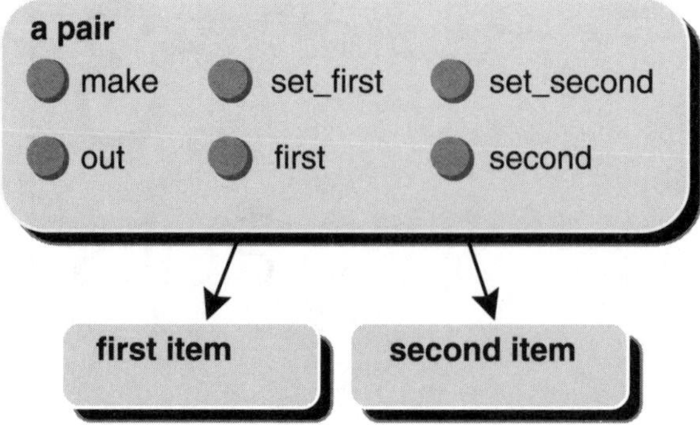

Figure 3.2 The outside view of an object of class *PAIR*.

With this skeleton, we immediately run into a problem: When we pass the objects as parameters to features *set_first* and *set_second*, we have to specify their types, but we do not know them. Similarly, we do not know what types of values features *first* and *second* return. We do not even know yet if the two objects will be of the same type! Since it is more flexible to allow them to be of different types, we will design *PAIR* that way. Obviously, whatever type *set_first* takes as its parameter must be the type of *first*, and the same goes for *set_second* and *second*. Thus, we will set up class *PAIR* to depend on two type parameters (called "generic parameters"), which we will call "*ITEM1*" and

```
class PAIR
creation make

feature
   first: ???;
         --First item.

   second: ???;
         --Second item.

   make is
         --Initialization.
      do
         .
         .
         .
      end; --make
```

Listing 3.1 Definition of class *PAIR,* take 1: feature list.

```
  set_first (an_item: ???) is
        --Track an_item as first item.
     do
        .
        .
        .
     end; --set_first

  set_second (an_item: ???) is
        --Track an_item as second item.
     do
        .
        .
        .
     end; --set_second

  out: STRING is
        --Printable representation of the pair.
     do
        .
        .
        .
     end; --out
end --class PAIR
```

Listing 3.1 *(continued)*

"ITEM2". The class declaration starts with "**class** *PAIR*[*ITEM1*,*ITEM2*]", and then uses *ITEM1* and *ITEM2* as the types of the first and the second item in the pair, respectively. (In general, we will use the term "item" to refer to an object kept track of by our object structure.) This leads to the class skeleton in Listing 3.2.

```
class PAIR[ITEM1,ITEM2] inherit
   ANY
      redefine
         out
      end;

creation make

feature
```

Listing 3.2 Definition of class *PAIR*, take 2: now using type parameters *ITEM1* and *ITEM2*.

```
    first: ITEM1;
            --First item.

    second: ITEM2;
            --Second item.

    make is
            --Initialization.
        do
            .
            .
            .
        end; --make

    set_first (an_item: ITEM1) is
            --Track an_item as first item.
        do
            .
            .
            .
        end; --set_first

    set_second (an_item: ITEM2) is
            --Track an_item as second item.
        do
            .
            .
            .
        end; --set_second

    out: STRING is
            --Printable representation of the pair.
        do
            .
            .
            .
        end; --out
end --class PAIR
```

Listing 3.2 *(continued)*

3.1.1 The Contract

Having established what a *PAIR* object should do, we must make it clear when it can be used and what can be expected of it. This clarification will form a **contract** between the programmer who writes class *PAIR* ("the supplier") and the programmer who uses objects of that class ("the user").

A **contract** consists of five components:

1. The names of public features;
2. The types of parameters the public features take and the types of values in which they result;
3. The preconditions of the public features, which specify what must be true when a feature is invoked (the user's obligation);
4. The **postconditions** of the public features, which specify what can be expected to be true after a feature is finished doing its work (the supplier's obligation); and
5. The class invariant, which specifies (using only the public information, of course) what must be true about any valid object of this class.

Postconditions are listed in an **ensure** section at the end of a feature declaration. Its syntax is identical to that of the **require** sections we used in Chapter 2 to list the preconditions.

Let us consider each feature's part of the contract. The first is *make,* a creation routine. What distinguishes creation routines from other features is their ability to work in situations where the object is not valid (i.e., the invariant is unsatisfied), as is often the case right after memory is allocated for the new object. A creation routine takes a blank blob of memory and turns it into a valid object. In fact, all features—not just creation routines—have to leave the object that executes them in a state where the class invariant is true.

Since *make* accepts its task under any circumstances, it has no preconditions and hence no **require** section. Since it does not promise anything more than the standard "the object is valid" condition, it has no postconditions and no **ensure** section.

Next is *set_first*. Since it is not a creation routine, it will be executed only by objects that are already valid. Should it require its parameter, *an_item*, to be valid also? Do we care if we are told to make the first item of a *PAIR* void? We don't if the user only plans to retrieve it back by requesting the feature *first*: In this case, we can just follow the "garbage in, garbage out" principle. Only if the user tries to get the string representation of the pair (using the *out* feature) will there be trouble, but the user may have no plans to do that. Thus, we will not insist on getting valid items through *set_first*, and put in a check for void items into feature *out*, displaying something reasonable in that case (we will attend to *out* a little later). This leaves *set_first* with no preconditions.

How about the postconditions? What can we promise to the user? We can definitely promise that after the *set_first(an_item)* is performed, a *first* request will result in the same *an_item*.

Can we promise anything about *second*? We can specify that there will not be any side effect on the second item in the pair. This would preclude the kind of pair-based structures in which the objects *first* and *second* are interconnected in a certain way, so in general we don't want to make such a promise. However, let us go ahead and make it just to see how it can be done.

We use the operator **old**, which returns the value of an expression as it was before the routine was invoked:

work in progress

```
ensure
    first_was_replaced: first = an_item;
    second_is_unchanged: second = old second;
```

(We label the assertions with the names "*first_was_replaced*" and "*second_is_unchanged*" so that if one of them is violated when we execute the program, the error message will include its label.)

So far so good, but *second_is_unchanged* is not quite right. All it says is that the reference to the item in the second position will be unchanged, i.e., that the entity *second* is tracking the same item as before. It does not say that the item's *value* will be unchanged. For that, we need to use the standard feature *is_equal*: "*second.is_equal*(**old** *second*)" (inherited from *ANY*). So, our next attempt at the postcondition is

work in progress

```
ensure
    first_was_replaced: first = an_item;
    second_is_same: second = old second;
    second_is_unchanged: second.is_equal(old second);
```

This assumes that *is_equal* is a feature of class *ITEM2*. Since *ANY* provides that feature to its heirs, that is a safe bet. If a class refuses to provide *is_equal*, its members cannot be tracked by our pairs.

Unfortunately, *second_is_unchanged* is still wrong. In fact, there are two problems with it. The first is that when *set_first* is requested of a newly made pair, *second* will not be tracking a valid item yet. And since we have decided to allow the user to track invalid items in pairs, this situation can happen at any time. But we cannot request *is_equal* of a void object! To guard against that situation, a way to say "item is void" is needed.

Eiffel provides, through class *ANY*, a standard object tracked by the feature "*Void*" that has a unique purpose: It is the only object that has the right—nay, obligation!—to be invalid. If an entity does not yet refer to a valid object (for example, when it is not initialized by a creation routine), it is automatically made to refer to *Void*'s object. In fact, to make entity *e* let go of the object of which it keeps track, we say "*e* := *Void*". Thus, an entity that keeps track of *Void*'s object is said to be "invalid" or "void" and we can use the test "*e* = *Void*" to identify that situation. If there is nothing else keeping track of the object that used to be identified by *e*, that object is automatically recycled: The memory it occupies is released for other uses (this automatic activity is known as **"garbage collection"**).

But can't an entity be tracking an object that is not void, but is invalid because it got messed up somehow? No. Impossible. If such was the case, the program would have stopped as soon as the class invariant of that object was violated. If it reached the point where we are using the object, it must be either valid or void.

Given the feature *Void*, there are two equivalent ways to express that *second* should be equal to **old** *second* whenever *second* is a valid item:

second_is_unchanged: *second* /= *Void* **implies** *second.is_equal* (**old** *second*);

("/=" means "does not equal" in Eiffel) and

second_is_unchanged: *second* = *Void* **or else** *second.is_equal* (**old** *second*);

Both **implies** and **or else** (as well as **and then**) only evaluate the expression on their right if the expression on the left does not decide the result. Thus, their meanings are as shown in Table 3.1. Using this kind of expression allows us to evaluate *second.is_equal*(**old** *second*) only when *second* /= *Void*. Since "*x* **implies** *y*" is logically equivalent to "**not** *x* **or else** *y*", the choice between them is a matter of taste. I prefer the "**implies**" form.

That takes care of the first problem. The second problem is more subtle. The tricky part is "**old** *second*". Since *second* merely stores the reference to the tracked object, **old** *second* is just the old value of that reference. If the object

Table 3.1 Eiffel operators that do not evaluate their right-hand side unless it is necessary.

Operator	*Meaning*
<left> **and then** <right>	Compute <left>. If it is **false**, then the answer is **false**, else compute <right> and use its answer.
<left> **or else** <right>	Compute <left>. If it is **true**, then the answer is **true**, else compute <right> and use its answer.
<left> **implies** <right>	Compute <left>. If it is **false**, then the answer is **true**, else compute <right> and use its answer.

changed but the reference to it didn't, then both *second* and **old** *second* refer to the same object, and of course it will report that it *is_equal* to itself! If we are to state that the object did not change, we will have to squirrel away a copy of it:

```
ensure
   first_was_replaced: first = an_item;
   second_is_same: second = old second;
   second_is_unchanged:
         second /= Void implies second.is_equal(old deep_clone(second));
```

The feature *deep_clone* is also provided by our ancestor *ANY*. That will do it for *set_first*.

Feature *first*, being either an entity (as in our current implementation) or a function, should not modify any entities of the *PAIR* object. Although we cannot specify postconditions for entities in Eiffel (preconditions and postconditions are only possible for routines), "nothing about this object changed" is always an assumed postcondition with entity and function features. (Eiffel programmers almost never allow their functions to change the object, although it is permitted by the language.)

What works for *set_first* and *first* also works for *set_second* and *second*, except that the roles of *first* and *second* are reversed in the postconditions.

While *first* and *second* do not care if the two items are valid, *out* does: If even one of the items is invalid, it will not be able to build a string representation for the pair. Thus, we would want the following preconditions for *out*:

Invalid for out

```
require
   first_not_void: first /= Void;
   second_not_void: second /= Void;
```

Too bad—we cannot have them. Since our *out* is a redefinition of the one inherited from *ANY*, it is not allowed to have preconditions that are more stringent than those of the original *out*. This restriction is due to the relationship between the contracts of a parent and an heir, which we will study in Chapter 4. Part of that relationship is that an heir cannot refuse to respond to a feature request under circumstances in which the ancestor would respond to it.

This means that we may be faced with void items. There are two ways to deal with a request to produce the string representation of a pair that contains a void item. The first is to let an error be generated when we request the *out* feature of the void item. This would only happen if one of the preconditions desired above had been violated. This, of course, is no solution: Since we did not tell the user in the contract not to invoke *out* when either of the items is void, we are responsible for making *out* work without crashing the program even with one or both items being void.

The other way is to fulfill the contractual obligation—buckle down and deal with it. We could use a predefined string to represent void objects. How about "`"-void-"`"? That is what we will do.

Because *out*, being a function, does not change the *PAIR* object or anything it tracks, it has the same implied postconditions as *first* and *second* and any other function.

Finally, we need to consider what to list in the class invariant for *PAIR*: nothing. As long as a pair exists as a *PAIR* object, it is valid (even, as we saw, if one or both of the items it tracks are void). Thus, we can omit the **invariant** section of the class definition.

Combined with the class skeleton we had earlier, all these assertions give us a skeleton that can serve as the contract (Listing 3.3).

This completes the **definition** of *PAIR*.

```
class PAIR[ITEM1,ITEM2] inherit
   ANY
      redefine
         out
      end;

creation make

feature
   first: ITEM1;
         --First item.

   second: ITEM2;
         --Second item.

   make is
         --Initialization.
      do
         .
         .
         .
      end; --make

   set_first (an_item: ITEM1) is
         --Track an_item as first item.
      do
```

Listing 3.3 Definition of class *PAIR*, take 3: the contract.

```
            .
            .
            .
        ensure
            first_was_replaced: first = an_item;
            second_is_same: second = old second;
            second_is_unchanged:
                second /= Void implies second.is_equal(old deep_clone(second));
        end; --set_first

    set_second (an_item: ITEM2) is
            --Track an_item as second item.
        do
            .
            .
            .
        ensure
            second_was_replaced: second = an_item;
            first_is_same: first = old first;
            first_is_unchanged:
                first /= Void implies first.is_equal(old deep_clone (first));
        end; --set_second

    out: STRING is
            --Printable representation of the pair
            --(void items replaced with "-void-").
        do
            .
            .
            .
        end; --out
end --class PAIR
```

Listing 3.3 *(continued)*

3.1.2 How Detailed Should the Contract Be?

On the one hand, the more detailed the contract is, the less potential there is for misunderstanding between the user and the supplier. As suppliers, we have a vested interest in making the preconditions as detailed as we can; it is in the interest of the users to make the postconditions as detailed as possible. It is also easier to test the program with detailed contracts: As a tester object exercises feature requests in our object structure, the preconditions and postconditions are checked automatically.

On the other hand, most of the postconditions are of the form "nothing changes" or "almost nothing changes." In the case of a *PAIR* object, where there were only two features that could have changed to begin with, it takes three postconditions each in two procedures to state that fact. As our object structures get more complicated, this could get out of control. There is, however, a shortcut in Eiffel that we can use, and we will consider it when the time comes (in Section 6.4.1).

As with any contract, it is very tempting to adopt global conventions and leave things unmentioned explicitly. As with any contract, doing so increases the risk of things going wrong.

In general, we want to make the contract as detailed as possible. One exception to this rule is the implicit "nothing changed" postcondition for any function. There are two reasons for this exception:

1. Writing a function that causes changes (also called "side effects") is very poor engineering: If such a function is used twice in one expression, one cannot be sure which request the compiler will issue first, and thus you may get different results from running the same program under different compilers.
2. Since you cannot attach a postcondition to an entity, attaching one to any feature advertises it in the contract as a function and not an entity. That, however, should remain an implementation decision: If at all possible, we want to leave open the option to store that feature as an entity within the object instead of computing it on-the-fly as a function.

Also, the elaborate scheme we have derived for specifying "nothing else changes" tends to be too restrictive and too cumbersome to be useful. It is a good illustration on how the keyword **old** can be used in postconditions, as well as how important it is to understand the distinction between a reference to an object and the object itself. However, it is rarely used by Eiffel programmers, and we will come back to it only once, in Section 6.4.1, when we look at another potentially useful but rarely used technique.

3.2 How a *PAIR* Does What It Does

Now that we have defined *what* a *PAIR* is and *what* it does (the definition), we can consider *how* it does it (an **implementation** of *PAIR*). Most object structures can be implemented in several good ways, but there is really only one good way in Eiffel to implement a pair of items of arbitrary types. Thus, we will only consider one implementation of *PAIR* in this text.

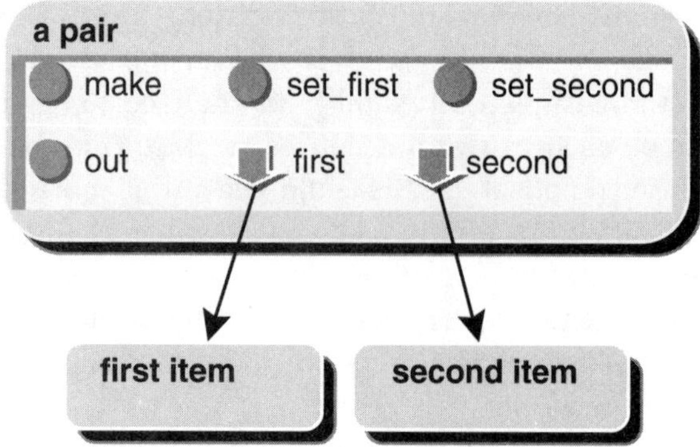

Figure 3.3 The inside view of an object of class *PAIR*.

3.2.1 The Representation

The way entities are set up inside an object structure is known as its **representation**. We represent the pair simply with one entity to track each item: *first* and *second* (Figure 3.3).

3.2.2 Expanded and Nonexpanded Classes

Compare the graphic notation used for *first* and *second* in Figure 3.3 with the one used for *character* in Figure 2.2. The reason for the difference is that there are two ways for an entity to identify an object, depending on how that class was declared.

Class *CHARACTER* is declared in standard Eiffel libraries as an **expanded class**. If an entity *e* is declared to be of a type that represents an expanded class ("expanded type" for short), then the object is actually expanded within the entity during assignment. Also, when the contents of one entity are assigned to another, the destination entity gets a copy of the object. Thus, if *e1* and *e2* are both of type *CHARACTER*, then the following sequence of statements results in the indicated sequence of figures:

```
    --Figure 3.4a
e1 := 'M';
    --Figure 3.4b
e2 := e1;
    --Figure 3.4c
```

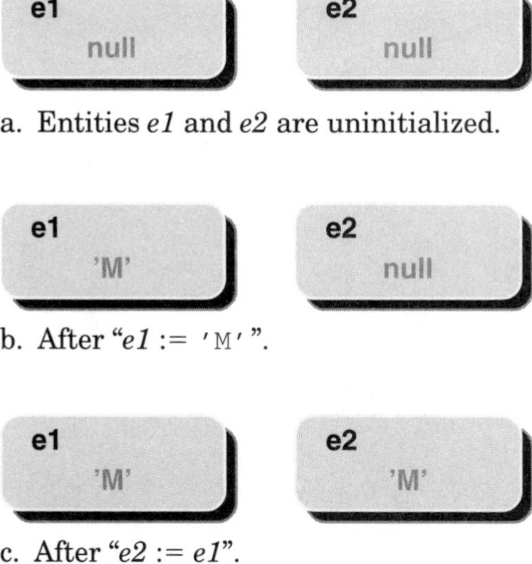

a. Entities *e1* and *e2* are uninitialized.

b. After "*e1* := 'M' ".

c. After "*e2* := *e1*".

Figure 3.4 Assignment of an object of an expanded class.

On the other hand, objects from regular, **nonexpanded** classes reside in memory outside the entities that keep track of them. The only thing stored inside the entity is information about how to locate that object in memory, the **reference** to the object—just as what is found on a line of a class list is the reference to a student (her name), and not the student herself. It is only that reference—and not the object itself—that is copied during an assignment. Therefore, if *e1* and *e2* are of any nonexpanded type (which we can safely assume about *ITEM1* and *ITEM2*), such as our type *LETTER*, we have the following situation:

```
    --Figure 3.5a
!!e1.make('M');
    --Figure 3.5b
e2 := e1;
    --Figure 3.5c
```

Since object structures keep track of objects without, generally, containing them, we will assume that we are always given nonexpanded item types.

Having decided on the representation, we can proceed to write the **do** sections of the class definition.

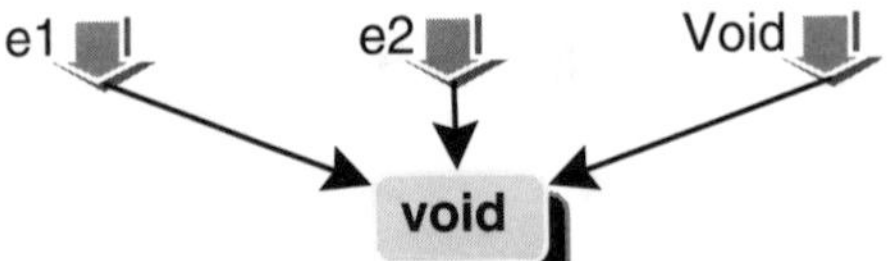

a. Entities *e1* and *e2* are uninitialized.

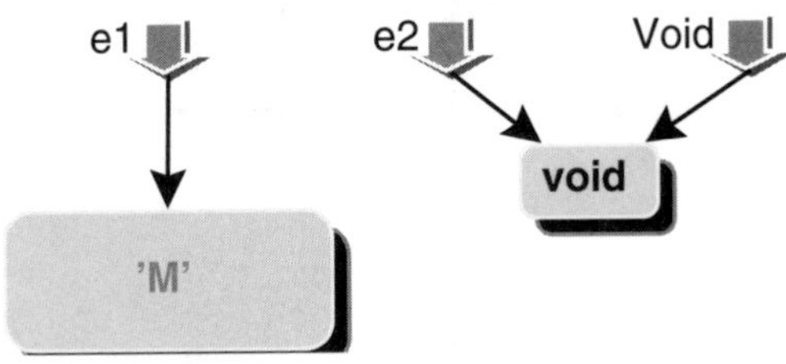

b. After "!!*e1.make*('M')".

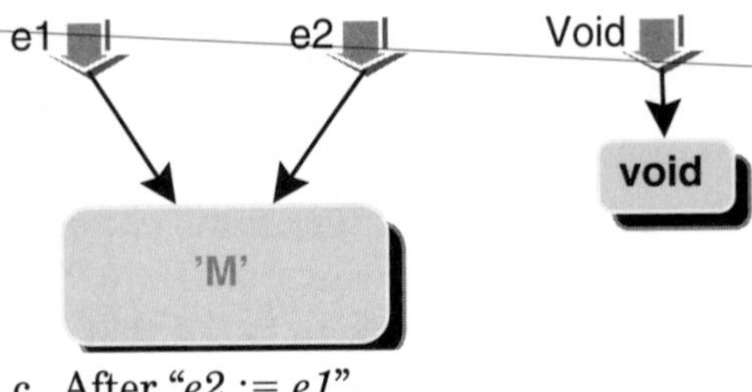

c. After "*e2* := *e1*".

Figure 3.5 Assignment of an object of a nonexpanded class.

3.2.3 Creating a *PAIR* Object

A creation routine's primary job is to make sure that the newborn object is a valid member of its class—namely, that it satisfies the class invariant. This is easy in the case of class *PAIR*, because there is nothing that needs to be done. All we have to put into the **do** section is a comment to that effect, so that it doesn't look like we forgot to write it.

3.2.4 The Insertion and Retrieval Features

All we need to do when an item is **inserted** into a pair (meaning that the pair starts to keep track of it) is assign it to the proper tracking entity. For example, *set_first* does:

```
do
    first := an_item;
```

Observe that this implementation will ensure the postconditions of the routine, and the *PAIR* object will still be valid after the routine is finished (i.e., the class invariant will be true for the object).

To retrieve an item from a position in a pair, we simply let the entity *first* be a feature.

The implementations of *second* and *set_second* are analogous.

3.2.5 Implementation of *out*

Feature *out* has to produce a string representation of the pair in the form "(<*first*>,<*second*>)". But to write a routine that does that, don't we need to know how to represent an *ITEM1* and an *ITEM2* as strings? No! We do not need to know that, and we do not *want* to know that! If it was our job to micromanage the string representation of *first* and *second*, we would have to know the details of representing as strings the objects of every possible class that we may be asked to track. Even if that was a reasonable task, we would have to edit the class definition of *PAIR* every time a new class was introduced into the system. That would be ridiculous.

It is not the job of class *PAIR* to know how to "*out*" objects of classes *ITEM1* and *ITEM2*, whatever they turn out to be. It is *their* job. In order for us to be able to represent a pair as a string, *first* and *second* need to know how to represent themselves as strings.

More specifically, we insist that they offer their own *out* features. Then we can implement the *out* feature for class *PAIR* as follows:

```
do
    Result := clone("(");[1]
    if first /= Void then
        Result.append_string(first.out);
    else
        Result.append_string("-void-");
    end;
    Result.append_string(",");
    if second /= Void then
        Result.append_string(second.out);
```

[1]We make *Result* refer to a clone of the *STRING* object "(", because otherwise "*Result.append_string*(. . .)" would change the value of "(" in some Eiffel systems.

```
else
   Result.append_string("-void-");
end;
Result.append_string(")");
```

We see now that we neglected to state an important provision in the contract: that *first* and *second* must both respond to *out*. In Eiffel, it is not possible to list that requirement in a precondition to *out*. Eiffel is a statically typed language, and the set of supported features is a property of a type. Fortunately, due to a technique known as **subclassing,** all classes in Eiffel respond to *out* requests. Subclassing deserves a thorough treatise of its own, so we will cover it in detail in Chapter 4. For now, please take it on faith that all programmer-supplied objects in Eiffel respond to the *out* feature request (though not necessarily resulting in a satisfactory string representation). We will not always be this lucky, but we *will* have a way of specifying such requirements when the need arises.

Listing 3.4 shows the full implementation of class *PAIR*.

```
class PAIR[ITEM1,ITEM2] inherit
   ANY
      redefine
         out
      end;

creation make

feature
   first: ITEM1;
         --First item.

   second: ITEM2;
         --Second item.

   make is
         --Initialization.
      do
         --Nothing needs to be done.
      end; --make
```

Listing 3.4 Definition of class *PAIR*, with implementation.

```
set_first (an_item: ITEM1) is
        --Track an_item as first item.
    do
        first := an_item;
    ensure
        first_was_replaced: first = an_item;
        second_is_same: second = old second;
        second_is_unchanged:
            second /= Void implies second.is_equal (old deep_clone (second));
    end; --set_first

set_second (an_item: ITEM2) is
        --Track an_item as second item.
    do
        second := an_item;
    ensure
        second_was_replaced: second = an_item;
        first_is_same: first = old first;
        first_is_unchanged:
            first /= Void implies first.is_equal (old deep_clone (first));
    end; --set_second

out: STRING is
        -- "(<first item>.out,<second item>.out)"
        --(void items replaced with "-void-").
    do
        Result := clone("(");

        if first /= Void then
            Result.append_string (first.out);
        else
            Result.append_string ("-void-");
        end;

        Result.append_string (",");

        if second /= Void then
            Result.append_string(second.out);
        else
            Result.append_string ("-void-");
        end;

        Result.append_string (")");
    end; --out
end --class PAIR
```

Listing 3.4 *(continued)*

3.3 Sifting Out the Inside to Get the Outside View

We have completed an implementation of class *PAIR*, but in doing so we have filled the outside view (Listing 3.3) with implementation details, winding up with the inside view (Listing 3.4). Since we reserve the right to change the inside view in any way that does not disturb the outside view, we may want to hide the inside view from our users (or only show it to them on a "need to know" basis).

```
class interface PAIR[ITEM1,ITEM2]
creation procedures

   make
         --Initialization.

feature specification

   first: ITEM1
         --First item.

   second: ITEM2
         --Second item.

   set_first(an_item: ITEM1)
         --Track an_item as first item.
      ensure
         first_was_replaced: first = an_item;
         second_is_same: second = old second;
         second_is_unchanged:
            second /= Void implies second.is_equal(old deep_clone(second));

   set_second(an_item: ITEM2)
         --Track an_item as second item.
      ensure
         second_was_replaced: second = an_item;
         first_is_same: first = old first;
         first_is_unchanged:
            first /= Void implies first.is_equal(old deep_clone(first));

   out: STRING
      --(void items replaced with "-void-").
end --class interface PAIR
```

Listing 3.5 The **short form** (outside view) of class *PAIR*.

This need is facilitated by an Eiffel utility called `short`. Basically, it sifts out the implementation details of a class and leaves the outside view. When applied to our class *PAIR*, its output looks similar to that of Listing 3.5. Note that there is a slight difference in notation between the short form of class *PAIR* and its full form: For example, "**class**" has been replaced with "**class interface**," and "**feature**" with "**feature specification**." This is done so that a short form of a class could not possibly be confused by the reader with the full form.

The short form of the class now serves as the contract, and can be handed out to users.

3.4 Testing Class *PAIR*

Before we hand off our *PAIR* implementation to a user, we should "play user" ourselves and try it out. To do that, we create a class called "*PAIR_TESTER*," and let its initialization routine create a *PAIR* object and address to it a sequence of feature requests. The full definition of *PAIR_TESTER* is given in Listing 3.6; we will step through each step of the test to reinforce our understanding of how *PAIR* objects operate. Note that we *do not* write code to check the preconditions and postconditions of each feature: They are tested automatically when the features start and finish their work. If a precondition is violated, an error condition is triggered in the user's routine; if a postcondition is violated, it is triggered in the supplier's routine.

Before stepping through the test routine, let us review what *print* does. Routine *print* (*x*), inherited from *ANY*, displays the result of *x.out* on the standard output device (usually, the display of your computer or terminal). Thus,

```
print (pair)
```

will display *pair.out*, and

```
print ("Second item set to 'b'.%N You should see '(a,b)': ")
```

will display

```
("Second item set to 'b'.%N You should see '(a,b)': ").out
```

which is defined in class *STRING*. That class's *out* feature interprets certain substrings instead of displaying them as they appear in the program. For instance, substring "%N" is not displayed, but a 'new line' command is sent to the display in its place.

```
class PAIR_TESTER
creation test

feature
  test is
      --Test a PAIR.
    local
      pair: PAIR[LETTER,LETTER];
      letter1: LETTER;
      letter2: LETTER;
    do
      !!pair.make;
      print("New pair created.%N You should see '(-void-,-void-)': ");
      print(pair);
      print("%N");

      !!letter1.make('a');
      pair.set_first(letter1);
      print("First item set to 'a'.%N You should see '(a,-void-)': ");
      print(pair);
      print("%N");

      !!letter2.make('b');
      pair.set_second(letter2);
      print("Second item set to 'b'.%N You should see '(a,b)': ");
      print(pair);
      print("%N%NTest done.%N");
    end; --test

end --class PAIR_TESTER
```

Listing 3.6 A class for testing *PAIR* objects.

Thus, here is what happens when this code is executed:

```
   --Figure 3.6a
!!pair.make;
   --Figure 3.6b
print("New pair created.%N You should see '(-void-,-void-)': ");
   --"New pair created," a 'new line' command and
   --"You should see '(-void-,-void-)': " are sent to the display
print(pair);
   --"(-void-,-void-)" is sent to the display
print("%N");
   --A 'new line' command is sent to the display
```

```
!!letter1.make('a');
    --Figure 3.6c
pair.set_first(letter1);
    --Figure 3.6d
print("First item set to 'a'.%N You should see '(a,-void-)': ");
    --"First item set to 'a'," a 'new line' command and
    --"You should see '(a,-void-)': " are sent to the display
print(pair);
    --"(a,-void-)" is sent to the display
print("%N");
    --A 'new line' command is sent to the display
!!letter2.make('b');
    --Figure 3.6e
pair.set_second(letter2);
    --Figure 3.6f
print("Second item set to 'b'.%N You should see '(a,b)': ");
    --"Second item set to 'b'," a 'new line' command and
    --"You should see '(a,b)': " is sent to the display
print(pair);
    --"(a,b)" is sent to the display
print("%N%NTest done.%N");
    --Two 'new line' commands, "Test done." and
    --another 'new line' command are sent to the display
```

For the moment, we have taken our first object structure as far as we can. The next chapter, as promised, studies the subclassing mechanism, which will clear up the question of from where all these "predefined" features come. It will also suggest some improvements to class *PAIR*.

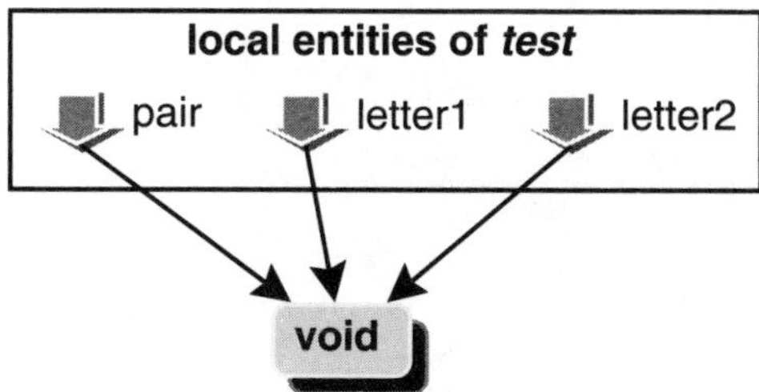

a. Local entities *pair*, *letter1*, and *letter2* are uninitialized.

Figure 3.6 What happens to the various entities while routine *test* executes.

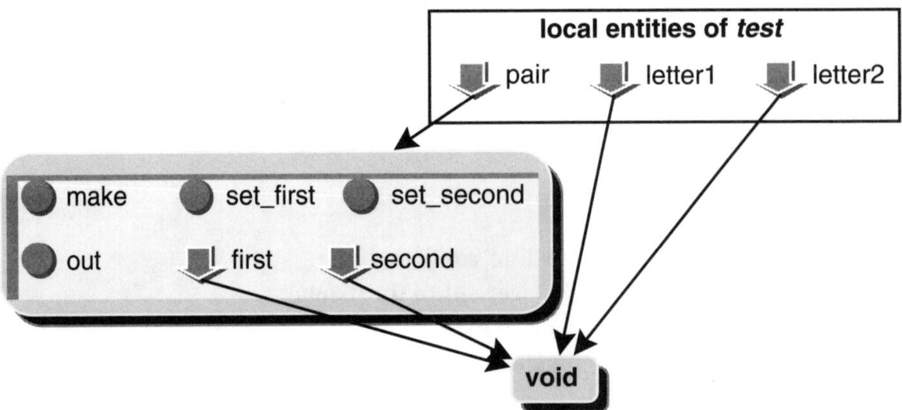

b. After "!!*pair.make*".

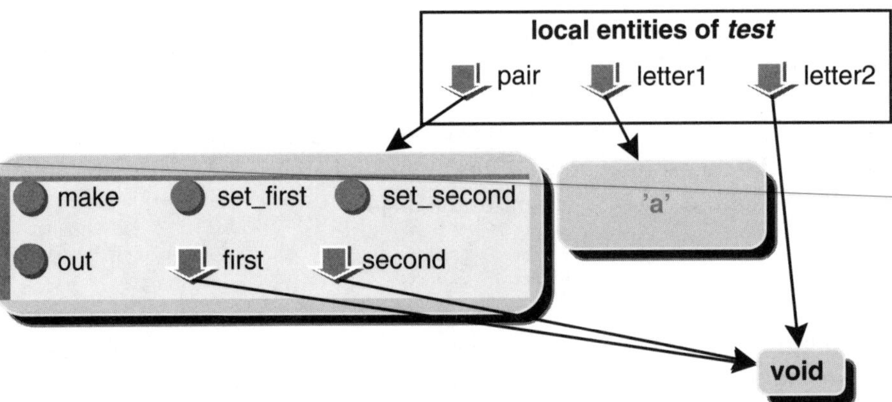

c. After "!!*letter1.make*('a')".

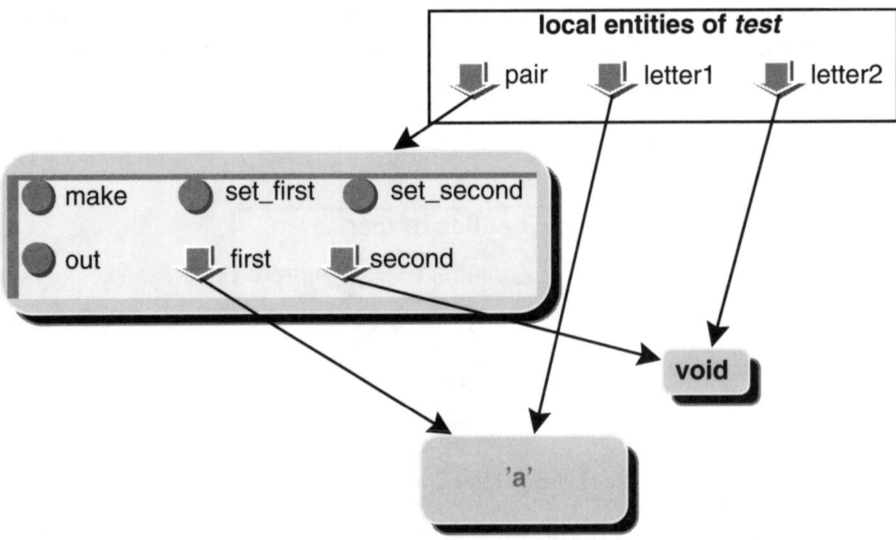

d. After "*pair.set_first*(*letter1*)".

Figure 3.6 (*continued*)

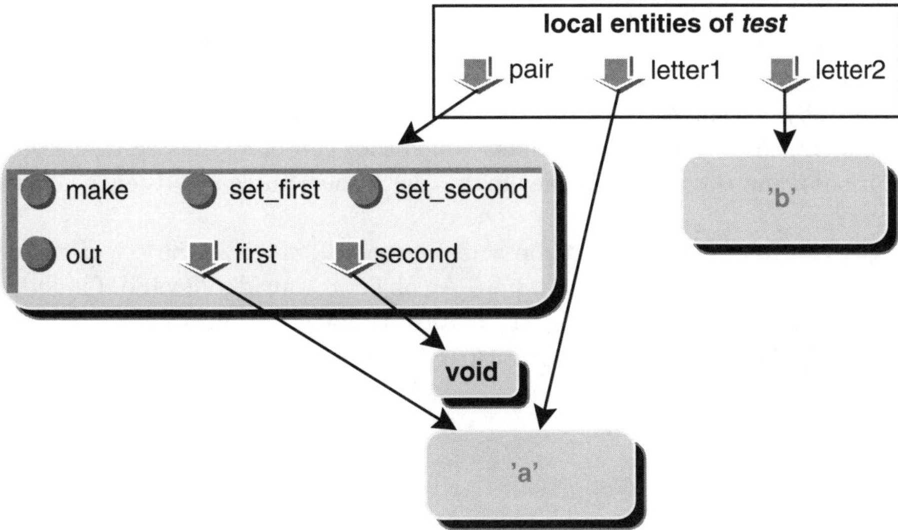

e. After "!!*letter2.make*('b')".

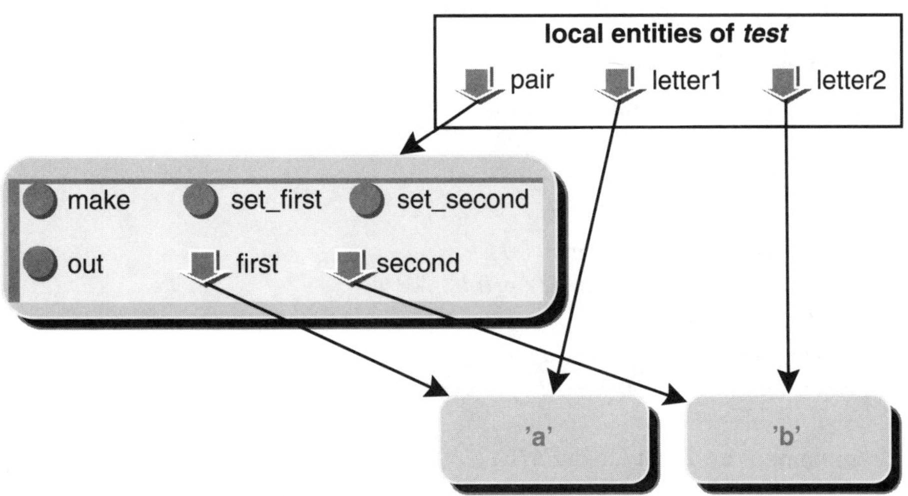

f. After "*pair.set_second*(*letter2*)".

Figure 3.6 (*continued*)

Summary

A *PAIR* is a simple object structure. It keeps track of two objects: the first object and the second object. It defines and implements its own features, and inherits some of the common features (such as *print*) from the predefined class

ANY. One of the inherited features (*out*) is redefined to provide an implementation that is more meaningful to pairs than the generic version provided by *ANY*.

The set of features provided by an object structure (or an object in general) is defined by its contract. The contract lists the names of the features and their parameters, the circumstances under which they can be requested (their preconditions), and the promises they make about their outcomes (their postconditions).

The contract also specifies the class invariant, which is the set of assertions made about the object as a whole. An object is considered valid if it obeys the invariant of its class. An object's feature is allowed to make the invariant temporarily false, but it must return it to the true state before it finishes execution.

Exercises

1. What output does the following code segment produce if *e1* and *e2* are entities of type *LETTER*, and *LETTER* is defined as

   a. an expanded class?

   b. a nonexpanded class?

```
e1.make('A');
e2 := e1;
print("At first e1="); print(e1);
print(" and e2="); print(e2); print(",%N");
e1.set_character('B');
print("Then e1="); print(e1);
print(" and e2="); print(e2); print(".%N");
```

2. Implement and test class *PAIR*.

4 Subclasses and Subcontracts

We now take a closer look at how classes may be related to each other. In particular, we will study the inheritance relationship, and what effect it has on the contract. In light of that study, we will consider how inheritance can be used and when it should be avoided. We will then revisit class *PAIR*, to make it a better heir to *ANY*.

4.1 A More Sophisticated *PAIR* Structure

The class *PAIR* presented in Chapter 3 gives us a good general pair object structure. But suppose we had a program that required something else of its pairs?

For example, we may need to keep track of which position in our object structure was modified last. Thus, we need a feature, call it *last_change*, that returns a 1 if the first position was changed last, and 2 if it was the second position. If *last_change* is requested before anything changed (i.e., after the pair is created but before either the first or the second position is set to track an object), it should result in a 0.

But this need was not anticipated when *PAIR* was written. We could hound the author of *PAIR* to add the feature for us. If we bought the class from another company, the reply we are likely to get is "Sure, we will include it in the next release of the system. It is due to come out in the second quarter of next year, and the upgrade will cost a mere $99.95. Per user. Per byte." You ask then, "If you could be so kind as to send me the source code for this one little class, I could make this tiny little change myself. . . ." To this they politely reply that they just cannot do that for these reasons:

1. It is against their company policy.
2. If they gave you the source, you could not really use it unless they gave you this and that and this other thing too, which is also against company policy.
3. Besides, their distribution and support system is not set up to send you all that stuff, because it is just *such* an unusual request.
4. Not that they think this could happen with *you,* but what if you screw up something in their class, then call their support number, and they won't be able to help you fix it because they don't know what you had done, and they don't get paid to fix your bugs, and it would reflect poorly on them if people think it's their bug when it's actually yours.
5. That is why it is against company policy.

Okay, okay, so I am exaggerating a little. However, almost anybody who has ever tried to get a *bug fix*—not to mention an enhancement, which is what we need—out of a large software vendor is familiar with this scenario.

Fortunately, object-oriented programming gives us a way to get what we want without disturbing the original *PAIR* class. Here is how we do it:

1. We define a new class—let us call it "*ENHANCED_PAIR*."
2. We proclaim *ENHANCED_PAIR* to be an **heir** to *PAIR*, thus inheriting its contract as well as all the guts and the smarts of it.
3. We add the feature *last_change* to *ENHANCED_PAIR*.
4. In our code that deals with pair objects, we create an *ENHANCED_ PAIR* object wherever we used to create a *PAIR* object.

The resulting class is shown in Listing 4.1.

```
class ENHANCED_PAIR[ITEM1,ITEM2] inherit
   PAIR[ITEM1,ITEM2]
      redefine
         set_first, set_second
      end;

creation make

feature
```

Listing 4.1 Definition of *ENHANCED_PAIR*, an heir to *PAIR* that adds a feature to the contract.

```
    last_change: INTEGER;
            --1 if the first position was changed last,
            --2 if the second,
            --0 if neither has been changed (i.e., both are void).
    set_first (an_item: ITEM1) is
            --Track an_item as first item.
        do
            first := an_item;
            last_change := 1;
        ensure then
            last_change = 1;
        end; --set_first
    set_second (an_item: ITEM2) is
            --Track an_item as second item.
        do
            second := an_item;
            last_change := 2;
        ensure then
            last_change = 2;
        end; --set_second
end --class ENHANCED_PAIR
```

Listing 4.1 *(continued)*

Note that we do not rewrite the whole class: We just add our new feature, *last_change*, and redefine *set_first* and *set_second* to keep it correct. All the other features are inherited from *PAIR* with no modification.

To test our new class, we can simply make a copy of *PAIR_TESTER* and fix it up to be *ENHANCED_PAIR_TESTER*, as shown in Listing 4.2. All we had

```
class ENHANCED_PAIR_TESTER
creation test
feature
    test is
            --Test an ENHANCED_PAIR.
        local
            pair: ENHANCED_PAIR[LETTER,LETTER];
            letter1: LETTER;
            letter2: LETTER;
```

Listing 4.2 Class *ENHANCED_PAIR_TESTER*, built out of a copy of *PAIR_TESTER*.

```
    do
        !!pair.make;
        print("New pair created.%N You should see '(-void-,-void-)': ");
        print(pair);
        print("%NLast position changed (you should see '0'): ");
        print(pair.last_change);
        print("%N");

        !!letter1.make('a');
        pair.set_first(letter1);
        print("First item set to 'a'.%N You should see '(a,-void-)': ");
        print(pair);
        print("%NLast position changed (you should see '1'): ");
        print(pair.last_change);
        print("%N");

        !!letter2.make('b');
        pair.set_second(letter2);
        print("%NSecond item set to 'b'.%N You should see '(a,b)': ");
        print(pair);
        print("%NLast position changed (you should see '2'): ");
        print(pair.last_change);
        print("%N%NTest done.%N");
    end; --test

end --class ENHANCED_PAIR_TESTER
```

Listing 4.2 *(continued)*

to do was modify the type of the local entity *pair*, and add the code that tests the new feature *last_change*.

4.2 The "Can Act As a" Relationship

It is certainly convenient to inherit from a parent class all the features that are already good enough to use with the heir class.[1] But it was mentioned earlier that an heir inherits the parent's contract too, which means that an object of the heir class must be able to do everything that its ancestor class's objects can,

---

[1]A common term for "heir class" is "**subclass**"; the parent class is frequently called the "**superclass**."

and do it under the same circumstances, and do it at least as well. *A user may always substitute an heir's object for an ancestor's object.*

Thus, by saying that one class is an heir of another, we say that objects of the heir class can act as objects of the ancestor class. For example, an *ENHANCED_PAIR* **can act as a** *PAIR*.[2]

For instance, objects of class *ENHANCED_PAIR* must be able to pass the *test* routine of *PAIR_TESTER*, since *PAIR* objects do. To do this test, we modify *PAIR_TESTER* in only one place: the line

```
!!pair.make
```

where we create a *PAIR* object and attach it to entity *pair*. What we want to attach to *pair* instead is an *ENHANCED_PAIR* object.

The Eiffel way to specify what class to use when creating a new object is to put that class's name between the two exclamation marks. In fact,

```
!!pair.make
```

is really just a shortcut for saying

```
!PAIR[LETTER,LETTER]!pair.make
```

If you do not specify a class name between the "! . . . !", then the class corresponding to the type of the entity is used. In this case, since *pair* is of type *PAIR[LETTER,LETTER]*, objects of class *PAIR[LETTER,LETTER]* are created by default.

However, since objects of class *ENHANCED_PAIR* can do whatever *PAIR* objects can, it is perfectly safe and legal to create an *ENHANCED_PAIR [LETTER,LETTER]* object instead of the *PAIR[LETTER,LETTER]* object:

```
!ENHANCED_PAIR[LETTER,LETTER]!pair.make;
```

The *PAIR_TESTER* class in Listing 4.3 is just like the one in Listing 3.6, but it tests an *ENHANCED_PAIR* object in its capacity as a *PAIR* object. Note that the entity *pair* is still of type *PAIR*, not *ENHANCED_PAIR*.

---

[2]Many object-oriented design texts state that the relationship is ". . . is a . . ." instead of ". . . can act as a . . . ." In Section 4.4 we discuss why that is an inaccurate description.

```
class PAIR_TESTER
creation test

feature
   test is
         --Test a PAIR.
      local
         pair: PAIR[LETTER,LETTER];
         letter1: LETTER;
         letter2: LETTER;
      do
         !ENHANCED_PAIR[LETTER,LETTER]!pair.make;
         print("New pair created.%N You should see '(-void-,-void-)': ");
         print(pair);
         print("%N");

         !!letter1.make('a');
         pair.set_first(letter1);
         print("First item set to 'a'.%N You should see '(a,-void-)': ");
         print(pair);
         print("%N");

         !!letter2.make('b');
         pair.set_second(letter2);
         print("Second item set to 'b'.%N You should see '(a,b)': ");
         print(pair);
         print("%N%NTest done.%N");
      end; --test

end --class PAIR_TESTER
```

Listing 4.3 Testing the ablity of *ENHANCED_PAIR* objects to act as *PAIR* objects.

4.3 Subcontracting: Obligations of the Heir

As the previous section illustrates, because an heir inherits the contract of its ancestor, its objects may be called on to act as subcontractors for the ancestor. Specifically, if in a given situation a user routine is allowed to request a feature of an ancestor object (i.e., that feature's precondition is satisfied), then it is also allowed to request that feature of an heir object in the same situation. Therefore, if the heir redefines that feature, it may not add more restrictive preconditions to its part of the contract.

On the other hand, the subcontractor is certainly allowed to accept the job under circumstances that the contractor would have rejected. For example, suppose you rent a dwelling from Olde Fashioned Rentals Corporation and the contract for the "accept my rent" feature (if you may call it that) says: "Rent is paid by check." If Olde subcontracts the management of your abode to Plastiphile Property Management, Inc., they may modify the requirement in your favor: "Rent is paid by check **or else** rent is paid by credit card." You would not complain about that, would you? If your regular routine is to pay by check, you will not be affected by the looser precondition.

Eiffel lets the heir class loosen the precondition of its heir for a routine by using a **require else** part. Since you are not permitted to completely disregard the heir's preconditions, a simple **require** part is not allowed in a redefined routine.

The opposite is true for postconditions. If Olde promised you a specific place to live as a postcondition of the "accept my rent" feature, Plastiphile will have to do at least that much. They are not allowed to say ". . . **or else** you get a clock radio." On the other hand, if they said ". . . **and then** you will have a place to park your car," that would hardly be cause for litigation.

So the **ensure** part is not allowed in a redefined routine, but an **ensure then** part is. For example, *ENHANCED_PAIR*'s *set_first* can add another promise to its part of the contract:

```
ensure then
    last_change = 1;
```

To summarize, when an heir (the subcontractor) redefines a feature,

- Its precondition may be the same as (no **require** part at all) or more forgiving than (a **require else** part) what it was in the parent (the contractor); and
- Its postcondition may be the same as (no **ensure** part at all) or stricter than (an **ensure then** part) what it was in the parent.

4.4 When Subclassing Should *Not* Be Used

It is tempting to call the "can act as a" relationship the "is a" relationship instead, and many texts do just that. After all, an *ENHANCED_PAIR* is a *PAIR*, is it not?

Yes, it is. But the "is a" relationship includes situations that the "can act as a" relationship excludes, and vice versa. For example, a square is a rectangle, but a square cannot subcontract for a rectangle: a rectangle may be asked to take on a 2:1 aspect ratio, but a square is incapable of doing that. So, defining *SQUARE* as an heir to *RECTANGLE* is impossible.

On the other hand, a rectangle can do anything a square can do, so declaring *RECTANGLE* as an heir to *SQUARE* is perfectly reasonable. Note, however, that while "a rectangle can act as a square" holds, it makes no sense to say that "a rectangle is a square."

It is unfortunate that many object-oriented texts claim that the relationship between an heir and a parent is "is a." That claim is just a really old but bad habit. One of the "godfathers" of object-oriented programming is the discipline known as "semantic networks," and connections between nodes of those networks were actually meant to indicate "is a" relationships. (In computer science, as in many things, if something does not make sense, look for historical reasons.)

So, don't worry about what is a what, and think in terms of subcontracting instead.

4.5 What *PAIR* Should Do As Subcontractor to *ANY*

So, we have written *PAIR* as an heir to the predefined class *ANY*. Recall that we did not have much choice in the matter: *every* programmer-written class in Eiffel inherits directly or indirectly from *ANY*.

So far, being an heir to *ANY* has been nothing but advantageous. Since *ANY* defines *out* in its contract, all other classes are obligated to support it, so we can write our *PAIR*'s *out* feature in terms of *ITEM1* and *ITEM2*'s *out* features. We don't know what results they'll provide, but we know they exist.

It has also eased our implementation: Because *ANY* implements a *print* feature that prints out the result of *out*, we did not have to do anything to implement *print* in *PAIR* or *LETTER*. With a good implementation of *out*, no class needs to redefine *print*, it can just inherit its implementation from *ANY*.

Thus, we took advantage of one inherited feature without redefining it, and redefined another one. We didn't *have to* redefine *out*: *ANY*'s implementation will result in something that represents the entities in the pair, but it may not be particularly legible, will probably not be visually attractive, and is certain not to look the way we expect a pair to look ("*(x,y)*").

But *print* and *out* were not the only inherited features that we used: We also used the entity *Void* and the feature *is_equal*. What other features are in *ANY*, and how do we know what they do? We may want to redefine some of them, just like we redefined *out*!

The answer lies in *The Eiffel Library Standard* [2]. Appendix B of this book reproduces the standard interface to *ANY* for easy reference. A detailed narrative of how some of these features interact with each other appears in Section 13.3 of *Reusable Software* [6].

Note that some of *ANY*'s features are marked with the keyword **frozen**. Heirs are not permitted to redefine those features. Why? Well, observe that many of these are just features of convenience, like *print*. For example,

equal (*a*,*b*)

is just a shortcut for

(*a* = *Void* **and** *b* = *Void*)
or else
((*a* /= *Void* **and** *b* /= *Void*) **and then** *a*.*is_equal* (*b*))

so it saves you the trouble of making sure that *is_equal* is not applied to a void entity, and defines two void entities as equal. Since this shortcut is the same for all objects, there is never a reason to redefine *equal* (which is why it is frozen). If the way to compare two objects of a new class is different from the inherited way, *is_equal* is the feature to redefine.

Another category of frozen features is that of features having names prefixed with "*standard_*". They are provided and frozen so that any heir class can get to *ANY*'s original way of doing things. In this way, a class that normally uses a redefined *is_equal* can easily get to *ANY*'s version by using *standard_is_equal*.

Finally, there are features that are frozen because Eiffel relies on a specific method of their operation. These include *default*, *tagged_out* and *do_nothing*.

Of what remains, besides some system-level stuff, there are features that deal with object comparison and those that deal with object copying. The two categories are intimately related:

- Shallow copying of an object results in an object that is shallowly equal to the original.
- Deep copying of an object results in an object that is deeply equal to the original.

Let us study them using *PAIR* as the example, and see if any of them needs to be redefined in *PAIR*.

4.5.1 Comparing Pairs

Two object structures are considered equal if they track the same items in the same order. Let us see if we already have something like that in our inheritance from *ANY*.

ANY provides for two levels of comparisons: deep equality (indicated by a "*deep_*" prefix in entity name) and shallow equality (no prefix). Two objects have shallow equality if each corresponding entity within them has the same value. For example, *PAIR* objects *a* and *b*, are shallowly equal if and only if[3]:

1. <*a*'s *first*> = <*b*'s *first*>, and
2. <*a*'s *second*> = <*b*'s *second*>.

Recall that since *first* and *second* are nonexpanded entities, the "=" means "track *the same* object," not "track an equal object." Thus, a shallow copy of a pair is another pair that tracks the same items in the same order—which is just what we want! We do not need to redefine *is_equal*.

Unlike shallow equality checking, deep equality does not stop at the level of the first object. Instead, each pair of corresponding entities is checked for deep equality. Thus, *deep_equal* (*a*,*b*) is true if and only if:

1. *deep_equal* (<*a*'s *first*>,<*b*'s *first*>), and
2. *deep_equal* (<*a*'s *second*>,<*b*'s *second*>).

We do not need to redefine that either. In fact, comparing all object structures for deep equality is done the same way. We will never have to redefine *deep_equal*. However, we will soon encounter structures where the shallow equality is too shallow and will need to be redefined.

4.5.2 Copying Pairs

The section of *ANY* that lists duplication features requires some explanation.

The feature that does actual work is *copy*. If anything needs to be redefined to support heir-specific copying, it is *copy*. The deep duplication routines, *deep_copy* and *deep_clone,* are frozen (and we would not want to mess with them anyway). The rest of the features in this portion of *ANY* are just shortcuts that call on *copy* to do real work.

The command

a.copy (*b*)

copies all entities of object *b* into the corresponding entities of object *a*. If *b* has entities that refer to nonexpanded objects, then only the references are copied,

[3] I avoid the notation "*a.first*" because it only makes sense when *first* is an exported feature. In this case, all of *PAIR*'s entities are exported, but we will have other object structures that keep some entities private. Equality checks apply to all entities, exported or private.

```
frozen clone(other: ANY): like other is
        --Void if other is void; otherwise new object equal to other.
    do
        if other /= Void then
            Result := <bit-by-bit copy of other's memory>;
            Result.copy(other);
        end; --else leave Result void.
    ensure
        equal: equal(Result,other);
    end -- clone
```

Listing 4.4 The frozen implementation of *clone*, inherited from class *ANY*. (The construct "**like** *other*" is explained in Section 4.6.)

not the objects. After such copying, the corresponding nonexpanded entities in *a* will refer to *the same* objects as do the entities in *b*.

As was the case with *is_equal*, *ANY*'s version of *copy* does just what we need for *PAIR*:

1. <*a*'s *first*> := <*b*'s *first*>;
2. <*a*'s *second*> := <*b*'s *second*>.

After these assignments, *a*'s *first* and *second* entities track the same objects as *b*'s *first* and *second*, respectively, which is exactly what we wanted.

Listing 4.4 shows the typical implementation of feature *clone*.

It appears that *clone* is doing the copying twice, doesn't it? Indeed it does. It has to, because *copy* is not a creation routine, so it needs to be requested of an object that is already valid. Routine *clone* has no concept of how to make *Result* refer to a valid object, because all it knows about the result is that it is a member of some heir of *ANY*—in other words, of any class whatsoever. Thus, *clone* has no way of knowing what creation routine to use to initialize *Result*.

However, it knows that *other* is a valid object, so it plagiarizes *other*'s current state. In this way, *Result* refers to a valid object, even though it is just a duplicate of *other*.

Why does *clone* call *copy* then, which does the same thing? Because you may want to redefine *copy*, so that it does something more suitable for your class.

All right then, why doesn't the default version of *copy* just do nothing, since *clone* has already done the shallow copy? Because then the default implementation of *copy* would not be usable outside of *clone*.

The default *copy* implementation and its interaction with *clone* are suitable for *PAIR*, but in more complex object structures we will need to redefine *copy*, and in doing so we will have to take into account the exact manner in which *clone* uses it.

4.6 Specifying Types with the like Keyword

You may have noticed that in most cases, *ANY* actively avoids naming the types for its features and their parameters. Instead, it uses type specifications "**like** <entity or parameter>." For example, the interface to *copy* is:

copy (*other*: **like** *Current*)

This means that the type of *other* is the same as the type representing the class of the current object. When a *PAIR* object responds to *copy*, *other* will be of type *PAIR* (meaning that it will accept an object of class *PAIR* or one of its heirs); when *copy* is performed by a *LETTER*, *other* will be of type *LETTER* (so it will accept an object of class *LETTER* or one of its heirs), and so on.

The need for such declarations should be apparent: It is fair to expect a *LETTER* object to copy another *LETTER* object onto itself, but telling it to copy a *PAIR* onto itself is unreasonable.

4.7 Types, Classes, and Assignment

We have seen three kinds of entities:

1. Features (visible to the whole class, and perhaps requestable by other classes);
2. Locals (visible only within a feature); and
3. Parameters (visible only within a feature).

All three come with a type declaration. When we declare an entity *e* to be of type *T* ("*e*: *T*"), we tell the compiler that any object attached to *e* is capable of responding to the features provided by class *T*. To enforce this promise, the compiler will only allow assignments of compatible objects to this entity. Only objects from class *T* or from classes that are heirs to *T* are guaranteed to respond to requests for all features provided by *T*. Therefore, only such objects are allowed to be assigned to *e*.

Delving into this example a little, suppose that class *B* is an heir of class *A*, and the following code is encountered:

```
local
   a: A;
   b: B;
do
```

```
  !!a.make; --Legal
    --a may track a new object of class A.
  !!b.make; --Legal
    --b may track a new object of class B.
  a := b; --Legal
    --a tracks a B object, which can do anything an A object can.
  b := a; --Illegal
    --b's object may be asked to do things that an A object cannot do.
  !B!a.make; --Legal
    --a may track a new B object, since it can do anything an A can.
  !A!b.make; --Illegal
    --b's object may be asked to do things that an A object cannot do.
end
```

Passing an object into a parameter has the same effect—and hence the same restrictions—as making an entity track a newly made object or assigning one entity's object to another.

Summary

Inheritance is used in object-oriented programming to derive one class from another. The heir class inherits the contract from its ancestor together with the implementations of its features.

An object of the heir class must be able to act as an object of the ancestor class. This means that it must accept the same requests with the same or easier preconditions, and perform them with the same or stricter postconditions.

Since class *ANY* is an automatic heir to all classes in Eiffel, all classes are subcontractors for *ANY*. It is generally desirable to review *ANY* while writing a new class, and redefine some of the inherited features in a way that better suits the class.

Exercises

1. Implement and test *ENHANCED_PAIR*, including all applicable **require else** and **ensure then** parts.
2. When using *PAIR_TESTER* to test *ENHANCED_PAIR* as a subcontractor to *PAIR*, we did not change the type of local entity *pair*, we just created an *ENHANCED_PAIR* object and attached it to *pair*. But when we tested

ENHANCED_PAIR with *ENHANCED_PAIR_TESTER*, we did change *pair*'s type to *ENHANCED_PAIR*. Was that necessary? Why or why not?

3. Much of the code in *ENHANCED_PAIR_TESTER*'s *test* routine is a repetition of *PAIR_TESTER*'s *test*. Can inheritance be used to alleviate this duplication? If so, sketch the resulting classes and discuss the trade-offs between using inheritance and just copying the class and modifying it. If not, explain why not.

4. If *PAIR* does not redefine *out*, what does your Eiffel system produce if you *print* a pair object? (If you have access to several Eiffel systems, try it on all of them and compare the results.)

5. Draw a single diagram representing the following object structures:

   a. Entity *a* tracks a *PAIR* tracking two distinct *LETTER* objects.

   b. Entity *b* tracks a shallow copy of *a*'s object (for example, one obtained by doing "*b* := *clone* (*a*)").

   c. Entity *c* tracks a deep copy of *a*'s object (e.g., one obtained by doing "*c* := *deep_clone* (*a*)").

6. Determine if the following claims are true or false and justify your answers.

   a. "*equal* (*a*,*b*)" implies "*deep_equal* (*a*,*b*)".

   b. "*deep_equal* (*a*,*b*)" implies "*equal* (*a*,*b*)".

7. Fill in the blank with a statement that demonstrates why the statement before it is illegal.

```
local
    s: ENHANCED_PAIR[LETTER,LETTER];
do
    !PAIR[LETTER,LETTER]!s.make;
    ______________________________
end
```

8. *Void* is defined in *ANY* as a feature of type *NONE*. The assignment "*x* := *Void*" is always legal, regardless of the type of *x*. What does this say about the relationship of *NONE* to all other classes in an Eiffel system?

9. Modify *PAIR_TESTER* to test the comparison and duplication routines that *PAIR* inherits from *ANY*.

Part II

Linear Object Structures

5 Arrays

Arrays are the one object structure in this text that we will not be implementing because it is already provided to us in standard Eiffel libraries, and described in the language and library references [5, 6]. We will, however, discuss one possible way to implement it. We study class *ARRAY* because we will be using it to implement other object structures in later chapters.

5.1 What an *ARRAY* Is and What It Does

An array keeps track of objects by their relative **positions** within the array. The positions are numbered consecutively, and the range of position numbers is specified when an array is created. For example, after the entity declaration

```
x: ARRAY [SOME_TYPE];
y: ARRAY [SOME_OTHER_TYPE];
```

the statement

```
!!x.make (1,100);
```

creates an array of 100 positions ("capacity 100"), in which position number 1 ("lower bound") is first, and position number 100 ("upper bound") is last, and attaches it to entity *x*. Similarly,

```
!!y.make (−3,3);
```

attaches to *y* a new array of capacity 7 (don't forget to count position 0!), where the lowest numbered position is number −3, and the highest is number 3.

To make position n of an array x refer to object *obj1*, we use the "*put* (<what>,<where>)" feature, for example:

x.put (*obj1*,75);

makes position 75 of array x track object *obj1*.

Feature *item* (n) returns the object tracked by position n. For example,

print (*x.item* (75));

requests the *out* feature of object at position 75 and displays the result. As a shortcut, we say that an object is "at position n in array x" if it is tracked by that position of that array.

Other features of class *ARRAY* have to do with its dimensions: *lower* and *upper* result in the number of the lowest numbered position (the lower bound) and the highest numbered position (the upper bound); *count* returns the number of positions in the array (its capacity, always equal to *upper* – *lower* + 1); and *resize* (*new_lower,new_upper*) changes the bounds of an *ARRAY* object, copying it to a less crowded spot in memory if needed (as discussed in Section 5.2). Figure 5.1 shows an example of such an array.

The full interface to the standard *ARRAY* class is given in *The Eiffel Library Standard* [2] and reproduced in Appendix B.

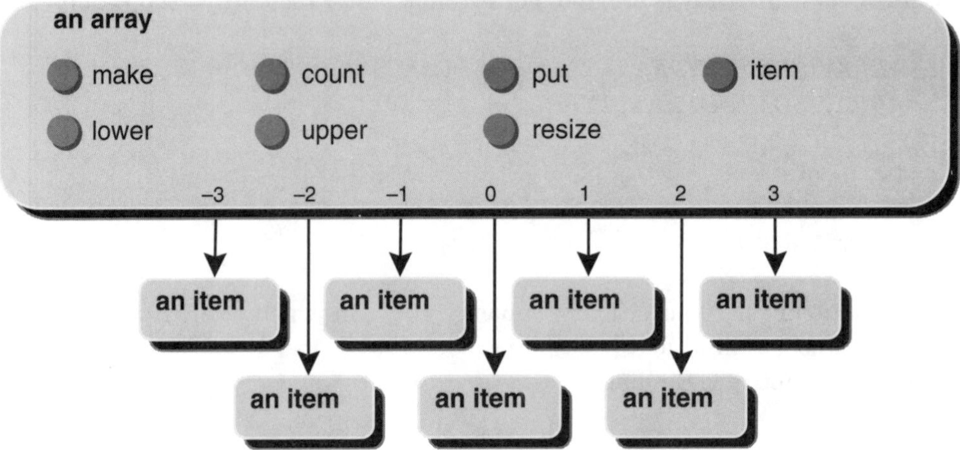

Figure 5.1 An external view of a typical *ARRAY* object. This one was created using "*make* (−3,3)" and then an item was put into each of its positions.

5.2 One Way for an *ARRAY* to Do What It Does

We do not know exactly how *ARRAY* does what it does. Implementation of class *ARRAY* is up to the supplier of the Eiffel compiler. However, most array implementations use similar techniques, and we can describe them in general.

Consider laying all the positions of array x in memory, starting at memory location a. Suppose that each array position occupies w memory units (for example, 4 bytes). Then, position $x.lower$ is at location a, position $x.lower + 1$ is at location $a + w$, position $x.lower + 2$ is at location $a + 2w$, $x.lower + 3$ is at $a + 3w$, and so on. The highest numbered position of x will be at location $a + (x.count - 1)w$.

Thus, position p of array x will be at memory location

$$a + (p - x.lower)w$$

Given a position number, subtracting the lower bound gives us how many positions from the beginning of the array one must move to get to that position. If we multiply that number by the width of each position, we get the distance from the beginning of the array in memory to the position we seek (as demonstrated in Figure 5.2).

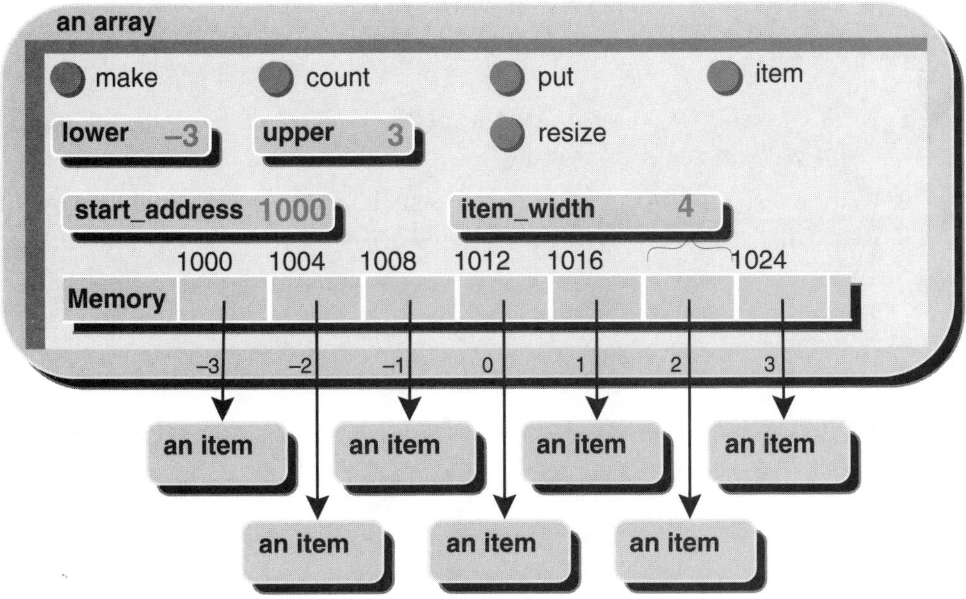

Figure 5.2 A typical internal view of the *ARRAY* shown in Figure 5.1.

This mechanism is very fast, and it works for position *x.lower* as quickly as for *x.upper* or any position between. Most array implementations use this technique.

However, in order for it to work, all positions must be lined up in a continuous segment of memory. Usually, this is not a problem. The only place this restriction is noticeable is in the implementation of *resize*: If the new lower bound is lower than the old one, or if the new upper bound is higher than the old one, a different location for all the positions may have to be found (since there may not be any vacant memory immediately below or above the space occupied by the array), requiring us to move all those object references to the new location. This is a slow operation, and it gets slower as the array gets larger (the time it takes to perform it is directly proportional to the size of the array). Thus, *resize* should be used sparingly.

Summary

An *ARRAY* keeps track of objects by numbering them. Class *ARRAY* is part of the base class library in Eiffel. It is implemented in such a way that object number *n* can be located directly, without scanning the array.

Exercises

1. What can a *PAIR* object do that an *ARRAY* object of capacity 2 (e.g., the result of "!!*a.make* (1,2)") cannot?
2. Write a class *ARRAY_TESTER* and test the class *ARRAY* that came with your Eiffel system.

6 Lists

Lists are the first nontrivial object structure we will write. In this chapter, we will consider *what* a list is and does, and then look at one variation of *how* it can do it: by using an array. In Chapter 7, we will do two more implementations.

Eiffel systems usually come with at least one *LIST* class; we will be creating our own instead of using those. Our version of *LIST* was inspired by their predecessor, presented in [3], but it offers a slightly different interface.

6.1 What a *LIST* Is and What It Does

While an *ARRAY* keeps track of objects by an *absolute* position (e.g., "the object at position 7"), a *LIST* organizes them by *relative* position ("the object immediately to the right of this object"). Positions in a *LIST* are *not* numbered.

To support this type of interface, we need to be able to, figuratively, put a finger on a position in the list and say "I want *this* one!" How can we do that without numbering the positions and specifying the number?

Consider a radio. Nowadays, there are radio tuners where one can simply punch in the frequency of a station (e.g., "89.5"), or even just its call letters ("KENW"). That is the equivalent of just saying "object at position 7" (well, position 89.5 in this case).

Believe it or not, radios were not always like that. They looked like the one shown in Figure 6.1. A long strip of paper had the stations' positions marked on it, but they were so imprecise that the best one could use them for was educated guessing. It was not possible to just point to a place on this rough scale and get the desired station. Instead, there was a needle that claimed that if you interpolated between the nearest markings on the scale and figured out what number would appear right under the needle, you would get the frequency of the carrier wave that was bringing you the noise you were hearing. To select a different station, you turned a knob. If you turned it clockwise, the

Figure 6.1 A good old-fashioned radio.

needle would move to the right; turning it counterclockwise would move the needle to the left. You knew you were at a station when the proportion of music to noise was at its best.

In fact, the radio was perfectly operable without the scale: just turn the knob to change stations in either direction. Even if you found yourself in a strange city with a receiver in which the scale had fallen off, you could still make perfectly good use of the radio: Move the needle all the way to the left, so that it is off the scale on the left side ("off-left," for short), then move it one station to the right, see if you want to listen to it, and keep moving to the right, one station at a time, until you find one you like.

We can use a similar user interface to navigate through a *LIST*: We start out on the left side (off-left), and move to the right until we are at the item we want—for whatever reason we want it. We may end up going all the way off-right. Inside the *LIST* we also have a needle, but, being sophisticated computer scientists, we call it a "cursor" instead of a "needle." (A **cursor** is something that indicates current position.)

6.1.1 Moving the Cursor

Thus, we start out with an external view of a *LIST* shown in Figure 6.2, with features *move_left* and *move_right*. The precondition for *move_left* is that we can be anywhere but off-left, and for *move_right*, we can be anywhere but off-right. To be able to specify these preconditions, and to give our user a way to check whether or not the cursor is off-left or off-right, we supply Boolean features *is_off_left* and *is_off_right*. This leads us to the skeleton in Listing 6.1. Note

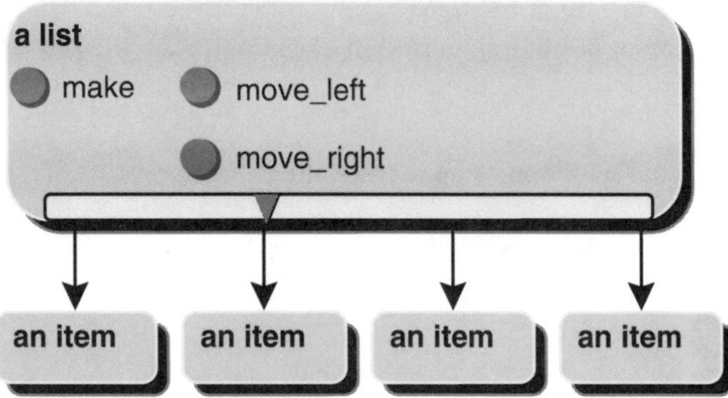

Figure 6.2 External view of a *LIST* object, take 1: obvious movement routines. (This one tracks four items, the cursor is on the second one.)

```
class LIST[ITEM]
creation make

feature
   is_off_left: BOOLEAN is
         --Is the cursor off-left?
      do
         .
         .
         .
      end; --is_off_left

   is_off_right: BOOLEAN is
         --Is the cursor off-right?
      do
         .
         .
         .
      end; --is_off_right

   move_left is
         --Move the cursor one step to the left.
      require
         not_off_left: not is_off_left;
      do
         .
         .
         .
      ensure
```

Listing 6.1 Definition of class *LIST*, take 1: essential movement routines.

```
            not_off_right: not is_off_right;
            --The cursor is one step to the left of where it was.
        end; --move_left

    move_right is
            --Move the cursor one step to the right.
        require
            not_off_right: not is_off_right;
        do
            .
            .
            .
        ensure
            not_off_left: not is_off_left;
            --The cursor is one step to the right of where it was.
        end; --move_right

invariant
    not_both_off_left_and_off_right: not (is_off_left and is_off_right);
end --class LIST
```

Listing 6.1 *(continued)*

that we have not yet committed ourselves to deciding whether *is_off_left* and *is_off_right* will be functions or entities: That is an implementation decision.

These four routines are all the user needs to move around the list. However, there are two other movements that are often useful: moving all the way off-left and moving all the way off-right. We do not *have* to provide them, because the user can simply use what we already offer in a loop (we will discuss Eiffel loops in detail in Section 6.3.3), for example:

```
from
until the_list.is_off_left
loop
    the_list.move_left;
end
```

Yet, for convenience and efficiency, we can provide routines *move_off_left* and *move_off_right* that do the job. These features are common enough that by supplying them in class *LIST* we can save users from repeating loops like the preceding one in their code, thus making the whole system easier to maintain and debug. Besides, when we get to implementing them, we will find that we

```
move_off_left is
        --Move the cursor to the off-left position.
    do
        .
        .
        .
    ensure
        off_left: is_off_left;
    end; --move_off_left

move_off_right is
        --Move the cursor to the off-right position.
    do
        .
        .
        .
    ensure
        off_right: is_off_right;
    end; --move_off_right
```

Listing 6.2 Additional movement routines for the definition of class *LIST*.

can do it much more efficiently than stepping through the whole list. (Even in the radio analogy, one can just spin the knob to the left until the needle stops off-left—there is no need to stop at every station on the way!)

Thus, we add the routines in Listing 6.2 to the skeleton in Listing 6.1, giving us the external view in Figure 6.3.

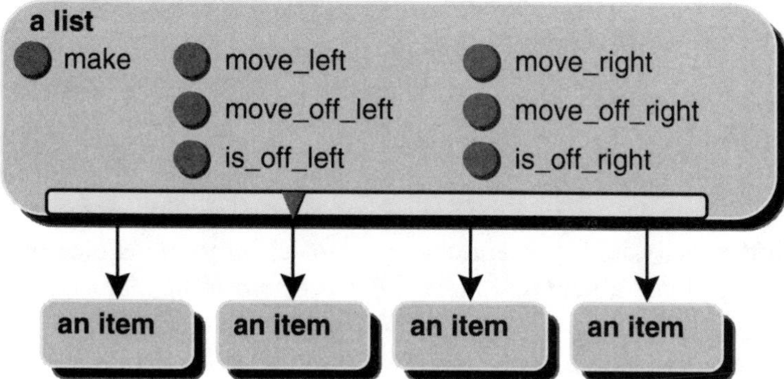

Figure 6.3 External view of a *LIST* object, take 2: all features that support movement.

6.1.2 What an Empty *LIST* Looks Like

Having described how *move_left*, *move_right*, *move_off_left*, *move_off_right*, *is_off_left*, and *is_off_right* interact, we can specify what an empty *LIST* looks like. If a *LIST* is empty, then:

1. There are no items in it;
2. It is either off-left or off-right (since there are no items for the cursor to be on);
3. If it is off-left and *move_right* is requested, it will become off-right; and
4. If it is off-right and *move_left* is requested, it will become off-left.

The four features that are most affected by these observations are *make*, since it has to make a new empty list; *is_empty*, which reports if the list is empty; *wipe_out*, which empties a list; and *length*, which reports how many items are in the list (the first observation could be written as "*length* = 0").

Before we use these properties in pre- and postconditions of specific routines, let us see if any of them relate to a *LIST* object as a whole, so that we can list them in the class invariant. Since the invariant is a Boolean expression, it can only contain requests of features that are entities or functions (and not procedures, since procedure calls cannot appear inside an expression). This restriction eliminates from consideration the *move_*. . . features and leaves *is_off_left*, *is_off_right*, *is_empty*, and *length*. Indeed, these *are* related for all objects, so we upgrade the class invariant to the following:

```
invariant
    not_both_off_left_and_off_right: not (is_off_left and is_off_right);
    not_on_item_if_empty: is_empty implies (is_off_left or is_off_right);
    empty_iff_zero_length: is_empty = (length = 0);
    length_not_negative: length >= 0;
```

Now we can look at postconditions of *make*. The first and most obvious one is that the list is empty. According to the class invariant, this automatically means that its length is zero. But is it off-left or off-right? We must either make a choice and specify it in the contract, or not specify our choice at all, thus forcing the user to do an explicit *move_off_left* or *move_off_right* right after the *make*. Since any choice we make in the first option is arbitrary, the second option is the most general one. However, having *make* leave the new *LIST* object in an unknown state makes me nervous, so let us choose *is_off_left* as a postcondition of *make*.

For consistency, we make the same choice for *wipe_out*. This adds the features in Listing 6.3 to the class skeleton.

```
make is
        --Initialize to get an empty, off-left list.
    do
        .
        .
        .
    ensure
        empty: is_empty;
        off_left: is_off_left;
    end; --make

wipe_out is
        --Make this list empty and off-left.
    do
        .
        .
        .
    ensure
        empty: is_empty;
        off_left: is_off_left;
    end; --wipe_out

is_empty: BOOLEAN is
        --Is this list empty?
    do
        .
        .
        .
    end; --is_empty

length: INTEGER is
        --The number of items currently in this list.
    do
        .
        .
        .
    end; --length
```

Listing 6.3 Routines that deal with an empty list.

6.1.3 Moving Items In and Out of the Lists

To add a new item to the list, we insert it near the cursor. We cannot insert it exactly *under* the cursor, since there is something there already: either an item, or an off-left or off-right delimiter. We can, however, insert the new item immediately to the left or immediately to the right of the cursor. Not knowing whether the insert-on-left or insert-on-right behavior will be more convenient to our user, we will provide both features: *insert_on_left* and *insert_on_right*. Of course, restrictions apply to when these features may be requested: One cannot insert to the left of an off-left cursor or to the right of an off-right cursor; and it is impossible to insert into a list that is already full (we will need to provide an *is_full* feature to make the latter an enforceable precondition). Finally, we need to specify what happens to the cursor after the insertion: Does it stay with the same item, or move to the new one? Let us make it stay with the same item. The skeleton of these features is shown in Listing 6.4.

Feature *delete* deletes the item under the cursor from the list. For this to work, the cursor can be neither off-left nor off-right. Also, it has to move a step either to the left or to the right, because it cannot stay with the deleted item; since the choice is, once again, arbitrary, we will move it a step to the right. This routine's skeleton is also shown in Listing 6.4.

```
is_full: BOOLEAN is
        --Is there no room in this list for one more item?
    do
        .
        .
        .
    end; --is_full

insert_on_left(new_item: ITEM) is
        --Insert new_item to the left of the cursor.
    require
        not_full: not is_full;
        not_off_left: not is_off_left;
    do
        .
        .
        .
    ensure
        one_more_item: length = old length + 1;
        --The cursor is on the same item as it was before.
    end; --insert_on_left

insert_on_right(new_item: ITEM) is
        --Insert new_item to the right of the cursor.
    require
        not_full: not is_full;
        not_off_right: not is_off_right;
```

Listing 6.4 Routines that move items in and out of the list.

```
    do
        .
        .
        .
    ensure
        one_more_item: length = old length + 1;
        --The cursor is on the same item as it was before.
    end; --insert_on_right
delete is
        --Remove the item under the cursor from the list.
    require
        not_off_left: not is_off_left;
        not_off_right: not is_off_right;
    do
        .
        .
        .
    ensure
        one_less_item: length = old length - 1;
        --The cursor is on the item to the right of the deleted one.
    end; --delete

item: ITEM is
        --The item under the cursor.
    require
        not_off_left: not is_off_left;
        not_off_right: not is_off_right;
    do
        .
        .
        .
    end; --item

replace (new_item: ITEM) is
        --Replaces the item under the cursor with new_item.
    require
        not_off_left: not is_off_left;
        not_off_right: not is_off_right;
    do
        .
        .
        .
    ensure
        item_replaced: item = new_item;
        length_unchanged: length = old length;
    end; --replace
```

Listing 6.4 *(continued)*

Note how the pre- and postconditions and the class invariant cooperate: It is not necessary to state "**not** *is_empty*" in the precondition of *delete*, since the conjunction of assertions *not_off_left* and *not_off_right* in the precondition and *not_on_item_if_empty* in the invariant is logically equivalent to "**not** *is_empty*."

Similarly, it would have been redundant to state "**not** *is_empty*" in the postcondition of *insert_on_left* and *insert_on_right*, since the conjunction of *length_incremented* with *length_not_negative* and *empty_iff_zero_length* is equivalent to "**not** *is_empty*."

If the user needs to replace an item that is under the cursor with a new one, the following combination of steps can be taken:

```
the_list.delete;
the_list.insert_on_left(new_item);
```

However, it is both nice and more efficient to provide a routine to replace the item, so we added its skeleton to Listing 6.4.

Finally, we need a function that returns to the user the item that is under the cursor. We will simply call it *item*, as shown in Listing 6.4.

6.1.4 The String Representation

Next, we provide the routine *out*, which returns the string representation of its object. Among other things, it will allow the user to say "*print*(*the_list*)" and get consistent and meaningful output. For a list, we will have *out* result in a string of the form

"< <1st item>.*out* <2nd item>.*out* . . . <last item>.*out* >"

As we did with class *PAIR*, we allow void items into the list, and replace them with `"-void-"` in *out*'s result.

6.1.5 Comparing and Duplicating

As usual, we provide the *is_equal* feature. Two lists are equal if they keep track of *the same* (not just equal) items in the same order. We do not insist that their cursors match too—for that we provide a separate *cursor_matches* feature, which determines whether the two lists' cursors are the same number of steps away from the left edge of their respective lists. (We have to measure the distance from a specified end of the list, since the lists may not be of the same length.)

A copy of a list is a new list that is interchangeable with the original. That means that the copy and the original are equal (but not the same list), and their cursors match. As we discussed in Chapter 4, only *copy* needs to be redefined; *clone* calls it to do the copying.

We add these skeletons to the class, as shown in Listing 6.5.

```
out: STRING is
        --Returns "< <1st item>.out . . . <last item>.out >".
    do
        .
        .
        .
    end; --out

is_equal (other: LIST): BOOLEAN is
        --Do this list and other keep track
        --of the same items in the same order?
    do
        .
        .
        .
    end; --is_equal

cursor_matches (other: like Current): BOOLEAN is
        --Is this list's cursor the same distance
        --from off-left as other's cursor?
    do
        .
        .
        .
    end; --cursor_matches

copy (other: like Current) is
        --Copies other onto Current.
    do
        .
        .
        .
    ensure then
        copy_same_cursor: cursor_matches (other);
    end; --copy
```

Listing 6.5 String representation, comparison and copying features.

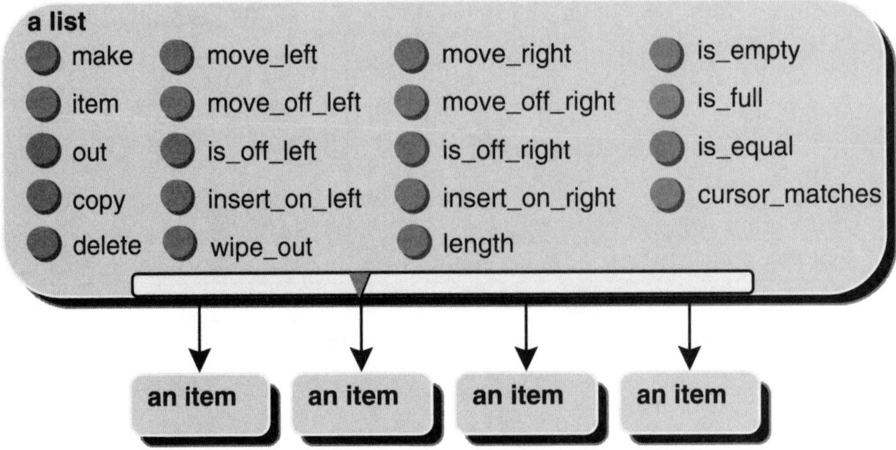

Figure 6.4 Complete outside view of a *LIST* object.

6.1.6 The Contract

This concludes our specification of a *LIST*. The resulting outside view is shown in Figure 6.4. Putting all these skeletons together, we get the contract. To save printing space, we present it after discussing deferred classes in the next section.

6.2 How a *LIST* Does What It Does: Multiple Implementations

The *LIST* is the first object structure for which we will provide multiple implementations. First, let us address the logistics of doing that.

One way to do multiple implementations is to have a copy of the class *LIST* for each implementation, and simply compile in the one we want to use. The problem with this approach is that if we do make changes in the interface (the contract), we will have to remember to make them in all three versions. Alas, experience shows that human memory is not a tool suitable for keeping multiple versions of software synchronized.

6.2.1 Using a Deferred Class to Keep the Contract

Instead, what we can do is set up a little hierarchy of classes. At the top will be a **deferred** class called "*LIST 1*", which will be the keeper of the contract, but will have no implementation. For each implementation, we will create a subclass of *LIST*. As subcontractors, objects in those classes will have to follow contracts that are compatible to *LIST* objects (see the section on subcontracting).

The resulting class *LIST* is shown in Listing 6.6. While we were at it, we reorganized the routines under several **feature** sections.

```
deferred class LIST[ITEM] inherit
   ANY
      undefine --to make them deferred
         out, is_equal, copy
      redefine --to add comments or improve the contract
         out, is_equal, copy
      end;

feature --Creation and initialization
   make is
         --Initialize to get an empty, off-left list.
      deferred
      ensure
         empty: is_empty;
         off_left: is_off_left;
      end; --make

feature --Moving through the list

   move_left is
         --Move the cursor one step to the left.
      require
         not_off_left: not is_off_left;
      deferred
      ensure
         not_off_right: not is_off_right;
         --The cursor is one step to the left of where it was.
      end; --move_left

   move_right is
         --Move the cursor one step to the right.
      require
         not_off_right: not is_off_right;
      deferred
      ensure
         not_off_left: not is_off_left;
         --The cursor is one step to the right of where it was.
      end; --move_right
```

Listing 6.6 Deferred class *LIST* with the contract.

```
move_off_left is
        --Move the cursor to the off-left position.
    deferred
    ensure
        off_left: is_off_left;
    end; --move_off_left

move_off_right is
        --Move the cursor to the off-right position.
    deferred
    ensure
        off_right: is_off_right;
    end; --move_off_right

is_off_left: BOOLEAN is
        --Is the cursor off-left?
    deferred
    end; --is_off_left

is_off_right: BOOLEAN is
        --Is the cursor off-right?
    deferred
    end; --is_off_right

feature --Moving items into and out of the list

insert_on_left(new_item: ITEM) is
        --Insert new_item to the left of the cursor.
    require
        not_full: not is_full;
        not_off_left: not is_off_left;
    deferred
    ensure
        one_more_item: length = old length + 1;
        --The cursor is on the same item as it was before.
    end; --insert_on_left

insert_on_right(new_item: ITEM) is
        --Insert new_item to the right of the cursor.
    require
        not_full: not is_full;
        not_off_right: not is_off_right;
    deferred
    ensure
        one_more_item: length = old length + 1;
        --The cursor is on the same item as it was before.
    end; --insert_on_right
```

Listing 6.6 *(continued)*

```
delete is
        --Remove the item under the cursor from the list.
    require
        not_off_left: not is_off_left;
        not_off_right: not is_off_right;
    deferred
    ensure
        one_less_item: length = old length - 1;
        --The cursor is on the item to the right of the deleted one.
    end; --delete

wipe_out is
        --Make this list empty and off-left.
    deferred
    ensure
        empty: is_empty;
        off_left: is_off_left;
    end; --wipe_out

replace (new_item: ITEM) is
        --Replaces the item under the cursor with new_item.
    require
        not_off_left: not is_off_left;
        not_off_right: not is_off_right;
    deferred
    ensure
        item_replaced: item = new_item;
        length_unchanged: length = old length;
    end; --replace

item: ITEM is
        --The item under the cursor.
    deferred
    end; --item

feature --Sizing

is_empty: BOOLEAN is
        --Is this list empty?
    deferred
    end; --is_empty

is_full: BOOLEAN is
        --Is there no room in this list for one more item?
    deferred
    end; --is_full
```

Listing 6.6 *(continued)*

```
   length: INTEGER is
         --The number of items currently in this list.
      deferred
      end; --length

feature --Comparisons and copying

   is_equal (other: like Current): BOOLEAN is
         --Do this list and other keep track
         --of the same items in the same order?
      deferred
      end; --is_equal

   cursor_matches (other: like Current): BOOLEAN is
         --Is this list's cursor the same distance
         --from off-left as other's cursor?
      deferred
      end; --cursor_matches

   copy (other: like Current) is
         --Copies other onto current.
      deferred
      ensure then
         copy_same_cursor: cursor_matches (other);
      end; --copy

feature --Conversions

   out: STRING is
         --"< <1st item>.out ... <last item>.out >".
      deferred
      end; --out

invariant

   not_both_off_left_and_off_right: not (is_off_left and is_off_right);
   not_on_item_if_empty: is_empty implies (is_off_left or is_off_right);
   empty_iff_zero_length: is_empty = (length = 0);
   length_not_negative: length >= 0;

end --class LIST
```

Listing 6.6 *(continued)*

6.3 An Implementation Using an *ARRAY*

In our first implementation, we use an *ARRAY* object inside the *LIST* object to keep track of the items. Recall that in Eiffel, *ARRAY* objects are resizable, but the resizing can be very expensive. Thus, we want to avoid automatic resizing: Chances are that if the user picked the array implementation, they know the maximum size they will need. All we have to do is provide a way for them to specify the list's capacity when they create it.

For compatibility with the contract, we will have a *make* routine with no parameters that picks its own capacity. In addition, we will provide routines *make_capacity* and *resize* that take capacity as a parameter, allowing our user to specify and explicitly (since it is expensive) change the capacity of a list.

Now that we have decided to use an array of a given capacity (let us name it "*items*") and that the capacity may change during execution (if the user calls *resize*), we know that we need an entity, *capacity*, whose value is the current capacity. Also, since we will not be using the entire array all of the time, we need an entity to keep track of the current length of the list—but we already have it: We can use the feature *length* that we inherited from class *LIST*. Thus, the items in the list may be accessed as *items.item* (1), . . . , *items.item* (*length*). The current position of the cursor is just a number in the range [1, . . . , *length*], and we will create an entity called "*cursor*" to hold it. This gives us the internal view of a list as shown in Figure 6.5.

We now have enough information to get started on writing the code, in particular: to redefine inherited features *is_empty* and *is_full*; to define new private features *items* and *cursor* and a new public feature *capacity* as entities; and to define the inherited feature *length* as an *INTEGER* entity.

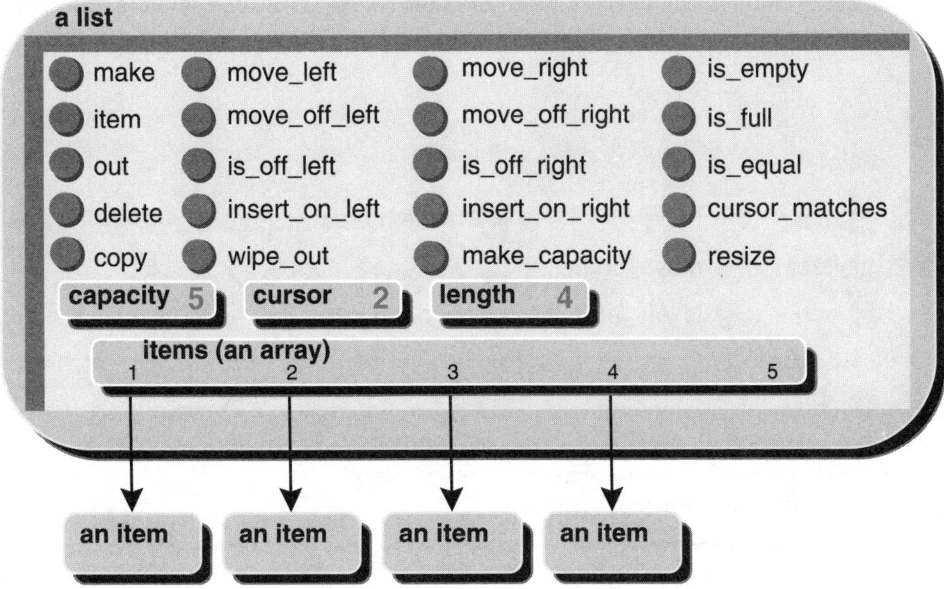

Figure 6.5 The internal view of a *LIST_ARRAY* object. This particular list is of capacity 5, has 4 items in it (in positions 1 through 4), and the cursor is on the item in position 2.

6.3.1 Off-Left, Off-Right, and Empty *LIST*

Before we can write *make*, though, we need to visualize the empty *LIST_ARRAY*. It would have some capacity; the length would be 0; and the cursor would be either off-right or off-left . . . for which we have no position numbers! How do we indicate "off-left" and "off-right?"

To answer that question, we need to first implement *move_left* and *move_right*. Then, using *move_left* when the cursor is on the leftmost item (position 1 in this implementation) should yield an off-left cursor; similarly, using *move_right* when the cursor is on the rightmost item (position *length*) should give us an off-right cursor.

To move a cursor one step to the left, we simply need to decrement the *cursor* entity, and increment it to move one step to the right. Now we see that the list is off-left when $cursor = 0$ and off-right when $cursor = length + 1$, so the range of the *cursor* entity is actually $[0, \ldots, length + 1]$.

6.3.2 Creating a *LIST*

Now we are ready to write *make* and *make_capacity*: They need to create an object that looks like the one in Figure 6.6. In fact, the implementations of *resize*, *is_off_left*, *is_off_right*, *move_off_left*, and *move_off_right* also fall into place. The result is the early version of class *LIST_ARRAY*, which is shown in Listing 6.7.

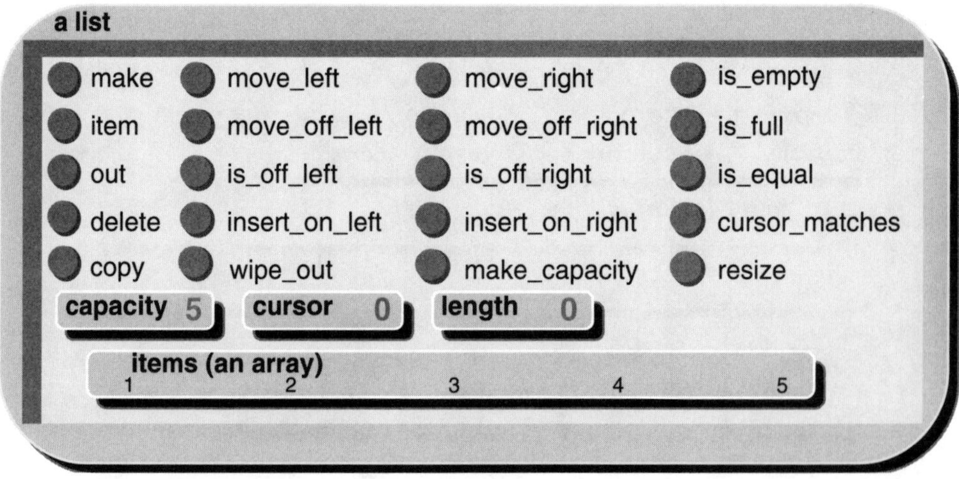

Figure 6.6 An empty *LIST_ARRAY* object of capacity 5. This one is off-left, as would be made by *make* according to its postcondition.

```
class LIST_ARRAY[ITEM] inherit
   LIST[ITEM]
creation make, make_capacity
feature {LIST_ARRAY} --Visible only to similar lists
   items: ARRAY[ITEM];
         --The array tracking the items.
   cursor: INTEGER;
         --Index within items of the item under the cursor.
feature --Creation, initialization, resizing
   make is
         --Initialize to get an empty, off-left list
         --of default capacity.
      do
         make_capacity(100); --Default capacity.
      end; --make
   make_capacity(initial_capacity: INTEGER) is
         --Initialize to get an empty, off-left list
         --of capacity initial_capacity.
      require
         initial_capacity >= 0;
      do
         capacity := initial_capacity;
         !!items.make(1,initial_capacity); --First item is always at index 1.
         length := 0; --Start out empty.
         cursor := 0; --Start out off-left.
      end; --make_capacity
   resize(new_capacity: INTEGER) is
         --Resizes the list to new_capacity. Could be very expensive.
      require
         new_capacity > = 0;
      do
         capacity := new_capacity;
         items.resize(1, new_capacity); --First item is always at index 1.

         --May have to truncate this list to fit the new array.
         if cursor > capacity+1 then
            cursor := capacity + 1;
         end;
         if length > capacity then
            length := capacity;
```

Listing 6.7 Initial sketch of class *LIST_ARRAY*: features dealing with initialization, sizing, and movement through lists.

```
            end;
        end; --resize

    feature --Sizing

        capacity: INTEGER;
                --Current capacity.

        length: INTEGER;
                --The number of items currently in this list.

        is_empty: BOOLEAN is
                --Is this list empty?
            do
                Result := length = 0;
            end; --is_empty

        is_full: BOOLEAN is
                --Is there is no room in this list for one more item?
            do
                Result := length = capacity;
            end; --is_full
    feature --Moving through the list

        move_left is
                --Move the cursor one step to the left.
            do
                cursor := cursor - 1;
            end; --move_left

        move_right is
                --Move the cursor one step to the right.
            do
                cursor := cursor + 1;
            end; --move_right

        move_off_left is
                --Move the cursor to the off-left position.
            do
                cursor := 0;
            end; --move_off_left

        move_off_right is
                --Move the cursor to the off-right position.
            do
                cursor := length + 1;
            end; --move_off_right
```

Listing 6.7 *(continued)*

```
    is_off_left: BOOLEAN is
            --Is the cursor off-left?
        do
            Result := cursor = 0;
        end; --is_off_left

    is_off_right: BOOLEAN is
            --Is the cursor off-right?
        do
            Result := cursor = length+1;
        end; --is_off_right

invariant

    capacity_not_negative: 0 <= capacity;
    length_in_range: length <= capacity;
    cursor_in_range: 0 <= cursor and cursor <= length+1;
    good_array: items /= Void and then
                    items.count = capacity and items.lower = 1;

end --class LIST_ARRAY
```

Listing 6.7 *(continued)*

Particular care has to be taken with *resize*. What do we do when the new capacity is smaller than the list's current length? There are two options:

1. No problem, just truncate the list; or
2. This is an error.

This should be discussed with the user. If the first option is preferred, then the implementation of *resize* used in Listing 6.7 is appropriate: just truncate the list to fit the smaller capacity.

On the other hand, if it is an error to remake the list into one too small to continue tracking the same items, then the precondition "*new_capacity*>= *length*" must be added to the description of *resize* in *LIST_ARRAY*'s contract. (This will not disturb *LIST*'s contract, since *resize* is not mentioned there at all. A user who relies on *LIST*'s contract for list creation will not attempt to resize it.)

The invariant in Listing 6.7 is different from invariants we have seen before, in that it talks about hidden features: *cursor* and *items*. This is known as an **implementation invariant.** When the program `short` extracts the interface of this class, it leaves out assertions that talk about hidden features (we do not want to tie our hands by giving out details of our current implementation, do we?). They are *not* part of the contract; they are just safety checks we put in for our own benefit. Our user will never see them (unless we show him or her our source code).

6.3.3 Inserting and Deleting *ITEMs*

With *move_left* and *move_right*, we started with a routine that would work in the middle of the list, and then adapted the internal object structure so that the same routines work at both ends (thus defining "off-left" and "off-right"). We will use the same strategy with *insert_on_left*, *insert_on_right*, and *delete*.

Let us consider *insert_on_left* first. We start with the list in Figure 6.7a. To insert *new_item* to the left of the cursor, we need to make room for it. The easiest way to do this is to "smudge" the object references by one position to the right, as shown with the arrows. Great care must be taken in the order in which this copying to the right is done: If we start with *cursor* and copy its item to the right, then we will lose the connection to the item that was on the right of the cursor! We will end up with the cursor's item smudged all the way to off-right. Instead, we must copy the last item's reference one position to the right, then the one before it, then the one before it, and so on, as shown in the figure. This results in Figure 6.7b. Finally, we attach *new_item* to the slot we made available, giving us Figure 6.7c.

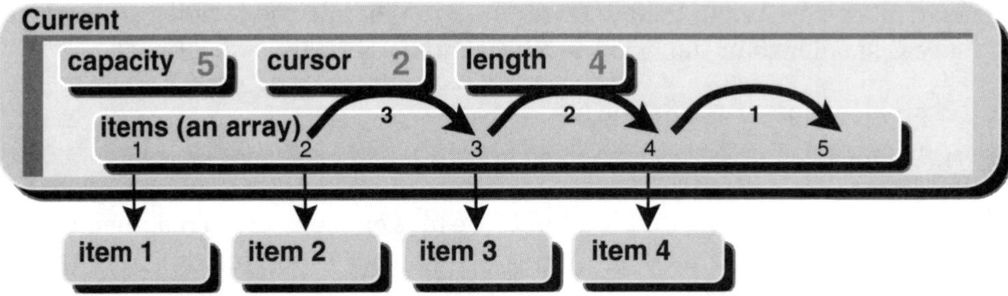

a. The order of copying needed to make room for *new_item*.

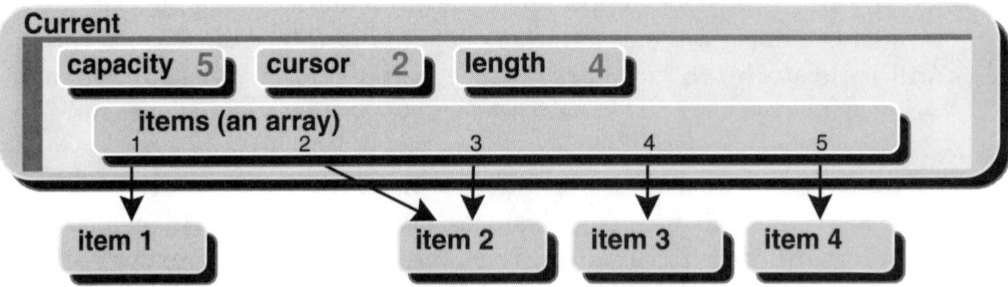

b. Room has been made for *new_item* to the left of *cursor*.

Figure 6.7 Responding to request "*insert_on_left*(*new_item*)". (The object's routines are still there, they were omitted to save page space.)

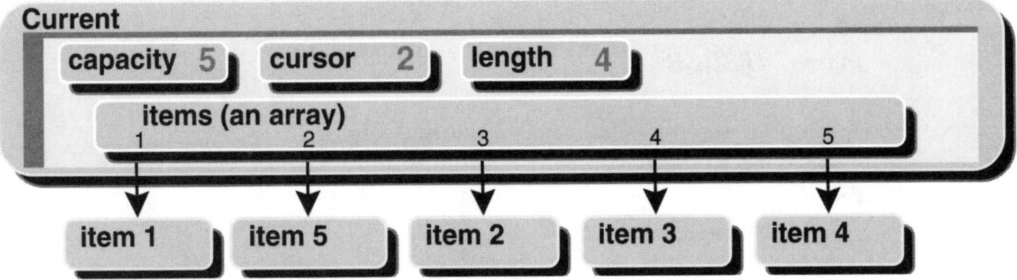

c. Item *new_item* is in the correct place.

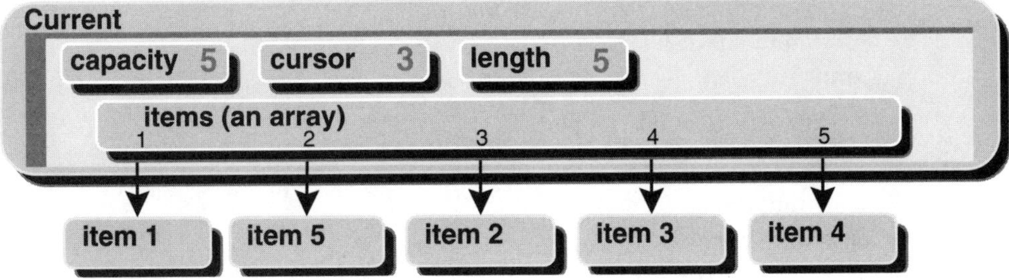

d. A promise is a promise.

Figure 6.7 *(continued)*

Are we done? Well, let's check the postconditions:

1. *length* = **old** *length* + 1 (oops!)
2. ––The cursor is on the same item as it was before (oops again!)

We are not done yet. We need to increment *length* to keep up with the new list length, and increment *cursor* to keep it at the same item as it was before. This takes us into Figure 6.7d. Now are we done? That depends on whether we are still obeying the class invariant (otherwise, we cause the list to be invalid). A check of the class invariant shows that it was not affected by these changes.

Knowing what needs to be done, we write the Eiffel routine *insert_on_left*, as shown in Listing 6.8.

The repetitive copying of object references within the array is done using the Eiffel **loop** statement. Its form is[1]

from
<things to do before the loop starts>
until
<exit condition>

[1]This is a simplified form of **loop**. The complete form is presented in Section 12.2.1.

```
insert_on_left (new_item: ITEM) is
        --Insert new_item to the left of the cursor.
    local
        index: INTEGER;
    do
        --Smudge the items between cursor and length
        --one step to the right.
        from
            index := length;
        until
            index < cursor
        loop
            items.put (items.item (index), index+1);
            index := index - 1;
        end;

        --Put new_item into its place.
        items.put (new_item, cursor);

        --Fulfill the postconditions.
        cursor := cursor + 1;
        length := length + 1;
    end; --insert_on_left

delete is
        --Remove the item under the cursor from the list.
    local
        index: INTEGER;
        void_item: ITEM;
    do
        --Smudge the items between cursor+1 and length
        --one step to the left.
        from
            index := cursor + 1;
        until
            index > length
        loop
            items.put (items.item (index), index-1);
            index := index + 1;
        end;

        --Disconnect the rightmost item from its former position
        --(for future garbage collection).
        items.put (void_item, length);

        --Fulfill the postconditions.
        length := length - 1;
        --cursor is already where it belongs.
    end; --delete
```

Listing 6.8 Features *insert_on_left* and *delete* of class *LIST_ARRAY*.

loop
<things to do repeatedly until the exit condition is true (loop body)>
end

You may have programmed in a language where the loop has an automatic increment mechanism; Eiffel **loop** does not have one. If we want *index* to be incremented by 1 before the body of the loop is executed again, we put an explicit "*item*:=*item*+1" statement at the end of the loop body.

Deleting the item under the cursor requires that the same steps be taken in reverse order, as shown in Figure 6.8. The Eiffel code for that operation is shown also in Listing 6.8.

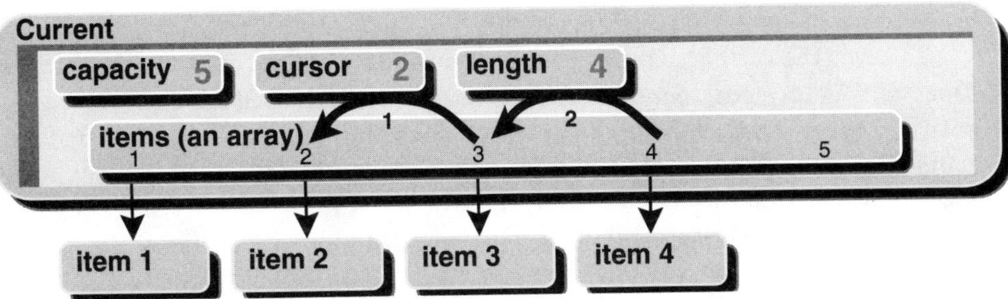

a. The order of copying needed to remove the hole that would be left by deleting the item under the cursor.

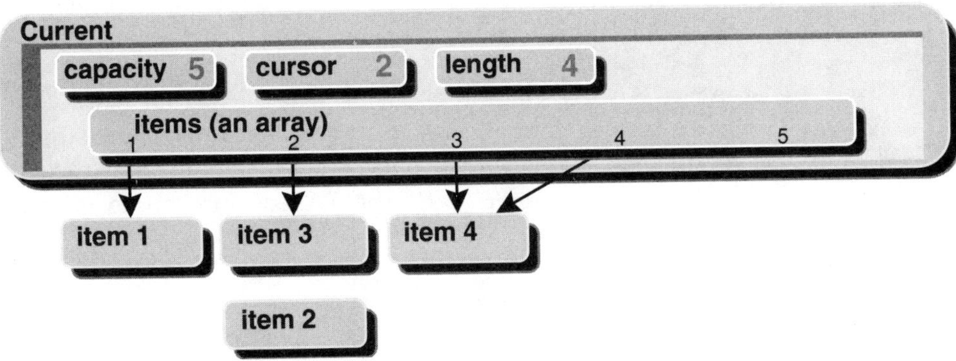

b. The item that was under the cursor has been removed from the list and cast adrift (if there are no entities tracking it, it will be picked up by the garbage collector). Due to the nature of the compaction, the value of *cursor* is such that the cursor is over the item to the right of the one that got deleted, which is what the postcondition requires.

Figure 6.8 Responding to request "*delete*". (The object's routines are not shown to save page space.)

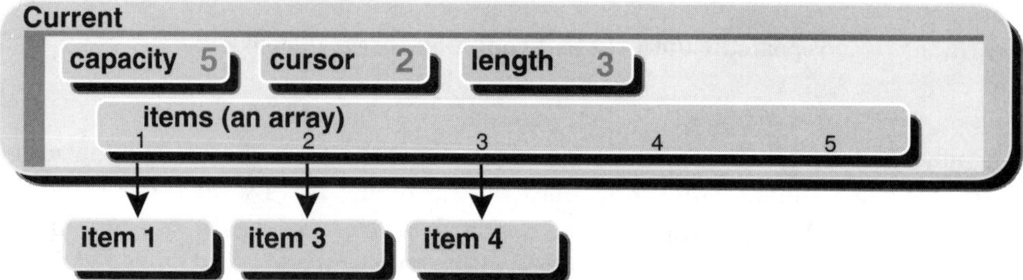

c. The tracking information in the last position has been wiped out. The remaining postcondition has been taken care of.

Figure 6.8 *(continued)*

To sever the connection from the last position of the array to the rightmost item, *delete* puts *void_item* into that position. The local feature *void_item* is an entity of type *ITEM* that is left at its initial value (void). We cannot just use "*Void*" in its place, because of a deep-rooted rule in the Eiffel language; let us just leave it at that.[2]

Finally, consider *wipe_out*. There are three things to do there:

1. Reset the length to zero.
2. Reset the cursor to off-left.
3. Set adrift the items that the array had been tracking (some of them may get garbage-collected at this time).

Since the standard *ARRAY* class does not provide a *wipe_out* feature, we would have to write a loop to do the last step. It is easier to just recreate the array! But if we do that, we end up with a routine that is just like *make_capacity*, except it does not change *capacity*. So the easiest thing to do is to let *make_capacity* do the work:

```
wipe_out is
        --Make this list empty and off-left.
    do
        make_capacity(capacity); --Start from scratch, same capacity.
    end;--wipe_out
```

[2]Some Eiffel systems actually do allow *Void* to be used here, but the "void entity of type *ITEM*" solution *always* works.

6.3.4 *Is_equal*

Two lists are equal if they track the same items in the same order. At first glance, it may seem that all we need to do is ask the arrays inside them if they are equal. If we do, however, we may not get the right answer, since we do not want to compare *all* positions in those arrays. We only care about comparing items that are within the lists: positions 1 through. . . *length*? But the lists could have different lengths! Well, if they do, they are not equal. We can check this condition before we even bother comparing respective items. Listing 6.9 shows the implementation.

6.3.5 Copying and Cloning

We saw in Section 4.5.2 how *clone* first makes its *Result* a bit-by-bit copy of the original object, and then requests "*Result.copy* (<original>)" (Listing 4.4). That bit-by-bit copy has a major (and unpleasant) influence on how we redefine *copy*.

```
is_equal (other: like Current): BOOLEAN is
        --Do this list and other keep track
        --of the same items in the same order?
    local
        index: INTEGER;
    do
        if length /= other.length then
            --Can't be equal, so no sense going through the loop.
            Result := false;

        else

            from
                Result :=true; --Equal until proven unequal.
                index := 1;
            until
                Result = false --Exit as soon as inequality is detected
                or index > length --or when the list ends.
            loop
                Result := items.item (index) = other.items.item (index);
                index := index + 1;
            end;

        end;
    end; --is_equal
```

Listing 6.9 Feature *is_equal* of class *LIST_ARRAY*.

```
copy (other: like Current) is
        --Copy other onto Current.
    local
        index: INTEGER;
        void_item: ITEM;
    do
        --Start from scratch.
        make_capacity (other.capacity);

        length := other.length;
        cursor := other.cursor;

        --Copy all the item references.
        from
            index := 1;
        until
            index > length
        loop
            items.put (other.items.item (index), index);
            index := index + 1;
        end;
    end; --copy
```

Listing 6.10 Feature *copy* for class *LIST_ARRAY*.

If it was not for *clone*, copying *other* onto *Current* would mean resizing *items* if necessary to *other.length*, copying the item references from *other*, and wiping out the item references in positions between *other.length* and *Current*'s old length.

But if *copy* has been called from *clone*, then *Current*'s *items* is a reference to the same array as *other.items*! Whatever we do to *items* will just be done to *other.items*, no real copying happens. This situation, when several entities unexpectedly refer to the same object, is called **aliasing** (more on that in Section 15.5).

So to account for the possibility that *copy* is executing by request from *clone*, we have to disconnect *items* from the aliased array, and create a new one, using "!!*items*." The resulting routine is given in Listing 6.10.

6.3.6 String Representation

Just as we could not use *items.is_equal*, we could not use *items.out* even if class *ARRAY* provided a good *out* feature (which it does not). It is up to us to write a feature that results in a string of the form specified in *out*'s description. One such implementation is shown in Listing 6.11.

```
out: STRING is
        --Returns "< <1st item>.out . . . <last item>.out >".
    local
        index: INTEGER;
    do
        Result = clone("< "); --Left delimiter.
        from
            index := 1;
        until
            index > length
        loop
            Result.append_string(items.item(index).out); --Item's representation.
            Result.append_string(" "); --Space between item representations.
            index := index + 1;
        end;
        Result.append_string(">"); --Right delimiter.
    end; --out
```

Listing 6.11 Feature *out* of class *LIST_ARRAY*.

6.4 Testing List Implementations

Listing 6.12 presents a tester object for testing this list implementation. The parts that are implementation dependent are marked with "**--imp**." Note that there are only three such places in the program!

```
class LIST_TESTER

creation test

feature {NONE}

    full_at_4: BOOLEAN is false; --imp: set to true if list fills up at 4

    --The following lines control which implementation is being tested.
    list1: LIST_ARRAY[LETTER]; --imp: use make_capacity in test
    --list1: LIST_DOUBLY_LINKED[LETTER]; --imp: use make in test
    --list1: LIST_SINGLY_LINKED[LETTER]; --imp: use make in test

    list2: like list1;

    write_cursor(the_list: like list1) is
            --Displays information about the cursor.
        do
            if the_list.is_off_left then
                print("off-left");
```

Listing 6.12 *LIST_TESTER*, a class to test list classes.

```
            elseif the_list.is_off_right then
               print("off-right");
            else
               print("at the ");
               print(the_list.item);
            end;
         end; --write_cursor

      display(the_list: like list1; name: STRING) is
            --Displays informations about the list.
         do
            print("The list "); print(name); print(" is...%N");
            print(the_list);
            print("%N...and its cursor is "); write_cursor(the_list);
            print(".%N");
         end; --display

      step_right(through_list: like list1; list_name: STRING) is
            --Steps through the list from off-left through off-right.
         local
            count: INTEGER;
         do
            print("Moving off-left in "); print(list_name);
            print(" and stepping through the whole list...%N");
            print(" the length is "); print(through_list.length);
            through_list.move_off_left;
            print(" step 0, cursor is "); write_cursor(through_list);
            from
               count := 1;
            until
               count > through_list.length + 1
            loop
               through_list.move_right;
               print(" step "); print(count);
               print(", cursor is "); write_cursor(through_list);
               print("%N");
               count := count + 1;
            end;
            print("%N");
         end; --step_right

      step_left(through_list: like list1; list_name: STRING) is
            --Steps through the list from off-right through off-left.
         local
            count: INTEGER;
```

Listing 6.12 *(continued)*

```
      do
         print("Moving off-right in "); print(list_name);
         print(" and stepping back through the whole list...%N");
         print(" the length is "); print(through_list.length);
         through_list.move_off_right;
         print("%N step 0, cursor is ");
         write_cursor(through_list);
         from
            count := 1;
         until
            count > through_list.length + 1
         loop
            through_list.move_left;
            print("%N step "); print(count);
            print(", cursor is "); write_cursor(through_list);
            count := count + 1;
         end;
         print("%N%N");
      end; --step_left

feature

   test is
         --Test the list class.
      local
         item: LETTER;
      do
         print("Creating list list1...%N");
         !!list1.make_capacity(4); --imp: for LIST_ARRAY
         --!!list1.make; --imp: for LIST_DOUBLY_LINKED
                           --and LIST_SINGLY_LINKED
         print("...done.%N%N");
         check
            list1_not_void: list1 /= Void;
            list1_not_full: not list1.is_full
         end;
         display(list1, "list1");

         print("%NMoving to off-left in list1...%N");
         list1.move_off_left;
         print("...done.%N");

         !!item.make('A');
         print("%NAdding an 'A' to list1...%N.");
         list1.insert_on_right(item);
```

Listing 6.12 *(continued)*

```
print("...done.%N%N");
display(list1, "list1");
check
   list1_not_full: not list1.is_full;
   list1_off_left: list1.is_off_left
end;

!!item.make('B'); --Lets go of old item and creates a new one.
print("%NAdding a 'B' to list1 at the right end...%N");
list1.move_off_right;
list1.insert_on_left(item);
print("...done.%N%N");
display(list1, "list1");
check
   not list1.is_full;
   not list1.is_off_left;
   list1.is_off_right
end;

!!item.make('C');
print("%NAdding a 'C' to list1 at the left end...%N");
list1.move_off_left;
list1.insert_on_right(item);
print("...done.%N%N");
display(list1, "list1");
check
   not list1.is_full;
   list1.is_off_left;
   not list1.is_off_right
end;

!!item.make('D');
print("%NAdding a 'D' to list1 after the 'A'...%N");
list1.move_off_left; list1.move_right; list1.move_right;
list1.insert_on_right(item);
print("...done.%N%N");
display(list1, "list1");
check
   list1.is_full = full_at_4;
   not list1.is_off_left;
   not list1.is_off_right
end;

step_right(list1, "list1");
step_left(list1, "list1");
```

Listing 6.12 *(continued)*

```
print("%NMoving off-left twice in a row...%N");
list1.move_off_left; list1.move_off_left;
print("...done.%N%N");
check
    not list1.is_empty;
    list1.is_full = full_at_4
end;

print("Moving off-right twice in a row...%N");
list1.move_off_right; list1.move_off_right;
print("...done.%N%N");
check
    not list1.is_empty;
    list1.is_full = full_at_4;
end;

display(list1, "list1");
print("%NMaking list2 a clone of list1...%N");
list2 := clone(list1);
print("...done.%N");
display(list2, "list2");
print("%N");

print("Letting go of list2.%N");
list2 := Void;
print("%NDeleting the second item from list1...%N");
list1.move_off_left; list1.move_right; list1.move_right;
list1.delete;
print("...done.%N%N");
display(list1, "list1");
check
    not list1.is_empty;
    not list1.is_off_left;
    not list1.is_off_right
end;

print("%NDeleting the first item from list1...%N");
list1.move_off_left; list1.move_right;
list1.delete;
print("...done.%N%N");
display(list1, "list1");
check
    not list1.is_empty;
    not list1.is_off_left;
    not list1.is_off_right
end;
```

Listing 6.12 *(continued)*

```
        print("%NDeleting the last item from list1...%N");
        list1.move_off_right; list1.move_left;
        list1.delete;
        print("...done.%N%N");
        display(list1, "list1");
        check
            not list1.is_empty;
            not list1.is_off_left;
            list1.is_off_right
        end;

        print("%NMaking list1 empty...%N");
        list1.wipe_out;
        print("...done.%N%N");
        display(list1, "list1");
        print("%N");

        step_right(list1, "list1");
        step_left(list1, "list1");

        print("%NTest done.%N");

    end; --test

end --class LIST_TESTER
```

Listing 6.12 *(continued)*

6.4.1 Stronger Assertions with strip()

When we were writing our implementations, we came to appreciate how preconditions keep the routine simple. When we write the tester object, good postconditions begin to pay off.

Until now, we have avoided listing in the postconditions all things about the object that do *not* change, because it would have been distracting. Even now, it would be too tedious to enumerate all the unchanged features of the object—and, remember, we not only created our own features, we inherited many, too!

To make this task possible, Eiffel provides a "strip expression." The expression

strip(*a*,*b*, . . .)

results in an array whose elements are all the entities of the current object except *a*,*b*, ...

The strip expression allows us to write much stronger postconditions. For example, the postcondition for *move_right* can now be written as

ensure
  not_off_left: **not** *is_off_left*;
  --The cursor is one step to the right of where it was.
  strip(*cursor*).*is_equal* (**old** *deep_copy* (**strip**(*cursor*)));

With one line, we specified that no entity except the cursor changed about this object.

A limitation of **strip**() is that it only works on features that are entities. Thus, the new assertion above will check that *length* stayed the same only if *length* is implemented as an entity and not a function.

As was mentioned in Section 3.1.2, the "nothing else changes" postconditions are rarely used for practical reasons, and the presence of **strip**() does not change that. Consider *LIST_ARRAY*'s routines, for example: If *items* does not change, we would need to *deep_copy* the whole array every time! This would leave us no choice but to turn off postcondition checking to have reasonable performance—which brings us to the next topic.

6.5 Performance of the Array Implementation

The two important aspects of software performance are how much time it consumes and how much space (usually in memory) it requires. Neither aspect should be measured in absolute terms: We cannot say that a certain piece of code will run in x seconds, because absolute performance depends on plenty of other factors, starting with the speed of the computer. Instead, we care about how performance changes as the number of items in the object structure changes. If we have ten times more items in the list, will it take us the same amount of time to move off-right? twice as long? ten times as long? twenty? one hundred? The same questions can be asked about how much more space overhead will be required.

In other words, if there are N items in an object structure, we want to know in what way the time it takes to do a specific operation is proportional to N. This is known as the **time complexity** of that operation. Similarly, the **space complexity** is an expression that indicates how the amount of additional space needed to run the operation is related to N.

By evaluating performance of algorithms as a function of N, we have what we need to compare competing implementations of routines, so that we can choose the best one for the job.

Formal analysis of a routine usually uses **recurrence relations**, which yield a precise measurement, such as "$\frac{3}{2}N^2 + 9N - 1$". This text does not use recurrence relations: They are considered overkill for our purposes, and there are better places to study them (such as in a course on algorithm analysis or on discrete mathematics). Recurrence relations are too precise for our purposes. Instead of going through the trouble of deriving the formula above, we say that the complexity is "$O(N^2)$" (pronounced "order N squared"). This is known as "**big O notation.**" To get from a precise measurement to an order-of measurement, we take the following steps:

1. Discard everything except the fastest growing term.
2. Discard the constant factor and dress up what's left in "O(. . .)."

In the preceding example, step 1 leaves us with "$\frac{3}{2}N^2$," and step 2 turns it into "$O(N^2)$." But . . . aren't we throwing away valuable information? Well, no. First of all, we probably do not need it. Second, if we do need it, we know where to find it.

The precise measurement is often unnecessary for comparing two implementations. Consider two implementations, one of which (call it A) is $O(N)$, while the other (B) is $O(N^2)$. Suppose that the actual measurement for A is $10N + 10{,}000$, while for B it is $0.01N^2$. If we plot them out (Figure 6.9), we see that despite the penalizing factor and the bias of the second term, the $O(N)$ A still overtakes the less efficient, $O(N^2)$ B. The extra information merely tells us how large N has to be to make the implementation with the lower order of complexity more desirable.

We *do* need the discarded information if the two implementations we are comparing have the same order of complexity. Practically, however, the recur-

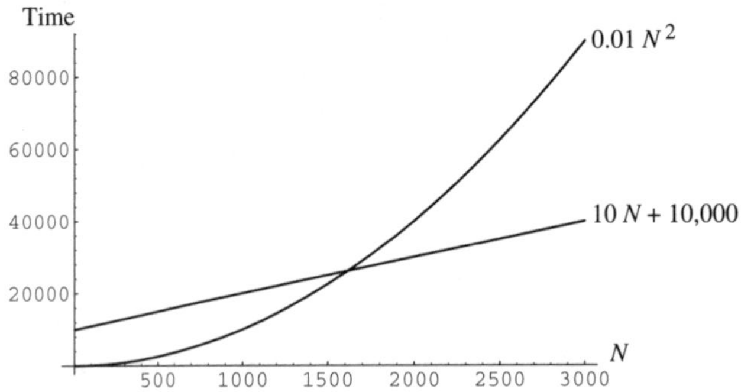

Figure 6.9 Regardless of the discarded constants and slower growing terms, an $O(N)$ implementation is always better than an $O(N^2)$ implementation for large enough N.

rence relation does not give us a sufficiently precise result because there are too many factors beyond the boundaries of the algorithm that can influence the actual performance: locality of memory reference, performance of the memory management system and other disk interfaces, etc. The most practical way to choose among two algorithms of the same order of complexity is to test them both in action on the real input and measure their absolute performances. The choice may vary from system to system, and from input set to input set. What is best for one of your customers may not be the best for another.

Object structure features tend to have one of the following complexities, in increasing order: O(1) (meaning that the complexity of the operation is not dependent on N at all, so it is O(N^0)); O(log N); O(N); O(N log N); and O(N^2) (this list is by no means exhaustive). O(1) is often called "constant complexity," O(log N) is "logarithmic complexity," O(N) is "linear," and O(N^2) is "quadratic." Since we tend to discuss time complexity much more frequently than space complexity, the reference to time is often omitted: If we talk about a feature's complexity without specifically naming *space* complexity, then *time* complexity is the subject of discussion.

6.5.1 Complexity of Features of *LIST_ARRAY*

Most features of class *LIST_ARRAY* do not depend on the length of the list, so they are O(1). For example, *move_left* and *move_right* just increment and decrement an integer, so they are O(1). So are *move_off_left* and *move_off_right*, since they just assign an integer.

Some of the features, however, must step through the whole list to do their job. Since they visit every item exactly once, they are all O(N). Feature *out* is one of these.

Routine *make* just needs to make a few assignments, and request *items.make*. On most systems, *make* in class *ARRAY* is O(*count*), so our *make* is O(*capacity*). So is *copy*, since it must start from scratch because of the aliasing that occurs when it is called from *clone* (see Section 6.3.5).

While *is_equal* is similar in its loop to *out*, it does not *have* to go through the whole list. The best case scenario is when the lists are not of the same length—then the feature is O(1). The trouble with best case scenarios is that they clash with Murphy's Law. If the lists are of equal length, we must look through them until we either find corresponding positions that hold different items or until we reach the end of the list. Thus, the worst case is when the two lists are indeed equal, in which case the feature is O(N). Not knowing anything about the nature of the problem, we can venture a guess that on the average, we may have to search through half the list before finding an unmatched pair of items. Thus, the average case complexity is also O(N). (There is no such thing as "O($\frac{N}{2}$)", since the constant $\frac{1}{2}$ is discarded when we use the big O notation.)

Similar situations arise with *insert_on_left*, *insert_on_right*, and *delete*. In these routines, the time-consuming part is moving to the left (during deletion) or to the right (during insertion) all the item references that are to the right of the target position. Thus, the worst case is when we insert into or delete from the leftmost position of the list: We have to move O(N) item references. The best case is when we are working with the rightmost position of the list: There is nothing to move, so the operation is O(1). On the average, we will be working somewhere in the middle of the list, which is still O(N).

The O(N) complexities of *out* and *is_equal* cannot be helped: The very nature of these operations demands that we deal with O(N) items.

Not so with insertion and deletion. The only reason we are getting O(N) performance with those is that we chose to store our item references in consecutive positions of an array, with one end of the list nailed down to one end of the array. This implementation is just fine if we usually work on the cheap end of the list (the right end, in our case) and avoid the expensive (left) end. If we know that our object structure will be used in circumstances where most of the inserting and deleting happens on the left side of the array, we can easily derive an implementation in which the list is nailed down on the right instead of on the left, thus giving O(1) performances on the left and O(N) on the right.

On the other hand, if we do many insertions or deletions in the middle portions of the array, choosing an end to nail down will do us no good. We need a representation with which we can do insertions and deletions in O(1) time. We will study it in the next chapter.

Summary

A list is an object structure that keeps track of each object based on its position relative to its neighbors. Our list model is based on the notion of a "current position" (indicated by the cursor), and the list provides operations to move the cursor to the left or to the right. Items can be inserted as left or right neighbors of the object under the cursor, and the item under the cursor may be deleted from the list. These operations are embodied in the contract, which is kept in class *LIST*.

LIST is a deferred class, because it defers the implementation of the routines in its contract to its heirs. One such heir is *LIST_ARRAY*, which uses an *ARRAY* to keep track of the objects. It provides good (O(1)) performance in movement routines, but average and worst case time complexity for insertion and deletion are poor (O(N)).

Exercises

1. a. Implement deferred class *LIST*.

   b. Implement and test class *LIST_ARRAY*.

2. Use the **strip**() expression to strengthen the postconditions of the routines in each list implementation that you have written. Can *LIST_TESTER* be simplified now? If so, simplify it.

3. You have a list implemented as *LIST_ARRAY*.

   a. It is tracking 1,000,000 items, you insert an item at its left end, and it takes x seconds. How long would you expect to wait if the list had 2,000,000 items?

   b. It is tracking 1,000,000 items, you insert an item at its right end, and it takes x seconds. How long would you expect to wait if the list had 2,000,000 items?

   c. It is tracking 1,000,000 items, you insert an item in the middle of it, and it takes x seconds. How long would you expect to wait if the list had 2,000,000 items?

4. Suggest a way to speed up *delete* in the array implementation. What features have to be modified? Are they adversely affected?

5. What is the time complexity of *LIST_ARRAY*'s *wipe_out*? Can it be improved? If so, discuss the trade-offs involved. If not, explain why not.

7 Linked Implementations of Lists

Now we look at a different way to implement a list, by making its structure more **dynamic.** This method is a little harder to program, but it will provide a much more efficient implementation in many cases—two implementations, in fact. We will see how inheritance can be utilized to share code between two similar classes, and consider the trade-offs between sharing a feature in the parent class versus implementing it separately in the heirs.

7.1 Linked Implementations

We discussed in Chapter 5 that an *ARRAY* accomplishes its O(1) performance (though we did not call it that at the time) for features *item* and *put* by arranging all its positions in consecutive memory locations. While it was perfect for an array, that design decision is what forced us to do all that copying of item references when we did insertion and deletion with *LIST_ARRAY*.

Suppose the item references were not all stored in consecutive memory locations. How would we be able to get from one item to the next? For each item, we would need to keep track not only of the item, but of at least one of its neighbors, thus making a chain of item references, as shown in Figure 7.1a. Traditionally, each element of such a chain is called a "**node.**"

Effectively, the array of items that we used in the array implementation of lists was also a chain of nodes: The right neighbor was immediately to the right in memory, and the left neighbor was immediately to the left. In a linked chain,

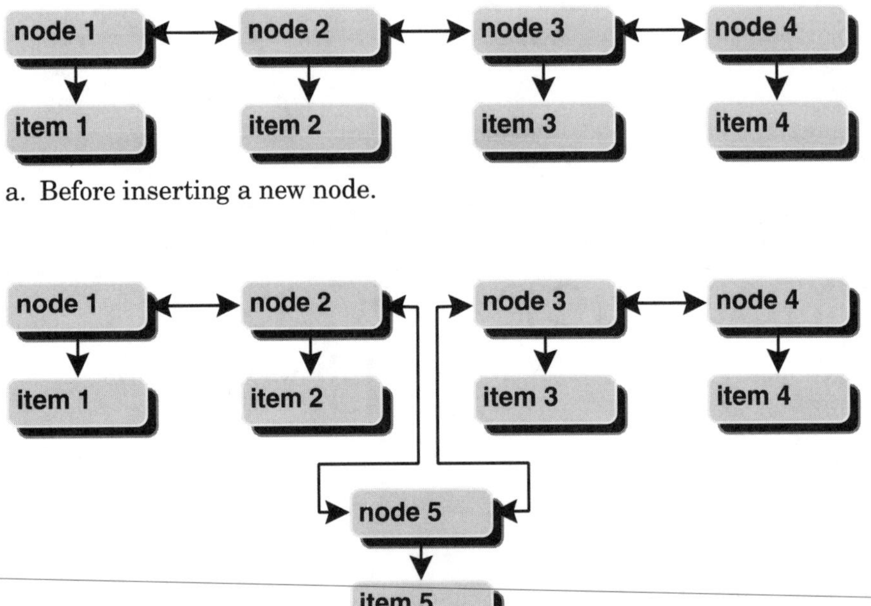

a. Before inserting a new node.

b. After inserting a new node and the item it tracks.

Figure 7.1 A chain of *NODE* objects with the items they track.

the neighbors could be anywhere in memory, so each node tracks its neighbors explicitly.

The chief advantage of this approach is that there is no need to squeeze in a new node between two neighbors. To add a new node, all we need to do is make sure that it knows where its neighbors are, and let them know that it is now their new neighbor. For example, after inserting a new node between nodes 2 and 3 into the chain of Figure 7.1a, we get the chain of Figure 7.1b. Nothing needs to be moved aside, so the operation requires the same number of steps regardless of the length of the chain—an O(1) operation!

7.1.1 The Contract for Class *NODE*

There are a couple of common ways to implement a *NODE* object, and we will deal with them in Section 7.2. The detailed external view of a *NODE* is shown in Figure 7.2, and its interface (as it would be produced by `short`) is given in Listing 7.1. Note that the contract allows us to set any of the three references (to the item and to either neighbor) to *Void*.

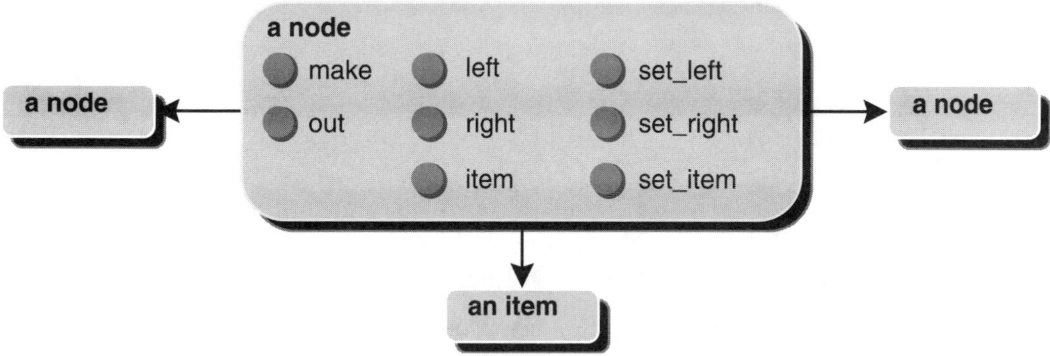

Figure 7.2 The outside view of a *NODE* object.

class interface *NODE*[*ITEM*]
creation procedures

make
--Standard initialization.
ensure
item_is_void: *item* = *Void*;
left_is_void: *left* = *Void*;
right_is_void: *right* = *Void*;

exported features

left: **like** *Current*
--The left neighbor.
right: **like** *Current*
--The right neighbor.
item: *ITEM*
--The tracked object.

set_left (*new_left*: **like** *Current*)
--Make *new_left* this node's left neighbor.
ensure
left_updated: *left* = *new_left*;

set_right (*new_right*: **like** *Current*)
--Make *new_right* this node's right neighbor.
ensure
right_updated: *right* = *new_right*;

set_item (*new_item*: *ITEM*)
--Make this node track *new_item*.
ensure
item_updated: *item* = *new_item*;

end --class interface *NODE*

Listing 7.1 The interface and contract of class *NODE*, take 1.

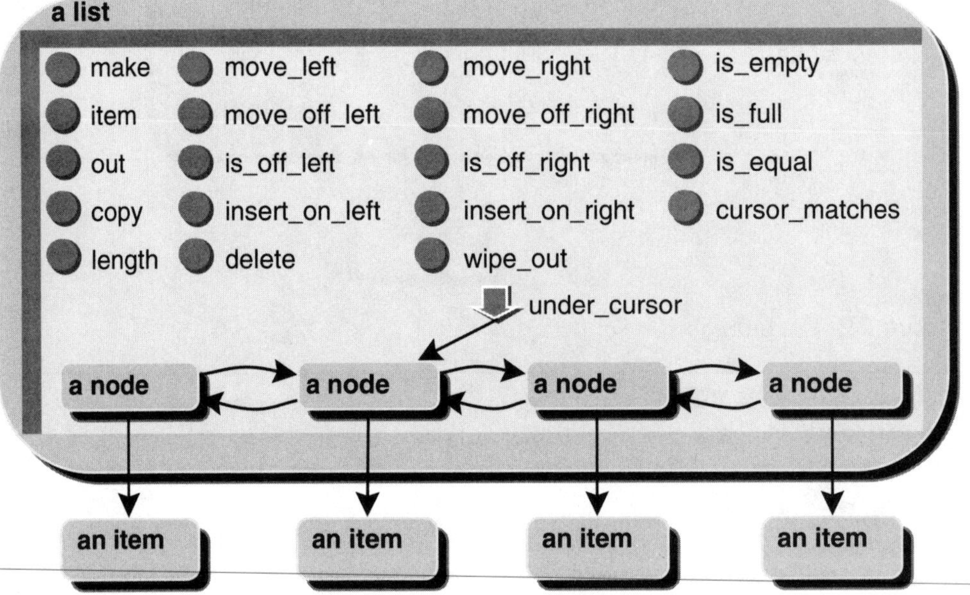

Figure 7.3 The inside view of a *LIST_LINKED* object, take 1.

7.1.2 A Linked Representation of a List

Given a contract for *NODE*, we can sketch an internal view of a linked implementation of a list, and we do just that in Figure 7.3. Instead of storing the number of the position in an array that tracks the item under the cursor, attribute *under_cursor* tracks the *NODE* object that tracks that item.

7.1.3 Moving Left and Right

This linked representation of a list makes *move_left* and *move_right* easy: All we have to do is make *under_cursor* track the left or the right neighbor, respectively, of the node that it is currently tracking. For instance, *move_right* is simply

```
move_right is
        --Move the cursor one step to the right.
    do
        under_cursor := under_cursor.right;
    end; --move_right
```

and *move_left* is analogous.

7.1.4 Inserting and Deleting an Item

We already saw in Figure 7.1 what needs to be done to insert a new item, so all we need to do now is make it fit our list implementation. We will use *insert_on_right* as the example. We start out with the list in Figure 7.4a. Then we create a new node and use a local entity called *new_node* to track it. Before we forget, we hook *new_item* to it. That gives us Figure 7.4b. Then, while the two

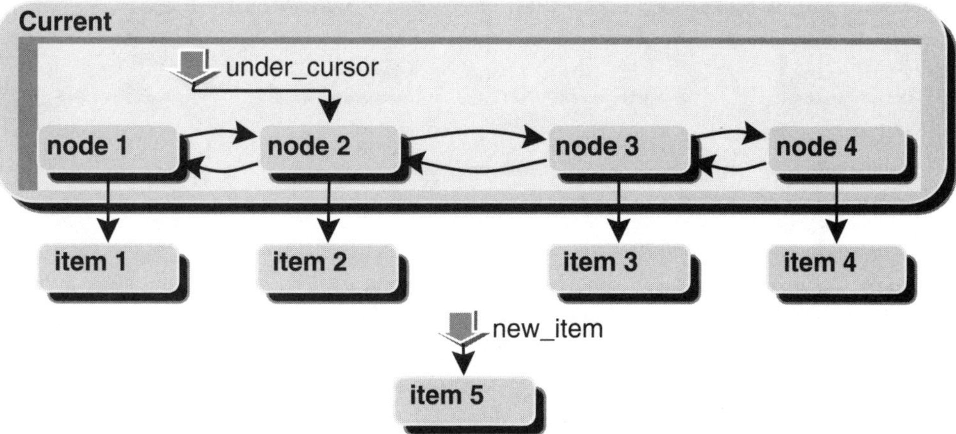

a. The list with which we started.

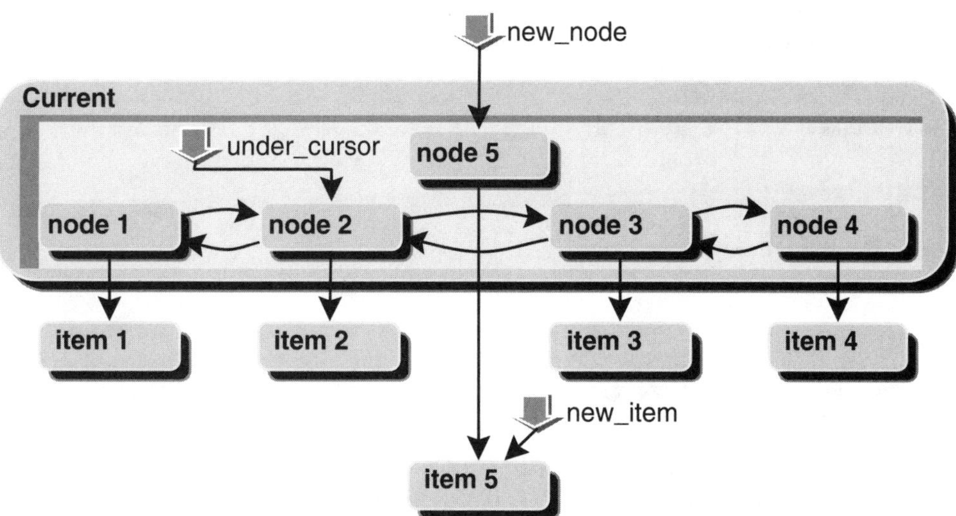

b. *New_node* has been made and is tracking *new_item*.

Figure 7.4 Responding to request "*insert_on_right*(*new_item*)". (The object's routines are not shown in order to save page space.)

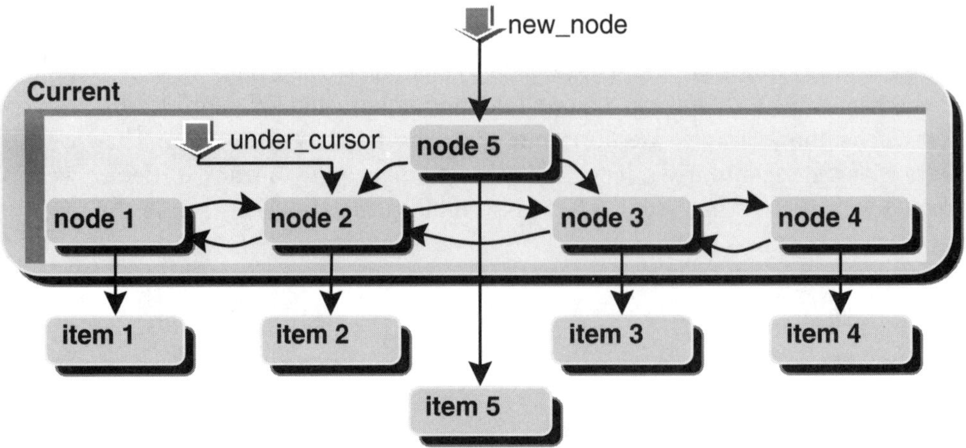

c. *New_node* has been told about its neighbors.

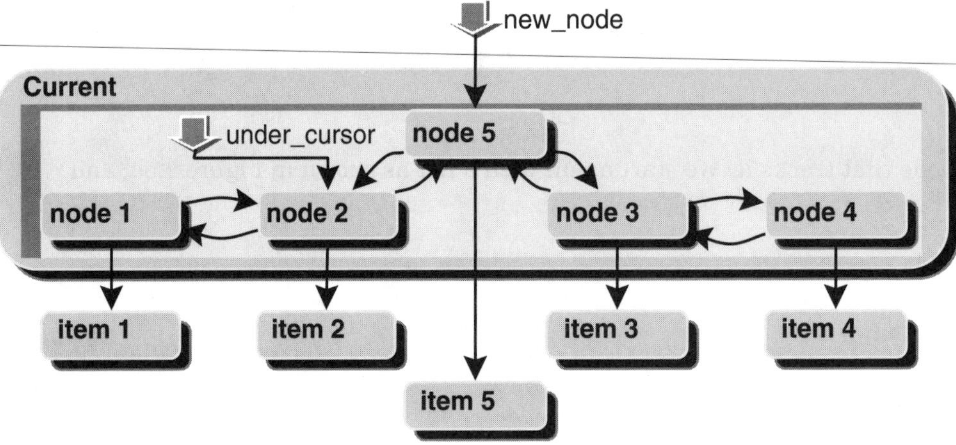

d. *New_node*'s neighbors have been told about *new_node*.

Figure 7.4 *(continued)*

nodes between which we will insert *new_node* still remember each other, we let *new_node* know that they are its left and right neighbors; now we have Figure 7.4c. Next, we tell *new_node*'s left and right neighbors that *new_node* is now their right and left neighbor, respectively, yielding Figure 7.4d.

Checking our postconditions, we see that the cursor is already over the same item as in the old list, and the length . . . we have not defined *length* yet, so we will have to check that postcondition again after we have done so. The code for *insert_on_right* is given in Listing 7.2.

```
insert_on_right(new_item: ITEM) is
        --Insert new_item to the right of the cursor.
    local
        new_node: NODE[ITEM];
    do
        --Make a new node and make it track new_item.
        !!new_node.make;
        new_node.set_item(new_item);

        --Let new_node know about its neighbors.
        new_node.set_left(under_cursor);
        new_node.set_right(under_cursor.right);

        --Let new_node's neighbors know about it.
        new_node.left.set_right(new_node);
        new_node.right.set_left(new_node);
    end; --insert_on_right
```

work in progress

Listing 7.2 Linked list implementation's *insert_on_right*.

Deleting an item from a linked list is as simple as making the chain bypass the node that tracks it. We start again with a list as shown in Figure 7.5a, and simply tell the neighbors of the node under the cursor that they are each other's neighbors instead (Figure 7.5b). Now we have to make entity *under_cursor* track another node—according to the postcondition, the one to the right. Doing that results in Figure 7.5c.

Now, how do we expel the unnecessary node from the list? We do not have to. Nothing in the list is tracking it anymore, so it is not part of the list anymore.

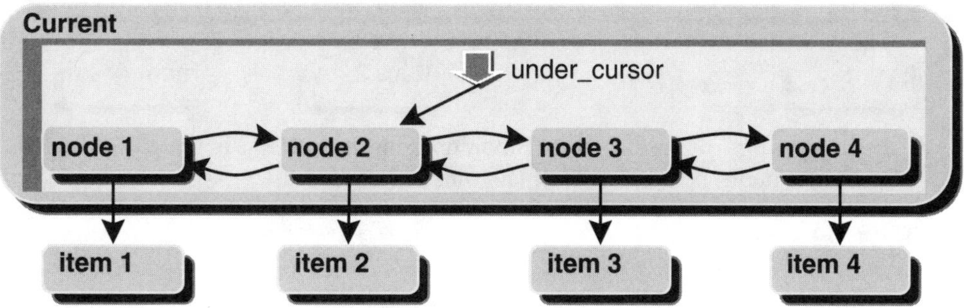

a. The list with which we started.

Figure 7.5 Responding to request "*delete*". (The object's routines are not shown in order to save page space.)

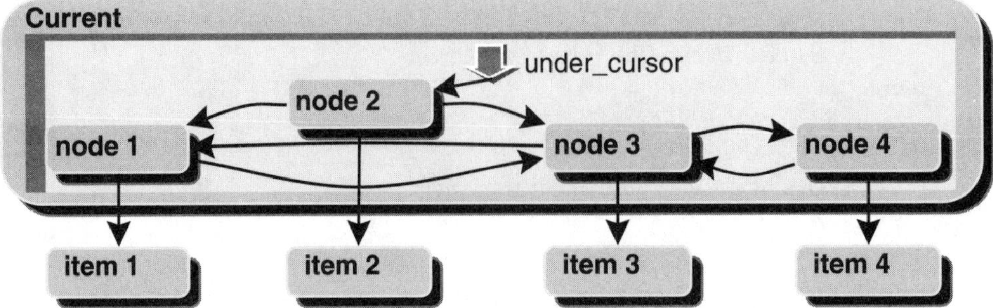

b. *Under_cursor*'s neighbors have been told to bypass *under_cursor*.

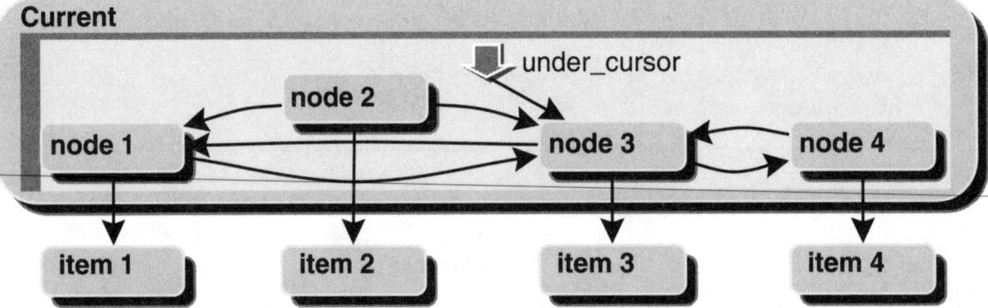

c. The entity *under_cursor* is made to track the node to *under_cursor*'s right.

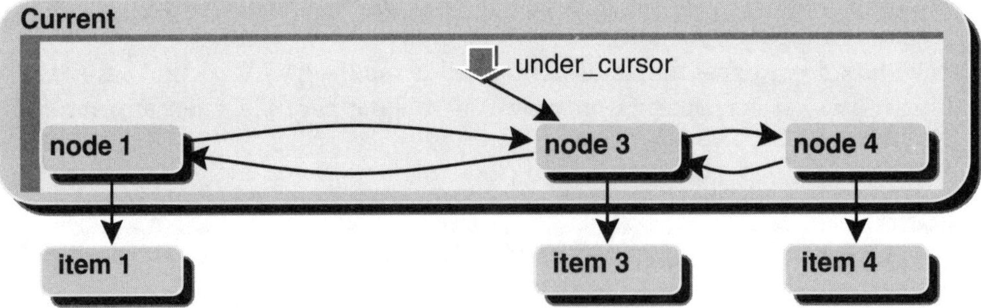

d. Just cleaning up the diagram. Since nothing in this list is tracking the bypassed node, it is not part of the picture anymore.

Figure 7.5 *(continued)*

Since nothing outside the list is tracking it either, the garbage collector will recycle it. When that happens, it may be that the item it tracked is also unreferenced, in which case that item will also be recycled. Just cleaning up our mental picture of the list, we get Figure 7.5d. The code to do that is shown in Listing 7.3.

```
delete is
        --Delete the item under the cursor.
    do
        --Make under_cursor's neighbors track each other
        --instead of under_cursor.
        under_cursor.left.set_right(under_cursor.right);
        under_cursor.right.set_left(under_cursor.left);

        --Advance the cursor one step to the right.
        under_cursor := under_cursor.right;
    end; --delete
```

Listing 7.3 Linked list implementation's *delete*.

7.1.5 Making It Work at the Endpoints

These versions of *insert_*. . . and *delete* work when there is a node on each side of the target node. What do we do if we want to insert to the right of the rightmost item or to the left of the leftmost one? How do we delete the leftmost or the rightmost item? And now that we are considering the ends of the list, how do we determine if the list is off-left or off-right?

We simply modify our internal representation so that the routines do work at the endpoints of the list: We add an empty node to the left of the node that tracks the leftmost item, and another one to the right of the node that tracks the rightmost item. These nodes make natural off-left and off-right markers. We add hidden entities to track them, so that we can go off-left and off-right quickly (in O(1) time). This gives an inside view of a *LIST_LINKED* as shown in Figure 7.6.

This little change answers many implementation questions. The *insert_*. . . and *delete* routines we have written already will work at the endpoints as well as in the middle. We know now what an empty list looks like (see Figure 7.7), so we can write *make* and *wipe_out*. We know how to write *move_off_left* and *move_off_right*. Some of these routines are given in Listing 7.4; I will let you fill in the rest.

A few notes are in order here. First, observe how simple the *wipe_out* implementation is. This simplicity is made possible by the garbage collection system. If our language did not support automatic garbage collection (and such languages are numerous), it would be our job to loop through all the nodes between *off_left* and *off_right* and manually deallocate the space they occupy. Otherwise, those useless nodes would be occupying memory—a mistake known as a "memory leak." (If you have friends who learned how to do linked lists in a language that doesn't offer automatic garbage collection, ask them how many points they lost because of this on their assignments, or how much it cost their company to send out bug fix releases that plugged up such leaks.)

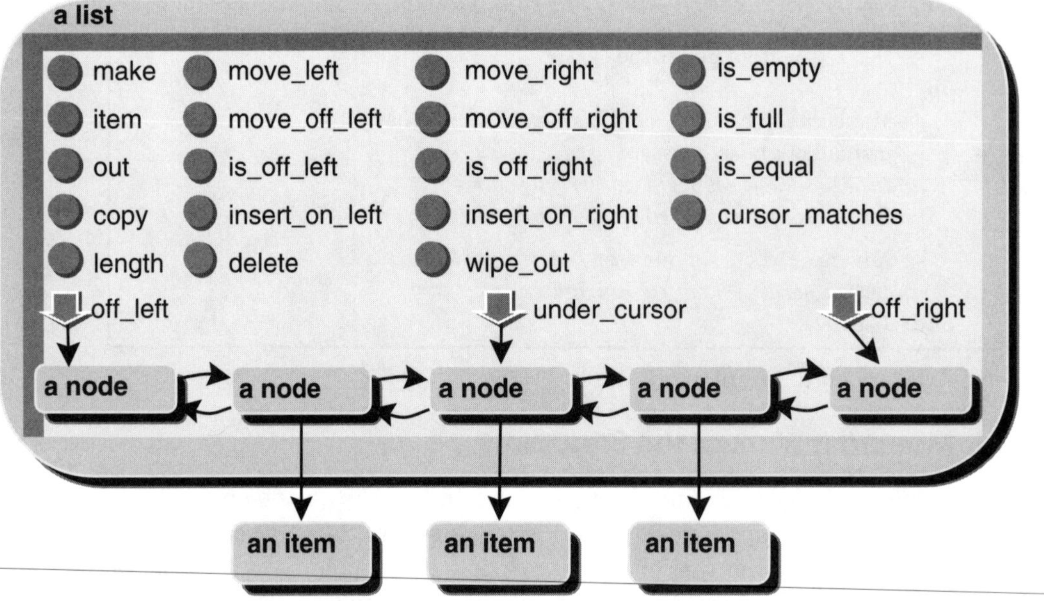

Figure 7.6 The inside view of a *LIST_LINKED* object, take 2.

Second, note how the features' implementations and their pre- and post-conditions interoperate. For instance, if we try to use *insert_on_right* when the cursor is on the rightmost node (the empty one), it will fail. *But it is not expected to work in that situation,* because that is the *is_off_right* condition, and

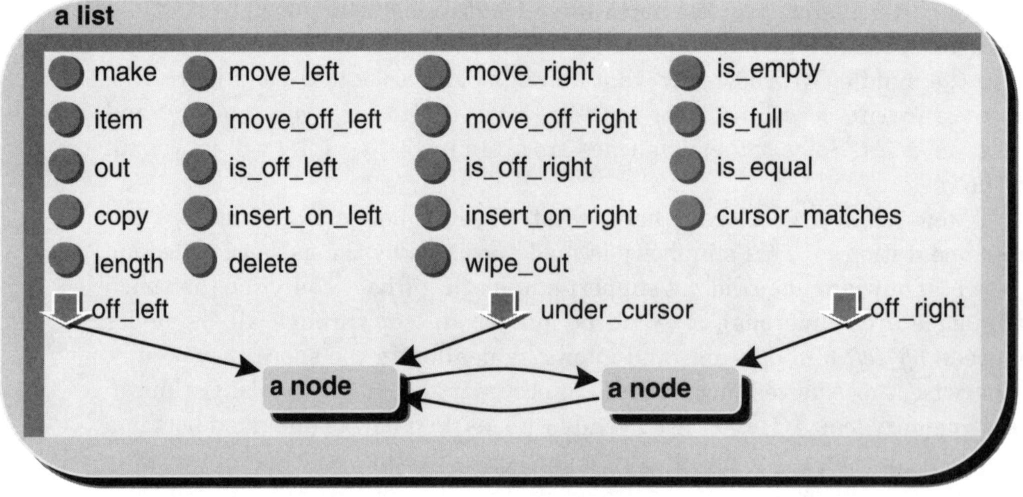

Figure 7.7 The inside view of an empty *LIST_LINKED* object.

```
feature {LIST_LINKED} --Entities visible only to linked lists
   off_left: NODE[ITEM];
         --Off-left marker (an empty node).
   off_right: like off_left;
         --Off-right marker (an empty node).
   under_cursor: like off_left;
         --Tracks the node under the cursor.
feature
   wipe_out is
         --Make this list empty and off-left.
      do
         off_left.set_right(off_right);
         off_right.set_left(off_left);
         under_cursor := off_left;
      end; --wipe_out
   make is
         --Initialize to get an empty, off-left list.
      do
         !!off_left.make;
         !!off_right.make;
         wipe_out;
      end; --make
   move_off_left is
         --Move the cursor to the off-left position.
      do
         under_cursor := off_left;
      end; --move_off_left
   move_off_right is
         --Move the cursor to the off-right position.
      do
         under_cursor := off_right;
      end; --move_off_right
```

Listing 7.4 Features dealing with the endpoints of the list.

the preconditions for *insert_on_right* rule it out. Many of the features will not work when the cursor is one of the end markers, but all of them are exempted by their preconditions from working under these circumstances. This is not cheating on our part: We defined the preconditions because they made sense, not to make our implementation easier—we had not even considered the implementation at that time! Yet it is a good illustration of how a set of well-defined preconditions makes implementation easier.

7.1.6 Dealing with *is_full*

A full list is one into which no more items can be inserted. It was easy to write *is_full* for the array implementation, because we knew the capacity of the array inside the list. When all positions in the array are in use, the list is full.

In a linked list, we can insert new items as long as there is enough memory available to make nodes for them. Thus, the straightforward way to implement *is_full* is to make it ask the memory management system if there is enough room left for another node. Unfortunately, that is not enough.

Since "**not** *is_full*" is a precondition to the insertion routines, we have to set things up so that the following code always works for the user:

```
if not a_list.is_full then
   a_list.insert_on_right(new_item);
end
```

Thus, as soon as we return *false* as the result of *is_full*, we are committed to making one insertion into that list work as promised. But we cannot get that guarantee by asking the memory management system if there is more space, since other parts of the system may be competing for memory with this program: The memory may be available during the execution of *is_full*, but may disappear before execution of *insert_on_right*.

It is not enough to check if room is available, we must also make a reservation.[1] It would be bad form to make that reservation during the evaluation of *is_full*: It is a function and should not have any side effects. The program should run the same way whether or not *is_full* is called. Since it is called from within the **ensure** clause of the insertion routines, we could run into this nasty situation:

1. Precondition checking is turned off, and the program runs out of memory during list insertion and crashes.
2. We turn on precondition checking, and the program gets past the point in which it crashed because the precondition calls *is_full* and makes a reservation, but may run out of memory and crash at a different point.

Instead, we will make our reservation as soon as we create the list. We will make each list carry a "spare tire"—a spare node. If during an insertion we run out of memory, we will use the spare. Thus, the list is not full as long as the

---

[1]This is going to get complicated. On your first try to implement a linked list, you may want to just make *is_full* always result in *false*, and hope that you never run out of memory—not a bad risk if you are just doing this as an exercise for an object structures course on a system with virtual memory.

spare is available. When we delete an item, we check to see if we had consumed the spare. If we had, we make the node that used to track the deleted item our new spare, otherwise we cast it adrift and let the garbage collector recycle it.

Thus, we revise *make*, *insert_on_right*, and *delete* into the ones shown later in Listing 7.6. To make their new implementation possible, we create private features *spare* and *another_node*, shown in Listing 7.5.

The private feature *another_node* attempts to create another node. If there is memory for it, the new node is the result, and the insertion routines use it to track the new item. When the system is unable to oblige us with more memory, it generates an error condition—"raises an **exception**" in programmer talk. You have probably encountered other situations in which an exception is raised; requesting a feature of a void entity is a common example, as is dividing a number by zero.

Normally, an exception causes the program to "crash." But what does that *mean?* Does the whole computer come to a halt? Well, maybe; if yours does, you may want to shop around for a decent operating system. Usually, though, only your program terminates, and the rest of the system hums along. The system provides an **exception handler,** which is a piece of code that gets executed

```
feature {NONE} --Visible only to this list

   spare: like off_left;
         --Spare node to guarantee safe is_full.

   another_node: like off_left is
         --A node for use in insertion.
      local
         already_tried: BOOLEAN;
      do
         if not already_tried then
            --Try creating another node.
            !!Result.make;
         else
            --No more memory, so use the spare.
            Result := spare;
            spare := Void;
         end;
      rescue
         already_tried := true;
         retry;
      end; --another_node
```

Listing 7.5 Versions of *is_full, make, insert_on_right*, and *delete* that use a "spare tire."

```
feature

   make is
         --Initialize to get an empty, off-left list.
      do
         !!off_left.make;
         !!off_right.make;
         !!spare.make;
         wipe_out;
      end; --make

   insert_on_right(new_item: ITEM) is
         --Insert new_item to the right of the cursor.
      local
         new_node: like off_left;
      do
         --Make a new node and make it track new_item.
         new_node := another_node;
         new_node.set_item(new_item);

         --Let new_node know about its neighbors.
         new_node.set_left(under_cursor);
         new_node.set_right(under_cursor.right);

         --Let new_node's neighbors know about it.
         new_node.left.set_right(new_node);
         new_node.right.set_left(new_node);
      end; --insert_on_right

   delete is
         --Delete the item under the cursor.
      do
         --Keep under_cursor as the spare if necessary.
         if spare = Void then
            spare := under_cursor;
         end;

         --Make under_cursor's neighbor track each other instead of
         --under_cursor.
         under_cursor.left.set_right(under_cursor.right);
         under_cursor.right.set_left(under_cursor.left);

         --Advance the cursor one step to the right.
         under_cursor := under_cursor.right;
      end; --delete
```

Listing 7.6 Versions of *is_full*, *make*, *insert_on_right*, and *delete* that use a "spare tire."

```
is_full: BOOLEAN is
        --Is there no room in this list for one more item?
    do
        Result := spare /= Void;
    end; --is_full
```

Listing 7.6 *(continued)*

when the error occurs. Generally, the standard handler prints out an error message and exits the program.

In many languages, including Eiffel, it is possible for the programmer to provide more specialized exception handlers. A specific handler could be as simple as one that prints a more accurate error message and exits the program. However, it may also be capable of doing some damage control so that the program may continue operation.

Here is how this works in Eiffel. A feature may have a **rescue** section between the **do** and **ensure** sections. If an exception happens while the **do** part of the feature is running, the **rescue** part will get an opportunity to clean up the mess. The **rescue** section does not have to perform miracles. Its purpose is to see that even though the feature fails (and it *does* fail, causing an exception in the routine that invoked it), the object is still valid (i.e., the invariant is true).

But for those who refuse to accept failure, a **rescue** section may contain the command **retry**, which causes the **do** part to be run all over again. If we use this technique, we need to make sure that the same exception does not keep happening while we retry the feature over and over again.

In the case of *another_node*, there are two courses of action. The first is to create another node. The backup plan—for the **retry** action—is to use the spare. All we need is to be able to tell in the **do** part which time around we are executing it. The way to do this is to take advantage of automatic initialization of entities:

- Object-tracking entities are initialized to *Void*.
- Numeric entities are initially zero.
- Boolean entities start out *false*.

The last one is just what we need. We use a local Boolean feature called *already_tried*. The first time through the **do**, it is *false*. If the "!!*Result.make*" fails, an exception is raised and the **rescue** part is invoked, setting *already_tried* to *true* and doing a **retry**. This time around the **do**, we know that we have already tried making a new node, so we use the spare.

7.1.7 Checking If Cursors of Two Lists Match

In *LIST_ARRAY*, feature *cursor_matches* simply checked to see if the values of entity *under_cursor* in the two lists were equal. That is insufficient in the linked implementation: The only way for two cursors to be equal is if both refer to the same node, which only works if they are both within the same list object. In general, we have to step through both lists from the left, and look for a cursor in either list at that distance from off-left. As soon as we find a cursor, we can stop the looping. If both lists have a cursor at that position, then the cursors of the two lists match, otherwise they do not. This routine is shown in Listing 7.7.

A similar loop can be used to implement *is_equal*.

7.1.8 Cloning

As we did with the array version, we need to write feature *copy* to support cloning.

```
cursor_matches (other: like Current): BOOLEAN is
        --Is this list's cursor the same distance
        --from off-left as other's cursor?
    local
        node_in_current: like off_left;
        node_in_other: like off_left;
    do
        --Find a distance from off-left in which
        --at least one of the lists has its cursor.
        from
            node_in_current := off_left;
            node_in_other := other.off_left;
        until
            node_in_current = under_cursor
                or node_in_other = other.under_cursor
        loop
            node_in_current := node_in_current.right;
            node_in_other := node_in_other.right;
        end;

        Result :=
            node_in_current = under_cursor and
            node_in_other = other.under_cursor;
    end; --cursor_matches
```

Listing 7.7 Linked list implementation's *cursor_matches*.

Copy (other) can simply follow a loop similar to the one in Listing 7.7 to build a copy of *other* and leave *under_cursor* in the same loop step where we find *other.under_cursor*. We will do something along those lines later, but first, we consider a twist on the linked implementation.

7.2 Singly vs. Doubly Linked Lists and Their Class Hierarchy

There are two common ways to implement class *NODE*. The most straightforward way is to simply make it track both of its neighbors. A list that is implemented using such nodes is known as **doubly linked.**

The other way is to track only one of the neighbors—by convention, the one on the right—and find the neighbor on the left by scanning the list. A list organized this way is called "**singly linked.**" There are problems in which lists are usually (or even always) traversed in only one direction. For such implementations, it makes little sense to store references to both neighbors in each node. If the list is long, using singly linked nodes can result in considerable space savings.

We have two very similar implementations here. They are so similar that many of the routines—those which do not use the *left* feature of class *NODE*—are going to be the same for both implementations! It would not be productive to have two independent classes for singly and doubly linked lists if many of the routines will be duplicated. Somehow, we should be able to "factor out" the similar parts, and accommodate only the differences in separate classes.

The simplest way to do this would be to have just one class for linked lists, and make it take either a singly linked or a doubly linked node as a parameter. A doubly linked node tracks both of its neighbors using entities *left* and *right*; a singly linked node tracks only the neighbor to its right with entity *right*, but its feature *left* searches the list for its left neighbor every time it is called.

There are two problems with this solution: (1) it limits reusability and (2) it does not work. It reduces reusability of class *NODE*, because it assumes that it is a node in a linked list. Later, we will want to use nodes in a different object structure, one for which "searching the list for the node's left neighbor" is a meaningless activity. Even when the action makes sense, the way it is carried out would be different from one object structure to another. A node should not be concerned with what structure encloses it.

It does not work because a node does not have enough information to find its left neighbor: It does not know what list it is in, so it cannot know where to start looking!

No, we need two distinct (though related) classes to do the two versions of linked list implementations. The doubly linked version asks its nodes for their left neighbors; the singly linked version finds them itself. To save space, the singly linked version uses an implementation of nodes that does not track the left neighbor.

Let us take another look at what types of nodes we have. For a singly linked list, we need a node that tracks its right neighbor; let us call it *NODE_R* ("R" for "right"). For a doubly linked list, we need a node that tracks its right neighbor and also tracks its left neighbor, let us call it *NODE_LR* ("L" for "left" and "R" for "right"). Do you think we should define *NODE_L* while we are at it? Be my guest, but we do not need it for now.

How are *NODE_R* and *NODE_LR* related? Are they related by inheritance? If so, then one should be able to subcontract for the other. A *NODE_R* cannot subcontract for a *NODE_LR*, since the latter may get a request for feature *left*, and a *NODE_R* object cannot handle it.

On the other hand, a *NODE_LR* can do whatever a *NODE_R* can do, plus it has its own talents (knowing where its left neighbor is). Thus, class *NODE_LR* is an heir of class *NODE_R*. Stating it in terms of the "can act as a" relationship: A *NODE_LR* (node that tracks its left and its right neighbors) can act as a *NODE_R* (node that tracks its right neighbor).

The implementations of *NODE_R* and *NODE_LR* are given in Listing 7.8.

```
class NODE_R[ITEM]

creation make

feature

   make is
         --Initialize the node to track nothing and have no neighbors.
      do
         --Nothing needs to be done.
      end; --make

   right: like Current;
         --The right neighbor.

   item: ITEM;
         --The tracked object.

   set_right(new_right: like Current) is
         --Make new_right this node's right neighbor.
```

Listing 7.8 Implementation of classes *NODE_R* and *NODE_LR*.

```
        do
            right := new_right;
        ensure
            right_updated: right = new_right;
        end; --set_right

    set_item (new_item: ITEM) is
            --Make this node track new_item.
        do
            item := new_item;
        ensure
            item_updated: item = new_item;
        end; --set_item

end --class NODE_R

class NODE_LR[ITEM] inherit NODE_R[ITEM]

creation make

feature

    left: like Current;
            --The left neighbor.

    set_left (new_left: like Current) is
            --Make new_left this node's left neighbor.
        do
            left := new_left;
        ensure
            left_updated: left = new_left;
        end; --set_left
end --class NODE_LR
```

Listing 7.8 *(continued)*

Note that *make* has nothing to do (all entities will be set to *Void* automatically), but is provided in case a future heir will want to redefine it with a more active one.

How, then, are the singly and doubly linked list classes related? The answer to this question is not quite as obvious. They both implement the same set of features, with the same pre- and postconditions. Either one could serve as a subcontractor for the other, but neither adds functionality to the other.

Instead, we can do something similar to what we did with class *LIST* with respect to its implementations. First, we make class *LIST_LINKED*, which implements those features that the singly and doubly linked implementations

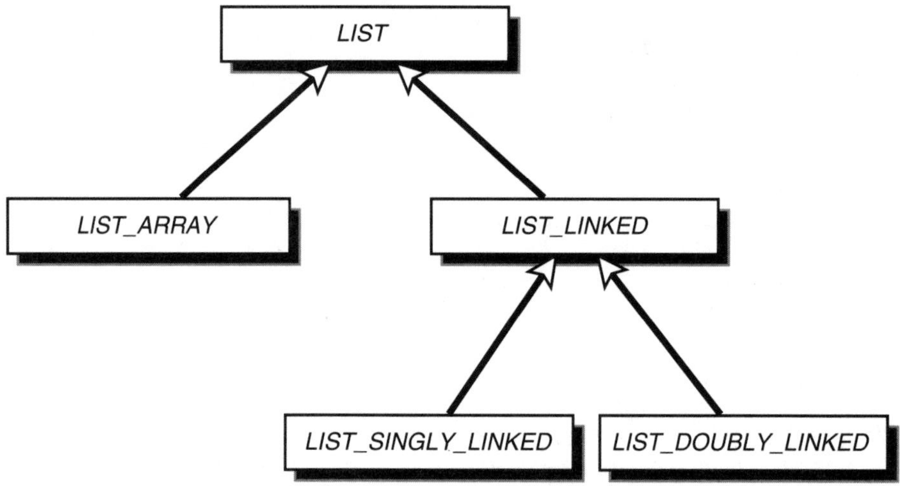

Figure 7.8 The hierarchy of list classes.

do the same way and defers all the rest. Then we define for it subclasses *LIST_SINGLY_LINKED* and *LIST_DOUBLY_LINKED*, which implement their respective versions of routines in which they differ. The resulting inheritance hierarchy is shown in Figure 7.8.

We have looked at what happens with double linking. We will consider the special aspects of single linking next. Then we will contemplate which features go into the deferred class *LIST_LINKED* and which belong in the specific classes.

7.3 Implementing a Singly Linked List

For convenience, an inside view of a singly linked list is given in Figure 7.9 (it differs from Figure 7.6 only in directionality of the arrows between nodes).

Some routines do not need to refer to a node's left neighbor in the singly linked implementation. Consider, for example, *insert_on_right*. Since there is never a reason to look left of the cursor, there is no need to find the left neighbor of the node under the cursor. Since the left neighbors are not tracked, there is no need to ever call *set_left*. The steps taken by *insert_on_right* in a singly linked list are shown in Figure 7.10, and the code for it is in Listing 7.9.

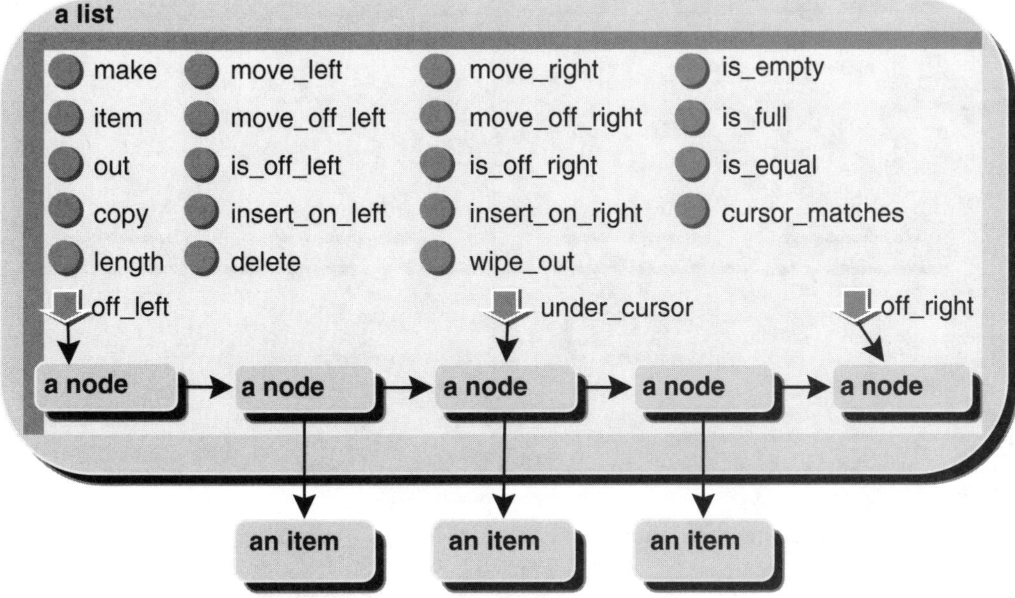

Figure 7.9 The inside view of a *LIST_SINGLY_LINKED* object, take 1.

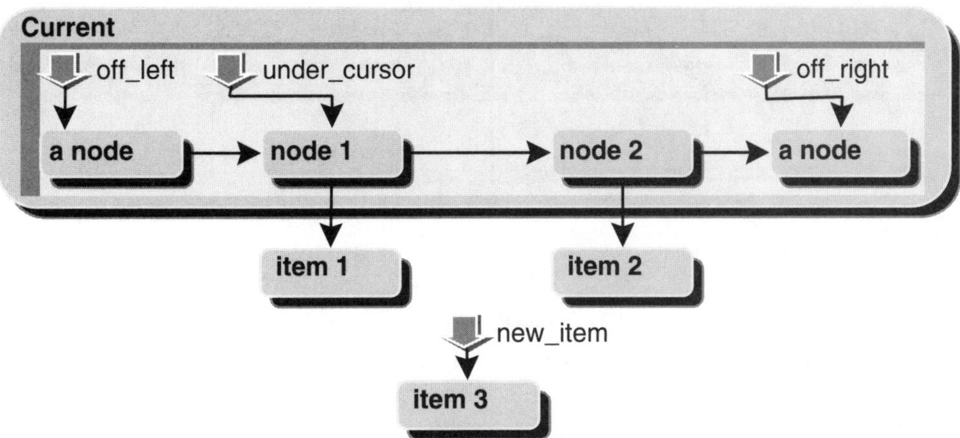

a. The list with which we started.

Figure 7.10 A singly linked list responds to request "*insert_on_right*(*new_item*)". (The object's routines are not shown in order to save page space.)

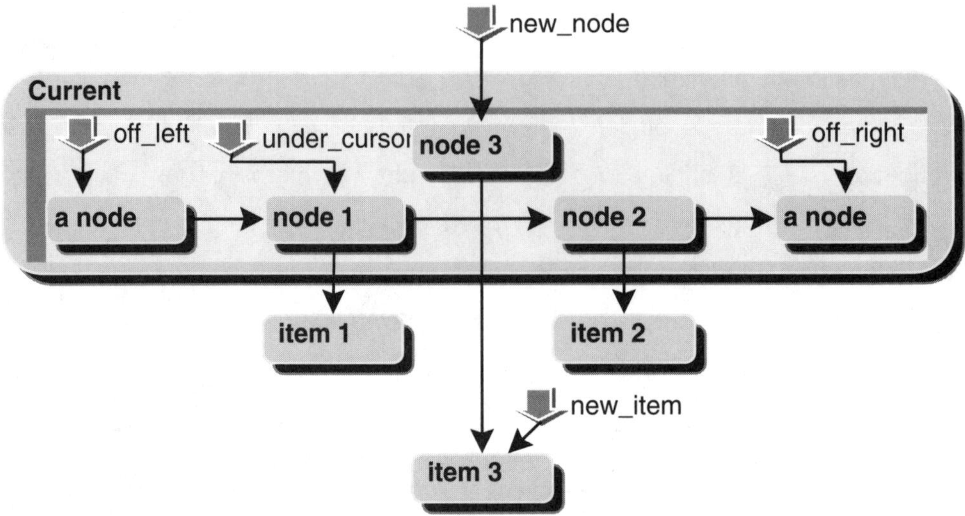

b. *New_node* has been made and is tracking *new_item*.

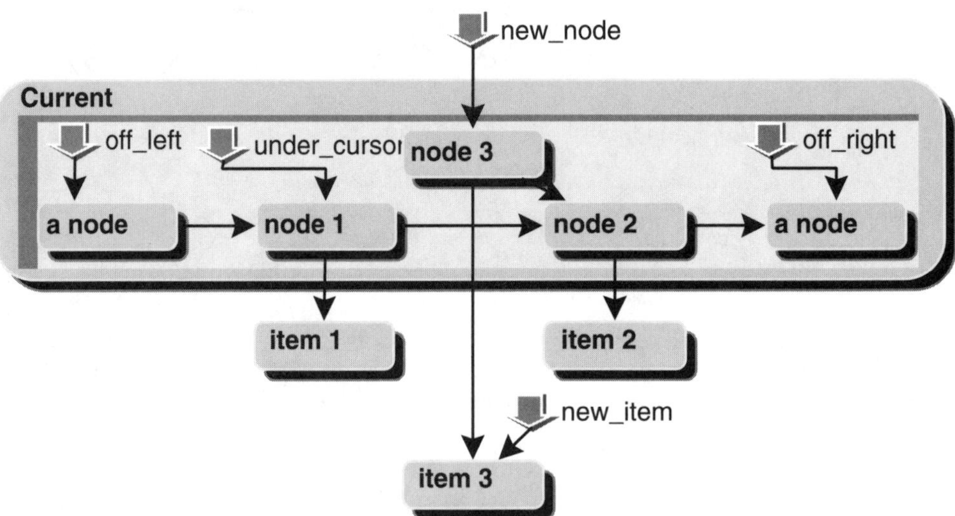

c. *New_node* has been told about its right neighbor.

Figure 7.10 *(continued)*

Observe that without tracking the last item of the list (or the off-left marker in an empty list), the off-right marker has nothing to do: It tracks no item and it never has a right neighbor to track. All it has to do is "be there," so that we know when we have reached the right end of the list. That being the case, there is no need to create a whole new node: Comparing an entity with a

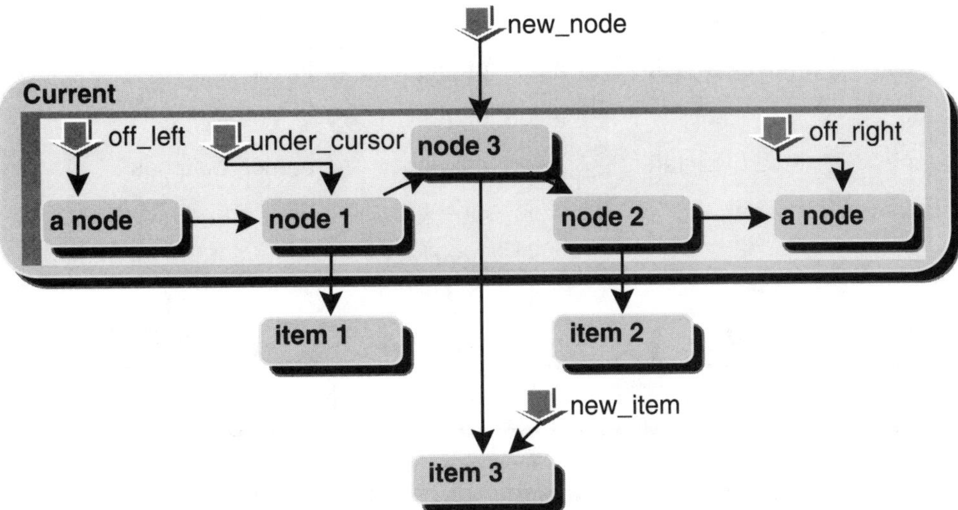

d. *New_node*'s left neighbor has been told about *new_node*.

Figure 7.10 *(continued)*

reference to *Void* is just as good as comparing it with a specially allocated but otherwise unused node. This gives us a just slightly more efficient representation of a singly linked list as shown in Figure 7.11.

On the other hand, *delete* does require looking to the left of the node under the cursor in order to set up a bypass from the left neighbor to the right neighbor, as shown in Figure 7.12.

```
insert_on_right(new_item: ITEM) is
        --Insert new_item to the right of the cursor.
    local
        new_node: like off_left;
    do
        --Make a new node and make it track new_item.
        !!new_node.make;
        new_node.set_item(new_item);

        --Let new_node know its right neighbor.
        new_node.set_right(under_cursor.right);

        --Let new_node's left neighbor know about it.
        under_cursor.set_right(new_node);
    end; --insert_on_right
```

Listing 7.9 Singly linked list's implementation of *insert_on_right*.

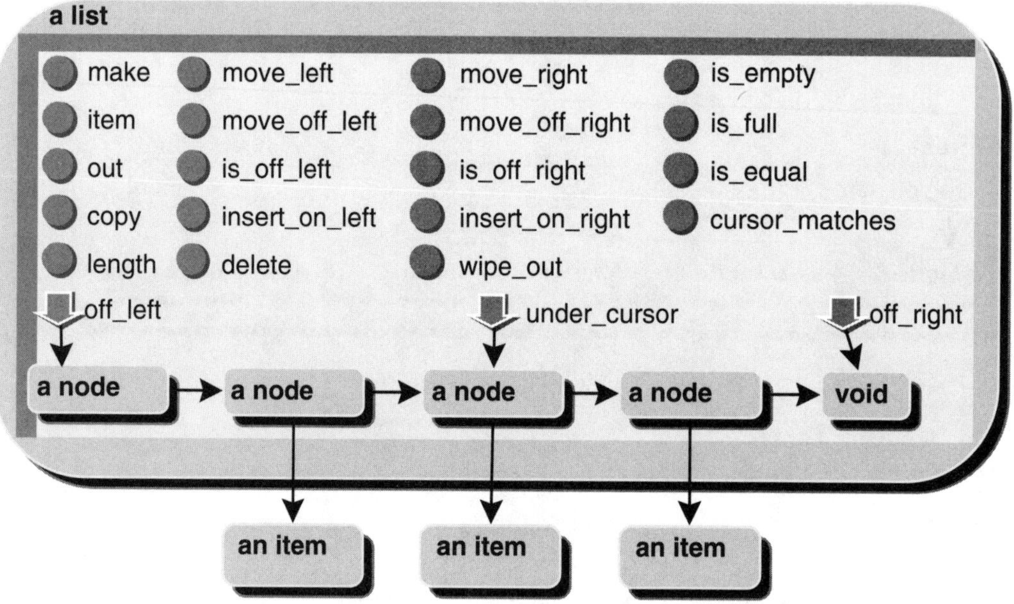

Figure 7.11 The inside view of a *LIST_SINGLY_LINKED* object, take 2.

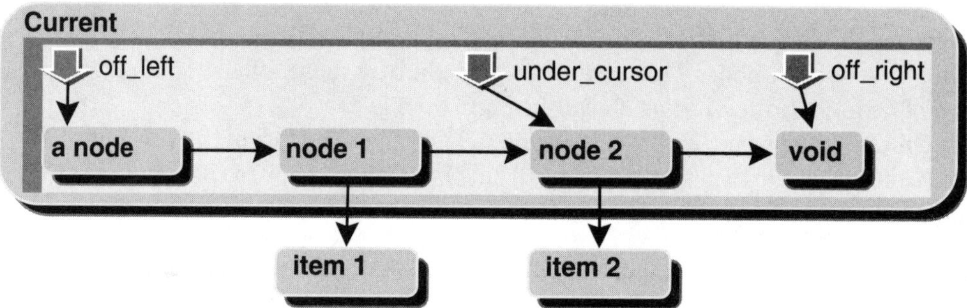

a. The list with which we started.

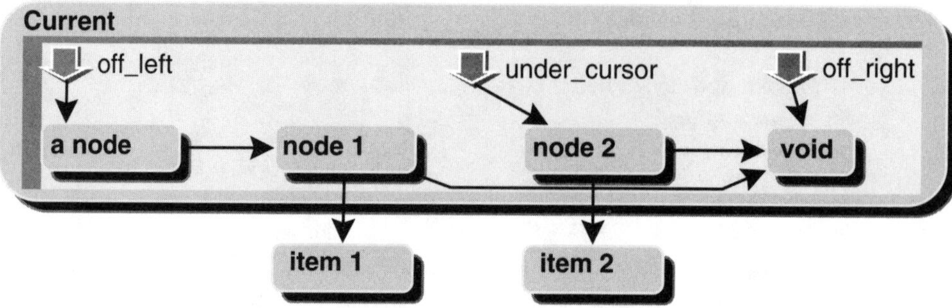

b. *Under_cursor*'s left neighbor has been told to bypass *under_cursor*.

Figure 7.12 A singly linked list's response to request "*delete*". (The object's routines are not shown in order to save page space.)

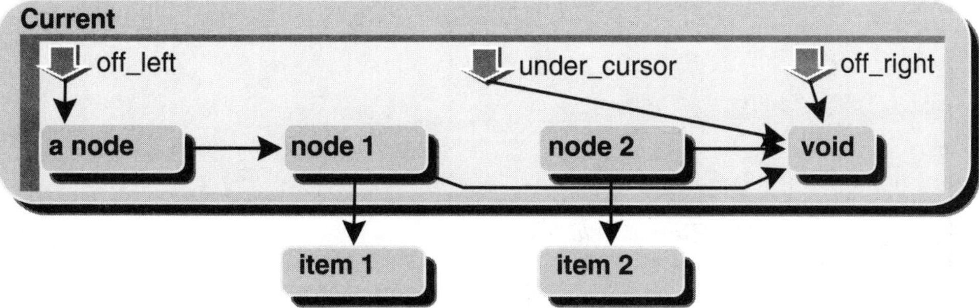

c. The entity *under_cursor* is made to track the node to *under_cursor*'s right.

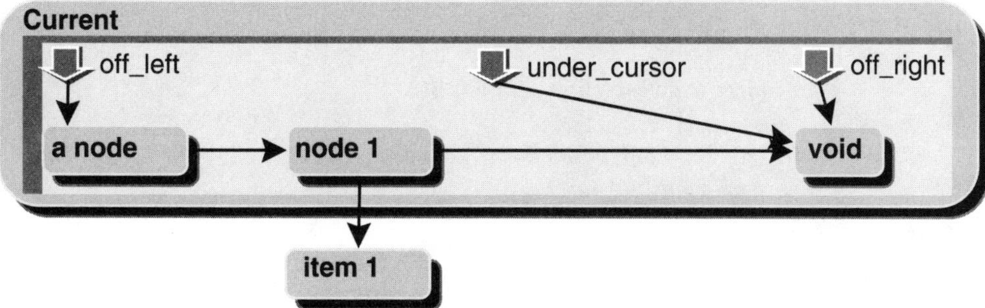

d. Just cleaning up the diagram. Since nothing in this list is tracking the bypassed node, it is not part of the picture anymore.

Figure 7.12 *(continued)*

Since a singly linked list cannot ask a node to identify its left neighbor, the list has to do the job itself. We create a private feature for that task and call it "*left_of*(<node>)." Its code is shown in Listing 7.10, together with *make* and *delete*.

Using *left_of*, conversion of the routines described in Section 7.1 is straightforward.

```
class LIST_SINGLY_LINKED[ITEM]
inherit LIST_LINKED[ITEM]
creation make
feature {NONE}

    left_of(node: like off_left): like off_left is
            --The node to the left of node in this list.
        require
```

Listing 7.10 A beginning of class *LIST_SINGLY_LINKED*.

```
            --node is somewhere in this list
        do
            from
                Result := off_left
            until
                Result.right = node
            loop
                Result := Result.right;
            end;
        ensure
            Result.right = node
        end; --left_of

feature
    make is
            --Initialize to get an empty, off-left list.
        do
            !NODE_R[ITEM]!off_left.make;
            --Leave off_right = Void.
            wipe_out;
        end; --make

    delete is
            --Delete the item under the cursor.
        do
            --Make under_cursor's left neighbor track under_cursor's right neighbor
            --instead of under_cursor.
            left_of(under_cursor).set_right (under_cursor.right);

            --Advance the cursor one step to the right.
            under_cursor := under_cursor.right;
        end; --delete
end --class LIST_SINGLY_LINKED
```

Listing 7.10 *(continued)*

7.4 Factoring Out Implementation Commonalities

The implementations of arrayed lists and linked lists had very little in common. The only thing they shared was the external view, so their common ancestor, *LIST*, deferred all implementations to them.

In contrast, *LIST_SINGLY_LINKED* and *LIST_DOUBLY_LINKED* are quite similar in their implementations. This gives us an opportunity to place some common code into *LIST_LINKED* (Figure 7.13).

Several considerations are relevant to deciding which routines to factor out of the more specific classes into their common ancestor.

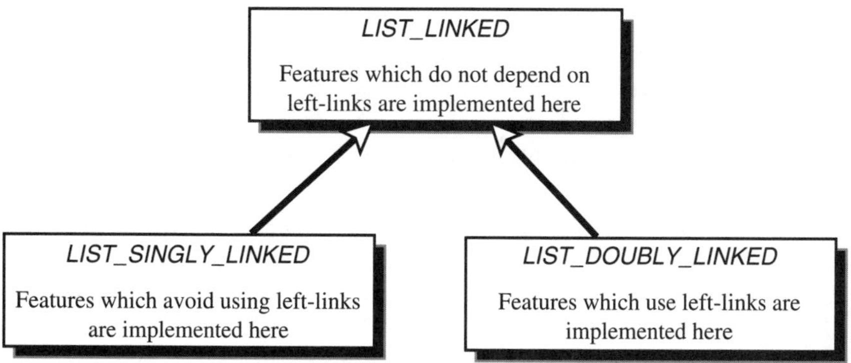

Figure 7.13 A plan for distributing feature implementations among the linked list classes.

1. *Avoiding code duplication.* All other things being equal, it is better to have something implemented once rather than twice. If there is a bug in the code (not that this ever happens to *you,* but hypothetically speaking), it is more likely to be caught during testing if it is used in twice as many situations. If you fix it in one place, two classes are fixed at once.
2. *Does the common ancestor have everything it needs to implement a routine?* Since implementations of the specific classes do differ, putting a feature into the common ancestor may require it to use features that are implemented in the more specific classes. This may take some additional planning.
3. *Is there an unacceptable loss of performance?* If an implementation of a feature in the ancestor would be *significantly* slower, then it should be done in the heirs instead, the previous two considerations notwithstanding.

7.4.1 Simple Example: *move_left* and *move_right*

Let us look at some of the features of *LIST_LINKED* and decide the level at which to implement them. *Move_left* and *move_right* are excellent examples of how to apply the three considerations.

All *move_right* does is advance the cursor one step to the right:

```
under_cursor := under_cursor.right;
```

That code is identical for both singly and doubly linked lists. Thus, it is a good candidate for being factored out into *LIST_LINKED*. Before we make that decision, we need to determine what its pre- and postconditions need. The precondition is "**not** *is_off_right*" and the postcondition is "**not** *is_off_left*." Does this mean that we need to implement *is_off_left* and *is_off_right* in *LIST_LINKED*? Not at all. They need to be *defined,* but they already are (in *LIST*). Their implementation, though, may be left to the specific classes. When *move_right* is requested of a *LIST_SINGLY_LINKED* object, it will use its own implementation of *is_off_left* and *is_off_right*, at whichever level that was defined. That does not mean that we must not define them at the *LIST_LINKED* level, but we do not have to. Thus, *move_right* goes into *LIST_LINKED*.

The singly and doubly linked implementations of *move_left* are quite different. *LIST_DOUBLY_LINKED*'s version cannot possibly be used on a singly linked list, because *NODE_R* objects do not provide the *left* feature. *LIST_SINGLY_LINKED*'s version must start off-left and seek out the node to the left of *under_cursor*. Now, we *could* use that version on doubly linked lists too, but that is a perfect example of why we have consideration 3: Searching for the left neighbor from off-left is an O(*N*) operation, while asking a *NODE_LR* for it is O(1)—how's that for unacceptable loss of performance? No, *move_left* better stay in the more specific classes.

7.4.2 A More Subtle Example: *out*

Since *out* builds the list's string representation left-to-right, it would seem a good candidate for being factored out of the specific classes into *LIST_LINKED*. Let us write it and see. Listing 7.11 is the result.

```
out: STRING is
      --"< 1st_item.out ... last_item.out >".
   local
      node: like off_left;
   do
      Result := clone("< "); --Left delimiter.
      from
         node := off_left.right;
      until
         node = off_right
      loop
         Result.append_string(node.item.out); --Item's representation.
         Result.append_string(" "); --Space between item representations.
         node := node.right;
      end;
      Result.append_string(">"); --Right delimiter.
   end; --out
```

Listing 7.11 Feature *out* of class *LIST_LINKED*.

```
feature {LIST_LINKED}

    off_left: NODE_R[ITEM] is
            --The off-left marker.
        deferred
        end; --off_left

    off_right: like off_left is
            --The off-right marker.
        deferred
        end; --off_right
```

Listing 7.12 Making *off_left* and *off_right* known in class *LIST_LINKED*.

If we rush off to compile this now, we will get a blunt reminder that *off_left* and *off_right* are not defined at this level. Of course, we already knew that. So, can we define it here for both of the heir classes? It would be easier not to do that at this time. For instance, *off_right* will need to be a *NODE_LR* in *LIST_DOUBLY_LINKED* but a *NODE_R* in *LIST_SINGLY_LINKED*. So, let us just define them as deferred features of the most general type of node we have: *NODE_R* (as shown in Listing 7.12).

I will let you work out how to spread the rest of the features between the two levels of the class hierarchy. When I did it, I ended up with a *LIST_LINKED* class consisting of three deferred features and a fully implemented one in the "**feature** {*LIST_LINKED*}" section, and 14 fully implemented features visible by all classes. That left eight features to be added in *LIST_SINGLY_LINKED* and *LIST_DOUBLY_LINKED*, and, of course, the three features that were deferred in the ancestor had to be defined too.

7.5 Choosing an Implementation: Performance Analyses

It is time to step back and look at the "big picture." Given three implementations (deferred classes do not count), when does it make sense to use each one?

7.5.1 Time Considerations

First, let us summarize the worst case and average time complexities of each feature in each implementation in Table 7.1 (average and worst case time complexities do not always coincide, but they do in these classes).

Table 7.1 Average and worst case time complexities for implementations of lists. N = *length*, M = *other.length*.

Feature	*Array*	*Singly Linked*	*Doubly Linked*
make	O(*capacity*)	O(1)	O(1)
move_left	O(1)	O(*N*)	O(1)
move_right	O(1)	O(1)	O(1)
move_off_left	O(1)	O(1)	O(1)
move_off_right	O(1)	O(1)	O(1)
is_off_left	O(1)	O(1)	O(1)
is_off_right	O(1)	O(1)	O(1)
is_empty	O(1)	O(1)	O(1)
is_full	O(1)	O(1)	O(1)
item	O(1)	O(1)	O(1)
replace	O(1)	O(1)	O(1)
insert_on_left	O(*N*)	O(*N*)	O(1)
insert_on_right	O(*N*)	O(1)	O(1)
delete	O(*N*)	O(*N*)	O(1)
wipe_out	O(*capacity*)[a]	O(1)[b]	O(1)[b]
out	O(*N*)	O(*N*)	O(*N*)
copy	O(*capacity*)	O(*M*)	O(*M*)
is_equal	O(*N*)	O(*N*)	O(*N*)
cursor_matches	O(*N*)	O(*N*)	O(*N*)
length	O(1)	*See Exercise 7.4*	

[a] See Exercise 6.5.
[b] The garbage collector *may* have to do O(*N*) work to recycle the discarded nodes.

The doubly linked implementation appears to be the clear winner: In the array and the singly linked implementations, each feature has either the same or worse complexity. Why, then, don't we simply use the doubly linked version and not bother with the other two?

Well, for one thing, the user may not *need* the expensive (O(*N*)) routines. For example, if user code never requests the *move_left*, *insert_on_left*, and *delete* features, then the singly linked implementation is as fast as the doubly linked one. As we will discuss in Section 7.5.2, the singly linked implementation requires less space.

The other consideration is *where* within the list the cursor is when a feature is requested. Table 7.2 shows the best case complexities for the various features, and the circumstances under which they happen.

Fine, but when are we lucky enough to have the user request features only under the best circumstances? Very rarely. However, in later chapters we will be using linear object structures where we only support insertions at one end of a list and place a similar restriction on removals. When that happens, we will revisit this analysis, rather than trying to figure it all out again.

Table 7.2 Best case time complexities for implementations of lists, and the situations in which they occur. $N = length$, $M = other.length$.

Feature	*Array*		*Singly Linked*		*Doubly Linked*	
make	O(*capacity*)		O(1)		O(1)	
move_left	O(1)		O(1)	On first item	O(1)	
move_right	O(1)		O(1)		O(1)	
move_off_left	O(1)		O(1)		O(1)	
move_off_right	O(1)		O(1)		O(1)	
is_off_left	O(1)		O(1)		O(1)	
is_off_right	O(1)		O(1)		O(1)	
is_empty	O(1)		O(1)		O(1)	
is_full	O(1)		O(1)		O(1)	
item	O(1)		O(1)		O(1)	
replace	O(1)		O(1)		O(1)	
insert_on_left	O(1)	Off-right	O(1)	On first item	O(1)	
insert_on_right	O(1)	On last item	O(1)		O(1)	
delete	O(1)	On last item	O(1)	On first item	O(1)	
wipe_out	O(*capacity*)		O(1)		O(1)	
out	O(*N*)		O(*N*)		O(*N*)	
copy	O(*capacity*)		O(*M*)		O(*M*)	
is_equal	O(1)	Lengths differ	O(1)	1st differ	O(1)	1st differ
cursor_matches	O(1)		O(1)	Both off-left	O(1)	Both off-left
length	O(1)			See Exercise 7.4		

7.5.2 Space Considerations

Now let us look at how much space overhead these implementations require. Let us call the amount of space taken up by one reference to an object "*R*." At the time of this writing, *R* is typically 32 bits (4 bytes).

The array implementation will occupy $R \times capacity$, plus a little more space for other attributes in the object (e.g., *length*). It does not matter how many items are in the list; enough room is reserved for *capacity* items. Thus, the space complexity of the array implementation is O(*capacity*).

A singly linked representation uses two references per node: a reference to the item and a reference to the node's right neighbor. But since nodes are allocated only when needed, the number of nodes is approximately *N* (plus a small, constant number of nodes for the end markers and the spare, if any). Thus, the space utilization is about $2R \times N$, which is O(*N*).

The doubly linked implementation is similar in its space consumption, except that there is an additional reference in each node for tracking its left neighbor. Thus, the space consumption is roughly $3R \times N$, also O(*N*).

With complexities so similar, we do have to pay attention to the constants. All other considerations aside, paying attention only to space use, when does it make sense to use which implementation?

Suppose we have an array-based list with capacity 1,000,000. If it tracks 10 items, we are using 1,000,000R bytes (or whatever memory units we use) for the job. A singly linked representation would only use 20R bytes, and a doubly linked—30R. On a system with 4-byte R, the array representation loses by almost 4 megabytes.

On the other hand, suppose it is tracking 999,990 items. In the array representation, we are still using the same 1,000,000R bytes, but a singly linked representation uses 1,999,980R, and the doubly linked—2,999,970R! On a machine with 4-byte references, the array representation beats the singly linked representation by almost 4 megabytes, and the doubly linked list by almost 8 megabytes!

The break-even points are easy to compute. For array vs. singly linked, we have:

$$2R \times N = R \times capacity$$
$$N = \frac{capacity}{2}$$

For array vs. doubly linked, we get $N = \frac{1}{3}\,capacity$. When N is smaller than the break-even point, the linked representation is more space efficient; above the break-even point, the array representation wins.

An important thing to consider is whether it is important to use only enough memory to track the current number of items. On a multi-purpose system, it is important not to "hog" memory that you are not using. However, if the object structure resides in a fixed amount memory that nobody else wants (for example, a buffer box), then we might as well allocate the whole thing for the array, and thus be capable of tracking twice as many items as with the singly linked representation, and three times as many as with the doubly linked version.

7.5.3 Is Time or Space More Important?

That, of course, depends on the circumstances. That is why there are different implementations to consider. There is always a trade-off.

If the system is restricted in memory space (for example, it could be an oscilloscope or a cheap personal computer), then memory considerations prevail. If, on the other hand, the system is loaded with physical memory, then space efficiency may be sacrificed to get more speed.

Why just "physical memory"; isn't virtual memory just as good? Well, if you think that space efficiency is not important on a virtual memory system (as most general-purpose operating systems now are), think again. If your object structure is spread over too many memory pages, the system will have to do swapping with the hard disk to access parts of it. There is no easier way to slow down the execution of your program than by having to wait for disk access to complete: Disk access is thousands of times slower than memory access.

Summary

Linked lists use interconnected nodes to keep track of objects. Insertion and deletion entail manipulating node references, and are potentially O(1) in time complexity.

Linked lists can be singly linked or doubly linked. In a doubly linked list, a node has references to both of its neighbors; in a singly linked list, only to one neighbor. Singly linked lists occupy less space, and their implementations of some of the features are simpler. However, moving in the direction opposite of the node reference chain is an O(*N*) operation, so all operations that require it become O(*N*) or worse. Doubly linked lists have the best time complexity, but require more space per node.

Classes *SINGLY_LINKED_LIST* and *DOUBLY_LINKED_LIST* have enough feature implementations in common to warrant the creation of a shared parent class, *LINKED_LIST* (which is an heir to *LIST*).

Exercises

1. Consider the "spare tire" implementation of linked lists.
   a. Draw an empty list.
   b. Draw the result of inserting an item into the list you drew in part (a), assuming that there is room for another node in the system.
   c. Draw the result of inserting an item into the list you drew in part (b), assuming that there is not enough room for another node in the system.
   d. Draw the result of deleting an item from the list you drew in part (c).
2. Suppose we did want to have a class *NODE_L*. How would it fit in with the other node classes discussed in this chapter? Suggest a class hierarchy for these classes, stating which methods are implemented and which (if any) are deferred in each class. (*Note:* A class may have more than one parent.)
3. Which features should be implemented in class *LIST_LINKED*, and which should be deferred to *LIST_SINGLY_LINKED* and *LIST_DOUBLY_LINKED*?

4. Sketch two different ways of implementing feature *length* in class *LIST_LINKED* (deferring it does not count). Discuss the trade-offs between the two implementations.

5. a. Implement deferred class *LIST_LINKED*.

   b. Implement class *LIST_DOUBLY_LINKED*.

   c. Implement class *LIST_SINGLY_LINKED*.

   d. Changing only the lines marked "--**imp**" in *LIST_TESTER*, test classes *LIST_DOUBLY_LINKED* and *LIST_SINGLY_LINKED*.

6. Consider the typical implementation of *ARRAY* discussed in Chapter 5. What are the time complexities of the operations *item*, *put*, and *resize*? Explain your answers.

8 Stacks

Now that we have thoroughly studied the linear object structure in its most general form, we take a couple of chapters to examine two structures that have more specific behaviors. Both of them keep track of objects in an order determined by the time at which they were asked to track each one. They start tracking an object in a specific way, and they provide access to them only in the prescribed order.

In this chapter, we look at **stacks,** which give access only to the last object to be inserted into the object structure. We will consider three implementations for it: using a list, an array, and a linked representation designed specifically for stacks.

8.1 What a *STACK* Is and What It Does

A stack is a linear object structure that can only be accessed and modified on one end. To understand the terminology computer scientists use for stacks, imagine a cylinder with a spring-loaded piston at the bottom, and a latch at the top (Figure 8.1). Objects are stacked inside, and the latch prevents the spring from shooting all the objects out of the cylinder. The **top** object is visible from outside the cylinder.

If you tap the latch, the top object will **pop** off, and the object that was just under it will become the top object (Figure 8.2). The latch only lets through one object at a time and then it snaps back.

To insert an object into the cylinder, **push** it onto the stack of objects inside (Figure 8.3). The latch will let it through and snap back.

Note that the last object to go onto the stack is always the first to come off. The stack is a **last in, first out** (**"LIFO,"** pronounced "LIFE-oh") object structure. It is used in situations where most recently tracked objects are of the most interest.

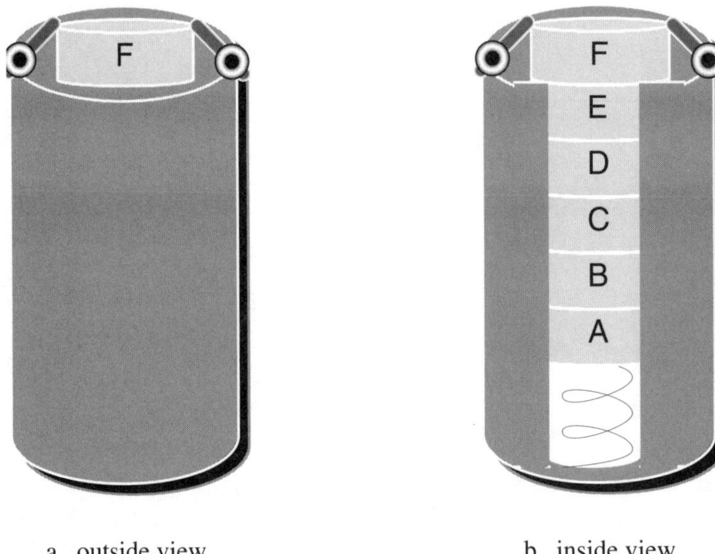

Figure 8.1 A metaphor for the *STACK* object structure.

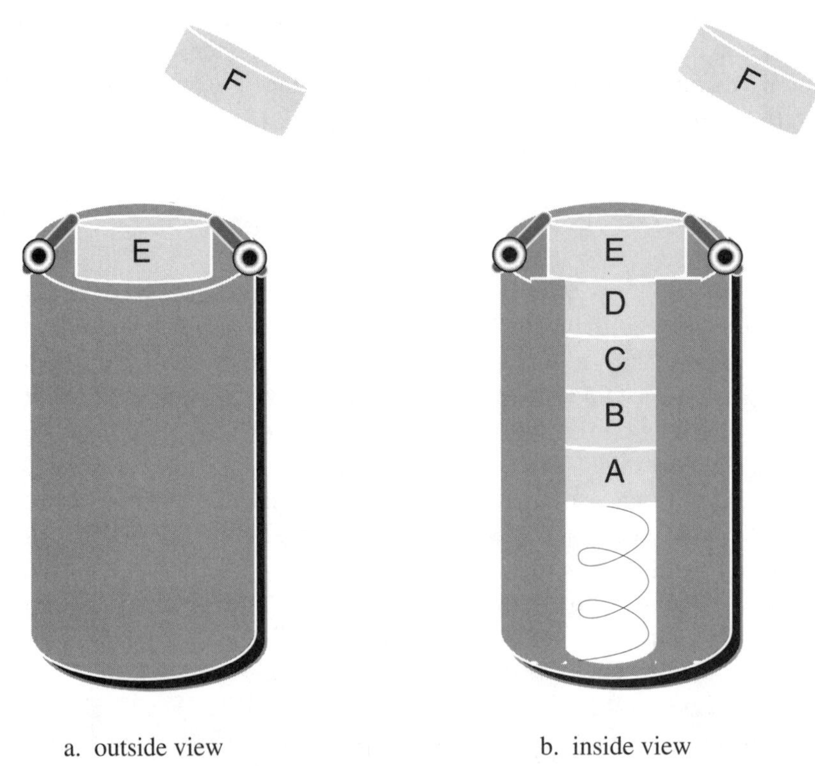

Figure 8.2 The result of popping the stack in Figure 8.1.

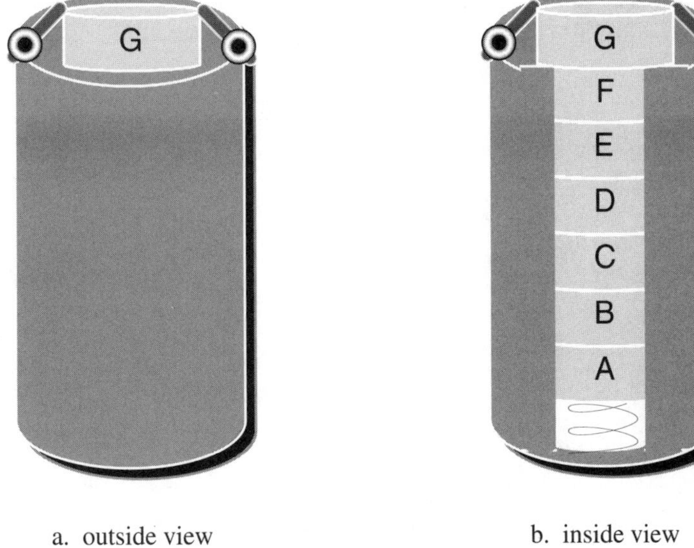

a. outside view b. inside view

Figure 8.3 The result of pushing object *G* onto the stack in Figure 8.1.

8.1.1 The Contract

Because the only way to insert an item into a stack is to push, the only way to remove one is to pop, and the only way to access one is through the top, the interface with a *STACK* is considerably simpler than the interface with a *LIST*. Thus, the contract will be simpler. Listing 8.1 provides the complete contract. (Compare that with *LIST*'s contract in Listing 6.6.)

Many of the specifications in Listing 8.1 are analogous to their *LIST* counterparts. There is a slight change in terminology: Whereas a list has length, we traditionally talk about a stack's *size*.[1] Another minor change is in *out*'s delimiters: a bar at the top and a bracket at the bottom.

The features for moving items into and out of the stack are the only ones that are significantly different from those we defined for lists. There are only three of them, and their postconditions are simpler because there is no cursor location to worry about. There is one thing that we can say about *push* that had no convenient equivalent in the *insert_*. . . routines for lists: the postcondition

new_item_on_top: *top* = *new_item*

---

[1] If you like "length" more than "size," hold on until the next chapter: We will be back to "length" with queues. There is a school of thought that similar features should have the same name in all classes, regardless of the tradition; for example, the ISE library uses the name "count" for each class's sizing feature.

```
deferred class STACK[ITEM] inherit
   ANY
      undefine --to make them deferred
         out, is_equal, copy
      redefine --to add comments
         out, is_equal
      end;

feature --Creation and initialization

   make is
         --Initialize to get an empty stack
      deferred
      ensure
         empty: is_empty;
      end; --make

feature --Moving items into and out of the stack

   push(new_item: ITEM) is
         --Push new_item onto this stack.
      require
         not_full: not is_full;
      deferred
      ensure
         one_more_item: size = old size + 1;
         new_item_on_top: top = new_item;
      end; --push

   pop is
         --Remove the top item.
      require
         not_empty: not is_empty;
      deferred
      ensure
         one_fewer_item: size = old size - 1;
      end; --pop

   top: ITEM is
         --The top item.
      require
         not_empty: not is_empty;
      deferred
      end; --top
```

Listing 8.1 Deferred class *STACK* with the contract.

```
   wipe_out is
         --Make this stack empty.
      deferred
      ensure
         empty: is_empty;
      end; --wipe_out

feature --Sizing

   is_empty: BOOLEAN is
         --Is this stack empty?
      deferred
      end; --is_empty

   is_full: BOOLEAN is
         --Is there is no room on this stack for one more item?
      deferred
      end; --is_full

   size: INTEGER is
         --The number of items currently on this stack.
      deferred
      end; --size

feature --Comparisons and copying

   is_equal(other: like Current): BOOLEAN is
         --Do this stack and other keep track
         --of the same items in the same order?
      deferred
      end; --is_equal

feature --Simple input and output

   out: STRING is
         --"| <top item>.out ... <bottom item>.out ]" or
         --"[ <bottom item>.out ... <top item>.out |".
      deferred
      end; --out

invariant

   empty_iff_zero_size: is_empty = (size = 0);
   size_not_negative: size >= 0;

end --class STACK
```

Listing 8.1 *(continued)*

promises that one of the results of *push* (*new_item*) will be that *top* will return *new_item*. (In *LIST*'s contract, the position of the cursor with respect to the new item had to be promised in a comment instead of a checkable assertion.)

8.2 How a *STACK* Does What It Does

We will consider three different ways to implement a *STACK*: using a *LIST*; with an *ARRAY*; and through a linked object structure.

8.3 Using a *LIST* to Implement a *STACK*

A *STACK* lays its items out in a straight line, as does a *LIST* (though we picture lists as going from left to right and stacks as going from top to bottom). Thus, it is worth considering whether we can reuse all that work we have done for *LIST* classes for our *STACK* implementation.

First, let us consider if we can make *STACK_LIST* an heir to *LIST* or to one of *LIST*'s heirs. We ask the question,

Can a *STACK* act as a *LIST*?

No. For one thing, a *STACK* must not allow insertion of an item into its middle, or it will not be a LIFO structure. So a *STACK* object cannot subcontract to a *LIST* object.

While we cannot reuse *LIST* through inheritance, we can still take advantage of its implementations by putting a *LIST* object inside our *STACK* object, as illustrated in Figure 8.4 (just as we used an *ARRAY* object inside a *LIST_ARRAY* object). That *LIST* will be used to track the *STACK*'s items. The *STACK* object's features will utilize the *LIST*'s features to do most of the work.

For example, if we call the internal *LIST* object "*items*," feature *size* becomes simply

```
size: INTEGER is
        --The number of items currently on this stack.
    do
        Result := items.length;
    end; --size
```

Thus, we reuse the work we have put into the *LIST* implementation for keeping count of the tracked items. Many of the features will be as simple as that.

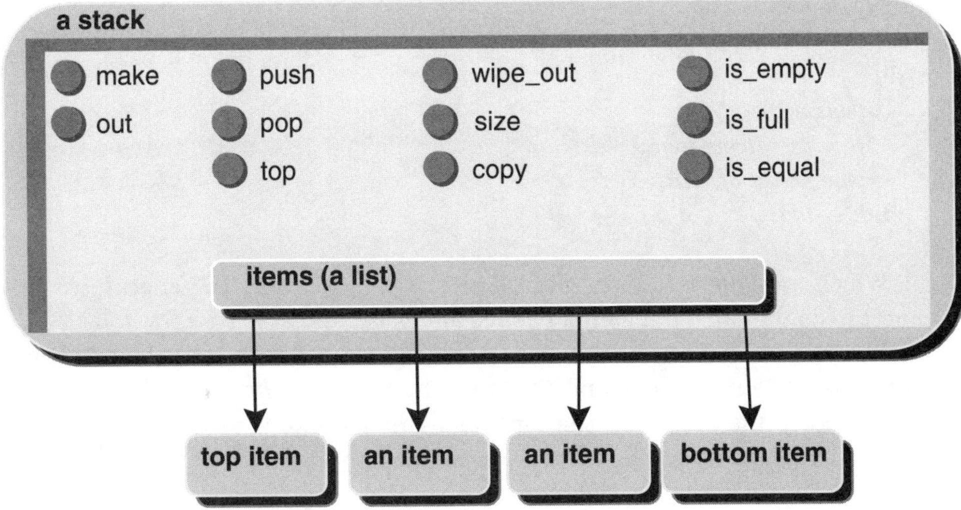

Figure 8.4 The inside view of an implementation of *STACK* that uses a *LIST* object.

8.3.1 Moving Items In and Out

The *LIST* object allows insertion and deletion anywhere, but a *STACK* needs to use its *LIST*'s features to operate only on the end that we designate as the top of the stack. Let us arbitrarily pick the left end of the list as the top of the stack (we will discuss the performance implications of this choice later).

Consider *push*. It has to insert the new item in such a way that it becomes the leftmost item. We have two ways to do that:

1. Go off-left and then insert on right.
2. Go to the leftmost item and insert on left.

The first way is more convenient: Both *insert_on_left* and *insert_on_right* leave the cursor where it is. Thus, the first method will leave the cursor off-left and ready for the next *push* without any cursor movement. The second method, however, will leave the cursor at what is now the second item from the top, and we will need to do a *move_left* to get back to where we can do another *insert_on_left*.

So, to speed up *push*, we can adopt the convention that the list is always off-left. However, if we do that, we will need to do cursor movement for *top* and *pop*, because both require the cursor to be right on the top item. For example, *top* becomes

```
top: ITEM is
        --The top item.
  do
    items.move_right;
    Result := items.item;
    items.move_off_left;
  end; --top
```

Which is requested more often, *push* or *pop* and *top*? In general, we can expect to do the same number of *push*es and *pop*s, and at least a few *top*s. (Why would our users bother stacking up items if they never look at them?) Thus, there should be more *pop*s and *top*s than there are *push*es, so it makes more sense to keep the cursor on the top item. Unfortunately, we have no efficient Boolean expression to indicate that, so we have to turn that part of the implementation invariant into a comment:

```
invariant
  have_list: items /= Void;
  --The cursor in items is on the leftmost item,
  --or off-right if items.is_empty.
```

To support this invariant, we make sure that all routines leave the cursor one step right of off-left. For example, *make* as shown in Listing 8.2 creates an empty list object that is off-right (which is one step to the right of off-left in an empty list).

```
class STACK_LIST[ITEM] inherit
  STACK[ITEM]
creation make
make is
        --Initialize to get an empty stack.
  do
    !!items.make;
    items.move_off_right;
  end; --make
feature --Sizing
  size: INTEGER is
        --The number of items currently on the stack.
```

Listing 8.2 A partial implementation of *STACK_LIST*.

```
      do
         Result := items.length;
      end; --size

feature --Moving items into and out of the stack

   push (new_item: ITEM) is
         --Push new_item onto this stack.
      do
         --Put new_item into its place.
         items.insert_on_left (new_item);

         --Fulfill the invariant.
         items.move_left;
      end; --push

   pop is
         --Removes the top item.
      do
         items.delete; --We rely on the "cursor moves right" postcondition.
      end; --pop

invariant

   have_list: items /= Void;
   --The cursor in items is on the leftmost item,
   --or off-right if items.is_empty.

end --class STACK_LIST
```

Listing 8.2 (*continued*)

8.3.2 A Programmer to One Structure, a User to Another

When we were implementing *LIST_ARRAY*, we were a user for *ARRAY*. We did not write *ARRAY*, so behaving like a user was not hard. Now, however, we are users of one of our own structures (*LIST*). For example, look at the *out* feature in Listing 8.3. It reads like a tester routine for *LIST*!

When programmers use one of their own structures to implement another, they may be tempted to modify the old structure to better accommodate the new one. For instance, I was tempted to add an *is_on_leftmost_item* feature to *LIST* just to make the *STACK_LIST* class invariant codable in Eiffel. Such temptation should be resisted: If a feature or a behavior did not seem necessary before, it is often better to work around it and leave the old structure alone. Remember, any class modification needs to be followed by more testing; the longer a class has gone with no modifications other than bug fixes, the less likely it is to contain mistakes.

```
feature --Conversions

  out: STRING is
      --"| <top item>.out ... <bottom item>.out ]".
    do
      Result := clone("| "); --Top delimiter.
      from
        --Start at the top item (already there).
      until
        items.is_off_right
      loop
        Result.append_string(items.item.out);
        Result.append_string(" ");
        items.move_right;
      end;
      Result.append_string("]"); --Bottom delimiter.

      --Move back to the top item.
      items.move_off_left;
      items.move_right;
    end; --out
```

Listing 8.3 Feature *out* illustrates how a programmer of one object structure (*STACK_LIST*) acts as a user of another (*LIST*).

8.3.3 Deciding Which *LIST* Implementation to Use

Since *LIST* is a deferred class (the keeper of the contract and not a complete implementation), we cannot actually create an object of class *LIST*. Listing 8.2 uses *LIST_DOUBLY_LINKED*, but that was an arbitrary choice. Let us put some thought into it.

Our choices of list implementations are *LIST_ARRAY*, *LIST_DOUBLY_LINKED* and *LIST_SINGLY_LINKED*. The features we have requested of them so far are *make*, *move_off_left*, *move_off_right*, *move_left*, *move_right*, *is_off_right*, *length*, *insert_on_left*, and *delete* (you will run into others as you write the class). Of these, *insert_on_left*, *move_left*, *delete*, and *item* are of greatest concern to us, since they are used in *push*, *pop*, and *top*, the most frequently used stack features.

Table 8.1 summarizes the average and worst case time complexities of those features (abstracted from Table 7.1). Judging by that table, it would seem that *LIST_DOUBLY_LINKED* is the only good choice. Not so.

What makes those O(*N*) features in the singly linked implementation slow? In the case of *move_left*, it is having to start at the left end of the list to find the previous node (since each node tracks its right neighbor but not its left). But if the cursor is on the leftmost node, that is only a one-step loop! This is the best

Table 8.1 Average and worst case time complexities for critical features of the three list implementations.

Feature	*Used In*	*Array*	*Singly Linked*	*Doubly Linked*
insert_on_left	*push*	O(*N*)	O(*N*)	O(1)
move_left	*push*	O(1)	O(*N*)	O(1)
delete	*pop*	O(*N*)	O(*N*)	O(1)
item	*top*	O(1)	O(1)	O(1)

case scenario, and the complexity is O(1), not O(*N*). The same situation applies to *insert_on_left* and *delete*.

Best case situations rarely arise randomly, but they can be made to happen by design (or, in this case, by a lucky fifty–fifty choice).

What makes those O(*N*) features in the array implementation slow? Deleting and inserting an item into the array implementation requires all items to the right to be moved over, hence the O(*N*) complexity. If we are operating on the left end of the list, we have to move *all* of the other items—the worst case scenario.

Thus, the array column is unchanged, the singly linked column is updated, and we get Table 8.2. Now it looks like the singly linked implementation is the best, since the doubly linked implementation has more space overhead (because each node tracks its left neighbor as well as the right one).

Well, do not write off the array implementation just yet.

Recall that the decision to align the left end of the list with the top of the stack was arbitrary. What if we aligned the top with the right end instead? The rightmost item would be the top item, so all of our routines would be mirror images of the ones presented above: *push* would use *insert_on_right* followed by *move_right*, *pop* would do *delete* followed by *move_left* (since *delete* moves the cursor to the right and we need it to move to the left), and so on.

The reason this rearrangement makes a difference is that the best case conditions are on the right end in the array implementation of lists. If we are at the right end of the list, there are no items on the right to move, so the operations are O(1).

Table 8.2 Time complexities for critical features operating on the left end of the three list implementations.

Feature	*Used In*	*Array*	*Singly Linked*	*Doubly Linked*
insert_on_left	*push*	O(*N*)	O(1)	O(1)
move_left	*push*	O(1)	O(1)	O(1)
delete	*pop*	O(*N*)	O(1)	O(1)
item	*top*	O(1)	O(1)	O(1)

Table 8.3 Time complexities for critical features operating on the right end of the three list implementations.

Feature	*Used In*	*Array*	*Singly Linked*	*Doubly Linked*
insert_on_right	*push*	O(1)	O(1)	O(1)
move_right	*push*	O(1)	O(1)	O(1)
delete	*pop*	O(1)	O(*N*)	O(1)
move_left	*pop*	O(1)	O(*N*)	O(1)
item	*top*	O(1)	O(1)	O(1)

The rearrangement hurts the singly linked implementation: *move_left* is O(*N*) at the right end of the list, since it has to traverse the entire list left-to-right to find the node to the left of the rightmost node. This does not affect *push* since it does not need *move_left* anymore, but *pop* does. The complexities in the "top is on the right" alignment are summarized in Table 8.3.

8.4 Using an *ARRAY* to Implement a *STACK*

Using a list inside a stack is a quick way to implement stacks—if you already have lists. Does that mean that if you need a stack you need to write list classes first? Obviously not; instead of using an array implementation of a list we could manipulate an array directly, and we can write a linked stack as easily as a linked list (even easier, since there are fewer features in a stack). If good list classes are unavailable, or if measurements show that going through a list's interface is too slow for the purpose at hand, it is better to just write lower level implementations of stacks. We start by writing a *STACK_ARRAY* class, and will do *STACK_LINKED* later.

We use an array called *items* and put the bottom item into position 1, the second from the bottom item into position 2, and so on, up to the top object in position *size*, as shown in Figure 8.5. Thus, we can get the top object by using the *size* feature:

```
top: ITEM is
        --The top item.
  do
    Result := items.item(size);
  end; --top
```

To push a new item, we increment *size* and make the new *size* position track the new item:

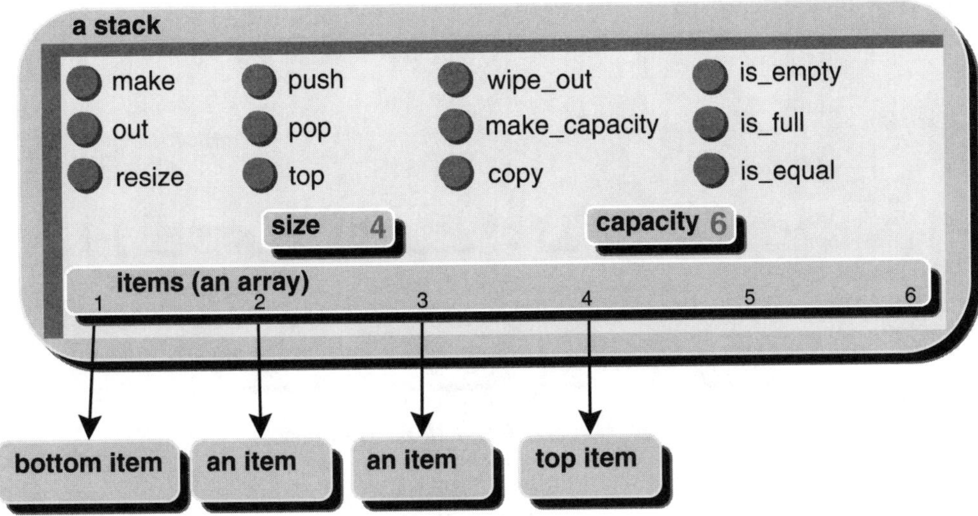

Figure 8.5 The inside view of an implementation of *STACK* that uses an *ARRAY* object.

```
push (new_item: ITEM) is
        --Push new_item onto this stack.
    do
        size := size + 1;
        --Put new_item into its place.
        items.put (new_item, size);
    end; --push
```

To pop an item, we set the top item adrift by disconnecting it from the array, and then decrement size:

```
pop is
        --Remove the top item.
    local
        void_item: ITEM;
    do
        items.put (void_item, size); --Set the old top item adrift.
        size := size - 1;
    end; --pop
```

Nice, simple, and O(1). The remaining features are analogous to their counterparts in *LIST_ARRAY*.

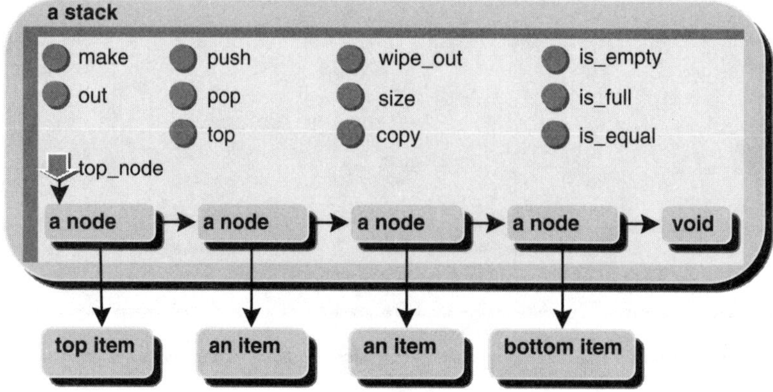

Figure 8.6 An inside view of a *STACK_LINKED* object.

8.5 A Singly Linked Implementation of *STACK*

We observed earlier that a singly linked structure is sufficient to push, pop, and get the top in O(1) time, as long as the top is aligned with the leftmost node. Thus, we will not bother with a doubly linked implementation. Instead, we will just write a singly linked implementation of stacks and call it "*STACK_LINKED*."

Using the example of *LIST_SINGLY_LINKED* (Figure 7.11), we design the inside view of *STACK_LINKED* shown in Figure 8.6.

To push a new item onto such a stack (Figure 8.7a), we create the new node and make it track the new item (Figure 8.7b), make the new node track the for-

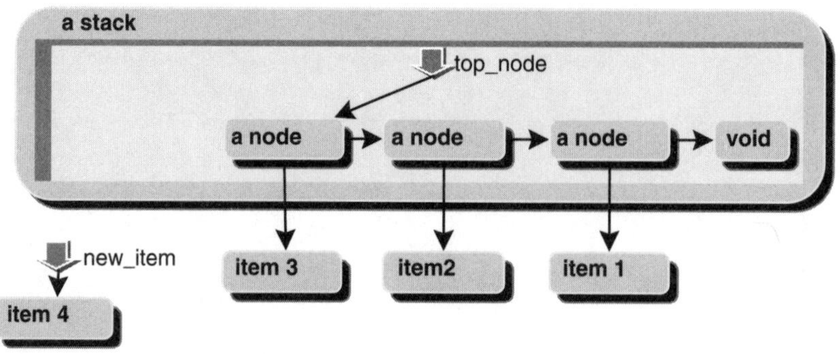

a. The stack with which we started.

Figure 8.7 Responding to request "*push* (*new_item*)". (Routines are not shown in order to save page space.)

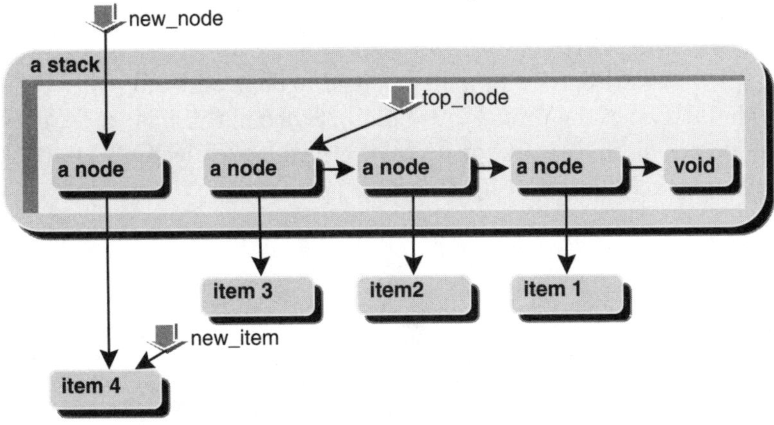

b. *New_node* has been made and is tracking *new_item*.

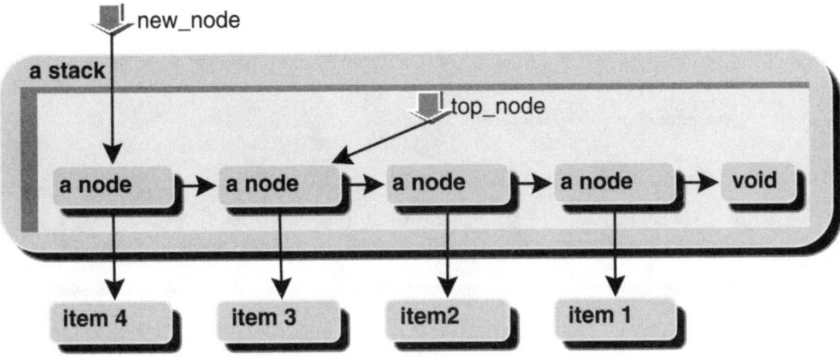

c. *New_node* now tracks the old top node.

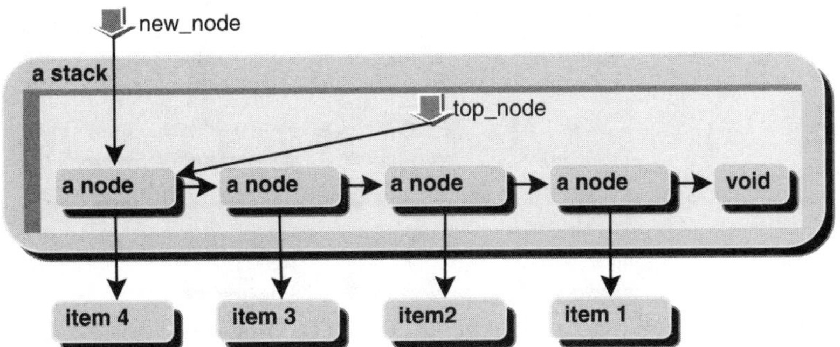

d. *Top_node* now tracks *new_node*, making *new_item* the top item on the stack.

Figure 8.7 *(continued)*

mer top node as its right neighbor (Figure 8.7c), and then make *top_node* track the new node (Figure 8.7d).

To pop the stack (Figure 8.8a), all we need to do is make *top_node* track the second node instead of the first (Figure 8.8b). Since nothing is tracking the former top node anymore, it is swept up by the garbage collector, as is its item if nothing else is tracking that (Figure 8.8c).

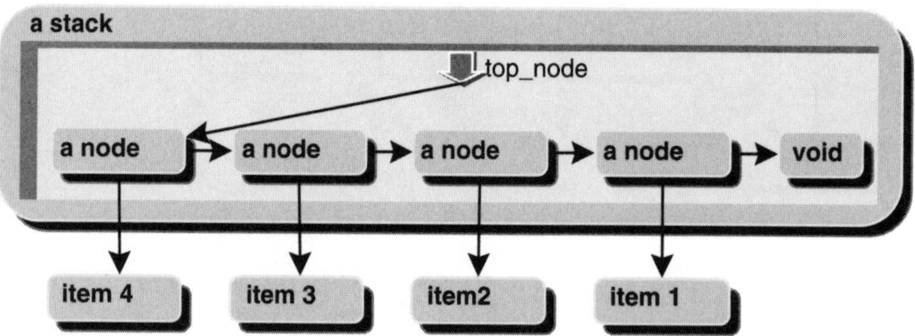

a. The stack with which we started.

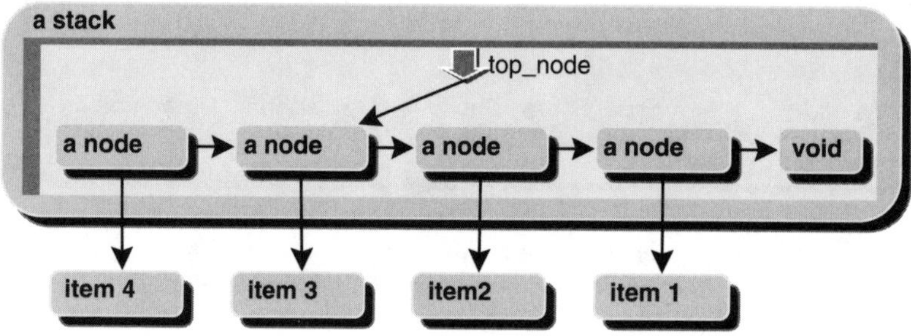

b. *Top_node* tracking the second node.

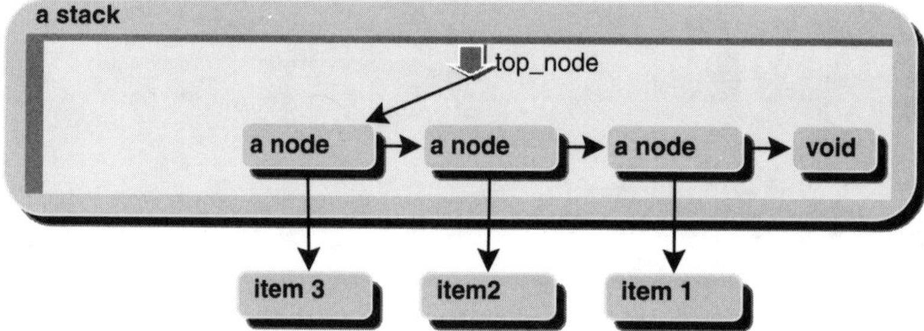

c. Just cleaning up the diagram. Since nothing in this stack is tracking the former top node, it is not part of the picture anymore.

Figure 8.8 Responding to request "*pop*". (Routines are not shown in order to save page space.)

8.6 Choosing the Best *STACK* Implementation for a Given Use

We have seen several *STACK* implementations that have O(1) time performance in the most frequently used routines (*push*, *pop*, and *top*). How do we pick one?

Since modifying a counter is faster than allocating memory and setting tracking information, the array implementations (using either an *ARRAY* or a *LIST_ARRAY*) may be a little faster—as long as there is no need to resize the array. But as soon as we hit the capacity, we take a tremendous penalty in performance. Thus, the array implementations are desirable from the speed point of view only when we can avoid resizing them, which occurs when we know the maximum size of the stack we will need.

From the space efficiency point of view, an array implementation is more efficient if the stack is usually at least half full. If it is less than half full, it is more efficient to use a singly linked implementation, even though the latter has twice as much tracking information per item. It is also a question of what else could be done with that space: If nothing else could possibly use the space, we might as well use it all in one big array.

We will not discuss the time complexities of the other features, because it is important for you to work them out for at least one implementation by yourselves (see the end-of-chapter exercises). You may want to refer back to the discussion of the list implementation time complexities for examples.

8.7 Who Needs It?

Most object structures in this book have straightforward uses. In fact, we use some of them ourselves to build higher level structures—for example, an array is used to implement a stack in *STACK_ARRAY*, and a list is used to implement it in *STACK_LIST*. We will continue using them throughout the book.

The applicability of chronological structures (the stack and the queue, which is discussed in Chapter 9), however, is not as apparent.

Starting with Chapter 13, we implement some of our structures' features **recursively:** The feature will request the current or a different object of the same class to execute the same feature (probably with different parameters). Though recursion does not involve the stack classes we have written in this chapter, the Eiffel run-time system uses a stack to keep track of what object requested what feature at what time, and what the values were of the feature's local entities at the time of the call. I refer you to a compiler design course for details; let me just say now that most (if not all) modern programming languages support recursion and thus utilize a run-time stack.

The stack that supports recursion is invisible to the programmer, but there are plenty of cases where *STACK* object structures are needed. In Chapter 10, for instance, we will build a program that utilizes stacks in two different ways, neither of which has anything to do with recursion.

Summary

A stack is a last in, first out (LIFO) object structure. Objects are pushed onto the stack through the top, and popped from the top of the stack. It is useful in situations where the most recently encountered object is the object of interest.

If implemented correctly, the stack performs its time-critical operations (*push*, *pop*, and *top*) in O(1) time.

Exercises

1. Using *LIST_TESTER* as an example, write *STACK_TESTER*.
2. Implement (efficiently, of course) class *STACK_LIST* using a *LIST_SINGLY_LINKED* object.
3. Implement class *STACK_LIST* using a *LIST_ARRAY* object.
4. Draw the inside view of an empty *STACK_ARRAY*.
5. Implement class *STACK_ARRAY*.
6. Draw the inside view of an empty *STACK_LINKED*.
7. Implement class *STACK_LINKED*.
8. Make a table of time complexities for each routine
   a. in the *STACK_LINKED* implementation, and
   b. in the *STACK_ARRAY* implementation.
9. How can *STACK_LINKED* be written to make the time complexity of its *size* feature O(1)? What are the trade-offs involved? When is it worth it?
10. Note how similar some of the routine implementations in *STACK_ARRAY* and *LIST_ARRAY* are. Can you think of a way to use inheritance to factor them out? (*Hint:* A class may have more than one parent!)

9 Queues

Just as LIFO structures have their uses, computer science has a niche for **first in, first out** (**"FIFO"**) object structures. These are known as **queues.** As we did with stacks, we briefly look at an implementation using a list, and then study the linked and the array versions in detail.

9.1 What a *QUEUE* Is and What It Does

The term "queue" means exactly the same thing in computer science as it does in everyday English: "a line to wait in." When an object is added to the queue, it is placed at the back. Objects are removed from the front.[1] The feature that adds a new item to a queue object structure is traditionally called "*enqueue*," and the object removal feature is named "*dequeue*."[2] There is also a feature called "*front*" that results in the object currently at the front of the queue—the object that is next in line to be dealt with.

9.1.1 The Contract

It is your turn to write the contract. A couple of considerations before you start:

- Tradition dictates that while a stack has "size," a queue has "length."
- I recommend "> <back item>.*out* . . . <front item>.*out* >" or "< <front item>.*out* . . . <back item>.*out* <" for the string representation.

---

[1]Actually, our queues are a little more predictable than the ones in real life, since objects do not try to cut into the line or leave from the middle of the queue when they get tired of waiting.

[2]"*Add*" and "*remove*" are also used sometimes.

9.2 How a *QUEUE* Does What It Does

As we did with stacks, we will first use a *LIST* to implement a *QUEUE*. Then we will look at doing a linked representation. We will do the array representation last (it happens to be the one needing the longest explanation).

9.3 Using a *LIST* to Implement a *QUEUE*

The inside view of this implementation shown in Figure 9.1 is very similar to *STACK_LIST*'s inside view (Figure 8.4). It reflects an arbitrary decision to enqueue objects into the left end of the list, and dequeue them from the right.

9.3.1 Moving Items In and Out

Since we cannot keep the *LIST*'s cursor at both ends at once, we will not try to keep it positioned in the right place for the next feature request, as we had done with stacks. Instead, we will move it to the left end when responding to *enqueue* requests, and to the right end in response to *dequeue* and *front* requests. If the internal *LIST* object is called "*items*," we get the features shown in Listing 9.1.

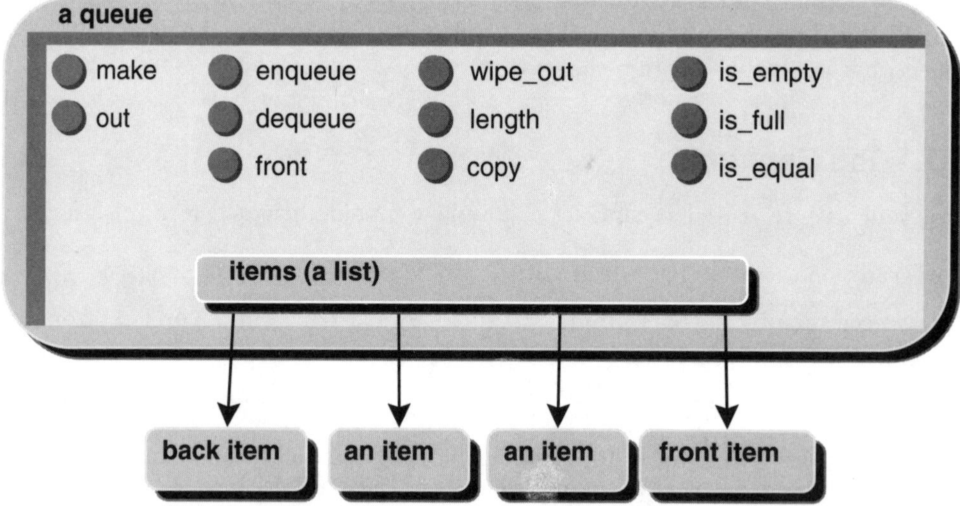

Figure 9.1 The inside view of an implementation of *QUEUE* that uses a *LIST* object.

```
feature --Moving items into and out of the queue

  enqueue(new_item: ITEM) is
        --Add new_item to the back of this queue
     do
        --Put new_item into its place.
        items.move_off_left;
        items.insert_on_right(new_item);
     end; --enqueue

  dequeue is
        --Remove the front item.
     do
        --Place the cursor over the front item.
        items.move_off_right;
        items.move_left;

        --Do the work.
        items.delete;
     end; --dequeue

  front: ITEM is
        --The front item.
     do
        --Place the cursor over the front item.
        items.move_off_right;
        items.move_left;

        --Do the work.
        Result := items.item;
     end; --front
```

Listing 9.1 Features for moving items into and out of a queue, using a *LIST* object.

9.3.2 Deciding Which *LIST* Implementation to Use

With *STACK_LIST*, we could use an array list if we aligned the top with the right end, and a singly linked list if we aligned the top with the left end. Both allowed us to work on their respective best case ends of the list.

Since we work on both ends of the list in *QUEUE_LIST*, either *enqueue* or *dequeue* and *front* will be on the worst case end of the list, no matter how we align the front of the queue.

Consider the singly linked list version. If we align the front with the right end, as we did in Figure 8.4, then the *items.move_left* and the *items.delete* in *dequeue* make it an O(*N*) operation. If we make the left end the front and replace *enqueue* with its mirror image, then the *items.insert_on_left* while in off-right position is an O(*N*) operation.

A similar problem occurs if we use *STACK_ARRAY*: Either the insertion or the deletion will be done on the left end of the list, where it is O(*N*).

There is only one implementation of *LIST* that is suitable for use in *STACK_LIST*: *LIST_DOUBLY_LINKED*, where all the features we need are O(1).

9.4 A Singly Linked Implementation of *QUEUE*

We cannot use *LIST_SINGLY_LINKED* to efficiently implement a stack, but is it possible to use a singly linked structure if we bypass *LIST*'s interface, like we did with *STACK_LINKED*? Can we set things up in a way that avoids the O(*N*) operations? They were slow because we needed to move one node left in the list. Suppose we keep track of that node instead of looking for it every time?

Sticking to our "front is on the right" alignment, we get the inside view in Figure 9.2. Does it speed up *front* and *dequeue*? It certainly does speed up *front*: It just becomes "*Result* := *front_node.item*".

It does not help *dequeue*, though, since it would have to move *front_node* one step to the left, which is still O(*N*).

Time to try the "front is on the left" alignment (Figure 9.3). The *top* implementation is still as trivial. To *dequeue*, we just make *front_node* track *front_node.right*. But that is the cheap end of the list anyway; it is *enqueue* that is vulnerable now. Well, since *enqueue* adds the new node to the right of the one under *back_node*, it becomes an O(1) operation too. This alignment allows us to

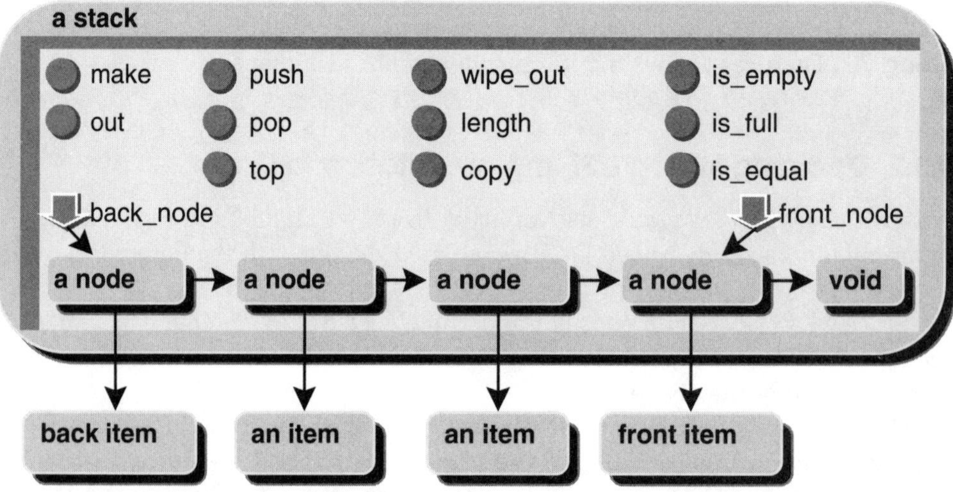

Figure 9.2 Inside view of *QUEUE_LINKED,* with the front of the queue aligned with the right end of the chain of nodes.

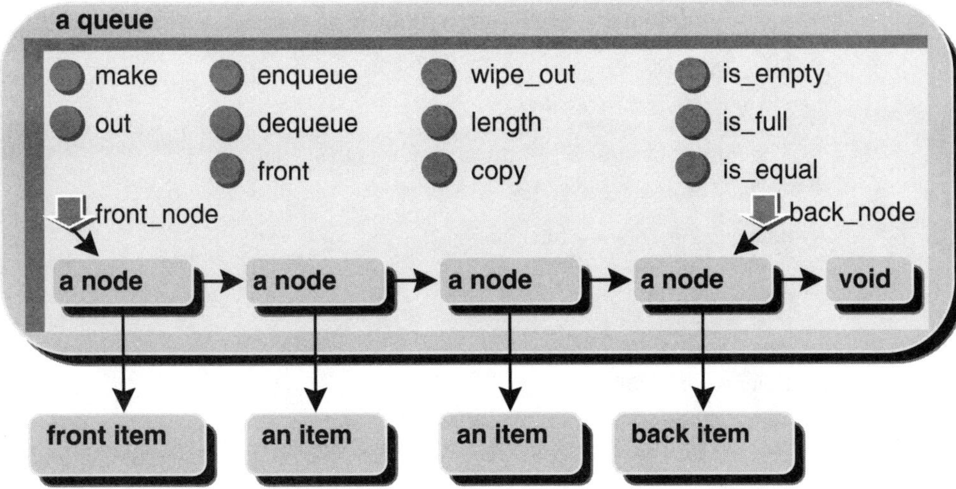

Figure 9.3 Inside view of *QUEUE_LINKED,* this time with the front of the queue aligned with the left end of the chain of nodes.

have O(1) on both ends of the queue, since both *enqueue* and *dequeue* move from left to right, as does the tracking information.

Before we write the code for these routines, let us consider the purpose of the convention of putting a *Void* reference at the right end of the chain. In *LIST_SINGLY_LINKED*, it was there to give the internal *off_right* feature a value, so that *LIST_LINKED* routines that use *off_right* still work; we do not need it for this purpose in *QUEUE_LINKED*. In *STACK_LINKED*, it was used to denote the bottom of the stack, and the stack was empty when *top_node* = *Void*. How do we indicate an empty queue? We could use *top_node*=*bottom_node*=*Void*, but that only solves half of our problem.

Consider the implementations of *enqueue* and *dequeue* given in Listing 9.2. If *back_node* = *Void* when the queue is empty, then *enqueue* will crash on *back_node.set_right*(. . .). In order for *enqueue* to work on an empty queue, we need to have a dummy node at the end of the chain. The queue is then empty when *front_node* and *back_node* both track the dummy.

```
feature --Moving items into and out of the queue

   enqueue(new_item: ITEM) is
         --Add new_item to the back of this queue.
      local
         new_node: like front_node;
```

Listing 9.2 Features for moving items into and out of a *QUEUE_LINKED,* take 1.

```
      do
         --Make a new node and make it track new_item.
         !!new_node.make;
         new_node.set_item(new_item);

         --The former back node's right neighbor is new_node.
         back_node.set_right(new_node);

         --new_node is the new back node.
         back_node := new_node;
      end; --enqueue

   dequeue is
         --Remove the front item.
      do
         --Make front_node track the second node from the front,
         --casting the former front node adrift.
         front_node := front_node.right;
      end; --dequeue

   front: ITEM is
         --The front item.
      do
         Result := top_node.item;
      end; --front
```

Listing 9.2 *(continued)*

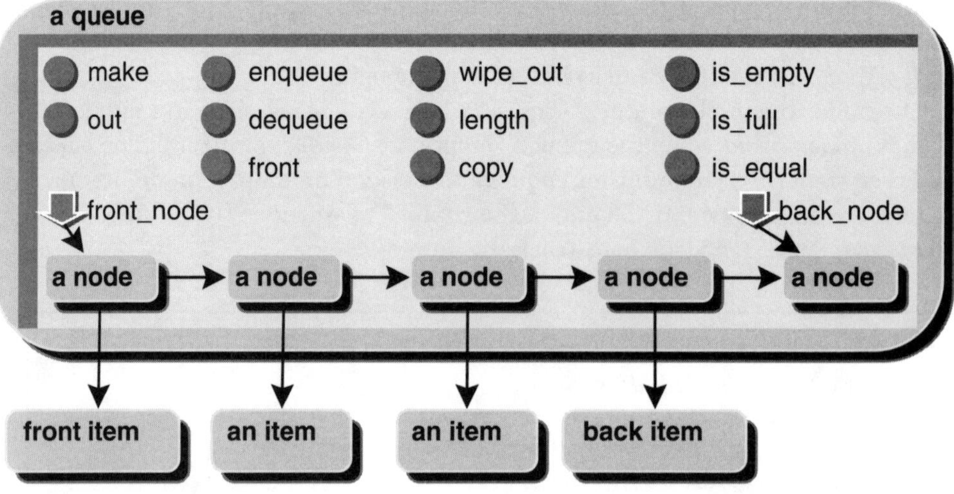

Figure 9.4 Inside view of a *QUEUE_LINKED* object, the final edition.

```
enqueue (new_item: ITEM) is
        --Add new_item to the back of this queue.
    local
        new_node: like front_node;
    do
        --Make a new dummy node and attach it on the right end.
        !!new_node.make;
        back_node.set_right (new_node);

        --The former dummy gets to track new_item.
        back_node.set_item (new_item);

        --The new dummy is the new back node.
        back_node := new_node;
    end; --enqueue
```

Listing 9.3 A modified *enqueue* that deals with the dummy node at the end.

Once we do that, we need to put some "dummy avoidance" code into our routines. If we leave *enqueue* unmodified, then it will keep adding nodes on the right, and the dummy will always be at the front of the queue. We would need to modify both *front* and *dequeue* to avoid it and work on the second node from the left instead.

Another option is to modify *enqueue* so that the dummy is always at the right end of the chain—in fact, we can use it as the end marker instead of comparing with *Void*. This gives us, finally, the inside view in Figure 9.4. The modified *enqueue* is shown in Listing 9.3, and Figure 9.5 illustrates its operation.

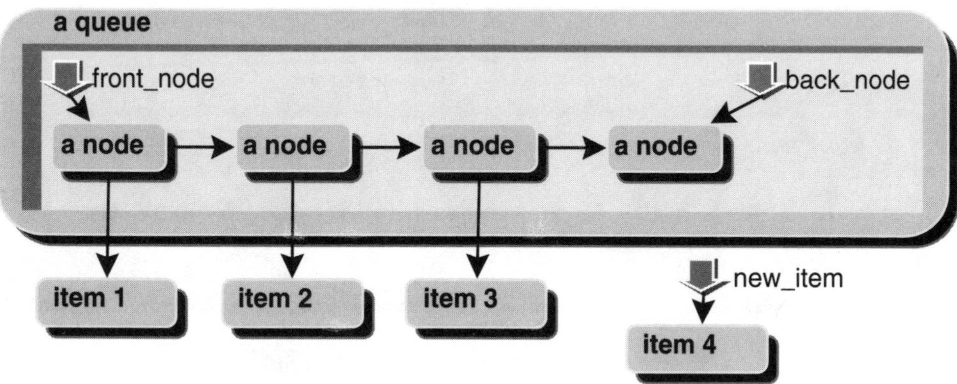

a. The queue with which we started.

Figure 9.5 Responding to request "*enqueue* (*new_item*)". (Routines are not shown in order to save page space.)

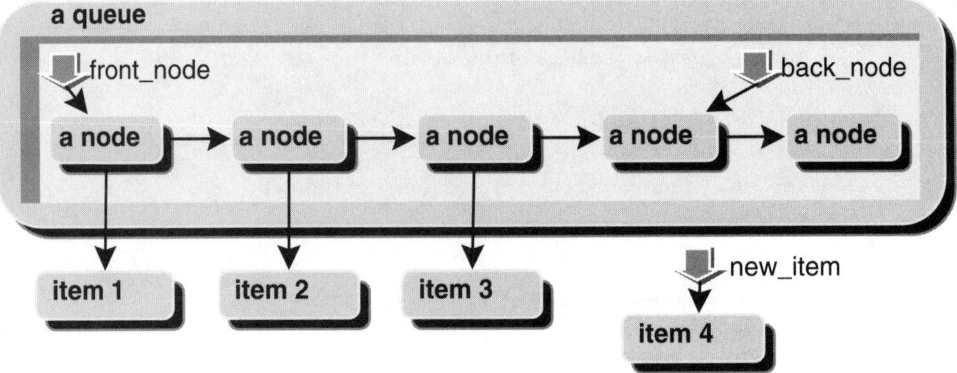

b. The new dummy node has been made and linked up.

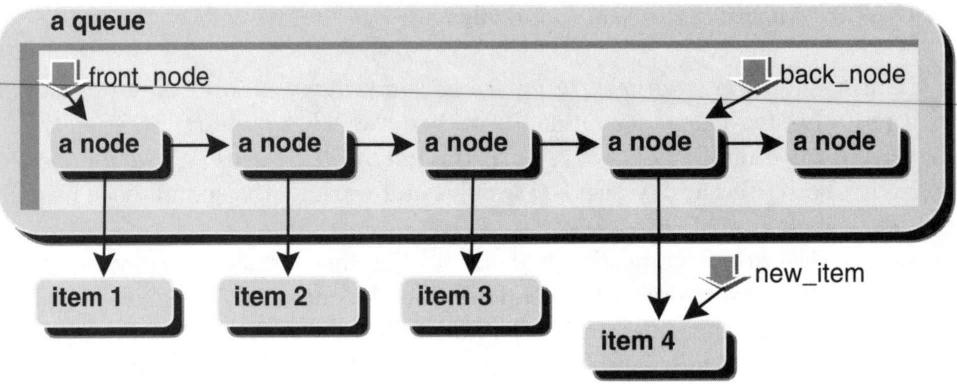

c. The former dummy node is now tracking *new_item*.

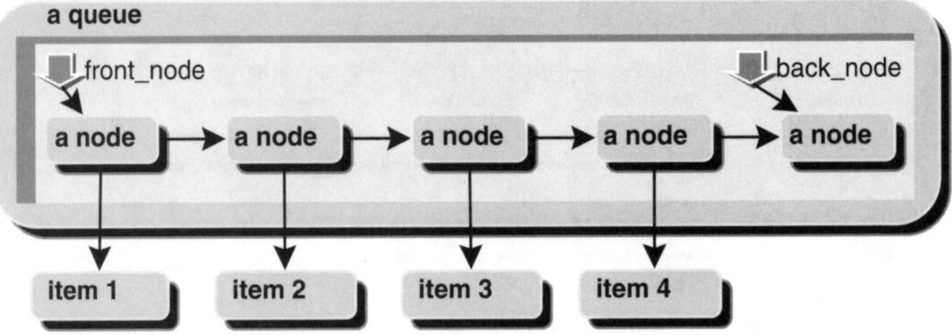

d. *back_node* is now tracking the new dummy.

Figure 9.5 *(continued)*

9.5 Using an *ARRAY* to Implement a *QUEUE*

In *STACK_ARRAY*, we nailed the bottom of the stack down to the left end of the array, and let the top extend toward the right end, where best case conditions existed for adding and removing items.

In *QUEUE_ARRAY*, if we nail the front to the left end and let the back extend to the right, we will get O(1) *enqueue* but O(*N*) *dequeue*. If we nail the back down to the left end and let the front extend to the right, we will get O(1) *dequeue* but O(*N*) *enqueue*.

Suppose we use an array implementation that mimics the linked representation we just finished discussing? Then both the front and the back of the queue will advance along the array as *dequeue* and *enqueue*, respectively, are requested. The first attempt at this representation is shown in Figure 9.6, and the *enqueue* and *dequeue* routines for it are given in Listing 9.4.

The problem with this approach is that if our user does enough *enqueues*, we will have our *back_index* against the wall. We will be unable to enqueue more items no matter how many times *dequeue* has been requested. For example, suppose the object in Figure 9.6 gets one *enqueue* and one *dequeue*. That will make its *back_index* = 6 and its *front_index* = 3. The queue is not full yet (the length of the queue is only 4, while the capacity is 6), but another *enqueue* attempt will crash.

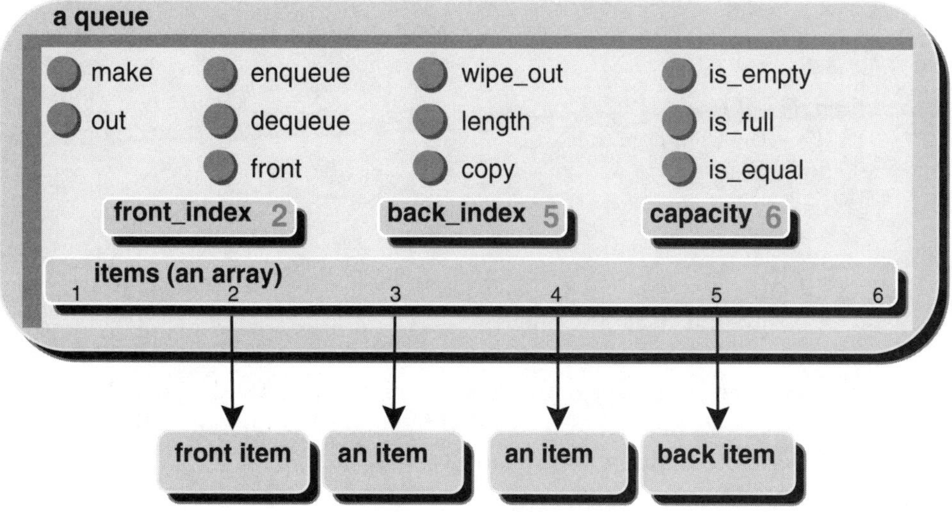

Figure 9.6 A first attempt at the inside view of a *QUEUE_ARRAY* object.

```
feature --Sizing

   capacity: INTEGER;
         --Current capacity.

feature {QUEUE_ARRAY} --Visible only to similar queues

   front_index: INTEGER;
         --Index of the front item.

   back_index: INTEGER;
         --Index of the back item.

   items: ARRAY[ITEM];
         --The array tracking the items.

feature --Moving items into and out of the queue

   enqueue(new_item: ITEM) is
         --Add new_item to the back of this queue.
      do
         back_index := back_index + 1;
         items.put(new_item, back_index);
      end; --enqueue

   dequeue is
         --Remove the front item.
      local
         void_item: ITEM;
      do
         items.put(void_item, front_index); --Set the old front item adrift.
         front_index := front_index + 1;
      end; --dequeue

   front: ITEM is
         --The front item.
      do
         Result := items.item(front_index);
      end; --front
```

Listing 9.4 A first attempt at *QUEUE_ARRAY* features for moving items into and out of the queue.

What we need is an array that does not have a right edge, but that wraps itself back so that its index 6 is followed by index 1 again (since that is where the next available position is). We have two options:

1. Create class *CIRCULAR_ARRAY*.
2. Treat our *ARRAY* object as if it were circular.

The first option is more appealing aesthetically, since it is easy to envision *CIRCULAR_ARRAY* as a self-contained class. However, creating a good *CIRCULAR_ARRAY* requires a study of circular object structures, which is outside the scope of this text. Instead, we will follow the second option.[3] We will use a linear array in a circular manner.

9.5.1 Making Array Indices Go in Circles

Take a circle of circumference C units. Take any two points on that circle and call them a and b. If you always follow the circle in one direction—say, counterclockwise—you have an infinite number of ways to get from a to b:

0. Go from a and stop when you reach b.
1. Go from a one full circle and keep going until you reach b.
2. Go from a two full circles and keep going until you reach b.
3. Go from a three full circles and keep going until you reach b.
4. Etc.

So to get from a to b, one can travel for $(b - a)$ units, or $(b - a) + C$ units, or $(b - a) + 2C$ units, or $(b - a) + 3C$ units, etc. In short, the distance along the circle from a to b is

$$nC + (b - a)$$

where n is any integer, including zero and the negatives ($-1C$ is one trip around the circle in the opposite direction).

If we are told that $C = 10$ and some trip t from a to b took 64 units, how do we determine the shortest distance from a to b along the circle? We throw away all those extra nC's:

$$64 = n \times 10 + (b - a)$$

means that $n = 6$ and $(b - a) = 4$. Namely, $n = \lfloor \frac{t}{C} \rfloor$ and

$$(b - a) = \text{remainder of } \frac{t}{C}$$

Note that when $a = 0$, all "$(b - a)$" become just "b."

[3]The second option also happens to be slightly more efficient, but that was not the reason for choosing it.

So much for the review of trigonometry—now back to arrays. Suppose we have an array that is shaped like a circle and its indices range from 0 to 9, and that x is index 5 of that array.

If y is the index that is 2 slots away from x, what is it? It is 7, of course, since $5 + 2 = 7$. But if y is 9 slots away from x, what is y? $5 + 7 = 12$ and 12 is outside of the index range of the array, so that cannot be right. A simple count shows that the answer is 2, but let us see how we can do it without counting with our fingers.

In the past, we have found it convenient to start our arrays at index 1, but this time the array starts at 0. The reason is that if the array starts at 0, then each index is also the distance from the array's beginning: position 0 is 0 slots away from the beginning of the array, position 5 is 5 slots away from the beginning, etc. Since the array is a circle, asking for the index of the $(5 + 7)$'th position is like asking how far it is from the beginning of the circle. Since the circle starts at 0 and its circumference is 10 (0 through 9 is ten positions), the answer is

$$\text{remainder of } \frac{5+7}{10}$$

which is 2.

The way to write "$\lfloor \frac{a}{b} \rfloor$" in Eiffel is "$a$ // b," and "remainder of $\frac{a}{b}$" is written as "a \\ b." Since the Eiffel notation is shorter, we will use it from now on.

To summarize, to compute the index of the position in array *items* that is d positions away from index x in the same array, we can simply compute

$$(x + d) \verb|\\| \textit{items.count}$$

provided that the first index of *items* is 0.

This observation leads us to the modified *enqueue* and *dequeue* in Listing 9.5.

```
enqueue (new_item: ITEM) is
        --Add new_item to the back of this queue.
    do
        back_index := (back_index + 1) \\ items.count;
        items.put (new_item, back_index);
    end; --enqueue

dequeue is
        --Remove the front item.
```

Listing 9.5 Features *enqueue* and *dequeue* modified to treat the *items* array as a circular structure.

```
    local
        void_item: ITEM;
    do
        items.put(void_item, front_index); --Set the old front item adrift.
        front_index := (front_index + 1) \\ items.count;
    end; --dequeue
```

Listing 9.5 *(continued)*

9.5.2 Detecting Full and Empty Queues

A *QUEUE_LINKED* is empty when *front_node* and *back_node* are equal and tracking the dummy node. In *QUEUE_ARRAY*, when *front_index* and *back_index* are equal, we get a queue of length 1 instead, as shown in Figure 9.7a. Doing a *dequeue* gives us the empty queue in Figure 9.7b.

Aha, so the queue is empty when *front_index* gets one step ahead of *back_index*! That means that *is_empty* is

```
is_empty: BOOLEAN is
        --Is this queue empty?
```

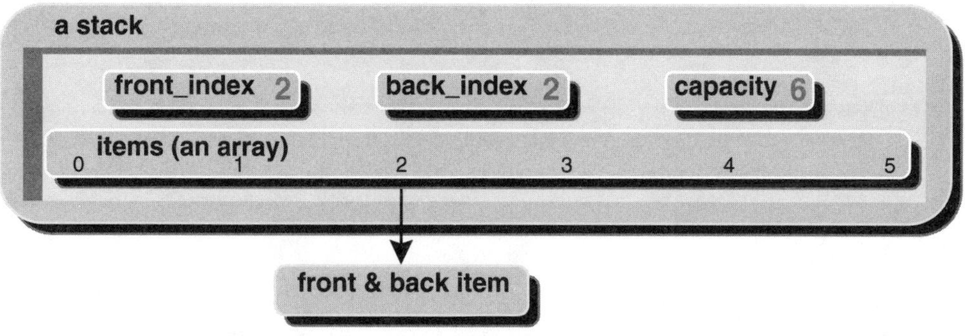

a. A queue of length 1.

b. Result of a *dequeue* request.

Figure 9.7 Going from a length 1 *QUEUE_ARRAY* to an empty one.

```
do
   Result := front_index = (back_index + 1) \\ items.count;
end; --is_empty
```

Let us consider the full queue condition the same way. If we start with the empty queue in Figure 9.7b and enqueue five objects in a row, we will get the almost full queue shown in Figure 9.8a. Then the sixth *enqueue* gives us Figure 9.8b.

We now see that the *is_full* condition occurs when . . . *front_index* is one step ahead of *back_index*. Unfortunately, we have already made that our *is_empty* condition.

There are two common solutions to this problem:

1. Make *length* an attribute, increment it in each *enqueue*, decrement it in each *dequeue*, and compare it with *capacity* in *is_full*.

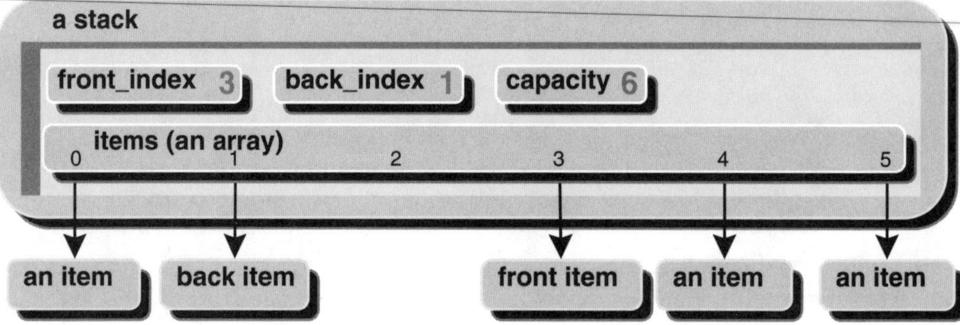

a. A queue that is almost full.

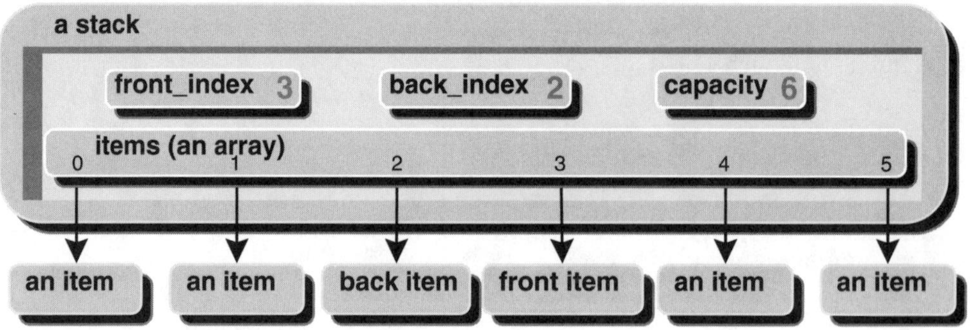

b. Result of an *enqueue* request.

Figure 9.8 Going from an almost full *QUEUE_ARRAY* to a full one.

2. Consider the queue in Figure 9.8a to be full, making "*front_index* is two steps ahead of *back_index*" the *is_full* condition.

There is not much difference in the efficiencies of the two techniques. The space occupied by the unused position in the array is about equal to the space occupied by *length* as an attribute. Counting the length up and down in each *dequeue* and *enqueue* does slow them down a bit, but that may or may not be noticeable. Let us use the second method—simply because it is more interesting.

First, if we want our queue to have capacity X, we need an array inside of capacity $X + 1$. That means that the array will have indices 0 through *capacity* instead of 0 through *capacity* $- 1$.

Second, since we are not counting the length up and down, we need to compute it on demand. If the queue does not go across the array boundary (where the index restarts at 0), then the length is simply

$$back\_index - front\_index + 1$$

(try it on Figure 9.7a).

If the queue crosses the array boundary, then *front_index* is a greater integer than *back_index*, so the preceding formula will yield a negative length, because instead of measuring the distance from *front_index* to *back_index*, it measures its complement (the distance from *back_index* to *front_index*). We can compensate for it by adding one full circle to the answer:

$$back\_index - front\_index + 1 + items.count$$

(try it on Figure 9.8a).

We can combine these two into one formula by always adding the full circle, and then chopping it off with the remainder operator in case the answer was positive at the beginning. This gives us the following *length* feature:

```
length: INTEGER is
        --The number of items currently in the queue.
  do
    Result :=
        (back_index - front_index + 1 + items.count) \\ items.count;
  end; --length
```

We have finally zeroed in on the appropriate inside view of *QUEUE_ARRAY* objects. It is given in Figure 9.9.

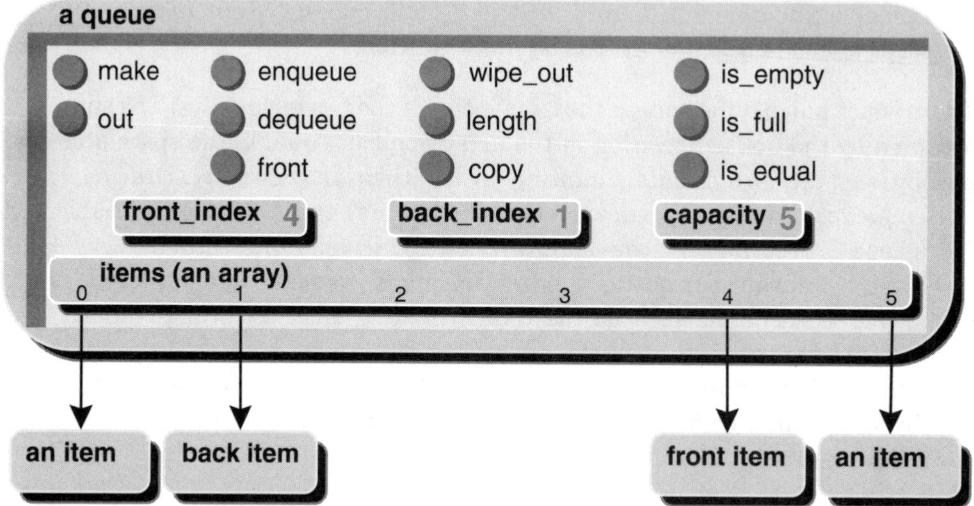

Figure 9.9 The inside view of a *QUEUE_ARRAY* object, with appropriately numbered array indices. The queue's capacity is one less than the array's capacity to allow *is_empty* and *is_full* to differ from each other.

9.5.3 Testing for Equality

The last feature of *QUEUE_ARRAY* that deserves special attention is *is_equal*. Comparing *QUEUE_ARRAY*s is almost as straightforward as comparing *STACK_ARRAY*s or *LIST_ARRAY*s. The only difference is that two equal queues do not have to start at the same index in their respective arrays. Also, their arrays may not be of equal capacity, which means that while advancing the index in *other*'s array, we have to remember to use "*x* \\ *other.items.count*" instead of "*x* \\ *items.count*." These concerns appear in other features as well, so Listing 9.6 shows the implementation of *is_equal* as an example.

```
is_equal(other: like Current): BOOLEAN is
        --Do this queue and other keep track
        --of the same items in the same order?
    local
        current_index: INTEGER;
        other_index: INTEGER;
    do
        if length /= other.length then
```

Listing 9.6 Feature *is_equal* of class *QUEUE_ARRAY*.

```
            --Can't be equal, so no sense going through the loop.
            Result := false;
    else
        from
            Result := true; --Equal until proven unequal.
            current_index := front_index;
            other_index := other.front_index;
        until
            --Exit as soon as inequality is detected
            Result = false
            --or when queues end.
            or else current_index = (back_index + 1) \\ items.count
        loop
            Result :=
                items.item(current_index) = other.items.item(other_index);
            current_index := (current_index + 1) \\ items.count;
            other_index := (other_index + 1) \\ other.items.count;
        end;
    end;
end; --is_equal
```

Listing 9.6 *(continued)*

9.6 Choosing the Best *QUEUE* Implementation for a Given Use

The trade-offs among the three *QUEUE* implementations are almost identical to the trade-offs among their *STACK* counterparts. All three offer O(1) performance in the critical features (*enqueue*, *dequeue*, and *front*). *QUEUE_ARRAY* is better if the maximum capacity can be predicted, and if the queue is usually at least half full or that memory is not needed for anything else. If the queue length is too unpredictable, *QUEUE_LINKED* is better. If pressed for development time and a doubly linked list is available, use it to implement *QUEUE_LIST*.

9.7 Who Needs It?

Queues are most useful in multiprocess programming, where they serve as buffers in transmission of objects from one process to another. However, there are uses for it that have nothing to do with parallelism.

In the calculators we will build in Chapter 10, we will be using queues to organize parsed (partially compiled) arithmetic expressions. In Section 15.3.3, we will use a queue to implement a breadth-first traversal of a tree.[4]

Summary

A queue is a first in, first out (FIFO) object structure. Objects are enqueued at one end of it and dequeued at the other.

If implemented correctly, *enqueue*, *dequeue*, and *front* have a time complexity of O(1).

Exercises

1. Write the contract for queues in the form of a deferred class *QUEUE*.
2. Using *STACK_TESTER* or *LIST_TESTER* as an example, write *QUEUE_TESTER*. When testing the array implementations, make sure it makes the queue cross the array boundary at least once (for example, fill it to capacity, then dequeue twice, then enqueue twice).
3. Implement and test *QUEUE_LIST*.
4. Implement and test *QUEUE_LINKED*.
5. Implement and test *QUEUE_ARRAY*.
6. Show how the **if** statement in *is_equal* can be combined with the **loop**.

---

[4] If you do not know yet what the terms "breadth-first," "traversal," and "tree" mean, please wait until Chapter 15.

10 Application: Calculators

Stacks and queues are used practically everywhere in computer science. If you are a computer science practitioner, I do not need to tell you that. If you are relatively new to the field, however, you may be impatient to see a good use for them, and justifiably so.

This chapter presents the design and implementation of two calculators: a postfix calculator (also called "Reverse Polish Notation," or "RPN") and an infix calculator (one that uses customary arithmetic notation).

We will not be evolving the code as we did in other chapters—the program is presented as a finished product.

10.1 Postfix Notation (RPN)

"Reverse Polish Notation" calculators have no parentheses and no '=' key. To calculate "33 + 22," the user enters "33" and hits the 'enter' key to say that the next digit belongs to a different number, then enters "22" and then hits the '+' key to say "add the last two values." Such calculators were popularized by Hewlett-Packard, and were idolized by engineers: Not only were they built to last forever, but they were also as mystical to most laypeople as were the slide rules they replaced.[1]

They do not need an '=' key, because the operator keys ('+', '−', '×', *etc.*) invoke computation, using the last values that had been seen. If the operator is

[1]Let me state for the record, lest this provoke a deluge of hate mail, that I myself favor RPN calculators, and love my HP-16C.

binary, it takes the last two values; if it is unary, such as 'CHG' (change sign, or negate) or '$\sqrt{x}$,' then it takes just the last value. It then replaces all the values it took with the result.

They do not need parentheses because the order of evaluation is explicit: You do not tell the calculator to perform an operation until all the values it needs are ready. For example, suppose we need to evaluate "10 − 2 × 4." We enter "10," and the value to be subtracted from it is the answer to "2 × 4." That value has not been computed yet, and we cannot press '−' until it is available. Thus, we leave "10" where it is and enter "2" next to it: "10 2." The "2" is to be multiplied by 4, so we need to enter "4" and then hit '×': "10 2 4 ×." Since '×' is an operator, it immediately evaluates its result: "10 8." Now we can enter the '−': "10 8 −," which produces "2."

Thus, the RPN version of the expression "10 − 2 × 4" is "10 2 4 × −." RPN notation is also called "**postfix**" because the operator appears after its operands; the customary arithmetic notation is "**infix**."

10.2 Converting from Infix to Postfix

There is a mechanical way of determining a postfix equivalent of an infix expression. Operands are appended to the postfix expression as soon as they are encountered, but evaluation of operands is delayed by pushing operators onto a stack. If the new operator is lower precedence than the ones that are at the top of the stack, then it is time to evaluate them, so they are popped and appended to the postfix expression. When the operator at the top is of lower precedence than the new one, then it will have to wait, and the new one is pushed onto the top. (This algorithm is embodied in feature *postfix* of class *INFIX_CALCULATOR*, discussed later.)

10.3 The Design

A program that implements a postfix calculator needs to read in the expression from the keyboard, separate it into individual entries (numbers and operators), and use a stack to compute the result.

A program that implements an infix calculator needs to read in the expression from the keyboard, separate it into individual entries, convert it into postscript notation, then use the stack to evaluate the result.

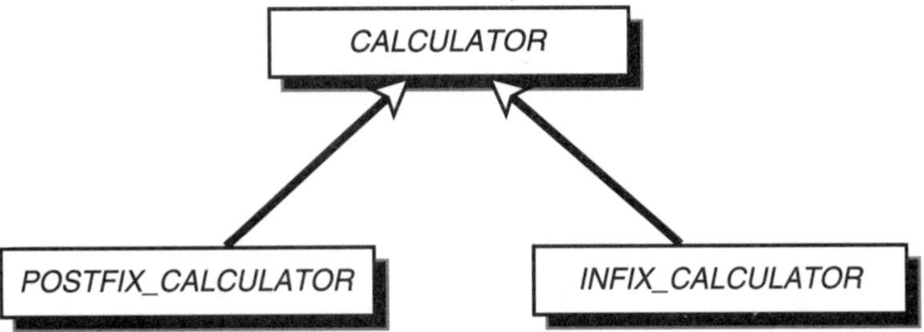

Figure 10.1 The hierarchy of calculator classes.

The two have enough in common to take advantage of a common ancestor. Thus, there are three calculator classes: the parent *CALCULATOR*, and its heirs *POSTFIX_CALCULATOR* and *INFIX_CALCULATOR* (Figure 10.1).

The calculator builds up a queue of *CALCULATOR_ENTRY* objects in postfix form, then creates an *EXPRESSION* from that queue and asks for its *value*. There are two kinds of calculator entries: *OPERAND* and *OPERATOR*. There are two kinds of operators: *UNARY_OPERATOR* and *BINARY_OPERATOR*. Finally, each specific kind of operator (plus, minus, negate, etc.) is an heir to either the binary or the unary operator class. This class hierarchy is shown in Figure 10.2.

10.4 The Implementation

Since the rest of this chapter is mostly Eiffel code, with a few explanations thrown in, the boxed listing format we have been using is too awkward. Instead, the code is presented as normal text flow, with short explanations before or after the code, and with guiding notation in the margins.

10.4.1 *CALCULATOR*

This is the main class of the program. It is a deferred class that provides the running framework for its subclasses, *POSTFIX_CALCULATOR* and *INFIX_CALCULATOR*. The main loop of the calculator is in routine *run* (the subclasses inherit it and make it their creation routine).

It defers to the specific calculator features *greeting* (a string telling the user which calculator is being run) and *postfix* (the parsed expression in postfix form).

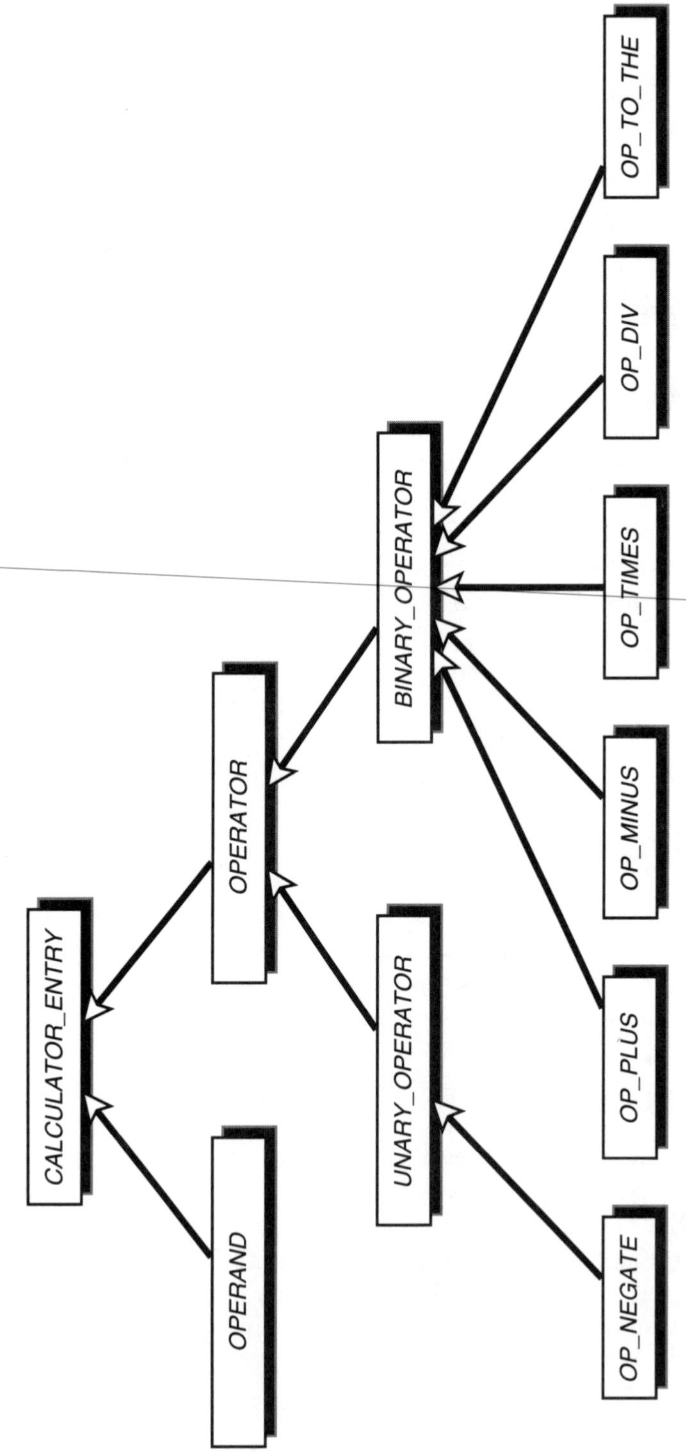

Figure 10.2 The hierarchy of calculator entry classes.

The input features that it uses are summarized in Appendix B.

```
deferred class CALCULATOR

feature

  run is
      --Main loop of the calculator.
    local
      user_input: QUEUE_LINKED[CALCULATOR_ENTRY];
      postfix_input: QUEUE_LINKED[CALCULATOR_ENTRY];
      expression: EXPRESSION;
    do
      print(greeting);
      from
      until
        io.end_of_file
      loop
        io.read_line;
        user_input := parsed(io.last_string);

        if user_input.is_empty then

          print("Blank lines are ignored. To exit, give me end
          of file.%N");
        else

          print("Input: "); print("user_input"); print("%N");

          postfix_input := postfix(user_input);
          print("Postfix: "); print(postfix_input); print("%N");

          !!expression.make(postfix_input);
          print("Value: "); print(expression.value); print("%N");

        end;

      end;

    end; --run

feature {NONE}

  greeting: STRING is
      --What to print to welcome the user.
    deferred
    end; --greeting
```

io.read_line *leaves the line in* io.last_string.

```
postfix (input: QUEUE_LINKED[CALCULATOR_ENTRY]):
                              QUEUE_LINKED[CALCULATOR_ENTRY] is
      --The postfix version of the input queue.
   deferred
   end; --postfix

parsed (line: STRING): QUEUE_LINKED[CALCULATOR_ENTRY] is
      --A queue of the individual entries on the input line.
   local
      index: INTEGER;
      last_number: INTEGER;
      line_length: INTEGER;
      parsing_a_number: BOOLEAN;
      last_character: CHARACTER;
      entry: CALCULATOR_ENTRY;
      zero_code: INTEGER;
   do
      zero_code := ('0').code;
      from
         index := 1;
         line_length := line.count;
         !!Result.make;
      variant
         line_length - index
      until
         index > line_length
      loop
         last_character := line.item (index);

         if last_character >= '0' and last_character <= '9' then

            last_number := last_number * 10 + (last_character.code-zero_code);
            parsing_a_number := true;

         else

            entry := Void;

            if parsing_a_number then
               !OPERAND!entry.make (last_number);
               Result.enqueue (entry);
               parsing_a_number := false;
               last_number := 0;
               entry := Void;
            end;
```

Loop variants are discussed in Section 12.2.1. They do not affect loop execution, thus can be safely ignored.

```
            inspect
               last_character
            when '+' then
               !OP_PLUS!entry.make;
            when '-' then
               !OP_MINUS!entry.make;
            when '~' then
               !OP_NEGATE!entry.make;
            when '*' then
               !OP_TIMES!entry.make;
            when '/' then
               !OP_DIV!entry.make;
            when '^' then
               !OP_TO_THE!entry.make;
            else
               --Skip it.
            end;

            if entry /= Void then
               Result.enqueue(entry);
            end;

         end;

         index := index + 1;
      end;

      if parsing_a_number then
         !OPERAND!entry.make(last_number);
         Result.enqueue(entry);
      end;

   end; --parsed

end --class CALCULATOR
```

10.4.2 *POSTFIX_CALCULATOR*

Since with a postfix calculator the user is entering a postfix expression, feature *postfix* has nothing to do in class *POSTFIX_CALCULATOR*. This makes for a very simple class.

```
class POSTFIX_CALCULATOR inherit CALCULATOR

creation run --inherited
```

A string can be split between two lines by putting a % at the end of the first part and at the beginning of the second.

```
feature {NONE}

   greeting: STRING is
      "Enter a postfix (RPN) expression and hit RETURN%N%
      %Hit end-of-file (control-d in Unix) to exit.%N";

   postfix(input: QUEUE_LINKED[CALCULATOR_ENTRY]):
                     QUEUE_LINKED[CALCULATOR_ENTRY] is
         --Same as input.
      do
         --The parsed line is already in postfix.
         Result := input;
      end --postfix

end --class POSTFIX_CALCULATOR
```

10.4.3 *INFIX_CALCULATOR*

The infix calculator is, basically, the postfix calculator with an infix-to-postfix conversion. The conversion is performed by feature *postfix*, which scans its input queue and tells each entity in it to modify the resulting queue and the operator stack appropriately.

An operand will immediately enqueue itself into *Result*. An operator will pop all items of greater (or perhaps equal—see the discussion in Section 10.4.7) precedence off the operator stack, enqueuing them into *Result*, and then push itself onto the stack. After the last entry has done its part, feature *postfix* transfers the operators still on the stack to the end of the postfix expression.

```
class INFIX_CALCULATOR inherit CALCULATOR

creation run --inherited

feature {NONE}

   greeting: STRING is
      "Enter an arithmetic expression and hit RETURN%N%
      %Hit end-of-file (control-d in Unix) to exit.%N";

   postfix(the_input: QUEUE_LINKED[CALCULATOR_ENTRY]):
                     QUEUE_LINKED[CALCULATOR_ENTRY] is
      local
         waiting_operators: STACK_LINKED[OPERATOR];
         input: like the_input;
      do
         --Make a local copy of the_input to prevent side effects.
         input := clone(the_input);
```

```
from
    !!Result.make;
    !!waiting_operators.make;
variant
    input.length
until
    input.is_empty
loop
    input.front.modify_infix(Result, waiting_operators);
    input.dequeue;

    debug
        print(Result); print("%N");
        print(waiting_operators); print("%N");
    end;
end;

--Flush out the operators still waiting.
from
variant
    waiting_operators.size
until
    waiting_operators.is_empty
loop
    Result.enqueue(waiting_operators.top);
    waiting_operators.pop;

end;

end; --parsed

end --class INFIX_CALCULATOR
```

Statements bracketed with ***debug . . . end*** *are executed only if the class was compiled with debugging enabled in the Ace file (see Appendix D).*

10.4.4 *EXPRESSION*

An expression consists of the calculator entries in postfix order. It is made out of a queue that is already in that order, which it clones for future reference. Its feature *make* also evaluates the expression, using a stack.

The evaluation is done by creating an empty stack of operands, and then telling each entry in the queue to modify it according to its own definition: Operands will just push themselves onto the stack; operators will pop the right number of operands, use them in computation, and push the result.

```
class EXPRESSION inherit
   ANY
      redefine
         out
      end;

creation make

feature {NONE}

   queue: QUEUE[CALCULATOR_ENTRY];
         --So that out knows the original expression.

feature

   value: INTEGER is
         --The result of computing this expression.

   make(postfix: QUEUE[CALCULATOR_ENTRY]) is
         --Create a new expression out of the entries of postfix,
         --and compute its value.
      require
         input_not_empty: not postfix.is_empty;
      local
         results: STACK_LINKED[OPERAND];
      do
         --Keep a copy of the queue.
         queue := clone(postfix);

         from
            !!results.make;
         variant
            postfix.length
         until
            postfix.is_empty
         loop
            debug
               print(results); print("%N");
            end;

            postfix.front.modify_postfix(results);
            postfix.dequeue;
         end;

         check
            one_result_left: results.size = 1;
         end;
```

```
      value := results.top.value;
    end; --make

  out: STRING is
      --Same as out of the original queue.
    do
      Result := queue.out;
    end; --out

invariant

  have_queue: queue /= Void;

end --class EXPRESSION
```

10.4.5 *CALCULATOR_ENTRY*

Every feature in *CALCULATOR_ENTRY* is deferred to its heirs. It only provides the contract for operators and operands.

The two primary routines it defines are *modify_postfix*, which operates on a stack of operands (it is used while computing the value of a postfix expression), and *modify_prefix*, which operates on a stack of operators and adds to the queue that holds the postfix expression.

The remaining routines are there only to allow the heirs to specify meaningful preconditions.

```
deferred class CALCULATOR_ENTRY inherit
  ANY
    undefine
      out --Force subclasses to implement out.
    end;

feature --Dealing with the postfix-to-value stack

  modify_postfix(stack: STACK[OPERAND]) is
        --Modify the operand stack appropriately.
    require
      stack_not_void: stack /= Void;
      stack_big_enough: postfix_stack_is_big_enough(stack);
      stack_small_enough: postfix_stack_is_small_enough(stack);
    deferred
    end; --modify_postfix
```

```
postfix_stack_is_big_enough (stack: STACK[OPERAND]): BOOLEAN is
        --Are there enough items on the stack for this entry to work?
    require
        stack_not_void: stack /= Void;
    deferred
    end; --postfix_stack_is_big_enough

postfix_stack_is_small_enough (stack: STACK[OPERAND]): BOOLEAN is
        --Is there enough room on the stack for this entry to work?
    require
        stack_not_void: stack /= Void;
    deferred
    end; --postfix_stack_is_small_enough

feature --Dealing with the infix-to-postfix queue and stack

modify_infix (postfix: QUEUE[CALCULATOR_ENTRY];
              waiting: STACK[OPERATOR]) is
        --Modify the postfix queue and the waiting operator stack appropriately.
    require
        queue_not_void: postfix /= Void;
        queue_small_enough: infix_queue_is_small_enough (postfix,waiting);
        stack_not_void: waiting /= Void;
        stack_small_enough: infix_stack_is_small_enough (waiting);
    deferred
    end; --postfix_stack_is_small_enough

infix_stack_is_small_enough (stack: STACK[OPERATOR]): BOOLEAN is
        --Is there enough room on the stack for this entry to work?
    require
        stack_not_void: stack /= Void;
    deferred
    end; --infix_stack_is_small_enough

infix_queue_is_small_enough (queue: QUEUE[CALCULATOR_ENTRY];
                             stack: STACK[OPERATOR]): BOOLEAN is
        --Is there enough room in the queue for this entry to work?
    require
        queue_not_void: queue /= Void;
    deferred
    end; --infix_queue_is_small_enough

end --class CALCULATOR_ENTRY
```

10.4.6 *OPERAND*

An operand has a numeric value (an integer in this example). During evaluation of the postfix expression, it pushes itself onto the stack. During infix-to-postfix conversion, it enqueues itself into the postfix queue.

```
class OPERAND inherit CALCULATOR_ENTRY
creation make
feature
   make (the_value: INTEGER) is
         --Make a new operand with value the_value.
      require
         value_not_void: the_value /= Void;
      do
         value := the_value;
      end; --make
   value: INTEGER;
         --The numeric value of this operand.
   out: STRING is
         --value.out.
      do
         Result := value.out;
      end; --out
feature --Dealing with the postfix-to-value stack
   modify_postfix (stack: STACK[OPERAND]) is
         --Push the operand onto stack.
      do
         stack.push (Current);
      end; --modify_postfix
   postfix_stack_is_big_enough (stack: STACK[OPERAND]): BOOLEAN is
         --The stack is always big enough.
      do
         Result := true;
      end; --postfix_stack_is_big_enough
   postfix_stack_is_small_enough (stack: STACK[OPERAND]): BOOLEAN is
         --Is there room for one more operand?
      do
         Result := not stack.is_full;
      end; --postfix_stack_is_small_enough
```

```
feature --Dealing with the infix-to-postfix queue and stack

   modify_infix (postfix: QUEUE[CALCULATOR_ENTRY];
                 waiting: STACK[OPERATOR]) is
         --Add the operand to postfix.
      do
         postfix.enqueue (Current);
      end; --modify_infix

   infix_stack_is_small_enough (stack: STACK[OPERATOR]): BOOLEAN is
         --The stack is not used, so it is always small enough.
      do
         Result := true;
      end; --infix_stack_is_small_enough

   infix_queue_is_small_enough (queue: QUEUE[CALCULATOR_ENTRY];
                                stack: STACK[OPERATOR]): BOOLEAN is
         --Is there room for one more?
      do
         Result := not queue.is_full;
      end; --infix_queue_is_small_enough

invariant

   value_not_void: value /= Void

end --class OPERAND
```

10.4.7 *OPERATOR*

Class *OPERATOR* defers *modify_postfix* to the specific operator classes. Feature *modify_infix* performs this operator's part in the infix-to-postfix conversion scheme described in Section 10.4.3.

An important detail of the priority scheme is that most operators are left-associative, which means that when two operators of the same precedence appear side by side, the one on the left is to be performed first, but some are right-associative, meaning that among equal-precedence operators the one on the right is done first. For example, '+' and '−' are the same priority and left-associative, so "1 − 2 + 3" means "(1 − 2) + 3," not "1 − (2 + 3)." On the other hand, exponentiation ("^") is right-associative, so "2^{3^4}" means "$2^{(3^4)}$," not "$(2^3)^4$."

Thus, when a left-associative operator is popping the stack, it needs to pop off all items of greater or equal precedence, while a right-associative operator needs to pop off items of strictly greater precedence.

```
deferred class OPERATOR inherit CALCULATOR_ENTRY

feature --Dealing with the postfix-to-value stack

  postfix_stack_is_small_enough (stack: STACK[OPERAND]): BOOLEAN is
        --Will be popping at least as many as pushing.
     do
        Result := true;
     end; --postfix_stack_is_small_enough

feature --Dealing with the infix-to-postfix queue and stack

  precedence: INTEGER is
        --In infix expressions, higher precedence operations are done first.
     deferred
     end; --precedence

  is_right_associative: BOOLEAN is
        --When two of these are in a row, does the one on the right have precedence?
     do
        Result := false; --Good default for most operators.
     end; --is_right_associative

  modify_infix (postfix: QUEUE[CALCULATOR_ENTRY];
                waiting: STACK[OPERATOR]) is
        --Pop operators that are higher in precedence than this one from waiting
        --and add them to postfix, then push this operator onto waiting.
     do
        from
        variant
           waiting.size
        until
           waiting.is_empty
           or else precedence > waiting.top.precedence
           or else (is_right_associative
                    and then precedence = waiting.top.precedence)
        loop
           postfix.enqueue (waiting.top);
           waiting.pop;
        end;

        waiting.push (Current);
     end; --modify_infix

  infix_stack_is_small_enough (stack: STACK[OPERATOR]): BOOLEAN is
        --Will either pop or need room for one more.
```

```
    do
        Result := stack.is_empty
                        or else precedence < stack.top.precedence
                        or else not stack.is_full;
    end; --infix_stack_is_small_enough

  infix_queue_is_small_enough (queue: QUEUE[CALCULATOR_ENTRY];
                               stack: STACK[OPERATOR]): BOOLEAN is
        --May need to add as many as stack.size vacancies in queue.
    do
        --There is no easy way to check if there are enough vacancies in
        --queue. The condition below is better than nothing, but
        --the result may be true when it should have been false.

        Result := not queue.is_full;
    end; --infix_queue_is_small_enough

end --class OPERATOR
```

10.4.8 Binary Operator Classes

During the evaluation of a postfix expression, all of the binary operators do the same thing to the operand stack: pop off two operands, use them to determine the answer, and push the answer back onto the stack. Thus, *modify_postfix* is implemented in *BINARY_OPERATOR* using the private deferred feature *answer* to compute the actual answer to push. The specific *OP_. . .* classes implement function *answer* as is appropriate for each operator.

```
deferred class BINARY_OPERATOR inherit OPERATOR

feature

  make is
        --Initialization.
    do
        --Nothing.
    end; --make

feature --Dealing with the postfix-to-value stack

  modify_postfix (stack: STACK[OPERAND]) is
        --Replace top two items with the answer.
    local
        left: OPERAND;
        right: OPERAND;
        the_answer: OPERAND;
```

```
    do
        right := stack.top; stack.pop;
        left := stack.top; stack.popn;

        !!the_answer.make (answer (left.value,right.value));
        stack.push (the_answer);
    end; --modify_postfix

  postfix_stack_is_big_enough (stack: STACK[OPERAND]): BOOLEAN is
    --Are there at least two operands?
    do
        Result := stack.size > 1;
    end; --postfix_stack_is_big_enough

feature {NONE}

  answer (left: INTEGER; right: INTEGER): INTEGER is
        --Redefined by heirs to do the actual computation.
    deferred
    end; --answer

end --class BINARY_OPERATOR


class OP_PLUS inherit BINARY_OPERATOR

creation make

feature

  precedence: INTEGER is 2;

  out: STRING is
        --"+".
    do
        Result := clone ("+");
    end; --out

feature {NONE}

  answer (left: INTEGER; right: INTEGER): INTEGER is
        --left + right.
    do
        Result := left + right;
    end; --answer

end --class OP_PLUS
```

It does not matter what numbers are used for precedence, as long as that of '~' is greatest, followed by '^', then '' and '/', then '+' and '−'.*

```
class OP_MINUS inherit BINARY_OPERATOR

creation make

feature

   precedence: INTEGER is 2;

   out: STRING is
         --"-".
      do
         Result := clone("-");
      end; --out

feature {NONE}

   answer(left: INTEGER; right: INTEGER): INTEGER is
         --left - right.
      do
         Result := left - right;
      end; --answer

end --class OP_MINUS
```

```
class OP_TIMES inherit BINARY_OPERATOR

creation make

feature

   precedence: INTEGER is 5;

   out: STRING is
         --"*".
      do
         Result := clone("*");
      end; --out

feature {NONE}

   answer(left: INTEGER; right: INTEGER): INTEGER is
         --left * right.
      do
         Result := left * right;
      end; --answer

end --class OP_TIMES
```

```
class OP_DIV inherit BINARY_OPERATOR

creation make

feature

   precedence: INTEGER is 5;

   out: STRING is
         --"/".
      do
         Result := clone("/");
      end; --out

feature {NONE}

   answer(left: INTEGER; right: INTEGER): INTEGER is
         --left // right.
      do
         Result := left // right;
      end; --answer

end --class OP_DIV


class OP_TO_THE inherit BINARY_OPERATOR

creation make

feature

   precedence: INTEGER is 8;

   is_right_associative: BOOLEAN is
         --Exponentiation is right-associative.
      do
         Result := true;
      end; --is_right_associative

   out: STRING is
         --"^".
      do
         Result := clone("^");
      end; --out

feature {NONE}

   answer(left: INTEGER; right: INTEGER): INTEGER is
         --left ^ right.
```

```
      do
         Result := (left ^ right).floor;
      end; --answer

end --class OP_TO_THE
```

10.4.9 Unary Operators

Unary operators are very similar to binary operators, except they only pop one operand off the stack and base the answer on just that one operand. The division of labor between *UNARY_OPERAND* and its heirs (only *OP_NEGATE* in this example) is the same as it was with binary operators and their parent class.

```
deferred class UNARY_OPERATOR inherit OPERATOR

feature

   make is
         --Initialization.
      do
         Nothing.
      end; --make

feature --Dealing with the postfix-to-value stack

   modify_postfix(stack: STACK[OPERAND]) is
         --Replace top item with the answer.
      local
         operand: OPERAND;
         the_answer: OPERAND;
      do
         operand := stack.top; stack.pop;

         !!the_answer.make(answer(operand.value));
         stack.push(the_answer);
      end; --modify_postfix

   postfix_stack_is_big_enough(stack: STACK[OPERAND]): BOOLEAN is
         --Is there at least one operand?
      do
         Result := not stack.is_empty;
      end; --postfix_stack_is_big_enough

feature {NONE}

   answer(operand: INTEGER): INTEGER is
         --Redefined by heirs to do actual computation.
```

```
        deferred
        end; --answer
end; --class UNARY_OPERATOR
class OP_NEGATE inherit UNARY_OPERATOR
    precedence: INTEGER is 10;
creation make
feature
    out: STRING is
            -- "~".
        do
            Result := clone("~");
        end; --out
feature {NONE}
    answer(top: INTEGER): INTEGER is
            -- -top.
        do
            Result := -top;
        end; --answer
end --class OP_NEGATE
```

Exercises

1. Convert by hand (without using the computer)
   a. the infix expression "$9 - 4 \times 2 + 5^2$" to postfix;
   b. the postfix expression "1 2 3 4 * − / 2 ^" to infix.
2. Add the binary operator "remainder" to the calculators. Use the symbol '\' (e.g., the infix expression "5\2" should evaluate to 1). Its precedence is the same as that of multiplication and division, and it is left-associative.
3. The classes presented in this chapter are very intolerant to user errors. Modify them so that a user mistake results in a polite error message instead of a crashed program.
4. Add the ability to handle parentheses to the infix calculator.
5. Create a prefix calculator.

Part III

Sorting and Searching

11 Dictionaries and Associations

In the remainder of this book, we will concentrate on object structures that are organized in ways that make it easy to find specific objects. The best metaphor for an object structure that is used for looking up specific objects is the dictionary.

11.1 Dictionaries

A dictionary is a structure that organizes definitions (or translations) in such a way that they can be quickly found.

What makes a typical dictionary easy to search is the fact that all entries in it are sorted. This allows a reader to pick a page and see whether the definition being sought appears on it, before it, or after it. Namely, if we see a definition for a word that lexicographically follows the word whose definition we seek, then the definition we need appears earlier than the one we are looking at now. If the definition is for a word that is identical to the one we are looking up (allowing a few spelling mistakes on our part), then we take that definition. Otherwise, we look for the definition in the remainder of the dictionary.

This activity is called "looking up a word," but that is misleading. We already *know* the word. What we are looking up is *the definition,* using the word to identify it.

Moving a generation ahead in the dictionary technology, we get the electronic dictionary. All we do to search one of those is type in a word, and out comes the definition.

The implementers of a dictionary in its book form do not have a choice regarding a dictionary's organization: If it were not sorted alphabetically by the defined word, it would be useless. A book is a data structure rather than an object structure: Its users have to perform the operations themselves, so they need to know its internal organization. By age-old convention, that organization is that of an array of (<word>, <definition>) pairs, sorted by the <word>.

On the other hand, the electronic dictionary gives no clue as to how it is organized inside. It may well use an array of sorted (<word>, <definition>) pairs (as we will see in Chapter 14), but it could use something else. For instance, if the dictionary allows users to add their own entries, then the array representation may be too slow.

The implementation of the digital dictionary is the implementers' business; the contract with the users ("type in a word and hit the 'define' button, and the result will be a definition if the word is in the dictionary") is all that is needed to operate it.

11.2 The *DICTIONARY* Object Structure

Traditional dictionaries let people use words to find definitions. Dictionary object structures have a more general role: to use any type of object to locate any other kind of object. The object that is used to identify the goal of the search is called the "**key**," and the object that is identified by it is called the "**value**."

We can set up the contract for *DICTIONARY*[*KEY,VALUE*] right now. As we did with the various versions of *LIST*[*ITEM*], we will make *DICTIONARY* a deferred class. Specific fully implemented subclasses will be discussed in Section 11.5 and Chapter 14, after we develop a few tools.

But first, we need to consider how keys and values are tied together.

11.3 Associations

The first thing we need is a class of objects to tie together a key and a value. In Chapter 3, we had a class of objects to tie two objects together: *PAIR*. Unfortunately, we cannot use it directly. The first problem is that a pair *is_equal* to another if *first* of both tracks the same item and *second* of both tracks the same item. That is too strong to be used to identify an association in a dictionary: If we had the *same* key and value objects to put into an association for comparison purposes, we would not need to look for the value object in the dictionary. An association's *is_equal* needs to compare only the keys—and compare them for equality, not identity: If we want to look up the translation for the word "mother," we should be able to use any *STRING* object whose value equals `"mother"`, not just the one that is part of the association in the dictionary.

The second problem is that there is no way to compare *PAIR* objects that tells us which should precede the other in a dictionary. There is, however, a deferred class in the standard Eiffel library called *COMPARABLE* that defines the ordering features we need (see Appendix B). These features are **infix** "<", **infix** "<=", **infix** ">", and **infix** ">=" (the last three are defined in terms of "<" and *is_equal*).

The **infix** declaration allows expressions of the form

comparable1 < *comparable2*

which means "tell the object tracked by *comparable1* to execute the feature '<' using the object tracked by *comparable2* as its single parameter."

Thus, we need *ASSOCIATION* objects to act like both *COMPARABLE* and *PAIR*. We define the class to be an heir to both (see Figure 11.1), redefining features from either as needed. While we are at it, we can use Eiffel's **rename** instruction to give *first*, *second*, *set_first*, and *set_second* names that are more appropriate for associations: *key*, *value*, *set_key*, and *set_value*, respectively. The resulting class is shown in Listing 11.1.

Since *ASSOCIATION*'s **inherit** section is more complicated than the ones we have previously encountered, it deserves a closer look. First, there are two parent classes, each with its own **rename-undefine-redefine-end** structure. Second, the **rename** section for *PAIR[KEY, VALUE]* provides new names to the features inherited from *PAIR*. If an association object is addressed through an entity of type *ASSOCIATION*, new names are used; if it is addressed through a *PAIR* entity, then the old names are used. For example, the following code segment is perfectly legal:

```
local
    p: PAIR[STRING,STRING];
    a: ASSOCIATION[STRING,STRING];
do
    !!a.make;
    a.set_key("aardwolf");
```

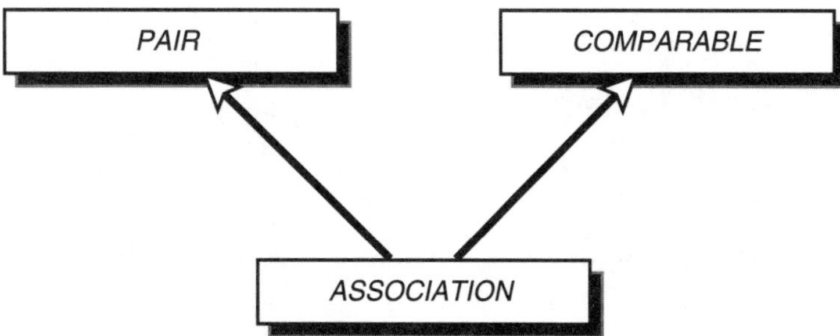

Figure 11.1 Class *ASSOCIATION* is an heir to both *PAIR* and the predefined class *COMPARABLE*.

```
class ASSOCIATION[KEY -> COMPARABLE, VALUE] inherit
   PAIR[KEY,VALUE]
      rename
         first as key, second as value,
         set_first as set_key, set_second as set_value
      redefine
         is_equal
      end;
   COMPARABLE
      undefine
         out, is_equal
      redefine
         infix "<"
      end;
creation make
feature
   is_equal(other: like Current): BOOLEAN is
         --Same as key.is_equal(other.key).
      do
         Result :=
            (key = Void and other.key = Void) or else
            ((key /= Void and other.key /= Void) and then key.is_equal(other.key));
      end; --is_equal
   infix "<"(other: like Current): BOOLEAN is
         --Same as key < other.key.
      do
         Result := (key /= Void and other.key /= Void) and then key < other.key;
      end; --infix "<"
end --class ASSOCIATION
```

Listing 11.1 Class *ASSOCIATION*.

```
   !ASSOCIATION[STRING,STRING]!p.make;
   p.set_first("platypus");
end
```

The feature that sets the first item of the pair is being called, regardless of what name is used to invoke it.

The third thing to consider is the fact that when a class has more than one parent, two (or more) different features with the same name could be inherited.

In the case of *COMPARABLE* and *PAIR*, there is a conflict with *out*. For instance, class *COMPARABLE* inherits the standard *out* from *ANY*, but *PAIR* redefines it to be a different feature. *ASSOCIATION* would inherit both features, which would be perfectly fine if they didn't have the same name. To avoid the conflict, we have to either rename one of them or undefine one of them. Since we have no use for the feature that *COMPARABLE* calls "*out*," we undefine that one. The same reasoning applies to *is_equal*.

The last new bit of Eiffel in class *ASSOCIATION* is in the **class** section itself: "*KEY->COMPARABLE*". This notation indicates that the type that is plugged in for *KEY* when the association object is created is *constrained* to type *COMPARABLE*. In other words, the key of an association must be an object of class *COMPARABLE* or one of its subclasses. We require this so that we can be sure that expressions like "*key<other.key*" are safe to use. If we leave off the "-><type>" part, then "->*ANY*" is assumed.

A simple tester for class *ASSOCIATION* is given in Listing 11.2.

```
class ASSOCIATION_TESTER

creation test

feature

  test is
        --Test ASSOCIATIONs.

     local
        assoc1: ASSOCIATION[STRING,STRING];
        assoc2: ASSOCIATION[STRING,STRING];
        assoc3: ASSOCIATION[STRING,STRING];
     do
        !!assoc1.make;
        assoc1.set_key("dictionary");
        assoc1.set_value
           ("a book containing words along with their definitions");
        print("Assoc1 created:%N");
        print(assoc1);
        print("%N%N");
        !!assoc2.make;
        assoc2.set_key("dictionary");
        assoc2.set_value
```

Listing 11.2 Class *ASSOCIATION_TESTER*. (Definitions adapted from *The NeXT Digital Edition of Webster's Ninth New Collegiate Dictionary*, Copyright 1988 Merriam-Webster, Inc., and NeXT Computer Inc.)

```
        ("a book giving for words of one language equivalents%
%in another");
      print("Assoc2 created:%N");
      print(assoc2);
      print("%N%N");
      check
        assoc1_equals_assoc2: assoc1.is_equal(assoc2);
        assoc1_not_less_than_assoc2: not (assoc1 < assoc2);
        assoc1_not_greater_than_assoc2: not (assoc1 > assoc2);
      end;
      !!assoc3.make;
      assoc3.set_key("diction");
      assoc3.set_value("vocal expression: enunciation");
      print("Assoc3 created:%N");
      print(assoc3);
      print("%N%N");
      check
        assoc1_not_equal_assoc3: not assoc1.is_equal(assoc3);
        assoc1_not_less_than_assoc3: not (assoc1 < assoc3);
        assoc1_greater_than_assoc3: assoc1 > assoc3;
      end;
      print("Test done.%N%N");
    end; --test
end --class ASSOCIATION_TESTER
```

Listing 11.2 *(continued)*

11.4 The Contract for *DICTIONARY*

All that a dictionary needs to do is keep track of associations of keys and values. If the key shows up in the dictionary *only once,* then a function *value*(<key>) can be provided for retrieving the value associated with that key. But that is not an assumption to be made lightly.

First, it appears to be a rather severe restriction: Real-world dictionaries contain several descriptions or translations for many of the words. This, however, can be easily worked around: Just make each value an array of translations instead of individual translations.

Second, it is expensive to enforce. The bullet-proof way to ensure that no duplicate keys exist is to treat the key analogously to the index in an *ARRAY*: When you *put*(<value>,<key>) it replaces whatever value was associated with that key, if any—just as *put*(<value>,<position>) does in class *ARRAY*.

The problem is that this forces us to perform a search inside each *put*, an expensive process that will have to be repeated O(*N*) times as a dictionary of size *N* is initially filled.

The second alternative is to allow multiple associations to the same key within the dictionary. Then inserting associations is no problem, but looking them up is. Either we can write a *values*(<key>) function, which builds and returns an array of values, or we need to write a set of features that allows the user to find all the values for that key, and then traverse them in a loop, getting the next value each time. The latter solution is wasteful, because it forces us to duplicate the traversal facilities that are already present in *ARRAY* (and, for that matter, in *LIST*).

Writing a *values* function that results in an array or a list of values is also problematic. If we return an *ARRAY* or a *LIST_ARRAY*, we need to make a good estimate about the size of the array, or resizing it will kill our performance. This may be acceptable if we know something about the dictionary: For example, if no more than five definitions are ever present per key, *values* can always create five-item arrays, and then resize them down if necessary.

Alternatively, we could have *values* always result in a *LIST_LINKED*, but that would mean that class *LIST_LINKED* and at least one of its undeferred subclasses must be present in the system even if the rest of the dictionary is completely array based.

So given several not quite satisfactory solutions, here is what we are going to do. We will provide the users with Boolean feature *has*(<key>) for determining if a key is already in the dictionary, and put "**not** *has*(*key*)" into *put*'s precondition. If precondition checking is enabled, this will still perform searching during every *put*, but at least the user can easily disable it.

Given a *has* feature, we can insist on *has*(*key*) as a precondition to *value*(*key*), or we can have *value* return *Void* if the key is not found. We can use the same precondition to *delete*(*key*), or we can make it ignore requests to delete a missing key. Since there is a harmless way to deal with the missing key situations, my preference is for allowing it, though it does complicate the postconditions somewhat.

The remainder of the features are the familiar *out*, *wipe_out*, and *copy*. The whole contract is shown in Listing 11.3.

```
deferred class DICTIONARY[KEY->COMPARABLE, VALUE] inherit
   ANY
      undefine
         is_equal, out, copy
```

Listing 11.3 The contract for *DICTIONARY* in the form of a deferred class.

```
        redefine
            is_equal, out
        end;

feature --Creation and initialization

    make is
            --Create a new, empty dictionary.
        deferred
        end; --make

feature --Adding, removing, and checking associations

    has(key: KEY): BOOLEAN is
            --Is there an association for key in this dictionary?
        deferred
        end; --has

    put(new_value: VALUE; key: KEY) is
            --Insert an association of key and new_value into this dictionary.
        require
            unique_key: not has(key);
            enough_room: not is_full;
        deferred
        ensure
            has_after_put: has(key);
            size_after_put: size = old size+ 1;
        end; --put

    delete(key: KEY) is
            --Delete the association for key (if any) from this dictionary.
        deferred
        ensure
            size_after_delete: size = old size - 1 or else
                                (size = old size and then not old has(key));
        end; --delete

    value(key: KEY): VALUE is
            --The value associated with key in this dictionary.
            --Void if there is no such association.
        deferred
        end; --value

    wipe_out is
            --Make this dictionary empty.
        deferred
        ensure
            empty: is_empty;
        end; --wipe_out
```

Listing 11.3 *(continued)*

```
feature --Sizing
   size: INTEGER is
         --The number of associations currently in this dictionary.
      deferred
      end; --size
   is_empty: BOOLEAN is
         --Is this dictionary empty?
      deferred
      end; --is_empty
   is_full: BOOLEAN is
         --Is there no room in this dictionary for one more association?
      deferred
      end; --is_full
feature --Comparisons and copying
   is_equal(other: like Current) is
         --Do this dictionary and other associate the same values
         --with the same keys?
      deferred
      end; --is_equal
feature --Simple input and output
   out: STRING is
         --"< (<key 1>.out,<val 1>.out) . . . (<key n>.out,<val n>.out) >".
      deferred
      end; --out
invariant
   empty_iff_zero_size: is_empty = (size = 0);
   size_not_negative: size >=0;
end --class DICTIONARY
```

Listing 11.3 *(continued)*

11.5 Linear Search Implementation

The simplest way to do a dictionary given the structures we have already seen is to keep an unsorted list of associations. To locate an association, we can simply loop through the list until we find an association whose key *is_equal* to the one we want to match. This is called a "**linear search**." Class *DICTIONARY_LINEAR*, shown in Listing 11.4, uses this technique.

The list of associations is named "*associations*." An internal feature *locate*(*key*) is used to move *associations*' cursor to the association for *key* if it is the dictionary, or all the way off-right if it is not. It is used then in *value*, *has*, *put*, and *delete*.

```
class DICTIONARY_LINEAR[KEY->COMPARABLE, VALUE] inherit
   DICTIONARY[KEY, VALUE]

creation make

feature {DICTIONARY_LINEAR}

   associations: LIST_DOUBLY_LINKED[ASSOCIATION[KEY,VALUE]];
         --The list of associations.

   locate(key: KEY) is
         --Move associations' cursor to the association for key
         --or off-right if there is no such association.
      do
         from
            associations.move_off_left; associations.move_right;
         until
            associations.is_off_right or else key.is_equal(associations.item.key)
         loop
            associations.move_right;
         end;
      end; --locate

feature --Creation and initialization

   make is
         --Create a new, empty dictionary.
      do
         !!associations.make;
      end; --make

feature --Adding, removing, and checking associations

   value(key: KEY): VALUE is
         --The value associated with key in this dictionary.
         --Void if there is no such association.
      local
         void_value: VALUE;
      do
         locate(key);

         if associations.is_off_right then
            Result := void_value;
         else
            Result := associations.item.value;
         end;
      end; --value
```

Listing 11.4 Class *DICTIONARY_LINEAR*—a dictionary implementation that uses a linear search.

```
  has (key: KEY): BOOLEAN is
        --Is there an association for key in this dictionary?
     do
        locate (key);

        Result := not associations.is_off_right;
     end; --has

  put (new_value: VALUE; key: KEY) is
        --Insert an association of key and new_value into this dictionary.
     local
        association: ASSOCIATION[KEY,VALUE];
     do
        !!association.make;
        association.set_key (key);
        association.set_value (new_value);

        --Less trouble to go to off-left than to check for off-right.
        associations.move_off_left;
        associations.insert_on_right (association);
     end; --put

  delete (key: KEY) is
        --Delete the association for key from this dictionary.
     do
        locate (key);

        if not associations.is_off_right then
           associations.delete;
        end;
     end; --delete

  wipe_out is
        --Make this dictionary empty.
     do
        associations.wipe_out;
     end; --wipe_out

feature --Sizing

  size: INTEGER is
        --The number of associations currently in this dictionary.
     do
        Result := associations.length;
     end; --size
```

Listing 11.4 *(continued)*

```
   is_empty: BOOLEAN is
         --Is this dictionary empty?
      do
         Result := associations.is_empty;
      end; --is_empty

   is_full: BOOLEAN is
         --Is there no room in this dictionary for one more association?
      do
         Result := associations.is_full;
      end; --is_full

feature --Comparisons and copying

   copy (other: like Current) is
         --Copy other onto Current.
      do
         --Start from scratch.
         make;

         associations.copy (other.associations);
      end; --copy

   is_equal (other: like Current): BOOLEAN is
         --Do this dictionary and other associate
         --the same values with the same keys?
      local
         other_value: VALUE;
      do
         if size /= other.size then
            Result := false;
         else
            from
               Result := true;
               associations.move_off_left; associations.move_right;
            until
               Result = false or else associations.is_off_right
            loop
               other_value := other.value (associations.item.key);
               Result := other_value /= Void and then
                           associations.item.value.is_equal (other_value);

               associations.move_right;
            end;
         end;
      end; --is_equal
```

Listing 11.4 *(continued)*

```
feature --Simple input and output

   out: STRING is
         -- "< (<key 1>.out,<val 1>.out) . . . (<key n>.out,<val n>.out) >".
      do
         Result := associations.out;
      end; --out

invariant

   have_list: associations /= Void;

end --class DICTIONARY_LINEAR
```

Listing 11.4 *(continued)*

Most features in *DICTIONARY_LINEAR* are straightforward, but the implementation of *is_equal* is significantly different from the way we have done it for *LIST*, *STACK*, and *QUEUE*. Since *associations* is not sorted, it is possible to have two dictionaries that are equal even though they do not store the equal associations in the same order. Thus, instead of going through the two lists in parallel and compairing the keys and the values of associations, we go through *Current.associations* and see if each key appears in *other* (no matter where) and is associated with the same value there. (The local entity *other_value* is used so that *other* does not have to be searched twice: once to establish that it contains the key, and once to get the associated value.)

11.6 Performance Analysis

Having to search through the list of associations is quite expensive. As Table 11.1 shows, while building the dictionary is quick (O(1) for each insertion), the features that look up associations are slow (O(N)). Dictionaries tend

Table 11.1 Average and worst case time complexities for the linear implementation of dictionaries (using a doubly linked list). N = *size*.

Feature	*Linear*	*Feature*	*Linear*
make	O(1)	*size*	O(N)
value	O(N)	*is_empty*	O(1)
has	O(N)	*is_full*	O(1)
put	O(1)	*copy*	See Exercise 10.2
delete	O(1)	*is_equal*	See Exercise 10.3
wipe_out	O(1)[a]	*out*	O(N)

[a] The garbage collector *may* have to do O(N) work to recycle the discarded nodes.

to be built once, and then accessed for lookups many times, so this is not a particularly efficient implementation.

Consider the book dictionary again. If every time you had to look up a word, you had to scan the whole dictionary from the beginning to the end, how long would it take? It would be foolish to do dictionary searches that way. The same situation applies to dictionary object structures: If the list of associations was sorted, we could zero in on the needed association much quicker.

We will do such an implementation in Chapter 14, after learning how to sort lists in Chapters 12 and 13.

Summary

Associations are specialized pairs. They associate a key with a value. They are intended for use in dictionaries, where the key is used to find the associated value.

Dictionaries are collections of associations. In this chapter, only linearly searched dictionaries were considered. Searching such a dictionary is an $O(N)$ operation.

Exercises

1. Write class *DICTIONARY_TESTER*. Use it to test *DICTIONARY_LINEAR*.
2. What is the time complexity of *copy* in *DICTIONARY_LINEAR*?
3. What is the time complexity of *is_equal* in *DICTIONARY_LINEAR*?
4. If *DICTIONARY_LINEAR* used *LIST_ARRAY* instead of *LIST_DOUBLY_LINKED*,

   a. on which end of the list should new associations be inserted?

   b. what would be the time complexity of *delete*?
5. If *DICTIONARY_LINEAR* used *LIST_SINGLY_LINKED* instead of *LIST_DOUBLY_LINKED*,

   a. on which end of the list should new associations be inserted?

   b. what would be the time complexity of *delete*?

12 Sorting

To facilitate more intelligent searching for an association in a list, we need to have a sorted list, according to the comparison methods we discussed in Chapter 11. Let us look at three ways to do that, and think about their time complexities.[1]

12.1 Sortable Lists

A list is sorted if for any two adjacent items tracked by it, the item on the left is **infix** "<=" to the item on the right. There are two approaches to this:

1. Replace *insert_on_left* and *insert_on_right* with an *insert* feature that places the new item into a position in which it is **infix** ">=" its left neighbor and **infix** "<=" its right neighbor.
2. Allow insertion anywhere, and provide features *sort* and *is_sorted* so that the user can sort the list on demand.

The first approach results in a list that is always sorted: "list is sorted" is part of its invariant. Since it discards the semantics of insertion either to the left or the right of the cursor, it cannot be an heir to class *LIST*.

The second method gives us a class of objects that can act as *LIST*s, and just adds a sorting facility. Let us use this approach.

Following the example of *COMPARABLE*, we create a deferred class called *SORTABLE*, which holds the contract for sortable object structures, as shown in Listing 12.1.

---

[1]The words and definitions used in the examples in this and the following chapter are from *The Deeper Meaning of Liff: A Dictionary of Things There Aren't Any Words for Yet—But There Ought to Be* by Douglas Adams and John Lloyd, copyright 1990 by Serious Productions Ltd. and John Lloyd. Used by permission.

```
deferred class SORTABLE[ITEM -> COMPARABLE] inherit
   ANY
      undefine
         out, is_equal, copy
      end;

feature

   is_sorted: BOOLEAN is
         --Is this structure currently sorted?
      deferred
      end; --is_sorted

   sort is
         --Sort this structure.
      deferred
      ensure
         sorted: is_sorted;
      end; --sort

end --class SORTABLE
```

Listing 12.1 Deferred class *SORTABLE*, providing the contract for all sortable object structures.

A sortable list is an heir to classes *SORTABLE* and *LIST*. Since *LIST* is deferred, if we inherit from it directly we will lose the three implementations we have written in Chapters 6 and 7. Instead, we will have class *SORTABLE_LIST_ARRAY*, which inherits from *LIST_ARRAY* and *SORTABLE* on the array-implementation side. For linked implementations, there is class *SORTABLE_LIST_SINGLY_LINKED*, which inherits from *SORTABLE_LIST_LINKED*, which in turn is an heir to *LIST_SINGLY_LINKED* and *SORTABLE*. We will skip the study of *SORTABLE_LIST_DOUBLY_LINKED*: if you can sort a singly linked list, you can figure out how to sort a doubly linked list (see the exercises).

Since we will be studying several ways to sort a list, feature *sort* will stay deferred in *SORTABLE_LIST_ARRAY* and *SORTABLE_LIST_SINGLY_LINKED*. For each sorting algorithm, we will have a subclass that implements *sort* in that specific way. Figure 12.1 shows the list class hierarchy with which we will end up at the end of this chapter.

Listing 12.2 shows deferred class *SORTABLE_LIST_ARRAY*. It implements *is_sorted* fully, but defers the implementation of *sort* to its algorithm-specific heirs. It does, however, place an additional postcondition on them: After the list is sorted, the cursor must be placed off-left (it needs to be placed into *some* predictable spot).

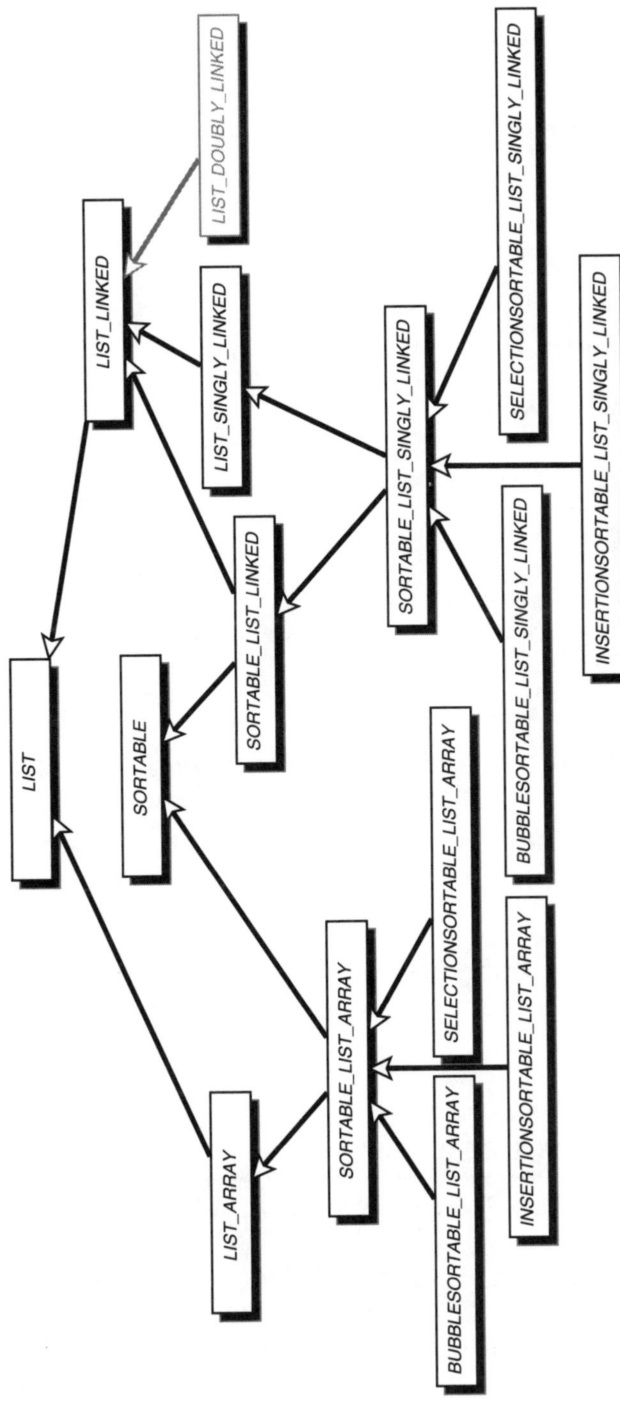

Figure 12.1 The hierarchy of sortable list classes used in this chapter.

```
deferred class SORTABLE_LIST_ARRAY[ITEM -> COMPARABLE] inherit
   LIST_ARRAY[ITEM];
   SORTABLE[ITEM]
      redefine
         is_sorted, sort
      end;
feature
   is_sorted: BOOLEAN is
         --Is this list currently sorted?
      local
         index: INTEGER;
      do
         from
            index := 1;
            Result := true;
         variant
            length - index
         until
            index >= length or Result = false
         loop
            Result :=
               (items.item(index) /= Void and items.item(index+1) /= Void)
               and then items.item(index) <= items.item(index+1);
            index := index + 1;
         end;
      end; --is_sorted
   sort is
         --Make this list sorted and off-left.
      deferred
      ensure then
         off_left: is_off_left;
      end; --sort
end --class SORTABLE_LIST_ARRAY
```

Listing 12.2 Deferred class *SORTABLE_LIST_ARRAY*.

Deferred class *SORTABLE_LIST_LINKED* is left as an exercise (12.1). All that *SORTABLE_LIST_SINGLY_LINKED* (Listing 12.3) does, for now, is inherit everything from *SORTABLE_LIST_LINKED* and *LIST_SINGLY_LINKED*. Nothing is added at this stage: *SORTABLE_LINKED_SINGLY_*

```
deferred class
   SORTABLE_LIST_SINGLY_LINKED[ITEM -> COMPARABLE]
inherit
   LIST_SINGLY_LINKED[ITEM];
   SORTABLE_LIST_LINKED[ITEM];
end --class SORTABLE_LIST_SINGLY_LINKED
```

Listing 12.3 A convenient class that combines the parental qualities of *SORTABLE_LINKED_LIST* and *LIST_SINGLY_LINKED*.

LINKED is just a convenient ancestor for the algorithm-specific sortable singly linked list classes.

12.2 Insertion Sort

The first algorithm we will consider is perhaps the closest to the method most people intuitively use to sort a stack of papers:

1. Sort the first two sheets.
2. Take the third sheet and insert it into the correct place among the first two sheets.
3. Take the fourth sheet and insert it into the correct place among the first three sheets.
4. Etc., until the last sheet has been inserted into the correct place.

To make the algorithm more consistent, we note that step 1 is not much different from the rest of them, and we rewrite it as

1. Take the second sheet and insert it into the correct place among the first one sheet.

As an English sentence it stinks, but it makes it clear that we have a nice, general loop on our hands.

This loop looks at each unsorted item, and puts it in its proper place among the sorted items. The sorted portion starts out with just one item in it (a list of only one item cannot help being sorted), and grows longer by one item each time through the loop.

Let us first look at the array version of this algorithm.

12.2.1 Insertion Sorting a *SORTABLE_LIST_ARRAY*

In a *LIST_ARRAY* object, the internally tracked array called *items* is used to line up the references to all the items in positions [1, . . . , *length*]. Thus, sorting from left to right, we use a local entity called *leftmost_unsorted* to store the index of the next item that needs to be placed.

The sorted region of the array is in positions

$$[1, \ldots, leftmost\_unsorted - 1]$$

This is *always* true about this loop: It is true upon each entry into the loop and also true right after the loop terminates. Such a property is called the **loop invariant,** and Eiffel provides a place for it in the loop statement itself. We have been omitting loop invariants until now, but they will come in handy when trying to understand sorts, where iterations can get quite convoluted. Figure 12.2 shows the state of a list with ten items at the entry into the loop with *leftmost_unsorted* = 5.

Listing 12.4 shows the complete class *INSERTIONSORTABLE_LIST_ARRAY*. The main loop is in feature *sort*, and two hidden features are invoked from within that loop. Let us look at the main loop first.

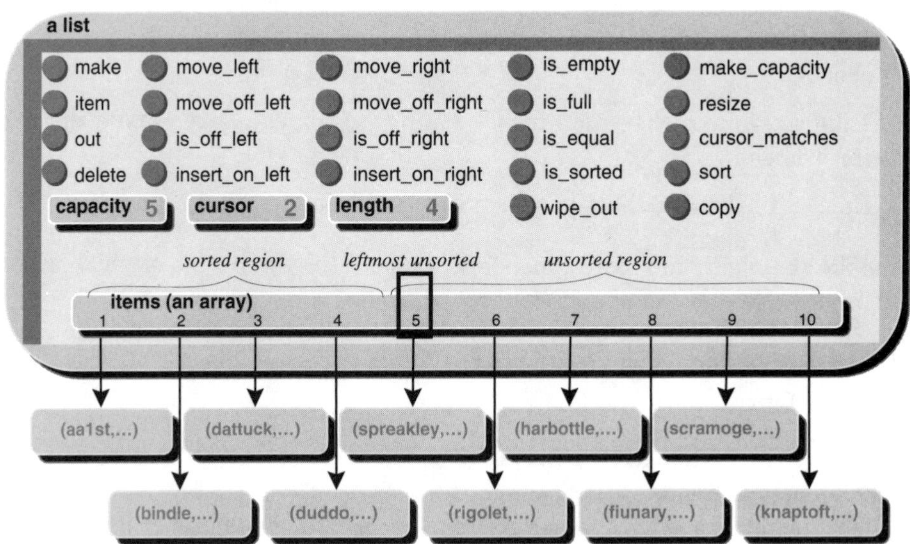

Figure 12.2 A partially sorted *INSERTIONSORTABLE_LIST_ARRAY*. Upon this entry into the loop (when *leftmost_unsorted*=5), the left four positions have already been sorted.

```
class INSERTIONSORTABLE_LIST_ARRAY[ITEM -> COMPARABLE]
inherit
   SORTABLE_LIST_ARRAY[ITEM]
      redefine
         sort
      end;

creation make, make_capacity

feature {NONE}

   position_for (unsorted_item: ITEM): INTEGER is
         --First index such that unsorted_item <= items.item (Result).
      require
         --unsorted_item is tracked by items.
      do
         from
            Result := 1;
         until
            unsorted_item <= items.item (Result)
         loop
            Result := Result + 1;
         end;
      end; --position_for

   shift_right (from_index: INTEGER; to_index: INTEGER) is
         --Shift all items between from_index and to_index
         --inclusively one step to the right.
      local
         index: INTEGER;
      do
         from
            index := to_index;
         variant
            index - from_index
         until
            from_index > index
         loop
            items.put (items.item (index), index+1);

            index := index - 1;
         end;
      end; --shift_right
```

Listing 12.4 Class *INSERTIONSORTABLE_LIST_ARRAY*.

```
feature

  sort is
        --Make this list sorted and off-left.
     local
        leftmost_unsorted: INTEGER;
        saved_item: ITEM;
        new_position: INTEGER;
     do
        from
           leftmost_unsorted := 2;
        invariant
           --items.item (1), . . . ,items.item (leftmost_unsorted-1) are sorted
        variant
           length - leftmost_unsorted
        until
           leftmost_unsorted > length
        loop
           new_position := position_for (items.item (leftmost_unsorted));

           if new_position /= leftmost_unsorted then
              --Rotate items.item (new_position), . . . ,items.item (leftmost_unsorted)
              --one position to the right.
              saved_item := items.item (leftmost_unsorted);
              shift_right (new_position, leftmost_unsorted-1);
              items.put (saved_item, new_position);
           end;

           leftmost_unsorted := leftmost_unsorted + 1;
        end;

        move_off_left;

     end; --sort

end --class INSERTIONSORTABLE_LIST_ARRAY
```

Listing 12.4 *(continued)*

We start with *leftmost_unsorted* set to 2, since everything to its left is already sorted (because there is only one item there). So the loop invariant holds. We leave the invariant as a comment, but we could have written a hidden feature *is_sorted_between* (<left index>,<right index>) and put "*is_sorted_between* (1,*leftmost_unsorted*−1)" into the **invariant** part of the loop. (Since that check is O(*N*), it would be very expensive to use it at every entry into the loop, so it would probably be disabled most of the time.)

The next section of this loop is the **loop variant,** which we have also been omitting. A variant of a loop is an integer number that gets smaller each time the loop is entered, but never becomes negative. Why does a loop need a variant? Well, it does not *need* one, in the sense that stating the variant does not alter the execution of the loop at all (just like stating the invariant does not alter the execution). The question is whether a variant for a given loop exists. Is there an integer expression that becomes smaller every time through the loop, but never turns negative? If there is, that means that the loop will finish its work after a finite number of iterations. If there is no such expression, then the loop is potentially infinite.[2]

Putting a **variant** section into a **loop** tells the compiler what its variant is, so that it can be checked at run time: If the variant does not decrease between two loops, or if it becomes negative, then an exception is triggered. Since the Eiffel **loop** statement does not have an automatic increment section, it is rather easy to forget to put an "*index*:=*index*+1" type statement at the end of the loop; many Eiffel programmers use the **variant** section to flag such problems and detect accidental infinite loops.

The loop in *sort* does two things:

1. Finds the proper position for *items.item* (*leftmost_unsorted*) in the range [1, . . . , *leftmost_unsorted*] (it may already be in its proper place, if all items to its left are less than it). This is done using hidden feature *position_for*.
2. Slides all items between that position and where it is now one step to the right, and then makes *items* track it in that position. Hidden feature *shift_right* assists that operation.

Features *position_for* and *shift_right* are often expanded within *sort*, to speed things up, since on most (but not all) computers each feature invocation costs a noticeable time delay, which adds up when you invoke the feature in a loop that runs O(*N*) times. This text separates them for the sake of clarity.

Feature *position_for* itself uses a loop that steps through *items* from the left edge until it finds an item that is greater than the unsorted item. That is the spot into which the unsorted item will have to be inserted. Note that

---

[2] Infinite loops are not necessarily bad. For example, a traffic light controller operates in an infinite loop: red, green, yellow, red, . . . Sorting loops are never infinite, so they always have a variant.

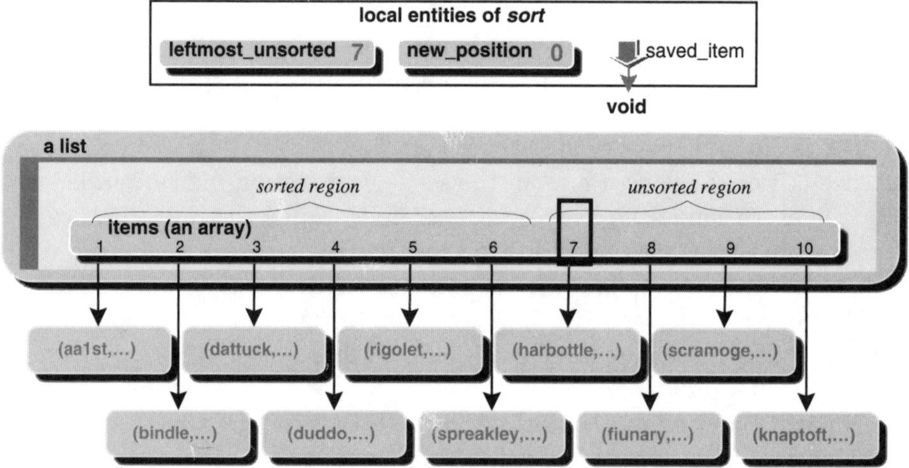

a. The loop is entered with *leftmost_unsorted*=7.

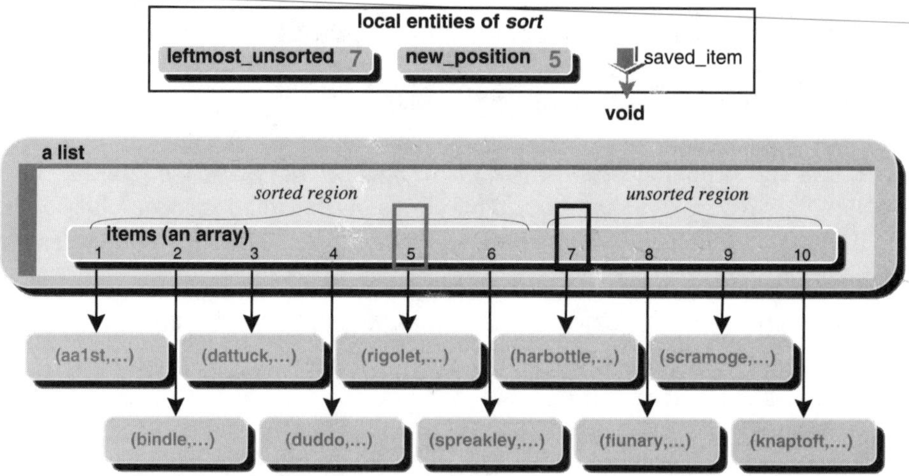

b. The result of *position_for* (*items.item* (7)) is 5.

Figure 12.3 The sixth pass through the loop in *INSERTIONSORTABLE_LIST_ARRAY*'s *sort*.

if it happens that *items.item* (*leftmost_unsorted*) is already greater than everything to its left, then the loop in *position_for* will stop when the search hits the leftmost unsorted item itself, and result in the position that it already occupies.

One pass through this loop is illustrated in Figure 12.3.

```
creation make

feature {NONE}

    left_neighbor_for (unsorted_item: ITEM): like off_left is
            --First node such that unsorted_item <= Result.right.item.
        require
            not is_empty;
            --unsorted_item is in this list's node chain.
        do
            from
                Result := off_left;
            until
                unsorted_item <= Result.right.item
            loop
                Result := Result.right;
            end;
        end; --left_neighbor_for

feature

    sort is
            --Make this list sorted and off-left.
        local
            rightmost_sorted: like off_left;
            leftmost_unsorted: like off_left;
            new_left_neighbor: like off_left;
        do
            --If length < 2, then the list is already sorted.
            --Avoid it, or Void.right and Void.item will happen.
            if length >= 2 then

                from
                    rightmost_sorted := off_left.right;
                invariant
                    --The chain up to rightmost_sorted is sorted.
                --variant
                    --The length of the unsorted part of the list
                until
                    rightmost_sorted.right = off_right
                loop
                    leftmost_unsorted := rightmost_sorted.right;

                    --Where does leftmost_unsorted.item belong?
                    new_left_neighbor := left_neighbor_for (leftmost_unsorted.item);

                    if new_left_neighbor = rightmost_sorted then
```

Listing 12.5 *(continued)*

```
                --The item in question is already where it
                --belongs, so now it is the rightmost sorted item.
                rightmost_sorted := leftmost_unsorted;
            else
                --Remove the leftmost unsorted item's node from the chain.
                rightmost_sorted.set_right(leftmost_unsorted.right);
                --Insert it to the right of new_left_neighbor.
                leftmost_unsorted.set_right(new_left_neighbor.right);
                new_left_neighbor.set_right(leftmost_unsorted);
                --rightmost_sorted is still over the rightmost sorted item.
            end;
        end;
    end;
    move_off_left;
  end; --sort
end --class INSERTIONSORTABLE_LIST_SINGLY_LINKED
```

Listing 12.5 *(continued)*

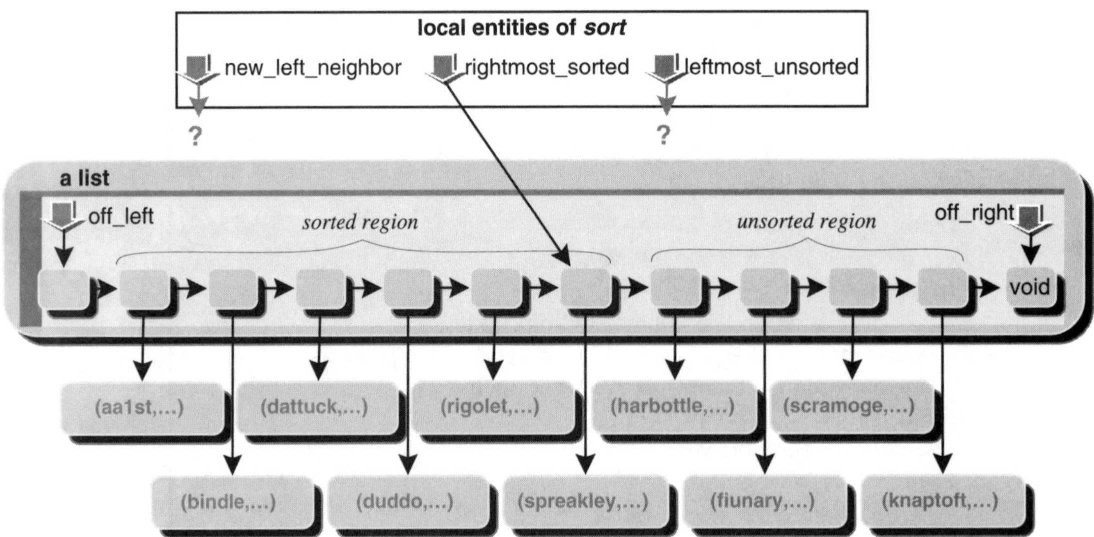

a. The loop is entered with *rightmost_sorted* tracking the node that tracks (harbottle, . . .).

Figure 12.4 The sixth pass through the loop in *INSERTIONSORTABLE_LIST_SINGLY_LINKED*'s *sort*.

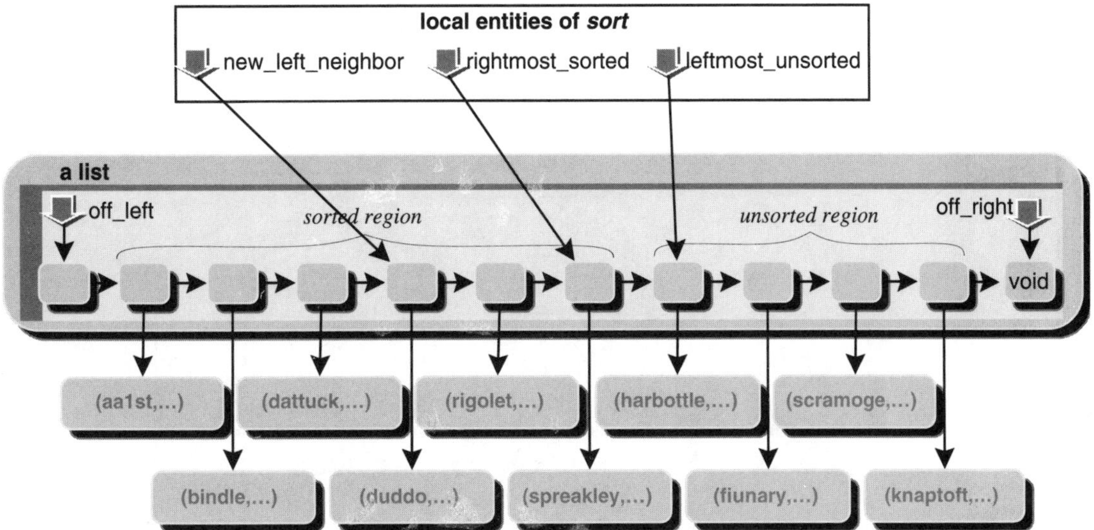

b. The result of *left_neighbor_for* (*leftmost_unsorted.item*) tracks the node that tracks (duddo, . . .).

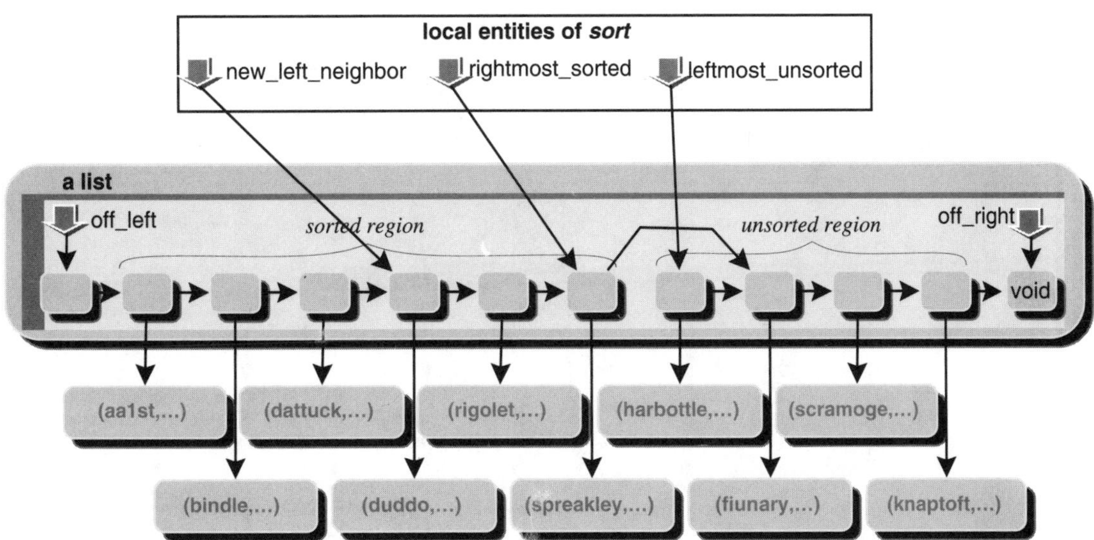

c. The leftmost unsorted item's node (the right neighbor of *rightmost_sorted*) has been bypassed.

Figure 12.4 (*continued*)

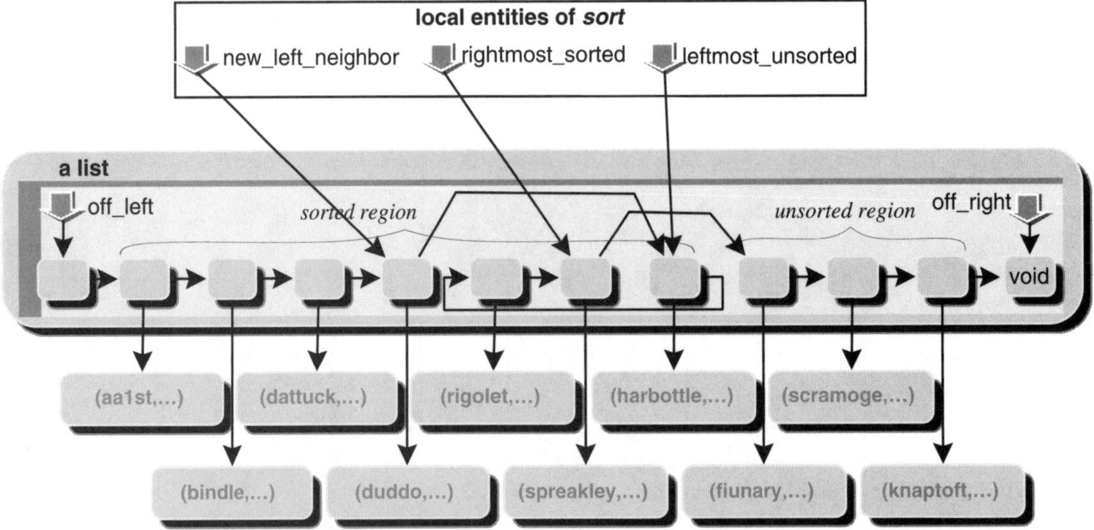

d. The leftmost unsorted item's node has been linked into the chain to the right of *left_neighbor_for* (*leftmost_unsorted.item*).

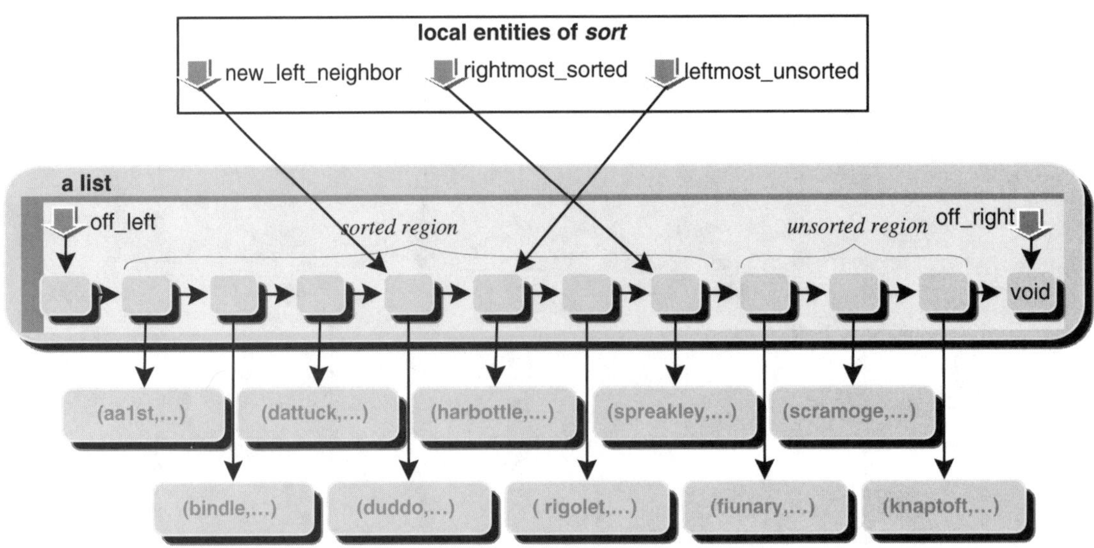

e. Same state, just cleaning up the diagram.

Figure 12.4 (*continued*)

12.2.3 Performance Analyses

We have been very careful, in both the array and the singly linked implementation, to avoid in our loops all list operations that take longer than O(1). In previous chapters, that gave us an $O(N)$ implementation for the loop. In the case of insertion sorting, it does not work that way, since we have loops within loops. In fact, it has been shown that it is impossible for a sorting algorithm that works by comparing pairs of items to be as fast as $O(N)$: The best possible time complexity for such an algorithm is $O(N \log N)$ (see Ref. 1, Theorem 2.7).[3]

To see what happens during an insertion sort, let us consider the array implementation, and what the loops have to do. We draw the array, and trace the execution of *sort* and its friends by leaving a trail of markers everywhere they go:

1. During the first pass through *sort*'s loop, the loops in *position_for* and *shift_right* visit positions 1 and 2. So we put markers under positions 1 and 2 of the array, as shown in Figure 12.5a.
2. During the second pass through *sort*'s loop, the loops in *position_for* and *shift_right* visit positions 1, 2, and 3. On the line below, we put markers under positions 1, 2, and 3 (Figure 12.5b).
3. Etc. We keep doing this until *sort*'s loop is finished.

When we are done, we will end up with a chart that has $N - 1$ rows of markers, one row for each pass through *sort*'s loop. The width of each row is equal to the value of *leftmost_unsorted*, so the last row is going to be N markers wide. This chart is shown in Figure 12.5c.

The total number of these markers, in terms of the length of the list, is the time complexity of *sort*. Recall that with the big O notation, we just want the proportion, so there is no need to get the precise count. The quickest way to get the "on-the-order-of" count of the markers is shown in Figure 12.6: Look at the triangle formed by the markers, and name its area in terms of N. Why area? Well, as we learned in calculus, the area within certain bounds is the accumulation of the areas of all the little squares you can stuff into those bounds.[4] If each of those squares happens to be 1×1, then the area of each square is 1, so the accumulation of those areas is equal to the number of the squares, which is what we seek.

---

[3]There are algorithms that work faster for keys that have a certain kind of internal structure, but they do not work when keys are arbitrary objects.

[4]Calculus books tend to express this idea a bit differently.

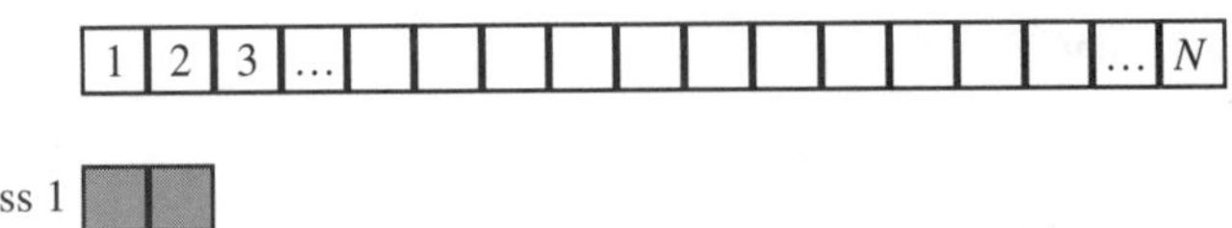

a. Positions of the array visited during the first pass through *sort*'s loop.

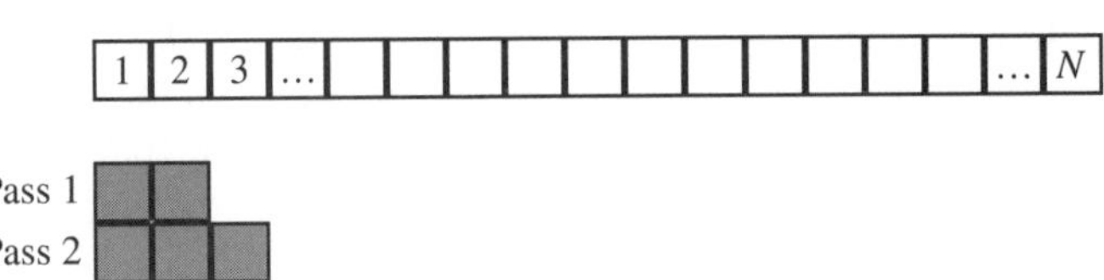

b. Positions of the array visited during the first two passes through *sort*'s loop.

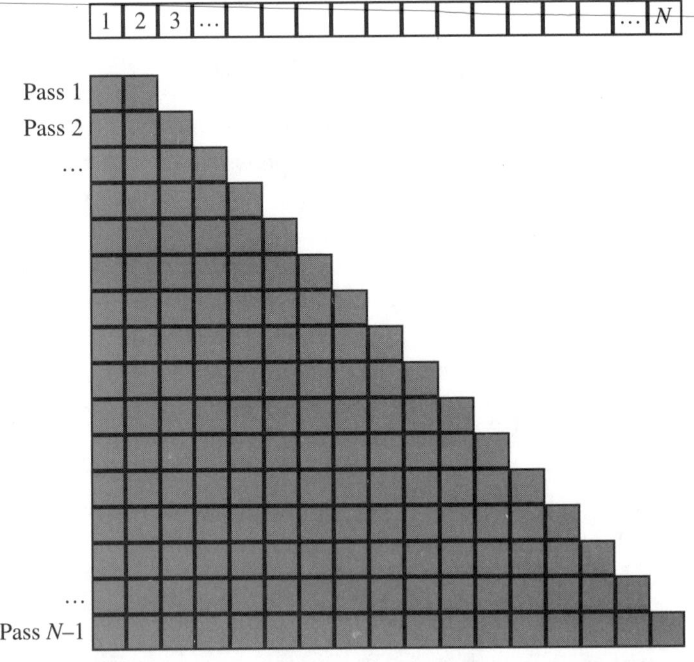

c. Positions of the array visited during all of the passes through *sort*'s loop.

Figure 12.5 The execution chart for the *INSERTIONSORTABLE_LIST_ARRAY*'s *sort* routine.

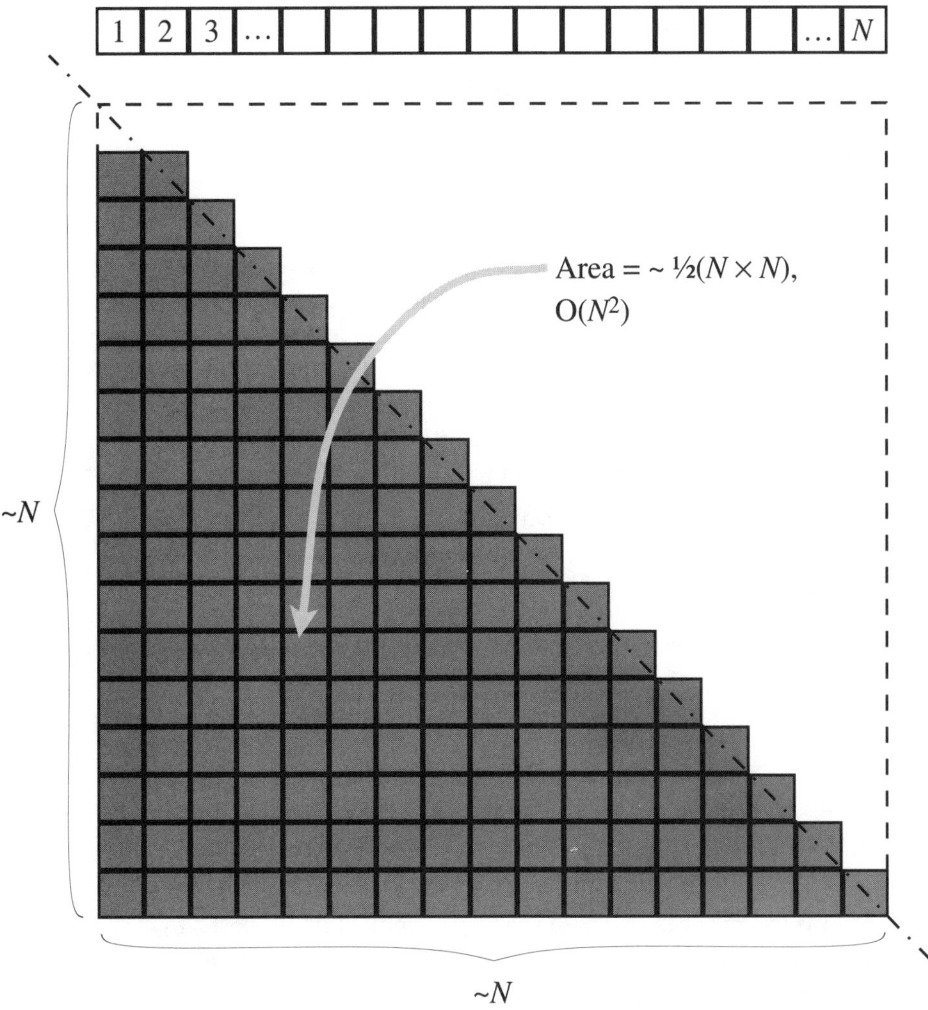

Figure 12.6 Tallying up the item visiting markers to get the time complexity of *sort* in *INSERTIONSORTABLE_LIST_ARRAY*.

The quickest way to get the area of the triangle is to recall that it is a rectangle sliced in half diagonally, so the area is "one-half the base times the height." The base of the rectangle is approximately equal to the longest trek taken by *position_for* and *shift_right* (about N), and the height is approximately equal to the number of passes through *sort*'s loop the algorithm takes (also about N). Thus, the number of position visitations performed by the *sort* routine is roughly $\frac{1}{2}N^2$, which is $O(N^2)$.

If we chart the progress of *sort* in *INSERTIONSORTABLE_LIST_SINGLY_LINKED*, we only get the full triangle in the worst case scenario, which is when everything in the sorted portion is always **infix** "<" the unsorted item, so *left_neighbor_for* has to go all the way through the sorted portion every time. Ironically, this worst case happens when the list is already sorted and each key is unique.

In the average case, we can expect that the *left_neighbor_for*'s loop will go through half of the sorted region before the proper spot for the leftmost unsorted item is found, which will give us roughly $\frac{1}{4}N^2$ markers, which is still $O(N^2)$.

There is a variation of the algorithm for insertion sorting an array that works better with sorted or partially sorted lists: Instead of having *position_for* search the sorted region from left to right, have it search it from right to left. In this way, the marker path taken by *position_for* and *shift_right* is identical—in fact, the two can be done in one loop: Compare the leftmost unsorted item to its left neighbor and swap them if they are out of order, and keep doing that until it percolates left to its proper spot. If the list is partially sorted, there is a good chance that the leftmost unsorted item is greater than everything in the sorted region, and the percolation stops immediately. With this algorithm, insertion sorting a list that is already sorted becomes $O(N)$—provided, of course, that moving left in the list is $O(1)$, so doing this in a singly linked list is difficult (but not impossible: it can be done by making a reverse copy of the node chain).

12.3 Bubble Sort

Whereas insertion sort mimicked the way humans tend to perform manual sorting, bubble sort takes a brute-force whack at the definition of the problem. To sort a list means to produce a list that is sorted. A list is sorted if no two consecutive items in it are out of order. Bubble sort looks for consecutive pairs of items that are out of order and swaps them. Figure 12.7 demonstrates how this operation is performed on an unsorted list. The first two items happen to be in order, so they are left alone. Items in positions 2 and 3 are out of sequence, so they are swapped. So far, it looks like everything to the left of the position being checked is sorted, but the next step proves that wrong: The item that is moved to the left during a swap will definitely be "<=" its new right neighbor, but that says nothing about its relationship with items to its left (see Figure 12.7d).

What does happen, however, is that the greater item keeps moving to the right, until it meets with an item that is even greater (Figure 12.7e). At that point, *that* item starts moving to the right. At the end of the sweep, we know that the greatest item, "(spreakley, . . .)" has bubbled up to the right end of the unsorted region (Figure 12.7f). All of its left neighbors are "<=" to it. Thus,

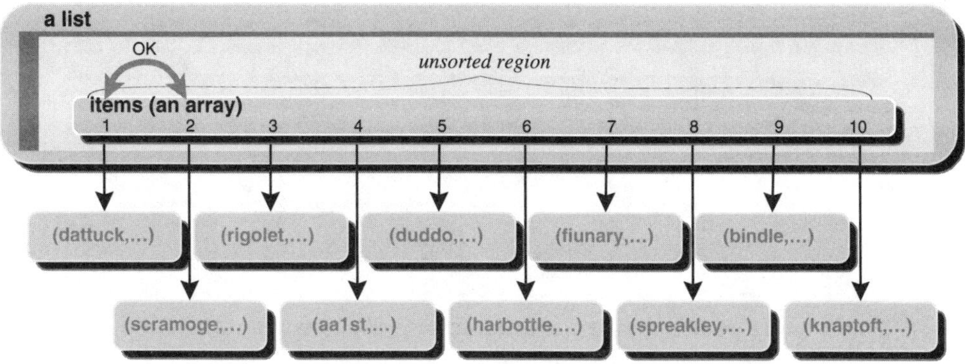

a. Items in positions 1 and 2 are in order.

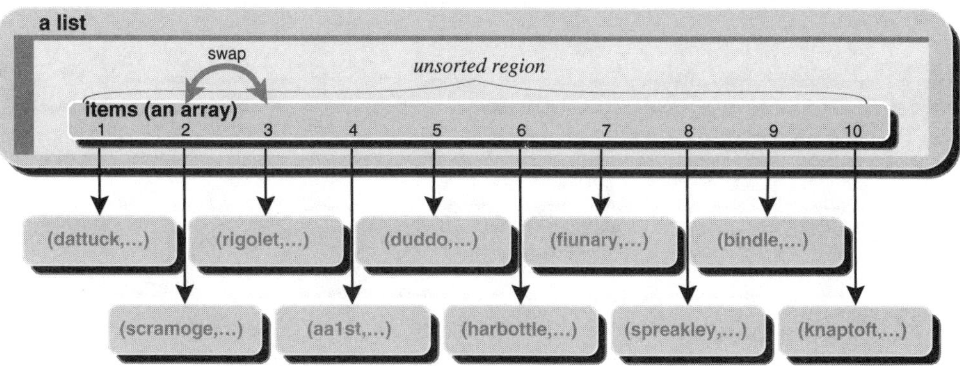

b. Items in positions 2 and 3 must be swapped.

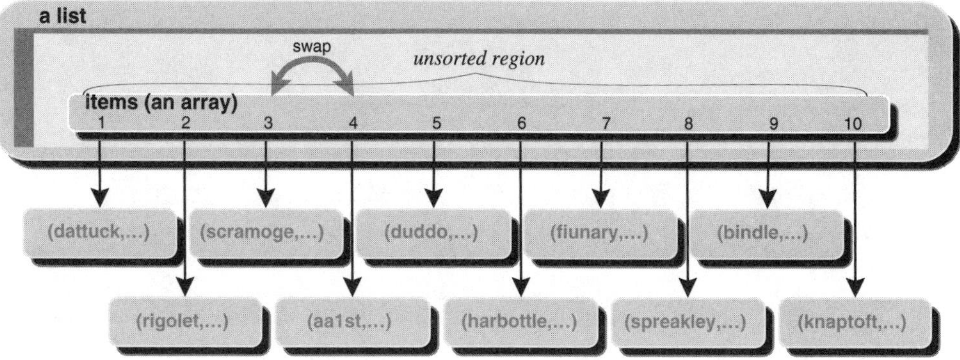

c. Items in positions 3 and 4 must be swapped.

Figure 12.7 One left-to-right sweep through the items, exchanging those that are out of sequence.

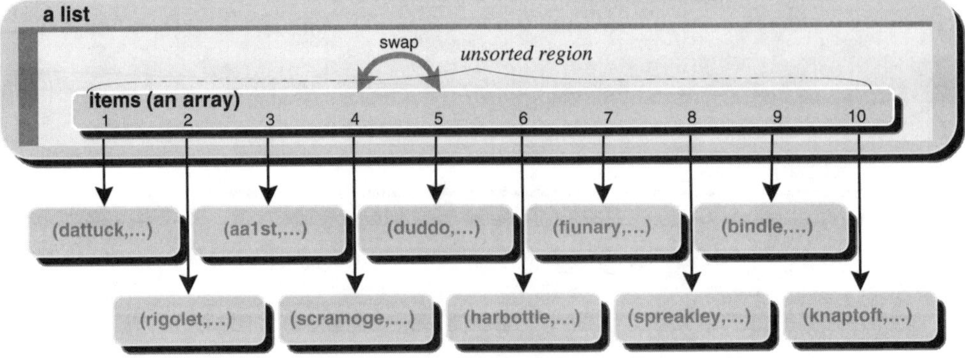

d. The region to the left of the swapping activity is demonstratively *not* sorted. Items in positions 4 and 5 must be swapped.

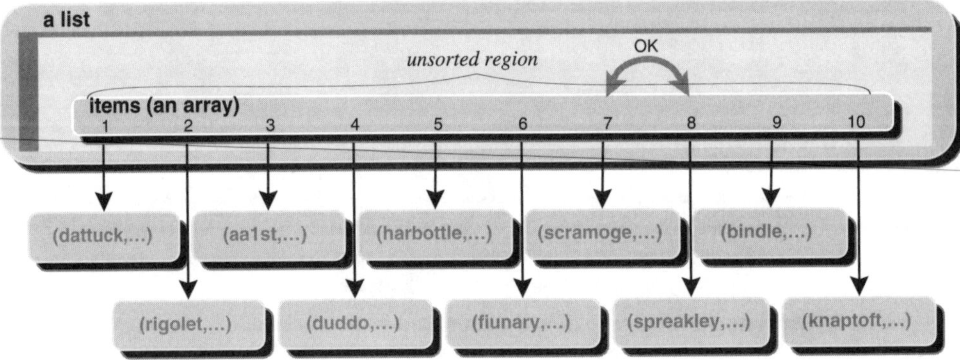

e. After two more steps (not shown), "(scramoge, . . .)" stops moving to the right because an even greater item, "(spreakley, . . .)" is encountered. No swapping here.

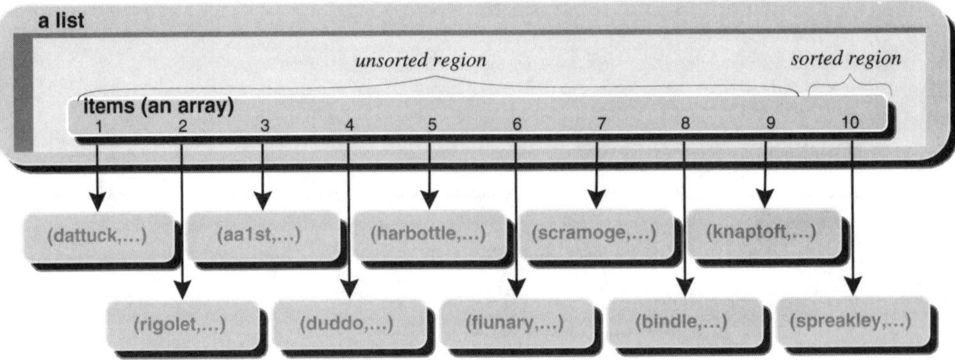

f. Two steps later (not shown), the greatest item has bubbled up to the right end of the unsorted region.

Figure 12.7 *(continued)*

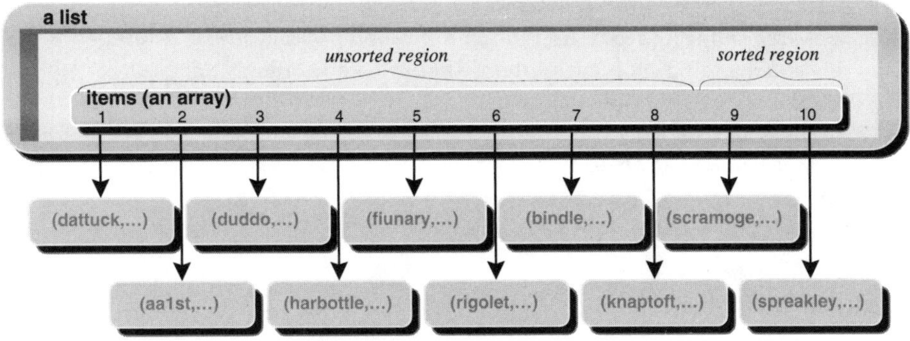

Figure 12.8 The list in Figure 12.7 after the second sweep.

there is no reason to ever move it again—it is, for what little it is worth, our sorted region.

Obviously, one sweep is not enough to sort the list, but if we perform another sweep, then the second greatest item, "(scramoge, . . .)" will bubble up to the right end of the unsorted region, coming to rest in front of "(spreakley, . . .)," thus joining the sorted region (Figure 12.8). In fact, since we know that everything in the sorted region is ">=" the greatest item in the unsorted region, we can stop the sweep at the end of the unsorted region. In this example, since there are 10 items, the first sweep stops after 9 comparisons, the second—after 8 comparisons, the third—after 7, and so on.

The algorithm then consists of two loops: a loop to make one sweep of comparisons and exchanges, and a loop around it to make enough sweeps to sort the entire list. The resulting routine *sort* (this time self-contained, though we could have separated the two loops as we had in the insertion sortable classes) is shown in Listing 12.6. Its singly linked list counterpart is left as an exercise (*Hint:* Never go left).

```
class BUBBLESORTABLE_LIST_ARRAY[ITEM -> COMPARABLE] inherit

   SORTABLE_LIST_ARRAY[ITEM]
      redefine
         sort
      end;

creation make, make_capacity

feature {NONE}
```

Listing 12.6 Class *BUBBLESORTABLE_LIST_ARRAY*.

```
   sweep (sweep_length: INTEGER) is
         --Make one sweep from position 1 through position sweep_length,
         --exchanging consecutive items that are out of order.
      local
         position: INTEGER;
         saved_item: ITEM;
      do
         from
            position := 1;
         invariant
            1 <= position and position <= sweep_length
         variant
            sweep_length - position
         until
            position = sweep_length
         loop
            if items.item (position) > items.item (position+1) then
               --Swap them.
               saved_item := items.item (position);
               items.put (items.item(position+1), position);
               items.put (saved_item, position+1);
            end;
            position := position + 1;
         end;
      end; --sweep
feature
   sort is
         --Make this list sorted and off-left.
      local
         unsorted_length: INTEGER;
      do
         from
            unsorted_length := length;
         invariant
            --Items to the right of position unsorted_length are sorted
            --and >= all items in positions 1 through unsorted_length.
         variant
            unsorted_length - 1
         until
            unsorted_length = 1
         loop
```

Listing 12.6 *(continued)*

```
            sweep (unsorted_length);
            unsorted_length := unsorted_length - 1;
        end;
        move_off_left;
    end; --sort
end --class BUBBLESORTABLE_LIST_ARRAY
```

Listing 12.6 *(continued)*

12.3.1 Performance Analysis

Figure 12.9 shows the execution trace of the routines in Listing 12.6. The singly linked version, if properly written, will have exactly the same trace. As was the case with insertion sorting, the trace takes the shape of an equilateral right triangle with base of approximately N, indicating $O(N^2)$ time complexity.

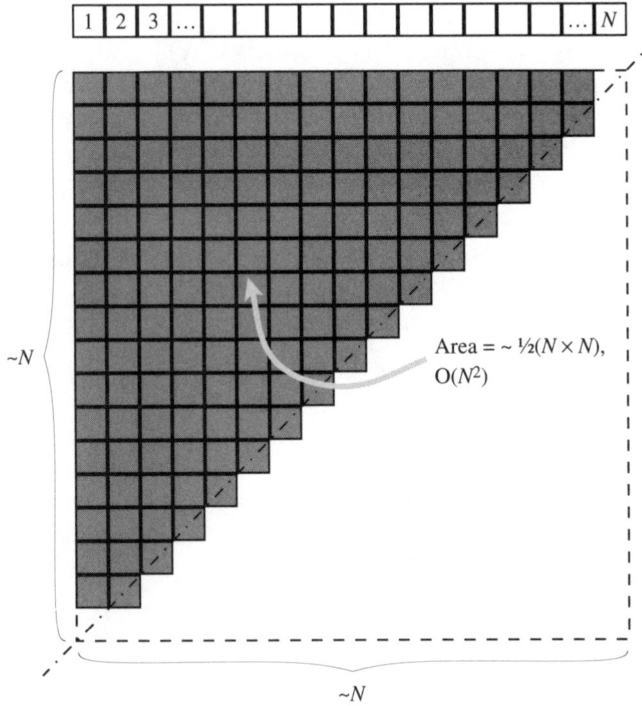

Figure 12.9 The tally of execution markers of the bubble sort algorithm.

12.3.2 Counting the Swaps

Both insertion sort and bubble sort have a time complexity of $O(N^2)$, because that is how many comparisons they perform. But while the number of comparisons is about the same, the number of object references that get moved around is quite different. Swapping object references in memory is cheap, so this is not a critical consideration for us. However, there are other sorting situations where swapping items is significantly expensive, and the number of swaps needs to be minimized (rearranging large files on disk, for example).

Consider insertion sort in the array implementation. The worst case situation is when the list starts out sorted in reverse: Then each new insertion goes into position 1, forcing the rest of the previously sorted region to move. If we place a marker at each spot where an object reference was moved, we get exactly the triangle of Figure 12.6. Thus, there are $O(N^2)$ object reference movements.

If the objects start out in random order, then the insertion will happen, on the average, halfway through the sorted region. This gives us a right triangle with the horizontal edge being half the vertical one, but it is still $O(N^2)$ (it is half the area of the comparison tracing triangle, but the constant $\frac{1}{2}$ does not matter).

The linked list implementation is much more efficient in terms of object reference swapping, because each insertion is $O(1)$, and one insertion is done on each pass, so the total number of insertions is $O(N)$.

Bubble sorting, on the other hand, performs many object reference swaps on every sweep (on the average, roughly half of the pairs in the unsorted region will be out of order), giving us the triangle again. Performing one swap is $O(1)$ in both the array and the linked implementation (if you did it correctly), so both implementations perform $O(N^2)$ swaps.

If the goal is to work the greatest item to the right end of the unsorted region of the list, why not just select it and put it there, instead of bubbling it through all the others, swapping half the time, on the average?

12.4 Selection Sort

The third and last sorting algorithm in this chapter does just that: It sweeps the unsorted region, remembering which element is the greatest, and moves it to the right end of the region, where it is adjoined to the sorted region.

Both the array and the singly linked versions of this algorithm are left up to you. I suggest using a hidden function that results in the position of the greatest item within a range. Then swap the item at that position with the rightmost unsorted item—especially in the array implementation, this is *much* cheaper than shifting everything to the left ($O(1)$ instead of $O(N)$).

Summary

Three sorting algorithms were considered in this chapter: insertion sort, bubble sort, and selection sort.

Insertion sort works by repeatedly inserting items into their proper place within the sorted portion of the list.

Bubble sort works by bubbling the greatest item to one end of the list, then repeating the process with the shorter unsorted region.

Selection sort is similar to bubble sort, but instead of bubbling greater items to one side, it first finds the greatest item of the unsorted region and then swaps it with the one at the end of the unsorted region.

All three of these algorithms have average and worst case performance of $O(N^2)$. Selection sort may be advantageous in situations where swapping is expensive. Insertion sort can be programmed to perform better than others on lists that are already mostly sorted.

Exercises

1. Write the deferred class *SORTABLE_LIST_SINGLY_LINKED*.
2. Modify *INSERTIONSORTABLE_LIST_ARRAY* to improve its performance with partially sorted lists.
3. If the algorithm in Exercise 2 was used in *INSERTIONSORTABLE_LIST_SINGLY_LINKED*, what would be its worst case time complexity?
4. Implement bubble sort with singly linked lists.
5. Add the sortable doubly linked classes to Figure 12.1.
6. Implement selection sort with array-based lists. What is the time complexity of your implementation?
7. Implement selection sort with singly linked lists. What is the time complexity of your implementation?
8. Implement insertion sort with doubly linked lists.
9. Implement bubble sort with doubly linked lists.
10. Implement selection sort with doubly linked lists.
11. Use inheritance to factor out the common code in classes *BUBBLESORTABLE_LIST_ARRAY* and *BUBBLESORTABLE_LIST_SINGLY_LINKED*.

12. Each of the *sort* routines listed in this chapter makes a call to a hidden feature (e.g., *left_neighbor_for* and *sweep*) to do the inner loop. Unless the compiler is very clever at optimizing, each one of these feature calls will take some time to set up and return from. Execution of the *sort* routines can be sped up by expanding the code of the hidden feature within the loop inside *sort*.

    a. Does this optimization change the time complexity of the routine? If so, how?

    b. Rewrite one of the *sort* routines presented in this chapter using this optimization.

13. Draw the execution chart of feature *delete* of *DICTIONARY_LINEAR* (see Listing 11.4).

14. Eiffel language rules insist that the loop variant must be an integer expression. Could real expressions be allowed? Explain.

13 Faster Sorting

The three sorting algorithms we discussed in Chapter 12 (insertion sort, bubble sort, and selection sort) have the time complexity of $O(N^2)$—acceptable for short object structures, but bogging down considerably as the structures grow longer. There are also three commonly used sorts that have a much lower complexity. We will study two of them (**merge sort** and **quick sort**) in this chapter, but we have to postpone the third (**heap sort**) until Chapter 16. We will conclude this chapter with a discussion on how to pick the best sorting algorithms for given circumstances.

13.1 Merge Sort

Suppose you had two lists that were already sorted. How would you merge them into one sorted list? Easy: Pick the lesser of the leftmost items of the two lists, then pick the lesser of the leftmost unpicked items of the two lists, and so on. Using the *LIST* contract, we can do it as shown in Listing 13.1.

Fine, but what does that have to do with sorting? Well, suppose we had a list whose left half-list was sorted and whose right half-list was sorted. Then we can use the same algorithm to merge the two sorted half-lists into the sorted full list. Of course, we cannot tell our users that our *sort* routine only works for lists in which the left half is already sorted and the right half is already sorted.

So how do we get a list with a sorted left half-list and a sorted right half-list? Well, suppose we had half-lists where the left quarter-lists were sorted and the right quarter-lists were sorted. Then we could merge the respective sorted quarter-lists into sorted half-lists. And we get those by merging sorted eighth-lists, and so on. In other words, we can use the same algorithm to sort

```
merged_list (list1, list2: LIST): LIST is
    require
        lists_sorted: list1.is_sorted and then list2.is_sorted;
    do

        --As long as both lists are not off-right, keep appending the lesser
        --of the two lists' items to the right end of Result.
        from
            !!Result.make;
            list1.move_off_left; list1.move_right;
            list2.move_off_left; list2.move_right;
        until
            list1.is_off_right or list2.is_off_right;
        loop
            if list1.item < list2.item then
                Result.insert_on_right (list1.item);
                list1.move_right;
            else
                Result.insert_on_right (list2.item);
                list2.move_right;
            end;
            Result.move_right;
        end;

        --Get the rest of list1, if any.
        from
        until
            list1.is_off_right
        do
            Result.insert_on_right(list1.item);
            list1.move_right;
            Result.move_right;
        end;

        --Get the rest of list2, if any.
        from
        until
            list2.is_off_right
        do
            Result.insert_on_right(list2.item);
            list2.move_right;
            Result.move_right;
        end;
    ensure
        result_sorted: Result.is_sorted;
    end; --merged_list
```

Listing 13.1 An algorithm for building a sorted list out of two sorted lists.

the smaller sublists. When do we stop? When we get a sublist that is empty or that only has one item in it—a list like that is already sorted.

In pseudocode (that's computerese for "just an outline of the algorithm, don't even try compiling it"), the *merge_sort* feature looks like this:

```
merge_sort (<range within this list>) is
        --Sort this range of this list.
  do
    if <length of the range> > 1 then
      <find the middle of the range>;
      merge_sort (<left half of the range>);
      merge_sort (<right half of the range>);
      merge (<left half of the range>, <right half of the range>);
    end;
  end; --merge_sort
```

This is called a **recursive** algorithm. An algorithm is a script for performing a task; any algorithm that breaks its task into smaller tasks and uses the same script to perform at least one of them is recursive. In order for a recursive algorithm to bring its task to completion ("to terminate" in computer science slang), two things must be true about it:

1. Every time the script is recursively invoked, it must be given a smaller problem to solve.
2. It must include at least one way to solve sufficiently small problems *without* recursively invoking the script.

The merge sort algorithm gets smaller problems every time: The range it gets is half as long as before. It also has a way to sort ranges that are short enough without using recursion: Ranges that are empty or only have one item in it are already sorted, so the algorithm does nothing—which certainly does not involve invoking the script again.

13.1.1 The Array Version

The merge sort algorithm is easy to use with the array implementation of lists. A sublist is simply denoted with the range of array indices that it overlays. To find the middle of the sublist, we simply find the mean index of the range:

$$\langle\text{middle index}\rangle = \left\lfloor \frac{\langle\text{leftmost index}\rangle + \langle\text{rightmost index}\rangle}{2} \right\rfloor$$

If the range contains an even number of positions, the exact middle falls between two indices (position "x.5"), so we just truncate the ".5" and call the index immediately to the left of the exact middle "the middle index." The Eiffel operator for integer division, which truncates the fractional part, is "//" (and the remainder operator is "\\").

First, let us do the hidden routine *merge*. The algorithm wants two sublists, so the simple thing to do is pass it the boundary indices of those ranges as four parameters. However, since we know that in merge sort we are always merging adjacent sublists, it's enough to pass three parameters—*first_left*, *first_right*, and *last_right*—knowing that the last index in the left subrange is *first_right* − 1.

The routine, shown in Listing 13.2, creates a spare array to keep the object references in sorted order. After the merging is done, those references are copied back into *items*.

```
merge (first_left, first_right, last_right: INTEGER)
        --Merge the sorted regions [first_left, . . . ,first_right−1] and
        --[first_right, . . . ,last_right] into one sorted region [first_left, . . . ,last_right].
    local
        merged: like items; --Temporary array to track merged items.
        left_index, right_index, merged_index: INTEGER;
    do
        !!merged.make (first_left, last_right);

        --Merge them while they are both unempty.
        from
            left_index := first_left;
            right_index := first_right;
            merged_index := first_left;
        invariant
            --merged.item (first_left), . . . ,merged.item (merged_index−1)
            --are sorted.
        variant
            last_right − merged_index
        until
            left_index >= first_right or right_index > last_right
        loop
```

Listing 13.2 Hidden routine *merge* of class *MERGESORTABLE_LIST_ARRAY*.

```
        if items.item (left_index) < items.item (right_index) then

            merged.put (items.item (left_index),merged_index);
            left_index := left_index + 1;

        else

            merged.put (items.item (right_index),merged_index);
            right_index := right_index + 1;

        end;

        merged_index := merged_index + 1;
    end;

    --Copy whatever remains in the left subrange.
    from
        --Everything is ready.
    invariant
        --merged.item (first_left), . . . ,merged.item (merged_index-1)
        --are sorted.
    variant
        first_right - left_index - 1
    until
        left_index >= first_right
    loop
        merged.put (items.item (left_index), merged_index);
        left_index := left_index + 1;
        merged_index := merged_index + 1;
    end;

    --Copy whatever remains in the right subrange.
    from
        --Everything is ready.
    invariant
        --merged.item (first_left), . . . ,merged.item (merged_index-1)
        --are sorted.
    variant
        last_right - right_index
    until
        right_index > last_right
    loop
        merged.put (items.item (right_index), merged_index);
        right_index := right_index + 1;
        merged_index := merged_index + 1;
    end;
```

Listing 13.2 *(continued)*

```
        --Copy the merged references back.
        from
            merged_index := first_left;
        invariant
            --merged.item (first_left), . . . ,merged.item (merged_index-1)
            --are sorted.
        variant
            last_right - merged_index
        until
            merged_index > last_right
        loop
            items.put (merged.item (merged_index), merged_index);
            merged_index := merged_index + 1;
        end;

    end; --merge
```

Listing 13.2 *(continued)*

The next thing to do is write the recursive *merge_sort* routine (also hidden). Shown in Listing 13.3, it is a straightforward translation of the algorithm.

What little remains to be written of class *MERGESORTABLE_LIST_ARRAY* is left up to you.

```
merge_sort (leftmost, rightmost: INTEGER) is
        --Merge-sort the region [leftmost, . . . ,rightmost].
    local
        middle: INTEGER;
    do
        if leftmost < rightmost then

            middle := (leftmost + rightmost) // 2;

            --Sort the two halves of this range.
            merge_sort (leftmost, middle);
            merge_sort (middle+1, rightmost);

            --Merge the two sorted halves of this range.
            merge (leftmost, middle+1, rightmost);
        end;
    end; --merge_sort
```

Listing 13.3 Hidden routine *merge_sort* of class *MERGESORTABLE_LIST_ARRAY*.

13.1.2 Performance Analysis of the Array Version

Before attempting the linked list version of the merge sort algorithm, let us analyze the time complexity of what we have so far. Unlike the algorithms in Chapter 12, this time we do not have a sequence of passes or sweeps to record. What *do* we have? We have levels of recursion.

At the first level of recursion, the middle is found, which is a simple division by two, which is O(1), and requires no marker. Then the algorithm has to wait for *merge_sort* of the left half-list to terminate. We don't know yet how many markers that is going to take, so let us just draw a blank box under the left half of the list; we will fill it in later. Then we have to wait for *merge_sort* of the right half-list to terminate—another blank box. Now we merge the two half-lists, an action that touches every item (as its reference is copied into the merged array and later as it is copied back). So we place one marker under each array position, resulting in Figure 13.1a.

Let us now fill in the two level 2 boxes. Every *merge_sort* of a half-list has to find the middle, then wait for *merge_sort* of the left quarter-list (a blank box), then wait for *merge_sort* of the right quarter-list (another blank box), then merge the quarter-lists ($\frac{N}{2}$ items). This gets us Figure 13.1b.

Filling in the level 3 boxes, in each level 2 box we find the middle, wait for two level 4 blank boxes, then merge $\frac{N}{4}$ items (Figure 13.1c).

a. Execution trace of the first level of recursion.

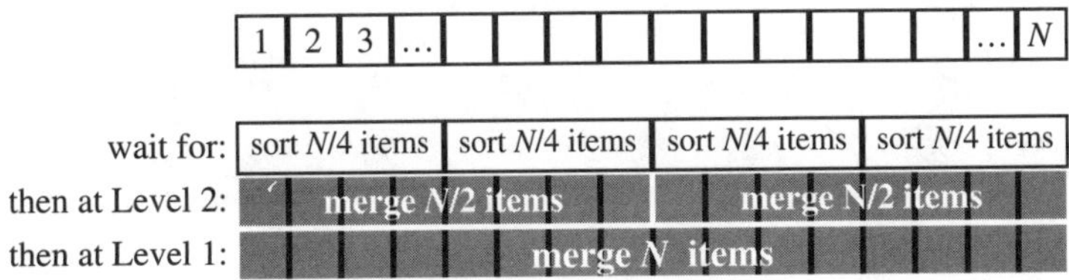

b. Execution trace of the first two level of recursion.

Figure 13.1 The execution chart for the *MERGESORTABLE_LIST_ARRAY*'s *merge_sort* routine.

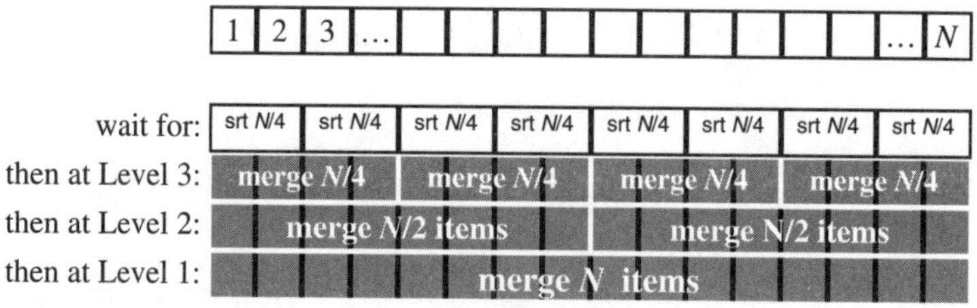

1	2	3	...											...	N

wait for:	srt $N/4$	srt $N/4$	srt $N/4$	srt $N/4$	srt $N/4$	srt $N/4$	srt $N/4$	srt $N/4$
then at Level 3:	merge $N/4$		merge $N/4$		merge $N/4$		merge $N/4$	
then at Level 2:	merge $N/2$ items				merge $N/2$ items			
then at Level 1:	merge N items							

c. Execution trace of the first three level of recursion.

Figure 13.1 *(continued)*

We keep doing that until all the boxes get to be only 1 item wide (or empty), where there is no waiting involved.

Tallying up the markers, we see that at every level we have a total of N markers. How many levels are there? At every level, the range length is cut in half. We start with N items, so how many times can N be divided by two, before we get to ranges of size 1? We are looking for x such that

$$\left(\frac{1}{2}\right)^x N = 1$$

That is easy enough to solve:

$$N = 2^x$$
$$\log_2 N = x$$

So the tally diagram looks like Figure 13.2. The markers form a rectangle $O(N)$ across and $O(\log_2 N)$ high, for a total time complexity of $O(N \log_2 N)$.

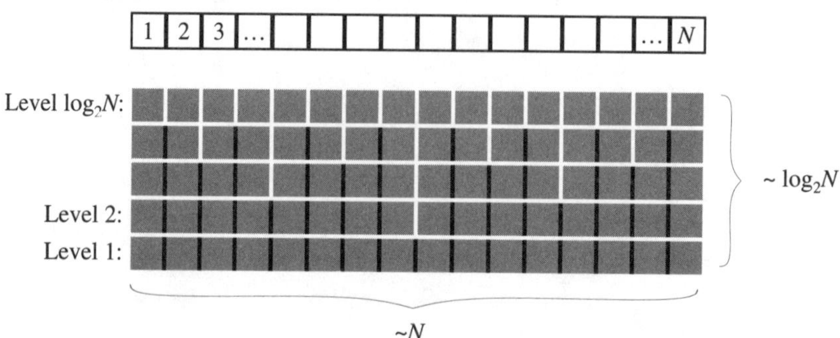

Figure 13.2 Tallying up execution markers.

How does that compare with the performance of the algorithms in Chapter 12? All of those were $O(N^2)$ routines. If a list had a million items, it would take on the order of a trillion (a million million) steps to sort them with an $O(N^2)$ algorithm. With an $O(N \log_2 N)$ algorithm, it would take on the order of . . . now, put away that calculator, a computer scientist should be able to do base-2 logarithms in his or her head. It's easy—all you need to remember is that 1K (1024) is exactly 2^{10}. So a million is about 1M, which is 1K $\times$ 1K, which is 2^{20}. Thus, $\log_2 1M = 20$.

So, to merge sort a million items would only take about 20 million steps—much better than the 1,000,000 million steps that, say, bubble sort would take.

While we are on the subject of logarithms, let us take a simplifying step. Instead of writing "$O(\log_2 N)$," we can simply write "$O(\log N)$." There are two reasons for it:

1. As computer scientists, we deal with powers of 2 more than with powers of 10 or e, so we usually talk about base-2 logarithms, not base-10 or natural (base-e) logarithms.
2. With the big O notation, it does not matter what the base of the logarithm is, since it only changes a constant ($\log_a x = k \log_b x$ for any a and b), and constants are discarded.

13.1.3 The Singly Linked Version

Merge sorting a linked list is similar to merge sorting an array-based list, but there are a few details to consider.

The first detail is delimiting the range. In the array-based version, we used the index of the leftmost item and the index of the rightmost item. The list analog to that is using references to the leftmost and the rightmost nodes. If we sort the range by moving the nodes around, we are likely to lose track of the range because the leftmost and rightmost nodes may move. So instead we identify the range by the node just left of the leftmost node (we need it anyway to avoid insertions on left) and the length of the range (i.e., the number of nodes to the right of the left-of-leftmost node that form the range).

The second detail is finding the middle of the range. Since the items are not numbered, we cannot just compute the average of the leftmost and rightmost positions. Instead, we have to move right, counting off to half of the range's length.

The code that does that is given in Listing 13.4. It should be studied as an example of how many engineering decisions might still be needed after the basic algorithm is understood. While you are studying it, draw the execution

```
feature {NONE}

  merge_sort (left_of_first: like off_left; sublist_length: INTEGER) is
        --Merge sort the region of sublist_length
        --to the right of the node tracked by left_of_first.
    local
      left_length: INTEGER; --Length of the left half of the range.
      last_left: like off_left; --Last node of the left half-range.
      counter: INTEGER;
    do
      if sublist_length > 1 then

        --Identify and sort the left half of the sublist.
        left_length := sublist_length // 2;
        merge_sort (left_of_first, left_length);

        --Identify and sort the right half of the sublist.
        from
          last_left := left_of_first;
          counter := 0;
        variant
          left_length - counter - 1
        until
          counter = left_length
        loop
          last_left := last_left.right;
          counter := counter + 1;
        end;
        merge_sort (last_left, sublist_length-left_length);

        --Merge the two halves.
        merge (left_of_first, last_left, sublist_length-left_length);

      end;

    end; --merge_sort

  merge (left_of_first_left, last_left: like off_left; right_length: INTEGER) is
      --Merge the sorted regions [left_of_first_left.right, . . . ,last_left]
      --and right_length items to the right of last_left into one sorted region.
    local
      last_merged: like off_left; --Tracks last merged node.
      next_left: like off_left; --Next nodes to compare.
      next_right: like off_left;
      right_counter: INTEGER;
```

Listing 13.4 Sorting routines for class *MERGESORTABLE_LIST_SINGLY_LINKED*.

```
do
    --Merge them while they are both unempty.
from
    last_merged := left_of_first_left;
    next_left := left_of_first_left.right;
    next_right := last_left.right;
    right_counter := 1;
invariant
    --left_of_first_left.right.item, . . . ,last_merged.item are sorted.
--variant
    --Sum of unmerged segments of the two subranges
until
    next_left = last_left.right or right_counter > right_length
loop

    if next_left.item < next_right.item then

        last_merged.set_right (next_left);
        last_merged := next_left;
        next_left := next_left.right;

    else

        last_merged.set_right (next_right);
        last_merged := next_right;
        next_right := next_right.right;
        right_counter := right_counter + 1;

    end;
end;

--Attach whatever remains to the merged sublist
--and attach the rest of the list to its end.
if next_left = last_left.right then

    last_merged.set_right (next_right);
    --The rest of the list is already attached to the end of the right sublist.

else

    last_merged.set_right (next_left);
    --next_right is now one step beyond the right half-range.
    last_left.set_right (next_right);

end;

end; --merge
```

Listing 13.4 *(continued)*

trace chart for it and convince yourself that this implementation's time complexity is also O(N log N).

13.2 Quick Sort

Another commonly used recursive sorting algorithm is **quick sort.** The basic algorithm is this:

```
quick_sort (<range within this list>) is
        --Sort this range of this list.
    do
        if <length of the range> > 1 then
            <pick a "pivot" item p from within the range>
            <put all items <= p into the left subrange>;
            <put all items >= p into the right subrange>;
            quick_sort (<the left subrange>);
            quick_sort (<the right subrange>);
        end;
    end; --quick_sort
```

If the picking of p and the partitioning of the range into the "<=" and ">=" subranges can be done in the time proportional to the length of the subrange, then we can get an execution trace very similar to that of merge sort (Figure 13.2). Assuming that p was picked so that the range is split down the middle (in other words, p is the median object of the range), we get the picture in Figure 13.3a. Unfortunately, if we always pick the worst p—either the least or the greatest object in the range—we wind up with Figure 13.3b, which is O(N^2).

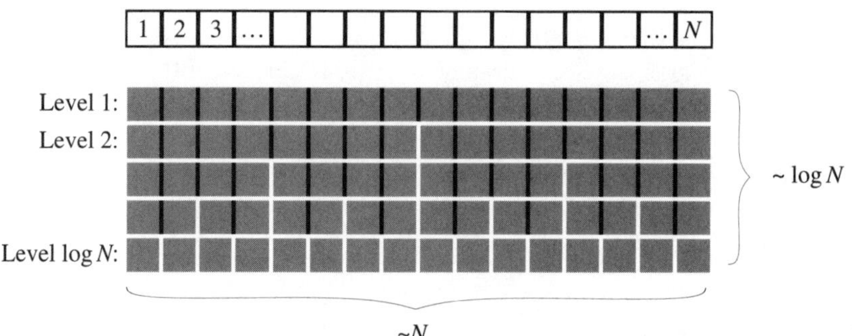

a. Best case: the median is always picked as the pivot.

Figure 13.3 Execution charts for the quick sort algorithm.

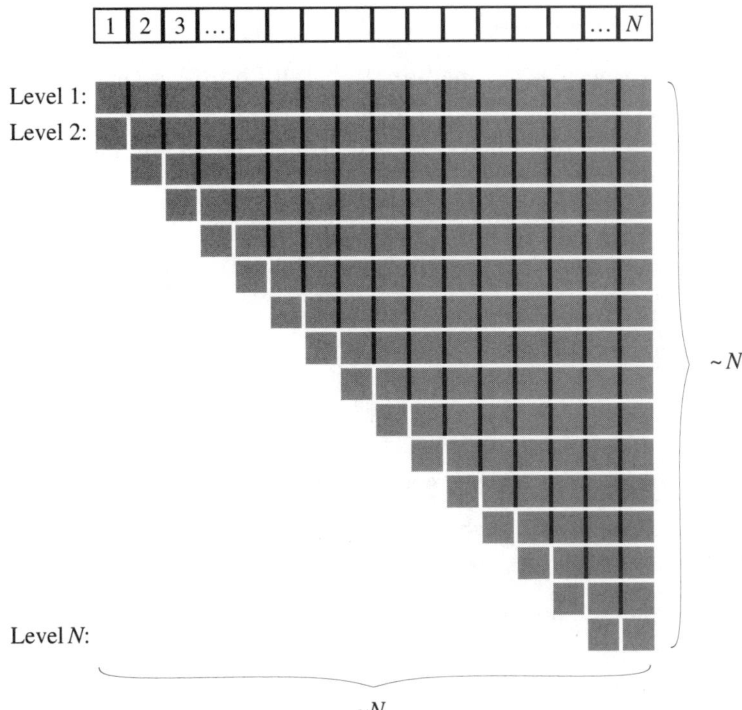

b. Worst case: the least item is always picked as the pivot. (Picking the greatest one is just as bad.)

Figure 13.3 *(continued)*

Merge sort is always O(N log N), while quick sort tends to be O(N log N) but can get as bad as O(N^2). The obvious question is "Why not just stick to merge sort?" The answer is practical: When quick sort does perform in O(N log N) (as it usually does), it can work faster than merge sort. They have the same time complexity, but quick sort can be written to have a significantly smaller constant.

Much research has gone into finding the quickest version of quick sort. It has concentrated on two questions:

1. How can one quickly pick a good pivot item?
2. How can one quickly partition a range around a pivot?

The answers that we will use, at least for the array implementation, are the ones discussed by Robert Sedgewick [9] and Mark Allen Weiss [11], with a slight modification.

13.2.1 The Array Version

Ideally, the pivot would be the median item, but finding the exact median takes too much time. A compromise that has proven to work well in practice is to compare the leftmost, the middle, and the rightmost items, and pick the median of just those three.

The partitioning of the range is rather straightforward:

1. Scan the range from left to right until an item that is ">=" than the pivot is found.
2. Scan the range from right to left until an item that is "<=" than the pivot is found.
3. Swap those two items.
4. Repeat until the left-to-right scan meets the right-to-left scan.
5. Where the scans meet is where the partition needs to be. Swap the boundary item with the pivot.

To find the median of the leftmost, middle, and rightmost items, we need to write an intricate **if** statement that checks for the various combinations of the comparisons between each pair of the three items. While we are doing all that work, we may as well do some sorting: Instead of just comparing those three items, we can sort them among themselves. Routine *sort_3* in Listing 13.5

```
sort_3 (position1, position2, position3: INTEGER) is
        --Sort the items tracked by position1, position2, and position3 of items.
    do
        if items.item (position1) > items.item (position2) then
            swap (position1, position2);
        end;

        if items.item (position1) > items.item (position3) then
            swap (position1, position3);
        end;
        if items.item (position2) > items.item (position3) then
            swap (position2, position3);
        end;
    ensure
        sorted: items.item (position1) <= items.item (position2)
                and then items.item (position2) <= items.item (position3);
    end; --sort_3
```

Listing 13.5 A routine to sort three items for class *QUICKSORTABLE_LIST_ARRAY*.

serves that purpose (using a short routine *swap*, which exchanges items tracked by two positions of the internal array *items*).

Let us now study routine *quick_sort* itself (Listing 13.6). This routine provides two ways out of the recursion:

1. If the range is empty or is of length 1, then it is already sorted, so nothing is done.
2. If the range is of length 2 or 3, then a simple call to *sort_3* is used to sort it.

```
quick_sort (leftmost, rightmost: INTEGER) is
        --Quick sort the region [leftmost, . . . ,rightmost].
    local
        middle: INTEGER;
        left_index, right_index: INTEGER;
        pivot: ITEM;
    do
        if leftmost + 3 < rightmost then
            middle := (leftmost + rightmost) // 2;

            --Presort the leftmost, the middle, and the rightmost items.
            sort_3 (leftmost, middle, rightmost);

            --Items in positions leftmost and rightmost are now in correct
            --partitions. Swap the rightmost item still to be partitioned (in position
            --rightmost−1) with the pivot, and partition items in positions
            --leftmost+1 through rightmost−2.
            pivot := items.item (middle);
            swap (middle, rightmost−1);

            from
                left_index := leftmost; --Set up for pre-incrementing loops.
                right_index := rightmost − 1;
            invariant
                --items.item (leftmost), . . . ,items.item (left_index) <= pivot
                --items.item (right_index), . . . ,items.item (rightmost) >= pivot
            variant
                right_index − left_index
            until
                left_index > right_index
            loop
                --The inner loops must pre-increment, otherwise when pivot,
                --items.item (left_index) and items.item (right_index)
                --are all equal, the outer loop becomes infinite.
```

Listing 13.6 Routine *quick_sort* for class *QUICKSORTABLE_LIST_ARRAY*.

```
            from
               left_index := left_index + 1;
            until
               items.item (left_index) >= pivot
            loop
               left_index := left_index + 1;
            end;

            from
               right_index := right_index - 1;
            until
               items.item (right_index) <= pivot
            loop
               right_index := right_index - 1;
            end;

            if left_index <= right_index then
               swap (left_index, right_index);
            end;
         end;

         --Place the pivot between the two partitions.
         swap (left_index, rightmost-1);

         quick_sort (leftmost, left_index-1);
         quick_sort (left_index+1, rightmost);

      elseif leftmost < rightmost then

         --Range length is either 2 or 3. Just use sort_3 on it.
         sort_3 (leftmost, leftmost+1, rightmost);

      end;
   end; --quick_sort
```

Listing 13.6 *(continued)*

If the range length is greater than 3, then it is partitioned as we discussed earlier and the two subranges are recursively sorted. The portion of the **if** statement that performs the partitioning and the recursive calls (the first in Listing 13.6) is thus the most complicated one. It is illustrated in Figure 13.4.

First, we find the middle of the range and use *sort_3* to sort the middle, leftmost, and rightmost items in the range, and use the new middle item as the pivot (Figure 13.4a). After that is done, we know that the item in the leftmost position is "<=" the pivot (which is now in the middle position), and the item in the rightmost position is ">=" the pivot. In other words, they are already in the correct partitions. The rest of the partitioning process only needs to work on the range [*leftmost* +1, . . . ,*rightmost* − 1].

The next thing we do is get the pivot out of the way for the time being, by swapping it with the rightmost item still to be partitioned—the one tracked by

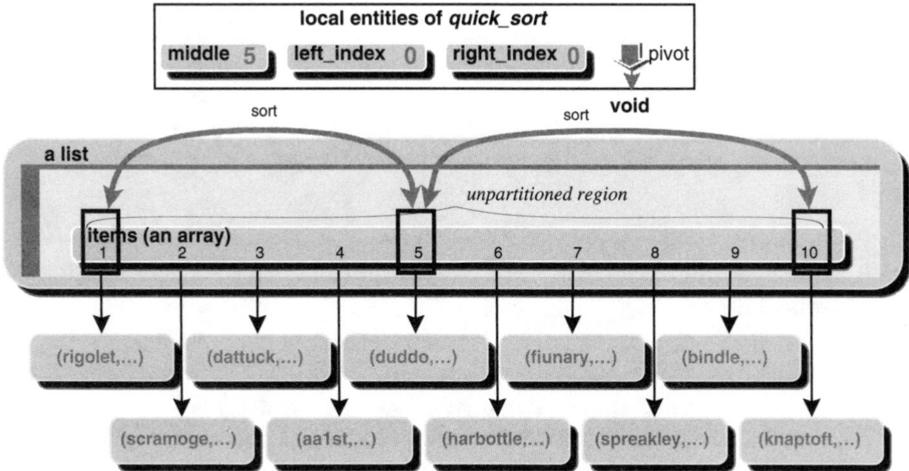

a. The middle is located. It will be sorted with the leftmost and rightmost items in the range.

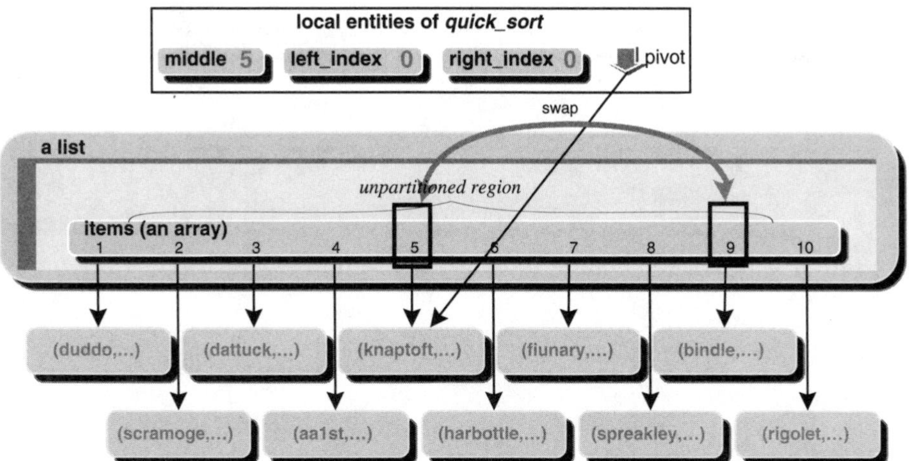

b. The median of the leftmost, middle, and rightmost items is now the pivot. The unpartitioned section has narrowed by one on each side, since the leftmost and rightmost items are where they belong. The pivot will be swapped with the rightmost unpartitioned item to get it out of the way.

Figure 13.4 Quick sort partitioning process.

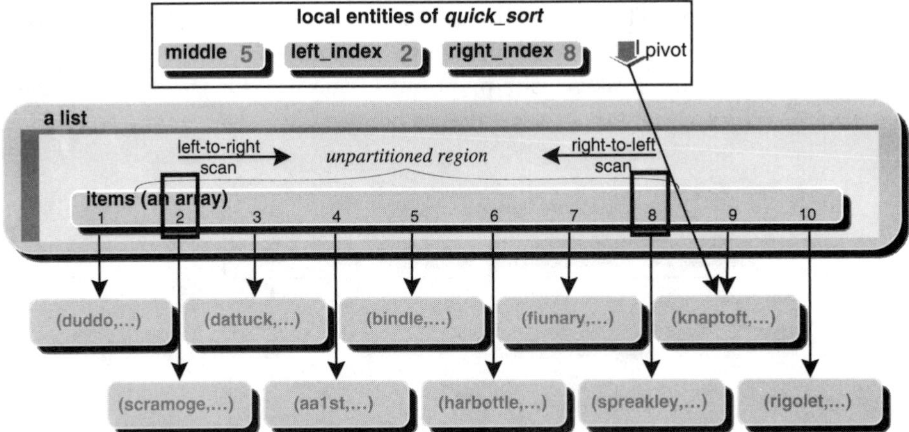

c. With the pivot out of the way, scan left-to-right and then right-to-left for out-of-place items.

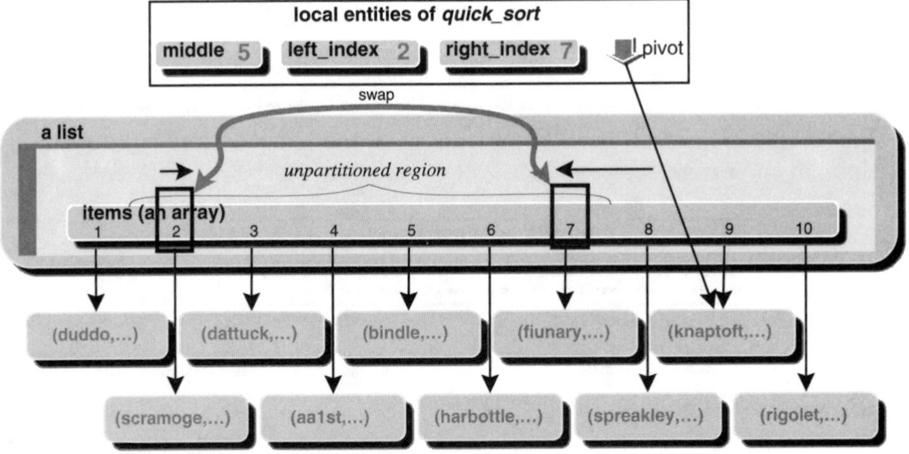

d. An item >=*pivot* was found to the left of an item <=*pivot*. They will be swapped.

Figure 13.4 *(continued)*

position *rightmost*−1 (Figure 13.4b). Then we loop from left to right looking for an item that belongs in the right partition, and right to left looking for an item that belongs in the left one, and swap them (Figure 13.4c–d). The looping stops when the left-to-right loop and the right-to-left one cross—at the boundary between the two partitions (Figure 13.4e).

The tricky part of this nested loop is making sure that the inner loops always advance by at least one step. It would have been more straightforward to start

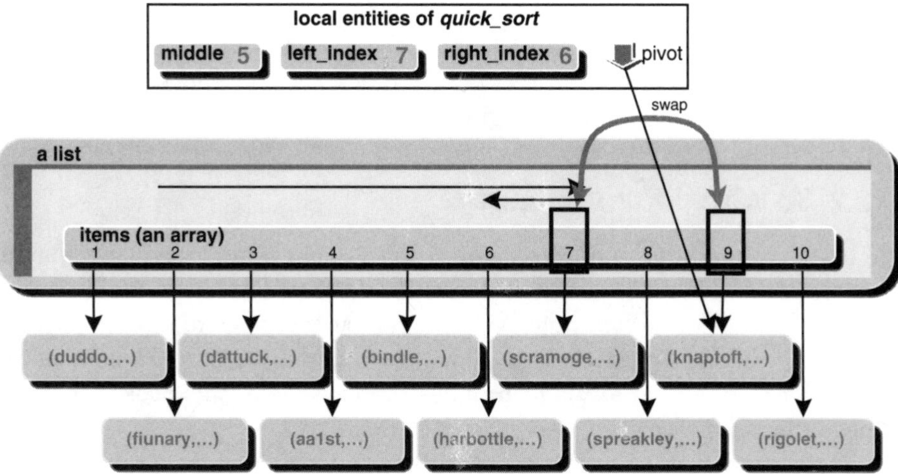

e. In an attempt to find two more items out of place, the scans cross. Where the left-to-right scan stopped is the leftmost item of the >=*pivot* subrange. It will be swapped with the pivot.

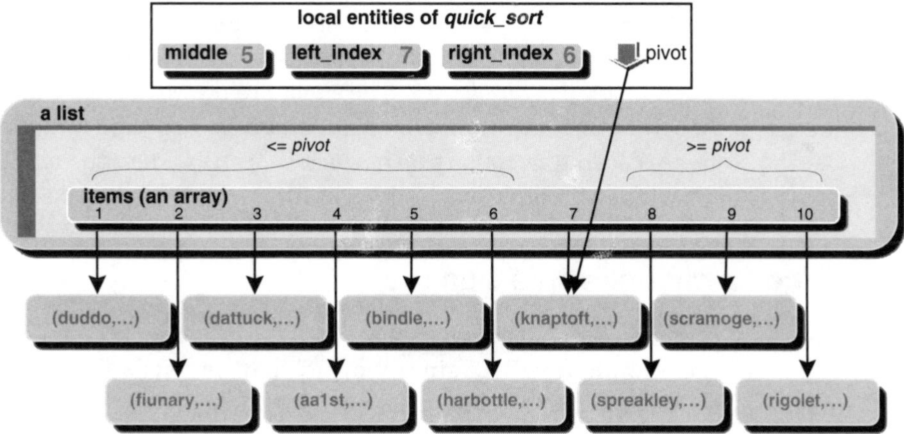

f. The range has been partitioned.

Figure 13.4 *(continued)*

the outer loop with *left_index* at *leftmost*+1 and *right_index* at *rightmost*−2, and leave the **from** parts of the inner loops empty. But suppose we were to hit a situation where *items.item*(*left_index*)*.is_equal*(*pivot*) and *items.item*(*right_index*)*.is_equal*(*pivot*)—both inner loops would exit immediately without changing *left_index* or *right_index*, and the outer loop would become infinite!

After the outer loop terminates, we place the pivot item at the boundary by swapping it with the leftmost item in the right subrange, which is exactly at position *left_index*, where the left-to-right loop failed its **until** condition and terminated (Figure 13.4f).

Now all that remains is to recursively quick sort the left subrange ([*leftmost*, . . . ,*left_index*−1]) and the right ([*left_index*+1, . . . ,*rightmost*]).

13.2.2 So What Makes It Quick?

O(N log N) is the best time complexity that a general-purpose object sorting algorithm can have, but the big O notation says nothing about the discarded constant. Quick sort's advantage is that it can be best tweaked to increase the speed of the partitioning and thus decrease that constant. This tweaking requires more precise analysis techniques than we use in this book, backed up by measured experiments.

A common optimization in quick sort is to avoid it altogether when the length of the range is small. As we saw back in Figure 6.9, the constants involved in algorithms of different big O complexities may make a difference up to a certain N, but for large enough N the lower big O complexity algorithm will win. The flip side of that coin is that for small enough N, an O(N^2) algorithm may work faster than an O(N log N) *algorithm*. That is what tends to happen with quick sort and insertion sort, so when the range gets to be small enough, *insertion_sort* is called instead of *quick_sort*. The exact break-even range length depends on exactly how both algorithms are coded, and how a specific compiler optimizes that code. According to Robert Sedgewick [9, p. 124], lengths of 5 to 25 tend to be good switchover points.

13.2.3 The Singly Linked Version . . .

. . . is left as an exercise to you. The basic algorithm is the same, but you will need a different partitioning method, since moving right-to-left is the kiss of death in singly linked lists.

13.3 Space Complexity

Time complexity tells us how much time an algorithm needs as a function of N. But there is another consideration: How much *space* does it use (also in terms of N)?

Let us clarify one thing: We only care about *maximum additional memory* needed to perform the algorithm, just as with time complexity we only cared about the time the algorithm added to the whole program's execution. The space occupied by the object structure itself does not count.

To count space usage, we need to take into account these details:

1. Every time a routine is called, a constant amount of space is used. A fixed amount of space is needed for:

   a. The return address (so that execution can resume in the right place within the calling routine);

   b. The passed parameters (if any); and

   c. The **local** entities.

   All this space is freed up when the routine exits. This is a *big* distinction from time complexity measurement: Space can be returned, but once time is used up, it is gone.

2. Every time an object is created (with the "!!" operator), enough space to hold all of its attributes is consumed. That space is restored when the object is garbage-collected.

3. Objects can be instructed to grab more space. Operations *make* and *resize* in *ARRAY*, *make_capacity* and *resize* in *LIST_ARRAY*, *insert_on_left* and *insert_on_right* in *LIST_LINKED*, *push* in *STACK_LINKED*, and *enqueue* in *QUEUE_LINKED*—all of these pick up space.

4. Objects can be instructed to let go of space. (They cannot actually deallocate it: only the garbage collector can do that.) The routines listed in the previous item have counterparts that release space.

Thus, there are four possible reasons for a routine to have a space complexity other than O(1):

1. It repeatedly creates objects and puts them into an object structure (so that they do not become disconnected from the root object and garbage-collected).

2. It creates an object structure of an initial size proportional to N (for example, an *ARRAY* object of length *length* or *length* // 2).

3. It forces an object structure to grow.

4. It is recursive. Item 1 in the previous list starts with the words "every time a routine is called," and routines are called many times during recursion.

Looking over the insertion sort, bubble sort, and selection sort algorithms, it should be clear that none of the preceding four reasons holds, so those three algorithms have a space complexity of O(1).

Let us skip merge sort for the moment and look at quick sort. It is recursive, so space is added at each level of the recursion. It does not create objects or utilize object structures, so reasons 1–3 do not hold, therefore the amount of space added at each level of the recursion is constant. The maximum number of levels we can encounter with luckily chosen pivots is $O(\log N)$, times $O(1)$ space used at each level, which gives us a space complexity of $O(\log N)$. With unluckily chosen pivots, we get a worst case space complexity of $O(N)$.

Both of our implementations of merge sort are also recursive. The singly linked one avoids reasons 1–3 too, and its recursion consistently goes down $O(\log N)$ levels, so we get consistent $O(\log N)$ space complexity.

Our array-based implementation of merge sort is more interesting. At level 1 of the recursion, we merge N items using an additional array of N, after two sets of $\frac{1}{2}N$ items are sorted. That additional array is allocated inside routine *merge*, which *merge_sort* calls after both recursive *merge_sort* calls return. Thus, by the time the array of size N is created, both arrays of size $\frac{1}{2}N$ have been released to the garbage collector. Those arrays do not accumulate during the recursion.

At the deepest level of recursion, the parameters and local entities accumulate $O(\log N)$ of space, but at the time the array is very short, only 2 items. At the shallowest level of recursion, the array is $O(N)$ in length, but there is only $O(1)$ local entities and parameters accumulated. Since the $O(\log N)$ consumption and the $O(N)$ consumption cannot occur at the same time, we just take the maximum of the two: $O(N)$.

13.4 Choosing the Best Sorting Algorithm for a Given Use

There is no single "best" sorting algorithm—if there was, we would not bother discussing five of them, and there are others from which to choose.

In general, for large N and objects about which we know nothing, an $O(N \log N)$ algorithm should be picked over $O(N^2)$ algorithms. Quick sort tends to do quite well on large lists. When it divides the list down to small lists, it should use a lower cost routine, such as insertion sort, to finish that part of the job.

Another interesting question is what happens if the items are already mostly (or even completely) sorted before the sorting algorithm is invoked.

Consider, for instance, the array version of merge sort. At each level of recursion, the merge involves moving the entire range into a temporary array and then back. It does not matter at all if the whole range is already sorted (i.e., the rightmost item of the left subrange is "<=" than the leftmost item of the right subrange).

The singly linked version of merge sort is similar, but it only goes through the left subrange and then attaches the right subrange in one step.

The quick sort version we studied will work very well on mostly sorted lists, since the median of the leftmost, middle, and rightmost items will tend to be the median of the whole list; it will be *the* median of the whole list if the list is fully sorted. (There are versions of the algorithm that always simply take the leftmost item as the limit. These versions will display the miserable $O(N^2)$ time and space complexity if the range is already sorted.)

Insertion sort, in its right-to-left scanning form, does wonderfully on fully sorted lists. The inner loop always quits right away, so the whole sort is done in $O(N)$ time. Suppose that only one item is out of place. Let us say that the least item is all the way at the right end of the list, while the rest of the list is sorted. Then the outer loop zips through the whole list in $O(N)$ time, and then finally hits the out-of-place item. The last time through the outer loop, the inner loop will have something to do: Move the least item all the way to the left, another $O(N)$ operation. Thus, the whole thing was done in $O(N)$ time.

Suppose, on the other hand, that the greatest item was all the way at the left end of the list, while the rest of the list was sorted. As far as the outer loop is concerned, that greatest item is the initial sorted section. The item in position 2 then has to be inserted into the sorted region—but it only has one step left to move. Then the item in position 3 has to be inserted, but it also only has one step left to move, and so on. When all is said and done, the array is sorted in $O(N)$ time.

These, of course, are extreme cases of "mostly sorted." But the fewer items out of place, the closer to $O(N)$ insertion sort gets.

Selection sort ends up with its predictable $O(N^2)$ time complexity no matter how sorted it is, because the inner loop always has to go all the way to the right end.

Bubble sort, though, can be easily made to recognize sorted lists: If no swap was performed during an inner loop, then the whole list must be sorted. It is easy to add an **if** statement that detects that situation and signals the outer loop to bail out. If your application frequently deals with mostly sorted lists, this may be a good solution; otherwise adding the **if** would just slow down your sort for no good reason. So for short lists that may or may not be mostly sorted, you may want to stick to insertion sort.

Summary

The two sorting algorithms discussed in this chapter have the average performance of $O(N \log N)$. Merge sort is $O(N \log N)$ in the worst case as well, but quick sort's worst case behavior is $O(N^2)$.

Merge sort works by recursively sorting two halves of the list, and then merging them into one sorted list.

Quick sort works by partitioning the list into two parts—with items less than or equal to a selected pivot item in the left part, and those greater than or equal to the pivot in the right—and then sorting the two parts recursively.

Exercises

1. Complete class *MERGESORTABLE_LIST_ARRAY*.
2. In Listing 13.3, a new array is created every time so that merged object references can be copied into it and then back into *items*. Since Eiffel guarantees that everything new is initialized (in case of object references, to *Void*), making an array is an O(*N*) operation. Modify class *MERGESORTABLE_LIST_ARRAY* so that the spare array is created only once during the entire run of *sort*.
3. Complete class *MERGESORTABLE_LIST_SINGLY_LINKED*.
4. Draw the execution chart for the *merge_sort* routine in class *MERGESORTABLE_LIST_SINGLY_LINKED* and show that its time complexity is O(*N* log *N*).
5. Routine *merge* in Listing 13.4 rearranges the node chain within the list. Another way of sorting the list is by leaving the node sequence unchanged, but moving their item references around. Write a version of *MERGESORTABLE_LIST_SINGLY_LINKED* that works that way.
6. Complete class *QUICKSORTABLE_LIST_ARRAY*.
7. A common speedup for quick sort is to call insertion sort for subranges that are small enough.
   a. Add this optimization to class *QUICKSORTABLE_LIST_ARRAY*. Consider ranges of length 20 to be small enough. (You will need to modify *SORTABLE_LIST_TESTER* to use a longer list.)
   b. Modify the *LIST_ARRAY* class hierarchy so that the insertion sort code is not duplicated between *INSERTIONSORTABLE_LIST_ ARRAY* and *QUICKSORTABLE_LIST_ARRAY*.
8. Devise a quick sort partitioning algorithm that works on singly linked lists in O(*N*) time. Implement it in class *QUICKSORTABLE_LIST_SINGLY_LINKED*.

14 Faster Dictionaries

In Chapter 11, we played with linear search, but saw that it was inefficient. In this chapter, we look at two other ways to search for items. The first works on sorted object structures in a manner similar to the way humans search book dictionaries. It works much faster than a linear search—as long as we use the array implementation of lists.

The second way tends to perform well statistically, if the nature of the key is known in advance and taken into account—but, again, only with arrays.

We will look at efficient ways to search for associations in linked object structures in Part IV.

14.1 Binary Search

So, how do humans search paper dictionaries? Most people start by taking a guess about the page the word is on. If the word sought precedes alphabetically the words on that page, they make another guess among the preceding pages. If it follows those words, they make another guess among the following pages. They keep doing it until they zero in on a page where they expect the sought word to be, and scan that page for it.

Well, our dictionary objects do not have pages, so we can make the algorithm simpler and more efficient. In fact, we have a much better analogy for it: the "higher/lower" game. You pick a number between, say, 1 and 100, and I have to guess it. You tell me if each of my guesses is higher or lower than your number. The fastest way for me to zoom in on your number is to keep dividing the range in half and asking you about the number in the middle of the range.

That is exactly how the binary search algorithm works. The recursive version of it is:

```
location (<an item>, <a range>): INTEGER is
        --Location of the item within the range.
  do
    if <the range is empty> then
      Result := <a number that indicates "not found">;
    elseif <the item>.is_equal (<item in the middle of the range>) then
      Result := <the middle index>;
    elseif <the item> < <item in the middle of the range> then
      Result := location (<the item>, <left half of the range>);
    else
      Result := location (<the item>, <right half of the range>);
    end;
  end; --location
```

Looking back at class *DICTIONARY_LINEAR* in Listing 11.4, we see that it can be modified into a *DICTIONARY_BINARY*. In fact, most of the features are unaffected, as long as we keep using a *LIST* to track the items—for example, *delete* will work exactly the same way, regardless of whether the version of *locate* it calls performs a linear search or a binary one. So let us start by factoring the common routines (most of them) into a common ancestor, deferred class *DICTIONARY_LIST*, as shown in Listing 14.1. That class defines *associ-*

```
deferred class DICTIONARY_LIST [KEY -> COMPARABLE, VALUE] inherit
  DICTIONARY[KEY, VALUE]

feature {DICTIONARY_LIST}

  associations: LIST[ASSOCIATION[KEY, VALUE]];
        --The list of associations.

  locate (key: KEY) is
        --Move associations' cursor to an association for
        --key or off-right if there is no such association.
    deferred
    end; --locate

feature --Adding, removing, and checking associations

  <same as in Listing 11.4, but without put>
```

Listing 14.1 Deferred class *DICTIONARY_LIST*, the common ancestor of *DICTIONARY_LINEAR* and *DICTIONARY_BINARY*.

```
feature --Sizing
    <same as in Listing 11.4>
feature --Comparisons and copying
    <same as in Listing 11.4>
feature --Simple input and output
    <same as in Listing 11.4>
invariant
    have_list: associations /= Void;
end --class DICTIONARY_LIST
```

Listing 14.1 *(continued)*

ations as *LIST*[*ASSOCIATION*[*KEY,VALUE*]], so that the subclasses can redefine it as the appropriate subclass of *LIST*.

The new version of class *DICTIONARY_LINEAR*, as shown in Listing 14.2, is very short. It redefines *associations* to be the subclass of *LIST* best suited to the task. (I have chosen the doubly linked version to keep *delete* at O(1); other choices may be better in other circumstances.) It provides a version of *put* that

```
class DICTIONARY_LINEAR[KEY -> COMPARABLE, VALUE] inherit
  DICTIONARY_LIST[KEY, VALUE]
    redefine
      associations, locate, put
    end;
creation make
feature {DICTIONARY_LIST}
  associations: LIST_DOUBLY_LINKED[ASSOCIATION[KEY,VALUE]];
        --The list of associations.
  locate(key: KEY) is
        --Move associations' cursor to an association for key
        --or off-right if there is no such association.
    do
      from
        associations.move_off_left; associations.move_right;
      until
        associations.is_off_right or else key.is_equal(associations.item.key)
```

Listing 14.2 Class *DICTIONARY_LINEAR* as an heir to *DICTIONARY_LIST*.

```
         loop
            associations.move_right;
         end;
      end; --locate

feature --Creation and initialization

   <same as in Listing 11.4>

feature --Adding, removing, and checking associations

   put(new_value: VALUE; key: KEY) is
         --Insert an association of key and new_value into this dictionary.
      local
         association: ASSOCIATION[KEY,VALUE];
      do
         !!association.make;
         association.set_key(key);
         association.set_value(new_value);

         --Less trouble to go to off-left than to check for off-right.
         associations.move_off_left;
         associations.insert_on_right(association);
      end; --put

end --class DICTIONARY_LINEAR
```

Listing 14.2 *(continued)*

is optimized for that type of list, and the linear version of *locate*. (The reason *make* is here and not in the common ancestor is that in class *DICTIONARY_LIST* it would be interpreted as an attempt to create an object of class *LIST*, which is a deferred class and thus cannot have any created objects.) You should test the new version with *DICTIONARY_TESTER*, which you wrote in Exercise 11.1.

With the easy part out of the way, we can attend to *DICTIONARY_BINARY*. The first thing we need is to pick a better class for *associations*. We need a subclass of *LIST* that allows us

1. To sort it;
2. To find its middle quickly; and
3. To specify subranges in it.

We do not have such a subclass, but we can easily make one by inheriting from one of the *SORTABLE_LIST_ARRAY* classes and adding features for zooming the cursor directly to the middle. Such a class is shown in Listing 14.3. Inheritance is useful for enhancing our own classes, not just those of vendors.

```
class
   INSERTIONSORTABLE_INDEXED_LIST_ARRAY[ITEM -> COMPARABLE]
inherit
   INSERTIONSORTABLE_LIST_ARRAY[ITEM]

creation make, make_capacity

feature

   lower: INTEGER is
         --The leftmost array index.
      do
         Result := items.lower;
      end; --lower

   upper: INTEGER is
         --The leftmost array index.
      do
         Result := items.upper;
      end; --upper

   move_to_index (index: INTEGER) is
         --Move the cursor to the item in position index.
      require
         index_in_range: lower <= index and index <= upper
      do
         cursor := index;
      end; --move_to_index

end --class INSERTIONSORTABLE_INDEXED_LIST_ARRAY
```

Listing 14.3 A sortable arrayed-based list class that makes binary searching possible.

This leads us to class *DICTIONARY_BINARY* in Listing 14.4. The attribute *associations* is an *INSERTIONSORTABLE_INDEXED_LIST_ARRAY*. Routine *locate* makes sure *associations* is sorted and starts the recursive binary search routine *binary_locate*. Since we are restricted to use of an array version of list, we may as well let the user set the dictionary's capacity during creation,

```
class DICTIONARY_BINARY[KEY -> COMPARABLE, VALUE] inherit
   DICTIONARY_LIST[KEY, VALUE]
      redefine
         associations, locate, put, is_equal
      end;
```

Listing 14.4 Class *DICTIONARY_BINARY*, which uses binary search to locate keys.

```
creation make, make_capacity

feature {DICTIONARY_LINEAR}

  associations: INSERTIONSORTABLE_INDEXED_LIST_ARRAY
                    [ASSOCIATION[KEY,VALUE]]
        --The list of associations.

  binary_locate (key: KEY; leftmost, rightmost: INTEGER) is
        --Move to the association with key if it is in the range
        --[leftmost, . . . ,rightmost], or off-right if it is not in the range.
    local
      middle: INTEGER;
    do
      if leftmost > rightmost then

        --It is not there.
        associations.move_off_right;

      else

        middle := (leftmost + rightmost) / / 2;

        associations.move_to_index (middle);

        if key < associations.item.key then

          --Look for it in the left half of the range.
          binary_locate (key, leftmost, middle-1);

        elseif key > associations.item.key then

          --Look for it in the left half of the range.
          binary_locate (key, middle+1, rightmost);

        end;
      end;
    end; --binary_locate

  locate (key: KEY) is
        --Move associations' cursor to the association for key
        --or off-right if there is no such association.
    do
      if not associations.is_sorted then
        associations.sort;
      end;

      binary_locate (key, associations.lower,
                    associations.lower+associations.length-1);
    end; --locate
```

Listing 14.4 *(continued)*

```
feature --Creation and initialization

   make is
         --Create a new, empty dictionary.
      do
         !!associations.make;
      end; --make

   make_capacity (initial_capacity: INTEGER) is
         --Create a new, empty dictionary of capacity initial_capacity.
      do
         !!associations.make_capacity (initial_capacity);
      end; --make_capacity

feature --Adding, removing, and checking associations

   put (new_value: VALUE; key: KEY) is
         --Insert an association of key and new_value into this dictionary.
      local
         association: ASSOCIATION[KEY,VALUE];
      do
         !!association.make;
         association.set_key (key);
         association.set_value (new_value);

         --Insert at the cheap end.
         associations.move_off_right;
         associations.insert_on_left (association);
      end; --put

   is_equal (other: like Current): BOOLEAN is
         --Does this dictionary and other associate the same values
         --with the same keys?
      local
         association, other_association: ASSOCIATION[KEY,VALUE];
      do
         if size /= other.size then
            Result := false;
         else
            if not associations.is_sorted then
               associations.sort;
            end;
            if not other.associations.is_sorted then
               other.associations.sort;
            end;
```

Listing 14.4 *(continued)*

```
            from
               Result := true;
               associations.move_off_left; associations.move_right;
               other.associations.move_off_left; other.associations.move_right;
            until
               Result = false or else associations.is_off_right
            loop
               association := associations.item;
               other_association := other.associations.item;

               Result :=
                  association.is_equal(other_association) and then
                  association.value.is_equal(other_association.value);

               associations.move_right;
               other.associations.move_right;
            end;
         end;
      end; --is_equal
end --class DICTIONARY_BINARY
```

Listing 14.4 *(continued)*

so we provide a trivial *make_capacity* routine. Routine *put* is similar to the one in the linear dictionary, but it inserts items on the right end of the list, since that is the cheap end for the array-based implementation.

A nice benefit of the sortable list implementation is that we can get a much more efficient implementation of *is_equal*. Since duplicate keys are disallowed (this is important because association comparisons only look at keys), two equal association lists will align into parallel lists. Then a single loop that compares the keys and associations pairwise can determine if the association lists are equal.

14.1.1 Performance Analysis

The linear search algorithm is O(N) in time: If we charted its execution, we would get a straight line of markers under the array. Its space complexity is O(1), since it uses no variable-length object structures and no recursion. What are the complexities of the binary search algorithm?

As the execution chart in Figure 14.1 shows, at each level of recursion we visit one list position (the one in the middle). Each time we go down a level, we cut the problem in half. We can do that O(log N) times before the list becomes empty, so the time complexity is O(log N).

Since the recursion gets O(log N) levels deep and a constant amount of space is used at each level, the space complexity is also O(log N). However, unlike the

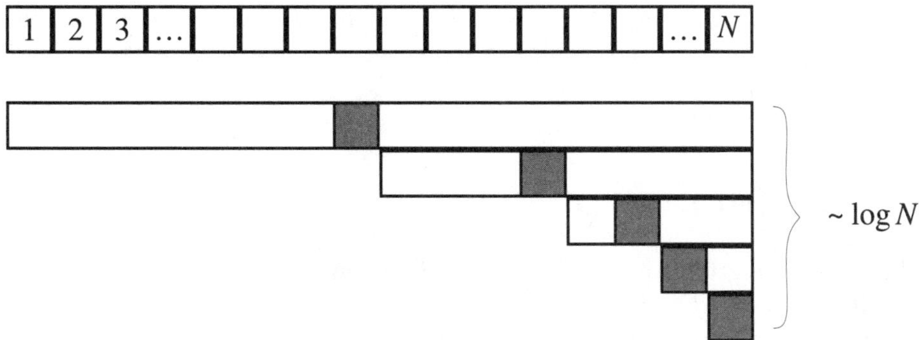

Figure 14.1 A worst case execution chart for the binary search algorithm.

sort algorithms in Chapter 13, the binary search algorithm can be easily done nonrecursively, with a single loop, resulting in O(1) space complexity.

14.1.2 Linked Implementation Is Useless

It would be easy to have a binary search dictionary that uses an indexed sortable linked list instead of an indexed sortable array-based list. However, even if we are very, very clever about it, moving to the middle of a range will take half as many steps as the length of that range. (If we are not clever about it and just implement a "move to position p" feature as we did with the array, the performance gets even worse.)

As Figure 14.2 shows, the time complexity of the linked implementation of the binary search algorithm is O(N). Given that the linear search is O(N) too

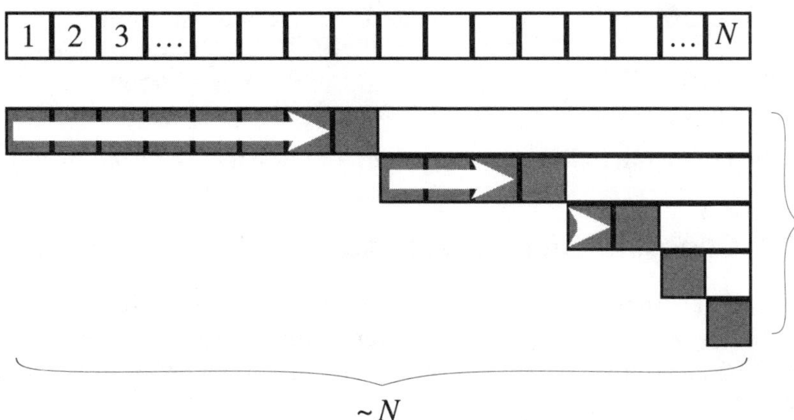

Figure 14.2 The binary search is O(N) in time for a linked list implementation. (The white arrows indicate the search for the middle of each subrange.)

and much simpler, binary search is useless for this implementation. But there is a way to do binary search on linked structures in O(log N), and we will study it in Chapter 15.

14.2 Hashing

While we are on the subject of array-based dictionaries, let us indulge in some wishful thinking. Binary search gives us O(log N) performance, which is the second best we have seen so far. But suppose we had a function that took the key and in O(1) time resulted in the index at which the association with that key resides. In goes the key, out comes the correct index—wouldn't it be nice?

Well, in extremely rare cases we are lucky enough to have a key for which such a function exists. For example, if we run a car dealership, and we need to look up the technical characteristics of a car, we may be able to rig up a function that converts a model name into a number between 1 and, say, 75 (or whatever the number of possible models is). Then we just use an array of size 75, and we get O(1) performance. This is called a "**perfect hash function**."

In general, we will not be able to find a perfect hash function for our keys. An imperfect hash function is one that maps more than one key to the same array index. For example, if our keys are "person" objects, their years of birth could be used as the hash values. This would schedule people born within the same year for the same array position. Just how imperfect is this function? If we need to keep track of historical figures, it is pretty good. If we are keeping track of this year's class of kindergarten students, then it is horrible: It will send them all into two or three array positions.

So when we are hashing, we need to worry about two things:

1. Finding a hash function that results in the fewest collisions (i.e., assigning a key to a position that is already occupied).
2. When there is a collision, finding another place for the incoming association.

14.2.1 Choosing the Hash Function

If a function is to provide array indices, its results must be integers within the index range of the array. That means, for example, that we cannot have it just generate 32-bit integers, unless we want a 4 billion position array, and have a system that can accommodate it.

However, if we can map our key to *some* integer, then there is a common trick to cutting it down to size: Divide that number by the length of the array, and use the remainder as the index (similar to the way we forced the indices to fit in the circular array implementation of queues in Chapter 9). In fact, that is the most commonly used solution in situations where nothing is known about the keys.

How a key is converted to an integer depends on the class of the key. It is done by the standard[1] feature *hash_value* (inherited from class *ANY*) which returns a nonnegative integer number.

For class *INTEGER* this feature is quite easy—just return the integer's value. For other classes it may be trickier. Since we have been using *STRING* keys in our examples, you may want to look at your vendor's implementation of *hash_value* in class *STRING* (if its source code is available). An easy thing to do is to add up the character codes of all the letters in the string.

Once the hash value is obtained, the index is computed as the hash value modulo the length of the array provides the index. For example, if the length of the array is 100, then keys 9816104, 171970, 4904907, and 465404 will be assigned to indices 4, 70, 7, and 4, respectively (thus, there is a collision). Thus, if the array length is 100, only the last two decimal digits of the number are used. That cannot be helped, it is the nature of the remainder operation; besides, we only have 100 positions to fill in the array anyway.

We would like, however, to make sure that the numbers are distributed among the array positions as evenly as possible, to minimize the likelihood of collision. We can control that by carefully choosing the array length.

Suppose we have a 12-position array (indices 0 through 11, since we are using the remainder function). Let us see how certain subsets of integers will map onto it, starting with keys whose hash values are multiples of 5:

Hash value	0	5	10	15	20	25	30	35	40	45	50	55	60
Index	0	5	10	3	8	1	6	11	4	9	2	7	0

We see that the hash values are assigned to distinct indices until we hit 60, at which point the assignment cycle starts at 0 again. But the period of this cycle is 12, which is the length of the array—we did not get a collision until the whole array was filled! This is as good as it gets.

If we try the set of multiples of 7, we get a similar situation:

Hash value	0	7	14	21	28	35	42	49	56	63	70	77	84
Index	0	2	9	4	11	6	42	1	8	3	10	5	0

[1]Actually, it is not in the standard at the time this is written, but is likely to be in its 1996 vintage.

But now let us look at multiples of 2:

Hash value	0	2	4	6	8	10	12
Index	0	2	4	6	8	10	0

This is a cycle with a much shorter period—only 6—and half of the array is untouched! But it gets worse. With multiples of 3 we get a cycle period of only 4:

Hash value	0	3	6	9	12
Index	0	3	6	9	0

with $\frac{2}{3}$ of the array wasted. With multiples of 6 we get a cycle period of only 2:

Hash value	0	6	12
Index	0	6	0

And with multiples of 12 we get the shortest possible cycle period:

Hash value	0	12
Index	0	0

If we are looking at how multiples of n behave with an array of length M, the greater the common divisor of n and M is, the shorter the cycle (culminating in a cycle period of 1 when $n = M$, so M is the greatest common divisor). Thus we get the longest cycles when n and M are relatively prime.

This means that we should *always use prime numbers for the length of the array*—that way we will get the maximum cycle period for multiples of everything except M itself.

14.2.2 One Way to Deal with Collisions

Having done our best to minimize collisions, we need to accommodate the cases when they *do* occur. There are two common ways to deal with them.

The first is to make the array track not associations, but object structures containing associations. For example, we could use an *ARRAY*[*LIST_SINGLY_LINKED*[*ASSOCIATION*[KEY,VALUE]]. When an association gets assigned to a position, we just insert it into the list tracked by that position. There is no collision because there is plenty of room at that position for all comers.

When a lookup is done, the hash value modulo table length ("M" as we called it in the previous section) tells us which list to search. It is a linear search, but if the hashing distributed the array indices evenly, then each list will be roughly $\frac{N}{M}$ in length. If $M \geq N$, then the performance should approach O(1): Most lists would be either empty or have only one association each, and the more "crowded" ones should still have only two or three associations in them.

The worst case is when all keys get mapped to the same index. In that situation, all associations fall into the same position in the hash table and the search degenerates to a linear search.

Of course, a singly linked list is not the only kind of object structure we can use with the hash table's array. We could use more complicated structures with better search time complexity. However, with a decent hash function and a sufficiently large table, the lists should be short enough for the singly linked version to suffice.

14.2.3 Another Way to Deal with Collisions

The second method for accommodating collisions is to redirect the incoming association to another position within the same array. The algorithm for finding the available position is:

```
from
   position := key.hash_value \\ associations.length;
until
   associations.item(position) = Void
loop
   position := (position + offset) \\ associations.length;
end
```

The several variations on this theme have to do with how the value of *offset* is chosen.

The simplest thing to do is to use *offset*=1. The hash function directs us to a position. If that position is occupied, we try the one immediately to its right. We keep moving one step to the right (wrapping around the edge of the array) until we find an empty spot. During the search, we start at the mapped position and keep looking to the right until we find an equal association.

This approach is OK, but it has a vulnerable spot. If several associations are mapped into the same index, they will cluster together right at that position and to its right. Any associations mapped into that cluster will have to be placed at its end, making the cluster longer yet. Searches for those associations will be slowed down by collision of associations to the left of their intended positions. (Consider what happens when a big game ends and all the spectators get in their cars and onto the nearby highway; not only is that particular highway entrance crowded, but so are several entrances downstream.)

For example, if five associations are mapped into position 0, they will be placed into positions 0, 1, 2, 3, and 4. If an association is then mapped to position 1, then the loop will try to place it into positions 1, 2, 3, and 4 before managing to drop it into position 5.

The clustering problem can be eased a little by picking wider offsets. Again, we want the offset to be relatively prime with respect to the array length, otherwise we will get shorter period cycles, but since we have picked a prime length, we do not have to worry about that.

However, constant offsets do not solve the clustering problem completely. Suppose we use *offset*=2 and we hit position 0 with five associations. They will be placed into positions 0, 2, 4, 6, and 8. Then if an association is mapped into position 1, it is not affected—an improvement. But if one is mapped into position 2, the loop will try positions 2, 4, 6, and 8 before finally placing the new association into position 10—no improvement at all.

A common solution to this problem is to make *offset* depend on the key. We compute it by sending the key through a *secondary hash function*. That function must be carefully written so that it does not result in a multiple of the array size, lest the loop become infinite. This pitfall is impossible to avoid inside class *KEY*, because the latter in general knows nothing about hash tables and their sizes. Thus, the function is part of the hash table class:

offset := *secondary_hash_value* (*key*)

(and not "*key.secondary_hash_value*").

As long as *associations.length* is prime, a good secondary hash function is

1 + *key.hash_value* \\ (*associations.length* − 1)

I refer you to Derick Wood's *Data Structures, Algorithms, and Performance* [13, Section 9.3.2] for details.

14.2.4 Implementation Details

Since the array size is crucial to decent hash table performance, it is essential to include feature *make_capacity* in the contract for class *HASH_TABLE*. The default feature *make* can be provided, as long as it calls *make_capacity* with a prime number.

There is no reason to make *HASH_TABLE* deferred: A default implementation of *secondary_hash_value* can simply result in a constant (probably 1, 2, or 3). Users can easily redefine it in a subclass to compute a value based on the key.

Summary

This chapter introduced two methods for fast searching. Binary search works on sorted arrays by comparing the median with the item sought. The comparison eliminates one-half of the region as the possible place to find the item, and the item is recursively sought in the other half. This method's time complexity is O(log *N*).

Hashing provides performance approaching O(1), if done carefully. A function is applied to the key to get an array index. Since several keys may get mapped to the same index, it may be necessary to try for another index, several positions away, and so on. The distance between the successive attempts can be a constant, or determined by a secondary function of the key.

Exercises

1. Write a nonrecursive version of routine *binary_locate*.
2. a. Write classes *HASH_TABLE* and *HASH_TABLE_TESTER*.

   b. Write a subclass of *HASH_TABLE* that uses the function

   1 + *key.hash_value* \\ (*associations.length* − 1)

   as the secondary hash function. Test it with *HASH_TABLE_TESTER*.
3. Write a hash table class that uses *SINGLY_LINKED_LIST*s to handle collisions.

Part IV

Trees

15 Binary Search Trees

We saw in Chapter 14 how effective binary search can be on a sorted array, but how the advantage is lost on linked lists (see Section 14.1.2). Well, we do not have to lose that advantage. We can have the best of both worlds.

15.1 Two-Dimensional Linking

What slowed us down in Section 14.1.2 was finding the middle of the range: We had to start at the left end and move right to half of the range's length. What we need is a shortcut—a reference straight to the middle node, as shown in Figure 15.1a (the object references that were there before are shown in gray, to keep them out of the way of this discussion). From there we may need to go halfway to the left or halfway to the right. Let us make the middle node track both of the half-range middle nodes (Figure 15.1b).

Suppose we checked the node at the middle of the list, and saw that the key we seek is "<" its key. That means that the association we want is in the left half-list (if it is in the list at all). Next we find the middle of the left half-list, which is an O(1) operation now. If we do not hit the association we want, we will need to find the middle of either the left quarter-list, or the right quarter-list, depending on how the keys compare. So we make the mid-half-list node track the two mid-quarter-list nodes (Figure 15.1c), and so on.

When we finish threading the list this way, we get the structure shown in Figure 15.1d.

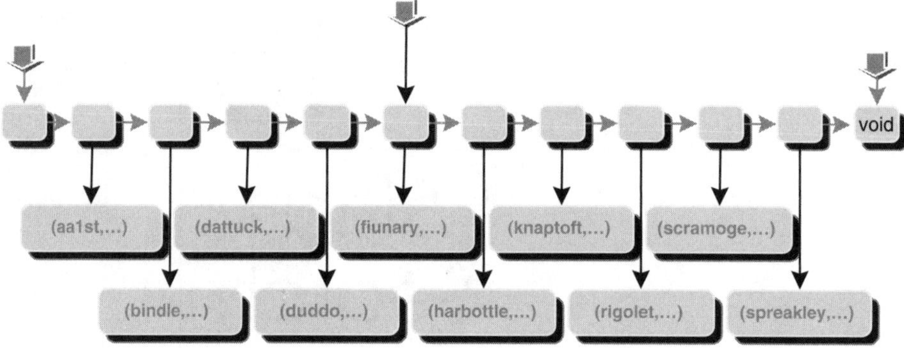

a. Track the middle of the list.

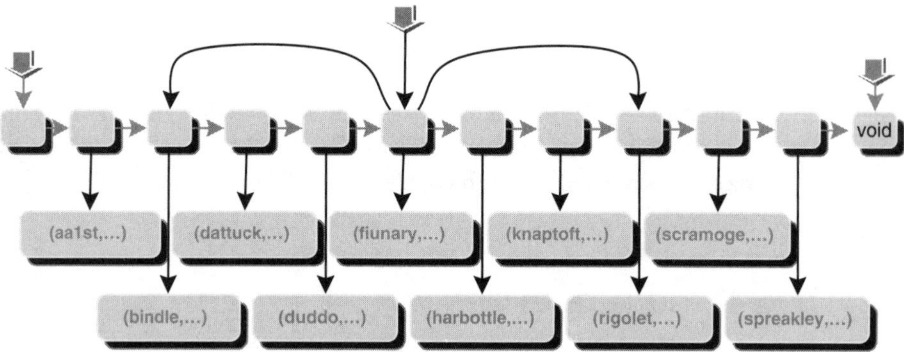

b. The middle node tracks the middles of the two half-lists . . .

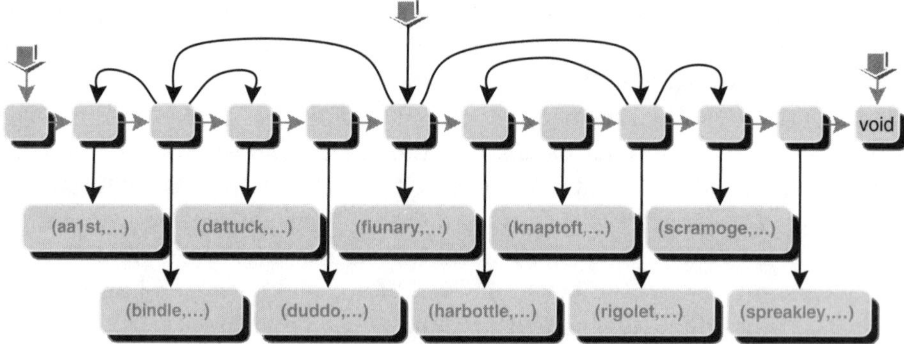

c. . . . and those nodes track the middles of the quarter-lists . . .

Figure 15.1 The derivation of a binary search tree.

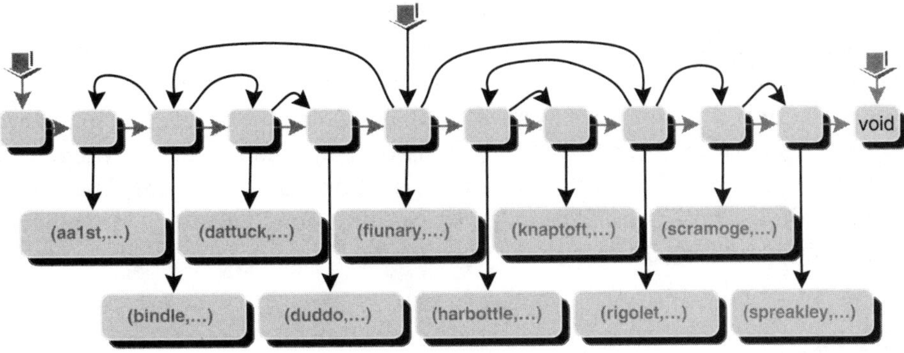

d. . . . and so on.

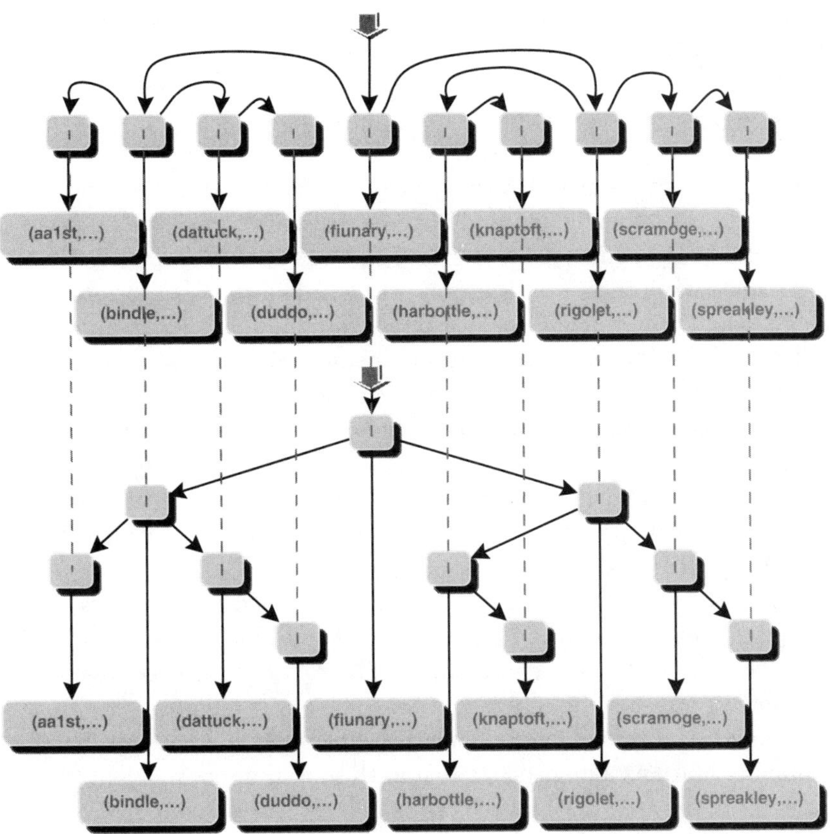

e. Cleaning up the diagram, we get a **binary search tree.**

Figure 15.1 *(continued)*

If we use this structure only for searching, then only the new links, shown in black, are needed. The old, gray links, which each node uses to track its immediate left and right neighbors, can be dropped. With those out of the way, we can stretch the structure vertically to make the new links easier to see (envision constraining the nodes to moving only up and down, and then grabbing the incoming link to the middle of the list and pulling it up). The result, shown in Figure 15.1e, is one possible representation of a **binary search tree** (commonly abbreviated "BST").

15.2 Tree Terminology

Though we arrived at this representation purely pragmatically by solving a problem with binary searches of linked structures, there are other kinds of trees, other representations of trees, and other purposes for trees. Let us nail down a few of the definitions.

15.2.1 Trees

A **tree** is a structure in which there is exactly one node that cannot be reached from any of the other nodes in the tree—this node is called "the **root** of the tree"—and every node except the root can be reached from exactly one other node. This means that in a diagram of the linked representation of a tree, all nodes except the root will have one arrow going to them. There is no restriction on the number of arrows coming from a node: a node can be tracked by at most one other node in the same tree, but it can track several nodes in it, or none at all (a tree node that tracks no others is called a "**leaf**"). This is what makes Figure 15.1e a tree.

When node n_1 tracks nodes n_2 and n_3, n_1 is called the "**parent**" of n_2 and n_3. Following through with this terminology, n_2 and n_3 are **children** of n_1 and each other's **siblings.**

If n_1 is the root of tree t_1, then n_2 and n_3 are roots of **subtrees** of t_1. (A root of a tree cannot be tracked by a node in the same tree, but we never said that it cannot be tracked by an outside object. The root of a subtree has no parent in that subtree, but has one in a larger tree.)

The **size** of a tree is the number of items in it, and the **height** of a tree is the number of items along the longest path from the root to a leaf (for example, the height of the tree in Figure 15.1e is 4).

That wraps up our list of general tree buzzwords.

We can use the subtree concept to define trees more precisely and compactly. A tree is either

1. Empty, or
2. A root plus a list of subtrees (each subtree is itself a tree).

(Using this definition, a leaf is a tree in which all subtrees are empty.) Note that this is a recursive definition. As with binary search, recursion is very useful for binary trees—in fact, for all trees. Furthermore, while in a binary search, recursion is easily replaced with a loop, in tree operations it is practically indispensable.

15.2.2 Binary Trees

A **binary tree** is a tree where:

1. No node has more than two children.
2. Every child of a node is designated as either its left child or its right child. (This is important when a node has only one child: the child cannot just hang directly below the parent, it must be below and to the left, or below and to the right.)

Rephrasing this definition in terms of subtrees, a binary tree is either

1. Empty, or
2. A root plus a left subtree plus a right subtree, where each subtree is a binary tree.

15.2.3 Binary Search Trees

Finally, a **binary search tree** is a binary tree that is set up for binary searching: If its root tracks item i_1, then its left subtree is a binary search tree that holds only items that are $< i_1$, and its right subtree is a binary search tree that holds only items that are $\geq i_1$.[1]

15.3 What a *BINARY_SEARCH_TREE* Is and What It Does

There are two good ways to model a tree. The first is to use the cursor concept with its set of *move_*... commands, just as we did with lists. The other is to follow the recursive definition, and use a recursive model. Let us do the latter.

---

[1]We could have chosen to put equal items into the left subtree instead of the right subtree. The choice does not matter as long as we use it consistently.

15.3.1 The *BINARY_TREE* Contract

Because binary search trees are just one type of binary tree, we can anticipate a future need for class *BINARY_TREE* from which *BINARY_SEARCH_TREE* and others can inherit. The definition says that the tree can be either empty, or be a root item and a left subtree and a right subtree. Thus, we provide features *is_empty*, *root_item*, *left*, and *right*.

These are the essential operations for traversing a populated binary tree. But how do we add items to it? Well, that depends on what kind of a binary tree it is. For binary search trees, we want a simple *insert*(<item>) operation; the tree will know where to put the item. For other kinds of trees, we may want to provide *set_root_item*, *set_left*, and *set_right* operations—but we do not want them in *BINARY_TREE* because we do not want *BINARY_SEARCH_TREE* to inherit them (unlike sortable lists, a BST is always sorted, so we cannot allow its users arbitrary tree manipulation). Thus, we must leave *BINARY_TREE* with just read-only features. There are enough of those to make a useful contract.

A number of other useful features are available that can not only be specified in the contract, but provided with a default implementation (no problem as long as they use the deferred routines *left*, *right*, and *root_item* instead of relying on a specific representation). These are *out*, *size*, and *height*.

Most of deferred class *BINARY_TREE* is given in Listing 15.1; the rest is left as an exercise.

```
deferred class BINARY_TREE[ITEM] inherit
  ANY
    undefine
      copy
    redefine
      out, is_equal
    end;

feature --Creation and initialization

  make,wipe_out is
        --Make this an empty tree.
    deferred
    ensure
      empty: is_empty;
    end; --make,wipe_out

feature --Accessing the components
```

Listing 15.1 A contract with a partial implementation for *BINARY_TREE*.

```
  left: like Current is
        --The left subtree.
     deferred
     end; --left

  right: like Current is
        --The right subtree.
     deferred
     end; --right

  root_item: ITEM is
        --The item at the root.
     deferred
     end; --root_item

feature --Sizing

  is_empty: BOOLEAN is
        --Is this tree empty?
     deferred
     end; --is_empty

  size: INTEGER is
        --The number of items in this tree.
     --Left as an exercise.

  height: INTEGER is
        --The number of levels in this tree.
     do
        if is_empty then
           Result := 0;
        else
           Result := 1 + left.height.max(right.height);
        end;
     end; --height

feature --Comparisons and copying

  is_equal(other: like Current): BOOLEAN is
        --Do this tree and other have identical structures
        --and track the same items at the corresponding nodes?
     --Left as an exercise.

feature --Simple input and output

  out: STRING is
        -- "(left.out / root_item.out \ right.out)" or "" if empty.
     do
        if is_empty then
           Result := "";
```

Listing 15.1 *(continued)*

```
        else
            Result := clone("(");
            Result.append_string(left.out);
            Result.append_string("/");

            Result.append_string(root_item.out);

            Result.append_string("\");
            Result.append_string(right.out);
            Result.append_string(")");
        end;
    end; --out

invariant

    empty_if_size_zero: is_empty = (size = 0);
    size_not_negative: size >= 0;

end --class BINARY_TREE
```

Listing 15.1 *(continued)*

Look at the implementations of *out* and *height*, and observe how the recursive model of the tree lends itself to easy recursive solutions:

- What is the height of a binary tree? For an empty tree it is 0, otherwise it is 1 plus the larger of the heights of the two subtrees (*left.height.max*(*right.height*)—integer objects inherit feature *max* from class *COMPARABLE*).
- What is the string representation of a binary tree? For an empty tree it is the empty string, otherwise it is the string representation of the left subtree (*left.out*), followed by the string representation of the root item (*root_item.out*), followed by the string representation of the right subtree (*right.out*), with a few delimiters thrown in.

As an exercise, write the *is_equal* feature for *BINARY_TREE*. When are two binary trees equal? When they are both empty or when their roots track the same item and their left subtrees are equal and their right subtrees are equal. (Note that this definition of equality checks the *shape* of the tree as well as its contents.)

15.3.2 The *BINARY_SEARCH_TREE* Contract

The primary purpose of a binary search tree is to look up items. Thus, we provide a feature that takes an item and finds an equal item in the tree, *item_equal_to*. (If we want to use the tree in a dictionary, we can just make it a tree of associations.) If there are several items equal to its parameter, it results in the first one it finds.

At this point, we can also add the insertion and deletion routines to the contract. Routine *insert* takes an item to insert and puts it into a place that preserves the binary search tree ordering. Routine *delete* takes an item equal to the one we want deleted. If more than one item in the tree is equal to the parameter, *delete* deletes the first one it encounters.

It is possible to provide a general implementation of *item_equal_to* at this point, using the deferred features *left*, *right*, and *root_item*. It would be a straightforward coding of the binary search algorithm. What is the item equal to *equal_item* in this tree? For an empty tree, it is void; if *equal_item.is_equal (root_item)*, then it is *root_item*; otherwise it is the *item_equal_to (equal_item)* from either the left subtree or the right subtree, depending on whether *equal_item* is "<" or ">" *root_item*.

As we did with *BINARY_TREE*, we can spruce up deferred class *BINARY_SEARCH_TREE* with a couple of implemented routines. In particular, we can easily provide the *least* and the *greatest* items in the tree (one of which, it turns out, we will need in at least one implementation of *delete*).

The resulting class is shown in Listing 15.2.

```
deferred class BINARY_SEARCH_TREE[ITEM->COMPARABLE] inherit
   BINARY_TREE[ITEM];

feature --Adding, removing, and finding items

   item_equal_to (equal_item: ITEM): ITEM is
         --An item in this tree which is_equal (equal_item);
         --Void if no such item exists.
      require
         not_void: equal_item /= Void;
      local
         void_item: ITEM;
      do
         if is_empty then
            Result := void_item;
         elseif equal_item.is_equal (root_item) then
            Result := root_item;
         elseif equal_item < root_item then
            Result := left.item_equal_to (equal_item);
         else
            Result := right.item_equal_to (equal_item);
         end;
      end; --item_equal_to
```

Listing 15.2 A contract with a partial implementation for *BINARY_SEARCH_TREE*.

```
has(equal_item: ITEM): BOOLEAN is
        --Is there an item in this tree that is_equal(equal_item)?
    require
        not_void: equal_item /= Void;
    do
        Result := item_equal_to(equal_item) /= Void;
    end; --has

insert(new_item: ITEM) is
        --Insert new_item into its proper place in this tree.
    require
        not_void: new_item /= Void;
    deferred
    ensure
        size_after_insert: size = old size + 1;
        has_after_insert: has(new_item);
    end; --insert

delete(equal_item: ITEM) is
        --Remove an item that is_equal(equal_item), if any, from this tree.
    require
        not_void: equal_item /= Void;
    deferred
    ensure
        size_after_delete: (size = old size and then not old has(equal_item))
                           or else
                           (size = old size - 1 and then old has(equal_item));
    end; --delete

least: ITEM is
        --The least (leftmost) item in the tree.
    local
        void_item: ITEM;
    do
        if is_empty then
            Result := void_item;
        elseif left.is_empty then
            Result := root_item;
        else
            Result := left.least;
        end;
    end; --least

greatest: ITEM is
        --The greatest (rightmost) item in the tree.
```

Listing 15.2 *(continued)*

```
      local
         void_item: ITEM;
      do
         if is_empty then
            Result := void_item;
         elseif right.is_empty then
            Result := root_item;
         else
            Result := right.greatest;
         end;
      end; --greatest

feature --Sizing

   is_full: BOOLEAN is
         --Is there no room in this tree for another item?
      deferred
      end; --is_full

end --class BINARY_SEARCH_TREE
```

Listing 15.2 *(continued)*

15.3.3 Tree Traversals

Several of the operations that we have discussed do their work by systematically visiting every node in the tree. Such operations are called "**traversals** of the tree." We used traversals with linear object structures too, but there they were too boring to discuss: You just start at the left end and move right until you reach the right end. Trees, on the other hand, are two-dimensional structures, so they require two-dimensional traversals.

There are four common traversal schemes. **Postorder** traversal is what we did in *height*:

1. Traverse the left subtree postorder (e.g., get the left subtree's height).
2. Traverse the right subtree postorder (e.g., get the right subtree's height).
3. Visit the root (e.g., add it in to compute the height of *this* tree).

Figure 15.2a illustrates the sequence in which a postorder traversal proceeds. The diagrams in Figure 15.2 use a generic tree diagram for clarity; we will get back to object structure diagrams in the next section. The nodes are marked with circles, their items not shown, and the children of a node are drawn below it.

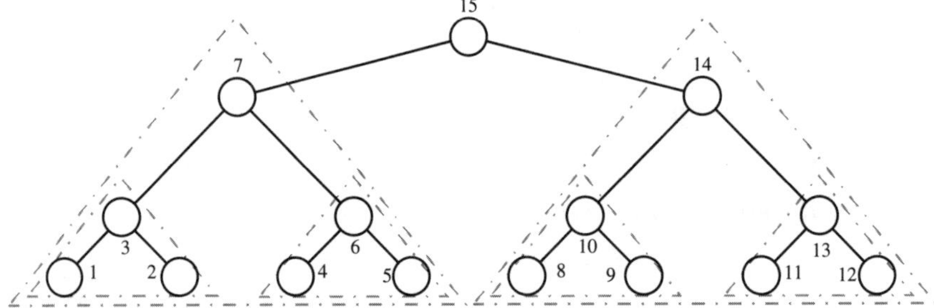

a. Postorder traversal: Visit the root *after* traversing both subtrees.

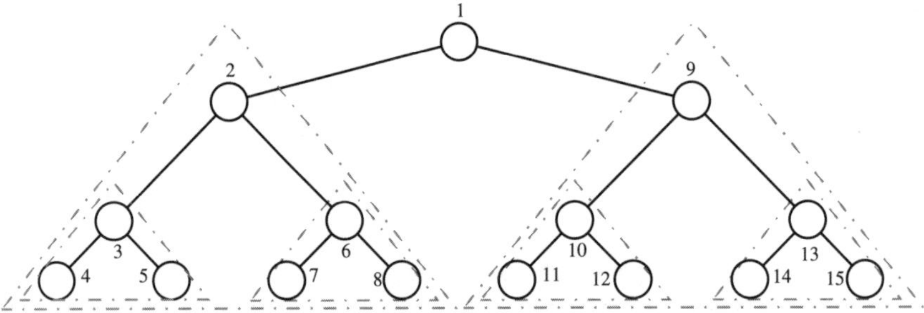

b. Preorder traversal: Visit the root *before* traversing both subtrees.

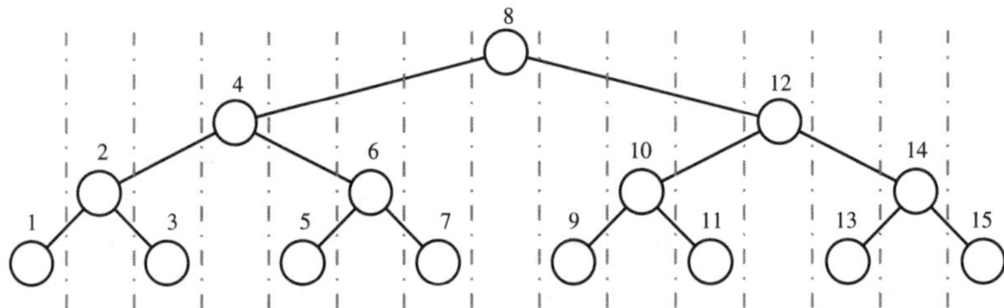

c. Inorder traversal: Visit the root *in between* traversals of the subtrees.

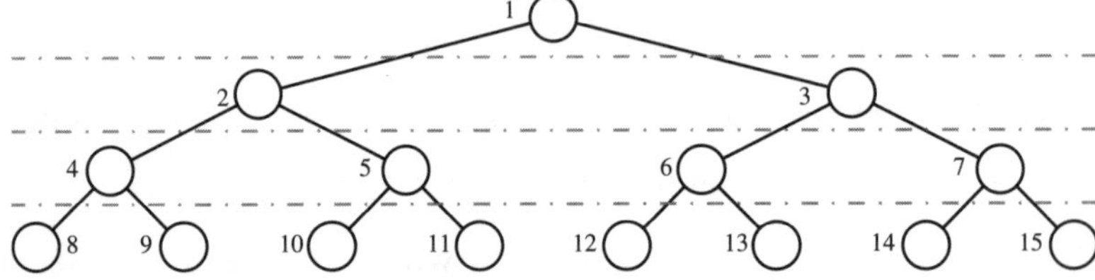

d. Breadth-first traversal: Visit the nodes of each layer left-to-right, starting with the root's layer.

Figure 15.2 Four methods of traversing a binary tree.

In a postorder traversal, before visiting the root we must wait for the left subtree to get traversed and then for the right subtree to be traversed. Thus the traversal dives straight for the bottom left node, and builds the result of the traversal from the bottom up. This is why it is appropriate for *height*.

The opposite of the postorder traversal is the **preorder** traversal, where the root is visited before either of the subtrees is traversed:

1. Visit the root.
2. Traverse the left subtree preorder.
3. Traverse the right subtree preorder.

A preorder traversal is illustrated in Figure 15.2b.

The **inorder** traversal was used in *out*:

1. Traverse the left subtree inorder (e.g., create the left subtree's string representation).
2. Visit the root (e.g., append the root item's string representation).
3. Traverse the right subtree inorder (e.g., append the right subtree's string representation).

An inorder traversal is illustrated in Figure 15.2c.

In effect, an inorder traversal traverses the tree "left to right." This means that an inorder traversal of a search tree will be visiting the items in sorted order (you will see that if you look at the result of *out*, ignoring the subtree delimiters).

We have not needed to do a *preorder* traversal yet, but it is useful when the results of a traversal propagate top-down instead of bottom-up. (For example, it can be used to compute the depth of a node—its distance from the root.)

As an exercise, let us write feature *out_preorder*. It will be a simplified version of *out*: the string representing the tree in preorder, with the parentheses and slashes omitted (the slashes would not be particularly useful anyway). The feature, shown in Listing 15.3, is a very straightforward coding of the traversal algorithm—the only detail is that "visit" means "append *root_item.out* to the result."

All of the preceding algorithms traverse whole subtrees at once. This behavior is called "**depth-first** traversing." A **breadth-first** traversal, on the other hand, ignores the concept of subtrees and scans each layer of the tree left-to-right, as shown in Figure 15.2d.

There is a nice algorithm [13, Section 5.3.2] that performs breadth-first traversals, and it serves as a testament to the usefulness of queues even when no multiprocess programming is involved. The trick is to use the queue to

```
out_preorder: STRING is
      -- "<Preorder traversal>", with no delimiters.
   do
      if is_empty then
         Result := "";
      else
         Result := clone(root_item.out);
         Result.append_string(" ");
         Result.append_string(left.out_preorder);
         Result.append_string(" ");
         Result.append_string(right.out_preorder);
      end;
   end; --out_preorder
```

Listing 15.3 Feature *out_preorder* for class *BINARY_TREE*: an illustration of preorder traversals.

remember which nodes need to be visited next. We start by enqueuing the root of the tree. At each step of the traversal we visit the node at the front of the queue, then dequeue it and enqueue its children.

In the example shown in Figure 15.2d, we start with the queue just having node 1 in it: <1<. We visit and dequeue node 1 and enqueue nodes 2 and 3, so the queue becomes <2 3<. We visit and dequeue node 2, and enqueue its children: <3 4 5<. Visit and dequeue 3, enqueue its children: <4 5 6 7<. Visit and dequeue 4, enqueue 4's children: <5 6 7 8 9<. And so on. The algorithm stops when the queue is exhausted.

The code for this algorithm is in Listing 15.4.

```
out_breadth_first: STRING is
      -- "<Breadth-first traversal>", with no delimiters.
   local
      to_do: QUEUE_LINKED[like Current];
      subtree: like Current;
   do
      Result := clone("");
      if not is_empty then
         from
            !!to_do.make;
            to_do.enqueue(Current);
```

Listing 15.4 Using a *QUEUE* to implement a breadth-first traversal.

```
        until
            to_do.is_empty
        loop
            subtree := to_do.front;
            to_do.dequeue;

            Result.append_string(subtree.root_item.out);
            Result.append_string("  ");

            if not subtree.left.is_empty then
                to_do.enqueue(subtree.left);
            end;

            if not subtree.right.is_empty then
                to_do.enqueue(subtree.right);
            end;
        end;

    end;
end; --out_breadth_first
```

Listing 15.4 *(continued)*

15.4 How a *BINARY_SEARCH_TREE* Does What It Does

By far the most straightforward implementation of a binary tree is the linked version, which has been our motivation. That is the implementation we will do first. Then we will do an implementation using an array.

15.4.1 A Linked Implementation of *BINARY_SEARCH_TREE*

Filling in the implementation gaps for *BINARY_SEARCH_TREE_LINKED* is easy. Features *left* and *right* are just entities tracking smaller *BINARY_SEARCH_TREE_LINKED* objects, and *root_item* is just an entity tracking an *ITEM*. An empty tree is one where all three of these entities are void (see Listing 15.5).

The inside view of a binary search tree thus represented is shown in Figure 15.3. Note that each subtree is a tree in its own right.[2]

How do we insert an item into this representation of a tree? We need to put it into a spot where *item_equal_to* can find it. Basically, we have to follow the path *item_equal_to* takes:

---

[2]Do not be alarmed if this structure looks "heavy." Only the entities of each object (in this case, the references inside *left*, *right*, and *root_node*) occupy space for each and every tree node; the routines are only stored once for the whole class.

```
feature --Accessing the components

   left: like Current;
         --The left subtree.

   right: like Current;
         --The right subtree.

   root_item: ITEM;
         --The item at the root.

feature --Creation and initialization

   make,wipe_out is
         --Make this an empty tree.
      local
         void_item: ITEM;
      do
         root_item := void_item;
         left := Void;
         right := Void;
      end; --make,wipe_out
```

Listing 15.5 Representation details of class *BINARY_SEARCH_TREE_LINKED*.

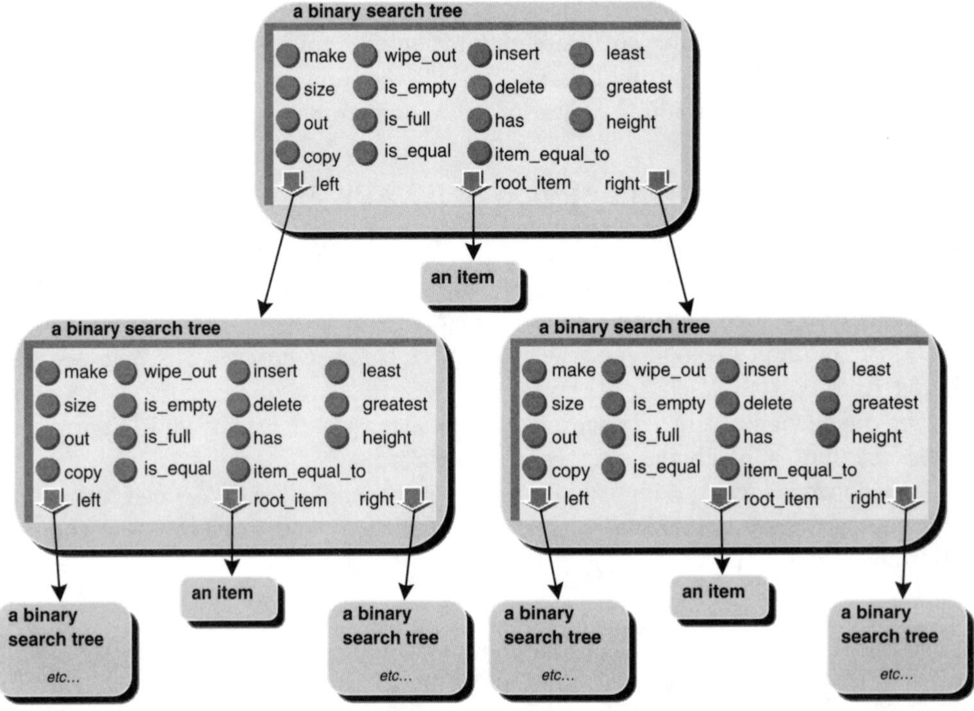

Figure 15.3 The inside view of a linked binary search tree.

1. If *new_item* < *root_item*, then it belongs in the left subtree, so we just tell the left subtree to insert *new_item* into itself.
2. If *new_item* >= *root_item*, then it belongs in the right subtree (or at the root, but the root is already tracking an item), so we just do *right.insert* (*new_item*).
3. The recursion stops when we are trying to insert into an empty tree. If that happens, there is no *root_item* to compare, but we know what needs to be done instead: The empty tree must become a leaf, with *new_item* tracked by the root, and both subtrees empty (as opposed to void).

The resulting routine *insert* is in Listing 15.6.

Deleting an item is trickier. The *delete* routine is given an item equal to the one we want to delete, so first we have to search for it. This is the easy, recursive part:

1. If *equal_item* < *root_item*, tell the left subtree to delete *equal_item*.
2. If *equal_item* > *root_item*, tell the right subtree to do it.

In the remaining case, *equal_item.is_equal* (*root_item*), we need to delete *root_item*. The trick is to do it in such a way, that we still have a binary search tree at the end—we cannot just void out *root_item*.

```
insert (new_item: ITEM) is
        --Insert new_item into its proper place in this tree.
    do
        if is_empty then

            --This tree is no longer empty . . .
            root_item := new_item;

            --. . . but its subtrees are.
            !!left.make;
            !!right.make;

        elseif new_item < root_item then

            left.insert (new_item);

        else

            right.insert (new_item);

        end;

    end; --insert
```

Listing 15.6 Routine *insert* for class *BINARY_SEARCH_TREE_LINKED*.

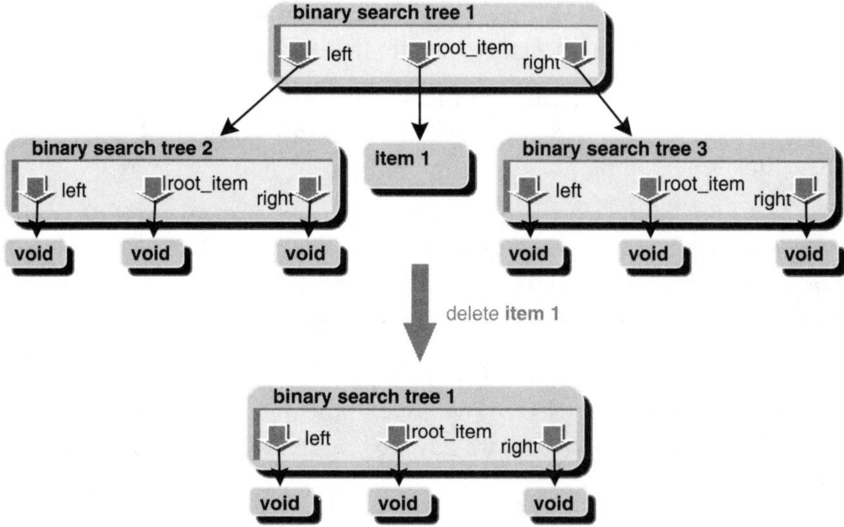

Figure 15.4 Deleting the root item of a leaf results in an empty subtree.

In fact, there are three distinct cases to handle (well, four, but two of them are almost the same). The first case is the easiest: when the tree has no subtrees.

If we are deleting the root node of a leaf, then we can simply convert this tree into an empty tree (the inverse of what we did in *insert*), by setting *left*, *right*, and *root_item* to *Void*, as shown in Figure 15.4.

The next easiest case is when this tree has one empty and one nonempty subtree. Here we want to just move the whole nonempty subtree up one level, overwriting the current root (Figure 15.5).

This leaves the most difficult case: removing the root item of a tree with two nonempty subtrees. We cannot just promote one of the subtrees, because that would result in a tree with three subtrees (the subtree that wasn't promoted plus the left and right subtrees of the promoted one would want to be tracked by the same node). If it is not a binary tree, it is not a binary search tree.

Nor can we just void *root_item*, because then we would be unable to search past that node. If it is not a search tree, it is not a binary search tree. But we are on the right track.

The way out of the dilemma is to replace *root_item* not with *Void*, but with another item from the tree. But which one?

Recall that the inorder traversal of a binary search tree always visits the items in sorted order (Section 15.3.3), and that we get the inorder traversal by reading the tree's items left-to-right. If we delete an item, the result would also

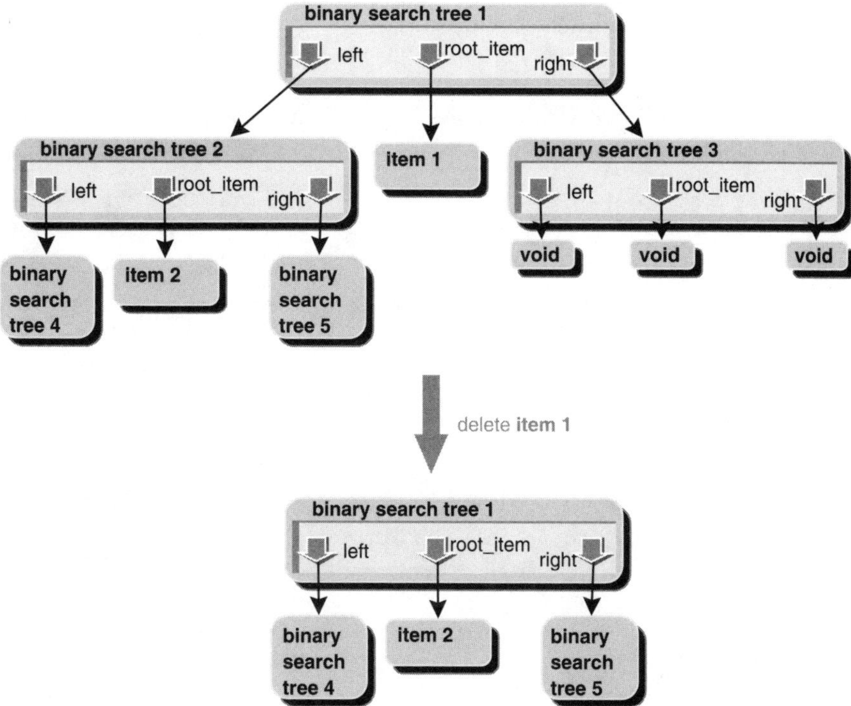

Figure 15.5 To delete the root item of a tree with one empty subtree, the non-empty subtree is promoted up one level.

be a binary search tree, so its inorder traversal must be sorted the same way—it will just skip the item that we deleted.

Thus, the item that must take the place of *root_item* must be one of its neighbors in the inorder traversal: either the rightmost item of the left subtree (obtained using the request *left.greatest*), also known as the **inorder predecessor** of *root_item*, or the leftmost item of the right subtree (the **"inorder successor,"** *right.least*). Let us pick the inorder successor (the choice will become clear in a moment).

If we do "*root_item* := *right.least*", we get a result that is quite close to the tree that we want. The only problem is that the inorder successor is now in two places in this tree: at the root and at the leftmost position of the right subtree. This is easily solved by requesting *right.delete* (*root_item*). The complete operation is illustrated in Figure 15.6.

How do we know that it will delete *that* item and not just an equal one? After all, *delete* deletes the first equal item it finds, and we specifically need to delete the leftmost item in the subtree. Well, since we split our tree with "<"

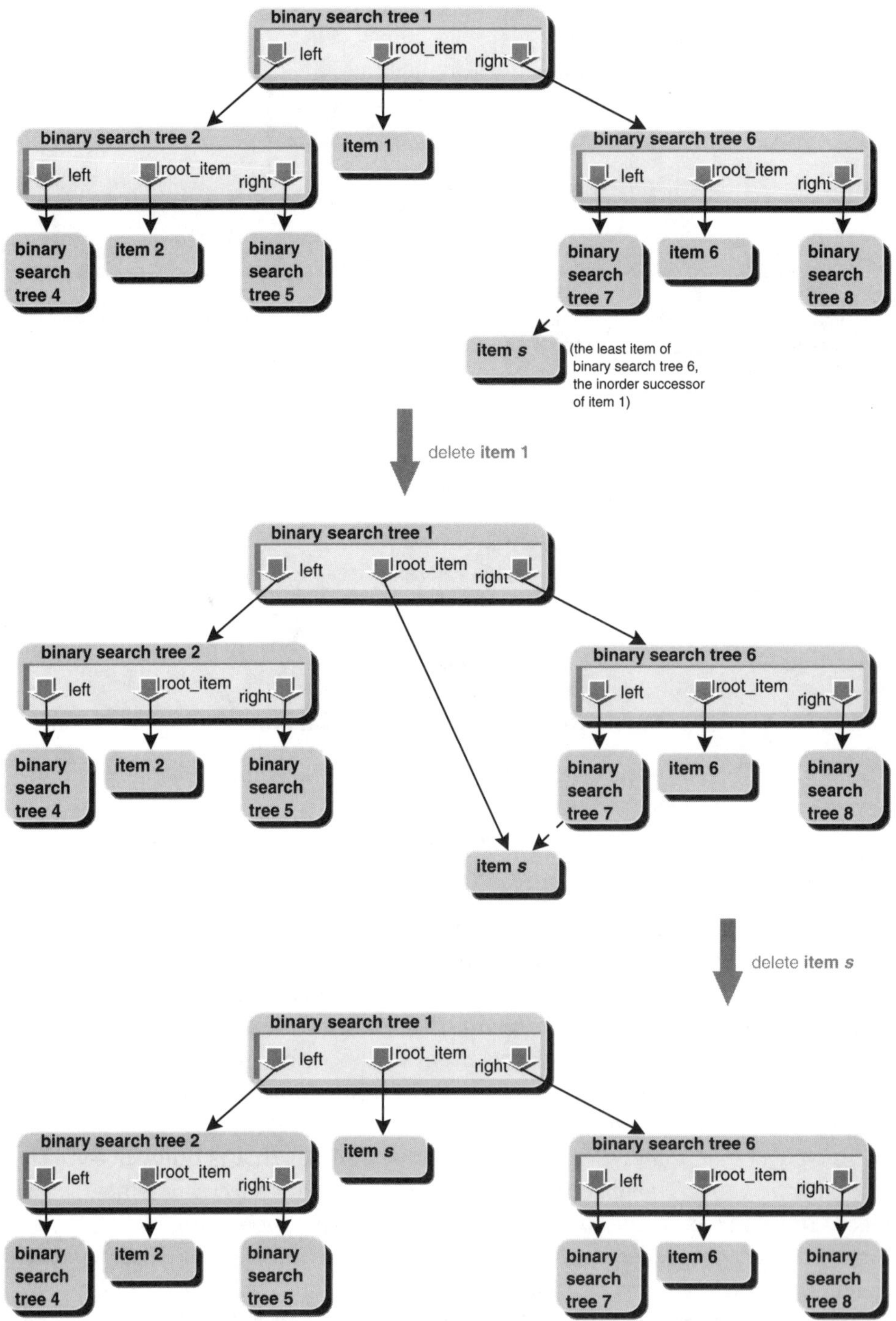

Figure 15.6 To delete the root item of a tree with two nonempty subtrees, make the root track the inorder successor of the deleted item, then tell the right subtree to delete the inorder successor.

items on the left of the root and ">=" items on the right, it is impossible to have a tree whose root item is equal to its leftmost item and is not the leftmost item itself: If they were two distinct but equal items, then the leftmost item would have to go into the root's right subtree, and then it couldn't be the leftmost item, could it?

Note that if we had decided to use the inorder predecessor (*left.greatest*) instead of the inorder successor, we would not be able to delete it from the left subtree this easily, since then we *could* be deleting an equal item that is higher in the tree. So the inorder successor choice goes with the "<, >=" sorting scheme to which we had agreed. If our tree used the "<=, >" sorting scheme, we would want to promote the inorder predecessor instead.

The coding of this algorithm is left as an exercise.

15.4.2 Using an *ARRAY* to Implement a *BINARY_SEARCH_TREE*

Linked object structures are traversed by following object references; array-based object structures are traversed by manipulating array indices. For an array-based tree, this means using the index of the root item to find the root items of the subtrees.

The easiest way to lay out a tree to fit the shape of an array is to use one of the traversals (Figure 15.3.3). Which of the four will give us the easiest way to compute a child's index from a parent's index? A bit of head-scratching over Figure 15.2 yields the answer: the breadth-first traversal.

If we use the relative position of a node within the breadth-first traversal as the array index, then it is very easy to find the children given the parent's index: If the parent is in position p, then its left child is in position $2p$, and its right child is at index $2p + 1$. The mapping of tree nodes to array indices is illustrated in Figure 15.7.

So, what exactly, is the representation of a tree? It is the array of items, plus the index of the tree's root. The inside view of a *BINARY_SEARCH_TREE_ARRAY* object is shown in Figure 15.8.

The implementation of *root_item* is obvious: The result is merely *items.item* (*root_index*). But how do we implement *left* and *right*? It is not enough to just return *root_index**2 and *root_index**2+1; those are integers, but *left* and *right* are trees!

What we need to do in *left* and *right* is to build tree objects for the result. But we do not want to copy item references for a subtree from one array to another, for two reasons.

The first is that it would destroy our performance, making each *left* and *right* request O(*capacity*) in time. If we cannot do them in O(1) time, we cannot get O(log *N*) performance out of our tree.

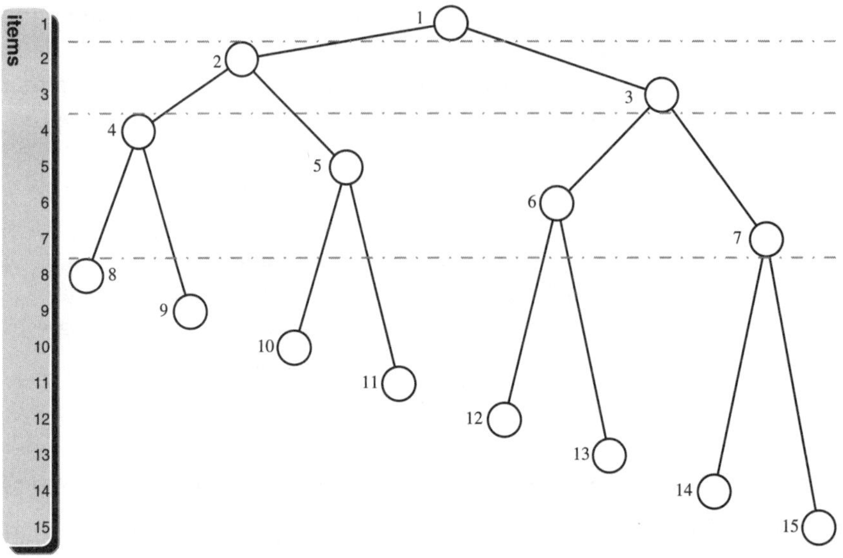

Figure 15.7 Binary tree nodes are mapped onto the array in breadth-first order.

The second, even more important, reason is that we want the tree and its subtrees (and their subtrees, etc.) to be a nested object structure instead of a group of independent ones. Otherwise, our recursive algorithms will not work at all. For example, when we insert a new item into a tree, we delegate the

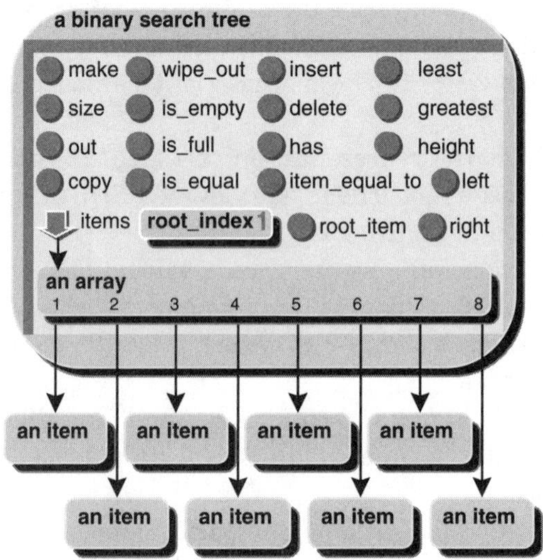

Figure 15.8 The inside view of a *BINARY_SEARCH_TREE_ARRAY* object.

insertion to the left subtree or the right subtree, depending on how it compares with the root item. When it gets inserted into that subtree, it is also inserted into the main tree. A tree is not conceptually independent from its subtrees, it must reflect all the changes in them.

With the linked tree, this was easily accomplished: *left* and *right* simply resulted in the same references to the subtree objects that the tree itself used. In effect, the user was provided with shortcuts into the middle of the tree.

With the array-based implementation, to nest the trees, we must make the tree objects share the array. The tree objects will share the array tracked by their respective *items* entities, and will be distinguished by the *root_index* value only.

Figure 15.9 illustrates objects that are results of *left* and *right* features.

Listing 15.7 shows a way to perform this operation. A creation procedure, *make_subtree*, is made available only to other *BINARY_SEARCH_TREE_ARRAY* objects. When a new object is told to use that routine to initialize itself, it is told which object is its supertree, and whether it is the left subtree of that tree (if not, it is the right subtree, obviously). It then makes its *items* track the supertree's *item*, and computes its *root_index* based on the supertree's *root_index*. Features *left* and *right* then simply create their results using *make_subtree*.

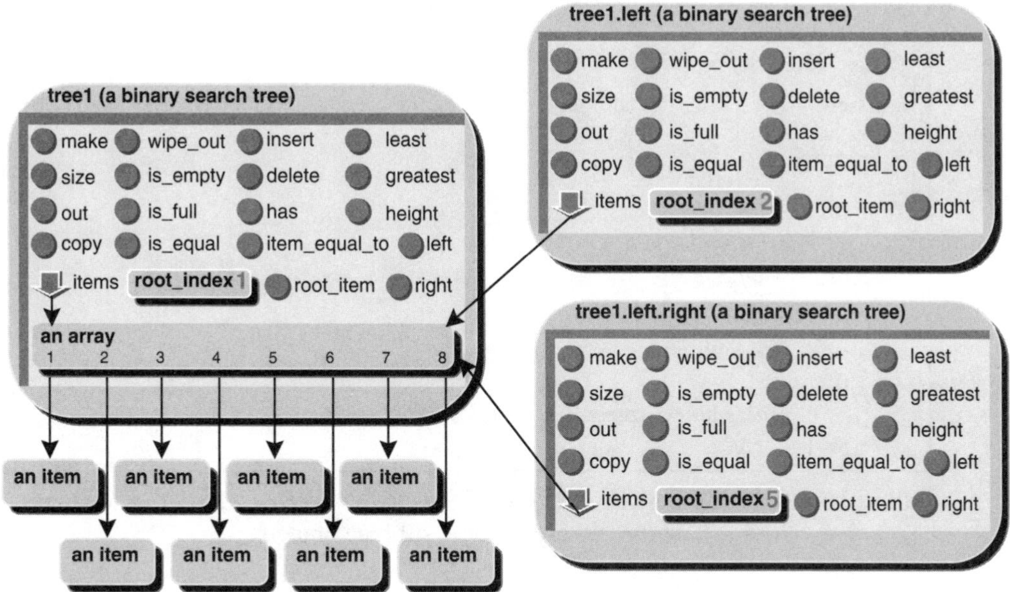

Figure 15.9 Subtrees of a *BINARY_SEARCH_TREE_ARRAY* share its internal array and use *root_index* to identify their beginning within it.

```
class BINARY_SEARCH_TREE_ARRAY[ITEM -> COMPARABLE] inherit
   BINARY_SEARCH_TREE[ITEM]
      redefine
         left, right, root_item, make, wipe_out, insert, delete, is_empty, is_full
      end;

creation make, make_capacity, make_subtree

feature {BINARY_SEARCH_TREE_ARRAY}

   items: ARRAY[ITEM];
   root_index: INTEGER;

   make_subtree(supertree: like Current; is_left_subtree: BOOLEAN) is
         --Make this tree the left subtree of supertree if is_left_subtree is true,
         --and its right subtree otherwise.
      require
         array_starts_at_1: supertree.items.lower = 1;
      do
         --Share the array with the supertree.
         items := supertree.items;

         if is_left_subtree then
            root_index := supertree.root_index * 2;
         else
            root_index := supertree.root_index * 2 + 1;
         end;
      end; --make_subtree

feature --Accessing the components

   left: like Current is
         --The left subtree.
      do
         !!Result.make_subtree(Current, true);
      end; --left

   right: like Current is
         --The right subtree.
      do
         !!Result.make_subtree(Current, false);
      end; --right
```

Listing 15.7 A portion of class *BINARY_SEARCH_TREE_ARRAY*, showing how *left* and *right* create new subtree objects.

Most of the other operations are analogous to those in *BINARY_SEARCH_TREE_LINKED*, but two areas warrant additional discussion.

The first is the treatment of *is_full*. In the array-based implementations of other structures, we used the size of the internal array to determine if it was full. We never automatically resized the array, because resizing is an expensive operation, so we left the decision to do it to the user. Unfortunately, we cannot do that in *BINARY_SEARCH_TREE_ARRAY*.

The problem is this. We define "full" to mean "no more insertions are possible." With lists, stacks, and queues, the full state happens when all positions of the array are occupied (or perhaps one empty position exists in the case of queues). But with binary search trees, we are always inserting into the appropriate empty subtree, wherever it may be within the array. We may exceed the boundary of the array without filling up all the slots. For example, suppose the array capacity is 8 and we insert into the tree only four items in sorted order: `"aalst"` (into position 1), `"bindle"` (position 3), `"dattuck"` (position 7), and `"duddo"` (position 15—out of bounds).

Since we have no way of providing a meaningful *is_full*, we have to make its result always false, and resize the array automatically when necessary. Listing 15.8 shows the routines most affected by this decision.

The second area of interest is the deletion algorithm. The one we used in the linked implementation took advantage of the situation where the tree whose root item is being deleted had only one nonempty subtree. In that case, we would effectively slide the nonempty tree up one level.

In the linked implementation, promoting a whole subtree up one level is cheap: We merely reassign three object references. In the array-based implementation, it is expensive: We actually have to copy item references to other indices within the array.

Instead of doing that, we move the inorder successor up to the root if the right tree is not empty, whether the left tree is empty or not (thus combining two cases from the algorithm for the linked version), and move the inorder predecessor up if the right tree is empty but the left tree is not. As we discussed in Section 15.4.1, we cannot just use *delete* to remove the inorder predecessor from the left subtree (there could be an equal item higher in the tree that will get deleted instead). This problem is easily solved, however, by starting the deletion at the predecessor node itself.

Listing 15.9 shows the code for *delete* and the new private routine needed to find the predecessor's subtree, called "*greatest_subtree*."[3]

---

[3] I am not too crazy about this name. Suggestions for a better one are gladly accepted at Jacob@ToolCASE.com.

```
feature --Adding, removing, and finding items

   insert (new_item: ITEM) is
         --Insert new_item into its proper place in this tree.
      do
         if is_empty then

            --This is where we insert it. Resize if necessary.
            if root_index > items.count then
               items.resize (1, root_index);
            end;

            items.put (new_item, root_index);

         elseif new_item < root_item then

            left.insert (new_item);

         else

            right.insert (new_item);

         end;

      end; --insert

feature --Sizing

   is_empty: BOOLEAN is
         --Is this tree empty?
      do
         Result := root_index > items.count
                    or else items.item (root_index) = Void;
      end; --is_empty

   is_full: BOOLEAN is false;
         --Cannot predict jumping out of the array,
         --so will have to resize as necessary.
```

Listing 15.8 Features of class *BINARY_SEARCH_TREE_ARRAY* that deal with the array boundary.

The function *greatest_subtree* provides a shortcut for the deletion of the inorder predecessor from the left subtree. This brings up an interesting question: Do we want to use this shortcut for deleting the inorder successor from the right subtree as well? We did not do that because the request *right.delete (right.least)* used the routines already in the contract (in fact, *least* was inherited from *BINARY_SEARCH_TREE*). Would it be better to provide *least_subtree* and *greatest_subtree* in the contract instead of *least* and *greatest*? After all, the job of *least* can be accomplished with *least_subtree.root_item*, and then we could conveniently use the deletion shortcuts in both the linked and the array-based implementations of *BINARY_SEARCH_TREE*. What do you think?

```
feature {BINARY_SEARCH_TREE_ARRAY} --Adding, removing
                                   --and finding items

  greatest_subtree: like Current is
        --Like greatest, but the result is not just the rightmost item,
        --but the subtree at the root of which it resides.
     require
        not_empty: not is_empty;
     do
        if right.is_empty then
           Result := Current;
        else
           Result := right.greatest_subtree;
        end;
     end; --greatest_subtree

feature --Adding, removing, and finding items

  delete(equal_item: ITEM) is
        --Remove an item that is_equal(equal_item) from this tree.
     local
        void_item: ITEM;
        predecessor_subtree: like Current;
     do
        if is_empty then

           --Nothing.

        elseif equal_item < root_item then

           left.delete(equal_item);

        elseif root_item < equal_item then

           right.delete(equal_item);

        else

           --Found it. Deleting.

           if left.is_empty and then right.is_empty then
              --This is a leaf. Easy.
              items.put(void_item, root_index);
           elseif not right.is_empty then
              --Adopt the inorder successor item and
              --remove it from the right subtree.
              items.put(right.least, root_index);
              right.delete(root_item);
```

Listing 15.9 Routines for deleting an item from a *BINARY_SEARCH_TREE_ARRAY*.

```
else
    --Find the subtree for which the inorder predecessor is root,
    --adopt it in this root and delete it from that subtree.
    --(Can't just remove the greatest item from the left subtree,
    --since a subtree's root item may be equal to its greatest item,
    --and the wrong item would get deleted.)
    predecessor_subtree := left.greatest_subtree;
    items.put(left.greatest_subtree.root_item, root_index);
    predecessor_subtree.delete(predecessor_subtree.root_item);
end;

end;

end; --delete
```

Listing 15.9 *(continued)*

15.4.3 Trade-Offs Between the Two Implementations

The two implementations have the same time complexities (this time you get to determine the complexities; see the exercises) when no array resizing is needed. The trade-offs lie entirely in space management—and space consumption comparison is not as straightforward as it was with the linear object structures.

With the linked version it is easy. For each item, we have a node that stores three object references (to the root item, and to the left and right subtrees). In addition, we have one such node for each empty subtree.

The array-based version is the convoluted one. For each node, the array stores only one object reference, that to the item itself. So if the array is more than $\frac{1}{3}$ full, it is utilizing space more efficiently. But those full positions may not be consecutive within the array.

A binary search tree tends to grow near its bottom, by adding items into the empty trees. Each time we go down a level, we double the index, thus skipping many array positions. If the array is relatively small, it is not hard to force a resizing, which can slow down *insert* considerably. The only general way to avoid it is to keep the array relatively large, but then there will be many unused positions in it.

There are other places where the array version has more overhead. For instance, every time *left* or *right* is requested, a new object with two attributes (the reference to the array and the integer for *root_index*) is created, at least temporarily. Another place where the linked implementation is more efficient is the single-subtree case of *delete*: It is faster to slide a subtree up a level in the linked version than to move and remove the inorder successor or predecessor in the array-based one.

But it is the unpredictable space utilization within the array that makes *BINARY_SEARCH_TREE_ARRAY* unattractive in practice. In fact, most object libraries do not bother to provide it. However, there are cases where its internal representation is very *à propos:* when the tree is filled not arbitrarily, but in the breadth-first order. Then all of the occupied positions are arranged sequentially at the left side of the array, and resizing is only necessary when there are more items in the tree than positions in the array (allowing us again to have a meaningful *is_full* routine).

This situation does not arise with binary search trees (unless the user arranges the insertions very, very carefully), but in Chapter 16 we will study an object structure that takes advantage of the array representation so well that it is the linked version of it that is rarely used.

15.5 Caveat: Aliasing

The recursive model of trees is simple and elegant, but it has one danger zone: When several objects (trees and subtrees) share parts of an object structure, changes in one of them can screw up the others (this is known as the "**aliasing**" problem). For example, consider the following code:

```
!!tree.make;
tree.insert("rigolet");
tree.insert("duddo");
tree.insert("aalst");
subtree := tree.left;
```

After it is performed, *tree* is `"(((/aalst\)/duddo\)/rigolet\)"` and *subtree* is `"((/aalst\)/duddo\)"`. If next we do

```
tree.wipe_out;
```

what will be the value of *subtree*? What *should* its value be?

Well, in an ideal world, the object tracking information stored in the entity *subtree* would be automatically invalidated at this point (but that cannot be done in Eiffel). We made *left* and *right* result in trees so that we could recursively use the same operations on subtrees as on the main tree, not so that our users could set up entities to track the subtrees. After the main tree changes, references to what used to be its subtrees should be discarded.

This limitation is not enforceable by preconditions, and requires programming discipline on behalf of the users. The best we can do is document it in the contract as comments for *left* and *right*.

```
left: like Current is
        --The left subtree.
        --WARNING:
        --1. The result may become stale if the parent tree changes.
        --2. Modifications must not be made directly to the result,
        --   except as part of a recursive modification of the parent tree.
    require
        not_empty: not is_empty;
    deferred
    end; --left
```

Listing 15.10 An aliasing problem warning in class *BINARY_TREE*. The same warning applies to *right*.

So what does happen if the user ignores our warning and tries to use the left subtree after the parent tree has been wiped out? The fastest implementations of *wipe_out* for the linked and array-based versions will yield different results. In the linked version, the subtree would still exist and have the same value, but it would become disconnected from the parent tree. In the array-based version, the subtree would become empty.

The two implementations could be made to yield a consistent result, but that would significantly slow down *wipe_out* for the main tree in at least one of them. Consistent handling of "stale" object references is just not worth sacrificing the speed of the legitimate use of *wipe_out*.

Users must also avoid bypassing the main tree to work on subtrees. If operations are performed directly on a subtree, the integrity of the parent tree cannot be guaranteed. For example, suppose we used the tree we built in the above example to do this:

```
subtree.insert("spreakley");
```

The result would be that *tree* is no longer a binary search tree, since "spreakley" is now in the left subtree of "rigolet".

The bottom line is that the results of *left* and *right* are to be used *only in recursive or read-only operations* on the main tree. An example of the warning in the contract is given in Listing 15.10.

15.6 Using a Binary Search Tree in a Dictionary

Listing 15.11 shows class *DICTIONARY_BST*, which uses a binary search tree to do its work. Its routines simply put together associations that the binary search tree requires. The BST does the rest.

```
class DICTIONARY_BST[KEY -> COMPARABLE, VALUE] inherit
   DICTIONARY[KEY, VALUE]

creation make

feature {DICTIONARY_BST}

   associations:
      BINARY_SEARCH_TREE_LINKED[ASSOCIATION[KEY, VALUE]];
         --The binary search tree of associations.

feature --Creation and initialization

   make is
         --Create a new, empty dictionary.
      do
         !!associations.make;
      end; --make

feature --Adding, removing, and checking associations

   value(key: KEY): VALUE is
         --The value associated with key in this dictionary.
         --Void if there is no such association.
      local
         pattern: ASSOCIATION[KEY, VALUE];
         match: ASSOCIATION[KEY, VALUE];
      do
         !!pattern.make;
         pattern.set_key(key);

         match := associations.item_equal_to(pattern);

         if match /= Void then
            Result := match.value;
         end; --else leave Result void.
      end; --value

   put(new_value: VALUE; key: KEY) is
         --Insert an association of key and new_value into this dictionary.
         --If the dictionary already contains an association for key, replace it.
      local
         pattern: ASSOCIATION[KEY, VALUE];
         match: ASSOCIATION[KEY, VALUE];
      do
         !!pattern.make;
         pattern.set_key(key);

         match := associations.item_equal_to(pattern);
```

Listing 15.11 Class *DICTIONARY_BST*, which uses a binary search tree to keep track of its associations.

```
      if match = Void then

         !!match.make;
         match.set_key(key);
         match.set_value(new_value);

         associations.insert(match);

      else

         match.set_value(new_value);

      end;
   end; --put

 delete(key: KEY) is
      --Delete the association for key from this dictionary.
   local
      pattern: ASSOCIATION[KEY, VALUE];
   do
      !!pattern.make;
      pattern.set_key(key);

      associations.delete(pattern);
   end; --delete

 wipe_out is
      --Make this dictionary empty.
   do
      associations.wipe_out;
   end; --wipe_out

feature --Sizing

 size: INTEGER is
      --The number of associations currently in this dictionary.
   do
      Result := associations.size;
   end; --size

 is_empty: BOOLEAN is
      --Is this dictionary empty?
   do
      Result := associations.is_empty;
   end; --is_empty

 is_full: BOOLEAN is
      --Is there no room in this dictionary for one more association?
   do
      Result := associations.is_full;
   end; --is_full
```

Listing 15.11 *(continued)*

```
feature --Comparisons and copying

   copy (other: like Current) is
         --Copy other onto Current.
      do
         associations := clone (other.associations);
      end; --copy

   is_equal (other: like Current): BOOLEAN is
         --Do this dictionary and other associate the same values
         --with the same keys?
      do
         Result := associations.out.is_equal (other.associations.out);
      end; --is_equal

feature --Simple input and output

   out: STRING is
         --"< (<key_1>.out,<value_1>.out) ... (<key_n>.out,<value_n>.out) >".
      do
         Result := clone ("< ");
         Result.append_string (associations.out);
         Result.append_string (" >");
      end; --out

invariant

   have_list: associations /= Void;

end --class DICTIONARY_BST
```

Listing 15.11 *(continued)*

Summary

A binary search tree is a two-dimensional object structure that directly supports binary searching. It is a binary tree in which each subtree's root item serves as the separator between the left subtree, which tracks items that are less than the separator, and the right subtree, which tracks the rest.

Binary trees can be implemented as linked or array-based structures. The array-based implementation follows the breadth-first traversal, which will prove very useful in the following chapter.

Exercises

1. Write feature *size* for class *BINARY_TREE*. What is its time complexity if *left* and *right* are both O(1)? (Draw the execution chart.)
2. Write feature *is_equal* for class *BINARY_TREE*.

3. Write features *out_inorder* and *out_postorder* for class *BINARY_TREE*.
4. Using pencil, paper, and the *insert* algorithm of class *BINARY_SEARCH_TREE_LINKED*, insert the following sequence of *STRING* objects into a tree that is initially empty:

   a. `"fiunary"`, `"bindle"`, `"aa1st"`, `"dattuck"`, `"rigolet"`, `"duddo"`, `"harbottle"`, `"knaptoft"`, `"scramoge"`, `"spreakley"`.

   b. `"aa1st"`, `"bindle"`, `"dattuck"`, `"duddo"`, `"fiunary"`, `"harbottle"`, `"knaptoft"`, `"rigolet"`, `"scramoge"`, `"spreakley"`.

   What is the time complexity of *item_equal_to* on the tree created in part (a)? What is its time complexity on the tree created in part (b)?
5. Using the deletion algorithm described in Section 15.4.1, delete the following strings from the tree you drew in part (a) of the previous exercise. Do them in sequence (first part (a), then part (b), *etc.*).

   a. `"aa1st"`

   b. `"duddo"`

   c. `"harbottle"`

   d. `"fiunary"`
6. Show that the time complexity of *insert* and *delete* in both *BINARY_SEARCH_TREE_LINKED* and *BINARY_SEARCH_TREE_ARRAY* is O(log *N*). (In the case of the array-based version of *delete*, show it for the cases where resizing is not necessary.)
7. Write feature *wipe_out* for *BINARY_SEARCH_TREE_ARRAY* so that it works in O(*N*) time (and not O(*capacity*)). Which traversal did you use?
8. Write a faster *is_equal* implementation for *BINARY_SEARCH_TREE_ARRAY*.
9. Complete class *BINARY_SEARCH_TREE_LINKED*.
10. Complete class *BINARY_SEARCH_TREE_ARRAY*.
11. A general traversal feature would perform an arbitrary operation at each node. In Eiffel, it is impossible to pass an arbitrary routine to a feature, since routines do not exist outside objects. Suggest an alternative way to write a general binary tree traversal routine.
12. Suggest a redefinition of *out_breadth_first* for *BINARY_SEARCH_TREE_ARRAY*. Does it improve the time complexity of the routine? the space complexity?
13. What would happen if *to_do* in *out_breadth_first* was not a queue but a stack?

16 Heaps

Searching for an equal object is not always what is needed. For example, we may want the first object to arrive at the scene (remember queues?), or perhaps the object considered to be of greatest importance. Let us see how that can be done with linear object structures, and then see how using a tree can speed up things.

16.1 Priority Queues

An interesting variation of a queue is a **priority queue.** It is similar to the queues we studied in Chapter 9, but with one distinction: Items in it are conceptually sorted by their "greatness," so that if an item is at the front of the queue, no item behind it is ">" it.

I say "conceptually sorted" because *how* a priority queue is implemented is only the implementer's business. It may actually be a sorted linear structure inside, but it does not have to be. All it needs to do is make sure that *front* results in the greatest item (or one of the greatest items if there are equal items in the queue).

16.1.1 Linear Versions

If we did implement the queue as a linear structure, we would not need to use any of the sort algorithms to keep it in sorted order. We could simply have *enqueue* start at the end of the queue and move the new item forward until it is behind an item that is ">=" the new item.

For example, suppose you are in a martial arts class, and the instructor is reviewing the techniques of individual students today. The instructor reviews students in the order of their rank, so when you arrive, everybody who got there before you is already lined up by rank. To enqueue yourself, you move through the line until you are behind a person of your own or higher rank.

This is an $O(N)$ operation, which is better than the $O(N \log N)$ a real sort would require. (Well, insertion sort would also be $O(N)$ in this case, because it would be using essentially the same algorithm.)

Alternatively, we could let *enqueue* be $O(1)$ by just adding the new item to the end, and letting *front* and *dequeue* search the queue for the greatest item. This would also be $O(N)$, though with a higher average-case constant, since to determine the highest item in a list that is sorted only chronologically, it is always necessary to scan the entire list. (In the worst case, the *enqueue* in the keep-it-sorted method will also scan the whole queue.) In our example, the instructor would just scan the queue to find the frontmost student of the highest rank still in the queue.

However, we do not have to settle for an $O(N)$ implementation. Now that we know about trees, we have a way to do it in $O(\log N)$ time.

16.1.2 A Tree Version

Suppose instead of one line to wait in, there were two sorted lines. To pick the next student to evaluate, the instructor could look at the two front people, and call the one with the higher rank (recall the merge operation in merge sort). But in the martial arts culture, students do not make their instructors do work that the students can do themselves. So the two front people look at each other, and the one with higher rank steps forward and stands between the two lines, ready for dequeuing. Everybody behind the newly vacated spot then moves up a step. The *enqueue* operation would pick a line and do as before, but this time the line is only half as long (if the lines are balanced).

Let us proceed with this optimization. Suppose the two half-lines were split into two quarter-lines. The higher ranked of the two left lines moves forward, and the highest ranked of the two right lines moves forward. Now we have the two highest ranking students up front, and we have already covered what they do to make the instuctor's life easier. The *enqueue* routine now only has about $\frac{1}{4}N$ positions to traverse.

If we continue this process, we wind up with a binary tree, with its root being the front of the queue. The tree is sorted, but not the way binary search trees in Chapter 15 were. The ordering is now "the root item of a tree is '>=' the root items of both subtrees." A tree like that is shown in Figure 16.1. With this arrangement, *front* is $O(1)$, since the front item is right there at the root.

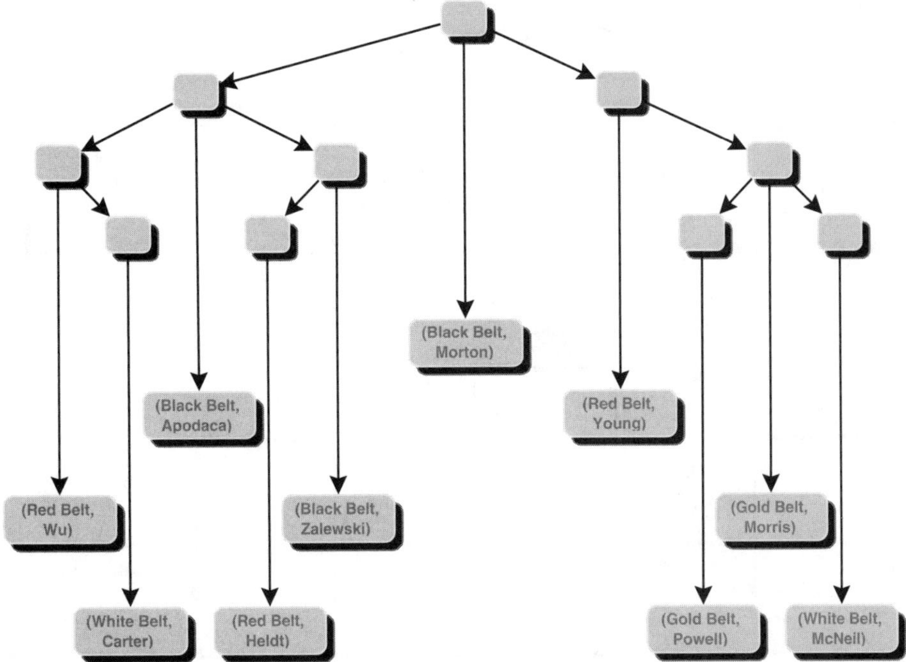

Figure 16.1 A priority queue. The belts are ranked as follows: White < Gold < Green < Blue < Red < Black.

An *enqueue* starts by adding the new item into an empty subtree, and then moving it up (trading places with its parent) until its parent is ">=" it. Thus, the time complexity of *insert* is the height of the tree, which is O(log *N*) if the tree is balanced.

The *dequeue* takes the front item. This creates a vacancy at the root, which is filled by promoting the greater of the root items of the two subtrees, and the process is repeated recursively. Its time complexity is also O(*height*) which is O(log *N*) if the tree is balanced.

Fortunately, unlike the case with binary search trees, there is a way to keep priority queues balanced. We need to be clever about how enqueuing and dequeuing work.

First, a couple of new definitions. We have been talking about balanced trees, but never really defined them. A **balanced** binary tree is one in which, for every node, $|left.height - right.height| \leq 1$. (When we talk of a tree as "less balanced" or "more balanced," we refer to how close that tree is to this ideal.)

A binary tree is **full** if the only way to add a node to the tree is to start a new level. A full tree looks like a triangle with no holes in it. All of its leaves

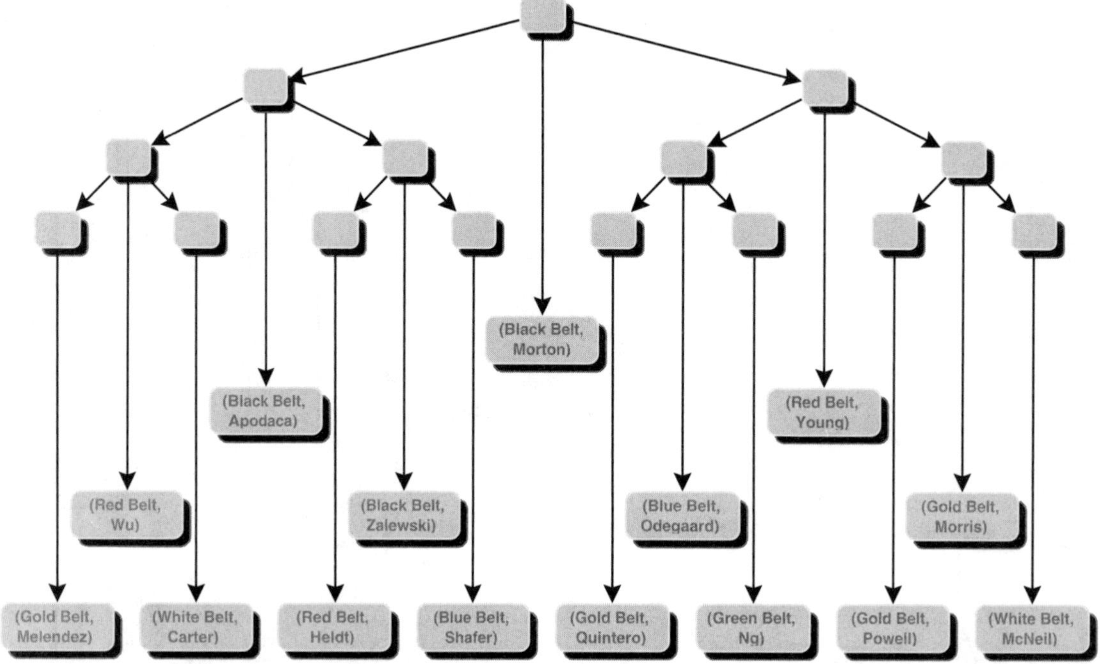

Figure 16.2 A full tree.

are lined up at the bottom level (for example, see Figure 16.2). A full tree is as balanced as it gets. However, only binary trees of certain sizes can possibly be full: trees with 1 item, 3 items, 7 items, 15 items, etc.—in other words, trees with $2^n - 1$ items. For other sizes, we need balanced trees that are a little less restrictive in form.

A binary tree is **complete** if when you do its breadth-first traversal, you encounter no holes. As the example in Figure 16.3 shows, a complete tree looks like a full tree with the right side of the bottom layer cut off. (Note that a full tree is complete too.)

If a binary tree is complete and for every node in it, the root item is ">=" the root items of both subtrees, then it is a **heap.** (For example, the trees in Figure 16.2 and Figure 16.3 are heaps.)

Heaps make a natural representation for priority queues, but they serve other purposes as well (for example, in Section 16.3 we will use a heap for sorting). Thus, instead of going over how to implement priority queues specifically, let us concentrate on heaps. Implementations of linear and heap-based priority queues are too straightforward for us to study at this point.

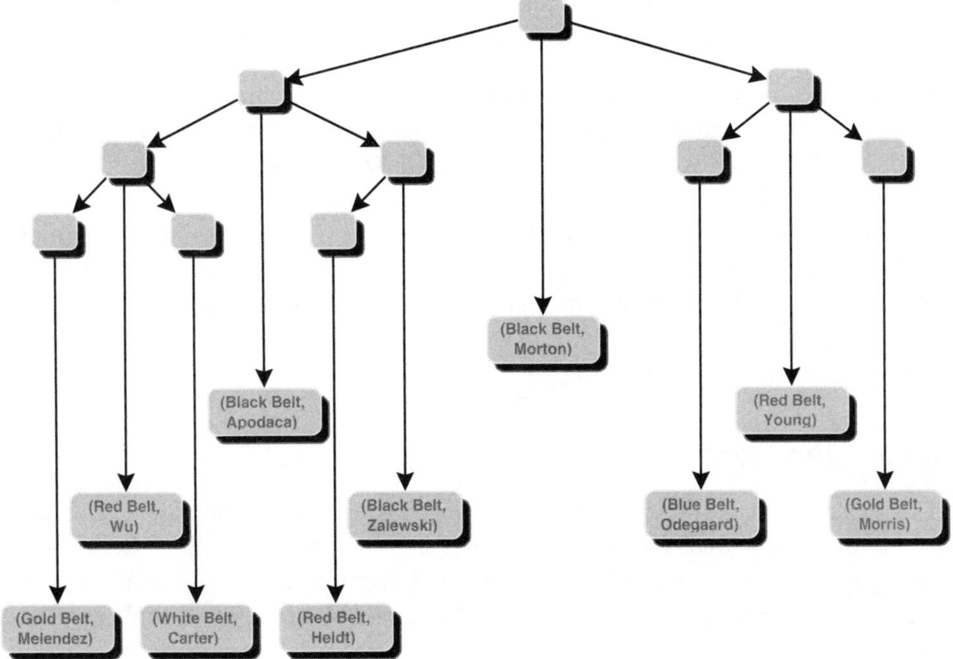

Figure 16.3 A complete tree.

16.2 Heaps

As we said in the previous section, heaps are complete binary trees in which the item at every node is ">=" the items at that node's children. The item at the root (at the top of the heap) is thus one of the greatest items (items below it may be equal to it, but not greater).

There is no reason to assume the heap is to be used as a priority queue, so instead of the queue terminology (*front*, *enqueue* and *dequeue*), we will stick to the ordered tree terminology we used in Chapter 15: *root_item*, *insert*, and *delete*.

Routines *insert* and *delete* must preserve the qualities of the tree that make it a heap. In the case of *insert*, that means two things:

1. The new item must end up as a child to an item that is ">=" it.

2. Since the new tree will be a complete tree too, it will be shaped so that the leftmost unoccupied space in the bottom layer becomes occupied. (If the

tree had been full, then the additional node would be in the leftmost position of a newly opened bottom layer.)

A heap's *delete* always removes the root item. The constraints of the heap mean that after the root item is deleted, the spot occupied by the rightmost item in the bottom layer is the one to vacate while preserving the "parent is '>=' both children" ordering.

Although it is possible to implement heaps as linked trees, the heap algorithms were created for the array version. The linked-version algorithms are clever adaptations of the array-based ones (see, for example, Section 4.14 in L. C. Paulson's *ML for the Working Programmer* [7]). We will only study the array-based version in this chapter.

16.2.1 The Contract

In a priority queue, only access to the front item is allowed; but there is no prohibition against traversing a heap as a binary tree. In fact, a *HEAP* can do anything a *BINARY_TREE* can, so we can use inheritance to save ourselves some work. The contract, shown in Listing 16.1, inherits *BINARY_TREE*'s contract (as well as the default, high-level implementations of routines such as *out*), and adds to it the features *insert*, *delete*, and *is_full* (compare it with the contract for *BINARY_SEARCH_TREE* in Listing 15.2).

```
deferred class HEAP[ITEM -> COMPARABLE] inherit
      BINARY_TREE[ITEM];

feature --Adding, removing, and finding items

   insert (new_item: ITEM) is
         --Insert new_item into this heap.
      require
         not_void: new_item /= Void;
         not_full: not is_full;
      deferred
      ensure
         size_after_insert: size = old size + 1;
      end; --insert

   delete is
         --Delete the root item.
      require
         not_empty: not is_empty;
```

Listing 16.1 The contract for heaps.

```
        deferred
        ensure
            size_after_delete: size = old size - 1;
        end; --delete

feature --Sizing

    is_full: BOOLEAN is
            --Is there no room in this heap for another item?
        deferred
        end --is_full

end --class HEAP
```

Listing 16.1 *(continued)*

16.2.2 The Array-Based Implementation

An implementation of heaps must provide two sets of features: those that are general to binary trees (since we have inherited the *BINARY_TREE* contract) and the ones specific to heaps.

Since *BINARY_SEARCH_TREE_ARRAY* is also an array-based implementation of a binary tree, it and *HEAP_ARRAY* have much in common:

- They both use an array (*items*) and an integer identifying the root index (*root_index*).
- They both implement *left* and *right* as features that create tree objects that share *items* with the parent tree.
- They use the same algorithms for copying, comparing, and wiping out trees.

Looks like we need a common ancestor for these two classes! Well, since you have done all that work in the exercises for Chapter 15, I will provide this one. The entire class *BINARY_TREE_ARRAY* is given in Listing 16.2.

Note that although the features *left* and *right* are implemented identically in *HEAP* and *BINARY_SEARCH_TREE_ARRAY*, they cannot be factored out into *BINARY_TREE_ARRAY*. The reason is that they do "!!*Result.make_subtree*," for which *make_subtree* needs to be a creation routine. But *BINARY_TREE_ARRAY* is a deferred class, so it is not allowed creation routines (since it is impossible to create an object of a deferred class).

That is why *left* and *right* must be duplicated in the two fully implemented subclasses. Feature *make_subtree* itself can be shared via the superclass, but the subclasses are the ones that declare that it is a creation routine.

The task of class *HEAP_ARRAY* is to inherit everything from both *HEAP* and *BINARY_TREE_ARRAY*, and add implementations for *insert* and *delete*,

```
deferred class BINARY_TREE_ARRAY[ITEM -> COMPARABLE] inherit
   BINARY_TREE[ITEM];

feature {BINARY_TREE_ARRAY}

   items: ARRAY[ITEM];
   root_index: INTEGER;

feature {BINARY_TREE_ARRAY } --Creation and initialization

   --This is really a creation routine, but it is illegal to declare
   --it as such in a deferred class. Fully implemented subclasses
   --need to declare "creation make_subtree," and implement left
   --and right that use it as a creation routine.
   make_subtree (the_items: like items; the_root_index: like root_index) is
         --Make this tree share the array the_items and start at the_root_index.
      do
         items := the_items;
         root_index := the_root_index;
      end; --make_subtree

feature --Accessing the components

   root_item: ITEM is
         --The item at the root.
      do
         Result := items.item (root_index);
      end; --root_item

   is_empty: BOOLEAN is
         --Is this tree empty?
      do
         Result := root_index > items.count
                   or else items.item (root_index) = Void;
      end; --is_empty

   is_full: BOOLEAN is
         --Cannot predict jumping out of the array,
         --so will have to resize as necessary.
      do
         Result := false;
      end; --is_full

   wipe_out is
         --Make this tree empty.
      local
         void_item: ITEM;
         subtree: like Current;
```

Listing 16.2 Class *BINARY_TREE_ARRAY*, a common ancestor to *BINARY_SEARCH_TREE_ARRAY* and *HEAP_ARRAY*.

```
      do
         subtree := left;
         if not subtree.is_empty then
            subtree.wipe_out;
         end;

         subtree := right;
         if not subtree.is_empty then
            subtree.wipe_out;
         end;

         items.put(void_item, root_index);

      end; --wipe_out

feature --Cloning and comparing

   copy(other: like Current) is
         --Copy other onto this tree.
      do
         if root_index = 1 then

            --Chances are that we were called from clone, which had aliased
            --our items to other.items. Remake that array, just in case.

            !!items.make(1, other.items.count);

         end;

         if not is_empty then
            wipe_out;
         end;

         if not other.is_empty then
            --Track the same item at the root.
            items.put(other.root_item, root_index);

            --Clone other's subtrees.
            left.copy(other.left);
            right.copy(other.right);
         end;
      end; --copy

invariant

   have_array: items /= Void;
   empty_if_no_item: is_empty = (root_item = Void);
   root_index_positive: root_index > 0;

end --class BINARY_TREE_ARRAY
```

Listing 16.2 *(continued)*

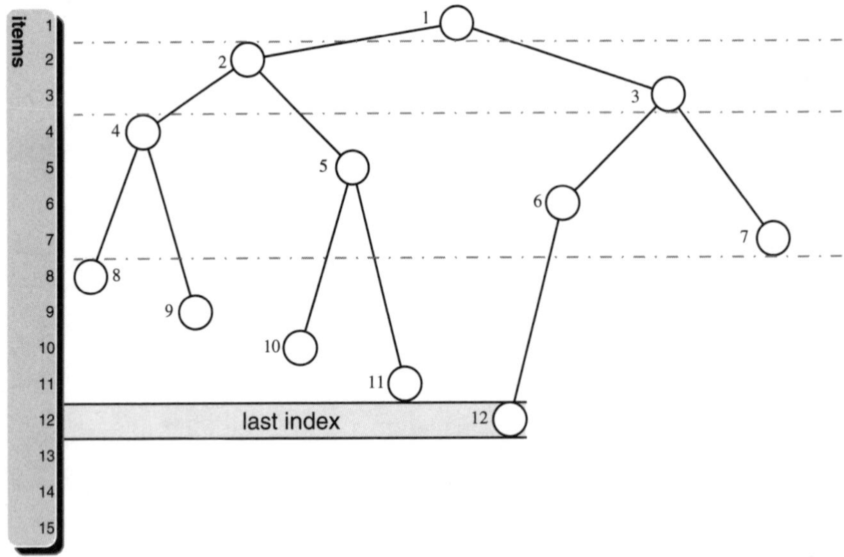

Figure 16.4 The mapping of a 12-item heap onto an internal array.

creation routines *make* and *make_capacity*, and navigation features *left* and *right* (since they cannot go into *BINARY_TREE_ARRAY*, as we have just discussed).

We have set ourselves up to use the same representation as we did in *BINARY_SEARCH_TREE_ARRAY*, but we can actually improve on it in *HEAP_ARRAY*, thanks to the fact that heaps are always complete trees.

For a complete tree, the breadth-first mapping of its nodes onto the array *items* looks like the one in Figure 16.4. The items line up nicely, from position 1 through the position corresponding to the rightmost node in the bottom layer, with no holes. This allows us to keep track of the last array index associated with the heap.

An immediate advantage of this improvement is that we can do a meaningful *is_full* with heaps: The heap is full if the last index of the heap is equal to the size of the array. So we redefine the *is_full* from the implementation that we inherited from *BINARY_TREE_ARRAY* to the more precise one that uses the new private feature *last_index* (Listing 16.3).

Let us now attend to *insert*. We know that after the insertion, the heap will extend to position *last_index*+1, as shown in Figure 16.5 (or it would not be a complete tree anymore).

The trouble is that if we just drop the new item into position *last_index*+1, we may have a complete tree that is not a heap, since the new item could be ">" the item at its parent node. Well, if that happens, we can exchange them. In the example in Figure 16.5, we would compare the items in positions 13 and 6, and exchange them if they are out of order.

```
class HEAP_ARRAY[ITEM -> COMPARABLE] inherit
   HEAP[ITEM]
      redefine
         insert, delete
      end;
   BINARY_TREE_ARRAY[ITEM]
      redefine
         is_full
      end;
creation make, make_capacity, make_subtree
feature {HEAP_ARRAY}
   last_index: INTEGER is
         --Cannot use size, since that has to work for subtrees too.
feature --Sizing
   is_full: BOOLEAN is
         --Is there no room in this heap for another item?
      do
         --Any subheap is full if the main heap is full.
         Result := last_index >= items.count;
      end; --is_full
```

Listing 16.3 The redefinition specifications and features *last_index* and *is_full* of class *HEAP_ARRAY*.

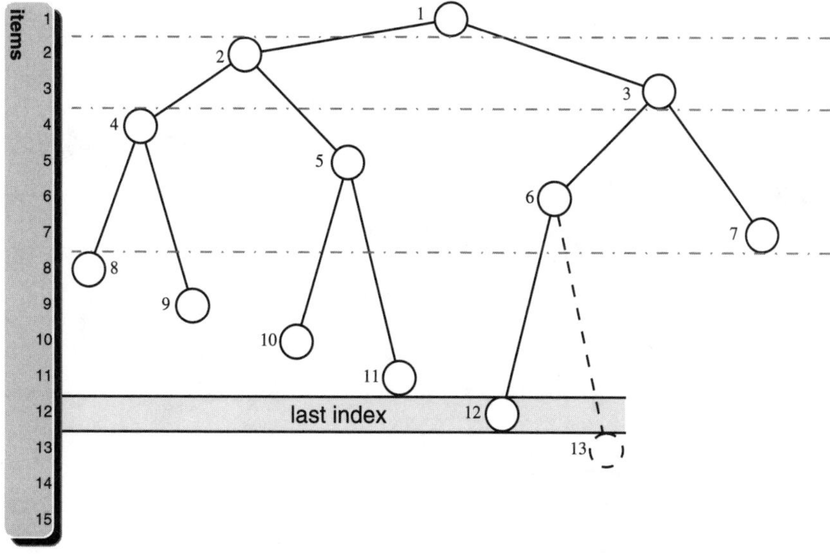

Figure 16.5 If there is an insertion, the shape of the resulting heap will extend to position *last_index*+1.

That would assure that the subtree rooted at index 6 is a heap. Since we had a heap before *insert* started its work, the item that was in position 6 was ">=" its other child (in position 12). If we swap the items in positions 13 and 6, it is because the new item was ">" the item in position 6, so it must also be ">" its former sibling in position 12.

However, if we had to do a swap and put the new item into position 6, we might still not have a heap. What if the new item is ">" the item in position 3? Well, if it is, we swap them. We keep tumbling the new item up until it either comes to rest below a greater or equal parent, or becomes the root of the whole heap. This process is illustrated in Figure 16.6.

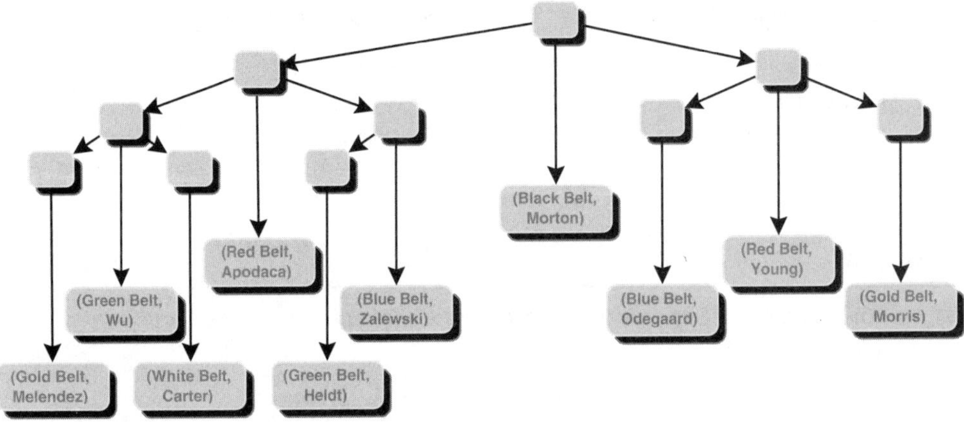

a. Into this heap, (Black Belt, Baker) will be added.

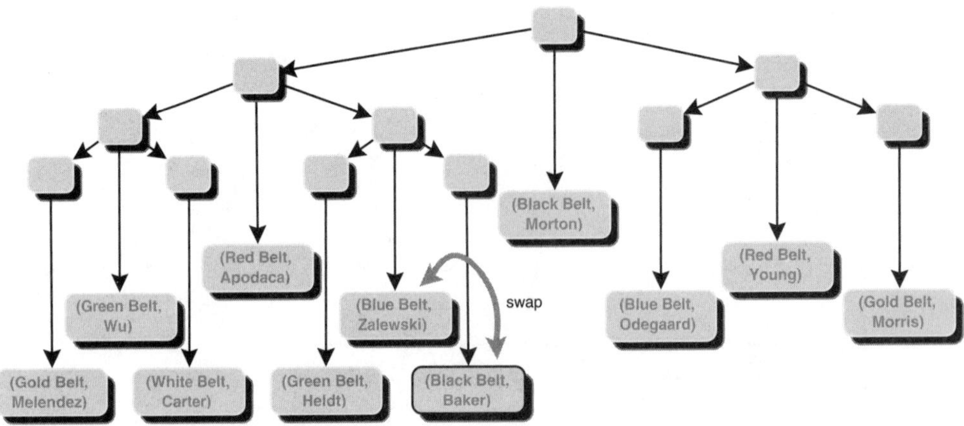

b. Place the new item in the next available complete tree slot. It is ">" its parent's item, so they will have to be exchanged.

Figure 16.6 Inserting a new item into a heap. (The new item is marked with a black border.)

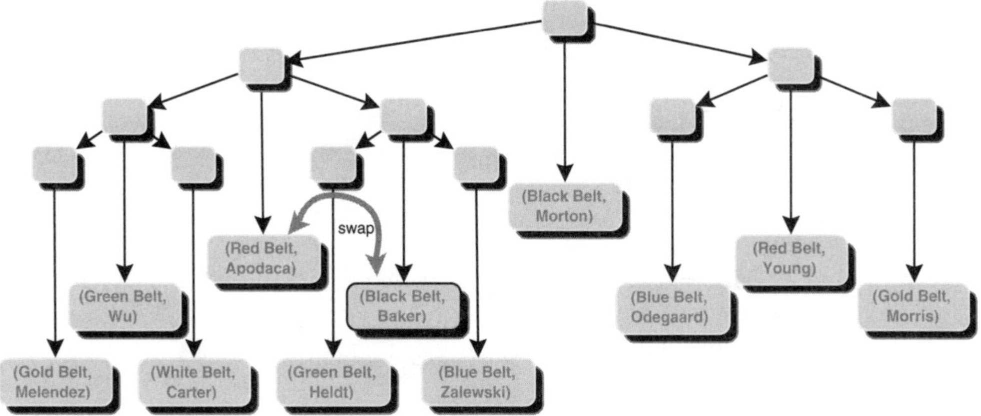

c. It is “>” its new parent’s item, so they will have to be exchanged.

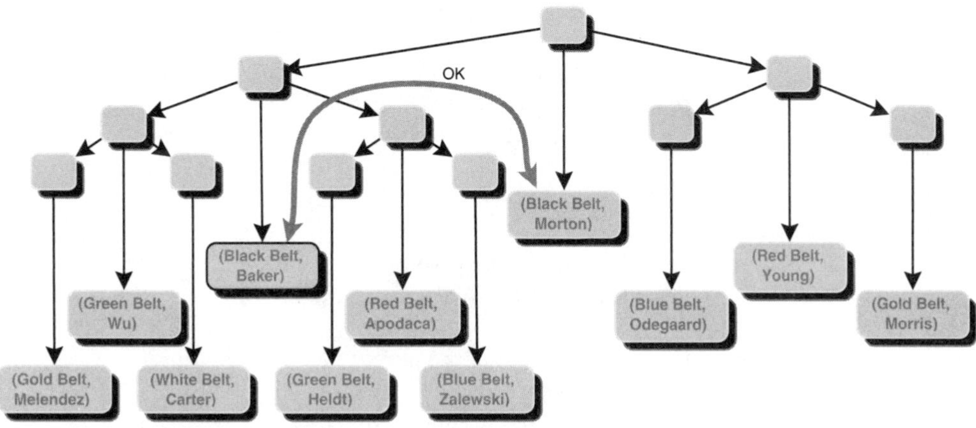

d. It is “<=” its new parent’s item, so we are done.

Figure 16.6 *(continued)*

This tumbling-up progresses from a leaf toward the root, against the arrows. In a linked tree, this would be inefficient, but the array representation makes it just as easy to go up as to go down. If to compute a child’s index we multiply the parent’s index by 2 and then add 1 if it is the right child, then to compute the parent’s index from the child’s index we just divide by 2 and drop the remainder. In other words,

<parent’s index> := <child’s index>//2

An implementation of *insert* that uses this technique is provided in Listing 16.4.

```
insert(new_item: ITEM) is
        --Insert new_item into this heap.
    local
        index: INTEGER;
        parent_index: INTEGER;
        saved_item: ITEM;
    do
        --Start at the end.
        last_index := last_index + 1;
        items.put(new_item, last_index);

        --Move it up until it runs into a greater parent.
        from
            index := last_index;
            parent_index := index // 2;
        invariant
            item_ge_left_child: index*2 <= last_index implies
                                items.item(index) >= items.item(index*2);
            item_ge_right_child: index*2+1 <= last_index implies
                                items.item(index) >= items.item(index*2+1);
        variant
            index
        until
            parent_index < root_index or else
            items.item(index) <= items.item(parent_index)
        loop
            --Swap the item with that of the parent node.
            saved_item := items.item(index);
            items.put(items.item(parent_index), index);
            items.put(saved_item, parent_index);

            index := parent_index;
            parent_index := index // 2;
        end;
    end; --insert
```

Listing 16.4 Routine *insert* of class *HEAP_ARRAY*.

A similar approach is taken with *delete*. The root item is always the one being removed, but it is the last position in the breadth-first traversal that must be vacated. So we simply move the item from the last position to the root (Figure 16.7a).

It could be out of place in its new position, so we compare it with its children. If it is "<" at least one of its children, then it must be swapped. We

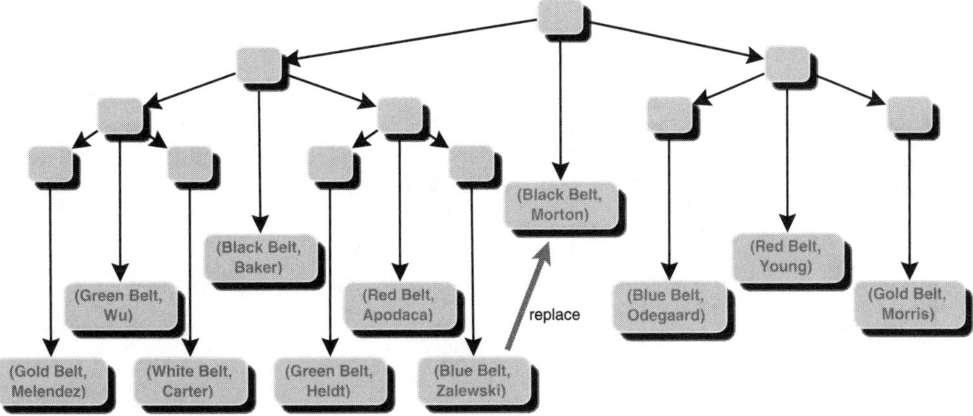

a. The last-indexed item will be moved to the root.

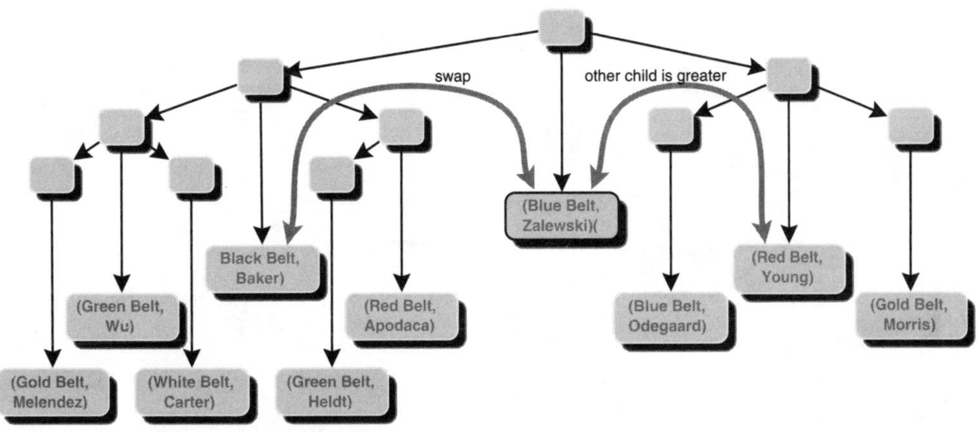

b. It is "<" at least one of its children, so it must be exchanged with the greater child.

Figure 16.7 Deleting the top item from a heap. (The item being moved is marked with a black border.)

swap it with the greater of its children (because if we swapped it with the lesser one, the lesser one would become the parent of the greater one, violating the heap's definition of order), as shown in Figure 16.7b. We keep tumbling it down the heap (Figure 16.7c) until it finds itself ">=" all of its children (Figure 16.7d).

The coding of this routine is left as an exercise.

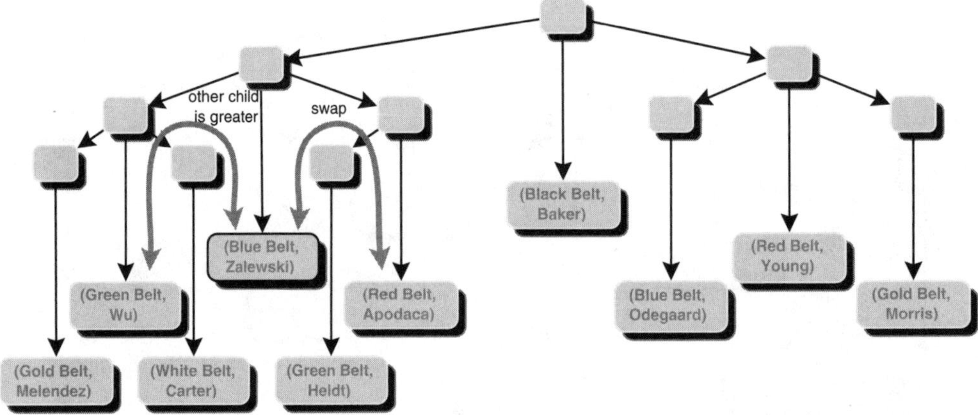

c. It is "<" at least one of its children, so it must be exchanged with the greater child.

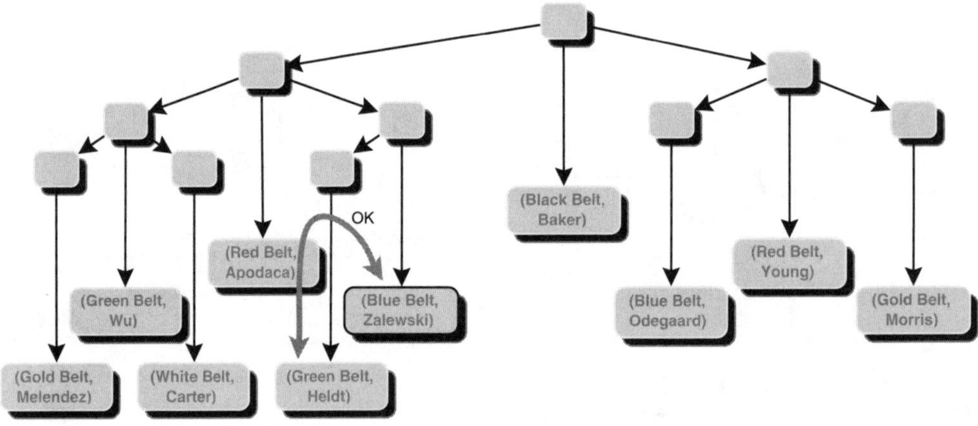

d. It is ">=" all of its children, so we are done.

Figure 16.7 *(continued)*

16.3 Heap Sort

There is a clever sorting algorithm that uses the heap structure to sort the array onto which it is mapped. It works through a variation of the *delete* algorithm.

The idea is simple. Suppose the whole array of length n was overlaid with a heap, as in Figure 16.8a. Position 1 is the root of the heap, so it is tracking the greatest item. In a sorted array, the greatest item belongs in the last position of the array, not the first. No problem. We do a *delete*, thus removing the root item from the heap and making the heap overlay only array positions through $n - 1$.

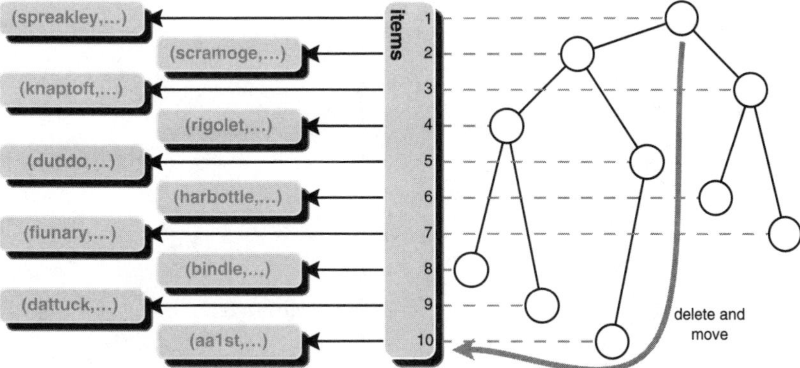

a. Starting with a 10-item heap, *delete* and move the deleted item to the newly vacated position 10.

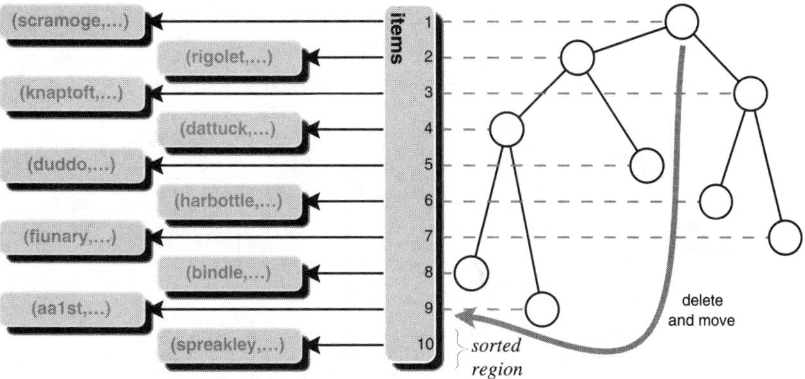

b. Again *delete* and move the deleted item to position 9.

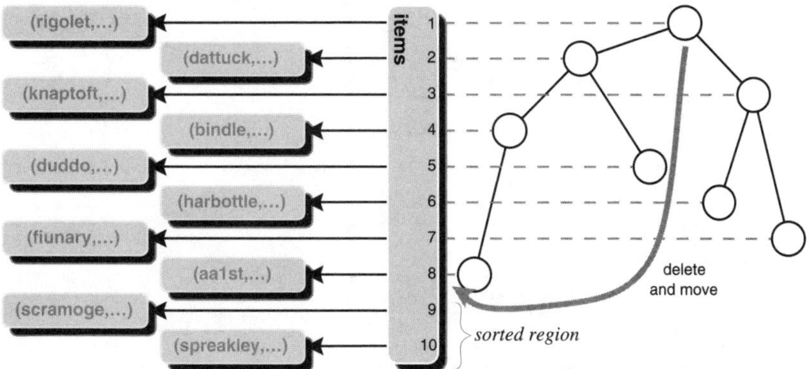

c. Move the next deleted item to position 8.

Figure 16.8 Execution of heap sort on a 10-item array.

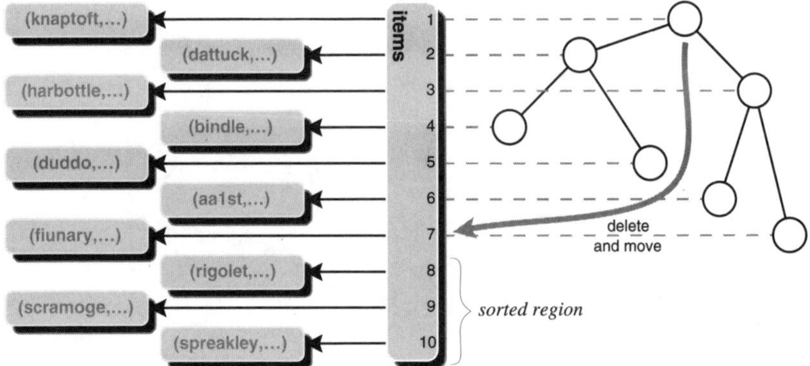

d. . . . to position 7.

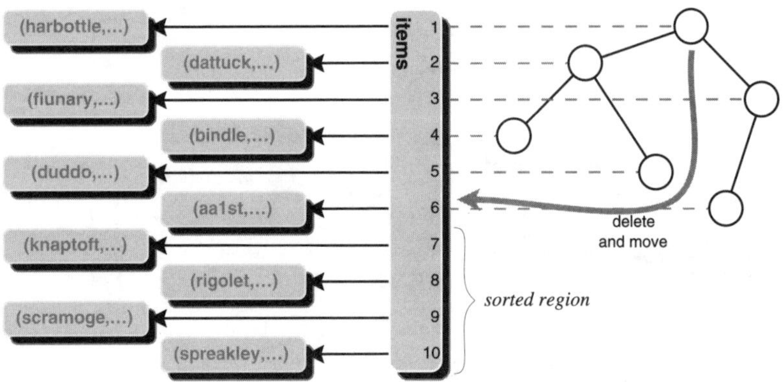

e. . . . to position 6.

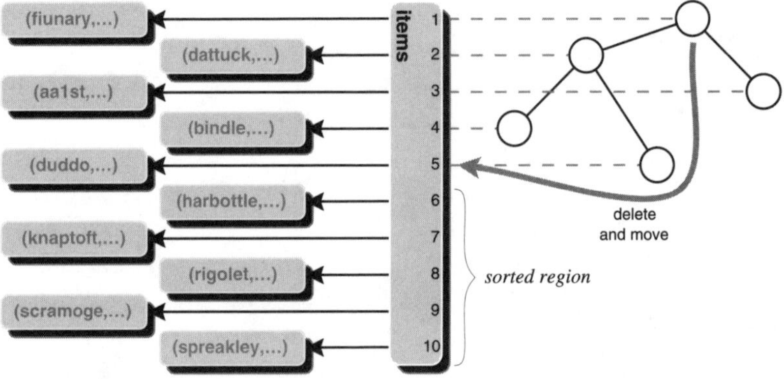

f. . . . to position 5.

Figure 16.8 *(continued)*

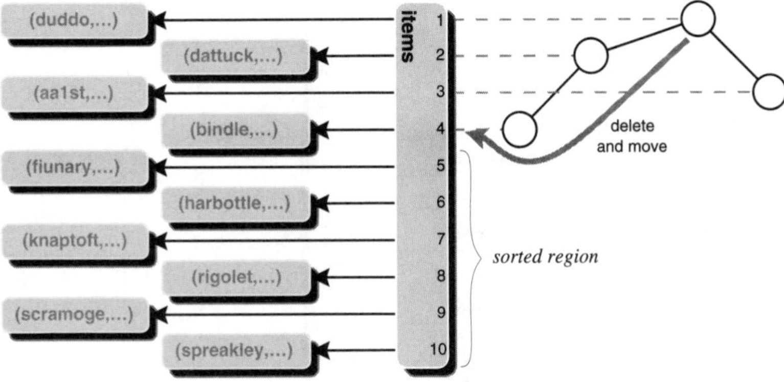

g. . . . to position 4.

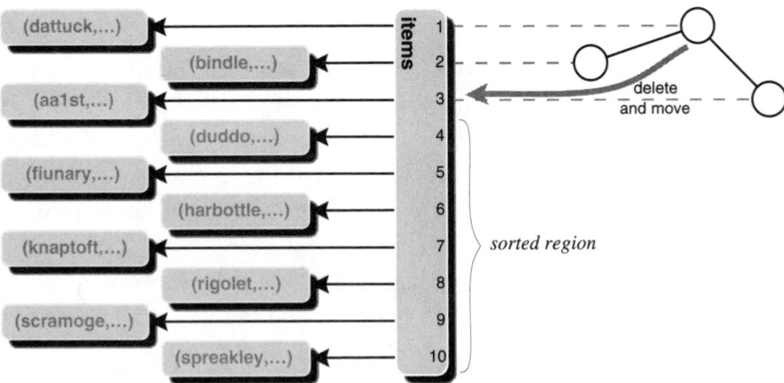

h. . . . to position 3.

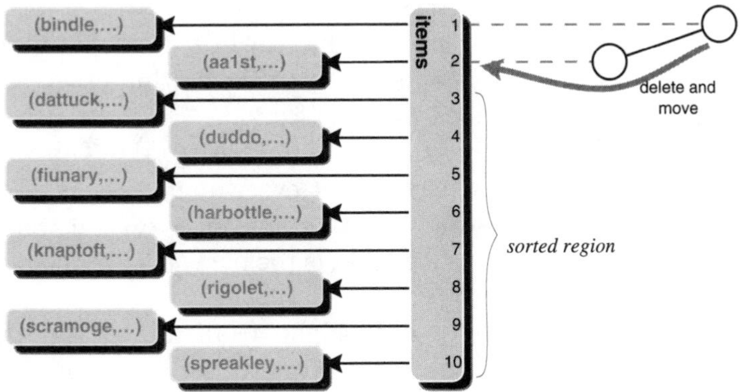

i. . . . to position 2.

Figure 16.8 *(continued)*

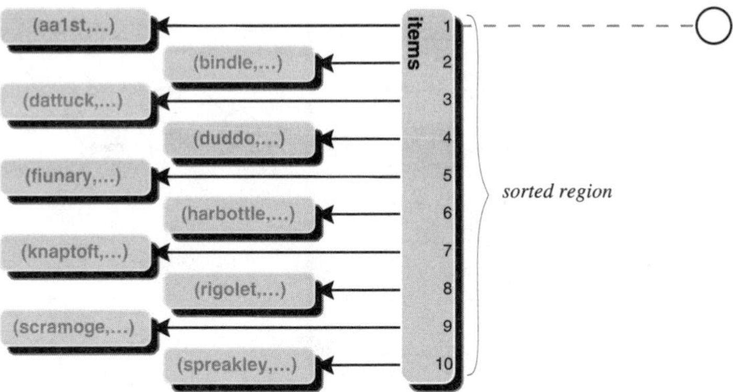

j. The array is fully sorted.

Figure 16.8 *(continued)*

The item that was removed from the heap is placed into the newly vacated position n. That one position is now the sorted region of the array (Figure 16.8b).

Now the second greatest item of the array is at the root of the heap, in position 1. We do another *delete*, moving that item to the newly vacated position $n - 1$. Positions $1, \ldots, n - 2$ are now representing a heap, and positions $n - 1, \ldots, n$ are sorted (Figure 16.8c).

This goes on (Figure 16.8d–i) until the heap shrinks to contain just the smallest item of the array (Figure 16.8j), and the whole array is sorted. Heap sort is thus very similar to selection sort, except in the latter we had to look for the next greatest item linearly, while in heap sort it is propagated to the root at every step.

Let us determine the time complexity of this process. It performs *delete* O(N) times, so the total sorting time will be roughly the sum of the time each *delete* takes. We cannot take for granted that the answer is "N times the complexity of *delete*," because the heap shrinks as the sorting progresses, giving *delete* shorter and shorter trees on which to work.

So, let us count the steps that the algorithm has to take. This time, rather than leaving little square bread crumbs at every step, we will just draw an example tree and mark each node with the number of steps it would take to tumble it up to the proper place (since that is the part of *delete* that varies with the height of the tree).

Figure 16.9a shows a full tree of height 4 (15 items). The *delete* that vacates the last position of the tree (the rightmost position in the bottom level) will take up to log 15 (three) swaps (after the former last item is moved to the root). So we put "log 15" next to that node. The next *delete* will vacate the position just to its left, and will take log 14 (still three) swaps in the worst case, so we mark it with a log 14 (Figure 16.9b).

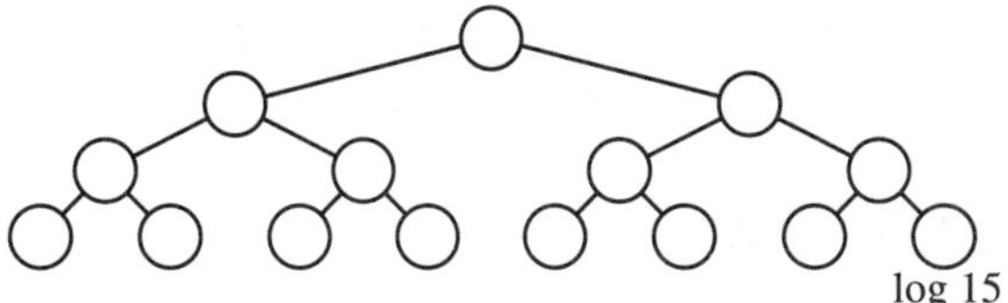

a. With a 15-item heap, *delete* takes log 15 steps.

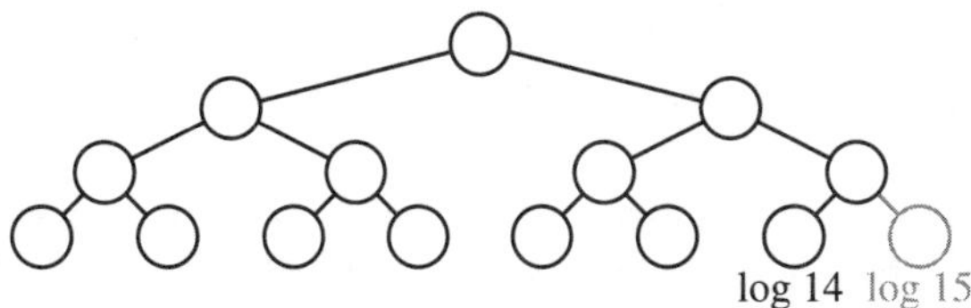

b. Log 14 more for the smaller heap, etc.

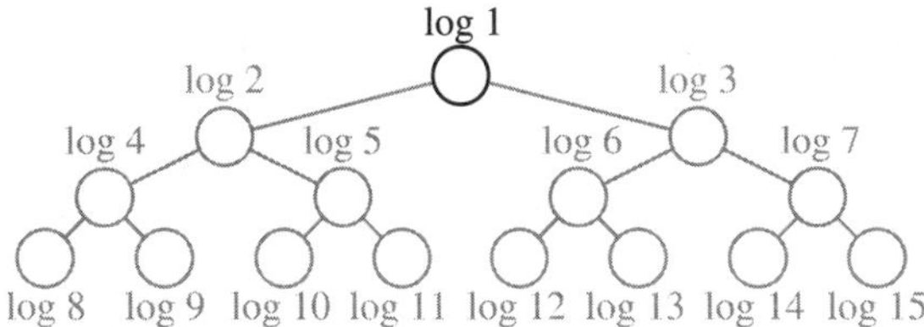

c. At the end, the tally is $\sum_{i=1}^{15} \log i$.

Figure 16.9 Counting the number of swaps performed by the sorting stage of heap sort.

This process continues until there is only one item left, which takes no effort at all ($\log 1 = 0$), resulting in Figure 16.9c.

So, if the heap is of size N, the first deletion will take $\log N$ steps. The remaining heap will be of size $N - 1$, so the next *delete* will take $\log(N - 1)$ steps. The third deletion will take $\log(N - 2)$ and so on, until we get down to the one-item heap, which takes log 1 steps (i.e., zero). So we need to add all of these up:

$$\log N + \log(N - 1) + \cdots + \log 2 + \log 1$$

or, more compactly,

$$\sum_{i=1}^{N} \log i$$

Since the time when we began figuring out algorithm complexities back in Section 6.5, we have used intuitive techniques to count up the steps. Unfortunately, *this* case is one where intuition hits a dead end, and rigorous mathematics is needed to determine that this sum is O(N log N). (For a proof, see Herbert S. Wilf's *Algorithms and Complexity* [12, Eqs. 1.1.1–1.1.7].)

16.3.1 Building the Heap

We are not done with the heap sort algorithm yet. Our discussion started with the words "suppose the whole array was overlaid with a heap." Well, we cannot just tell our users "Make sure you list the objects to sort in breadth-first heap order!", can we? We need a way to convert an array of arbitrarily organized items into a heap.

One way would be to perform the preceding sorting process in reverse: Start with a heap of size 1, then insert the element from position 2 into it, then insert the element from position 3 into it, and so on.

The time complexity of this operation is

$$O(\log 1 + \log 2 + \cdots + \log(N - 1) + \log N)$$

which is the same as it was for the sorting portion of the algorithm: O(N log N). With two consecutive O(N log N) parts, the total time complexity of heap sort is O(N log N).

But there is a faster way to turn the array into a heap. The algorithm is based on the observation that the reason *delete* can work in O(log N) time is that the tumbling-down process starts with a structure that is almost a heap already: Both of its subtrees are heaps, we are just not sure if the new root item is in the right place (such a structure is called a "**semiheap**"). Thus, when we tumble it down to a spot where it is ">=" both of its children, we know that it is ">=" *all* items in both subtrees.

The build-the-heap algorithm works by building little heaps at the bottom of the tree, and then it takes advantage of the fact that two sibling heaps plus their parent form a semiheap. Then it tumbles the parent down to form a larger heap. To make this process systematic, it starts at the last nonleaf node in the breadth-first traversal (i.e., the last position in the array that is not a leaf), and moves backward toward the root of the main heap.

For example, Figure 16.10a shows an unsorted 10-position array and the complete binary tree structure that overlays it. Our task is to turn that binary tree into a heap. The first thing to do is turn the subtree with root at position 5 into a heap. That is achieved by tumbling its root down, just as in *delete*, giving us the tree in Figure 16.10b.

Then we move on to the tree rooted at position 4, and turn it into a heap by tumbling down its root. This gives us the tree in Figure 16.10c. Repeating the process for trees with roots at positions 3–1, we get figures Figure 16.10d–f.

So what makes this algorithm faster than just inserting N items? We are looping $\frac{N}{2}$ times (the number of nonleaves in the tree), and doing a *delete*

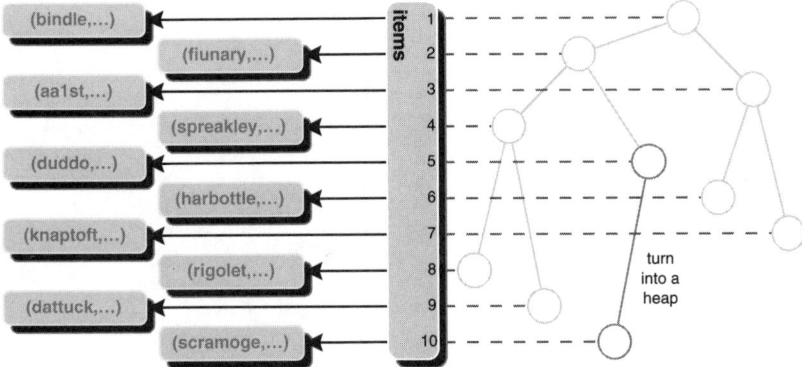

a. Start with the last nonleaf position (position 5).

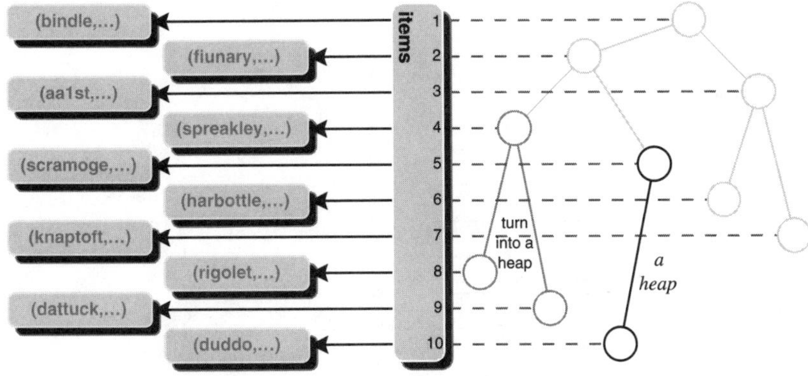

b. Tumble that item down and move on to position 4.

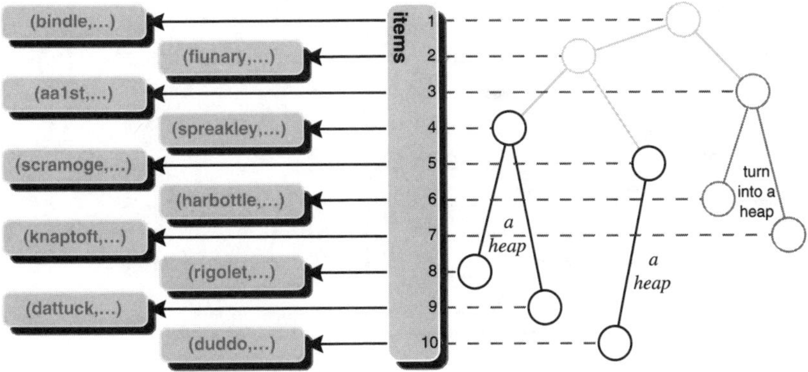

c. Tumble down and move to position 3.

Figure 16.10 Building a heap out of an unsorted tree.

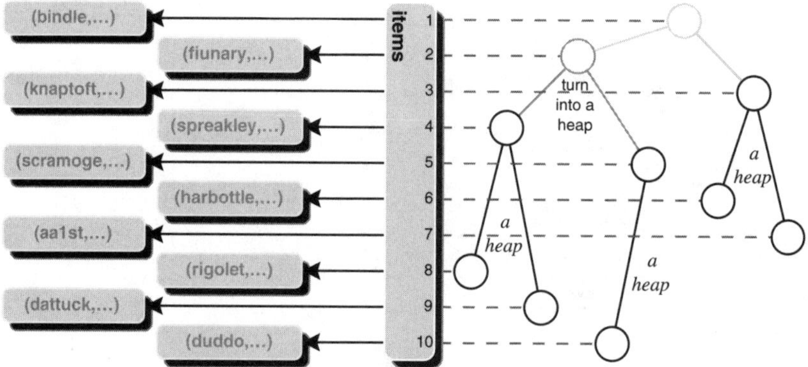

d. Tumble down and move to position 2.

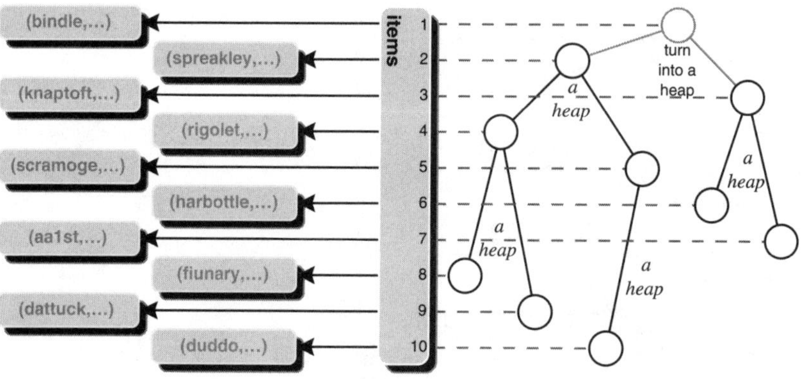

e. Tumble down and move to position 1.

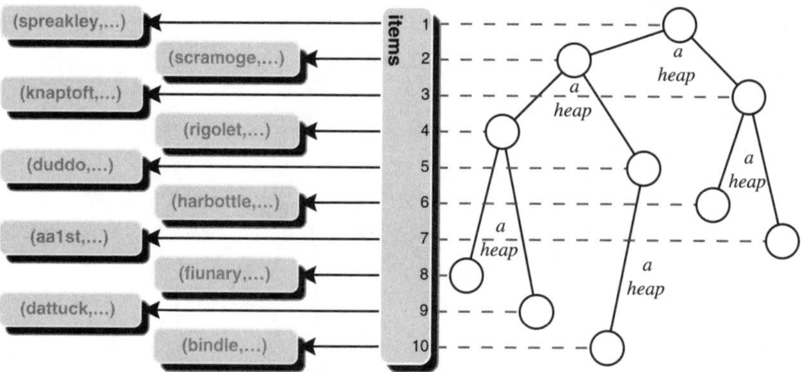

f. Tumble down. The whole tree is now a heap.

Figure 16.10 *(continued)*

equivalent at each step. Doesn't that add up to $O(N \log N)$? Perhaps, but we cannot take that for granted, for the same reason we could not in the analysis of the sorting portion of heap sort: The tree height is not fixed at N.

Figure 16.11a shows the number of swaps needed to build a 15-node heap by starting with an empty heap and inserting 15 items (the top-down approach). The number at each node is the maximum number of swaps needed to insert an item into a heap so that it extends to that position. This illustration is the same as Figure 16.9c, except the "log *i*" have been replaced with their numeric values.

The bottom-up approach gives us a different picture. It takes zero swaps to turn the bottom row (level 4) into eight heaps, because being leaves, all of those nodes are heaps already. Turning the trees rooted in level 3 into heaps takes at most one swap each. Trees with their roots in level 2 will take no more than two swaps to turn into heaps, and tumbling the main root down will take a maximum of three swaps. Comparing the resulting tally diagram (Figure 16.11b) with the one of the top-down technique (Figure 16.11a), it is clear that the bottom-up method takes fewer steps. It may even be possible that it has lower time complexity, so let us look at it closer.

Adding up the numbers in Figure 16.11b (starting at the bottom), we have

$$8 \times 0 + 4 \times 1 + 2 \times 2 + 1 \times 3$$

or

$$2^3 \times 0 + 2^2 \times 1 + 2^1 \times 2 + 2^0 \times 3$$

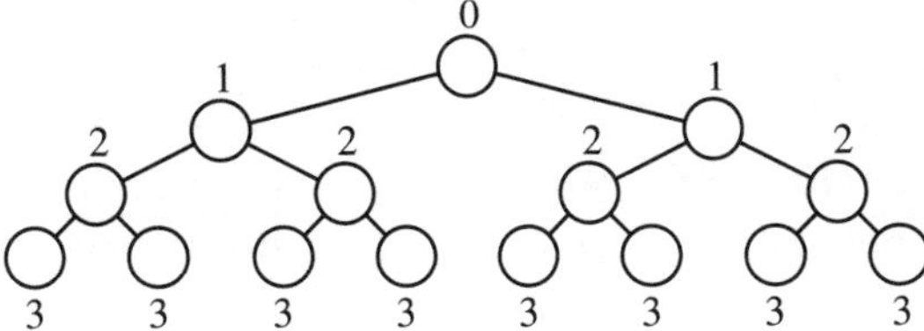

a. top-down

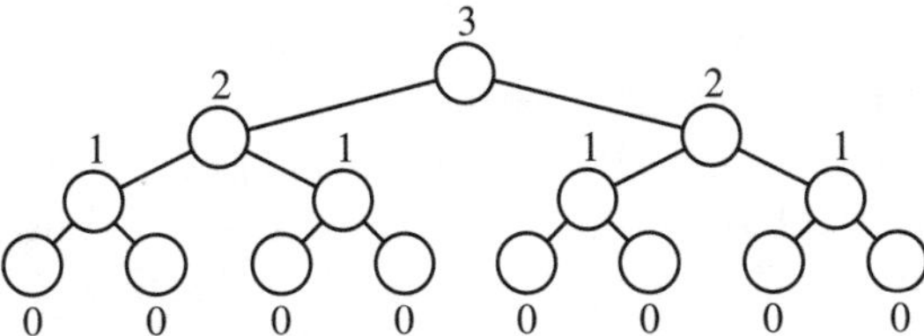

b. bottom-up

Figure 16.11 The number of swaps needed to build a heap top-down (start empty and insert all items) and bottom-up.

So as the exponent of 2 goes down by 1, the number of steps needed to tumble the root down from that level goes up by 1.

How does N fit into the picture? In the example, $N = 15$, or $2^4 - 1$. A full tree of height h always has $2^h - 1$ nodes. So the first factor in our example (2^3) is approximately $\frac{N}{2}$. The second is about $\frac{N}{2^2}$; the third, $\frac{N}{2^3}$ and so on.

So in general, for a full tree of size N, the sum is approximately

$$\frac{N}{2^1} \times 0 + \frac{N}{2^2} \times 1 + \frac{N}{2^3} \times 2 + \cdots + \frac{N}{2^{h-1}} \times (h-2) + \frac{N}{2^h} \times (h-1)$$

where h is the height ($h = \log N$).

If we factor out N, we get

$$N\left(\frac{0}{2^1} + \frac{1}{2^2} + \frac{2}{2^3} + \cdots + \frac{h-2}{2^{h-1}} + \frac{h-1}{2^h}\right) \tag{16.1}$$

So if the sum in parentheses is less than O(log N), then bottom-up heap building has better time complexity than top-down heap building.

Let us take a brief mathematical detour, to establish a fact that turns out to be quite a useful tool for software writers. Not infrequently, one runs into the sum

$$\frac{1}{2} + \frac{1}{2^2} + \frac{1}{2^3} + \frac{1}{2^4} + \cdots$$

To what does that add up? There is an infinite number of terms, but they keep getting smaller and smaller, so the answer may not be "infinity."

Consider an empty glass. Add to it half a glass of water ($\frac{1}{2}$). The result is a glass that is half empty.[1] Add to it a quarter glass ($\frac{1}{2^2}$); now it is only a quarter empty. Add to it an eighth of a glass ($\frac{1}{2^3}$); now there is only one-eighth of a glass left to fill. Add $\frac{1}{2^4}$ of a glass; $\frac{1}{2^4}$ of a glass is left. And so on.

The more of the terms of the sum you add, the closer you will get to a full 1, but you will never get exactly 1, and you will certainly never go over it. So

$$\frac{1}{2} + \frac{1}{2^2} + \frac{1}{2^3} + \frac{1}{2^4} + \cdots < 1 \tag{16.2}$$

(You may recall that we got approximately the same result by counting squares in the linked list version of binary search, Figure 14.2.)

End of detour, back to Eq. (16.1). Can we use Eq. (16.2) to solve it? Well, it starts at $\frac{1}{2^2}$ instead of $\frac{1}{2}$, but it is easy to compensate for that. We can just subtract $\frac{1}{2}$ from the answer (in other words, use a half-size glass). The tricky difference lies in the fact that the numerators in Eq. (16.2) are all 1, while in Eq. (16.1) they keep increasing.

---

[1]No, I am not a pessimist. Just read on.

Let us rewrite the sum in Eq. (16.1) a little, by splitting up the terms to get a sum where every numerator is 1: Replace "$\frac{2}{2^3}$" with "$\frac{1}{2^3} + \frac{1}{2^3}$," "$\frac{3}{2^4}$" with "$\frac{1}{2^4} + \frac{1}{2^4} + \frac{1}{2^4}$," and so on.

$$\frac{1}{2^2} + \frac{1}{2^3} + \frac{1}{2^3} + \frac{1}{2^4} + \frac{1}{2^4} + \frac{1}{2^4} + \cdots$$

[The sum in Eq. (16.1) is finite while this one is infinite, so if this sum has a limit, the one we seek will be bound by it too.] Do you see the sum from Eq. (16.2) lurking in it?

Let us rewrite it two dimensionally, putting the terms with the same power of 2 under each other instead of consecutively:

$$\begin{array}{lllll}\frac{1}{2^2} & + \frac{1}{2^3} & + \frac{1}{2^4} & + \frac{1}{2^5} & + \cdots \\ & + \frac{1}{2^3} & + \frac{1}{2^4} & + \frac{1}{2^5} & + \cdots \\ & & + \frac{1}{2^4} & + \frac{1}{2^5} & + \cdots \\ & & & + \frac{1}{2^5} & + \cdots \\ & & & & \ddots \end{array}$$

Well, well, well. Not only is Eq. (16.2) lurking in this sum, but it appears in every row! The sum of row 1 is $< \frac{1}{2}$ [subtracting $\frac{1}{2}$ from both sides of Eq. (16.2)]; the second row adds up to almost $\frac{1}{2^2}$; the third approaches $\frac{1}{2^3}$; and so on.

If we add up the sums of the rows, we get

$$\frac{1}{2} + \frac{1}{2^2} + \frac{1}{2^3} + \frac{1}{2^4} + \cdots$$

in which Eq. (16.2) does not have to lurk.

So the sum in Eq. (16.1) will be a number between 0 (if the tree is of size 1) and 1 (if the tree is infinite in size). Thus, the time complexity of the bottom-up heap building algorithm is $O(N)$.

16.3.2 Heap Sort vs. Other O(*N* log *N*) Sorts

Heap sort consists of two parts: building the heap and sorting. The time it takes to do a heap sort is the sum of the times it takes to do each part, which is $O(N + N \log N)$, which is $O(N \log N)$.

In Chapter 13, we looked at two other algorithms that can perform with equally low time complexity: merge sort, which is consistently $O(N \log N)$ but has a rather high constant, and quick sort, which tends to be a quicker $O(N \log N)$ but can get as bad as $O(N^2)$.

Heap sort is always O(N log N), so its worst case is much better than quick sort's worst case. In the average case, though, quick sort can be coded to be a little faster.

In the worst case, heap sort is the same as merge sort. On the average, heap sort is still O(N log N), but the constant gets lower. Merge sort keeps the same constant in the average case as in the worst case, so it tends to be slower than heap sort.

Summary

A balanced tree is one where for every node, the difference between the heights of its subtrees is no greater than 1. A complete tree is one whose breadth-first traversal has no holes (thus, a complete tree is balanced). A heap is a complete tree that obeys priority queue ordering: For every subtree, the root item is ">=" the root items of its children. This chapter presented an O(N) algorithm for building a heap, and O(log N) algorithms for building a heap, and inserting and deleting items.

Heap sort overlays a breadth-first heap structure over a list, and works by removing the greatest item from the heap's root (the leftmost item of the list) and exchanging it with the item in the last breadth-first position of the old heap (the rightmost item of the unsorted region). It is similar to selection sort, except the heap is used to select the greatest item. Heap sort's performance is O(N log N), and on the average it tends to perform better than merge sort but not quite as well as quick sort.

Exercises

1. Write feature *delete* for class *HEAP_ARRAY*.
2. Complete class *HEAP_ARRAY*.
3. What is the time complexity of *insert*?
4. Show that the time complexity of *delete* is O(log N).
5. Design and implement priority queues:
   a. Write deferred class *PRIORITY_QUEUE*.
   b. Write class *PRIORITY_QUEUE_HEAP* using *HEAP_ARRAY*.
6. Make *BINARY_SEARCH_TREE_ARRAY* take advantage of *BINARY_TREE_ARRAY*.
7. How well does heap sort perform on a mostly sorted array?
8. Write class *HEAPSORTABLE_LIST_ARRAY*.

17 B-Trees

We saw in Chapter 15 how binary search trees provide O(log N) performance when they are balanced, but we also saw how easy it is to unbalance them. Heaps, on the other hand, were always complete and thus always balanced, but they are not suitable for searching for a specific object. There are several ways to keep search trees balanced, and we examine one of them in this chapter.

17.1 What a *B_TREE* Is and What It Does

The name **b-tree** is short for "balanced tree." It is not a *binary* search tree, but rather a **multiway search tree.** In a binary one, each node has two ordered subtrees and one separator item between them. When we seek an item, we compare it with the separator, and go to the left subtree if the separator is greater, and to the right subtree if the separator is less. For example, if our binary search tree was a dictionary, having a `"mother"` item between the two subtrees told us that all items in the left subtree were "<`"mother"`," and all items in the right subtree were ">=`"mother"`."

A multiway search tree uses a more flexible organization: A node has m subtrees, and there are $m - 1$ separator items between them, as shown in Figure 17.1. The subtree bracketed by items `"mother"` and `"niece"` tracks items that are ">=`"mother"`" and "<`"niece"`." The leftmost subtree tracks items that are "<" the leftmost separator; the rightmost subtree tracks items that are ">=" the rightmost separator. The binary search tree is just a two-way search tree, i.e., a multiway search tree in which $m = 2$.

A b-tree is a multiway tree where the number of trees per node is not fixed, but varies within limits. The maximum number of subtrees a b-tree node is allowed to have is called "the **degree** of the b-tree." While the degree can be

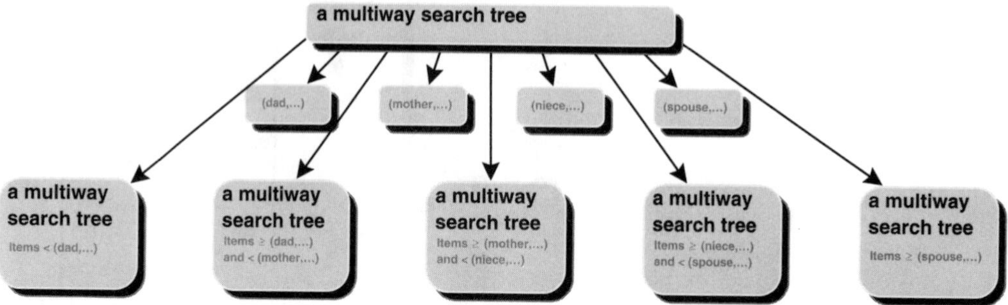

Figure 17.1 A multiway search tree node.

any positive integer, we will only look at odd-degree b-trees. The assumption that the degree is odd will simplify our algorithms and the discussion, and this limitation is easy to accommodate in practice.

The following rules apply for a b-tree of degree m, where m is odd:

1. The maximum number of subtrees is m. Therefore, the maximum number of separator items is $m - 1$.
2. The minimum number of subtrees is $\lceil \frac{m}{2} \rceil$. The minimum number of separator items is thus $\lfloor \frac{m}{2} \rfloor$.[1]
3. The root of the whole b-tree is exempt from rule 2 (otherwise, it would be impossible to start a b-tree from scratch). The roots of the subtrees must follow rule 2 (otherwise, it would be legal to have just one humongous node, which would be no better than using a sorted array).
4. There must be an item between any two adjacent subtrees.
5. For any node that is not a leaf, there must be a subtree to the left of any item, and a subtree to the right of any item. (This implies that all leaves must be at the bottom level of the tree.)

Since only the root is allowed to have fewer than $\lfloor \frac{m}{2} \rfloor$ items, we cannot define leaves as "nodes all of whose subtrees are empty": Only the main tree is allowed to be empty; empty subtrees are forbidden by rule 2. Thus, in a b-tree, a leaf is a node with no subtrees.

Figure 17.2 shows a b-tree of degree 5. All the leaves are at the bottom level, each node has no more than 5 subtrees (4 separator items), and each

[1] Since m is odd, $\frac{m}{2} = \lfloor \frac{m}{2} \rfloor + 0.5$, so $\lceil \frac{m}{2} \rceil - 1 = \lfloor \frac{m}{2} \rfloor$.

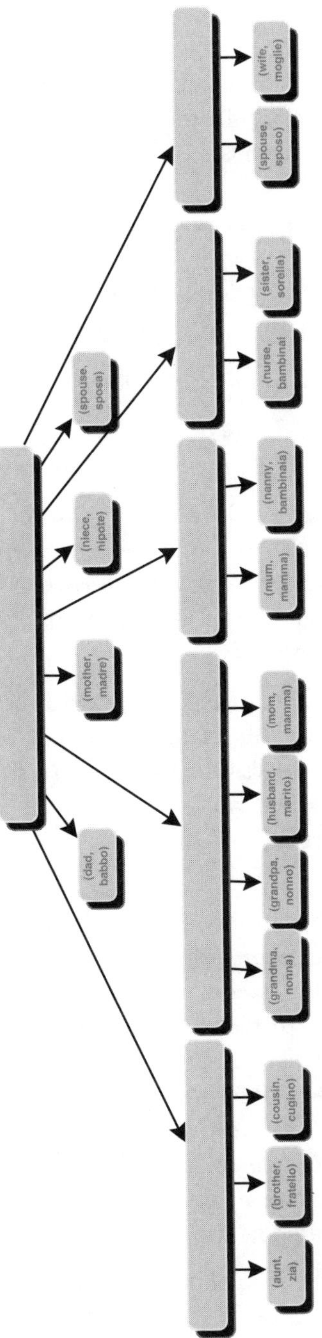

Figure 17.2 A b-tree of degree 5.

nonleaf node except the root has at least 3 subtrees (2 items). Leaves have at least 2 items and no subtrees.

To maintain these rules, b-trees must use insertion and deletion algorithms that are considerably more complicated than those of binary search trees. We will examine them after we state the contract.

17.1.1 Preliminary Contract

Listing 17.1 contains a contract for b-trees. It is an extension of the binary search tree contract (Listing 15.1), with the following differences:

1. Feature *degree* is used to indicate the degree of the tree. It must be an odd positive integer.
2. Feature *make* is told what degree b-tree to make.
3. Feature *root_width* indicates the number of items the root node is tracking. In general, the condition "*degree* // 2 ≤ *root_width* < *degree*" must hold, but for the root of the whole tree, *root_width* can be as low as 0. The preliminary contract avoids specifying this condition; we will get back to it when we consider an implementation.
4. Since only the main tree can have root width below *degree* // 2, only the main tree can be empty. This means that it is impossible to have empty subtrees attached to the leaves. In *BINARY_TREE*, we allowed empty subtrees everywhere, and a leaf was simply a node with two empty subtrees; here, we provide feature *is_leaf* to identify leaves. Subtrees of leaves are not empty, they are void.
5. With binary trees, there was only one root item and only two subtrees. Features *root_item*, *left*, and *right* provided them to the user for external tree traversals. A b-tree has up to *degree* − 1 root items and up to *degree* subtrees, so we need to refer to root items and subtrees by number. Ideally, we would number our subtrees "1, 2, 3, . . . , *degree*" and number the items "1.5, 2.5, 3.5, . . . , *degree* − 0.5," but fractional item numbers are impractical. So instead we adopt the convention that an item's number coincides with the number of the tree to its right (which tracks greater or equal items). Thus, our nodes track subtree 0, then item 1, then subtree 1, then item 2, then subtree 2, etc., as illustrated in Figure 17.3.
6. It is time to give up on the idea of having *out* build a string where the whole tree is displayed in one line. That was already hard to read with binary trees, and it would be hopeless with the shape of the b-tree. Instead, we will have *out* result in such a string that when we print it and turn the page 90 degrees clockwise, we will be able to visualize the tree.

In other words, the result would be

```
        subtree (root_width).out
item (root_width).out
        subtree (root_width−1).out
        .
        .
        .
        subtree (1).out
item (1).out
        subtree (0).out
```

```
deferred class B_TREE[ITEM −> COMPARABLE] inherit
   ANY
      undefine
         copy
      redefine
         is_equal, out
      end;
feature −−Creation and initialization
   make (the_degree: INTEGER) is
         −−Make a new, empty tree of degree the_degree.
      require
         odd_degree: the_degree \\ 2 = 1;
         wide_enough: the_degree > 0;
      deferred
      ensure
         empty: is_empty;
         leaf: is_leaf;
      end; −−make
   wipe_out is
         −−Make this tree empty.
      deferred
      ensure
         empty: is_empty;
      end; −−wipe_out
feature −−Sizing
   degree: INTEGER is
         −−The degree (maximum number of subtrees per node) of this tree.
      deferred
      end; −−degree
```

Listing 17.1 A preliminary contract for b-trees.

```
is_empty: BOOLEAN is
        --Is this tree empty?
    deferred
    end; --is_empty

is_full: BOOLEAN is
        --Is there no room for another item in this tree?
    deferred
    end; --is_full

height: INTEGER is
        --The number of levels in this tree.
    deferred
    end; --height

size: INTEGER is
        --The number of items in this tree.
    deferred
    end; --size

feature --Accessing the components

root_width: INTEGER is
        --The number of items (or number of subtrees - 1) tracked
        --by the root node of this tree.
    deferred
    end; --root_width

item (position: INTEGER): ITEM is
        --The item at position position
        --(between the subtrees at positions position-1 and position).
        --
    require
        in_range: 1 <= position and position <= root_width;
    deferred
    end; --item

subtree (position: INTEGER): like Current is
        --The b-tree at position position
        --(between the items at positions position and position+1).
        --Void if this is a leaf.
        --
        --WARNING: The result may become stale if the parent tree changes.
        --Modifications must not be made directly to the result,
        --except as part of a recursive modification of the parent tree.
```

Listing 17.1 *(continued)*

```
    require
        in_range: 0 <= position and position <= root_width;
    deferred
    end; --subtree

  is_leaf: BOOLEAN is
        --Does this node have no subtrees?
    deferred
    end; --is_leaf

feature --Adding, removing, and finding items

  item_equal_to(equal_item: ITEM): ITEM is
        --An item in this tree for which is_equal(equal_item) is true;
        --Void if no such item exists.
    require
        item_not_void: equal_item /= Void;
    deferred
    end; --item_equal_to

  has(equal_item: ITEM): BOOLEAN is
        --Is there an item in this tree that is_equal(equal_item)?
    require
        item_not_void: equal_item /= Void;
    deferred
    end; --has

  least: ITEM is
        --The least (leftmost) item in the tree.
    deferred
    end; --least

  greatest: ITEM is
        --The greatest (rightmost) item in the tree.
    deferred
    end; --greatest

  insert(new_item: ITEM) is
        --Insert new_item into this tree.
    require
        not_full: not is_full;
        item_not_void: new_item /= Void;
    deferred
    ensure
        size_after_insert: size = old size + 1;
        has_after_insert: has(new_item);
    end; --insert
```

work in progress

Listing 17.1 *(continued)*

work in progress

```
   delete(equal_item: ITEM) is
         --Delete an item equal to equal_item from this tree.
         --Do nothing if there is no such item.
      require
         item_not_void: equal_item /= Void;
      deferred
      ensure
         size_after_delete: (size = old size;
                                    and then not old has(equal_item))
                                 or else
                                 (size = old size - 1
                                    and then old has(equal_item));
      end; --delete

feature --Comparisons and copying

   is_equal(other: like Current): BOOLEAN is
         --Do this tree and other have identical structures and track
         --the same items in the same order at the corresponding nodes?
      deferred
      end; --is_equal

feature --Simple input and output

   out: STRING is
         --Inorder traversal of the tree,
         --indented so that it can be read sideways.
      deferred
      end; --out

invariant

   odd_degree: degree \\ 2 = 1;
   --items.item(1), . . . ,items.item(root_width) are sorted.

end --class B_TREE
```

Listing 17.1 *(continued)*

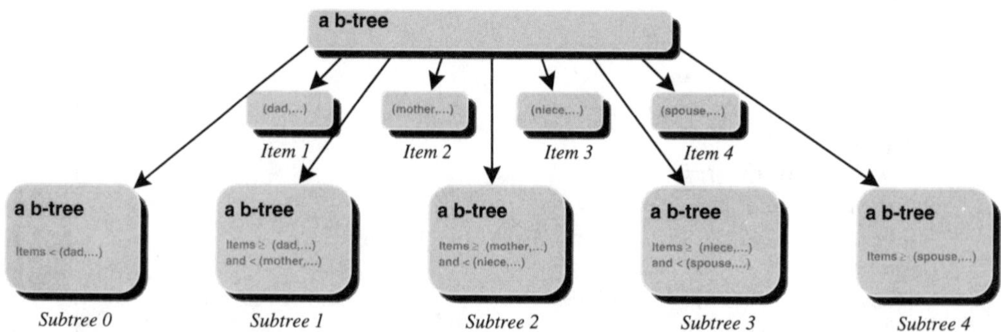

Figure 17.3 The item and subtree numbering convention.

17.2 How a *B_TREE* Does What It Does

We will study a specific implementation of b-trees in Section 17.5. First, though, we must answer a general question: How do we keep a b-tree balanced?

With binary search trees, we simply let *insert* and *delete* modify the shape of the tree as necessary. That did not ensure balanced trees.

With heaps, we worried about the shape of the tree first, keeping it complete, and then swapped items within the tree until they were in the proper order. But the heap organization was that of a priority queue, not a search tree. It *could* be done for a search tree, but with greater difficulty. But this cannot be how a b-tree does it, since a b-tree cannot be shaped as a complete tree: In a complete tree, not all leaves are at the same level (unless it happens to be a full tree).

Well, let us see what needs to be done.

17.2.1 Insertion Algorithm

Suppose we take the tree in Figure 17.4, and ask it to insert (cousin, cugina). The first thing that comes to mind is putting it into the root node, between subtree 0 of the root node and the item (dad,babbo). However, then we would have no subtree between (cousin,cugina) and (dad,babbo), which is illegal in a nonleaf.

So we must go down a level, into subtree 0. Now we are looking at a leaf, so there is no rule against inserting (cousin,cugina) into the proper place within this node. It can go on either side of (cousin,cugino); let us be consistent with the way things worked out with binary search trees, and put the new item to the right of the old one. This gives us the tree in Figure 17.5.

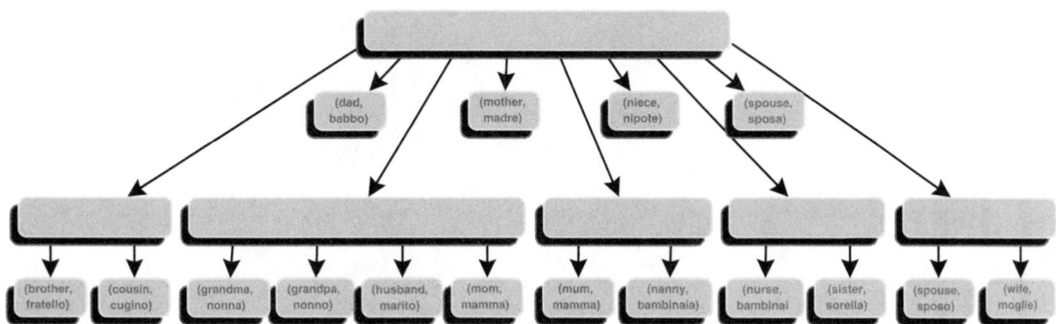

Figure 17.4 A b-tree to illustrate the insertion process.

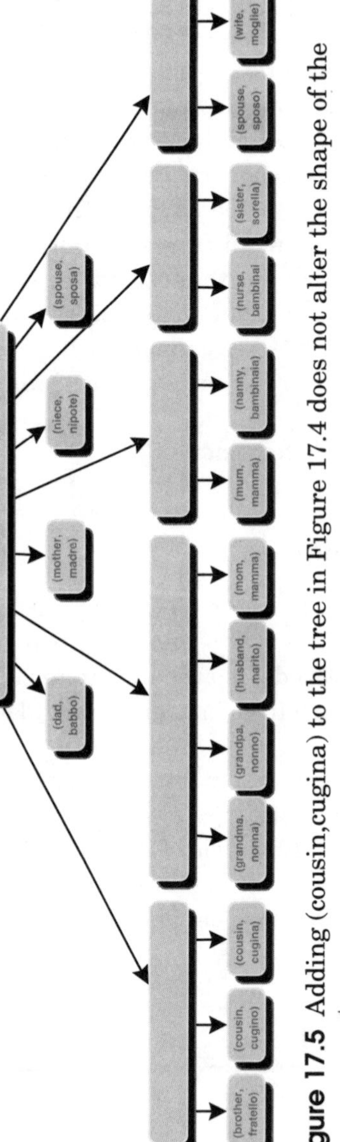

Figure 17.5 Adding (cousin,cugina) to the tree in Figure 17.4 does not alter the shape of the tree.

Observe that rule 5 will cause all new items to be inserted into a leaf. This is almost the way binary search trees behave, except that with BSTs, "inserting at the bottom" meant "inserting into an empty subtree," whereas with b-trees, it means "adding another item to a leaf node."

However, rule 1 prevents us from adding items to a node indefinitely. For example, consider what happens when the tree in Figure 17.5 is told to insert (dad,papà). Its place in the leaf is to the left of (grandma,nonna), as shown in Figure 17.6a. Since we have no choice in the placement of the new item, we go ahead and put it there—but now that node is too wide for a b-tree of degree 5.

Ignoring the rest of the tree for the moment, let us split that node directly down the middle by taking out the middle item. We get two nodes: {(dad, papà), (grandma,nonna)} and {(husband,marito), (mom,mamma)}. The item that was in the middle, (grandpa,nonno), can be used to separate them (Figure 17.6b). So in the parent node, we replace subtree 1 with the two new subtrees and the new separator item, as shown in Figure 17.6c.

Since this procedure adds an item (and a subtree) to the parent node, it is possible that the parent node is now too wide (as it is in our example). If that is the case, we do the same thing with the parent node: Split it into two subtrees, use the former middle item as the separator between them, and replace the original subtree in its parent node with this grouping. If the split node used to be the root of the whole tree, this process creates a new root, as in Figure 17.6d.

This is how we keep all leaves at the bottom level. A tree becomes a level taller by growing a new root at the top, not by growing below the bottom level.

In more detail, the insertion algorithm described earlier is:

```
location := <number of the rightmost item that is <= new_item>

if <this node is a leaf> then
    <inject new_item into location+1>
else
    <insert new_item recursively into subtree number location>
end

from
    node := <this node>
until
    <node is not too wide>
loop
    <split node into two subtrees and a separator item>
    <inject the resulting (subtree,item,subtree) cluster into node's parent>
    node := <node's parent>
end
```

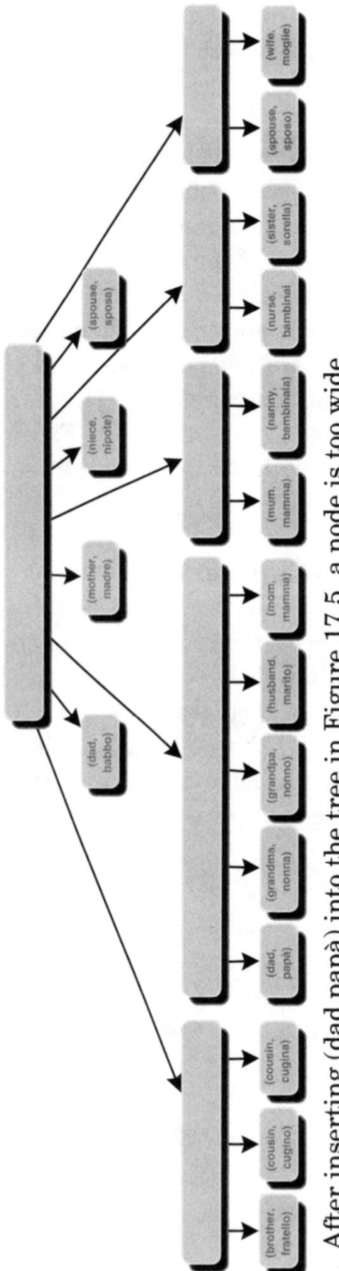

a. After inserting (dad,papà) into the tree in Figure 17.5, a node is too wide.

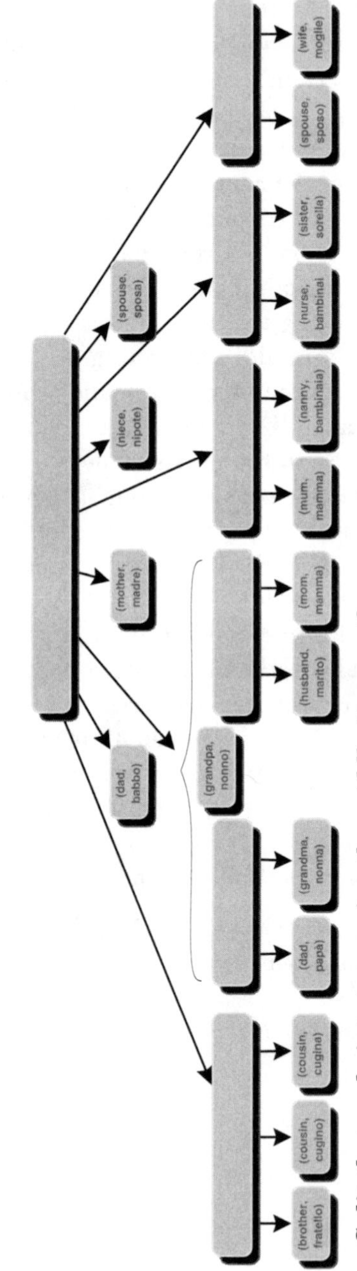

b. Split that node into two, using the middle item as the separator.

Figure 17.6 Dealing with a node that is too wide.

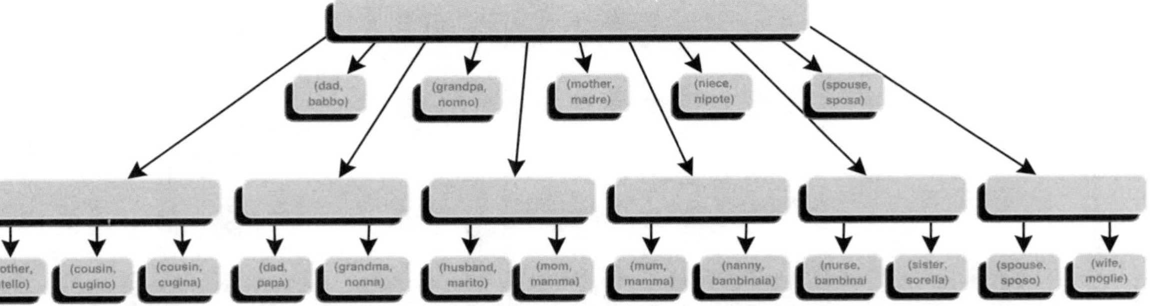

c. Replace the old subtree in the parent node with the new subtrees and their separator item. Now the parent node is too wide.

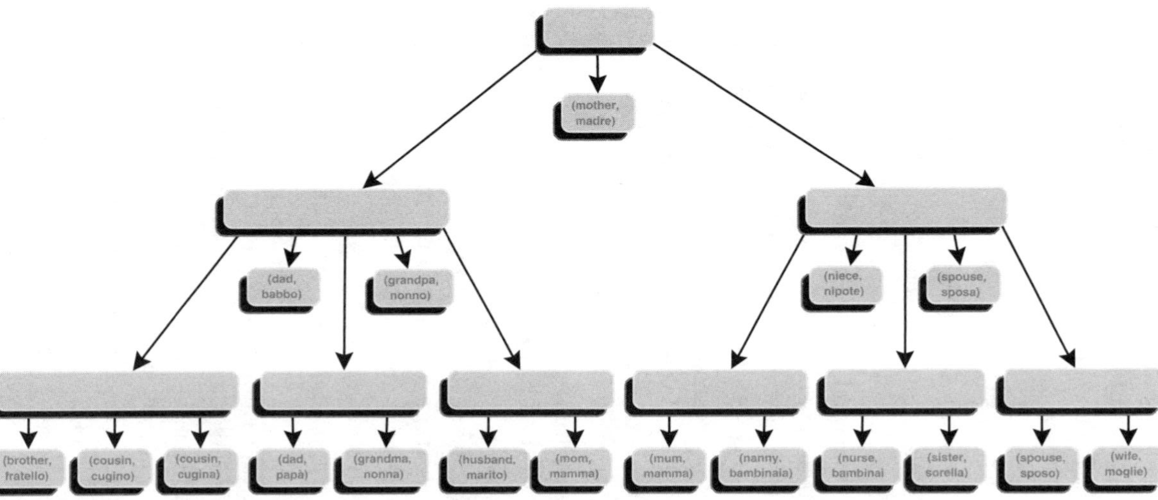

d. Split the parent node too. This creates a new root.

Figure 17.6 *(continued)*

This algorithm is usable as it is, but it is not recursive. In Section 17.5, we will be using a recursive b-tree object structure, so we will study a recursive variation on this algorithm at that time.

17.2.2 Deletion Algorithm

Insertion always started in a leaf. Deletion, of course, does not have that luxury: We delete an item from wherever it happens to be. Suppose we started with the b-tree in Figure 17.7 and told it to delete (dad, . . .). We cannot just drop the item (dad,babbo), because then we would be left with two subtrees with no item to separate them. What do we do when the shape of the tree prevents us from simply omitting an item? Well, we have already seen that situation with binary search trees for the case in which both subtrees are not empty.

We use exactly the same solution now with b-trees: We put the inorder successor (the least node from the subtree to the right of the deleted item) in place of the deleted item, and then recursively delete the newly promoted item from that subtree (as illustrated in Figure 17.8a). In our example, this gives us the tree in Figure 17.8b.

In the process of deleting a nonleaf item, we also demonstrated what can happen when a leaf item is deleted (only leaves may have no leftmost subtree, so the least item of a tree is always the leftmost item in its leftmost leaf). In our example, (grandma,nonna) had to be deleted from subtree 1 of the main tree after it got promoted. That left behind a node with two items in it, which is still wide enough.

Suppose that the tree is now asked to delete (grandpa, . . .). Just dropping that item gives us the tree in Figure 17.9a, which has a node that is too narrow. The first thing that comes to mind is to do the opposite of what we did during insertion: Merge the narrow node with one of its neighbors (and with the separator item between them). Good idea, but it will not work in this case; merging that node with either its left or its right neighbor will create a subtree with 5 items in it—one too many. Well, that's OK, we will be able to use this idea later.

When the narrow node cannot be merged with a neighbor, that neighbor must have $\lceil \frac{m}{2} \rceil$ or more items. Thus, it can lose an item and not become too narrow. So, we widen the narrow node by narrowing its neighbor.

Let us do this in our example with the narrow node and its right neighbor. We cannot just transfer (mother,madre) one node to the left, since that will destroy the sorted inorder traversal. To preserve the traversal ordering, we first transfer the separator, (mom,mamma), to the narrow node. It now needs a subtree on its right. Where do we get one? Well, it is the leftmost subtree of the neighbor, which is where the items that are ">(mom,mamma)" and "<=(mother, madre)" belong. So we move that subtree over the the formerly

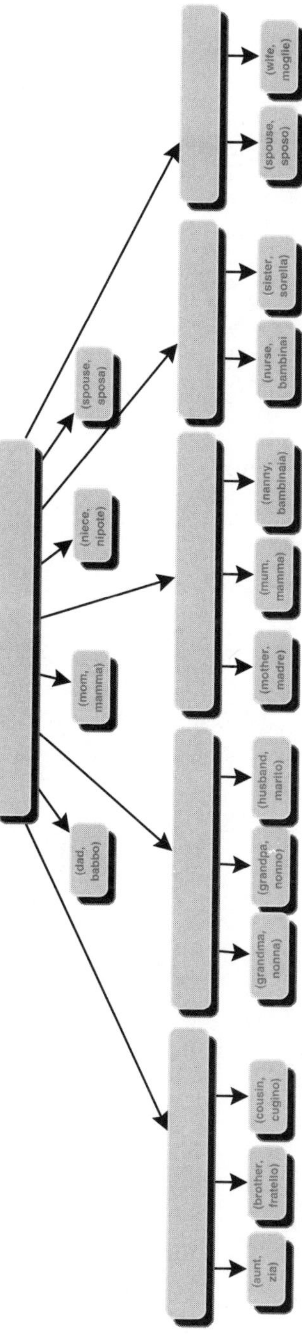

Figure 17.7 A b-tree to illustrate the deletion process.

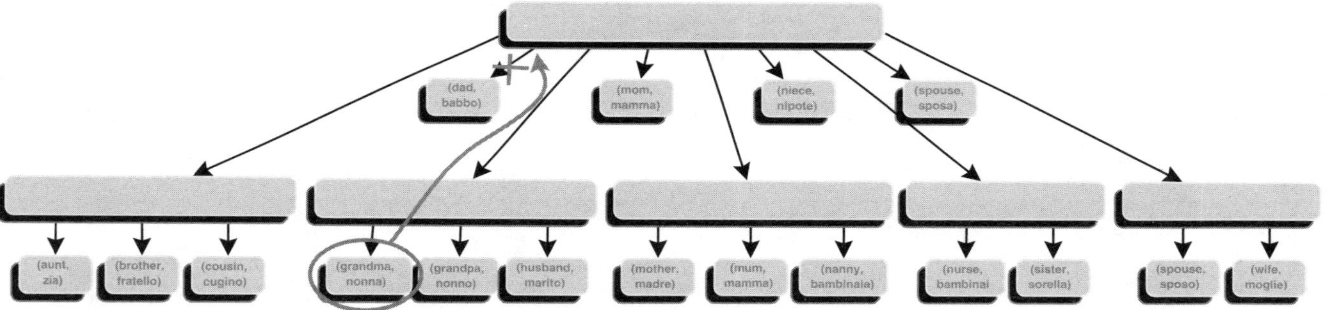

a. Replace the item with its inorder successor.

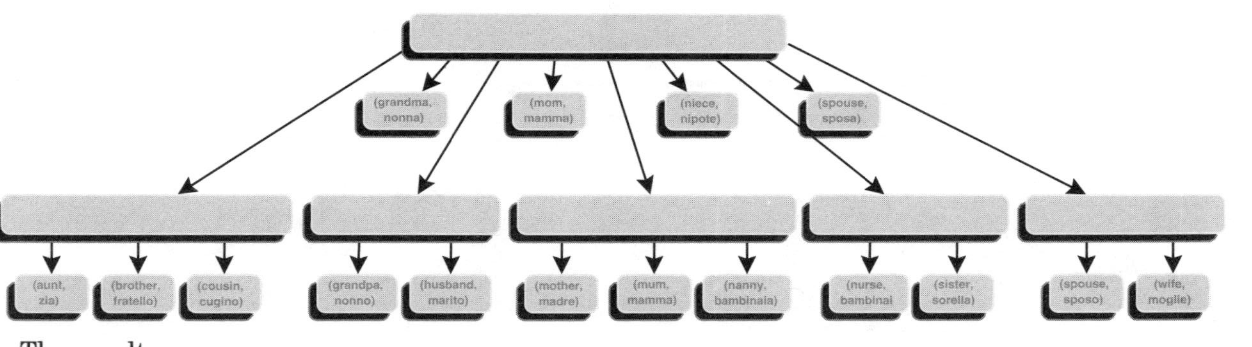

b. The result.

Figure 17.8 Deleting item (dad, . . .) from a nonleaf node.

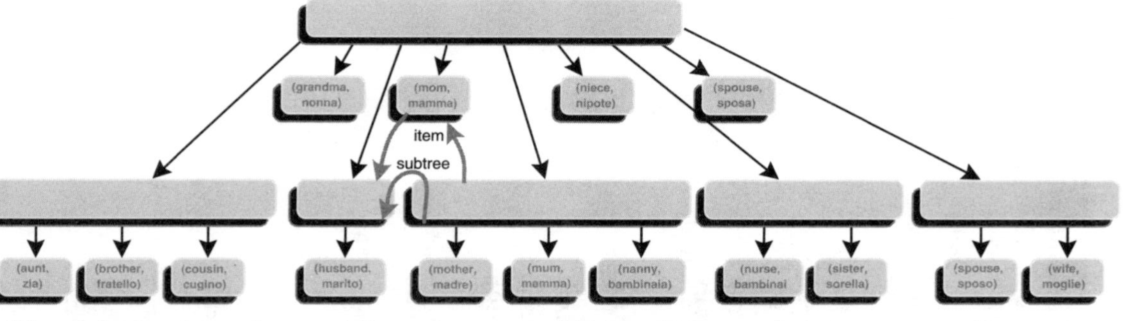

a. After deleting (grandpa, . . .) from the tree in Figure 17.8, a node is too narrow. Rotate in an item from a neighbor.

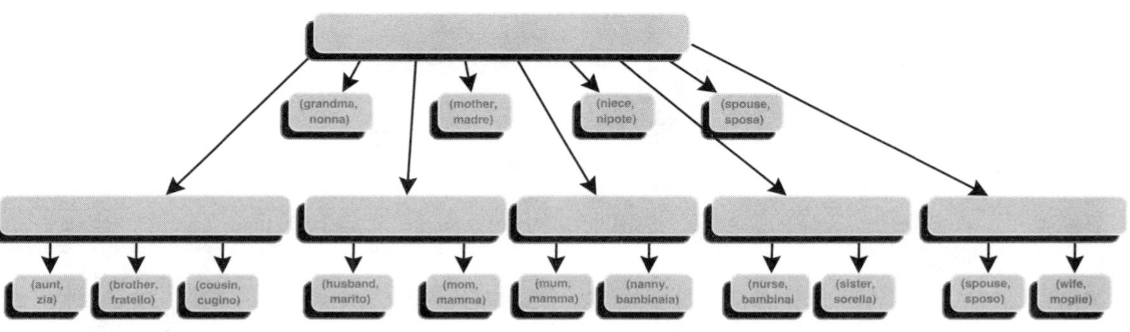

b. The result of the rotation.

Figure 17.9 Using rotation to deal with a node that is too narrow.

narrow mode.[2] Finally, we move (mother,madre) to the parent, where it becomes the new separator item. This operation, summarized in Figure 17.9a, is called a "**rotation,**" and its result is shown in Figure 17.9b.

If we were to delete (nurse, . . .) now, we would not be able to rotate in an item from either neighbor, because they are both at a minimum width already. That, however, implies that we are able to merge the narrow node with either neighbor: the resulting number of items will be $\lfloor \frac{m}{2} \rfloor - 1$ from the narrow node plus $\lfloor \frac{m}{2} \rfloor$ from the neighbor plus 1 for the separator, which adds up to $m - 1$ since m is odd. So performing this merge, as illustrated in Figure 17.10a, gives us the tree in Figure 17.10b.

A merge makes the parent node narrower. If it is not a root, it may become too narrow. If it does, then we do the same thing with this node: either rotate in an item from a neighbor, or merge it with a neighbor.

The described algorithm can be summarized roughly as follows:

```
location := <number of the rightmost item that is <= equal_item>

if item (location).is_equal (equal_item) then
   if <the node is a leaf> then
      <drop item (location)>
      from
         node := <this node>
      until
         <node is the main root> or <node is not too narrow>
      loop
         if <an item can be rotated from one of node's neighbors> then
            <do the rotation>
         else
            <merge node with one of its neighbors>
         end
         node := <node's parent>
      end
   else
      <make subtree (location).least the new separator>
      <delete the new separator from subtree(location)>
   end
else
   <delete equal_item from subtree (location)>
end
```

[2]Unfortunately, in our example there is no subtree there because we are working with leaves, so it is easy to miss the need to transfer the subtree that would have been to the left of (mother,madre) if it wasn't in a leaf.

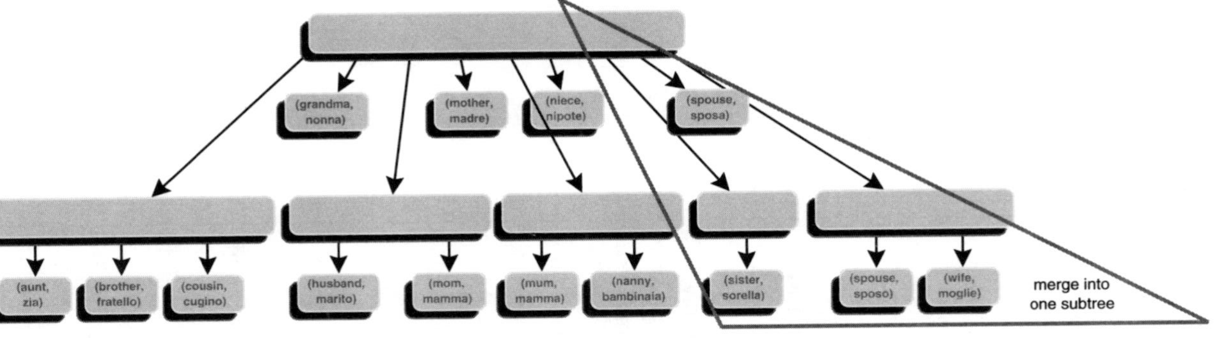

a. After deleting (nurse, . . .) from the tree in Figure 17.9b, a node is too narrow. Merge it with a neighbor.

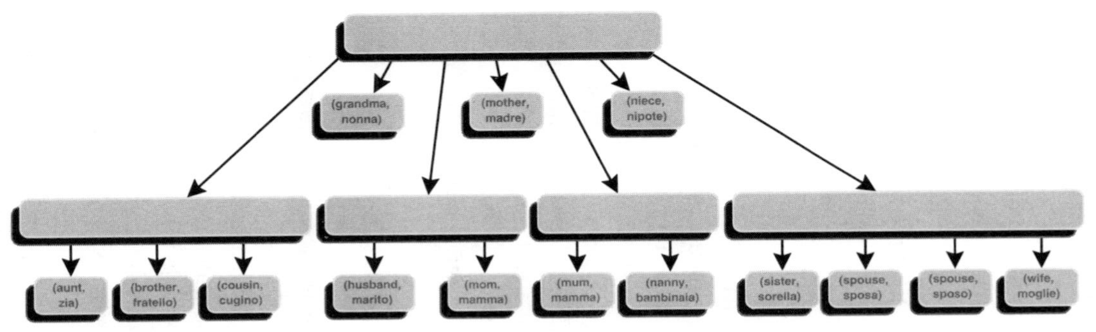

b. The result of the merge.

Figure 17.10 Merging nodes to deal with a node that is too narrow.

17.2.3 An Improvement to the Insertion Algorithm

In the insertion algorithm in Section 17.2.1, we did not utilize rotation, because it was never necessary. A node that is too wide can always be split, regardless of the width of its neighbors. However, now that we have discovered the rotation technique, we should note that it can help insertion too: Instead of always splitting the node, we can first try to rotate an item to a neighbor. This will delay the time when another level must be added, slightly improving future search performance.

17.3 Revised Contract

In the contract in Listing 17.1, we promised that after an *insert*, the tree size will increase by 1, and after a *delete*, the tree size will decrease by 1 (unless no equal item is found in the tree). That is true for the main tree. However, our subtrees are of class *B_TREE* too, and this promise is too restrictive for them. Items and subsubtrees move from subtree to subtree during rotations; subtrees are split and merged—there is no good assertion to make about the change in size of any given subtree.

The same problem occurs with postcondition *has_after_insert*. The new item will be *somewhere* in the main tree, but it may not be in the specific subtree, due to a split or a rotation.

Thus, we drop postconditions *has_after_insert*, *size_after_insert*, and *size_after_delete* from the contract.

17.4 General B-Tree Routines

When we were writing binary search trees, we first wrote the linked implementation, then the array version, and then we identified common elements and factored them out into the ancestor classes. Having done that with BSTs, we can recognize routines that can be implemented in class *B_TREE* and shared through inheritance by the fully implemented subclasses. These are the routines that navigate the tree using the features *subtree* (<number>), *item* (<number>), and *is_leaf* instead of utilizing the representation details.

For example, the size of the tree can be computed that way, and feature *size* in Listing 17.2 does just that. The same thing can be done with *height*, which is left as an exercise.

Note that *size* for b-trees is analogous to *size* for binary trees: Recursively compute the sizes for all the subtrees, and sum them with the number of items at the root. Likewise, features *least* and *greatest* are analogous to their counterparts in *BINARY_SEARCH_TREE*. Find the leftmost (for *least*) or rightmost (for *greatest*) item in the tree. Listing 17.3 shows the implementation of *least*.

```
size: INTEGER is
        --The number of items in this tree.
    local
        index: INTEGER;
    do
        Result := root_width;
        if not is_leaf then
            from
                index := 0
            variant
                root_width - index
            until
                index > root_width
            loop
                Result := Result + subtree(index).size;
                index := index + 1;
            end;
        end;
    end; --size
```

Listing 17.2 Feature *size* can be implemented in the deferred class *B_TREE* this way.

Similar analogies exist with *has*, *copy*, and *is_equal*, all of which can be done generically in *B_TREE* (all are left as exercises for you).

The deferred binary tree classes also provided default implementations for *out* and *item_equal_to*. *B_TREE* can do the same. Let us look at *out* first.

```
least: ITEM is
        --The least (leftmost) item in the tree.
    do
        if is_empty then
            --Leave Result void.
        elseif is_leaf then
            Result := item(1);
        else
            Result := subtree(0).least;
        end;
    end; --least
```

Listing 17.3 Feature *least* of deferred class *B_TREE*.

We promised in the contract to print out the tree so that when the sheet is turned 90 degrees clockwise, the tree structure is visible. That means that the upper level items need to be closer to the left edge of the sheet, and the rightmost item will be closest to the top. In other words, *out* needs to build a string that represents the right-to-left inorder traversal, with each level indented further from the left edge.

The reverse inorder traversal is done recursively easily enough, but to handle the indentation we need to pass a parameter to *out* that tells it at what level that particular subtree starts. We are not allowed to add a parameter to *out* (its contract is inherited from *ANY* and is not under our control), so we create a private feature (visible only to objects of class *B_TREE* and its subclasses) to do the recursion. It and *out* are given in Listing 17.4. Feature *out* starts the recursion by invoking *out_indented* and passing it an empty string of

```
feature --Simple input and output

   out: STRING is
         --Inorder traversal of the tree, indented so that it can be read sideways.
      do
         Result := out_indented("");
      end; --out

feature {B_TREE} --Simple input and output

   out_indented(indent_string: STRING): STRING is
         --Indented string representation.
         --indent_string is the right number of spaces to indent at this level.
      local
         index: INTEGER;
         next_indent_string: STRING;
      do
         next_indent_string := clone(indent_string);
         next_indent_string.append_string("     ");

         --Build right-to-left, so that the page can be turned
         --90 degrees clockwise and read left-to-right.
         from
            index := root_width;
            Result := clone("");
         variant
            index - 1
         until
            index = 0
         loop
```

Listing 17.4 *B_TREE*'s *out* uses a supplementary recursive routine to handle indentation.

```
        Result.append_string(indent_string);
        if not is_leaf then
            Result.append_string(subtree(index).out_indented(next_indent_string));
        end;
        Result.append_string(indent_string);
        Result.append_string(item(index).out);
        Result.append_string("%N");
        index := index - 1;
    end;
    if not is_leaf then
        Result.append_string(indent_string);
        Result.append_string(subtree(0).out_indented(next_indent_string));
    end;
end; --out_indented
```

Listing 17.4 *(continued)*

blanks. When *out_indented* tells a subtree to recursively execute *out_indented*, it passes it a longer string of blanks. The string of blanks is appended at the beginning of each line (i.e., after a `"%N"`) and then the item's *out* is appended.

17.4.1 Searching the B-Tree

To find an item in a b-tree, we first look for it in the root node. If it is there, we are done; if not, we find the subtree in which it belongs and tell it to find the item.

If the item we seek (by trying to match it with the parameter *equal_item*) is not in the root node, we do not have to search the node again for the subtree. How do we find the right subtree? Since the items in the node are sorted, we can establish that the item is not tracked by the node but is tracked by *subtree*(*n*) when we find a consecutive pair of items (*item*(*n*) and *item*(*n* + 1)) such that

$$item(n) < equal\_item < item(n+1)$$

So a private feature that finds the location of the rightmost item that is "<*equal_item*" would do.

How do we find an item that *is* tracked by the root node? We look for the item *item*(*n*) such that *item*(*n*).*is_equal*(*equal_item*). So a private feature that finds the location of the rightmost item that "*is_equal*(*equal_item*)" would do.

We can save some searching time (and programming time) by combining these into a private feature that returns the location of the rightmost item that is "<=*equal_item*." Either the item is at that location (if it is equal to *equal_item*), or it is in the subtree at that location (since that is the subtree to the right of the item at that location). Such a feature, called "*location_for*", is shown in Listing 17.5.

```
feature {B_TREE} --Adding, removing, and finding items

  location_for(equal_item: ITEM): INTEGER is
        --The index of the rightmost item that is <= equal_item,
        --or 0 if equal_item < item(1).
     do
        from
           Result := root_width;
        invariant
           Result < root_width implies equal_item <= item(Result+1)
        variant
           Result - 1
        until
           Result < 1 or else item(Result) <= equal_item
        loop
           Result := Result - 1;
        end;
     end; --location_for
```

Listing 17.5 Private feature *location_for*, used by *item_equal_to*, *insert*, and *delete*.

```
feature --Adding, removing, and finding items

  item_equal_to(equal_item: ITEM): ITEM is
        --An item in this tree that is_equal(equal_item);
        --Void if no such item exists.
     require
        item_not_void: equal_item /= Void;
     local
        location: INTEGER;
     do
        location := location_for(equal_item);

        if location > 0 and then equal_item.is_equal(item(location)) then

           Result := item(location);

        elseif not is_leaf then

           Result := subtree(location).item_equal_to(equal_item);

        end; --else leave Result void

     end; --item_equal_to
```

Listing 17.6 Feature *item_equal_to* of class *B_TREE*.

Feature *item_equal_to*, shown in Listing 17.6, does the recursive search, using *location_for* to search the individual nodes.

17.5 Linked B-Trees

Now we are ready to consider a specific implementation of b-trees. We will use a recursive linked representation in this section, and briefly discuss a very useful variation of the array-based representation in Section 17.6.

We use two private arrays to keep track of items and subtrees:

- *items*: *ARRAY*[*ITEM*], index range from 1 to *degree*+1, and
- *subtrees*: *ARRAY*[**like** *Current*], index range from 0 to *degree*+1.

The extra position is needed for the insertion algorithm, in which a node may temporarily become too wide.

17.5.1 Insertion Features

Let us consider feature *insert* first. We discussed an insertion algorithm in Section 17.2.1, but it is not directly implementable with this representation, because the recursion it uses flows from the leaf toward the root, whereas our representation is set up for recursion from the root down to the leaves.

Instead of the child node doing its insert and then, if necessary, splitting and recursively telling the parent to insert the new separator, the parent node is the one playing the major role. The parent's script is:

1. Tell the child to insert the new item.
2. Ask the child if the insertion made it too wide, and if so,
    a. Tell the child to split into two subtrees and a separator.
    b. Insert the separator and the new subtree into myself.

After this operation, the parent node may have become too wide. If it is not the root of the whole tree, then there is no problem, since its own parent is waiting in the middle of the same script, and will see to this subtree's splitting. However, if it *is* the root, then it needs to be transformed into a smaller root with two subtrees.

Listing 17.7 contains the feature *insert* for class *B_TREE_LINKED*. It invokes a number of supporting features in both itself and one of its subtrees; we will discuss all of them shortly. For now, treat the features that we have not yet defined as pseudocode.

```
insert (new_item: ITEM) is
        --Insert new_item into this node.
    local
        location: INTEGER;
        void_subtree: like Current;
        new_left: like Current;
    do
        location := location_for (new_item);
        if is_leaf then
            insert_at (location+1, new_item,
                       location+1, void_subtree);
        else
            subtrees.item (location).insert (new_item);
            adjust_after_insertion (location);
        end;
        if is_main_root and then is_too_wide then
            --Split into two nodes.
            split;
            --Current will have to become the new root, so copy it to a new node.
            !!new_left.make_node_copy (Current, 0, root_width);
            wipe_out;
            subtrees.put (new_left, 0);
            items.put (spawned_separator, 1);
            subtrees.put (spawned_subtree, 1);
            root_width := 1;
        end;
    end; --insert
```

Listing 17.7 Feature *insert* of class *B_TREE_LINKED*.

Let us study the details of Listing 17.7. First, *location_for* is called to find the place where we want the new item to be. Recall that *location_for* will return either the index of an equal item in *items*, or the destination for the new item in *subtrees* if there is no equal item in this node. For the purposes of insertion, it does not matter if there is an equal item in this node or not:

- If this is a leaf, then the new item belongs in this node, just to the right of where *location_for* stopped its loop (it does not matter if *item* (*location*) <*new_item* or *item* (*location*).*is_equal* (*item*)).
- If this is not a leaf, then we have to go into the subtree regardless of whether the item that stopped *location_for*'s loop was equal to or less than *new_item*.

To inject *new_item* into the current node, we use a private routine called "*insert_at*," which works similarly to *insert_on_left* in *LIST_ARRAY*, except that it lets us insert an item and a neighboring subtree at the same time. Since we may want the subtree to be inserted on either side of the item, *insert_at* will take the intended locations of the item and the subtree as separate parameters, but its precondition specifies that the two are adjacent. Feature *insert_at* is shown in Listing 17.8.

```
feature {B_TREE_LINKED} --Support for insertion
  insert_at(item_position: INTEGER; new_item: ITEM;
        subtree_position: INTEGER; new_subtree: like Current) is
      --Insert new_item into position item_position
      --and new_subtree into position subtree_position.
    require
      adjacent: item_position = subtree_position or
            item_position = subtree_position + 1;
      --The insertion would maintain a b-tree ordering.
    local
      index: INTEGER;
    do
      from
        index := root_width;
      variant
        index - item_position
      until
        index < item_position
      loop
        items.put(items.item(index), index+1);
        subtrees.put(subtrees.item(index), index+1);
        index := index - 1;
      end;
      if subtree_position < item_position then
        --One more subtree to move.
        subtrees.put(subtrees.item(subtree_position), subtree_position+1);
      end;
      items.put(new_item, item_position);
      subtrees.put(new_subtree, subtree_position);
      root_width := root_width + 1;
    ensure
      new_width: root_width = old root_width + 1;
    end; --insert_at
```

Listing 17.8 Private feature *insert_at* of class *B_TREE_LINKED*.

If this node is not a leaf, then we have to tell the proper subtree to insert the new item. If the subtree becomes too wide, we rotate an item out of it if possible, and split it if not. Rather than clutter up the code of *insert*, we use a private routine called "*adjust_after_insertion*" to handle the details. It is shown in Listing 17.9.

Routine *adjust_after_insertion* introduces yet more private features:

- To determine if the subtree needs splitting, it is asked if it *is_too_wide*.
- Routines *rotate_left* and *rotate_right* handle the details of rotation.
- To split a subtree, we first tell it to *split*. That routine splits off the right half of the subtree and makes it available via the feature *spawned_subtree*, and the new separator item is provided by feature *spawned_separator*. The new value of the subtree itself is its former left half.

Listing 17.10 shows the *rotate_left* routine; *rotate_right* is analogous.

```
adjust_after_insertion (location: INTEGER) is
        --If subtree (location).is_too_wide, rotate an item to a sibling, or split it.
    local
        destination_subtree: like Current;
    do
        destination_subtree := subtree (location);

        if destination_subtree.is_too_wide then

            if location > 0 and then
              subtree (location−1).can_take_an_item then

               rotate_left (location);

            elseif location < root_width and then
                   subtree (location+1).can_take_an_item then

               rotate_right (location+1);

            else

               destination_subtree.split;
               insert_at (location+1, destination_subtree.spawned_separator,
                          location+1, destination_subtree.spawned_subtree);

            end;
        end;

    end; --adjust_after_insertion
```

Listing 17.9 Private routine *adjust_after_insertion* of class *B_TREE_LINKED*.

```
rotate_left(pivot: INTEGER) is
        --Perform sibling←separator←sibling rotation.
    require
        in_range: 1 <= pivot and pivot <= root_width;
    local
        right_subtree: like Current;
        left_subtree: like Current;
        left_width: INTEGER;
    do
        right_subtree := subtree(pivot);
        left_subtree := subtree(pivot-1);
        left_width := left_subtree.root_width;

        left_subtree.insert_at(left_width+1, items.item(pivot),
                               left_width+1, right_subtree.subtree(0));

        items.put(right_subtree.item(1), pivot);

        right_subtree.delete_at(1, 0);

    end; --rotate_left
```

Listing 17.10 Private routine *rotate_left* of class *B_TREE_LINKED*.

Note that *is_too_wide*, *split*, *spawned_subtree*, and *spawned_separator* are performed by the subtree, while *rotate_left* and *rotate_right* are performed by the current tree. Since both are objects in class *B_TREE_LINKED*, that is the class where all of these routines are defined (though we may later decide to move a few routines up to *B_TREE*).

Finally, the routine *split* and its companion features *spawned_subtree* and *spawned_separator* are given in Listing 17.11. Only two new private features are introduced in *split*: *make_node_copy* is a creation routine used to initialize

```
spawned_subtree: B_TREE_LINKED[ITEM];
        --After a split, this is the right half of the old node.

spawned_separator: ITEM;
        --After a split, this is the item separating
        --the left and the right halves of the old node.

split is
        --Split this node in half, leaving the left half in Current, the right half
        --in spawned_subtree, and the item separating them in spawned_separator.
```

Listing 17.11 Private features *split*, *spawned_subtree*, and *spawned_separator* of class *B_TREE_LINKED*.

```
      require
         wide_enough: is_too_wide;
      local
         void_item: ITEM;
         middle: INTEGER;
      do
         --The median is the new separator.
         middle := (1 + root_width) // 2;

         spawned_separator := items.item(middle);

         --The right half is the new subtree.
         !!spawned_subtree.make_node_copy(Current, middle, root_width);

         --Break the connections from the right half.
         items.put(void_item, middle);
         wipe_out_range(middle, root_width);

         root_width := middle - 1;

      ensure

         new_subtree: spawned_subtree /= Void;
         new_separator: spawned_separator /= Void;
         root_widths: root_width + spawned_subtree.root_width + 1
                        = old root_width;
         leaves: is_leaf = spawned_subtree.is_leaf;
         --spawned_separator = old items.item(old root_width//2+1)

      end; --split
```

Listing 17.11 *(continued)*

the new right subtree (tracked by feature *spawned_separator*) to the right half of the current node, and *wipe_out_range* is then used to wipe out the right half of the current node. I will let you code both of them.

We now resume our depth-first study of feature *insert* at the last **if** statement in it. For convenience, it is repeated in Listing 17.12.

First, we need to decide if the current node is the root of the main tree. Since we have no way to look up from a node, what we do is use a private feature called "*is_main_root*" to keep track of each node's status. That feature is set to *true* when *make* initializes the first node of the tree, and to *false* in *make_node_copy* (which initializes all other nodes in the tree).

If the current node is the root of the main tree and it is too wide, then we need to grow a new root. Conceptually, we want simply to *split* the current node and create a new root with *Current* as its subtree 0, *spawned_separator* as item 1, and *spawned_subtree* as subtree 1. Unfortunately, if we do that, then our

```
if is_main_root and then is_too_wide then

    --Split into two nodes.
    split;

    --Current will have to become the new root, so copy it to a new node.
    !!new_left.make_node_copy(Current, 0, root_width);

    wipe_out;
    subtrees.put(new_left, 0);
    items.put(spawned_separator, 1);
    subtrees.put(spawned_subtree, 1);
    root_width := 1;

end;
```

Listing 17.12 The portion of feature *insert* (Listing 17.7) that handles the creation of a new root.

users will never know that there is a new root—they are tracking *Current*, so to them *Current* is the root of the tree regardless of what other node tracks it.

We do split the current node, truncating *Current* to the left half of its former self, but then we create a duplicate of it (tracked by local entity *new_left*). That frees up *Current* to become the new root, with *new_left* as its subtree 0, *spawned_separator* as item 1, and *spawned_subtree* as subtree 1.

17.5.2 Deletion Features

We move on to the routine *delete*, shown in Listing 17.13. It uses *location_for* to try to find an item equal to *equal_item* in the current node. If the result is a location at which there is an equal item, then that is the item to remove.

```
delete(equal_item: ITEM) is
        --Delete an item equal to equal_item from this tree.
        --Do nothing if there is no such item.
    local
        location: INTEGER;
        successor: ITEM;
    do
        if not is_empty then

            location := location_for(equal_item);
```

Listing 17.13 Feature *delete* of class *B_TREE_LINKED*.

```
            if location > 0 and then equal_item.is_equal(item(location)) then
                if is_leaf then
                    delete_at(location, location);
                else
                    successor := subtree(location).least;
                    items.put(successor, location);
                    subtree(location).delete(successor);
                    adjust_after_deletion(location);
                end;
            elseif not is_leaf then
                subtree(location).delete(equal_item);
                adjust_after_deletion(location);
            end;
        end;
    end; --delete
```

Listing 17.13 *(continued)*

To remove an item from the current node, we have to do one of two things:

- If the current node is a leaf, then we simply remove the item (using private routine *delete_at*, the dual of *insert_at*).
- Otherwise, we bring up the inorder successor and delete it from its subtree. If that subtree becomes too narrow, we deal with it in private routine *adjust_after_deletion*.

If there is no equal item in this node, then *location_for*'s result tells us which subtree to tell to *delete*(*equal_item*). If that subtree becomes too narrow, *adjust_after_deletion* deals with the problem.

Basically, *adjust_after_deletion* (Listing 17.14) does the opposite of what *adjust_after_insertion* would do. It asks the subtree if it is too narrow (private

```
    adjust_after_deletion(location: INTEGER) is
            --If subtree(location).is_too_narrow,
            --rotate into it or merge it with a neighbor.
        local
            the_subtree: like Current;
        do
            the_subtree := subtree(location);
```

Listing 17.14 Private routine *adjust_after_deletion* of class *B_TREE_LINKED*.

```
if the_subtree.is_too_narrow then
   if location > 0 and then
     subtree(location-1).can_spare_an_item then

      --Give it an item by shrinking its left sibling.
      rotate_right(location);

   elseif location < root_width and then
          subtree(location+1).can_spare_an_item then

      --Give it an item by shrinking its right sibling.
      rotate_left(location+1);

   elseif is_main_root and root_width = 1 then

      --Shedding the root.
      merge_root;

   elseif location > 0 then

      --Merge it with its left sibling.
      subtree(location-1).merge(item(location),the_subtree);
      delete_at(location,location);

   else

      --Merge it with its right sibling.
      the_subtree.merge(item(location+1),subtree(location+1));
      delete_at(location+1,location+1);
   end;

 end;

end; --adjust_after_deletion
```

Listing 17.14 *(continued)*

feature *is_too_narrow*). If the answer is "yes," it rotates in an item and the corresponding subsubtree from a neighbor if it can (using *rotate_left* and *rotate_right*, which we have already written for insertion), and if rotation is impossible, it merges the subtree with one of its neighbors.

Listing 17.15 shows the private routine *merge_with*. Since we cannot operate directly on a subtree, the subtree is told to merge with the separator on its right and with its right neighbor.

The absorption of the root during deletion is implemented in a different manner from the creation of a root during insertion. In *insert*, we adjusted the subtrees in the regular manner, and then recognized the fact that the current node was the root, so if it does not split itself up, no other node will (since there is no parent to take care of it).

```
merge_with (separator: ITEM; right_sibling: like Current) is
      --Make this node the concatenation of itself, separator and right_sibling.
   require
      separator_not_void: separator /= Void;
      sibling_not_void: right_sibling /= Void;
      in_order: items.item (root_width) <= separator and then
                  separator <= right_sibling.items.item (1);
      small_enough: can_merge_with (right_sibling);
   local
      index: INTEGER;
      right_width: INTEGER;
   do
      --Copy the separator and the subtree to its right.
      root_width := root_width + 1;
      items.put (separator, root_width);
      subtrees.put (right_sibling.subtree (0), root_width);

      --Copy the rest of the items and subtrees.
      from
         index := 1;
         right_width := right_sibling.root_width;
      variant
         right_width - index
      until
         index > right_width
      loop
         items.put (right_sibling.item (index), root_width+index);
         subtrees.put (right_sibling.subtree (index), root_width+index);

         index := index + 1;
      end;
   end; --merge_with
```

Listing 17.15 Private routine *merge_with* of class *B_TREE_LINKED*.

During deletion, however, it is easier to handle the disappearing root during the adjustment process: If the subtree is too narrow and cannot be widened through rotation, then it will be merged with a neighbor, and the effect will be to make the current node narrower by one item. If the current node is the main root, then this action would make a node with no items but one subtree, which is not allowed. In this situation, instead of merging the right subtree into the left subtree, private routine *merge_root* (Listing 17.16) is invoked to merge both subtrees into the root, thus making the tree one level shorter.

```
merge_root is
        --Merge this node's subtrees and their separator item onto this node.
        --Used to shed the root and a level in height.
    require
        narrow_enough: root_width = 1;
        is_root: is_main_root;
    local
        index: INTEGER;
        left_subtree: like Current;
        right_subtree: like Current;
        left_width: INTEGER;
        right_width: INTEGER;
    do
        --Hold on to the original subtrees.
        left_subtree := subtree(0);
        right_subtree := subtree(1);

        --Widen this node.
        left_width := left_subtree.root_width;
        right_width := right_subtree.root_width;
        root_width := left_width + right_width + 1;

        --Move the item to its new place.
        items.put(item(1), left_width+1);

        --Adopt the left subtree's items and subtrees.
        subtrees.put(left_subtree.subtree(0), 0);
        from
            index := 1;
        variant
            left_width - index
        until
            index > left_width
        loop
            items.put(left_subtree.item(index), index);
            subtrees.put(left_subtree.subtree(index), index);
            index := index + 1;
        end;
        --Adopt the right subtree's subtrees.
        subtrees.put(right_subtree.subtree(0), left_width+1);
        from
            index := 1;
```

Listing 17.16 Private routine *merge_root* of class *B_TREE_LINKED*.

```
    variant
        right_width - index
    until
        index > right_width
    loop
        items.put (right_subtree.item (index), left_width+1+index);
        subtrees.put (right_subtree.subtree (index), left_width+1+index);
        index := index + 1;
    end;
end; --merge_root
```

Listing 17.16 *(continued)*

17.5.3 Getting It All Organized

Well, that was quite a list of private features. Many of them are not specific to the linked implementation, so they can be moved up to the deferred class *B_TREE*.

Several features have to do with size constraints (*is_too_narrow*, *can_spare_an_item*, etc.), and these can be used for writing class invariant assertions that are not too restrictive to allow the tree to operate: If we just asserted the b-tree rules, we would not be able to have a node that is temporarily too wide or too narrow.

My final contribution to the exercise of creating b-tree classes is the short form of *B_TREE* (Listing 17.17) and of *B_TREE_LINKED* (Listing 17.18). As you may recall, the short form of a class is a listing of its interface and assertions. These listings enumerate all the features that need to be written, and their distribution between the partially and the fully implemented classes. (The features of *B_TREE* that are not identified as deferred in the short form provide a default implementation in that class.)

These short forms include private features (those exported to other *B_TREE* and *B_TREE_LINKED* objects), so they should not be used as the contract with the users.

```
deferred class interface B_TREE[ITEM -> COMPARABLE]
feature specification --Creation and initialization
    make (the_degree: INTEGER)
            --Make a new, empty tree of degree the_degree.
        require
            odd_degree: the_degree \\ 2 = 1;
            wide_enough: the_degree > 0;
        deferred
```

Listing 17.17 A short form of class *B_TREE*.

```
    ensure
        empty: is_empty;
        leaf: is_leaf;

    wipe_out
        --Make this tree empty.
    deferred
    ensure
        empty: is_empty;

feature specification --Sizing

    degree: INTEGER
        --The degree (maximum number of subtrees per node) of this tree.
    deferred

    root_width: INTEGER
        --The number of items (or number of subtrees - 1) tracked
        --by the root node of this tree.
    deferred

    is_empty: BOOLEAN
        --Is this tree empty?
    deferred

    is_full: BOOLEAN
        --Is there no room for another item in this tree?
    deferred

    height: INTEGER
        --The number of levels in this tree.

    size: INTEGER
        --The number of items in this tree.

feature specification --Accessing the components

    item (position: INTEGER): ITEM
        --The item at position position
        --(between the subtrees at positions position-1 and position).
        --
    require
        in_range: 1 <= position and position <= root_width;
    deferred
```

Listing 17.17 *(continued)*

```
subtree (position: INTEGER): like Current
        --The b-tree at position position
        --(between the items at positions position and position+1).
        --Void if this is a leaf.
        --
        --WARNING: The result may become stale if the parent tree changes.
        --Modifications must not be made directly to the result,
        --except as part of a recursive modification of the parent tree.
    require
        in_range: 0 <= position and position <= root_width;
    deferred

is_leaf: BOOLEAN
        --Does this node have no subtrees?
    deferred

feature specification {B_TREE} --Adding, removing, and finding items

location_for (equal_item: ITEM): INTEGER
        --The index of the rightmost item that is <= equal_item,
        --or 0 if equal_item < item (1).

feature specification --Adding, removing, and finding items

item_equal_to (equal_item: ITEM): ITEM
        --An item in this tree for which is_equal (equal_item) is true;
        --Void if no such item exists.
    require
        item_not_void: equal_item /= Void;

has (equal_item: ITEM): BOOLEAN
        --Is there an item in this tree that is_equal (equal_item)?
    require
        item_not_void: equal_item /= Void;

least: ITEM
        --The least (leftmost) item in the tree.

greatest: ITEM
        --The greatest (rightmost) item in the tree.

insert (new_item: ITEM)
        --Insert new_item into this tree.
    require
        not_full: not is_full;
        item_not_void: new_item /= Void;
    deferred
```

Listing 17.17 *(continued)*

```
delete (equal_item: ITEM)
        --Delete an item equal to equal_item from this tree.
        --Do nothing if there is no such item.
    require
        item_not_void: equal_item /= Void;
    deferred

feature specification {B_TREE} --Size constraints

    is_main_root: BOOLEAN
        --Is this node the root of a main b-tree
        --(and thus exempt from the minimum width constraint)?

    min_width: INTEGER
        --Minimum legal number of items per node.

    max_width: INTEGER
        --Maximum legal number of items per node.

    is_too_wide: BOOLEAN
        --Is this node too wide?

    is_too_narrow: BOOLEAN
        --Is this node too narrow?

    can_spare_an_item: BOOLEAN
        --Can this node lose an item and still be wide enough?

    can_take_an_item: BOOLEAN
        --Can this node gain an item and still be narrow enough?

    can_merge_with (sibling: like Current): BOOLEAN
        --Can this node and sibling be merged?

feature specification --Comparisons and copying

    is_equal (other: like Current): BOOLEAN
        --Do this tree and other have identical structures and
        --track the same items in the same order at the corresponding nodes?
    require
        other_not_void: other /= Void;

feature specification --Simple input and output

    out: STRING
        --Inorder traversal of the tree, indented so that it can be read sideways.

feature specification {B_TREE} --Simple input and output

    out_indented (indent_string: STRING): STRING
        --Indented string representation.
        --indent_string is the right number of spaces to indent at this level.
```

Listing 17.17 *(continued)*

```
invariant
    only_root_may_be_empty: is_empty implies is_main_root;
    odd_degree: degree \\ 2 = 1;
    --items.item (1), . . . ,items.item (root_width) are sorted.
    wide_enough: is_too_narrow
                        = not is_main_root and root_width < min_width;
    narrow_enough: is_too_wide = root_width > max_width;
end interface --class B_TREE
```

Listing 17.17 *(continued)*

```
class interface B_TREE_LINKED[ITEM -> COMPARABLE]
creation
    make, make_node_copy
feature specification {B_TREE_LINKED}
    items: ARRAY[ITEM]
    subtrees: ARRAY[like Current]
feature specification {B_TREE_LINKED} --Creation and initialization
    make_node_copy (other: like Current;
                    from_subtree: INTEGER; thru_subtree: INTEGER)
        --Initialize Current to be a node-shallow copy of the segment of other
        --between subtrees number from_subtree and thru_subtree inclusively.
    wipe_out_range (from_subtree: INTEGER; thru_subtree: INTEGER)
        --Disconnect this range of this node from its items and subtrees.
feature specification --Creation and initialization
    make (the_degree: INTEGER)
        --Make a new empty root node of degree the_degree.
      require
        odd_degree: the_degree \\ 2 = 1;
        wide_enough: the_degree > 0;
      ensure
        empty: is_empty;
        leaf: is_leaf;
    wipe_out
        --Make this tree empty.
      ensure
        empty: is_empty;
```

Listing 17.18 A short form of class *B_TREE_LINKED*.

```
feature specification --Sizing

  degree: INTEGER
        --The degree (maximum number of subtrees per node) of this tree.

  root_width: INTEGER
        --The number of items (or number of subtrees - 1) tracked
        --by the root node of this tree.

  is_empty: BOOLEAN
        --Is this tree empty?

  is_full: BOOLEAN
        --Is there no room for another item in this tree?

feature specification --Accessing the components

  item (position: INTEGER): ITEM
        --The item at position position
        --(between the subtrees at positions position-1 and position).
     require
        in_range: 1 <= position and position <= root_width;

  subtree (position: INTEGER): like Current
        --The b-tree at position position
        --(between the items at positions position and position+1).
     require
        in_range: 0 <= position and position <= root_width;

  is_leaf: BOOLEAN
        --Does this node have no subtrees?

feature specification {B_TREE_LINKED} --Support for insertion and deletion

  rotate_right (pivot: INTEGER)
        --Perform sibling→separator→sibling rotation.
     require
        in_range: 1 <= pivot and pivot < root_width;

  rotate_left (pivot: INTEGER)
        --Perform sibling←separator←sibling rotation.
     require
        in_range: 1 <= pivot and pivot <= root_width;

feature specification {B_TREE_LINKED} --Support for deletion

  delete_at (item_position: INTEGER; subtree_position: INTEGER)
        --Delete the item at position item_position and
        --subtree at position subtree_position.
```

Listing 17.18 *(continued)*

```
    require
        adjacent: item_position = subtree_position or
                  item_position = subtree_position + 1;
    ensure
        new_width: root_width = old root_width - 1;

  merge_with (separator: ITEM; right_sibling: like Current)
        --Make this node the concatenation of itself, separator and right_sibling.
    require
        separator_not_void: separator /= Void;
        sibling_not_void: right_sibling /= Void;
        in_order: items.item (root_width) <= separator and then
                  separator <= right_sibling.items.item (1);
        narrow_enough: can_merge_with (right_sibling);

  merge_root
        --Merge this node's subtrees and their separator item
        --onto this node. Used to shed the root and a level in height.
    require
        narrow_enough: root_width = 1;
        is_root: is_main_root;

  adjust_after_deletion (location: INTEGER)
        --If subtree (location).is_too_narrow,
        --rotate into it or merge it with a sibling.

feature specification {B_TREE_LINKED} --Support for insertion

  insert_at (item_position: INTEGER; new_item: ITEM;
             subtree_position: INTEGER; new_subtree: like Current)
        --Insert new_item into position item_position and
        --new_subtree into position subtree_position.
    require
        adjacent: item_position = subtree_position or
                  item_position = subtree_position + 1;
        --The insertion would maintain a b-tree ordering.
    ensure
        new_width: root_width = old root_width + 1;

  spawned_subtree: B_TREE_LINKED[ITEM]
        --After a split, this is the right half of the old node.

  spawned_separator: ITEM
        --After a split, this is the item separating
        --the left and the right halves of the old node.

  split
        --Split this node in half, leaving the left half in Current,
```

Listing 17.18 *(continued)*

```
        --the right half in spawned_subtree,
        --and the item separating them in spawned_separator.
    require
        wide_enough: is_too_wide;
    ensure
        new_subtree: spawned_subtree /= Void;
        new_separator: spawned_separator /= Void;
        root_widths: root_width + spawned_subtree.root_width + 1
                    = old root_width;
        leaves: is_leaf = spawned_subtree.is_leaf;
        --spawned_separator = old items.item (old root_width // 2+1);

  adjust_after_insertion (location: INTEGER)
        --If subtree (location).is_too_wide, rotate an item to a sibling, or split it.

feature specification --Adding, removing, and finding items

  insert (new_item: ITEM)
        --Insert new_item into this leaf.
    require
        not_full: not is_full;
        item_not_void: new_item /= Void;

  delete (equal_item: ITEM)
        --Delete an item equal to equal_item from this tree.
        --Do nothing if there is no such item.
    require
        item_not_void: equal_item /= Void;

feature specification --Comparisons and copying

  copy (other: like Current)
        --Copy other onto this tree.
    require
        other_not_void: other /= Void;
        conformance: other.conforms_to (Current);
    ensure
        result_is_equal: is_equal (other);

invariant

  items_length_ok: items.count >= degree - 1;
  subtrees_length_ok: subtrees.count >= degree;
  --is_leaf implies subtrees.item (0), . . . ,subtrees.item (root_width) = Void
  --not is_leaf implies subtrees.item (0), . . . ,subtrees.item (root_width) /= Void
  --items.item (0), . . . ,items.item (root_width) are sorted

end interface --class B_TREE_LINKED
```

Listing 17.18 *(continued)*

17.6 B-Trees for Disk-Based Indexing

We have been working on the assumption that our object structures fit in our computer's memory. There are mechanisms for storing them on disk (this is known as "object **persistence**") and reading them back into memory, but they are outside this book's scope.

However, suppose that the structure is so gigantic—for example, terabytes in size—that it is not realistic to read it into memory in its entirety. In that case, we would be forced to leave it on disk, and retrieve only those nodes that are needed, when they are needed.[3] In this situation, we have an additional set of trade-offs to consider.

The controller of the disk accesses the recorded data in fixed-sized **blocks**. The most important features in its contract are as follows:

read (*block_number*: *INTEGER*, *memory_location*:*ADDRESS*)
  --Copy the contents of block number *block_number* into the consecutive
  --bytes of main memory starting at *memory_location*.

write (*memory_location*:*ADDRESS*, *block_number*: *INTEGER*)
  --Copy the consecutive bytes of main memory starting at
  --*memory_location* into block number *block_number*.

Thus, a disk appears as an array of blocks to the rest of the system. The block size is set when the disk is formatted; typical block sizes are 512 bytes ($\frac{1}{2}$ kilobyte or 0.5KB) and 1024 bytes (1KB), but larger block sizes (always a power of 2) are also used.

The important point here is that it is physically impossible to read less than a block of data at a time. If the block size is 1KB, you have to read the whole kilobyte, even if the node you need is only 60 bytes (which is roughly the space a node of degree 5 takes on a 32-bit system).

With a regular binary search tree, making the search more efficient would mean trying to assign neighboring nodes into the same block—a generally hopeless task, because the tree branches out so quickly.

With b-trees, there is a much easier and more reliable solution: Make each node so wide that its representation occupies the whole block.

The representation itself would need to be slightly different. First, to address a subtree we need a block number rather than a subtree object reference. The feature *subtrees*, therefore, is an array of integers. Feature *subtree* (*n*)

---

[3]It is true that virtual memory alleviates this necessity, but paging in the whole structure would waste a lot of time.

reads block number *subtrees.item* (n) from disk, builds an object out of it, and returns that object as the result.

Keeping track of separator items is a slightly trickier problem. For fastest searching, their keys should be stored in the same block (associated values can be stored elsewhere, since we retrieve the value only once, at the end of the search). If the keys are character strings, as they have been in our example, this scheme places a limit on the sum of their lengths (to ensure that the whole node fits into the block).

In our example, if the average key occupies 10 bytes and the block size is 1KB, we would want the degree to be roughly 71 (the exact number would need to be measured for a specific Eiffel runtime system).[4]

17.7 Special Case: 2–3 Trees

A 2–3 tree is simply a b-tree of degree 3. It is called a "2–3 tree" because its nodes have either 2 or 3 subtrees.

The nodes of 2–3 trees are not wide enough to make them good disk-based indices, so they tend to be used as balanced in-memory search trees.

Summary

A multiway search tree is a tree in which each node has several subtrees, with one separator item between each two adjacent subtrees. The degree of such a tree is the maximum number of subtrees a node may have. A b-tree is a multiway search tree in which each node must have either no subtrees at all, or at least $\lceil \frac{1}{2}\, degree \rceil$ subtrees with a separator item between each two. (The root of the whole tree may have fewer than the minimum number of subtrees.)

Inserting an item into a b-tree involves first injecting it into a leaf, then if that exceeds the maximum width of the node, adjusting the tree by either rotating an item from the leaf to one of its neighbors, or splitting it into two subtrees and injecting the former median item into the parent node as a separator between the new subtrees. This process may cause the root of the tree to split, creating a new root above the two halves of the old one.

Conversely, deleting a node may involve adjusting for too-narrow nodes by either rotating a spare item in from one of the neighbors, or merging with one of the neighbors. This process may cause a single-item root and its two subtrees to merge into a single root node.

---

[4] Pardon me for not drawing a degree 71 b-tree in this book.

Since these procedures always keep all leaves at the same level, the tree is always balanced.

B-trees are particularly suitable for on-disk indices, since each node can be made wide enough to take full advantage of the size of the disk block (which has to be transferred no matter how little of it is used by the program).

Exercises

1. Consider feature *item_equal_to*.

   a. What is its time complexity?

   b. What is its space complexity?

   c. How does its use of feature *location_for* affect its time and space complexities?

2. Under what circumstances would the height of a b-tree decrease?

3. Write an O(log *N*) default implementation of feature *height* for class *B_TREE*.

4. Complete the implementation of classes *B_TREE* and *B_TREE_LINKED*.

5. What happens if you change

   next_indent_string := *clone* (*indent_string*);

   to

   next_indent_string := *indent_string*;

   in feature *out_indented*?[5] Why?

6. Add an indented version of *out* to binary search trees.

[5] The answer may be different on various Eiffel systems.

18 Application: Hacker's Dictionary

Search structures are for searching, so let us look at one of the most straightforward applications for them: a real dictionary. We will use the public domain *The On-Line Hacker Jargon File, version 2.9.9, 01 APR 1992*, edited by Eric Raymond (see the beginning of the included file for its history and full credits). That file contains most of the entries in *The New Hacker's Dictionary* [8].

18.1 Format of the Input

Our dictionary gets its entries from the raw jargon file. The entries in the file look like this:

```
:adger: /aj'r/ [UCLA] vt. To make a bonehead move with
   consequences that could have been foreseen with a
   slight amount of mental effort. E.g., "He started
   removing files and promptly adgered the whole project".
   Compare {dumbass attack}.

:admin: /ad-min'/ n. Short for 'administrator'; very
   commonly used in speech or on-line to refer to the
   systems person in charge on a computer. Common
   constructions on this include 'sysadmin' and 'site
   admin' (emphasizing the administrator's role as a site
   contact for email and news) or 'newsadmin' (focusing
```

```
specifically on news). Compare {postmaster}, {sysop},
{system mangler}.
```

Thus, entries are identified by the ':' at the beginning of a line. Everything up to the next ':' is the key, and then everything up to an empty line is the value (translation) for that key.

18.2 The Implementation

The dictionary design is so simple (only two new classes) that it does not warrant a separate section. Let us proceed to a study of the implementation.

In previous examples, we had all assertion checking enabled. In this example, running with assertion checks turned on may be unacceptably slow. I recommend turning them all off in the Ace file ("*assertion* (*no*)").

18.2.1 *HACKERS_DICTIONARY*

The main routine of the system is feature *run* of class *HACKERS_DICTIONARY*. It creates a *DICTIONARY_B_TREE* and loads it with the entries from the file. Then it repeatedly asks the user for a key and reports the matching value.

build is passed the path from the current directory to the jargon file.

```
class HACKERS_DICTIONARY

creation run

feature

   run is
         --Main loop for the hacker's dictionary.
      local
         value: STRING;
      do
         print("Building the dictionary (this may take a while)...%N");

         build("jargon/jargon");

         print("Dictionary ready.%N%
               %Enter a word and I will give you its definition.%N%
               %Hit end-of-file (control-d in Unix) to exit.%N");

         from
         until
```

```
            io.end_of_file
        loop
            io.read_line;

            value := dictionary.value (io.last_string);

            if value = Void then
                print ("'");
                print (io.last_string);
                print ("' is not in this dictionary.%N");
            else
                print (value); print ("%N");
            end;
        end;

    end; --run

feature {NONE}

    dictionary: DICTIONARY_B_TREE[STRING,STRING];

    build (file_name: STRING) is
            --Build the dictionary from the jargon file named file_name.
        local
            file: FILE;
            parsing_an_entry: BOOLEAN;
            line: STRING;
            end_of_key: INTEGER;
            key: STRING;
            value: STRING;
            entry_number: INTEGER;
        do
            !!file.make_open_read (file_name);

            !!dictionary.make_degree (33);

            from
            until
                file.end_of_file
            loop
                --Skip to the first definition
                from
                    parsing_an_entry := false;
                until
                    file.end_of_file or else parsing_an_entry
```

Class FILE is presented in Appendix B.

You may want to experiment with the degree.

```
loop
   file.read_line;
   line := file.last_string;
   parsing_an_entry := line.count > 0 and then
                              line.item (1) = ':';
end;

if parsing_an_entry then

   --Find the matching ":".
   from
      end_of_key := 2
   variant
      line.count - end_of_key
   until
      end_of_key > line.count or else
      line.item (end_of_key) = ":"
   loop
      end_of_key := end_of_key + 1;
   end;

   key := line.substring (2, end_of_key-1);

   --Start the value with the rest of this line.
   if end_of_key < line.count then
      value := line.substring (end_of_key+1, line.count);
   else
      value := clone ("");
   end;

   --Append the rest of the lines from this paragraph to value.
   from
   until
      not parsing_an_entry or else file.end_of_file
   loop
      file.read_line;
      line := file.last_string;
      parsing_an_entry := line.count > 0;

      if parsing_an_entry then
         value.append ("%N");
         value.append (line);
      end;
   end;

   dictionary.put (value, key);
```

```
            debug
                entry_number := entry_number + 1;
                if entry_number \\ 50 = 0 then
                    print(entry_number);
                    print(" entries (last key: ");
                    print(key); print(") %N");
                end;
            end;
        end;
    end;
    file.close;
    debug
        print(entry_number);
        print(" entries in the dictionary.%N");
    end;
  end; --build
end --class HACKERS_DICTIONARY
```

If debugging is enabled in the Ace file, give progress reports every 50 entries.

18.2.2 *DICTIONARY_B_TREE*

DICTIONARY_B_TREE is very similar to *DICTIONARY_BST* (see Listing 15.11). In fact, it is so similar, that a common ancestor (such as *DICTIONARY_SEARCH_TREE*) may be called for—but that I leave as an exercise for you.

```
class DICTIONARY_B_TREE[KEY -> COMPARABLE, VALUE] inherit
  DICTIONARY[KEY, VALUE]
creation make, make_degree
feature {DICTIONARY_B_TREE}
  associations: B_TREE_LINKED[ASSOCIATION[KEY,VALUE]];
        --The b-tree of associations.
feature --Creation and initialization
  make is
        --Create a new, empty dictionary using a b-tree of default degree.
    do
        make_degree(5);
    end; --make
```

```
make_degree (b_tree_degree: INTEGER) is
        --Create a new, empty dictionary using a b-tree of specified degree.
    do
        !!associations.make (b_tree_degree);
    end; --make_degree

feature --Adding, removing, and checking associations

  value (key: KEY): VALUE is
        --The value associated with key in this dictionary.
        --Void if there is no such association.
    local
        pattern: ASSOCIATION[KEY, VALUE];
        match: ASSOCIATION[KEY, VALUE];
    do
        !!pattern.make;
        pattern.set_key (key);

        match := associations.item_equal_to (pattern);

        if match /= Void then
            Result := match.value;
        end; --else leave Result void.
    end; --value

  put (new_value: VALUE; key: KEY) is
        --Insert an association of key and new_value into this dictionary.
        --If the dictionary already contains an association for key, replace it.
    local
        pattern: ASSOCIATION[KEY, VALUE];
        match: ASSOCIATION[KEY, VALUE];
    do
        !!pattern.make;

        pattern.set_key (key);

        match := associations.item_equal_to (pattern);

        if match = Void then

            !!match.make;
            match.set_key (key);
            match.set_value (new_value);

            associations.insert (match);

        else
```

```
            match.set_value(new_value);
        end;
    end; --put

  delete(key: KEY) is
        --Delete the association for key from this dictionary.
    local
        pattern: ASSOCIATION[KEY, VALUE];
    do
        !!pattern.make;
        pattern.set_key(key);

        associations.delete(pattern);
    end; --delete

  wipe_out is
        --Make this dictionary empty.
    do
        associations.wipe_out;
    end; --wipe_out

feature --Sizing

  size: INTEGER is
        --The number of associations currently in this dictionary.
    do
        Result := associations.size;
    end; --size

  is_empty: BOOLEAN is
        --Is this dictionary empty?
    do
        Result := associations.is_empty;
    end; --is_empty

  is_full: BOOLEAN is
        --Is there no room in this dictionary for one more association?
    do
        Result := associations.is_full;
    end; --is_full

feature --Comparisons and copying

  copy(other: like Current) is
        --Copy other onto Current.
    do
```

```
            associations := clone (other.associations);
        end; --copy

    is_equal (other: like Current): BOOLEAN is
            --Do this dictionary and other associate the same values
            --with the same keys?
        do
            Result := associations.out.is_equal (other.associations.out);
        end; --is_equal

feature --Simple input and output

    out: STRING is
            --"< (<key_1>.out,<value_1>.out) ... (<key_n>.out,<value_n>.out) >".
        do
            Result := clone ("< ");
            Result.append (associations.out);
            Result.append (" >");
        end; --out

invariant

    have_list: associations /= Void;

end --class DICTIONARY_B_TREE
```

Exercises

1. Experiment with the degree of the tree to see how it affects performance.
2. Create a common ancestor for classes *DICTIONARY_BST* and *DICTIONARY_B_TREE*.
3. Modify *HACKERS_DICTIONARY* so that the user can specify the name for the jargon file (for example, on the command line—you may need to peruse the manuals for your specific compiler and system for that).
4. Modify the program so that it ignores the case of the key (i.e., the user can type in the key in either uppercase, lowercase, or mixed case, and still match the key stored in the dictionary). (*Hint:* Look at class *STRING* in Appendix B.)

Appendix A | Tester Classes

Chapters 2, 3, 6, and 7 included listings of testers for the presented classes. In Chapters 4, 5, 8, 9, 11, and 14, writing the tester class was an exercise. In the rest of the chapters, whether or not the testers should be written by the reader is a pedagogical toss-up.

Thus, I leave that decision to the reader (or to the teacher, as the case may be). The tester classes are provided in this appendix, but readers may want to ignore them and write their own.

A.1 *SORTABLE_LIST_TESTER*

Tester for classes <algorithm>*SORTABLE_LIST_*<implementation> (e.g., *BUBBLESORTABLE_LIST_ARRAY*), Chapters 12 and 13.

```
class SORTABLE_LIST_TESTER

creation test

feature {NONE}

   list: QUICKSORTABLE_LIST_ARRAY[ASSOCIATION[STRING,STRING]];
         --imp

   --list: MERGESORTABLE_LIST_SINGLY_LINKED[ASSOCIATION
   [STRING,STRING]];
         --imp

   add(key: STRING; value: STRING) is
         --Insert association of key and value into the list.
      local
         association: ASSOCIATION[STRING,STRING];

      do
         print("Inserting "); print(key); print("...%N");

         list.move_off_right;

         !!association.make;
         association.set_key(key);
         association.set_value(value);
```

```
            list.insert_on_left(association);

            print("...done.%N%N");
        end; --add

    feature

        test is
                --Test a sortable list.
            do
                print("Creating list...%N");
                --!!list.make_capacity(20); --imp
                !!list.make; --imp
                print("...done.%N%N");

                print("(All insertions are done at the end of the list.)%N%N");

                list.move_off_right;

                add("dattuck","One who performs drum solos on his knees.");
                add("spreakley","Irritatingly cheerful in the morning.");
                add("rigolet",
                    "As much of an opera as most people can sit through.");
                add("aa1st",
                    "One who changes his name to be nearer the front.");
                add("duddo",
                    "The most deformed potato in any given collection of%
                    %potatoes.");
                add("harbottle",
                    "A particular kind of fly which lives inside double%
                    %glazing.");
                add("fiunary",
                    "The safe place you put something and forget where it%
                    %was.");
                add("scramoge","To cut onself while licking envelopes.");
                add("bindle","To slip foreign coins into a customer's%
                    %change.");
                add("knaptoft",
                    "The mysterious fluff placed in your pockets %
                    %by dry-cleaning firms.");

                print("The list is:%N");
                print(list); print("%N%N");

                print("Sorting list...%N");
                list.sort;
                print("...done.%N%N");
```

```
      print("The list is:%N");

      print(list); print("%N%N");

      print("Test done.%N");
   end; --test

end --class SORTABLE_LIST_TESTER
```

A.2 *BINARY_SEARCH_TREE_TESTER*

This class can be used to test binary search trees (Chapter 15). It builds the tree in such a way that all branches of *delete* can be tested.

One can also use *DICTIONARY_TESTER* in conjunction with *DICTIONARY_BST* (Listing 15.11).

```
class BINARY_SEARCH_TREE_TESTER

creation test

feature {NONE}

   tree1: BINARY_SEARCH_TREE_ARRAY[ASSOCIATION[STRING,STRING]];

   put(value: STRING; key: STRING) is
         --Insert (key,value) into tree1.
      local
         association: ASSOCIATION[STRING,STRING];
      do
         print("Inserting (");
         print(key);
         print(",");
         print(value);
         print(") into tree1...%N");

         !!association.make;
         association.set_key(key);
         association.set_value(value);
         tree1.insert(association);

         print(tree1);
         print("%N...done.%N%N");
      end; --put

   delete(key: STRING) is
         --Delete (key, <anything>) from tree1.
```

```
        local
            association: ASSOCIATION[STRING,STRING];
        do
            print("Deleting (");
            print(key);
            print(",...) from tree1...%N");

            !!association.make;
            association.set_key(key);

            tree1.delete(association);

            print(tree1);
            print("%N...done.%N%N");
        end; --delete

feature

    test is
            --Test a BINARY_SEARCH_TREE.
        local
            tree2: like tree1;
        do
            !!tree1.make;
            print("Tree1 created.%N");

            put("rana", "frog");
            put("gente", "folk");
            put("manta", "blanket");
            put("espejo", "mirror");
            put("velocidad", "speed");
            put("payaso", "clown");

            print("%NNow a few duplicates.%N%N");

            put("Frosch", "frog");
            put("Volk", "folk");
            put("Hanswurst", "clown");

            print("Making tree2 a clone of tree1%N");
            tree2 := clone(tree1);
            print(tree2);
            print("%N...done. Tree1 is%N");
            print(tree1);
            print("%Nbreadth-first:%N");
            print(tree1.out_breadth_first);
            print("%N%N");
```

```
        delete("speed"); --a leaf
        delete("blanket"); --right subtree only
        delete("mirror"); --left subtree only
        delete("frog"); --two subtrees

        print("Wiping out tree1...%N");
        tree1.wipe_out;
        print(tree1);
        print("%N...done.%N%N");

        print("Test done.%N%N");
    end; --test

end --class BINARY_SEARCH_TREE_TESTER
```

A.3 *HEAP_TESTER*

This class may be used to test heaps (Chapter 16). Class *SORTABLE_LIST_TESTER* (Section A.1) together with *HEAPSORTABLE_LIST_ARRAY* (Exercise 16.8) may also be used for this purpose.

```
class HEAP_TESTER

creation test

feature {NONE}

  heap1: HEAP_ARRAY[STRING];

  insert(value: STRING) is
        --Insert value into heap1.
    do
        print("Inserting %""); print(value); print("%" into heap1...%N");

        heap1.insert(value);

        print(heap1);
        print("%N...done.%N%N");
    end; --insert

  delete is
        --Delete the root value from heap1.
    do
        print("Deleting %"");
        print(heap1.root_item);
        print("%" from heap1...%N");
```

```
            heap1.delete;

            print (heap1);
            print ("%N...done.%N%N");
        end; --delete

feature

    test is
            --Test heaps.
        local
            heap2: like heap1;
        do
            !!heap1.make;
            print ("Heap1 created.%N");

            insert ("Eventually");
            insert ("Urgent");
            insert ("Important");
            insert ("Avoid doing");
            insert ("Very urgent");

            --Now a few duplicates.
            insert ("Important");
            insert ("Eventually");
            insert ("Eventually");
            insert ("Very urgent");

            print ("Making heap2 a clone of heap1...%N");
            heap2 := clone (heap1);
            print (heap2);
            print ("%N...done%N%N");

            delete; delete; delete; delete; delete;
            delete; delete; delete; delete;

            check
                clone_not_aliased: not heap2.is_equal (heap1);
            end;
            print ("Heap2 is still%N");
            print (heap2);

            print ("%N%NTest done.%N");

        end; --test

end --class HEAP_TESTER
```

A.4 *B_TREE_TESTER*

This is a tester class for b-trees (Chapter 17).

```
class B_TREE_TESTER

creation test

feature {NONE}

   tree1: B_TREE_LINKED[ASSOCIATION[STRING,STRING]];

   put(value: STRING; key: STRING) is
         --Insert (key,value) into tree1.
      local
         association: ASSOCIATION[STRING,STRING];
      do
         print("Inserting (");
         print(key);
         print(",");
         print(value);
         print(") into tree1...%N");

         !!association.make;
         association.set_key(key);
         association.set_value(value);
         tree1.insert(association);

         print(tree1);
         print("(height "); print(tree1.height); print(")%N");

         print("...done.%N%N");
      end; --put

   delete(key: STRING) is
         --Delete (key, <anything>) from tree1.
      local
         association: ASSOCIATION[STRING,STRING];
      do
         print("Deleting (");
         print(key);
         print(",...) from tree1...%N");

         !!association.make;
         association.set_key(key);
```

```
            tree1.delete(association);

            print(tree1);
            print("%N...done.%N%N");
        end; --delete

    lookup(key: STRING) is
            --Find the matching value.
        local
            equal_association: ASSOCIATION[STRING,STRING];
            found_association: ASSOCIATION[STRING,STRING];
        do
            print("Seeking (");
            print(key);
            print(",...) in tree1...%N");

            !!equal_association.make;
            equal_association.set_key(key);

            found_association := tree1.item_equal_to(equal_association);

            print("Value: ");
            if found_association = Void then
                print("-void-");
            else
                print(found_association.value);
            end;
            print("%N...done.%N%N");
        end; --lookup

feature

    test is
            --Test a b-tree.
        local
            tree2: like tree1;
        do
            !!tree1.make(5);
            print("Tree1 (of degree 5) created.%N");

            put("zia", "aunt");
            put("fratello", "brother");
            put("babbo", "dad");
            put("cugina", "cousin");
            put("cugino", "cousin");

            delete("dad");
            put("babbo", "dad");
```

```
    put("nonno", "grandpa");
    put("marito", "husband");
    put("mamma", "mom");
    put("madre", "mother");
    put("mamma", "mum");

    put("bambinaia", "nanny");
    put("nipole", "niece");
    put("bambinaia", "nurse");
    put("sorella", "sister");
    put("sposa", "spouse");

    put("sposo", "spouse");
    put("moglie", "wife");

    lookup("wife");
    lookup("husband");
    lookup("aunt");
    lookup("dad");
    lookup("mum");
    lookup("nurse");
    lookup("pet");

    print("Making tree2 a clone of tree1...%N");
    tree2 := clone(tree1);
    print("tree2 is:%N");
    print(tree2);
    print("%Ntree1 is still:%N")
    print(tree1);
    print("%N...done.%N%N");

    print("Wiping out tree2...");
    tree2.wipe_out;
    print(tree2);
    print("%N...done.%N%N");

    delete("husband");
    delete("mom");
    delete("niece");
    delete("sister");
    delete("dad");

    print("%NTest done.%N");

  end; --test

end --class B_TREE_TESTER
```

Appendix B | Essential Predefined Classes

Eiffel systems come with class libraries. Some of them are vendor specific, some are standard and have interfaces defined by NICE (the Nonprofit International Consortium for Eiffel). This appendix reproduces interfaces to those standard classes that are needed for designing and writing object structures studied in this book.

These interface listings are from *The Eiffel Library Standard: Vintage 95*, copyright Nonprofit International Consortium for Eiffel (NICE), 1995. Used by permission.

These are "flat-short" interfaces, meaning that they list not only features defined in the class itself, but also contract clauses and important features inherited from their ancestors (this is called "**flattening**" the class). Inherited features are identified as such in their comments.

B.1 *ANY*

What looks to the programmer like class *ANY* is really broken into two parts. The first part is defined by the standard, and is supplied by the vendor of the Eiffel compiler system. This part is factored out into class *GENERAL*.

Class *ANY* itself inherits *GENERAL* and defines the second part: site-specific features that are to be inherited by all programmer-defined classes. It is empty when the compiler system is first installed.

Thus, for standard features inherited from *ANY*, see the listing of class *GENERAL* (Section B.6).

indexing

description: "Project-wide universal properties. This class is an ancestor to all developer-written classes. *ANY* inherits from *GENERAL* and may be customized for individual projects or teams."

class interface *ANY*

end --class interface *ANY*

B.2 *ARRAY*

indexing

description: "Sequences of values, all of the same type or of a conforming one, accessible through integer indices in a contiguous interval"

class interface *ARRAY*[*G*]

creation

make (*minindex*, *maxindex*: *INTEGER*)
 --Set index interval to *minindex*..*maxindex*; reallocate if necessary;
 --set all values to default. (Make array empty if *minindex* > *maxindex*.)
 ensure
 no_count: (*minindex* > *maxindex*) **implies** (*count* = 0);
 count_constraint: (*minindex* <= *maxindex*) **implies**
 (*count* = *maxindex* − *minindex* + 1)

make_from_array (*a*: *ARRAY*[*G*])
 --Initialize from the items of *a*; reallocate if necessary.
 --(Useful in proper descendants of class *ARRAY*,
 --to initialize an array-like object from a manifest array.)

feature --Access

entry (*i*: *INTEGER*): *G*
 --Entry at index *i*, if in index interval.
 --(Redefinable synonym for *item* and **infix** "@".)
 require
 good_key: *valid_index* (*i*)

frozen *item* (*i*: *INTEGER*): *G*
 --Entry at index *i*, if in index interval.
 require
 good_key: *valid_index* (*i*)

frozen infix "@"(*i*: *INTEGER*): *G*
 --Entry at index *i*, if in index interval.
 require
 good_key: *valid_index* (*i*)

feature --Measurement

count: *INTEGER*
 --Number of available indices.

```
lower: INTEGER
        --Minimum index.

upper: INTEGER
        --Maximum index.

feature --Comparison

    is_equal (other: like Current): BOOLEAN
            --Is array made of the same items as other?
            --(Redefined from GENERAL.)

feature --Status report

    valid_index (i: INTEGER): BOOLEAN
            --Is i within the bounds of the array?

feature --Element change

    enter (v: G; i: INTEGER)
            --Replace i-th entry, if in index interval, with v.
            --(Redefinable synonym for put.)
        require
            good_key: valid_index (i)
        ensure
            inserted: item (i) = v

    force (v: like item; i: INTEGER)
            --Assign item v to i-th entry.
            --Always applicable: resize the array if i falls out of
            --currently defined bounds; preserve existing items.
        ensure
            inserted: item (i) = v;
            higher_count: count >= old count

    frozen put (v: like item; i: INTEGER)
            --Replace i-th entry, if in index interval, with v.
        require
            good_key: valid_index (i)
        ensure
            inserted: item (i) = v

feature --Resizing

    resize (minindex, maxindex: INTEGER)
            --Rearrange array so that it can accommodate indices down to
            --minindex and up to maxindex. Do not lose any previously entered item.
```

```
        require
            good_indices: minindex <= maxindex
        ensure
            no_low_lost: lower = minindex.min (old lower);
            no_high_lost: upper = maxindex.max (old upper)

feature --Conversion

    to_c: POINTER
            --Address of actual sequence of values, for passing to external (non-Eiffel)
               routines.

feature --Duplication

    copy (other: like Current)
            --Reinitialize by copying all the items of other.
            --(This is also used by clone.)
            --(From GENERAL.)

invariant

    consistent_size: count = upper - lower + 1;
    non_negative_count: count >= 0

end --class interface ARRAY
```

B.3 *CHARACTER*

```
indexing

    description: "Characters, with comparison operations and an ASCII code"

expanded class interface CHARACTER

feature --Access

    code: INTEGER
            --Associated integer value

    hash_code: INTEGER
            --Hash code value
            --(From HASHABLE.)
        ensure
            good_hash_value: Result >= 0

feature --Comparison
```

```
infix "<" (other: like Current): BOOLEAN
        --Is other greater than current character?
        --(From COMPARABLE.)
    require
        other_exists: other /= Void
    ensure
        asymmetric: Result implies not (other < Current)

infix "<=" (other: like Current): BOOLEAN
        --Is current character less than or equal to other?
        --(From COMPARABLE.)
    require
        other_exists: other /= Void
    ensure
        definition: Result = (Current < other) or is_equal (other);

infix ">=" (other: like Current): BOOLEAN
        --Is current object greater than or equal to other?
        --(From COMPARABLE.)
    require
        other_exists: other /= Void
    ensure
        definition: Result = (other <= Current)

infix ">" (other: like Current): BOOLEAN
        --Is current object greater than other?
        --(From COMPARABLE.)
    require
        other_exists: other /= Void
    ensure
        definition: Result = (other < Current)

max (other: like Current): like Current
        --The greater of current object and other.
        --(From COMPARABLE.)
    require
        other_exists: other /= Void
    ensure
        current_if_not_smaller: (Current >= other) implies (Result = Current)
        other_if_smaller: (Current < other) implies (Result = other)

min (other: like Current): like Current
        --The smaller of current object and other.
        --(From COMPARABLE.)
```

require
other_exists: *other* /= *Void*
ensure
current_if_not_greater: (Current <= other) **implies** (*Result* = *Current*)
other_if_greater: (*Current* > *other*) **implies** (*Result* = *other*)

three_way_comparison (*other*: **like** *Current*): *INTEGER*
--If current object equal to *other*, 0; if smaller, −1; if greater, 1.
--(From *COMPARABLE*.)
require
other_exists: *other* /= *Void*
ensure
equal_zero: (*Result* = 0) = *is_equal* (*other*);
smaller_negative: (*Result* = −1) = *Current* < *other*;
greater_positive: (*Result* = 1) = *Current* > *other*

feature --Output

out: *STRING*
--Printable representation of character.
--(From *GENERAL*.)

invariant

irreflexive_comparison: **not** (*Current* < *Current*)

end --class interface *CHARACTER*

B.4 *COMPARABLE*

indexing

description: "Objects that may be compared according to a total order relation"

note: "The basic operation is '<' (less than); others are defined in terms of this operation and *is_equal*."

deferred class interface *COMPARABLE*

feature --Comparison

infix "<" (*other*: **like** *Current*): *BOOLEAN*
--Is current object less than *other*?
require
other_exists: *other* /= *Void*

```
    deferred
    ensure
        asymmetric: Result implies not (other < Current)

infix "<=" (other: like Current): BOOLEAN is
        --Is current object less than or equal to other?
    require
        other_exists: other /= Void
    ensure
        definition: Result = (Current < other) or is_equal (other);

infix ">=" (other: like Current): BOOLEAN
        --Is current object greater than or equal to other?
    require
        other_exists: other /= Void
    ensure
        definition: Result = (other <= Current)

infix ">" (other: like Current): BOOLEAN
        --Is current object greater than other?
    require
        other_exists: other /= Void
    ensure
        definition: Result = (other < Current)

is_equal (other: like Current): BOOLEAN
        --Is other attached to an object considered equal to current object?
        --(Redefined from GENERAL.)
    require
        other_not_void: other <= Void
    ensure
        symmetric: Result implies other.is_equal (Current);
        consistent: standard_is_equal (other) implies Result;
        trichotomy: Result = (not (Current < other) and not (other < Current))

max (other: like Current): like Current
        --The greater of current object and other.
    require
        other_exists: other /= Void
    ensure
        current_if_not_smaller: (Current >= other) implies (Result = Current)
        other_if_smaller: (Current < other) implies (Result = other)
```

```
min (other: like Current): like Current
        --The smaller of current object and other.
    require
        other_exists: other /= Void
    ensure
        current_if_not_greater: (Current <= other) implies (Result = Current)
        other_if_greater: (Current > other) implies (Result = other)

three_way_comparison (other: like Current): INTEGER
        --If current object equal to other, 0; if smaller,-1; if greater, 1.
    require
        other_exists: other /= Void
    ensure
        equal_zero: (Result = 0) = is_equal (other);
        smaller_negative: (Result = -1) = (Current < other);
        greater_positive: (Result = 1) = (Current > other)

invariant

    irreflexive_comparison: not (Current < Current)

end --class interface COMPARABLE
```

B.5 *FILE*

```
indexing

    description:  "Files viewed as persistent sequences of characters"

class interface FILE

creation

    make (fn: STRING)
            --Create file object with fn as file name.
        require
            string_exists: fn /= Void;
            string_not_empty: not fn.empty
        ensure
            file_named: name.is_equal (fn);
            file_closed: is_closed

    make_create_read_write (fn: STRING)
            --Create file object with fn as file name and open file
            --for both reading and writing; create it if it does not exist.
```

```
    require
        string_exists: fn /= Void;
        string_not_empty: not fn.empty
    ensure
        exists: exists;
        open_read: is_open_read;
        open_write: is_open_write

make_open_append (fn: STRING)
        --Create file object with fn as file name
        --and open file in append-only mode.
    require
        string_exists: fn /= Void;
        string_not_empty: not fn.empty
    ensure
        exists: exists;
        open_append: is_open_append

make_open_read (fn: STRING)
        --Create file object with fn as file name
        --and open file in read mode.
    require
        string_exists: fn /= Void;
        string_not_empty: not fn.empty
    ensure
        exists: exists;
        open_read: is_open_read

make_open_read_write (fn: STRING)
        --Create file object with fn as file name
        --and open file for both reading and writing.
    require
        string_exists: fn /= Void;
        string_not_empty: not fn.empty
    ensure
        exists: exists;
        open_read: is_open_read;
        open_write: is_open_write

make_open_write (fn: STRING)
        --Create file object with fn as file name and open
        --file for writing; create it if it does not exist.
```

```
        require
            string_exists: fn /= Void;
            string_not_empty: not fn.empty
        ensure
            exists: exists;
            open_write: is_open_write

feature --Access

    name: STRING
            --File name.

feature --Measurement

    count: INTEGER
            --Size in bytes (0 if no associated physical file).

feature --Status report

    empty: BOOLEAN
            --Is structure empty?

    end_of_file: BOOLEAN
            --Has an EOF been detected?
        require
            opened: not is_closed

    exists: BOOLEAN
            --Does physical file exist?

    is_closed: BOOLEAN
            --Is file closed?

    is_open_read: BOOLEAN
            --Is file open for reading?

    is_open_write: BOOLEAN
            --Is file open for writing?

    is_plain_text: BOOLEAN
            --Is file reserved for text (character sequences)?

    is_readable: BOOLEAN
            --Is file readable?
        require
            handle_exists: exists
```

```
is_writable: BOOLEAN
        --Is file writable?
    require
        handle_exists: exists

last_character: CHARACTER
        --Last character read by read_character.

last_double: DOUBLE
        --Last double read by read_double.

last_integer: INTEGER
        --Last integer read by read_integer.

last_real: REAL
        --Last real read by read_real.

last_string: STRING
        --Last string read by read_line, read_stream, or read_word.

feature --Status setting

close
        --Close file.
    require
        medium_is_open: not is_closed
    ensure
        is_closed: is_closed

open_read
        --Open file in read-only mode.
    require
        is_closed: is_closed
    ensure
        exists: exists;
        open_read: is_open_read

open_read_append
        --Open file in read and write-at-end mode;
        --create it if it does not exist.
    require
        is_closed: is_closed
    ensure
        exists: exists;
        open_read: is_open_read;
        open_append: is_open_append
```

open_read_write
--Open file in read and write mode.
require
is_closed: *is_closed*
ensure
exists: *exists*;
open_read: *is_open_read*;
open_write: *is_open_write*

open_write
--Open file in write-only mode; create it if it does not exist.
ensure
exists: *exists*;
open_write: *is_open_write*

feature --Cursor movement

to_next_line
--Move to next input line.
require
readable: *is_readable*

feature --Element change

change_name (*new_name*: *STRING*)
--Change file name to *new_name*.
require
not_new_name_void: *new_name* /= *Void*;
file_exists: *exists*
ensure
name_changed: *name.is_equal* (*new_name*)

feature --Removal

delete
--Remove link with physical file; delete physical file if no more links.
require
exists: *exists*

dispose
--Ensure this medium is closed when garbage-collected.

feature --Input

read_character
--Read a new character. Make result available in *last_character*.
require
readable: *is_readable*

```
read_double
        --Read the ASCII representation of a new double from file.
        --Make result available in last_double.
    require
        readable: is_readable

read_integer
        --Read the ASCII representation of a new integer from file.
        --Make result available in last_integer.
    require
        readable: is_readable

read_line
        --Read a string until new line or end of file.
        --Make result available in last_string.
        --New line will be consumed but not part of last_string.
    require
        readable: is_readable

read_real
        --Read the ASCII representation of a new real from file.
        --Make result available in last_real.
    require
        readable: is_readable

read_stream (nb_char: INTEGER)
        --Read a string of at most nb_char bound characters or until end of file.
        --Make result available in last_string.
    require
        readable: is_readable

read_word
        --Read a new word from standard input.
        --Make result available in last_string.

feature --Output

put_boolean (b: BOOLEAN)
        --Write ASCII value of b at current position.
    require
        extendible: extendible

put_character (c: CHARACTER)
        --Write c at current position.
    require
        extendible: extendible
```

```
put_double (d: DOUBLE)
        --Write ASCII value of d at current position.
    require
        extendible: extendible

put_integer (i: INTEGER)
        --Write ASCII value of i at current position.
    require
        extendible: extendible

put_real (r: REAL)
        --Write ASCII value of r at current position.
    require
        extendible: extendible

put_string (s: STRING)
        --Write s at current position.
    require
        extendible: extendible

invariant

    name_exists: name /= Void;
    name_not_empty: not name.empty;
    writable_if_extendible: extendible implies is_writable

end --class interface FILE
```

B.6 GENERAL

```
indexing

    description:   "Platform-independent universal properties. This class is an
                    ancestor to all developer-written classes."

class interface GENERAL

feature --Access

    generating_type: STRING
            --Name of current object's generating type
            --(type of which it is a direct instance).

    generator: STRING
            --Name of current object's generating class
            --(base class of the type of which it is a direct instance).
```

```
id_object (id: INTEGER): INTEGER
        --Object for which object_id has returned id; void if none.

object_id: INTEGER
        --Value identifying current object uniquely;
        --Meaningful only for reference types.

stripped (other: GENERAL): like other
        --New object with fields copied from current object,
        --but limited to attributes of type of other.
    require
        conformance: conforms_to (other)
    ensure
        stripped_to_other: Result.same_type (other)

feature --Status report

frozen conforms_to (other: GENERAL): BOOLEAN
        --Does type of current object conform to type of other
        --(as per Eiffel: The Language [5], Chapter 13)?
    require
        other_not_void: other /= Void

frozen same_type (other: GENERAL): BOOLEAN
        --Is type of current object identical to type of other?
    require
        other_not_void: other /= Void
    ensure
        definition: Result = (conforms_to (other) and other.conforms_to (Current))

feature --Comparison

frozen deep_equal (some: GENERAL; other: like some): BOOLEAN
        --Are some and other either both void
        --or attached to isomorphic object structures?
    ensure
        shallow_implies_deep: standard_equal (some, other) implies Result;
        same_type: Result implies some.same_type (other);
        symmetric: Result implies deep_equal (other, some)

frozen equal (some: GENERAL; other: like some): BOOLEAN
        --Are some and other either both void or attached
        --to objects considered equal?
    ensure
        definition: Result = (some = Void and other = Void) or else
                    ((some /= Void and other /= Void) and then
                    some.is_equal (other));
```

```
is_equal (other: like Current): BOOLEAN
        --Is other attached to an object considered equal to current object?
    require
        other_not_void: other /= Void
    ensure
        consistent: standard_is_equal (other) implies Result;
        same_type: Result implies same_type (other);
        symmetric: Result implies other.is_equal (Current)

frozen standard_equal (some: GENERAL; other: like some): BOOLEAN
        --Are some and other either both void or attached to field-by-field identical
        --objects of the same type? Always uses the default object comparison
        --criterion.
    ensure
        definition: Result = (some = Void and other = Void) or else
                        ((some /= Void and other /= Void) and then
                         some.standard_is_equal (other))

frozen standard_is_equal (other: like Current): BOOLEAN
        --Is other attached to an object of the same type as
        --current object, and field-by-field identical to it?
    require
        other_not_void: other /= Void
    ensure
        same_type: Result implies same_type (other);
        symmetric: Result implies other.standard_is_equal (Current)

feature --Duplication

frozen clone (other: GENERAL): like other
        --Void if other is void; otherwise new object equal to other.
    ensure
        equal: equal (Result, other)

copy (other: like Current)
        --Update current object using fields of object attached to other,
        --so as to yield equal objects.
    require
        other_not_void: other /= Void;
        type_identity: same_type (other)
    ensure
        is_equal: is_equal (other)

frozen deep_clone (other: GENERAL): like other
        --Void if other is void; otherwise, new object structure
        --recursively duplicated from the one attached to other.
```

```
        ensure
            deep_equal: deep_equal (other, Result)

    frozen standard_clone (other: GENERAL): like other
            --Void if other is void; otherwise new object field-by-field
            --identical to other. Always uses the default copying semantics.
        ensure
            equal: standard_equal (Result, other)

    frozen standard_copy (other: like Current)
            --Copy every field of other onto corresponding field of current object.
        require
            other_not_void: other /= Void;
            type_identity: same_type (other)
        ensure
            is_standard_equal: standard_is_equal (other)

feature --Basic operations

    frozen default: like Current
            --Default value of current type.

    frozen default_pointer: POINTER
            --Default value of type POINTER.
            --(Avoids the need to write p.default for some p of type POINTER.)
        ensure
            Result = Result.default

    default_rescue
            --Handle exception if no rescue clause. (Default: do nothing.)

    frozen do_nothing
            --Execute a null action.

    frozen Void: NONE
            --Void reference.

feature --Output

    io: STD_FILES
            --Handle to standard file setup.

    out: STRING
            --New string containing terse printable representation of current object.

    print (some: GENERAL)
            --Write terse external representation of some on standard output.
```

frozen *tagged_out*: *STRING*
--New string containing printable representation of current object,
--each field preceded by its attribute name, a colon, and a space.

invariant

reflexive_equality: *standard_is_equal* (*Current*);
reflexive_conformance: *conforms_to* (*Current*);
involutive_object_id: *id_object* (*object_id*) = *Current*

end --class interface *GENERAL*

B.7 *INTEGER*

indexing

description: "Integer values"

expanded class interface *INTEGER*

feature --Access

hash_code: *INTEGER*
--Hash code value.
--(From *HASHABLE*.)
ensure
good_hash_value: *Result* >= 0

one: **like** *Current*
--Neutral element for '*' and '/'.
--(From *NUMERIC*.)
ensure
Result_exists: *Result* /= *Void*;
value: *Result* = 1

sign: *INTEGER*
--Sign value (0, −1 or 1).
ensure
three_way: *Result* = *three_way_comparison* (*zero*)

zero: **like** *Current*
--Neutral element for '+' and '−'.
--(From *NUMERIC*.)
ensure
Result_exists: *Result* /= *Void*;
value: *Result* = 0

```
feature --Comparison

    infix "<" (other: like Current): BOOLEAN
            --Is other greater than current integer?
            --(From COMPARABLE.)
        require
            other_exists: other /= Void
        ensure
            asymmetric: Result implies not (other < Current)

    infix "<=" (other: like Current): BOOLEAN
            --Is current object less than or equal to other?
            --(From COMPARABLE.)
        require
            other_exists: other /= Void
        ensure
            definition: Result = (Current < other) or is_equal (other);

    infix ">=" (other: like Current): BOOLEAN
            --Is current object greater than or equal to other?
            --(From COMPARABLE.)
        require
            other_exists: other /= Void
        ensure
            definition: Result = (other <= Current)

    infix ">" (other: like Current): BOOLEAN
            --Is current object greater than other?
            --(From COMPARABLE.)
        require
            other_exists: other /= Void
        ensure
            definition: Result = (other < Current)

    max (other: like Current): like Current
            --The greater of current object and other.
            --(From COMPARABLE.)
        require
            other_exists: other /= Void
        ensure
            current_if_not_smaller: (Current >= other) implies (Result = Current)

    other_if_smaller:
            (Current < other) implies (Result = other)
```

```
  min (other: like Current): like Current
        --The smaller of current object and other.
        --(From COMPARABLE.)
     require
        other_exists: other /= Void
     ensure
        current_if_not_greater: (Current <= other) implies (Result = Current)
        other_if_greater: (Current > other) implies (Result = other)

  three_way_comparison (other: like Current): INTEGER
        --If current object equal to other, 0; if smaller, -1; if greater, 1.
        --(From COMPARABLE.)
     require
        other_exists: other /= Void
     ensure
        equal_zero: (Result = 0) = is_equal (other);
        smaller: (Result = 1) = Current < other;
        greater_positive: (Result = -1) = Current > other

feature --Status report

  divisible (other: like Current): BOOLEAN
        --May current object be divided by other?
        --(From NUMERIC.)
     require
        other_exists: other /= Void
     ensure
        value: Result = (other /= 0)

  exponentiable (other: NUMERIC): BOOLEAN
        --May current object be elevated to the power other?
        --From NUMERIC.
     require
        other_exists: other /= Void
     ensure
        safe_values: (other.conforms_to (Current) or
                        (other.conforms_to (0.0) and (Current >= 0)))
                      implies Result

feature --Basic operations

  abs: like Current
        --Absolute value
     ensure
```

```
        non_negative: Result >= 0;
        same_absolute_value: (Result = Current) or (Result = -Current))

infix "*" (other: like Current): like Current
        --Product by other.
        --From NUMERIC.
    require
        other_exists: other /= Void

infix "+" (other: like Current): like Current
        --Sum with other.
        --From NUMERIC.
    require
        other_exists: other /= Void
    ensure
        result_exists: Result /= Void;
        commutative: equal (Result, other + Current)

infix "-" (other: like Current): like Current
        --Result of subtracting other.
        --From NUMERIC.
    require
        other_exists: other /= Void
    ensure
        result_exists: Result /= Void

infix "/" (other: like Current): DOUBLE
        --Division by other.
    require
        other_exists: other /= Void;
        good_divisor: divisible (other)
    ensure
        result_exists: Result /= Void

infix "//" (other: like Current): like Current
        --Integer division of Current by other.
        --(From '/' in NUMERIC.)
    require
        other_exists: other /= Void;
        good_divisor: divisible (other)
    ensure
        result_exists: Result /= Void
```

```
infix "\\" (other: like Current): like Current
        --Remainder of the integer division of Current by other.
    require
        other_exists: other /= Void;
        good_divisor: divisible (other)
    ensure
        result_exists: Result /= Void

infix "^" (other: NUMERIC): DOUBLE
        --Integer power of Current by other.
        --From NUMERIC.
    require
        other_exists: other /= Void;
        good_exponent: exponentiable (other)
    ensure
        result_exists: Result /= Void

prefix "+": like Current
        --Unary plus.
        --From NUMERIC.
    ensure
        result_exists: Result /= Void

prefix "-": like Current
        --Unary minus.
        --From NUMERIC.
    ensure
        result_exists: Result /= Void

feature --Output

out: STRING
        --Printable representation of current object.
        --(From GENERAL.)

invariant

irreflexive_comparison: not (Current < Current);
neutral_addition: equal (Current + zero, Current);
self_subtraction: equal (Current - Current, zero);
neutral_multiplication: equal (Current * one, Current);
self_division: divisible (Current) implies equal (Current/Current, one)
sign_times_abs: equal (sign * abs, Current)

end --class interface INTEGER
```

B.8 *STD_FILES*

indexing

description: "Commonly used input and output mechanisms. This class may be used as either ancestor or supplier by classes needing its facilities."

class interface *STD_FILES*

feature --Access

default_output: *FILE*
--Default output.

error: *FILE*
--Standard error file.

input: *FILE*
--Standard input file.

output: *FILE*
--Standard output file.

standard_default: *FILE*
--Return the *default_output* or *output* if *default_output* is void.

feature --Status report

end_of_file: *BOOLEAN*
--Has an EOF been detected?

last_character: *CHARACTER*
--Last character read by *read_character*.

last_double: *DOUBLE*
--Last double read by *read_double*.

last_integer: *INTEGER*
--Last integer read by *read_integer*.

last_real: *REAL*
--Last real read by *read_real*.

last_string: *STRING*
--Last string read by *read_line*, *read_stream*, or *read_word*.

feature --Element change

put_boolean (*b*: *BOOLEAN*)
--Write *b* at end of default output.

put_character (*c*: *CHARACTER*)
        --Write *c* at end of default output.

put_double (*d*: *DOUBLE*)
        --Write *d* at end of default output.

put_integer (*i*: *INTEGER*)
        --Write *i* at end of default output.

put_new_line
        --Write line feed at end of default output.

put_real (*r*: *REAL*)
        --Write *r* at end of default output.

put_string (*s*: *STRING*)
        --Write *s* at end of default output.
    require
        s /= *Void*

set_error_default
        --Use standard error as default output.

set_output_default
        --Use standard output as default output.

feature --Input

read_character
        --Read a new character from standard input.
        --Make result available in *last_character*.

read_double
        --Read a new double from standard input.
        --Make result available in *last_double*.

read_integer
        --Read a new integer from standard input.
        --Make result available in *last_integer*.

read_line
        --Read a line from standard input.
        --Make result available in *last_string*.
        --New line will be consumed but not part of *last_string*.

read_real
        --Read a new real from standard input.
        --Make result available in *last_real*.

```
read_stream (nb_char: INTEGER)
        --Read a string of at most nb_char bound characters from standard input.
        --Make result available in last_string.

to_next_line
        --Move to next input line on standard input.

end --class interface STD_FILES
```

B.9 *STRING*

```
indexing
    description: "Sequences of characters, accessible through integer indices in a
                  contiguous range."
class interface STRING
creation
    frozen make (n: INTEGER)
            --Allocate space for at least n characters.
        require
            non_negative_size: n >= 0
        ensure
            empty_string: count = 0

    make_from_string (s: STRING)
            --Initialize from the characters of s.
            --(Useful in proper descendants of class STRING,
            --to initialize a string-like object from a manifest string.)
        require
            string_exists: s /= Void

feature --Initialization

    from_c (c_string: POINTER)
            --Reset contents of string from contents of c_string,
            --a string created by some external C function.
        require
            C_string_exists: c_string /= Void

    frozen remake (n: INTEGER)
            --Allocate space for at least n characters.
        require
            non_negative_size: n >= 0
```

```
    ensure
        empty_string: count = 0

  make_from_string (s: STRING)
        --Initialize from the characters of s.
        --(Useful in proper descendants of class STRING,
        --to initialize a string-like object from a manifest string.)
    require
        string_exists: s /= Void

feature --Access

  hash_code: INTEGER
        --Hash code value.
        --(From HASHABLE.)
    ensure
        good_hash_value: Result >= 0

  index_of (c: CHARACTER; start: INTEGER): INTEGER
        --Position of first occurrence of c at or after start; 0 if none.
    require
        start_large_enough: start >= 1;
        start_small_enough: start <= count
    ensure
        non_negative_result: Result >= 0;
        at_this_position: Result > 0 implies item (Result) = c;
        --none_before: For every i in start..Result, item (i) /= c
        --zero_iff_absent: (Result = 0) = For every i in 1..count, item (i) /= c

  item (i: INTEGER): CHARACTER
        --Character at position i.
    require
        good_key: valid_index (i)

  substring_index (other: STRING; start: INTEGER): INTEGER
        --Position of first occurrence of other at or after start; 0 if none.

  infix "@" (i: INTEGER): CHARACTER
        --Character at position i.
    require
        good_key: valid_index (i)

feature --Measurement

  count: INTEGER
        --Actual number of characters making up the string.
```

```
    occurrences (c: CHARACTER): INTEGER
            --Number of times c appears in the string.
        ensure
            non_negative_occurrences: Result >= 0

feature --Comparison

    is_equal (other: like Current): BOOLEAN
            --Is string made of same character sequence as other?
            --(Redefined from GENERAL.)
        require
            other_exists: other /= Void

    infix "<" (other: STRING): BOOLEAN
            --Is string lexicographically lower than other? (False if other is void.)
            --(From COMPARABLE.)
        require
            other_exists: other /= Void
        ensure
            asymmetric: Result implies not (other < Current)

    infix "<=" (other: like Current): BOOLEAN
            --Is current object less than or equal to other?
            --(From COMPARABLE.)
        require
            other_exists: other /= Void
        ensure
            definition: Result = (Current < other) or is_equal (other);

    infix ">=" (other: like Current): BOOLEAN
            --Is current object greater than or equal to other?
            --(From COMPARABLE.)
        require
            other_exists: other /= Void
        ensure
            definition: Result = (other <= Current)

    infix ">" (other: like Current): BOOLEAN
            --Is current object greater than other?
            --(From COMPARABLE.)
        require
            other_exists: other /= Void
        ensure
            definition: Result = (other < Current)
```

```
max (other: like Current): like Current
        --The greater of current object and other.
        --(From COMPARABLE.)
    require
        other_exists: other /= Void
    ensure
        current_if_not_smaller: (Current >= other) implies (Result = Current)
        other_if_smaller: (Current < other) implies (Result = other)

min (other: like Current): like Current
        --The smaller of current object and other.
        --(From COMPARABLE.)
    require
        other_exists: other /= Void
    ensure
        current_if_not_greater: (Current <= other) implies (Result = Current)
        other_if_greater: (Current > other) implies (Result = other)

three_way_comparison (other: like Current): INTEGER
        --If current object equal to other, 0; if smaller, -1; if greater, 1.
        --(From COMPARABLE.)
    require
        other_exists: other /= Void
    ensure
        equal_zero: (Result = 0) = is_equal (other);
        smaller_positive: (Result = -1) = Current < other;
        greater_positive: (Result = 1) = Current > other

feature --Status report

empty: BOOLEAN
        --Is string empty?

valid_index (i: INTEGER): BOOLEAN
        --Is i within the bounds of the string?

feature --Element change

append_boolean (b: BOOLEAN)
        --Append the string representation of b at end.

append_character (c: CHARACTER)
        --Append c at end.
    ensure
        item_inserted: item (count) = c;
```

```
        one_more_occurrence: occurrences (c) = old occurrences (c) + 1;
        item_inserted: has (c)

    append_double (d: DOUBLE)
        --Append the string representation of d at end.

    append_integer (i: INTEGER)
        --Append the string representation of i at end.

    append_real (r: REAL)
        --Append the string representation of r at end.

    append_string (s: STRING)
        --Append a copy of s, if not void, at end.
      ensure
        new_count: s /= Void implies count = old count + s.count
        --appended: For every i in 1..s.count, item (old count + i) = s.item (i)

    fill (c: CHARACTER)
        --Replace every character with c.
      ensure
        --all_replaced: For every i in 1..count, item (i) = c

    head (n: INTEGER)
        --Remove all characters except for the first n; do nothing if n >= count.
      require
        non_negative_argument: n >= 0
      ensure
        new_count: count = n.min (old count)
        --first_kept: For every i in 1..n, item (i) = old item (i)

    insert (s: like Current; i: INTEGER)
        --Add s to the left of position i.
      require
        string_exists: s /= Void;
        index_small_enough: i <= count;
        index_large_enough: i > 0
      ensure
        new_count: count = old count + s.count

    insert_character (c: CHARACTER; i: INTEGER)
        --Add c to the left of position i.
      ensure
        new_count: count = old count + 1
```

```
left_adjust
        --Remove leading white space.
    ensure
        new_count: (count /= 0) implies (item (1) /= ' ')

put (c: CHARACTER; i: INTEGER)
        --Replace character at position i by c.
    require
        good_key: valid_index (i)
    ensure
        insertion_done: item (i) = c

put_substring (s: like Current; start_pos, end_pos: INTEGER)
        --Copy the characters of s to positions start_pos..end_pos.
    require
        string_exists: s /= Void;
        index_small_enough: end_pos <= count;
        order_respected: start_pos <= end_pos;
        index_large_enough: start_pos > 0
    ensure
        new_count: count = old count + s.count - end_pos + start_pos - 1

right_adjust
        --Remove trailing white space.
    ensure
        new_count: (count /= 0) implies (item (count) /= ' ')

tail (n: INTEGER)
        --Remove all characters except for the last n; do nothing if n >= count.
    require
        non_negative_argument: n >= 0
    ensure
        new_count: count = n.min (old count)

feature --Removal

remove (i: INTEGER)
        --Remove i-th character.
    require
        index_small_enough: i <= count;
        index_large_enough: i > 0
    ensure
        new_count: count = old count - 1
```

```
wipe_out
        --Remove all characters.
    ensure
        empty_string: count = 0;
        wiped_out: empty

feature --Resizing

    resize (new_size: INTEGER)
        --Rearrange string so that it can accommodate at least new_size characters.
        --Do not lose any previously entered character.
    require
        new_size_non_negative: new_size >= 0

feature --Conversion

    to_boolean: BOOLEAN
        --Boolean value; "true" yields true, "false" yields false (case-insensitive).

    to_double: DOUBLE
        --"Double" value; for example, when applied to "123.0", will yield 123.0
          (double).

    to_integer: INTEGER
        --Integer value; for example, when applied to "123", will yield 123.

    to_lower
        --Convert to lowercase.

    to_real: REAL
        --Real value; for example, when applied to "123.0", will yield 123.0.

    to_upper
        --Convert to uppercase.

feature --Duplication

    copy (other: like Current)
        --Reinitialize by copying the characters of other. (This is also used by clone.)
        --(From GENERAL.)
    ensure
        new_result_count: count = other.count;
        --same_characters: For every i in 1..count, item (i) = other.item (i)

    substring (n1, n2: INTEGER): like Current
        --Copy of substring containing all characters at indices between n1 and n2.
```

```
    require
        meaningful_origin: 1 <= n1;
        meaningful_interval: n1 <= n2;
        meaningful_end: n2 <= count
    ensure
        new_result_count: Result.count = n2 - n1 + 1
        --original_characters: For every i in 1..n2-n1, Result.item(i) =
            item(n1+i-1)

feature --Output

    out: STRING
            --Printable representation.
            --(From GENERAL.)
        ensure
            result_not_void: Result /= Void

invariant

    irreflexive_comparison: not (Current < Current);
    empty_definition: empty = (count = 0);
    non_negative_count: count >= 0

end --class interface STRING
```

Appendix C | Eiffel Syntax

The complete treatise on the language Eiffel is *Eiffel: The Language* by Bertrand Meyer [5]. Appendix J of that book is reproduced here for convenience. Copyright Bertrand Meyer, 1992. Reprinted with permission. For any recent updates see the latest version of the diagrams at http://www.eiffel.com.

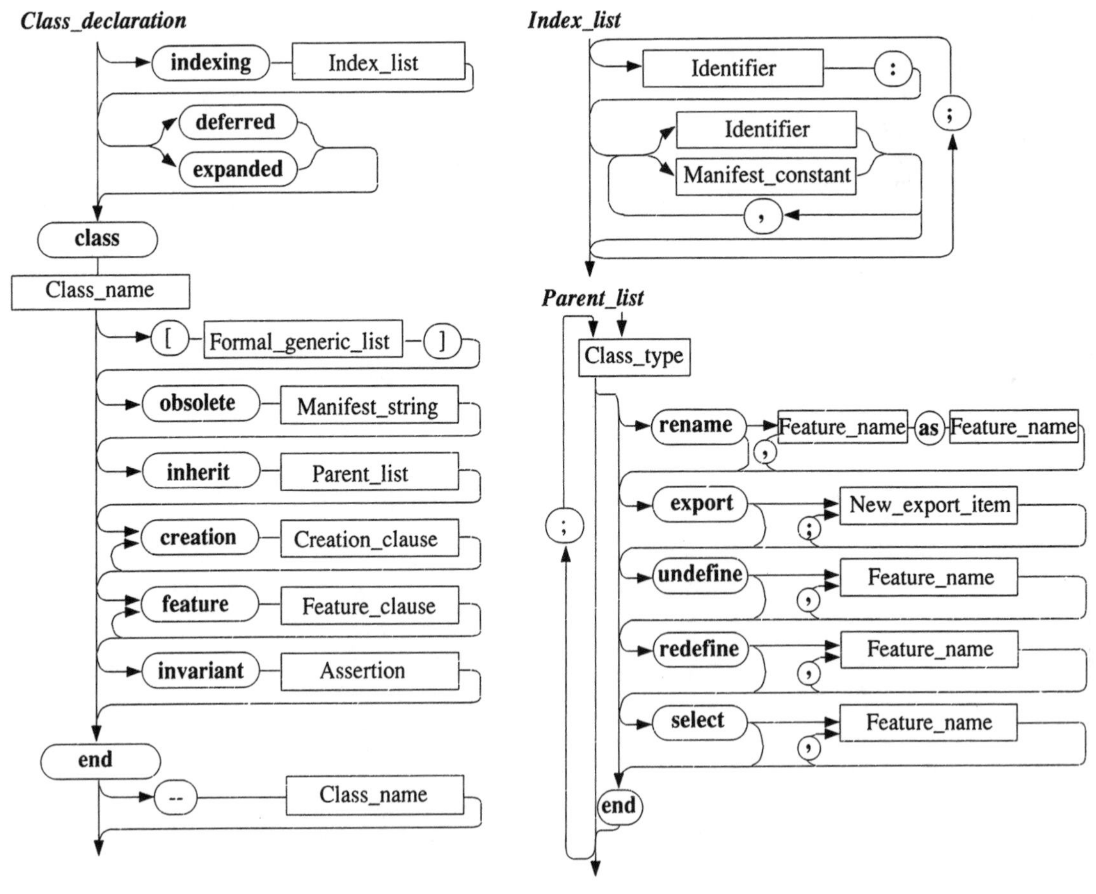

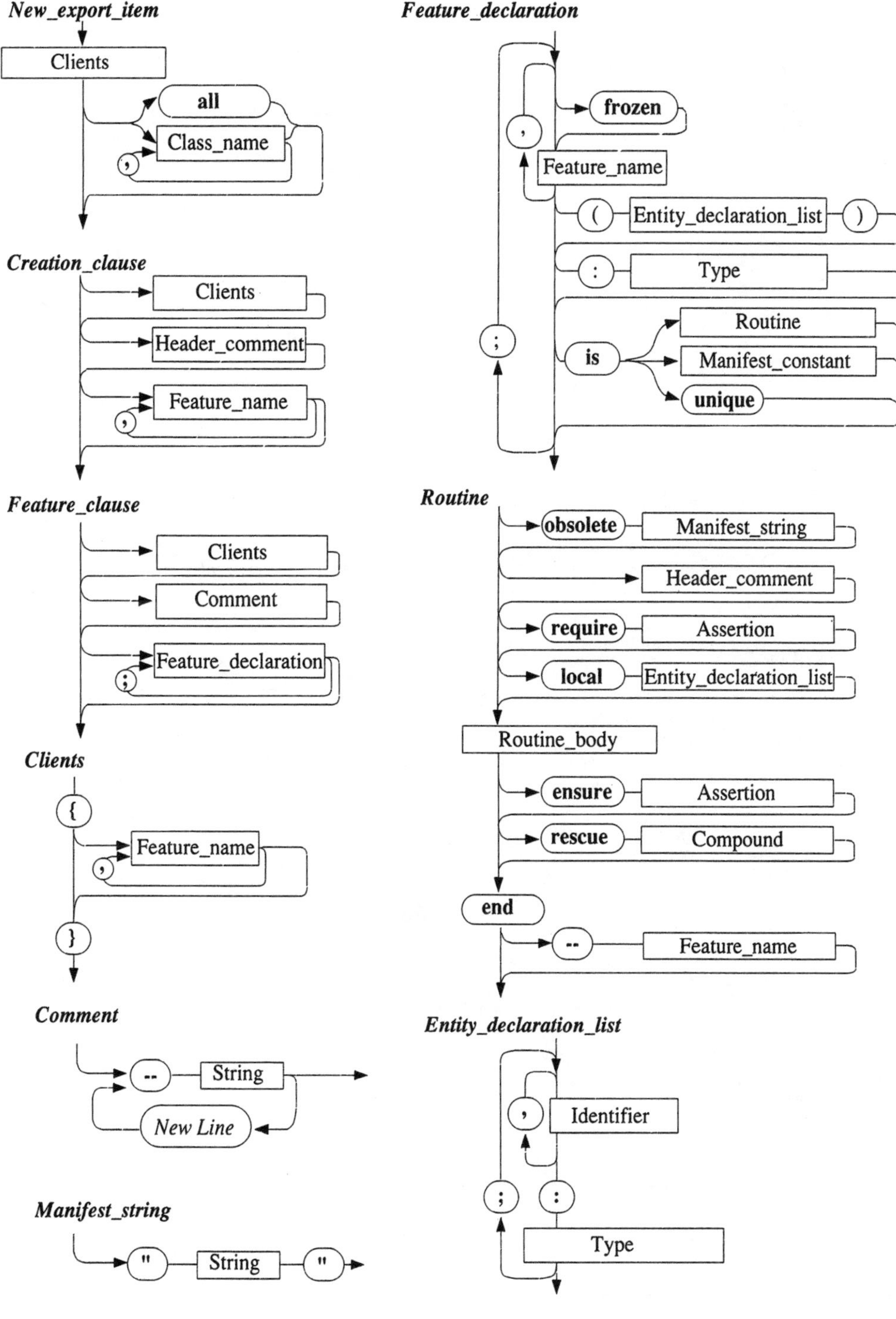
New_export_item
Clients
all
Class_name
,
Creation_clause
Clients
Header_comment
Feature_name
,
Feature_clause
Clients
Comment
Feature_declaration
;
Clients
{
Feature_name
,
}
Comment
--
String
New Line
Manifest_string
"
String
"
Feature_declaration
frozen
,
Feature_name
(
Entity_declaration_list
)
:
Type
;
is
Routine
Manifest_constant
unique
Routine
obsolete
Manifest_string
Header_comment
require
Assertion
local
Entity_declaration_list
Routine_body
ensure
Assertion
rescue
Compound
end
--
Feature_name
Entity_declaration_list
,
Identifier
;
:
Type

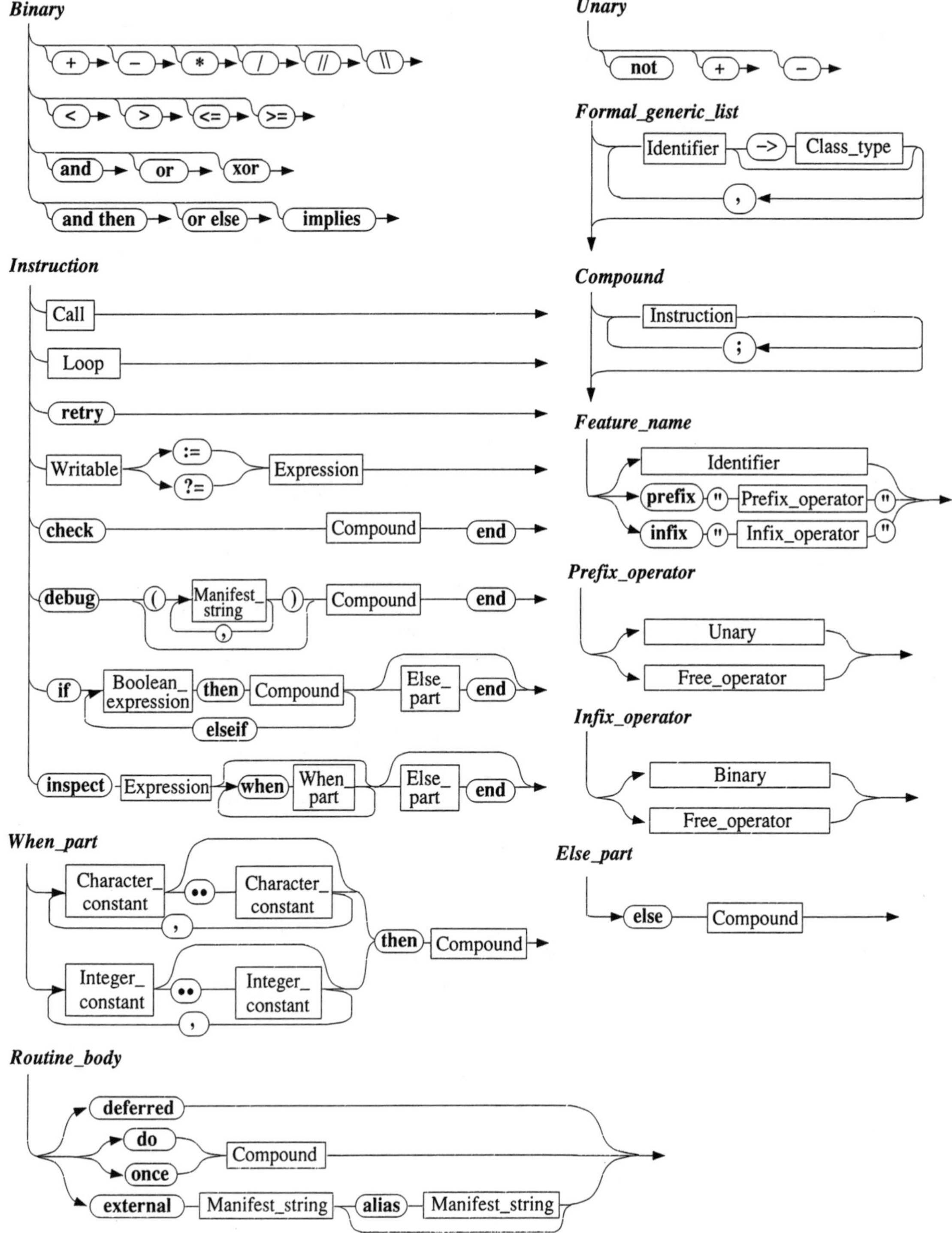

Binary
+
−
*
/
//
\\
<
>
<=
>=
and
or
xor
and then
or else
implies
Instruction
Call
Loop
retry
Writable
:=
?=
Expression
check
Compound
end
debug
(
Manifest_ string
,
)
Compound
end
if
Boolean_ expression
then
Compound
elseif
Else_ part
end
inspect
Expression
when
When part
Else_ part
end
When_part
Character_ constant
••
Character_ constant
,
Integer_ constant
••
Integer_ constant
,
then
Compound
Routine_body
deferred
do
once
Compound
external
Manifest_string
alias
Manifest_string
Unary
not
+
−
Formal_generic_list
Identifier
->
Class_type
,
Compound
Instruction
;
Feature_name
Identifier
prefix
"
Prefix_operator
"
infix
"
Infix_operator
"
Prefix_operator
Unary
Free_operator
Infix_operator
Binary
Free_operator
Else_part
else
Compound

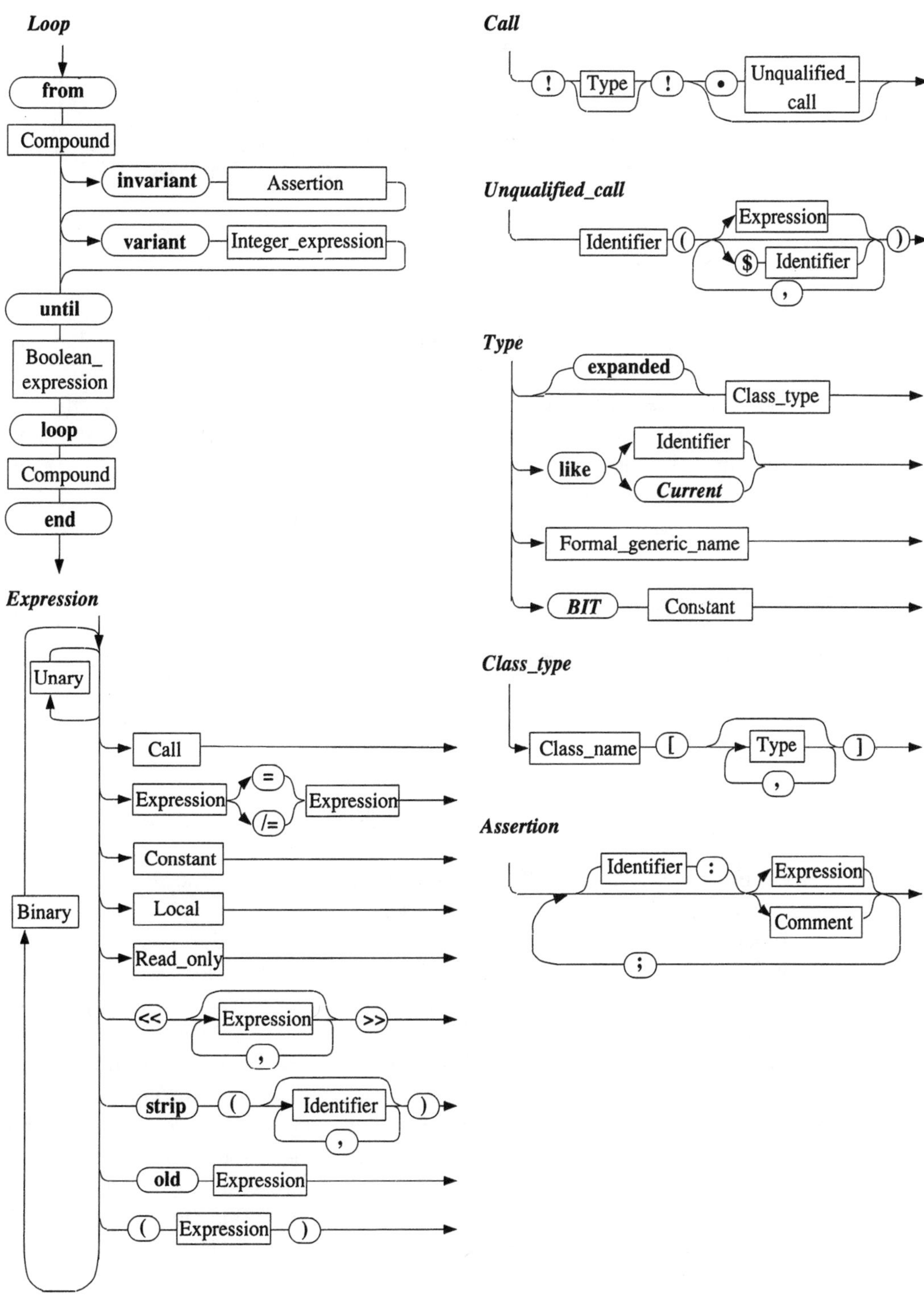
Loop
from
Compound
invariant
Assertion
variant
Integer_expression
until
Boolean_expression
loop
Compound
end
Expression
Unary
Binary
Call
Expression
=
/=
Expression
Constant
Local
Read_only
<<
Expression
,
>>
strip
(
Identifier
,
)
old
Expression
(
Expression
)
Call
!
Type
!
•
Unqualified_call
Unqualified_call
Identifier
(
Expression
$
Identifier
,
)
Type
expanded
Class_type
like
Identifier
Current
Formal_generic_name
BIT
Constant
Class_type
Class_name
[
Type
,
]
Assertion
Identifier
:
Expression
Comment
;

Appendix D | Making the Examples Work with Specific Compilers

Before reading this appendix, note that files listed in it, as well as the listings in the text, are available at `http://www.aw.com/`. At that World Wide Web site, there are files for MS-DOS and UNIX that will ease the tasks described here. Also located there are "readme" files that may contain more up-to-date information, and better instructions for MS-DOS (this appendix is written using the UNIX file naming conventions).

D.1 Overview of the Tasks

The examples in this book were tested with three Eiffel compiler systems:

- Eiffel 3 from Interactive Software Engineering (Goleta, California, `queries@eiffel.com`).
- TowerEiffel from Tower Technology (Austin, Texas, `tower@twr.com`).
- Eiffel-1.3S from SIG Computer GmbH (Germany, `order@eiffel.de`).

As this is written, the Eiffel Library Standard (ELS), some of the classes of which are listed in Appendix B, is in its infancy. Eiffel compiler vendors are still in the process of converting their libraries to the standard.

The examples in this text stick to the ELS definitions, so a certain amount of modification may be required to make the examples work. Whenever possible (unless the vendor had requested otherwise), it is the Eiffel library that gets modified, and not the examples. This way, an instructor or a system administrator can see to the changes, and the students do not have to worry about them. Once in a while, however, a specific compiler system will require a change to be made to the example itself. Hopefully, as new revisions of the libraries come out, more and more of these changes will become unnecessary.

The library modifications presented here are minimal: They are sufficient for the examples in the book. It is not my goal to make the libraries completely ELS compliant.

Nothing in this appendix is meant to express preference for a specific system on my part (don't even read anything subliminal into the order of presentation; it is alphabetical). I commend all Eiffel vendors on agreeing on a standard, even where it forces them to make extensive modifications to shipping libraries.

D.2 ISE

The information in this section applies to the latest system currently available, Release 3.3 (specifically, 3.3.7).

There are two levels at which the system needs to be prepared: The centrally installed compiler environment needs to be set up, and then the individual programmers' accounts must be configured. Then some of the examples will need to be modified.

D.2.1 Preparing the Shared Area

First, go to the directory in which the Eiffel system resides (for example, `/usr/local/Eiffel3`). All file names are given with respect to that directory.

- Identify your standard precompiled base library.
  - List the contents of subdirectory `precomp/spec`. It will contain a subdirectory for each platform on which your compiler runs. Pick the one that corresponds to the system you are using right now (in my case, it is `linux`). Let us call that "$PLATFORM" (you may want to define that as an environment variable).
  - Inside subdirectory `precomp/spec/$PLATFORM`, there is a subdirectory called "`base`". That is where the regular precompiled base library resides.

We will build a slightly modified version of the base library and precompile it. Our version will exclude all predefined object structures that can be avoided without having ill effects on the supplied kernel library classes, and bring the behavior of *clone* in line with what is described in Section 6.3.5.

- Edit the file `library/base/kernel/any.e`:
  - Change

inherit
    PLATFORM

to

```
inherit
   PLATFORM
      redefine
         setup
      end;
```

- Add the following routine:

```
setup (other: like Current) is
      --Do the same thing Tower and SIG do in their clone:
      --start out with a field-by-field copy.
   do
      standard_copy (other);
   end; --setup
```

- Create subdirectory `precomp/spec/$PLATFORM/base-objstructs` and go into it.
- Create a file called "`Ace.ace`" with the following contents:

```
system EiffelBase

root

   ANY

default

   assertion (require)

cluster

      access:      "$EIFFEL3/library/base/structures/access";
      cursors:     "$EIFFEL3/library/base/structures/cursors";
      kernel:      "$EIFFEL3/library/base/kernel";
      list:        "$EIFFEL3/library/base/structures/list";
      storage:     "$EIFFEL3/library/base/structures/storage";
      support:     "$EIFFEL3/library/base/support";
      traversing:  "$EIFFEL3/library/base/structures/traversing";
      tree:        "$EIFFEL3/library/base/structures/tree"
         exclude
            "binary_search_tree.e"
         end;

end
```

(If you did not get this file off the Web site mentioned earlier, you may want to copy `../base/Ace.ace` to the current directory and modify it.)

- Issue the command `'es3 -precompile'`. (This will take a while.)
- Go into subdirectory `EIFGEN/W_code`. Issue the command `'finish_freezing'`. (This will take a while.)

D.2.2 Preparing the User's Area

- I recommend creating a separate directory for this work, for example, `object_structures`. Create it if you wish, and go into it.
- The exercises call for creation of numerous files. It will be easier to keep them straight by separating them into subdirectories. Create subdirectories `letters`, `pairs`, `lists`, `stacks`, `queues`, `calculators`, `dictionaries`, `binary_search_trees`, `heaps`, `b_trees`, and `jargon`.
- Edit your account's startup files to set the following environment variables:

Variable	*Set It to*	*Examples*
EIFFEL	Location of the Eiffel compiler system	`/usr/local/Eiffel3`
PLATFORM	The platform code for your system	`linux, ibm6000`
PATH	$PATH:$EIFFEL/bench/spec/$PLATFORM/bin	

(If you were not the one who installed the Eiffel compiler system on your computer, ask whoever did it which exact values for EIFFEL and PLATFORM you should use.)

- Create a file called Ace with the following contents:

```
system
    tester
root
    LETTER_TESTER: "test"
default
    assertion (all);
    debug (yes);
    precompiled ("$EIFFEL3/precompiled/spec/$PLATFORM/base-objstructs");
```

```
cluster
  letters:        "./letters";
  pairs:          "./pairs";
  lists:          "./lists";
  stacks:         "./stacks";
  queues:         "./queues";
  calculators:    "./calculators";
  dictionaries:   "./dictionaries";
  bsts:           "./binary_search_trees";
  heaps:          "./heaps";
  btrees:         "./b_trees";
  jargon:         "./jargon";
end
```

This file is set up to compile and run the example in Chapter 2. As you progress, you will need to change the root class name from *LETTER_TESTER* to whichever one is applicable.

I recommend using either the `ebench` program under X Windows, or '`es3-loop`' on a terminal or in a terminal window. I also recommend simply "melting" (partially interpreting) the programs: They are too short to justify the time it takes to "freeze" (fully compile) them.

It is easiest to go into the directory containing the Ace file before running `ebench` or `es3`.

D.2.3 Changes to the Examples

- The ISE-supplied classes *LIST* and *BINARY_TREE* could not be omitted from the shared area (see Section D.2.1), because too many of the other precompiled classes depend on them. Thus, you have to use different names for these classes.
  - Use the name *XLIST* instead of *LIST* in `./lists/list.e`.
  - Classes *LIST_ARRAY* and *LIST_LINKED* need to inherit from *XLIST* instead of *LIST*.
  - Class *DICTIONARY_LIST* needs to declare feature *associations* as an *XLIST* instead of *LIST*.
  - Use the name *XBINARY_TREE* instead of *BINARY_TREE* in `./binary_search_trees/binary_tree.e`.
  - Classes *BINARY_SEARCH_TREE*, *BINARY_TREE_ARRAY* and *HEAP* need to inherit from *XBINARY_TREE* instead of *BINARY_TREE*.

- When compiling classes *CALCULATOR* in Chapter 10 and *HACKERS_DICTIONARY* in Chapter 18, if your version of the system still complains about the feature invokation "*io.end_of_file*", change it to "*io.input.end_of_file*".
- When compiling class *HACKERS_DICTIONARY* in Chapter 18, if your version of the system still complains about trying to create an object of a deferred class (*FILE* is a deferred class in Version 3.3), use *PLAIN_TEXT_FILE* instead of *FILE*.

D.3 SIG

SIG Computer GmbH has two major releases of their Eiffel compiler system at this time: 1.3S, which is shareware, and 2.0. Release 2.0 is advertised as ELS compliant, but I have not had an opportunity to test the examples with it.

Steps described in this section will make all examples except the hacker's dictionary of Chapter 18 work with Release 1.3S.

D.3.1 Preparing the Shared Area

First, go to the directory in which the Eiffel system resides (for example, `/usr/local/eiffel_s`). All file names are given with respect to that directory.

- Make a copy of directory `library/basic`, call it "`library/basic-objstructs`". Go into the new subdirectory.
- There is a directory called "`elks95`" at the above-mentioned Web site, which contains files `general.e`, `std_file.e`, `rt_fm_95.e`, and `lib.pdl`. Copy these to the current directory.
- In file `char_ref.e`, change the feature declaration *to_integer* to *code,to_integer*. That is, the line

  to_integer: *INTEGER* **is**

  should read

  code,to_integer: *INTEGER* **is**

D.3.2 Preparing the User's Area

- I recommend creating a separate directory for this work, for example, `object_structures`. Create it if you wish, and go into it.

- The exercises call for creation of numerous files. It will be easier to keep them straight by separating them into subdirectories. Create subdirectories `letters`, `pairs`, `lists`, `stacks`, `queues`, `calculators`, `dictionaries`, `binary_search_trees`, `heaps`, `b_trees`, and `jargon`.
- Edit your account's startup files to set the following environment variables:

Variable	*Set It to*	*Examples*
EIFFEL_S	Location of the Eiffel compiler system	`/usr/local/eiffel_s`
PATH	$PATH:$EIFFEL_S/bin	

(If you were not the one who installed the Eiffel compiler system on your computer, ask whoever did it which exact values for EIFFEL_S you should use.)

- Create a file called `tester.pdl` with the following contents:

```
program tester
root
  LETTER_TESTER: "test"
cluster
  "./letters"
  end
  "./pairs"
  end
  "./lists"
  end
  "./stacks"
  end
  "./queues"
  end
  "./calculators"
  end
  "./dictionaries"
  end
  "./binary_search_trees"
  end
```

```
    "./heaps"
    end
    "./b_trees"
    end
    "./jargon"
    end
    "$EIFFEL_S/library/basic-objstructs"
    find
        "boolean_ref"        in "bool_ref.e",
        "character"          in "characte.e",
        "character_ref"      in "char_ref.e",
        "comparable"         in "compar.e",
        "environment"        in "environ.e",
        "exception"          in "except.e",
        "file_system"        in "file_sys.e",
        "integer_ref"        in "int_ref.e",
        "system_time"        in "sys_time.e",
        "object_structure"   in "objstruc.e",
        "part_comparable"    in "partcomp.e",
        "std_files"          in "std_file.e",
        "arguments"          in "argument.e",
        "std_files"          in "std_file.e"
    end
end
```

This file is set up to compile and run the example in Chapter 2. As you progress, you will need to change the root class name from *LETTER_TESTER* to whichever one is applicable.

To compile, issue the command '`ecc tester`'. The generated program will be called "`tester`".

D.3.3 Changes to the Examples

- Class *LETTER* (Chapter 2) violates an unnecessary restriction in the current definition of Eiffel: It is illegal to name a feature "*character*". The SIG compiler, at least in release 1.3S, enforces this restriction, so a different name must be used (for example, "*char*").
- Release 1.3S of the SIG compiler does not allow a deferred feature to be redefined with an attribute. Such declarations must be replaced with functions. For example, if an ancestor class declares *is_full* as deferred, and the heir class has the code

```
is_full: BOOLEAN is false
        --This version never gets full.
```

then it must be changed to

```
is_full: BOOLEAN is
        --This version never gets full.
    do
        Result := false;
    end;
```

Here is the checklist of affected features:

- *is_full* in *LIST_LINKED* (Chapter 7)
- *is_full* in *STACK_LINKED* (Chapter 8)
- *is_full* in *QUEUE_LINKED* (Chapter 9)
- *is_full* in *B_TREE_LINKED* (Chapter 17)
- *is_full* in *BINARY_SEARCH_TREE_LINKED* (Chapter 15)
- *is_full* in *BINARY_SEARCH_TREE_ARRAY* (Chapter 15)
- *precedece* in *OP_DIV* (Chapter 10)
- *precedece* in *OP_MINUS* (Chapter 10)
- *precedece* in *OP_NEGATE* (Chapter 10)
- *precedece* in *OP_PLUS* (Chapter 10)
- *precedece* in *OP_TIMES* (Chapter 10)
- *precedece* in *OP_TO_THE* (Chapter 10)
- *greeting* in *INFIX_CALCULATOR* (Chapter 10)
- *greeting* in *POSTFIX_CALCULATOR* (Chapter 10)

- In class *SORTABLE_LIST_SINGLY_LINKED* (Chapter 12), change the lines

```
inherit
    LIST_SINGLY_LINKED[ITEM];
    SORTABLE_LIST_LINKED[ITEM];
```

to

```
inherit
   LIST_SINGLY_LINKED[ITEM];
   SORTABLE_LIST_LINKED[ITEM]
      undefine
         item
      end;
```

- Do not do the extended example in Chapter 18: Class *FILE* in Release 1.3S is too different from the one defined in ELS and used in the example.

D.4 Tower

The information in this section applies to the system currently available to me, Version 1.5 (specifically, 1.5.1.0). At this time, it is the latest release.

There are two levels at which the system needs to be prepared: The centrally installed compiler environment needs to be set up, and then the individual programmers' accounts must be configured. A minor modification to one example may still be required.

D.4.1 Preparing the Shared Area

First, go to the directory in which the Eiffel system resides (for example, `/usr/local/tower`). All file names are given with respect to that directory.

- Make a copy of directory `clusters/kernel`, call it "`clusters/kernel-objstructs`". Go into the new subdirectory.
- In file `string.e`, change the feature declaration *append* to *append_string, append*. That is, the line

  append (*s*: *STRING*) **is**

  should read

  append_string,append (*s*: *STRING*) **is**

- In file `file.e`, change the feature declaration *make_read* to *make_open_read,make_read*. Add *make_open_read* to the **creation** clause.
- Issue the command '`ebatch .`' (note the dot!) to precompile the kernel cluster. (This will take a while.)

D.4.2 Preparing the User's Area

- I recommend creating a separate directory for this work, for example, `object_structures`. Create it if you wish, and go into it.
- The exercises call for creation of numerous files. It will be easier to keep them straight by separating them into subdirectories. Create subdirectories `letters`, `pairs`, `lists`, `stacks`, `queues`, `calculators`, `dictionaries`, `binary_search_trees`, `heaps`, `b_trees`, and `jargon`.
- Edit your account's startup files to add the directory of Eiffel binaries to your PATH environment variable. That directory is a subdirectory of the form `bin/`<platform name> of the Eiffel system directory—for example, on my system it is

  ```
  /usr/local/tower/bin/m68k-nextstep
  ```

  If you were not the one who installed the Eiffel compiler system on your computer, ask whoever did it which exact directory you need to add to your PATH.
- Create a file called `Ace` with the following contents:

```
system
    letter_tester
root
    LETTER_TESTER: "test"
default
    assertion (all);
    debug (yes);
cluster
    letters:        "./letters"
    pairs:          "./pairs"
    lists:          "./lists"
    stacks:         "./stacks"
    queues:         "./queues"
    calculator:     "./calculators"
    dictionaries:   "./dictionaries"
```

```
        bsts:           "./binary_search_trees"
        heaps:          "./heaps"
        btrees:         "./b_trees"
        jargon:         "./jargon"

        kernel:         "$EIFFEL/clusters/kernel-objstructs"
            default
                assertion (require)
            end

    end
```

This file is set up to compile and run the example in Chapter 2. As you progress, you will need to change the root class name from *LETTER_TESTER* to whichever one is applicable, and the system name from *letter_tester* to whatever name you choose for the compiled program.

D.4.3 Changes to the Examples

While compiling class *OP_TO_THE* in the calculator example of Chapter 10, if the compiler complains about applying feature *floor* to an *INTEGER* object, simply remove the "*.floor*" call. (The NICE Libraries Committee is discussing the specification of feature "^" as this is written; the standard as it is published right now requires the "*.floor*" request to be there, but that may change.)

Bibliography

[1] Sara Baase. *Computer Algorithms.* Addison-Wesley, Reading, MA, 2nd edition, 1989.

[2] *The Eiffel Library Standard.* The Nonprofit International Consortium for Eiffel (NICE). Goleta, CA, vintage 95 edition, 1995.

[3] Bertrand Meyer. *Object-Oriented Software Construction.* Prentice-Hall, Englewood Cliffs, NJ, 1988.

[4] Bertrand Meyer. Design by contract. In Dino Mandrioli and Bertrand Meyer, editors, *Advances in Object-Oriented Software Engineering,* Chapter 1. Prentice-Hall, Englewood Cliffs, NJ, 1992.

[5] Bertrand Meyer. *Eiffel: The Language.* Prentice-Hall, Englewood Cliffs, NJ, 1992.

[6] Bertrand Meyer. *Reusable Software: The Base Object-Oriented Component Libraries.* Prentice-Hall, Cambridge, UK, 1994.

[7] Laurence C. Paulson. *ML for the Working Programmer.* Cambridge University Press, Cambridge, UK, 1991.

[8] Eric S. Raymond, editor. *The New Hacker's Dictionary.* MIT Press, 2nd edition, 1993.

[9] Robert Sedgewick. *Algorithms.* Addison-Wesley, Reading, MA, 2nd edition, 1988.

[10] Robert Switzer. *Eiffel: An Introduction.* Prentice-Hall, Englewood Cliffs, NJ, 1993.

[11] Mark Allen Weiss. *Data Structures and Algorithm Analysis.* Benjamin/Cummings, Redwood City, CA, 1992.

[12] Herbert S. Wilf. *Algorithms and Complexity.* Prentice-Hall, Englewood Cliffs, NJ, 1986.

[13] Derick Wood. *Data Structures, Algorithms, and Performance.* Addison-Wesley, Reading, MA, 1993.

Index

C

D

E

F

S

S0-BJH-877

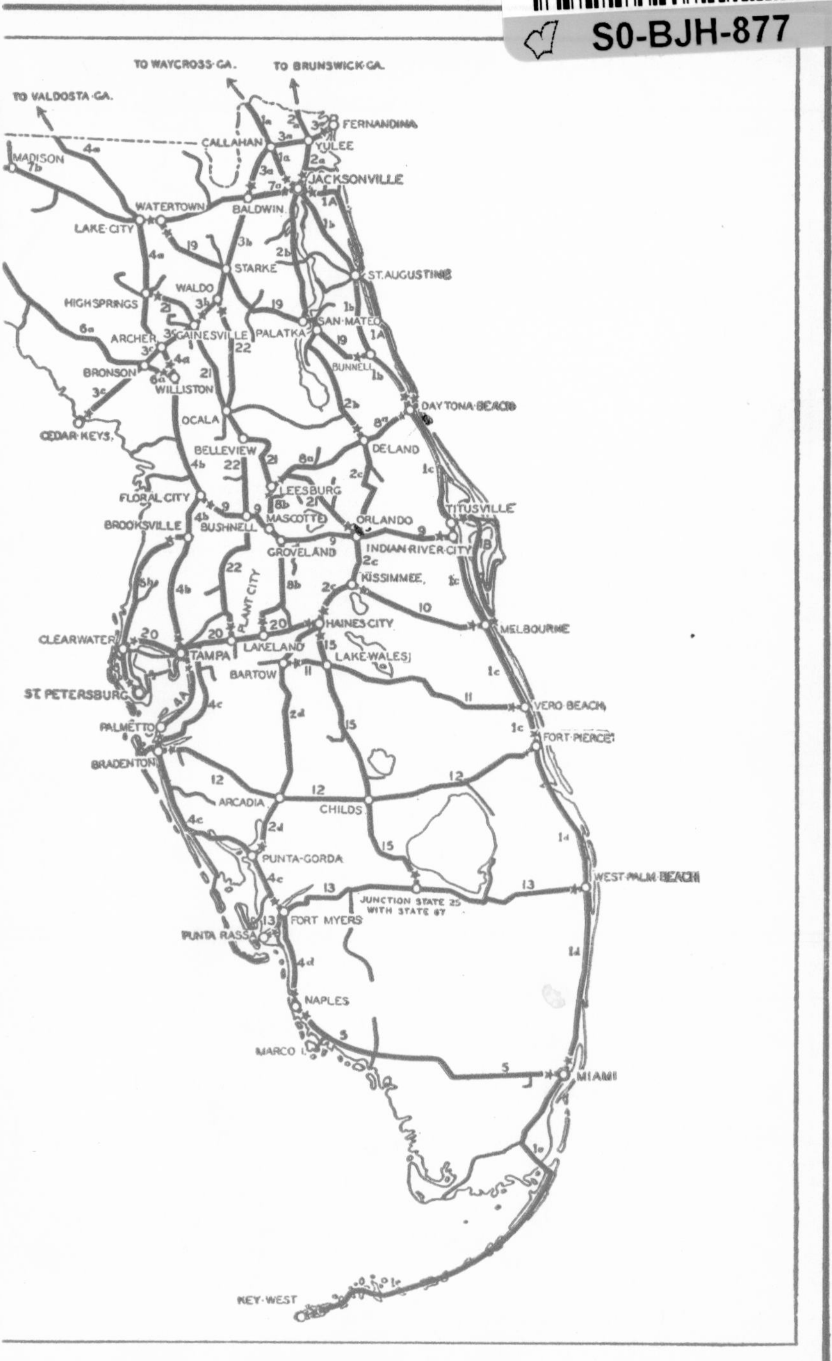

TO WAYCROSS·GA.
TO BRUNSWICK·GA.
TO VALDOSTA·GA.
FERNANDINA
CALLAHAN
YULEE
MADISON
JACKSONVILLE
WATERTOWN
BALDWIN
LAKE·CITY
STARKE
ST. AUGUSTINE
WALDO
HIGHSPRINGS
SAN·MATEO
ARCHER
GAINESVILLE
PALATKA
BRONSON
WILLISTON
BUNNELL
CEDAR·KEYS
OCALA
DAYTONA·BEACH
BELLEVIEW
DE·LAND
FLORAL·CITY
LEESBURG
BROOKSVILLE
BUSHNELL
MASCOTTE
ORLANDO
TITUSVILLE
GROVELAND
INDIAN·RIVER·CITY
KISSIMMEE
PLANT CITY
HAINES·CITY
MELBOURNE
CLEARWATER
TAMPA
LAKELAND
LAKE·WALES
BARTOW
ST. PETERSBURG
VERO·BEACH
PALMETTO
FORT·PIERCE
BRADENTON
ARCADIA
CHILDS
PUNTA-GORDA
WEST·PALM·BEACH
JUNCTION STATE 25 WITH STATE 67
FORT MYERS
PUNTA RASSA
NAPLES
MARCO I.
MIAMI
KEY·WEST

FLORIDA

A Guide to the Southernmost State

ST. MARY'S COLLEGE OF MARYLAND
ST. MARY'S CITY, MARYLAND

C56781

FLORIDA

A GUIDE TO THE SOUTHERNMOST STATE

Compiled and Written by the Federal Writers' Project
of the Work Projects Administration
for the State of Florida

AMERICAN GUIDE SERIES

ILLUSTRATED

Sponsored by State of Florida Department of Public Instruction

OXFORD UNIVERSITY PRESS · NEW YORK

COPYRIGHT 1939 BY STATE OF FLORIDA DEPARTMENT OF PUBLIC INSTRUCTION

NINTH PRINTING, 1965

FEDERAL WORKS AGENCY
WORK PROJECTS ADMINISTRATION

F. C. HARRINGTON, *Commissioner*
FLORENCE KERR, *Assistant Commissioner*
ROY SCHRODER, *State Administrator*

PRINTED IN THE UNITED STATES OF AMERICA

All rights are reserved, including the right to reproduce this book or parts thereof in any form.

Foreword

FLORIDA, the southernmost State, is frequently referred to as the last American frontier. Four centuries of varying culture under five flags may be noted as one is guided, through the pages of this book, from quaint old St.Augustine to metropolitan Miami, or from the exclusiveness of *ante bellum* Tallahassee to the exclusiveness of modern Palm Beach. For the many Floridians who may wish to read a comprehensive story of their land, as well as the million or more visitors who come to us each year, the *Florida Guide* will be a source of pleasurable information.

JOHN J. TIGERT, *President*
University of Florida

Preface

So many individuals and agencies have contributed to this State guide for Florida that it may properly be described as a co-operative product. The Federal Writers' Project acted both as a clearing-house for information and as a creative group. After extensive and adequate files of Floridiana had been accumulated, our work became that of selecting, compiling, writing, and editing the book.

More than 400 experts on special topics served as consultants. Statistical and factual data came from many sources, particularly from historical societies, civic groups, newspaper files, the State and local chambers of commerce; rail, auto, and air transportation companies; governmental and private agencies, colleges, libraries, and churches. All branches of the Florida WPA lent their assistance. Perhaps the most significant aspect of the work has been the general awakening of interest in many phases of Florida life heretofore treated only in technical publications. This common interest promises rich educational returns.

The Federal Writers' Project wishes to thank the many specialists listed in the bibliography for their valuable additions to the guide material. As indicated in the list of illustrations the Florida Federal Art Project supplied all sketches and the American Philosophical Society granted permission for use of certain archeological material. Our thanks are also due Alfred A. Knopf, Inc., for permission to reprint the lines from Wallace Steven's *Harmonium*, found in the essay on literature.

CARITA DOGGETT CORSE, *State Director*

Contents

Part III. The Florida Loop

Part IV. Appendices

Illustrations

Pen-and-ink sketches by Robert Delson, Florida Art Project.

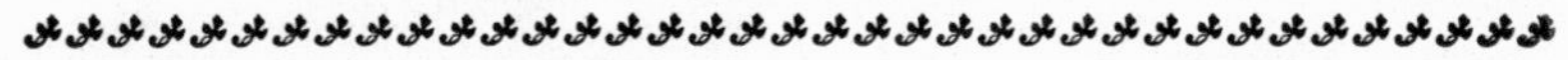

Maps

General Information

Railroads: Atlantic Coast Line R.R., Florida East Coast Ry., Georgia Southern & Florida Ry., Louisville & Nashville R.R., Seaboard Air Line Ry., St.Louis, San Francisco Ry., Georgia & Florida R.R. Other lines have less than 100 miles of track each. The ACL and FEC penetrate the Everglades, meeting at Lake Harbor, south of Lake Okeechobee.

Bus Lines: Florida Motor Lines, Atlantic Greyhound Lines, Southeastern Greyhound Lines, Pan-American Bus Lines, Union Bus Co. Lesser lines offer intrastate service.

Highways: Fifteen Federal highways, eight having international connections. State highway patrol. State gasoline tax 7¢.

Passenger Steamship Lines: Clark Steamship Co. (Miami) to Jamaica; Clyde-Mallory Line (Jacksonville, Miami) to New York, Charleston, and Galveston; Merchants & Miners Transportation Co. (Jacksonville, Miami) to Boston, Philadelphia, Baltimore, Norfolk, and Savannah; Mobile Oceanic Line (Tampa) to Europe; Munson Lines (Miami) to New York, Nassau, and Havana; Pan-Atlantic Co. (Tampa) to New York and New Orleans; Peninsula & Occidental Co. (Port Tampa, Key West, Miami) to Havana; Waterman Line (Tampa) to Mobile, New Orleans, and Puerto Rico.

Air Lines: Eastern Air Lines (Miami to New York and Chicago) stops at West Palm Beach, Vero Beach, Daytona Beach, Orlando, Tampa, and Jacksonville. National Airlines (New Orleans to Jacksonville) stops at Pensacola, Marianna, and Tallahassee; National Airlines (Daytona Beach to Miami) stops at Orlando, Lakeland, Fort Myers, Sarasota, Tampa, and St.Petersburg. Pan American Airways connects Miami with the West Indies and South and Central America.

Accommodations: Acceptable living quarters and meals for transients in all sections of Florida. Prices generally higher in winter.

Recreational Areas: Main year-round resorts are in south and central Florida, along the Gulf and Atlantic coasts. Summer resorts on the upper Gulf and Atlantic coasts. Adequate amusement facilities. (*See Sports and Recreation.*)

Fishing Laws: Fresh-water game fish are defined as black bass, bream, jack, redbreast, shellcracker, speckled perch, and warmouth perch. There are more than 40 leading varieties of salt-water game fish.

Open Season: Open throughout year, except where closed by county commissioners or by special laws.

Licenses: Required of all persons over 15 and under 65 years of age when fishing in fresh water; no license required for salt-water fishing. Resident, $2.25; nonresident, $5.50; nonresident 3-day continuous, $1.75. Issued by county judges.

Limits (daily): Black bass (not less than 12 in. in length), 12; speckled perch (7 in.), 30; shellcrackers, 30; warmouth perch, 30; redbreast, 30; jack, 15; pike, 30; mixed string, 40.

Prohibited: Sale of black bass. Use of nets, baskets, traps, gigs, dynamite or other deleterious substances, in fresh water.

Hunting Laws: Game birds are defined as brant, coot, doves, ducks, geese, jacksnipe, marsh hens, quail, wild turkey; game animals are alligator, bear, deer (bucks only), fox, muskrat, opossum, otter, panther, rabbit, skunk, squirrel, wildcat.

Open Season (dates inclusive): Deer, Nov. 20–Dec. 31, except where altered by special county laws. Quail, squirrel, wild turkey, doves, Nov. 20–Feb. 15. Ducks, geese, brant, jacksnipe, coot, Nov. 20–Dec. 19. Raccoon, muskrat, otter, Dec. 1–Mar. 1. Skunk, fox, bear, panther, opossum, open year round.

Licenses: Resident home county, $2.25. Resident other than home county, $3.25. Resident State, $5.50. Nonresident State, $25.50. Nonresident 10-day continuous, $10.50. Issued by county judges.

Limits: Deer (bucks only), 1; quail, 15; squirrel, 15; wild turkey, 2; doves, 20; ducks, 10; geese, brant, 4; marsh hens, jacksnipe, 15. Possession of game prohibited during closed season, except 5 days immediately following the open season. Possession of more than 2-day bag limit prohibited at all times.

Prohibited: Sale of game prohibited, except reindeer meat imported and sold as such. Shooting of migratory game birds over baited areas, and the use of live decoys. Unlawful to shoot game birds between

4:00 p.m. and 7:00 a.m. Only shotguns permitted in taking migratory game birds; if automatic loading or hand-operated repeating gun, it must be reduced to 3-shell capacity by plug that cannot be removed. Unlawful to hunt wild turkeys with dogs, or kill quail on ground. Unlawful to molest or kill deer while swimming.

Note: Hunting and fishing laws are altered frequently and many counties have special laws. Tourists are cautioned to procure from county judges the latest digest of laws available before hunting or fishing in any county.

Climate and Equipment: Weather usually warm from April to November and variable from December to March. There are periods of cold weather, seldom lasting more than three days, during winter months. June, July, August, and September are the months of heaviest rainfall, and the dry season comes in winter. Ocean breezes over all parts of the peninsula. September is the month when hurricanes may be expected. Topcoats are often needed in winter, while sport clothes and light linens are suitable for the rest of the year.

Information for the Motorist: Nonresident owners or operators of motorcars have the full use of Florida highways. Florida registration laws extend reciprocal privileges to the motorist of any other State; but the motorist must purchase a license plate immediately upon becoming gainfully employed, engaging in any trade or profession, or placing children in school. License tags can be purchased at county courthouses, or branch license bureaus in various cities. The registration authority for the State is Commissioner, Motor Vehicle Dept., Tallahassee. Driver's license 50¢.

Legal Speeds: 15 m.p.h. in business districts, 25 m.p.h. in residential districts, and 45 m.p.h. elsewhere. Motorists habitually drive faster than 45 m.p.h. on the open road when traffic and road conditions are satisfactory. In addition to State highway police, most counties have highway patrols.

General Rules of the Road: The first rule of the Florida road is for the motorist to exercise caution when approaching livestock, particularly cattle, which roam most of the State's principal highways. In case of injury or death to livestock, Florida law enables the owner to collect damages from the motorist equal to the value of the livestock. Passing another motorist on a hill is illegal. There are prohibitions against parking on highways, coasting in neutral, passing stopped streetcars, and the use of windshield stickers. Some municipalities have ordinances governing hitch-hiking. The use of spotlights is permitted. The motorist is required to use a rear reflector, and to dim his headlights when passing another motorist on the highway. There are local ordinances against driving under the influence of intoxicating liquors, driving with muffler open, and using sirens.

Caution to Tourists: Do not enter bushes at sides of highway in rural districts; snakes and redbugs usually infest such places. Do not eat tung nuts; they are poisonous. Do not eat green pecans; in the immature stages the skins have a white film containing arsenic.

Calendar of Annual Events

('nfd' means *no fixed date*)

January		
1	Miami	Orange Bowl Football Game
1	St. Petersburg	Kumquat Bowl Football Game
1	Fort Myers	New Year's Regatta
6	Tarpon Springs	Greek Epiphany Ceremony
10 to Mar. 10	Leesburg	National Fresh-Water Bass Tournament
17–22	Winter Haven	Florida Orange Festival
31	Tampa	South Florida Fair and Gasparilla Carnival
nfd	Bowling Green	Hardee County Strawberry Festival
nfd	Miami	All-American Air Maneuvers
nfd	Eustis	Winter Vandalia Trap-Shooting Tournament
nfd	West Palm Beach	Sailfish Derby
nfd	Daytona Beach	American Motorcycle Races
February		
7–10	Miami	Midwinter Trap-Shooting Tournament
11	St. Petersburg	State Shuffleboard Association Tournament
10–12	Fort Myers	Edison Day
11	Lake Wales	Ste. Anne Pilgrimage
12–13	New Smyrna	Winter Regatta
14–16	St. Petersburg	St. Petersburg Trap-Shooting Tournament
14–19	Orlando	Central Florida Exposition
17	Tampa	Cigar City Special Trap-Shooting Tournament
22–26	Ormond Beach	South Atlantic Women's Golf Tournament

24	Key West	El Grito de Yara (Cuban Independence Day)
26–27	Belleair	West Coast Open Golf Tournament
26–27	Clearwater	International Snipe Boat Races
nfd	Orlando	State and International Lawn Bowling Tournament
nfd	Orlando	National Shuffleboard Tournament
nfd	Mount Dora	Yacht Club Regattas
nfd	Winter Park	Animated Magazine (Founders' Week)
nfd	Palm Beach	Yacht Club Regatta
nfd	Palm Beach	Romany Chorus
nfd	Palm Beach	Flower Show
nfd	Fort Myers	Southwest Florida Fair
nfd	St.Petersburg	International Midwinter Lawn Bowling Tournament
nfd	Sanibel Island	Sea Shell Fair
nfd	Key West	La Semana Alegre (Week of Joy)
nfd	Miami	International Miami-Nassau Yacht Race
nfd	Lakeland	Outboard Motor Regatta
nfd	Palatka	Azalea Festival

March

1–5	Plant City	Strawberry Festival
8–10	Tampa	National Midwinter Pistol Meet
10–12	Tampa	Verbena del Tobaco Fiesta
nfd	Sarasota	Pageant of Sara de Soto and Sarasota County Fair
nfd	Ruskin	Florida Tomato Festival
nfd	St.Augustine	A Day in Old Spain
nfd	Tampa	Horse Show
nfd	Miami	Midwinter Sailing Regatta
nfd	St.Petersburg	Festival of States and Outdoor Bridge Tournament
nfd	St.Petersburg	Sunshine Rifle and Pistol Club State and National Tournament
nfd	Pensacola	Camellia Show
nfd	Daytona Beach	Stock Car Races

nfd	Daytona Beach	International Senior Golf Tournament
nfd	Miami	Sir Thomas Lipton Cup Race
nfd	Miami	Florida Year-Round Club Golf Tournament
nfd	Miami	Greater Miami Fishing Tournament
nfd	Miami	Miami-St.Petersburg Yacht Race
April		
nfd	Tampa	Florida High School Music Festival
nfd	Cypress Gardens	Gardenia Festival
nfd	Orlando	Orlando Yacht Club Regatta
nfd	St.Petersburg	St.Petersburg-Havana Yacht Race
nfd	Miami	Pan-American Day
nfd	Jacksonville	Jacksonville Outboard Club Regatta
Easter	Jacksonville, Tampa, and Miami	Sunrise Services
Low Sunday	St.Augustine	Pilgrimage to Shrine of Nuestra Señora de la Leche
May		
1	Tallahassee	May Day Celebration
1	Fort Ogden	May Day Picnic
May to Aug.	Sarasota	International Tarpon Tournament
May to Sept.	Tampa	Hillsborough Fish and Game Protective Association Tarpon Tournament
June		
June to Aug.	St. Petersburg	Tarpon Roundup
July		
4	Pensacola	Southern Yachting Association Regatta
4	La Belle	Rodeo
August		
1–15	Quincy and Live Oak	Tobacco Festivals

October		
28	Masaryktown	Czechoslovakian Independence Day
nfd	Tampa	Old Timers' Picnic
November		
nfd	Gainesville	Homecoming Day, University of Florida
nfd	Dade City	Tin Can Tourists' Homecoming Celebration
December		
12–24	Arcadia	Tin Can Tourists' Yuletide Celebration
15–Feb. 15	Clearwater	Fresh-Water Bass Tournament
15–Apr. 15	Mountain Lake	Bok Tower Carillon Recitals. Special recitals on the Eves of Easter, Christmas, and New Year's
nfd	Miami	Miami-Biltmore Open Golf Tournament
nfd	Orlando	Florida Field Trials

PART I

Florida's Background

Contemporary Scene

ACROSS the wide strip of its upper area, from the Atlantic to within a short distance of the Mississippi border, Florida is at once a continuation of the Deep South and the beginning of a new realm in which the system of two-party politics reasserts itself. Narrowing abruptly to a peninsula, it drops through five degrees of latitude and a constantly accentuated tropical setting, until the tip of its long Roman nose pokes very nearly into the confines and atmosphere of Latin America. Equatorial waters move up from the south along its coasts, to temper its climate and confuse its seasons; every winter a tidal wave of tourists moves down from the north, to affect its culture, its economy, its physical appearance. Throughout more than four centuries, from Ponce de Leon in his caravels to the latest Pennsylvanian in his Buick, Florida has been invaded by seekers of gold or of sunshine; yet it has retained an identity and a character distinctive to itself. The result of all this is a material and immaterial pattern of infinite variety, replete with contrasts, paradoxes, confusions, and inconsistencies.

Politically and socially, Florida has its own North and South, but its northern area is strictly southern and its southern area definitely northern. In summer the State is predominantly southern by birth and adoptions, and in winter it is northern by invasion. At all seasons it is divided into Old and New Florida, separated by the Suwannee River. The political thought that controls it originates in a united minority above the Suwannee and reaches down into the more populous peninsula to impose the diminishing theory that Florida should be preserved for Floridians rather than exploited for visitors.

Religious intolerance marked the conquest and early settlement of Florida, but the State has long since embraced practically all cults and religions, and licenses the occult and the supernatural. Yet its melting pot is a brew of conflicting ideas, which enables the native to dictate State policies and politics. And so the Florida Cracker runs the courthouse and assesses, collects, and spends the tax money.

The background traditions of Florida are of the Old South; and though the Republican Party regularly appears on the ballot, only once since Reconstruction days has the State switched from its Democratic allegiance. In 1928, when prohibition and religion confused the issues, the electorate supported Herbert Hoover.

To the visitor, Florida is at once a pageant of extravagance and a land of pastoral simplicity, a flood-lighted stage of frivolity and a behind-the-scenes struggle for existence. For the person with a house car it is a succession of trailer camps and a vagabond social life. For the Palm Beach patron it is a wintertime Newport made up of the same society, servants, and pastimes. For migratory agricultural labor it means several months of winter employment in the open under pleasant skies; and for the Negro turpentine worker, an unvarying job in the pine woods.

The derivation of the name Florida has not been overlooked in publicity literature, the rhetoric of which has lent itself to a major misconception. Nature, though lavish, has not been flamboyant enough to make the great variety of native flowers and plants notably obvious except to naturalists, scientists, and botanists. Spectacular settings have been devised by man, but since Florida remains primitive in many respects these splashes of color are comparatively isolated and, in some cases, hidden. Swamps and jungles have been enclosed and converted into Japanese, cypress, Oriental, and many other kinds of gardens, to which an admission fee is charged. Here have been assembled extensive collections of native and exotic plants.

On the other hand, florid rhetoric has not exaggerated the State's much publicized scent—the perfume from a half-million-acre bouquet of citrus groves. A border region of localized smells, however, suggests that all is not fragrance in the land of flowers. From sponge and shrimp fleets, menhaden fertilizer factories, and the stacks of paper mills drift malodorous fumes that lade the sea breezes with unsung vapors. A neutralizing incense, the aromatic smoke from burning pine woods, has steadily lessened with the expansion of forest-fire control, but occasionally there is a pall as well as a moon over Miami from Everglades muck fires.

Attempts to romanticize Florida's playground features have resulted in an elaborate painting of the lily. Coast resorts have been strung into a bejeweled necklace that sparkles on the bosom of a voluptuous sea; all is glamour and superficiality. This superimposed glitter diverts attention from Florida's more characteristic native life.

The pioneer settler came from the same stock as the Appalachian mountain dweller, and long existence in the flat pine woods tended to perpetuate his original pattern of thought. He knew little of life beyond his own small clearing and saw only a few infrequent visitors, until a network of highways left him exposed to many persons in motorcars. This traffic affected his economy and aroused his instinct to profit. He set up a roadside vegetable display, then installed gasoline pumps and a barbecue stand, and finally with the addition of overnight cabins he was in the tourist business.

The highways even mechanized his mountain music. To attract patronage, he installed a 'jook organ' that would dispense Bronx-composed records of hillbilly laments at the drop of a nickel. Real hillbilly bands, that regularly come to Florida, scorn the rural areas and become street minstrels in the larger towns or play in bars and night clubs for collections. To their music is added a sidewalk overtone from guitars, zithers, accordions, and harmonicas played by mendicants who follow the tourist crowds.

Ten thousand miles of roads that crisscross the State have streaked it with what might be described as roadside culture and commerce, with each section revealing a characteristic quality. In the staid plantation territory of northern Florida, placards on gate posts chastely admit, 'Guests Accepted,' and tourist camps offer 'Cabins for Travelers Only.' Everywhere are 'dine and dance' places, which, as the highways extend southward into the established tourist belt, more and more resemble midways. Vegetable stands add citrus fruit, and then about everything likely to catch the motorist's eye: carved coconuts, polished conch shells, marine birds made of wood or plaster, cypress 'knees,' pottery, bouquets made from tinted seashells or dyed sea oats, and an endless assortment of other native and imported handicraft. Agrarian preoccupations turn from corn, cotton, and tobacco to alligator and lion farms, reptile ranches, botanical gardens, and Indian villages. Here and there are the 'pitches' of palm readers and astrologers; but, to maintain the contrast, long stretches of uninhabited pine woods intervene with warning signs, 'Open Range—Beware of Cows and Hogs.'

In one notable instance, where the United States Army and a hundred years of persuasion failed, a highway has succeeded. The Seminole Indians surrendered to the Tamiami Trail. From the Everglades the remnants of this race emerged, soon after the trail was built, to set up their palm-thatched villages along the road and to hoist tribal flags as a lure to passing motorists. Like their white brethren, they sell articles of handicraft and for a nominal fee will pose for photographs.

This concentration of the Seminole, however, by no means represents the extent of their influence. Seminole names are more numerous and widespread in Florida than are the living members of the race. Such names were even more plentiful before the railroads interceded in behalf of train callers—as one example among many, the 'jawbreaker' Ichepuckesassa was changed to Plant City. The Indians themselves have made the most of one profitable name. Since they discovered that the story of Osceola is popular among tourists, that fiery war chief has acquired many descendants, and most of the present-day Osceolas display their names along the Tamiami Trail.

Although signboards ruin many beautiful stretches of country, they are, in fact, a significant part of the Florida scene. In rural upper Florida one sees crude notices of patent medicines or of 'Mules for Sale.' In the vicinity of St.Augustine a great deal of early history is presented on roadside signs, and farther south the flora and fauna are similarly publicized for commercial purposes. Nearly everywhere gastronomy and distance are combined in directional markers that announce '11 miles to Guava Paste' or '13 miles to Tupelo Honey.' The name of a popular brand of malaria medicine appears on tin signs attached to thousands of trees, but the manufacturer complains that business has been 'terrible' since mosquito control became effective.

The signboard plays an important role in that it introduces the Yankee to the Cracker and quickly establishes the fact that the two have much in common although their customs differ. The native Floridian may offer specious replies to what he considers oversimple questions, but he is likely to be puzzled at the abysmal ignorance that causes the Yankee to refer to orange groves as 'orchards,' sandspurs as 'sandburs,' and sandflies as 'sandfleas.' Neither does he see any reason to exclaim over a bullfrog chorus in February or the call of the whippoorwill at twilight in early March. In his own behalf he is fluently persuasive on the virtues of his particular locality; but the Yankee in Florida has become a roving visitor determined to see the entire State regardless of regional blandishments.

The first-time visitor is primarily a sightseer. He is the principal customer for the admission places along the road. He learns very soon how far Florida is supposed to project from the Old South by the discovery that a turpentine still with its Negro quarters has been turned into a tourist attraction and advertised as a survival of bygone plantation days.

Clockwise and counterclockwise the sightseeing newcomer makes the circuit of the State, filling the highways with a stream of two-way traffic. If traveling southward by the Gulf coast route, he stops to partake of a Spanish dinner in the Latin quarter of Tampa, to sit on the green benches of St.Petersburg, to view the Ringling Circus animals and art museum at Sarasota, to admire the royal palms at Fort Myers. Thence he follows the Tamiami Trail through the ghostly scrub cypress and primitive silence of the Everglades, to encounter at last the theatrical sophistication of Miami. As a side trip from the latter city, he may proceed down the long overseas highway to Key West, once the State's most populous city and an important defense base, but since its recent rehabilitation by the Federal Government something of a public curiosity, a place favored by artists and writers, and noted for its green-turtle steaks.

On his return up the Atlantic coast, the traveler may concede that publicity word-pictures of the resorts from Miami Beach northward have not been greatly exaggerated, but he is impressed by the long intervening stretches of woodland, suggesting that Florida is still very largely an empty State. From Palm Beach, which has long been the earthly Valhalla of financial achievement, he may detour inland to discover the hidden winter-vegetable kingdom on the muck lands along the southern shore of Lake Okeechobee, where Negro workers harvest thousands of carloads of beans and other fresh food supplies; or farther north he may swing inland by way of Orlando, through the great citrus groves of the hilly lake region and the thriving strawberry country around Plant City; then up to Ocala, where he can look through the glass bottoms of boats at water life in the depths of crystal-clear springs. Returning to the east coast, he inspects the far-famed natural speedway at Daytona Beach and the old Spanish fort at St.Augustine before he reaches the northern terminal city of Jacksonville. Frequently at the end of the tour, the visitor announces that he is never coming back.

His second excursion into Florida is somewhat different. On his first trip, unconsciously or deliberately, he had selected a spot where he thought later on he might want to live and play, and when he comes again he usually returns to that chosen place for a season. Ultimately, in many cases, he buys or builds a home there and becomes by slow degrees a citizen and a critic.

The evolution of a tourist into a permanent resident consists of a struggle to harmonize misconceptions and preconceptions of Florida with reality. An initial diversion is to mail northward snapshots of himself reclining under a coconut palm or a beach umbrella, with the hope that they will be delivered in the midst of a blizzard. At the same time, the tourist checks weather reports from the North, and if his home community is having a mild winter he feels that his Florida trip has been in part a swindle. Nothing short of ten-foot snowdrifts and burst waterpipes at home can make his stay in the southland happy and complete. On the other hand, he is firmly convinced that with his departure in the spring the State folds up and the inhabitants sizzle under a pitiless sun until he gets back, official weather reports and chamber-of-commerce protests to the contrary. Eventually he takes a chance on a Florida summer and makes the discovery that the average summer temperature in Florida is lower than in the North; he tries to tell about it at home, and for his pains receives a round of Bronx cheers. He is now in the agonies of transition, suspected by friends and shunned by strangers. His visits to Florida thereafter shift to visits back home, and these latter become less frequent; but 'back home' has left an indelible imprint, which he proposes to stamp on Florida.

An expansive mood is one of the most familiar and sometimes costly first responses to a Florida winter sun. The person noted for taciturnity in his home community often becomes loquacious, determined that those about him shall know that he is a man of substance. This frequently makes him an easy prey to ancient confidence games; sometimes leads to unpremeditated matrimony; and almost inevitably results in the acquisition of superfluous building lots.

Already something of a solipsist, he becomes an incurable nonconformist, vigorously defending his adopted State and indignantly decrying it by turns. He refutes the tradition that life in the South is a lackadaisical existence adapted to an enervating climate. He comes here to play and to relax but at the slightest provocation he resumes his business or profession, if for no other reason than to demonstrate that the sound economic practices of his home State will pull Florida out of the doldrums he perceives it to be in. If he opens a shop, the back-home instinct is likely to reassert itself in choosing a name, so that Florida abounds in Michigan groceries, Maryland restaurants, Ohio dry-cleaners, Indiana laundries, and New York shoe shops.

Along with business and professional theories, the Northerner brings to Florida a great deal of his local architectural tradition. This assures a structural variant to the repetitious designs of filling stations at the four corners of all the crossroad villages and of chain stores along the main streets in the larger towns.

While Florida's tourist population is drawn to the State largely by the prospect of play and recreation in a beneficent climate, the distribution of its population is influenced to a great extent by personal inclination. The newcomer usually gravitates to the locality where his individual preferences can best be realized, and in so doing he helps to identify these preferences with his adopted community. This tends to emphasize the strikingly diverse characteristics of Florida's cities. For example, there is the commercial metropolis of Jacksonville, with its converging railroads and northern bustle; and, close by, antique St.Augustine, with its historical background and buildings and its horse-drawn sightseeing conveyances; St.Petersburg with its clublike foregathering of elderly folk, where fire and police lines are sometimes needed to handle the throngs of Sunday morning worshipers; and Miami, where employees in public establishments are fingerprinted as a police precaution to safeguard the crowds that fill its hotels, race tracks, and night clubs.

Regardless of individual circumstance and preference, one desire seems to be common to all—the desire to improve Florida. But man's subduing efforts seldom extend much beyond the cities or penetrate very far from the highways; and if those efforts were relaxed for a generation, much of Florida would become primeval territory again. In combating nature and in trying to reconcile divergent ideas, the citizen performs a public service, and if the climate, as advertised, adds ten years to his life, the dispensation is utilized to the advantage of the State.

Natural Setting and Conservation

FLORIDA is bounded on the north by Georgia and Alabama, and on all other sides by the salt waters of the Atlantic Ocean, the Straits of Florida, and the Gulf of Mexico, except for about 50 miles on the west where the Perdido River forms a boundary between this State and lower Alabama. The State's tidal shore line—including the Ten Thousand Islands off the west coast, and all bays, estuaries, and other tidal reaches—extends 3,751 statute miles from the northern boundary on the Atlantic to the western boundary on the Gulf. Florida's area of 58,666 square miles, of which 3,805 are water surface, is more than large enough to contain Maine, Vermont, New Hampshire, Connecticut, and Rhode Island. Jacksonville, in northeast Florida, is in the same latitude as Cairo, Egypt, and Shanghai, China, and the entire peninsula lies hundreds of miles nearer than Rome to the equator.

Viewed from the air, with its broken coast line and its innumerable lakes, canals, and rivers, Florida looks like a frayed and perforated green mat spread upon a blue sea. Inland the mat develops a ridge composed of round-shouldered limestone hills, that tapers off from the north into the prairie region above Lake Okeechobee. Below the lake appear the Everglades, a half-submerged waste of sawgrass studded with cypress hammocks and oasislike palm islands. In profile, as seen from offshore, the land of Florida becomes a soft pastel line separating sky and water.

The Atlantic coast sweeps in an even curve to the end of the peninsula, where it breaks into segments; from there the Florida Keys extend like coral steppingstones into southern waters. The Gulf coast, deeply marked with bays and bordered with rank growths of hardwood, makes a great arching swing southward, and finally crumbles into the Ten Thousand Islands, a labyrinth of uncharted waterways.

Geographically, the State can be divided into four sections: the east-coast strip, bordering the Atlantic from Fernandina to Key West; the lake or central-ridge district; the west-coast area, of which Tampa is the hub; and the panhandle of west Florida, which includes the rolling country along the north shore of the Gulf.

The east coast is protected from the open sea by a ribbon of sand bars and islands, on which have been built many leading tourist towns, notably Ormond, Daytona Beach, Palm Beach, and Miami Beach. Although the business districts are often on the mainland, the resort sections lie beyond salt-water lagoons on barrier beaches. Inland from the coast, a wedge-shaped area of pine and palmetto flatwoods reaches from the Georgia border on the north to a point between the Everglades and the Atlantic on the southern tip of the peninsula.

The Everglades—until 1842 an unexplored, mysterious region known only to the Seminole who found sanctuary there from invading whites—form a vast area, much of which is under water throughout the year, and nearly all during the rainy summer season.

Big Cypress Swamp, that portion of the Everglades nearest the west coast, has considerably less surface water than the eastern half of the region. Its northern section, known as Okaloacoochee Slough, has been used as pasture for open-range cattle since the War between the States. The Tamiami Trail, running east and west, bisects the Everglades and skirts the southern part of the Big Cypress Swamp.

Fringing the lower Gulf coast are the Ten Thousand Islands, a group of mangrove-covered islets divided, and often submerged, by swift-running tidal channels. No railways or highways link these keys, and because of their inaccessibility they have been the refuge of many picaresque characters since the late 1880's. North of the Ten Thousand Islands the coast is blanketed with pine forests and hardwood hammocks. Several drowned river valleys and the absence of reefs, except along its upper reaches, indicate that this section is probably older than the east coast.

The topography of much of northwest Florida has little to differentiate it from the red clay hills of Georgia and Alabama across the border, but along the Gulf coast great swamps cut deep into the land, and tourist resorts of this section are built on bay fronts or islands overlooking the Gulf.

The lake or central-ridge section is rolling land pitted with lakes and springs. Le Heup Hill, 4 miles south of Dade City, with an elevation of 330 feet, is one of the highest measured points in the State. The estimated 30,000 lakes scattered throughout Florida range in depth from 2 to 27 feet, and in size from ponds of a few acres' extent to Lake Okeechobee, with an area of 717 square miles, the second-largest body of fresh water lying wholly within the United States. Free-running artesian wells are found chiefly along the coast and in central Florida, but in the lake district the water supply is obtained by pumping. North of Lake Okeechobee the Kissimmee Prairies, covered with grass and patches of palmetto, and interspersed with scattered hammocks, represent the State's largest cattle ranges.

The major part of Florida's shallow surface soil is underlaid by a deep limestone foundation. Sinks or potholes, varying in size from one to hundreds of acres, occur where the crust is broken. The huge Florida springs, the lakes, and many of the surface streams also result from breaks in the limestone. Underground watercourses often cause the earth's surface to cave in, exposing streams such as the one at Falmouth Spring, the Santa Fe and Alapaha Rivers, and Bear Creek, which disappear only to reappear miles beyond. The disappearance of lakes is also a familiar occurrence. One explanation of this phenomenon is that logs, stumps of trees, and other refuse clog openings in the limestone bottoms of the lakes. In time the debris rots and the water escapes into subterranean channels, but suction from escaping water draws other floating refuse and sediment to plug the holes again and allow the lakes to refill. Lake Iamonia, north of Tallahassee, has gone through this process several times within the past century. Lake Neff, in Hernando County, has disappeared and returned three times since 1917.

Florida's 27 major springs range in flow from about 14,000 to 800,000,000 gallons per day. Silver Springs, southeast of Ocala; Rainbow Springs, near Dunnellon; and Itchetucknee Springs, south of Lake City, in the order named, are the largest. Wakulla Spring has the largest volume from a single fissure in the earth. Some rivers—the Suwannee, the Withlacoochee, and the St. Johns—rise in swampy ground and are later swelled by the flow from springs. Rivers west of the Suwannee have their sources in the hills of Georgia and Alabama and become deeper after receiving the inflow from west Florida springs. Among these, the Apalachicola, Escambia, and Choctawhatchee Rivers were important trade routes before the development of highways and railroads connecting the *ante-bellum* plantations of south Georgia and Florida with the Gulf of Mexico.

The largest and most important river in the State, the St. Johns, flows northward, parallel to the east coast, and empties into the Atlantic Ocean east of Jacksonville. Dredging has opened the river to navigation by ocean liners as far as Jacksonville, a distance of 26 miles, but since 1841 small steamers have been plying the river as far south as Sanford, 200 miles from the sea.

Projecting into subtropical water, the Florida Peninsula enjoys a mild atmospheric drift from the Atlantic to the Gulf, and its climate in consequence is unusually pleasant and uniform. Below-freezing temperatures are rare, and snowfall is a subject for historians. Temperatures in January, the coldest month, average about 58.7° F., and in the warmest months, July and August, about 81° F.; the average for the year is 69.4°. In central and south Florida the average extreme range lies between 90° and 43°, while in north Florida the mercury sometimes drops below 32° for short periods. In summer the salt waters of Florida become lukewarm, and in winter their temperature is about the same as that of the north Atlantic in summer. But atmospheric warmth above Florida waters in the winter months is, of course, less than that above northern waters in summer, and at times winter sun bathing on Florida beaches is a somewhat chilly pastime.

Evaporation from the thousands of lakes and the encircling waters contributes to an annual average rainfall of 58 inches. Much of this precipitation occurs from April to November, usually when it is most needed to insure good crops and lower summer temperatures. The peninsula has a daily average of sunshine in excess of six hours.

The warm Gulf Stream curves around the peninsula's southern tip and flows north along the Atlantic coast. This factor, however, is not as important to Florida's climate as was once believed; geographers explain that the general marine influence and latitudinal position of the State would assure mild temperatures, apart from the proximity of the Gulf Stream. For short intervals each winter cold waves invade the State, bringing frost, delaying maturity of crops, and sometimes damaging fruit trees. The winds bearing this cold come overland from the northwest, and are not tempered by the Gulf Stream.

Florida and other South Atlantic States lie in the general path of tropical hurricanes, arising mostly in the Caribbean Sea in the fall of the year; but many of these storms blow themselves out before reaching land, or they come ashore with their destructive forces greatly spent. For the most part they describe a clockwise arc into the Gulf or up the Atlantic coast, although sometimes they reverse themselves. These atmospheric disturbances, caused by wind rushing toward a low-pressure area, take the form of a huge doughnut, with high wind revolving around a calm center or core. Because of this formation, the storm passes through three stages at any given spot in its path: first a furious gale in one direction, then a dead calm during the passage of the core, and finally a wind equal in velocity to the first but in the opposite direction. It is during the period of calm that inhabitants unfamiliar with the structure of the storm often leave their shelters, and are caught in the last stage. Buildings weakened by strain during the first wind are frequently wrecked by the second blast. Torrential rains usually accompany a hurricane, and water blown into unroofed buildings accounts for much property damage. Loss of life in the past has been chiefly because of poor housing and unpreparedness; one storm struck in the Everglades before Lake Okeechobee was diked, forcing that body of water over a wide territory to the south, where many laborers housed in flimsy shacks were drowned.

Government weather stations now chart the approximate path of all disturbances, and newspapers and radios give ample warning. Though the revolving wind may exceed 100 miles an hour in velocity, the forward movement of a hurricane seldom exceeds 20 miles, and this leaves plenty of time for those in danger to board up buildings or vacate the territory.

GEOLOGY AND PALEONTOLOGY

The far-reaching Floridian Plateau includes not only the State but an even greater surrounding area that lies less than fifty fathoms beneath the Atlantic Ocean and the Gulf of Mexico. Primarily an offspring of the sea and bearing the marks of its marine parentage, the plateau was built up largely during the most recent of the five geologic eras; it is the youngest part of the United States, a land infant but 45,000,000 years old.

During the convulsive age of mountain building the Floridian Plateau remained comparatively calm, only rising and falling in a rolling motion, with a down dip into the Gulf of Mexico. This process still continues; in the last 25,000 years the plateau, tipping on an axis that runs obliquely up the peninsula from Key West to a point below Fernandina, has lifted 6 feet at Miami and dropped 30 feet at Pensacola.

In the Paleozoic era of earth history, the area that is now the Mississippi Valley was a vast sea, and east of this, in the Appalachian region, lay the land mass to which is now attached the Floridian Plateau. But the hills of Florida are not a part of the Appalachian Mountains; they stand out principally because surrounding material has settled or eroded away. The crystalline rock that outcrops in Georgia is not found in Florida, except for deeply buried fragments. Neither do the subsurface waters that feed the State's springs and artesian wells originate in the Appalachian Mountains. Nor is the peninsula a great coral reef, as was once believed. Less than one per cent of its structure is coral.

Although the foundation rocks of Florida are covered with a stone blanket of marine deposit at least 4,000 feet deep, geologists surmise that they are probably folded and wrinkled in much the same way as are similar rocks in the Piedmont Plateau, which extends from the Hudson River to Alabama. The layers of marine sediment that rest upon the basement rocks were formed when the entire section was beneath the sea, and are composed for the most part of the skeletons of microscopic sea animals. During the Triassic, Jurassic, and Lower Cretaceous periods of the Mesozoic era, the State area was above the waters, but was submerged many times during the Cenozoic (Recent), the age of mammals. At no time, so far as can be learned, did the land ever rise very high above sea level, or did the sea ever cover the land to any great depth.

The warm shallow seas that repeatedly covered the area were ideally suited to foraminifera. These tiny marine animals, some too small to be seen by the naked eye, lived and died by the millions in tropic waters. While alive they were protected by shells of lime; when they died the shells sank to the floor of the ocean to form layers of limestone, each hundreds of feet thick. During the Eocene and Oligocene epochs the strata were composed almost entirely of this matter, and the formations of these periods are nearly pure limestone. During the Miocene, however, fine sand was washed down from the mountains of Georgia and Alabama and was deposited on the Floridian Plateau to form sandy limestone; and later much clay drifted south to settle over the State area and complete its stratified layers. Thus the foundation rocks are separated from the earliest exposed strata by a mass of limestone 4,000 feet thick and by layers of red, white, and black clay.

A gentle up-arching of the Eocene and older rocks had begun before the last of these deposits was made, and this doming finally gave the structure a list which, despite torrential rains that battered and slashed to beat it down, left it 150 feet above sea level to form an island around present Ocala. Eventually, when the Suwannee Strait to the north closed, this became a peninsula less than half the size of the Floridian Plateau, and part of the North American land mass.

The tip of the peninsula extended at one time only to the lower rim of Lake Okeechobee, but far to the south of that point another formation emerged from the up-building of live coral on submerged oolitic rock. Gradually wind and waves rolled up barriers along the Atlantic and Gulf coasts, extending the peninsula toward the coral reefs and eventually forming dunes that shut out the sea. The enclosed area, rank with marine plant life, became a fresh-water basin, and its decaying vegetation through the centuries turned into the peatlands that now comprise the Everglades.

A survey made along the Florida Reef in 1846 by Timothy Abbott Conrad, and followed by Louis Agassiz, gave original ground for the belief that the entire peninsula of Florida was of coral formation; and this theory was incorporated by Joseph LeConte in his excellent textbook, *Elements of Geology*, in 1878. This belief continued until 1886, when Angelo Heilprin determined that the progressive growth of the peninsula as far south as Lake Okeechobee was due to a combination of sedimentation and upheaval.

Geologically, Florida's strata date back only to the Tertiary or later periods of the Cenozoic era, embracing the Eocene, Oligocene, Miocene, and Pliocene epochs. Under familiar names these layers supply an inexhaustible source of road material, give Florida its lucrative phosphate industry, account for its pitted topography, and provide underground reservoirs that assure to all sections an independent supply of fresh water from local rainfall.

Ocala limestone, of the Eocene epoch, the oldest exposed sediment in the State, outcrops over a large section around Ocala, reaching north to the Suwannee River and south to the Withlacoochee River. This limestone underlies the entire State except for the extreme western portion. It is a pure-white to cream-colored granular rock, varying in thickness from 50 to 500 feet, and consists almost entirely of carbonate of lime. Chiefly composed of foraminifera, as are the older strata upon which it rests, it also contains fossil coral, sea urchins, molluscs, and occasionally a vertebrate sea mammal known as *Zeuglodon*, an early ancestor of the whale.

Marianna and Glendon limestones and Byram marl rest on the Ocala limestone, and belong to the Oligocene epoch. They correspond to the strata known as the Vicksburg group in Mississippi and Alabama, and appear in Florida only in the vicinity of Marianna, with the exception of a curved strip of the Glendon stone on either side of the Suwannee River near Ellaville. The Marianna limestone, a soft white rock, weathers to a dirty gray; Glendon limestone is hard, and its color runs from yellow to a pinkish hue; Byram marl consists of soft, fine-grained, sandy yellow limestone. The first two, quarried on a small scale, are used in the construction of chimneys.

The era of mountain building in the western part of North America, during the Miocene epoch, brought few changes in the contour and general outline of Florida. Six different layers of limestone, sand, and marl were then deposited: the Tampa limestone, widespread, but missing in many areas; the Shoal River formation; the Chipola formation; the Oak Grove sands in the northwestern part of the State; the Choctawhatchee formation, found both in the panhandle and inland from Charlotte Harbor; and the Hawthorn formation, also widespread, but thin, and much of it eroded away.

The most important Miocene strata are the cream-to-white colored limestones of the Tampa and the Hawthorn formations, both exposed over large areas. The former is essentially a marine and estuarine formation;

the latter, chiefly a land deposit. Tampa limestone is used in the manufacture of cement, and both are used for making quicklime. The Hawthorn contains commercial deposits of fuller's earth.

Pliocene deposits are divided into Caloosahatchee marl, the Citronelle formation, Bone Valley gravel, and the Alachua formation. The first of these, consisting of fine sand, lime ooze, and shells, was laid down in shallow salt water when the State was submerged by a calm sea. The Citronelle formation appears to have been deposited as a large delta, and the Bone Valley gravel similarly from an estuarine source. The Bone Valley and Alachua formations contain a great number of land-animal bones and phosphatic material from the Hawthorn decayed-phosphate deposits, such as calcium phosphate, calcium carbonate, and other minerals, derived from the fossil remains of extinct land and water animals. The Alachua deposits, mined in the Dunnellon region, supply hard rock phosphate, while from the Bone Valley gravel, in the Bartow region, comes pebble phosphate. Phosphate was discovered on Peace River in 1884 by J.Francis LeBaron, but was not commercially developed until 1887, when Colonel T.S.Moorehead managed to raise capital where LeBaron had failed.

The Pleistocene, first epoch of the Quaternary period of the Cenozoic era, and also known as the age of man, saw the formation of both land and water deposits. Muck, peat, alluvium, and wind-blown sand were laid down away from the ocean; while in the sea were built up shell marl, the coquina that furnished the early Spaniards with an easily worked building stone, soft oolitic rock, and coral-reef limestone. The greater part of the population of Florida occupies the Pensacola terrace, a formation of Pleistocene origin. On this terrace are the cities of Fernandina, St.Augustine, Jacksonville, Miami, Fort Myers, Bradenton, Tampa, St.Petersburg, and Pensacola.

Florida has its share of geological mysteries. One that gave rise to much speculation was a column of smoke and a red glare that appeared in the sky above the impenetrable Wakulla Swamp in August 1886 and that disappeared immediately after the Charleston earthquake. Geologists infer that it was caused by the ignition of escaping natural gas by lightning, and that the earthquake sealed the vent and thus extinguished the flames.

More difficult to explain, though unspectacular, is a row of round holes a few miles north of Brooksville, each about 36 inches in diameter and filled almost to the top with drifted sand and decayed vegetation. These 'chimneys,' as they are locally named, are blackened around the top, but show no indication of volcanic heat.

At Ballast Point near Tampa, geodes are frequently uncovered. These are little knots of stone with quartzlike interiors, running from light agate tints to jet black. The geode is a detached formation, and its accidental presence in the silex beds at Ballast Point is attributed to a tendency of nature to form concretions out of whatever substance is at hand. The only known similar specimens are found in the Mediterranean and Aegean Seas.

During the first two periods of the Tertiary era the only living creatures in Florida were marine animals, although the Tertiary produced in other parts of the continent the dinosaurs that are associated with prehistoric life. The Florida area was submerged at this time, and the corresponding formation—Ocala limestone—contains evidence of but one mammal, a whalelike sea monster known as *Basilosaurus*.

Formations of the last two periods of the Tertiary (Miocene and Pliocene) contain evidence that the State was then inhabited by strange beasts that found their way to the peninsula from many parts of the world. In the Alum Bluff beds of the Hawthorn formation in Leon, Gadsden, and Alachua Counties have been found the bones and teeth of deer, three-toed horses, camels, giant pigs, and rhinoceroses. These were not predatory types, however, and had man inhabited the State at this time he would have feared but one carnivorous animal, a prowling beast akin to both the modern wolf and the dog.

A number of significant plant fossils have been found in the Alum Bluff bed between the Chipola and Choctawhatchee formations. Among the thirteen species positively identified are fan palm, breadfruit, satinwood, ironwood, camphor, buckthorn, elm, and persimmon, all of which are adapted to the present habitat of the region. The species indicate that the flora was predominantly tropical, with additions from a temperate climate.

The Miocene three-toed horse, known as *Parahippus*, can be traced through several varieties to the *Hipparion*, the three-toed horse of the Pliocene. *Hipparion*, however, was not in the direct line that led to the development of the modern horse, but a branch that has since disappeared. It is not until the Pleistocene that fossils of *Equus*, the prehistoric one-toed horse that is often called the '*homo sapiens*' of the horse family, appear in Florida deposits.

The Pliocene deposits, following in point of geological time directly after the Miocene, contain an even greater abundance of fossil animal remains. The phosphate mines of Alachua, Levy, and Polk Counties have yielded rich stores to the Florida paleontologist. The fauna of this age differs greatly from that of modern times. It was in the Pliocene that the mastodons made their way from the Old World by way of Asia; even at the very beginning of the age they were firmly established on the peninsula. The serrate-toothed mastodon, a great elephantlike creature with a short trunk and four tusks, wandered from India halfway around the world before reaching Florida.

With the Pleistocene era there came such a multitude of both great and small animals as will probably never be found in one region again. The great ice sheet at this time was advancing south from the North Pole; and covering the northern part of the United States and all of Canada was a glacial mass that destroyed vegetation and drove animal life before it. Herbivorous beasts sought green pastures in the warmer territories to the south, and countless thousands invaded Florida. Camels, horses, mammoths, huge sloths, armadillos, and peccaries roamed the State, cropping grass and stripping leaves from the Pleistocene trees. After them came the beasts of prey—saber-toothed tigers, wolves, and lions—which made life precarious for the vegetarians. Many of these animals bear a resemblance to the modern fauna of South America and Africa, and students of ancient life present this as evidence for the theory that camels originated in America and later made their way to the Old World long before man, possibly following the animal trail, found his way to the New World.

The most important deposits of the Pleistocene era in the State are the Melbourne bone beds, a series of patches along the east coast containing the bones of extinct animals just as they were buried thousands of years ago beneath beds of shifting sand. Investigation of these beds has been carried on from time to time, but the deposits are so rich that it will be many years before all the material can be assembled and classified.

Geological information on Florida is not to be obtained from mountains, where outcroppings can be studied with comparatively little effort and expense, but from strata thousands of feet below the surface. Usually the expense of such operations has made geological research in the State an incident of commercial enterprise, as in the deep-well borings of Marion County. Thus only intermittently have geologists been able to study that part of the earth's history written in the rocks, soils, and waters of Florida.

THE ISLE OF FLOWERS

Florida, regarded by Ponce de Leon as 'the Isle of Flowers,' is entirely within the temperate zone but is influenced by subtropical waters. As a result, most of its tropical plants bloom in summer and many of the temperate zone varieties bloom in winter—a reversal of the usual order. This, together with the State's four distinct growing seasons, produces an unusual mingling of vegetation.

High and low 'hammocks,' fresh and salt marshes, sand and clay hills, and rich muck beds are well suited to both native and imported plant life, but the distribution of the many species is greatly influenced by topography. Native plants are especially sensitive to elevation. In the flat pine woods a shallow depression reaching water level usually results in the appearance of a cypress dome; a rise of from six to eight feet frequently means a change from pine to scrub blackjack oak.

Mark Catesby, an English naturalist, collected specimens of Florida plant life as early as 1731, and published prints of many that he found. In the last quarter of the eighteenth century, William Bartram, son of John Bartram, botanist to the King of England, created something of a sensation both here and abroad by his published description of Florida plants. Only recently a rare bulbous plant described by him, the blue ixia, was rediscovered growing on the roadside between Jacksonville and St.Augustine. André Michaux, who was sent to Florida by the French Government to gather botanical specimens, arrived in 1788; part of his herbarium is now in the Jardin des Plantes in Paris. Dr. Henry Perrine, a distinguished pioneer in the study of subtropical plants, met his death on Indian Key at the hands of Indians in 1840. Dr. Alvan Wentworth Chapman of Apalachicola narrowly escaped capture by Indians while he was searching near St.Marks for the feathery blooms of the titi, a native tree. His *Flora of the Southern United States*, published in 1860, is still a standard work. As a result of studies by these and many other distinguished botanists, more than 3,000 varieties of indigenous flowering plants have been identified, ranging in size from the magnolia to the delicate terrestrial orchid, and in many cases found nowhere else in North America. Together with thousands of imported tropical or subtropical plants, they make Florida a favorite field for the botanist and the amateur flower lover.

In general, Florida vegetation is distributed among seven more or less distinct habitats—flatwoods, scrub lands, grassy swamps, savannas, salt marshes, hammocks or hardwood forests, and high pinelands. Collectively, these contain about half of the tree species found north of Mexico, and more varieties of native trees than any similar region in America north of the Tropic of Cancer. Yet only five—oak, pine, cypress, palm, and mangrove—are the familiar trees of Florida.

Flatwoods, common throughout the State, consist of poorly drained level areas, with a sour boggy soil. Although open forests constitute their chief vegetation, they contain an abundance of flowers that bloom many months of the year. Most noteworthy in the low and wet fields of lower Florida are the terrestrial orchids, of which there are 64 varieties. Here also are the insect catchers—pitcher plants, sundews, and yellow and purple Pinguicula—together with red lilies and several species of milkwort. Among the more showy native species are the liatris, commonly called the blazing star, whose nodding purple spikes decorate the landscape in late summer and fall, and the gray-leaved, pale-blue lupine that covers the hills and roadsides as early as February.

The scrub lands, identified by small sand pines, include much of the ridge district in the central part of the peninsula, together with the sand dunes along the coasts. The ridge area, abounding in lakes and springs, is characterized by dense growths of saw palmetto, evergreen, live oaks, blackjack, and water oaks, interspersed with varieties of evergreen shrubs, hollies, and such members of the heath family as huckleberries, sparkleberries, and fetter-bush. Many species of cactus are common. Throughout the central and lower east-coast section grows a cycad, the coontie of the genus *Zamia*, roots of which provide a kind of arrowroot. From these roots the Indians often made bread during the Seminole Wars, when they could not remain in one locality long enough to raise corn. Most of this region is fragrant from early March to June with the blossoms of commercially grown grapefruit, tangerine, and orange trees. (The orange blossom is of interest not only to citrus growers and wedding parties—it has been chosen as the State flower.) During the same season, fields of white and red morning-glories, sunflowers, and black-eyed Susans are conspicuous.

In the savannas of central Florida, water lettuce forms a heavy aquatic growth, and spectacular displays of the yellow American lotus may be seen on several of the fresh-water marshes. The major marine grasses are the turtle, eel, and manatee varieties. The cabbage palm predominates in palm savannas over the State. Floating water hyacinths cover many small lakes and streams, often growing thickly enough to impede navigation. On the east coast, and for a distance along the lower Gulf coast, are flourishing growths of Spanish bayonets, seagrapes, lantanas, and blue verbena (*Verbena maritima*).

The larger plant growth in north Florida is longleaf and other pines, cypresses, magnolias, bays, gums, and oaks. Two trees native to the northwest area, Tumion cedar and Floridian yew, grow only along the Apalachicola River. Chapman's rhododendron is found exclusively in the sandy pinelands of west Florida.

Near the coast in lower Dade County and extending to the western edge of Homestead, an area of 500 square miles, is a region of pineland without a close counterpart elsewhere in the world. In the absence of sufficient topsoil, the trees take root directly in the soft honeycombed lime rock that outcrops here. Much of the native vegetation of southern Florida (which is free from severe frosts) occurs nowhere else in the United States. Here cypresses, mangroves, mahoganies, ferns, lianas, and aerial plant growths flourish, as well as several of the State's most decorative palms.

Of a half-dozen varieties of oak, the laurel, water, and live oaks (the latter an evergreen species) attain great size. Many of the State's towns and villages may be recognized immediately as older settlements by the water oaks, with their straight trunks and high branches, that shade the streets. It has been said of the live oak that a man can always rest his hand on a lower bough. The trunk is short and thick, and the spread of the tree is often greater than its height. Some of the moss-hung live oaks in Florida today were standing when America was discovered.

Although the palm is Florida's much exploited emblem, the pine is its commonest tree. From the stunted sand variety to the tall open-crown longleaf type, the pine ranges over the peninsula on upland and plain, and masses luxuriantly in the flatwoods. The quick-growing slash is the crop pine, and with the loblolly supplies raw material to Florida's paper mills.

Florida has but 15 native palms, among which only the cabbage palmetto grows naturally throughout the State; but to these more than a hundred species have been added from every palm-growing country in the world. The majority of the natives, which include four palmettoes, are palmate or fan-flared; and only two, the royal and the coconut, bear pinnate or feather leaves. The royal palm, now largely transplanted, grows wild on the muck lands near the lower Gulf coast. The coconut palm, also transplanted, is widespread on the Florida Keys, extending to Key West; its presence here is attributed to the buoyancy of its fruit, which drifted up from the American tropics and took root on the island reef. Other palms, small and mostly of the thatch varieties, grow on the reef.

The palmettoes, with their recumbent trunks and enormous root systems, form impenetrable mats that blanket the dry waste spaces throughout the State. They are usually of a yellow-green color; but one variety of saw palmetto takes on a startling glaucous blue on the high dunes along the Atlantic coast.

The royal is the sovereign palm for ornamental planting, but in cooler central Florida it abdicates in favor of a plumy palm, popularly miscalled *Cocos plumosa*, a hardy feather-leaf importation from Brazil. The Washingtonian palm, from Mexico, is another much used for street planting; it attains great height but does not shed its fronds, and unless trimmed it disports a gray 'hula' skirt of dried leaves that reaches nearly to the ground. Among the curious importations is the traveler's palm, an apparently two-dimensional fan-shaped tree, the fronds of which are said to point naturally north and south. It can be tapped for drinking water, and therefore serves both as a font and a compass for the wayfarer in desert countries.

Dense thickets of red, white, and black mangroves cover the greater portion of Florida's lower coast. Mangroves grow from floating seeds shaped somewhat like elephant tusks that anchor themselves in shallow places. These strange trees rise from tide-washed sand flats where, with their exposed perpendicular roots, they give the impression of a forest marching on stilts. The mangrove is a land builder; its aerial roots collect quantities of drifting earth and debris, and gradually the shore line back of the trees is extended. The greatest of mangrove forests are those on the Ten Thousand Islands, a wild and partly submerged region south of Marco on the Gulf coast.

The largest swamp and savanna area of the State is the Everglades, a section occupying nearly all the southern interior of the peninsula and covered for the most part with tall grasses and sedges, the most common being a tawny sawgrass. On elevations and islands are patches of live oak surrounded by fringes of coco plum. The custard apple, a species of the *Annona*, often forms dense thickets here; but where the land is low, cypress is the common tree. The Big Cypress Swamp of Collier County, embracing 2,400 square miles west of the Everglades, is the largest of its kind in Florida. The buttressed trunk of the cypress spreads wide at its base for greater support, and projecting into the air, sometimes at a considerable distance from the roots, are 'knees,' believed to be of use in aerating the tree. Known to manufacturers as the 'wood eternal,' the cypress dates back to the ice age; specimens excavated from ancient rock strata were neither decayed nor petrified. Known also as the oldest living thing on the earth, attaining an age of 6,000 years, the cypress grows slowly, adding but an inch to its radius in 30 years. The living patriarch of these trees in Florida is 'Old Senator' at Longwood, estimated to be 3,500 years old. Duckweed, floating heart, sagittaria, bonnets, and bladderwort grow luxuriously in the shallow water, and air plants thrive among the tree tops. The Tillandsia or Spanish moss, of the pineapple family, is the most conspicuous of the epiphytic or air-growing plants.

Contrasting vividly with the fresh green of new cypress foliage are the spider orchid, with fragrant, narrow-petaled, large white flowers; the shell orchid, with its showy larkspurlike spike; and the chintz orchid, bearing odd-looking mottled flowers. Great orchids (*Cyrtopodium punctatum*), some of them almost unbelievably huge, have been found in the Everglades. Expeditions from the New York Botanical Gardens have reported specimens with as many as a thousand blossoms, and one, estimated to be 500 years old, so large that four men were needed to lift it.

Hammocks are defined by J.K.Small, the botanist, as dense growths of trees and shrubs, mostly broad-leaved, sometimes occupying whole circumscribed portions of a geological formation, or occurring as 'islands' surrounded by pine woods or prairie. Hammock soil is rich in humus and is arable when cleared. In the hardwood hammocks of northern Florida, looping vines of rattan, wild grape, and Spanish moss festoon cabbage palms, magnolias, and oaks.

Florida's jungles are made up mostly of hardwood growths—oaks, gums, bays, and magnolias—intertwined with tenacious creepers, hostile vines, and bristling plants that bar passage. One of the latter is the thorny *Cerus pentagonus*, of which Charles Torrey Simpson, the naturalist, has written: 'I have abused it elsewhere but it is sufficiently villainous to call for more condemnation. I cannot conceive how it would be possible to devise a more devilish plant. Not frequently it almost fills the vacant space in the forest, thrusting its long, lithe stems through the thickest growth and appearing in the most unexpected places. Its stems may be three or five angled, and each is lined with terrific spines an inch or more in length. They are so sharp and strong that they easily pierce the heaviest leather. The explorer may be ever so alert but he is certain to run into dozens of them. He is equally sure to carry away a fine collection of its thorns, which have a vicious way of breaking off in the body.'

Two native rubber trees of the jungles are the so-called strangling or strangler fig, and a shortleaf variety which resembles the banyan of India. The strangling fig derives its name from the fact that it often germinates on trunks and branches of other trees, sending down root stems that encircle and eventually strangle the host tree.

More than a hundred ferns and plants closely related to ferns are found in the State. Fronds of the largest tropical varieties are from 10 to 18 feet in length. Of the two great fern areas in Florida, one is in the west-central lime sink region, the other in the extreme southern portion of the State.

An immense variety of rare, odd, and beautiful plants has been introduced by the U.S. Plant Introduction Garden at Cocoanut Grove, Miami, by numerous private nurseries, and by owners of large private estates. Purple and magenta bougainvillea and the golden bignonia, or flame vine, embellish walls and gateways. Hedges and clusters of flowering oleander, Turk's-cap, and hibiscus are seen everywhere. The rapid-growing Australian pine is not a true pine, but belongs to the same group as the European paradise plant. Although not so sturdy as the native pine, the tree thrives in dry sandy soil, and is seldom damaged by salt spray. It is tall, symmetrical, and pointed, an importation of recent years used for windbreaks and street planting. Exotic fruits, silk oaks, the feathery bamboo, the jacaranda, the poinsettia, and the variegated crotons are favorites among the cultivated trees and plants.

ANIMAL LIFE

Pioneers and explorers recorded centuries ago that Florida was immensely rich in animal life. Today much of the State retains its early wilderness character and, in a great variety of natural habitats, affords refuge and retreat for numerous species. Moderate winters and ample sunshine have helped to produce a particularly abundant aquatic life.

Eighty-four species of land mammals are found in Florida. Black bear, deer, gray fox, wildcat, bay lynx, and puma inhabit the extensive areas of swamp and forest. The puma, or Florida panther, leads an isolated life in the Big Cypress country of lower Florida, more than a thousand miles from its nearest relative, the mountain lion, or western cougar. The Florida species is slightly smaller than the mountain lion.

The majority of the small animals are those common to all Southern States, but they are particularly numerous here: squirrels, cottontail rabbits, raccoons, and opossums. An unusual type is the marsh rabbit, a relative of the woods rabbit of Central and South America, which is known locally as the 'pontoon.' It is somewhat smaller than the cottontail and may be distinguished by its smaller ears, shorter hind legs, and nearly unicolored tail. Except for the swamp rabbit, this is the only species of rabbit that will take to the water. The small rodent oddly termed 'salamander' is actually the pocket gopher, while the so-called 'Florida gopher' is a land turtle. The salamander builds the countless little white mounds of sand that are a familiar sight in Florida. The mounds appear mysteriously overnight, but the industrious creatures that build them are seldom seen. The manatee, or sea cow, is another rarity, a marine mammal that was once particularly abundant along the Indian and Manatee Rivers. Otter and mink, once plentiful, have been greatly reduced by trapping.

The wild razorback hog, though still present and untamed, has been abolished by law; an act of the 1937 legislature declared the wild razorback legally nonexistent in order to do away with a common defense in cases of hog theft—that the culprit thought the filched beast was wild and therefore ownerless.

More than 400 species and subspecies of birds have been recorded, counting the numerous migrants that winter in Florida. The mockingbird was chosen Florida's State bird by a vote of the school children, and made officially so in 1927 by an act of the legislature. An old argument as to the relative singing ability of the mockingbird and the European nightingale was settled in 1931 at Bok Tower, near Lake Wales, when imported nightingales demonstrated their talent in competition with mockingbirds of the neighborhood. The latter at once appropriated the song of the nightingales and made it a part of their own repertoire.

Among the common land birds nesting in Florida, the bald eagle and the turkey buzzard are the largest. Woodlands abound in titmice, catbirds, kingbirds, and butcher birds; tiny humming birds; gnatcatchers and chickadees; colorful orchard orioles, cardinals, summer tanagers, brown thrashers, blue birds and painted buntings; a multitude of warblers, including the pine warbler, the bark-creeping black and white warbler, the parula, palm and myrtle varieties. Common blue jays, Florida wrens and English sparrows are familiar to every householder. The blackbirds are: the redwing, the Florida grackles, common and fish crows, and the purple martin—a member of the swallow family, whose color is very nearly black. At night appear 'chuck will's widow' and his less numerous cousin, the northern whippoorwill; the swooping bull bat; barred, and screech owls. The most common of woodpeckers are the redheaded, redbellied, flicker and downy species. The almost extinct ivory-billed woodpecker is known to exist in tropical jungles, and the rare pileated woodpecker is occasionally seen in various parts of the State.

Quail, doves, and other game birds are plentiful. Wild turkeys, now protected between hunting seasons, have increased, and can be found in remote swamps and hammocks. More than 35 species of duck have been noted.

The savannas and marshes are inhabited by redwings, rails, gallinules, ibises, and several species of heron and egret. The handsome white egret, once nearly extinct, is now protected and, with the little blue and Louisiana herons, again ranges the State in large numbers. The great white heron, a Florida native, nests on the keys and coral reefs near Cape Sable. The sandhill crane, often four feet tall, is the only true crane here, and because of its loud cry is sometimes mistaken for the whooping crane, a type no longer found. The white ibis, or Spanish curlew, habitant of the mangrove swamps, the central lake regions, and the fresh-water marshes of the upper St. Johns River, is becoming increasingly numerous. Two other spectacular birds, once abundant, are the roseate spoonbill, which is almost extinct, and the scarlet flamingo, now to be found in the State only in captivity. A strange and fascinating kind of aquatic bird is the limpkin, with its hobbling gait and the wailing cry of a maniac.

Along the coasts and salt marshes, gulls, pelicans, cormorants, and particularly ospreys, or fish hawks, are common. A visitor to the southern part of the State is the magnificent frigate, or man-o'-war bird, which nests in the Bahamas and West Indies. This creature sails gracefully over its hunting ground on outspread motionless wings, waiting for a chance to descend on gulls, terns, pelicans, and other fishing birds. A migratory bird of unusual range is the Arctic tern, which journeys between a summer home in the Arctic and a winter home in the Antarctic, an annual round trip of 22,000 miles, with stops both ways in Florida.

A diurnal burrowing owl inhabits the dry prairie regions of the peninsula, where it nests in the soil. This species is closely related to a similar bird found on the western plains, and has aroused much controversy among ornithologists on the circumstances of its separation from the western type. Another unusual species, found chiefly in the scrub-oak belt, is the Florida, or 'scrub' jay, a cousin of the blue jay and distinguished from the latter by its uncrested head. This attractive bird is surprisingly easy to tame. Audubon's caracara, a migrant from South America, ranges north as far as the prairies of south central Florida. Somewhat intermediate between the hawk and the vulture, the caracara spends much of its time on the ground capturing turtles and small rodents.

Among the State's finest natural rookeries are those around Lake Okeechobee, in the marshes of the upper St. Johns, the Kissimmee Prairie, the Florida Keys, Big Cypress Swamp, and the Shark River region. Among the rarest of Florida birds are the Everglades kite, the latest Audubon Society count showing only about 30 remaining. A similar census indicates only 100 roseate spoonbills, 500 burrowing owls, and 600 great white herons. Other birds, some rare, some grotesque, but all attractive, include white pelicans, white, glossy and wood ibises, snowy and American egrets, Audubon's caracaras, black-necked stilts, little blue and Louisiana herons, Caspian terns, herring and laughing gulls and cormorants.

In the reptile family, the alligator and the crocodile are often popularly confused. The alligator is widespread and fairly numerous, while the crocodile ranges only through the brackish coastal inlets from Biscayne Bay to Cape Sable. The alligator is black with a yellowish belly; it has a broad snout, heavy body, prominent eyes, and raised articulations along the spine. Its diet includes several species of turtle that are destructive to valuable game fish, and for this reason the alligator's presence is regarded as desirable. An unmolested alligator seldom attacks men, but the active and savage crocodile will readily charge a human foe. The crocodile has a long narrow snout, double-hinged jaws (unlike those of the alligator), a slender greenish-gray body splotched with black, and a light gray belly.

Snakes, frogs, and toads are abundant. Only four of the snakes commonly found in Florida are poisonous: the diamondback rattler, the cottonmouth moccasin, the harlequin or coral snake, and the pigmy rattler, usually called 'ground rattler.' The pigmy rattler's bite is seldom deadly. The poisonous copperhead is occasionally found in Jackson County. Venomous reptiles are becoming less numerous in the more settled districts, especially in counties where bounties are paid for their destruction. Rattlesnakes are easily killed; an injury to their spine or overexposure to intense sunlight causes death. The hog is the natural enemy of snakes and, where permitted to roam, is very effective in eliminating rattlers. Canned rattlesnake meat recently has been accepted as a delicacy for human consumption. Water snakes, often resembling the dangerous cottonmouth, are numerous, but nine out of ten are harmless. The nonpoisonous king snake, one of the most conspicuous reptiles, and the formidable 9- to 10-foot indigo, or gopher snake, feed largely on other snakes and are credited with keeping down the number of rattlesnakes. About 40 species of snakes inhabit Florida.

Of the true and edible frogs, the strictly aquatic Florida bullfrog is most common. The familiar frog choruses, however, usually come from tree frogs—small, emerald-green amphibians that climb by means of tiny suction cups on the tips of their toes. Curiosities are the sapo, or Cuban toad, a nocturnal nonhibernating creature, and the spade-footed toad that burrows underground with its horny feet.

Turtles found in Florida are the common alligator snapper, the loggerhead, the soft-shell, the mud turtles, and a land terrapin which is peculiar to the State. Green and loggerhead turtles are captured in large nets for the market. In Key West is a 'turtle crawl'—a fenced-in corral where turtles—most of them caught off the coast of Central America by natives of Grand Cayman—are confined for shipment alive to various markets, or await conversion into canned meat and soup. A marine turtle weighs from 100 to 500 pounds, and during mating season lays several batches of one hundred or more eggs on outlying dunes and isolated beaches.

Several species of lizard abound in the State. The common green lizard, miscalled the 'chameleon,' is capable of changing its color to a dull brown and thus adapting itself to its environment. Another lizard is the so-called 'grass' or 'glass' snake. Several of the brighter-colored lizards, sometimes termed 'scorpions,' are erroneously considered to be poisonous, but no Florida variety need be feared on that account.

Spiders and insects are comparatively numerous, particularly butterflies, moths, katydids, dragonflies, grasshoppers, and beetles. More than 300 native butterflies have been identified, a number increased to approximately 700 by migrants and foreign species. Butterflies frequently seen are monarchs, Gulf fritillaries, cloudless sulphurs, viceroys, buckeyes, zebras, great southern whites, painted ladies, minute skippers; commas, which bear the Greek question mark in silver color; '88's,' also named for their wing decorations; blue morphoes, imported from South America and said to be the bluest things in nature; and orange dogs, which are citrus pests. A butterfly farm in Pensacola has introduced a number of foreign varieties. The day-flying pink variety is one of the more common moths. Some of the spiders are unbelievably large and brilliantly marked. The black widow, so-named because of its shining blackness and the female's habit of devouring its mate, is the only Florida spider considered capable of inflicting a fatally poisonous bite. It is fairly large in size and distinguished by reddish markings, shaped like an hourglass, upon the belly. The black widow lives in rubbish, in lumber piles, and around unkempt human habitations.

Florida nuisances are tiny sandflies that are felt rather than seen on windless summer days; redbugs, encountered in underbrush; and scorpions, whose sting is more painful than that of a wasp. Municipal, State, and Federal Governments have sponsored drainage and irrigation projects for the purpose of combating the once formidable mosquito menace, but this insect continues to be a nuisance over wide areas during the summer.

More than 700 species of fish have been identified in the lakes, rivers, and coastal waters of Florida. According to Barton W. Evermann, ichthyologist and author of *The Fishes of North and Middle America* (1896–1900), Florida has more kinds of fish than any other part of the country, with 300 species along the Gulf coast, 174 along the east coast, and 290 in Key West waters. One hundred of these are edible, more than twice the number in any other region in the United States.

Commercial fishing, one of the State's largest industries, concerns itself principally with mullet, red snapper, Spanish mackerel, speckled trout, and grouper. The small menhaden is used in the manufacture of lubricating oil, chicken feeds, and fertilizer. Leading salt-water food fishes are pompano, bluefish, and flounder, favored by epicureans; and bass, sheepshead, and kingfish. The mullet is the only variety, it is said, that fishermen regard highly enough to use for a steady diet.

In the big-game group are tarpon, 'silver kings' of the sporting world; marlin, swordfish, sailfish, sawfish, dolphin, and the savage sharp-toothed barracuda. Smaller salt-water game fish include snook, bluefish, bonefish, mackerel, and speckled trout. Fresh-water fighters are the much-sought, yet plentiful, large-mouthed and small-mouthed black bass; record specimens of both have been taken from Florida lakes and rivers. The small-mouthed bass is an importation whose size increased rapidly when placed in the State's waters. Despite the natural abundance of fish, State hatcheries are maintained for the propagation of bass, bream, crappie, and shad, and the breeding of tropical fish for study and observation. Many privately operated hatcheries supply rare tropical fish to aquariums throughout the country.

Other salt-water fish are grunts, snappers, trunkfish, and porkfish; angelfish in blue, black, and yellow varieties; French rock beauties, amberjack, and wahoo. Colorful tropical fish are cow pilots or sergeant majors (yellowish-green banded with indigo); four-eyed blue and brown squirrelfish, turquoise-blue parrotfish, red goatfish, black pilots, muttonfish, lanes, mangroves, and red mahoganies. And there are queen triggerfish, commonly called 'old wenches' because of shrewish wrinkles etched in blue on the background of their yellow faces; 'flying robins' that walk on their ventral fins; sea porcupines, or hedgehog fish; and schoolmasters—flashing silver, red, orange, yellow, black, green, and blue. A native 'Conch' of Key West, acting as guide for a scientist, disdainfully disposed of tropical fish: 'Them's no 'count. I'd ruther hev one good sheepshead than all the painted rubbage from Largo to the Markees.'

The broad flat-bodied rays are encountered in shallow water along the coast; in some varieties the long thin tail is equipped with a sting. The giant devilfish or manta, a deep-sea nightmare, is a ferocious fighter when harpooned and often tows a boat for miles. A specimen weighing a ton and a half was captured in 1936 after a prolonged battle off Mayport, near Jacksonville. The gar is a predatory fresh-water fish that dates back to the Silurian period.

Chief of Florida crustaceans are shrimp, crabs in many varieties—king, horseshoe, stone, hermit, land, and fiddler—and Key West crawfish, known in the market as 'Florida lobster.' Shrimp are perhaps the most commercially valuable inhabitants of coastal waters. Molluscs are represented by oysters, clams, scallops, and conchs, whose hard shells were once used by the Indians as cutting tools. The donax, or coquina—a tiny edible clam—is found on sandy beaches in tremendous numbers.

Growing coral reefs, found nowhere else in the United States, lie in clear shallow water for 200 miles along the southern tip of the peninsula. Under a microscope these living polyps are revealed as fragile creatures, yet their skeletons form vast reefs that often resemble submerged castles. The reef at Elliott Key is exquisite in its structure; and reefs equally beautiful occur at Virginia and Biscayne Keys. The brain coral, fashioned like a limestone model of the human brain, and the pepper coral that stings the hand are common types. The brain coral is valued as a voodoo charm.

Inhabiting the reefs are black porcupine sea urchins, with long vicious quills that can penetrate a man's shoe. Sea fans and plumes, or gorgonians, wave in graceful wands of tan and purple.

Marine worms, flowerlike organisms of the sea anemone family, sprout from interstices of the reefs and trap minute animals in their tentacles. Valuable sheepswool sponges, as well as grass and wire varieties, are taken from the deep water of the Gulf north and west of Tarpon Springs and, in smaller quantities, from shallow beds in the vicinity of Key West.

CONSERVATION

An unforeseen consequence of the conquest of the Florida wilderness—largely achieved within the present generation—is the serious depletion of natural resources. The State today is faced with several pressing conservation problems, chief of which is reforestation. A population, tripled since 1900, has required the destruction of vast timber tracts in the development of housing facilities and industry. Because of ceaseless timber cutting, forest fires, and evasion of conservation laws, the peninsula retains but one-fourth of its original supply of merchantable lumber. About eight million acres of submarginal land, more suitable for reforestation than any other purpose, were tax-delinquent and idle in 1938. The State planning board recommended to the 1937 legislature an act to permit reclamation of this land, but it was not passed.

Many forest conservation agencies operate in the State. The Florida Forest Service, under the supervision of the State board of forestry, administers five State forests, totaling 30,142 acres, and co-operates with landowners and counties in the control of fires on approximately 3,128,000 acres. Adding to this total the public forest lands under the jurisdiction of the U.S. Forest Service, the Farm Security Administration, and the U.S.

Biological Survey, more than 5,400,000 acres were under protection in 1938. A State nursery is maintained at Olustee, but the reforestation of private lands depends largely on the number of persons who pay for seedling stock. The general effectiveness of the board of forestry is limited likewise by the number of forest owners co-operating with conservation agencies.

The U.S. Forest Service is custodian of four national forests in the State, totaling more than one million acres, where it maintains reforestation and fire control service. The National Park Service co-operates with the State park service in the development of State parks, seven of which have been designated, and in the acquisition of a portion of the Everglades as a national park. The Civilian Conservation Corps, during 1936, operated 24 camps in Florida. A total of 4,776 workers aided in the fight against forest destruction by building firebreaks, patrolling the forests, planting seedling stock, and checking erosion.

A forestry project of the Works Progress Administration carries on an intensive educational program, particularly within the schools, that stresses the advantages of protection as compared to the annual losses from forest fires. As another effective method of fire prevention, the WPA employs men to patrol their neighborhoods in the various timber sections. These men strive to demonstrate to cattle owners the waste and folly of burning forest lands, widely practiced in Florida for the purpose of creating new pasturage. They point out that the valuable Bermuda grass is killed, and that only weeds and worthless wire grass grow back. WPA labor is held constantly in readiness to assist in fire fighting.

Methods used in the past by the naval-stores industry also contributed to the depletion of forests. In scraping pine trees for turpentine gums, it was frequently the practice to scrape away the bark over too great an area and as a consequence the trees were greatly injured. Many trees were scraped, or 'bled,' while too young, and left unprotected against fire. Too few were spared for seed purposes. Today the operators are usually scientific and careful in their work. Instruction by the U.S. Forest Service has eliminated much of the excessive 'bleeding' of trees and other injurious practices. Fire protection is more generally understood and effectively undertaken. The results are increased yields and higher qualities of resins over longer periods of production. Related to the general forestry problem is the diminishing supply of wild life, caused by destructive methods of hunting and trapping, and the willful burning of forests.

Another conservation problem is the safeguarding of Florida's abundant supply of salt- and fresh-water fish, one of the State's main assets both from a commercial and recreational standpoint. This is in charge of the State board of conservation, which maintains a division of shellfish, a division of salt-water fish, and a division of geology. The board also administers all conservation measures relating to the shrimp and sponge industries, crawfish, crabs, the manatee, and some varieties of turtles and terrapins. The board sponsors radio broadcasts, lectures, fair exhibits, and a monthly magazine. Acting upon the recommendation of the board, the 1935 legislature passed a law requiring a conservation course to be included in the curricula of high schools in the State.

A separate commission of game and fresh-water fish, created in 1935, administers all laws pertaining to game and nongame birds and animals and fresh-water fish. Its division of more than a hundred conservation officers is active throughout the year in enforcing regulations, and in protecting the State breeding grounds and wild-life refuges. These sanctuaries, comprising three million acres, are closed to hunting at all times.

The Federal Government has expended millions of dollars to save Florida resources, largely in co-operation with State conservation agencies. Steps have been taken to eradicate the oyster leech from the valuable Apalachicola oyster beds; new oyster beds have been planted along the coast, the sponge industry has been regulated, a crawfish and stone-crab hatchery established in Key West, and three large fresh-water fish hatcheries put into operation at Welaka, Winter Haven, and Wewahitchka. The hatcheries replenish the supply of black bass, bream, and shad. In 1935 the State prohibited the sale of black bass, and in 1937 provided a closed season on this game fish during its spawning time.

The agricultural 'mining' of arable land, by which the soil is deprived of the minerals needed for plant growth, is a matter of increasing seriousness. Although less than 10 per cent of the State's 30 million acres of farmland is under cultivation, there is a growing need for scientific farming and soil conservation of the cultivated acres. Such measures are largely directed by the school of agriculture and the U.S. experiment station at the University of Florida. These agencies offer free advice and bulletin service to farmers on up-to-date soil protection methods. By means of radio programs, literature, demonstrations, club work, and county fairs, they advance scientific farming methods in all communities. The school of agriculture is teaching Florida's future farmers the importance of improved techniques.

Underground waters, utilized in the form of artesian wells, are Florida's main source of a potable water supply and are also used extensively in farming. These wells are made possible by an abundant rainfall, Florida having more than most other States, an average of 52.8 inches annually. This insures a permanent and adequate water supply. Geologists state that rain seeps through Florida's surface soil to an under layer of limestone, where it is absorbed and held in cell-like pockets, just as water is held when it soaks into a porous brick. The downward seepage of water creates the pressure needed for artesian wells. When the land is drained of an unusual quantity of water by surface streams, natural springs, and wells, the pressure of the run-off is often reduced, but only in the immediate area. Engineers have estimated that only about one-tenth of Florida's rainfall finds an outlet in springs, rivers, and wells. The remainder seeps through the limestone and into the ocean by way of crevices in the underwater portions of the Floridian Plateau. When opponents of the National Gulf-Atlantic Ship Canal contended that its construction would lower the water table throughout the State, U.S. army engineers investigated the problem and reported that the canal would reduce water pressure only in the immediate vicinity of the cut. It was also pointed out in this survey that the canal would not pierce the main body of limestone substratum.

In co-operation with the National Resources Committee, the Florida State planning board conducted a comprehensive survey of Florida's water resources during the latter part of 1936. This survey contained recommendations for conserving the water supply, and pointed the way for further investigation of the underground and surface waters of the State.

Too rapid drainage of the peatlike Everglades has created another localized conservation problem. Spontaneous combustion and brushwood fires have caused the burning and loss of large areas of valuable soil that, before artificial drainage, were normally under water. Various agencies, including the State forest service and local fire departments, co-operate in guarding this immensely fertile region against destructive ground fires. Airplanes often spot and report fires while en route across the 'Glades.

The question of erosion is of minor importance, principally because the State has an abundant natural flora and a gentle topography. According to U.S. Department of Agriculture records, eastern and southern Florida are the largest areas in the Nation that are virtually free from soil erosion. A fringe along the northwestern boundary of the State is the only region where the loss of soil is serious. The 1937 legislature passed a bill authorizing the State's co-operation with the Federal Government in a national erosion program.

A last but vital conservation problem has resulted from the exploitation of mineral resources, particularly of phosphate. About 60 per cent of the world's supply of phosphate is mined here, chiefly for foreign consumption. A recent report of the National Resources Committee concludes that America cannot afford to waste or export its precious phosphate rock, but conservation of this material and other minerals is a problem linked with the future regulation of mining. Florida ranked twenty-fifth among the States in income from mining activities in 1928; although most of its minerals are comparatively low in value, their utility is great. The principal minerals are fuller's earth, phosphate, kaolin, titanium oxide, diatomite (or infusorial earth), silica, limestone, and coral rock. A State-sponsored geological survey, established in 1907 and operating as a division of the State board of conservation, conducts annual geological surveys, locates mineral deposits, and assists in the development of private mineral industries.

The State planning board in 1939 was in the preliminary stage of making an inventory of the State's conservation problems and requirements, including a detailed record and classification of natural resources.

Archeology and Indians

IN THE last decade of the nineteenth century an extensive investigation of the shell and sand mounds of Florida was financed and directed by the archeologist, Clarence Bloomfield Moore. Prior to this time there had been little but amateur investigation of Florida's rich archeological remains. Relics had been carried off as souvenirs, shell mounds used to build road foundations, and bones and pottery scattered by plows and harrows. But thousands of mounds and earthworks in relatively inaccessible places have been preserved. Earthworks stand in swamps or on offshore islands in west Florida; along the southwest coast, burial mounds and heaps of shell, thrown up by the ancient Calusa to form dwelling platforms, are in mosquito- and snake-infested portions of the Ten Thousand Islands; sand and shell heaps remain unexcavated in the depths of the Everglades.

The work of Moore and the investigations (1895–96) of F.H.Cushing of the Federal Bureau of Ethnology gave the first authoritative information on Florida's pre-Columbian tribes. Moore found that the existing mounds were built of sand or shell and were of four types: ceremonial, foundation, kitchen midden (refuse), and burial. Contents of refuse mounds reveal the varieties of food, methods of cooking, and a number of the implements and weapons used by the tribe. The size and number of mounds in some sections along the coast indicate that at certain seasons of the year the aborigines consumed extraordinary quantities of shellfish. The unusually heavy bone structure of the Florida aborigines is attributed by Dr.Ales Hrdlicka, curator of the National Museum of Anthropology, to the predominance of sea food in their diet.

Moore's initial investigations were in the sand mounds in the panhandle section. Some of the mounds in west Florida, between the Perdido River and Tallahassee, were 80 feet across the base and 8 feet in height, and contained as many as 100 burials. Most of the skeletal material was fairly complete. Many bodies were orientated with the heads towards the center of the mound; some were flexed, lying on one side with the folded legs at right angles to the vertebrae; others were extended, and lay either on one side or face upwards. The absence of some bones in many of the skeletons tends to support the theory that these Indians removed the flesh from bodies before interment, leaving only the sinews to hold the bones together. This was done either by exposure to the weather or by cooking. This custom may have given rise to the early belief, now doubted by most authorities, that the Florida Indians were cannibals.

Implements found in west Florida were few and in many cases crude, but there were some ornaments and weapon points fashioned of bone, chert, or slate that were finely worked. These, together with the small pieces of copper found with them, may have been brought from northern sections where the Indians had gained greater proficiency.

The mounds of this section yielded ornamented clay vessels, similar to those described by Alvar Nuñez Cabeza de Vaca, who in 1528 stated that the Indians of west Florida were very poor, but 'before their houses were many clay pitchers of water.' Some of those found were elaborate, having as many as five compartments, built up into the form of a human body or an animal, and fashioned so that the head protruded and served as a handle. The majority were ornamented on the outer wall with incised or printed lines, whorls, and dots to form a geometric design or formalized drawing of some bird or animal; and in many cases the lines were filled with an unidentified white substance in order to bring out the designs more sharply.

Receptacles here indicated a definite change in religious ideas over a period of time. An early custom was to break a hole in the bottom of a vase that was to be buried with the dead, and thus 'kill' the vessel so that its soul might escape and join that of the deceased. Pots thus destroyed were found with many burials, sometimes placed over the skull, sometimes buried in caches. Later it became the thrifty custom to construct for funeral purposes an artistic reproduction of the utilitarian vessels, with ready-made holes as part of the design. Among these the best portrait vases are found.

Moore's investigations in the northeast portion of the State, particularly in the vicinity of the St. Johns River, were not as productive as those in the northwest. The sand mounds excavated here yielded artifacts, pottery, and skeletal material, but in small amounts and in poor condition. The results of the exploration seemed to show that the works were built before contact with the whites, but in some places articles of European manufacture were found, indicating possibly that the historic Indians had used an early mound to include later burials. Notable finds were a number of conch shells with holes bored at the base for the insertion of handles. The conclusion reached was that such a shell was used as a domestic tool rather than as a weapon, for the hole would not admit a handle of sufficient size to permit the striking of a heavy blow without the handle's breaking.

The earth and shell mounds of the southwest and southeast coasts, investigated by Moore, Cushing, Hrdlicka, and later archeologists, were interesting more because of their form and manner of construction than for their content. Most heaps yielded few or no remains, and seem to have been built mainly for dwelling platforms above the high-water mark of a swampy country. Artifacts were crude, most of them constructed of shell, while pottery was simple and without elaborate decoration. Living on and by the sea, the natives built an elaborate system of canals and basins to transport their canoes between dwelling platforms and the open water. Breakwaters and causeways surrounded and connected village sites. An interesting custom noted here was the decoration of the bases of some mounds with a low wall of conch shells. These shell walls gave rise to early stories of aboriginal stone structures on the keys.

Some burials in this section were found embedded in a solidified matrix of sand and shell, and at first it was believed that the remains were of great age; now it is thought that the matrix was hardened quickly by the infiltration of water carrying minerals in solution, and that the deposits are of no greater age than those found in higher and drier burials.

Perhaps the greatest find in this section was the collection of carved wooden objects unearthed by Cushing in 1895 in the muck of Key Largo. These, probably made of cypress, of good workmanship, are thought to have been used for ceremonial purposes. In 1921 a wooden idol and two flat carved objects of wood called 'altar slabs' were plowed up in the muck in reclaimed land north of Lake Okeechobee.

J.S.Fewkes in 1924 excavated a group of mounds at Weeden Island in Tampa Bay. The pottery here seemed to show a level of culture higher than that found in most parts of the section and resembled in design the claywork of northwest Florida. Fewkes reported that he found three levels of culture; the lowest, Antillean; the middle, Muskhogean; and the upper layer, modern. There was no evidence of European influence, although Spanish trading beads were uncovered.

In 1928 Henry B. Collins,Jr., of the National Museum, explored mounds south and west of Lake Okeechobee, doing the most extensive excavation in the shell and sand heaps on Captiva Island, south of Charlotte Harbor. A burial mound on this island, although destroyed in part by early treasure seekers, yielded more than 70 skulls. Some of these, in the bottom of the mound, had been cemented together by a mixture of muck

Natural Setting

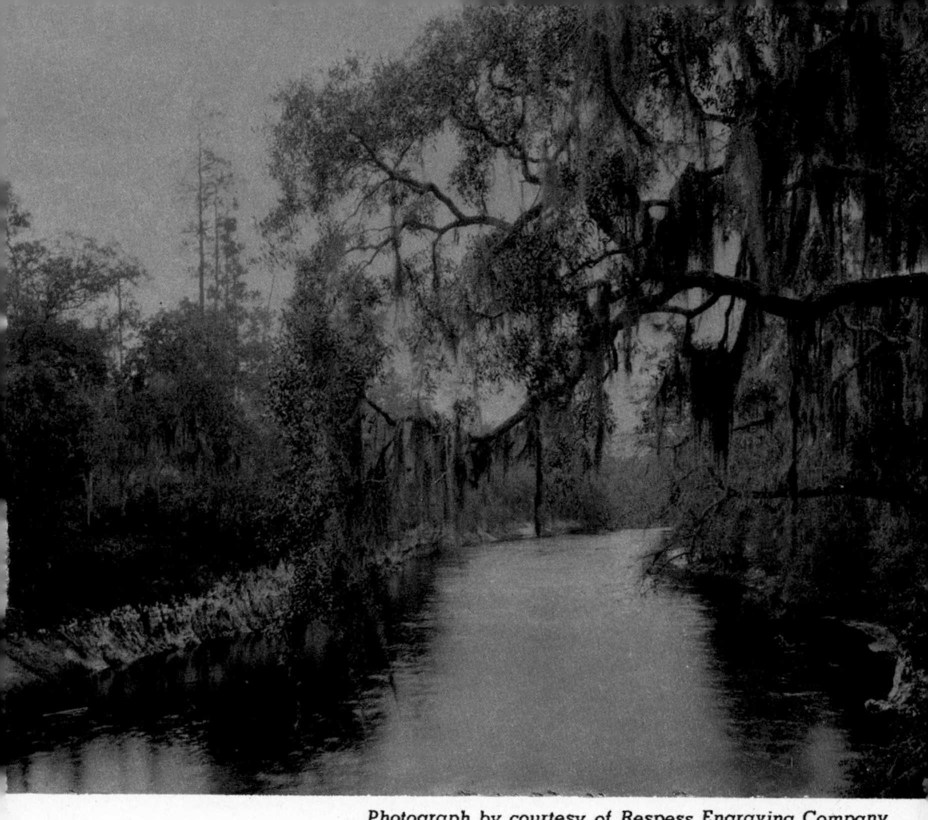

Photograph by courtesy of Respess Engraving Company

SUWANNEE RIVER

Photograph by courtesy of Farm Security Administration

THE COUNTRYSIDE, NEAR LAKE OKEECHOBEE

HIGHWAY, NEAR PALM BEACH

Photograph by courtesy of Farm Security Administration

Photograph by courtesy of United States Sugar Corporation

SUGAR CANE FIELDS IN THE EVERGLADES

BEACH SCENE NEAR THE JETTIES, JACKSONVILLE

Photograph by Virgil Moore

Photograph by courtesy of Tampa Chamber of Commerce

SPANISH MOSS

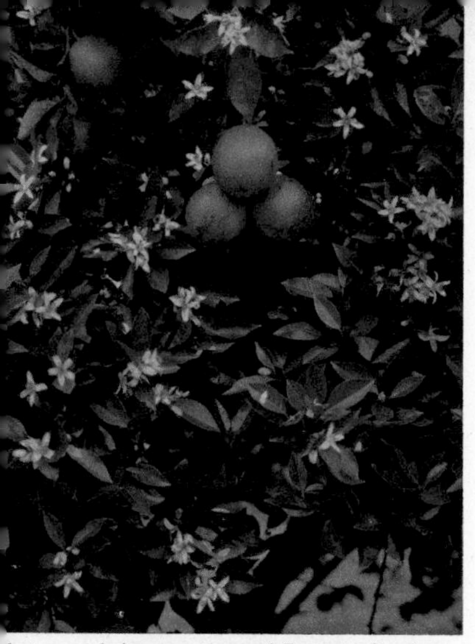

hotograph by courtesy of Burgert Brothers

ORANGE BLOSSOMS

TUNG BLOSSOMS

THE LAND-BUILDER — MANGROVE TREE

Photograph by G. W. Romer

ROYAL PALMS

Photograph by Darel McConkey

Photograph by G. W. Romer

THE OLD ROAD, MIAMI

Photograph by Ebbett

IBIS

and water and were well preserved; others, lying in the loose sand at the surface of the mound, considered to be secondary burials, were in poor condition.

A large oval mound with three projecting arms 40, 100, and 300 feet long respectively, and somewhat resembling the effigy mounds of the Northern States, was also reported by Collins, east of Fort Myers near Citrus Center. It was partly inclosed by an embankment. Beginning less than a mile away and extending westward for more than a mile and a half was a canal of aboriginal construction that apparently had some connection with the mound. Excavation produced nothing more than a few potsherds.

The Smithsonian archeological projects, conducted in 1934 under the Federal Emergency Relief Administration, investigated mounds in southeast and southwest Florida. Excavations in the vicinity of Belle Glade, on the shore of Lake Okeechobee, revealed the same culture at all levels. Shell and bone implements as well as muck pottery were abundant. Several carved bird heads of wood and parts of two wooden plaques were found deep in the sand. Since 1935 some remarkable effigy carvings in fine-grained sandstone have been discovered.

The native population of Florida at the time of the Spanish conquest comprised approximately 10,000 Indians, divided into four major tribes who lived in the four quarters of this region. The Calusa in the southwest were mariners and fishermen who sailed their canoes as far as Cuba and Hispaniola and lived on the abundant oysters and fish along the coast. It is possible that they were of Carib stock and had crossed from the islands to make a new home in Florida long before the coming of the white men. Attempts to land in their territories were fiercely resisted, and it was from a wound inflicted by one of their arrows that Ponce de Leon died after returning to Cuba from the west coast of Florida. Because of their attacks, no Spanish colony or mission ever succeeded in long holding a foothold in this part of the State.

East of the Calusa and south of Cape Canaveral dwelt the Tegesta, a people as hostile to the white man as their neighbors, although not as warlike. Spanish missions were established among them, and many claimed to have been converted to the new faith, yet the Tegesta were long a source of trouble. They protested friendship for the Spanish settlers, but there were continual reports of shipwreck victims being murdered while attempting to make their way up the coast to St.Augustine. Letters from that city to Spain tell of cruelty and breach of faith, and beg that the Indians be enslaved and sent away, in order to insure safety in the future.

The Timucuan, who lived in central and northeast Florida, had reached a stage of civilization superior to that of the southern Indians. They cultivated extensive cornfields, constructed substantial houses, and traded with the tribes to the north. More is known of the Timucuan than of other early Florida tribes. Because their language was understood in all parts of the peninsula, it was used as a sort of *lingua franca* by the Spanish missionaries who needed a general dialect to carry on their work. Catechisms and texts were published in Timucuan to simplify the instruction of the different tribes, and the language became a medium of communication in most of Florida.

In 1564 the French artist LeMoyne accompanied the Huguenots who built Fort Caroline. He made pictures of the native villages and customs, and his drawings, supplemented by the narrative written by leaders in the colony, are today a valuable source of information of this extinct tribe. Added to these are the works of Father Pareja, a missionary who lived among these Indians for many years, and left behind him books rated among the earliest and most valuable of Americana.

The Apalachee in northwest Florida were as civilized as the Timucuan and more powerful because their chiefs were united in a strong league. 'Keep on, robbers and traitors,' the southern Indians warned the soldiers of De Soto, 'in Apalache you will receive the chastisement your cruelty deserves.' The Apalachee area was reputed to be the richest country in Florida.

All these tribes were sun worshipers. On the dawn of a certain day every spring a stag's head, garlanded with flowers, was set upon a pole facing east. As the first rays of light touched the antlered head, the tribe bowed in prayer. If the crops were not plentiful, first-born children and captives were often sacrificed to appease the sun god.

Moon and sun worship were analogous. The moon was associated with moisture and the Indians' water worship included many rites. For example, when the people wished to overcome illness, they bathed three times in clear running water, and sometimes, as in the case of measles, this treatment resulted in appalling fatalities.

Descent among these tribes was through the mother, so that a chief was succeeded by his sister's son, rather than by his own. Likewise, when a man said he was going home he meant that he was going to his mother's house. There were also instances where women ruled the tribes, as in the case of Dona Maria, the chieftainess who ruled Nombre de Dios near St.Augustine in 1592.

What clothes these early Floridians wore were for ornament; men wore brilliant feathered mantles, metal breastplates, and leather breechclouts. The typical brave wore inflated fish bladders, dyed red, in his ears, and his long hair was piled high in a knot at the top of his head. Fingernails and toenails were worn long. Elaborate tattooing covered the warrior's body, and his neck, arms, and legs were strung with beads and rattles.

An Indian woman wore a moss skirt and mantle, and her hair was unbound. Upon the death of her husband her hair was cut short, and she was not permitted to remarry until it covered her shoulders again.

Many of these people became Christians through the heroic efforts of Spanish missionaries. During the seventeenth century, Indian villages in Florida presented a remarkable picture of civilized community life. Indian children learned to read and write, and adults went to church dressed in European fashion. No white people except the priests were allowed to live near these villages, and trade in firearms and liquor was unlawful.

The progress of Indian civilization was rudely interrupted in the beginning of the eighteenth century. The Creek of Georgia sided with the English against the Spanish, and, beginning in 1702, made raids into Florida as far south as the Everglades, carrying thousands of cattle and Indian captives to Charleston. The Spanish Indians were sold as slaves in New England and the West Indies, where they were highly valued for their training. Those who escaped fled to the protection of the French at Mobile, or to the Spanish forts at St.Marks and St.Augustine. By 1706, the towns of the Spanish trail across north Florida were almost deserted.

Slave-raiding parties from the north were usually composed of a few hundred Creek led by a small band of their British friends. As the land was laid waste and the natives were carried off, the Creek invaders took over the fields and settled here. When Florida became a British Territory, the English colonists who replaced the Spanish found their old Indian allies from Georgia firmly established in the State and banded together in a strong confederation. They had broken with their old nation in the north and were now known as the Seminole or 'Runaways.'

After the Revolution, when Georgia became a part of the United States and Florida again became a Spanish possession in 1783, the ranks of the Seminole were continually being swelled by fugitive Negro slaves who found refuge and freedom among the Indians, to whom they paid tribute in corn. Attempts by planters of Georgia to recapture the runaways resulted in friction between Florida and the United States, and Seminole animosity against the Americans was inspired by the British. These continuing disturbances culminated in the short Florida campaigns of Andrew Jackson in 1814 and 1818, the latter known as the First Seminole War. Four years later, when Florida became a part of the United States, the Government realized that measures were necessary to check the hostilities between Seminole and white settlers, and a movement was started to send the Indians to reservations west of the Mississippi.

In 1832 a delegation of chiefs traveled to the western reservation to inspect the land. They were persuaded to sign a treaty that committed their tribe to immigration, but the Seminole disavowed the treaty. Attempts to move the Indians by force and the seizure of Osceola's wife as a fugitive slave were among the incidents that precipitated the Second Seminole War, a seven-year struggle (1835–42) involving great losses in life and property.

The principal figure in this war was Osceola, or, more correctly, As-se-he-ho-lar, a name meaning Black Drink, which was bestowed because of his prowess in drinking a ceremonial brew. Osceola was the stepson of William Powell, a white trader; his mother was an Indian woman of the Red Stick tribe, a branch of the Creek. His white blood came from a Scotch grandfather. In 1808, when the second secession from the Creek occurred, Osceola, at that time about four years old, came to Florida with his mother and finally settled on Peace Creek. When he appeared at Fort King shortly before the Seminole War, he had reached manhood.

The young quarter-breed was tall and erect, with an expressive countenance. His light eyes showed his mixed parentage. In his dealings with the whites he was proud to the point of arrogance. Osceola was not a chief and, according to Indian custom, had no voice in the councils of his tribe; but his natural talent for leadership soon asserted itself, for the nominal chief, Micanope, an irresolute and phlegmatic man, soon fell under the influence of this spirited, more determined warrior.

The unfair treatment accorded Che-cho-ter (Morning Dew), Osceola's wife, was one of the chief causes for his open hostility towards the whites. Although Che-cho-ter had been married long enough to bear Osceola four children, a trace of Negro blood gave white settlers an excuse to carry her off as a slave. Osceola never forgave what he considered a blood insult to his people and himself.

During the first half of the Second Seminole War, Osceola was the real, if not the nominal, leader of the Indians. The spirit of his leadership is well expressed in a message which he sent to General Clinch. 'You have guns, so have we. You have powder and lead, and so have we. Your men will fight, and so will ours till the last drop of Seminole blood has moistened the dust of his hunting ground.'

In 1837, at a council with General Hernández, Osceola and his friends were surrounded and taken as prisoners to St.Augustine, but were later removed to Fort Moultrie, South Carolina. Here Osceola, although suffering from quinsy, to which he succumbed soon afterwards, posed for a portrait by Catlin. His last wish was that he should die as a Seminole brave in the war dress of his tribe.

Coacoochee (Wild Cat), one of the chiefs imprisoned with Osceola at Fort Marion, escaped and became the most influential leader of the latter half of the war. General William J. Worth finally won the friendship of this chief in 1841, and through him persuaded about 500 Seminole and their Negroes to emigrate.

The majority of the Seminole were transported west, where they formed one of the Five Civilized Tribes of Oklahoma, but about 150 fled to the unexplored wilderness of the Everglades.

The Seminole in Florida today are divided into two tribes: the Muscogee, numbering about 140, who live north and east of Lake Okeechobee, and the 446 Micosukee, who occupy the region south of the lake and the Big Cypress swamp on the west. Customs and habits vary, but to the casual observer there is little except dialect to distinguish the tribes.

The center of the modern Seminole encampment is the 'fireplace' built of eight or ten dry logs arranged like the spokes of a wheel. The fire is built at the hub, and as the innermost ends are consumed, the logs are moved toward the blaze. In this manner the Indian gathers enough wood at one time to last several days; this does away with the necessity of chopping and splitting large logs, and, incidentally, by making use of the unburned ends of the wood, provides the entire family with convenient seats near the hearth at mealtime and in the evening.

If the camp is being set up for any length of time, the Indian erects over his fire a roof thatched with palmetto leaves supported by four uprights set in the ground. In addition to protecting the fire, these structures serve as kitchen house and shelter in bad weather. Rafters form convenient rails on which the family pots and pans are hung when not in use, and smoke from the campfire tends to preserve and dry the meat and herbs suspended from the ridgepole. The mortar, hollowed from the head of a large log, and the wooden pestle, used for hashing dry venison and pounding corn, have an important part in domestic economy. Living quarters are grouped about the hearth.

The Seminole hut, known as a *chikee,* is built in the same manner as the kitchen shelter, except for a platform of saplings elevated a few feet above the ground upon which occupants sleep. A blanket serves as mattress and covering. There is practically no furniture, but few establishments are without a hand-operated sewing machine so necessary for the making of clothing. The first machines were introduced about 50 years ago by an enterprising salesman, whose wife, Minnie Moore Wilson, accompanied him on his travels and gathered material for her books on the modern Seminole.

The Indians live well. They are not held subject to the hunting and fishing laws of the State, but civilization has made inroads on their game supply. Turkeys, curlews, herons, gophers, and venison find their way into the Seminole kettle, but the staple food is *sofkee*, a mush made of ground corn meal. From the jungles come coontie and chinabrier, from which a flour is made. Corn, sweet potatoes, squash, melons, and cowpeas are raised on cleared ground near permanent settlements; coco-plums, sea-grapes, gopher apples, and sour oranges grow wild and are gathered throughout the year. The bud of the cabbage palm, eaten raw or cooked, is a delicacy. For sweetening, the Indian depends upon syrup obtained from his small patch of sugar cane. The time of cane boiling is observed as a minor nonreligious fiesta, and the entire community joins in harvesting the crop, extracting the juice, and tending the kettles. There are no fixed meal hours; the sofkee pot is on the fire all day, to be dipped into whenever a member of the family is hungry.

The present Seminole clothing was adopted around 1900; it is both distinctive and colorful, and tedious to make. Material for women's garments is composed of hundreds of patches of cloth pieced into strips which, when sewed together, form horizontal varicolored bands that reach from the waist to the ground. The upper part of the body is covered by a bolero with long sleeves that is slipped over the head and falls loosely from the shoulders to the top of the skirt. Sometimes the jacket and skirt do not meet by an inch or two, allowing the copper-colored skin to show at the waistline. The freedom and comfort of these simple garments, however, are offset by a weight of constricting necklaces. A Seminole girl is given a string of colored glass beads when she reaches the age of puberty. On birthdays strings are added for acts of virtue, or as gifts in times of financial prosperity, until her neck up to the chin is buried deep beneath a gorget of many strands. After a woman has passed middle life, the necklaces are removed strand by strand until the first present is reached. This first and last ornament is worn to the grave. A woman's hair is never covered; but a large 'rat,' after the mode of the early 1900's, is used to bolster her pompadour.

Seminole men wear a tunic composed of colored strips, which falls to the knees and is caught in at the waist by a belt, or, less frequently, by a bright red sash. The old, close-fitting deerskin leggings, with their fringed seams and cuffs, are rapidly giving way to store-bought blue denim or serge trousers. The turban, once the customary headdress of every Seminole brave, has been replaced in many cases by the 'ten-gallon' Stetson. The old turban was built up of numerous bandannas wrapped around the head. Originally it was fastened with a pointed bone, later with an ornamental clasp made of a hammered-out silver coin; but since the advent of the dime stores, these have been supplanted by garish, bejeweled pins. Most Seminole men today, when not dressed for tourist exhibition purposes, go bareheaded.

Hunting and trapping are still the Indian's principal source of revenue; hides of otter, coon, skunk, and alligator find a ready market, and the tanned skins of deer sometimes bring as high as $2 a pound. Added to this is the money that comes in during the hunting season, for the Seminole's knowledge of the best hunting grounds and his ability to follow trails through the Everglades make him an excellent guide.

Some families gather in 'camps' in Miami, West Palm Beach, and at points along the Tamiami Trail, where they live during the winter months, charging admission to visitors and making extra money through the sale of handmade ornaments, dolls, and souvenirs. These funds are usually spent for guns, ammunition, cotton cloth, sewing machines, second-hand cars, beads, and tobacco.

The Seminole differ from other North American tribes in their treatment of women. No severe agricultural labor is imposed upon them and they are shown great consideration. Marriage laws are regarded as sacred, and divorces are permitted only in case of incompatibility. Either party may remarry, but the marriage must be approved by the tribal leaders.

The Seminole have a dual conception of God. Ishtoholo is the Indian's symbol of God as the embodiment of greatness, purity, goodness, and the love of the 'Great Spirit.' The other god is 'Yo-He-Wah,' whose name is never mentioned in common speech, but is chanted around the sacred fires of religious festivals. This god is believed to command demons, pronounce curses, and bring on pestilences and calamities, and he can be placated only by rites, sacrifices, and ceremonials.

To appease Yo-He-Wah, the Seminole make sin offerings twice a year, and hold the *Shot Cay Taw* (Green Corn Dance) on the first day after the appearance of the first new moon of the vernal equinox, the beginning of their New Year. The sin offering of the hunt is the rite of burning the first deer killed in a new season in the woods where it fell, an act which it is believed will bring health to any ailing member of the hunter's family, as well as forgiveness for his sins. Another sacrifice is the custom of burning a small portion of every deer slain on or near the campgrounds, before the meat is prepared for a stew. When the stew is made, the Indians dip their middle fingers into the broth and sprinkle it over the graves of the women and children in the burial ground to ward off evil spirits. All adult males are interred in the depths of the jungle.

The Cypress and Okeechobee clans hold separate Green Corn Dances on a schedule permitting the tribes to attend both ceremonies. However, only 60 per cent of the Indians have the time or interest to attend the annual celebrations, and comparatively few join in any of the dances.

All tribal matters are heard and adjusted during the Green Corn Festival. Judicial powers within the reservation are in the hands of a council of medicine men, which decrees penalties for violations of its rules. Banishment from the tribe is considered the worst form of punishment. The death penalty among the Seminole is extremely rare and has been imposed only twice since 1886.

The last case of this sort occurred during the spring of 1938 and was widely publicized by the press. A young Indian man was killed by John Osceola, one of the six chiefs of the Seminole Nation. According to newspaper accounts, a council of chiefs had previously commanded the slaying, because of the Indian's criminal record. The execution occurred off the reservation, and Osceola was exonerated by a Miami coroner's jury. When Osceola faced trial a second time at the Seminole Green Corn Dance in May 1938, the Indians officially approved his action.

Today the Green Corn Dance is conducted much as it was a hundred years ago, and all events having to do with the Seminole existence are depicted in its many dances. Indian families gather far in advance of the opening and await the coming of the medicine men, who open the sacred festival with the ceremony of the 'black drink.' This concoction, made from ilex cassine, acts as an emetic and cleanses the persons who are to take part in the events to follow. After the black drink is administered the medicine men open the dance, which continues for five nights. The second day is one of feasting for the males, who are served with a variety of foods carefully prepared by the women and deposited near the eating house. The women then withdraw, for they are not permitted to remain within sight of the feasting braves. The day after the banquet is one of fasting. In the autumn the Indians conduct a Hunting Dance similar in character to their Green Corn Dance.

The Florida legislature has concerned itself with the Seminole only to the extent of setting aside reservations for his use. He is tried in civil courts but shown the utmost leniency in his transgressions. There is a tacit understanding with Federal authorities that Indian tribal law shall prevail on the reservation. The U.S. Seminole Agency, located at Dania since 1926, protects the Indians in their property and political rights. A truce between the Seminole and the United States Government was signed in 1934, publicized as bringing to a close the longest war in history. Another such treaty was signed in 1937. A story has it that one of the Indians present on this occasion kept muttering a word that no one understood until an interpreter translated it: 'He say "lotta bull."'

History

AND believing that this land was an island, they named it *La Florida,* because it has a very beautiful view of many cool woodlands, and it was level and uniform; and because, moreover, they discovered it in the time of the Feast of Flowers.'

So wrote Antonio de Herrera, royal historiographer of Spain, of the day in March 1513, when Juan Ponce de Leon first sighted the shores of Florida from the deck of his flimsy caravel. Ponce de Leon, companion of Columbus on his second voyage to the New World, had listened to a story by the Puerto Rican Indians of a wonderful land to the northwest, rich in gold and having a magic fountain that restored youth. The West Indians had believed this story and had even explored and named sections of the coast. Many times they left Puerto Rico in canoes to search for the fabled spring on the mainland. Some were lost, but others reached southeastern Florida and were allowed by the natives to settle there. Andreas the Bearded, a West Indian, told the Spanish historian, Peter Martyr, that his father had found the spring in Florida and had returned home, restored to health and vigor.

Ponce de Leon, at this time a robust man of fifty and ambitious to add to his reputation, received a royal patent to explore and colonize 'Bimini' (the Indian word used to designate the land to the northwest of the Bahamas). On March 5, 1513, he set sail with three ships from Puerto Rico and after three weeks of leisurely journeying came within sight of Florida on March 28. On April 2, he took his bearings off the coast a little north of St.Augustine, and the next morning landed to claim the country for Spain. He sought a harbor and stayed six days in the vicinity, finally sailing southward along the coast. As he passed among the Florida Keys he named them 'The Martyrs,' because they looked like men suffering. He continued up the coast, probably as far as Apalachicola. After a six months' vain quest for gold and the fountain, he returned to Puerto Rico, on the way making the valuable discovery of the Bahama channel, later used by fleets plying between the Colonies and Spain.

Belief in the island persisted until 1519, after which the name Florida was applied by Spanish historians not only to the peninsula but to the unknown coastal region extending northward and eastward. The words *Terra Florida* appear on a map attributed to Leonardo da Vinci (*c.*1515). Bartolome de Las Casas, in his account of the New World, wrote in 1540: 'The name Florida is applied to all the coast from the great cape which he (Ponce de Leon) discovered, as far as Bacallaos or Labrador.' Other powers did not acknowledge Spanish claims, except to those parts actually settled. The ensuing contests for possession of the Atlantic coastal region formed an important part of Florida's history.

Unauthorized raids, to obtain slaves for labor in the West Indies, spread hatred of Europeans among the Indians of Florida. Although Ponce de Leon protested officially against these infringements of his patent, it was eight years before he could assert the exclusive right to settle the land he had discovered. In 1521, he sailed with two shiploads of colonists, cattle, and seeds, landing finally in the vicinity of Charlotte Harbor. The colony lasted but five months, because of illness and constant clashes with the Indians. When Ponce de Leon received a wound so serious that he departed for Cuba to obtain treatment, the whole colony returned with him. He died soon after reaching the island, and his heirs lost claim to Florida through their failure to settle.

In a determined effort to hold Florida, the Spanish sent two other great expeditions to the west coast, but Indian resistance defeated them. Panfilo de Narvaez organized an expedition in 1528, landing in the vicinity of Tampa Bay and marching north in search of rich cities. A third of his 300 soldiers perished before the force reached the site of St.Marks on the Gulf coast, and the rest clamored to return to their ships. They built crude rafts and attempted to sail along the shore, but a storm scattered them, and Narvaez and most of his followers were drowned.

One of the survivors, Alvar Nuñez Cabeza de Vaca, with two other Spaniards and a Negro slave, wandered for eight years among the Indian tribes of the interior. When he returned to Spain, he told a wonderful tale of his adventures, which had taken him as far as the Gulf of California. His story probably heightened the interest of the next explorers, who came under the leadership of Hernando de Soto.

On May 30, 1539, De Soto landed in the Tampa area with 600 foot soldiers and more than 100 cavaliers, marching north and west in search of the golden cities. Four years later the remnants of the army reached Mexico with news of the death of its commander on May 21, 1542. The soldiers had buried De Soto's body in the Mississippi River to save it from the Indians.

After the failure of two similar expeditions, under Fray Luis Cancer in

1549 and Tristan de Luna in 1559, the King of Spain abandoned the idea of Florida settlement and by advice of the Council of Indies refused to grant any more patents for that purpose.

Other nations had watched with envious eyes, however, the riches pouring out of Mexico and South America into Spain. So numerous became the English and French corsairs who preyed on this trade that convoys were organized to escort treasure ships sailing twice a year by a route through the Bahama channel and along the Florida coast.

Failure to guard this coast brought complications. When word reached Spain in 1563 that in the previous year a French Huguenot colony had been planted by Jean Ribaut on what is now the South Carolina seaboard, Philip II of Spain protested to Catherine de Medici, Queen Mother of France. He said that in Pope Alexander's Bull of Demarcation, in 1493, the New World fell within the territory given to Spain. France had officially sanctioned the Ribaut colony, but at this time did not dare to challenge openly the Pope's authority. Catherine protested that, while colonists would go to the Newfoundland fishing banks of the Bretons, they would not go to Florida. The Ribaut venture was a failure, but in 1564 another Huguenot colony was started even nearer the route of Spanish trade, on the St.Johns River. Any thought that 'Lutherans' should convert Indians and control the country so close to the arteries of Spanish trade disquieted the richest, most powerful, and most devout monarch of Europe and stirred his uncompromising resistance.

Don Pedro Menéndez de Avilés, Captain General of the Spanish treasure fleets, undertaking to rid Florida of the French, presented plans for fortifying the coast and converting the Indians. King Philip commissioned Menéndez to equip the expedition, practically at his own expense, as was customary at that time. Before Menéndez could attack, René de Laudonnière, the French commander, had spent a year strengthening Fort Caroline, his defense on the St.Johns River, and Ribaut brought further reinforcements in September 1565. When part of the Spanish fleet, under Menéndez, reached the St.Johns River, they found the French united and prepared to fight. The Spanish retreated to St.Augustine to await the arrival of the remainder of their forces, and as they were unloading stores from Menéndez' ship, the French fleet drew up to give battle.

Menéndez probably escaped capture only because a low tide prevented the Frenchmen from following him into the harbor. Before the tide turned, a great storm arose and drove the French vessels southward to Cape Canaveral, where they were shipwrecked. On September 20, however, Menéndez captured Fort Caroline by a surprise attack, killing nearly all the occupants except the women and children; afterwards he found and executed all but a few of the survivors of the shipwrecked French fleet. His action was the subject of much criticism by the Protestant nations.

During the seven years Menéndez spent in Florida, he founded St. Augustine (1565), the first permanent white settlement, established a line of posts from Tampa Bay to what is now Port Royal, South Carolina, and explored the interior of a large part of the present North Carolina, South Carolina, and Florida. In 1567, he returned to Spain and was received as a hero. During his absence from Florida, an expedition of revenge for the destruction of Fort Caroline was undertaken by the French under Dominique de Gourgues, who executed everyone in the Spanish garrison on the St. Johns River. Menéndez, on his return from Spain, however, ruthlessly suppressed French efforts to secure another foothold in Florida. That this was a political as well as a religious issue is shown by the fact that, 17 years after Fort Caroline fell, a group of English Catholics was banned from Florida as emphatically as were the French Huguenots.

Menéndez was untiring in his efforts to convert the Indians, a task in which he showed tact and patience. At first obliged to use soldiers as teachers, he persuaded Philip, in 1566, to send three Jesuit priests. One was killed, but the other two were established at Tampa Bay and Charlotte Harbor. Menéndez traveled as far north as the Potomac River in 1571, to avenge the massacre of the priests he had sent to establish a mission not far below what is now Washington. He left Florida for the third and last time in 1572, and died two years later.

Within the next few years, English depredations upon Spain's New World empire surpassed the previous exploits of the French Huguenots. When Francis Drake returned in 1580 from his trip around the world, bringing booty worth £1,500,000 from Spanish settlements, he was knighted by Queen Elizabeth on board his flagship at Deptford. From then on, England's course was officially to deny hostility toward Spain but to press English colonization in America in the face of Spanish claims. Sir Walter Raleigh was granted the right to colonize what he called Virginia, and sent over colonists in 1585, 1586, and 1587. In 1586, Sir Francis Drake again raided the Spanish towns of the West Indies and burned St. Augustine. Hailed as a hero in England, he went on to greater glory in England's supreme effort of 1588, when she crippled the 'Invincible Armada' of Spain.

With the defeat of the Armada, the mastery of the ocean passed gradually to England, making possible the advance of English colonies on the Atlantic seaboard during the next century. But the Spanish stubbornly disputed this seizure of what they considered their property. Santa Elena, a Spanish fort at the present site of Hilton Head, South Carolina, established by Menéndez in 1566, was rebuilt in 1577, and other Spanish defenses were erected at strategic points farther south on the coast to resist encroachments by other European nations.

With increasing assurance England ignored Spain's protests. An unsuccessful attempt to settle in New England was made in 1607, but in the same year, with the settlement of Jamestown by another English company, the permanent occupation of Virginia began. In 1629–30, Charles I of England gave one of his ministers, Sir Robert Heath, a patent to the region between Albemarle Sound and the St.Johns River in Florida (lat. 36° to 31° N.). Heath made no use of this grant, but Virginians reached out in 1653, and some New Englanders in 1662, into what is now North Carolina.

In 1663, Charles II of England made another proprietary grant of the Heath territory. To it the new proprietors, the Earl of Clarendon and seven others, gave the name Carolina. In 1665, their grant was enlarged and extended south to latitude 29° N. and westward to the Pacific, thus including Georgia and the northern half of the peninsula of Florida.

Spain could do little to resist the encroachment on its Florida domain, for its hold on the Atlantic coastal region had weakened considerably in the century since Menéndez' time. St.Augustine, in 1665, was described as a place where 200 Spaniards and Indians 'were in hiding.' Spanish defenses in the region became so weak that by the terms of a treaty in 1670, Spain for the first time acknowledged the right of England to a portion of North America. An immediate result was the establishment in 1670–71 of the English colony of Charleston.

The French began closing in on the west, and in 1699 Pierre le Moyne Sieur d'Iberville succeeded in planting a French colony at Biloxi on the Gulf. At this time relations between the French and Spanish were cordial, because of their common fear of English colonial power, though there were occasional conflicts between the French of Mobile and the Spanish of Pensacola. The treaty of 1670 did not restrain the English long in their southward advance. In 1733, Savannah was built south of the treaty line. Steady inroads of French on the west and English on the north cut deeply into Spanish territory, until Spanish Florida was confined to the peninsula.

The defense of St.Augustine and Pensacola became increasingly difficult. San Marcos, a great stone fort at St.Augustine begun in 1672, withstood three major attacks of the English. At Pensacola, Fort San Carlos, built in 1698, was destroyed by the French in 1719; possession of the site was disputed by the French and Spanish until 1723, when it was returned to Spain.

During the seventeenth century much of Spain's energy for colonization went into conversion of the Indians. Mission towns flourished along the east coast, south from St.Catherine's Island as far as the present site of Miami, and across the northern border of Florida from St.Augustine to the present site of Tallahassee. The greatest number of Florida missions were located along a westerly trail from St.Augustine to the Gulf. The trail crossed the St.Johns River at Picolata where two forts guarded the river pass; skirting the shore of Santa Fe Lake, it turned northwest to the present Monticello, then north at Tallahassee, where stood Fort San Luis. After the destruction of this fort in 1704, the trail was continued to Fort San Marcos de Apalache, erected on the Gulf in 1718.

No Spaniard was allowed to live in the mission towns except the resident priest, who not only instructed his charges in Christian doctrine but taught them to herd cattle and plant crops. He drew a soldier's pay from the Spanish Crown and commanded the Indians in the defense of their territory. But this defense was made difficult by the refusal of Spain to give firearms to the Indians, and a number of successful raids were made by both the French and English.

James Moore, Governor of the Council of South Carolina, laid siege to St.Augustine in 1702, but withdrew after three months, unable to take it. He carried away many Florida Indian slaves, however, who were sold in the Charleston markets, and the success of this enterprise caused Moore and other Carolinians to repeat their raids, which carried them from the Tallahassee area as far south as Lake Okeechobee. Palmer in 1728 and Oglethorpe in 1740 likewise devastated north Florida and also laid unsuccessful siege to St.Augustine. Many of the Indians of Georgia accompanied these raiders and settled in the villages that had been despoiled of their inhabitants.

The rule of Spain in Florida was slowly dying because of her lack of sea power, and English freebooters harried the Spanish treasure fleets. One of these, a buccaneer called Davis, sacked St.Augustine in 1668. Spanish holdings were finally reduced to a few Indian towns under the protection of the forts at St.Augustine, St.Marks on the Gulf, and Pensacola. But Florida was still a thorn in the side of the British colonies. Slaves from the Carolina plantations, escaping to Florida, were protected by the Spanish governor and allowed to man Fort Moosa, an outpost of St.Augustine. In 1762, Havana fell before a British attack, and by the Treaty of Paris (February 10, 1763) Spain agreed to trade Florida for the Cuban capital.

English financiers took up vast grants of land and offered inducements to settlers. In 1767, the largest colony ever brought in one body to British America was established by Dr. Andrew Turnbull, a Scotchman, who settled at New Smyrna with 1,500 colonists from Italy, Greece, and the island of Minorca. The New Smyrna colony lasted nine years and was finally broken up as a result of a quarrel, personal and political, between Turnbull and Governor Tonyn of Florida.

In 1765, Denys Rolle, Member of Parliament, started a settlement on the St.Johns River (*see Tour 2b*) after the plan of Oglethorpe's Georgia colony. In the same year the Kings Road was built from New Smyrna, through St.Augustine, to the Georgia line, thus establishing overland communication with the other English colonists. Famous travel writers and botanists, among them John and William Bartram, came to Florida to explore and describe the new territory. The English had little trouble with the Indians because the Seminole, as the Creek tribes from Georgia were called, were now dominant among the Florida natives. The Creek had always been allies of England and were favored under the British administration.

Under English rule the first serious effort was made to define the actual limits of Florida, and the territory was divided for administrative purposes into two units, East and West Florida. East Florida's northern boundary extended from the mouth of the St.Marys River westward to the junction of the Chattahoochee and Flint Rivers; the western boundary was the Apalachicola River, and the eastern was the Atlantic Ocean from the mouth of the St.Marys to Dartmouth Inlet (now Miami Inlet) at Cape Florida. These lines were established by William Gerard de Brahm, His Majesty's surveyor. West Florida included the area west of the Apalachicola River to the Mississippi and as far north as 32° 28′. After the purchase of Florida by the United States, the western boundary of the State was set at the Perdido River.

The American Revolution added to East Florida's prosperity. Some of the leading Tory families of the South came in small coastal vessels or high piled wagons to the last loyal British province south of Canada. St.Augustine was thronged with refugees, and feeling against the Revolutionists waxed high. Captain F.G.Mulcaster, a half-brother of George III, was stationed there as army engineer. After the fall of Charleston, 61 leaders of the Revolution, including Middleton, Rutledge, and Heyward, signers of the Declaration of Independence, were sent to the old city as prisoners of war. General Robert Howe invaded Florida in 1778 with an army of 3,000 Americans. The British, aided by Florida woodsmen and Indians, repulsed them with 1,210 men, mostly British regulars.

West Florida was attacked by Spain in 1779 and captured in 1781. After the English departed, Pensacola was almost deserted, for few Spanish colonists returned. But East Florida continued to flourish until it became impossible for England to hold the colony between the hostile new United States on the north, the Spanish strongholds on the south, and the French and Spanish on the west. So, in 1783, it was ceded back to Spain, whereupon more than 15,000 English moved to the West Indies, leaving most of the plantations to Indians, robbers, and the quick-growing tropical jungles.

Spain found little but trouble during her second tenure of Florida. In an effort to resettle the plantations left by the English, inducements were offered to Americans, and they poured over the border, literally conquering the country by colonization. Clashes with Spanish officials soon developed, for many of these turbulent new settlers were descendants of English frontiersmen who had invaded Florida under Oglethorpe. The United States lent moral support to American pioneers on the border who urged the purchase of Florida from Spain. In 1812, a Republic of Florida was organized by these settlers with the aid of American troops. Finally an agreement was made with the Spanish authorities granting local self-government to northeast Florida. Spain, weakened by the spread of revolutions in her American colonies, had little strength left for the defense of Florida. The Seminole Indians held aloof from Spanish authority, hoping for a return of English rule, and buccaneering adventurers, among them William Bowles, incited the natives against the American and Spanish settlements. Finally the pretense of Spanish authority was shattered by General Andrew Jackson's two invasions of the peninsula at a time of tension between England and the United States. The English, threatening New Orleans in 1814, used the Spanish Pensacola harbor as a base for their ships and drilled Seminole Indians in the public square. Jackson took the city by storm. In 1818, Jackson made another punitive expedition into Florida, operating largely in the region between Pensacola and the Suwannee River. He burned many Indian towns, seized Fort St.Marks on the Gulf, and executed two English traders accused of inciting the Indians against American settlements. At Pensacola, Jackson removed the Spanish civil authorities and substituted Americans who remained in control for several months.

By the treaty of February 22, 1819, Spain—unable to police the region effectively—sold Florida to the United States for $5,000,000 and a rectification, in Spain's favor, of the boundary between Spain and the United States in the southwest. No money was paid, however, the United States simply assuming the indemnities owed to American property owners in Florida for damages incurred during the unsettled times following the establishment of the Republic of Florida. This transfer to the United States ended a 300-year period in which Florida was an international pawn among nations striving for control of the Gulf of Mexico.

On March 3, 1821, the two Florida provinces were formed into one territory with General Andrew Jackson as military commander. He took charge upon the change of flags in July 1821. The Territory of Florida was created and civil government was established by the act of March 30, 1822. William P. Duval was appointed first Territorial Governor and Joseph M. Hernandez the first delegate to Congress. In 1824, Tallahassee was selected as the site of the new capital.

The Seminole Indians were the first great problem of American settlers who moved to Florida. Placated for years by the English and Spanish authorities, the Indians occupied the best lands in the interior of the State and viewed the Americans with hatred and fear. Both settlers and Indians made efforts to keep the peace, but outrages committed by some of the white men were promptly avenged by the Indians. Attempts to claim as slaves Negroes living with the Indians added bitterness to the dispute. Clashes with the Indians spread until Florida was plunged into the long ruinous Seminole Wars, 1835–42, which cost the United States the lives of 1,500 soldiers and of many settlers and more than $40,000,000 in expenditures and property damage. Sporadic outbreaks continued until 1858.

A spirit of optimism was evident among the new settlers, and development of the Territory was rapid. Beginning in 1828, banks and insurance companies were chartered with little restriction of the power of directors. The Territory issued bonds for the Union Bank of Tallahassee to the amount of $3,000,000, and these were sold in the North and abroad. Money flowed freely until the panic of 1837 when a decline in cotton prices, the prolonged Seminole War, and a frost which destroyed the citrus crop contributed to the downfall of credit. Many banks failed, including the Union Bank, and so widespread was the reaction that the constitution was amended, making it unlawful for the Government to go into debt or for bankers to hold office. (The prohibition regarding State debt is still in force, but that affecting bankers has been nullified.)

By the middle of the 1830's there was considerable agitation in favor of statehood. In February 1837, the Territorial legislative council authorized an election to determine popular opinion on the matter, and the election held in April showed a majority in favor. Consequently, the council authorized an election of members to a constitutional convention. Thus originated the historic Convention of 1838, which met at St. Joseph in December 1838 and remained in session through January 1839.

Under the constitution framed by the Convention of 1838 Florida was admitted to statehood on March 3, 1845. This constitution limited the franchise to white males more than 21 years old who were enrolled in the State militia, and provided for an annual session of the legislature, composed of 17 senators and 41 representatives to be elected by popular vote. Of the executive officers only the governor was elected by the people. The State treasurer, comptroller, and attorney general were elected by the legislature, as were the justices of the supreme court and the chancellors and judges of the circuit courts. One representative to the Congress of the United States was elected from the State at large by popular vote; the two senators were elected by the legislature, since the seventeenth amendment to the Federal Constitution had not yet been passed.

To keep a balance between the free and slave States, Florida was admitted as a slave State and Iowa as a free State. William D. Moseley was the first State Governor, David L. Yulee and James D. Westcott, Jr., the first United States Senators, Edward C. Cabell and William H. Brockenbrough the first United States Representatives.

By this time there were great plantations of cotton and of sugar cane; cattle and hogs were raised, especially in west Florida; orange culture was beginning to be important; settlers and visitors were attracted in large numbers. Forty counties were created between 1820 and 1860, as the population spread over a wide area. Between 1840 and 1860, Florida cotton plantations produced a crop totaling half of the wealth of the State.

In addition to the Negro slaves of the plantations and those who had found refuge with the Indians, there was a small group of free Negroes in Florida. Some of these had acquired property during the easy-going Spanish era but, as early as 1826, legislation restricting their privileges was passed by the Territorial council. In 1840, the 76 free Negroes and 96 slaves in Key West were forbidden to appear on the streets after sundown without written permission, from the mayor for free Negroes, and from their masters for slaves. The penalty for violators was whipping or forced labor on the streets. By 1860, laws had become so stringent that many free Negroes emigrated and some even sought voluntary servitude.

Cotton had become the basis of Florida's economic life by 1860, and it was to be expected that Florida would secede with the other Southern States. The Ordinance of Secession was passed on January 10, 1861, Florida being the third State to join the Confederacy. Fifteen thousand Floridians served in the Confederate army, a number greater than the voting population of the State. While no decisive engagements were fought on its soil, Florida was a major source of food supplies for the Southern army. In 1862, John Hay, President Lincoln's personal representative, tried to provide for civil government at Jacksonville, and in 1864 General Sherman made a similar attempt, but neither of them succeeded.

After the war, President Johnson set up a provisional government in Florida, and appointed William Marvin Governor. Marvin called a constitutional convention which met on October 25, 1865, annulled the secession ordinance, and adopted a new constitution. On November 5, 1865, the convention ratified the Thirteenth Amendment and gave the governor power to appoint a commission to make recommendations, chiefly on the problem of assimilating the Negro into the new government. The State legislature, which convened in June 1866, ratified the Fourteenth Amendment and passed laws that safeguarded most of the Negroes' civil rights but denied them the vote. This position, similar to the policy of the other Southern States, was unsatisfactory to the radical element in Congress. Accordingly, when ex-Governor Marvin of Florida was presented for a seat in the Senate, Charles Sumner opened his attack on the Johnson plan of Reconstruction by challenging the eligibility of Marvin, on the ground that many Florida citizens had been disfranchised. The Senate refused to seat Marvin, and the Congressional Reconstruction Acts were passed on March 21, 1867. Florida became a part of the Third Military District, administered under General John Pope.

In November 1865, a branch of the Freedmen's Bureau had been established in Florida, with Thomas W. Osborne of the Federal army as Assistant Commissioner for the State. In 1867, Osborne organized the Lincoln Brotherhood, a 'secret league' to secure participation of the Negro in politics. Osborne's intention was to make his Negro constituents voters but not holders of high office. In the same year, the Loyal League of America was established by a Negro from Baltimore, William M. Saunders, who sought to secure offices for Negroes. In November, Florida voted for a constitutional convention, nine-tenths of the votes in its favor being cast by Negroes. The constitution, however, carried out Osborne's ideas by making the requirements for higher offices such that the Negro could not qualify.

The Reconstruction Period in Florida was darkened by suffering and poverty, though it was not characterized by the harshness experienced in other Southern States. An immediate adjustment was made between planters and the Freedmen's Bureau, and by 1866 nine-tenths of the Florida Negroes were at work in the fields, while employers were asking for more laborers from other States. Though the bureau was empowered to establish courts to protect the Negro, this was not done in Florida and both civil and penal suits were tried in the regular courts. Finally the work of the bureau in establishing schools for Negroes was supported by the planters, many of whom, according to the 1866 report of the State superintendent of Negro schools, offered to pay half the expense. Public schools were established for Negroes by the bureau in Jacksonville, St.Augustine, and other cities.

In 1867, General John Pope reported that he expected trouble in Alabama and Georgia but none in Florida, while Edward King and Harriet Beecher Stowe stated that the freedmen were in much better condition in Florida than in the Carolinas or Georgia. About 1870, Florida experienced a period of lawlessness, particularly in the turpentine sections of middle Florida, evidenced by an unusually active Ku Klux Klan; but even this disturbance disappeared by 1871. When the Republicans gained a share of political offices for Negroes, Jonathan C. Gibbs, a Negro, was made Secretary of State in 1869 and State superintendent of education in 1872; J.Walls became Florida's only Negro Congressman in 1872. The Negro vote had begun to turn to the Democrats by 1874 and their candidate, Charles W. Jones, was elected United States Senator, one of the first Democrats to be seated in 14 years.

With a view to freeing Florida from military rule, a fourth State constitution was framed in February 1868, ratified by the people in May, and accepted by the Federal Government. The State was readmitted to representation in Congress on June 25, and the Reconstruction government gave way on July 4, 1868, to regular State officials, headed by Harrison Reed as Governor. Military control, however, was not finally abolished until 1876. Florida functioned for almost 19 years under the 1868 constitution, which extended the franchise to all male citizens of 21 years or older, including Negroes. It also provided that the governor, the lieutenant governor, members of the legislature, and constables be elected by popular vote. The governor and the senate appointed the State supreme court, composed of a chief justice and two associates, who held office for life or during good behavior; they also appointed the other judicial and executive officials. The constitution under which the State still functions was framed in 1885, ratified by popular vote in 1886, and became effective in January 1887.

In 1881, when the nearly bankrupt State sold 4,000,000 acres of land to Hamilton Disston 'and associates' for $1,000,000 the intensive development of Florida began. Although its population had almost tripled in thirty years, growing from 140,424 in 1860 to 391,422 in 1890, its urban centers were not large. St.Augustine, a sleepy fishing village just beginning to attract tourists, had a population in 1890 of 4,742. Key West, the largest city, with 18,000 inhabitants, was a prosperous naval base as well as the center of the sponge and cigar industries. Jacksonville, with 17,201 inhabitants was the second largest city, its prosperity depending on lumber and naval stores. Pensacola, with a population of 11,750, was still an important Gulf port; Tampa, half the size of St. Augustine, was experiencing its first boom with the coming of the cigar manufacturers from Key West to Ybor City. Miami and Palm Beach were not yet in existence.

The major part of the State was an unexplored wilderness. A few plantations in the north and west produced quantities of cotton, corn, and tobacco; orange groves in the northeastern section were assuming commercial importance; and vast phosphate deposits in the center of the State had recently been discovered; but modern transportation and communication facilities were still in their infancy.

A State bureau of immigration had been established in 1868. Many railroad companies launched extensive programs of land development, especially featuring the profits of the citrus industry. As a result, a number of English colonist groups, such as the one which founded Avon Park, came to Florida and a citrus boom developed in northeast and central Florida; this collapsed after the severe freeze of 1895.

Cuban immigrants brought their political troubles along with their cigar business to Florida. Over a period of 50 years before the Spanish-American War, Florida was the sounding board for Cuban grievances. Refugees at Key West published newspapers and organized expeditions to invade Cuba, notwithstanding efforts of United States authorities to control their propaganda. In the years immediately preceding the war, filibusterers in Florida carried ammunition and volunteers to the Cuban revolutionists, despite a double blockade of American and Spanish warships. Although 5,000 Floridians volunteered, few of them saw action in the Spanish-American War.

In the 1870's the greater part of the tourist travel was by way of the St.Johns River to middle Florida. After railroad and hotel developments were initiated in the 1880's by Henry M. Flagler and H.B.Plant, pioneer Florida financiers, the volume of travel was turned to the east and west coasts. But this diversion of tourist trade did not retard the development of the interior of the State in the period between the Spanish-American War and the World War. Drainage of the Everglades was begun in 1906 as a State project under the State board of drainage commissioners; rapid progress was made after 1910. Medical research made possible preventive measures for the control of yellow fever and malaria. North Florida developed a large turpentine and naval-stores industry, after the center of citrus culture was moved from the St.Johns River valley to middle and south Florida following the destructive winters of 1895–96. Pebble phosphate was discovered in 1884 and hard rock phosphate in 1889; the former is still a source of wealth for the State. In some sections phosphate offered a substitute industry for timber, depleted by sawmills. Sixteen new counties were formed between 1909 and 1921, the greatest number since before the War between the States.

The World War broke commercial ties valuable to Florida, but tourist trade prospered and many persons who had formerly traveled to foreign resorts spent their vacations in the State. After the United States entered the War, an important army training camp was established at Jacksonville, a naval training school at Pensacola, and student flying fields at Arcadia and Miami. An army post was maintained at Key West and coastal defenses strengthened.

After the World War reports of large profits in real estate brought speculators by the hundreds of thousands to Florida. The hysterical buying and selling of land so inflated prices that it was profitable in many cities to dredge sand from the bottom of bays and build artificial islands. People rushed in by train, auto, and boat, intent upon making a fortune in a few days. As a result, between 1920 and 1925, population increased four times as fast as in any other State. One and a half million visitors came annually in the early 1920's, and seven new counties were formed in 1921. At the peak of the real-estate craze in 1925, 2,500,000 people entered the State. The bubble burst in the spring of 1926. Banks failed, and individuals who had made millions became penniless overnight. Thus Florida experienced a depression in advance of the rest of the country.

A great natural catastrophe occurred in the same year—the hurricane in mid-September, which caused the death of several hundred. Thousands more were injured or left temporarily homeless. The damage caused by the September hurricane of 1928 was more serious; 1,810 persons were killed and 1,849 injured, according to estimates given by the American Red Cross. A third disastrous storm swept the Florida Keys in September 1935, destroying the railroad between Florida City and Key West. Red Cross estimates set the number of dead or missing at 425. One hopeful result of the earlier disasters was the increased attention given to modern building construction in restoring the devastated areas and in developments in other parts of the State. It was found during the more recent storms that the hurricane damage was relatively slight where modern construction had been used. Also a hurricane research station has been set up at Gainesville, through the co-operation of the local radio station, the University of Florida, and the WPA.

The inflow of money from the tourist trade helped Florida toward a partial recovery between 1926–29, but the Nation-wide depression, dating from the stock-market crash of October 1929, for a time destroyed the prosperity of many of the tourist and recreation centers. In 1930, public-bond debts approximated $550,000,000. The State itself owed no part of this sum, for the debts were the obligations of counties, cities, drainage districts, and special school-tax districts. An apparently insatiable bond market in the north and persuasive bond brokers seeking new issues to sell had induced some towns to incur debts in excess of $1,000 per capita. This was accomplished by raising assessed valuations of property to create the illusion of security.

Bond defaults began in 1930 and this introduced the era of bondholder committees, who entered into refunding agreements. Action by the legislature, assisted by the Federal Government, helped to restore the badly shaken financial structure. The State then turned to the development of tangible resources. Introduction of paper mills led to extensive reforestation, port improvements to the installation of pre-cooling plants for the more orderly marketing of perishable fruits and vegetables, and the resumption of building took into account utility rather than effect. Co-operative farm groups were organized, co-operative farm markets constructed, the citrus-fruit industry was regulated by law. As industry expanded, the number of local labor unions increased; on the other hand, many employers banded together in an organization known as Associated Industries of Florida.

Violence broke out in 1936 when Earl Browder, Communist candidate for President, was attacked at a Tampa political rally. This incident and the 1938 parades of the Ku Klux Klan at Jacksonville, Lakeland, Miami, St.Petersburg, and Starke engaged the attention of labor unions and groups organized for the protection of civil liberties. By 1939 organized labor had gained a number of advantages for the workers. A liberal trend was indicated in 1935 in the passage of a Workman's Compensation Law and the creation of a Florida industrial commission and a State welfare board.

In 1930 Florida had a population of 1,468,211, with about 50,000 more urban than rural inhabitants. Of the 1,035,205 white Floridians, 976,148 were native born and 59,057 foreign born. Negroes made up 431,828 of the total. Approximately 100,000 of the native whites were of foreign or mixed parentage, including 13,136 from England, 5,886 from the Irish Free State, 9,038 from Canada, 17,084 from Germany, 8,053 from Italy, and 5,975 from Spain.

Since 1934, extensive improvements, either partly or wholly undertaken by Federal emergency agencies, have greatly added to the physical equipment of the State. Outstanding among these are land reclamation and the building of courthouses, post offices, roads, bridges, and recreation centers. Cultural, educational, and welfare projects have greatly widened interest in these fields and increased the number of participants in the activities.

GOVERNMENT

Florida's present constitution, adopted in 1885 and made operative in 1887, was concerned chiefly with the preservation of State sovereignty. Drafted shortly after the close of the Reconstruction period, it represented a compromise between the necessities of the times and the political philosophy of the Old South. More specifically, it was conceived with the problems in mind of the north Florida agricultural area, occupied by most of the State's population at that time. It has since, by numerous amendments, been expanded to meet economic changes, but the sectional political control contemplated by its authors has remained intact.

Under this constitution the common and statute laws of England enacted before July 4, 1776, not inconsistent with the Constitution and laws of the United States and with the legislative acts of Florida, are part of the common law of the State. The constitution provides for the usual three departments of government—executive, judicial, and legislative—and expressly limits their respective functions. Provisions relating to the executive department represented a distinct advance toward democratic government, requiring for the first time in Florida history that all members of the cabinet be elected by the people. The members are the treasurer, comptroller, attorney general, secretary of state, commissioner of agriculture, and superintendent of public instruction. It further provides that county administrative officials be elected by citizens of the several counties.

The governor, elected for a four-year term, has broad executive powers. He recommends measures to the legislature, signs all grants and commissions, and has the power to suspend officers who are not liable to impeachment. He may either veto bills passed by the legislature or disapprove any items that call for appropriations. Another important power of the governor is that he may demand of the supreme court an interpretation of provisions of the State constitution upon any question affecting his executive powers. The governor's power has been further enlarged through the creation of boards and bureaus by legislative act.

The governor is prohibited from immediately succeeding himself in office, but other State officials have continued to 'carry over.' In 1939, for example, the commissioner of agriculture had been in office since 1923 and the treasurer had been a member of the cabinet as either treasurer or comptroller for 23 out of 34 years. In effect, the chief executive finds himself with a ready-made cabinet over which he has little jurisdiction, except through his influence on the legislature, which controls appropriations. It is the duty of the legislature to appropriate funds to run the executive branch. The lack of a civil-service commission, however, gives the governor extensive appointive powers. The constitution does not provide for a lieutenant governor, but in the event of the governor's death, incapacity, or impeachment, the president of the senate fills his unexpired term.

The judicial branch of Florida government is vested in a supreme court, 16 circuit courts, 11 special courts, 67 county judges' courts, magistrates' courts, and 16 county courts (in Broward, De Soto, Gadsden, Glades, Indian River, Jefferson, Lee, Manatee, Martin, Okeechobee, Osceola, Pasco, Pinellas, Sarasota, Seminole, and St.Lucie Counties). The State supreme court, consisting of six judges, appears to follow the constitution more closely than other departments, but to its original and appellate jurisdiction has been added an advisory power: that of giving an opinion on the constitutionality of legislative acts.

Justices of the supreme court are elected at large for a term of six years, and appointments by the governor can be made only to fill unexpired terms; frequently such an appointment is bestowed upon the current attorney general. The chief justice is elected by members of the court.

As the population increased, the number of circuit courts was also increased, until in 1935 there were 28 circuits. In that year the number was reduced to 16 by the legislature, in recognition of easier transportation facilities among heretofore isolated communities. While circuit judges are appointed by the governor and such appointments are confirmed or rejected by the State senate, candidates (by statute provision) first submit to a primary election in their respective circuits. Although not bound to do so, the governor invariably follows the mandate of the voters. A constitutional amendment of 1912 provided an additional circuit judge for Duval County; unlike the other circuit judges of Florida, who are paid by the State, this judge is paid by the county. Each circuit is also provided with a State's attorney and an assistant. State's attorneys, like circuit judges, are selected at primaries, then appointed by the governor and confirmed by the senate. Counties elect a clerk of the circuit court for a term of four years, even though a judicial circuit may include several counties. As a county official, the clerk operates the delinquent tax-redemption department, in some cases serves as county treasurer, and acts as clerk of the county court. Prosecuting attorneys and clerks are paid by fees within a limitation fixed by law. It is customary to submit the names of candidates or appointees for the State judiciary to the State bar association for approval before nomination or appointment.

Each of Florida's 67 counties has a county judge's court, and 16 have county courts; the former handles probate cases, the latter handle criminal misdemeanors involving penalties not to exceed one year in jail. The judge of the county judge's court serves on the bench of county courts, and also as a committing magistrate. The county judge appoints the clerk of the county judge's court. Justices of the peace are elected from districts within a county and their powers are limited to their districts. The county sheriff or any constable acts as executive officer of the magistrate's court. Eleven special courts, such as criminal courts of record and civil courts of record, have been created in eight of the more populous counties: Dade, Duval, Escambia, Hillsborough, Monroe, Orange, Palm Beach, and Polk Counties.

Economic and social conditions in Florida have changed greatly since 1885; population has increased and shifted, and many new problems have arisen. Yet the legislative branch of the State government has been able to retain a number of features originally desired by the authors of the constitution, especially the one providing for sectional political control.

At the first session under the new constitution, in 1887, the legislature was made up of 68 representatives and 32 senators. The 1937 legislature consisted of a lower house of 95 representatives and a senate of 38 members. The senatorial increase was by constitutional amendment in 1923, creating new senatorial districts. Additions to the house were brought about through the creation of new counties, each of which is entitled to from one to three representatives according to population. Every ten years the lower house is automatically reconstructed on a basis of three members for each of the five largest counties, two members for each of the next eighteen, and one for each remaining county. In 1935, the date of the last revision, west Florida lost a member and south Florida gained one. According to the 1930 census, the three so-called 'big' counties, which include Florida's three largest cities—Jacksonville, Tampa, and Miami—had a population of 451,977, nearly one-third of the State's total. These three counties—Duval, Hillsborough, and Dade—have nine representatives and three senators, whereas the three smallest senatorial districts, comprising four counties with a combined population of only 30,000, have four representatives and three senators.

Any attempt to bring about reapportionment through a constitutional convention probably would fail, since representation at such a convention would be precisely the same as that in the legislature, which has opposed a shift of power. Advocates of reapportionment, therefore, foresee no rewriting of the constitution for this purpose.

Representatives are elected for two years, but they actually serve but one session, which is held biennially beginning in April of the odd-numbered years. Senators are elected for a term of four years. As only 19 of the 38 are elected at one time, there is never a completely new senate. The 19 hold-over senators nominate a president for the next term from among those who must submit to a general election to retain their seats. Nomination for the presidency is equivalent to election, if the nominee is successful at the polls. The speaker of the house of representatives is elected by that body. Subordinate officers are elected from nonmembers by each body and receive the same pay as members, $6 a day while the legislature is in session.

Municipalities operate under legislative charters, and consequently many laws pertaining to city government are enacted in the legislature through what are known as local bills. These consume a great deal of the time and energy of members, often to the neglect of general legislation. To correct this condition, the 1935 session passed a joint resolution to submit an amendment to the people that would allow cities to enact local legislation under their own charters. This amendment was ratified by the voters in 1936, but has never been put into effect.

A more serious aspect of the local-bill evil, its opponents contend, is that candidates for the legislature run on local issues, thus creating as many separate platforms as there are offices to fill. State-wide legislation takes second place and successful candidates are not bound to support or oppose general measures that appear after the sessions convene. This situation has arisen from the failure of the controlling party to adopt a State platform since the beginning of the twentieth century.

General legislation since 1933 has been in the direction of public welfare; boards to administer old-age pensions have been created, medical clinics established, and workmen's compensation laws and laws regulating the fruit industry enacted. A trend toward price-fixing in specialized trades and businesses began with the passage of an emergency milk-control act in 1933. Similar laws have been enacted, applying to barbers, beauticians, dry-cleaners, and laundries, each setting up a board with price-fixing authority. The milk-control act was enacted into a permanent law in 1939, but the barber law has been declared unconstitutional and the laundry legislation is now (1939) under attack in the courts.

In 1937 the poll tax as a prerequisite to voting was abolished, but the white Democratic primary system prevails and nomination in the Democratic primary is tantamount to election. Negroes are not admitted to the polls for the Democratic Party primaries, but they frequently vote in the general election and, under charter provisions, take part in municipal nominations and elections in several Florida cities.

Transportation

BEFORE the coming of the railroads, transportation in Florida depended chiefly on streams and coastal waters. Overland travel presented a dreary and discouraging prospect; with the exception of the Kings Road along the upper east coast and the Spanish Trail between St.Augustine and Pensacola, land routes were little more than paths. The St.Johns River, emptying into the Atlantic, and the Apalachicola, leading into the Gulf of Mexico, were the main channels of commerce. From the headwaters of navigation, goods were transported in wagons drawn by eight or ten yoke of oxen. Five or six heavily loaded wagons made a train, the coming of which was announced by the cracking of drivers' whips long before the caravan came into sight.

For a long time after its discovery, explorers believed Florida to be an island rather than a peninsula, and many efforts were made to find a natural waterway across the State. During the temporary occupation of St.Marks and Pensacola by American forces in 1818–19, the Secretary of War directed an examination of the sources of the St.Marys and Suwannee Rivers. Shipping interests wished to connect these streams with a canal, and thus obviate the necessity for ocean traffic around the peninsula. The era of the steam railroad had not yet begun, and the idea of canals occupied the minds of persons working for improved transportation.

Various minor canals were projected in Florida, but few ever developed beyond the phase of promotion. The Chipola Canal Company was incorporated in 1829 to construct a ditch or railroad from the Chipola River to St.Andrews Bay, and to finance its operations the company was authorized to raise $50,000 by a lottery. Another effort to reach the interior from the Gulf was that of the Wacissa & Aucilla Navigation Company, incorporated in 1831. Shortly before the War between the States, a survey was made for a cross-State canal, after numerous shipping disasters on the Florida Reef had produced a strong agitation for an inland passage. During the period from 1848 to 1857 a total of 499 vessels, valued at $16,266,426, met disaster on the reefs.

Florida's earliest railroad, chartered in 1834 and at first dependent upon mule power, had meanwhile begun operations. It consisted of a 22-mile stretch between Tallahassee and Port Leon, and the mule-drawn train made the initial 'run' in five hours. Steam was introduced in 1834. This was the humble beginning of the Tallahassee Railroad Company, a predecessor of the Seaboard Air Line Railway. The second railroad, even shorter than the first, was built between Apalachicola and St. Joseph's Bay in an attempt to divert river commerce to the boom port of St. Joseph. A third line was established between St. Joseph and Iola, a farming settlement on the Apalachicola River. The prospects of St. Joseph in marine commerce failed to materialize and both lines were abandoned, the Apalachicola road in 1839 and the Iola in 1841. These and other early railroads were narrow-gage lines using light wooden rails faced with iron straps. Most of them were built between a seaport and a cotton or orange-growing section a few miles inland. Passenger equipment consisted of flatcars with wooden benches.

Steam locomotives, when first introduced in Florida, were not popular, but, by 1861, railroads linked most of the important cities in the northern part of the State. The Florida Railroad in 1860 connected Fernandina on the Atlantic Coast with Cedar Keys on the Gulf, forming the first cross-State line. Another line, from Jacksonville to Tallahassee, passed through Lake City, and from Tallahassee a short branch ran to St. Marks on the Gulf. A financial merger of these and other small lines was accomplished in 1880 under the name of the Florida Central & Peninsula Railroad. The new company included the Florida Railroad, although this line did not become a physical unit of the system until 1888. In 1903 these properties were acquired by the Seaboard Air Line and added to the system.

Railroad construction, however, did not discourage the advocates of inland waterways. The Apopka Canal Company was authorized in 1879 to connect Lake Eustis and Lake Apopka with a canal for navigation and drainage. This canal was dug and operated. Others linked railheads with natural waterways, and railroads in turn filled in gaps between protected waterways along the Atlantic coast of Florida. Operations started in 1882 by the Florida Coast Line Canal & Transportation Company eventually provided inland water communication from Daytona Beach to Titusville on the Indian River, the southern terminus of the Florida East Coast Railway, and to Jupiter Inlet, from which the Jupiter & Lake Worth Railroad continued the route southward to Lake Worth. Subsequently, a canal was cut between Jupiter and Lake Worth, and in 1896 another canal was completed for the 27-mile haul between Juno and the mouth of the Miami River.

A line of steamers established in 1889 on the Indian River operated from Titusville to Jupiter, and many independent boats plied this tidewater lane. The transportation of nonperishable freight southward and of pineapples and oranges northward became a paying business. During the pineapple season competition among the river boats was intense, and the captains would hoist a broomstick at the smokestack to indicate a full cargo aboard.

This enthusiasm for expanding transportation opened up much territory; but by guaranteeing many rail and canal bonds, the State in the process had been pushed to the verge of bankruptcy. Paradoxically, then, it was the most pretentious plan of all for developing inland water commerce that extricated Florida from its financial distress. In 1881 Hamilton Disston, a Philadelphia saw manufacturer, purchased 4,000,000 acres of so-called swamp and overflow land at 25¢ an acre, and the State with this $1,000,000 cash liquidated the most pressing of its bond defaults. Public funds, then tied up in the courts, were released.

Disston's purchase extended from the Gulf nearly across central Florida, and in this territory he began to dig a great network of canals that, among other things, connected Kissimmee, a railhead on Lake Tohopekaliga in the middle of the State, with the Gulf by way of the Kissimmee River, Lake Okeechobee, and the Caloosahatchee River. Through this passage he brought boats from the Mississippi River to Kissimmee, which was to be the hub of his ambitious waterways empire. Shipyards were built there, and a boiler factory; but a few years later rails were extended by the Plant System from Kissimmee to the Gulf, and Disston's waterways found little use except as drainage canals.

Coastwise sailing packets were still in use and enjoying good business, but steam was rapidly replacing the sail, and in the late 1870's and early 1880's steamboat traffic on the larger rivers prospered as never before. Large and luxuriant side-wheelers were built for the accommodation of tourists; the St. Johns River provided the favorite route for water excursions.

The Brock Line, established by Jacob Brock in 1852, was the principal steamboat company operating on the St. Johns until 1876, when Frederick de Barry started the De Barry Line. This was later combined with the Baya Line, and operated 13 steamers. The De Barry-Baya Line ran between Jacksonville and all points on the St. Johns, obtained the mail contracts, and later placed steamers on the 'Sea Island Route' to Savannah. In 1889 the business was sold to the Clyde Line, which, in 1886, had built the *S.S. Cherokee* and *S.S. Seminole* for the first through service by water from Jacksonville to New York. The registry of St.Johns River traffic, in 1885, listed a total of 74 vessels, aggregating 8,168 tons.

By now Florida's two spectacular railroad builders, Henry M. Flagler and Henry B. Plant, had their grandiose plans well under way. Flagler, with his East Coast Railway, had begun to penetrate and develop the east coast, and Plant, by carrying his lines across the State, was opening up the lower Gulf coast. Each sought to install port terminals that would capture Central and South American water commerce, and each erected in Florida, as railroad feeders, amazing hotels that still tower as monuments of lavishness. Plant combined railroads and boat lines in his program, while Flagler confined himself to rails, eventually extending them to the sea to establish a rail and port terminal at insular Key West. From there he operated a train ferry to Cuba.

Plant, the head and principal owner of the Southern Express Company, with headquarters at Atlanta, Georgia, entered upon railroad building after he had purchased, in 1879–80, several small Georgia lines that were bankrupt after the War between the States. In 1881 he took over the East Florida Railroad, which had been built from Jacksonville to the St.Marys River to connect at the State boundary with the Waycross Short Line in Georgia. With these properties and his newly organized Savannah, Florida & Western Railroad, Plant entered Florida, and then laid his plans for crossing the State to the Gulf coast.

Land bonuses were plentiful, and traffic in railroad charters carrying these grants became a profitable business. Plant purchased such a charter for $30,000 and under it completed his cross-state line from Kissimmee to Tampa. The charter, covering a stretch of 75 miles, carried a grant of 5,000 acres per mile, but its unexpired term, to January 24, 1884, covered only seven months. Construction was therefore pressed at feverish speed, and the road, costing an estimated $375,000, was completed with 63 hours to spare. This was known as the South Florida Railroad. From Tampa, Plant inaugurated a steamship service to Key West and Cuba. Other boat lines operated by the Plant Investment Company, parent concern of various rail, ship, land, and hotel enterprises, included the People's Line on the St.Johns River, connecting at Jacksonville with Plant's Savannah, Florida & Western Railroad, and at Sanford with his South Florida Railroad and a line of steamers on the Apalachicola River and its tributaries.

Plant was to acquire from a less fortunate promoter another cross-state railroad, roughly paralleling his own to the north. Peter Demens (Piotr Alexeitch Dementieff), a Russian political exile of noble birth who had come to Florida in 1880 to engage in lumber milling, built a short logging railroad for his mill near Sanford. He also purchased an inoperative railroad charter, acquired some land grants, and in 1888 completed what became known as the Orange Belt Line, terminating at the town site of St.Petersburg on the Pinellas Peninsula. Demens, however, experienced a succession of troubles. Rainy weather, mosquitoes, and an epidemic of yellow fever conspired to delay work. Land bonuses had to be forfeited because of this delay, to the hindrance of credit and underwriting. Labor disputes completed Demens' tragedy. Rolling stock was chained to the tracks under judgments obtained by creditors; unpaid workmen threatened to lynch Demens; and, as a climax, when he finally brought his line to the site of St.Petersburg, half of which was to go to the railroad, a wrangle between the landowner and Demens tied up the property, causing both to lose the profits resulting from real-estate activity stimulated by the entrance of the railroad. A creditor syndicate, headed by E.T.Stotesbury, a Philadelphia financier, took over and operated the road until 1895, when a freeze destroyed the citrus groves that supplied freight to the Orange Belt. Ten days after this disaster Plant absorbed the crippled line. The Plant System, in 1902, became a part of the existing Atlantic Coast Line.

Flagler, an associate of Rockefeller in the Standard Oil Company, was one of the first of a long line of retired millionaires who came to Florida to play and remained to work. At the age of 53 he visited St.Augustine, where he was struck with the lack of modern facilities for visitors. He gained control of the Jacksonville-St.Augustine Line to bring in materials for his Ponce de Leon Hotel, the first of a series of hotels which he built at points from St.Augustine to Key West. In 1888 he acquired a narrow-gage road running from Tocoi Junction to East Palatka, and a logging railroad extending from East Palatka to Daytona. With these as a nucleus he rapidly laid rails southward in a system that became known as the Florida East Coast Railway. Train service was established to New Smyrna in 1892, to Fort Pierce in January 1894, and to Palm Beach three months later. By 1896, continuous rail facilities had been completed from Jacksonville to Miami, a distance of 366 miles. Not until 1912, a year before his death, did Flagler complete the last and most spectacular extension of the Florida East Coast Railway, connecting the Florida Keys en route to Key West by overseas bridges. After the Labor Day hurricane of 1935, when 38 miles of this track were destroyed, the 'overseas' railroad was abandoned.

The principal figure in railroad building, after Flagler and Plant, was

S.Davies Warfield, president of the Seaboard Air Line. Under his leadership the Seaboard invaded the previously undisputed territory of the Florida East Coast by building in 1924 a cross-state line from Coleman to West Palm Beach, a distance of 204 miles, and thence to Miami and Homestead in 1926. This line provided the first direct rail connection between the prosperous lower east coast and the rapidly developing west coast, and saved the long, indirect journey through Jacksonville from one south Florida coast to the other. Warfield was responsible for the consolidation of many small roads with the Seaboard and for extensive construction activities during 1920–27, when approximately 500 miles of trackage were added to the system in Florida.

During the boom period of 1925–26 the Atlantic Coast Line, to compete with the Seaboard's through passenger service from the west coast, built the Perry cutoff, connecting a short gap in its system between Perry and Monticello in northwest Florida. This made it unnecessary to route passenger traffic from Tampa and other Gulf cities through Jacksonville for points west and north. The Seaboard, in conjunction with the Southern Railway and the Georgia, Southern & Florida, already had established a direct route north through Hampton that eliminated Jacksonville. Thus, with the completion of the Perry cutoff, Jacksonville ceased to be the railroad gateway to west Florida.

Shortly after this the St.Louis & San Francisco Railroad invaded Florida at Pensacola, terminating the port monopoly enjoyed there for many years by the Louisville & Nashville, and at the same time providing another outlet from the north and west.

It was also during the boom period that the Atlantic Coast Line double-tracked its main line from Richmond to Jacksonville, and the Florida East Coast Railway double-tracked from there to Miami. Still the railroads were swamped with freight. Demand for building materials and machinery was such that freight yards became snarls of rolling stock. Thousands of empty cars, occupying available sidings, were blocked by hundreds of incoming loaded cars, and this tie-up finally resulted in a railroad embargo. Carload shipments into Florida were allowed thereafter only by permit, and the long delays that ensued had much to do with bringing water shipping back into its own.

Steamship lines, like the railroads, acquired new equipment and expanded their services. The Clyde Line's *Apache*, first passenger steamer to enter Biscayne Bay, made an initial run from New York to Miami in 1924. This line had formerly operated only to Jacksonville. The Peninsular & Occidental Steamship Company, founded by Plant and operated by the Atlantic Coast Line, built new ships and added a service between Miami and Havana to its regular run from Tampa to Key West and Cuba. But the urgent demand was for materials to keep Florida's fantastic building program going, and to meet this nearly everything seaworthy was pressed into service. Sailing ships resurrected from marine graveyards during the World War again saw service, and these old-timers jockeyed with fleet steam freighters to disgorge cargoes in Florida's bustling, congested ports. Lumber from Puget Sound came by way of the Panama Canal, and more from South America, Canada, and Europe. All this inspired extensive port developments around the coast of Florida.

When this activity ceased, almost as quickly as it began, ports were deserted, and railroads resumed normal operations. As a by-product, tramp steamers have done a fair business exporting the junk metal of deserted equipment to Japan, and hauling this scrap to shipside has provided railroads with considerable intrastate freight. It was after the boom that bus and truck lines grew into an important factor in transportation. Previously the need for fast and reliable carriers to market perishable produce in the North had given the railroads an advantage. Refrigerated fruit expresses for years handled the bulk of this business; but the installation of pre-cooling plants at port terminals and the introduction of refrigerator ships divided the fruit business. Truck service, however, penetrated many communities not served by rail or water, made direct deliveries, and eliminated the necessity for refrigeration, a costly item in handling perishables. To meet this competition the railroad interests sponsored a law, enacted by the 1937 Florida legislature, allowing rail lines to operate truck pick-up-and-delivery systems, as well as to use trucks to complete short hauls and fill in gaps in their lines. Passenger-bus lines reach practically every section of Florida, and their affiliations with out-of-State systems provide through transportation to all parts of the country.

Practically all the modern roads in Florida have been built since 1915, when the State legislature created the State road department. Prior to that time such construction was in the hands of the several counties, and as a result there was no co-ordinated system. Beginning in 1919, the State road department was given its first necessary funds for carrying out a comprehensive program. Road construction advanced until, during the boom period, expenditures reached as high as $18,000,000 annually. More than $250,000,000 had been spent on highway improvements by 1938, providing about 9,000 miles of hard-surfaced roads. Six cents of the 7¢

Florida gasoline tax is applied in equal parts to new road construction and the retirement of county highway bonds.

Perhaps the major achievement of the State road department since 1935 has been the completion of a 170-mile highway from Miami to Key West. The causeway of the Florida East Coast Railway, extending into the ocean from Lower Matecumbe Key to Big Pine Key, and unused since the 1935 Labor Day hurricane, was purchased by the State in 1936 at a cost of $640,000. Two ferries formerly carried motor vehicles across this stretch of open water. A $3,600,000 loan from the Public Works Administration enabled the State to construct a highway 20 feet in width over the abandoned causeway; it was begun in 1937 and completed in 1938. With the opening of this, the longest 'overseas' thoroughfare in the world, US 1 became an unbroken highway extending from Maine to Key West.

Motorists now can circle south Florida by traveling from Miami to Gulf-coast cities over the Tamiami Trail through the Everglades. The trail, built of rock blasted out of submerged ground, was completed in 1928. The trench formed by the removal of road-building material serves as a drainage canal and as a watercourse for Seminole canoes.

The State road department has succeeded in improving the appearance of roadsides, as part of its new program for making thoroughfares wider and safer. In laying out new roads, provision has been made for two-channel highways divided by a parkway to reduce the menaces of bright lights and head-on collisions. The value of this device has been demonstrated by a short stretch of double-channel highway already in operation along the lower east coast on US 1, and another north of Tampa.

Commercial aviation in Florida began with the establishment in 1914 of a 22-mile demonstration flying service over Tampa Bay between St.Petersburg and Tampa. Prior to this, four aviation schools had been established in the State at Pensacola, Jacksonville, St.Augustine, and Miami.

The Tampa-St.Petersburg air line, launched primarily to gain publicity, was later authenticated by aeronautical societies as the first scheduled air service in the world. Inaugurated January 1, 1914, with a single plane, the line maintained two daily round-trip flights for 28 consecutive days. The first passenger ticket was auctioned, and Mayor A.C.Pheil of St.Petersburg paid $500 for the privilege of making the initial trip. Tony Jannus, who piloted the plane during the brief existence of the line, shortly afterward joined the Czar's flying corps and lost his life in Russia. The Tony Jannus Administration Building at the Tampa airport perpetuates the name of this aviator.

Commercial aviation after the Jannus flights was not resumed until more than 20 years later, when individual pilots attempted scheduled trips between resort cities, catering to tourist trade. Some of these, incorporated as local lines, were soon displaced by larger interstate companies. The National Airlines, Inc., organized in St.Petersburg, is the only Florida airway operating out of the State.

In 1939, there were three scheduled air lines in Florida, the Pan American, Eastern, and National, and approximately 150 airports with modern facilities and emergency accommodations. Marking the airways in the State are 35 rotating beacons, 30 of them along the Atlanta and New York routes from the State line through Jacksonville, to Miami by way of St.Augustine, Daytona Beach, Titusville, Cocoa, Melbourne, Vero Beach, Stuart, and West Palm Beach. Across the center of the State, from Daytona Beach to St.Petersburg, beacons designate the course at Sanford, Orlando, Lakeland, Tampa, and St.Petersburg. Twenty-two airports in Florida are illuminated for night flying.

The Pan American's commercial marine air base, largest in the world, is in Miami. More than 60,000 air travelers bound to and from Latin America pass through it annually. This city has seven land and two sea airplane bases, one combined land-and-sea base, and a mile-square dirigible field equipped with mooring mast. In all, aviation facilities in the Miami area cover a territory of 3,500 acres. In mid-December each year, during the All-American Air Maneuvers, aircraft assemble here from all parts of the United States and from Latin America.

New forms of transportation have caused the abandonment of some short stretches of railroad in the State, but in 1938 the Atlantic Coast Line and the Seaboard formed an interlacing pattern over Florida, with the East Coast Line extending its rail tentacles inland down the Atlantic coast. These three roads, with two other main lines entering north Florida, and 17 local roads, have a combined trackage in excess of 4,500 miles. Through trains into Florida have been air-conditioned, and in December 1938 the Seaboard operated the first chair coach streamline train, the *Silver Meteor*, between New York and Miami. For this service the Seaboard contracted for three Diesel-electric locomotives, each generating 6,000 horsepower and declared by the company to be the largest and most powerful in the world.

Florida is a maritime State, on one of the main traffic lanes of world trade, over which freighters from the seven seas come to load and discharge their varied cargoes. A dozen deep-water ports space its shores, and 40 rivers with more than 1,000 miles of navigable waters penetrate its interior. Its thousands of lakes still offer expedient routes for connecting canals. In 1935, a $5,000,000 start was made on a $140,000,000 cross-State canal, which would have connected the Atlantic and Gulf and bordering intercoastal waterways, but construction was later suspended. Nine million dollars have been spent on the protected passage for pleasure craft, between reefs and mainland, down the east coast of Florida to Key West.

Agriculture

IN THE ornate script of LeMoyne, a French artist-explorer who lived at Fort Caroline on the St. Johns River in 1564, it is recorded that the Indians of Florida 'cultivate the earth diligently and the men know how to make a kind of hoe from fishbone, which they fit to wooden handles and prepare the soil, which is light.' Unfortunately the French settlers in Florida failed to learn from their neighbors how to raise crops, and a shortage of food drove their soldiers to raid Cuban shipping. This act focused the attention of the Spanish on the lone French colony, Fort Caroline, and so contributed to the destruction of its fort.

Late in the sixteenth century the Spanish Crown offered cattle and bounties on crops to persons who would colonize Florida, but most Spanish settlers preferred Mexico. Failing to induce its subjects to locate here, the Crown sent missionaries to convert the Indians, in the hope that Christian allies would enable Spain to hold the land. The missionaries brought oranges, lemons, figs, and sugar cane, planted them in mission gardens, and encouraged the Indians to settle near by. They also taught the Indians to herd the cattle and horses imported from Europe, which throve on the green Florida prairies. One reason for English raids into Florida in the early eighteenth century was a need for livestock and experienced Indian slaves for the Carolina plantations.

When England acquired the entire Florida Peninsula in 1763, many large land grants were parceled out to British colonists, who established prosperous plantations on the coast of northeast Florida. The Kings Road, extending from New Smyrna to Colerain, Georgia, traversed this area. Because of the large bounty offered for its cultivation, indigo was a popular crop, and the blue dye may still be seen in stained old vats, hidden in overgrown fields.

During the second Spanish occupation, 1783–1819, many Americans received Spanish grants, and their acreage was principally devoted to sea-island cotton and sugar cane, crops that could be produced profitably with slave labor. Importation of slaves from Africa continued in notoriously large numbers long after Florida became American territory and the slave trade was prohibited. Territorial agriculture was mainly an extension of the cotton kingdom; cattle ranked second in importance. Settlement of the land was a slow process until the Seminole Wars ended in 1842. Following the War between the States, a great number of planters in north Florida lost their lands through high taxation and lack of revenue; but new railroads and improved water transportation after 1880 gave impetus to agriculture in the central and southern parts of the State.

A tremendous advance was made in the agricultural development of Florida in the period from 1880 to 1935. Then, as now, the major part of the State's 35,000,000 acres consisted of forest land. In 1880 there were only 23,000 farms, aggregating 3,000,000 acres of improved farming land; by 1935 the number of farms had risen to 72,000 and the acreage of farming land to 6,000,000, but less than half of this acreage was under cultivation.

Florida, extending 500 miles into the ocean and gulf, has a range of more than six degrees in latitude and six degrees in average annual temperature between its northern and southern borders; thus the growing season progresses from south to north, and many tender crops mature in south Florida weeks earlier than in counties adjacent to Alabama and Georgia. Another factor in shaping the character of Florida agriculture is the curious pattern of soils that vary from clay and coarse sand to peat. These peculiarities of climate and soil divide the State into four distinct farming regions—south, central, north, and west Florida. With few exceptions, all four produce the same crops, but the importance of certain crops changes from one region to another. For example, vegetables lead in south Florida, but farming in central Florida is dominated by citrus. General farming is a minor occupation in peninsula-Florida, where vast stretches of pine land are broken by few clearings; but in the *ante-bellum* plantation region of upper Florida the scene is strikingly northern: farmhouses line the highways, fields are fenced, and livestock graze on the hills.

South Florida, with the rich Everglades muck lands, is one of the winter 'market baskets' of the States east of the Mississippi. Vegetables became the leading crop within a relatively short period, during which governmental and private research proved the adaptability of the local soils to crops formerly confined to the central and northern producing areas of the State. This development has lengthened Florida's growing season without creating serious competition with other shippers, many of whose peak crops go to market in other months of the year.

The harvest season starts in September when the grapefruit ripen, and the first carloads of vegetables are shipped in October. Irish potatoes, string beans, peppers, lima beans, green corn, cabbages, cucumbers, eggplants, tomatoes, celery, lettuce, English peas, and other varieties of garden truck are harvested throughout the winter and spring. The growing of avocadoes, coconuts, and papayas repays the producer, lends color to the Florida scene, and has considerable value as a tourist attraction. Vegetable shipments reach a peak in March and decline thereafter until May; a few mixed carloads go out to eastern markets in June and July, leaving only August and September when no carload shipments are made. About 18,000 carloads of fresh vegetables were shipped from south Florida in the 1936–37 season, about four times the quantity of citrus shipped from the same area.

General farming is relatively unimportant in this vegetable garden of south Florida, where crops are usually planted, grown, and matured with two main objects in view: an out-of-season market and a quick and high cash return on the investment. Corn, sweet and Irish potatoes, and forage crops for home consumption are the principal staples grown.

Cane, a bumper crop of the Everglades, is converted into sugar and syrup. At Clewiston, on the southern shore of Lake Okeechobee, approximately 25,000 acres of cane are cultivated by a single company for the manufacture of raw sugar.

South Florida's dairying industry has expanded rapidly since 1930, following the partial elimination of the cattle-fever tick and the introduction of Brahma stock for cross-breeding with the native herds. A great part of rural Florida is open range on which an estimated one million beef and dairy cattle graze. The south and central Florida counties that lie within the lush Kissimmee Valley north of Lake Okeechobee constitute the largest beef-producing region. Florida beef is priced lower than prime western grades, but the veal is considered equal to the western product. Poultry raising is another paying venture, and most of the present output is consumed locally, especially during the winter months when south Florida more than doubles its population.

Agriculture in south Florida largely owes its recent advance to the vast work, practically complete, which has been done in controlling the waters of Lake Okeechobee and in draining sections of the Everglades. Lacking a natural outlet to the sea, the lake has for centuries flooded its southern hinterland, the Everglades, at the return of each rainy season. Plans to reclaim portions of this rich land date back to 1845, but the work was actually begun in 1881. Since then Federal and State Government special tax districts and private interests have jointly borne the expense of building around the lake a 66-mile dike and a system of pumping stations, spillways, hurricane gates, locks, levees, and canals, the last of which drain excess water into the Gulf of Mexico and the Atlantic Ocean. Year by year, the huge tasks of flood control and reclamation of submerged lands have been carried toward completion.

Enormous yields per acre are produced with hothouse rapidity on the reclaimed muck lands of this region, with snap beans a major crop. Unlike citrus-fruit production, which required years for the development of groves and a substantial outlay for equipment, the growing of vegetables can be carried on at relatively little expense. The producers who operate individually are often called 'one-season gamblers,' because they stake their money on one planting, sell the harvest at auction in the fields, and move on. If the market is good, the planter will have cashed in on three months of effort. He may even have planted the ground without owning or leasing it, since much of the country around Lake Okeechobee belongs to persons who live elsewhere and are frequently in tax arrears. The corporate producers, many of them controlling thousands of acres, must depend on the same speculative market for their returns. Because of its general remoteness from the main highways, little is seen of the truck-growing industry; but the navigable waters in this region are crowded from December to March with barge trains moving winter vegetables to the Atlantic seaboard for reshipment.

A different agricultural picture exists in central Florida, a region of lakes, sandy loam hills, and river valleys. Here citrus is king. Beginning in the late 1880's, when better methods of water and rail transportation were offered the grower, citrus rapidly became the leading industry. The first carloads of grapefruit roll to market in early September. These are followed by a steady rise in the shipments of oranges until a peak of 6,000 cars is reached in January; then the crop gradually dwindles until June. Citrus-fruit shipments from this region during the 1936–37 season totaled approximately 32,000,000 boxes, or three-fourths of the State crop.

Citrus fruits are not immune to damage from severe cold weather in central Florida. A Federal radio service informs growers of impending frosts, and a dangerous drop of the mercury is a signal for the bonfires and oil pots that create a protective smoke ceiling over the groves. The many lakes of the region afford some natural aid against frost, which makes grove land near water more desirable.

Insects that menace citrus are combated and largely controlled by methods developed by the Federal and State Departments of Agriculture. They have been especially successful in eradicating citrus canker. The Mediterranean fruit fly, a European scourge, was discovered at Orlando in 1929, but prompt action by governmental agencies, including a quarantine of affected areas and the destruction of infected fruit, resulted in the stamping out of this pest in little more than a year.

Citrus-fruit growing is usually an individual undertaking, although marketing is carried on through co-operatives and corporations. The business is largely dominated by the packers and shippers who move the crop to Northern auctions.

Citrus products are exported to many European countries, but Great Britain and its dominions are the principal foreign buyers. The State maintains a citrus control commission that regulates the grading and advertising of all citrus fruits.

Both fruit and truck farms are highly industrialized, with packing houses and canning and processing plants taking the place of sheds, barns, and silos. Migratory labor is employed for short periods, mostly white for fruit picking and Negro for vegetable harvesting; much of this labor comes from Georgia between the growing seasons there. Second to citrus culture in central Florida is the production of other fruits and winter and early-spring vegetables. The growing season for a number of tender crops is several weeks later in the year than that of south Florida. In addition to watermelons, cantaloupes, and great quantities of strawberries, almost all varieties of common garden vegetables are grown.

Florida produces about 40 per cent of the total celery shipments of the Nation. Approximately 8,000 carloads are shipped annually, chiefly from the neighborhood of Sanford, in Seminole County, but in increasing quantities from Sarasota County. This crop requires careful cultivation. By placing tiles throughout the fields, celery farmers have developed an admirable type of subirrigation control. The average yield is more than one carload per acre.

The sweet and Irish potatoes, corn, sugar cane, peanuts, field peas, and forage crops produced in central Florida are chiefly for State and home consumption. The lesser farming enterprises include dairying, poultry farming, viticulture, and the growing of ferns and flower bulbs for Northern markets.

In north Florida, subtropical crops are few and general farming is the rule. Although the farmer does not receive the same high rate of profit as the farmer in south and central Florida, his chances of crop failure are not so great. This older farming region, where low-priced and low-yield crops are produced, was the last to get the benefit of cash markets. Here the farmer produced little more than enough for his own needs and was therefore limited to local barter. In 1937, however, with State and Federal funds, co-operative farm markets were established, where livestock and other products in less than truck or carload lots could be exchanged for cash. Within a year these co-operatives began to solve some of the problems of growers to whom currency had almost become an abstraction. The benefits of similar outlets for tobacco growers in this same region already had been demonstrated. The Suwannee River Valley in 1921 produced only six acres of tobacco. Through the installation of marketing warehouses at Live Oak, doing away with expensive transportation to distant buyers, planting in the valley had increased by 1938 to 3,600 acres. Sales from this and neighboring territory exceeded 11,000,000 pounds in the same year. Smaller markets do business at Lake City and Quincy.

The agriculture of north Florida is more nearly self-sustaining than that of the rest of the State, and the farmers have few specialized crops other than tobacco and cotton. A composite picture would contain a farm with milk cows and barnyard poultry, enough hogs for home consumption, patches of sweet potatoes and watermelons, a small grove of pecan trees, fields of corn and peanuts, forage crops, sugar cane, many rows of cotton, and a few acres of tobacco. More than half the sweet potatoes raised are disposed of through local channels, and less than 50 carloads are shipped to other markets. Sugar cane is sold in the form of cane syrup. Peanuts, Satsuma oranges, pecans, watermelons, cotton, Irish potatoes, and tobacco are the principal crops that reach consumers outside the State.

An average of 14,000,000 pounds of tobacco is grown in north Florida each year. Two types of leaf are produced: burley, a bright leaf used in cigarettes, and Sumatra, in demand for cigar wrappers. Among the colorful autumn events in the State are the tobacco auctions. The short staple variety of cotton is produced mainly in Madison and Suwannee Counties. Sea-island cotton, a long staple variety, was the leading crop of the State a generation ago, but inroads of the pink boll weevil forced farmers to abandon its planting. Since 1935 a method for combating the boll weevil has been perfected by entomologists and this may restore sea-island cotton to its former importance. More than 4,000 bales of this variety were ginned in the State in 1937. A total of 40,000 bales of short and long staple cotton was produced during the same year, and an estimated total of 28,000 bales in 1938.

Of the 7,000,000 bushels of corn harvested annually in the State, 2,000,000 are produced in north Florida. This section also leads in the production of Irish potatoes. Alachua, Clay, Flagler, Putnam, and St. Johns Counties ship approximately 3,000 carloads of potatoes to Northern markets every year. Alachua and Putnam Counties, bordering on central Florida, produce more citrus fruits and vegetables than other north counties. Watermelons are next in importance as a shipping crop, and 2,000 carloads move to market in June and July. Jefferson County produces tons of watermelon seed and ships them to all parts of the United States.

In an effort to develop a native supply of Chinese tung nuts for the manufacture of paints and varnishes, approximately 16,000 acres of tung trees have been set out in several north-Florida counties and in other sections of the State. One-quarter of the United States' production of tung oil comes from Florida. The growing of tung nuts may become an important branch of Florida agriculture, if the growers replace the single-type tree with the better yielding cluster-type.

West Florida, the fourth farming region, was noted for its agricultural products long before the War between the States. Physically, it is divided into two parallel strips running east and west. On the north, touching Alabama and Georgia, are red clay foothills that have been cultivated longer than any other acreage in the State. The southern strip comprises lowlands bordering the Gulf of Mexico. Cattle ranges and cut-over pine and hardwood forests cover much of the flatlands, and farms dot the foothills.

West Florida is comparable to north Florida in growing seasons and general farm crops. Corn is the principal staple, with more than 2,500,000 bushels produced annually. Cotton, tobacco, peanuts, sweet and Irish potatoes, sugar cane, and forage crops are grown on a moderate scale.

A late-season truck-farming belt of limited proportions has been developed in this area since 1925. Carload shipments of cabbages, Irish potatoes, string beans, peppers, English peas, onions, and watermelons reach the market in summer months. Cucumbers for pickling are raised in several small farming communities, placed in brine, and shipped to factories for bottling. Peanut farming keeps a number of factories busy shelling, cleaning, and grading the nuts, which are salted for the retail trade or used by candy manufacturers. Mills in the area handle from 300,000 to 400,000 tons of peanuts annually. Eggs and poultry are shipped to all Florida points. Hog raising is an integral part of west Florida's agricultural economy, although the production figures are not high. Dairy products and a few range cattle, slaughtered for beef, are absorbed by local markets. Pecans, peaches, pears, blueberries, blackberries, and plums are grown on all the farms in this section. Satsuma oranges, a variety that withstands low temperatures, are shipped in small quantities in October and November. Tupelo honey, a clear, white, nongranular type, is a distinctive product of this section, where the tupelo gum trees flourish. Apiarists from distant points bring their bees here when the tupelo blooms.

Gulf County, the leader in honey production, ships approximately 2,000 barrels a year.

The gross income, for the 1936–37 season, from farming activities over the long sweep of the Florida Peninsula clearly showed the relative importance of different products. Citrus farming headed the list with a gross income of $68,838,000; this was followed by a return of $39,090,000 from vegetables, strawberries, and melons. Revenue from livestock, poultry, and dairying totaled more than $30,000,000, while the income from staples—corn, cotton, tobacco, peanuts, and forage crops—came to approximately $12,579,000. The grand total of all agricultural revenue was close to $160,000,000. Florida exports more than $100,000,000 of food products annually.

Better farming practices—crop rotation, a definite system of cover crops, more animals to help build up the soil—would improve greatly the State's agricultural economy. The extent of importation of feeds, beef, poultry, dairy products, and other staples is out of proportion to the potentialities of production within the State. In 1936, for example, Florida consumed, in addition to the local production, $15,000,000 worth of butter, eggs, poultry, meat, and sweet and Irish potatoes. Also, certain products that are now imported from other countries could be introduced as new crops on Florida soils.

While farm tenancy is widely regarded as the key problem of Southern agriculture, because it affects about half of all Southern farmers and naturally depresses the whole Southern economy, the same emphasis can hardly apply in Florida. (The proportion of tenant-operated farms in 1935 for the State was 28 per cent, in contrast to an average of 48.7 per cent for the 16 Southern States during the same year.) Tenancy in Florida exists, chiefly, in the north and west sections of the State.

Lessees of the muck lands south of Lake Okeechobee and the thousands of laborers, imported to work in that area and also in the fruit- and truck-growing districts of central Florida, constitute a population that comes within the scope of farm tenancy in the sense that they do not own the land they work. But, since the members of these groups do not establish (or attempt to establish) homes, the problem raised is one of industrialized farming rather than of tenancy.

The number of Florida farmers in 1935, according to the U.S. Bureau of Census, was 72,857, of whom 60,093 were white and 12,764 were Negro. Of the 60.093 white farmers, 42,627 or 70.9 per cent were owners, 2,989 or approximately 5 per cent were managers, and 14,477 or 24.1 per cent were tenants. Of the 12,764 Negro farmers, 6,792 or 53.2 per cent were owners, 50 or .4 per cent were managers and 5,992 or 46.4 per cent were tenants.

Floridians take encouragement from the fact that tenant-purchase allotments for 1938–39 under the Bankhead-Jones Farm Tenant Act amounted to only $154,057, the lowest sum applied for by any Southern State. The next lowest sum asked for was about seven times as much. Of the 20,399 tenant farmers in Florida, 547 made loan applications in 1938.

Although the greater part of the State is not afflicted with the twin evils of tenancy and the one-crop system, Florida has special problems in agriculture that still await solution. A bewildering variety of soils and crops demands scientific measures that cannot now be undertaken by tenant and small farm owners. The substandard living conditions of migrant and resident farm laborers who harvest the citrus and truck crops constitute a serious problem. An unstable national market for winter produce and costly freight differentials lower the farmer's margin of profit; moreover, because of the nature of their crops, many Florida farmers must have reserve capital to tide them over a bad season if they are to win at this risky agricultural game.

Industry and Commerce

LESS well known than its winter resorts and oranges are the varied industries of Florida. Among these are naval-stores production, lumbering, fishing, fruit packing, mining, cigar making, and sponge fishing. A survey by the U.S. Bureau of Foreign and Domestic Commerce placed the value of all products manufactured in 1935 at $162,359,000. For the same year, tourists spent an estimated $300,000,000, and the citrus crop was valued at $53,189,000.

Florida plays host each winter to a population greater than its own. The movement of tourists to Florida begins with the first nip of frost in the North and continues well into spring, taxing the capacity of railroads, busses, and steamship lines, and crowding the arterial highways of the State with automobiles and trailers. At the peak of the 1936 season more than 10,000 railroad passengers passed through Jacksonville in a single day. The State has been popularized also as a summer resort, and many thousands of visitors, principally from the other southeastern States, spend their summer vacations on the Gulf and Atlantic beaches.

The flamboyant tourist invasion is the lifeblood of resort Florida and stimulates business in less favored localities. Moderately priced hotels, apartment houses, and trailer and tourist camps do capacity business from early December until late April, but as a rule expensive hotels, clubs, fashionable sanatoria, and cabaña colonies open during the Christmas holidays for an average season of 12 weeks. It is ostensibly for the tourist that citizens tax themselves to provide paved highways, landscape their towns, improve recreational facilities, enlarge schools, and arrange a galaxy of annual festivals.

The tourist industry, however, is a comparatively recent addition to Florida enterprises; it did not become a big business until after the World War, whereas natural resources had long before been put to profitable use. The Spaniards found the moss to which they gave their name a fine stuffing for cushions and horse collars, the English undertook the production of indigo, and to the aboriginal pursuits of fishing and farming, early nineteenth-century settlers added cattle raising and lumbering.

Cuba furnished a ready market for cattle, and in return supplied dressed boards and other building material. Almost up to the time of the War between the States little currency except Spanish gold circulated along the Gulf coast. With the coming of sawmills in north Florida, coastwise sailing packets delivered lumber down the coast and took on cattle for Key West and Cuba, and out of this commerce grew one of the larger present-day shipping concerns. Captain James McKay, who operated a cattle boat from Tampa, obtained much of his cargo from Dr.Howell Lykes, a pioneer stockman of the region, and from this business relation and a subsequent intermarriage originated the Lykes Brothers Steamship Line.

The great pine forests of Florida had contributed products of value to marine commerce for nearly two centuries before the sawmill made its appearance. The first were pitch and tar produced from the sap of the pine tree. Because carpenters used them to caulk the seams of wooden ships pitch and tar were called 'naval stores,' and the present products of pine-tree sap—turpentine and rosin—are still known by that name. Sir John Hawkins, the English sea fighter, reported in 1565 that Florida was a possible source of naval stores; and it was not long before the Spaniards were chipping the pine trees of the State to obtain them. One of the reasons the leading maritime nations of Europe desired colonies in America was to obtain a source of naval stores.

With the advent of iron ships, chemical research found new uses for the pine gums. Turpentine now thins the paint that colors American houses, and is used extensively in the manufacture of polishes, perfume bases, waterproof cement, and sealing wax, and for various medicinal purposes. Rosin, once discarded as a practically valueless by-product of turpentine, is today the principal ingredient of the varnish that covers floors and furniture, and is also used in the manufacture of soap, insulating material, writing paper, printing ink, sealing wax, plastics, and linoleum.

The work of gathering pine sap in the field is done in the vicinity of turpentine camps, each with its own still and quarters where the manager, woods riders, and laborers are housed (*see Tour 3b*). Florida produces 20 per cent of the world's supply of these products. The forest management, or 'operators,' bleed the trees, collect and distil the gum, and barrel the turpentine and rosin. The 'factors,' or middlemen, then finance, transport, grade, and assemble the products in market centers. Eighty per cent of the pine area of Florida now carries a natural second growth of trees valued at $10,000,000.

Although many varieties of trees are found in Florida, the longleaf and slash pine are the most abundant and valuable, followed by the cypress and some hardwoods. The value of products from the lumber industry amounts to more than $125,000,000 annually and provides a yearly pay roll of $31,000,000. The forest wealth of the State has been depleted to less than one-fourth its original volume, because of indiscriminate cutting, overcupping for gum, and fires and lack of reforestation. These conditions have made it necessary for Florida to import part of its lumber.

An important quantity of lumber is used in marketing the State's agricultural and citrus crops. More than 100,000,000 board feet are used annually in the manufacture of fruit and vegetable containers, in addition to the lumber required for barrels, cigar boxes, and containers demanded by other industries. There are many reduction plants where waste wood and stumps are ground into small bits by powerful machines and cooked in huge vats. A variety of by-products is then extracted, including turpentine, rosin, and pine oil. Some of these extraction plants make charcoal, a popular fuel for cooking and heating.

Another important use for the lumber of the State is the manufacture of paper. One mill at Panama City uses over 40 carloads of pulp a day. Mills have recently been established at Port St. Joe, Jacksonville, and Fernandina.

Although the fish, shrimp, and oysters taken from Florida waters were a ready source of food to early settlers and the Indians, it was not until the coming of the railroads, with fast transportation and improved methods of handling, and later the perfecting of a quick-freezing process, that fishing became important commercially. Investment in this industry has increased from approximately $1,000,000 in 1900 to $10,000,000 in 1938. The catch—principally mullet, snapper, mackerel, and bream—has risen from about 34,000,000 to 125,000,000 pounds during the same period. Florida oysters, found chiefly in the Apalachicola, Fernandina, and Crystal River areas, though small, are tender and delicate in flavor. All oyster beds are owned by the State and leased to the oyster farmers. In former years, when beds were privately owned, men built watchtowers and protected their holdings with powder and ball.

Pensacola, Apalachicola, Cape Canaveral, Fernandina, New Smyrna, and the mouth of the St. Johns River are centers of the shrimp-fishing industry in Florida, and the waters of the State each year yield 20 per cent of all shrimp caught in North America. At sunset the fishing craft, with nets drying at the masts, can be seen returning to port, trailed by thousands of screaming gulls feeding on shrimp heads that are cast overboard. Packing houses are busy long after dark, cleaning the catch and preparing it for iced shipment to all parts of the United States. Most of the cleaning is done by Negro women who receive approximately 15¢ a bucket for their labor, and average from 10 to 15 buckets a day. An estimated 12,000 buckets are cleaned daily for shipping and canning purposes.

Along the southwest coast of Florida is one of the largest beds of hard clams in the United States. This covers more than 150 square miles of sea bottom, and clams are so plentiful that the dredges used in digging them work in one small area for months at a time. After being dug, the clams are shucked and canned at Marco and Caxambas in the form of chowder, minced and steamed clams, and clam juice.

The principal marine turtle market in Florida is at Key West, where three different species are handled: the green turtle, whose meat is used for soup and steaks; the loggerhead, inferior in quality, which serves as food chiefly for local markets; and the hawksbill, caught solely for its shell. Most turtles brought to Key West are captured at sea in large nets. Turtles shipped alive on the coastwise steamers have their flippers bound and are loaded back-down, for the under-shell is not strong enough to support the great weight for long periods.

The crawfish, or 'Florida lobster' as it is known on the market, finds an important place in the Key West fishing industry. Caught in traps and hand nets in coral-reef waters, crawfish are shipped, alive or boiled, to markets along the entire Atlantic seaboard.

Stone crabs, found along the lower east and west coasts, have become scarce, and shipments out of the State are prohibited. The meat of their extraordinarily large claws is eaten, and the other portions are discarded.

By-products of fisheries are important commercially. The nonedible menhaden are used in the manufacture of fish oil and fertilizers. Oyster shells are used for road building, and crushed shells are shipped to poultry growers here and abroad. Five hatcheries in the State distribute millions of fresh-water fingerlings for restocking lakes and streams.

Florida's cigar industry began at Key West in 1831, when W.H.Hall chose the island city as a site for a factory, because of its climate and its proximity to Cuban tobacco fields. In 1868, with open revolution and business demoralization in Havana, many cigar makers migrated to Key West, where established factories offered employment. When fire swept the city in 1886, destroying the larger factories, and labor disputes further disrupted production, the majority of the manufacturers moved their plants to a district east of Tampa which they named 'Ybor City' for Vicente Martínez Ybor, one of their leaders.

Since that time, Tampa's Latin quarter has supplied a world market with fine cigars. Wrapper tobacco comes from the United States, but the better grade used for the filler is imported from Cuba. In Tampa, the finer brands are still rolled by hand, at long benches where three workers form a team to turn out coronas, royals, perfectos, and panatelas, as the different sizes and shapes are termed. In former years the monotonous work was relieved by a reader, or lector, who sat on a platform and read plays, stories, and the current news from Spain and Cuba to the workers; but later, when readers were accused of spreading strike propaganda, they were banned by factory owners. Radios are now used to entertain the workers.

Ybor City, with 122 factories employing approximately 10,000 workers, has an annual pay roll of $8,000,000. The factory output was 258,465,000 cigars in 1936, an increase of 15.1 per cent over 1935, the industry's best year since 1931. One large factory in Jacksonville, employing more than 2,000 workers, mostly young white women, has an annual pay roll of $1,250,000. It is entirely mechanized and produces 400,000,000 cigars yearly.

The sponge industry probably originated some 4,000 years ago in the Mediterranean Sea, where sponges were called *zoffitan* by the Greeks (meaning half plant and half animal). The Florida industry started in 1849 at Key West, where spongers in small boats 'hooked' the growths from the shallow sea beds with long-handled, three-pronged spears. With the improvement of the diving suit it became possible to work at greater depths, and when virgin beds were discovered farther north in the Gulf, the major part of the industry moved to Tarpon Springs in 1905.

Working in deep water, sponge divers alternate with each other and seldom stay down longer than 30 minutes at a time, because they are exposed to a hazard known as the 'bends,' a paralysis caused by a too rapid change in air pressure after diving. In addition to divers, the sponge crew consists of a captain, engineer, lifeline tender, cook, and two or more deck men, according to the size of the boat. In lieu of wages, the crews are given a percentage of the profits after the costs of the voyage have been deducted (*see Tour 6b*).

Florida phosphate was discovered in the winter of 1884–85 by J.Francis LeBaron on the Peace River near the present city of Arcadia. A few years later larger deposits were found to the south of Plant City and east of Tampa. Between 1888 and 1892, shipments from the State increased from 1,000 to 345,327 tons. In 1936, about 2,920,000 tons were mined, valued at approximately $10,000,000.

Limestone, the most abundant and widely deposited mineral of the State, is crushed for lime, cement, and building and road materials. A total of 1,778,263 tons, valued at $1,969,745, was produced in 1934. Coquina, a native rock composed of hard molluscan shells, mined in Volusia, Flagler, and St. Johns Counties, is another popular building material.

A valuable clay—fuller's earth—is mined near Ocala and Quincy. More than $1,000,000 worth of the Florida product is sold annually to the petroleum industry for use in filtering processes. Other Florida clays having commercial importance are grouped into kaolin and brick clays. Kaolin, found principally in Putnam and Lake Counties, is used for fine chinaware.

Deposits of diatomite, composed largely of the skeletons of microscopic marine plants, occur in Lake, Polk, and Santa Rosa Counties. Diatomite is chiefly employed by chemists as a filtering medium in the manufacturing of an insulating material; because of its unusual capacity for absorbing moisture, it is also used in the manufacture of salt-shaker tops.

The State's extensive culture of citrus fruits is the basis for another industry—the packing and canning of fruits and their by-products. Packing houses operate throughout central Florida during the citrus-picking season. In the case of individually owned groves, the crop is bought on the tree and the purchasing company sends its own crew to pick and transport the fruit to the packing houses. Here it is washed, dried, sprayed with wax for protection against moisture, and polished and graded by machinery. Oranges are individually wrapped and packed by hand in wooden crates for shipment. Culls are sold to canneries and local markets.

Central Florida has a large yearly output of canned grapefruit and grapefruit juice, canned oranges and orange juice, candied or crystallized grapefruit and orange peel, and marmalades and jellies, as well as jellies and pastes made from guava and other noncitrus fruits. Two factories in Tampa supply containers to the central-Florida canning plants. Florida grapefruit brandy, grapefruit cordial, and orange wine are increasing in popularity. Citrus hulls are used for cattle food or for the extraction of pectin and oils. In the 1935–36 season, the gross value of Florida's canned citrus products amounted to $2,884,800.

Sporadic attempts were made to develop the sugar cane industry in the Everglades as early as the middle 1880's, but large-scale commercial production in this area dates from January 1929, when the first cane was delivered to the pioneer sugar mill at Clewiston. During the nine harvests since that year, more than 600,000,000 pounds of raw sugar were produced. Black strap molasses, a by-product, is used in manufacturing cattle food and grain alcohol (*see Tour* 13).

After the real-estate deflation in 1926, the volume of Florida business and commerce dropped sharply for almost a decade, but economic conditions improved by 1934, and a business recovery, partly due to Government aid, was evident in 1936. The State's economic development over a period of years is best shown by a comparison of bank resources. Standing at $50,000,000 in 1907, they trebled by 1917, and soared to more than $500,000,000 in 1927. Two years later they fell to $400,000,000 and continued downward until the early 1930's. Bank resources in 1936 stood at approximately $339,228,000. An index of the current business life of the State is seen in the comparative volume of retail sales, which dropped from $504,523,000 in 1929 to $288,804,000 in 1933, and then rose to $485,000,000 during 1936.

Building contracts awarded during 1936 were 35 per cent greater than for 1935, mounting from $53,843,000 to $72,587,000; and real-estate transactions were higher in 1936 than for any year since 1929. The continued activity in real estate and the building trades is attributed largely to four factors: the recent industrial expansion in Florida; loans to local public agencies by the Public Works Administration; the co-operation of Federal agencies with home owners in refinancing, building, or repairing their homes; and the general stimulus of an increase in consumer purchasing power, through the program of the Works Progress Administration.

Electric power consumption increased from 718,256,000 kilowatt hours in 1935 to 801,774,000 in 1936, testifying to Florida's industrial expansion and the growing demand for electrical household appliances. The volume of foreign trade has grown substantially. The development of better port facilities and the extension of trade with South and Central American countries, Europe, and the Orient have occurred since 1920. Jacksonville, Tampa, Pensacola, and Miami, ranking in the order named, are the four leading ports. Imports were 33 per cent higher in 1936 than 1935, advancing from $14,312,000 to $19,036,000. Exports for the same years rose from $36,466,000 to $39,185,000. In 1935 operating revenues of railroads in the State amounted to $30,824,000, and revenues of automobile transportation companies, to $9,897,000. Many factories are expanding; new industries, such as paper and pulp production, are erecting large plants and virtually building new communities around them; and the dredging of ship channels has brought better port accommodations and increased water commerce to seaboard cities.

Labor

PRIVATE enterprise in Florida employed 349,339 workers in 1935, according to a business census of the United States Department of Commerce. Of these workers, 215,855 were engaged in industry and 133,484 in agriculture. The total represented approximately 22 per cent of the State's population of 1,606,842.

Earnings of business and industrial employees in the State then averaged $859 per worker as compared with $1,171 for the Nation. (No figures were made available on the earnings of agricultural workers.) U.S. Department of Labor figures for Florida in July 1936 showed an average hourly wage for common labor of 26¢; for the entire South, 33¢; and for the Nation as a whole, 43¢.

The seasonal nature of Florida employment causes a heavy influx of skilled and unskilled labor to the resort cities during the winter season, with a corresponding increase in rents. In communities less affected by the tourist trade, and among certain low-wage groups, living costs change little throughout the year. This particularly applies to the one-quarter million Negroes normally employed in Florida. Economic opportunities for Negroes are well-defined and limited, and are even further reduced in times of depression when many manual occupations are taken over by white labor. One-third of the Negroes employed are women, who are engaged for the most part in domestic work. Male Negro employment falls into three categories: agriculture, commerce, and domestic service.

In almost all Florida industries the wage scale is low. This is particularly true of the naval-stores industry, which employs the commissary system and, in addition, makes a practice of advancing small sums of money to Negro turpentine hands. Once in debt, the Negroes are hindered by some counties from leaving their employers until all obligations are paid. Phosphate mine operators also utilize this plan. Negro women, available at low wages, are being increasingly employed to replace men in processing phosphate.

One of the obstacles in the way of organizing unskilled labor has been the migration of workers in this class. Few Florida industries give year-round work to the resident population. As a result, thousands of people become itinerant jacks-of-all-trades and never attain a settled or substantial mode of living. Transients move in from the adjoining States and from the North, and many of them accept low wages for the sake of living temporarily in a pleasant climate. Thousands help to move Florida's fruit and winter vegetables to market. Thousands more come to work in hotels and the various enterprises connected with the tourist trade. In the latter group the average earning is about $300 per single man and about $400 per family during the season. These people belong to a semi-tourist class that seeks only enough to finance a winter's stay. A third group is composed of indigents, who were once excluded by a border patrol; a fourth is composed of health and pleasure seekers who, without sufficient funds to carry them through the season, seek employment at small wages to provide the balance.

Florida's first labor organization was composed of Latin-Americans, who moved with the cigar industry from Cuba to Key West, and there in the 1880's formed a union. The Spanish factory owners had left Cuba because of revolutionary movements and labor troubles there; but they discovered that their problems were apparently inescapable and the industry in 1886 began a second migration—this time to Tampa—and within a decade the Key West factories were deserted. But the problems that had troubled the cigar workers in Havana and in Key West were no easier to solve in Tampa. During the 1900's, changing economic conditions and the militancy of the Latin-American workers accounted for periodic outbreaks in the cigar industry. In 1910, nearly a thousand cigar makers went on strike for nine months, and the disorders that occurred in connection with the strike resulted in three deaths. The hiring of women, more dexterous at certain operations than men, caused vigorous objection, and more recently the introduction of machines aroused protest.

Cigar workers are now represented by seven locals in the International Cigar Makers' Union. The first of them, Tampa Local No.336, became affiliated with the American Federation of Labor in 1898. Several independent unions existed for short periods, but all had been chartered by the A.F. of L. in 1938, when the membership exceeded 8,000 men, 20 per cent of whom were unemployed. During the same year many workers demanded that these locals transfer to the CIO, in order to make all employees, skilled and unskilled, eligible for union membership. As a consequence, the officers of the Tampa locals were suspended by the A.F. of L. In January 1939 the idea was abandoned and these men were reinstated in their unions, but not to their former offices.

In 1886, shortly after Reconstruction days, the agriculturalists of northern Florida organized a Farmers' Alliance at Chipley, and with this backing the Populist Party in 1892 adopted a farmer-labor platform and put a candidate in the field for governor. Lonnie Weeks, the Populist candidate, received only 14,000 votes to the winning Democratic nominee's 22,000, but this showing of strength made organized labor a political force to be dealt with, and indirectly led to much beneficial labor legislation.

The huge construction program launched in the State in the 1920's stimulated membership in the building-trades unions of the A.F. of L., because in the wild scramble to get houses built, many apprentice painters and carpenters were pressed into service. The great wave of unemployment following the real-estate crash caused a tightening up of standards in the building trades, and by means of city ordinances something of a monopoly in jobs and contracts has been created.

During the years prior to 1932, active labor organizations were largely represented by cigar makers and those engaged in the building trades, but with the advent of NRA the movement spread. Little was accomplished during the brief life of the business codes beyond organizing small groups in the unskilled occupations. Efforts to organize the citrus-fruit industry were on several occasions countered with violence, while threats of violence were numerous, as in the case of a vigilante committee that was formed by Orlando citizens in 1937 to repel CIO organizers. Several years before, Frank Norman of Orlando, who had attempted to enlist citrus workers in an independent union, was abducted and his fate has remained a mystery.

Florida's first labor paper was *El Internacional*, started in 1906 as the official organ of the cigar-makers' unions at Tampa. It began as a monthly, was later issued twice a month, and is now a weekly.

Eight other labor papers were published in the State in 1938; *Labor Journal* at Jacksonville, Miami *Citizen* at Miami, *Florida Labor Advocate* at Tampa, *Union Labor News* at West Palm Beach, *Union News* at Daytona Beach, the *Advocate* at St.Petersburg, and the *Florida Federationist*, a State-wide publication issued at Miami. All these papers express A.F. of L. opinion. Many of the daily newspapers regularly publish a page devoted to union activities, where such matters are freely discussed by union spokesmen.

From 1916 until 1932, during which period 31,625 labor disputes were recorded in the United States, Florida had but 159, or less than half of one per cent of the total.

As early as 1910, streetcar-company employees in Jacksonville struck for the right to organize. A second strike was called in 1912 to enforce a demand for increased wages and improved working conditions. Strikebreakers were imported from New York and the State militia ordered out, but the strikers were able to effect a settlement that carried several benefits. A third strike occurred in 1918, but local women who proclaimed that strikes in wartime were unpatriotic took over the jobs of the workers. So infectious was the war hysteria that this walkout quickly ended.

Florida longshoremen and dock workers, organized in 1935, joined in a South Atlantic strike, which began in October 1937 and for three weeks tied up the water fronts of Jacksonville, Fort Pierce, Miami, and Tampa. The strikers, Negro and white, numbered more than 4,000. Few disorders occurred, and the walkout was settled after arbitration among the steamship-company officials, workers, and mayors of the cities involved. The workers gained small wage increases and shortened hours of labor.

The Joseph Shoemaker kidnaping and murder case at Tampa in 1935 that attracted nation-wide attention was denounced by the Civil Liberties Union and organized labor. Shoemaker, Eugene Poulnot, and Dr. Samuel Rogers, members of an organization called the Modern Democrats which made a local campaign issue of honest elections, were arrested at a meeting in a private home. The men were held for investigation and, when no evidence of illegal activity could be found against them, were released. Just outside the police station they were seized by a masked band, taken in cars to an isolated place and beaten—Shoemaker so violently that he died of the injuries. Eleven men were indicted, including six Tampa policemen; all obtained acquittals after two years of court procedure.

Two Miami newspapers were involved in a labor dispute early in 1937, when typographical workers went on a sit-down strike and won an increase in wages after 48 hours of arbitration. During the same period, Miami was also the scene of brief strikes by members of the building-trades unions, who demanded and gained substantial wage increases. In July 1937 the Workers Alliance called strikes on WPA projects in Daytona Beach and Tampa.

Before 1935 organized labor in Florida had been limited almost entirely to urban industrial workers, but in November 1938, after an organization drive among the fruit pickers by the United Cannery, Agricultural, Packing, and Allied Workers of America (a CIO international union), the members of the Lake Alfred local struck against a reduction of wages for 'clean-up' picking in the orange, tangerine, and grapefruit groves. The fruit pickers were joined in the strike by the packing-plant employees of six firms in Winter Haven, making a total of approximately 500 men and women in opposition to the Lake Alfred Citrus Growers' Association and the Winter Haven packers. It happened at the time that a glutted fruit market made the closing of the plants desirable rather than detrimental, and the strike did not succeed.

At the end of 1938, organized workers represented roughly 20 per cent of the total number gainfully employed throughout Florida and slightly more than 4 per cent of the State's total population. The Brotherhood of Sleeping Car Porters, an A.F. of L. all-Negro union, is strongly entrenched. Its international president, A.Philip Randolph, was born in Crescent City and educated in Jacksonville. The white transport unions, including the railroad brotherhoods, have a total membership of several thousands.

The A.F. of L. in 1937 estimated that its membership included 65,000 craft unionists in 400 locals affiliated with the State Federation of Labor. Some of these unions admit only white members. A few Negro locals are affiliated directly with the national offices of the A.F. of L. The strength of organized craft workers is concentrated around three population centers—Jacksonville, Miami, and Tampa.

The Workers Alliance has a membership of 3,500 among the 35,000 WPA workers, mostly in Jacksonville, Tampa, Miami, Daytona Beach, Ocala, and Orlando.

The CIO, which admits Negro workers, has gained a foothold in several Florida industries. In 1938, its membership in the State numbered 1,925 workers, distributed among 5 groups as follows: United Cannery, Agricultural, Packing and Allied Workers, 1,400; American Newspaper Guild, 25; National Maritime Union, 300; American Communications Association, 100; and the Inland Boatmen's Union, 100.

A State child-labor law, enacted in 1913 and amended in 1915, established minimum wages and maximum hours for the employment of children and specified a State labor inspector to be charged with its enforcement. The proposed child-labor amendment to the Federal Constitution, however, was voted down by the 1937 Florida legislature. Boiler inspection and other safety measures have been passed at different times by State and municipal law-making bodies. A State workmen's compensation law enacted in 1935 provides, with exceptions, for medical care, compensation, and other assistance to workers receiving injuries while gainfully employed; the law does not apply to elected governmental officials, Federal employees, and workers engaged in agricultural pursuits or domestic service, or to firms employing three workers or less. A Florida industrial commission, created in 1935, supervises the enforcement of this act and exercises general authority over industrial employment.

****

Education

IN THE seventeenth-century Spanish mission schools, Indian youths were instructed in the Spanish language and taught the catechism. Many of the *padres* were scholars, and all were earnest in their endeavor to convert and civilize the natives. It is difficult to evaluate their work, as the contentions of Spanish, English, and French explorers over a period of some two centuries mystified and confused the aborigines, while active warfare between the whites precluded any progress in formal education.

While mission education was given to all promising children, Spanish or Indian, whom the priests considered eligible for their schools, the plan of education introduced by the English colonists in the eighteenth century benefited only the children of the wealthier classes. This restriction, coupled with the apathy of the poorer white people and the handicaps of the indentured servants, produced a large illiterate group. A Catholic parochial school, supported by public funds and free to all children of St.Augustine, was opened in 1786 and continued, with some lapses, until cession of the territory to the United States. Negro children were allowed to attend if they sat apart near the schoolhouse door.

In 1831 a group of prominent citizens met in Tallahassee and organized the Florida Educational Society. Later they sought to stimulate a desire for education by establishing branches in several towns, but the attempt was unsuccessful, and the society finally disbanded. Children of the well-to-do attended private schools or were instructed by private tutors, while those of the poor 'improved rapidly in dissipation and vice,' according to John Lee Williams, authority on territorial Florida. By 1840 there were 69 private schools and academies in the Territory. The concept of free education for all, regardless of ability to pay, was quite foreign to the South of that time; free education was synonymous with pauper education to most Southerners.

By an act of Congress in 1845, supplementing the act admitting Florida and Iowa into the Union, the new State of Florida was given each sixteenth section of land within its boundaries for the support of common schools and two sections of land to be used for seminaries of learning. This theoretical increase of culture was of little consequence; few of the State's political leaders wanted public schools.

The education of Negro slaves, where it existed at all during the early nineteenth century, was conducted partly for sentimental reasons and partly on material grounds. It is recorded that as early as 1817 Zephaniah Kingsley, who lived on Fort George Island and was one of the largest slave owners of his day, gave instruction to his slaves and thus increased their per capita valuation. The free Negroes were generally more fortunate. A few were sent away by their white fathers to be educated, and others were allowed to attend schools kept by privileged members of their race.

The first State constitution perpetuated the use of the seminary lands and the funds derived from them, and further legislation gave the State the right to sell school lands and invest the proceeds in bonds. In 1852 a public school was established in Tallahassee. According to the Federal census of 1860, there were 2,132 pupils in public schools and 4,486 in private schools of the State. The War between the States seriously hampered educational progress; during its course there were few competent teachers, no good textbooks, and an almost total lack of provision for public schools.

It was during the Reconstruction Period, 1865–76, that the concept of free education for all classes may be said to have developed. The Freedmen's Bureau established public schools, primarily for educating the Negroes; among them was the institution that became Bethune-Cookman College. White children were free to attend, but their parents were reluctant to allow this. Nora Clark, a Negro woman in St. Augustine, kept a day school until it was closed by the whites. Finally the idea of free education bore some fruit, although practice lagged behind theory. Legislation in 1869 provided for the office of State superintendent of public instruction and a board of education and appropriated funds to maintain schools. Counties were required to augment State funds. Jonathan C. Gibbs, a Negro who served as Florida's Secretary of State from 1869 to 1872 and as Superintendent of Public Instruction for the following two years, is described by one historian as 'probably the most outstanding character in the early life of the Florida public school system.' It was about fifteen years, however, before the general public was ready to benefit by these laws, such was the economic and social distress of the times.

Higher education fared better. Two public seminaries were founded, the first in 1852 at Ocala, to the east of the Suwannee River, and the second in 1857 at Tallahassee, to the west of the river. With various changes and removals, these finally became the University of Florida and the Florida State College for Women. Denominational colleges were established here

Industry

Photograph by courtesy of Tampa Chamber of Commerce

TRANS-SHIPMENT OF BANANAS, TAMPA

RAILROAD TERMINAL, JACKSONVILLE

Photograph by courtesy of Respess Engraving Company

Photograph by courtesy of Farm Security Administration

COMMERCIAL FISHING FLEET AT KEY WEST DOCK

AIR VIEW OF COMMERCIAL DOCKS, MIAMI

Photograph by courtesy of Farm Security Administratio

CITRUS PACKING PLANT, FORT PIERCE

ROLLING HANDMADE CIGARS IN A TAMPA FACTORY

Photograph by courtesy of Tampa Chamber of Commerce

Photograph by courtesy of Farm Security Administration

INSPECTING SPONGES, KEY WEST

◀ A BEAN CANNING FACTORY, DANIA

Photograph by courtesy of Farm Security Administration

Photograph by courtesy of Department of Agricultu

PHOSPHATE MINE, POLK COUNTY

PULP MILL, FERNANDINA

Photograph by courtesy of Respess Engraving Compan

Photograph by courtesy of Farm Security Administration

TURPENTINE PLANT, NEAR MARIANNA

Photograph by Gereck

PAN AMERICAN AIRWAYS OFFICE, MIAMI

and there. The most notable for its continuance in spite of difficulties was the school founded at DeLand in 1883 by H.A.DeLand of Fairport, New York. In 1885 it passed under control of the Baptist State Association and the next year became known as DeLand Academy and College. It was chartered as DeLand University in 1887 and two years later given its present name, Stetson University. Rollins College at Winter Park, now noted for its interesting experiments in educational methods, was incorporated in 1879, but did not open until 1885. It is nonsectarian in policy, although in the past it was connected with the Congregational Church.

The history of some four or five other institutions is confused by removals from town to town, as well as by changes of name and administration. Schools for special groups were established comparatively late: the Florida State School for the Deaf and Blind at St.Augustine in 1883, a school for delinquent boys at Marianna in 1915, a similar school for girls at Ocala in 1917, and a colony for feeble-minded children at Gainesville in 1921.

Vocational education was tried unsuccessfully in Tallahassee as early as 1831, but it was not until 1887 that steps were taken to inaugurate the vocational education which has since been adopted by the populous urban counties.

In 1905 the legislature enacted the Buckman Act, one of the most constructive laws in the history of Florida education. This act abolished the State-supported institutions of higher learning then in existence and created instead three colleges: one for white males, the University of Florida, at Gainesville; one for white females, the Florida State College for Women, at Tallahassee; and the other for Negroes of both sexes, the Florida Agricultural and Mechanical College, at Tallahassee. The results of concentrating available funds on these institutions have been most gratifying. Equipment and standards of scholarship compare favorably with similar institutions in other parts of the South.

The University of Florida, which opened at Gainesville in 1906 with fewer than 100 students, now has an average enrollment of 3,000 students. The teaching personnel and equipment are of a high order, and the university's record of expansion in some ways typifies the history of State education. A Phi Beta Kappa chapter was founded in 1938. Agricultural experiment stations operated in conjunction with the university have had an important part in the development of scientific agriculture in Florida, carrying out experiments not only in citrus culture but in tropical plants, long-staple cotton, pine products, and general forestry. Summer schools for adult rural education have resulted in widespread cultural improvement both in Florida and in neighboring states that send students to the lectures and conferences conducted at the university.

One of the most progressive educational units in the State is the P.K. Yonge Demonstration School, administered by the University of Florida. It is attempting to devise methods of instruction that will develop intellectual curiosity in pupils of kindergarten, grade-school, and high-school age. A point of departure from tradition is its method of basing the curriculum on the children's capabilities, needs, and desires rather than on a prearranged system of courses. The school's aim is to graduate students 'whose activities will bring society to a higher level.'

The Florida State College for Women, founded in 1905, now has an average enrollment of approximately 2,000 students, and has the distinction of being the first State women's college to be admitted to membership in the Southern Association of Colleges and Secondary Schools, and the first in the South to be placed on the approved list of the Association of American Universities. Its Phi Beta Kappa chapter was founded in 1934. This college, one of the three largest women's colleges in the United States, has had an important influence upon the professional and cultural life of women in Florida.

The Florida Agricultural and Mechanical College for Negroes, established as a normal school in 1887, is the leading Negro educational institution in the State, with an enrollment of 860 for the 1938–39 term. The State department of education has accredited this college and given it a standard rating. Appropriations by the State and Federal Governments for its support are sometimes supplemented by contributions from the general educational fund.

No tuition fee is required of State residents at the University of Florida or at the State College for Women, but for nonresidents the tuition fee is $100 at both schools. The Florida Agricultural and Mechanical College requires a $35 entrance fee of all students. Tuition costs are moderate at the leading privately endowed institutions: Stetson University, the University of Miami, the University of Tampa, Rollins College, and Florida Southern College at Lakeland.

There are three junior colleges for white students, all coeducational. The Ringling Junior College, endowed by John Ringling, was established at Sarasota in 1931; the St.Petersburg Junior College, founded in 1927, receives an annual appropriation of $10,000 from the city of St.Petersburg; Palm Beach Junior College, at West Palm Beach, established in 1933, is controlled by the county government.

Junior colleges for Negroes are also coeducational. The Florida Normal and Industrial Institute in St.Augustine, a Baptist institution founded in 1892, became a junior college in 1933. Edward Waters College in Jacksonville had its beginning in 1883 as a high school founded by the African Methodist Episcopal Church. The school became a junior college in 1926. The Bethune-Cookman College at Daytona Beach is an outgrowth of the Daytona Normal and Industrial Institute, founded by Mrs. Mary McLeod Bethune in 1904, and the Cookman Institute, established in 1872. In 1923 the two schools were merged under the board of education of the Methodist Episcopal Church.

Despite its delayed beginning and slow growth, the public-school system of Florida includes 2,523 buildings, a total investment in all school property of $75,484,656, and a personnel of 12,409 teachers for the 385,763 children of school age. Free public education is provided in virtually all elementary and secondary schools, as well as some free vocational training for children of both races. All counties require out-of-State residents whose children enter public schools to purchase Florida automobile licenses for their cars, and Miami also charges a nominal tuition fee for each nonresident pupil.

In addition to State and county public schools, Florida has 61 private educational institutions, many accredited by the National Education Association. This is exclusive of private kindergartens and commercial schools. The constitution of 1885 contains the provision: 'White and colored children shall not be taught in the same school but impartial provision shall be made for both.' The principle of segregation has been carried out, but educational facilities for Negro and white children are far from equal. The report of the Florida superintendent of public instruction for the two years ending June 30, 1936, (the latest issued at this writing, 1939) states that there are 1,494 buildings for white students and 1,029 for Negroes. The value of white school property is $70,543,001; of Negro property $4,941,655. The report says quite frankly that: 'In a few south Florida counties and in most north Florida counties many Negro schools are housed in churches, shacks, and lodges, and have no toilets, water supply, desks, blackboards, etc. Counties use these schools as a means to get State funds and yet these counties invest little or nothing in them.'

There are 9,513 white teachers and 2,896 Negro teachers. The average annual salary for white teachers is $1,029 and for Negroes, $492; 22 whites and 530 Negroes hold temporary certificates. All 67 counties have facilities for white students in the high-school grades, but only 28 counties make similar provisions for Negroes.

Every county provides transportation for white students, and 39 counties also transport Negroes. In 1936 transportation for 71,376 white students cost $1,579,824, and for 1,664 Negroes, $24,815. The superintendent's report states further: 'In 1934-35 the State average per capita cost of instructing white children was $40.72, whereas the State average per capita cost of instructing Negro children was $14.78.' The work of the State and Federal Governments and of religious organizations in the interests of Negro education has been aided by outstanding contributions from the Rosenwald, Slater, and Jeanes Funds, and the General Education Board, a Rockefeller foundation. The Rosenwald Fund has spent nearly $1,500,000 to help build 125 rural schools. The Slater Fund has fostered normal and industrial training in institutions which do not have accredited four-year high-school courses. It has also co-operated with the Jeanes Fund in maintaining 27 Negro teachers who, as county supervisors, have developed better Negro schools in the rural districts. The General Education Board has given much financial aid to institutions of higher learning.

Compulsory school attendance was not inaugurated in Florida until 1919. Distribution of free school books was begun in 1911, but was limited to pupils under 15 years of age who were orphans or the children of indigent parents; this was extended in 1925 to include all children in the public schools in the first six grades, and in 1935 to include basic textbooks in junior and senior high schools.

The State average per capita cost for white children is less than half the average per capita cost for the Nation. Using the per capita cost of instructing children in the Nation as an index, it would seem that the quantity and quality of education provided for white children in Florida is inadequate. By the same index the quantity and quality of education provided for Negroes is even more inadequate. Yet Florida's effort to support education, measured by the percentage of annual income spent for education, is greater than the average for the Nation.

A substantial addition to school facilities has been made by the WPA, at an expenditure of approximately $3,700,000. By the end of 1938 the construction of new buildings and enlargement of existing ones had provided 5,236 classrooms to relieve badly overcrowded conditions in some counties.

Public Health and Social Welfare

THE yardstick of reality can well be applied to Florida by measuring the public-health facilities and social services available to the common citizen. The State's population has multiplied at an amazing rate since 1900, and, though great advances have been made toward an adequate public program, the problems of development, engineering, and construction—to meet obvious and pressing needs—have taxed public energies to the relative detriment of public health and social welfare.

The State board of health was created in 1889, chiefly for the purpose of combating a yellow-fever epidemic. As the cause of the disease was unknown, medical authorities attempted to stamp it out by quarantine measures. Counties maintained 'shotgun quarantine' against one another; armed guards even held up the shipment of flatcars of iron rails and boxcars of ice. It was not until after the Spanish-American War that Walter Reed, William C. Gorgas, and other medical officers in the United States army succeeded, with the aid of enlisted men, in discovering the deadly 'yellow jack.' The only other duty specifically assigned to the board was the task of enforcing a quarantine of smallpox and cholera patients. Maritime quarantine of these diseases was not transferred to the Federal Government until 1893. Cholera has never been prevalent in the State, and smallpox has taken comparatively few lives. The latter fact explains why a mandatory vaccination law, though needed, has never been passed in Florida.

Had the board confined itself to quarantine activities, its usefulness would soon have been outgrown; but following the general trend toward a wider concept of public health and the progressive example of other States, it adopted a liberal construction of power and a broadened program. The work of the board of health is carried out through nine bureaus, all directly responsible to the State health officer, who in turn is responsible to the members of the State board of health. The bureaus are: administration, vital statistics, local health work, epidemiology, laboratories, public-health nursing, health education, sanitary engineering, maternal and child health.

A division of narcotic and drug inspection is operated under the bureau of administration. Drug and narcotic violations account for 90 per cent of this division's work, and drugstore inspection for the remainder. The bureau of local health work is concerned with the establishment of full-time local health departments in all counties of the State. One of the functions of the bureau of public-health nursing is the licensing of midwives, for whom it maintains a continuous teaching course. This bureau supervises all nursing projects of the WPA, promotes health education through newspaper publicity, moving pictures, popular health pamphlets, exhibit material and library service, and the monthly bulletin, *Health Notes*. Under the bureau of maternal and child health is a division of dental health, which carries on a program of education through the schools.

While the value of the board of health in Florida's government is generally conceded, its operating funds are still too meager to allow it to cope effectively with public-health and sanitary problems. For the period of 1937–39, the legislature appropriated $225,000 annually for use of the board. This sum, together with funds that the State received under the National Social Security Act (Titles 5 and 6), has resulted in an increase of county health units from 3 in 1935 to 15 in 1938.

Lack of adequate hospitals furnishes another significant clue to public-health conditions of Florida. There are 87 privately and publicly financed hospitals, and five Federal institutions—including one of the largest veterans' homes and hospitals in the South (*see Tour 6b*). But not all of these serve the general public, because the list includes such special hospitals as Moosehaven, East Coast Railroad hospital, the hospital at the State prison, and two college infirmaries.

With an appropriation by the 1937 legislature and a PWA loan, a State tubercular institution was built near Orlando with 312 rooms, providing for 400 patients, white and Negro. The WPA by the end of 1938 had built or improved 13 hospitals, providing 896 additional beds, at a cost of more than $700,000. Nevertheless, 36 of the State's 67 counties have neither general hospitals nor hospital facilities for the treatment of indigents. Only 10 hospitals have out-patient clinics, and only 16 are entirely supported by their municipalities or counties. Patients without funds and in need of hospitalization must often go outside their counties for treatment; and even there overcrowding greatly reduces the value of available services. This is particularly true where patients require prolonged and expensive treatment.

Exclusive of hospitals not open to the general public, Florida's rate of about 6 beds in general hospitals per 1,000 population compares favorably with the national standard of 4.6 beds; but the State's provision for nervous and mental patients is 3.4 beds per 1,000 of population, in comparison with the national standard of 5.6. It should be noted, however, that Florida's annual expenditure of 18¢ per person for public-health and sanitary services in 1930 compared favorably with the average national rate of 9¢ for the same year. In 1934, the Florida health expenditures were lowered to 12¢. Public-health authorities estimate that there can be no adequate public-health service without a minimum annual expenditure of $1 per capita.

Co-operative medical service was launched in Tampa more than 50 years before 'socialized medicine' became a controversial national issue. Soon after the Cuban cigar industry migrated to Tampa in 1886, a Cuban physician, Dr. Guillermo Machado, was conducting a mutual benefit society for medical aid. For 10¢ a week, members of *La Iguala* (The Equal) were entitled to medicine and services. This example was followed by the Spanish, Cuban, and Italian clubs that later appeared in Tampa for social and mutual benefit purposes. In 1906 the *Centro Español* erected a $60,000 hospital where members could obtain medical care and hospitalization in return for their dues of $1.50 a week. An offshoot of this organization, the *Centro Asturiano*, erected a large modern hospital in 1928. About 83 per cent of its income is used for medical services.

The Florida State Hospital for the Insane, founded at Chattahoochee in 1876 (*see Tour 7c*), is the only hospital in the State free to all indigent residents regardless of race. But it is so understaffed and overcrowded (with more than 4,000 patients) that many persons mentally ill but not requiring mechanical restraint are confined in county jails. The Florida farm colony for feeble-minded and epileptic children, established at Gainesville in 1919, admits white patients only.

Florida's recorded death rate per 1,000 population was 12.8 in 1935 as compared with 10.9 for the country as a whole. A large percentage of those deaths was caused by preventable diseases. The maternal death rate is second highest in the Nation; the incidence of malaria is six times as high as the Nation's average, or 20.3 per cent as compared with 3.5. Tuberculosis and syphilis are alarmingly prevalent, especially among Negroes, as is shown by rates of 109.4 and 67.6 respectively, compared to national rates of 55.0 and 9.1. During 1935 the rate of deaths from syphilis per 100,000 population in Florida was 26.0 for whites and 67.6 for Negroes; the tuberculosis rate was 56.3 for whites and 109.4 for Negroes. The general resident death rate for Negroes in 1935 was 15.1 as compared with 11.8 for whites.

Despite the prevalence of disease and high death rate among Negroes, only seven counties (Dade, Duval, Hillsborough, Palm Beach, Pinellas, Putnam, and Volusia) have general hospitals that provide care for them; 28 other hospitals in the State, including the State Tuberculosis Hospital near Orlando, and the Florida State Hospital for the Insane at Chattahoochee, make some provision for Negroes.

In recent years, two small but well-equipped hospitals for Negro tubercular patients have been established: one in Pensacola, with a capacity of 50 patients, a branch of the Escambia County Tubercular Sanitarium; the other, the Tubercular Rest Home in Jacksonville, with 50 beds. In Miami, a white specialist conducts annual clinics for Negro physicians of Florida. At the Florida Agricultural and Mechanical College for Negroes in Tallahassee, a yearly clinic in general medicine attracts Negro practitioners from all parts of the country.

Brewster Hospital, in Jacksonville, is outstanding among the dozen or more private and semi-private hospitals and training schools for nurses and interns that are operated by and for Negroes. It has been approved by the American Medical Society and American College of Surgeons. The hospital was opened in 1931 by the Methodist Episcopal Women's Home Missionary Society.

With the aid of WPA funds, the city of Tampa in 1938 completed a 60-bed hospital for Negroes at a cost of $125,000. It is equipped with laboratory and X-ray department, and employs a staff of white and Negro physicians and surgeons. The brick structure is set in a landscaped park, overlooking the Hillsborough River.

Support for the active social agencies and institutions in Florida comes both from private sources and from Federal, State, county, and municipal funds. Public agencies are the more important in point of general usefulness and the number of persons served. In most instances, however, private agencies have pioneered in the field of social service and developed many general policies and technical procedures that serve as a foundation for public welfare activities.

The early laws of Florida providing for social services read well enough, but they were not immediately put into effect. In Article X, Section 1, of an early State constitution (1868), provisions were made to 'establish such institutions for the benefit of the insane, blind, and deaf and other benevolent institutions as the public good may require.' Section 2 provided for a 'penitentiary and a house of refuge for juvenile offenders.' The spirit of this provision is now carried out in the school for boys at Marianna and for girls at Ocala. Section 3 provided that the counties of the State should care for 'the inhabitants who by reason of age, infirmity, or misfortune may have claims upon the aid and sympathy of society.' Thus the constitution divided social responsibility: the State was to care for the handicapped, delinquent, and criminal classes, while the counties were in some way to provide for the aged, infirm, and dependent.

Various progressive laws affecting social service were enacted during the next 60 years, notably in the fields of mothers' pensions and child welfare; but the need for public social services on a State-wide basis was not fully realized until the economic depression, beginning in 1929, drained the resources of counties, municipalities, and private welfare agencies. After making strenuous efforts, they conceded in 1931 that the task was beyond their power. Several communities attempted unsuccessfully to stem the rising tide of destitution by appointing committees on unemployment relief, by enlisting community resources, and by making special appropriations for relief purposes.

The first Federal funds were available under the Emergency Relief and Construction Act of 1932. The need for them was evident in the rapid swelling of relief rolls to approximately 100,000 cases within a few months. The Civil Works Administration and the Federal Emergency Relief Administration met the most pressing needs of the State during 1933-34. By the early part of 1935, approximately one-fifth of the State's population was receiving either direct relief or work relief from the FERA. By August 1935, the newly created WPA, providing work relief for unemployed, began to take the place of the older organization. In November of that year, with the FERA discontinued, the WPA assumed responsibility for the majority of the employable workers on the Florida relief rolls.

Other agencies of the Federal Government have provided valuable social services in Florida during the emergency period. Outstanding for their benefits to the unemployed are the Civilian Conservation Corps, the Resettlement Administration, the Federal Surplus Commodities Corporation, the National Youth Administration, and the Public Works Administration.

The necessity for a co-ordinated program resulted in the passage of a social welfare act by the 1935 legislature. This law represented the State's first effective provision for a comprehensive program of social services. Simultaneously, the legislature submitted a proposed amendment to the constitution that would permit appropriation of State funds for relief purposes. It was ratified in November 1936 by a twelve-to-one majority.

The 1935 act created a State welfare board of 7 members and 12 district boards, with power to administer relief and other welfare activities as well as Federal social-security funds. Until ratification of the amendment, however, no funds could be appropriated to match Federal grants for public assistance as provided in the United States Social Security Act.

This situation resulted in a proposal that Florida counties provide funds for a temporary old-age assistance program limited to needy persons 70 years of age and over. After months of negotiations by the State welfare board with county commissioners and the Social Security Board, the plan was inaugurated on October 1, 1936, a month before the amendment was ratified. Nine months before State funds were available, many counties voluntarily appropriated them for public-assistance purposes. Under this program 9,922 aged received yearly payments aggregating $816,979; one-half of this sum represented grants-in-aid from the Federal Government.

The 1937 legislature, empowered by the amendment, appropriated $3,800,000 annually for old-age assistance, aid to dependent children and the blind, and other welfare services. Relief for those not included in social-security categories remained a responsibility of the counties, but the latter were not required to participate in costs of the three Federal-State assistance programs. An initial survey in 1936–37 indicated that there were 27,304 residents more than 65 years of age eligible for old-age assistance, 1,200 for assistance to the blind, and 25,037 children eligible for aid to dependent children.

Private welfare agencies in Florida are relatively few in number and small in size, but their work is of great value. Fraternal organizations, service clubs, religious orders, and other private agencies alleviate social and economic distress in many ways. They are active in providing free summer camps for children of the poor, hospitalization for invalids, correction of physical defects, maternity care, day nurseries, low-cost food and shelter for transients, and vocational training.

There are more than 30 orphanages and detention homes for white children in the State, a few supported by county funds, and the majority by church and fraternal organizations. Homes for unmarried mothers are located in Tampa and St.Petersburg. Church and fraternal groups also maintain several homes for the aged. The counties of Brevard, Dade, Escambia, Hillsborough, Manatee, Pinellas, and Volusia support homes for the aged out of public funds.

Provision for the Negro seems even less adequate in the field of social welfare than in public health. Several private and semi-private institutions, some of which are supported by community chests and similar enterprises, care for the Negro sick and indigent. In Jacksonville the Negro Welfare League, which is probably the Negro Floridian's most comprehensive social agency, contributes to an old-folks home, a child-placement bureau, a juvenile-detention home for boys, and the Clara White Mission. Tampa has a well-managed day nursery for the children of working mothers. Three similar nurseries are conducted in Jacksonville, two of them by the WPA and a third with the assistance of community chest funds. In St.Augustine several welfare associations for Negroes are aided by the Buckingham Smith Benevolent Association, which was incorporated to administer the bequest of Buckingham Smith, a white philanthropist who left his estate 'for the benefit of the black people of St.Augustine.' In 1871, the year of the bequest, the property was valued at approximately $20,000, but by wise administration it has been made to yield an annual income of $10,000.

Florida's former penal system has been described as one of 'aimless experimentation, followed by about 30 years of a lease system.' The lease system, abolished in 1919, enabled private contractors to rent labor from the State at the rate of $1 a day per convict. The State supported the convicts and provided guards. The present greatly improved penal system began to take shape when the 1911 legislature appropriated funds to establish a prison farm at Raiford. This was completed in 1914, and the lash and sweatbox were outlawed in 1923. A State prison fund, derived from a levy of three-eighths of a mill on the dollar of all taxable property, supplements the small revenue from the State prison farm. Women and the physically unfit are retained at the farm, while others, with the exception of those who work on the premises, make up the convict road force.

Negro prisoners are lodged in the State prison at Raiford, the various road camps scattered throughout the counties, and in the city and county jails. At Raiford, where conditions are probably the best, the buildings are well constructed, regular occupations are permitted the prisoners, some educational opportunities are provided, and Negro religious services are given under the direction of a registered Negro chaplain.

The Florida Federation of Women's Clubs, making a survey of 13 county jails in 1931, found conditions far from ideal, and in some cases worse than those surveyed nine years before. Among the more objectionable features noted were inadequate medical care, the total lack of education and rehabilitation measures, enforced idleness of prisoners, and the fee system, whereby sheriffs received 65¢ a day for the board of each inmate. Fortunately, some of these conditions have been remedied in many counties. New jails with modern equipment are replacing unsanitary structures, and the welfare of the prisoners is given increasing attention.

Yet unfavorable prison conditions were but one of the many problems that confronted the State when it attempted to consolidate the economic and population gains that resulted from the great expansion program of the 1920's. Public health and social welfare emerged, during the 1930's, as matters to be treated not as a private liability, but as a public responsibility; and this the State has undertaken in increasing measure through education, legislation, and financial assistance.

Sports and Recreation

PROJECTING into subtropical seas, yet lying within overnight reach of many millions of people, Florida has become a winter playground for half a continent. It is more extensively used for recreation than any other area east of the Rocky Mountains. From the great bay at Pensacola in northwest Florida, and from Fernandina on the Atlantic coast, down to the island of Key West, a program of play activities practically overshadows the workaday side of the State's life.

Climate and accessibility, of course, have much to do with the great winter migration, but Florida's beaches, lakes, and forests offer many natural facilities for recreation. The kinds of recreation are but a matter of personal preference. They may be simply sitting in the sun, observing plant or animal life, playing a game of chess in the shade of a banyan tree, listening to an open-air band concert or an opera by radio on the deck of a cruiser, golfing, fishing, hunting, swimming, or, for the 'form' player, watching the 'bangtails' finish at the race tracks. The opportunity to indulge in these preferences in the open under almost continuous sunshine, adding the factor of health to play, accounts largely for the presence of the millions who annually patronize Florida.

Many persons seeking health are drawn by the abundance of sunlight. Florida's daily average of more than six hours is greater than that of any other territory in the eastern United States. But warmth, which can be enjoyed elsewhere in enervating comfort by a fireside, is not the principal lure for the health seeker; the opportunity to absorb vertical rays of clear sunlight at sea level is an important factor in Florida's winter monopoly.

Since the rewards of thrift and industry frequently come late in life, a high percentage of visitors in Florida are beyond middle age. But this neither diminishes their fun, nor seems to lessen their energy. Organized into clubs for lawn bowling, shuffleboard, roque, horseshoe pitching, checkers, dominoes, and bridge, these elderly contestants usually exceed in numbers the gallery of spectators. Mass participation is the formula in Three-Quarter Century clubs and like organizations. One shuffleboard club in St.Petersburg claims 4,000 active members, and an annual card party in a public park in the same city attracts 3,000 or more players.

Florida, accordingly, is a playground for the many rather than for the wealthy few; nevertheless, it is around the latter that recreation has been publicized into the State's most prominent industry. To foster this, much costly and elaborate paraphernalia has been installed in the resorts. Commercialized recreation, with its attendant spotlighting, nearly obscures the State's other interests and pursuits, and resort patrons consequently have little acquaintance with these.

Scarcely known, for example, are 'syrup boilings' in the pine woods, when neighbors join a farmer in turning to good use his patch of sugar cane; the gatherings for chicken pilau—made with rice—which corresponds socially to a wiener roast elsewhere; the combined barbecues and rodeos in the cattle-raising sections; and the country fish fries, where hundreds gather to feast and hear political orations. More familiar are the festivals, fairs, and diverse celebrations that mark the end of harvest time in the tobacco, strawberry, and fruit regions. These are widely advertised and to an extent have become tourist attractions. Least known are the Negro 'jooks,' primitive rural counterparts of resort night clubs, where turpentine workers take their evening relaxation deep in the pine forests.

Greatest resources for sport and play, of course, are Florida's fresh and salt waters. Bays and sounds are plentiful for small-boat racing, deep harbors for ocean-going yachts, and distributed along the State's coast are nearly 800 miles of operating or potential bathing beaches. Swimming has universal appeal, and for good reasons fishing lures thousands.

'I have fished in every State in the Union but three,' declared Barton W. Evermann, ichthyologist with the U.S. Bureau of Fisheries for more than twenty years, 'and from the Bering Sea to the Gulfs of Mexico and California, and, all things considered, I regard Florida as unequalled in the richness and variety of its attractions for all sorts of sport with rod and reel.'

Accounting for the fish indigenous to each of Florida's coasts, Evermann explained that, 'The warm waters of the Florida Keys serve as a more or less effective barrier to the passage of fishes living in colder waters. As a result many species are found on the east coast of Florida which do not occur on the Gulf coast and vice versa.'

Tarpon and sailfish are the leading game fish in coastal waters. The silver-scaled tarpon migrates from South American shores to the lower east and west coasts of Florida; its most promising grounds are the swift-running passes leading into Tampa and Sarasota Bays, Boca Grande, the Caloosahatchee River, the Ten Thousand Islands, and the waters off Miami, Fort Lauderdale, and Palm Beach. Full-moon nights are preferred by experienced anglers, since sunburn is avoided and the tremendous leaps of the 30- to 150-pound hooked warrior seem more spectacular. No less valiant is the sailfish, whose habitat is the warm Gulf Stream. International sportsmen compete annually in tarpon and sailfish tournaments sponsored by several Florida cities.

Other favorite game fish are kingfish, sea trout, robalo or snook, sheepshead, cabia, flounder, pompano, bluefish, marlin, amberjack, and a host of the bizarre species found only in tropical seas. The State requires no license of the salt-water fisherman, provided his catch is not sold, since his fishing grounds are under Federal jurisdiction. Up and down the coast, cabin launches and motorboats are available for hire at reasonable rates in all seasons.

The numerous lakes, rivers, and 'runs' from springs are stocked with game fish. The black bass is the prize fresh-water fighter. Less combative species include the speckled perch, bluegill, redbreasted sunfish or bream, rock bass, and pickerel. Among bodies of water that are noted for the size and variety of fishes are Lakes Okeechobee, St.George, and Apopka, and the St.Johns, Indian, Kissimmee, Choctawhatchee, and Apalachicola Rivers. Professional guides and amateur advisers for fishermen are in evidence throughout the State. Local chambers of commerce issue fishing booklets with maps spotting the best grounds; newspapers in the larger communities carry a column listing charter boats, guides, fees, and tide charts. Regularly scheduled broadcasts dealing with the sport, its prize catches and experiences, are featured by radio stations in several cities. Seasonal fishing has long been outdated in Florida; the Izaak Walton zealot can enjoy his pastime twelve months of the year. (*For Fishing and Hunting Regulations, see General Information.*)

Clear streams in several sections of the State wind through the dense jungles and lead campers to occasional bluffs on either side, which afford an unspoiled view of Florida's natural woodlands that the highway traveler misses. There are many rivers over which the paddler can travel, but the best known extended canoe trip is the 469-mile tour of north Florida. From White Springs on the Suwannee the route skirts Suwannee Sound on the Gulf, continues up the tropical Withlacoochee River to Lake Panasoffkee, then follows portage to Lake Griffin; from there it goes down the swift Ocklawaha to the St.Johns, and northward with the current into Jacksonville.

Amateur sailors find opportunities for winter yachting and boating, and competition among all types of craft is an outstanding sport. Major events drawing wide attention are the Miami-Nassau Sailing Races, the Bermuda

Race, the St.Petersburg-Havana Yacht Race, and the annual Biscayne Bay Sailing Regatta at Miami. International motorboat tournaments are held at Miami, New Smyrna, Palm Beach, and Tampa. Perhaps no one factor has been more responsible for arousing interest in small-boat sailing than the activities of the Melbourne Sailing Club. Active member clubs of the Florida East Coast Yachting Association are found in practically all cities along the Atlantic, and races between them are held throughout the year. Aquaplaning is popular on inland lakes and in sheltered bays.

For those who wish to view water life from the surface, glass-bottomed boats are available at Miami for trips over the coral beds of the Atlantic, and at the docks of Florida's largest springs.

Low-lying sand islands, reached by bridges and causeways, parallel both coasts and form most of the Florida beaches. Where the white sand is firmly packed, the beaches serve as motorways and playgrounds. The beaches of the quiet Gulf, from Pensacola to Fort Myers, compete with those along the surf-rolling Atlantic as summer resorts. Swimmers and divers are attracted to the many rivers, springs, lakes, and salt- and sulphur-water pools. Meets are held throughout the year, enabling the State to develop world's champions in these sports. Swimming is by far the most popular sport with children.

Panther, wildcat, and black bear are hunted in several of the Gulf hammocks and in the Everglades. Deer also abound in the Everglades and in the national forests. An experimental deer-breeding farm for restocking purposes was maintained for a time by the State at Welaka, and several private preserves—one of which claims to have 5,000 deer under fence—are established in the west, central, and northern parts of the peninsula.

The hunter finds a profusion of small fur-bearing animals, including red and gray fox, skunk, raccoon, muskrat, and opossum. The otter is less plentiful. In late fall, natives and visitors take to the field with their dogs to flush quail and doves, both found in all parts of the State. Wild turkeys inhabit isolated interior localities, while streams, lake regions, and the coast are the haunts of marsh hens, ducks, and snipe.

In territories near the supply headquarters at Jacksonville, Tallahassee, Winter Haven, Miami, and Orlando are five leading hunting grounds that include the virgin wilds of Florida's national forests. State foresters, assigned to the Ocala, Osceola, Apalachicola, and Choctawhatchee National Forests, co-operate with hunters in the selection of camping grounds, the best 'stands,' and the observance of game laws. For those primarily interested in marksmanship, numerous trap and skeet tournaments are held throughout the State.

Scenic attractions along the State's 9,000 miles of hard-surfaced roads vary from the hilly, roller-coaster terrain of the west and central sections to the vast prairie lands that extend through the south-central portion of the State. Off the main routes are roads and trails leading into State parks, national forests, tropical gardens, and along glistening stretches of ocean beach. Florida's historical background is revealed in the old Spanish forts and buildings of St.Augustine and Pensacola, the Mission ruins at New Smyrna, and the time-mellowed Georgian homes of Tallahassee and vicinity. Hotels, apartments, and tourist and trailer camps are available in every section of the State.

Several State parks, which offer a variety of low-cost recreation to the tourist, were developed and improved in 1936–38 by CCC workers, under the direction of the State park service. Florida Caverns State Park, in Jackson County, has a natural limestone bridge over the Chipola River and caves with stalagmite and stalactite formations. Torreya State Park, set in the hilly region of west Florida, has many historical points of interest, as well as large stands of the rare Torreya tree. Fort Clinch State Park, on Amelia Island near Fernandina, includes the fort and 1,200 acres of subtropical scenery. In north Florida, Gold Head Branch State Park has fishing and swimming facilities, picnic grounds, and many miles of woodland paths. In Hillsboro River State Park, near Tampa, are overnight cabins, trails, roads, and a museum. Set in a region having an abundant flora and fauna, Myakka River State Park, an area of 25,000 acres between Sarasota and Arcadia, is fully equipped with camping facilities. Perhaps the largest virgin hammock left in Florida is located in Highlands Hammock State Park, which lies between Sebring and Zolfo Springs. Royal Palm Park, more than six square miles in area, is west of Miami in the wildest portion of the Everglades. It is owned and administered by the Florida Federation of Women's Clubs and forms a part of the proposed Everglades National Park. Accommodations for visitors are available on Paradise Key within the park.

In mid-November an army of trailer-tourists rolls its homes into Florida for the winter season. These visitors live in the hundreds of camps that have been established for them throughout the State. Their most representative organization, the Tin Can Tourists of the World, which was formed in 1920 at Tampa, in 1938 had a membership of 30,000. These tourists assemble at Dade City for Thanksgiving and move to Arcadia for Christmas, where they celebrate the season with a community Christmas tree and a Santa Claus for the children. In January, the colony changes its residence for an annual convention, usually at Sarasota; in

1939 this was held at Tampa. A spirit of comradeship, often lacking in the more expensive tourist centers of the State, is evident as the trailer folk gather in their camps and exchange tales of Nation-wide wanderings.

Both seashore and inland resorts provide golf and tennis. Many of America's golfing classics attract professional and amateur champions to Florida cities during the winter. A majority of the State's 200 golf courses are open to public play at nominal greens fees. Numerous tennis courts are municipally owned and operated for the benefit of tourists and residents. Annual State and National shuffleboard and horseshoe-pitching tournaments are held at Lake Worth and St.Petersburg.

Florida offers many exciting spectator sports: horse and dog races, air and auto races, boxing and wrestling, basketball, baseball, football, diamond ball, polo, and jai alai. Miami's two horse-racing tracks compare favorably in capacity, maintenance, and speed with those in the North. A horse track, said to be the fastest in the country, was opened at Hollywood in 1939 for a brief meet. The Hialeah track, with its royal palms, landscaped grounds, and rare collection of pink flamingoes and black swans, makes an exotic picture. Dog tracks in several of the larger cities, together with horse-racing tracks where pari-mutuel betting is legal, operate during a 100-day winter season. Annual air maneuvers are held in Miami. Many speed records have been established on the natural automobile speedway at Daytona Beach. Polo matches are regularly scheduled at Miami and Palm Beach. Miami is one of the few places in the United States where jai alai may be seen; this exciting sport, brought from Cuba, is played on a paved court, like handball.

Florida claims to have originated diamond ball, now known as softball, played by more than 3,000 teams throughout the State. Interscholastic football, basketball, and track and field events are held in fall and winter.

In March, Florida's baseball month, spring training camps are established by a dozen big-league and numerous minor-league clubs. Exhibition games are played on an advertised schedule, and participating teams make up what is known as the 'Grapefruit League,' a name bestowed by sports writers. Regular league umpires officiate, and box scores are studied by club managers and others to obtain a preview of players' performances.

Although Negroes make up nearly 30 per cent of Florida's population, they share little in the organized sports of the State. Negro schools and colleges, as far as their limited facilities permit, have interscholastic and intra-mural sports activities—football, basketball, baseball, and tennis. Projects established by the NYA and WPA, such as Bethune-Cookman's Cypress 'Cabin' and the recreation training institute at Dunbar High

School in Fort Myers, are helping to expand these recreational opportunities.

Fishing, which costs little and gives a return in food, is a favorite occupation among Negroes. A possum hunt likewise combines sport and the possibility of a savory dish, and the baying that announces a treed raccoon is the musical prelude to a feast. Negro churches sponsor concerts, picnics, and fish fries; social clubs provide opportunities for dancing and sometimes for games of chance such as skin (a card game), bolita, and dice. Motion-picture theaters and night clubs in the city, and 'jooks' in the country are operated for Negroes. At Jacksonville, a Negro club maintains a 9-hole golf course, a swimming pool, a shooting range, picnic grounds, and recreational equipment for children. The entire property, covering 36 acres, has been improved by the WPA and NYA.

In the use of Florida's improved beaches the Negroes are definitely handicapped; few cities have provided bathing facilities for them. At Fernandina, near Jacksonville, the employees of the Afro-American Life Insurance Company have established American Beach, a tract of more than twenty acres, with electrically lighted streets, modern homes, and summer cottages.

The WPA, maintaining a division of recreational projects operated on a State-wide basis, is active in promoting organized play. Some of its most notable work has been among underprivileged children. Facilities installed in scores of cities up to 1939 included 207 parks and playgrounds, 78 community houses, 6 swimming pools, 20 golf courses, 6 yacht basins, and 14 piers, representing an outlay of nearly $6,000,000. Plays of the Federal Theater, classes conducted by the Federal Art Project, and concerts sponsored by the Federal Music Project have been well attended.

City recreation departments, in co-operation with school authorities and civic clubs, supervise children's sports, arrange tourist dances, and sponsor card parties, excursions, and community 'sings'; these services are extended to visitors and citizens alike. In some cities the ocean beaches are used for playgrounds and for physical culture classes.

Newspapers and Radio

A TORY die-hard, William Charles Wells, published Florida's first newspaper at St.Augustine in 1783—the *East Florida Gazette,* an inflammatory weekly that stormed at Americans for affronting the English Crown. Wells came from Charleston a year before the British evacuated that city in 1784, but found little peace in St.Augustine, for shortly after he arrived Great Britain relinquished Florida to Spain. That left her loyal subject with no apparent choice but to return to London, but in the bitterness of defeat Wells demonstrated that he was first of all a newspaperman by rushing to press an extra that emblazoned the outcome of the Revolutionary War. Three issues of his *East Florida Gazette,* were discovered in London in 1926, and photostatic copies of these are in possession of the Florida Historical Society. One issue bears the date, 'From Saturday, February 22, to Saturday, March 1, 1783.'

No other newspapers were attempted until the United States obtained Florida from Spain in 1821. In that year Richard W. Edes started the *Florida Gazette,* also in St.Augustine, but it was as short-lived as Wells' paper, lasting only from July 14 until October 15, when Edes died of yellow fever.

Meanwhile, the *Floridian* made its appearance on August 18, 1821, at Pensacola. Cary Nicholes and George Tunstall, the editors and owners, kept this paper going until 1824, when they sold the press and equipment to W.Hasell Hunt, who launched the Pensacola *Gazette and West Florida Advertiser.* In 1822 St.Augustine's third paper, the *East Florida Herald,* was founded by Elias B. Gould and occupied an uncontested local field for thirteen years.

Florida now had two newspapers, one in each of its former capitals under Spanish rule, with approximately 400 miles of sparsely inhabited wilderness separating them. This situation soon inspired both publications to advocate territorial division. The first legislative council met in Pensacola in 1821, the second in St.Augustine in 1822, and the difficulties of overland travel to these sessions intensified the campaign for separation. Unity was preserved only by the selection of a neutral site midway between these two cities for a new capital, and here Tallahassee was founded in 1823.

Two years later the *Florida Intelligencer* made its appearance in Tallahassee, sponsored by Hunt and his associates, who shipped the equipment from Pensacola.

An early issue of the *Intelligencer* prophesied accurately that Tallahassee, 'with its advantages and prospects will soon necessarily increase in respectability, in wealth and population.' Great plantations developed, and the capital and its environs became the Territory's cultural, economic, and political center. Fourteen papers were published in Tallahassee and its surrounding villages, including weeklies at Quincy, Magnolia, Port Leon, Newport, Monticello, Apalachicola, and St.Joseph.

Hunt once explained in his papers that a delayed issue of the *Florida Intelligencer* at Tallahassee was occasioned by the priority of legal printing. He likewise recorded something of the state of politics in 1829 by alleging that he had been booted out of Pensacola's postmastership for not shouting, 'Huzza for Jackson! The Hero of New Orleans! Down with Adams and Clay, the Hartford Conventionist and the Prince of Intriguers!' Hunt sold out, and his former newspaper properties were consolidated in the Pensacola *Gazette*, one of three dominant papers that survived territorial days. The others were the *Floridian* of Tallahassee, founded in 1828, and the *Florida Herald* of St.Augustine, started as the *East Florida Herald* in 1822 and still in the Gould family when Florida became a State in 1845. The paper was conservative under Elias Gould, its founder, but when it was taken over by his son James in 1824 it became an outspoken advocate of the Democratic Party. The name was shortened to the *Florida Herald* in 1829, and nine years later the subtitle *and Southern Democrat* was added. The *Herald* flourished without opposition until D.W.Whitehurst in 1838 brought out *The News*, a Whig journal, which became a Democratic organ in 1845 when ownership passed to Albert A. Nunes. These St.Augustine papers, perhaps more than any others, recorded the political strife and maneuverings of their day. The Pensacola *Gazette*, Democratic under Hunt, and a paper notable for its historical content, revealed Whig leanings under the guidance of Benjamin D. Wright. Most influential of the three was the Tallahassee *Floridian*, strongly Democratic from its inception, but most ardently so during secession and the War between the States.

For nearly a decade journalism was confined to northern and northwestern Florida, but in 1829 Thomas Eastin, after a brief and futile attempt to oppose the Pensacola *Gazette* with the *Argus*, drifted down to Key West and founded the *Register*. This paper lasted but a short time, and no copy is extant. Then, on March 21, 1831, the Key West *Gazette* appeared and ran for little more than a year, to be followed by the *Inquirer*, edited and published for two years by Jesse Atkinson. Although salt, cigars, and ship salvage made Key West an important commercial city, its sparse population offered little financial return to publishers, and after the *Inquirer* died, the island city was without a newspaper for 13 years.

Meanwhile, the plantations in north Florida were producing huge cotton crops and creating two port cities. Apalachicola was the original port of the territory, but a defective title to much of the town site and surrounding country eventually resulted in the development of a competitor. When the courts awarded the disputed title to the Apalachicola Land Company, successor to the English pioneer trading firm of Panton, Leslie & Company, many indignant citizens, reduced to the status of squatters, moved to near-by St.Joseph Bay and there founded the city of St.Joseph. With them went R.Dinsmore Westcott, who had started the Apalachicola *Advertiser* in 1833 and now continued it as the St.Joseph *Telegraph*. The victorious land company replaced the *Advertiser* with a paper of its own, the Apalachicola *Gazette*, and in 1836 imported Cosam Emir Bartlett, New Hampshire born but at the time engaged in newspaper work in Georgia, to run it. Bartlett made the *Gazette* into a daily in 1839 and sustained it on that basis for three months. This was the first daily in Florida and the only one during the territorial period.

Efforts of St.Joseph to divert shipping business from Apalachicola were unsuccessful, and in 1842 the Apalachicola *Journal*, successor to the *Gazette*, declared: 'St.Joseph with her artificial resources and beautiful bay has sunk into an everlasting commercial slump.' Nevertheless, St.Joseph had secured Florida's first constitutional convention in 1838–39, and in the *Times* of that city, formerly the *Telegraph*, appears a full account of these proceedings. Under the editorship of Peter W. Gautier,Jr., the *Times* became the most widely quoted paper in the territory.

In 1844, the Apalachicola *Commercial Observer* published 11 scientific articles written by Dr. John Gorrie, inventor of the first patented ice machine (*see Tour 7a*). The articles were signed 'Jenner,' his pen name.

Mortality among territorial papers was high. From 1822 to 1845, when Florida joined the Union, 45 papers existed, a larger number than is usually found in new, thinly settled regions. Tallahassee led with 11, and Apalachicola had 10. Of the total of 6,800 issues published before 1845, none of more than four pages, about 3,600 have been preserved. Subscription prices varied from $4 to $5 annually, and readers were few. The Pensacola *Gazette* began printing in 1824 with 75 subscribers. The general rate of increase by 1850 was indicated in the combined circulation of 10 newspapers, amounting to 5,750. This figure had increased by 1860 to 15,500, representing the total circulation of 22 papers, a substantial figure for a State with but 77,746 white inhabitants. Negroes in the State numbered 66,777, but few of them were allowed the privileges of schooling.

James Owen Knauss, in his *Territorial Florida Journalism*, points out that editors and publishers of those days also filled many other positions; they were postmasters, port collectors, United States marshals, ministers of the gospel, magistrates, and members of the territorial council.

The slavery question agitated the press long before Florida became a State. In 1832, scarcely a decade after the purchase of Florida, the Key West *Inquirer*, somewhat incoherently, as no doubt befitted the temper of the editor, expressed itself on this subject:

> We have always thought that the value of our Union consisted in affording equal rights and equal protection to every citizen; when, therefore, its objects are so perverted as to become the means of impoverishment to one section, whilst it aggrandizes another, when it becomes necessary to sacrifice one portion of the States for the good of the rest the Union has lost its value to us; and we are bound, by a recurrence to first principles, to maintain our rights and defend our lives and property. If we are oppressed, it is a matter of perfect indifference whether that oppression be inflicted by a foreign power or our next door neighbor. Upon the same principles we are compelled to resist both—'even unto death.'

The issue had become so important by 1835 that a meeting was held at Tallahassee to protest abolition; threats were made to dissolve the Union if slavery were abolished. No abolitionist papers appeared in Florida. Although Whitehurst, editor of the St.Augustine *News*, interested himself in an African colonization society and advocated return of the Negroes to Africa and the West Indies, St.Augustine papers were united against abolition and quarreled only about local and territorial matters. Despite the Yankee nativity of many Florida editors, most of them denounced the abolitionists. By 1860, the imminence of war between the North and South was reflected in the savagery of editorial opinion. The Tampa *Peninsular* of November 17, 1860, carried the following onslaught:

> The election of Abraham Lincoln as President and Hannibal Hamlin as Vice President is beyond per-adventure. Sovereigns of Florida! Will you submit to a Black Republican administration? Will you become pensioners of Black Republicanism for the right to hold and protect your property? Will you sacrifice your *Honor* and sell your birthright for a mess of pottage?

At the outbreak of the war, with the exception of the papers of Key West, journalism had penetrated no further south than Tampa. When Florida became a State, Key West had once more entered journalistic ranks with the *Light of the Reef*, a paper that apparently lasted but a few months. The *Key of the Gulf*, appearing the same year, also had a short life, but was revived in 1857 under the editorship of William H. Ward, champion of secession. The only other paper in peninsular Florida at that time was at Ocala. A contemporary paper of the period, the *Sunny South*, published at Tampa in the 1850's, listed 16 weeklies in 14 cities as follows: the *Family Friend*, Monticello; *Floridian & Journal*, Tallahassee; the *Florida Sentinel*, Tallahassee; *Weekly East Floridian*, Fernandina; *St.John's Mirror*, Jacksonville; the *Examiner*, St.Augustine; *Florida Home Companion*, Ocala; the *Sunny South*, Tampa; the *Florida Peninsular*, Tampa; *Key of the Gulf*, Key West; *Cotton States*, Micanopy; *Eastern Herald*, Lake City; *Florida Dispatch*, Newnansville; *Madison Messenger*, Madison; *West Florida Enterprise*, Marianna; and the *Florida Tribune*, Pensacola.

The *Key of the Gulf* was suppressed in 1861 when Union forces took Key West. For two years thereafter Key West gleaned its local news from a Union paper, the *New Era*, published by R.B.Licke, an officer of the 90th New York Volunteers. After the war, the *Key of the Gulf* was twice revived, and a half-dozen other papers came and—through mergers or suspensions—went. The present-day Key West *Citizen* was founded in 1904.

Jacksonville's first paper, established in 1835, was the *Courier*, rapidly succeeded by the *East Florida Advocate*, the *Tropical Plant*, and the *Florida Statesman*, all short-lived. On December 31, 1864, J.K.Stickney issued the *Florida Union*, a four-page war news sheet upholding Northern views. A year later it changed hands, became a tri-weekly, attempted to become a daily, and finally passed in 1873 to Walton, Fowle & Company, a printing firm, who turned it over to W.W.Douglas and the Reverend H.B.McCallum. This pair switched it from Republican to Democratic, marking the end of Reconstruction influence. The present *Florida Times-Union* (which is the State's oldest surviving daily and bears its original masthead) first appeared on the morning of February 4, 1883.

Timothy Thomas Fortune, the 'Dean of Negro journalists,' born of slave parents in Marianna, Florida, became a nationally known editor in the last quarter of the nineteenth century. Beginning his career as an office boy with the Marianna *Courier*, he later worked in the composing rooms of the Jacksonville *Courier* and several other publications. He went to New York City in 1878 and eventually found a place there on the *Evening Sun* editorial staff. He is best known, however, for his books on race relations and for his political writings in the New York *Freeman*, a Negro newspaper which he edited. A noted Negro contemporary, Mathew M. Lewey, former mayor of Newnansville and a member of the State legislature, founded the *Florida Sentinel* at Gainesville in 1887.

The early Florida editor, regardless of erudition, took his journalism raw. There were no 'weasel-word' qualifications, such as 'it is alleged,' or 'it has been charged.' If an editor believed a man to be a scoundrel he called him that and very likely a blackguard and coward as well. Consequently the life of a newspaperman was at times both exciting and hazardous. Libel laws eventually toned down the phraseology, and so rigid did restrictions finally become that the mere printing of testimony in a criminal trial made a paper liable for damages if the person under charges were acquitted.

Teeth were extracted from the law in 1935, but in the meantime twentieth-century journalism had made newspapers thoroughly respectable and soft-voiced in their sentiments, although intensely sectional. Local boosting and bias took the form of ignoring rather than disparaging other communities, and became so obvious that one newly arrived editor made an appeal to include, along with praise for the home town, a good word for the State. Since 1910 the St.Petersburg *Independent* has done its part for the climate by giving away an entire edition every day the sun fails to shine before the paper goes to press in the early afternoon.

The chamber of commerce trend began with a taboo on the news of hurricanes, freezes, and anything calculated to scare off visitors, but in recent years the Florida press has treated such events more in accordance with their news value. Where once an editor, through the magic of printer's ink, subdued a howling gale into a caressing breeze, he now decorates the gale with all the tested and approved circulation getters. This editorial appeared in a Florida daily in September 1937:

> The widest of publicity is being given anything that even looks like it might turn into a tropical disturbance or hurricane. Which is well. The old system of hushing up storm news really did more harm than good in that often a community was not warned sufficiently of an approaching storm's perils until it was too late. Now an efficient storm warning service gives ample time to board up windows and otherwise prepare for these autumnal visitations of what used to be called the gentle zephyrs.

Flamboyant claims have mostly given way to constructive criticism of local affairs. Among the beneficial reforms resulting from this criticism are medical examination of food handlers and a more outspoken approach to the problem of venereal diseases.

The mechanical makeup, syndicate features, wire service, editorial dress, and general appearance of the Florida papers, introduced in the early 1920's during real-estate booms, has been retained. In 1925–26, the Miami *Herald* carried more advertising lineage than any newspaper in the world for that period, and the St.Petersburg *Times* ran a close second. The world's largest single edition of a standard-size newspaper was published by the Miami *Daily News* July 26, 1925, with 504 pages, weighing 7½ pounds. Many of the great presses that were brought in still operate in the larger cities. Frequent suspension or relocation of newspapers followed the collapse of real-estate prices, although several of the surviving publishers invested in more elaborate buildings and equipment.

Many of the city dailies of Florida have special issues, called 'star editions,' that carry from one to three pages of Negro news of schools, churches, clubs, and other social and civic activities. The Negroes publish five weekly papers in the State, the Miami *Times*, the St.Petersburg *Public Informer*, the Tampa *Bulletin*, the West Palm Beach *Florida News*, and the St.Augustine *Post*.

Among the labor newspapers, all weeklies, are the *Labor Journal* of Jacksonville, the *Advocate* of St.Petersburg, the *Florida Labor Advocate* of Tampa, and the *Union Labor News* of West Palm Beach (*see Labor*).

The Latin-American colony of Tampa supports two daily papers published in Spanish: *La Gaceta* and *La Prensa-La Traducción*. These folk also subscribe heavily to Cuban newspapers. The only other foreign language paper in the State, the weekly *Florida Deutsches Echo* of Miami, is published in German and English.

The number of daily newspapers in Florida has steadily increased since 1880 when only three existed. In 1899, there were 11 dailies. By 1919, the number had risen to 35, and at the end of 1938 a total of 41 was being published in 31 cities. These dailies with 21 Sunday editions had a combined daily and Sunday circulation of 761,000. For 1937, the weekly papers, totaling 153, covered 127 towns and cities, and had a combined circulation of approximately 240,000. Publishers of the dailies and many of the weeklies are organized into the Florida State Press Association. The Suwannee River Press Association is a smaller organization of west Florida newspaper owners.

In 1938, the *Florida Newspaper News*, a journal devoted to the newspaper profession, listed 20 papers of continuous publication over half a century, although many of them had undergone change of name and ownership in that time. These publications appear in Jacksonville, Ocala, Jasper, Palatka, Lake City, Leesburg, Starke, Gainesville, Titusville, Bushnell, Key West, Eustis, Live Oak, Plant City, St.Petersburg, Fernandina, Taveres, Mayo, and Pensacola.

RADIO: Florida's part in the development of the radio broadcasting systems began in 1921, when station WQAM at Miami went on the air. Nearly a score of public and private stations were in operation in 1938.

WJAX, in Jacksonville, and WSUN, in St.Petersburg, are municipally owned; WRUF, operated by the University of Florida in Gainesville, is owned by the State and has been rated by the Federal Communications Commission as one of the four leading educational stations in the country. Not dependent upon commercial programs, WRUF is able to give broadcasts of public information and instruction, including daily market reports to farmers, police reports, lectures on home economics and the domestic sciences, and courses in music appreciation, elocution, and child psychology. Fourteen of its staff of 18 employees in 1938 were students in training for radio careers.

Fourteen privately-owned radio stations broadcast from the larger cities of the State, and two of these, in Palm Beach and Tampa, are equipped for ship-to-shore communications. Federal stations at Jupiter, St.Augustine, Key West, and Pensacola are engaged in handling naval messages. The United States Coast Guard has ship-to-shore stations at Jacksonville Beach and Fort Lauderdale, and stations at Miami and St.Petersburg for communications with aircraft. During the winter season a number of radio stations designed to carry Federal frost warnings broadcast special temperature bulletins to citrus and truck farmers whenever there is a possibility of a frost. The U.S. Department of Commerce maintains a network of seven short-wave stations in Florida, which are used to broadcast climatic changes to aircraft pilots and weather bureaus.

In co-operation with station WRUF at Gainesville, and the University of Florida's engineering college, a hurricane research station of the WPA maintains short-wave radio communication with Puerto Rico. By photographing static, the Gainesville station is able to determine the approximate location, direction, and speed of hurricanes, and to forecast when and where they can be expected to strike. When a hurricane impends, bulletins are broadcast hourly as long as there is danger.

Folklore

THE folklore of Florida is in great measure a heritage from the 'cracker,' the Negro, the Latin-American, and the Seminole. From these four strains has been woven a pattern of beliefs and superstitions that dictate many of the ways of Florida life.

The cracker, a pioneer backwoods settler of Georgia and Florida, has come to be known as a gaunt, shiftless person, but originally the term meant simply a native, regardless of his circumstances. Belief that the name may have been shortened from 'corn cracker' is given credence in Georgia, but in Florida it derives from the cracking of a whip. It is a name honorably earned by those who made bold talk with their lengthy, rawhide bullwhips in the days when timber and turpentine were the State's chief industries. Those enterprises involved heavy-haul jobs, with oxen the motive power, bullwhips to keep them moving, and the pistol-shot crack of these whips to signal the wearisome progress of the haul through the woods. Cracking the whip became, in fact, an art and a means of communication—an art of making a noise without permitting the whip to touch the animals, and a signal system by which conversations were held across miles of timber barrens. Today the whip crack echoes through the pines only when cowboys are rounding up their herds, and at rodeos and barbecues when the crackers demonstrate their skill.

The cracker's wants are simple—his garden plot, pigpen, chicken coop, and the surrounding woods and near-by streams supply him and his family with nearly all the living necessities. Fish is an important item of diet, and when the cracker is satiated with it he has been heard to say: 'I done et so free o' fish, my stommick rises and falls with the tide.' Any small income from his place is spent at the general store, and Saturday is the day to go to town and stock up with 'bought vittles.' His one luxury is tobacco. Snuff-dipping is still prevalent among the older womenfolk, though they scorn cigarettes as immoral.

Teas and brews from native plants and herbs supply remedies for most of the cracker's ills, although few households are complete without a drug-store malaria medicine, usually a volatile draught of cathartic and quinine to cure 'break-bone' fever. Panther oil, when it can be obtained, is prized for easing stiff joints and rheumatism.

Superstition rules the life of the cracker; hunting or fishing or planting—almost everything he undertakes—is done according to accepted formula. He would no more set fence posts in the light of the moon than he would plant potatoes or other crops that mature underground.

Any windfall, or a considerable profit from crops, goes for an automobile, preferably a Ford, since the old Model T proved to be the most trustworthy on woods trails. His economic status therefore is known by his transportation, which falls into four categories: mule, Model T, Model A, and V-8; but the garage is the same, an open shed or lean-to.

Experience taught the cracker to resent intrusion and be suspicious of unfamiliar things and persons, particularly strangers who do not speak his idiom. Anyone approaching with a 'How do you do?' is likely to be answered by an eloquent and disdainful expectoration. Generations of contact with hardship and poverty have made him undemonstrative, and he seldom displays any but the strongest emotions. He has appropriated the defensive guile of the Negro and turned it to good account in his dealings. Consequently he drives a hard bargain with soft words. The Yankee is his special prey and to best a Yankee by any device is legitimate. 'In the winter,' the cracker boasts, 'we live on the Yankee, and in the summer on fish.' Yet with all his bargaining craft, he is often cheated.

The Florida cracker has a fondness for social gatherings and for his kinfolks. The latter being numerous as a rule, and observance of birthday and wedding anniversaries being an inviolate custom, occasions for celebrating are frequent. Quiltings and hog-killings serve equally well for neighborhood get-togethers, but a chicken pilau is perhaps the most appetizing excuse for an outing. The men build fires and put on large pots of rice; the women clean and boil chickens. Later, chicken and rice are cooked together with rich seasoning. While this goes on, the men may go hunting and fishing, or just sit and swap news. Also, the Sunday preaching may be prolonged into an all-day 'sing' or picnic on the church grounds.

The speech of the cracker is a mixture of Old English provincialisms, local slang, and a variety of home-invented words, including 'Heifer on my haslet,' meaning 'Well, I'll be damned!' Orthodox 'cussing,' however, when occasion seems to demand, attains a scope and degree of inflection that blight any hope of imitation. The cracker's humor, for the most part, originated from the limitations and hazards of his existence, and so he may declare that 'I done drunk outa fruit jars so long I got a ridge acrost my nose.'

With more embellishments, there is the cattle-country story of Burwell Yates and the syrup kettle. 'One time,' the tale goes, 'Yates loant his syrup kettle to Bill Stevens down at Ox Pond. Bill kept the kettle for three years, so finally Yates drove down to get it. Bill's wife warn't goin' to let him have it and took to squalling, so Yates grabs him a cypress shingle, gets after her, and takes the kettle anyway. When Bill Stevens hears this he takes down his shot gun, straddles his hoss, and sets out for Canoe Creek to see Yates. When Bill gets there, Yates is drivin' a nail in a porch post to hang up a bridle. Bill throws up his gun and pulls the trigger, and the load cuts a staple fork out of Yates' ear and ruins his hearin'. A year later one of the Partins from Fort Christmas is a huntin' for stray cattle, but none of the boys admits they'd seed any till Elmer Johns asks about their mark. "Staple fork in the right ear," says the Partins. "That's different," says Elmer. "They's a old deef bull with that mark ranging up around Canoe Creek."'

Long before the advent of the white man in America, West Indian natives made expeditions to Florida in the belief that one of its many springs held miraculous properties, and so the myth of the Fountain of Youth was current here when early European maps, drawn before Columbus sailed from Spain, located a similar spring in the Far East.

Eternal youth was not to be found in the crystal depths of Florida's springs, but their mysterious caverns provided a source of much lore among the now-extinct Indian tribes. From them came water gods and many legends. One legend was that on moonlight nights hundreds of little people only four inches in height came and danced around the deeply submerged inflow of Wakulla springs until a huge Indian warrior in a stone canoe appeared to drive them away—an illusion perhaps created by waving water plants and the moving shadow from a projecting rock in the springs. Scores of these legends, collected in book form, give a romantic overtone to the wonders viewed by tourists through glass-bottomed boats.

The Seminole, who moved into Florida after the white man, brought more practical beliefs and applied them to his daily life. The making of a dugout canoe is still attended by great ceremony. After a powwow in camp, the leader guides his tribe into the swamp to select the cypress tree that is to be converted into a *pich-li*, a craft often 30 feet long. Singing and dancing take place around the tree; then the men selected for the task fell the tree, remove the branches and bark, and bury the *ash-a-vee* (cypress log) in a wet mud bank where it is left for 18 months to age. The unearthing of the log involves more ceremony and feasting. After about a week of drying, work begins on shaping and hollowing out with a *pit-a-chen-a-lo-*

gee, which resembles a hand adz. As the work progresses the children join in, squatting around the canoe and beating on it with sticks. From the sound of this tattoo the cutters can tell when the desired thinness has been obtained.

Seminole beliefs are largely associated with warnings; to places and objects strange powers are attributed, and portents are seen in many things. The blooming of the sawgrass in the Everglades is notice of a forthcoming hurricane, and the Seminole thereupon migrates to higher ground. This belief has been widely accepted by white men, even though the sawgrass is known to bloom regularly without regard to tropical storms.

Since voodooism is an unwritten form of the occult, it varies greatly according to the environment. Its commonest exponent is the 'root doctor.' His medications may run from harmless nostrums to lethal powders, the latter to be given an enemy with appropriate abracadabra. A side line is usually amulets and charms. In Jacksonville a 'conjure' shop does a thriving business in trinkets and devices for warding off evil and illness. For the same purpose drugstores in the Negro section of Miami stock such ingredients as Guinea pepper, rock incense, sandalwood, and Irish moss. For those adhering to Hispano-Christian beliefs, a heart-shaped scrap of red flannel is dispensed as the 'Sacred Heart of Jesus.' Placed on the bed of the afflicted, it is supposed to work a cure or at least delay death.

The placing or removal of cures and the dispersion of evil spirits often develops into a profitable business. In 1936, a Negro voodoo doctor named Brundas Hartwell was reported to be rendering such services to the credulous people of his race at Chester, near Fernandina. At the rate of $25 a treatment he stripped his patients and burned their clothes, then immersed them in a creek and 'cussed' the evil spirits out of them.

In the vegetable muck lands around Okeechobee, Negro bean pickers from the Bahamas and the West Indies indulge in voodoo ceremonials and dances, and at night the rhythmic throb of the tom-tom spreads to the far horizons of the Everglades. These manifestations are sincere and far removed from curious eyes. Voodoo rituals in Tampa have been witnessed up to their ultimate frenzies, from which outsiders are excluded.

Although lucky pieces, powders, and potents are made in Tampa to expedite matters of love, finance, and health, many articles of this nature are imported by salesmen who solicit from door to door. Widely popular is a cone of incense which, when burned, reveals in the ash at its base a number supposed to foretell the current bolita winner. Bolita, introduced to Tampa by the Cubans in the 1880's, means 'little ball.' A hundred balls, consecutively numbered, are tied in a bag and tossed from one person to another. One ball is clutched through the cloth and this bears the winning number. Played by Negroes and whites alike in Jacksonville, Key West, Miami, Tampa, and surrounding towns, bolita has sponsored a great variety of superstitions. Some of these, traceable to the Chinese, who brought the game to Cuba, include Oriental interpretations of dreams. As a result the sale of all dream books as well as publications on astrology and numerology has boomed. For thousands of Tampa folk bolita has invested nearly all the commonplace occurrences of life with the symbolism of figures. House addresses, auto licenses, theater stubs, steps, telephone poles, or anything that can be counted, added, subtracted, or divided, are grist for bolita. Equipped with the additional resources of voodooism, the Cuban Negro can begin with virtually any incident and arrive at a bolita number. He is equally adroit at explaining his miscalculations.

The Afro-American Negro has similar sources to explain many of his troubles. 'Witches have been ridin' me all night' may account for his morning-after 'miseries.' Burning paper in the corners of a room is thought to be a help in such cases, but a more effective way to thwart a witch is to use her own weapon, a broom. If the broom is placed across the doorway to a sleeping room, the witch must stop and pluck the straws one by one before she can enter, a task almost impossible to finish before daylight. A still more ingenious handicap is to cover the floor with mustard seed, all of which must be picked up before the witch can reach the bed.

Muscular prowess is a tradition with the Negro, and feats of strength have become an important part of his lore. Long before Roark Bradford developed John Henry into a black Paul Bunyan, Old Pete, a railroad roustabout, was performing physical miracles at Port Tampa. Christened Henry Peterson, Old Pete set the pace for Bradford's character. For 5¢ he would permit coconuts to be cracked on his skull, and for 50¢ he would engage a goat in a butting contest. Reputed to have a skull an inch thick, Old Pete is said to have fallen asleep on a railroad track and derailed a freight car. After the front wheels had passed over his cranium, fellow workers rushed forward and dragged the 'body' from the tracks. This aroused Old Pete, and when informed what had happened, he rubbed his eyes, yawned and remarked, 'Dawg-gone, my haid do feel kinda funny.' Old Pete's fame has since expanded greatly in the telling. Among other feats he used a ship's anchor for a pickaxe, lifted a locomotive back on the rails, and pulled up a tree by the roots, 'toted' it home, and chopped it into four cords of firewood. He died in 1934 at the age of seventy-seven.

A legend of a different kind, fraught with realistic dread, was the renewal of life years ago in a mulberry tree, which is said to have taken place in the town of Mulberry. Negroes there say the place received its name from this particular tree. It was the custom of lynch mobs, the story goes, to hang the victims from this tree and then riddle their bodies with bullets. This gunfire finally killed the tree. For many years it stood bare and apparently dead, until one spring it again sprouted leaves. The news spread rapidly among Negroes, who saw in it an omen of more lynchings, and many of them fled to other sections. In 1938, the hollow and battered trunk still supported a live bough, but further lynchings had not yet occurred.

To the Florida Negro is attributed the coinage of the word 'jook,' now in general use among Florida white people. First applied to Negro dance halls around turpentine camps, the term was expanded with the repeal of prohibition to include roadside dine-dance places, and now to go 'jooking' means to attend any night club. Will McGuire, in his 'Note on Jook,' published in the *Florida Review*, says the word was originally applied to Negro bawdy houses. It gained legal recognition in connection with a murder case in the prairie cattle country of Florida. Witnesses testified that the killing took place in a 'jook joint,' and the term was later incorporated in a State supreme court decision.

From Cuba, Spain, and Italy, the Latin-Americans of Ybor City and Tampa have imported their own customs and traditions which survive mostly in annual festivals. The Cubans found good political use for voodoo beliefs brought by slaves from Africa to the West Indies and there called *Carabali Apapa Abacua*. Prior to the Spanish-American War, Cuban nationalists joined the cult in order to hold secret revolutionary meetings, and it then received the Spanish name, *Nanigo*. In 1882, *Los Criminales de Cuba*, published in Havana by Trujillo Monaga, described Cuban Nanigo societies as fraternal orders engaged in petty politics. Initiation ceremonies were elaborate, with street dances of voodoo origin. Under the concealment of the dances, political enemies were slain; in time the dance came to signify impending murder, and the societies were outlawed by the Cuban Government. When the cigar workers migrated from Cuba to Key West and later to Tampa, societies of 'notorious Nanigoes,' as they were branded by Latin opposition papers, were organized in these two cities. The Nanigo in Key West eventually became a social society that staged a Christmas street dance. A murder during one of these affairs served to dissolve the organization, and the last of the street dances was held in 1923.

Tampa has adopted José Gaspar, the infamous Gasparilla, as its patron rogue, and perpetuates his name in an annual Gasparilla carnival. In celebration of the cigar industry, Latin-Americans in Tampa stage an annual fiesta known as *Verbena del Tabaco.* Cuban, Spanish, and Italian clubs take part, with street dances and strolling entertainers in native costumes. A feature is the famous folk dance of Cuba known as *Comparsa*, originally a slave feast dance from which the rhumba is said to have developed. Other dances include the *Tarantella*, *Danza Montaneza*, *Tango Andalus*, *Fandango*, and *Esemble Fantasia*.

Stories of buried treasure are no doubt the most enticing legacy inherited from the Spanish. Pirates at one time practically controlled the coasts of Florida, and tales of their plundering invariably included caches of loot, hastily buried and lost. Black Caesar and Gasparilla were real enough pirates, but the mystery of their wealth has remained unsolved. Little gold has been recovered by treasure expeditions, but the quest continues.

The Greek sponge fishermen at Tarpon Springs retain many European customs, such as the observance of the Feast of Epiphany, introducing the medieval pageantry of the Greek Orthodox Church, and diving for a golden cross tossed into the waters of Spring Bayou.

The Conchs are a group almost as hard to define as the crackers. Although the term is now applied to anyone living on the Florida Keys, bona fide Conchs at least have in common a Bahaman ancestry. The great majority of those in Florida live in Key West, and are Anglo-Saxon descendants of Cockney Londoners who migrated there via the Bahamas. The Conch colony at Riviera includes persons of mixed Cockney and Negro blood, a result of miscegenation.

After a century of living in Florida, both Conch groups retain much of their Cockney English lore, with an evident Negroid influence apparent at Riviera. One story is an adaptation of Jack-and-the-bean-stalk. A Conch fisherman climbed the stalk to Heaven, only to see the stalk wither and die and leave him stranded there. The virgins in lower Heaven came to his rescue by piecing together their celestial robes to make a rope ladder, but this was not quite long enough and the fisherman had to jump. He landed head first in the sand on the beach and buried himself to the waist. 'There he struggled in vain to get out, but he couldn't manage it. So he went to a near-by barn, got a grubbing hoe, and came back and dug himself out.' And there are riddles and riddling rhymes:

Two O's, two N's, an L and a D,
Put them together and spell them to me.
Answer: L-o-n-d-o-n.

A few mother-country customs still prevail among several small foreign groups. The Austro-Hungarian farm colony in west Florida holds weekly gatherings that perpetuate peasant folk dances; the Swedish settlement in

Dade County observes *Martinmas*, Saint Martin's feast day; and at Korona, near Daytona Beach, Polish families hold a special Easter service. Children carry baskets of flowers to the priest to be blessed; their elders, after being anointed with water and wine, administer to one another a half-dozen lashes.

Literature

WRITINGS with Florida as the theme began to accumulate soon after Ponce de Leon's first voyage in 1513. Peter Martyr, historiographer of Spain in 1520, interviewed returning explorers at the Spanish Court, and wrote of their adventures in Florida and other parts of the New World. Many dignitaries of the Church considered Martyr a vulgarian, but Pope Leo X enjoyed his tales. Because of his intimate style, historians have compared Martyr to Samuel Pepys.

The tragic Florida expeditions of Narvaez and De Soto were recorded by scribes who accompanied the soldiers. Cabeza de Vaca, one of the four survivors of Narvaez' company, wrote a dramatic story of his seven-years' wanderings, and despite De Vaca's boasting and exaggerations, this old chronicle is valuable for its description of Indian life.

The *Relation of the Gentleman of Elvas*, anonymously written by an officer in De Soto's expedition, gave a factual account of the four years' wandering by that ill-fated party in the wilderness. First published in Portuguese in 1557, it was later translated by Richard Hakluyt into English and published in London in 1609 to promote British colonization in America. A recent translation was made by James A. Robertson, and issued in 1932 in a limited edition by the Florida State Historical Society.

An account of the De Soto expedition by Garcilaso de la Vega, based on stories related by members of the party, was a much more fanciful version, picturing battles with howling savages and encounters with pearl-bedecked princesses. Written by a Spanish historian born the year after De Soto helped Pizarro sack Peru, this book was described by Robert Southey as 'one of the most delightful narratives in the Spanish language.' Its material has been freely used by historical writers, including Grace King in her book on De Soto, but no complete translation into English existed until 1938, when one was made for the De Soto Commission that had been appointed by President Roosevelt to determine the landing place in Florida of the old Spanish explorer and his route through the southern United States.

During the attempted settlement of Florida by the French, there were memoirs, journals, and letters in great number, many of them written for the purpose of confounding the Spanish accounts of unsuccessful French ventures. One of the best is *The Memoir of Challeux*, published in 1566. After escaping from Fort Caroline during an attack by the Spanish, Challeux recalled the massacre and subsequent events, mixing fact, fancy, and argumentation in a way that revealed the author as keenly observant, sensitive, and definitely inclined to moralizing.

The letters of René de Laudonnière, the French commander, in his *Notable History of Florida*, edited in 1586 by M.Martine Basanier, told of the voyage of Ribaut, the building of Fort Caroline, and its destruction by the Spanish. Laudonnière also drew an apparently faithful word picture of the Timucuan tribes as they existed during the French occupation, and thereby preserved priceless information about a vanished race.

As early as the sixteenth century, English sea dogs made sport of French and Spanish accounts of Florida. Persons overcredulous of the riches and adventure to be found here were told facetiously to disregard 'pirates, or the natives, or the alligators, or the Spaniards,' and the country was referred to as 'Stolida, the Land of Fools,' and 'Sordida, the Land of Muckworms.' Here (from the Ashmolean Manuscript in the Bodleian Library at Oxford, England) is a tipsy sailor, talking to a friend in a tavern:

Have you not hard of floryda,
  A coontre far bewest,
Where savage pepell planted are
  By nature and by hest,
Who in the mold
  Fynd glysterynge gold
And yet for tryfels sell?
  with hy!

Yet all alonge the watere syde,
  Where yt dotne eb and flowe,
Are turkeyse founde and where also
  Do perles in oysteres growe,
And on the land
  Do cedars stand
Whose bewty do (th) excell
  with hy!
trysky, trym, go trysky wun
  not a wallet do well?

Divers Voyages Touching the Discoveries of America, more familiarly known as *Hakluyt's Voyages*, collected by Richard Hakluyt and published in 1582, contains the first descriptions of North America in the English language and is written in excellent Elizabethan prose. The author of 'one Voyage,' John Sparke, a shipmate of Sir John Hawkins when the two adventurers stopped at Fort Caroline in 1565, comments on the queerness of

Frenchmen who smoked tobacco. The *Voyages* contains an account of Sir Francis Drake's descent upon St.Augustine and a description of Florida, written by Pedro Morales, a Spaniard captured by Drake.

Spanish missionaries, during their flourishing days, produced some scholarly writing in the precise ethnic records which they kept while trying to convert the Indians. In books published in Mexico as early as 1612, Father Pareja, one of these resident missionary authors, relates the customs of the Timucuan Indians. Through his study of Indian dialects he was able to write the first treatise on American Indian languages ever published. Pareja's writings rank with the rarest and most valuable of Americana.

Jonathan Dickenson, a member of a group of Quakers shipwrecked near Hobe Sound on the east coast of Florida in 1696, converted this experience into a book, *God's Protecting Providence*, published in 1720, which ran through many editions. Seized by the Indians, who stripped them of their clothes, the party of men, women, and children finally reached St.Augustine after months of hardship in the wilderness. Describing the Indians, Dickenson wrote, 'When these men-eaters' fury was at its height, their knives in one hand, and the poor ship-wrecked peoples' heads in the other, their knees upon their shoulders, and their looks dismal; on a sudden, the savages were struck dumb, and their countenances changed. . . .' This change, which saved their lives, Dickenson attributed to God's protecting providence.

When England gained control of Florida, the British people evinced a lively curiosity in the new colony, and books and pamphlets on the subject began to appear in London. In the year of the cession, 1763, *An Account of the First Discovery and Natural History of Florida* was written by William Roberts in collaboration with the English Geographer Royal. Although of slight literary value, the work met with enough success and public praise to run through several editions. Florida's natural history, despite the name of the book, is mentioned nowhere except on the title page.

John Bartram, a Pennsylvania Quaker whom Linnaeus called 'the greatest botanist in the New World,' published a journal of his Florida travels, later included in William Stork's *An Account of East-Florida with a Journal by John Bartram* (1776). His son William, who accompanied him, was a more facile writer and had a wider range of interests. The son returned to Florida alone a decade later, and wrote his famous *Travels*, which has gone through many editions, the latest published in 1928. William Bartram's book drew the attention of the English literary world. Samuel Taylor Coleridge called it the last book 'written in the spirit of the old travellers.' From Bartram, William Wordsworth derived his 'Seminolies,' and Coleridge, it is thought, was indebted to the *Travels* for some of the imagery in *Kubla Khan*:

> Where Alph, the sacred river, ran
> Through caverns measureless to man
> Down to a sunless sea.

Preserved in the Harvard Library is a lengthy manuscript by William Gerard de Brahm, which contains many comments on Florida during the English occupation and provides an especially good description of the customs and people of St.Augustine from 1763 to 1771. De Brahm was the British surveyor for the southern district of North America. In detailing for George III the fruits of his labor, he displayed a rich fund of scientific knowledge; but his dogmatic interpretations somewhat mar an otherwise delightful report.

Bernard Romans' *Natural History of East and West Florida*, written during the English occupation and published in 1775, has been widely accepted as a standard authority on the manners and customs of eighteenth-century Florida. Romans, who worked as a draftsman in De Brahm's surveying party, produced a book of greater literary merit than that of his employer. Although the personal pronoun 'I' is written throughout Romans' book as 'i,' the author's egotism remains undisguised. Discursive, original, and occasionally bombastic, Romans boldly presents many biased opinions. Practices among the Indians that he judged abnormal drew his attention particularly.

Romans' picture of Dr.Andrew Turnbull, the English colonizer, as a harsh exploiter of defenseless humanity, has largely set the pattern for subsequent writers dealing with the mutinous New Smyrna Colony. This account apparently was the basis of Stephen Vincent Benét's novel, *Spanish Bayonet* (1926), which has to do with the ruthless treatment by English masters of Minorcan, Italian, and Greek colonists. A different version of this pre-Revolution misadventure is *Dr.Andrew Turnbull and the New Smyrna Colony* (1919), by Carita Doggett Corse, a history based on hitherto unpublished original documents and letters, known as the Shelburne papers. According to this account, Turnbull's troubles were manifold, between trying to hold in check more recruits than he had bargained for and making trips to England in an effort to protect his land contracts, which were threatened by political shifts in the government there. While he was absent on one of these excursions, members of the colony, incited by political enemies, burned the settlement and marched to St.Augustine, where a Minorcan group remained to become pioneers of the present city.

Florida was nearly barren of literary men during the second period of

Spanish control, 1783–1821. Cultured travelers in the province were rare, and intelligent interests were directed more toward land grant disputes and difficulties between the United States and Spain in regard to boundaries, than to the production of prose or poetry. The bulk of Florida writing for these years is found in current Government documents, ponderous and didactic.

An immediate, widespread demand for information regarding the new Territory was created when the United States acquired Florida in 1821. The same year saw the publication of *Sketches of the History and Topography of Florida*, written by James Grant Forbes, an authority on the Territory because of his travels and his familiarity with many unpublished documents relating to it. His book, according to Daniel G. Brinton, the famous American archeologist and ethnologist, received much praise at the time of its publication, but was later unjustly denounced as a 'wretched compilation from old works.' An anonymous work, *Notices of East Florida with an Account of the Seminole Nation of Indians*, was published the following year (1822) in Charleston. It contained a minutely descriptive diary of a journey through northern Florida, and an account of the Seminole Indians, with a vocabulary of their language. It was later learned that the writer was Dr. William H. Simmons, one of the two commissioners appointed to select the site of a capital for the Territory of Florida. Many of Dr. Simmons' predictions concerning Florida and its future have proved remarkably accurate, especially in regard to the development of population centers.

One of the fullest accounts of this period was written by Colonel John Lee Williams, the other commissioner chosen to select the capital site. His *View of West Florida* (1827) and *Territory of Florida* (1837), descriptions of the eastern section, were the result of years of laborious investigation and difficult travel. Surprisingly, in view of his extensive knowledge of the Territory, Colonel Williams doubted the existence of Lake Okeechobee and neglected to place it on a map of Florida which he prepared.

In the 1820's, St. Augustine became a rendezvous for travelers, artists, and magazine writers from the North. Many pages of diaries, periodicals, and personal letters were filled with praise of the city's climatic and architectural charms. Ralph Waldo Emerson visited there in 1827 to recover his health and, upon returning home, wrote in gratitude the poem beginning:

> There liest thou, little city of the deep,
> And always hearest the unceasing sound
> By day and night, in summer and in frost,
> The roar of waters on thy coral shore.

Another distinguished visitor, Washington Irving, wrote a lifelike sketch of Florida's first Territorial Governor, William P. Duval, who was his stagecoach companion during one summer. In this short piece, 'Early Experiences of Ralph Ringwood,' Irving incorporated some of the Governor's witticisms and anecdotes.

Prince Achille Murat, eccentric nephew of Napoleon, settled on a plantation near Tallahassee, where he wrote *A Moral and Political Sketch of the United States of North America* (1833). This titled immigrant filled his book with dissertations on American customs, expressing an especially great surprise at the American enthusiasm for voting. Any astonishment that Prince Murat felt in regard to the customs of his Florida neighbors must have been equaled by their amazement at his omniverous appetite, if stories concerning him are true. It is reported that he would eat anything that crawled, swam, or flew, except, as he declared, 'ze turkey boozard, and she are no good.'

About the same time, John James Audubon, the great ornithologist, made a rich contribution to the knowledge of the customs and natural history of Florida through letters written while traveling here in the winter of 1831–32. These brilliant, yet simply written, descriptions of the Territory appear in the first three volumes of his *Ornithological Biographie* (1831–35).

Indian warfare in Florida during the first half of the nineteenth century has been a favorite subject for many writers, whose treatment of the matter varies greatly in point of view and in degree of literary and historical value. Captain John T. Sprague's *The Origin, Progress and Conclusion of the Florida War*, published in 1848, is accepted by historians as a standard authority on the 1835–42 period. An active participant in the Seminole War, Captain Sprague drew a vigorous pen-portrait of this bloody conflict, remarkably impartial for one who was personally concerned in its prosecution.

Another account of the American conquest of the Seminole and their Negro allies, *The Exiles of Florida* (1858) by Joshua R. Giddings, closely approaches the standards of belles-lettres. Including a history of the runaway slaves who found asylum in Spanish Florida early in 1800, Giddings' work is a plea for understanding of the Negroes who intermarried with and became allies of Indians in the long struggle against white authority. Because of the strongly partisan tone of the book, critics have differed widely in evaluating it.

Two noteworthy contributions were made to Florida travel description in 1850, when William Cullen Bryant's *Letters of a Traveller* and Charles

Lanman's *Haw-Ho-Noo, or, Records of a Tourist* were published. Bryant, in cool, severe prose, described northern Florida and St.Augustine, where he had sojourned for a period; while Lanman's work is an ingratiating collection of stories about Florida fishing, rattlesnakes, barbecues, and local customs.

Daniel G. Brinton in his *Notes on the Floridian Peninsula, Its Literary History, Indian Tribes and Antiquities*, published in 1859, added new material to Florida literature, which up to that time had been devoted mainly to the fields of history, war, personal reminiscences, and travel. Brinton, who later became president of the American Association for the Advancement of Science, by virtue of diligent research and capable presentation of his material, provided an excellent bibliography of books on Florida. Alvan Wentworth Chapman further broadened the field of Florida literature with his *Flora of the Southern United States*, published in 1860 and still considered an authoritative volume.

Historical works regained their popularity in 1868 when Theodore Irving's *Conquest of Florida* was published. This nephew of Washington Irving used a graceful, flowing style for his history of De Soto's expedition. The book has the dramatic force, sustained interest, subtle humor, and sharp character delineation of a well-constructed novel. De Soto's march through Florida also fills three lengthy chapters of George R. Fairbanks' *History of Florida* (1871), a lucid book that covers the period from 1513 to the conclusion of the second Seminole War in 1842. Fairbanks' *The History and Antiquities of St. Augustine* (1858) tells of the establishment of French and Spanish settlements, the activities of Spain in Florida, and the gradual growth of St.Augustine.

A few years after the War between the States, Harriet Beecher Stowe, author of *Uncle Tom's Cabin*, made her home in Mandarin on the St.Johns River. It was here in the turbulent Reconstruction Period that she wrote *Palmetto Leaves* (1873), a volume of tranquil sketches describing this section and its people. Other writings published during Reconstruction were for the most part violent polemics.

In 1875, a railway line commissioned the Georgia poet, Sidney Lanier, a visitor in Jacksonville (then a village of 8,000), to write a guidebook of the State. His *Florida, Its Scenery, Climate and History*, published in 1876, in spite of the fact that it is the work of a poet writing prose under the stress of financial necessity, has Lanier's characteristic charm of expression.

Barnard Shipp's *The History of Hernando de Soto and Florida*, published in 1881, was the most comprehensive work up to that time on the life of this dashing explorer.

Constance Fenimore Woolson (1848–94), one of the first American writers to use local color in her novels, lived in Florida for several years, where she wrote articles for various periodicals. In 'The Ancient City,' a lengthy travel article, she described a trip from New York to Jacksonville and Tocoi, and thence by mule-train to St.Augustine. In *East Angels*, a novel published in 1886, she pictures the effect upon human personality of the exotic surroundings of St.Augustine.

Tallahassee, with its hills and prim customs, in no sense exotic, is the scene of Maurice Thompson's novel, *A Tallahassee Girl* (1881). The supposition is that the title was inspired by the sight of a graceful young lady, probably the daughter of Governor Call, strolling on the grounds of the executive mansion.

Kirk Munroe drew upon Florida's rich historical background for material for several of his most popular books. *Flamingo Feather* (1887) is a quasi-historical novel of the Spanish period in the sixteenth century; his novel of adventure, *The Coral Ship* (1893), is a tale of the Florida Reef. Munroe settled at Cocoanut Grove, and there re-created the Florida country as a setting for many of his stories for boys.

Stephen Crane visited Florida shortly after his Civil War story, *The Red Badge of Courage* (1895), had lifted him from obscurity to international fame. Crane lived in Jacksonville for a while and there met Cora Taylor, who later nursed him through a serious illness and became his wife. Prior to the Spanish-American War, Crane went on a filibustering expedition to Cuba in 1896. He was shipwrecked off the Florida coast, and this experience formed the basis of one of his greatest short stories, 'The Open Boat,' published in 1898.

At the beginning of the twentieth century George Gibbs wrote *In Search of Mademoiselle*, a swashbuckling tale of the struggle between Spanish and French colonists for dominion over Florida. The plot chosen by Eugene O'Neill in 1923 for his play, *The Fountain*, also employed Florida as locale, Ponce de Leon for the central character, and the fantasy of the fountain of youth as a theme. In the early 1930's, Robert W. Chambers directed his attention to Fernandina and the slave-smuggling days for a series of stories.

The beginning of the twentieth century brought more historical works. Woodbury Lowery published in 1901 *The Spanish Settlements within the Present Limits of the United States*, 1513–61, a scholarly résumé of that period; and in 1905 a second book, *Spanish Settlements within the Present Limits of the United States: Florida*, 1562–74. In this same year Edward Gaylord Bourne, professor of history at Yale University, brought forth the

Narrative of the Career of Hernândo de Soto in the Conquest of Florida, a compilation of practically all the source materials on the discoverer of the Mississippi River. A monograph, *The Civil War and Reconstruction in Florida* by William Watson Davis, a painstaking history of a tragic and sordid era, appeared in 1913. *Flight into Oblivion* (1938), by Professor A.J.Hanna of Rollins College, is a well-documented account of the experiences in Florida and elsewhere of Confederate officials and army officers who fled their posts after Lee's surrender at Appomatox.

The Florida Historical Society publishes an interesting quarterly and gives valuable assistance to Florida historians. Another organization, the Florida State Historical Society, published in 1923 *Pedro Menendez de Aviles* by Jeannette Thurber Connor, a biography of the man who founded St.Augustine and developed the Spanish claims to the Atlantic seaboard.

Charles Torrey Simpson, Florida naturalist, shows literary talent comparable to his recognized ability as a scientist in his account of tropical Florida, *In Lower Florida Wilds* (1920). His *Out of Doors in Florida* (1923) contains a series of essays on flora, fauna, and geology, and his *Florida Wild Life* (1932) covers the same subjects with particular attention to climate and environment.

Contemporary writers, native and transient, have explored the gilded coast resorts, or sought near-by extremes in primitive surroundings. Palm Beach, symbol of wealth and exclusiveness, has lured both the literary sophisticate and the sociological writer. Elmer Davis summarized his impressions in *White Pants Willie* (1932). Joseph Hergesheimer, a master of surface detail, paid the resort meticulous attention in his *Tropical Winter* (1933), in which he skillfully enumerated the superficialities of those who make play a serious occupation. Arthur Somers Roche appropriated Palm Beach to give his murder mysteries a resplendent setting, while his wife, Ethel Pettit, in her book *Move Over* (1927) revealed absurdities of the 'small talk' among the wealthy. Few writers who have developed a well-known character leave him behind when they visit Florida, and the character inevitably invades Palm Beach. Even Porky Neale, a phlegmatic detective accustomed to the New York slums, was allowed a season of sleuthing there by his creator, Roland Phillips.

The west coast of Florida, equally important as a resort section, has inspired different treatment and subjects. Spring training camps of major-league ball teams, particularly the St.Petersburg headquarters of the New York Yankees, have been used as background by Heywood Broun, Grantland Rice, Quentin Reynolds, and many more. Ring Lardner's 'Golden

Wedding,' considered by some critics his greatest short story, was a St.Petersburg tale.

Sewell Ford, who wrote the 'Shorty McCabe' and 'Torchy' stories, lived for many years at Clearwater. Edison Marshall has a winter home at Perry, but seldom writes of Florida. Eustace Adams at Tarpon Springs has used the Greek sponge fleet for numerous stories, and Charles Rawlings' *The Dance of the Bends* is also a story of the Greek sponge fishers.

Rex Beach, who grows bulbs and celery at Sebring, has written two Florida novels, *The Mating Call* (1927) and *Wild Pastures* (1935), both well removed from the resorts. Earl Derr Biggers' novel, *Love Insurance* (1914), is a romance of St.Augustine. Edwin Granberry brings the flavor of mysticism into his St.Augustine story, *Erl King* (1930). Far different is Granberry's *Strangers and Lovers* (1928), a tale of the south Florida cattle country dealing with a girl's struggle against the brutality of her environment. Equally distant from familiar resort trimmings is Percival Wilde's psychological novel, *There Is a Tide* (1932). Irving Addison Bacheller, of Winter Park, exposes in *Uncle Peel* (1933) the injustice done to Florida by real-estate gamblers of the boom period, who 'left the State loaded with debts incurred for their benefits.'

Merian C. Cooper of Jacksonville, globe-trotter and soldier of fortune, made literary use of some of his experiences in *Grass* (1925), which is the story of an epic migration of the Baktyari tribe across the lofty mountains of Persia. John Anderson, New York dramatic critic, born at Pensacola, has written two books, *Box Office* (1929), a critical survey of the theater, and *The American Theater* (1938), a history.

Writers of post-boom Florida tend to avoid the beaten tracks of the tourist, and by so doing have uncovered parts of Florida little changed from pioneer days. Marjorie Kinnan Rawlings has practically staked out a domain of her own, the interior scrub country and its elemental people, in her three novels, *South Moon Under* (1933), *Golden Apples* (1935), and *The Yearling* (1938). Her faithful reproduction of 'cracker' speech and backwoods customs, destined soon to disappear with the invasion of modern highways, becomes a presentation of the conflict between man and nature. The State's wood lore and wild life is, in *The Yearling*, unfolded before the eyes of a sensitive youth who achieves maturity through his acceptance of nature on its own terms. *The Yearling* was awarded the Pulitzer Prize in 1939.

MacKinlay Kantor, in *The Noise of Their Wings* (1938), with the vanished passenger pigeon as his subordinate theme, penetrates the Ten Thousand Islands in south Florida, and shows the disastrous impact of sudden wealth on a primitive fisherman. T.S.Stribling in a short story, 'Yankees Don't Know Nothin',' developed in serio-comic style the efforts of the flatwoods dwellers in northwest Florida to 'go industrial' along with the pulp mills.

Ernest Hemingway used Key West, where his home is located, as a background for *To Have and Have Not* (1937), a novel of uncompromising realism. The life of Harry Morgan, the book's central character, pictures the path that leads from unrelieved poverty to lawlessness. Hemingway strengthens his moral by the device of contrasting decadent wealthy visitors (those who have) and native Key West families (those who have not). In a powerful climax Morgan realizes that his 'rugged individualism' contributed to his defeat and death. Many of Hemingway's short stories and magazine articles also have had a Key West setting, and his Spanish writings have been finished here between visits to Madrid.

The Negro's part in Florida literature has progressed from the simple recording of slave days to thoughtful self-expression. In the 1840's, Jonathan Walker, a white carpenter, tried before a Pensacola court and found guilty of abducting slaves, wrote an eloquent account of his misfortunes and of the early struggles between slave and free States in the *Trial and Imprisonment of Jonathan Walker*. In addition to a jail sentence, Walker was branded on the right hand with the letters 'SS,' meaning 'Slave Stealer.' The book, published in Boston, was read and widely praised by Abolitionists. Shortly after Walker's release from a Florida jail and his return to Massachusetts, John Greenleaf Whittier wrote an indignant poem, 'The Branded Hand,' in which he eulogized Walker's actions.

Reconstruction days were vividly portrayed in *Carpetbag Rule in Florida* (1888) by John Wallace, a self-educated Jacksonville Negro, who served in the State senate during those tumultuous times. Dispassionately written, the book undertakes to show how the Negro became the pawn of those who professed to befriend him. Wallace was nearly blind when he began to teach himself to read and write.

Jacksonville was the birthplace of another Negro writer, the gifted and versatile James Weldon Johnson, who died in 1938. His *Autobiography of an Ex-Colored Man* (1927), recites the tragic ostracism by the white race of a person with Negro blood, one who was a close friend of Johnson. In *God's Trombones* (1927), a book of seven Negro sermons in verse, Johnson pictures the old-time Negro preacher. *Along This Way* (1933), Johnson's autobiography, illuminates with quiet irony and a wealth of humorous detail his career as lawyer, poet, musical comedy composer, diplomatic official, author, editor, orator, and educator. *Negro Americans, What Now?*

(1934) examines the status of Negro citizens in the United States, and argues that their wisest course is to work as a group toward integration within the Nation.

A widely read contemporary Negro writer, Zora Neale Hurston, resides at Eatonville, Florida's only incorporated Negro town. Her first book, *Jonah's Gourd Vine* (1934), is a simple story about her people. In *Mules and Men* (1935) she presents a collection of Negro songs and an initiate's account of the practices, formulae, and paraphernalia of voodooism. Another work on this subject, *Tell My Horse* (1938), is set in Haiti and Jamaica, where the author took part in native rites. Her novel, *Their Eyes Were Watching God* (1937), reaches its emotional and dramatic climax in a description of a hurricane in the Everglades and its devastating effect on the lives of her characters.

Poets have always been aroused by Florida, and the 'public forum' departments of the State press overflow during the winter with spontaneous verse from exuberant visitors. Several cities have poetry clubs and conduct poetry contests. Wallace Stevens, one of America's best modern poets, is a regular visitor to Florida. *Harmonium*, published in 1923, contains several poems that reflect his appreciation of the special quality of Florida; among these is the characteristic 'Nomad Exquisite':

As the immense dew of Florida
Brings forth
The big-finned palm
And green vine angering for life,

As the immense dew of Florida
Brings forth hymn and hymn
From the beholder,
Beholding all these green sides
And gold sides of green sides,

And blessed mornings,
Meet for the eye of the young alligator,
And lightning colors,
So, in me, come flinging
Forms, flames, and the flakes of flames.

George Dillon, one of the most important Floridians in contemporary poetry, is the author of the 1932 Pulitzer prize volume, *The Flowering Stone.* He collaborated in 1936 with Edna St.Vincent Millay in a translation of Baudelaire's *Fleurs de Mal.* Formerly an associate of Harriet Monroe on the editorial staff of *Poetry*: *A Magazine of Verse* (Chicago), Dillon became editor of the magazine in 1937 after Miss Monroe's death.

Eunice Tietjens of Cocoanut Grove, connected for many years with the same magazine, is the editor of an anthology of classic secular poetry of the East, *Poetry of the Orient*, published in 1928, and the author of *Profiles from China* (1917), *Body and Raiment* (1919), and *Leaves in Windy Weather* (1929), all verse. Jessie Rittenhouse Scollard, a resident of Winter Park, is author of several volumes of poetry, editor of *The Rollins Book of Verse* (1929) and other anthologies of modern verse, and the founder of the Poetry Society of Florida. Gilbert Maxwell, another Florida poet, is best known for his *Stranger's Garment*, a volume of verse published in 1936.

Music and Theater

LITTLE is known of the music of the Indians who occupied Florida before the Seminole except from the drawings of Jacques LeMoyne, the French artist, who pictured Indian groups in 1564 blowing trumpets made of bark and shell, hung with oval balls of gold, silver, and brass. When such instruments were played, the Indians were marching on missions of peace, but there is no record of their melodies.

Study of the Seminole tribe reveals that folk songs have survived for generations deep in the Everglades. The music of the Green Corn Dance and the songs, 'The Night of Love' and 'The Hunting Song,' are Seminole classics, as are the musical legends, 'Little Red Rabbit' and 'Story of the Little Coon.' The instruments still in use are small water drums, gourd and tortoise-shell rattles, and the flute.

An early instance of musical influence occurred in Florida when Jean Ribaut and his company of French Huguenots were massacred in 1565 by the Spanish governor, Menéndez. The fifers, drummers, and trumpeters, and several men who professed to be Catholics were spared, and the musicians were taken to St.Augustine where they became members of the garrison band.

Twenty years later, Sir Francis Drake sighted St.Augustine from the sea and made ready to attack with his freebooters. One of these same French musicians paddled out alone in a canoe to meet the British, fluting the 'March of the Prince of Orange' as loudly as he could. Hearing the familiar tune, Drake befriended the musician before beginning an assault upon the town.

Differing greatly from the primitive music of the Seminole are the Negro spirituals and secular tunes. These have been given their present character by improvisers, work-gang choruses, religious groups, dance bands, and music clubs. Perhaps the most vital aspect of music in Florida today, this growing Negro art reaches back to African and to Indian music and out toward the Cuban; it influences—and is influenced by—contemporary musical composition. Music always has been an emotional outlet for the Florida Negro, and his songs have multiplied and shaped themselves to his tasks, his tribulations, and his irrepressible spirits. A chanty or rowing song, sung by Fernandina slaves in the late 1850's, compressed this into a few lines:

Jump, Isabel, slide water,
Ho, my aunty, ho!
Jump, Isabel, slide water,
Ho, my aunty, ho!

I wash my shirts
An' I nebber rench 'em
Ho, my aunty, ho!
Mosquito eat a-plenty
O' my buckwheat dough
Ho, my aunty, ho!

In Florida's turpentine or sawmill camps, at the docks, prison farms, wherever Negroes work in gangs, singing lightens the drudgery. Songs often punctuate the swing of the axe, thrust of the shovel, or swipe of the hoe. Composed in time of sorrow, joy, work, or imprisonment, they illustrate the Negro's relief in rhythm.

Little corn, UGH!
Yellow gal, UGH!
Little fight, UGH!
Lotta time, UGH!

The grunt concluding each line marks the bite of the logging crew axes, or the swipe of the hoes in the weed-cutting or potato-digging gang. Although only one person may be chanting, all the hoes or axes fall in unison.

Among the sawmill gangs, the accent of the song is often marked by the huge saw slashing into a log.

OH—HO—In the morning;
OH—HO—In the evening;
OH—HO—Hallelujah!
Ain't gonna be here all my days.

In the turpentine crews, where scores of men frequently work over wide areas, songs are pitched to carry long distances through the woods.

When I left de State of old Virginia,
I left in de winter time;
Where you guin Nigger?
I'se guin to Florida, I'se guin to Florida,
Guin to Florida to work in de turpentine.

Perhaps the best-known and best-loved song among Negro laborers is 'Uncle Bud,' which begins:

Uncle Bud is a man, a man in full,
His back is strong like a Jersey bull;
Uncle Bud, Uncle Bud, Uncle Bud, Uncle Bud.

Occasionally in a Negro song contrast and embellishment are obtained by stress and accent in the tune, rather than by a change of words:

> Love ain't nothing but the *EASY–GOING* heart disease,
> *OH LOVE* ain't nothing but the easy-going heart *DISEASE*,
> *LOVE* ain't *NOTHING* but the *EASY–GOING HEART DISEASE.*

The Florida Negro's religious music, which is as popular as his work songs, ranges from the hymns and spirituals of the larger churches in cities to the 'semi-jazz' of the backwoods meetings. The swing type of music, with its insistent rhythm, has been increasingly used in some of the city churches, especially those of the 'store-front' variety.

> Sinner you can't fool God,
> Sinner you can't fool God,
> Sinner you can't fool God,
> He's got His eyes on you.

Two of the best-known Negro swing bands are the Hartley Toots Orchestra of Miami, and Ace Harris and his Sunset Royal Orchestra, of West Palm Beach. Both of these have been organized for a number of years, and arrangements of their music have been recorded.

An eminent present-day Negro composer, J.Rosamond Johnson, a native of Jacksonville, has written the music to numerous lyrics, spirituals, and Broadway musical-comedy successes. His song, 'Lift Every Voice and Sing,' is known as the Negro national anthem, and his dialect song, 'Li'l Gal,' is considered a classic in its field. A volume of Johnson's music, *Rolling Along in Song*, was published in 1937. Many lyrics in this collection were written by his gifted brother, the late James Weldon Johnson.

The influence of Negro melodies on the English composer Frederick Delius (1863–1934) is evident in much of his work, though he lived in Florida for only two years. Born in Bradford, England, of wealthy German parents who wanted their son to enter business, Delius persuaded his father to send him to Florida to become an orange grower. He came to Solano Grove on the St.Johns River in 1884, at the age of 21, ostensibly to take up this occupation, but in reality to pursue his interest in music free from unsympathetic parental control. In a boat on the St.Johns and at his house, he listened to an old Negro playing on the banjo and singing plantation and old slave songs. One of these, beginning 'Oh Honey, I am going down the river in the morning,' Delius later introduced into *Appalachia*, a tone poem for orchestra and chorus, suggesting forests and mighty waters.

In 1885, Delius moved to Jacksonville, where he found ample recognition of his talent. William Jahn, a German professor of music, gave him piano lessons, and Thomas F. Ward, organist of that city, taught him composition, harmony, and organ. When his allowance from home was cut off, Delius found employment as organist in a Jewish synagogue. Many of his early compositions were dedicated to another friend, Mme Bell-Ranski, of near-by Picolata, who gave him much encouragement. An early work, *Zum Carnival*, was published in Jacksonville. Delius returned to England in 1886, and visited Florida only once again, twelve years later. But vivid memories of Floridian life inspired his opera *Koanga*; *Sea Drift*, for chorus and orchestra; and *Florida*, an orchestral suite.

'In Florida, through sitting and gazing at Nature,' Delius wrote, 'I gradually learnt the way in which I should eventually find myself.' Richard Strauss once said of his work: 'I never dreamed anybody except myself was writing such good music.'

Mana-Zucca, a resident of Miami, has written sonatas, chamber music, études, and songs. Best known of her songs are 'I Love Life,' 'Rachem,' and 'Nichavo'; her compositions for piano, 'Bolero de Concert' and 'The Ocean,' are favorite concert pieces. Mana-Zucca has been active in local musical organizations for years, and has brought to Miami some of the world's best artists.

Appreciation and encouragement of music in Florida has received stimulus during recent years from the rapid growth of civic music clubs, organists' guilds, choral groups, and student and other musical organizations. Several symphony orchestras of consequence have been organized during the last decade, and colleges and universities of the State have also developed orchestras and bands.

Rollins College conservatory of music, under the direction of Christopher O. Honaas, and the music department of Stetson University, directed by Dr. W. E. Duckwitz, are fully accredited music schools. The University of Miami conservatory, the school of music of the Florida State College for Women, and the Jacksonville College of Music are also rated highly.

State music festivals are held each year in Tampa, Winter Park, and DeFuniak Springs; the first sponsored by the University of Tampa, the second by Rollins College, and the third by the Federal Music Project of the WPA.

The Symphony Society of central Florida at Winter Park was organized by Mary Leonard in 1926. Its orchestra, composed of members of the faculties of Rollins College and Stetson University and professionals from the local radio station, is conducted by Alexander Bloch. Dr. John Palmer Gavit, former editor of the New York *Evening Post*, has presented the orchestra with a set of educational sound films illustrating functions of various instruments, and designed for use in the public schools. The Friday Musicale Orchestra, Jacksonville, is conducted by George Orner. There are student orchestras and bands at Stetson University, Florida State College for Women, Rollins College, University of Florida, and the University of Miami. At the last-named institution Arnold Volpe was conductor. The Florida Symphony Orchestra of the Federal Music Project, John Bitter, conductor, has given many concerts in its State-wide tours from Pensacola to Key West. An outgrowth of four major symphony units organized by the project in 1935, this orchestra has played to more than 3,000,000 people.

Tampa's Thalians regularly produce Gilbert and Sullivan operettas, the Tampa Civic Opera Association stages light opera, and the Latin-American Opera Company, of Tampa, using local Spanish and Italian talent, frequently gives performances with renowned artists. A professional opera group, organized by the Federal Music Project in 1935, has given performances throughout the State, with most of the properties and costumes designed in its own workshops. Several New York artists have appeared with this group, and a number of young Florida singers have made their debuts under its sponsorship.

Through the Federal Music Project, about 20,000 lessons in voice or instrument are given weekly in the public schools and to persons unable to pay for instruction, often in isolated rural sections. The project also maintains a composers' forum, to encourage embryonic composers. Those showing promise are helped in a number of ways to develop their talent.

THEATER

The first recorded dramatic entertainments in Florida were the religious pageant processions of St.Augustine. Seven *confradios*, or religious brotherhoods, established there before 1600, presented plays and entertainments in support of Santa Barbara, the first hospital of the city. Of one of these pageants, Governor Pedro Ybarro wrote in 1607 to the King of Spain: 'The caciques [Indian chiefs] have returned to their country, dressed and very happy, and edified with the religious services and processions they have witnessed.'

A century later, a disgruntled English actor, Tony Ashton, wrote a play based on his adventures while taking part in Governor Moore's siege of St.Augustine (1703). 'I returned to Charleston after the siege full of lice, shame, nakedness, poverty, and hunger,' he wrote. 'I turned player and poet and wrote a play on the subject of the country.'

The next record of the drama is found in an advertisement published during the Revolution in a Tory paper, the *East Florida Gazette* at St.Augustine. It announced that two plays, *The Beaux Stratagem* and *A Miss in Her 'Teens*, would be given for the benefit of distressed refugees—Tories from the United States—on Monday evening, March 3, 1783. The characters were to be played by young British officers quartered in St.Augustine.

Gayer times evidently followed when the Spanish regained Florida, judging from the testimony of an Englishman who visited St.Augustine in 1817. He described a carnival in full swing there at the time: 'Masks, dominoes, harlequins, punchinellos and a great variety of grotesque disguises, on horseback, in carts, gigs and on foot, paraded the streets with guitars, violins and other instruments, and in the evenings, the houses were open to receive masks, and balls were given in every direction.'

An early example of the theatrical precept, 'the show must go on,' occurred in 1840 at St.Augustine in connection with the staging of *Honeymoon*, memorable less for its histrionics than for the dramatic arrival of the players. 'Feminine members of the troupe,' the local newspaper reported, 'were in the first section of the party and reached the city in safety. The men of the cast, however, were waylaid by Indians while en route from Picolata by stagecoach. One actor was slain. Despite this tragic prelude, the play was presented before a large and enthusiastic audience.'

Indians later became actors and toured with road shows. At Pensacola, the Indian Amphitheater Troupe played in 1842 with the star advertised as 'Beautiful Squaw Alazuma, daughter of Camuncks, Chief of Sack and Fox Nations, appearing at each performance.'

Pensacola, where the mention of a theater dates back to 1821, saw many famous players of the late nineteenth century. In 1869, Fay Templeton, then a child of six, appeared with her father's company in a makeshift theater composed of rough planks laid among cotton bales and coffee sacks in an old warehouse. Thomas and Lawrence Keene and Fanny Davenport played Pensacola in 1878 in a remodeled one-story building. A large theater, called the Opera House, was begun in 1882, while Pensacola was in the midst of a yellow-fever epidemic, and completed a year later. Its acoustics were admirable, and its interior 'modern' in every way. The second, or 'peanut,' gallery was set aside for Negroes, and a section of 15 seats was reserved for the demimondaine of the town. Behind the gas footlights of the Opera House appeared Pavlova, the famous dancer, and many notable actors, including Charlotte Thompson in *Jane Eyre*, Minnie Maddern Fiske, Joseph Jefferson, Lillian Russell, Billie Burke, May Robson, George M. Cohan, and Grace George.

Jacksonville became known throughout Florida and southern Georgia as a show town and gathering point for theater patrons in the 1880's. Before its first theater was built in 1884, empty stores and school buildings were used by one-night stand companies. The first theater, destroyed by fire, was promptly rebuilt in 1887, and notices of the opening, which featured a production of *Faust* with Minnie Hank and her company, were telegraphed to all parts of the Nation. The Duval Theater was established a few years later, and here Richard Mansfield, Joseph Jefferson, Sarah Bernhardt, Modjeska, and many other distinguished actors played. It was also here that the Divine Sarah once decided not to appear; this whim resulted in a suit by the Duval Theater for breach of contract that caused a great deal of unsolicited press comment throughout the country. The average theatrical vehicles of those days were such ephemeral pieces as *The Fast Mail*, *Our Country Cousin*, *A Breezy Time*, and *Poor Jonathan*.

Small theatrical companies visited Florida intermittently from 1900 until the early 1920's, but, in general, the population centers were too small to insure profit for the large, first-rate attractions. Although the boom (1924–26) remedied this difficulty for a time, the decline of the road shows was felt in Florida, as elsewhere.

Since 1925, interest in the stage has been revived by little theater organizations, which have been greatly aided by the recreational projects of the WPA in nearly every county in the State. These projects foster dramatic productions and pageants, and conduct drama classes for the purpose of forming additional little-theater groups.

The Miami Civic Theater erected a playhouse in 1929 and has produced many popular plays. The group takes an active part in encouraging all forms of dramatic production in Miami. The little-theater group of Jacksonville, established in the 1920's, designed and built its own theater in 1937, and has presented hundreds of standard dramas. The Bandbox Players and a little-theater group in St.Petersburg give mainly light comedies of the type of *Charlie's Aunt*; Clearwater has an active little-theater group and its own playhouse, the Francis Wilson Theater, dedicated to the memory of the actor of that name who lived in retirement there. In Tampa the Spanish, Cuban, and Italian clubs give amateur and professional performances in their native languages. Few cities of any size are without similar organizations, but practically all confine themselves to familiar plays.

Professional drama has been largely limited to the Federal Theater Project of the WPA. This project, besides furnishing employment to professional actors, has given excellent productions of dozens of popular plays.

In 1939, before it was discontinued, the Federal Theater had three separate acting companies: an outstanding dramatic repertory company in Miami; a revue and musical-comedy company in Tampa; and a touring company with headquarters in Jacksonville.

The company in Miami, housed in the Scottish Rite Temple theater, successfully produced some of the famous old American and Continental plays, as well as Shakespeare and modern comedy. But it was *Altars of Steel*, a play about steelworkers by Thomas Hall Rogers, that won it high critical praise.

The Tampa company occupied its own building, the old Rialto Theater, with a new interior designed and executed by WPA artists. Composed largely of former musical-comedy and vaudeville players, many of them Americans of Latin extraction, this unit has produced Cuban, Spanish, and American revues, most of them written by members of the project. Among the productions were *El Mundo en el mano* (The World in Your Hand), *It Can't Happen Here* (Spanish version), *The Old Rip*, and *Ready! Aim! Fire!*

The Jacksonville company, after a year and a half of locally presented repertory, made a State-wide educational tour in 1938, presenting an *Animated History of the Drama*. Plays representative of great periods of drama history were given in high schools, civic centers, and commercial theaters. Each drama was supplemented with a specially prepared study outline. In Miami and Jacksonville, the Federal Theater had also established marionette units that presented plays and variety programs on State-wide tours. The Miami unit conducted regular Saturday morning performances for children.

Nearly all the colleges and universities in Florida have active dramatic art departments and producing groups. The Annie Russell Theater at Rollins College, in addition to giving many plays produced by students, has a professional artists' series every season, presenting well-known actors, musicians, and dancers.

Art

THE first professional art produced in America consisted of drawings by the French artist, LeMoyne, who lived in Florida in 1564–65. From him it is learned that primitive Indian art was devoted mainly to personal adornment: dyed pelts, gay bird plumage, and trinkets fashioned from bone and shell. Aboriginal use of copper ornaments was also indicated by LeMoyne, but this has been disputed by anthropologists. The Jacksonville public library possesses a volume of the *Narrative of LeMoyne*, translated from the Latin of Theodore De Bry, with heliotype reproductions of De Bry's engravings from the LeMoyne originals.

The development of art in Florida was long delayed by the fact that three times the territory was emptied of its settlers. Inexpensive church pieces comprised most of the art of the early Spanish mission period, and most of these were hastily concealed, carried away, or destroyed when the English burned the missions. Fragments of three brass altar candlesticks, buried in the ruins of the Franciscan missions at New Smyrna, were recovered in 1885.

Pictorial art of the mission period seems to have been limited to the 'illumination' of reports with crude pen drawings by Spanish missionaries and officials. One report, having to do with the shipment of 100 Indians from Mexico to Florida in the sixteenth century, is embellished with figures of Spanish soldiers wearing plumed hats and carrying spears and shields. Other drawings show Indians imprisoned in stocks, and undergoing various punishments for offenses described in the report.

Art was meager during the brief English occupation from 1763 to 1783. A powder horn, combining art and utility, is now in the J.H.Grenville Gilbert collection of American powder horns in the Metropolitan Museum, New York City. Listed as the St.Augustine horn, it is described in a museum bulletin as 'engraved with the British arms, a general view of the town with its red roofs standing out conspicuously, the fort with the British flag flying triumphantly, and sailboats which give color and action to the picture. It bears the inscription: "An Exact Prospect of St.Augustine from the Light House, the Metropolis of the Province of East Florida."'

Another reminder of this period is an anonymous portrait, now in a Jacksonville home, of Gracia dura Bin, wife of Dr.Andrew Turnbull, founder of the New Smyrna colony in 1767.

After 1783 the territory, once more under Spanish rule, became the domain of Indians and pirates. Itinerant portrait painters, who traveled about the new Nation in the North, shunned Florida. It was therefore many years before the influence of American art penetrated this frontier.

Meanwhile Florida had served as a laboratory for study and research in natural science, with pictorial art employed as a recording medium. Mark Catesby's *Natural History of Carolina, Florida and the Bahama Islands*, in two large folio volumes, was published in London between 1731–48 after years of preparation. It contained colored drawings of birds, animals, fish, serpents, insects, and plants. An original may be seen under glass in the Webb Memorial Library at St.Augustine, and, though now more than 200 years old, the plates still retain remarkable freshness of color.

A hundred years later the great ornithologist, John James Audubon, arrived in Florida to make studies for his *The Birds of America*. A mimeographed copy of *A Naturalist's Excursion in Florida*, written by Audubon at Bulowville in 1831, is owned by Rollins College.

By the time Florida was acquired from Spain in 1821, colonial portraitures had been left behind, and American artists were embarking on the new movement in landscape painting which later became known as the 'Hudson River School.' Florida, then busy fighting Indians, took little part in this development. Its only notable contribution at this time was a series of Seminole Indian portraits, executed by George Catlin for the United States Government. Included in the series is the famous painting of Osceola, reproduced in school histories and books on the Seminole; it now hangs in the Indian section of the Smithsonian Institution at Washington.

The first great painter to reside in Florida was George Inness, who built a home and studio on the Anclote River at Tarpon Springs in 1877. A master of atmosphere, Inness in Florida ignored the characteristic palm and painted the drab pine woods, which in early morning mists or in the soft glow of evening were found to possess an unexpected beauty. His *Early Morning—Tarpon Springs*, in the Art Institute of Chicago, is an example of Inness' Florida work. His paintings, now in many museums and private collections throughout the country, are rare in Florida.

George Inness,Jr., who succeeded to the Tarpon Springs home, finally gained recognition as an artist in his own right, despite the handicap of an illustrious father. At first a painter of animals, he eventually adopted his father's technique; he began to paint landscapes which increasingly became studies in atmosphere, the details tending to lose themselves in the general effect. Confining his work to studio problems, and seldom troubling himself with observation and analysis, the younger Inness developed an extreme facility. Many of his pictures hang in Florida homes. During the prosperous days of the early 1920's, small canvases brought him from $2,000 to $5,000, and in a short time he made more money than his father did in a lifetime. In Tarpon Springs, the Church of the Good Shepherd has been dedicated as a shrine to the memory of George Inness, Jr. Here are examples of his earlier efforts, as well as one of his last and most notable paintings, the *Only Hope*, which aroused a great deal of comment on its travels abroad.

Winslow Homer, one of America's foremost artists, who painted many pictures in the South after the War between the States, was a frequent visitor to Key West between 1888 and 1903. Some of his best-known works, *A Norther, Key West, The Gulf Stream, Taking on Wet Provisions*, and *Palms in the Storm*, are said to have been produced here. Homer's pictures of Key West waters focused attention on this insular outpost, which has become popular among present-day artists. Old waterfront structures, fishing boats, quaint streets, and weathered houses provide inexhaustible material. Docks and beaches are constantly visited by artists who hope to capture the translucence of the many-hued seas. When the Federal Government launched its rehabilitation program for Key West in 1933, many artists were given employment under a program for beautifying the city. Art consequently flourishes there in public buildings, restaurants, night clubs, bars, filling stations, and roadside stands. Sloppy Joe's bar has a mural depicting local characters, including the proprietor and Ernest Hemingway, the author, crowned with a Bacchus-wreath of grapes.

While the elder Inness was still painting in his obscure Anclote studio, Florida suddenly received a tremendous consignment of art. Trainloads of works, imported for the embellishment of the spacious railroad hotels erected by Flagler and Plant, descended among a people struggling for existence in a raw country. Lavishness was the keynote: pictures with ponderous gilt frames, floor coverings of breath-taking expanse, and furniture and decorative bric-a-brac in an amazing profusion of styles.

Plant outdid Flagler in the quantity of his collection. For two years prior to the opening of the Moorish-style Tampa Hotel in 1891, Plant scoured Europe, collecting art objects. Despite the vast size of his establishment, the purchases he made overflowed the place, and the surplus had to be disposed of at auction. One authentic piece of sculpture stands before the grand main entrance to the hotel, a fountain symbolizing *Transportation*, executed by George Gray Barnard shortly after he received acclaim in Paris in the early 1890's. Much of the original art and furnishings in Plant's Tampa Bay Hotel has been removed, but a wing of the building, set aside as a museum, still contains a bewildering assortment of rococo bronzes, furniture, clocks, tapestries, paintings, and vases; one vase being a gift from the Emperor of Japan.

Flagler showed an extensive interest in murals, and, through commissions for the walls of his Ponce de Leon Hotel at St.Augustine, perpetuated the academic tastes of the 1880's. Symbolic and allegorical themes, interspersed with Florida landscapes and Shakespearean scenes, cover the walls of his hotel. In the dining room, cupids with outstretched hands, bearing wine cups, bread, and grapes, depict *The Feast.* Above them sail Spanish caravels of the era of Ponce de Leon. Around the dome are figures representing *Spring*, *Summer*, *Autumn*, and *Winter*, alternating with coats-of-arms of Spanish provinces. At the head of one stairway is *Columbus Discovering America*, and at the head of another, *The Introduction of Christianity to the Huns of Charlemagne.* Balcony paintings include a Florida landscape, and portraits of Cortez, the Spanish explorer, and Osceola, the Seminole war leader. Four standing figures in fresco represent *Air*, *Fire*, *Water*, and *Earth*, and four seated ones, *Adventure*, *Discovery*, *Conquest*, and *Civilization.* The Shakespearean heroines, Desdemona and Ophelia, share a drawing room with *A Bit of Old Mexico*, *A Trip on the Bosphorus* (a group of harem beauties), *The Sultan's Favorite*, and *A Girl in the Woods*; Juliet, Rosaline, Anne Page, Beatrice, and Titania, queen of the fairies, occupy another room; and *Off for a Row*, and *Consternation*, a young woman with a surprised expression, grace a third. These hotels, and others built subsequently by Flagler and Plant, had the effect, one might say, of carrying the banner of art down the peninsula of Florida, and of drawing to art the attention of members of the new leisure class who built winter homes there; in turn, these newcomers brought valuable art-treasures to the State.

Palm Beach, Miami Beach, and Miami have the largest private collections. It would be difficult, in fact, to find any city in Florida that lacks an art collection. All principal cities have art leagues or clubs, and, in 1927, a State federation was formed to stimulate and unify these activities. Results are shown in the increasing amount of art literature available in public and school libraries in the State.

Art instruction has also become widespread. Courses in fine and applied arts are given at the University of Florida, Gainesville; Florida State College for Women, Tallahassee; Stetson University, DeLand; Rollins College, Winter Park; the University of Tampa; and the Florida Agricultural and Mechanical College (Negro), Tallahassee. Many private schools and studios also offer courses in art. Notable among art schools in the South is that of the John and Mable Ringling Art Museum at Sarasota. The museum, bequeathed to the State by its founder, John Ringling, contains a collection of more than 700 works, including important examples of the Italian, French, Dutch, Spanish, and English schools, and a group of paintings, tapestries, and a sculptural work by Rubens. Around the museum and the privately owned school, a thriving art colony has grown up. Sarasota, with its Ringling Museum and Ringling Circus quarters, offers to students the unique opportunity of studying old masters as well as an amazing assortment of wild animals. It is a common sight to see artists at work on the circus grounds.

During the real-estate boom (1924–26) many artists were drawn to the prosperous resorts, hoping to profit from the lavish spending. With the arrival of the national depression, however, most of these artists were deprived of support and ultimately found themselves on relief. Under the Federal Art Project, which continued the work of earlier Government agencies, much permanent art has been produced for Florida buildings. Project work includes bas-relief designs of Florida fauna, carved in native stone on the Coral Gables Library; murals in the Orlando Chamber of Commerce; over-mantel decorations in the student union building at the University of Florida; seven murals in the Tony Jannus Administration Building at the Tampa airport; and many murals in school buildings. An outstanding piece is the memorial monument on Matecumbe Key to those who lost their lives in the 1935 hurricane; a rectangular shaft of Key limestone bears a carved panel, showing in simple lines palm trees streaming in a high wind.

Through gallery exhibits, lectures, art centers, and classes, including a Negro unit, the Federal Art Project in Florida has carried on an educational campaign in appreciation and practice of fine and craft arts. Its Index of American Design division has contributed approximately 200 reproductions of early textile designs, samplers, coverlets, spreads, costumes, carvings, and other manifestations of folk and popular art. Perhaps the most interesting among these are the old circus-wagon designs, copied at the Ringling headquarters in Sarasota from famous old circuses that have long departed from the American scene. The elaborate figures and ornamental carvings on this rapidly deteriorating equipment have been recorded on faithfully drawn colored plates.

The Treasury Department Art Project is another Government agency for the encouragement of art. It has awarded several mural commissions for Florida buildings on the basis of regional competitions.

Many of the country's leading artists have found Florida a pleasant place in which to live and work; and their presence has tended to overshadow any local style that may be striving to emerge. Artists continue to frequent the resorts, producing, as a rule, impressions of Florida scenery for sale to tourists. St.Augustine has the most Bohemian of these colonies: Aviles Street, one of the original narrow lanes of the old city, with antique stucco houses, has been largely taken over by studios, and has become a tourists' attraction. Here the artists display their work on outside walls and do much painting in the open. St.Augustine's historic buildings are the favorite theme, and early historical events, especially the landing of Ponce de Leon, are popular.

Recreation

Photograph by courtesy of Miami Beach News Service

ALONG THE ATLANTIC, MIAMI BEACH

VENETIAN POOL, CORAL GABLES

Photograph by courtesy of G. W. Romer

Photograph by courtesy of City of West Palm Beach

IN THE GULF STREAM, OFF PALM BEACH

HUNTERS IN THE EVERGLADES

Photograph by courtesy of Burgert Brothers

Photograph by courtesy of Burgert Brothers

FISHING IN ST. JOHN'S RIVER

Photograph by courtesy of Respess Engraving Compan[y]

TRAILER CAMP, MIAMI

Photograph by courtesy of John Lodwick News Service

GOLF COURSE, PASADENA, ST. PETERSBURG

)LLYWOOD BEACH

Photograph by courtesy of the Hollywood Chamber of Commerce

START OF THE RACE, GREYHOUND TRACK, JACKSONVILLE

RACE TRACK, HIALEAH

Photograph by courtesy of G. W. Romer

LAWN BOWLING, ST. PETERSBURG

CHESS GAMES, ST. PETERSBURG

Photograph by Gerec

FEEDING A PORPOISE, MARINE STUDIOS, NEAR ST. AUGUSTINE

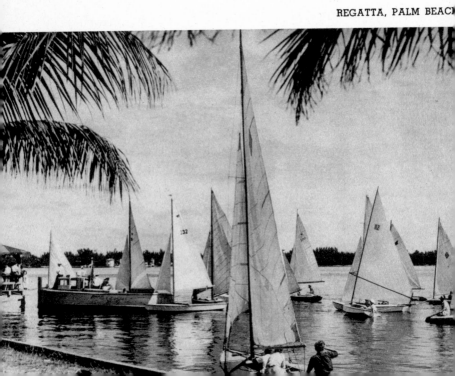

REGATTA, PALM BEAC

Architecture

THREE centuries of building in Florida, ranging from medieval dungeons to ephemeral vagaries, have recorded the historical, political, and economic evolution of the State in terms of architecture. This span links present-day Florida with early European culture and has brought into startling conjunction, and sometimes conflict, many schools of architecture, and perhaps a few innovations without academic ancestry. The composite result therefore may lack definition but certainly not diversity.

Nothing of aboriginal construction in Florida is left save numerous shell mounds, the largest collections of which are found in the Tampa Bay region. Early Indian tribes in Florida chiefly used perishable materials. Writings of Spanish explorers, however, describe the use of stone by Indians for what must have been ceremonial structures, and De Bry's engravings of LeMoyne's drawings also show the use of stone; but no trace of such buildings exists in Florida. Oviedo, a Spanish writer, stated that the Indian houses had 'walls of lime and stone (which lime they make of shells of sea oysters) and these are one and one-half times as high as a person.'

Nearly all the missions built of wood and stone by priests who came with the early Spanish expeditions have also disappeared. Two exceptions exist in the crumbling ruins of the missions in the vicinity of New Smyrna. Built by Indian labor under the direction of Franciscan priests, these missions, Jororo and San Antonio de Anacape, were utilized for material by the Turnbull colony to build sugar mills, but the stone walls and arches that were spared have withstood the inroads of centuries.

Most substantial examples of early Spanish architecture are medieval Fort Marion (Castillo de San Marcos) and Fort Matanzas, at St.Augustine, and Fort San Carlos at Pensacola. Fort Marion, begun in 1672 and completed in 1756, was built of large blocks of coquina rock, quarried on near-by Anastasia Island by exiles and Indian slaves, many of whom were sentenced to their task for life. The cost of San Marcos Castle, as it was called, was estimated at $30,000,000, a sum that prompted the King of Spain to exclaim: 'Its curtains and bastions must be made of solid silver.'

Fort Matanzas, built in 1736 of coquina rock, is much smaller. It was erected to replace a watch tower at the entrance to the Matanzas Inlet.

Fort San Carlos at Pensacola represents a much later period. The original fort, built of pine logs in 1698, was burned, later rebuilt, blown up in 1719, rebuilt a second time, and then reconstructed of brick between 1783 and 1796, after England had returned Florida to Spain. In recent years it became a national park, and its masonry was completely restored. Although sacked and burned several times, Pensacola and St.Augustine have retained indelible imprints of the Spanish engineer and architect. Sometimes no more remains of this early work than the original building blocks used in British and American reconstruction.

Original Spanish homes in St.Augustine survive in a few rectangular, two-story buildings with the first story constructed of coquina rock and covered with a plaster made of burnt oyster-shell lime. North walls were usually left windowless as a protection against cold winds, and second stories were fashioned of hewn cedars. It is said that the idea of a first story of stone and a second of wood was worked out in the West Indies as a protection against earthquakes and hurricanes. In Florida this construction provided a ground-floor refuge in case of storms, and if the superstructure were blown away, it could easily be replaced. These early houses had thatched roofs. Chimneys were added by successive English and American occupants.

The 'Oldest House,' now a historical museum, is thought to have been built in the late sixteenth century and has been certified by an unbroken chain of titles since 1763. It has arched doorways and, at each end, a second-story ornamental porch. No nails were used in the original construction. Other examples of early Spanish architecture at St.Augustine include the Llambias House, built previous to 1763; and the Public Library, erected prior to 1785. The City Gates, once part of Fort San Marcos and now St.Augustine's most familiar landmark, were erected in 1745 and rebuilt in 1804. The Catholic Cathedral, built in 1793, was damaged by fire in 1885 and restored the same year.

The Spaniards were building with stone in Florida fifty years before William Strachey, recorder of the Jamestown colony, described in 1618 the wigwams of that settlement; before the Dutch West India Company issued instructions to its American colonists in 1650 on how to build a house by digging a hole in the ground, using sod for side walls and boughs for thatched roofs; and more than a hundred years before the Provincial Executive Council of Philadelphia in 1685 ordered those dwelling in caves along the river to come out by a certain date so that Front Street could be opened. Yet Florida, because of its wars and changes in ownership, was to start over again with the most primitive type of wooden dwelling at the beginning of the nineteenth century.

Following the purchase of Florida from Spain in 1821 and the erection of a chain of forts for protection against the Indians, settlers from Georgia and other states to the north developed a utilitarian wooden structure, known as a 'shotgun' house. This consisted of two houses under a single roof, with an open passage or ventilating airway between. Porches were later added on all sides. The houses probably were so named because of the fact that a shotgun could be fired through the passage without hitting the walls. This was supposed to be an advantage in combating Indians, but in reality the open passage was for ventilation. The survival of many shotgun houses suggests that the pioneer builders used native materials and common-sense methods of construction in recognition of climatic conditions. These houses, built of fat pine, were set on high land and well off the ground, thus providing for a windsweep beneath to prevent dry rot, a scourge of later building in Florida. The James McMullen homestead, a two-story log house at Coachman on the Pinellas Peninsula, since converted into a historical landmark by the Daughters of the American Revolution, is a well-preserved example of the shotgun period.

Another distinctive type appeared about the same time in Key West, where the salvage of cargoes from stranded ships (or 'wrecking' in local parlance) was an important business. Much of the building was done by ship carpenters, and occasionally houses were constructed of mahogany, possibly because Honduras was more accessible for material than were the northern pine forests. Today no mahogany houses survive, but some interior mahogany trim remains in the older structures, salvaged mostly from the cabinet work of ships that foundered on the Florida Reef.

Early Key West houses were entirely of wood, for the most part following the styles of New England and the British colonials of the Bahamas. Minor detail showed Cuban influence, but Spanish architecture was almost completely lacking. They were designed to meet the lack of shade and fresh water, but in another respect ignored the elements. Although sturdily built and anchored with bolts to the native rock to withstand high winds and waves, many of them were two stories in height with porches and balconies and steep-pitched roofs, making them fair targets for hurricanes. All openings were shuttered to keep out heat and glare. For additional ventilation 'scuttles' were installed on roofs along with a platform or 'mirador,' from which to sight ships in distress. Porch posts of a later period are mostly slender lathe-turned wooden supports; and in some cases the roofs of two-story houses extend down to shelter ground-floor porches, thereby hiding from view upper-story windows. The multiplicity of gables, the presence of numerous above-ground square concrete cisterns, and a general lack of paint give Key West the appearance of a weathered settlement of excessive roofs and surplus foundations. Chimneys were unknown there before the introduction of brick and cement in 1844 for the building of Fort Taylor. After masonry came into general use, a familiar American type, the two-story brick house with wooden porches, appeared.

Brick had been extensively used in north Florida long before it reached Key West. In 1837 a newspaper at Apalachicola boasted that the town's business street along the waterfront 'had 2,000 feet of continuous brick stores, three stories high, 80 feet deep, and all equipped with granite pillars.' The most prodigious use of brick, however, occurred west of Key West on that lonely outpost of the Florida Reef, the Dry Tortugas. Here was constructed Fort Jefferson, once known as the Gibraltar of the Gulf of Mexico, and now a national monument under the care of the National Park Service. The structure was begun in 1851 and work on it ceased in 1865.

Before the conclusion of the Seminole Wars in 1842 plantations developed in northern Florida, and with them came the pretentious Maryland and Virginia late Georgian Colonial mansions. Some of these were destroyed during the War between the States, but characteristic examples of brick construction are still extant, especially around Tallahassee; among them are 'Goodwood,' built in 1839, and the century-old Governor Call mansion, now the Grove Hotel. The latter is a good example of the early Greek Revival style. Less pretentious but well proportioned are at least a dozen more in the *ante-bellum* towns of Madison, Monticello, Quincy, and Marianna, nearly all of them built in the 1830's. These are of the Southern Planter type with two-story galleried porches and, with but one or two exceptions, square boxed columns and plain doorways, suggesting the lack of expert wood carvers in Florida during this period. The Nichols Inn at Marianna, which has round fluted columns, is one of the exceptions.

Other notable structures of these earlier days, still in good repair, are the Fleming home, at Hibernia on the St.Johns River, built in 1825; the Methodist parsonage in Quincy, begun in 1830 and completed in 1835 for J.S.Smallwood; Ma'am Anna's House on Fort George Island (*see Tour 2a*); and the Gamble mansion, near Bradenton, built in 1850 (*see Tour 4c*).

During the prosperous days of the 1880's and early 1890's more elaborate homes began to appear in central and south Florida. With the arrival of sawmills, turning lathes, and similar devices, permitting wide latitude in the ornamental use of wood, classic columns yielded to spindle supports and jigsaw traceries. This period lasted until its spectacular possibilities had been exhausted.

It was in the 1880's that Florida acquired the first of its huge resort hotels, those extravagant structures built by Flagler and Plant. Beginning at St.Augustine, Flagler finally ended his hotel chain at Key West. One of his railroad hotels launched Palm Beach, but his outstanding achievement was the Ponce de Leon at St.Augustine. Other Flagler buildings in St.Augustine are the Alcazar Hotel and Memorial Church. Plant on the west coast built the Tampa Bay Hotel at Tampa and the Belleview at Belleair on the Pinellas Peninsula. From the standpoint of general lavishness no modern hotel in Florida—not even the grand-scale hostelries of the 1920's, such as the Miami-Biltmore at Coral Gables, the Roney Plaza at Miami Beach, the Breakers at Palm Beach, and the Vinoy Park at St.Petersburg—has surpassed Flagler's Ponce de Leon or Plant's Tampa Bay Hotel.

Early in 1884, as a preliminary to building in St.Augustine, Flagler sent two young New York architects to Spain to study and absorb ideas, John M. Carrere and Thomas W. Hastings. For two years they made sketches and collected data, after which they returned and set to work. The architectural results made the pair famous, but it would seem that they had exhausted their Spanish inspiration on these mammoth hotels, for they designed only one other building in the Spanish style. Their Ponce de Leon Hotel, occupying a city block, is a monolithic structure of concrete composed of six parts of coquina shell to one part of cement. As the architects stated: 'It is not exact to say that the hotel was built; it was cast. The coquina, found almost on the very spot, was a suggestion of nature not to be overlooked.' In design the Ponce de Leon is a rich and colorful adaptation of early Spanish Renaissance motifs and details, with an admixture of Italian Renaissance; the latter is exemplified particularly in the grand gateway, following closely that of the Certosa at Pavia. The neighboring Alcazar Hotel lacks the setting and grand plan of the Ponce de Leon. Plant's Tampa Bay Hotel, 'a thousand feet long,' was built of brick with Moorish horseshoe-arched windows, a design carried out in the intricate woodwork of a lengthy veranda. Its silvered domes and minarets, emerging from tropical shrubbery on the west bank of the Hillsborough River, give an oriental quality to Tampa's sky line. The building now houses the University of Tampa.

Railroads held a monopoly on resort hotel construction until after 1900, and few other grand-scale hotels were built for the next two decades. Meanwhile, many comfortable native fortunes had accrued from phosphate, cattle, timber, and turpentine, and these were evidenced by a recurrence of classic columns. This desire to perpetuate an architectural tradition overlooked the more plentiful but less substantial houses in the lowlands of the South, and revived the feudalistic symbols that occupied the elevations. The reproductions included Palladian windows and porticos, but good proportion apparently was often sacrificed to display. An example of this ostentation is a former private residence in Jacksonville (now the quarters of the Y.W.C.A.), four stories in height, with three tiers of Corinthian columns. Gradually, however, this period waned and architecture, like the people, grew more cosmopolitan.

South Florida did not experience a marked architectural renaissance until about 1920, but long before that time Palm Beach became an established winter resort and attracted the builders of many magnificent private estates. Nothing that was constructed there, however, approached one of these estates, Viscaya, the home of the late James Deering, on Biscayne Bay, south of Miami. This magnificent residence was completed in 1920, after seven years of work, at a cost of $15,000,000. Enclosed by high walls, it became a place of mystery, and whispered stories were circulated of hidden panels and secret passageways. These beliefs were dispelled when, after the owner's death, Viscaya became a public museum for a short period and was opened for inspection; but what the estate lacked in mystery was more than made up for in splendor, for here was the realization of a multi-millionaire bachelor's dream—a fabulous home in fabulous gardens. The main house is Italian Baroque in style and reminiscent of a villa at Stra near Venice. It was built of stuccoed concrete, with doors and windows trimmed with native coral stone. There is a central courtyard arcaded on three sides and a second story with open balconies which serve the bedrooms. A swimming pool, half outside the house and half under it, is sheltered by a ceiling with marine decorations, painted by Robert W. Chanler. The gardens are an array of terraces, balustrades, and fountains, with natural and clipped shrubbery. The interior, reflecting incredible extravagance, includes many historical pieces and paintings from Venice, Florence, and deserted villas and palaces along the Brenta. The tile roof originally covered an entire Cuban village. The architects were F.Burral Hoffman and Paul Chalfin.

Addison Mizner exerted a dominant influence upon Florida architecture, particularly at Palm Beach. Collaborating there with Paris Singer, a son of the sewing-machine magnate, he designed and constructed the

Everglades Club. Upon completion of the club, he accepted a commission to build a house for the Stotesbury family of Philadelphia; this definitely established Mizner and inspired many imitators. While he studied Old World architecture in Spain and Central America for Florida adaptation, Mizner's followers, for the most part, gave their attention to superficial Spanish effects. To soften the glare of Florida's brilliant sun, Mizner used quiet pastel tints, and with multitones achieved a more vibrant texture. Immediately there ensued a cycle of surface treatments that exhausted the spectrum. The territory from Palm Beach to Miami became a kaleidoscopic flow of color that required ten years of subsequent painting to subdue to varying shades of buff. But much of this 'high-visibility' construction lacked permanence, as it ignored methods and materials suitable to Florida's climate.

Mizner was among the first to recognize that the flat country of coastal Florida provided only sky for a background, and this inspired his bold treatment of outline. One of his principal modifications of authentic Spanish architecture was in the treatment of windows; he removed the iron bars and enlarged the window openings. He has been credited with the original use of pecky cypress for interior finish, a pitted wood from trees usually not less than 125 years old. Sawed into boards, this material showed apparently rotted streaks. These were cleaned out with the aid of a blow torch and wire brushes, and the surface treated with acids and stains to simulate a pleasing antique finish. Pecky cypress formerly had been used for piling and fence posts, but after Mizner's innovation it became popular and trebled in price. The unfinished town of Boca Raton, now a private club, undoubtedly would have been his most ambitious work had not the real-estate boom collapsed. Jacksonville has one example of his work, the Riverside Baptist Church, and among his last efforts was the Williams home at St.Petersburg, in construction at the time of his death.

The 1924–26 period reflected the concentration of American wealth in a Florida setting. Magnitude and ostentation were indices to the culture of Yankee 'conquistadores' in the 1920's. A new scale of grandeur was achieved, but no new type of architecture. Heretofore, public buildings had run pretty much to a pattern, such as the State Capitol at Tallahassee with its fat classic columns, the State University and the State College for Women, with their familiar 'Collegiate Gothic,' and county courthouses with their clock towers. The square red-brick courthouses, however, have undergone a half-century of historic change. They register the migration of brick down the peninsula; they indicated by their design when many counties were formed, and by their pretentiousness, the expanding pride of an improved economy. So by 1938 they ranged from the one surviving wooden structure at Crawfordville in north Florida to the lofty gray stone tower of the Dade County Courthouse at Miami, the tallest building in the State. In the process of evolution these structures acquired classic porticos, and their clock towers grew into expansive domes, but both these features disappeared with the arrival of the neoclassic style and the use of cast stone and marble. Then the boom brought stucco and, to an extent, the abandonment of standard patterns. The Sarasota Courthouse, for example, took the form of a Venetian campanile, with detached wings joined by open colonnades.

Another of the more obvious, and somewhat ludicrous, by-products of that time was the erection of ten-story buildings in three-story towns. Lofty hotels and lone business structures jutted up obelisklike in surroundings of vacant lots, bungalows, and small business blocks, as in Panama City, Lake Wales, and Haines City.

More widely scattered monuments of the boom period are the real-estate subdivision gateways. Many of these stand forlornly in weed-grown fields along the highways as sole reminders of what were to be magnificent developments. Aside from their decorative function, they once served as barometers of realty prices. Building lots behind wooden frames covered with plaster in imitation of solid masonry were likely to represent the lower market levels. As gateways improved in size, material, and design, prices mounted accordingly. Likewise size and ornamentation increased and prices rose with the temperature. In northern Florida entrances were fairly simple, but, as the prospective lot purchasers moved southward into a balmier climate, these gradually attained an atmosphere of opulence and grandeur. Pylons grew into heroic arches of triumph, resplendent with ceramic tile and sculptured cast stone, or into turrets and towers, connected overhead by rainbow 'bridges of sighs' (not literally apparent at the time), and finally into practical structures penetrated by driveways. Subdivision portals reached their architectural climax in the grand entrance to Coral Gables, with a block-long building designed by Denman Fink and Phineas Paist.

To achieve an imposing effect and an air of stability was the goal, and architecture the device—a time-honored one. Just as financiers, with granite, bronze, and bookkeeping, created the illusion of cash deposits far in excess of existing currency, the promoters, by borrowing a page from the bankers, the motion-picture industry, and Barnum, created the illusion of adjacent high land values. The fictitious values were doomed to shrink, but many of the buildings, though in the nature of stage sets, outlasted some of the banks that helped to finance them. As a result, fruit stores and garages now occasionally occupy buildings with heroic marble fronts.

When familiar styles were depleted the exotic from remote lands appeared and buildings took form without precedent except in the *Arabian Nights*. The boom town of Opa Locka, near Miami, in advance of building the city, erected a city hall that pierced the sky with an acre of bulbous domes and needlelike minarets. The Florida landscape was spotted with pretentious buildings around which towns were supposed to grow, but sometimes these were left stranded in grand and startling isolation and found uses vastly different from those for which they were intended. One of the larger unfinished hotels in the Miami area was turned into a poultry ranch, and thousands of chickens perched in the lofty guest chambers. Perhaps the most incongruous phase of boom construction was the use of century-old tile, stripped from houses and barns in Cuba and Spain, to cover artificially aged reproductions.

Nevertheless, Florida gained interesting adaptations of academic European designs. The Singing Tower at Mountain Lake, erected by Edward Bok, is one of the foremost. This marble shaft, dominating a high elevation, has been called a successful union of architecture and sculpture. Its polished walls of many tints, combined with native limestone trim, terminate in foliated openings cut in marble around the carillon. The sculptured detail was designed and executed by Lee Lawrie and forty associates. The bronze door to the crypt at the base, which contains the body of the builder, was the work of Samuel Yellin.

The Ringling Museum at Sarasota is another notable addition. Built of Italian marble, it incorporates architectural details from many historic European structures. Some rooms are finished completely with original paneling from abroad. The loggia contains eleventh-century marble columns and an inlaid doorway from Florence, Italy. Similar architectural antiques have been reassembled throughout. Another good adaptation is the Florida Military Academy at St.Petersburg. Designed around an open court to represent a Spanish village, the grouping includes a chapel, a granary, and a reproduction of the golden tower of Seville. The Civic Center at Lakeland provides an interesting architectural treatment of a lake border, with a concrete sea wall rising on one side against a bluff to form a plaza and colonnade. Other noteworthy buildings are the Knowles Memorial Chapel and the Annie Russell Theater at Winter Park.

After the boom there was a departure from spurious effects and a more general use of native woods, stone, and brick. Coquina rock and Key limestone, particularly the latter, have found popular favor in the newer public buildings, such as the post office at Fort Myers, the Federal Building at Key West, and the municipal airport at Tampa. This material, quarried on the Florida Reef and sawed into slabs, quickly turns from a light cream to a soft weathered gray, and its surface is an almost continuous lacework of marine fossils.

An innovation of the building revival was utility; houses were built to live in, not to promote lot sales. French and British Caribbean colonial types appeared with the resumption of home building in Florida in 1932. This newer construction avoided the almost standard buff tints in favor of white, and eliminated protruding ornamental detail. Stucco bungalows sometimes extended the white finish to the tile roofs, an idea borrowed from Bermuda. The scores of new hotels erected at Miami Beach and elsewhere in Florida after 1935 also had sheer walls of dazzling white, unmarked except for flutings and incised geometric design. This cubicle type of building, more commonly associated with industrial architecture, with its flat surfaces and large windows of steel and glass, had invaded all parts of the State by 1939.

The cabaña, a comparatively modern beach structure, has developed into a rather elaborate facility for seashore comfort. From a primitive, single dressing room, it has expanded into a continuous composition with scores of units, including a lounging room, dressing rooms, and baths, constructed in a half-circle around a pool and attached to a central luxuriously equipped club house. Chiefly Spanish in style at first, with shaded loggias and arcades facing an open court and the sea, the cabaña has since undergone many changes, but all the variations strive for riotous color effects, gay and exotic. One of the most pretentious is the Surf Club at Miami Beach.

City zoning and planning had been in effect for many years in some cities, but the speculative era went far toward ignoring these restrictions. A notable exception was Coral Gables, which started off with fully developed city plans that have since been rigidly enforced. The business area of Coral Gables is restricted to buildings of the Mediterranean and Spanish types, with rock, stuccoed tile, and concrete as approved materials. Outlying sections are zoned to Colonial, French (urban and country), Dutch East African, and even Chinese compound types. The plans of all buildings, even to color and awnings, must be approved by a city-employed architect before their construction.

Florida's three largest cities, Jacksonville, Tampa, and Miami, portray architecturally several generations. Burned in 1901, Jacksonville practically rebuilt its business area, giving it something of the atmosphere of the financial district in a Northern city. Miami has the spectacular flare characteristic of a resort city of enormous and ornate hotels. Tampa, on the other hand, with a few tall buildings is an industrial city spotted with many flat-topped, two- and three-story red-brick cigar factories. In all three cities, outmoded business structures of the bay window, cupola, and turret era still loom among the severe glittering modern fronts that are gradually replacing them.

Architects have two organizations in Florida: the Florida Association of Architects, concerned mainly with the legal and business aspects of building, and three chapters of the American Institute of Architects, which consider the ethical, cultural, and professional phases of architecture. The State board of architecture is a law enforcement body. Practically all cities have enacted rigid building codes under which orderly construction proceeds. Factors that have proved costly in the past, such as dry rot, inadequate windstresses and termite damage, now receive consideration along with design. Florida has recognized the fact that sound construction is an essential element in architectural beauty.

PART II

Principal Cities

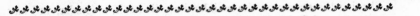

Daytona Beach

Railroad Station: 400 block Magnolia St. for Florida East Coast Ry.
Bus Stations: 115 Volusia Ave. for Florida Motor Lines; 118 Volusia Ave. for Pan-American Lines.
Airport: Municipal Airport 2.5 m. W. on US 92 for Eastern Air Lines and National Airlines; taxi 75¢.
Taxis: 10¢ and upward according to distance and number of passengers.
Local Busses: Fare 5¢ within city limits, 10¢ to Port Orange.
Traffic Regulations: R. turns on red in business district. Beach driving for 1 m. each side of pier, 10 m.p.h.

Accommodations: 39 hotels, numerous tourist homes on mainland and peninsula.

Information Service: Chamber of Commerce, 356 S.Beach St.; Peabody Community House (Tourist Headquarters), 28 N.Wild Olive Ave.; Broadwalk Registration Booth, Oceanfront; City Recreation Dept., City Island.

Radio Station: WMFJ (1420 kc.).
Motion Picture Houses: 5; one for Negroes.
Swimming: Daytona, Ormond, and Port Orange Beaches on Atlantic Ocean; bathhouse facilities 25¢ and 50¢; lifeguards in bathing zone.
Calisthenics: On beach June to Sept. 7–7:30 a.m. daily except Sundays, free.
Golf: Daytona Golf and Country Club, 1.5 m. S. on Ridgewood Ave., 18 holes, greens fee $1.50; Daytona Highlands Golf Course, Volusia Ave. and Lakeshore Dr., 9 holes, greens fee 75¢; Seabreeze Golf Course, 2 m. N. on Atlantic Ave., 18 holes, greens fee $2; Rio Vista Golf Course, N.Ridgewood Ave. between Holly Hill and Ormond, 9 holes, greens fee 50¢.
Fishing: From all bridges in city, free; ocean pier 25¢.
Shuffleboard: Peabody Community House, 28 N.Wild Olive Ave.; City Island Playground, foot of Orange Ave., $1.50 annual fee.
Lawn Bowling: Daytona Lawn Bowling Club, S. end Riverfront Park; Peabody Lawn Club, 28 N.Wild Olive Ave.
Band Concerts: Oceanfront Park, between Ocean Ave. and the Broadwalk (summer) Sun., Tues., and Thurs. evenings; (winter) daily Jan.–Mar.

Annual Events: Trap Shoot, Municipal Gun Club, N. side of DeLand Rd. Jan.; National Motorcycle 200-m. beach race, Mar.; Annual Stock Car Races, beach, Mar.; International Senior Golf tournament, Daytona Golf and Country Club, Mar.; Halifax Summer Frolics and local Mardi Gras celebration, July; Annual Labor Day Festival; mothboat races at intervals during summer and winter seasons.

DAYTONA BEACH (7 alt., 16,598 pop.) is a city with a triple waterfront, one on the Atlantic Ocean and one on each side of a tidewater lagoon known as the Halifax River. The western division, on the mainland, contains the larger business and shopping district, and many homes of year-round residents. The eastern section, on the peninsula, reached by four bridges—one a concrete span supported by wooden piles—contains a residential section along the riverfront and ocean, and the lively beach colony on the ocean shore.

Shading the streets on the mainland are live oak, magnolia, and bay trees, species of the hardwood forests that once flourished in this territory. To these have been added extensive plantings of native palms and the hardier subtropical trees and shrubs. The city is noted for its oleanders, which grow abundantly throughout the area and are in full pink and white blossom from March until late summer.

Beach Street, paralleling the river, is the principal mainland thoroughfare; its two- and three-story brick and stucco business buildings, occupying the west side of the street, overlook the mile-long Riverfront Park. In the heart of the shopping district, its broad lawn enclosed by a stone fence, stands the two-story Burgoyne residence, an ornate structure of coquina rock and faded green shingles, one of the city's oldest landmarks. In the river at the foot of Orange Avenue, separated by a narrow channel, lies City Island, once known as Railroad Island when used by Henry Flagler as a river freight terminal for his railroad. Donated to the city in 1897, it was enlarged and developed as a recreation center.

Ridgewood Avenue, following the crest of a low ridge from which the city slopes to the river, and sheltered for the most part by huge overhanging live oaks, is the oldest residential street. The broad avenue is lined by dwellings built in the early 1890's and by those of more recent construction.

The city's Negro settlement, comprising 33 per cent of the city's total population, lies west of the railroad, and has its churches, small mercantile establishments, and typical one- and two-room frame dwellings. Negro orchestras are in demand at white entertainments. The greater number of inhabitants are employed as domestics and unskilled labor, and during the tourist seasons many are in service at resort hotels as cooks, waiters, porters, and bellboys.

The majority of estates on the eastern shore of the Halifax River have their own piers and boathouses, and the river provides a basin for yachts, houseboats, and small craft, as well as a course, south of the bridges, for mothboat races held frequently throughout the year. Recreational and community activities, however, are centered about Oceanfront Park, with its spacious coquina rock stadium, concrete broadwalk, and privately operated amusement pier.

In the business district of the oceanfront section of the city are many retail shops that display curios, exciting bathing togs and appurtenances to water sports. Daytona Beach is both a summer and winter resort, and for practically twelve months of the year the sidewalks and streets here are hosts to a throng of sun-tanned men and women—with an occasional sheepish, white-skinned newcomer—arrayed in bright and scanty beach regalia. Activities in this half-mile area present a colorful cross-section of Florida's resort life.

Period architecture in the Daytona Beach territory is limited to private residences. Although pseudo-Mediterranean types prevail, there are examples of the Italian Renaissance type with turned columns of polished native stone, and of Spanish Colonial design. Certain other traditional features have been incorporated in the design of local buildings, such as the steep roofs, sturdy walls, wooden shutters, and massive chimneys of French provincial types.

Concerts, musicals, festivals, and art exhibits are a large part of each season's program. Since 1932 the city has conducted outdoor interdenominational services of short sermons and congregational singing on the ocean front each Sunday evening during the summer months. For Negroes, there is a social and educational center at Bethune-Cookman College.

The city of Daytona Beach lies in the area known provincially as the Halifax country, originally inhabited by the Timucuan Indians. Franciscan friars established missions in the area about 1587 and converted many to Christianity. In 1702 the English colonists, with their allies, the Creek Indians, swept down from Georgia, destroying the missions and killing the natives or taking them into slavery.

A dormant period followed until 1765, when the British settlers came to take up plantations along the Halifax River. The Indians were friendly and settlers prospered until the outbreak of the Revolution. The majority of the English moved to the West Indies when Florida was ceded to Spain in 1783, and their plantations, taken over by American pioneers during the second Spanish and American territorial periods, failed because of clashes with the Indians. Before 1821, through grants offered by Governor Nespedes of St.Augustine, practically all the land in the vicinity of Daytona was taken up by American colonists from Georgia. The majority of the grants were for sugar plantations, but a few were given for the cutting of timber.

Permanent settlement on the site of Daytona Beach began about 1870 when Mathias Day, of Mansfield, Ohio, bought a tract for $1,200, laid out the original plat of the town, and named the settlement Daytona. Alfred Johnson of New Jersey, who had preceded Day, built the first residence, a log cabin, at the corner of First Avenue and North Beach Street. Among the first large buildings was the Colony House, designed as a hotel to accommodate settlers until they could build for themselves. Despite the activity and enthusiasm of the pioneers, the town grew slowly, because of limited transportation facilities.

Transportation in English times was principally by sea from Jacksonville, and by the Kings Road, but this highway was neglected and overgrown at the beginning of the American territorial period. In 1876 a stage road was opened west of Daytona to Volusia Landing, near DeLand, on the St.Johns River, which shortened the route considerably. By 1881 a ferry was established across the Tomoka River, 11 miles north of Daytona, connecting with the reconstructed Kings Road into St.Augustine. Five years later the St.Johns and Halifax River Railroad was extended to the Tomoka River. This stream, bridged in 1887, permitted the first train to enter Daytona. The same year the Halifax River was spanned, making the peninsula and ocean beaches more accessible.

Henry M. Flagler, who played an important part in the development of the Florida east coast, extended his railroad south from St.Augustine in 1888 and purchased a large hotel at Ormond from John Anderson and Joseph D. Price, its builders. Daytona took on a new lease of life with the influx of winter visitors and soon had a population of 2,000. Although developed almost solely as a resort, the area is the center of a prosperous citrus industry. The more recent growing of the papaya and the preparation of products made from this melonlike fruit is a flourishing industry. This territory marks the approximate northernmost limits for its commercial cultivation.

Up to 1914, Beach Street was a narrow shell road along the Halifax River, fringed with tall pines and cabbage palms. In that year the sea wall and esplanade were built and presented to the city by C.C.Burgoyne, a pioneer resident.

Until 1926 the city of Daytona occupied only the west shore of the Halifax River. On the opposite side lay Seabreeze and Daytona Beach, separate municipalities. During the boom period of 1924–26, Daytona and the small community of Port Orange began wrangling over the annexation of the peninsula south of Daytona Beach. Landowners in the disputed territory demanded that they be included in Daytona. This was done in 1924, and the Daytona confines were extended to the southern end of the peninsula. Two years later Seabreeze and Daytona Beach voted for annexation and the three cities, with a single municipal government, were united under the name of Daytona Beach.

The magnificent ocean beach, 23 miles of white sand, 500 feet wide and beaten to the smoothness and hardness of a pavement by incoming tides, is internationally recognized as a natural motor speedway. Its modern history is linked with the development of the automobile, for pioneers of the motor industry conducted speed trials here over a period of 35 years. The first driver to break a world's record on the beach was Alexander Winton, who, in 1903, piloted his machine at the speed of 68 miles an hour. The same year R.E.Olds drove a measured mile in one minute, six seconds.

In 1905 John Jacob Astor, William K. Vanderbilt, Henry M. Flagler, Rollin White, and other wealthy racing enthusiasts and motorcar builders were attracted to the spot. Henry Ford, at that time perfecting his car, which he drove himself, was forced to withdraw from a race owing to lack of funds for necessary repairs. In the next decade the names of L.Malford Dusenberg, Jimmy Murphy, Ralph De Palma, H.O.D.Seagrave, and Barney Oldfield flashed on the racing horizon. Frank Lockhart and Lee Bible met spectacular deaths while attempting to set new records. In March 1935 Sir Malcolm Campbell, the English sportsman, drove his *Bluebird* along the measured mile at the rate of 276 miles per hour.

POINTS OF INTEREST

RIVERFRONT PARK, S.Beach St. between Orange and Fairview Aves. and extending to the Halifax River, is a landscaped area planted with Washingtonian palms, cedars, banana trees, and many native and exotic flowers and shrubs. There is a drinking fountain in a colonnaded Corinthian pavilion near the center of the park, and flowing artesian wells provide water for lily ponds and a brook spanned by arched stone foot bridges.

SUGAR MILL MACHINERY, on the lawn of a house at the SW. corner of S.Ridgewood and Loomis Aves., includes the flywheel and cylinder of a large sugar mill of the early nineteenth century. The origin and ownership are undetermined, and it is not known how long it has been on the site.

ST.PAUL'S ROMAN CATHOLIC CHURCH, SW. corner N.Ridgewood Ave. and Cypress St., was built in 1927, Gerald Barry, Chicago, architect. It is a buff stucco structure with red tile roof and dome designed in a modified Spanish-Italian Renaissance style with a lace-paneled pecky-cypress door framed by twisted columns of a composite order, topped with finials, a broken pediment and a niched figure of St.Paul. The dome, topped with a cupola and cross, dominates the Daytona Beach skyline. The design of the two massive doors is based upon that of the portals of the Basilica in Valencia, Spain. The church is the repository for a relic of Saint Teresa, brought from Rome, which consists of a bone, a strand of hair, and a fragment of the Saint's garments.

THE BETHUNE-COOKMAN COLLEGE (Negro), on both sides of 2nd Ave. between McLeod and Lincoln Sts., operated by the Methodist Episcopal Church, has a campus shaded by moss-draped oaks and cabbage palms. Two- and three-story rectangular red brick buildings with white-columned entrances house the various departments of the college. The institution was founded in 1904 by Mary McLeod Bethune, a Negro, as the Daytona Normal and Industrial Institute for Girls, and became co-educational in 1922 when merged with Cookman Institute. The latter school was established in Jacksonville in 1872. Bethune-Cookman was the first private school in Florida to offer Negroes an education above the elementary grades.

The college places special emphasis on Negro teachers' training, recognized as one of the State's greatest needs. The institution was expanded from a rented frame cottage to 14 brick and stucco buildings occupying a 58-acre campus. There is a faculty of 30 and an average yearly enrollment of 700 students.

OCEAN BEACH, on the eastern limits of the city, is a broad stretch of sand and surf accessible from a number of streets on the peninsula. The bathing zone between Silver Beach Avenue and University Boulevard is protected by lifeguards, and has first aid and rescue facilities. The beach is lined with wooden umbrellas painted red, yellow, blue, and green, contrasting vividly with the white sand. When the tide is low the beach is popular for driving, and rows of cars park on the sand above the wide driving area and the surf. Bicycles and motor scooters are popular conveyances, and colorfully clad bathers go far out on the gradually sloping shelf of sand into the surf. The well-known Daytona Beach speedway is an 11-mile stretch, 500 feet wide at low tide, extending from Ormond Beach on the north to Ponce de Leon Inlet on the south.

THE MUNICIPAL BROADWALK, a concrete promenade 50 feet wide and 1,680 feet long, extends along the beach front between Ora and Main Sts. Amusement devices border the land side of the walk, and steps lead down to the beach at intervals.

OCEANFRONT PARK lies below the street level between Ocean Ave. and the Broadwalk. Landscaped with flowerbeds and palms and criss-crossed with walks, the park contains a row of concession stalls under Ocean Avenue, and facing the beach, sun shelters, and ornamental fountains. At the northern end are a large coquina-rock bandshell and a stadium seating 6,500. In the center of the park rises a tall, obelisk-shaped clock tower. In place of numerals on the four faces of the clock dial, the 12-letter name of Daytona Beach is spelled out. Residents often give an alphabetical rendition of the time, saying: 'It is H after Y,' instead of the conventional, '25 minutes after 12.' Pedestrian tunnels beneath Ocean Avenue connect the park with several cross-street intersections.

The DAYTONA BEACH BOAT WORKS (*open daily*), 701 S.Beach St., covering about 10 acres, contains a landlocked yacht basin, parkway, machine shop, foundry, marine railway, and a drydock accommodating boats up to 600 tons. There are separate clubs for officers and sailors of visiting yachts.

DAYTONA BEACH PIER (*open 6 a.m.–7 p.m. daily; adm. including museum 10¢; for fishing 25¢*), E. end of Main St., extends 1,200 feet into the ocean. It has facilities for fishing and supports a casino where there is dancing Tuesdays and Saturdays. The MUSEUM on an upper floor has a small collection of mounted Florida fishes, birds, and animals.

POINTS OF INTEREST IN ENVIRONS

Ormond Tropical Gardens, 5.9 *m.*; New Smyrna, 14.5 *m.*; Ponce de Leon Lighthouse, 16.1 *m.* (*see Tour 1b*).

❧❧

Jacksonville

Railroad Station: Union Terminal, 1000 W.Bay St., for Atlantic Coast Line R.R., Seaboard Air Line Ry., Southern Ry., Florida East Coast Ry., and Georgia-Southern and Florida R.R.
Bus Stations: Union Bus Station, Bay and Hogan Sts., for Southeastern Greyhound Lines, Florida Motor Lines, McJunkin Bus Line, and Beach Motor Transit Co.; 16 N.Hogan St. for Pan-American Lines.
Airport: Municipal, 7 m. N. on US 17 for Eastern Air Lines and National Airlines, taxi $1.25, 1 to 5 passengers, time 20 min.
Taxis: Jitney cabs, 10¢ and upward according to distance and number of passengers; meter cabs, 35¢, 1 to 5 passengers in 3-mile zone.
Busses: Fare 8¢, 3 tokens 20¢, weekly 20-ride pass $1, school children, 10 tickets 40¢.
Piers: St.Johns River, S. end of Liberty St. for Clyde-Mallory Line; 800 E.Bay St. for Merchants and Miners Line.
Toll Bridge: S. end of Broad St. to S.Jacksonville and points S., autos 25¢, pedestrians 1¢, yearly tag $1, trucks according to tonnage.
Traffic Regulations: R. turns on red. One-way streets: E. on Forsyth, Monroe, and Church Sts.; W. on Adams, Duval, and Ashley Sts. Follow traffic lanes on Riverside Viaduct and St.Johns River bridge approach.

Accommodations: 28 hotels, 3 for Negroes; tourist camps on US highways in environs; rates higher during winter.

Information Service: Tourist and Convention Bureau, Hemming Park NE. corner W.Monroe and Hogan Sts.; Jacksonville Motor Club, Windsor Hotel, Hogan and W.Monroe Sts ; Jacksonville Tourist Club, Waterworks Park, 1st and Main Sts.; Florida State Hotel Assn., 224 W.Forsyth St.; Chamber of Commerce, 52 W.Bay St.
Radio Stations: WJAX (900 kc.); WMBR (1370 kc.).
Motion Picture Houses: 13; 3 for Negroes.
Swimming: Sunshine Pool, S.Jacksonville, foot of Flagler Ave.; Springfield Pool, 7th St. and Blvd.; Stockton Pool, Stockton St. near McCoy's Creek, Riverside; Lackawanna Pool, Lennox and Day Aves.; Jacksonville, Atlantic, and Neptune Beaches, 20 m., all free: regular bus service, 25¢.
Tennis: Boone Park, 3700 Park St.; Riverside Park, Gilmore St. between College and Park Sts.; Springfield Park, Perry and 4th Sts.; Southside Park, Hendricks Ave. between LaSalle and Cedar Sts. All $1 membership fee, 30¢ an hour daytime, 40¢ at night.
Golf: Municipal Links, 1450 Golfair Blvd., greens fee 75¢; Hyde Park Country Club, San Juan Ave. and 64th St., greens fee 75¢; Timuquana Country Club, Venetia, near Camp Foster, greens fee $2; Ponte Vedra Country Club, Jacksonville Beach, greens fee $1.50; San Jose Golf Course, San Jose Blvd., S.Jacksonville, greens fee $1; all 18-hole courses.
Riding: Stables and riding school, 64th St., Lake Shore; Orange Park Rd. at Yukon.
Dog Races: McDuff Ave. N. of Beaver St., adm. 25¢, Dec.–Apr.

Annual Events: Mid-winter Trap Shoots, Jan.; Flower Show, Apr.; Easter Sunrise Services (Ribaut Monument, Mayport); Jacksonville Outboard Club Regatta, Apr. and Sept.; Seminole Canoe Club, Ortega, tournaments and long distance trips in spring and fall.

JACKSONVILLE (25 alt., 129,459 pop.), the State's largest city and a leading commercial center of the South Atlantic seaboard, is sometimes referred to as a working son in the Florida family of playboys. It is in the northeast corner of the State, where the St. Johns River turns eastward to the Atlantic. This broad stream divides Jacksonville from South Jacksonville, and dictates the layout of business and residential sections. Spanning the river is one of the Nation's largest vertical-lift bridges. A viaduct, branching west, leads above a web of railroad tracks to areas where landscaped estates extend to the water's edge. Eastward along the north bank, where the river twists into a lazy 'S,' are five miles of wharves, terminating at municipal piers.

Within four blocks of the city's palm-fringed square, ocean liners, banana boats, globe-girdling freighters, and occasionally noble four-masted schooners dock, and at the near-by fishhouse wharf, weatherbeaten smacks and crab and shrimp boats discharge their cargoes. Purple flowering hyacinths clot the boat slips and basins, and out in midstream floating islands of them from the upper reaches of the river sail down to sea. A dozen or more streets of the business section, ending at the waterfront, afford a maritime vista of gleaming superstructures, towering spars, and wind-whipped flags of many nations.

Bay Street, paralleling the waterfront, was once a sandy trail lined with pine shacks. Despite paving and other attempts at modernization, the street retains much of the salty flavor that prevailed during the heyday of Jacksonville's river traffic. Here are the city's older commercial structures, and west of the bridge, where the street approaches the railroad terminals, is a succession of bars, pawnshops, and upstairs hotels. Few of these buildings have stood more than a third of a century, for the fire of 1901 swept away nearly all of this downtown area.

Rising from the waterfront is the modern business and shopping district, a six-block square area of metropolitan stores, lofty hotels, and office buildings that presents an impressive skyline. Yet within this section remain examples of once fashionable clapboard residences with dormer windows and rambling galleries supported by wooden columns, now converted into rooming and boarding houses. Many of their cramped yards are bright with jasmine, dogwood, and crape myrtle; flowering gardens edge brick walks, and coral vines and wisteria cover trellised nooks. Along some downtown streets evergreen oaks, camphor trees, and native palms relieve the stone and concrete backgrounds.

Plaques and tablets marking historic sites crop up unexpectedly on cornerstones and at street intersections. Mendicants are more plentiful than in tourist cities of Florida. Busses have replaced trolley cars, and an anti-noise campaign is responsible for the neon 'quiet' sign that decorates overhead traffic lights.

The city is awakened each morning at 7 o'clock by 'Big Jim,' a stentorian whistle atop the waterworks. It also proclaims the noonday respite, sounds again at five o'clock, and is a tocsin in times of disaster. The morning whistle is broadcast by a local radio station. This powerful, copper chime whistle was designed by John Einig and cast here in 1880 by James Patterson, for whom it was named. Funds for its manufacture were raised by public subscription through local labor unions, and it was donated to the city.

Main Street is a pioneer thoroughfare that marks the eastern boundary of the business area. Traversing residential districts on the outskirts, it runs between ramshackle buildings of faded brick and wood, threads a short neon-lighted stretch of chain stores, and halts amid a clutter of wharves and warehouses at the river. A boisterous street, its sidewalks are thronged far into the night, when the more sedate avenues adjoining are dim and deserted.

The more substantial Jacksonville homes are south and southwest of the business district. Here, along quiet, oak-shaded streets, and in estates where terraced lawns descend to the river bank, scarlet hibiscus and oleander hedges, trumpet vine, and purple bougainvillea drape brick walls and gateways.

At the western rim of the business area, Broad Street, an avenue of motley shops, is the outpost of the slum district. It is a strip of US 1 ending at the busy approach to the St. Johns River Bridge. A tall red-and-white brick temple erected by the Negro Masonic order, the most imposing edifice along the thoroughfare, contains offices of Negro professional men. The Negro settlements, extending west from Broad Street, redeemed in part by an extensive slum-clearance project, comprise a territory that represents less than 2 per cent of the city's 35-square-mile area.

Although the majority of local Negroes, 30 per cent of the total population, are engaged in domestic service or supply the unskilled labor market, others operate businesses that include restaurants, theaters, funeral establishments, and three insurance companies, one with assets of a million dollars. Their many churches range from the store-front type, with a few dozen worshippers, to a substantial edifice with a congregation of nearly 2,000. The Stanton High School has an average enrollment of 1,500 Negroes and the Edward Waters College for Negroes provides advanced educational facilities. Brewster Hospital serves the city's Negro population.

Jacksonville has more than 450 industries producing as many different commodities. The city has the largest naval-stores yard and the largest wholesale lumber market on the Atlantic coast. It stands second on the South Atlantic seaboard as a distribution port for petroleum products. Having the world's largest cigar factory under one roof, it supplies a tenth of all cigars consumed in America. Jacksonville also has the only dry-ice plant and the only glass factory in Florida.

The boom had little effect upon the city; it remained financially sound throughout depression years, and continues to be the banking center of the State. Its docks, terminals, cotton compress, naval-stores warehouses, and water and light plant are municipally owned. A towering sign over the light plant urges civic-minded citizens to 'Do It Electrically,' and a more modest one above the City Hall doorway reminds passers-by that to cook with electricity is the clean and economical way. In addition to furnishing current at the lowest rate in Florida, profits of the $10,000,000 light plant have averaged more than $1,500,000 annually, making it possible to give the city the lowest tax rate of any community of its size in the United States.

Jacksonville is a focal point of land, water, and air transportation in the South. A hundred passenger trains enter and depart daily in the winter season from the Union Terminal; 20 regularly scheduled commercial planes and numerous transient planes land every 24 hours at the municipal airport, and an average of 5 ocean-going and coastwise vessels tie up at the river piers during the same period. Three Federal highways converge at Jacksonville, and the greater number of tourists visiting the State pass through the city or remain overnight before scattering to resorts more typical of Florida's advertising literature. Twice each year—in early winter when the sun-trek South begins, and in early spring when the tourist exodus is under way—Jacksonville plays overnight host to more than half a million visitors. Shop windows display a limited amount of sporting togs, but local people do not wear 'whites' in winter, although as near as St.Augustine, 40 miles south, this is the custom.

The city operates an educational project known as the Jacksonville Plan that has won wide repute. Through arrangements with employers and parents, pupils in the two upper classes at high school may enter various plants co-operating with the school. These apprentices, working 4 hours a day in a 5-day week, obtain practical training in chosen occupations under experts, but as the training is purely an educational project, the pupils receive no salaries.

The city has the *a capella* choir of St.Johns Episcopal Church, the Friday Symphony Orchestra, and a Choral Guild of 300 voices. The Civic Music Association of more than 1,500 members offers a series of winter concerts.

In the literary field, George Dillon, a native, was awarded the Pulitzer prize in 1932 for his poem 'The Flowering Stone.' Harriet Beecher Stowe wrote several accounts of the St.Johns River in the vicinity of Jacksonville, where she spent many winters after the War between the States, and Stephen Crane was a resident during 1896, soon after publication of his most successful novel, *The Red Badge of Courage*. One of his short stories, 'The Open Boat,' written here deals with his experiences in Florida. Prominent among the local Negro writers are Thomas H. B. Walker, author of *Man without Blemish*, and the late James Weldon Johnson, who wrote many books and memoirs and poetry, the best known being the *Autobiography of an Ex-colored Man*, and the lyrics of 'Lift Every Voice and Sing,' a Negro anthem, nationally accepted, sung for the first time in Jacksonville, and written when he was principal of Stanton High School. His brother J.Rosamond Johnson, composer of many musical-comedy scores, and perhaps best known for his popular song, 'Under the Bamboo Tree,' spent the early years of his life in the city. Paul Laurence Dunbar and W.E.Dancer, Negro poets, were at one time Jacksonville residents.

The Florida Historical Society, originally organized in 1856, has for its objective the preservation of all material pertaining to the history of the State. The Society's library is in Jacksonville.

In 1816 Lewis Zachariah Hogans built a log cabin on his Spanish grant, overlooking the St.Johns River, and the field he tilled is now the heart of Jacksonville. In 1818, John Brady maintained a rowboat ferry across the river at the foot of present-day Liberty Street, where, years before, cattle were swum across the stream. This ford had been named Wacca Pilatka (cows crossing over) by the Indians, but the spot was known as the Ferry of St.Nicholas by the Spanish who in about 1740 built Fort St.Nicholas on the south shore to guard the crossing. The English, however, called the settlement Cowford, a name that persisted until 1822.

Taking advantage of the ford, the Kings Road, built in 1765 and leading from St.Augustine to Georgia, crossed the river at this point. Fort St.Nicholas was burned in 1812 by the Patriots of Florida during their operations against St.Augustine.

Upon the purchase of Florida by the United States in 1821, order was restored in the province by General Andrew Jackson, Territorial Governor. A section of Cowford on the north bank of the St.Johns River, platted in 1822 by Isaiah D. Hart, his brother Daniel, and Zachariah Hogans, was given the name of Jacksonville in honor of Florida's governor, although the nearest Jackson ever came to the town was the Suwannee River. Streets were laid out and named, but it was eight years before the town claimed a population of 300. The city was incorporated in 1832, but the charter was repealed in 1840, and until a new one was drawn 11 months later, Jacksonville was without a city government.

The first newspaper, the short-lived *Courier*, appeared in 1835 with a sentimental poem occupying the first column. Several proposed railroads were incorporated, and although none was built, the town developed rapidly as a market for cotton and naval stores, and with the introduction of the steam sawmill, lumber became an important industry.

The Seminole War followed a series of Indian depredations that terrorized the Jacksonville area. Business was paralyzed, and to crown the succession of disasters, a freeze in 1835, with the mercury dropping to 7° above zero, killed the orange groves of the St.Johns River section. At the end of the war in 1842, a 20-year period of prosperity ensued. Steamship lines inaugurated weekly services to Savannah and Charleston, and as far up the St.Johns as Enterprise. The harbor, crowded with schooners loading longleaf yellow pine for domestic and foreign markets, was described as resembling a forest of towering masts, and Bay Street, with its bars, gambling houses, and dance halls, patronized by roistering, hard-bitten seafarers, became almost as notorious as San Francisco's Barbary Coast.

While transportation by water flourished, a visitor stated that he saw only two vehicles in the city, a dray and a secondhand hearse, each pulled by aged mules and driven by a Negro. In 1851 the State legislature authorized the construction of a plank toll road between Jacksonville and Lake City, then known as Alligator. Prior to the building of a railroad to that point, the sole means of transportation between Jacksonville and the State capital at Tallahassee was by stage, a four-day journey.

At the outbreak of the War between the States, although having many wealthy northern citizens, Jacksonville sympathies were largely with the South, and when the State joined the Confederacy the local light infantry was first to offer its services. Blockade runners made the city a base. On four separate occasions Jacksonville was occupied for brief intervals by Union forces. Upon withdrawal of the northern troops in 1863, refugees returning to the city found their homes burned, trenches instead of streets, and outlying farms desolate. All ferry and dock facilities were destroyed; there was no commerce, no currency, no river transportation. At one time, according to the report of a Union officer, the town had less than two dozen inhabitants. During the Reconstruction period, however, Jacksonville grew into a popular winter-resort city. The first theater and several large hotels were built. The St. James, referred to as the Fifth Avenue Hotel of Florida, opened in 1869, and 14 years later the first electric lights in the State were installed on the premises—8 in the lobby and 8 outside. Population in 1870 reached 6,912, an increase of 300 per cent in a decade.

It was during this period that newspaper ventures showed signs of permanency, and predecessors of the two present Jacksonville dailies were established. The early 1880's marked progress in the development of the port of Jacksonville, when the channel was deepened and jetties built at the mouth of the river, an undertaking aided by Federal funds and supervised by Government engineers. The volume of river traffic soared; by 1885 upwards of 74 vessels were in port service, accounting for an annual business of $2,000,000. The peak value of bottoms and cargoes was estimated in excess of $38,000,000.

It was not until 1883 that a railroad began operation southward from the city. This was a narrow gauge line with a terminal on the south shore of the St. Johns River, running a daily combination passenger and freight train to St. Augustine. Until the completion of a bridge in 1890, passengers from Jacksonville and northern points were ferried across the river.

Prior to the Spanish-American War, Jacksonville became a refuge for many Cuban exiles. Filibustering vessels, among them the tugboat *Three Friends*, repeatedly smuggled arms and men into Cuba, eluding U.S. Revenue cutters and Spanish cruisers. Upon declaration of war, 40,000 American troops encamped near the city, and the river was mined as a precaution against raids by enemy gunboats.

The city's greatest catastrophe, the fire of 1901, swept an area of 148 blocks, destroyed 2,368 buildings and left 9,000 homeless; but upon the devastated area a new Jacksonville was built, and within a decade more than $25,000,000 had been expended to replace the burned structures. Rebuilding followed sounder standards of design and construction. The city is predominantly one of single-family frame dwellings and there is an absence of the hybrid type of architecture known as Florida-Mediterranean.

In 1930 a city plan adopted by the council and still in force was judged by the City Planning Experts' Board of the United States as one of four outstanding in the Nation. Fifty-seven years of intensive work and expenditure of $18,000,000 in dredging the river channel and basins have made Jacksonville a great inland port. Its population more than doubled between 1915 and 1937. Jacksonville's bonds sell on a par with Government securities and its bonded indebtedness stands less than $80 per capita, a figure approached by no other city in the State.

POINTS OF INTEREST

1. HEMMING PARK, Hogan St. between W.Duval and W.Monroe Sts. and extending to Laura St., is a block-square area planted with date, Washingtonian, and cabbage palms, live oak and camphor trees, and landscaped with hardy shrubs and flowers. The curved walks, lined with green-slatted concrete benches, converge at a central plaza from which rises a tall CONFEDERATE MONUMENT, surmounted by the figure of a soldier, given to the city by Charles G. Hemming in 1898, for whom the park was named. Hemming was a member of the Jacksonville Light Infantry and Third Regiment that encamped in the city during the War between the States. Parking on Monroe Street and a portion of Hogan Street, opposite the information booth, is reserved for out-of-State motorists.

2. JACKSONVILLE PUBLIC LIBRARY (*open 9–9 weekdays*), NE. corner E.Adams and Ocean Sts., a limestone structure with a Corinthian façade, built in 1905, is the depository of 130,000 volumes, largest in the State. The building was the gift of Andrew Carnegie. The library is noted for its collection of Floridiana.

3. The SITE OF COWFORD, SE. corner Liberty and Bay Sts., is designated by a bronze marker on a metal pedestal against the Liberty Street side of a red brick building. It denotes the site of the original settlement of Jacksonville in 1790.

4. The MUNICIPAL STADIUM, Adams St. between Bridier and Haines Sts. and extending to E.Monroe St., with concrete and steel-and-wood bleachers, has a seating capacity of 21,000. The Jacksonville Choral Guild of 300 voices holds outdoor oratorios and operas here.

The MUNICIPAL DOCKS AND TERMINALS, on the St.Johns River between 8th and 21st Sts., are distinguished by long galvanized steel warehouses and railroad spurs running out on three piers 1,000 feet long and 200 to 300 feet wide. Here freighters with round, tin rat guards clamped on their cables lade and unlade cargo with cranes direct from railroad cars. The place hums with the cheerful movements and shouts of scores of Negro stevedores; gulls wheel about the broad, hyacinth-dotted river or fly down screaming to pick up bits of food from brick pavements; there is the clatter of cranes and winches, and the heavy impact of freight.

From the NAVAL STORES YARD, operated in connection with the docks, there is the odor of resin from hundreds of gray barrels, and squat silver-painted turpentine tanks are covered with loose-woven wire 'cages' to safeguard them from lightning risk and doubled insurance rates.

The terminals are flanked by oil and gasoline company stations and dotted with dark, greasy petroleum tanks, gasoline tanks aluminum-painted to ward off the sun's heat and possible explosion, and row upon row of tank cars; by molasses and fertilizer warehouses; a cypress lumber yard, from which comes the pungent odor of freshly cut timber; piles of rusty scrap iron; a pre-cooling plant for fresh fruit and vegetable carriers, and white piles of sand in a dredge depot of the U.S. Engineers, whose duty it is to maintain a 30-foot channel to the sea.

The docks and terminals, established in 1915, operate their own railroad

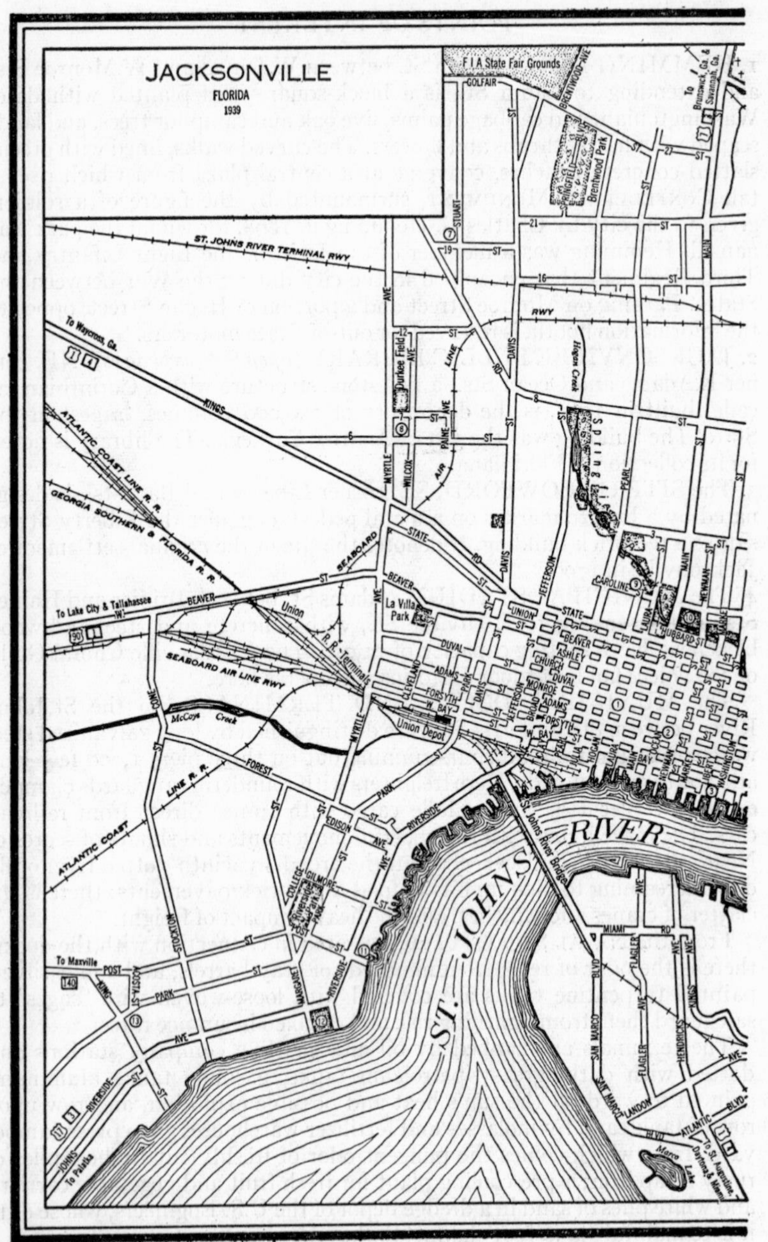

JACKSONVILLE
FLORIDA
1939
F I A State Fair Grounds
GOLFAIR
BRENTWOOD AVE
Brentwood Park
SPRINGFIELD PARK
To Brunswick, Ga. & Savannah, Ga.
STUART
ST. JOHNS RIVER TERMINAL RWY
RWY
To Waycross, Ga.
KINGS
Durkee Field
Hogan Creek
ATLANTIC COAST LINE R. R.
GEORGIA SOUTHERN & FLORIDA R. R.
MYRTLE
WILCOX
AIR LINE
PAINE AVE
DAVIS
PEARL
SEABOARD
STATE
RD
JEFFERSON
MAIN
NEWMAN
CAROLINE
LAURA
HUBBARD
BEAVER
To Lake City & Tallahassee
La Villa Park
Union R. R. Terminals
UNION
DUVAL
ADAMS
FORSYTH
W. BAY
CHURCH
ASHLEY
MONROE
CLEVELAND
SEABOARD AIR LINE RWY
CONE
McCoys Creek
Union Depot
BROAD
HOGAN
OCEAN
MARKET
LIBERTY
WASHINGTON
FOREST
PARK
EDISON
RIVERSIDE
ATLANTIC COAST LINE R. R.
St. Johns River Bridge
RIVER
ST. JOHNS
GILMORE
COLLEGE
Riverside Park
STOCKTON
MARGARET
To Maxville
POST
KING
ACOSTA
MIAMI
SAN MARCO
FLAGLER
HENDRICKS
KINGS
LANDON
ATLANTIC BLVD
Marco Lake
To St. Augustine, Daytona & Miami
JOHNS
To Palatka

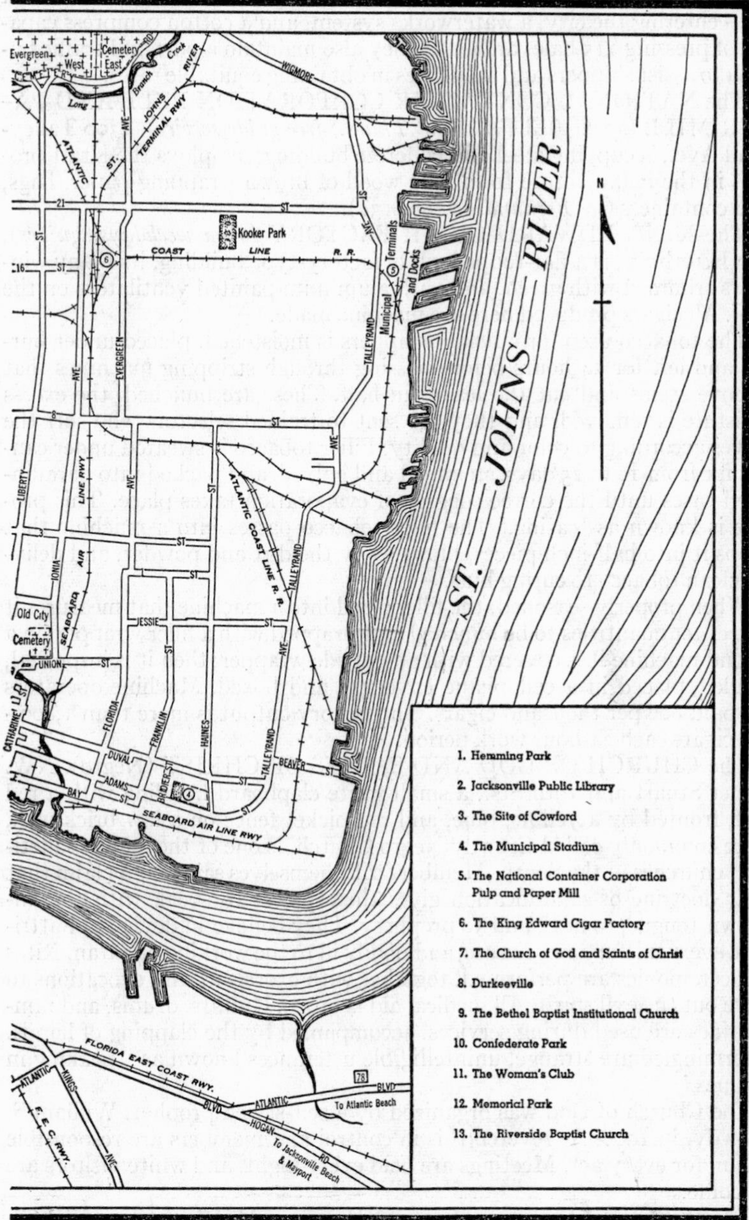
ST. JOHNS RIVER
N
Kooker Park
Terminals and Docks
Municipal
COAST LINE R.R.
ATLANTIC COAST LINE R.R.
SEABOARD AIR LINE RWY
FLORIDA EAST COAST RWY.
ST. JOHNS TERMINAL RWY
Evergreen
Cemetery West
Cemetery East
Long Branch Creek
Old City Cemetery
To Atlantic Beach
To Jacksonville Beach & Mayport
1. Hemming Park
2. Jacksonville Public Library
3. The Site of Cowford
4. The Municipal Stadium
5. The National Container Corporation Pulp and Paper Mill
6. The King Edward Cigar Factory
7. The Church of God and Saints of Christ
8. Durkeeville
9. The Bethel Baptist Institutional Church
10. Confederate Park
11. The Woman's Club
12. Memorial Park
13. The Riverside Baptist Church

system with 20 miles of tracks that have direct connection with all trunk lines entering the city, a waterworks system, and a cotton compress capable of pressing 115 bales an hour. They also maintain a port and traffic bureau to assist shippers and industries in obtaining equitable rates.

5. The NATIONAL CONTAINER CORPORATION PULP AND PAPER MILL (*open* 10–3 *Tues. and Thurs.; free guide service*), 4300 Talleyrand Ave., occupying steel and concrete buildings, employs the Kraft process in the manufacture from pine wood of brown wrapping paper, bags, and containers (*see Fernandina, Tour 3a*).

6. The KING EDWARD CIGAR FACTORY (*open weekdays; guides*), 459 E.16th St., is a flat-topped white factory-type building, its many windows trimmed with green, and with aluminum-painted ventilators on the roof. All cigars produced here are machine made.

The tobacco used for outside wrappers is moistened, placed under burlap and left for 24 hours before passing through stripping machines that remove stems and cut the leaves in half. These are bunched, the excess moisture is removed, and they are sent to trained selectors who sort the leaves according to color and quality. Filler tobacco is sweated under canvas for from 10 to 25 days, stemmed and halved, and packed into paraffin-lined cases until the correct degree of evaporation takes place. This process is known as 'casing.' The filler tobacco passes into a machine that chops it into half-inch pieces, blows away the dirt and powder, and delivers clean tobacco to curing bins.

When properly seasoned, the filler is fed into a machine that measures it into exact quantities to be bunched and wrapped with a filler wrapper; in a second machine it is covered with an outside wrapper; then it is inspected, banded, placed in a cellophane envelope, and boxed. Machine operators are paid 80¢ per thousand cigars. The factory output is more than 1,800,000 cigars each 24-hour work period.

7. The CHURCH OF GOD AND SAINTS OF CHRIST (Negro), NW. corner Stuart and 19th Sts., a small white clapboard building with a red roof, fronted by a yellow, blue, and red picket fence on a low brick wall, more commonly called Crowdy Negro Church, is one of the many 'sanctified' churches of the South. Members call themselves saints and claim that their doctrine of sanctification gives them power to speak with the unknown tongue, to heal, and to prophesy. They believe in devils and attribute every misfortune, disease, and bodily ill to the working of Satan. Rites and ceremonies are performed, together with exorcisms and evocations to drive out the evil spirit. All medical aid is taboo. Guitars, drums, and tambourines are used during services, accompanied by the clapping of hands. Intermingled are strange, unintelligible utterances known as 'speaking in tongues.'

The Church of God was organized by a self-styled prophet, William S. Crowdy, in 1908. A 'reverend' is in control and members are responsible to him for every act. Meetings are held every night, and white visitors are welcome.

8. DURKEEVILLE, main entrance NE. corner Myrtle Ave. and W.6th St., is a 20-acre low-rent, slum-clearance project for Negroes, undertaken

by the city in co-operation with the Federal Housing Administration. There are 34 one- and two-story reinforced concrete houses with red tiled roofs and concrete coal bins on each back stoop to provide fuel for cooking. Apartments range from two to five rooms, with individual porches and yards. The buildings cover less than 16 per cent of the ground area and ample space is available for playgrounds.

9. The BETHEL BAPTIST INSTITUTIONAL CHURCH, NW. corner Caroline and Hogan Sts., is the outstanding Negro church in the city. Of Romanesque design, it is built of grayish-yellow concrete blocks and a gray wooden belfry extends above the corner entrance to a black-shingled spire. The initial branch of the first church of the Baptist denomination was organized in Jacksonville in 1838 and was originally used by white and Negro worshippers. Its first meetings were held in the Government 'Block House,' near the site of the courthouse on Forsyth and Market Streets. In 1840 a chapel was built at the northeast corner of Duval and Newnan Streets, but this was sold to the Methodists in 1846. The fund purchased a plot of two acres in LaVilla, a residential section, where a small brick church was built. Pickets and outposts were stationed here during the War between the States whenever Jacksonville was occupied by Federal troops.

During the Reconstruction period an attempt was made to exclude Negroes from the organization. In court, it was decided that since the majority of the parishioners were colored, the church and its name belonged to them. As an aftermath, however, the Negroes sold the property to the white people, and bought a lot at Main and Union Streets where they built a frame building. In 1894 the church was incorporated by the State as the Bethel Baptist Institutional Church with authority to carry on social betterment and industrial training. It also has a publishing and tract-repository department. The present building was erected in 1903 and houses the second largest Negro congregation in the State.

10. CONFEDERATE PARK, Main and Hubbard Sts., bordering Hogans Creek on the south, is planted with date and cabbage palms, cedars, magnolias, and live oaks, and is landscaped with various shrubs and plants. Green-slatted concrete benches and occasional pieces of statuary line the winding walks. Swans and ducks swim on a small lake, and an island provides a sheltered nesting spot.

This site was the eastern end of Confederate trenches that extended to the present Union Terminal. As many as 14,000 troops were encamped here during the War between the States. On the west side of Main Street is WATERWORKS PARK, containing the municipal light plant, studios of the municipally owned radio station WJAX, a Tourist Center with shuffleboard courts, and a miniature golf course.

11. The WOMAN'S CLUB, NE. corner Riverside Ave. and Post St., is a two-story red brick Tudor-style vine-covered building with a steep-pitched red roof, casement windows, and two half-timbered gables on the Riverside Avenue side. The entrance is on Post Street. In the rear of the building a terraced lawn with marginal landscaping slopes down to the St. Johns River.

12. MEMORIAL PARK, Riverside Ave. between Margaret St. and

Memorial Park Dr., and extending to the St. Johns River, has an opening through the shrubbery on Riverside Ave. from which the winged WAR MEMORIAL FOUNTAIN is visible, silhouetted against the blue water and distant shore of the St. Johns River. The fountain, designed by Adrian Pillars, Jacksonville sculptor, has a winged bronze figure of a youth victorious, holding aloft a branch of laurel on a globe where child and adult figures are depicted caught in the terrestrial whirl.

The park has an open grassy center skirted by a circular promenade, around which are planted oaks, date palms, magnolias, and shrubs. Behind the fountain is a concrete balustrade and walk along the waterfront lined with classic concrete benches.

13. The RIVERSIDE BAPTIST CHURCH (*open* 8–12 *and* 1–5 *daily except Tues. and Fri. p.m.*), SE. corner King and Park Sts., is an octagonal structure of gray limestone blocks with a red tiled roof, embodying features of Spanish and Byzantine architecture. The building was erected in 1925, and Addison Mizner was the architect. Gable wings extend from four sides of the octagon, giving the structure the shape of a cross. The entrance into the front gable, on King Street, is through heavy carved pecky-cypress doors under a graven stone arch, above which is a series of three arched blue windows. Two other entrances into the side gables are through cypress doors under large blue rosette windows. All windows, placed in deep recesses in the thick walls, usually in groups of three, are of blue glass. The effect inside is that of calm blue light diffused from a great height over orderly pews. The only departure from the scheme of blue is a trinity of yellow windows on either side of the rear gable, that cast a golden light upon the choir, enclosed behind iron grillwork back of the pulpit. The central chandelier, copied from one in the Santa Sophia Mosque in Istanbul, has blue glass, to produce the same lighting effect by night as by day. Tile for the floors was brought from an ancient Spanish Cathedral.

14. ORIENTAL GARDENS (*open* 9–5:30 *daily; adm.* 40¢), 2 San Jose Blvd., includes 18 acres of brilliant subtropical plantings along the St. Johns River. Pools and winding streams reflect the massed colors of the many flower beds, and bridges, arches, and garden ornaments carry out the idea of a Chinese garden. The citrus grove here is the nearest spot to Jacksonville where visitors can see orange trees in fruit and bloom.

POINTS OF INTEREST IN ENVIRONS

Mandarin, 13 *m.* (*see Tour 1a*); Jacksonville Beaches, 18.6 *m.*; Ribaut Monument 22.5 *m.*; Mayport, 23.3 *m.* (*see Tour 1a*); Jacksonville City Zoo, 5.9 *m.*; Fort George Island, 21.4 *m.* (*see Tour 2a*).

Key West

Bus Station: Southard and Bahama Sts. for Florida Motor Lines.
Airport: Pan-American Airport, 3 m. NW. on S.Roosevelt Blvd. for Pan American Airways,Inc.; taxi 25¢.
Taxis: 25¢ per passenger, anywhere in city.
Piers: Trumbo Island for Peninsula & Occidental (P. & O.) Steamship Line.

Accommodations: 5 hotels; rooming and boarding houses; rates higher Dec. to Apr.

Information Service: Chamber of Commerce, La Concha Hotel, Fleming and Duval Sts.

Motion Picture Houses: 2.
Swimming: Yacht Basin Pier, S. end of Southard St.; pier off Roosevelt Blvd.N.; Rest Beach S. end of White St.; South Beach, S. end of Duval St.; Nelson English Beach (Negro), S. end of Whitehead St.; all free.
Tennis: Bayview Park, Division St. and North Beach, free daytime, small fee nights.
Golf: Key West Municipal Course, Stock Island, 5 m. E. on State 4A, 9 holes, greens fee $1.
Shuffleboard: Eaton and Simonton Sts., free; Jackson Square, Whitehead and Angela Sts., free.
Fishing: All bridges of the Overseas Highway; steamship docks. Deep-sea charter boats, Yacht Basin, S. end of Southard St.

Annual Events: El Grito de Yara (Cuban Independence Day), Feb. 24; La Semana Alegre (Week of Joy) Feb.

KEY WEST (7 alt., 12,831 pop.), the southernmost city in the United States, 100 miles off the Florida mainland, occupies a coral island barely four miles long and less than two miles wide, lying between the Atlantic Ocean and the Gulf of Mexico. Other keys are visible from the eastern end of the city, low emerald islands in a shimmering, painted sea beneath high-piled lavender clouds. Steamers and other craft work their way through the old Nor'west Channel, a charted course taken for centuries. Much of the vegetation that grows on the island—sapodilla, banyan, tamarind, East Indian palm, frangipani, night-blooming cereus, and a host of others—sprang from seed brought through this channel by seafaring men from far ports of the world. The natural, deep-water harbor is lined with sponge and fish docks, with turtle crawls and markets. Launches, dories, and sturdy smacks of commercial fishermen tie up here, often alongside battle cruisers and liners at anchor.

The sea is an ever-present consideration, yet most of the island is cut off from it by the fenced-in area around West Martello Tower and by the private hotel grounds and beach on the south; by the Fort Taylor fortifications on the west; by the Naval Station on the northwest; and by the docks and abandoned railroad terminal on the north. The city's skyline is low, broken only by two groups of tall radio towers, a large hotel, and the buff cone of a lighthouse.

North and South Roosevelt Boulevards, wide connecting drives planted with palms, rim the island on the east, affording beautiful marine views. Both of these, and Flagler Avenue between them, lead into the downtown area. Duval Street, the main business thoroughfare and the only one completely traversing the island, might be taken as a symbol of Key West. It extends northward from a bathing pier in the Atlantic Ocean through a combined business and residential section, and terminates at a steamship pier in the Gulf of Mexico. At each end of the street a sign reads: 'Stop! Thru Traffic!'

Streets in the business section are almost deserted during the heat of day, houses are shuttered, and dogs sleeping on the sidewalks are not disturbed by detouring pedestrians, none of whom is ever in a hurry. The iceman rings a bell to announce his approach (his product is made of distilled sea water), and occasionally an automobile, a bicycle, or a motor scooter passes, though deep-guttered intersections discourage rapid movement from one street to another. Before completion of the highway, a mule-drawn mail wagon met incoming and outgoing planes, boats, and busses, and between times resumed its regular schedule of hauling sponges. The downtown section comes to life on Saturday nights. Townspeople throng the streets and mingle with the fishermen who have come in for supplies and amusement. Inspired Negro 'Saints' carry on revival meetings at corners, and there is more than a hint of the Spanish promenade as men gather along the walks, their eyes following the ladies as they pass. Open-front cafés, coffee houses, and bars, nearly all erupting music, invite patrons. Many of these places have rear swinging doors labeled 'Club in Rear,' and embellished with an ace of clubs or a pair of dice.

Restaurants, nearly all owned by Cubans, feature Cuban-American cooking, and specialize in seafoods. Turtle steaks, conch steaks, and stews are popular foods, as are *bolichi* roast (beef stuffed with hard-boiled eggs), *alcaporado* (beef stew prepared with olives, raisins, and other ingredients), black bean and *garbanzo* soups, and *arroz con pollo* (chicken with yellow rice). Other dishes are stuffed *chaotas*, baked and fried plantains, preserved guavas, and baked guava duff with hard sauce. Since the island furnishes little forage for cows, and supports but one dairy and a flock of goats, evaporated milk is usually served.

There are no tearooms in Key West, but coffee shops are everywhere, serving black, sweetened coffee and buttered, hard-crusted bread that comes from the oven in two-foot loaves. Coffee is drunk at all hours of the day and night, not much at a time—*un buchito*—just a swallow. These shops are social institutions; here newspapers and magazines are read, problems of the day are discussed, and local gossip is exchanged.

Its isolation on the last of Florida's inhabited keys and its proximity to the West Indies have given Key West characteristics of friendliness and leisure, and tempered it with the Latin approach to life; the inhabitants are congenial and curious, ready with smile and conversation in a community where it is normal for everyone to know everyone else. The city is made up of a conglomeration of races speaking English and Spanish, each influenced by Negro dialects. Among the merchants, commercial fishermen, and artisans, are descendants of settlers who migrated here chiefly from Virginia, the New England States, and the West Indies. About one-fourth of the population is descended from Cubans and Spaniards that arrived with the establishment of the cigar factories in the 1860's, and from refugees of the Cuban Revolution of 1868 and 1898. Key West 'Conchs' are the offspring of two groups of cockney English; one group migrated to the Bahamas from London in 1649, another moved from Florida to the Bahamas when Spain regained Florida in 1783. Descendants of these two groups emigrated to the Florida Keys during the early 1800's when marine salvaging and fishing became profitable. Both white and Negro immigrants from the Bahamas speak with a cockney accent and use cockney words and phrases. The Negro population, confined to a section west of Duval Street, is almost wholly of Bahama origin, with a few immigrants from Cuba. Since slavery was abolished in the British territories long before it ended in the United States, there are few ex-slaves on the islands. Most of the Negroes are employed in fishing and turtle industries, and in domestic service, though some collect and sell large, rose-pink conch shells.

Houses in Key West differ little from those of the island's first settlers—pirates and seamen of foundered vessels who built homes similar to those they had seen in New England, New Orleans, or in the Bahamas. They used materials found close at hand—salvaged lumber, occasionally cedar and hardwoods from the upper keys and Cuba, and pine from Pensacola. Masonry made its appearance in 1844 when schooners arrived with great cargoes of brick and cement for the construction of Fort Taylor.

Then as now, the local builder, ever mindful of hurricanes, built staunchly. The typical Key West house, a one-and-a-half story frame structure put together with mortise and tenon joints, and secured by pegs and trenails, is anchored deep in the native coral rock. None has a basement because of the solid rock beneath the topsoil. Few are painted, for paint does not last long in the tropics. Roof area is of prime importance because the city depends solely on rain for its drinking water, as that obtained from drilled wells is brackish. Many houses have roofs with two and even three combs, and every inch of roof space is drained into pipes leading to backyard cisterns. Most houses have slatted shutters, which remain closed to keep out the glare, the slats permitting a free current of air. Many of the older houses were ceiled with wooden panels, and some of the interior trim is from cabins of ships wrecked on the near-by reefs.

Houses on the northern end of the island were constructed during the era of the city's greatest prosperity. Here wealthier citizens, some of them shipmasters, exceeded the average modest story-and-a-half dwelling and built dignified two- and three-story structures, often topped with a look-out platform or *mirador*. Two-story porches frequently extend around three sides of these houses.

It is probable that Ponce de Leon sighted Key West in 1513 when sailing south along the islands after landing in the vicinity of St.Augustine.

Other early Spanish adventurers threaded the maze of keys during that century, and named this island Cayo Hueso (Bone Key), because of the numerous human bones found here. Legend attributes the presence of these bones to a warring Indian tribe that pursued enemies over the Florida Keys and slaughtered them, leaving their skeletons to bleach in the hot sun. The island was later occupied by pirate crews that infested the neighboring seas, and by fishermen supplying Cuban markets, but the small settlement at Key West was abandoned when Florida fell into English hands in 1763.

Florida again became a Spanish possession in 1783, and in 1815 the King of Spain gave this island to Juan Pablo Salas, a young artillery officer of St.Augustine, for services rendered the Crown. Eight years later Salas sold it to John W. Simonton, an American, and in the same year the Government sent Commodore David Porter with his 'mosquito fleet' to rout buccaneers from the keys. Following his successful campaign, families from New England, Virginia, and South Carolina settled here, along with many Tories who had fled to the Bahamas during the American Revolution.

About this time many inhabitants turned to salvaging cargoes from vessels wrecked on outlying reefs, and ships were said to have been deliberately lured to destruction by false flares and beacons. A U.S. superior court, established on the island in 1828, issued salvage licenses, ruled that a cargo belonged to the first salvage crew reaching a doomed ship, and tried cases involving salvage questions. Wrecks boomed the town; professional 'wreckers' who had previously taken their cargoes from American waters to Nassau and Havana courts now made their headquarters here. Buyers came to bid on merchandise salvaged from ships lost on the reefs. In years of severe storms, salvage receipts often reached $1,500,000. Erection of Federal lighthouses (the first in Key West was built in 1825) brought aid to mariners and gradually diminished this business.

The U.S. Naval Station was enlarged during the Mexican War of 1846–48; construction of Fort Taylor was begun on the island, and that of Fort Jefferson, 60 miles west on Dry Tortugas. At the beginning of the War between the States the Government fortified Key West with the two Martello Towers. Local citizens were strong Confederate sympathizers, but the city, like other port towns of Florida, was held by Federal forces throughout the war. Nearly 300 blockade runners were captured, brought here, and tried in the admiralty court during this time.

Key West had become the world's largest cigar manufacturing center by 1870; and many Cuban patriots who fled to Key West prior to the Spanish-American War were employed in the factories. A cable was laid to Cuba in 1866; nuns opened a girls' school two years later, and a public-school system was established to supplement private instruction. The city had a population of 10,000 in 1880, which during the next decade grew to 18,000. Fire destroyed half of Key West in 1886, including Vicente Martinez Ybor's large cigar factory. This plant subsequently moved to Tampa where there existed a stable water supply, better transportation facilities, and some tax exemptions for factory owners.

During the Spanish-American War, Key West again became an important naval base. News of the sinking of the battleship *Maine* was brought by motor launch from Cuba and sent to American newspapers from Key West. Many of the dead and wounded were brought here, and an American fleet impatiently awaited sailing orders.

The Overseas Extension of the Florida East Coast Railway, a romantic engineering feat, completed in January 1912, linked Key West and intervening keys with the mainland. Freight trains were transported by ferry from the terminals to Havana; trade with Cuba thrived, and a year later Key West's population reached 22,000.

The World War added to the city's importance as a naval base. Patrol vessels, submarines, planes, and dirigibles were stationed here. Thomas Edison carried on extensive experiments near by with depth bombs. Throughout the prohibition era, with Cuba only 90 miles away, rumrunners played hide and seek with Government agents, and exciting chases recalled the activities of slave traders and hijackers of earlier years.

Trade with Cuba fell off rapidly after the Armistice, and only a few minor cigar factories continued operation. Steamship lines dropped the city as a port of call; increased tariff on Cuban pineapples closed local canning factories; the depression years soon destroyed markets for fish products, the sponge fishing industry was not entirely revived, and the tourist business vanished. Garrisons of the Naval Station and Army Post were removed, and the Coast Guard headquarters were transferred to St.Petersburg.

Whereas in the 1830's Key West was adjudged the richest city per capita in the United States, in 1934 it was bankrupt. There were no funds in the treasury, no market for its bonds, and public officials were unpaid. In July of that year the city council passed a resolution petitioning the Governor of Florida to declare a state of emergency for Key West. Because approximately 80 per cent of the inhabitants were on relief rolls, the Governor authorized the Florida Emergency Relief Administration to attempt rehabilitation of the stranded community. A program was originated whereby Key West was to be made the American winter resort of the tropics, competing with Bermuda and Nassau. Citizens volunteered and actually contributed 2,000,000 man hours of labor; streets were cleaned, beaches developed, adequate sanitation provided, houses renovated and redecorated. Hotels, long shuttered, were reopened, and fetes were devised to attract visitors.

This program, hailed as one of the Nation's most interesting experiments in community planning, made the city a proving ground for Government-sponsored cultural projects. FERA artists, transferred from other sections, covered walls of public buildings, cafés, and night clubs with murals, and recorded upon canvas and copperplate the manifold life of the island community. Classes in handicraft were organized to teach persons on relief new ways of livelihood through use of native raw materials. These products, on sale at a number of shops, include ash trays, buttons, buckles, and pins carved from the hard shell of coconuts; palm-fiber hats, purses, and rugs; novelties made from shells and fish scales, and Spanish drawnwork.

Pageants and operas were presented under the auspices of the Relief Administration; unemployed writers produced descriptive literature designed to attract the more conservative visitors who passed through on their way to the Bahamas. A housing service provided quarters for newcomers and arranged every detail from hiring servants and stocking pantries to preparing and serving the first meal. Forty thousand persons visited Key West the following winter.

Just as Key West seemed on the road to financial recovery the Labor Day hurricane of 1935 swept across the upper section of the keys, and though the city was unharmed, miles of the Overseas Railway tracks were destroyed, and much of the highway that paralleled parts of it was washed away. The railway company, already in receiver's hands, abandoned the extension and moved its ferries to Port Everglades near Fort Lauderdale; the island's commercial fishing industry, lacking quick transportation to mainland markets, was ruined.

Proposals for the Overseas Highway were resumed in order to eliminate ferry service established by the State and in 1936 the railway's right-of-way was taken over by the Monroe County Toll Bridge Commission. Utilizing long spans over which Flagler took his railway to sea, the system of highways and bridges, opened to traffic in 1938, brought the city within five hours of Miami by motor.

POINTS OF INTEREST

1. SPONGE PIER, N. end of Grinnell St. (*auction sales* 9 *a.m. Mon., Wed., Fri.*), is the headquarters for sponge dealers. Key West fishermen take sponges by grappling only. They assert that the Greek divers who formerly operated in this territory spoiled the beds by walking over them with weighted shoes, and add, without being asked, that no divers are permitted in these waters. The sponge dock is a lively place during its thrice-weekly auctions, recalling the 90's and before, when all commodities entering Key West were sold at auction.

2. The TURTLE CRAWLS (*open daily*), N. end of Margaret St., a row of pens built in the water beside a dock, normally contain large numbers of sea turtles. Butchering takes place at 8:30 a.m. from Monday to Thursday inclusive. Near by is a factory and cannery for preservation of turtle meat and soup. The animals are caught principally off the coast of Central America and brought to Key West on boats manned by natives of the Grand Cayman. Many of the turtles are estimated to be more than 100 years old, and weigh up to 300 pounds.

3. The FISH MARKETS, N. end of Elizabeth St., line the waterfront. Each has its wharf, and tied to the various docks are crates called 'fish cars.' Here fish are netted, killed, and dressed in the buyer's presence.

4. The AQUARIUM (*open* 7–6:30 *daily; adults* 15¢, *children* 5¢), N. end of Whitehead St., was built with CWA and FERA funds. Brilliantly-colored tropical fishes are on display in tanks, lighted and heated by the sun, through which salt water is pumped. The rare guitar fish can sometimes be seen here, and in contrast with the vividly colored tropical fishes are octo-

puses, sea turtles, sting rays, morays, and little purple Portuguese men o'war with their trailing stingers. Northern aquariums and dealers send to Key West for specimens. The aquarium has two murals of fishermen by Alfred D. Crim.

5. U.S. NAVAL STATION (*open 8–4:30 daily; no cameras allowed*), entrance W. end of Greene St., is distinguished from a distance by its three orange and black radio towers. The base operates a radio station, a fueling port for destroyers, and has various naval impedimenta in shops and on wharves. The station grounds are planted with many tropical trees and shrubs, all of them labeled. In the past, naval officers brought plants from Panama, Guam, Hawaii, and the Philippines and set them out here.

6. KEY WEST LIGHTHOUSE (*open daily, dawn to sunset*), Whitehead and Division Sts., a conical stuccoed brick tower with a lantern of 11,000 candlepower, has a light that is visible for 15 miles. It is said to be the only lighthouse in the United States entirely within the city limits of a community; an excellent view of Key West is obtained from its railed balcony. It was constructed in 1846 after a storm had washed away the first light, built in 1825 on Whitehead Spit where Fort Taylor now stands.

An AVIARY AND TROPICAL ARBORETUM is maintained on the grounds as a hobby of the lighthouse superintendent. Under a spreading India rubber tree are a sand pile for children and benches for those who want to linger in the cool shaded grounds. The plants include a cork tree, a wishbone tree with rounded green stems that branch somewhat like wishbones, a ribbon plant with many roots reaching out at odd angles; many kinds of cacti, West Indian almond, and other tropical plants. Most of the birds, some kept in a tall cage built over low trees, are native to the keys and Cuba. It is said that the only English sparrows in Key West frequent this vicinity.

7. The ERNEST HEMINGWAY HOUSE (*private*), SE. corner Olivia and Whitehead Sts., is a two-story white stucco residence with a flat roof and one of the few chimneys in Key West. Double porches have iron grillwork around three sides, and an outside green staircase ascends to the second-story porch. The arched windows are fitted with yellow slatted shutters. A high wall encloses the landscaped premises. Built shortly after the War between the States, it is one of the older houses in the city. The author, whose novel *To Have and Have Not* has a Key West background, is the present occupant (1939).

8. FORT TAYLOR (*open 2–4 Sun. and Wed., other days by permission of adjutant; no cameras allowed*), entrance W. end of United St., is a Coast Guard base with artillery mounted behind fortified ramps. Begun in 1844 and completed two years later, it was held by Union forces during the War between the States.

9. The HARRIS HOUSE (*private*), S. end of Duval St., an ornate red-brick structure with a tower, veranda, and second-story balcony, is the southernmost home in the United States.

10. The PUBLIC LIBRARY (*open 3–6 daily*), Duval St. between Virginia and Division Sts., housed in a white frame building, is operated by the Key West Woman's Club.

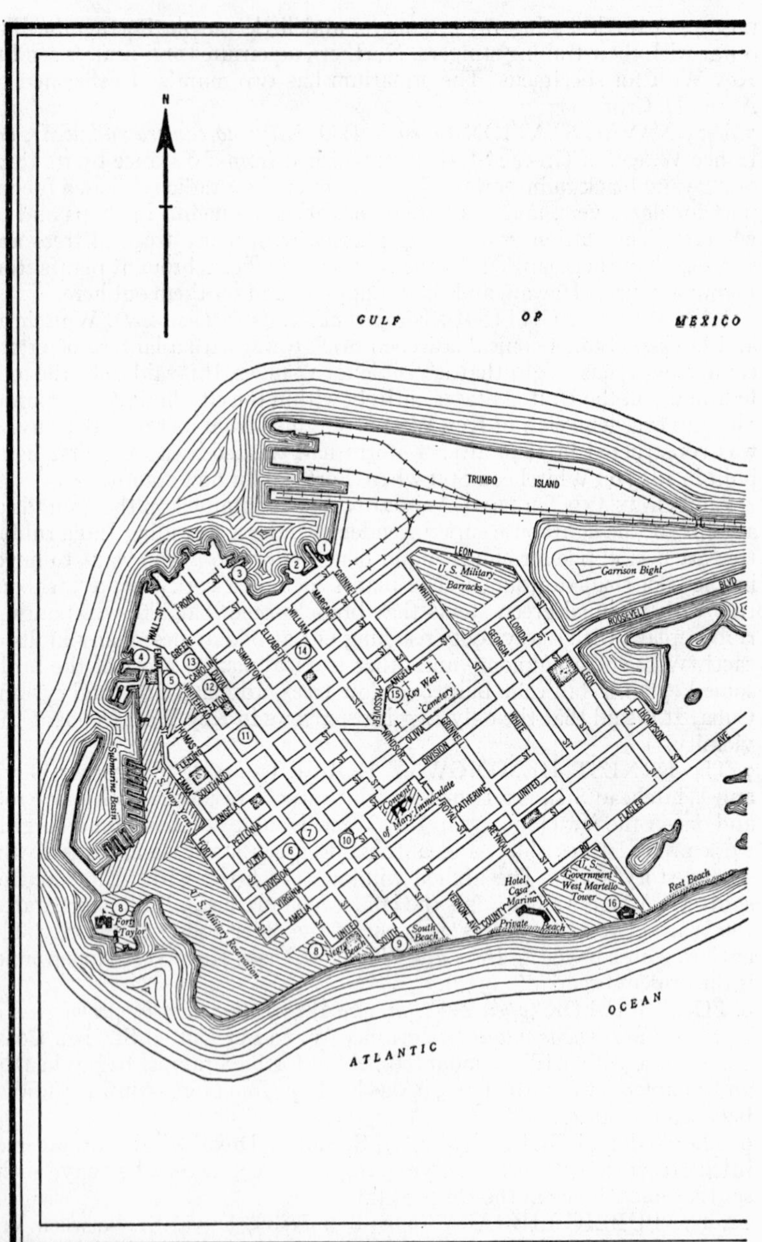
N
GULF OF MEXICO
TRUMBO ISLAND
Garrison Bight
U.S. Military Barracks
LEON
ROOSEVELT BLVD
FRONT
GREENE
CAROLINE
EATON
WHITEHEAD
THOMAS
FLEMING
EMMA
SOUTHARD
ANGELA
PETRONIA
OLIVIA
FORT
DIVISION
VIRGINIA
AMELIA
UNITED
SOUTH
MARGARET
WILLIAM
ELIZABETH
SIMONTON
DUVAL
GRINNELL
WHITE
GEORGIA
FLORIDA
PASSOVER
WINDSOR
Key West Cemetery
Convent of Mary Immaculate
CATHERINE
REYNOLDS
VERNON AVE
COUNTY
THOMPSON
FLAGLER AVE
Submarine Basin
U.S. Navy Yard
U.S. Military Reservation
Fort Taylor
Negro Beach
South Beach
Hotel Casa Marina
Private Beach
U.S. Government West Martello Tower
Rest Beach
ATLANTIC OCEAN

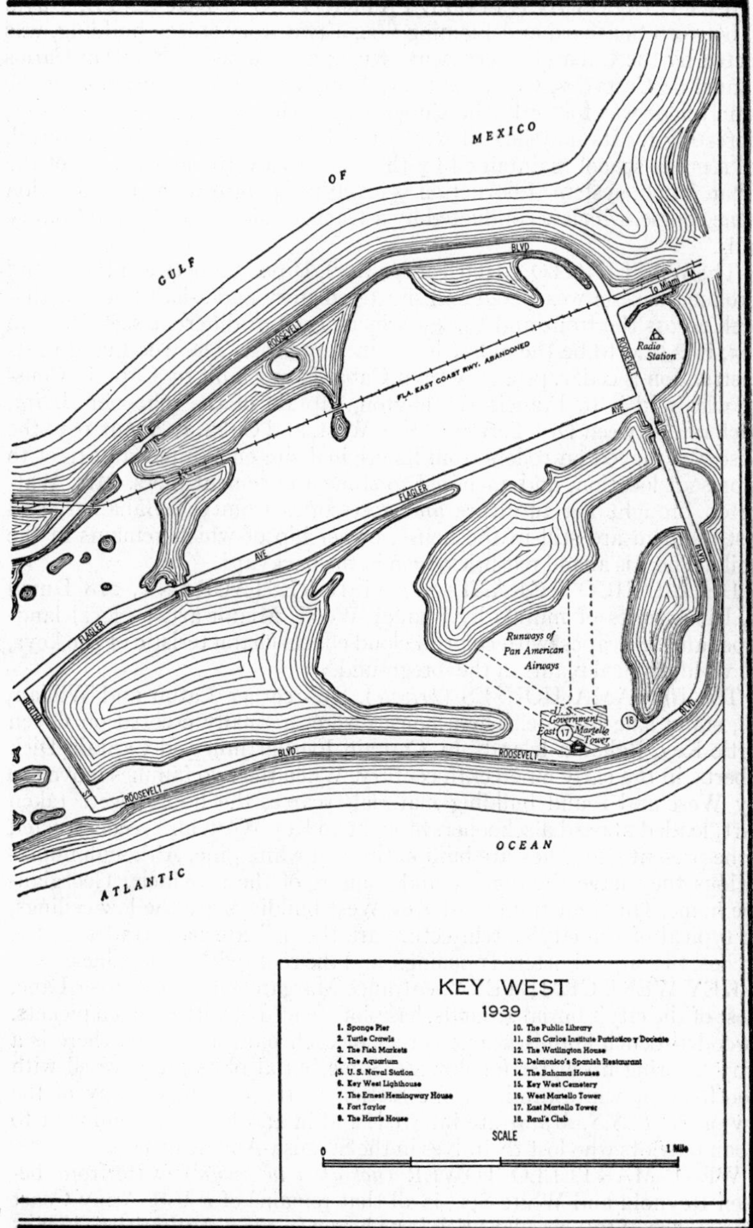
GULF OF MEXICO
ATLANTIC OCEAN
ROOSEVELT BLVD
FLA. EAST COAST RWY. ABANDONED
To Miami 4A
Radio Station
FLAGLER AVE
BERTHA ST
Runways of Pan American Airways
U. S. Government
East Martello Tower
17
18
KEY WEST
1939
1. Sponge Pier
2. Turtle Crawls
3. The Fish Markets
4. The Aquarium
5. U. S. Naval Station
6. Key West Lighthouse
7. The Ernest Hemingway House
8. Fort Taylor
9. The Harris House
10. The Public Library
11. San Carlos Institute Patriotico y Docente
12. The Watlington House
13. Delmonico's Spanish Restaurant
14. The Bahama Houses
15. Key West Cemetery
16. West Martello Tower
17. East Martello Tower
18. Raul's Club
SCALE
0
1 Mile

11. SAN CARLOS INSTITUTE PATRIOTICO Y DOCENTE, Duval St. between Southard and Fleming Sts., a two-story stucco building, was erected by the Cuban Government in 1924 and named in honor of Carlos Manuel de Cespedes, Cuban patriot. The Palace Theater occupying the ground floor was formerly the Cuban Opera House. On the second floor, interesting for its majolica tilework, are the offices of the Cuban consul, and a grade school maintained by the Cuban Government as part of the Cuban school system. Instruction is given in Spanish with the exception of one course, which is conducted by a teacher paid from Monroe County funds.

12. The WATLINGTON HOUSE (*private*), Duval St. between Eaton and Caroline Sts., is a weathered and shuttered story-and-a-half house with a porch across the front and three dormers, each of different size. Built in 1825, it is said to be the oldest house in Key West. The wood used in its construction is cedar, probably from Cuba. It was built by Captain Cousins, who sold it to Francis Watlington, captain of the schooner *Activa*, which ran between Dry Tortugas, Key West, and Cuba. In about 1832 the house was moved on rollers from its original site on Whitehead Street to its present location, and anchored to stone and cement piers. Mrs. Watlington brought her furniture and accessories from the Bahamas, and most of them are still in the house, ownership of which remains in the family. There is an old red-brick oven in the backyard.

13. DELMONICO'S GRAND SPANISH RESTAURANT, 218 Duval St., has a series of murals by Stanley Wood, Miami artist—local landscapes and seascapes, with colorful cloud effects characteristic of the keys, and vivid tropical plants in the foreground.

14. The BAHAMA HOUSES (*private*), SW. corner Eaton and William Sts., stand side by side. These houses were originally erected on Green Turtle Key, Bahama Islands, by Captain Joe Bartlum and Captain Dick Roberts, in the early nineteenth century. When the two families moved to Key West and found building materials scarce, the houses were taken apart, loaded aboard a schooner, brought to Key West, and reconstructed on the present site. They are built entirely of white pine. Although unpretentious they have the dignity and comfort of the provincial Georgian-type home. Different from most Key West buildings are the low ceilings, but typical of the city's architecture are the delicate balustrades on the porches, the large shuttered openings, and the roofs with twin gables.

15. KEY WEST CEMETERY, entrance Margaret St. at Passover Lane, oldest of the city's burial grounds, has plots fenced in with wooden pickets. A wooden bench stands in one corner of each plot, and often there is a pump to bring up water for flowers. Some burial plots are covered with smooth-swept white sand. In one section of the cemetery many of the crew of the *U.S.S. Maine* are interred; and in another is a monument to Cuban patriots who lost their lives in the Spanish-American War.

16. WEST MARTELLO TOWER (*not open to public*), waterfront between Reynold and White Sts., is all that remains of a U.S. Army Coast Defense, one of two circular brick forts begun in 1861. Authorities differ as to the origin of the name. Some claim it is derived from the Italian *mar-*

tello, or hammer, used to strike an alarm; others say the tower was named for a fort of this kind built on the coast of Corsica in the late 1790's.

17. EAST MARTELLO TOWER (*open by arrangement at airport*), S.Roosevelt Blvd., most imposing of Key West's old forts, was begun in 1861. Some of the Irish bricklayers who worked on the masonry settled in the town.

18. RAUL'S CLUB, S.Roosevelt Blvd., E. of East Martello Tower, has a series of murals by Avery Johnson in the main ballroom, depicting native dances of Africa, China, Cuba, and other nations. In the rear of the club building is a marine garden where many types of seashells and other specimens are displayed. A pool adjoining the garden contains fish that take food from the visitors' fingers and in some cases permit themselves to be stroked and removed from the water.

POINTS OF INTEREST IN ENVIRONS

FORT JEFFERSON (*open; reached by chartered boats only; no accommodations*), a ghost prison fortress, occupies 16 acres on Garden Key, one of a group of low-lying coral and sand bars known as Dry Tortugas, 60 miles west of Key West. Ponce de Leon first sighted the archipelago in 1513 on his voyage around the peninsula. Later, retracing his course, he landed and christened the keys Las Tortugas because of numerous turtles in adjacent waters. Surrounded by jagged reefs and shoals, and almost inaccessible, the islands were for three centuries the lair of pirates and smugglers. When the Tortugas were ceded to the United States with the rest of Florida in 1819, Garden Key was reserved for military purposes, because of its strategic position in the Gulf of Mexico, and in 1846 the Government began construction of the mammoth hexagonal, three-tiered, casemated fortification—a citadel intended to outrival all others.

Obstacles in the fort's construction were almost insurmountable. Ships, money, and cargoes were lost in making the hazardous 1,500-mile voyage from eastern seaports; workmen were difficult to obtain, and few, except Negro slaves, were able to withstand the tropical heat, disease, and poor food. The site was swept again and again by hurricanes. Temporary buildings were erected, and a section of the luxurious officers' quarters, three stories high, was partially completed, but the main structure was not begun until 1851. The outside walls were 5 feet thick, and each of the hexagonal sides 450 feet long and 60 feet high. The massive foundations rested on coral rock 10 feet below sea level.

A moat, 70 feet wide and 30 feet deep, open to the sea and infested by sharks and savage barracudas, encircled the fort. By 1865 the curtains and terreplein were carried to the point evident today. It is estimated that 40,000,000 bricks were used, at a cost of $1 each for transportation alone. Two hundred and forty-three large caliber guns were mounted, but not one of them was ever fired.

Among the fort's noted prisoners at the conclusion of the War between the States, were Dr.Samuel A. Mudd and three others charged with complicity in the assassination of President Lincoln. Although Mudd's acquaintance with John Wilkes Booth was purely casual, his act of setting the assassin's broken leg resulted in a life sentence. He was pardoned in 1869.

Neglected, stripped by vandals, swept by repeated tropical storms that crushed brick and concrete and bent steel girders, Fort Jefferson deteriorated rapidly. It remained unoccupied until 1898 when war with Spain was imminent. The American fleet was stationed here and the battleship *Maine* sailed from the fort for Havana.

In 1902 the property was transferred to the Navy Department, and coal rigs and water distilling plants were built. When these were destroyed by hurricanes in 1906, the fort was again abandoned. Two years later the entire group of islands was set aside as a Federal bird reservation. Until 1934 Garden Key and its crumbling ruins were merely a rendezvous for fishermen and tourists. In January 1936 President Roosevelt gave the fort the official status of Fort Jefferson National Monument and placed it under supervision of the National Park Service.

The TORTUGAS LABORATORY (*private*), Garden Key, maintained by the Carnegie Institution of Washington, D.C., was founded in 1907 by Dr.Alfred Goldsboro Mayor. Here each summer marine biologists and other scientists study the life of the coral reef, and the results of their investigations are published in the fall.

On Loggerhead Key, two and one-half miles west of Fort Jefferson, is LOGGERHEAD LIGHTHOUSE, said to be a greater distance from the mainland than any other light in the world.

Greater Miami

Railroad Stations: 200 NW.1st Ave. for Florida East Coast Ry.; 2210 NW.7th Ave. for Seaboard Air Line Ry.; both in Miami.
Bus Stations: Union Bus Station, 275 NE.1st St., for Florida Motor Lines, Greyhound, and Tamiami Trail Tours; 301 E.Flagler St., for Pan American Bus Lines; all in Miami. 2202 Ponce de Leon Blvd., Coral Gables, for Florida Motor Lines.
Airports: 2500 S.Bayshore Drive for Pan American Airways, taxi $1.15, bus from Columbus Hotel, Biscayne Blvd. and NE.4th St., 45 minutes before each plane departure, 50¢; 7 m. on NW.36th St. for Eastern Air Lines, taxi $1.50, time 30 minutes. Venetian Causeway, and NW.36th St. and NW.42nd Ave. Miami, and 380 Alton Road, Miami Beach, for charter land and seaplanes. Blimps leave County Causeway, Miami, for 20-minute trips daily, adults $3, children $1.50.
Taxi: Miami, 15¢ for first $\frac{1}{4}$ m., 5¢ each additional $\frac{1}{4}$ m. Miami Beach, 15¢ for first $\frac{1}{5}$ m., 5¢ for each additional $\frac{1}{5}$ m. Coral Gables, 15¢ for first $\frac{1}{4}$ m., 5¢ for each additional $\frac{1}{4}$ m. Jitney cabs to Miami Beach, 10¢ and 15¢.
City Busses: Miami, 10¢; Coral Gables, 5¢, to Miami Beach, 10¢.
Streetcars: Miami, 5¢ in city, 10¢ to Miami Beach. Transfers from streetcar to bus only in Miami Beach and the NW.7th St. bus in Miami.
Steamship Piers: NE.10th St. for Clarke S.S.Co. to Nassau, Clyde-Mallory S.S.Co. to New York, Jacksonville, and Galveston, and P. & O. Steamship Line to Key West and Havana; E. end of NE.12th St. for Merchants & Miners Line to Jacksonville, Savannah, Norfolk, Baltimore, Philadelphia, and Boston; E. end of NE.9th St. for Munson Line to Havana, Nassau, and New York; all in Miami.
Ferry: S. side County Causeway to Fisher Island, U.S. Quarantine Station, and W.K. Vanderbilt Estate, 10¢.
Traffic Regulations: Parking meters, 5¢.
Street Order and Numbering: The city is divided into NE., NW., SE., and SW. sections by Miami Ave. running N. and S., and by Flagler St., running E. and W., and all thoroughfares take the prefix of sections in which they lie. Streets, terraces, and lanes parallel Flagler St.; avenues, courts, and places parallel Miami Ave.

Accommodations: 413 hotels, rates higher Dec.–Apr. Tourist and trailer camps in environs.

Information Service: (Miami) Chamber of Commerce, 35 NW.2nd St.; Miami Motor Club, 242 Biscayne Blvd.; South Florida Motor Club (AAA), 1331 Biscayne Blvd.; (Miami Beach) Chamber of Commerce, 5th St. and Alton Road; (Coral Gables) Chamber of Commerce, Aragon Ave.

Radio Stations: WQAM (560 kc.); WIOD (610 kc.); WKAT (1500 kc.).
Motion Picture Houses: 30.
Tennis: (Miami) Municipal courts, NE.2nd Ave. and 19th St., free; NW.3rd St. and 9th Ave., 20¢ day, 50¢ night; NW.79th St. and 1st Court, free; NW.36th St. and 7th Ave., 20¢; NW.2nd Ave. and 34th St., free; Oak Ave. and Matilda St., free; NW.18th St. and NW.10th Ave., free. (Miami Beach) Flamingo Park, Meridian Ave. at 11th St.; Washington Park, Washington Ave. at 2nd St.; Lincoln Park, Lincoln Road at Washington Ave.; Municipal courts, Washington Ave. at Collins Canal, variable small fees. (Coral Gables) Salvadore Park, Columbus Blvd. and Andalusia Ave.; 997 Greenway Drive, small fees.
Golf: (Miami) Miami Country Club, 1345 NW.11th St., 18 holes, $1; Red Road Course,

Red Road and NW.36th St., 18 holes, 50¢ summer, $1 winter; West Flagler Course, W.Flagler St. and NW.37th Ave., 18 holes, $1. (Miami Beach) Municipal Golf Course, 848 Lincoln Road, 18 holes, 50¢ summer, $1 winter; LaGorce Golf Club, 5701 Alton Road, 18 holes, $3.25 (open in season only); Bayshore Golf Club, 2239 Alton Road, 18 holes, $2.25 (open in season only). (Coral Gables) Coral Gables Golf and Country Club, Greenway Drive and Coral Way, 9 holes, 50¢ summer, $1 winter; Riviera Golf Club, Bird Road, S. of Miami Biltmore Hotel, 9 holes, 50¢; Miami Biltmore Country Club, 18 holes, $3 winter, $2 summer.

Swimming Pools: (Miami Beach) Bouche Villa Venice, 23rd St. and Collins Ave.; Roman Pools, 23rd St. and Collins Ave.; Deauville Pool, 6701 Collins Ave., fees vary. (Coral Gables) Venetian Pool, De Soto Blvd. and Sevilla Ave., 50¢ winter, 25¢ summer.

Surf Bathing: (Miami Beach) between Biscayne and 14th Sts.; Surfside Park at 71st St., free (Coral Gables) Tahiti Beach, 25¢.

Fishing: All piers, docks, and bridges; deep-sea fishing boats at City Docks, Bayfront Park, Miami; Chamber of Commerce Docks and Floridian Hotel Docks, Miami Beach.

Shuffleboard, Roque, Chess, and Checkers: (Miami) NW.7th Ave. and NW.36th St.; NW.3rd Ave. between 2nd and 3rd Sts.; NW.10th Ave. and NW.18th St. (Miami Beach) Flamingo Park, Meridian Ave. and 11th St. (Coral Gables) Salvadore Park, Columbus Blvd. and Andalusia Ave.

Softball: (Miami), NW.20th St. and NW.11th Ave.; NW.3rd St. and NW.14th Ave.; NW.7th Ave. and NW.36th St., 10¢; SW.8th Ave. and SW.4th St., free; NW.2nd Ave. and NW.34th St.; NW.18th St. and NW.10th Ave., free, (Miami Beach) Flamingo Park, Meridian Ave. and 11th St., 10¢.

Jai Alai: Biscayne Fronton, 3500 NW.35th Ave. Miami, Dec.–Apr., 25¢.

Greyhound Racing: (Miami) W.Flagler St. and NW.37th Ave., 25¢; NE.2nd Ave. and NE.115th St., 25¢. (Miami Beach) South Beach on ocean front, 25¢. All Dec.–Apr.

Horse Racing: Hialeah Park, NW.79th St. and Bougainvillea Ave., $1.25; Tropical Park, 1½ m. W. of Coral Gables, $1.

Riding: (Miami) 3400 NW.62nd St., 5416 NW.12th Ave., 13575 NE.6th Ave.; (Hialeah) 48th St., 71 W.8th St.; 303 Giralda Ave., Coral Gables, $2 per hour.

Annual Events: (Miami) Orange Bowl Football Game, All-American Air Maneuvers, Jan.; International Flower Show, Glenn Curtiss Trophy Golf Tournament, Dixie Golf Tournament, Frost-Bite Dinghy Races, Feb.; Greater Miami Fishing Tournament, Mar. to May; Miami Yacht Club Sailboat Regatta, Biscayne Bay Regatta, Miami-St.Petersburg Yacht Race, Mar.; Pan American Day, Relay Olympics, Apr.; (Miami Beach) Fashion Show, Jan.; Miami-Nassau Yacht Races, Miami Beach Professional Tennis Tournament, Feb.; Lipton Cup Race, Mar.; (Coral Gables) Latin-American Institute, Jan.; Mixed Doubles Tennis Championship, Mar.; Miami-Biltmore $10,000 Open Golf Tournament, Dec.

GREATER MIAMI (Miami, 10 alt., 110,637 pop.; Miami Beach, 6 alt., 6,492 pop.; Coral Gables, 11 alt., 5,697 pop.; Hialeah, 11 alt., 2,600 pop.), southernmost resort area on Florida's mainland, covers approximately 90 square miles. Biscayne Bay, spanned by three causeways, separates Miami and Miami Beach, twin cities that in tourist eyes are one. Coral Gables merges imperceptibly on the west, but extends to the bay south of Miami, and Hialeah, adjoining on the northwest, tapers off into the Everglades, the source of the Miami River that winds through the heart of Miami and empties into the bay.

In less than a quarter century, miles of rainbow-hued dwellings, bizarre estates, ornate hotels, and office buildings have grown from mangrove swamp, jungle, coral rock, and sand dunes. Islands dredged from the bay are glorified by exotic plantings, and houses of many types and styles. Great wealth, lavishly spent on these synthetic isles and shores, has gone into the building of a winter playground designed to attract those, pleasure-bent, who follow the sun. To the first-time visitor its shining spires, its tropical foliage, the incredible blue of its waters, the cloud formations that tower in the background—all sharply etched under an intense, white sunlight—appear as ephemeral as a motion-picture set.

There is a Manhattanish touch to the gleaming white and buff skyscrapers—which are not needed, for there is room to expand horizontally—and the effect of the skyline, rising abruptly from the waterfront and floodlighted at night, is heightened by the flatness of the terrain. Residents pridefully point out the more expensive buildings, name their cost, and boast of the speed of their construction.

Henry Flagler's engineers, platting the resort over drawing boards in St.Augustine, were accountable for the predominance of narrow, one-way streets in the downtown area. In winter these thoroughfares are as crowded as a county fair and their attractions as varied as a midway. Cars bearing license plates from every State and many foreign lands clog traffic, for Miami's percentage of seasonal vehicular transportation is higher in proportion to population than any other American city.

Miami's show street, Biscayne Boulevard, a section of US 1, adorned with royal palms, is a four-lane motorway for almost a dozen blocks where it parallels a landscaped park overlooking the bay. At intervals broad causeways reach from island to island across to Miami Beach and provide bases for seaplanes, speedboats, and a blimp. Biscayne Bay, a roadstead shared by the cities, bristles with docks for coastwise liners, fishing and excursion boats, and a spacious harbor for yachts and houseboats.

Extending westward from the bay and waterfront park, Miami's shopping and theater district is confined to a dozen blocks, with Flagler Street the center. Open-front shops sell boxes of fruit, fruit juices, neckties, and innumerable souvenirs. Drugstores and department stores present the latest in show-window artistry: bewildering displays of sports equipment, beach togs and accouterments; Panama hats, shorts, and clothing suited to a subtropical climate. Seminole families sit in curio shops to attract patrons. Photograph galleries with canvas seashore backgrounds, or a boat lettered *Miss Miami*, invite passers-by who, if they prefer, can be snapped riding a stuffed alligator, holding up a huge mounted fish, or leaning nonchalantly against a prop palm. Pitchmen spiel endlessly to sell their wares. Astrologers read one's future—and pick winning horses—in the stars, and astronomers with portable telescopes show the wonders of the heavens, sometimes including the Southern Cross, for a dime.

Theater doormen, resplendent as admirals on dress parade, advertise orally the current screen attraction; policemen in navy blue uniforms with white belts and pith helmets direct traffic. Adult newsboys hawk their papers and racing forms like sideshow barkers, and stroll between cars held up by lights, a vociferous performance that continues far into the night. Pedestrians wear what they please. Sun glasses, eye shades, and lotions advertised to promote a quick tan are among the best sellers, for with the majority of newcomers a sepia complexion is a midwinter achievement.

Soaring planes and leisurely sight-seeing blimps are almost constantly overhead, for Miami, one of the important aviation centers in the South, is the base of two continental air lines and the international Pan American Airways. The army, the navy, and the coast guard have flying bases here. The municipal airport is the scene of the annual All-American Air Maneuvers, and not far from it is the dirigible mooring mast, one of five in the United States. The *Macon*, *Akron*, and the *Graf Zeppelin* have moored here.

To those preferring shuffleboard, band concerts, and shady benches in the park, Miami's neon glitter and pulse of Broadway are tempered by the languor of the tropics, and time is as negligible as yesterday's weather report. But to the spirited clan who descend upon the city at the beginning of the racing calendar, Miami is 100 days of perpetual carnival—New York's festive 40's transplanted, a Saratoga August multiplied by three prolonged Kentucky Derbies.

Miami's season of sports revolves around the race horse and the racing greyhound, but even jai alai has its pari-mutuels. Owners, trainers, touts, and hangers-on fill hotels and rooming houses, and throng the sunny streets, their patter concerned with odds, entries, and past performances. Paddocks and stands swarm with eager humanity each afternoon and evening. The playboy and plowboy, the dowager in pearls and the sylph in shorts, the banker on vacation and the grifter on prowl keep turnstiles clicking and feed staggering sums to the pari-mutuels. More than $34,000,000 was wagered at the horse tracks during the 1938–39 season, and nearly $10,000,000 at the dog tracks. The North American record for a winning daily double, $7,205, was made on March 15, 1935, at Tropical Park.

Gambling is both legal and illegal, for while it is quite within the law to buck pari-mutuels at the tracks, the same business with bookies is strictly illicit. Many grills are equipped with tickers and huge blackboards upon which racing entries and results here and at other tracks are chalked.

Miami Beach, once a 1,600-acre, jungle-matted sand bar three miles out in the Atlantic, grew to 2,800 acres when dredging and filling operations were completed. The island, 10 miles long and from 1 to 3 miles wide, is a world of moneyed industrialists, boulevardiers, and stars of stage and screen, its atmosphere gay, carefree, and expensive.

The older section of the city, around and south of the County Causeway approach, has the trappings and spirit of Coney Island with its preponderance of open-front bars, sandwich stands, bingo establishments, kosher restaurants, and delicatessen stores. On the tip of the island the greyhound track, the pier, and its burlesque theater overlook the ocean and the Government ship channel.

Northward along the Atlantic, where palatial hotels, apartments, and homes face Loomis Park and the beach, are terraces and swimming pools, bright with sun parasols and cabañas. Back from the beach and Collins Avenue that parallels it is Indian Creek, a placid, sea-walled lagoon winding southwest to the bay through a canal, which divides the island. Well-kept golf courses border the waterway, boulevards follow its irregular palm-fringed shores, gleaming yachts and houseboats moor in the sheltered coves, and broad stretches provide a course for speedboat races. On both sides are private piers and landing docks, some trellised with allamanda and bougainvillea, waterway entrances to winter estates of celebrities.

Lincoln Road, the principal east–west thoroughfare, is a street of theaters and exclusive shops, many of them branches of New York, Paris, and London establishments, and open only during the season. Its double sidewalks are gray. The outer walk is separated from an inner shoppers' walk along the store windows by a parkway bordered with royal and coconut palms. North of the road the residential sections and beaches are highly restricted.

Between Miami and the 'Glades lies Coral Gables, a boom-time city, blue-printed to the last detail before a palmetto was grubbed from the site. Its 'grand' entrance off Tamiami Trail, an imposing buff stucco archway in the medieval manner, forms part of a block-long building containing studios and apartments. The business area is restricted to buildings of Mediterranean design; their plans, color, and even awnings must be approved by the city architect. Palm-bordered drives bearing Spanish names, and coral-tinted sidewalks encircle numerous plazas, several golf courses, and the Venetian pool, a municipal development in an abandoned rock pit. A landscaped canal flows past a towering hotel and the University of Miami to a pseudo-Tahiti beach on Biscayne Bay where wind-tossed coconut trees and palm-thatched sun shelters attempt to capture a South Sea atmosphere.

Scarcely a fourth of Greater Miami's permanent population is native-born; some are from adjoining States, but the greater number hail from industrial centers and farm belts of the North and Midwest. Several thousand Latins reside or spend their vacations here, and many send their children to the University of Miami. They contribute to the sports and social life of the city, enjoy its winter tempo and sparkle, and are responsible for numerous Spanish and Italian restaurants. This influx has been brought about to a great extent by the Pan American Airways; its clipper ships to and from Caribbean, Mexican, Central and South American ports have made Miami an international city.

Miami Beach and Coral Gables are free of slums. Miami's restricted Negro district, bordering the tracks and representing 30 per cent of the city's population, virtually reaches into the heart of town, but halts abruptly at Fifth Street. A large number of residents are of West Indian stock, and many Filipinos live on the fringe of the settlement. Liberty Square, a Federal Housing project, provides modern accommodations for nearly 250 Negro families. The Booker T. Washington High School, with an average enrollment of 2,000, is the largest of the State's five accredited Negro high schools, and the St.Agnes Protestant Episcopal Church is the largest of its denomination in the South. The Negro population increases during the tourist season when resort hotels open and the unskilled-labor market reaches its peak.

The World War created a renaissance in south Florida, and the Miami area in particular, with a new affluent class fostering a demand for extravagant dwellings in harmony with climate and background. At the beginning, architects conceived a flamboyant style known as Florida-Mediterranean, and the boom era of building here resulted in a conglomerate of true and distorted Italian, Spanish, and Moorish designs. Cement block, coral rock, and stucco on lath, wire, and wallboard were the prevailing materials; paint pots of the world were dredged for fantastic colors. Old tile roofs were stripped from buildings in Cuba and Central American countries; floor and wall tiles, statuary and ornamental urns were brought from Spain and Italy. Full-grown exotic shrubs, palms, and other trees, many imported from the West Indies, transformed the flat, desolate sand and scrub land into a garden spot.

More recent houses are of modified English and French Caribbean and British Colonial types, sometimes referred to as Modern Tropical, with an occasional dwelling exhibiting walls of glass and flat roofs featuring sun decks and solariums. Only in the Coconut Grove section remain old houses native to Florida—stately and white columned, with balconies and lofty porticos.

Intermingled with the better architecture are clapboard houses of early builders, their ugliness sometimes concealed by heavy foliage. In sharp contrast to their surroundings are various groupings known as the Spanish Village, the French and Chinese Villages, and even the African Colonial Dwellings. With few exceptions, the hotels and commercial structures of Miami proper, where ornamental arcades are introduced, follow the lines of those in northern cities.

Infrequent tropical storms of late summer and early fall achieve headlines in northern papers but seldom more than 24-point type in the local press. Once it is certain the blow will strike the city, all precautions are taken to protect property and insure the safety of inhabitants; windows are boarded up, signs removed, and trees braced. Residents of insecure houses move into more substantial quarters and downtown hotels are filled. Favorite refuges for those of lesser means are the post office, municipal buildings, and churches, where families move in with bedding, kitchen utensils, and provisions to take squatters' rights until the danger has passed.

Because of its climate and natural advantages, the Miami site attracted settlers from earliest times; Indians long favored it, Spaniards coveted the territory but could not hold it, and the vicissitudes of the Seminole Wars compelled its temporary evacuation by Americans. The name Miami is reputedly a variant of the Indian words, *maiha*, translated as 'very large,' and *mih*, 'it is so.' On Spanish maps of the early seventeenth century, an area adjacent to Miami is marked *Aymai*, and *Mayami*.

William Brickell came to the site of Miami in 1870, and Julia S. Tuttle purchased property on both sides of the Miami River shortly afterwards. During the three decades that followed, the Everglades drainage project was begun to redeem productive land. The severe freeze of 1894–95 destroyed citrus groves of central Florida and threatened railroad earnings, but Mrs. Tuttle sent Flagler a bouquet of orange blossoms from Biscayne Bay, which was untouched by frost.

Flagler visited Mrs. Tuttle, and was impressed. Mrs. Tuttle deeded 100 acres to him, and, joined by Brickell, donated every alternate lot of her remaining acreage. Flagler installed a waterworks and other civic improvements. Miami at that time consisted of a dozen sand trails hacked through palmetto growths, and Flagler Street was lined with business enterprises in pine shacks and tents. Flagler's East Coast Railway reached the town from West Palm Beach in 1896 and his resort hotel, the Royal Palm, was opened. Miami was incorporated as a city that same year, with an estimated population of 1,500.

Throughout Miami's formative years, Miami Beach was a wilderness of mangroves, seagrapes, and scrub palmetto, infested with snakes and mosquitoes. Excursion boats carried picnic parties and bathers to the island where frame shelters along the beach served as bathhouses. An early attempt failed to develop the island as a coconut plantation, and John S. Collins, a New Jersey horticulturist, set out an avocado grove. To provide water transportation, Collins dredged the canal that bears his name, from Indian Creek to Biscayne Bay. When the fruit growing venture was abandoned, Collins organized the Miami Beach Improvement Company to promote a residential colony, and began construction across the bay to Miami of what was then the longest wooden bridge in the United States. It was opened in 1913, two years before Miami Beach was incorporated as a city.

Collins spent his funds and the late Carl F. Fisher of Indianapolis loaned him $50,000, with 200 acres of land as security. Fisher's money and enthusiasm revived the company. Miami Beach's first auction sale netted $65,000. Sometimes the auctioneer waved vaguely toward the mangrove swamps and explained that the lot being sold was 'off there somewhere.' Fisher's property, most of it under water, was made solid land by pumping in sand from the bottom of the bay, creating a yacht basin and several miniature islands.

During the early 1920's James Bright, Missouri ranchman, later joined by Glenn Curtiss, aeronaut and sportsman, founded Hialeah. The city is best known for the Hialeah Park race track, built by Joe Smoot in 1931, when pari-mutuel wagering was legalized.

The first symptoms of revived real-estate activities in 1922–23 brought an advance guard of investors. During the three years, before the boom collapsed in 1926, America became Florida conscious, and the Miami area held the center of the stage. A local newspaper issued a 504-page edition in 1925; northern periodicals carried special sections on Miami subdivisions and news stories on the fabulous real-estate values. Land in the flatwoods eight miles from the post office sold for $25,000 an acre; downtown business property found buyers at $20,000 a front foot; owners of a Flagler Street corner refused $6,000,000 for holdings that cost $350,000 in 1919. More than $100,000,000 was spent in building during the peak year.

Coral Gables came into existence like a magic city, and George Merrick, its founder, paid out $3,000,000 for advertising in 12 months. The demand for building material was so great that railroads were swamped and an embargo was declared on non-perishable Florida-bound freight. Water traffic increased tremendously and ships, unable to enter the congested harbor, were compelled to anchor outside for weeks awaiting their turn to discharge cargoes. The Seaboard Air Line Railway brought its cross-State extension into Miami in 1926, too late to share in the era of prosperity.

After the crash the Miami area marked time. First to feel the effects of the collapse, it was among the first to recover. Building permits reaching a 10-year low of $2,500,000 in 1932, rose to $14,000,000 in 1934, and exceeded $34,570,008 in 1939.

Greater Miami's leading industry is its tourist business, entertaining some 2,000,000 visitors annually. Since the dredging of the channel and harbor, coastwise freight and passenger vessels make the city a year-round terminal; several steamship lines operate to West Indian ports during the winter season, and ocean-going cruise ships make Miami a port of call. The 600 industrial firms are for the most part minor concerns manufacturing novelties and utilitarian products.

Fishing is perhaps the greatest Miami recreation, with practically every variety of game fish in near-by waters. The income of the charter fishing fleet and of equipment dealers increases annually. During the 100 days of winter fishing an estimated $500,000 is spent on boat hire alone.

POINTS OF INTEREST

(Downtown Miami)

1. BAYFRONT PARK, Biscayne Blvd. between SE.2nd St. and NE.6th St. and extending to Biscayne Bay, consists of 40 acres of land pumped from the bay in 1924 and landscaped with tropical shrubbery. Pelicans and gulls frequent a sand spit opposite the park.

The AMPHITHEATER was the scene in February 1933 of an attempt on the life of Franklin D. Roosevelt, then President-elect, which resulted in the death of Mayor Anton J. Cermak, of Chicago. A plaque to Mayor Cermak was unveiled in March 1939. The amphitheater is planted with royal and coconut palms and has a yellow stucco stage of oriental design with a gray platform, red-bordered brown curtain, and a series of paintings of Cairo street scenes on either side of the proscenium. A marquee with a dome painted green, yellow, orange, and red covers the central stage. The stucco structure is surmounted by two towers with onion-shaped domes painted attractively in colors of blue and silver, and open-air green benches seat 8,000.

The main PROMENADE, bordered by vivid flower beds, hedges of clipped pine, and royal palms, leads from the foot of E.Flagler St. to the bay. Benches line the promenade and bayfront. Strollers crossing the park should watch for almost invisible guy-wires that anchor large trees against the wind.

The park contains the OUTDOOR OBSERVATORY of the Southern Cross Astronomical Society, with two five-inch refracting telescopes erected on stands. Lectures are given on Sunday, Tuesday, and Friday nights, weather permitting. All stars visible in the northern hemisphere and those 60 degrees below the equator are seen here. The Southern Cross is visible during February and March, at about 2 a.m.

2. In the MUNICIPAL YACHT BASIN, N. of Bayfront Park at Bis-

cayne Blvd. and NE.6th St., pleasure boats and deep-sea fishing boats come and go. Here tickets are sold by barkers for sightseeing and fishing trips and glass-bottomed boat trips. People crowd the pier when the deep-sea fishing boats come in, bearing their catches of sailfish, barracuda, tarpon, and other game fish. A mechanically operated bulletin board is maintained for posting game-fish prizes.

3. The MIAMI AQUARIUM (*open* 8 *a.m. to midnight; adm.* 25¢) is a ship set in sand on Biscayne Blvd. at NE.5th St. At the entrance girl artists do portrait sketches for a tip, and two monkeys, chained to a revolving iron ladder, swing round and round. The vessel is the *Prinz Valdemar*, an old Danish barkentine. During the boom it sank in a storm, blocking Miami harbor when the city was in greatest need of lumber and supplies in ships waiting outside. The 1926 hurricane raised and beached the barkentine and it was converted into a 100-room hotel; in 1927 it was fitted out as an aquarium. Live exhibits include sea turtles, stone crabs, Florida lobsters, shrimp, morays, sharks, stingrays, alligators, crocodiles, and two manatees or sea cows, seldom seen in captivity. There are also numerous mounted specimens.

On the upper deck are tables for eating and drinking, and seats for those who wish to sit and look out over Biscayne Bay.

4. The MIAMI DAILY NEWS TOWER, Biscayne Blvd. at NE.6th St., is designed somewhat in the manner of the Giralda tower of Seville. The portals of this ochre-colored building are adorned with huge capped columns and scroll arch, with a Spanish shield or keystone. In the foyer are panels depicting the evolution of the art of painting.

5. DADE COUNTY COURTHOUSE, NE. corner W.Flagler St. and NW.1st Ave., a 28-story neo-classic structure, rests upon a high base, the lower floors adorned with Doric columns and a frieze. The upper stories are embellished with fluted columns of the Corinthian order. The building is topped with a temple-like octagonal upper story with pyramidal roof. The 16th to the 19th floors are occupied by the 'escape-proof' county jail. Completed in 1927 at a cost of $4,000,000, the building is illuminated at night and can be seen for miles.

6. FIRST PRESBYTERIAN CHURCH, SW. corner E.Flagler St. and SE.3rd Ave., is a white stucco structure with a neo-classic façade. A tower at the rear of the edifice resembles that of an old Scottish church. Miami's oldest church, it was completed in 1900. Extravagant offers for the land were made during the boom but Henry M. Flagler, the builder, specified that it was never to be sold.

7. The CITY CURB MARKET, SW.2nd Ave. and Miami River, is an open white building with a red tile roof. Stalls are piled with fresh, locally grown vegetables; small plants and flowers; tropical jellies and preserved fruits; fresh meats; fresh fruits—sapodilla, guava, mango, Surinam cherry, tangelo, kumquat, oranges, grapefruit, tiny lady-finger bananas, and strawberries. In an adjoining building on the river bank are the seafood stalls.

8. PFLUEGER'S MARINE MUSEUM (*open* 9–5 *daily*), 1367 N.Miami Ave., displays mounted specimens of south Florida marine life. Each case

has a painted reef scene as a background for the brilliantly colored fish such as the rainbow parrot, mud parrot, red-lined parrot, four-eye butterfly, angel, trigger, file, and many others.

9. MIAMI WOMAN'S CLUB BUILDING, NE.17th Terrace and Biscayne Bay, is a five-story buff stucco structure with a red tile roof. The club maintains the FLAGLER MEMORIAL LIBRARY (*open* 9:30–5:30 *daily except Tues. and Sat.* 9:30–9), largest of the six in the city.

(*Miami Bay Shore*)

10. The JAMES DEERING ESTATE (*private*), 3250 S.Miami Ave., was completed in 1916 at a cost of $15,000,000. The house of coraline stone, not visible from the road, dominates the lower bay. The roofing tile once covered an entire Cuban village. The grounds are enclosed by a pink concrete wall bearing carved primitive designs, topped with festoons of bougainvillea and orange flame vines. The massive seventeenth-century gateways are of pink marble and Istrian stone.

11. PAN AMERICAN AIRWAYS BASE (*open daily*), 2500 S.Bayshore Drive, built in 1928 on Dinner Key, is approached through an avenue of royal palms divided by a parkway planted with bougainvillea and other subtropical shrubs. The TERMINAL BUILDING on the bayfront is a smooth white stucco structure of modern design, two stories high in the center, with one-story wings. A yellow and white frieze of winged globes and rising suns circles the central two-story section, and is connected at the corners by sculptured eagles. The interior is decorated in quiet blues and grays. A 10-foot revolving globe in the concourse shows the air routes in colors. The beamed ceiling, two stories high, is decorated with signs of the zodiac surrounding a compass. A frieze traces the progress of aviation from Leonardo da Vinci's bird-shaped airplane design of 1490 to the Martin commercial ship of 1933. Around a balcony are offices, a restaurant, and a cocktail room overlooking Biscayne Bay. The architects were Delano and Aldrich, of New York. On bulletin boards announcing arrivals and departures are listed 32 West Indian and South American ports between which a fleet of 19-ton, 40-passenger clipper ships operate on regular schedule. From an outer second-floor promenade take-offs and landings can be watched.

In the HANGARS (*open* 8–4 *daily*), north of the terminal building, visitors are permitted to enter planes, and guides explain operations.

Miami has never recovered from the initial excitement of becoming a clipper-ship port, and it is the local custom to run down to the base around five in the afternoon, to see the planes come in.

12. COCONUT GROVE HOUSEKEEPER'S CLUB, 2985 S.Bayshore Drive, the oldest federated woman's club in Florida, is a two-story mission-style building with a front of rough, gray native rock. Founded in 1891 by Flora McFarlane, the club was the social center of the countryside; people came by boat, particularly from the community on the Miami River. They placed their small children in the nursery to sleep. At the close of the festivities the babies were picked up hurriedly, identified by their wraps. One night young Dick Carney, now Captain Richard Carney,

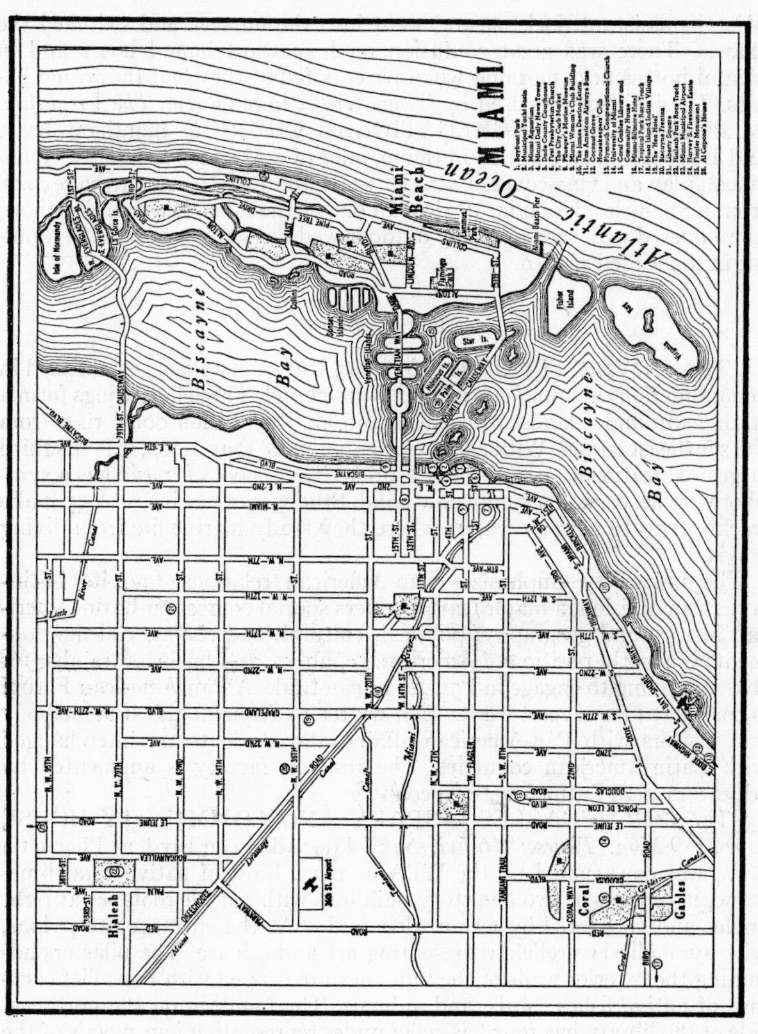
MIAMI
1. Bayfront Park
2. Municipal Yacht Basin
3. Miami Aquarium
4. Miami Daily News Tower
5. Dade County Courthouse
6. First Presbyterian Church
7. The City Curb Market
8. Pflueger's Marine Museum
9. Miami Woman's Club Building
10. The James Deering Estate
11. Pan American Airways Base
12. Coconut Grove Housekeepers' Club
13. Plymouth Congregational Church
14. University of Miami
15. Coral Gables Library and Community House
16. Miami-Biltmore Hotel
17. Tropical Park Race Track
18. Musa Island Indian Village
19. The "Hen Hotel"
20. Biscayne Fronton
21. Liberty Square
22. Hialeah Park Race Track
23. Miami Municipal Airport
24. Harvey S. Firestone Estate
25. Flagler Monument
26. Al Capone's House
Atlantic Ocean
Biscayne Bay
Biscayne Bay
Miami Beach
Hialeah
Coral Gables
Isle of Normandy
Fisher Island
Star Is.
Sunset Islands
Venetian Islands
Miami Beach Pier
36th St. Airport

Miami's assistant dock master, went into the nursery and switched the shawls. There was great confusion on homeward bound boats and in Miami homes next morning when parents found they had the wrong babies. The incident was used by Owen Wister in his novel, *The Virginian.*
13. PLYMOUTH CONGREGATIONAL CHURCH, Ingraham Hwy. and Devon Rd., is designed in the manner of a Mexican mission with basilican plan and vine-covered exterior walls; the doors are said to have come from a Spanish mission in Mexico. In one of the doors is a round cathole, now covered with screen. Many outdoor weddings are performed at a pulpit in the walled garden.

(*Coral Gables*)

14. The UNIVERSITY OF MIAMI, 515 University Place, established in 1926, functions in a buff stucco boom-time hotel. Three long wings form a triangle around a landscaped patio, and an observation dome rises from the southeast corner. With an enrollment of more than 1,000, it is the third largest educational institution in Florida. The school of music has a symphony orchestra and a symphonic band. Students in marine zoology make weekly trips to near-by waters where they study marine life from diving hoods.

The university emphasizes Pan-American relations, and its Latin-American division, a major feature, offers special courses on Latin-American history and geography; political, cultural, and commercial development; the world position of American republics, and business training for those planning to engage in Pan-American trade. A Pan-American Forum is conducted for several weeks each winter to acquaint the student body and visitors with Pan-American affairs, and students are interchanged with Latin-American countries. The resident faculty is augmented by educators from Latin-American countries.
15. The CORAL GABLES LIBRARY AND COMMUNITY HOUSE (*open* 1–9 *Mon.–Thurs.;* 9–6 *Fri.–Sat.*), Ponce de Leon Blvd. at Phoenetia Ave., was constructed by the WPA in 1937. Built of native coral limestone, it consists of two one-story buildings with red tile roofs set at right angles and connected by an arcaded patio. At the entrance are pylons, with symbolic bas-reliefs representing art and science. The pilasters adjoining the exterior walls of the buildings are capped with bas-relief carvings of native fishes, birds, and animals. The fountain on the northeast side of the library has four bas-relief nudes representing four moods of the sea. The hexagonal base of the fountain has bas-reliefs picturing waterfowl and marine life. The auditorium seats 500. The hand-hewn beams, murals, and sculpture are the work of the Florida Federal Art Project.
16. The MIAMI–BILTMORE HOTEL, Anastasia Ave. and Columbus Blvd., a massive tile-roofed concrete structure with rambling wings and a lofty central tower designed in the Mediterranean style, dominates the Coral Gables landscape. It was designed by Schultze and Weaver and built in 1925 at a cost of $10,000,000. The 150-acre grounds, traversed by a canal, include a country-club building and an 18-hole golf course. Guests

have membership privileges at the Roney Cabaña Club in Miami Beach, and the Anglers' Club at Key Largo. Free transportation is provided to the beach by aero-car, and to Key Largo by sea-sled and aero-car.

17. TROPICAL PARK RACE TRACK (*open daily; adm. during racing season* $1 *for grandstand*, $3 *for clubhouse*), 1.5 m. W. of Coral Gables on Bird Rd., was originally a dog track. In 1932 the grandstand, seating 3,500, then facing west, was reversed and the surrounding area landscaped. An Australian-pine hedge screens the track, and the clubhouse entrance is landscaped with clipped Australian pine, royal palms, and salvia.

(*Northwest Miami*)

18. MUSA ISLE INDIAN VILLAGE (*open* 9–6 *daily; adm.* 25¢), NW. 25th Ave. and NW.16th St. on the Miami River, presents the Seminole Indians as they live in their camps. A trading post displays Indian handiwork for sale. Within the village are the thatched-roofed platforms where the Indians live, a small zoo, and a museum. Men wrestle with alligators morning and afternoon, the exact time depending upon the attendance.

19. The 'HEN HOTEL,' NW.27th Ave. and NW.34th St., a huge unfinished building begun as a hotel in 1925, was named the 'million-dollar hen hotel' when a hatchery was established here during the early 1930's. The floor space accommodated more than 60,000 laying hens, 20,000 fryers, and 50,000 incubator chicks.

20. BISCAYNE FRONTON (*adm.* 25¢), 3500 NW.35th Ave., is a large, coral-tinted stucco building, its marquee supported by blue columns with red capitals. Night exhibitions of jai alai are played here throughout the season.

Jai alai (pronounced hi-li), a Spanish game similar to handball, is played with a *cesta*, or basket, strapped to the player's right hand. The curved, three-foot basket, woven from imported reed, has a maximum depth of 5 inches. A player often wears out three or four baskets during a contest. The hard, rubber-cored ball, or *pelota*, slightly smaller than a baseball, is covered with goatskin. Jai alai is 'faster than tennis and more dangerous than football.' The ball is driven with such speed that it sometimes breaks a leg or arm. In 1933 a star player died here from a fractured skull. There are few ball games calling for greater strength, endurance, and skill. It is said most jai alai players die young, for if not severely injured by the ball, their hearts give out. Featured players, who are always in rigid training, seldom appear more than twice a week. A stout net separates the *cacha*, or playing court, from spectators.

The server drops the ball, catches it on the rebound, and hurls it with a terrific forehand stroke against the wall. On the spacious court, 210 by 36 feet, players move like lightning, their *cesta*-lengthened hands reaching out miraculously to intercept and return bullet-like rallies of the ball. The *pelota* continues in play until it falls in illegal territory or a contestant fails to make good a return. Players are awarded purses for straight, place, and show, and there is pari-mutuel betting. Rules of the game are printed on programs sold at the fronton.

21. LIBERTY SQUARE, NW.14th Ave. between NW.62nd and NW. 65th Sts., a 62-acre Negro low-cost housing project built in 1936 by the FHA, was the first of its kind in the United States. Grouped around a white stucco administration building and recreation hall are 34 stormproof apartment buildings fronting on palm-planted courts.

(*Hialeah*)

22. HIALEAH PARK RACE TRACK (*open* 7–6 *daily; adm. during racing season* $1.25 *for grandstand*, $4 *for clubhouse*), entrance Bougainvillea Ave. and 23rd St., is approached through an avenue of royal palms, some 80 feet high and 150 years old, brought from the Everglades and Cuba. The vine-covered grandstand and the clubhouse, screened with clipped Australian pines, were built in 1931 and have a combined seating capacity of 10,500. The wide oval track rings a 92-acre area in lawns and flower beds surrounding a 32-acre artificial lake in which 300 pink flamingoes, seen from the stands, resemble a bed of pink water lilies. These birds, captured in southern Cuba, are kept in the park by clipping their wings. The first one hatched in the park, the only one then known to have been hatched in North America, lived three weeks and is mounted, together with an adult specimen, in a glass case on the southern pavilion.

The back of the grandstand is covered with a 250-foot trellis overgrown with purple bougainvillea. Behind the stands is the Australian totalizer, a large, electrically operated board, said to contain nearly 100,000 miles of wiring, that computes odds and pay-off prices, and displays results after each race. The race-track plant includes stables for about 1,500 horses.

23. MIAMI MUNICIPAL AIRPORT, NW.119th St. and LeJeune Road, the third airport established in the United States, was built in 1912 by a company headed by Glenn Curtiss, pioneer aviator. The annual All-American Air Maneuvers, designed to promote interest in light plane flying and to develop pilots for national defense, are held here. Army, navy, and commercial planes take part, and there is an exhibit of commercial planes.

From this field June 1, 1937, Amelia Earhart, with Captain Frederick Noonan as co-pilot, took off on a proposed 27,000-mile flight around the world, the first attempt ever made to encircle the globe at the middle latitudes. The route included Brazil, West Africa, India, Dutch East Indies, Australia, and New Guinea, whence the plane took off on a 2,556-mile hop to Howland Island. The last radio message, July 2nd, stated the plane was over the Pacific, position doubtful, with half an hour's fuel supply. More than 100 U.S. navy planes and 10 ships participated in a search that covered an estimated 250,000 square miles. Plane and pilots were given up for lost on July 18th. A bronze plaque honoring Miss Earhart, placed on the field by the Dade County Federation of Women's Clubs, was dedicated January 6, 1939.

(*Miami Beach*)

24. The HARVEY S. FIRESTONE ESTATE, Collins Ave. and 44th St., is at the point where Collins Ave. jogs one block from the ocean. The main

entrance, on the 44th St. side, is bounded by a low bougainvillea-covered wall, above which rises a high clipped Australian pine hedge. Back of this is a galvanized cyclone fence topped with barbed wire.

Fronting Collins Ave., about half way up the W. side of the estate, is a vine-draped pergola incorporated into boundary walls and hedges. The upper oval is open and affords a view of the vine-covered, many-chimneyed Georgian Colonial mansion with its glazed-tile roof. This estate is open once each spring for a charity garden tea.

25. FLAGLER MONUMENT (*accessible only by boat*), Bay Island, N. of Star Island, a square white shaft, illuminated at night, was erected in memory of Henry M. Flagler by Carl Fisher, Miami Beach pioneer.

26. AL CAPONE'S HOUSE (*private*), N. side of Palm Island, is a white mansion with a green tile roof barely visible over a high white wall. There are heavy wooden gates at the two entrances. Alphonse Capone purchased the house in 1928 and occupied it at intervals until he was sentenced May 1932 to 10 years imprisonment for violation of Federal income tax laws. He was transferred from Atlanta to Alcatraz, San Francisco Bay, in August 1934, and removed to Terminal Island, San Pedro Harbor, in January 1939.

✤✤✤✤✤✤✤✤✤✤✤✤✤✤✤✤✤✤✤✤✤✤✤✤✤✤✤✤✤✤✤✤✤✤✤✤✤

Orlando

Railroad Stations: Sligh Blvd. for Atlantic Coast Line R.R.; 79 W.Central Ave. for Seaboard Air Line Ry.
Bus Station: Terminal, 25 Wall St. for Florida Motor Lines.
Airport: Municipal Field, 2.1 m. E. on E.Central Ave., for National Airlines and Eastern Air Lines; taxi 25¢ per person, 10¢ extra baggage.
Taxis: Fare 15¢ up according to zone and number of passengers.
Local Busses: Fare 10¢, three tokens 25¢, within city limits.
Traffic Regulations: Right turns on red.

Accommodations: 17 hotels; numerous rooming and boarding houses, auto camps.

Information Service: Chamber of Commerce, 113 E.Central Ave.

Radio Station: WDBO (580 kc.).
Theaters and Motion Picture Houses: Municipal Auditorium, 203 W.Livingston Ave., concerts; five motion picture houses, one for Negroes.
Baseball: Tinker Field, 1500 W.Church St.; Sunshine Park, W.Livingston Ave., between Paramore and Garland Sts.
Swimming: Municipal Solarium, Lake Estelle, 25¢; Carolina Moon Beach, 303 N.Kentucky Ave., 25¢.
Tennis: Sunshine Park, W.Livingston Ave. between Paramore and Garland Sts., free; Eola Park, E.Central Ave., between Rosalind Ave. and Eola Drive, free. Tennis Club, Sunshine Park, annual fees $5 for men, $3 for women.
Golf: Orlando Country Club, Beardall Ave. at Country Club Drive, 18 holes, greens fee $1.50; Dubsdread Country Club, Edgewater Drive at city limits, 18 holes, greens fee $1.50.
Roque: Sunshine Park, annual fee $1.50.
Shuffleboard: Sunshine Park, annual fee $2.
Lawn Bowling: Sunshine Park, annual fee $2.50 to $5.

Annual Events: Orlando Air Party, Jan.; Central Florida Exposition, Feb.; Horse Show, Mar.; National Shuffleboard Tournament, Feb. and Mar.; State and International Lawn Bowling Tournament, Feb.; Casting Tournament (N.A.S.A.C. rules) Mar.; Choir Festival, Apr.; Amaryllis Show, Apr.; Yacht Club Regatta, early spring; Fishing Tournament, Dec. to Apr.; Florida Field Trials, Dec.

ORLANDO (111 alt., 27,330 pop.), in east central Florida, is the seat of Orange County and the State's largest inland city. It is in the ridge section on a watershed from which the St.Johns River flows north and the Kissimmee flows south. Orange County's thousand lakes, many of them spring-fed, temper the climate throughout the year. Lake shores in the city are extensively developed to the water's edge. Along their encircling boulevards landscaped parkways are shaded by live oaks, camphor trees, and a profusion of native and imported palms. Gardens are gay with subtropical shrubs, citrus trees, and winter-blooming flowers. In contrast are the dull red of brick-paved streets and the sparkling blue of lakes against this background of evergreen foliage. In less than half a century Orlando has grown from a trading post on a cow range to a city resembling a great cultivated park.

The business and shopping districts converge on Orange Avenue, the principal north and south thoroughfare. It resembles that of a substantial northern city in its architecture and its atmosphere of enterprise and activity. Sidewalks are narrow; traffic signal lights bear the admonition 'Quiet.' Fruit-juice stands and used-car lots, some in landscaped settings, appear between tall, year-round hotels, theaters, and department stores.

Architecturally the city varies from well-preserved two- and three-story brick business buildings and residences of the late nineteenth century with dormers, cupolas, and stamped metal cornices, to ornate structures of glazed tile embellished with chromium bands.

Frequently dwellings reflect that part of the country from which the owners came. Side by side are the plantation house with wide verandas and roof-high columns, the red brick English manor, the chaste New England cottage, and the flat-roof, gay-colored tropical house. Their variety of style is unified by landscaping. Coral and golden flame vines and exotic flowering shrubs grow in nearly every yard.

Social life is centered in homes, clubs, musical and theatrical groups, and around the parks and recreational facilities. Rollins College, six miles north, is the center of Orlando's academic life; speakers of note, many leading artists of concert and stage, and nationally known educators are heard there each winter.

Negroes, who comprise 25 per cent of the city's population, at one time owned and occupied property in the downtown area, principally along Church Street, but with the growth of the city they moved farther west. In a small Negro settlement in the western part of the city, is the L.C. Jones High School, named for a former principal. For his educational activities Jones was listed in *Who's Who in Colored America*. Except for a few business and professional men, local Negroes are employed on farms, in citrus groves and packing plants, turpentine camps, and domestic service.

The city is a shipping center for citrus fruits and winter vegetables cultivated on the thousands of fertile acres surrounding the city. Sales are handled through private and co-operative markets. One of the larger co-operatives is controlled by grower members according to the number of acres each owns. Thirteen nurseries specialize in citrus stock.

Dairying and poultry farming also form important units in Orlando's commerce. Nine sawmills and five naval-stores plants exploit the resources of surrounding pine forests. Amaryllis, gladiolus, and narcissus bulbs are grown and exported.

The settling of Orlando, like that of other towns in central Florida, was an aftermath of the Seminole Wars. Many volunteers, following the withdrawal of the regular army, remained to form a community. The site was selected for its proximity to Fort Gatlin, established about 1837 because of the excellence of the water and the habitable highlands of the area. Under protection of the garrison, settlers drifted into the Orlando area, unnamed until 1850. Among the first was Aaron Jernigan, of Georgia, who reached here with his family, slaves, and herds in 1842. Jernigan and most of the other pioneers that followed him were cattlemen.

In 1846, and again in 1849, this territory was menaced by Indian cattle rustlers. On both occasions Jernigan, then serving as Orange County's first representative in the State legislature, was called from Tallahassee to protect his herds. Cessation of hostilities by the Seminole led the army to abandon Fort Gatlin in 1848, but the settlers continued to carry arms, and Jernigan built a stockade on the west shore of Lake Holden. The stockade and the small settlement that grew around it was a convenient stopping place for travelers.

The stockade was granted a post office in 1850. Named Jernigan, it became the seat of Orange County by a legislative act of 1856, and was incorporated in 1875. Credit is given Judge V.D.Speer, a pioneer settler, for establishing Jernigan as the county seat. Towns competing for the honor were Fort Reed, called 'The Lodge,' and Apopka. The wily judge, aware that an American soldier at that time was entitled to vote wherever he might happen to be on election day, invited all soldiers stationed in Sumter County to be his guests at an old-fashioned picnic that day. They came, partook of his food and drink, promptly voted for his cause, and Jernigan became the county seat. Several versions are current for changing the name from Jernigan to Orlando. Judge Speer is said to have selected the name in honor of Shakespeare's hero in *As You Like It*; others assert it was named for Orlando Reeves, a runner between Mellonville and Fort Gatlin, slain by Indians on the site of the town.

During the War between the States, when a Federal blockade stopped all shipments of cattle from Florida to Cuba, Orlando stockmen sold their beef to the Confederates, delivering it on the hoof at Charleston, South Carolina.

Francis Eppes, grandson of Thomas Jefferson, and mayor of Tallahassee at the time the Army of Occupation took control, moved his impoverished family to Orlando in 1867. As lay reader he held the first Episcopal services in the district at his log cabin. For 14 years, until his death, Eppes was an intellectual and spiritual force in the community. In 1869 Will Wallace Harney, poet and journalist, editor of the Louisville (Kentucky) *Democrat*, and a member of the National Academy of Science, described in magazine articles the fertile farming land and ideal climate of Orlando, and the city had its first boom.

The first commercial citrus grove near Orlando was 100 acres planted during 1865–66 by W.H.Holden, from seeds of fruit trees found growing on his property. His crop was hauled to Mellonville, now Sanford, on the St.Johns River and carried by boat to Charleston. The long overland route brought a demand for better transportation facilities, and the South Florida Railroad was extended from Mellonville to Orlando in 1880. General U.S.Grant turned the first spadeful of earth.

During the early 1890's the State and railroad interests sold land in and about Orlando at approximately $1 an acre to English buyers, and large numbers migrated to the Lake Conway district and set out citrus groves. Nearly every home had its tennis court; a yacht club held periodic regattas; a polo team was organized in 1884, and the English Club was formed

Cities I

Photograph by Frank Turgeon, Jr.

VIA MIZNER, PALM BEACH

THE OLD SLAVE MARKET, ST. AUGUSTINE

PATIO, OLD SPANISH TREASURY, ST. AUGUSTINE
Photograph by J. Carver Harris

Photograph by F. W. Wolff

THE CATHEDRAL (1793), ST. AUGUSTINE

'VISCAYA,' THE DEERING ESTATE, MIAMI

Photograph by courtesy of Miami News Serv.

MIAMI

A PALM BEACH RESIDENCE

DAYTONA BEACH

DOWNTOWN SECTION, JACKSONVILLE

Photograph by Virgil Moore

Photograph by courtesy of Farm Security Administration

KEY WEST — DUVAL STREET, FROM THE ATLANTIC TO THE GULF

Photograph by courtesy of National Park Servi

MOAT, FORT MARION, ST. AUGUSTINE

two years later. The widespread planting of citrus gave agriculture in central Florida an importance that drove the cattle to ranges farther south, and marked the passing of frontier life in the community. However, stockmen and cowhands from Kissimmee Valley ranches are still seen at local sports events, and in the bars and mercantile establishments along West Church Street on Saturdays.

The freeze of 1895 ruined the citrus trees, but true to their traditions, the Englishmen played cricket during those harrowing hours. Later faced with disaster, more than half the growers abandoned their groves. Those who remained have been influential in the business and cultural life of the city.

In April 1929 grapefruit on a tree in the Orlando grounds of the Bureau of Entomology, U.S. Department of Agriculture, was found to be infested with a destructive insect pest. Specimens sent to Washington were identified as the Mediterranean fruit-fly by J.M.Aldrich, Associate Curator of the National Museum, and G.B.Merrill of the Florida State plant board made the same discovery a few days later. Plant board inspectors, after a quick survey, found 364 infested properties in the Orlando area. Federal emergency funds of $500,000 were provided and this sum was later increased by a Congressional appropriation of $4,250,000. The National Guard, employed in spraying and road patrol, remained on duty until July 1930, but the quarantine was not officially lifted until November (*see Tour 2c*).

During the past 30 years Orlando has been a favorite resort for a type of visitor, usually middle-aged and retired, appropriately called a perennial tourist. This man swears by Florida literature and believes his health and longevity depend upon orange juice and the local brand of sunshine. Although returning North or West from time to time he claims the city as his permanent residence and usually is an enthusiastic member of the Chamber of Commerce, his native State society, and the country club.

POINTS OF INTEREST

The CITY HALL, S.Orange Ave. between E.Jackson and South Sts., erected in 1905, a two-story structure with a heavy Corinthian portico, was one of the first white-sand brick structures built in the Orlando area.

The OLD COURTHOUSE, E.Central Ave. between Court and North Main Sts., an ornate dark red brick structure surmounted by a square clock tower, is of modified Romanesque design with steep gables and a massive turreted tower. Erected in 1892 it was considered one of central Florida's outstanding county buildings. It now houses municipal and WPA offices.

The ORANGE COUNTY COURTHOUSE, N.Main St. between E. Washington and E.Wall Sts., a four-story limestone and granite structure of neoclassic design with classic Tuscan colonnades and rusticated first story, was completed in 1927. Murray S. King of Orlando was the architect. A jail occupies the top floor. The grounds are planted with a variety of palms and ornamental subtropical shrubs. On the southeast corner of the lawn stands a chocolate or cacao tree. Brought from India and planted in 1892, it is marked by a bronze tablet.

ALBERTSON PUBLIC LIBRARY (*open 9–9 weekdays; 2–6 Sun.*), 165 E.Central Ave., of neoclassic design, opened in 1923, contains 70,000 volumes, including a rare-book section. The symmetrical façade is dominated by a high central section with pedimented Doric portico; a classic parapet crowns the long wings on either side. Murray S. King of Orlando was the architect. It was named for Captain Charles Albertson, who bequeathed his private library to the city.

The M.O.OVERSTREET RESIDENCE (*private*), E.Central and S. Rosalind Aves., is a red brick structure of classic design with two-story colonnaded porches on three sides. The pedimented porticoes are supported by Corinthian columns. It dominates the Lake Eola section and its landscaped grounds are among the most attractive in the city.

LAKE EOLA PARK, E.Central Ave. between Rosalind Ave. and Eola Drive and extending to Robinson Ave., with an area of 55 acres, is the largest park in the city. The lake is encircled by a concrete walk, its parkways landscaped with plumosa, date and cabbage palms, and live oaks. Scattered clumps of bananas and bamboos add to the tropical setting. This is a convenient place to study the swans, ducks, and sea gulls, particularly at feeding time. The swans inhabiting this and other municipal lakes are descendants of a pair imported in 1910 by Charles Lord, an Englishman, from the private preserves of Edward VII. They were named 'Mr. and Mrs. Bill.' It is claimed that 'Mr. Bill' drowned his mate when a setting of eggs failed to hatch. He died at the age of 78, was mounted, and is on display at the Chamber of Commerce building. The birds are fed by city employees each mid-afternoon, and sea gulls from Daytona Beach commute regularly to partake of the free meal.

The ORLANDO ZOO (*always open*), NE. corner W.Livingston Ave. and Garland St., exhibits Florida birds and animals in natural settings. Gravel paths lead between open-air cages that contain raccoons, monkeys, alligators, a wild cat, and a black bear. An elevated screened cage houses rattlesnakes and water moccasins; an aviary contains parrots, eagles, owls, geese, and a variety of herons; a natural rock pit is the home of the small Florida deer.

SUNSHINE PARK, W.Livingston Ave. between Paramore and Garland Sts. extending to Alexander Place, has large municipal recreation grounds with facilities for shuffleboard, roque, lawn bowling, and horseshoe pitching. The clubhouses are headquarters for tourists' societies and social gatherings .The Municipal Auditorium, seating 3,300, is used for organ recitals and varied entertainments during the winter. The adjoining Exposition Park embraces the grounds and permanent stucco buildings of the Central Florida Exposition.

POINTS OF INTEREST IN ENVIRONS

Winter Park (Rollins College), 1.7 *m.*; Eatonville, all-Negro town, 6 *m.*; 'The Senator,' huge cypress tree, 16 *m.* (*see Tour 2c*); Lake Apopka, 14.4 *m.* (*see Tour 9*).

✤✤✤✤✤✤✤✤✤✤✤✤✤✤✤✤✤✤✤✤✤✤✤✤✤✤✤✤✤✤✤✤✤✤✤

Palm Beach

Railroad Stations: S.Tamarind Ave. and Datura St., for Seaboard Air Line Ry.; E.Railroad Ave. and 5th St., for Florida East Coast Ry., both in West Palm Beach.
Bus Stations: 310 Evernia St. for Florida Motor Lines; 215 S.Olive Ave. for Pan American Bus Lines, both in West Palm Beach.
Airports: Municipal Field, 4 m. W. on Southern Blvd., West Palm Beach, for Eastern Air Lines, taxi 50¢.
Taxis: 25¢ per passenger per zone.
City Busses: Fare 10¢.
Ferry: W. end of Royal Poinciana Blvd. (Main St.), pedestrians only, fare 5¢.
Afromobiles: Breakers Hotel, E. end of Breakers Drive, Jan. to Apr.; along Lake Trail and Worth Ave. other months; fare $1.50 an hour, two passengers.

Accommodations: 13 hotels, majority open Jan. to Apr.

Information Service: Chamber of Commerce, Royal Palm Way and Lake Drive.

Motion Picture Houses: 2, open winter only.
Swimming: Lido pool, adm. 25¢, and Public Beach, ocean front, E. end of Worth Ave.
Golf: Palm Beach Country Club, N.County Rd. and Country Club Rd., 18 holes, greens fee $2.50. In West Palm Beach: Belvedere Golf Course, 2 m. W. on Belvedere Rd., 18 holes, greens fee 75¢; West Palm Beach Municipal Country Club, Southern Blvd. and Military Trail, 18 holes, greens fee $1.
Tennis: Poinciana Courts, N.Lake Trail near Cocoanut Walk.
Fishing: Rainbow Pier, foot of Worth Ave., adm. 25¢; charter boats for Gulf Stream fishing at numerous piers along the lake.

Annual Events: Yacht Club Regatta, Feb.; Southern Professional Tennis Tournament, Everglades Club, Feb.; Flower Show, Academy of the Society of the Four Arts, Feb.; Under-Privileged Children's Benefit, Feb.

PALM BEACH (10 alt., 1,707 pop.) is an exclusive resort town on the northern end of an 18-mile island between Lake Worth on the west and the Atlantic Ocean on the east. At no point is the island wider than three-quarters of a mile, and in places it is only 500 feet. Three bridges connect the city to West Palm Beach and the mainland: the concrete Flagler Memorial Bridge on the north, which replaces the wooden railroad trestle that led to the grounds of the now vanished Royal Poinciana Hotel; the imposing South Bridge in midtown, a continuation of Royal Palm Way; and the Southern Boulevard Bridge, which leads from the Bath and Tennis Club to the main highway that penetrates a section of the Everglades.

Royal Palm Way, the city's landscaped boulevard and principal east-west thoroughfare, extends from Lake Worth to the Atlantic Ocean, a three-quarter mile avenue bordered by double rows of royal palms. It divides a two-mile area that contains the business district, schools, clubs, brokerage offices, and unpretentious homes of year-round residents.

Worth Avenue, at the widest part of the island and the southern extremity of the shopping district, is a four-block street of smart shops, including branches of metropolitan stores. Lined by Australian pines and scarlet-flowered hibiscus, Wells Road forms the northern limit. North and south of this area are rich estates surrounded by vine-cloaked walls raised high to insure seclusion.

The restrained magnificence of these properties is the result of lavish expenditure, expert landscaping, and continuous care. They embrace acres of terraced lawns and formal gardens, dotted with tiled swimming pools and fountains, and glorified by exotic plants. Many of the flowering trees and shrubs are imported from the remote corners of the earth, and the ensemble has the variety and beauty of a tropical arboretum.

County Road, also known as Palm Beach Avenue, the city's main north–south highway, passes between many large estates. Front-page names are on many ornate gateways, but passers-by see little of the homes and only rarely the occupants. Lake Trail, paralleling the east shore of Lake Worth for several miles, a jungle-shaded lane beneath the palms, is reserved for pedestrians and afromobiles—two-wheeled wicker chairs, mounted on the front end of bicycles, accommodating two persons, and pedaled by Negroes. The lake, actually a salt-water lagoon and a section of the Intracoastal Waterway, was named for Brigadier General William J. Worth who served in the Seminole War. Barely half a mile wide, the gleaming blue water of the basin is, in season, a mirror for the many craft anchored there.

Wide, palm-fringed Ocean Boulevard, the resort's motorway and promenade, extends along the Atlantic and affords an unobstructed view of the ocean and tumbling surf. Many of the homes have passages under the boulevard, giving access to private beaches. A five-block ocean frontage between Brazilian and Hammon Avenues includes the public beach, swimming pool, casino, and a fishing pier.

Barely three miles off Palm Beach, its nearest approach to America's shores, the Gulf Stream runs 70 fathoms deep, while 30 miles out it reaches 400 fathoms. The current is so powerful that southbound vessels keep to its western edge, and white liners, rusty cargo ships, and oil tankers pass in review almost within hailing distance of the coast.

Palm Beach is regarded as the winter counterpart of Newport—cosmopolitan, individual, and independent. Its habitués constitute a fragment of international society seeking June in January and the pleasures afforded by right of social prestige and heavy purse. A municipal ordinance rules that all building operations cease by the middle of December so that incoming residents will not be disturbed, and the town planning board sees to it that trees and shrubbery are pruned, parkways cleared of rubbish, and beaches groomed.

A vanguard of servants descends from the North in December to set the stage. With the new year, private railroad cars are parked on West Palm Beach sidings and sumptuous houseboats and yachts from distant ports moor in the sheltered waters of Lake Worth.

Hotels offer every luxurious accommodation, but permanent winter residents have their own estates. For the organized coterie, the social whirl spins as regularly as the clock. The official day begins at eleven on the private beaches when the nomad citizenry assemble to devote a few hours to recuperation, and seek a coveted sun tan. During this period the ocean front is a panorama of brilliant bathing togs, bronzed bodies, painted wind breaks, and gay umbrellas. Luncheons, accompanied by music, are served in cabañas and upon canopied terraces that flank sea-water pools.

Restricted to members and their guests are a faultless golf course, many fast tennis courts, Bradley's Casino, and numerous clubs. At all times there are yachts cruising to remote Florida keys or the Bahamas, planes for Nassau and Havana, sea sleds for brief excursions up shallow tropical rivers and canals, motoring to Miami race tracks, and speedboats on the lake. But fishing remains the supreme sport, and quest of the valiant sailfish in the Gulf Stream provides the acme of thrills, a challenge to the skill and endurance of the deep-sea angler.

To lend zest to the eternal round of entertainment is the resort's winter colony of celebrities of stage, screen, and radio; playwrights, songsmiths, and producers. The annual charity benefits staged by the community, to which these stars contribute their services, are perhaps unrivaled in amusement circles. But with the ides of March gayety ends and the city becomes a ghost town given over to caretakers and artisans, its homes shuttered, its shops closed, its beaches practically deserted.

For many years no wheeled vehicles, with the exception of bicycles and afromobiles, were allowed in the city. Later motorcars were admitted, but rolling chairs and bicycles are still the popular conveyances. There are no commercial parking lots or tourist camps, and the parking of trailers is limited to one hour.

Palm Beach has no Negro settlement, and Negroes are not allowed on the streets after dark unless actively employed in the city.

To those of the literary world, many of whom are winter residents, Palm Beach has furnished alluring backgrounds. Joseph Hergesheimer's *Tropical Winter* has captured much that is characteristic of the city and its people. The island and environs have been the locale for numerous articles and short stories, and for novels by Elmer Davis, Arthur Somers Roche, and Ethel Pettit, his wife, and others. Prominent artists of magazine and newspaper fields make the city their winter vacation ground; matched with nationally known sports writers and novelists, their annual golf tournament is an event.

The early architecture of Palm Beach, running to steep-roofed, gable-typed frame houses with cupolas and turning-lathe ornamentation, was dominated by mammoth wooden hotels painted in the prevailing Flagler white and lemon yellow. Magnificent concrete structures have supplanted pioneer hostelries, but a few of the residences remain, some still occupied by owners who prefer their shingle-walled dwellings to the palatial estates that surround them.

It was Addison Mizner, artist-architect, prize fighter, and miner, who, shortly after the World War, introduced the Spanish vogue that resulted in a transformation of architecture along Florida's lower east coast. Mizner's houses, built with courtyards on various levels, were replete with arcades and lofty galleries; rooms featured exposed rafters and vaulted ceilings; tiled pools and mosaic murals resembled those of Pompeii. To obtain materials needed for his creations, Mizner established plants for the manufacture of tile, ironwork, furniture, and pottery. His pioneer Florida effort, the Everglades Club, was responsible for commissions to design homes for the Stotesburys and Vanderbilts, for Rodman Wanamaker II and Drexel Biddle, Jr.

Following the boom, with its extensive building program in the city, the Mizner vogue passed, and the British-Colonial-type house became popular; the pastel shades of the Mediterranean were in part replaced by the oyster white of the newer designs and by less bizarre ornamentation. Among more recent examples classed under the general term of Tropical Colonial are the West Indian and Bermudan, with whitewashed walls and green shutters.

Settlement of the Palm Beach area was of comparatively recent date; neither the Spanish, during three centuries of almost unbroken rule, nor the English left their imprints upon the lower east coast. It was not until the War between the States that Lang, a Confederate draft dodger, settled in what is now Palm Beach and built the first house. Lang vanished at the close of the war and in 1872 Charlie Moore from Miami took over the property. Others followed, and by 1873 four families had settled in the vicinity. Captain Elisha Newton Dimick, known as the founder of Palm Beach, reached the island in 1876 and built a house on land purchased from the State at approximately $1 an acre. His holdings, together with his father's, are a part of the property now occupied by Colonel Bradley's Casino and the Whitehall Hotel. Two miles of ocean front extending from what is now Sunset Avenue to McKenna Place, homesteaded by Melville Spencer of Pennsylvania in the early 1870's, was sold 40 years later to Samuel Untermeyer, New York lawyer. The land homesteaded by Captain Albert Geer was sold to Henry M. Flagler for $75,000 and became the site of the Royal Poinciana Hotel.

The resort proper perhaps owes its existence to the wreck of a Spanish barque in 1878. The vessel's cargo of coconuts washed ashore and took root; early settlers gathered many nuts and planted them on their property, and in time the barren sand key was transformed into a patch of South Sea loveliness.

After years of receiving mail in haphazard fashion, in 1880 the settlers were granted a post office under the name of Palm City. Afterwards, discovering that another town in the State had a prior claim to the name, the settlement was rechristened Palm Beach.

In 1893 Henry M. Flagler, whose railroad had reached as far south as Rockledge, attracted to the palm-covered island and quick to visualize its possibilities as a winter resort, purchased property on both sides of Lake Worth and began construction of the Royal Poinciana, Palm Beach's pioneer hotel. Shacks, tents, and boarding houses sprang up rapidly. Material for the hotel was shipped down the Indian River from Eau Gallie to Jupiter, thence 8 miles across country on the Jupiter and Lake Worth Railroad to Juno, where it was again transferred to boats on Lake Worth. Flagler visited here regularly, directed the layout of the township, installed waterworks, paved streets, and made other civic improvements, including an extensive landscaping program, at his own expense. The early arrivals were from Philadelphia—the Wanamakers, Stotesburys, and Wideners—families still prominent among colony leaders. With their approval, Palm Beach patronage increased, the capacity of the Royal Poinciana Hotel was doubled, and larger, more magnificent hotels and estates were built. Exclusive clubs with a membership fee of $10,000 came into being. To this slender ribbon of sand almost within sight of the Everglades has been transplanted the luxury of the world. It is a luxury tempered with good taste, and though the city is in many ways artificial, its beauty is genuine.

Several hurricanes have swept the city since its founding, the most severe one occurring September 16, 1928, causing an estimated damage of $10,000,000. Miles of ocean drives were washed away, trees and shrubbery destroyed, and homes ruined by water. Although there was no loss of life here or in West Palm Beach, more than 1,800 were drowned in the Okeechobee section west of the city.

POINTS OF INTEREST

1. MEMORIAL FOUNTAIN AND PLAZA, occupying the center of S. County Road between Brazilian and Australian Aves., was built in 1930 as a memorial to those who have taken a prominent part in the city's development. Behind a landscaped, oblong, sunken pool a series of steps lead to successive terraces. At the foot of the second flight are square-cut columns topped by ornamental urns bearing bronze memorial tablets. Upon the highest terrace is a circular, three-tier concrete fountain upheld by four rearing, winged horses. Addison Mizner contributed his services as designer; winter visitors and local business firms defrayed the cost of the structure, and the site was donated by the city. Only two names have so far been placed on the memorial tablets: Henry M. Flagler, railroad builder, and Elisha N. Dimick, pioneer resident and first mayor of Palm Beach.

2. VIA MIZNER and VIA PARIGI, Worth Ave. between Cocoanut Row and Hibiscus Ave., two roofless winding courts extending through to Peruvian Ave., are Mizner creations in the typical Mizner manner. The narrow, flag-paved streets, restricted to pedestrians and afromobiles, are bordered by shops displaying exotic wares, and by patio restaurants and open air cafés. Outside stairs lead to second floor apartments and studios, their casements opening upon iron-grilled balconies. Tropical trees, shrubs, and vines contribute to the Old World atmosphere.

3. The EVERGLADES CLUB (*private*), Worth Ave. at S. end of Cocoanut Row, a stucco building with a red tile roof, medieval turrets, and wrought-iron grille work, in the style of a Spanish monastery, was designed by Addison Mizner, his first venture in Palm Beach. The building, originally intended to serve as a country club with cottages for convalescent soldiers, was transformed into the first of the city's smart clubs following the World War.

4. BETHESDA-BY-THE-SEA, NE. corner S.County Road and Barton Ave., an Episcopal church of Gothic design, was built in 1925. It embraces a number of features of ecclesiastical design characteristic of fifteenth-century churches, when the embattlement tower was used for defensive purposes. The arched main entrance passes through the tower that is capped by a parapet with four corner finials. The nave, surrounded by large stained-glass windows, seats 500. Adjoining the tower is a cloister, formed by a series of decorated, foliated arches enclosing a quadrangle in the manner of open-air cloisters of medieval churches. The parish house alongside follows the same architectural design. The architects were Hiss and Weekes.

The CLUETT MEMORIAL GARDEN (*open daily*), adjoining the church, is noted for its tropical landscaping. It was presented to the church by Miss Nellie Agnes Cluett of Troy, New York, in memory of her parents.

This is the third church of the same name built in the city, all of which are standing. The original church on North Lake Trail, about a mile north of Bradley's Casino, was erected in 1889; its kneeling benches and book racks were built of rough pine boards and packing boxes. When a hurricane damaged the church in 1894, a second church was built near by. This is a gray shingled structure with a low arched veranda across the front and two octagonal towers. The larger tower, with curling eaves resembling a pagoda, contains a clock with gilt numerals and hands.

5. The BREAKERS, Ocean Walk, E. end of Breakers Drive, is a $7,000,000 hotel of Italian Renaissance design, built in 1925. It is of buff stucco, with twin towers on the west façade. The architects were Shultz and Weaver.

6. The WHITEHALL, S.Lake Trail at W. end of Cocoanut Walk, a $4,000,000 white stucco structure, is the city's second largest hotel. The nucleus of the building was the Henry Flagler residence. It was enlarged and reconstructed in 1925; Carrere and Hastings were the architects.

7. The SITE OF THE ROYAL POINCIANA HOTEL, S.Lake Trail between Royal Poinciana Blvd. and Cocoanut Walk, is associated with the early resort life of Palm Beach. Constructed as part of the Flagler East Coast development in 1894, the grandiose frame structure of more than 1,000 rooms was used until the season of 1929–30. It was demolished in 1936, but a wing of the great veranda still stands. The grounds and gardens remain intact and are considered among the most beautiful in America. The POINCIANA GREENHOUSE (*open daily*) contains a collection of rare tropical shrubs and trees.

8. BRADLEY'S BEACH CLUB (*private*), NE. corner Royal Poinciana Blvd. (Main St.) and N.Lake Trail, a rambling white clapboard house, universally known as Bradley's, is America's winter Monte Carlo. It was founded in 1898 by Colonel Edward R. Bradley, cowboy, scout, and miner, and chartered as a social club. All interior walls are white trimmed with green, the colors of the Bradley racing stables. Admittance to persons more than 24 years old and nonresident in Florida is by membership card or by introduction through a member.

9. ST.EDWARD'S ROMAN CATHOLIC CHURCH, NW. corner N.

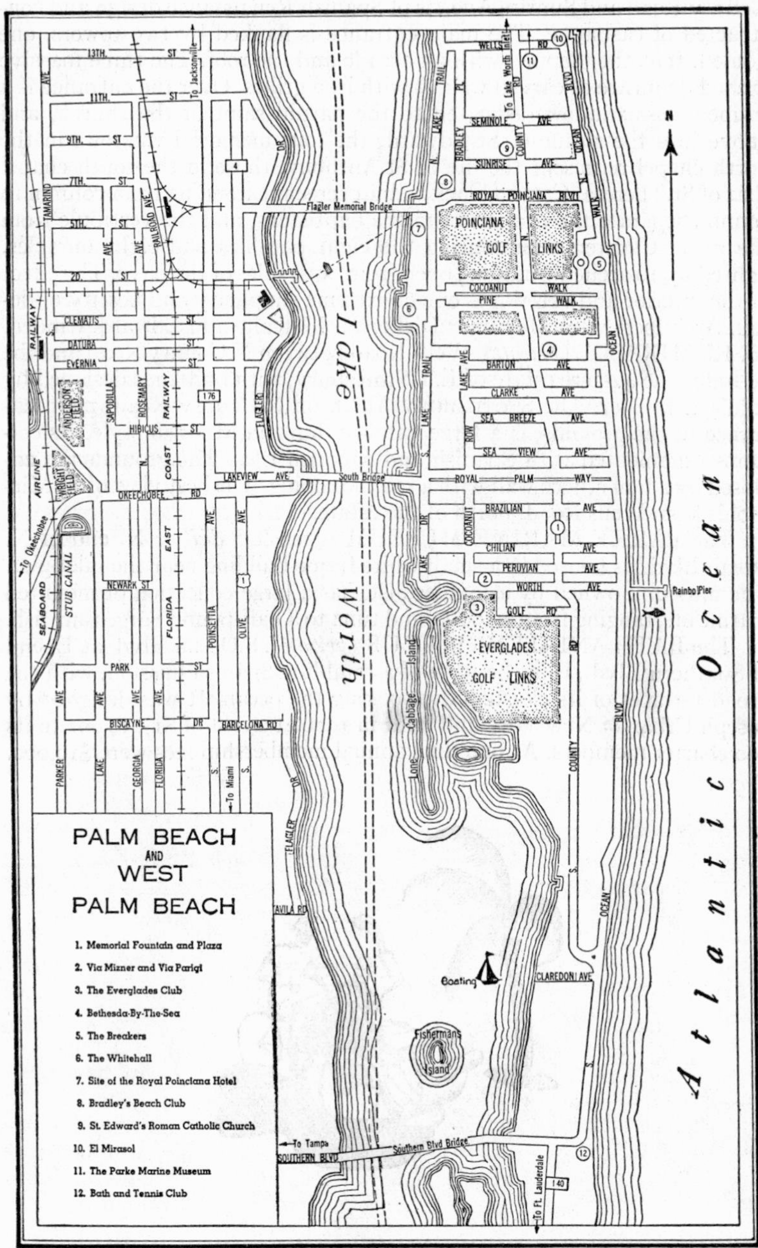
PALM BEACH
AND
WEST
PALM BEACH
1. Memorial Fountain and Plaza
2. Via Mizner and Via Parigi
3. The Everglades Club
4. Bethesda-By-The-Sea
5. The Breakers
6. The Whitehall
7. Site of the Royal Poinciana Hotel
8. Bradley's Beach Club
9. St. Edward's Roman Catholic Church
10. El Mirasol
11. The Parke Marine Museum
12. Bath and Tennis Club
Lake Worth
Atlantic Ocean
N
Flagler Memorial Bridge
South Bridge
Southern Blvd Bridge
POINCIANA GOLF LINKS
EVERGLADES GOLF LINKS
Lone Cabbage Island
Fishermans Island
Boating
Rainbo Pier
To Jacksonville
To Lake Worth Inlet
To Okeechobee
To Miami
To Tampa
To Ft. Lauderdale
ANDERSON FIELD
WRIGHT FIELD
STUB CANAL
SEABOARD AIRLINE RAILWAY
FLORIDA EAST COAST RAILWAY
ROYAL POINCIANA BLVD
COCOANUT WALK
PINE WALK
BARTON AVE
CLARKE AVE
SEA BREEZE AVE
SEA VIEW AVE
ROYAL PALM WAY
BRAZILIAN AVE
CHILIAN AVE
PERUVIAN AVE
WORTH AVE
GOLF RD
SEMINOLE AVE
SUNRISE AVE
WELLS RD
CLAREDON AVE
SOUTHERN BLVD
AVILA RD
LAKEVIEW AVE
OKEECHOBEE RD
CLEMATIS ST
DATURA ST
EVERNIA ST
HIBICUS ST
NEWARK ST
PARK ST
BISCAYNE DR
BARCELONA RD
13TH. ST
11TH. ST
9TH. ST
7TH. ST
5TH. ST
2D. ST
TAMARIND AVE
RAILROAD AVE
SAPODILLA AVE
ROSEMARY AVE
POINSETTIA AVE
OLIVE AVE
PARKER AVE
LAKE AVE
GEORGIA AVE
FLORIDA AVE
FLAGLER DR
N. LAKE TRAIL
S. LAKE TRAIL
COCOANUT ROW
LAKE DR
S. COUNTY RD
S. OCEAN BLVD
N. OCEAN BLVD
BRADLEY PL
N. COUNTY RD
N. OCEAN WALK
4
176
1
140

County Road and Sunrise Ave., is of Spanish Renaissance design and constructed of caststone. The main entrance is flanked by two towers, one domed, the other topped with an arcade and tile roof. The three massive arched doors are of carved walnut with iron grilles. Over the entrance is a stained-glass window dedicated to the patron saint of the church, and above it is the shrine of St.Edward; the four memorial windows in the north chapel represent the life of St.Anthony, those in the south chapel that of St.Theresa. Carved black walnut screens extending from column to column separate the chapels from the baptistery, and the vestibule from the nave. Cloisters representing the eight parables and eight miracles, lighted by 16 arched windows, open from both sides of the nave. The effect of the interior and exterior is one of extreme simplicity and beauty of detail. Architects were Mortimer Dickerson Metcalfe and Edward Minden.

10. EL MIRASOL (*private*), Wells Road between N.County Road and the ocean, is the 42-acre estate of E.T.Stotesbury, with buildings designed by Addison Mizner. The STOTESBURY ARCH, on N.County Road, main entrance to the grounds, is a large gateway built in Moorish style, its columns ornamented with Spanish and Moorish tiles. The grounds are enclosed by a buff stucco wall with a red tile coping. The best view of El Mirasol is from Wells Road, north of the estate.

11. The PARKE MARINE MUSEUM (*open* 9–5 *daily*), N. end of N. Ocean Blvd., is housed in a small white frame building near the inlet pier. The museum, owned by a taxidermist, has a large collection of mounted marine life, ranging from a 500-pound tuna to a half-pound Sargossum fish.

12. The BATH AND TENNIS CLUB (*private*), S.Ocean Blvd. at E. end of Southern Blvd., is in the form of a rambling Spanish mission, with the broad terraces of its cloisters overlooking the ocean. It was designed by Joseph Urban of New York and built in 1926 at a cost of $1,250,000 to its 300 charter members. At one time annual membership fees were $10,000.

Pensacola

Railroad Stations: 21 S.Coyle St. for Frisco Lines; SE. corner N.Alcaniz and Wright Sts. for Louisville & Nashville R.R.
Bus Stations: 121 N.Palafox St. for Greyhound Lines, St.Andrews Bay Transportation Co., and Teche Greyhound Lines; 17 E.Garden St. for Munroeville Bus Co.; Palafox and Gregory Sts. for local busses.
Taxis: Zone system, 10¢ fare.
Local Busses: Fare 5¢ in city; Fort Barrancas and Naval Air Station, 15¢.
Piers: L. & N. docks, S. end of Tarragona St., and Frisco docks, S. end of DeVilliers St. for North German, Dixie-Mediterranean, and Mobile Oceanic Lines.
Toll Bridges: Pensacola Beach, Santa Rosa Island, and State 53, 75¢ one way, 85¢ round trip; Lillian Bridge, Alabama points, 25¢.
Traffic Regulations: R. on red into S.Palafox St. only; all through streets marked by yellow signs.
Street Order and Numbering: Palafox St. is the dividing line for E. and W. Sts., Garden St. for N. and S. Sts.
Airport: 5 m. E. on 12th Ave. for National Airlines.

Accommodations: Five hotels; boarding houses and tourist camps.

Information Service: Chamber of Commerce, E.Garden and Brue Sts.; Municipal Advertising Board, San Carlos Hotel, W.Garden and N.Palafox Sts.

Radio Station: WCOA (1340 kc.).
Motion Picture Houses: Six.
Swimming: Bayview Park, E. end of Blount St., free; Pensacola Beach, Sonta Rosa Island, 8.3 m. SE. on State 53; Saunder's Municipal Beach, between I and J Sts.; Gulf Beach, 17 m. W. on State 93.
Shuffleboard: E.Garden St., opposite Chamber of Commerce.
Tennis, Checkers, and Dominoes: Bayview Park, E. end of Blount St.
Golf: Osceola Country Club, 4 m. N. on US 90, 18 holes, greens fee $1.
Fishing: Municipal pier, S. end of Palafox St., numerous piers and bridges for bay and river fishing, free; Pensacola Beach pier for surf fishing, 10¢. Charter boats, guides and equipment for deep-sea fishing along waterfront.

Annual Events: All Souls' Day Candle Lighting, St.Michael's Cemetery, week before Lent; Camellia Show, Mar.; Navy Carnival, May; Navy-Civilian Golf Tournament, May–June; Southern Yachting Association Regatta, July 4; Pensacola Tennis Association Tournament, July 4 and Labor Day; Pensacola Anglers' Club Fishing Rodeo, July; Navy Day Celebration, Oct.; Horse Show, Oct.; Escambia County Fair, Nov.

PENSACOLA (13 alt., 31,579 pop.) is built on the north shore of Pensacola Bay, the largest natural, landlocked, deep-water harbor in the State. On the east is Bayou Texar and on the west Bayou Chico, wide arms of the bay that reach inland on each side of the Pensacola peninsula. The ship channel winds past the U.S. Naval Air Station, Forts Barrancas and San Carlos, and enters the Gulf of Mexico between a barren sand spit and Santa Rosa Island.

The city rises from a level area, occupied by the business section and dominated by a block-square hotel, to North Hill and East Hill, the newer residential districts. From them is a view of the bay, more than 15 miles wide at places, with its irregular, tree-fringed bayous and ochre-yellow bluffs. It is spanned on the southeast by a long toll bridge connecting the city with Santa Rosa Island and the white Gulf beaches. The harbor, once crowded with ships when exports of lumber and naval stores made Pensacola an important Gulf port, shows little activity. Huge wharves, railroad coaling docks, and warehouses line the waterfront, obviously too large and numerous for the maritime commerce handled today.

In atmosphere and character, Pensacola is more an old Spanish town than an American city, and the old Spanish proverb, 'The night is made for sleep, and the day for rest,' is still quoted here. The names of streets—Zarragossa, Palafox, Tarragona, Intendencia, Moreno, Gonzales, and Alcaniz—are a heritage from early Spanish settlers.

The old city, extending six blocks north of the bay, presents a jumble of gables, pilasters, dormers, and colonnades. The plank walks and long flights of steps leading to second-story entrances have disappeared, but there remain high balconies, many ornamented with wrought-iron railings, and jutting balustrades reminiscent of New Orleans and Mobile, to which Pensacola is more closely related historically and architecturally than it is to other Florida cities.

Garden Street, a dividing line for north and south streets, served during the British occupation as a community garden and pasture. Although it has been converted into a two-way thoroughfare, a parkway landscaped with flower beds, shrubs, and pecan trees down the middle suggests its earlier use. Palafox Street, the principal business thoroughfare, is also divided for several blocks by a formal garden, and these two streets retain something of the color and charm of the easy-going 1700's, despite their intersection in the heart of the city's business district.

Intermingled along downtown streets are churches, monuments, and historical squares; store fronts of chromium and tile; faded two- and three-story frame and brick buildings with wood and metal awnings that have sheltered leisurely shoppers for more than a century. All are dwarfed by an eight-story gray stucco hotel with its patio and observation tower, the center of the town's social, civic, and political activities.

In residential areas overlooking the old town much of the natural growth of oak, magnolia, and other hardwood has been retained in small parks and spacious yards, and along the streets. The majority of the houses, built since the World War, are of Southern Colonial design; those of brick and stucco have not been influenced by the architecture or bright coloring introduced by the boom.

Unlike most Florida communities, there are no sharp dividing lines in the areas given over to the different racial groups and nationalities. In some white sections are numbers of Negro homes, and in other parts of the city where Negroes are most numerous, some white families live in harmony with their neighbors. The probable reason for this is that Pensacola is one of the few Southern cities where the dominant social group was originally Spanish. In fact, the customs and characteristics of southern Europe still prevail, and pure Latin types are frequently seen on the streets. Negro life in Pensacola is progressive, and members of this race seem better educated than is usual in the 'Deep South;' and though racial distinction is rigidly adhered to from a social standpoint, many Negroes hold trusted and responsible positions with firms operated by white men. There is a small professional group in the city, and some Negro establishments, particularly barber shops, are patronized by white customers.

There exists in Pensacola the remnant of a peculiar ethnic group calling themselves 'Creoles,' but who are not to be confused with the New Orleans Creoles of French and Spanish stock. The Pensacola Creoles are chiefly descendants of a much larger group, of Spanish and Negro admixture, who enjoyed great prosperity before the War between the States. A large percentage of them own their homes. Although they hold themselves aloof from the Negroes, they are not accepted on terms of social equality by the whites.

The economic life of the city is largely dependent on the Naval Air Station. Its officers and cadet aviators, and, to a lesser extent, the officers of the army post at Fort Barrancas, dominate the social life. Sailors, soldiers, and marines are abroad every afternoon and night. The gala occasions are the annual pre-Lenten coronation balls and Navy Day celebration, and the more boisterous festivities along the waterfront attending the return of red-snapper fishing boats.

There is evidence that Panfilo de Narváez and his men, leaving the vicinity of Apalachicola in a fleet of makeshift boats, passed close to the site of Pensacola during the winter of 1528; but its first recorded history begins with the arrival of Capitán Maldonado, commander of the fleet that brought De Soto to Florida shores, who entered the bay and christened it Puerta d'Anchusi, a name probably suggested by Ochus, as the bay was known to the Indians. By discovering the bay he completed a voyage westward along the Gulf coast seeking a harbor for De Soto, who was near Apalachee, 100 miles to the east. De Soto agreed to make the harbor his base of supplies, but intrigued by tales of gold he marched off to the north.

Nineteen years later, Philip II of Spain dispatched an expedition of 1,500 soldiers, colonists, Negroes, and Indians, in the command of Don Tristan de Luna, to the Pensacola region. The fleet reached the harbor in 1559, and De Luna renamed it Santa Maria. No historical data exist as to the exact spot upon which the settlement was established, but in 1561, after a storm destroyed the fleet, the colony was abandoned. This settlement on the shores of Pensacola Bay antedated by six years the founding of St.Augustine.

Gradually the name Santa Maria was replaced by the present name, reputedly derived from the Indian *panshi*, meaning hair, and *okla*, meaning people, a name conferred upon natives of this region who wore their hair long. Some historians, however, claim the settlement was named for the Spanish seaport Peniscola.

Formal possession of the site was re-established in 1698 by Don Andres d'Arriola, who, arriving with 300 soldiers and settlers, built a wooden fort in honor of Charles II, and erected houses and a church. The French, having established colonies to the west, captured the fort in 1719; it was retaken by the Spanish only to be surrendered to the French again when the town was burned and the fort blown up. Although a treaty was signed between the warring nations in 1720, it was not until 1723 that Pensacola was restored to Spain.

The new settlement was founded on Santa Rosa Island, a barren and uninhabited strip of land opposite the mainland, because its isolation promised security from Indian attacks. Destroyed by a hurricane in 1754, the settlement was re-established on the north side of the bay, the present site of Pensacola. Shortly after Florida became a British colony in 1763, the Spanish garrison and entire population were removed to Vera Cruz, Mexico, and Pensacola was made the capital of West Florida. A captain of the English forces occupying the deserted town, wrote that Pensacola consisted of '40 huts, thatched with palmetto leaves, and barracks for a small garrison, the whole surrounded by a stockade of pine posts.'

Many white settlers brought Negro slaves and established plantations. The first city plan was made—still discernible in the old sections of Pensacola—and streets were laid out through the swamp; the principal thoroughfare was named for George III, another for Queen Charlotte; a stockade was built in the center of town as refuge against Indian attacks. During the period of English rule, surrounding marshes were drained, cleared, and planted in gardens.

At the outbreak of the American Revolution, Pensacola became a haven for Tories. The most important commercial result of this immigration was the establishment of the Scottish firm of Panton, Leslie and Company, by its senior member, William Panton, America's first millionnaire and merchant prince, his object being to capture the Indian trade of West Florida. The Scotsman's interests were strengthened by the influential connection he formed with Alexander McGillivray, chief of the great Creek Confederation.

McGillivray was the son of Lachlan McGillivray, a youth of a good Scottish family, and of a French-Indian mother. He received an education in Charleston, South Carolina, and in 1776, at the age of 30, returned to his mother's people to become the chief of 6,000 Creek warriors. He held positions as Colonel in the British Army, Colonel in the Spanish Army, and Brigadier General in the United States Army. But McGillivray kept faith only with Panton and made the trading company more powerful than any government in the territory. The firm's trade with the Indians grew steadily, reaching as far as Tennessee.

This era (1772–81) was most prosperous, and Spain again coveted the harbor. A Spanish fleet under Don Bernardo de Gálvez, governor of New Orleans, besieged Pensacola from sea and land, until its surrender in May 1781. The Spanish governor was unsympathetic to all Protestant colonists, and most of the English left the city when Florida was ceded back to Spain in 1783. It was during this period that Fort San Carlos was built. After Napoleon sold Louisiana to the United States in 1803, Spanish Florida was surrounded by territory of its unfriendly neighbor, the United States.

By 1814 Pensacola had become a lawless and disorderly city, headquarters for filibusters, runaway slaves, and British agents. An English expedition under Colonel Edward Nichols entered the city in the summer of 1814 and received a hearty welcome from the Spanish governor. Soon the forts were repaired, arms and ammunition were distributed, and the flags of England and Spain floated in unison. Nichols busied himself in penning bombastic proclamations, and in enticing the Indians to join him. A visitor of that day wrote: 'Such scenes of preposterous costuming, of tripping over swords, of hopeless drill, and mad marching and countermarching as the common of Pensacola then witnessed can be imagined only by those who know precisely what sort of creatures Indians are. Captain Woodbine might as well have attempted to train the alligators of the Florida lagoons for the British artillery service.' These conditions induced Andrew Jackson to make an attack on Pensacola in November 1814, as a result of which the British withdrew.

Raids by Florida Indians on the Georgia border brought Jackson to Florida again in 1818, when he descended upon Pensacola and set up a military government. Severe criticism was directed at him for invading the territory of a nation with which the American Government was at peace, but Spain was told that West Florida would be returned when sufficient Spanish troops were sent to govern the unruly savages. This was done in 1819 and the province was surrendered. In 1821, with the transfer of Florida to the United States, Jackson was made provisional governor of the territory, and took up his residence in Pensacola. He accepted the appointment as a vindication of his Florida campaigns, but held it only four months. Neither he nor Mrs. Jackson understood the Latin population, and Jackson indulged in fiery tilts with retiring Spanish officials.

The first legislative council of the new Territory of Florida convened in Pensacola in 1822, but because of a yellow-fever epidemic the sessions were transferred to a plantation 15 miles from the city. Pensacola was chartered as a city in 1822. During 1825, owing to the strategic location and excellent harbor, the United States established a navy yard here, and the same year a New York syndicate projected the building of a railroad between Pensacola and Columbus, Georgia. Land auctions were held and lots changed hands rapidly; new buildings were erected. An editor of a local paper complained that 'The sound of carpenters' hammers, heard on every side, we regard as the greatest annoyance—a man can no longer adjust himself for an hour's siesta.'

Iron and cars for the railroad were imported from England; shiploads of laborers brought over from Ireland 'worked like beavers, but fought like devils,' and were replaced by Dutchmen. Half of these refused to stay in the city; the rest demanded their mid-morning and mid-afternoon beer, and until this privilege was granted laid down their tools.

In 1844 Jonathan Walker, abolitionist, was captured, tried in Pensacola for slave stealing, and sentenced to 15 days imprisonment, a fine of $150, and to be branded on the palm of his right hand with the letters 'SS' (slave stealer). Around this incident, John Greenleaf Whittier, in 1846, based his poem, 'The Branded Hand.'

At the outbreak of the War between the States, when United States arsenals and other property here were seized by the Confederates, Pensacola was the largest city in the State. The surrender of Fort Pickens on the western shore of Santa Rosa Island was demanded and refused, the Confederate decision being, 'We think no assault should be made, as possession of Fort Pickens is not worth one drop of blood to us. Bloodshed may be fatal to our cause.'

In February 1862 the Confederates were ordered to abandon the city; all supplies and ammunition were sent to Alabama, and the majority of troops moved to Tennessee. By May the greater number of citizens had departed, burning what they could not take with them, and on the 10th of the month Mayor Brosnaham surrendered the town to Federal military authorities.

The years immediately following the war found Pensacola a drowsy old town, 4 squares wide and 8 long, its streets deep in sand. A local newspaper protested the destruction of weeds that flourished in the areas, declaring they furnished the only signs of growth in the town. Upon recovery from the effects of the Reconstruction period, Pensacola enjoyed a second era of prosperity, due largely to railroad development of the territory and exports of timber and naval stores.

In the early 1870's began the development of the waterfront. The harbor was filled with steamboats and square-riggers from the ports of the world. Vessels, before loading cargo, discharged their ballast, which was hauled and dumped along the shore, and 60 acres of land were created in a few years. Thus Pensacola's reclaimed shoreline is made up of red granite from Sweden, blue stone from Italy, broken tile from France, and dredgings from the River Thames and the Scheldes of The Netherlands.

In 1880 fire gutted the business district, destroying more than 100 buildings. Rebuilding was slow. By the turn of the century Pensacola, with a population of 18,000, was the second largest city in the State. It did not grow proportionately through the early 1900's, and little of importance occurred until 1914, when the Government established its first training base for naval aviators. During the World War the Naval Air Base activities increased, and Pensacola datelines appeared regularly in the Nation's press. When the Armistice was signed, 438 officers and 5,559 enlisted men were stationed at the base.

Important industries in the Pensacola territory are those producing turpentine, rosin, and insulating wall board from pine stumps and wood waste, a furniture factory, and a large brewery. Vegetables, fruits, and poultry from the back country make the city an important agricultural trading center.

Pensacola is one of the leading points for commercial fishing, and 46 per cent of the red-snapper catch of the United States is shipped from here. Fishing boats, modeled after Gloucester smacks, sail to the snapper banks near Yucatan, remaining at sea for weeks and bringing back tons of fish. The snappers are caught by handlines often in water 25 fathoms deep. When a boat returns home, Pensacola's waterfront is a scene of merrymaking, with money flowing freely until spent. It is considered unlucky for a professional fisherman to set out on another trip with funds in his pockets.

POINTS OF INTEREST

1. PLAZA FERDINAND VII, S.Palafox St. between E.Government and E.Zarragossa Sts., is a remnant of the original Spanish Square. It is enclosed by a low stone fence and planted with oaks, cedars, magnolias, and cabbage palms. Old cannon are mounted at each corner, and a fountain and pool face Government Street. Here occurred the exchange of flags when Spain ceded West Florida to the United States in 1821, and a granite marker commemorates the event. The large monument in the center of the square is in memory of Colonel William D. Chipley (1840–97), soldier, statesman, and benefactor of West Florida.

2. SEVILLE SQUARE, S.Alcaniz St. between E.Government and E.Zarragossa Sts., is also a part of the original Spanish Square, which was broken up in 1802 and sold for building lots, only two city blocks being retained as public squares. This part was the center of the fashionable residential section of the city through the 1880's.

3. OLD CHRIST CHURCH (Episcopal), NW. corner S.Adams and E. Zarragossa Sts., erected in 1834, is the oldest church building in the city. It is a plain, rectangular brick structure with Gothic windows and a large square belfry. The church was used as a hospital and barracks by Union forces during the War between the States. Extensive repairs were made in 1879, including a 20-foot addition on the west side. The organ loft was removed, the flat ceilings were replaced by Gothic arches, and stained-glass windows substituted for plain ones. In 1902 the bell and the stained-glass windows were removed to the New Christ Church and some of the openings were bricked up.

The church was deserted from 1902 to 1936, when title to the property was given to the city for use as a PUBLIC LIBRARY (*open* 10–5 *weekdays*).

4. The BARCLAY HOUSE (*private*), S. end of S.Florida Blanca St., built in the late 1700's, is said to be the oldest residence in the city. Of stuccoed brick, with a large chimney on either end, it stands flush with the street and high off the ground. A large front gallery opens into a hall running through the building. The low second story is pierced by three dormers. The original floors, sills, window frames, and balustrades to the second floor are in an excellent state of preservation. Areas of broken plaster expose sections of hand-hewn lath. Tradition says a tunnel once ran from the basement to the Old Christ Church, a block and a half west.

5. ST. MICHAEL'S CEMETERY, Alcaniz St. between E.Chase and E. Romana Sts., the year of its establishment uncertain, is said to be the city's oldest cemetery and contains many historic graves, among them that of Dorothy Walton, wife of a signer of the Declaration of Independence, who died in 1832. On All Souls' Day candles are burned on many graves here.

6. The PERRY HOUSE (*private*), NE. corner N.Palafox and E.Wright Sts., now used as a Scottish Rite Temple, was the home of Governor Ed-

ward A. Perry. The two-story, stuccoed brick building with a balcony supported by a row of square white columns extending around three sides, is well preserved.

Edward Aylesworth Perry (1833–89) moved from Massachusetts to Pensacola in 1857, and at the outbreak of the War between the States enlisted in the Confederate army, where he was promoted to the rank of Brigadier General of the Florida Brigade. He was elected Governor of Florida in 1884; during his administration the State passed a Confederate Veterans Pension law.

7. FIRST METHODIST CHURCH, E.Wright St., adjoining the Perry House, established in 1821, was the first Protestant Church in Pensacola. The original structure occupied the site of the San Carlos Hotel. The present church, a brown stucco structure of Gothic design, was built in 1910.

8. NEW CHRIST CHURCH, NW. corner N.Palafox and W.Wright Sts., built in 1902, is a gray stucco structure with red tile roof. The entrance is between engaged Ionic columns that support a broken pediment. The façade rises to a bell gable topped with a concrete cross.

9. ST.MICHAEL'S ROMAN CATHOLIC CHURCH, SW. corner N. Palafox and W.Chase Sts., houses the oldest Catholic congregation (1781) in Pensacola. The gray stucco structure with Gothic doors and windows and a square belfry rising to a pyramidal spire was erected in 1888. The glass windows were imported from Munich, Bavaria.

10. DOROTHY WALTON HOUSE, 137 W.Romana St., built in 1805, is notable for an old-fashioned twin chimney piercing its low garret roof. The new roof extending over the porch is not in keeping with the plastered walls of oystershell, sand, and lime. This was the home of George Walton II, secretary of West Florida under Governor Andrew Jackson. A portion of the house is occupied by the DOROTHY WALTON MUSEUM (*open* 9–12 *and* 2–6 *daily; adm.* 10¢). Among the exhibits are old maps and engravings of Pensacola, ancient firearms, coins, and pottery, and cannon balls fired by the Spaniards in the bombardment of Fort George in 1781.

11. HULSE HOUSE (*private*), 210 W.Romana St., built in 1848, was originally occupied by Dr.Isaac Hulse, a surgeon in the United States navy, distinguished for his success in treating yellow-fever patients in Pensacola and in the French fleet anchored in the harbor during an early epidemic. The residence, a one-and-a-half story frame structure with a chimney at each end, has six wooden columns supporting a veranda roof, broken by three dormers, that extends across the front of the building. Four casement windows open upon the veranda. The building was used during the War between the States as a lodging house, and later by the Sisters of the Holy Cross as a convent school.

12. SITE OF GENERAL ANDREW JACKSON'S HOUSE, SE. corner S.Palafox and E.Intendencia Sts., is marked by a bronze tablet on a red brick business building. Mrs. Jackson viewed with horror the Sunday gambling and merrymaking of the gay Spanish populace, and when the city came under American rule observance of the Sabbath was strictly enforced, largely through her influence.

13. The SITE OF THE GRAVE OF ALEXANDER McGILLIVRAY,

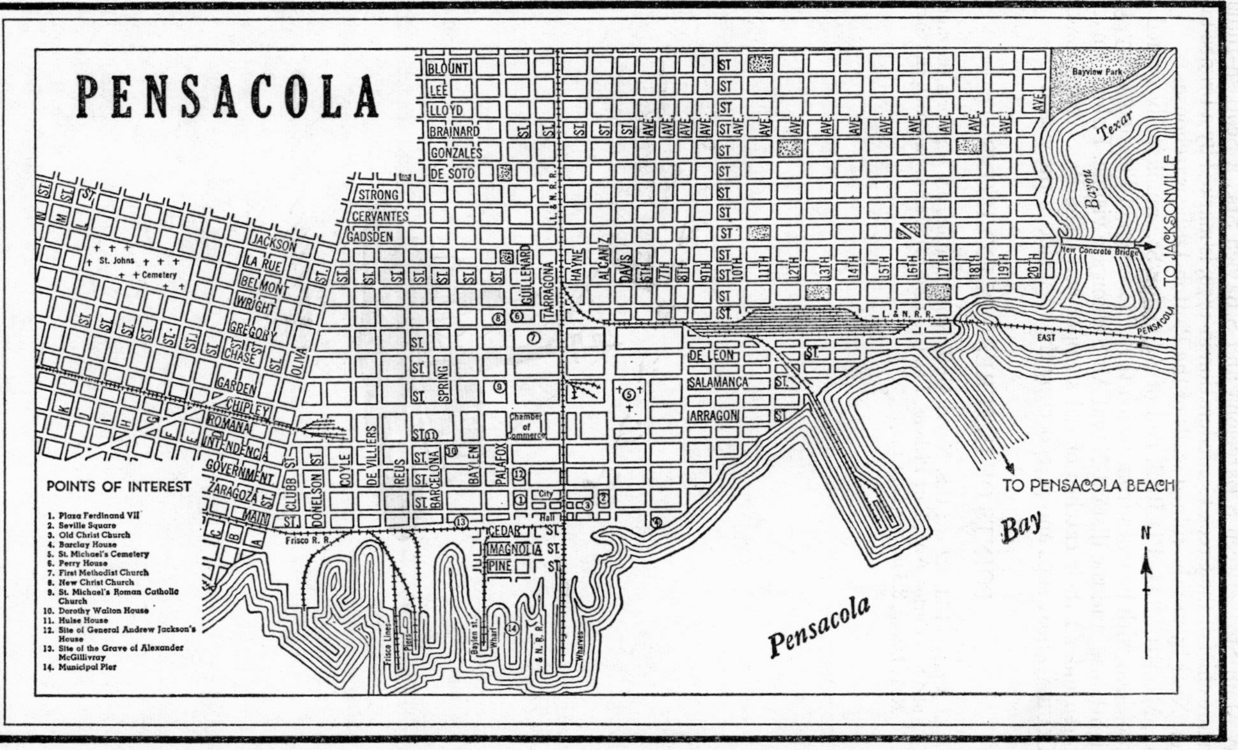

PENSACOLA
POINTS OF INTEREST
1. Plaza Ferdinand VII
2. Seville Square
3. Old Christ Church
4. Barclay House
5. St. Michael's Cemetery
6. Perry House
7. First Methodist Church
8. New Christ Church
9. St. Michael's Roman Catholic Church
10. Dorothy Walton House
11. Hulse House
12. Site of General Andrew Jackson's House
13. Site of the Grave of Alexander McGillivray
14. Municipal Pier
TO JACKSONVILLE
New Concrete Bridge
Bayview Park
Texar Bayou
TO PENSACOLA BEACH
Pensacola Bay
St. Johns Cemetery
Chamber of Commerce
City Hall
Wharves
Frisco Lines
Piers
Frisco R.R.
L. & N. R. R.

W.Main St., between S.Barcelona and S.Baylen Sts., a Scottish-Indian made chief of the Creek Confederation in 1776, is marked by a bronze tablet. Near by are the ruined walls of the Panton-Leslie warehouse.

14. MUNICIPAL PIER, S. end of S.Palafox St., municipally owned, is provided with benches from which the wide sweep of Pensacola Bay, the lighthouse, and the distant Naval Air Station are visible. Fishing smacks often unload their catches of red snapper here. The PENSACOLA YACHT CLUB, its boat slips and pier, occupy the west side of the wharf.

POINTS OF INTEREST IN ENVIRONS

Corry Field, 5.2 *m.*; U.S. Naval Air Training Station, 5.9 *m.*; Forts Barrancas and San Carlos, 6 *m.*; Fort Pickens, 7 *m.* (*see Tour 7d*). Pensacola Beach and Santa Rosa Island, 8.3 *m.* (*see Tour 14b*).

St. Augustine

Railroad Station: Malaga St. between Valencia and Ovieda Sts. for Florida East Coast Ry.
Bus Stations: Alhambra Hotel, King and Granada Sts. for Florida Motor Lines and Seminole Coach Co.; Gilbert Plaza Hotel for Pan-American Bus Lines.
Airport: Municipal Field, 4 m. N. on US 1; no scheduled service.
Taxi: 10¢ to 25¢ in city.
Hackmen: Negro; horse-drawn vehicles, $1.50 per hour. Stations 30 Granada St. and Ponce de Leon Hotel.
Traffic Regulations: Principal one-way streets, St.George and Aviles Sts. (S), Charlotte St. (N); numerous others, all marked.

Accommodations: 12 hotels; many cottages, rooming and boarding houses; rates higher Dec.–Mar.

Information Service: Chamber of Commerce, San Marco Ave. N. of City Gates. Licensed guides at Fort Marion entrance; city tour $1, including Anastasia Island, $1.50.

Radio Station: WFOY (1210 kc.).
Theaters and Motion Picture Houses: Cathedral Lyceum, 265 St.George St.; Civic Center Auditorium, adjoining Chamber of Commerce; two motion picture houses.
Swimming: North and South Beaches, Anastasia Island, free; YMCA indoor pool, Valencia and Ribera Sts. 15–25¢.
Tennis: Ponce de Leon Hotel, King and Valencia Sts., annual fees $10; Civic Center, San Marco Ave. N. of City Gates, 25¢; YMCA, 25¢.
Shuffleboard and Horseshoe Pitching: Civic Center, San Marco Ave. N. of City Gates, annual fee $3.
Golf: St.Augustine Links, 1 m. N. on US 1, 18 holes, $2; St.Augustine Municipal Course, 93 Cerro St., 9 holes, 50¢.

Riding: Garnett Orange Grove, St.Louis Ave. W. of San Marco Ave., $1 per hour.
Fishing: Vilano Bridge, Usina's Beach, City Pier, Lighthouse Park Pier, Matanzas Inlet Park, all free; boats, guides and equipment available along waterfronts; deep-sea fishing boats and guides at City Pier.

Annual Events: A Day in Old Spain, March; Pilgrimage to Shrine of Nuestra Señora de la Leche, Low Sunday (Pentecost).

For further information regarding this city consult *Seeing St.Augustine*, another of the American Guide Series, published in 1937 by the Record Co. and sponsored by the City Commission of St.Augustine.

ST.AUGUSTINE (7 alt., 12,111 pop.), is the oldest permanent white settlement in the United States. Time and sun and tropical rains have exacted toll from crumbling parapets and gateways, stucco and paint have covered age-mellowed walls and antique planking, but much remains to preserve the charm and memories of an old city.

The peninsular site was selected by the Spaniards in 1565 as a strategic point for defense because three rivers encircle all but the north side where Fort San Marcos, now Fort Marion, was built. The Matanzas and North Rivers, links in the Intracoastal Waterway, border on the east and south, the San Sebastian River on the west. All are salt-water lagoons lying behind Anastasia Island, which separates the city from the Atlantic Ocean.

On the north the City Gates, once the moated entrance to the town, open into narrow St.George Street, one of the principal thoroughfares. Guarding the channel on the east stands the gray stone fortress, a reminder of the settlement's early role as defender of Spain's claim to North America. Bay Street sweeps south of the fort along Matanzas Bay and past the bronze statue of Ponce de Leon, Florida's discoverer, overlooking the circle approach to the massive white Bridge of the Lions that crosses to Anastasia Island.

Here, in the heart of the ancient city, on opposite sides of the Plaza de la Constitucion, historic military parade grounds, are the Catholic Cathedral and Trinity Episcopal Church, occupying sites long used for religious activities. In the park west of the Plaza, once the site of the Spanish governor's palace, the balconied post office looks across to the red spires and tiled domes of the great Flagler hotels. Some distance beyond, past the yellow frame railroad station, are the busy docks of the shrimp-fishing fleet on the San Sebastian River.

Around the palm-fringed Plaza clusters the business district, an incongruous mixture of the old and new in structure and in wares. Although the majority of streets bear Spanish names, some are English and a few typically American. Here, side by side under overhanging balconies, are antique shops and cocktail lounges; a weathered cedar door adjoins one of gleaming chromium, and a rust-pitted iron grille, perhaps fashioned by slave hands, becomes a show window for the latest in radios. An office building shoulders an ancient cathedral; clustered flags and placards advertise points of interest; water tanks and neon signs break in on an Old World skyline, and machine-age traffic shatters the spell of drowsy, shadowed streets. The colors of Castile, emblazoned on municipal banners and on walls of ornate tourist hotels, are matched by the scarlet hibiscus and golden allamanda, blossoming in sheltered gardens and along city parkways.

Bicycles are still a favorite means of transportation. Horse-drawn surreys, driven by top-hatted Negroes who solicit fares for sight-seeing trips, are reminiscent of St.Augustine's early days as a tourist resort. On narrow, twisting side streets, Minorcan restaurants offer pilau (a highly seasoned potpourri of rice with boiled meat, fish, or fowl), fried shrimp, chowders, and gopher (land turtle) stew.

The art colony along Aviles Street displays its products on gray coquina garden walls, and the artists often work at easels beneath fig trees in open courtyards. Gardens throughout the city are bright with subtropical flowers. Many plots, secluded behind high walls, were laid out a century ago, and their patios are sheltered by pomegranate, fig, and sweet orange trees, fruits brought over at an early date by the Spaniards.

The western area of the town, paralleling the sluggish San Sebastian River and traversed by the railroad, with its docks, freight houses, warehouses, and clutter of shacks, presents an industrial aspect in sharp contrast to the city's older portion.

The Spanish flavor has remained dominant in the city's atmosphere as successive waves of non-Spanish settlers fell under its influence; climate, location, and background have contributed to the preservation of its charm. Although invading nations often razed old structures and salvaged stone to build new dwellings, they retained Spanish ideas in architecture. North walls remained windowless for protection against winter winds, while large southern casements and patios were retained. The English added steep gable roofs, chimneys, and porches to their houses, but kept intact the wooden second stories and walled-in gardens. Pioneering Americans found the buildings to their liking and moved in with but few changes. The newer structures in the old part of town suggest those of Granada and Seville, and native coquina rock used in their construction is as useful to modern builders as it was to the artisans who discovered and quarried the stone in 1580.

The residential districts have grown more since 1900 than during the previous three centuries. North of the City Gates are substantial homes of Southern Colonial type, surrounded by well-kept lawns shaded by palms, crape myrtles, and massive live oaks. Intermingled are conventional brick and frame bungalows and apartment houses, and a few houses of the Spanish Provincial styles. The oleander and hibiscus hedges, and bright flowering bignonia, bougainvillea, and coral vines that festoon fences and gateways, provide colorful suburban backgrounds.

Of St.Augustine's present-day population, the largest foreign group includes descendants of the Minorcans, transplanted by Dr.Andrew Turnbull from the Mediterranean island in 1767. Portuguese, Italians, and Scandinavians of the shrimp fleet make up a portion of foreign residents, as well as the Cubans, Greeks, and Armenians who operate many restaurants and curio shops.

Negroes have had an important place in St.Augustine's history. As slaves of the Spaniards brought over in the late 1500's, they were the property of the king and required to be of Catholic faith. In the first hospital in the United States, built here in 1597, a Negro woman waited on patients, including Negroes and Indians. During the Seminole War many Negroes allied with the Indians, causing much concern among St.Augustine slave owners. Shortly before the War between the States escaped slaves were aided in reaching Canada by a white family occupying a plantation near the city. This property is the site of the coeducational Florida Normal and Industrial Institute for Negroes, founded in 1892. The Negro colony, west of the railroad, has its stores, meeting houses, and recreational center. The inhabitants are employed in domestic service, as guides, as unskilled laborers in small manufacturing plants and on the shrimp fishing docks, and in hotels.

Extensive plans are under way for the preservation of the historic resources of the old town: St.Augustine is the subject of research by staff members of the Carnegie Institution at Washington, assisted by other historians and scientists. Excavations are revealing ancient landmarks, and old maps and documents are being used as the basis for the preservation of the important features of the city, under a program of the St.Augustine Restoration Committee.

On April 3, 1513, Ponce de Leon landed somewhere in the St.Augustine area and remained for five days. On September 8, 1565, Don Pedro Menéndez de Avilés, Spanish admiral, took possession of the territory along the river and founded the settlement, naming it St.Augustine because he first sighted Florida on August 28, St.Augustine's Day. The French fleet under Jean Ribaut, preparing to attack the town, was blown to sea by a hurricane.

St.Augustine became the Spanish military headquarters of North America, and its governors manned forts and policed the coast from Virginia to Florida for 40 years, repulsing efforts of other nations to establish colonies in the territory. One of the most formidable attacks on St.Augustine was made in 1586 by Sir Francis Drake, British admiral, who sacked and burned the town. The Spanish colonists fled to forest refuges during the raid, but later returned and rebuilt their homes.

St.Augustine was safer after it became the headquarters of missionary activities among southeastern Indians, and through its 40 or more mission towns controlled the natives and defended the frontier against the French and English. Following the founding of Charleston by the English, the Spaniards in 1672 began construction of a stone fort. From South Carolina in 1702, and again in 1728, the English descended to burn, plunder, and seize thousands of Indians for slaves. Although the fort withstood artillery attacks, the hospitals, monasteries, and the valuable Franciscan library were destroyed.

James Oglethorpe, Governor of Georgia, launched a series of attacks, the most formidable in 1740, and although he failed to capture the fort, he took all the outlying defenses. His victory on St.Simon's Island in 1742 ended the power of Spanish St.Augustine. Twenty years later, when the British took over Florida, they found a town of empty houses, most of its residents having fled to Cuba.

Under British rule (1763–83) St.Augustine enjoyed prosperity. The Indians were no longer a menace, great plantations were established in the vicinity, and the King's Highway was constructed to Georgia. During the Revolution, many slave-owning Tories found residence in the city, where anti-rebel sentiment was intense. John Hancock and Samuel Adams were burned in effigy in the public square, and later prominent dissenters, including Heyward, Rutledge, and Middleton—all signers of the Declaration of Independence—were imprisoned in the fort. The city became an important depot for British operations against the Southern Colonies, and gunboats patrolling the coast and the St.Johns River brought in numerous American prizes. A land attack against Savannah was launched from St.Augustine in 1777, and a naval venture in 1783 resulted in the capture of the Bahamas for England.

A rabid Tory paper, the *East Florida Gazette*, established here in 1783, ceased publication the year the war ended. When St.Augustine received word that Spain was again to control Florida, the British quickly evacuated. Abandoned houses gradually filled with Americans taking up Spanish land grants. A few years later American residents urged the annexation of Florida by the United States, and in 1812 a number of them joined a similar group from Fernandina for a time to support a Republic of Florida.

Another Spanish evacuation took place in 1821, when Spain transferred Florida to the United States. After the new American Government became operative, the second session of the legislature was held in St.Augustine, but later Tallahassee was chosen as the capital.

Among the visitors to the city during the next decade were Prince Achille Murat, nephew of Napoleon, and Ralph Waldo Emerson, who wrote that St.Augustine was a town of some 'eleven or twelve hundred people,' and that 'the Americans live on their offices, the Spaniards keep billiard tables, or, if not, send their Negroes to the mud to bring back oysters, or the shore to bring fish, and the rest of the time fiddle, mask, and dance.'

Throughout the Seminole War from 1835 to 1842, the city figured prominently in national news. Soldiers wrote letters to all parts of the country, giving their impressions of the old town; of forlorn refugees from the surrounding territory camping within the walls, and of pitiful Indian prisoners and hostages confined in the dungeons of the fort. Popular sentiment favored Osceola, Seminole leader, after his seizure in 1837 while en route to confer with American leaders 7 miles from St.Augustine. His death in prison at Fort Moultrie, South Carolina, served to increase the bitterness, but this and similar controversies lapsed at the close of hostilities.

Union troops held the fort and town of St.Augustine from 1862 to the end of the War between the States. For a period following the war the town was practically isolated from the rest of the State. River boats operated up the St.Johns River as far as Picolata, and passengers reached the city, a distance of 48 miles, after a 6-hour stage and ferry trip. Provisions were mostly brought in from Jacksonville by sea, and prices were exorbitant. In 1871 a mule-drawn railroad was built from Tocoi, on the St.Johns River, to St.Augustine, and it was 1874 before the first locomotive entered the city.

With improved transportation an increasing number of tourists visited the city. Letters and articles written by noted journalists and novelists began to appear in northern papers. Among those attracted in the 1880's was Henry M. Flagler of New York, retired oil man who, impressed by the beauty of the little Spanish community, began its development as a winter resort. Flagler erected two large hotels and extended a railroad southward. St.Augustine was made, and remains, headquarters of the Florida East Coast Railway and Hotel System.

Although surrounded by water, St.Augustine has been retarded in its development as a port by the constantly shifting sand bars at the mouth of the Matanzas River, channel to the sea, which form a barrier to all but shallow draft vessels. Some water commerce, however, has been developed through the Intracoastal Waterway.

POINTS OF INTEREST

1. FORT MARION (*open* 8:30–5:30 *daily, adm.* 10¢, *children under* 12, *free; guide service*) on Matanzas Bay at N. end of Bay St., oldest fort standing in the United States, was proclaimed a National Monument in 1924, and is administered by the National Park Service. The plan of this gray coquina fortress followed designs by Vauban, French military engineer. Construction of the quadrangular, four-bastioned, moated stronghold was begun in 1672, but the fort, known as Castle San Marcos, was not completed until 1756. St.Augustine was defended by wooden forts until Indian hostages, Negro slaves, soldiers, and inhabitants of the city erected San Marcos at a cost of millions of dollars. The outer walls, 12 feet thick at the base and tapering to 7 feet at the top, were built of coquina blocks quarried on near-by Anastasia Island and ferried to the site.

Seven years after completion the fort fell into British hands and during the 20 years of English occupancy it was known as Fort St.Marks. Again in possession of the Spanish, the old name was restored, but in 1825 after Florida became United States' territory, the stronghold was renamed Fort Marion in honor of General Francis Marion, Revolutionary patriot of South Carolina.

During the Seminole Wars the fort was used as a prison, and here Osceola, Coacoochee, Talmus Hadjo, and other Indians were confined. In the southwest corner room opening off the courtyard, Coacoochee and Hadjo were imprisoned, and made their escape through the high, narrow window.

A broad stairway, formerly a ramp up which heavy cannon were drawn to the terreplein, or roof, of the fort, is supported by a graceful elliptical arch considered remarkable by engineers because it sustained ramp and passage of ordnance without a keystone.

From the terreplein is a fine view of the fortification, the old sea wall, and the surrounding town. Granite arcs, upon which American guns were swung, are still in place, and below in the eastern earthworks is the hot shot oven where cannon balls were heated red before firing, in order to set fire to enemy ships.

2. The ZERO MILESTONE, between Bay St. and the City Gates, a coquina sphere six feet in diameter, was placed here in 1929. It marks the eastern terminus of an old Spanish trail that linked the missions between St.Augustine and Pensacola.

3. The CITY GATES, St.George St. at Orange St., consist of two square coquina pylons with concave peaks capped with representations of the Moorish pomegranate. The gates are attached to sections of an old coquina wall and a moat, and as part of the city defense system comprise one unit of Fort Marion National Monument. Construction of the original coquina gates, replacing earlier wooden ones, began in 1745, but the present more ornamental structures were erected in 1804, and for many years guarded the drawbridge over a moat.

4. The OLD WOODEN SCHOOLHOUSE (*open* 8–6 *daily; adm.* 10¢), 14 St.George St., a vine-clad, one-story clapboard structure of hand-hewn red cedar planks, with a coquina chimney and a dormer window, was built as

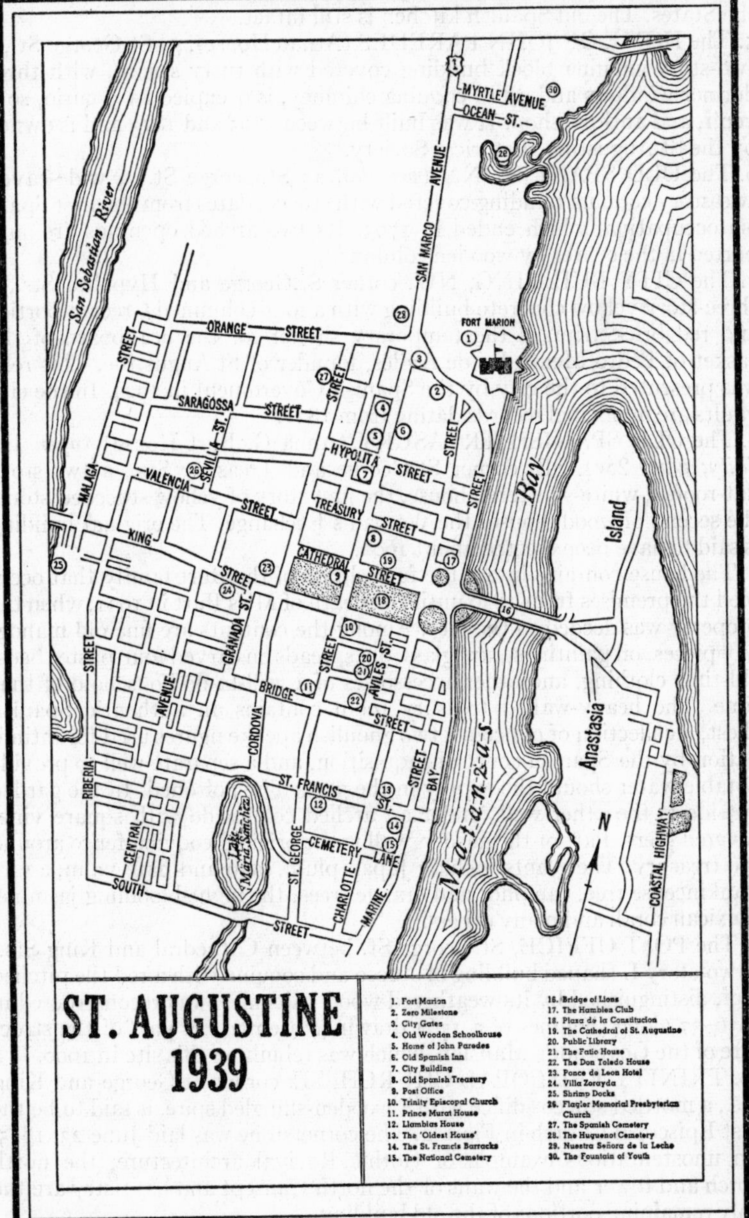
ST. AUGUSTINE
1939
1. Fort Marion
2. Zero Milestone
3. City Gates
4. Old Wooden Schoolhouse
5. Home of John Paredes
6. Old Spanish Inn
7. City Building
8. Old Spanish Treasury
9. Post Office
10. Trinity Episcopal Church
11. Prince Murat House
12. Llambias House
13. The 'Oldest House'
14. The St. Francis Barracks
15. The National Cemetery
16. Bridge of Lions
17. The Hamblen Club
18. Plaza de la Constitucion
19. The Cathedral of St. Augustine
20. Public Library
21. The Fatio House
22. The Don Toledo House
23. Ponce de Leon Hotel
24. Villa Zorayda
25. Shrimp Docks
26. Flagler Memorial Presbyterian Church
27. The Spanish Cemetery
28. The Huguenot Cemetery
29. Nuestra Señora de la Leche
30. The Fountain of Youth
San Sebastian River
Matanzas Bay
Anastasia Island
Lake Maria Sanchez
FORT MARION
MYRTLE AVENUE
OCEAN ST.
SAN MARCO AVENUE
ORANGE STREET
SARAGOSSA STREET
HYPOLITA STREET
VALENCIA STREET
TREASURY STREET
KING STREET
CATHEDRAL STREET
BRIDGE STREET
ST. FRANCIS ST.
CEMETERY LANE
SOUTH STREET
MALAGA STREET
SEVILLA ST.
GRANADA ST.
CORDOVA STREET
AVILES ST.
RIBERIA STREET
CENTRAL AVENUE
ST. GEORGE
CHARLOTTE
MARINE
BAY STREET
COASTAL HIGHWAY
N

a residence in 1778. It was used for a schoolhouse before the War between the States. The old Spanish kitchen is still intact.

5. The HOME OF JOHN PAREDES (Arnau House), 54 St.George St., a two-story coquina block building covered with rusty stucco, with three dormer windows and a tall coquina chimney, is occupied by a curio, souvenir, and antique shop. It was built between 1805 and 1813 and is owned by the St.Augustine Historical Society.

6. The OLD SPANISH INN (*private*), 43 St.George St., a wide-eaved two-story coquina building covered with stucco, dates from the first Spanish occupation, which ended in 1763. Its two arched openings are supported in the center by wooden columns.

7. The CITY BUILDING, NW. corner St.George and Hypolita Sts., a three-story yellow concrete building with a four-columned Grecian portico and red brick trim, is the temporary shelter for the headboard of the casket of Pedro Menéndez de Avilés, founder of St.Augustine. This relic was presented to the city by the Spanish Government in 1924. In the city vaults are municipal records dating from 1821.

8. The OLD SPANISH TREASURY (Anna G. Burt House) (*open* 1–5 *daily; adm.* 25¢), SE. corner St.George and Treasury Sts., a two-story flat-roofed, white-shuttered house, the first story of yellow stuccoed stone, the second of wood, houses the Woman's Exchange. The original building is said to have been erected about 1600.

The house contains intact the furnishings of the Burt family that occupied the premises from 1830 until the death of Miss Burt in 1931, when the property was deeded to the city. Among the contents are fine old mahogany pieces, oil paintings, rare glass, old spreads on carved four-poster beds, old-time clothing, and other accessories of a well-to-do household of that time. The heavy-walled treasury room contains an authentic Spanish chest, a collection of old coins, two ghoulish apelike figures used for intimidation by the Spanish court of inquisition, and a separate well to provide potable water should the supply in the garden be poisoned. In the garden outside is the other well, under an arched colonnade with square vine-covered piers. Part of the garden wall is the original coquina fence around the treasury. The plants include Japan plum, sago and date palm, a rare frankincense tree, camphor and orange trees, the night-blooming jasmine, Mexican coral, and many others.

9. The POST OFFICE, St.George St. between Cathedral and King Sts., a two-story L-shaped building of stucco and coquina with a red tile pitched roof, distinguished by its weathered wood balconies, was reconstructed in 1936–37 along the lines of a 1764 drawing. It embodies part of the structure of the Governor's Mansion, which was rebuilt on this site in 1690.

10. TRINITY EPISCOPAL CHURCH, SE. corner St.George and King Sts., a mottled stucco edifice with a wooden-shingled spire, is said to be the first Episcopal Church in Florida. The cornerstone was laid June 23, 1825. An unostentatious example of Gothic Revival architecture, the north porch and tower and the walls of the north transept and baptistry are the only remaining portions of the old building.

11. The PRINCE MURAT HOUSE, NW. corner St.George and Bridge

Sts., a two-story vine-covered building with two shingled dormer windows. Used as a coffee house, this coquina structure was built around 1815 and is believed to have been occupied by Prince Achille Murat during his residence in the city.

12. The LLAMBIAS HOUSE (*private*), 31 St.Francis St., a two-story coquina house with a red tile roof, green shutters, and overhanging balcony, built prior to 1763, was once owned by T.Llambias, member of the original Minorcan colony.

13. The 'OLDEST HOUSE' (*open 9–6 daily; 25¢ includes adm. to the Casa de Cannonosa and Webb Memorial Library and Museum*), 14 St.Francis St., was reputedly built in the late 1500's. The house abuts on the street, and thick coquina walls reach to the wooden second story, which terminates in small porches at each end. A hip roof adds to the massive appearance of the vine-covered structure. Notable features of the interior include low ceilings, huge fireplaces, crushed coquina floors in the old section, and hand-hewn cedar beams. Early accounts indicate the Franciscan Friars may have found refuge here during the six years they were rebuilding their monastery after the fire of 1599. A portion of the building was restored and the tower added in 1888. The St.Augustine Historical Society purchased the house in 1918.

WEBB MEMORIAL LIBRARY AND MUSEUM (*open* 10–12 *and* 2–4 *daily*), 16 St.Francis St., a stucco building adjoining the 'Oldest House,' was named in honor of Dr.Dewitt Webb, for 35 years president of the St.Augustine Historical Society. The library upstairs houses a collection of Floridiana valued at more than $50,000, including illustrated volumes by Catesby, 1743, on Florida plant and animal life.

CASA DE CANNONOSA (House of the Cannon Ball) (*open* 9–6 *daily*), 18 St.Francis St., a rectangular building with a vine-covered balcony, adjoins the library. It was so named because it is claimed one of the walls was pierced by a cannon ball from an Oglethorpe battery in the siege of 1740. During early American occupation the place served as a tavern.

14. The ST.FRANCIS BARRACKS (*open daily*), 108 Marine St., is a two-story yellow stucco building with a shallow balconied court topped with a flat balustrade. Officially designated as a barracks in 1881, it houses the State arsenal and executive offices of the Florida National Guard. On this site about 1577 the first Franciscans built their crude church, monastery, and convent. During the English occupation the chapel of the convent was adapted as barracks for the soldiery. When Florida became a territory of the United States the old cells were used as a jail. The main building, gutted by fire in 1915, was restored in 1921.

15. The NATIONAL CEMETERY, Marine St. and Cemetery Lane, bordered by a concrete wall, contains graves of many soldiers killed during the Seminole Wars, notably Major Dade and the 104 men massacred by the Indians in 1835. Their tombs are marked by three gray stone monuments known as the Dade Pyramids.

16. BRIDGE OF LIONS, continuation of Cathedral St., connects the mainland with Anastasia Island. Dedicated in 1927, the concrete span and drawbridge with its massive piers and symmetrical towers stretches in a

sweeping arc across Matanzas Bay. The bridge derives its name from two monumental marble lions guarding the city approach, a gift of the late Dr. Andrew Anderson.

17. The HAMBLEN CLUB (*two weeks free membership to tourists; dues* $1 *month*), Bay St. and plaza fronting on Cathedral St., is an ornate three-story stucco building with a variegated tile roof and a square tower topped by a blue dome, of typical boom-time Spanish architecture, with balconies and arched openings. It was willed by the late Charles F. Hamblen, local businessman, as a clubhouse for workingmen, and is operated as a social club.

18. The PLAZA DE LA CONSTITUCION (Place of the Constitution), Cathedral St. between Charlotte and St.George Sts., and extending to King St., is a landscaped parkway in the center of the town. It is named for the shaft erected in 1813 to commemorate the adoption in Spain of a liberal constitution. When in the next year Ferdinand VII was recalled to the throne of Spain he violated his pledge to abide by the new document, declared it null and void, and ordered the removal of monuments raised to it. However, the monument still stands in St.Augustine. The translated Spanish inscription on the base reads:

> Place of the Constitution. Promulgated in this city of Saint Augustine of East Florida on the 17th of October, 1812, the Brigadier Don Sebastian Kindalem, Knight of the Order of Saint James, being the Governor.
> For Eternal Memory. The municipal Government erected this monument under the supervision of Don Fernando de la Plza Arredondo the young senior Alderman and Don Francisco Robira.

Don Fernando's full name was Don Fernando de la Maza Arredondo, but tradition has it he was so active in trying to get the monument set up in the Plaza, that the Spanish jokingly called him 'Don Fernando de la Plaza.' The name on the monument, 'Don Fernando de la Plza,' is chiseled in such a manner that some think the sculptor started to inscribe the nickname, then thought better of it.

At the east end of the Plaza is the SLAVE MARKET, an open, shedlike structure built in 1824 to replace the original market on this site which dated back to 1598, and was used for public auctioning of provisions and slaves. The present structure, with its low gabled roof, square cupola, and simple square columns, is provided with tables for checkers, chess, and dominoes.

19. The CATHEDRAL OF ST.AUGUSTINE (*open daily*), Cathedral St. between Charlotte and St.George Sts., begun in 1793, was completed in 1797 and partially destroyed by fire in 1887. The structure has two fronts. The restored original front of stuccoed coquina rock is of Spanish mission style with pierced gable belfry and surmounting cross. The smallest bell is dated 1682. In a niche above the entrance portal is the aluminum-coated statue of St.Augustine. The portal is framed by coupled Doric columns and topped with a classic broken pediment.

The adjoining tower, built in 1887, has a choir entrance, over the door of which a sundial, stenciled on the façade, keeps time an hour earlier than Eastern Standard, having been placed there before Florida changed from

Cities II

Photograph by R. Kendall Williams

FISHING FROM MUNICIPAL PIER, ST. PETERSBURG

THE GREEN BENCHES, ST. PETERSBURG

Photograph by courtesy of United States Na

A PARACHUTE JUMP, PENSACOLA

CAMP SCENE, SPANISH AMERICAN WAR, TAMPA (189

Photograph by courtesy of Burgert Brother

Photograph by Dahlgren
WINTER HAVEN

ST. PETERSBURG

TAMPA

INTERIOR OF TAMPA THEATER

Photograph by courtesy of Burgert Brothers

UNIVERSITY OF TAMPA (FORMERLY TAMPA BAY HOTEL)

STATE CAPITOL, TALLAHASSEE

AGRICULTURAL BUILDING, UNIVERSITY OF FLORIDA, GAINESVILLE

REHEARSAL — CIRCUS WINTER QUARTERS, SARASOTA

RINGLING ART MUSEUM, SARASOTA

Central Standard time in 1919. Higher on the tower a blue-faced clock keeps the prevailing Eastern Standard time. Above the clock the tower changes from square to octagonal, with heavier ornamentation of pilasters and pediments, and is topped with a red tile roof surmounted by a gold cross. The belfry is heavily ornamented with carvings and brass work, now green with age.

In the interior stained-glass windows depict phases in the life of St.Augustine. Ventilators beside the pews along the outer walls are opened during hot weather. Adjoining the main entrance is the La Leche Shrine Shop, where figurines of the saints are for sale.

The Cathedral Parish of St.Augustine is the oldest in the United States, its records of births, marriages, and deaths dating from 1594.

20. The PUBLIC LIBRARY (*open* 9:30–5:30 *weekdays*), 5 Aviles St., owned by the St.Augustine Library Association, is a two-story coquina and wood structure erected prior to 1785. When Florida was ceded to the United States the house was rented to Joseph J. Smith, member of the Florida supreme court, and here was born Edmund Kirby-Smith, last of the Confederate generals to surrender. The garden and fountain in the rear patio are framed by Romanesque arches. The library contains 14,500 volumes in addition to the Ammidown Genealogical Collection, and the Caldecott Collection of original drawings.

21. The FATIO HOUSE (*open* 9–5 *daily*), adjoining the Public Library on the south, is a two-story stuccoed coquina building with a red tile roof, owned by the Colonial Dames in Florida. It was built by Andrew Ximenez between 1806 and 1821, in the style identified with the second Spanish occupation. Its old slave quarters, Spanish kitchen, patio, and balconies provide space for gift shops, artists' studios, and apartments.

22. The DON TOLEDO HOUSE (*open* 8–6 *daily; adm.* 25¢), NW. corner Aviles and Bridge Sts., a square, two-story coquina building with a low-pitched gable roof, a small overhanging balcony, and broad windows with faded red batten shutters, is typical of the houses erected during the second Spanish occupation. It is entered through a side door of the kitchen that opens upon a large room with a packed dirt and coquina floor. From the kitchen a jointed wooden stairway, to be drawn up at night, leads to an upstairs bedroom. The house contains relics, antiques, pictures, and furniture used by former residents of the city.

23. The PONCE DE LEON HOTEL (*open Jan. to Apr.*), Cordova St. between King and Valencia Sts. and extending to Sevilla St., together with its landscaped grounds enclosed by a chain fence with spiked iron balls in place of links, covers six acres. The monolithic concrete and coquina structure, with its red tile roof, many domes and spires, lavishly decorated arched gateways and interior ornamentation, was built by Henry M. Flagler. He sent Carrère and Hastings to study the architecture of Spain, many details of which they incorporated in their eclectic design. The Ponce de Leon opened in 1889, the first of the Flagler chain of Florida east-coast hotels, and established St.Augustine as a fashionable winter resort.

24. VILLA ZORAYDA (*open* 8:30–6 *daily; adm.* 25¢), 83 King St., a vine-

covered coquina and concrete structure of Moorish design, is trimmed in bright red, blue, and yellow, the Moorish colors. The house was erected in 1885 by its architect-builder, Franklyn W. Smith, who based his design on that of the Alhambra, as shown in the detail of the horseshoe arches and the arabesque ornaments on the interior. A museum, the collection of the owner, consists of inlaid and elaborately carved Oriental pieces, ancient Egyptian hangings, valuable rugs, ancient firearms, and many Oriental items.

25. The SHRIMP DOCKS, S. of King St. (US 1) on the San Sebastian River, are headquarters for the squat, pot-bellied boats of the shrimp fleet. The fleet comprises approximately 120 Diesel-powered boats ranging from 50 to 75 feet in length, with such names as *Natal*, *Diddy Wa Diddy*, *Old Glory*, and *Fortuna*. Manned by Scandinavian, Italian, Portuguese, Spanish, and Negro crews, the vessels often remain at sea for days.

With the arrival of loaded, net-festooned boats, each followed by a cloud of gulls, the docks present a colorful picture, best viewed from the King Street bridge over the San Sebastian River. An army of shouting Negro workers transfers the shrimp in great baskets from holds to the cleaning sheds on the docks where Negro women and children decapitate, shell, and clean the shrimp, receiving from 10¢ to 15¢ a bucket. A nimble-fingered worker can shell 15 buckets a day. From the sheds the shrimp are sent to near-by canning plants, or are loaded, fresh, into waiting trucks and refrigerator cars for shipment North. The industry employs 2,000 workers, and the annual cargo is valued at $1,200,000.

26. The FLAGLER MEMORIAL PRESBYTERIAN CHURCH (*open daily*), NW. corner Valencia and Sevilla Sts., was built in 1890 by Henry Flagler in memory of his daughter, Jennie Louise Benedict. This Venetian Renaissance style structure in yellow and white terra cotta and yellow brick, topped with a copper dome, is built in the shape of a Latin cross. Mosaic floors are of Siena marble, relieved by plaques of breccia violet marble. A domed MAUSOLEUM containing Flagler's remains adjoins the church.

27. The SPANISH CEMETERY, Cordova St. between Orange and Saragossa Sts., in a grove of oaks and cedars, was used as a burial place for Spaniards in 1794, and for others until 1878. Dark, weathered coquina crypts are built above the ground.

28. The HUGUENOT CEMETERY, NW. corner San Marco Ave. and Orange St., surrounded by a coquina wall, is overgrown with moss-hung cedars and magnolias. It was opened in 1821 during the yellow-fever epidemic. Despite the name, there is no record of Huguenot burials in the cemetery, but it may have been so named because it was a Presbyterian cemetery, and all Protestants were known to Spaniards as Huguenots.

29. NUESTRA SEÑORA DE LA LECHE (Our Lady of the Milk), Ocean St., one block E. of San Marco Ave., a small coquina chapel of Spanish mission type, built in a dense hammock on a tongue of land extending into an estuary of Matanzas Bay, commemorates the first mass (Sept. 8, 1565) said in the settlement. A shaded drive encircles the chapel and the slopes of the quiet hammock are dotted with mossy gravestones.

The original chapel near the present site, destroyed in 1728, was called *Nombre de Dios* (Name of God). When the miracle of the statue of the Lady of the Milk occurred in Spain about this time, the chapel obtained one of the statues that were adopted by many Catholic churches throughout the world. The present chapel, designed after the original structure, was erected in 1918.

At a little shop maintained in connection with the shrine, figurines of the saints and other religious objects are sold.

30. In the FOUNTAIN OF YOUTH PARK (*open* 7–7 *daily; adm.* 25¢), Magnolia Ave., foot of Myrtle Ave., are landscaped gardens, and a reproduction of an Indian stockade and communal house after a LeMoyne drawing of 1564, having an INDIAN BURIAL GROUND where more than 100 skeletons, uncovered and preserved, are displayed under green lights. These burials are believed to have been made after the founding of the city; crossed arms and other evidences indicate Christian interment. A well, in a missionlike grotto of coquina rock, is advertised as the Fountain of Youth that Ponce de Leon may have visited in 1513. A MUSEUM houses a collection of relics dating back to the sixteenth century.

POINTS OF INTEREST IN ENVIRONS

St. Augustine Lighthouse, 1.7 *m.*, Alligator Farm, 1.9 *m.*, Fort Matanzas, 13.9 *m.*, Marine Studios, 17.5 *m.* (*see Tour 1A*).

St.Petersburg

Railroad Stations: Atlantic Coast Line Station, 1st Ave.S. and 3rd St. for Atlantic Coast Line R.R.; Seaboard Air Line Station, 2nd Ave.S. and 9th St. for Seaboard Air Line Ry.
Bus Stations: Union Bus Station, Central Ave. and 1st St. for Florida Motor Lines and Tamiami Trails Motor Line; Transfer Station, Union Bus Station and Williams Park for Pass-A-Grille Bus Line, fare 25¢, 10-trip ticket $1.50. Uptown Union Bus Ticket office, Central Ave. and 5th St.
Airport: Albert Whitted Field, on Tampa Bay and 7th Ave.S., 10 blocks from business district for National Airline System and blimp hangar.
Taxis: Fares 15¢ per person for first zone, 10¢ each additional zone of 10 blocks for any number of passengers; same for each piece of hand baggage. City driving, $2 per hr. Rate card and zone map obtainable at Chamber of Commerce.
Streetcars and Municipal Busses: All cars and busses enter and depart from Central Transfer Station, Central Ave. and 6th St.; fares 10¢ until 6:30 P.M., afterwards 5¢; tokens, 4 for 30¢, 15-ride tickets, $1; pass for all day Sunday on all lines, 25¢; weekly pass, unrestricted, $1.
Ferry: Bee Line Ferry, slips S. end of 4th St.S., 5 m. from Post Office; connects with Tamiami Trail and points South; toll 10¢ per foot length of car; driver free; extra passengers over 14 yrs., 25¢ each.
Traffic Regulations: First alley N. of Central Ave. is E. only; first alley S. is W. only. Free parking except in spaces provided with parking meters. Meter charges for each half-hour or hour, 5¢, according to zone. Leaflet on regulations free at Police Dept., rear of Chamber of Commerce.

Accommodations: 85 hotels; rates higher, Dec.–Mar.; several large trailer camps.

Information service: Chamber of Commerce, 4th St. and 1st Ave.S.; A.A.A., 20 Beach Drive N.

Radio Station: WSUN (620 kc.).
Motion Picture Houses: 9, 3 equipped for legitimate performances. Negro gallery at Plaza theater.
Swimming: Municipal Indoor Pool, 2nd Ave.N., at entrance to pier, 35¢, with towel 40¢; Spa beach, adjoining, free; Municipal solarium, 35¢ (sun bathing), on Mole, 2nd Ave.N.; Gulf beaches, 10 m. W. from business district.
Tennis: Municipal Courts, on the Mole, free, but permits must be obtained from Recreational Bureau, 5th St. and 2nd Ave.N.; St.Petersburg Tennis Club, annual dues, adults $3, juniors $1.50, Bartlett Park, 4th St. and 18th Ave.S.
Shuffleboard: St.Petersburg Shuffleboard Club, annual dues $4, Mirror Lake Park, Mirror Lake Drive at 7th St.; Sunshine Pleasure Club, E. end of 1st Ave.S.
Roque: Roque Club, annual dues $10, Mirror Lake Park.
Bowling: Lawn Bowling Club, annual dues $10, Mirror Lake Park.
Chess: Chess Divan, annual dues $2, Mirror Lake Park.
Horseshoe Pitching: Sunshine Pleasure Club, annual dues $2.50, E. end of 1st Ave.S.
Gun Club: Sunshine Rifle and Pistol Club, annual dues $5, range 47th Ave., E. of 4th St.
Baseball and Diamond Ball: Waterfront Park, E. end of 1st Ave.S.
Golf: Clark's Sunset Golf Club, Snell Isle; Jungle Country Club, Park St. and 5th Ave.N.; Pasadena Golf Course, S. end of 64th St.S., Gulfport. All 18 holes, greens fee $1–$1.50 according to season.
Dog Racing: St.Petersburg Kennel Club, 6 m. N. on 4th St.N., Dec. to Apr.; adm. 25¢.

Annual Events: Kumquat Bowl football game, championship high-school teams, Jan.; International Mid-Winter Lawn Bowling Tournament, Feb.; Florida Shuffleboard Association State Tournament, Feb. and Mar.; Sunshine Rifle and Pistol Club, National and State Tournament, Mar.; Flower Show, Mar.; Festival of States, Apr.; St.Petersburg-Havana Yacht Race, Apr.; Tarpon Roundup, June through July.

ST.PETERSBURG (41 alt., 40,425 pop.), Florida's fourth largest city and the second in importance as a winter resort, occupies a semi-isolated area of 58 square miles on the southern tip of the Pinellas peninsula, a 25-mile projection between Tampa Bay and Boca Ciega Bay. US 19, entering from the north, is its only free trunk highway. A toll bridge provides connection with Tampa on the east, and a ferry, crossing the bay on the south, carries traffic from central and southern points. Because of tolls the city is sometimes referred to as a pay-as-you-enter playground.

St.Petersburg's front yard is a series of landscaped parks and driveways paralleling Tampa Bay, a filled-in stretch of two miles embracing the city's harbor, yacht basins, municipal pier, and major recreational attractions. North and west of the pier lie North Shore, the pioneer residential section, and Snell Isle. The latter, dredged from the bay, is reached by a short bridge over Coffee Pot Bayou. Both are planted with a variety of palms, Australian pines, and subtropical shrubs. Northward, following the irregular, pumped-in shores of Tampa Bay, is Shore Acres.

Five miles south around Pinellas Point, a newer residential district occupies the site chosen by the town's first white settler and overlooks the main ship channel leading into the Gulf. Bordering the bay to the southwest is Gulfport, a wedge-shaped municipality, its streets a continuation of St.Petersburg's, and served by the latter's trolley lines. Carved from the jungled western border of the peninsula, homes, many built upon Indian mounds, face shallow Boca Ciega Bay, across which lie the shimmering sand keys that are the city's Gulf bathing beaches. A green wall of citrus groves and open pine woods form much of the northern border.

Central Avenue, the city's 'White Way,' extends rulerlike for 7 miles across the peninsula, a 100-foot boulevard linking Tampa Bay with Boca Ciega Bay, and the dividing line for north and south streets. Along its lower reaches are faded brick and frame structures that make up the town's original business area of the late 1890's. Westward from the waterfront Central Avenue presents an abrupt mounting skyline; closely grouped hotels and business blocks of light brick and stucco emerge above the trees to give the city a profile. The brick-paved streets and bench-lined sidewalks are unusually wide, and although curbs are low, ramps are provided at nearly all downtown street intersections.

Here, in a compact area, open-air shops, often in ancient frame houses, false-fronted for business, elbow lofty hotels and office buildings—a contrast in style, size, and material rather than age, for the city is so young that its pioneers still take part in community life. Fruit stands and fruit-juice dispensaries abound; curio shops blossom with the tourist influx, offering, among other novelties, live alligators, miniature turtles, and doll-size green benches.

Branches of Fifth Avenue shops lift haughty eyebrows at less exclusive bazaars; health-food restaurants challenge glittering cafeterias, but do not provide the latter's bargain breakfasts, music, and lucky number drawings, nor do their menus include the ever-popular bowl of mush. In busy arcades one's blood pressure is taken for a dime; one can invest in an orange or tung-nut grove, dine at numerous nickel lunch counters, and have the future foretold by a pseudo-gypsy.

Beyond 9th Street, Central Avenue is lined with one- and two-story business buildings, filling stations, and residence property interspersed by vacant lots. It traverses a low area known as Goose Pond, devoted to the growing and selling of winter vegetables and flowers, and proceeds through sparsely settled territory to end abruptly at Sunset Park, bordering Boca Ciega Bay, where a small business district has developed around resort hotels and a community of suburban homes.

Methodist Town, clustered about a church of that denomination, and the adjoining colony on the south, both west of 9th Street, are Negro settlements containing schools, churches, mercantile establishments, recreational centers, and one of the seven exclusive Negro hospitals in the State. A few substantial brick and frame residences partly redeem the clutter of dilapidated shacks. The block paralleling the railroad tracks on Second Avenue is the night life bright-spot, with its upstairs dance halls, barbecue stands popular with white patrons, and an array of small shops. There is a limited Negro professional and business group, but the greater proportion of the inhabitants are engaged chiefly as laborers, in domestic service, and as waiters, bellboys, and porters in hotels. In 1939 a $1,000,000 Negro slum-clearance project was under construction, west of the southside Negro settlement.

St.Petersburg's architecture shows three distinct trends. Surviving are scattered examples of the early spindle and lathe period of frame construction; more pronounced is the effect of the pseudo-Spanish invasion that came in with the real-estate boom. Present-day types show a generous employment of stone, brick, and native woods, and a liberal use of the Romanesque design in public buildings, churches, and schools.

Conceived and publicized almost solely as a winter resort, St.Petersburg's leading industry is its tourist business, grossing more than $50,000,000 annually. Its healthful location was approved as early as 1885 by the American Medical Association, when one scientist completed records at Pinellas Point showing the peninsula to be one of the sunniest regions in the United States.

Although many Florida resorts have featured their abundant sunlight, St.Petersburg alone has been shrewd enough to capitalize on 'Old Sol' and to spend $1,000,000 advertising itself as the 'Sunshine City.' To make the name authentic, the publisher of the city's afternoon paper announced that he would give away his entire edition every day the sun failed to show its face up to 3 o'clock. In 26 years the paper was distributed free 123 times, an average of less than 5 editions a year. The record endurance contest was 546 days, ending on a Friday the 13th in 1935. Letters addressed 'Sunshine City' are sent to St.Petersburg.

Having advertised its place in the sun, St.Petersburg provided its visitors with ample means of absorbing the ultra-violet and infra-red rays. More than 5,000 green benches, in recreation centers and flanking the sidewalks of the principal thoroughfares, have converted the city into a park. Their color, size, and design are standardized by municipal ordinance. These slatted divans serve as mediums of introduction, with the weather the opening and principal topic. Operations, symptoms, and remedies run a close second. The benches are the open-air offices of the promoter, the hunting grounds of the real-estate 'bird dog,' a haven for the lonely, and a matrimonial bureau for many. They have figured in fiction, swindles, and divorce courts.

St.Petersburg's sunshine and green benches combine to create the illusion that life gets off to a good start at 75, not 40. Although persons of advanced years predominate, the majority of bench warmers are not strictly sedentary. The city is a place of energetic participation in outdoor recreation, and for the most part sitting is but an interlude. In fact those in the higher age brackets, including guests of the expensive hotels, and trailer-car transients, as well as those who own their winter homes, are banded together in the Three-Quarter Century Club, whose members top three-score years and fifteen. These oldsters stage their own dances, theatricals, boxing exhibitions, and ball games, always events of lively interest. So while the city offers interesting sights to the stranger, it is in reality one of organized activity rather than eye-filling vistas; lifetime habits of industry reassert themselves here in channels of recreation.

In addition to its recreational and sports attractions, St.Petersburg's cultural outlets offer a cosmopolitan blend found only in a city of diverse population. The range of music reaches from operatic concerts by metropolitan artists to daily band concerts in the downtown park. The band with its soloists is composed almost wholly of former members of Sousa's and Pryor's organizations and the Boston Symphony Orchestra. Eighty per cent of the members of the local Art Club are professionals. Several magazine illustrators and a number of leading comic-strip artists make St.Petersburg their permanent home and hold annual exhibitions.

The city has furnished locale and color for many professional writers. The late Ring Lardner's short story, *The Golden Wedding*, was a Sunshine City tale. Rex Beach, George Ade, and Sewell Ford have used St.Petersburg and its environs for fiction background. Since it plays host to two major-league ball clubs each spring—the New York 'Yankees' having trained here since 1924—St.Petersburg perhaps datelines more baseball copy than any other city in the State. Although it is the acknowledged winter baseball capital of the Nation, and ranks highest among Florida cities in gate receipts, including capacity Sunday exhibitions, nevertheless several churches hold double services twice a day on Sunday to accommodate the overflow of worshippers.

Narváez, Spanish explorer and commissioned governor of Florida, landed in 1528 somewhere along the Boca Ciega waterfront and marched across the peninsula to Tampa Bay, but the first recorded white settler did not arrive until 1843, when Antonio Maximo set up a fish 'rancho' on a point of land at the southern extremity of the peninsula, now called Maximo Point. When his holdings were swept away by a hurricane five years later he disappeared. The first house inside the present city limits was built in 1856 by James K. Hay, who came to look after hogs and cattle for Tampa stockmen.

Upon the outbreak of the War between the States, Union blockaders stopped fish shipments, shelled one of the houses, and drove most of the inhabitants to Tampa. A few returned at the end of the war, were joined by squatters, and resumed their former occupations of fishing and farming. Some of the first citrus groves were planted at this time. By 1876 a small community, christened Pinellas, had sprung up around Big Bayou, several miles south of Central Avenue; a post office was established, boat service to Tampa was inaugurated, and the settlement became the largest on the peninsula.

John C. Williams of Detroit, St.Petersburg's founder, acquired acreage in 1876 which became the nucleus of the city. Williams, later given the honorary title of 'General,' cleared some of the land and attempted to farm, but finally turned his efforts to urban development. He made a deal with Piotr Alexeitch Dementieff, a Russian exile of noble birth who simplified his name to Peter Demens upon his arrival in Florida, offering him an interest in the land to build a railroad into the territory. The Russian's road, known as the Orange Belt Line, reached St.Petersburg from Lake Monroe, near Sanford, in 1888, when the community had a population of 30.

Williams and Demens, according to the most popular story, tossed a coin to decide upon a name for the new town. The Russian won and the settlement was christened St.Petersburg in honor of Demens' birthplace. Later Williams built the first large resort hotel at the corner of Central Avenue and 2nd Street, calling it the Detroit, for his home town. Williams died in St.Petersburg in 1892; Demens went to California in the 90's and never returned to the city he named.

St.Petersburg, with a population of 300, was incorporated in 1892. Among early settlers were British from the Bahamas and Key West, later joined by pioneers who arrived in response to land-exploitation campaigns in England. From adjoining southern States came agriculturists, many of Scottish ancestry.

Except for its one railroad, which became a part of the Plant System and later was absorbed by the Atlantic Coast Line, the peninsula was still isolated. Known as West Hillsborough, it remained a part of Hillsborough County until 1911, when Pinellas County was created and the first major land boom got under way. Central Avenue and a streetcar line were extended westward to Boca Ciega Bay and the city took in a mile-wide strip paralleling it. Thousands of lots in this territory were sold from a plat at a tent auction, the most spectacular sale in the history of the city, not excepting those of 1924–26 boom days.

The resort remained a one-railroad town until 1914, when the Tampa and Gulf Coast Railroad, later taken over by the Seaboard Air Line, reached the city. By 1920 St.Petersburg claimed more than 14,000 inhabitants, and the population increased to 50,000 five years later. Miles of new roads were constructed, dozens of subdivisions laid out, and several million-dollar hotels erected. A ferry began operating to Manatee County, making possible a direct route to southern points, and the Gandy bridge, spanning upper Tampa Bay provided a short cut to Tampa. Two free causeways were built across Boca Ciega Bay to bring a belated boom to the long neglected islands. Building permits during 1924–25 reached a high total of $25,000,000. Meanwhile, in an extensive landscaping program, miles of Tampa Bay waterfront were filled in, improved with sea walls and promenades, and transformed into a string of municipal parks. In 1939 Central Avenue was extended by means of a causeway across Boca Ciega Bay to the island Gulf beaches.

FOOT OR WHEEL CHAIR TOUR

This tour, of about two miles, traverses the scenic waterfront of the city where the major points of interest are concentrated. All the avenues in the downtown area lead to Tampa Bay, along which follow parallel promenades, including a loop around the pier. It affords a pleasant trip on foot. Ramps are installed at intersections for wheel chairs and street names are posted.

(*North from Central Ave. on Beach Drive North*)

1. The ART CLUB OF ST.PETERSBURG (*open* 3–5 *daily*), occupies the upper floor of a two-story city-owned building and has an active membership of 100. Exhibits are continuous during season, representing applied and fine arts, local and transient, including originals of magazine and newspaper illustrations. Among prominent members and contributors was the late George Inness, Jr.

(*Right from Beach Drive North on 2nd Ave. North*)

The MOLE, a continuation of 2nd Avenue North, lying between two yacht basins, is the broad, landscaped fill that leads to the municipal pier.

2. MUNICIPAL BOAT SLIPS (R), extend the full length of the Mole, bordering the CENTRAL YACHT BASIN. Here yachts, sloops, and fishing and excursion boats are moored. Fishing trips and pleasure rides are offered at all hours, with information and tickets obtainable at the different slips. When the fishing boats return in the late afternoon, crowds collect to greet the anglers and appraise their catches. Proud fishermen hang up their largest fish or string of fish and strike a pose for the family photographer. Bets are paid off amid good-natured raillery in which spectators often join. Passengers carry home what fish they want, and licensed skippers dispose of the surplus cargo to shoppers, who are always on hand with their market baskets. Occasionally a shark, porpoise, or large whipray, harpooned on the day's trip, is strung up on a rack, an exhibit that attracts many prospective fares.

3. The ST.PETERSBURG HISTORICAL MUSEUM (L) (*open* 10–12, 2–5 *weekdays; adm.* 25¢), founded in 1920, is housed in a one-story stucco

building donated by the city for preservation of historical relics and records. Among the exhibits are fossils, collections of shells, pottery, ancient guns, butterflies, moths, and stamps; costumes of pre-Revolutionary origin, early almanacs and newspapers, antique dolls, and a collection of ladies' bonnets covering a period of 200 years. Archeological exhibits are from mounds within the St.Petersburg area. An unwrapped mummy, said to be that of an Egyptian princess, was brought into port by the captain of a tramp schooner.

4. CHILDREN'S PLAYGROUND (L), (*open* 8 *to dark daily*) is equipped with seesaws, swings, sand piles, and other amusement facilities.

5. MUNICIPAL SOLARIUM (L) (*open* 9–5 *weekdays; adm.* 35¢), a roofless enclosure with an Egyptian façade, provides facilities for nude sun bathing. Classes in physical culture, with lectures, are held during the season.

6. MUNICIPAL SPA AND BEACH (L) (*adm. to pool* 35¢) has an indoor heated fresh-water pool, facilities for medicinal baths and massages, and a white sand beach along the bay.

7. The SITE OF AIRLINE TERMINAL (R) is a triangular plot enclosed by a white picket fence and occupied by a small, one-story building. The first regularly scheduled American commercial air line was established here January 1, 1914, operating between Tampa and St.Petersburg. The first cargo was a ham. The pilot, Tony Jannus, lost his life while with the Russian air forces during the World War. On January 1, 1938, a bronze tablet dedicated to his memory and the historical flight was placed on a marker east of the blimp hangar.

8. MUNICIPAL PIER, foot of 2nd Ave.N., a steel and concrete structure extending 3,000 feet into Tampa Bay, has four motor lanes, a streetcar line, and wide promenades around the bench-lined pier head. Among other things, it is the city's fishing grandstand. Fishing balconies are provided along the pier. Feeding the pelicans, gulls, and ducks is a popular diversion.

The pier head supports a Spanish-type CASINO, a stuccoed, arcaded structure with red tile roof and low corner towers. It houses lunch and refreshment bars, indoor quarters for picnics and card parties, and booths for the sale of novelties. Fishing poles are for rent, and bait is sold. On the second floor is a large ballroom for tourist dances, where community sings are held each Sunday during the winter. Adjoining are the studios of the municipal broadcasting station, WSUN, affiliated with the National Broadcasting Company. Open balconies surrounding the station afford a view of the St.Petersburg skyline. Northeast across the main ship channel is Port Tampa with its towering phosphate elevators and oil storage tanks.

(*Circle Casino and retrace 2nd Ave. North; Left on Bayshore Drive*)

9. ST.PETERSBURG YACHT CLUB (R) Bayshore Drive between 1st Ave.N. and Central Ave. and overlooking Central Yacht Basin, is housed in a two-story stucco building with gay striped roof containing ballroom, dining room, bar and lounge. The club is headquarters for the Gulf Yachting Association.

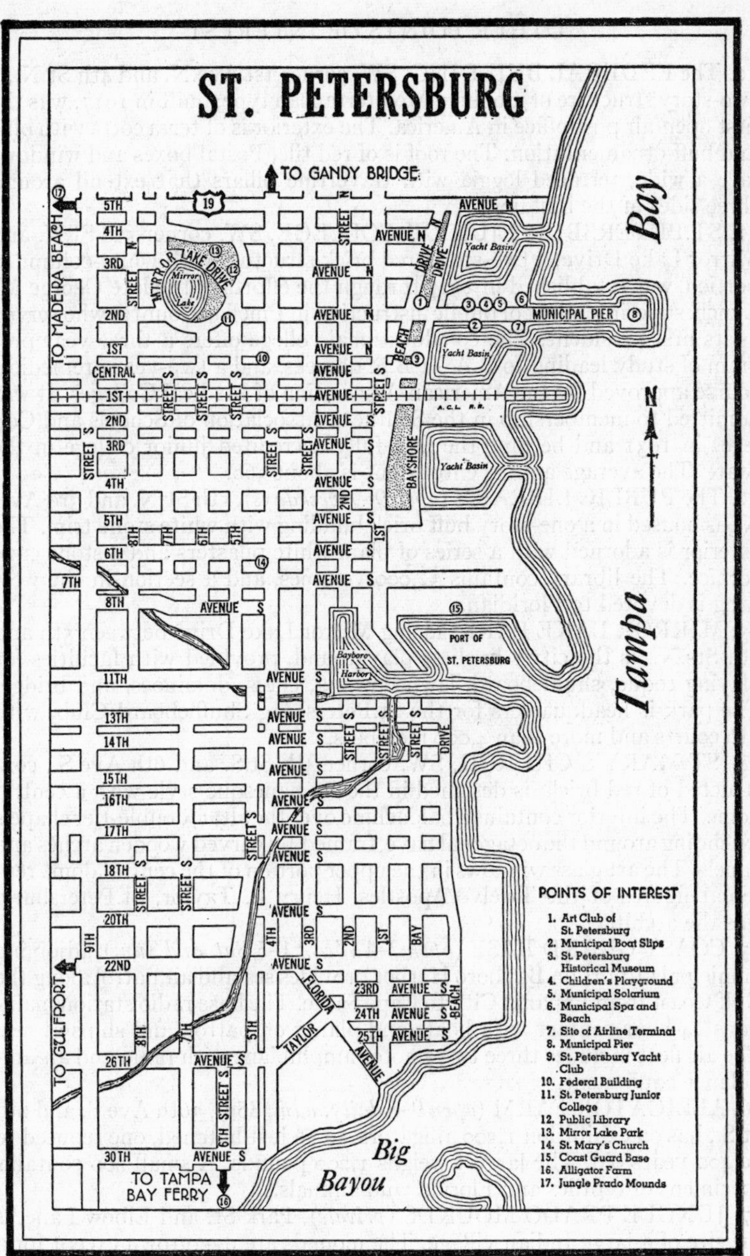
ST. PETERSBURG
TO GANDY BRIDGE
19
TO MADEIRA BEACH
TO GULFPORT
TO TAMPA BAY FERRY
Tampa Bay
Big Bayou
Mirror Lake
MIRROR LAKE DRIVE
Yacht Basin
MUNICIPAL PIER
PORT OF ST. PETERSBURG
Bayboro Harbor
BAYSHORE DRIVE
BEACH DRIVE
FLORIDA
TAYLOR AVENUE
CENTRAL AVENUE
A.C.L. R.R.
N
POINTS OF INTEREST
1. Art Club of St. Petersburg
2. Municipal Boat Slips
3. St. Petersburg Historical Museum
4. Children's Playground
5. Municipal Solarium
6. Municipal Spa and Beach
7. Site of Airline Terminal
8. Municipal Pier
9. St. Petersburg Yacht Club
10. Federal Building
11. St. Petersburg Junior College
12. Public Library
13. Mirror Lake Park
14. St. Mary's Church
15. Coast Guard Base
16. Alligator Farm
17. Jungle Prado Mounds

OTHER POINTS OF INTEREST

10. The FEDERAL BUILDING, SW. corner 1st Ave.N. and 4th St.N., a two-story structure of modified Mediterranean type, built in 1917, was the first open-air post office in America. The exterior is of terra cotta with blue and buff ornamentation. The roof is of red tile. Postal boxes and windows face a wide, terraced loggia with travertine pillars that extend around three sides of the building.

11. ST.PETERSBURG JUNIOR COLLEGE, SW. corner 5th St.N. and Mirror Lake Drive, a two-story, red brick structure with white-columned portico, was established in 1927 through the efforts of the late George M. Lynch, superintendent of public instruction in Pinellas County, who served as its first president. The co-educational college offers a three-year program of study leading to B.A. or B.S. degrees, and a two-year premedical course approved by the American Association of Medical Colleges. It was admitted to membership in the Southern Association of Schools and Colleges in 1931 and became the first fully accredited junior college in the State. The average annual enrollment is about 360.

12. The PUBLIC LIBRARY (*open 9–9 weekdays*), 5th St.N. and 3rd Ave. N., is housed in a one-story buff brick building with white stone trim. The exterior is adorned with a series of plain white pilasters and a stone cove cornice. The library contains 32,000 volumes, and a section in the west wing is devoted to Floridiana.

13. MIRROR LAKE PARK, facing Mirror Lake Drive between 5th and 7th Sts.N., is the city's liveliest playground, provided with facilities for playing roque, shuffleboard, lawn bowling, chess, dominoes, and bridge. The park is headquarters for the St.Petersburg Shuffleboard Club, with 116 courts and more than 4,000 members.

14. ST.MARY'S CHURCH, SW. corner 4th St.S. and 6th Ave.S., constructed of red brick, is designed in the Romanesque style with a central dome. The interior contains a baldachino over the altar, double-tier chapels extending around the octagonal nave, framed by carved wooden arches and panels. The art glass windows in the upper portion of the central dome represent figures of the Twelve Apostles. Henry L. Taylor, St.Petersburg, was the architect.

15. COAST GUARD BASE (*open 2–4 Wed.; 1–5 Sat. and Sun.*), adjoining municipal airport on Bayboro Harbor provides sea and air patrol along the Gulf Coast from Panama City to Cape Sable. The base radio station maintains 24-hour contact with boats and planes on patrol, and ships at sea. The air fleet includes three twin-motor amphibians with radio and air ambulance equipment.

16. ALLIGATOR FARM (*open 9–5 daily; adm. 35¢*), 36th Ave.S. and 6th St.S., has on exhibition 1,500 alligators, some just hatched, one reputed to be 400 years old. The largest weighs 1,200 pounds. A small zoo contains specimens of reptiles and Florida wild animals.

17. JUNGLE PRADO MOUNDS (*private*), Park St. and Elbow Lane, is the site of a large Indian village. The mounds are overgrown except for a small section where the street has been cut through. During this excava-

tion a number of skeletons and a broken Spanish sword were found. Somewhere in the immediate vicinity Narváez, Spanish explorer, landed in April 1528, marched across to the head of Tampa Bay, and northward to the neighborhood of Apalachicola, where he and his men built crude boats and attempted to sail for Mexico. Narváez and all but four of his men were lost at sea.

Sarasota

Railroad Stations: E. end of Main St. for Atlantic Coast Line R.R.; Lemon Ave. and 7th St. for Seaboard Air Line Ry.
Bus Station: 116 Central Ave. for Tamiami Trail Tours.
Airports: Municipal Field, 1.5 m. E. on State 18; no scheduled service. Seaplane base, Sarasota Bay, S. of Municipal Pier.
Taxis: 15¢ per passenger within city limits.

Accommodations: 17 hotels; numerous rooming and boarding houses, tourist camps on main highways. Trailer sites, Sarasota Tourist Park, Ringling Blvd. at Atlantic Coast Line R.R.; rates for two persons 50¢ a day, $1.50 per week; electric current 15¢ to 50¢ per day, 50¢ to $2 per week.

Information Service: Chamber of Commerce, Municipal Pier, W. end of Main St.; Point Welcome, 5 m. N. on US 41.

Motion Picture Houses: 2.
Swimming: Lido Beach, 2 m. W. on State 18, free; Sarasota Beach, Siesta Key, 5 m. SW. on US 41, free.
Golf: Bobby Jones Municipal Golf Course, E. end of 18th St., 18 holes, greens fee $1.
Tennis: Caples Park, Palm Ave. opposite Mira Mar Hotel; Gillespie Park, Osprey Ave. and 13th St.; Auditorium Park, Bradenton Road and W. 14th St.
Shuffleboard: Caples Park, Palm Ave. opposite Mira Mar Hotel, and Auditorium Park, Bradenton Road and W. 14th St.
Lawn Bowling: Gillespie Park, Osprey Ave. and 13th St.
Fishing: Numerous bridges and piers on mainland and islands; deep-sea fishing boats, guides, and equipment at Municipal Pier.

Annual Events: Pageant of Sara de Soto and Sarasota County Agricultural Fair, Mar.; Winter-Fishing Tournament, Nov. to Mar.; International Tarpon Tournament, May through July.

SARASOTA (18 alt., 8,398 pop.) is built along Sarasota Bay, an arm of the Gulf of Mexico. Its area of approximately 17 square miles includes landscaped islands, separating the bay from the Gulf, that provide miles of white-sand bathing beaches. The city is a clean-swept resort town, its wide thoroughfares and parks planted with royal, date, cabbage and coconut palms, and Australian oaks and pines. The pseudo-Spanish stucco houses, and the lofty tourist hotels that dominate the skyline, are for the most part set against a bright background of oleanders, crotons, and a variety of winter-blooming native and exotic shrubs.

In the heart of the business district around Five Points, permanent awnings shade many of the downtown sidewalks. In this area cafeterias, fruit and fruit-juice stands, and curio shops are wedged between imposing bank fronts and showy real-estate offices. The popular downtown tourist attraction is the Municipal Pier, entered under a stucco arch, where deep-sea fishing boats come and go, pelicans perform, and gulls wheel ceaselessly overhead. Beyond, spanning the blue bay, the Ringling causeway extends to Longboat and Lido Keys—low, palm-fringed islands that have become the newer residential section.

The late John Ringling selected Sarasota as winter quarters for his circus in 1929 and made his home here. The fortune derived from many seasons under the big top was spent on his art museum, his estate, the development and beautification of the islands in the bay, and widespread civic improvements. The city stirs into life each November with the arrival of long trains that roll 'home' after a summer on the road. During the winter the organization settles down to busy months of preparation and rehearsals for the next season, and many members of the circus family become home folk until the following April.

Sarasota's chief industry is its tourist business. The city is the home of a number of retired army and naval officers, and its resident winter colony of professional baseball players is the largest in the State. The outstanding natural attraction that contributed to the resort's early growth was, and remains, fishing. Anglers migrated here and pitched tents on the open beach before a house had been built. They cast their lines for mackerel, bluefish, kingfish, and that much sought sea warrior, the tarpon, and were seldom disappointed.

The city annually sponsors a Spanish fiesta and exposition known as the Pageant of Sara de Soto and the Sarasota County Agricultural Fair. The fiesta is based on a 'legend' concerning Sara, alleged daughter of De Soto, and her love for an Indian chief. During the celebration the city is gay with decorations; citizens and tourists don Spanish regalia; the circus contributes bands, clowns, elephants, and bespangled ladies to the glittering street parade.

The local Negro settlement, east of the railroad, has its shops, churches, recreation centers, and rows of shacks. The majority of inhabitants, 30 per cent of the city's total population, are engaged in agricultural pursuits, and a few find employment as hostlers and roustabouts with the circus, returning to Sarasota in the fall to pick up odd jobs in canning factories, packing houses, and as gardeners.

The origin of Sarasota's name has been variously attributed to Spanish and Indian sources. It is possibly a corruption of the Spanish expression, *sarao sota*, meaning 'place of dancing.' The Elino de la Puente map of 1768 designated the site as Porte Sarasote, and a map issued by Laurie and Whittle in 1794 marks the site as Sara Zota, a separation of the word Sarazota that appeared on the Bernard Romans map of 1774, which designated the inlet as Boca Sarazota.

In 1856, long before the advent of sportsmen to these shores, William Whitaker of Tallahassee homesteaded a tract on a bayou afterward named for him, and built a cabin there. During the War between the States he planted the pioneer orange grove in the vicinity with seed brought from Cuba. His half-brother, H.V.Snell, is credited with introducing the first guavas into Florida, setting out several acres on an island in the bay. Throughout this period Indian raids kept away all but the more venturesome settlers and little of the surrounding territory was occupied.

Much of the land in and around Sarasota was included in Hamilton Disston's 4,000,000-acre purchase in 1881, but no use was made of the property until three years later, when a Scotch syndicate, headed by Sir John Gillespie, of Moffatt, Dumfriesshire, bought 60,000 acres sight unseen, including the site of Sarasota. This induced 60 Scottish families to establish a colony on the holdings, adopting the name Sarasota by which the area previously had been known. A post office, two miles south, was moved to the new settlement, and the first hotel, the De Soto, was built. Transportation was almost entirely by water, a boat running to Palma Sola, where connections were made with steamers operating out of Tampa.

A son of Sir John, Colonel J.Hamilton Gillespie, arrived in Sarasota in 1886 to serve as resident manager of his father's organization. A veteran golfer, he built one of the early courses in the State, a four-hole affair, later expanded to nine holes, along Golf Street, east of Orange Avenue. With the twin attractions of golf and fishing, the settlement increased in popularity as a winter resort.

The first railroad, constructed in 1892, a crude pioneer line 12 miles long connecting Sarasota and Bradenton, had one wood-burning locomotive and a string of flatcars on which logs, freight, and passengers were carried. The road had been in operation three years when employees destroyed most of the track to force payment of overdue wages. As late as 1899 Sarasota was a community of only 20 houses without sidewalks, and its five, block-long streets began and ended in the flatwoods. The Seaboard Air Line Railway reached the city from Tampa in 1902. Seven years later electricity replaced kerosene street lights, Main Street was paved for several blocks, and a narrow, hard-surfaced road was built to Bradenton.

In 1911, Mrs. Potter Palmer, Chicago society leader, purchased 26,000 acres east of Sarasota and developed part of it into small farms. The program included road building, ditching and clearing the property, expert farm supervision, and co-operative marketing facilities. The soil was adapted to the production of early winter vegetables, particularly celery. Experienced farmers moved in, and the territory claimed its place in agricultural Florida. Although celery is the quick-money producer, citrus ranks first in crop area and returns. Sixty-seven per cent of the county's cultivated land—approximately 2,600 acres—is in orange, grapefruit, and tangerine groves.

In 1921 Sarasota County was severed from Manatee by an act of the legislature, and Sarasota was designated the county seat. During the boom period of 1924–26, population doubled and housing construction was unable to keep up with the demand. Large tourist hotels and business buildings were erected, recreational facilities expanded, a 4,000-foot harbor channel was dredged, and a causeway was built across the bay to connect with the islands, which were cleared and landscaped.

Sarasota industries include the packing and shipping of celery, averaging 1,200 carloads annually, other winter vegetables, and citrus fruits; production of fertilizers, and the manufacturing of automobile trailers. An unusual industry is the mining and preparation of dolomite, a carbonate of magnesium discovered in 1935, which serves as an antacid fertilizer.

POINTS OF INTEREST

The JOHN AND MABLE RINGLING MUSEUM OF ART (*open* 9–4:30 *daily; adm.* 25¢), four miles N. of downtown Sarasota, is the largest in the State. The showman spent 35 years collecting the 700 originals by old masters. Estimated value of building and contents, willed to the State in 1937, exceeds $14,000,000. The collection contains examples of the great periods of European art from classic to modern times, arranged according to schools of art and chronological sequence.

The building, of modified Italian Renaissance design, ranging in height from one to two stories, in itself a museum of architecture, was opened in 1931. J.H.Phillips of New York City was the architect. Its setting is a terraced waterfront, landscaped with tropical shrubs and native pines. Directly beyond the iron-gate entrance, steps lead to a sunken court bordered on three sides by cloistered wings. In the court are more than 80 original columns dating from the eleventh to the sixteenth centuries, the majority of the Florentine High Renaissance period. On the open side, terraces, balustrades, and fountains in which black swans swim separate the building from the forest and bay. A balustrade topped with rows of statues forms a parapet above the arcade. Along the frieze are architectural reliefs of an early date, and within the ambulatory are bronze and marble statues and fountain groups. The Fountain of the Turtles at the head of the court is noteworthy.

Masterpieces of painting of the Renaissance in Italy and the northern European countries are housed in the north wing, together with carved wood altar pieces and early terra cottas. On display are examples of Filippo Lippi, Luca Della Robbia, Uccello, Giordano, Raphael and Titian, a lively *Annunciation* of the school of Fra Angelico, and a fine head of the school of Duccio. The exhibition of northern schools includes two small heads by Lucas Cranach, and works by Frans Hals, Van Dyke, and Rembrandt, the latter represented by his *Descent from the Cross.*

The museum's greatest treasure is its spectacular collection of the works of Peter Paul Rubens, represented by a large exhibit of paintings, cartoons, tapestries, and a sculptured piece, after his design. The museum shares with the Louvre the distinction of owning cartoons and tapestries prepared and executed by Rubens at the request of Sloavey, prime minister to Philip IV of Spain, for the monks of the Carmelite Convent at Loesches. Some of the Rubens in this collection are magnificent examples apparently executed in their entirety by the master himself, one of the finest being the *Departure of Lot*; others, completed by his pupils, show in parts the power and vigor of the master's brushwork and the splendor of his color.

The south wing contains a collection of Spanish art, including examples of El Greco, Goya, Zurbaran, Murillo, a portrait attributed to Velasquez, together with a splendid example of Spanish wood carving. This wing also houses examples of French Renaissance and English-school seventeenth- and eighteenth-century paintings. Two complete rooms are incorporated in this wing: one in gold and white paneling from Fontainebleau and one from the Palmiere Palace near Florence, where Boccaccio wrote the *Decameron*.

The RINGLING BROTHERS–BARNUM AND BAILEY CIRCUS WINTER QUARTERS (*open* 10–4:30 *daily, Dec. to Apr.; adm.* 25¢), E. end of 18th St., have ample parking facilities within the fenced-in grounds. To the right of the long central road bisecting the area, the railroad yards form a huge triangle. Here the four show trains are repaired, refitted, and repainted during the winter.

The group of buildings consists of animal quarters, utility buildings and workshops, dormitories for workmen, executive offices, and a dining hall. The main animal barn, to the right of the roadway, beyond the railroad yards, is lined with cages, the majority opening upon outside runways. In the larger runways, occupied by lions, tigers, leopards, kangaroos, and other animals, the 'cats' are trained and put through their acts each afternoon at 2:30. On the upper floors are the tent, wardrobe, and harness-making departments. Canvas workers are employed the year round in the manufacture of 41 new tents required at the beginning of every season.

South of the animal house are outdoor cages for polar and American brown bears, pongurs (dwarf mules), and giraffes. Adjoining are special barns for 30 elephants, including pigmy species, that are rehearsed and exercised daily. Near by are quarters for rhinoceroses, orangutans, chimpanzees, and smaller varieties of the monkey family. Opposite is an aviary housing exotic birds. At the east end of the grounds are stables for 700 horses and practice rings, where daily rehearsals are held. Adjoining are runways for dromedaries, camels, and zebras.

The SARASOTA REPTILE FARM (*open* 9–6 *daily; adm.* 25¢), Fruitville Rd. and Tuttle Ave., has a large collection of birds and animals in cages, and reptiles in white-painted stone pens. Reptiles are most numerous, including alligators of all ages, rattlesnakes, water moccasins, copperheads, gila monsters, and many species of nonpoisonous snakes. The animal collection includes monkeys, wildcats, opossums, ground hogs, and squirrels. The bird cages contain love birds, parrots, pigeons, mourning doves, barn and screech owls, and eagles. Two pelicans walk amiably about the enclosure, or doze in the sun. Rattlesnake venom is extracted on Thursdays, the time of day depending on the weather.

SARASOTA TOURIST PARK, Ringling Blvd. at Atlantic Coast Line R.R., occupies a municipally-owned 30-acre tract set with Australian pines. Capacity of the park is 1,800 camping outfits, and as many as 4,000 persons have found accommodations here at one time. Numerous recreational facilities are provided, and an auditorium is devoted to theatrical and social activities. The camp has water, light, garbage disposal, and sanitary conveniences; police and fire protection, a post office, and stores.

In past years this park has been the site of the annual convention of the Tin Can Tourists of the World, an organization of trailer and house-car owners with a membership of 30,000. A giant parade of 'tincanners' and the showing of new model trailers, house cars, and equipment were integral parts of the convention.

A tourist camp presents a lively and typical American scene during the height of the season. Dusty cars and trailers bearing license tags of various States roll in toward evening and park in their allotted 'yards.' This is accompanied by a certain amount of haggling over rates and choice locations. Old acquaintances are hailed and new ones made. The iceman, baker, resort-plugger, and vendor of curios and myriad contraptions useful to the modern-day gypsies make their rounds. Between periods of gossiping, womenfolk attend to their sewing and laundry; washings soon flap on improvised lines; ironing boards are often set up in the open. Menfolk congregate to swap tales of the road, of their experiences en route, and to learn what accommodations are offered at anticipated destinations. Shuffleboard courts, horseshoe pitching lanes, and card games attract their devotees. Supper time is heralded by the clatter of dishes and the odor of cooking food. After dark the recreational hall is thronged with young and old who dance to new tunes and old, furnished, except on gala occasions when an orchestra is hired, by a nickel-in-the-slot phonograph. Other campers hurry into town to window shop, go to the movies, or attend more inviting nightspots.

MUNICIPAL AUDITORIUM, Bradenton Rd. and W. 14th St., a steel and reinforced concrete hangar-shaped building with a seating capacity of 3,200, is used for concerts, dances, and tourist conventions. The park surrounding the building contains 40 shuffleboard courts, 9 tennis courts, and 2 grass bowling greens, all lighted for night play. The auditorium and park were built in 1938 with WPA and city funds.

POINTS OF INTEREST IN ENVIRONS

Myakka River State Park, 8 *m.* (*see Tour 4c*).

Tallahassee

Railroad Station: Railroad Ave. for Seaboard Air Line Ry.
Bus Station: Terminal, 113 S.Adams St., for Southeastern Greyhound Lines, Gulf Crescent Motor Line, Coleman Motor Line, Adar Coach Line, Lee Coach Line, Rooks Coach Line, and Georgia Stages.
Airport: Dale Mabry Municipal Airport, 3.5 m. W. on US 19 for National Airlines, and Eastern Air Lines.
Taxis: 10¢ within 1 mile zone; 10¢ each additional passenger.
Street Order and Numbering: Park Ave. is the dividing line for N. and S. Sts., Monroe St. for E. and W. Sts.

Accommodations: 4 hotels; rooming and boarding houses; tourist camps.

Information Service: Chamber of Commerce, Floridan Hotel, NW. corner N.Monroe and Call Sts.

Radio Station: WTAL (1310 kc.).
Motion Picture Houses: 2.
Golf: Tallahassee Country Club, Country Club Estates, SE. of city, 18 holes, greens fee 50¢.
Tennis: City courts, W.Park Ave. and N.Monroe St., free.

Annual Events: Legislature convenes, Apr. of odd years; Flower Show, Apr.; May Day Celebration.

TALLAHASSEE (216 alt., 10,700 pop.), hilly capital of a lowland State, lies 30 miles north of the Gulf of Mexico and approximately midway between Pensacola and Jacksonville. The city has three conspicuous landmarks: the Capitol, the Florida State College for Women, and the Florida Agricultural and Mechanical College for Negroes, each built upon a hilltop.

The business district, confined to two wide streets, follows a ridge northward from Capitol Square, and cross streets, shaded by oaks and magnolias, drop off precipitously into residential districts. Within and surrounding the area are old homes with spacious lawns that date back to Territorial days, some of them converted into business property, and tall-steepled brick and stucco churches that once sheltered citizens during Indian raids. Out of the natural forest growth rise various State government buildings of gray sandstone and yellow brick.

Red clay streets intersect many paved thoroughfares, and horse- and mule-drawn vehicles are not uncommon sights. For two blocks, almost in the shadow of the Capitol dome, Adams Street is a noisy, crowded trading center on Saturdays when rural families attend to their weekly shopping. Store windows are plastered with signs, banners advertise bargain sales, and radios blare. Lunch counters and soft-drink stands do a brisk business. Parked along the high curbs are shining motors with liveried chauffeurs and rickety farm wagons acting as carry-alls for produce, groceries, and brown-faced children. Hitching posts and watering troughs still survive, and oats and baled hay are in demand along with gasoline.

Park Avenue, a two-way street separated by a parkway planted with live oaks, and extending seven blocks across the town, is the dividing line for north and south thoroughfares. Here the older homes of the columned plantation type have served as models for newer residences. Some of the suburban residential districts are occupied by bright-walled and tiled stucco houses of the conventional Florida-Mediterranean architecture introduced during the boom. But in general, Tallahassee, where an established society similar to that in other sections of the storied South existed in *ante bellum* days, has not succumbed to the cosmopolitanism of a tourist State.

In pockets between many of the hills, and along the clay streets leading toward the Agricultural College, are Negro colonies. Crowding the rear of the Governor's mansion is the principal Negro settlement, French Town, which owes its name to a French colony that once occupied the site. Many Negroes are employed in domestic service, in farming, and at unskilled labor, but some of the finest buildings in the city were erected by Negro artisans. On South Boulevard is a municipal curb market where on Wednesdays and Thursdays white and Negro farmers, occupying stalls on separate blocks, display their products on long counters beneath the oaks.

Tallahassee is predominantly an educational and political center; what the annual crop is to most agricultural towns, the convening of the State legislature and the opening of the colleges are to the city. For 60 days, beginning in April of odd years when the State legislature meets in biennial session, Tallahassee is a converging point for politicians, city and county officials, members of the press, lobbyists, and those who come merely to look on. Hotel accommodations are not to be had unless reserved months in advance, and citizens open their homes to paying guests. Night clubs and roadhouses in the outskirts unlock their doors, and with swing orchestras and floor shows inaugurate the two-month season.

The Indian meaning of Tallahassee is 'Old Town,' the name of the capital of the Apalachee Indians that was a flourishing settlement when De Soto and his men reached it in 1539. Following the Spanish explorer's departure in the spring of 1540, the territory was visited by a few missionaries and soldiers. In 1633 two Franciscan friars, led by a guardian from St.Augustine, arrived in the Apalachee region to begin missionary work. The rich farming land became a source of food supply for St.Augustine, and Fort San Luis, built about 1640, served as headquarters for seven missionary settlements.

Supply journeys were made by land from San Luis, and by water from San Marcos, on the near-by Gulf coast, to St.Augustine. Although the Indian population dominated, Spanish settlers moved in rapidly. The development of an extensive trade with Cuba ended with the English occupation of Florida.

Little was accomplished by the English between 1763 and 1783, except definition of the Tallahassee area as the dividing line between East and West Florida. Repeated raids by Indians south of the border brought Andrew Jackson into the area in 1818, where in retaliation he burned many villages.

After 1822, when the Territorial legislative body was formed, meetings were held alternately in St.Augustine and Pensacola, but in 1824 a site was chosen about a mile southwest of an area known as the Old Tallahassee Fields, and the new government seat was approved that year. Although no opposition was made by the Indians to the building of the government house for the new territory, Governor Duval, learning that Neamathla, a chief of the Seminole, was inciting his people to revolt, persuaded the Indians to evacuate the territory. After the Indians' departure, settlers came in rapidly, and in November 1825 Tallahassee was incorporated as a city. Streets were opened and named for national figures—Adams, Monroe, Calhoun, and Jefferson—a square for Nathanael Greene of Revolutionary fame, and another for Andrew Jackson. In January 1826 the cornerstone for the Statehouse was laid and one wing of the building completed.

During this era leading families from other Southern States, attracted by the possibilities for cotton culture, migrated here. In 1824, Prince Achille Murat, who before the overthrow of his father, the King of Naples, bore the title of Prince Royal of the Two Sicilies, came from Washington and bought a large plantation near Tallahassee (*see Tour 14a*). Shortly afterwards he met and married Mrs. Catherine Willis Gray, grandniece of George Washington.

The town became the center of a society reminiscent of the life of many other southern communities. Prince Murat, writing of the elaborate dinner parties, stated that the ladies attending were as beautiful and as well dressed as any in New York, and in a journal reports: 'No news in town except a wine party, or rather, eating, drinking, card playing, and segar smoking.' But Ralph Waldo Emerson, visiting the city in 1827, entered in his notebook: 'Tallahassee, a grotesque place, selected three years since as a suitable spot for the capital of the territory, and since that day rapidly settled by public officers, land speculators and desperados . . . Governor Duval is the button on which all things are hung.'

Tallahassee progressed industrially and culturally up to the time of the War between the States; it was the center of cotton marketing even prior to the building, in 1834, of Florida's first railroad, the Tallahassee-St.Marks' Railroad, which was operated by mule power during its first years. Cotton raised in middle Florida and much of that grown in Georgia and Alabama was carried to port over this sytem until traffic was disrupted by the war. Repeated attempts by Union troops on the coast to penetrate this section were repulsed by Confederate forces.

Following the war, families from Alabama, Georgia, and the Carolinas came to Tallahassee in increasing numbers, but as other sections of the State were populated the city assumed less importance as a marketing center. Northern politicians gained in power during the Reconstruction period and for the first time Negroes held political office. Jonathan Gibbs, a young Negro from Philadelphia, served four years under Governor Reed as Secretary of State, and in 1872 was named the first State superintendent of education. He served until his death, two years later. Throughout these years Negroes served in the State legislature, 19 holding seats at one time.

Development of the back country, the employment of more persons to direct State government activities, and an increasing enrollment at the colleges contributed to the city's growth. Since 1900, with the improvement and extension of highways throughout the surrounding area there has been widespread agricultural advancement. Aside from general farm crops, cotton and tobacco are the leading products, but considerable acreage has been given over to vineyards.

Selected as the capital of Florida when the site was a wilderness between Pensacola and St.Augustine, the two Territorial centers of population, Tallahassee has frustrated every attempt to remove the seat of Government to a more centralized portion of the State.

POINTS OF INTEREST

1. The STATE CAPITOL, S.Monroe St. between W.Pensacola and W. St.Augustine Sts., stands on a block-square terraced knoll overlooking the business district. The native growth of live oaks has been supplemented by magnolias, cabbage palms, bamboos, and oleanders. At the time the site was chosen as the seat of government no town existed, and the legislative council met here for the first time on November 8, 1824, in a crude log cabin set in a forest clearing.

In 1826 the cornerstone of a more durable building was laid, a wing of which was completed at a cost of $12,000, but work on the structure was suspended because of litigation between the Territory and the contractor. In March 1839 the Congress of the United States appropriated $20,000 to 'erect a suitable State house or public building for the use of the territorial legislature, for the offices of the secretary of the Territory and for keeping the public archives.' In January 1840, C.G.English, commissioner of the city of Tallahassee, reported to the legislature that he had effected a contract for the new capitol, and the building, though unfinished, was occupied by the legislature and executive officers in January 1841. It was completed in 1845, the year Florida was admitted to statehood, and remained without changes until additions were made in 1902. This was the only Southern capitol that did not fall into the hands of Northern troops during the War between the States.

In 1922 east and west wings were added, and the interior was redesigned. The spacious lobby and corridors, the marble stairs, the porticos and wide steps, as well as the house and senate chambers were designed by H.J.Klutho. The west portico was omitted to make room for the house chamber. In 1935 a north wing was added, to provide larger quarters for the house chamber. Leo Elliott was the architect.

As seen today, the building is greatly changed from the embryonic capitol of 1840. The general style of the edifice follows the Italian Renaissance mode, a symmetrical cross-shaped building with central portico, projecting end pavilions, and a massive central dome surmounted by a classical lantern or cupola. The main entrance through the east portico is reached by a flight of granite steps, flanked on each side by massive abutments. The pedimented portico is supported by six modified Doric columns with simple caps and shafts. In the pediment is the seal of the State of Florida, in stucco relief.

The building is planned with two principal stories above a raised basement or ground story. The outer walls, crowned with a heavy classic cornice and a balustraded parapet, are finished in buff painted stucco. The large central dome is raised on a square rusticated base and drum. The drum, pierced with triple windows, is adorned with Ionic columns, corner niches containing classic urns, and topped with a balustrade similar to that of the main structure. The design of the cupola, with its delicate arcading and bell-shaped dome, suggests a more direct reference to the Georgian Colonial mode than the rest of the exterior detail.

The west entrance, approached by a broad twin flight of steps, is accented by a slightly projecting pedimented portico supported by four coupled Doric columns.

The interior is designed in a simple classic style, with two central corridors running from the east and west entrances, and from the north to the south end of the building, intersecting under the dome. The floor of the corridors and a high wainscot on the walls are finished in polished marble. On the second floor is the STATE LIBRARY (*open* 8:30–1 *Mon.–Fri.*, 8:30–9:30, 12–1, *and* 4–5 *Sat.*), and other State offices. On the first floor are the governor's suite and offices of his cabinet.

The senate and house chambers are on the second floor. In the house chamber is a copy of a full-length Gilbert Stuart portrait of George Washington by Emmaline Buchholz, set in a pedimented wall screen behind the speaker's rostrum.

In the southeast corner of the grounds a granite block marks the site of the log cabin in which the first session of the legislative council was held in November 1824. Near by is a 10-foot gray granite obelisk erected to the memory of Captain John Parkhill, killed at Palm Hammock in 1857 while leading his company against the Seminole Indians. In the northeast corner of the grounds is a 10-foot white marble Confederate monument topped with a granite urn.

2. The MARTIN BUILDING, S.Adams St. between W.Jefferson and W. Pensacola Sts., a two-story buff brick structure of neoclassic design, contains offices of many State departments. The main entrance is flanked by two large white columns. The building, erected in 1927, bears the name of a former governor.

On the ground floor the MUSEUM OF THE STATE GEOLOGICAL SURVEY (*open* 8:30–1 *and* 2:30–5 *Mon.–Fri.;* 8:30–1 *Sat.*) houses collections of Florida minerals and soils, vertebrate and invertebrate fossils. Among the exhibits is an almost complete restoration of an American mastodon.

3. The COLUMNS, SW. corner N.Adams St. and W.Park Ave., built in 1835, is one of the oldest houses in the city. It is of red brick with a pitched roof, a columned entrance, and wide vine-covered chimneys rising from the gable ends. There is a tradition that a nickel was embedded in every brick.

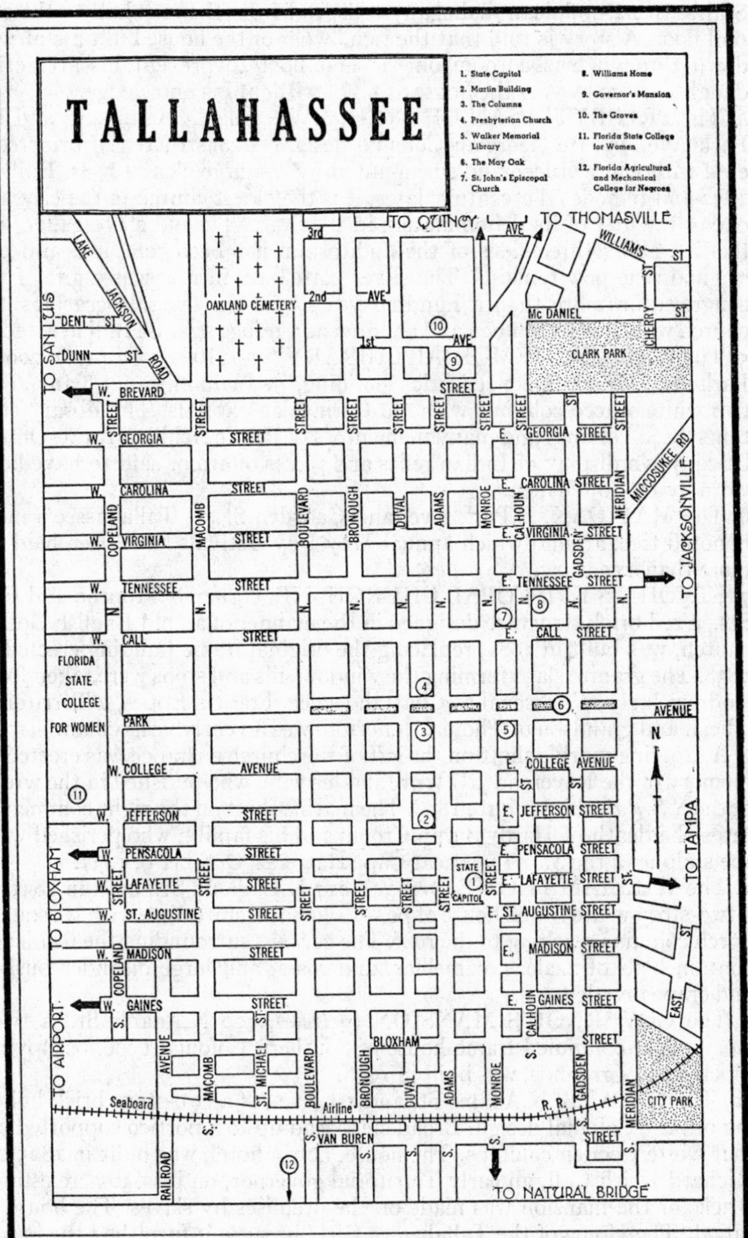
TALLAHASSEE
1. State Capitol
2. Martin Building
3. The Columns
4. Presbyterian Church
5. Walker Memorial Library
6. The May Oak
7. St. John's Episcopal Church
8. Williams Home
9. Governor's Mansion
10. The Groves
11. Florida State College for Women
12. Florida Agricultural and Mechanical College for Negroes
TO QUINCY
TO THOMASVILLE
TO SAN LUIS
TO JACKSONVILLE
TO TAMPA
TO BLOXHAM
TO AIRPORT
TO NATURAL BRIDGE
OAKLAND CEMETERY
CLARK PARK
CITY PARK
FLORIDA STATE COLLEGE FOR WOMEN
STATE CAPITOL
MICCOSUKEE RD
LAKE JACKSON ROAD
Seaboard Airline R. R.

Stairs with Dominican mahogany rails lead from the rear hall to the second floor. A story is told that the rich owner of the house built a stairway down through his bedroom on the first floor to prevent his attractive daughter from leaving the house at night without his knowledge.

4. The PRESBYTERIAN CHURCH, NW. corner N.Adams St. and W. Park Ave., in late Georgian Colonial design, is constructed of brick covered with white stucco and surmounted by a square clock tower. Built in 1832 and remodeled a century later, it is the oldest church in the city and one of the first of its denomination in the State. The old slave gallery extending along three sides of the auditorium has been retained, and one original pine pew remains. The silver plate, still in use, was a gift of the congregation more than a hundred years ago. On several occasions the church was used by women and children as a refuge against Indian attacks.

5. The WALKER MEMORIAL LIBRARY (*open* 10–4 *weekdays*), 209 E. Park Ave., is a boxlike red brick building, its main entrance flanked by two white stucco columns with red Corinthian capitals. The library contains 8,000 volumes and many mementoes of Prince Achille Murat. On the balcony is a display of Indian relics and pieces of armor said to have been worn by De Soto's men.

6. The MAY OAK, E.Park Ave. and Gadsden St., is Tallahassee's most honored tree, around which annual May Day festivals have been held for more than a century.

7. ST.JOHN'S EPISCOPAL CHURCH, NE. corner N.Monroe and Call Sts., a red brick structure designed in the manner of an old English Gothic church, was built in 1881, replacing the original frame building erected in 1838. The granite slabs forming the window sills and steps were taken from Andrew Jackson's arsenal at Chattahoochee. Francis Eppes, a Territorial official and grandson of Thomas Jefferson, was an early vestryman.

A tapering marble shaft on the left of the church entrance was erected in memory of the Reverend J.L.Wort and his wife, who perished in the wreck of the *S.S.Pulaski*, June 18, 1838. The marble shaft on the right commemorates the death of Hardy Bryan Croom and his family, who perished with the sinking of the *S.S.Home* near Cape Hatteras, October 9, 1837.

8. The WILLIAMS HOME (*private*), 217 N.Calhoun St., built in 1831, is a two-story white frame house of post-Colonial architecture with six square porch columns reaching to the roof. The gardens surrounding the residence contain beds of azaleas, camellias, and roses, and large oleander bushes and crape myrtle trees.

9. The GOVERNOR'S MANSION (*private*), 700 N.Adams St., a two-story white-columned frame house of Southern Colonial type, occupying block-square grounds, was built in 1908.

10. The GROVES, N.Adams St. and 1st Ave., is a two-story brick building of post-Colonial design. Broad steps lead up to a portico supported by four white wooden columns. The house, now a hotel, was built in 1825 by Richard Keith Call, an early Territorial governor, on his 640-acre estate. Brick for the mansion was made on the premises by slaves. The house is called 'The Home of the Tallahassee Girl,' because it furnished the locale for a novel, *The Tallahassee Girl*, written by Maurice Thompson in 1881.

11. FLORIDA STATE COLLEGE FOR WOMEN (*buildings open during school hours unless otherwise indicated*), occupies an 80-acre hilltop tract on W. Jefferson St. between Copeland St. and Woodward Ave. The rolling campus with a natural growth of pines and oaks, supplemented by hardy palms and subtropical shrubbery, provides a year-round green setting for 22 administration and school buildings. The red brick buildings, ranging from two to five stories, with red tile roofs, are of Collegiate Gothic design. The college grants A.B. and B.S. degrees in education, arts and sciences, commerce, accounting, and secretarial science, and offers a general business course. Student publications include the *Florida Flambeau*, a newspaper issued weekly during the college term, and the *Distaff*, published four times each school year. Enrollment for 1938–39 was 1,850.

At investiture services held early in the fall, seniors, accompanied by their 'sophomore sisters' dressed in white, march up to the auditorium stage where the college president places caps on the heads of the graduating class. On Class Day, during Commencement Week, students carry palm leaves, and at conclusion of the services the seniors remove caps and gowns and present them to their junior sisters. During the Torch Night Ceremony, conducted in the manner of a Greek pageant, sophomores pass glowing torches on to freshmen.

The State legislature in 1857 provided for the establishment of the two State colleges, one to be located east, the other west of the Suwanee River. The latter was established in Tallahassee that year and became the Florida State College, continuing until 1905, when by an act of the legislature male students were removed to Gainesville.

The James D. Westcott Memorial Building, facing a landscaped plaza on Copeland St., a five-story structure housing the administration offices, erected in 1910, is the oldest on the campus. In the west wing is an auditorium seating 1,800. The building was named for James D. Westcott, secretary of Territorial Florida (1830–34) and United States Senator (1843–49), who bequeathed much of his estate to the college upon his death in 1880.

The History Building, on Jefferson St., largest of the academic buildings on the campus, houses the departments of history, political science, geography, and journalism. The Augusta Conradi Theater on the first floor of the west wing is equipped for dramatic performances. It is also used for concerts, religious services, and as a workshop and production room for the department of speech and drama.

The Library Building (*open* 8:15–6 *and* 7:15–10 *weekdays;* 2:30–5 *Sun.*), adjoining on Jefferson St., contains 65,000 volumes. The collection of Florida material includes maps, documents, and original plantation records and diaries, in addition to books of history, travel, and fiction. An exhibition of historical subjects, maintained by the United Daughters of the Confederacy, is in the main reading room, and a geological exhibit is in the adjoining hall.

12. The FLORIDA AGRICULTURAL AND MECHANICAL COLLEGE FOR NEGROES, Palmer Ave. between Perry and S. Boulevard Sts., a group of 30 brick and frame buildings, occupies 375 acres on the

highest of Tallahassee's hills. Opened as a State Normal School in 1887, it was moved to the present site, formerly the plantation of Territorial Governor William P. Duval, in 1891, and placed under the management of the State Board of Control in 1905 as a co-educational college. It received its present name in 1909. Enrollment for 1938–39 was 860.

The ADMINISTRATION BUILDING, SE. corner S.Boulevard St. and Palmer Ave., a five-story red brick structure of Georgian Colonial design, erected in 1927, replaced a frame building destroyed by fire. The park opposite contains an open-air theater.

The LUCY MOTON PRACTICE SCHOOL, right of the administration building, a two-story red brick building of Georgian Colonial type, provides manual training, physical training, and home economics facilities for teachers. A LIBRARY (*open* 8–10 a.m., 1:30–5 *and* 7–9 *weekdays*) is in the east wing. The school was named for a former principal (1887) of the Minor Normal Training School of Washington, D.C., because of her educational work among the Negroes.

The CARNEGIE LIBRARY (*open* 8–10 a.m., 1:30–5 *and* 7–9 p.m. *weekdays*), center of the campus, built in 1906, is the oldest brick building on the grounds. It occupies the site of Governor Duval's house which was used by the college until burned in 1905. The library contains more than 12,000 volumes and bound editions of early magazines.

✤✤✤✤✤✤✤✤✤✤✤✤✤✤✤✤✤✤✤✤✤✤✤✤✤✤✤✤✤✤✤✤✤

Tampa

Railroad Stations: Union Station, E. end of Zack St., for Atlantic Coast Line R.R. and Seaboard Air Line Ry.
Bus Station: Marion and Twiggs Sts. for Florida Motor Lines, Tamiami Trail Tours, and Gulf Coast Motor Lines.
Airports: Peter O. Knight Airport, Davis Islands, for National Airlines and Eastern Air Lines.
Taxis: Jitney service 10¢ per passenger to principal points in city; private cabs 25¢ within 3-mile zone, 20¢ each additional mile.
Streetcars: Fare 5¢; to Port Tampa, 10¢.
Steamship Piers: Danzler Dock, Seddon Island, for Aluminum Line; Tampa Union Terminal, 13th and York Sts., for Waterman Line; Port Tampa docks, for P.&O. Line.
Traffic Regulations: R. turn on red light except where otherwise marked. One-way streets: Scott, Royal, Constant, Fortune.

Accommodations: 21 hotels, 2 for Negroes; tourist camps, rooming and boarding houses. Tampa Municipal Trailer Park, 2300 N.Oregon Ave., $1.50 per week for 2 persons, 50¢ per week for lights, 25¢ extra for more than 2 persons.

Information Service: Chamber of Commerce, and A.A.A., Lafayette and Morgan Sts.; Tourist Information Bureau, 429 W.Lafayette St.; Ybor City Chamber of Commerce, NW. corner 9th Ave. and 14th St.; West Tampa Chamber of Commerce, Rey Park, N.Howard Ave. between Palmetto and Cherry Sts.

Radio Stations: WDAE (1220 kc.); WFLA (620 kc.).
Auditorium and Motion Picture Houses: Municipal auditorium, Plant Park, lectures and concerts; 13 motion picture houses, 2 for Negroes.
Swimming: Y.M.C.A. pool, Zack St. at Florida Ave.; Sulphur Springs pool, Sulphur Springs, N. of city; Tampa Aquatic Club, Sligh and Ola Aves.; Davis Islands Pool, Davis Islands, reached by bridge from Bay Shore Blvd.; Cuscaden Park Pool, Columbus Drive between 14th and 15th Sts.
Golf: Macfarlane Municipal Park, Lisbon Ave. and Chestnut St., 9 holes, free; Airport Golf Course, Occident St. near Drew Field, 9 holes, 50¢; Davis Islands Club, 303 Bosporus Ave., 9 holes, 50¢; Forest Hills Golf and Country Club, 7 m. N. on Armenia Ave., 18 holes, 75¢; Temple Terrace Golf and Country Club, 12 m. NE. on Temple Terrace Highway, 18 holes, 50¢; Rocky Point Golf Club, 6 m. W. on Memorial Highway, 18 holes, $1; Palma Ceia Golf and Country Club, Lisbon Ave. and Aquilla St., 18 holes, $2.
Tennis: Davis Islands Municipal Tennis Club, annual fee $3; Robles Park, Central Ave. between Adalee and Emily Sts., free; Cuscaden Park, Columbus Drive between 14th and 15th Sts., free; Plant Park, Hillsborough River at Lafayette St., free; Macfarlane Municipal Park, Lisbon Ave. and Chestnut St., free; Hillsborough High School, Central Ave., at Wilder St., free; Rey Park, N.Howard Ave. between Palmetto and Cherry Sts., free.
Tourist Recreation Center: Community House, Plant Park, Hillsborough River at Lafayette St., reading and lounging rooms; chess, checkers, cards, roque, shuffleboard, horseshoe pitching. Registrations by States.
Skeet: Forest Hills Country Club, 7 m. N. on Armenia Ave., open Sun. p.m. Ammunition and clay pigeons for sale.
Greyhound Racing: Sulphur Springs Dog Track, Nebraska and Waters Aves., Dec. to Apr.; adm. 30¢.

Fishing: Tampa Bay. Boats, guides, and equipment at 22nd St., Causeway, Ballast Point Pier, Port Tampa Yacht Basin, Gandy Bridge, Davis Causeway.

Annual Events: Florida Fair, Plant Park, Feb., Gasparilla Carnival in connection with fair; Verbena del Tobaco Fiesta, Feb. or Mar.; Tampa Horse Show, Tampa Yacht and Country Club Riding Stable, Ballast Point, Mar.; Sailboat Races, Tampa Bay, Mar.; Tarpon Tournaments, May through Aug.; *U.S.S.Tampa* Memorial Observance, Plant Park, Sept. 15; Old Timers' Picnic, varying sites, Oct.; Annual Cabaret, Centro Asturiano, Ybor City, Nov.

TAMPA (15 alt., 101,161 pop.), third largest city in the State, is the Florida west coast's foremost port and industrial center. With a natural landlocked harbor at the head of Tampa Bay, it has shipping service to maritime countries in all parts of the world.

Tampa is politically southern, industrially northern, and has a distinct Spanish atmosphere. Although its port activities and cigar factories suggest a cosmopolitan industrial city set down in an environment usually dedicated to the sports and frivolities of a winter resort, Tampa has ample facilities for seasonal visitors and large hotels to accommodate them.

The Hillsborough River and an estuary form a maritime horseshoe around the city proper. In the estuary, an inner 'port within a port,' rust-streaked cargo boats of many nations, tramp schooners, sloops piled high with native fruits, fishing smacks, and often pretentious yachts rock side by side in the basins. Along the busy piers are huge warehouses and stevedore concerns that supply labor for loading and unloading vessels; harbor cranes load scrap metal into waiting holds, and chanting Negroes handle cedar and mahogany logs, bales of tobacco, timber, and barrels of turpentine and rosin. Inbound and outbound trucks rumble over waterfront streets, and above and around wheel screaming gulls.

In the midst of this is Tampa's retail district. Franklin Street, the principal shopping thoroughfare, bristles with neon and painted sidewalk signs, marble and glass chain-store fronts, wide metal awnings, tall office buildings, and portly bank structures. Scattered among them are two- and three-story structures of faded red brick, with stone turrets and tin cupolas, bay windows, and stamped metal cornices, some bearing names of pioneer residents and firms—names that reach back to the 1860's and form a visible web of Tampa's history. The venerable red brick courthouse, surmounted by dome and minaret and set in a palm-dotted square with bandstand and benches, dozes in the shade of a white city hall topped by a clock tower.

Drawbridges lift to permit passage of river craft; locomotives huff and puff across downtown thoroughfares, dragging strings of cars loaded with phosphate rock and oil to and from the Port Tampa piers. The absence of alleys, the numerous 'No Parking' signs in the retail section, and the strips of red painted curbing in the wholesale districts that practically surround the city add to the traffic problem.

The gleaming domes and minarets of the Tampa Bay Hotel, now occupied by the University of Tampa, rising above the oaks and palms that cloister its huge bulk, are visible from the shopping and near-by residential districts. The hotel had its effect in shaping the city's cultural growth, and symbolizes cherished memories and traditions. Hyde Park, adjoining the hotel grounds, was the original restricted residential section, and here are scrolled and spindled dwellings—most of them now genteel rooming and boardinghouses—fronting on quiet shaded streets.

Immediately south of Hyde Park, reached by a short bridge, are Davis Islands, a boom-time creation, and Tampa's newest close-in residential area. Landscaped parkways and drives provide a subtropical setting for hotels, apartments, and houses of pseudo-Spanish, Moorish, and Italian architecture. Bayshore Boulevard, sweeping south along Hillsborough Bay, with its double paving, landscaped parkways, and balustraded sea-wall promenades, traverses another urban residential section. Here substantial frame and brick houses of Georgian Colonial type are set back on deep, terraced lawns, overlooking the water.

Architecturally, Tampa records the waves of its growth. Old frame dwellings, many of them false-fronted for business purposes, are scattered throughout the retail district. Primitive one-story houses, occupied chiefly by Latin cigar workers and Negroes, surround the business section. In numerous subdivisions are typical American shingled and weatherboarded bungalows, and stucco and tile houses that came in with the boom. Some sections have been influenced by their Spanish, Cuban, and Italian populations, but the Latin trend has been more toward the Havana type dwelling than the Mediterranean—stucco, flat or tile roofs, grilled balconies, and courts and patios.

Tampa is noted for its cigar industry, established in 1886 when manufacturers in Key West, experiencing labor troubles, moved here with thousands of Spanish and Cuban employees. Ybor City, the pioneer colony founded by and named for Vicente Martinez Ybor, lies to the east of the business district, bordering Ybor estuary and McKay Bay. On the west, across the Hillsborough River, is newer West Tampa. Originally separate municipalities, both are now within Tampa city limits. They retain their native customs, their squalor and beauty, their picturesque festivals, and contribute to the city's gayety and color.

The majority of Tampa's 21,000 Negroes live in the thickly populated 'Scrub' section north of the business center; the name originally referring to its natural setting. Early settlers, building close to Fort Brooke, assigned less protected territory among the oaks to the Negroes. Later this group was augmented by Cuban and West Indian refugees and cargoes of contraband slaves. After the War between the States, southern planters brought freed slaves to Tampa because of the fishing and shipping industries.

The Scrub has its newspapers, schools, churches—Protestant and Catholic—a library, and municipal hospital. A theater features 'all-colored' productions, and numerous business enterprises are conducted by and for Negroes. Many of the inhabitants are skilled cigar makers and work in factories side by side with Cuban and Italian workers, but the greater proportion are employed as laborers and in domestic service. They have a jargon of English, Spanish, and Cuban, spiced with ancestral dialects and interpretations. The Tampa Urban League, a civic organization led by

Negroes, has the co-operation of the city government and acts as a clearing house for economic and social problems of the race in Tampa.

Ranking third among Gulf ports for inbound traffic, and eleventh in the United States for volume of exports in 1937, Tampa handles $86,000,000 worth of cargo annually. The average year's volume of traffic exceeds 3,600,000 tons. Approximately 90 per cent of Florida's canned grapefruit and 85 per cent of the world's mined phosphate are shipped from this port.

Each year in February during the Fair the pseudo-pirate, Gasparilla, and his motley 'crewe' descend upon the city from the Plant Park docks amid popping guns and corks, in festivities that mark the peak of Tampa's social season. Based on the life and alleged depredations of Captain José Gaspar, the celebration includes parades, pageants, and balls, climaxed by the crowning of a King and Queen who rule for the ensuing year.

The meaning and origin of the word Tampa is uncertain, and it is not known when Espiritu Santo Bay, so christened by De Soto, first became known as Tampa Bay. Fontenado included Tampa in a list of Indian towns in 1580, and De Laet's map of 1625 apparently applied the name to an Indian village.

The earliest authenticated arrival of white men in the Tampa vicinity was that of an expedition headed by Narvaez, commissioned governor of Florida, who reached here in 1528. His journey northward was the first white exploration into the interior of the United States. Even more extensive was the enterprise of De Soto, who sailed into Tampa Bay in 1539 and took possession of an Indian village.

Fort Brooke, a log fort, was established in 1823, marking the pioneer American settlement in the Tampa region. The fort was named for Colonel George Brooke, its first commander. His son, designer of the ironclad *Merrimac*, was born there. Protection of the garrison encouraged immigration and the settlement grew throughout the Seminole Wars. A post office called Tampa Bay was established in 1831, and the name was changed to Tampa three years later. The Government donated 40 acres of land north of Fort Brooke, a block of which was reserved for the courthouse and the remainder sold to finance its construction. Later, because of vast pastures and convenient water transportation, Tampa became the center of the territory's cattle industry. Trade with Cuba prospered until the outbreak of the War between the States.

Four companies left Tampa in 1861 to join the Confederate Army. The defenseless town was blockaded and shelled in 1863, and was later occupied by Federal forces in an effort to stop cotton-running to Cuban ports. Soldiers returned to Tampa after the war to find slaves free, money of little value, and plantations in weeds. Yellow fever swept the area in 1873, and Tampa suffered severely.

Population dwindled; the building of a railroad from Fernandina on the Atlantic to Cedar Keys on the Gulf shifted the economic order in the Tampa Bay region. For several years the city was merely a port of call for schooners operating between Cedar Keys and Key West.

A stagecoach line was established in 1877 between Tampa and Gainesville, but the comparative isolation of the town lasted until 1884 when

Henry Plant's narrow-gauge South Florida Railroad, later the Atlantic Coast Line, reached Tampa; it was extended 9 miles southwest to Port Tampa the following year. There Plant built a causeway and piers to deep water with capacity for berthing 26 ocean steamships.

In 1889 a wooden bridge across the Hillsborough River at Lafayette Street supplanted a hand-operated ferry, and a second railroad, the Florida Railway & Navigation Company, now the Seaboard Air Line, entered the city. From then on expansion was rapid. By 1890 population had increased to 5,000, and in the next decade reached 15,000. Discovery of neighboring phosphate fields gave impetus to its growth, for Tampa was the nearest deep-water port, and the greater portion of the product was exported. Meanwhile the cigar industry moved from Key West to Ybor City, and the pioneer factory attracted others. In 1891 Plant completed the building of his Tampa Bay Hotel, extravagant in size, plan, and furnishings. Determined to make the city a fashionable winter resort and outdo Henry Flagler on the east coast, he spent more than $3,000,000 on the hotel in less than two years. The opening, a social sensation, was attended by 2,000, among them princes, dukes and duchesses, and celebrities of the financial, theatrical, and literary world. The guests were entertained by a symphony orchestra and grand-opera artists, and toured the illuminated grounds in rickshaws. This was a red-letter day for a city of less than 6,000.

During the Spanish-American War, with some 30,000 troops encamped in and around Tampa, the hostelry was headquarters for American officers, among them Colonel Theodore Roosevelt, who trained his Rough Riders in the backyard of the hotel, now the South Florida Fairgrounds. Richard Harding Davis, war correspondent, strutted the hotel corridors and turned out copy for Hearst and the London *Times*. Accompanying him was Frederic Remington, doing his early pen and charcoal sketches.

Tampa was a source of front-page news, with a preponderance of Cuban sympathizers. All the town whistled and sang, 'There'll Be a Hot Time in the Old Town Tonight.' An epidemic of typhoid fever exacted heavy mortality among the troops, and its persistence hastened demobilization when peace was declared. Throughout this period, Clara Barton, founder of the Red Cross in the United States, maintained headquarters in the city.

Following the Spanish-American War began an era of rapid growth for the 'squalid, sand-blighted city,' as Richard Harding Davis described it. Population increased to 40,000. Steel and concrete bridges replaced wooden structures over the Hillsborough River, and the Government appropriated large sums for dredging and improving the harbor and deepening the main ship channel into the Gulf.

Cigar manufacturing reached its peak shortly before the World War, prior to the introduction of machines that revolutionized the industry, but Tampa continued to lead the world in production of high-class, handmade clear Havana cigars.

During the boom period numerous downtown hotels and apartment buildings were erected, Davis Islands were created, and increased recreational facilities were provided for tourists. Gandy Bridge, completed in 1924, spanning Tampa Bay and connecting with St.Petersburg, reduced the driving distance by half, and gave Tampa a direct highway to Gulf beaches. It also opened virgin territory on the west, which was rapidly developed for residential purposes. Davis Causeway across the northern end of Tampa Bay, opened in 1934, provided a short route to Clearwater and the Gulf beaches.

Owing to the increased production of winter vegetables, canned grapefruit, and grapefruit juice in the Tampa area, the American and Continental Can Companies erected plants here, and in 1938, after two decades of idleness, Tampa shipyards were awarded a $7,000,000 contract for the building of four large cargo boats.

POINTS OF INTEREST

(*Tampa*)

1. PLANT PARK, laid out in 1888 by Henry Plant as a setting for his Tampa Bay Hotel, occupies 20 acres in the heart of the city, fronting on the west bank of the Hillsborough River between Lafayette and Cass Streets. Purchased by the city in 1905, and converted into a municipal park, it is headquarters for tourist activities. Its live oaks, palms, bamboos, and other subtropical plantings are alive with songbirds, pigeons, and squirrels. Parking places are provided, but points of interest must be visited on foot.

The UNIVERSITY OF TAMPA, established in 1933, occupies the former Tampa Bay Hotel building, an ornate, sprawling red brick structure of Moorish architecture, two blocks long and varying from two to five stories in height, designed by J.A. Wood and completed in 1891. Its decorations of wood, stone, cement, and wrought iron culminate in an intricate wooden filigree of Moorish horseshoes that extends for hundreds of feet along its wide porches. The twelve domed towers and bulbous minarets are topped with silver crescents. The main entrance has clusters of slender columns forming a portico that rises in a maze of Moorish pendants. The building contains 402 rooms, a solarium, music and ballrooms, and lofty corridors, one of which runs the length of it. The university is co-educational, and has an average yearly enrollment of 500.

On the main floor is the TAMPA MUNICIPAL MUSEUM (*open* 10–3 *Mon.–Fri.*), containing exhibits of rare furniture, rugs, Venetian mirrors, paintings, and tapestries. A bronze figure of *Esmeralda*, the dancing girl in Victor Hugo's *Hunchback of Notre Dame*, stands in the rotunda.

The TAMPA BAY CASINO (*open by permission*) NE. of the university, a one-story cream-colored frame building, is occupied by the Tampa Post of the American Legion. It was formerly a playhouse and swimming pool for the Tampa Bay Hotel, and celebrities of the stage entertained guests here during the gay 90's.

The DE SOTO OAK stands opposite the E. entrance of the university. Under this tree legend says De Soto parleyed with the Indians. Underneath the oak is *Au Coup de Fusil*, by Maurice de Nonvilliers, a lifesize bronze of two dogs pointing for the shot.

The HENRY PLANT MEMORIAL, E. entrance of the university, a fountain designed by George Gray Barnard representing *Transportation*, is the source of a small stream that winds through the park. Along the stream are pens and cages of a small zoo, containing alligators, otters, and bears.

The MUNICIPAL AUDITORIUM, NW. of the university, a two-story octagonal buff brick building built in 1925, has a seating capacity of 2,500. On the second floor is the TAMPA BAY MUSEUM OF ANTIQUITIES AND NATURAL HISTORY (*open* 2–5 *Wed. and Fri.*) containing archeological, geological, and natural-history specimens.

The TOURIST RECREATION CENTER (*annual membership* $1–$2.50), N. end of Park, municipally owned, includes playgrounds, shuffleboard, roque, tennis, and croquet courts, and horseshoe-pitching lanes.

The FLORIDA STATE FAIR GROUNDS, adjoining the park on the NW., is a 50-acre tract containing 23 permanent exhibition and administration buildings, a race track, and an athletic field which is a spring training ground for big-league baseball clubs.

2. DAVIS ISLANDS, reached by bridge from Bay Shore Blvd. near the intersection of Plant Ave. and De Leon St., a group of three man-made islands, is Tampa's most spectacular real-estate development. These islands, covering 800 acres, separated by bridged lagoons and canals, were named for their creator, D.P.Davis. A concrete sea wall was built around submerged land at the mouth of the Hillsborough River and sand from the bottom of the bay pumped into the area. Deposits were made on lots still under water, and down payments at the opening sale amounted to $3,000,000. The exceptionally wide streets, a maze of interlacing curves, are bordered by palms, Australian pines, and subtropical plants. Mediterranean types of architecture prevail throughout the islands.

Tampa Municipal Hospital, the municipal yacht basin, a golf course, numerous parks, a swimming pool, and recreational centers are on the islands. The Peter O. Knight Airport and Seaplane Base occupies the southern tip of the property.

TONY JANNUS ADMINISTRATION BUILDING, completed in 1938, outstanding structure at the airport, is a two-story stone building faced with key limestone blocks and ornamented with coping bands of glazed black tile. The sawed surfaces of the limestone blocks, quarried on the Florida Keys, reveal cross-sections of shellfish, sea plants, and coral formations. An open balcony extends entirely around the second story of the building. The corners of the walls are adorned with projecting sculptures of eagles in flight, their wings flat against the surface, their heads emerging in full relief. The third story is formed by an octagonal, glassed-in observatory, above which a glass and metal lantern, designed to represent the lamp room of a lighthouse, supports an aerial beacon. The rotunda walls are decorated by seven murals by George Hill of St.Petersburg, commemorating the landing of Tony Jannus at Tampa, January 1, 1914, after the world's first commercial air flight (*see St.Petersburg*).

3. The SITE OF FORT BROOKE, SW. corner Platt and Franklin Sts., is indicated by a bronze plaque, marking the site of the first fort established in the Tampa area in 1823 for protection against the Indians.

4. SACRED HEART ROMAN CATHOLIC CHURCH, SE. corner

Twiggs St. and Florida Ave., dedicated in 1905, is distinguished by its marble front, Munich windows, and costly fittings. A huge arched loggia takes up two-thirds of the front; below are three smaller arches, one over each entrance, flanked by a cluster of four marble columns. At the sides of the main arch are octagonal towers of unpolished Georgia marble. The lower exterior walls are of granite, the upper walls of marble. Below the peaked gable in the upper circle of the big arch is a large rose window and above the central entrance is a heroic marble STATUE OF THE RISEN CHRIST. W.J.Clayton of Galveston, Texas, was the architect.

5. The ORANGE GROVE HOTEL BUILDING (*private*), 806 Madison St., is a two-story frame building now used by the Seaboard Air Line Ry. as freight offices. Built for a home in 1843 by William Hooker, one of the cattle kings of south Florida, it was later converted into a hotel, where Confederate and Union officers in turn were quartered during the War between the States. Here Sidney Lanier, poet of the South, wrote 'Tampa Robins'; J.A.Butterfield composed the music for 'When You and I Were Young, Maggie'; and Henry Wilde wrote 'My Life Is Like a Summer Rose,' a line of which reads: 'My life is like the prints which feet have left on Tampa's desert strand.'

6. OAK LAWN CEMETERY, a four-block area with an entrance on Harrison St. between Morgan and Pierce Sts., is enclosed by a brick and concrete wall, and the grounds are shaded by ancient oaks and cedars. During the yellow-fever epidemic in 1873, Tampa citizens died in such numbers that there was no time to dig graves, and bodies were buried in hastily dug trenches, now blank spaces surrounded by gravestones.

7. The TAMPA PUBLIC LIBRARY (*open* 9–9 *weekdays*), 7th Ave. between Tampa and Franklin Sts., erected in 1915, is a one-story-and-basement buff brick building, its entrance framed by a marble archway with white Doric columns. The library, founded by a Carnegie fund, contains 64,000 volumes. On exhibit is a clay tablet said to have been found in southern Babylonia, written in cuneiform characters about 2350 B.C. It records the receipt of various animals.

8. TAMPA UNION TERMINAL (*open* 10–3 *weekdays*) on waterfront at 13th St., is a mammoth plant, including cold-storage warehouses, where citrus fruit is graded and packed. Boxes for export are conveyed into ships' holds by endless belts. Other freight is shipped from the terminal at all seasons, and activities can be observed from an elevated walkway.

(*Ybor City*)

YBOR CITY (pronounced E-bore; colloquially E-bo), extending approximately two miles east from Nebraska Avenue, and south to Ybor estuary and McKay Bay, is the larger and older of Tampa's two Latin settlements. More than half of Tampa's 29,000 Latins live in this area of two square miles. With its clubs, restaurants, theaters, Spanish newspapers, and its own chamber of commerce, Ybor City is a self-contained unit. Spanish is the common tongue, and few outside the present generation speak or read English. In many shops are signs reading: 'English Spoken Here.'

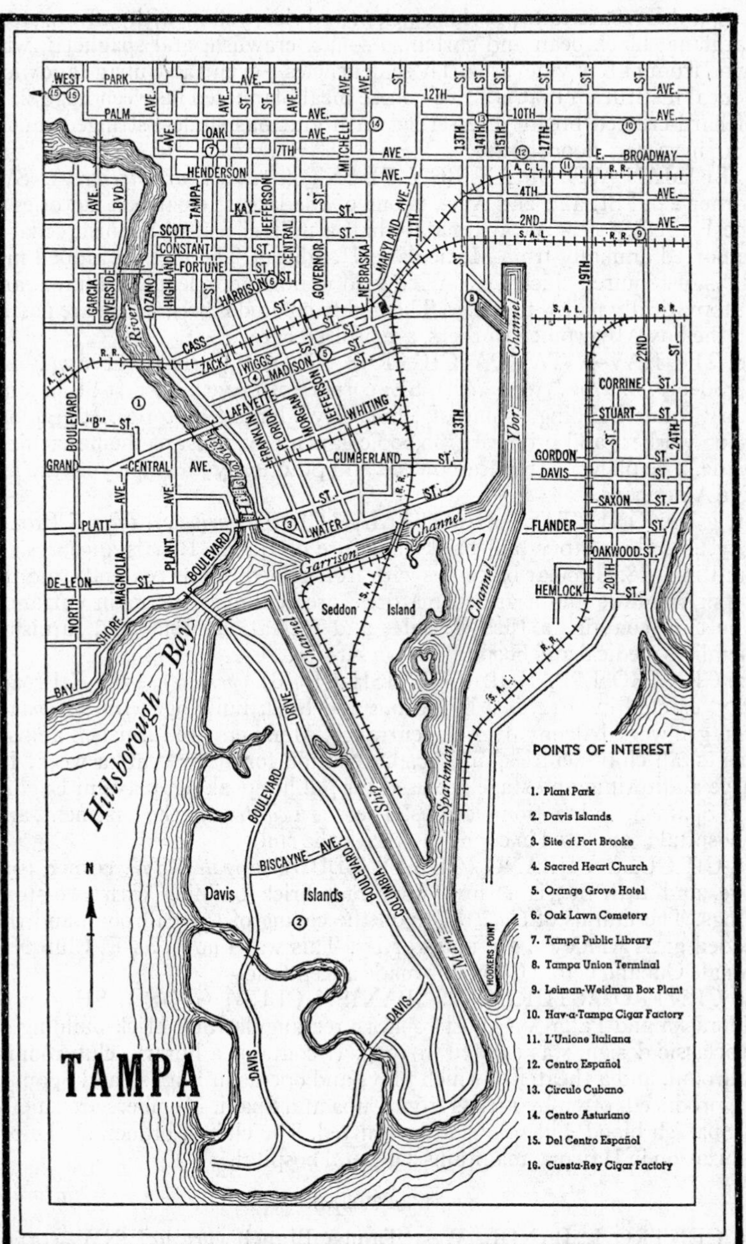
TAMPA
POINTS OF INTEREST
1. Plant Park
2. Davis Islands
3. Site of Fort Brooke
4. Sacred Heart Church
5. Orange Grove Hotel
6. Oak Lawn Cemetery
7. Tampa Public Library
8. Tampa Union Terminal
9. Leiman-Weidman Box Plant
10. Hav-a-Tampa Cigar Factory
11. L'Unione Italiana
12. Centro Español
13. Circulo Cubano
14. Centro Asturiano
15. Del Centro Español
16. Cuesta-Rey Cigar Factory
Hillsborough Bay
Davis Islands
Seddon Island
Garrison Channel
Ybor Channel
Sparkman Channel
Main Channel
Ship Channel
Hillsborough River
HOOKERS POINT

Spanish restaurants provide chicken and rice, yellow with saffron, steak catalana, black-bean and garbanzo soups, crawfish, and spaghetti, with wine from native vineyards. These delicacies—even the Cuban sandwich, a local institution that is a five-course meal blanketed between huge slabs of hard-crusted bread—are served with gracious smiles, stringed music, and, in season, floor shows.

9. LEIMAN-WEIDMAN BOX PLANT (*open by arrangement*), SW. corner 22nd St. and 2nd Ave., is one of the largest cigar-box factories in the United States. Approximately half a million feet of Spanish cedar is imported annually from Mexico and Honduras. The logs are ripped into slabs of required thickness, milled into uniform box lengths, buffed, and automatically nailed together. The highly colored labels, which are pasted on the boxes by women workers, are printed here.

10. The HAV-A-TAMPA CIGAR FACTORY (*open* 8-11 *a.m., and* 12:30-3 *p.m. weekdays; guides*), SE. corner 10th Ave. and 21st St., a four-story frame building, is one of Ybor City's largest factories. It employs 1,100 workers and produces 500,000 cigars a day, most of them machine-made. The plant is American owned and practically all employees are native Americans.

11. L'UNIONE ITALIANA (ITALIAN CLUB) (*private*), 1731 E.Broadway, is a three-story buff brick structure of Italian Renaissance design, built in 1918. Circular balconies with iron-grilled railings extend from the upper windows and a grilled marquee projects over the main entrance. The club contains a theater, cafe, and recreation room, and furnishes members medical and hospitalization service.

12. CENTRO ESPANOL (SPANISH CLUB) (*private*), 1536 E.Broadway, erected in 1912, is a block-long red brick building, with an ornate iron grillwork balcony over the entrance. Members are furnished amusements, all club facilities, and hospitalization for a few cents a week. Its large auditorium and stage are used for public speaking, plays in English and Spanish, and motion pictures. There is a *cantina* in the basement, and a hospital is operated in connection with the club.

13. CIRCULO CUBANO (CUBAN CLUB) (*private*), SW. corner 10th Ave. and 14th St., is a three-story buff brick building with two-story wings. The murals of *Cuba Libre* on the ceiling of the ballroom, and the leaded glass windows, are noteworthy. This was known as El Club Nationale Cubano before Cuba was made a Republic.

14. CENTRO ASTURIANO (SPANISH CLUB) (*private*), SE. corner Nebraska and Palm Aves., a two-story rectangular buff brick building of neoclassic design, was erected in 1913. It contains a library, club rooms, ballroom, and a theater in which plays and operas in English and Spanish are produced, often by artists from Cuba and Spain. Members are chiefly of Spanish blood, but others are admitted. The club, a branch of the organization in Havana, maintains a general hospital.

(*West Tampa*)

15. CENTRO ESPANOL, West Tampa Branch (*private*), NW. corner N.Howard Ave. and Cherry St., is a two-story red-brick Spanish club

building with a towerlike façade of modified Moorish design over the wide-arched main entrance. Interior facilities include a theater, presenting Spanish and American films, a ballroom, and recreation lounge.

16. CUESTA-REY CIGAR FACTORY (*open* 9–10 *a.m. and* 1–3 *p.m., Mon. to Fri.; guides*), SW. corner N.Howard Ave. and Beach St., a three-story brick building surrounded by a brick wall, is West Tampa's pioneer establishment. It produces handmade cigars almost exclusively, many of which are exported. This factory was commissioned as purveyor of cigars to the King and Court of Spain during the reign of Alfonso XIII, and its founder was knighted by the King in 1915.

The tobacco is brought from bonded warehouses and kept in air-conditioned rooms. A bale consists of 80 *manojos* or 320 *gavillas*, the latter known in English as 'hands,' each containing up to 50 leaves. Stems are removed from leaves by 'strippers' and the tobacco delivered to 'grabbers' or *boncheros* who make up the inside of the cigar known as the 'bunch,' filler, or *tripa*. The wrappers or choice leaves are picked by 'selectors' and passed on to the cigar makers, men and women, who make the finished product.

Cigar makers, or *tabaqueros*, work at long tables in double rows. These are grouped in units, each known as a *vapor*, the Spanish word for ship. Each worker is permitted to take out, free, three cigars a day, provided they are carried in plain sight, and allowed to smoke as many as he pleases on the job. The finished cigars are tied in bundles of 100, known as a *rueda* or 'wheel,' and graded by experts, *resagadors*, according to color that ranges from *claro claro*, very light, to *colorado*, red, and *maduro*, dark. The embossed bands and cellophane wrappers are applied by machines, and the cigars are packed into labeled boxes by hand. The tobacco left over from the making of cigars, called *mogolla*, is ground into small pieces for scrap or filler. All those who prepare the tobacco are known as clerks or *dependientes*. Readers, or *lectors*, who formerly read to the workers were abolished in 1933 because of the introduction of radical literature, but in many factories radios have replaced them.

A cigar that does not taper is called a 'straight,' and a tapering one is known as a 'shape.' The end of the cigar placed in the mouth is the *cabeza*, or head, the lighted end is the 'tuck,' the flare, or the *campana*, meaning bell. In making tapered cigars, a cutting process where the worker employs a special knife, a *chabeta*, is referred to as an 'operation.' Cigars are made in various shapes and sizes, the more popular known as 'blunts,' 'panetelas,' and 'perfectos.'

POINTS OF INTEREST IN ENVIRONS

Ballast Point, 5.4 *m.*, Rattlesnake Canning Plant, 11.3 *m.* (*see Tour* 20).

PART III

The Florida Loop

Tour 1

(Waycross, Ga.)—Jacksonville—St.Augustine—Daytona Beach—New Smyrna—Melbourne—Fort Pierce—West Palm Beach—Fort Lauderdale—Miami—Key West. US 1 and State 4A.

Georgia Line to Key West, 569 *m.*

Hard-surfaced roadbed throughout, mainly concrete- and asphalt-paved; watch for cattle along the highway.
Route paralleled by Atlantic Coast Line R.R. between Georgia Line and Jacksonville; by Florida East Coast Ry. between Jacksonville and Florida City; and by Seaboard Air Line Ry. between West Palm Beach and Homestead.
Accommodations of all kinds; numerous tourist camps.

US 1, and its extension State 4A south of Miami, the longest and most heavily traveled route in the State, enters north Florida over the St.Marys River, runs along the coast, and goes to sea to reach Key West, Florida's southernmost coral island, only 90 miles from Cuba. For most of its length it runs close to a chain of salt lagoons, separated from the ocean by low-lying islands and narrow reefs. These lagoons, connected by canals, form a section of the Intracoastal Waterway, a popular yacht and motorboat route to and from southern Florida waters.

With each mile, as the route proceeds southward, the vegetation becomes more tropical. Birds and marine life not found in other parts of the United States inhabit marshes and rivers. Almost every side road leads to a sandy bathing beach or to a resort with fishing and sailing facilities. And with each mile southward the temperature rises; the winter visitor, topcoated on entering the State, is often in shirt sleeves on reaching Miami.

Almost every Florida town along US 1 is a winter resort; boom towns of the 1920's stand between settlements that flourished in the 1700's; night clubs are within tee-shot of crumbling ruins built when Florida was a part of the Spanish Empire. Smoky pine woods, dense cypress hammocks, marshes, and glittering sand dunes relieve the flatness of the coastal region.

Section a. GEORGIA LINE to JACKSONVILLE; 38.7 *m.* US 1

In this section US 1 crosses a level region of pine forests and cut-over flatwoods; occasional hardwood hammocks mark the courses of sluggish streams. The country is sparsely settled, but near Jacksonville appear dairy and poultry farms, and filling stations of various sizes, colors, and styles.

The highway presents an interesting study of American roadside advertising. There are signs that turn like windmills; startling signs that resemble crashed airplanes; signs with glass lettering which blaze forth at night when automobile headlight beams strike them; flashing neon signs; signs painted with professional touch; signs crudely lettered and misspelled. They advertise hotels, tourist cabins, fishing camps, and eating places. They extol the virtues of ice creams, shoe creams, cold creams; proclaim the advantages of new cars and used cars; tell of 24-hour towing and ambulance service, Georgia pecans, Florida fruit and fruit juices, honey, soft drinks, and furniture. They urge the traveler to take designated tours, to visit certain cities, to stop at points of interest he 'must see.'

US 1 crosses the Georgia Line, 0 *m.*, on a bridge over the St.Marys River, 38 miles south of Waycross, Ga. (*see Georgia Guide, Tour* 4).

The St.Marys River is here a deep narrow stream, winding its way from its source in Okefenokee Swamp, Georgia, to Cumberland Sound, at Fernandina (*see Tour 3a*). Its waters move peacefully seaward in tiny swirls and eddies except after heavy summer rains when they become a raging torrent. Bay, oak, and cypress grow along the sandy banks. In the early eighteenth century ship chandlers made regular trips up the river to obtain water, selling it to ship masters at Fernandina docks for 1¢ a gallon. Because of its acid content, the water remains fresh for many months when placed in casks.

South of the bridge is (R) a small granite MONUMENT TO ROBERT E. LEE. The inscription on the bronze plaque states that this highway, here called the Dixie, is dedicated to his memory. At this point Florida soldiers departed to join other Confederate forces during the War between the States.

HILLIARD, 7 *m.* (66 alt., 550 pop.), a small poultry and truck-farming center, comprises a group of frame houses and stores on the crest of a low hill. The town began as a trading post in the early 1800's, when cotton and tobacco were the principal crops of the surrounding farms. Lumber and naval-stores industries have since supplanted agricultural pursuits.

South of Hilliard tall cabbage palms fringe a large hardwood swamp. The soil remains sandy, and the surface flat, covered with shortleaf, slash, and pond pines, which supply raw material for pulp mills at Fernandina (*see Tour 3a*). The countryside provides good grazing for free-range cattle.

CALLAHAN, 17.7 *m.* (26 alt., 637 pop.), the only community of any size between the Georgia Line and Jacksonville, has brick stores, attractive houses, and rich truck gardens. Here on narrow Alligator Creek, 300 American cavalry under Colonel Elijah Clarke attacked 450 British Redcoats on June 30, 1778, but were forced to withdraw with a loss of 13 men; the British lost 9.

Callahan is at the junction with State 13 (*see Tour 3a*).

An outdoor SWIMMING POOL (R), 20.3 *m.*, is popular with residents of the vicinity.

The pine forests south of Callahan are under fire protection of the Florida Forest Service (*see Tour 7a*); an occasional lookout tower rises above a group of white frame buildings. The tall broom sedge that grows in ditches on both sides of the highway is cut and sold to Jacksonville plants as fillers for brooms.

DINSMORE, 28 *m.* (26 alt., 708 pop.), consists of weathered frame houses, small stores, filling stations, and a turpentine camp (*see Tour 3b*).

Between Dinsmore and Jacksonville a forest of second-growth slash pine extends to a gently rolling area of taller pines and sycamores. Proximity to Florida's largest city is indicated by the increasing number of filling stations and tourist camps. Hitch-hikers of all ages and both sexes, with baggage and without, stand along the road, hoping to thumb a lift south in fall and winter, or a ride north in spring.

JACKSONVILLE, 38.7 *m.* (25 alt., 129,549 pop.) (*see Jacksonville*).

Points of Interest: Naval Stores Yard, Cotton Compress, Hemming Park, Memorial Park, and others.

Jacksonville is at the junctions with US 17 (*see Tour 2a and b*), US 90 (*see Tour 7a*), and State 78 (*see Tour 1A*).

Right from Jacksonville on State 47 is SAN JOSE, 7 *m.*, a suburb of Jacksonville, with attractive houses, carefully landscaped grounds and parkways. The former San Jose Hotel is now occupied by the BOLLES SCHOOL, a military academy.

At 11 *m.* is a junction with a paved road; R. here 2 *m.* is MANDARIN (16 alt., 645 pop.), on the east bank of the St.Johns River, a village founded during the English occupation of Florida (1763–83). In the vicinity stood Thimagua, an Indian town visited in 1564 by Laudonnière, French explorer of the St.Johns. During the Spanish regime in Florida, the village was known as San Antonio. It was named Mandarin for a variety of orange of that name introduced here from China.

Mandarin was not incorporated until 1841. During the latter part of the War between the States a Union gunboat shelled the village in an offensive against Confederates who sought to block transportation of Federal soldiers down the river. One cannon ball remains lodged in a tree. After the war the village flourished. In 1885 it had a population of 1,200, a boardwalk along the riverfront, large estates, and three steamer landings. As was true of Enterprise, Picolata, and other St.Johns River towns, a decline began with the cessation of heavy water traffic at the advent of railroads.

For many years Mandarin was the winter home of Harriet Beecher Stowe (1812–96), author of *Uncle Tom's Cabin*, who moved here in 1867. During following winters she completed *Palmetto Leaves*, *Our Plantation*, and other works. Mrs. Stowe and her husband, Professor Charles B. Stowe, taught in the Episcopal chapel, dedicated November 4, 1883. The one-room chapel of perpendicular pine siding, with an open conical belfry, contains a Tiffany window to the memory of Mrs. Stowe, contributed by popular subscription under the sponsorship of the magazine *Outlook*.

Section b. JACKSONVILLE to DAYTONA BEACH; 97.1 m. US 1

South of Jacksonville the route is bordered by pinelands, broken by occasional marshes and cypress hammocks. Cabbage palms grow thickly along rivers and creeks; the undergrowth is often dense and impenetrable. At intervals the road crosses low sandy ridges, forested with black-jack oaks, and skirts cypress ponds, their dark waters studded with tiny yellow flowers. Thistles, ferns, and blue flag flourish in roadside ditches. Cattle graze in the woods and the landscape is dotted with small white mounds thrown up by salamanders, an animal resembling the western gopher. The Florida gopher is a land turtle. Along the highway, all but lost among blatant neon lights flashing 'Whiskey' and 'Dance and Dine,' are crudely daubed warnings erected by itinerant evangelists, announcing that 'Jesus is soon coming,' or exhorting the traveler to 'prepare to meet thy God.'

In JACKSONVILLE, 0 *m.*, the route crosses the St. Johns River bridge (*25¢ car and passengers*), connecting the business section and South Jacksonville.

BAYARD, 17.9 *m.*, (25 alt., 225 pop.), was named by Henry M. Flagler, builder of the Florida East Coast Railway, for his friend, Thomas F. Bayard, Ambassador to Great Britain (1893–97), the first American of that rank at the Court of St. James's.

South of Bayard the route closely parallels the Florida East Coast tracks. Section houses, depots, and other railroad buildings are painted bright yellow with green trim. Blue iris, sacred to the Indians who used its roots for medicine, colors the marshes in spring. On higher ground grows the grenadilla, or passion flower, so called by Spanish missionaries to whom it symbolized the Passion of Christ. In the center of the blossom is a cross; the five stamens represent the five wounds of Christ, and the 72 filaments, the traditional number of thorns in His crown. Commonly known as maypop, the flower is a native of America; its succulent and edible fruit, large as a hen's egg, is highly perfumed.

The dense stands of pine between the road and the coast have long been slashed for turpentine and still provide a livelihood for wood choppers, tie cutters, and small sawmills. The highway cuts across a typical Florida flatwoods swamp, 25 *m.*; hammocks on both sides of the highway rise in towering pyramids of swamp flora from a fringe of low pinewoods and reedy cypress ponds. Tall trees crown dark masses of undergrowth; woody vines and gray Spanish moss form a canopy through which shafts of sunlight fall on white lilies floating in stagnant water amid a profusion of ferns and wild flowers. Among the trees are maple, gum, the bald cypress with fluted base, and the slender-trunked pumpkin ash.

The entrance to ST. AUGUSTINE MUNICIPAL AIRPORT (L), 33.7 *m.*, is marked by two coquina gate posts.

ST. AUGUSTINE, 39.4 *m.* (7 alt., 12,111 pop.) (*see St. Augustine*).

Points of Interest: Fort Marion, City Gates, Old Schoolhouse, Old Spanish Treasury, Oldest House, Slave Market, Fountain of Youth, and others.

St. Augustine is at the junction with State 78 and State 140 (*see Tour 1A*).

Right from St. Augustine on State 95 to the FLORIDA NORMAL AND INDUSTRIAL INSTITUTE, 2 *m.*, junior college for Negroes, a group of 12 brick and coquina buildings of Spanish design. The school has four divisions: liberal arts and science, teacher training, home economics, and high school. Enrollment in 1938 was 536. The institute was organized at Jacksonville in 1892 as the Florida Baptist Academy and removed here to the 1,000-acre Hanson plantation in 1917; its name was changed the following year. The Orange Blossom Quartette and the Jubilee Singers of the School are well known for their Negro songs and spirituals.

TOCOI (Ind., water lily) 17 *m.*, (8 pop.), is a fishing settlement on the site of an Indian village and Franciscan mission during Spanish occupation. Shortly after the War between the States, a crude combination mule-drawn and steam railway connected Tocoi and St. Augustine. This road caused the decline of Picolata (*see below*), but fell into disuse when Flagler completed a railroad from Jacksonville to St. Augustine.

Right from Tocoi, 6.5 *m.*, on an improved road is PICOLATA (Sp., broad bluff), a turpentine camp on the east bank of the St. Johns River, at a point where a Spanish trail once crossed the river. A square tower, 30 feet high, with a moat, guarded the crossing. On January 1, 1740, this site was captured by the English under Oglethorpe during an assault on St.Augustine. William Bartram, naturalist, had an indigo plantation here in 1766. During an Indian insurrection in 1835 a small wooden blockhouse was built for protection of settlers; some of the breastworks still remain.

MOULTRIE, 45.7 *m.* (500 pop.), on the bank of a tidal inlet bordered with salt marshes, was named for John Moultrie, lieutenant governor of Florida during the English occupation (1763–83), who lived near by in a large stone mansion on his plantation, Belle Vista. When England returned Florida to Spain in 1784, Moultrie moved to the Bahamas with many other British settlers.

Right from Moultrie on a sand road through dense pine woods to a marker (L), 0.8 *m.*, commemorating the capture of Osceola, great leader of the Seminole (*see Tour* 21). On October 20, 1837, Osceola and a party of 71 warriors, 16 women, and 4 Indian-Negroes, set out for Fort Peyton (*see below*) to confer with General Joseph M. Hernandez regarding the release of King Philip, imprisoned Seminole chief. Osceola had sent by Wild Cat, son of King Philip, a white plume and pipe, the Indian equivalent of a flag of truce, but the American commander, Thomas S. Jesup, instructed Hernandez to seize the Indians and bring them to St.Augustine. When Osceola realized that he had been tricked, he turned to a companion and said, 'You must talk; I am choked.' Public opinion denounced the flagrant breach of faith, and the New York *Herald* described it as the 'perfidious capture of Osceola, when the chieftain was engaged in an honest parley—which it is believed would have terminated the War.'

At 1.5 *m.* is the SITE OF FORT PEYTON. Nothing remains of the old wooden fort and blockhouse erected in 1836. William Tecumseh Sherman, who won distinction in the War between the States, was stationed here as a lieutenant during the last days of the Seminole War.

South of Moultrie the highway traverses a typical cypress swamp. One of the most symmetrical of trees, with silvery tapering trunk, the bald cypress reaches heights of 100 feet and attains great age. In its heavy branches herons and water turkeys often nest. The function of its 'knees,' smooth conical shapes rising from the main roots, is not definitely known; some have suggested that they absorb air for the root system.

BUNNELL, 71 *m.* (23 alt., 671 pop.), a lumber and turpentine town, lies in the heart of an extensive potato-growing area. From January to March an important industry is the cutting and shipping of palmetto leaves used in Palm Sunday ceremonies. Averaging 3 feet in length, the leaves are piled on wet sand and covered with damp burlap while awaiting shipment; so protected, they remain fresh for several months. The average price of leaves is $12 a thousand; approximately 350,000 are shipped from Bunnell annually.

Bunnell is at the junction with State 28 (*see Tour* 19).

Pine and palmetto thin out as the highway tunnels into dense hammock growth of moss-bearded oaks, cabbage palms hung with vines, and swamp cypress, with isolated citrus groves in occasional clearings.

KORONA, 77 *m.* (31 alt., 100 pop.), a potato and winter vegetable center, was settled in 1912 by a group of Polish families from Chicago and vicinity. As little has been done to maintain proper drainage, flood waters here destroy many crops. Polish families retain their Old World customs and still use their native language, although children are taught English.

The Ruins of Tissimi Mission (L), 81.4 *m.*, are almost hidden from view in an undergrowth of woods and vines. Reputedly built about 1696 by Franciscan Friars, the mission was one of a chain of 44 erected in Florida. The original structure, destroyed by the English in 1706, was later rebuilt and used as a sugar mill during the British occupation of Florida. Old fire boxes for sugar pans remain, along with pits supposedly used as ovens, and arches that may have framed windows in early days. Tall chimneys suggest gigantic gate posts; alongside are other flues, the purpose of which is unknown.

Broad reaches of salt marsh appear as US 1 crosses TOMOKA RIVER (Ind., lord, ruler), 86.3 *m.*, which offers good fishing (bass, perch, bream). In the lowlands along both banks live marsh hens, wild turkey, and deer. Herds of wild horses, called marshtackies, roamed this region as late as 1918. These horses, perhaps descended from the animals brought over by the first Spanish settlers, could traverse almost inaccessible swamps and lowlands, and were in demand by native stockmen who preferred them to western cow ponies. They were especially useful in rounding up the semi-wild Florida razorback hogs that forage the woods for acorns and roots.

Indian Burial Mounds, 87.6 *m.*, have been excavated by the Smithsonian Institution, and a number of skulls and bones recovered.

The highway runs under a continuous arch of large oaks, with the HALIFAX RIVER occasionally in sight (L) through the foliage. The river, like the city of Halifax in Nova Scotia, was named for George Montague Dunk, second Earl of Halifax (1716–71), who in 1747 was head of the Board of Trade of the American Colonies. In June 1751 he sought to have the West Indies placed under the jurisdiction of the Board with himself as third Secretary of State, in command of this territory, but the King refused. At his death Halifax was Secretary of State in the ministry of Lord North.

ORMOND, 91.2 *m.* (6 alt., 1,517 pop.), a quiet and conservative town, with pleasing houses and well-kept lawns and gardens, was established in 1875 by the Corbin Lock Company of New Britain, Conn., as a health center for employees threatened with tuberculosis. Originally called New Britain, the name was changed to Ormond in 1880 in honor of Captain James Ormond, a Scotsman from the Bahama Islands, who in 1815 settled a short distance to the north on a 2,000-acre plantation granted him by the Spanish Governor of Florida; Ormond was killed by a runaway slave in 1835.

The Ormond Tropical Gardens (*adm.* 25¢), Division St. and Granada Ave., comprise 116 acres planted with 250,000 subtropical and tropical trees and shrubs.

Left from Ormond across a wooden bridge spanning the Halifax River to ORMOND BEACH, 1.2 *m.*, (*see Tour 1A*).

HOLLY HILL, 93 *m.* (6 alt., 1,146 pop.), a suburb of Daytona Beach, named because of the holly trees that once grew here, is a part of the old Turnbull land grant (*see below*).

Right from Holly Hill to Holly Hill Jungle Gardens (*adm.* 25¢), 1 *m.*, a 7-acre tract containing one of the largest plantings of Easter lilies in America, producing 45,000 bulbs annually.

DAYTONA BEACH, 97.1 *m.* (7 alt., 16,598 pop.) (*see Daytona Beach*).

Points of Interest: Ocean Beach, Broadwalk, Pier, open-air Auditorium, Bethune-Cookman College (Negro), alligator and ostrich farms, and others.

Daytona Beach is at the junction with US 92 State 21 (*see Tour 8a*) and State 140 (*see Tour 1A*).

Section c. DAYTONA BEACH to FORT PIERCE; 136.2 *m. US* 1

This section of US 1 passes through the heart of the East Coast citrus country, celebrated for its Indian River oranges. The highway skirts Indian River, a broad reach of salt water separated from the ocean by outlying keys; the so-called river is part of the Intracoastal Waterway (*see Intracoastal Waterway*.)

Pine, palmetto, and cabbage palm still dominate the landscape; the fishing and tourist motif remains, but orange and grapefruit groves, dark green masses along the highway, appear more and more frequently, sometimes within towns and cities. In spring the blossoms perfume the countryside. Later, heavy trucks loaded with fruit rumble along the highway day and night, breaking the stillness of the pine woods. Two drivers usually alternate at the wheel and frequently resort to caffein and other pills to keep awake during long nonstop trips as far as Memphis, Chicago, and New York. At packing houses and city warehouses, where trucks line up for loading, drivers lean against their trucks, virtually asleep on their feet. Filling stations and refreshment stands remain open all night during the shipping season and seek to attract patronage of drivers by advertising free coffee.

Many citrus groves are bordered with Australian pine windbreaks; in some are beehives between the rows of trees; in others are stacks of pinewood ready to be lighted as a protection against frost. Some advertise 'All the fruit juice you can drink for a dime.' A few offer free orange juice to entice the motorist to stop and buy a box or red-meshed bag of fruit.

South of DAYTONA BEACH, 0 *m.*, US 1 passes a short distance west of the old Dixie Highway. The new highway traverses open sparsely settled territory, has few dangerous curves, and is not washed by the storm-driven seas that often damage sections of the old road.

PORT ORANGE, 4.9 *m.* (12 alt., 678 pop.), a shrimp and oyster center on the west bank of the broad Halifax River, was established in 1861. During the Seminole War the Battle of Dunlawton was fought along the riverfront at Port Orange. Under General Putnam the defenders, refugees of neighboring plantations, were forced to withdraw from the vicinity, while the Indians under King Philip destroyed a sugar mill and near-by settlements.

Although the citrus culture to which the town owes its name is still of consequence to the community, it has been superseded by the cultivation of oyster beds in the Halifax River, and by shrimp fishing.

In Port Orange (*follow markers*) are the RUINS OF THE DUNLAWTON SU-

GAR MILL (*adm.* 25¢), reputedly built during the early eighteenth century, later destroyed, rebuilt, and improved many times. Known to have been used as late as 1880, it is one of the largest coquina ruins in the vicinity. Two tall chimneys overtop the trees, and the walls are overrun with vines. Most of the machinery remains on its foundations, coated with rust. During the War between the States, Edward Archibald McDonald, founder of the settlement, transported salt water from the Halifax River and used the huge kettles of the mill to make salt for the Confederate forces.

Southward along the coast grows the coontie or komptie plant, a member of the cycad family, its roots providing an arrow-root starch used by the Seminole and by American pioneers to make bread when corn was not available. The roots were pounded in water, and the white sediment was dried and used as flour. The Indians regarded the coontie as sacred to the Great Spirit, and used it during their feast at the annual Green Corn Dance (*see Archeology and Indians*).

The highway winds around lagoons of the Halifax River; sea gulls float on the surface, and the low green growth of mangrove indicates the presence of salt water. Oyster beds are exposed at low tide, and sometimes a lone heron appears. The papaya fruit was discovered in Florida in this region. André Michaux, a French botanist, found it growing wild near the coast in 1778. In appearance and texture the papaya resembles a cantaloupe, having been described as 'the glorified melon that climbed a tree.' It is cooked as a vegetable when green, and served as a fruit when ripe. The presence of papain, a drug similar to pepsin, renders its juices remedial in stomach disorders. Tough cuts of meat become tender when wrapped for 24 hours in papaya leaves.

NEW SMYRNA, 14.5 *m.* (10 alt., 4,149 pop.), has a business section with square false-front buildings shaded by arcades of wood and corrugated iron to protect shoppers from sun and rain. Old frame houses, chiefly of the post-Victorian era, sit back from the street behind moss-hung oaks and Washingtonian palms. Fishing and shrimp fleets, citrus groves, packing houses, and the Florida East Coast Railway shops provide the income of New Smyrna residents.

Scattered through the town are many reminders of New Smyrna's long history—sunken stone piers, ruins of a Spanish mission, foundations of an old fort, and canals that start deep in heavy undergrowth and run through the town to the river. The first known settlement on the site was the Indian village of Caparaca. Spanish missionaries arrived in 1696 and established the Mission of Atocuimi (*see below*).

In 1767 Dr.Andrew Turnbull, a Scottish physician, brought 1,500 colonists here. About 1,200 were from the Island of Minorca, east of Spain; the others were Italians and Greeks. The British Government provided a sloop of war and gave a bounty of £4,500 to promote the settlement, which had many powerful backers. Lord Grenville, First Lord of the Treasury, was a partner *ex officio*. Grants of more than 100,000 acres of land were made to the colony. The colonists found pioneering anything but idyllic, but they accomplished a great deal in the nine years of settlement, building an elaborate system of canals to drain the rich hammock land. Indigo raised on the fertile soil found a ready market in England. Roads were laid out, some of which are still used.

By the time of the American Revolution many of the settlers had died, and discontent prevailed. Charges and counter-charges about the administration of the settlement flew thick and fast; troops were brought in to maintain order. With the appointment of Tonyn as governor in 1776, all who wished to do so were granted permission to leave the settlement; the majority moved to St.Augustine, where many of their descendants live.

In 1803 Spanish grants of land were given to the Martin and Murray families. Subsequently, though harried by Seminole raids and blockade-running in the War between the States, the town experienced a slow growth, stimulated by the advent of the railroad and later by highway improvements and the completion of the Intracoastal Waterway.

The FOUNDATIONS OF AN OLD FORT, Hillsborough St. between Washington and Julian Sts., were discovered in 1854 when an Indian mound was excavated. Their origin and history remain unknown.

The TURNBULL CANAL, 10 feet deep and 10 feet wide, excavated in places through solid coquina, extends 4 miles west from the boat slips at the river's edge and is still used for drainage purposes. In some parts of the city the canal is roofed over with sidewalks and streets.

The RUINS OF THE MISSION ATOCUIMI (*adm.* 25¢), Canal St., built in the 1690's, are owned by the Florida State Historical Society. In 1696 the Jororo Indians rebelled against an order of Fray Luis Sánchez, a priest, who forbade their observance of certain tribal customs. The priest and two of his Indian converts were slain, and the church ornaments stolen. The mission was used as a sugar mill during the British regime.

Left from New Smyrna over the Washington St. Bridge spanning the Halifax River and connecting several small mangrove islands to the ANGLERS' CLUB (*private*), 0.2 *m.*, a fishing and boating organization which holds annual meets from November to April. Ample dock facilities and a marine way are provided for small boats. In the club building (*open*) is a collection of Indian relics. At the east end of the bridge is (R) DUMMITT MOUND, named for Captain D.D.Dummitt (*see Tour 1B*), New Smyrna's first port collector, who lived at one time on the bluff.

Straight ahead on Flagler Ave., landscaped with palms, flowering shrubs, and Australian pines, to CORONADO BEACH, 1.6 *m.* (214 pop.), an ocean resort. Neighboring beaches are frequented by fishermen; a day's catch consists chiefly of channel bass, some of which weigh as much as 40 pounds. In the distance to the north, on the far side of Ponce de Leon Inlet, is PONCE DE LEON LIGHTHOUSE.

Right from CORONADO BEACH on Turtle Mound Road, 7 *m.*, to TURTLE MOUND, rising 50 feet above the beach, now under the protection of the Florida State Historical Society. Called Mount of Surruque by the Indians, it was charted on Florida maps as early as 1564, and Spanish galleons stopped here for repairs, wood, and water. A fishing camp and picnic grounds are near by.

A COAST GUARD AND LIFE-SAVING STATION, 12.5 *m.*, faces the ocean, and so narrow is the peninsula here that its rear door opens on the inlet.

In this area both Spanish and English colonists planted indigo, a bushy shrub of the pea family. It was cut with reaping hooks when in full bloom, immersed in vats of water until fermentation took place, decanted, treated with lime, and churned until blue flakes were precipitated in the form of a blue powdery sediment. Pressed into blocks and dried, this became the indigo of commerce. Formerly exported in large quantities, indigo was gradually supplanted by the more profitable cotton. Wild indigo, bearing both white and blue flowers, is found in many sections between the ocean and the St. Johns River.

During the English occupation of Florida, cochineal, a commercial dye, scarlet in color, was made from cooked bodies of the cochineal insect found on several species of cacti growing along the east coast above Palm Beach.

England urged her people to establish colonies in Florida, and as early as 1669 a pamphlet was issued in London entitled *A Brief Description of the Province on the Coasts of Florida*, undoubtedly the first promotion literature printed in English on Florida real estate. The pamphlet described with what profit indigo, tobacco, cotton, limes, oranges, and lemons could be grown in 'this place so desirable . . . seated in the most temperate clime, where the neighborhood of the golden light of heaven brings many advantages and his convenient distance secures them from the inconveniences of his scorching beams.'

Addressing itself to 'any younger brother whose spirit is elevated above the common sort, and yet the hard usage of our country hath not allowed suitable fortunes,' the circular suggested that he 'leave his native soil to advance his fortunes equal to his blood and spirit, and so . . . avoid the unlawful ways too many of our young gentlemen take to maintain themselves according to their high education.' The circular concluded: 'Those that desire further advice . . . let them repair to Mr. Mathew Wilkinson, the ironmonger, at the Sign of the Three Feathers in Bishopgate Street, where they will be informed when the ships will be ready.'

OAK HILL, 27.3 *m.* (18 alt., 457 pop.) packs citrus, and from apiaries in the vicinity ships many pounds of orange and palmetto honey annually.

At 29.5 *m.* is the junction with State 219, a paved road.

Left on this road is ALLENHURST, 8 *m.* (50 pop.), a settlement of fisherfolk. Here is the Haulover, a narrow channel dug to connect Mosquito Lagoon with upper Indian River. Formerly, small schooners bound from the lagoon into the Indian River were hauled almost a half mile across the sand by means of rollers and skids.

The road curves across a lowland meadow, over a concrete railroad overpass, and along a fill barely 3 feet above the water level. It traverses part of a vast salt marsh, yellow with sunflowers in spring, pink with rose mallow in the fall. Ibises, herons, and other waterfowl feed beside the causeway in the early morning and late afternoon. Kingfishers perch warily on telephone wires, plunging like a rocket for minnows. Tall graceful Australian pines appear at intervals, serving as windbreaks for citrus groves. From higher ground the Indian River (L) shimmers in the distance.

Sometimes at night, and especially before a heavy rain, the river glows with a phosphorescent light; waves whipped up by a stiff breeze resemble leaping flames; myriad fish appear to be bathed in fire; boats passing leave a luminous trail in their wake—a phenomenon caused by the presence of trillions of minute luminous organisms, both protozoa and protophyta.

Before 1600 the Indian River was known as Ais (Ind., deer), named by the Ais Indians who were among the earliest of Florida tribes. The river is actually a lagoon, from 1 to 5 miles wide, open to the Atlantic at many points, and extending to Stuart (*see below*) more than 100 miles south. For its entire length it is a section of the Intracoastal Waterway.

TITUSVILLE, 47 *m.* (14 alt., 2,089 pop.), seat of Brevard County, is one of many citrus shipping centers along the east coast. Large packing houses operate day and night throughout the season, and from December to April loaded trucks and trailers stream northward along the highway. Small dealers visit the packing houses daily to buy fruit and rush it to widely scattered points in the South.

The head of navigation on the Indian River, Titusville was a flourishing port in the 1880's, when a wooden-tracked railroad, powered by mules, carried goods as far inland as Sanford.

The town was named for Colonel H.T.Titus, an early resident. Local industrial plants include 5 citrus packing houses, a barrel factory, and a crabmeat packing plant. A Western Union relay station transmits messages from northern points to Miami, Cuba, and South America.

SAND POINT IMPROVEMENT PROJECT, a 67-acre park and recreation center built along the river on reclaimed swampland, contains a yacht basin and a swimming pool. Louis Coleman, a pioneer settler, was the owner of this property when Henry M. Flagler sought to buy it in the early 1890's. Coleman placed an extravagant price on it, and Flagler chose Palm Beach for his planned development.

Titusville is at the junction with State 119 (*see Tour 1B*).

Between Titusville and Indian River City, the highway parallels Indian River, bordered at intervals with tall oleanders.

INDIAN RIVER CITY, 50.9 *m.* (19 alt., 120 pop.) formerly called Clark's Corner, consists of a few stucco houses, filling stations, and a post office, overlooking the broad reaches of the river.

Indian River City is at the junction with State 22 (*see Tour 9*).

South of Indian River City dense growths of palms and pines flank US 1; palmetto thickets and low green shrubbery add to the beauty of the water views.

COCOA, 66.2 *m.* (26 alt., 2,164 pop.), is a citrus shipping center, with groves bordering some of its principal thoroughfares. Orange trees in nearby hammocks have borne fruit, it is said, since 1868. Incorporated in 1895 and named for the coco plum growing abundantly hereabouts, Cocoa was an outgrowth of Rockledge (*see below*). For more than a half-century the town has been popular with fishermen, who can be seen casting from the side platforms of the Indian River bridge, along the Banana River beyond, and in the ocean surf. Pine lands west of town offer a variety of small game.

Left from Cocoa on the old Dixie Highway is ROCKLEDGE, 1.1 *m.* (29 alt., 551 pop.), shaded by oaks and palms, named for its site on a coquina rock formation rising as high as 20 feet above the water.

South of Cocoa small palm-studded peninsulas jut out into Indian River, its quiet waters reflecting the ever-changing sky and cloud formations.

EAU GALLIE, 83.3 *m.* (19 alt., 871 pop.), a name compounded of French and Indian words meaning rocky water, was christened by W.H. Gleason, who, shortly after the War between the States, was commissioned by the Federal Government to make a topographical and agricultural survey of Florida for the purpose of ascertaining whether it was suitable for Negro colonization. Discovering that the natural resources of the country required capital for successful development, he reported adversely; but in 1866 he settled here himself.

Lying on the shores of Indian River and Elbow Creek, Eau Gallie was once a busy port; in 1890 material for Flagler's Royal Poinciana Hotel was brought by rail to this point and transshipped by water to Palm Beach (*see Palm Beach*).

MELBOURNE, 87.7 *m.* (22 alt., 2,677 pop.), named by an Australian for his native city, contains buildings more rococo in style than other Indian River communities. The town is a point of departure for hunting parties going inland to the headwaters of the St.Johns River, where small game and an occasional deer and bear are found (*guides available; inquire at sporting goods stores*). Both fresh- and salt-water fishing attract anglers throughout the year. Melbourne has a golf course (*greens fees* $1.50), and the annual International Motorboat Races are held here during the winter.

Melbourne is at the junction with US 192 (*see Tour* 10).

Left from Melbourne on a bridge across Indian River to INDIATLANTIC, 2.5 *m.* (*see Tour 1B*), and MELBOURNE BEACH, 4.5 *m.*, (72 pop.) (*see Tour 1B*).

Between Melbourne and Fort Pierce are scattered groups of cabbage palms and moss-bearded water oaks between the highway and the river; rows of oleanders have been planted here and there along the waterfront, and rickety piers project into the bayous. On the more substantial piers are fish markets and restaurants specializing in fish dinners. Gulls wheel over the water, and occasionally appears a solitary motionless heron, engaged in his own tireless vigil for fish. Many pleasure craft move southward along the Intracoastal Waterway early in winter, and north again after the season is over.

MALABAR, 94.6 *m.* (26 alt., 138 pop.), named for Cape Malabar on the African coast, consists of several white families and a colony of Negroes employed in a local sawmill.

MICCO (Ind., chief), 103.4 *m.* (25 alt., 100 pop.), has many old houses facing the river, each with its sulphur artesian well. Citrus culture and commercial fishing are the chief occupations.

The new concrete SEBASTIAN RIVER BRIDGE, 105 *m.*, replaced a narrow wooden span that proved to be the Waterloo of south Florida's most notorious band of desperadoes. In November 1924, John Ashley, Hanford Mobley, Ray Lynn, and Bob Middleton, members of the Ashley gang, met death here in a battle with deputy sheriffs after 14 years of bank robbing, highjacking, and rum-running; they were stopped at the bridge by a red lantern and chain, and shot when they resisted arrest.

The SEBASTIAN INLET (L) was dredged by the joint efforts of nearby communities, to provide convenient passage for small shrimp and fishing boats from ocean to river.

SEBASTIAN, 108.8 *m.* (21 alt., 386 pop.), named for St.Sebastian, is a tourist settlement. Tall cabbage palms and Australian pines grow along the waterfront. Piers, racks for drying nets, fish houses, and crab-picking shacks on the river bank contrast with the neat cottages and landscaped lawns that border the opposite side of the highway. In Sebastian, one of the oldest trading posts on the East Coast, river steamers formerly tied up at the foot of Main Street, where pilings of old docks still stand.

Opposite Sebastian is PELICAN ISLAND, a Government bird sanctuary, in which thousands of pelicans and terns spend the winter months.

WABASSO, 113.4 *m.* (20 alt., 300 pop.) is sustained by citrus groves, packing houses, and a sawmill. The Guale Indians migrated to this section from Ossabaw Island, Ga., and the name of the town is Ossabaw spelt backwards.

WINTER BEACH, 115.8 *m.* (31 pop.), surrounded by dark green groves protected by windbreaks of Australian pines, is a citrus center with several large packing plants. Many of the surrounding groves are owned by tourists who spend the winter here.

GIFFORD, 119 *m.* (19 alt., 500 pop.), was named for F.Charles Gifford, credited with having selected the site for Vero Beach (*see below*). He delayed the extension of the Florida East Coast Railway, so the story goes, by placing an excessive price on his land; in retaliation the railway started a settlement here exclusively for Negroes, and named it Gifford. The railroad was built around the Gifford holdings, and the town became the Negro section of Vero Beach.

VERO BEACH, 121.4 *m.* (19 alt., 2,268 pop.), seat of Indian River County, a citrus shipping point, extends across Indian River, known here as The Narrows, to the ocean. The broad streets of its residential section are bordered with coconut, royal and date palms, and a profusion of tropical shrubs.

Among skeletal remains found here along Van Valkenburg's Creek by Dr.E.H.Sellards in 1916 were those of the so-called 'Vero Beach Man,' who for a time was believed to be prehistoric and became the subject of much speculation and controversy among scientists. Later the bones were pronounced those of an Indian of Algonquin origin. Excavations, however, brought to light remains of many extinct mammals, including those of a mastodon.

POCAHONTAS PARK, 14th Ave., and 21st St., a tourist center, offers recreational facilities. An avenue lined with royal and coconut palms, hibiscus, and oleanders, crosses the Intracoastal Waterway to the ocean beach (*casino, bathhouses, fishing*).

Vero Beach is at the junction with State 30 (*see Tour 11*).

US 1 crosses one of several drainage canals, 123.3 *m.*, carrying overflow from bottom lands west of the road. These canals and lateral ditches are part of the Indian River Drainage District projects, covering more than 50,000 acres. The drained lands produce pineapples and winter vegetables.

The MCKEE JUNGLE GARDENS (*adm. $1; children under 14, free; guides for parties*), 124.2 *m.*, were opened in 1931 by Arthur G. McKee, an Ohio industrialist, who during his travels made a hobby of studying tropical plant culture. On an 80-acre tract of jungle here he cleared away only the trees and underbrush required to make room for 2,500 varieties of tropical and subtropical flora. Along winding paths grow thousands of exotic plants, brought from many parts of the world. In the jungle depths flourish rare varieties of orchids, ferns, and flowering vines. In the pools and lagoons float water lilies with unusually large pads. There is a bougainvillea glade, an azalea garden, a mirror pool, and a watery maze. Alligators, parrots, monkeys, and other denizens of the jungle live in an enclosure; many native birds have found sanctuary in the garden.

FORT PIERCE, 136.2 *m.* (24 alt., 4,803 pop.), seat of St.Lucie County, is a citrus and vegetable center; it ships large cargoes of fruit, winter vegetables, fish, and lumber, and receives incoming cargoes of miscellaneous goods for distribution along the central east coast. From a large new pier and warehouse, with pre-cooling facilities for perishable products, steamers sail regularly five times a week to Baltimore and New York. Fertilizer and seed stores, with farm implements displayed for sale, reflect Fort Pierce's interest in agriculture. Occasionally barefoot gayly skirted Seminoles visit the town to do their shopping, hurrying straight to the dime stores, their favorite haunts.

Sixteen cannon and four coral-encrusted anchors were salvaged in 1929 from wrecked vessels lying on a reef north of the town. Because of the heavy encrustations, it has been difficult to determine their exact origin. Dim mouldings on the cannon indicate that they may have been part of the armament of an early French or Spanish vessel. When raised, the cannon were covered with coral and oyster shells, which also encased several large round stones used as ballast in early days. The cannon and anchors were scraped, painted with aluminum, and mounted on the City Hall lawn, in various parks throughout the city, and before the Chamber of Commerce.

Fort Pierce received its name from the fortification built here in 1838 as a link in a chain of east coast defenses against the Indians. It occupied a strategic position on the St.Lucie Inlet, which afforded easy communication by water to the north. Settlers fought off Indian attacks and remained to set out citrus groves and cultivate winter vegetables. Prior to the World War, pineapples were grown extensively in the vicinity. Although disease and adverse tariffs practically ruined local pineapple growers, they have made a new start with the planting of hardier varieties, eradication of pests, and the use of colloidal phosphate fertilizer.

Fort Pierce is at the junction with State 8 (*see Tour* 12).

Section d. *FORT PIERCE to MIAMI;* 122.2 *m.* *US* 1

This section of the route runs the length of what is sometimes called 'Florida's Gold Coast,' a narrow strip of land between the Everglades and the ocean, the State's most popular tourist playground, marked frequently by an ostentatious display of wealth. For long stretches near the larger cities US 1 becomes a veritable Midway, with innumerable signs and loudspeakers ballyhooing sights and sites, amusements, foods, patent medicines, trailer camps, and roadside cabins ranging from one-room frame shacks to elaborate two- and three-room stucco dwellings. Souvenir stands offer carved coconuts, sea shells, honey, guava jelly, and a miscellany of bewildering edibles and mementoes; nurseries exhibit subtropical plants for sale; deep-sea fishing camps, Indian villages, and tropical gardens are blatantly advertised.

South of FORT PIERCE, 0 *m.*, the prevailing vegetation continues to be pine, scrub palmetto, and cabbage palm, varied occasionally with dwarf cedar. Prickly pear grows along the highway, bearing astonishingly large yellow blossoms early in spring. Dodder, a parasitic plant, extends its tangle of golden threads over weeds and undergrowth.

From August to October, Floridians of this section are hurricane-conscious. One day the newspapers report on an inside page the gathering of a tropical storm, usually somewhere in the West Indies, the hurricane incubator of the hemisphere. If the storm is of dangerous intensity and proceeding toward Florida, it 'makes' the front page the following day. As the storm approaches within a few hundred miles of the coast, the news is 'boxed,' accompanied with a diagram charting the storm's course. Radio programs are interrupted by announcements from the weather bureau. On the mainland the wind blows steadily toward the storm center, but the sun shines and people go quietly about their business. If the hurricane shows no signs of shifting its course or diminishing in volume, police and welfare agencies prepare for action. Trucks and busses are sent to evacuate people in outlying sections; they come with their bedding and cooking utensils to set up housekeeping in churches, auditoriums, and other buildings. Merchants remove signs and board up shop windows. Home owners brace their weaker trees, trim off limbs that might fall on roofs. Chimneys are capped and window and door crevices plugged, for the torrential rain does more damage than the wind. Bathtubs and all available receptacles are filled with water for drinking purposes in case the town's pumping plant is disabled; oil lamps and stoves are brought out and filled; stores sell candles by the dozens.

Few outward signs of excitement appear along the streets; citizens move about calmly, listen to sidewalk radio reports, and consult barometers. As the storm strikes inland, the towns along its path, one by one, are cut off from communication with the world as wires go down. A heavy sky and scurrying dirty gray clouds block out the sun. A drizzle begins and turns to rain, followed by a deluge as the wind gradually increases to a lashing gale, accompanied occasionally by lightning and a continuous rumble of thunder scarcely discernible above the roar of wind and rain. All electric power is cut off to avoid danger from live wires. Palms bend to the ground under the howling blast, shaking free their 'hula skirts' of dead fronds; pines are snapped or twisted off; sheds and flimsy roofs fly into space; streets become rivers; stalled cars are abandoned.

Some of the more reckless don bathing suits and venture out, but it is difficult to stand up against the wind. Guests in hotels gather in candle-lit lobbies and hold 'hurricane parties,' but most people remain at home to look after their property.

After a dozen hours at the most, the worst is over, but rain and unsettled weather may continue for several days. Householders and city trucks clean the debris from lawns and streets; fallen trees and poles are removed, and wires restrung. Roofing concerns do a rushing business, carpenters and painters work overtime, until reconstruction is completed. As a rule, the normal community routine is disrupted for several weeks.

WHITE CITY, 5.1 *m.* (32 alt.), second largest community in St.Lucie County, was settled shortly after 1893 by Danish immigrants from Chicago, who became interested in citrus culture here after reading a series of articles on the growing of oranges, written by a Danish newspaperman covering the Chicago World's Fair. They named their one street the Midway for the thoroughfare of that name at the fair, and called their little community White City, for Negroes were excluded. Children and grandchildren of the old settlers still tend the orange and grapefruit groves planted more than 40 years ago.

Between White City and Stuart, US 1 skirts (L), the JENSEN SAVANNA, a low grassy plain dotted with small lakes and ponds, and drained by creeks and branches of the St.Lucie River. This wild territory is popular with hunters of small game and fresh-water anglers (*guides available at Stuart*).

At 15.5 *m.* is the junction with State 140, paved.

Left on this road is JENSEN, 0.5 *m.* (23 alt., 419 pop.), a resort; in this vicinity Menendez (*see History*) established Fort Santa Lucia in 1568 and left a garrison. Indians killed so many of the soldiers that the survivors mutinied, abandoned the fort, and fled to St.Augustine.

The ST.LUCIE INLET, 17.1 *m.*, the southern end of Indian River, is the eastern terminus of the St.Lucie Canal, a link in the Cross-State Canal (*see Tour* 13), by which small craft of six-foot draft can pass from the Atlantic to Lake Okeechobee, and thence down the Caloosahatchee River to the Gulf.

STUART, 18.4 *m.* (14 alt., 1,924 pop.), is important for its fishing grounds. Shark fishing is a profitable occupation here. All varieties of shark—tiger, sand, nurse, hammerhead, and shovel-nose—are sought for their flesh, hides, teeth, bones, livers, fins, and eyes, the lens of which are crystallized and sold to a large market as insets for rings. Barreled in ice and shipped to extracting plants, shark livers yield from 2 to 14 gallons of oil, with higher vitamin-A content than cod liver oil. The tough thick hides are soaked in brine, tanned, and manufactured into novelties. The fins are shipped to China, where they are relished as a delicacy when properly aged and pickled. The flesh is chopped up and utilized as fertilizer.

Sea gulls assemble at the railroad bridge whenever passenger trains are due, impatient to pounce on scraps thrown from the dining cars. Long before a train is sighted by human eyes or before a whistle sounds, the gulls begin to assemble as if familiar with the timetable; freight trains are ignored.

South of Stuart the route traverses extensive sawgrass marshes crisscrossed by drainage ditches, their banks lined with cattails and willows; it bisects pine and palmetto flatlands scarred by fire, and proceeds through another marshy area, the haunt of white and blue herons, which stand in lagoons or roost in the tops of bushy mangroves. Crossing rolling sand dunes, white in the sun, the highway runs along the Intracoastal Waterway, fringed with cabbage palms and mangroves.

HOBE SOUND, 32 *m.*, bordered in places with Australian pines, appeared on maps under its present name as early as 1699. The name is probably a corruption of Jobe (Sp., Jupiter), although the Indians called it Hoe Sound.

At 39.4 *m.* is a junction with an improved road.

Left on this road to the red brick JUPITER LIGHTHOUSE, 0.5 *m.*, first lighted on July 10, 1859. The lighthouse occupies the SITE OF FORT JUPITER, built by early settlers in 1838. Here Thomas Jesup, a commander in the Seminole War, imprisoned 678 Indians and Negroes until they were transported to reservations in the West. The fort was abandoned about 1842, and construction of the light began in 1855. The lighthouse was dark from 1861 to 1865 when all lighthouses along Southern coasts ceased to function at the order of the Confederacy.

JUPITER, 39.9 *m.*, (12 alt., 176 pop.), on the south shore of Jupiter Inlet, is a small trading community (*fishing guides, boats, tackle*).

South of Jupiter the highway offers an almost unobstructed view of the ocean for several miles. The beach is wide and gently sloping, with a sweep of curling white surf; myriad gulls wheel and cry above the long rollers; farther out are fishing boats and often a school of porpoises. Coastwise vessels bound south stand in close to shore here to avoid the powerful current of the Gulf Stream. Sprawling sea grape and palmetto grow on the dunes below the highway. Fields of yellow sea oats ripple in the breeze; cut when fully headed and sprayed with many colors, this grass is sold in curio and souvenir shops. Inland, the dunes sweep up, wave upon wave, covered with scrawny pine, palmetto, and other low green growth, the whole resembling evergreens on an expanse of drifted snow.

A small stone MONUMENT TO THE CELESTIAL RAILROAD (R) commemorates the 8-mile, narrow-gauge road, so called because it connected Jupiter (*see above*) with the near-by settlements of Neptune, Mars, Venus, and Juno (seat of old Dade County from 1889 until superseded by Miami in 1891). A wood-burning locomotive pulled three or four cars up the line and backed them down again, for the road had no switches or turntable.

The SEMINOLE GOLF CLUB (*private*), 45 *m.*, borders the road (L); opposite (R) is the SEMINOLE POLO FIELD (*private*).

RIVIERA, 52.1 *m.*, (19 alt., 811 pop.), lies on the western shore of LAKE WORTH, actually a lagoon 18 miles long, named for Major General William J. Worth, who won the confidence of the Florida Indians and terminated the Seminole War.

The main street is lined with stores, souvenir stands, jooks, filling stations, and a post office. Along the lake front are fish houses, boat sheds, net racks, and wharves. Here lives a colony of Conchs, so named for the variety of shellfish they eat. Other Conchs inhabit the Florida Keys (*see Key West*); both groups are of English stock. Those on the Keys are part Spanish while some of the Riviera Conchs bear evidence of Negro blood, having dark skins, kinky hair, thick lips, and heavy features. Many are descendants of English fishermen who during and after the World War left the Bahamas and settled on Singer's Island, opposite Riviera. The Conchs left their island settlement and removed to the mainland here during the 1920's, when a 'land shark' extravagantly raised rents on Singer's Island.

The men are fishermen; the women and children weave native palmetto into baskets, rugs, purses, and head bands, and fashion fish scales into trinkets, delicate ornaments, and artificial flowers, for sale to tourists. They also import Nassau straw hats from the Bahamas on crawfish boats. These hats are woven from the tender inner fronds of the silver-top and the Bahama palmettoes, more durable than those of Florida. Shredded into long strips of the desired widths, the fronds to be woven into straw hats are first baked in rock ovens until white and properly cured, and then laid out in the open until night dews restore their pliability.

WEST PALM BEACH, 56.9 *m.* (14 alt., 26,610 pop.), occupies a ribbon of land 8 miles long and approximately 2 miles wide along the western shore of Lake Worth. Although it is the business and railroad center for Palm Beach (*see Palm Beach*) on the opposite shore, West Palm Beach, with its large hotels and recreational facilities, is a popular winter resort in its own right. Three ornamental bridges and a ferry connect the two communities.

Coconut palms flourish throughout the business and residential districts; thousands more are set out every year by civic organizations. Bicycles are a popular means of conveyance, but in the closely built-up business area, motorcar congestion has necessitated extensive one-way traffic regulations. Through traffic, southbound, passes over the Old Dixie Highway, and northbound, over US 1, one block to the east. Curio shops display articles fashioned locally of native woods, grasses, shells, and clays. Among the winter attractions is the sailfish fleet, with bases on both sides of the lake, which carries anglers to the Gulf Stream fishing grounds.

A small proportion of the population is of Scandinavian origin, descendants of artisans who were brought here to build the first Palm Beach hotels; others are descendants of New Englanders whose forbears pioneered the district. Negroes live in a colony west of the railroad and find employment as field hands, as gardeners and housemen on Palm Beach estates, and in the hotels of both cities during the winter season.

In 1880, Irving R. Henry homesteaded 130 acres of land embracing all of the present business section. His application for registry stated that his nearest neighbor was 3 miles away, that most of his land was a sandy waste encumbered with swamps, and that he had improved 5 acres at a cost of $500. Thirteen years later Henry Flagler, pioneer railroad builder, having selected the island opposite as the site of his new resort, Palm Beach, purchased Henry's tract and developed it as the commercial section of the new community.

Streets were laid out through the flatwoods; waterworks and other improvements were installed; a post office and schools were established. Stores sprang up rapidly, particularly after the coming of Flagler's East Coast Railway in 1893. When the settlement was incorporated in 1894, it had a population of approximately 1,000, composed almost wholly of workers engaged in building the Royal Poinciana Hotel at Palm Beach.

Wishing to exclude all business enterprises from Palm Beach, Flagler proposed to develop the new town merely as an adjunct to his fashionable colony, but West Palm Beach has long since outgrown its subsidiary position. Until Lake Worth was spanned in 1895, passengers leaving trains in West Palm Beach were ferried across to Palm Beach hotels. The wooden railroad bridge was replaced with the concrete FLAGLER MEMORIAL BRIDGE in 1938.

In 1909 Palm Beach County was created by division of Dade County, and West Palm Beach was designated as the county seat. Although the population grew from 1,700 in 1910 to more than 8,000 in 1920, it retained the atmosphere of a small town. In 1924–26, West Palm Beach shared in the real-estate boom. Approximately 100,000 visitors stormed the city and vicinity, many remaining to become permanent residents. Accommodations were inadequate in spite of the erection of 4,000 new houses, hotels, and apartments. Lots in the outskirts originally priced at $250, sold for $1,000, and then soared to $50,000. The population increased to 30,000. For a time the city limits, expanded to include mushroom developments laid out in flatwoods and on built-up swampy areas, embraced 11 miles of Lake Worth waterfront and included part of the Everglades.

Two projects contributed materially to the city's steady growth. In 1925–26 the WEST PALM BEACH CANAL (*see Tour* 13), extending from Lake Okeechobee to the Atlantic, made the community a focal point of the Everglades reclamation district. In addition to drainage facilities, the canal, deepest and widest in Florida, provided a short water route for small craft between the lake and east coast resorts. At the same time the Seaboard Air Line Railway built its cross-State extension, linking Tampa with the east coast cities; this line opened a rich and hitherto neglected agricultural territory, and West Palm Beach became the outlet for its products.

Tourist trade supplies the major part of the city's income, and the sailfish fleets provide a livelihood for a large number of people.

Tropical storms occasionally sweep the Palm Beaches; those of 1926 and 1928 were notably destructive, but loss of life was largely confined to the region around Lake Okeechobee (*see Tour* 13).

FLAGLER PARK, Flagler Drive between Poinciana and Myrtle Sts., given to the city by the Henry M. Flagler estate in 1907, contains recreational facilities, a municipal amphitheater seating 5,000 (*concerts during winter season*), and the Memorial Library (*open* 11–10 *weekdays*), dedicated in 1934 to local World War veterans. The library contains 15,000 volumes.

The CHRISTIAN SCIENCE CHURCH, foot of Okeechobee Rd., of neoclassic design, has walls of artificial limestone, manufactured locally, with grilles and exterior openings of wrought and cast bronze, and a roof of dark blue terra-cotta tile.

The DOCKMASTERS MUSEUM (*open daily* 8–6), on the Municipal Dock at the foot of 2nd St., has an exhibit of shells, coral, seagrasses, and sponges found in the vicinity.

The DIMICK MONUMENT, corner Railroad Ave. and 5th St., was erected in 1922 in honor of Elisha N. Dimick, 'A Pioneer Who Served His Community Well. Legislator, Developer, and Friend. 1849–1919.'

WOODLAWN CEMETERY, Acacia Rd. and S.Dixie Hwy., was deeded to the city in 1914 by the Henry M. Flagler estate. On the arch that spans the entrance is the inscription, 'That Which Is So Universal As Death Must Be A Blessing.' In the northwest corner of the cemetery a single headstone marks the graves of 69 persons who lost their lives in the Lake Okeechobee area during the hurricane of 1928.

West Palm Beach is at the junction with State 25 (*see Tour* 13).

LAKE WORTH, 61.5 *m.* (21 alt., 5,940 pop.), a tourist town of many bright-colored stucco residences, extends along both shores of the lake of the same name. A municipally owned CASINO (*bathhouses*) faces the ocean. Revenue from municipally owned ice, cold-storage, electric-light, and water plants pay almost all of the town's operating expenses. A municipal golf course (*greens fee* 75¢) is at the foot of Lucerne Ave. The main business section, consisting of several blocks of commercial structures, lies west of US 1.

An OSTRICH AND ALLIGATOR FARM (*adm.* 25¢), 63.2 *m.*, has alligators of all ages, ranging from babies just hatched to a battle-scarred veteran estimated to be 400 years old. Ostriches, crocodiles, monkeys, lemurs, kangaroos, and snakes are also to be seen.

LANTANA, 63.6 *m.* (11 alt., 188 pop.), a tourist community on Lake Worth, was named for a subtropical shrub, common throughout Florida, which bears umbellate heads of small red, yellow, and white flowers.

Left from Lantana 1 *m.* on a paved road and causeway crossing Lake Worth and Hypoluxo Island to LANTANA BEACH.

HYPOLUXO (Ind., *hapo*, mound, and *poloski*, round), 64.7 *m.* (12 alt., 43 pop.), settled in 1873 is one of the oldest communities on Lake Worth. Part of the village is built on a thickly wooded island of the same name, on which are several private estates.

BOYNTON, 67.7 *m.* (19 alt., 1,121 pop.), is a trading center on a sandy ridge in an area of rich farmland extending westward to the Everglades. Many Finnish farmers have settled here.

Left from Boynton 1 *m.* on State 195 across the Intracoastal Waterway to BOYNTON BEACH (*bathhouses, casino, refreshment stand*).

DELRAY BEACH, 72.2 *m.* (20 alt., 1,053 pop.), settled in 1901, is a tourist resort and the center of an area producing beans, peppers, tomatoes, sugar cane, and citrus fruit. Many Michigan farmers of German ancestry have bought farms in the vicinity.

On Atlantic Ave. is DELRAY COUNTRY CLUB AND GOLF COURSE (*greens fee* 50¢). CITY PARK, Atlantic Ave. and Canal, provides picnic and recreation grounds. MUNICIPAL BEACH, foot of Atlantic Ave., offers surf bathing and fishing (*boats and equipment available for deep-sea fishing*).

Left from Delray Beach on Ocean Boulevard to SUNKEN GARDENS (*adm.* 35¢; *guides*), 1.8 *m.*, exhibiting such curiosities as the dainty lipstick flower, the silk-cotton tree, the pelican flower, and the jack-knife tree, bearing fruit often 40 pounds in weight.

GULF STREAM, 2 *m.*, a small settlement, clusters about the wealthy GULF STREAM CLUB (*private*) and its 18-hole golf course. Roads branching from the boulevard are lined with tall Australian pines, coconut palms, and pink and white oleanders. Clumps of royal and cabbage palms grow along the fairways. West of the club is the POLO FIELD, and winding in and out among the trees and shrubbery are bridle paths leading to the stables maintained primarily for polo ponies.

BOCA RATON (Sp., rat's mouth), 80.3 *m.* (17 alt., 447 pop.), a resort, bears the name of an inlet just south of the community. On the landscaped waterfront (L) is the BOCA RATON CLUB (*private*), approached by a wide driveway planted with royal and coconut palms, crotons, bougainvilleas, hibiscus, and oleanders. Originally designed as a hotel by Addison Mizner (*see Palm Beach*), it is an excellent example of Spanish-Gothic architecture treated in the Mizner manner. The club has 650 rooms, 5 patios, an outdoor ballroom, and a swimming pool. A dredged channel connects Lake Boca Raton with the ocean, and permits yachts to moor at the clubhouse docks. The club maintains an 18-hole golf course, riding stables, and gun traps for its members.

DEERFIELD, 82 *m.* (15 alt., 1,483 pop.), center of a farming community producing green beans and peppers as its chief winter crops, was originally called Hillsborough, but adopted its present name about 1907 when deer were plentiful in the hammocks west of the town. Negroes brought here to work the once large pineapple plantations comprise about two-thirds of the population; many have prospered as land owners.

At 88.2 *m.* is the junction with a paved road.

1. Right on this road is POMPANO, 1.2 *m.* (15 alt., 2,614 pop.), originally a fishing village on the ocean but moved inland to its present site after suffering damage in the 1928 hurricane. An engineer surveying the area for the railroad in early days was so delighted with the flavor of a fish served him at dinner that, on learning it was called pompano and abounded in near-by waters, he wrote 'Pompano' on the map as the community's name. The pompano, also known as butterfish for its fine-textured flesh and delicious flavor, is Florida's rarest and choicest food fish, and brings the highest market prices. It can be caught with hook and line, but nets are usually employed. Pompano *papilotte*, baked in a sealed paper bag with an aromatic dressing of herbs, is a dish to please the most fastidious epicure. Somewhat belying the town's name, truck gardening is of first importance. When winter crops of beans and peppers are harvested, northern buyers arrive, and the town's loading platforms and warehouses, deserted for months, become centers of great activity.

2. Left on this road to HILLSBOROUGH LIGHTHOUSE, 3.7 *m.*, on Hillsborough Inlet, named for the Earl of Hillsborough, who was given large land grants here during the English occupation. The lighthouse, completed in 1907, and rising 136 feet above the water, contains a 5,500,000 candlepower light, marking the northern limit of the Florida reef, an underwater coral formation paralleling the lower east coast.

At 95 *m.* is the entrance to the CLYDE BEATTY JUNGLE ZOO, where wild animals are bred and trained for circuses. The animals roam at large in rock grottos, beside reflecting pools and in a Veldt area surrounded by a waterfilled moat, across which the animals never venture.

FORT LAUDERDALE, 97.2 *m.* (10 alt., 8,666 pop.), seat of Broward County, popular winter headquarters of yachtsmen and anglers, occupies the approximate site of a Seminole War fort constructed in 1838, and named for its commander, Major William Lauderdale. NEW RIVER, lined with many piers, flows through the city; its deep slow-moving waters mirror the white hulls, mahogany trim, and gleaming brass of numerous pleasure boats. Tarpon are occasionally caught within the city limits. New River Inlet did not exist until shortly before the American Revolution. William de Brahm (*see Literature*), surveyor for the king of England, described its creation, reporting that 'the great Rains . . . filled this River to its marshes with so much water that its weight within and the sea without, by force of the N.E. gales, demolished the N.E. bank and made this inlet between the 25th and 30th of May, 1765.'

More than 100 miles of natural and artificial waterways wind through Fort Lauderdale. Some canals were dug to stimulate commerce and agriculture; others were designed to enhance the charms of boom-time subdivisions containing artificial islands reached by Venetian bridges.

When the roads are dry in winter, Seminole come into Fort Lauderdale to sell hides and game, see the sights, and shop for food and such bright wares as the dime stores display. Along the streets the men, aloof and stolid, stride ahead of the women. The skirts of the women are fashioned of narrow strips of bright-colored cotton cloth, called *fock-see-kees*, and reach to their ankles. High-necked blouses of the same material and pattern fall in folds below the waist. Every woman coils her shining black hair, and wears strands of red, yellow, and blue beads around her neck; rhinestone brooches and jingling silver coins decorate her blouse. The men have adopted the white man's trousers and slouch hats, but cling to their own bright blouses. Shoes are seldom worn, and only by men. The dress of the children resembles that of their elders.

COLEE MONUMENT stands in a little wooded park on the shore of Tarpon Bend in the New River. Here, in the heart of Colee Hammock, now a residential section of Fort Lauderdale, occurred a massacre (1842) by Seminole Indians under the leadership of Arpeika, known also as Sam-Jones-be-Damned, a powerful medicine man of the Mikasuki. A member of the tribe had been friendly with the whites and was caught while trying to warn them of the attack; bound to a tree, he was forced to witness the slaying of his friends and then had his ears cropped, upper right and lower left. Deprived of his Indian name, Crop-ear Charlie, as he came to be called, was driven into the Everglades, with only a hunting knife and a few rags, and told that after seven years he might approach the camp and ask for another trial. Seven years later, in June, at the time of the Green Corn Dance, when the council met to pass on violations of tribal laws, Crop-ear Charlie appeared and was given permission to live near the tribe, although forbidden to eat, sleep, hunt, or marry with his people, and was denied his Indian name. To all questions about him the required answer was, 'I don't know anything.' Crop-ear Charlie lived beyond the century mark, dying in a shack near the present town of Dania (*see below*).

Near Las Olas Boulevard is the HOTEL AMPHITRITE, built of the remodelled superstructure of the *Amphitrite*, one of three monitors constructed by the Federal Government about 1893 for coastal defense. When monitors were found difficult to manage, the *Amphitrite* was sold and converted into a sea-going night club; as such, it plied up and down the Florida coast. In 1935, while anchored near the local Coast Guard Base, a hurricane tore it loose from its moorings, hurled it across the Intracoastal Waterway, and beached it high on the sand. In 1936 it was removed a few hundred feet east to its present site and transformed into a hostelry.

U.S. COAST GUARD BASE No.6, at Las Olas Beach, succeeded one of the houses of refuge constructed by the Federal Government in 1888 at 25-mile intervals along the lower Florida east coast, which was then poorly charted. The houses sheltered not only shipwrecked sailors, but travelers and local residents during hurricanes.

Left from Fort Lauderdale on the old Dixie Highway, which approximately follows the Capron Trail, built during the Seminole War. Cut bit by bit through dense jungle, the trail connected Fort Dallas (*see Miami*) with Fort Capron, erected by Captain Erastus Capron 5 miles north of Fort Pierce (*see above*). Having served its purpose in cutting the Seminole off from their source of supply in Cuba, the trail was abandoned at the end of the war and, in many places, became obliterated. Travel between Palm Beach and Miami continued to be very difficult until the building of the railroad in 1896. The traveler had either to go by boat or to walk 66 miles along a lonely beach. Those who walked usually accompanied the postman who carried the mail from Palm Beach to Miami on foot, for he was the only one who knew the trail, having boats hidden at the numerous inlets, across which he ferried his passengers. The postman received $5 from each traveler who made the trip.

At 99.1 *m.* is the junction with a rock paved road.

Left on this road to PORT EVERGLADES, 3 *m.*, a port of call for vessels in the European, Cuban, and South American trade. A swampy wasteland in 1926, Port Everglades has been transformed into one of Florida's more prosperous ports. Local contributions financed the $4,500,000 dredging and reclamation operations that have created here a 35-foot harbor, a large turning basin, and a channel 200 feet wide. Warehouses, gasoline tanks, and storage sheds line the waterfront; docks and piers, the largest 1,200 feet long, project into the harbor.

Unlike most Florida ports, Port Everglades is not engaged primarily in coastwise commerce. With the exception of petroleum products, the bulk of its traffic is with foreign ports, its freight moving usually in tramp steamers and ships under special charters, but it is a regular port of call for ships of the French Line plying to Antwerp and Marseilles, of the Pan American Steamship Company operating to Cuba, of the Refrigerated Steamship Line, and numerous tanker lines transporting oil for the Standard Oil Company, American Oil Company, Belcher Oil Company, and Shell Petroleum Corporation. Since 1935, when a hurricane washed away the railroad to Key West, Port Everglades has been the terminus of the Florida East Coast Railway car ferries to Havana, Cuba.

South of Fort Lauderdale appear outcroppings of Miami oölite, a limestone used as road material and railroad ballast. Limestone rarely supports much vegetation, but on higher and drier parts of this sandy, cross-bedded deposit grow forests of Caribbean pine and saw palmetto.

A BANYAN TREE (L), 99.7 *m.*, is known as the 'two-million-dollar tree.' This native of East India has a large smooth trunk, and from its limbs sends down slender, vinelike branches that take root and develop into secondary trunks, in time forming a whole grove. A boom-time yarn relates that a tourist offered $2,000,000 for the huge tree, provided that it could be transplanted to his estate in the north, and provided also that it survived the cold.

DANIA, 101.9 *m.* (12 alt., 1,674 pop.), a tomato-growing center, occupies part of an area known during the Seminole Wars as Five Mile Hammock. Of the many Danish families who migrated here in 1896 and subsequently named the town, little trace remains.

Right from Dania on Davie Road to the SEMINOLE INDIAN RESERVATION, 4 *m.*, where Indian affairs of the entire State are managed. THE DEPARTMENT OF INTERIOR BUILDING, a large white frame house with a high gabled roof, contains the office of the Indian agent. Its austere architecture contrasts sharply with the predominating styles in southern Florida. The dozen or more small, white, one-room-and-porch houses occupied by the Seminole here are totally unlike their palmetto-thatched huts in the Everglades (*see Tour* 5). The reservation has a businesslike air; here the Seminole are not on display, along with alligators and rattlesnakes, as in amusement parks in Miami. Jobs are provided for the Indians, who live here permanently or for as long as they desire.

THE FIRST SEMINOLE BAPTIST CHURCH was built by the Indians at the reservation with contributed materials, and dedicated in the summer of 1936. In charge of the ceremonies was Holy Canard, an Indian from Oklahoma, who distributed printed business cards declaring that he held a formal commission from the President as 'principal chief of the Creek nation.'

HOLLYWOOD, 104. 8 *m.* (7 alt., 2,869 pop.), founded in 1921 by Joseph W. Young and associates from California, is another 'tailor-made' city; the business and residential districts were platted before the mangrove swamps and salt marshes on which they rest were filled in. A city of hotels, apartment houses, attractive shops, pleasant houses, and beach cottages, Hollywood is a popular winter resort. The prevailing style of its houses and buildings in white, buff, and pink stucco, with gray and red roofs, is the conventional Florida-Mediterranean.

Hollywood's history is typical of that of many towns founded during the real-estate boom of the 1920's. Some have become ghost towns in the flatwoods; some of the more fortunate, like Hollywood, withstood the violent strain of deflation and have survived.

During early days of development here, 1,500 trucks and tractors were engaged in clearing land and grading streets; two blocks of pavement were laid each day. Hollywood Boulevard, the first to be cleared, was in its time the widest paved thoroughfare in Florida. A cement broadwalk two miles long was built along the waterfront; two yacht basins, designed by General George Washington Goethals, chief engineer in the construction of the Panama Canal, were dredged and connected with the Intracoastal Waterway. A large power plant was installed, and when the city lights went on for the first time, ships at sea reported that Miami was on fire, and their radio alarms and the red glow in the sky brought people to the rescue from miles around.

Hollywood had a fleet of 21 busses constantly on the road, traveling 1,000 miles and more to bring in prospective purchasers of lots, who were given free hotel accommodations, refreshments, and entertainment, 'with no obligation to buy.' They were driven about the city-to-be on trails blazed through palmetto thickets; so desolate and forlorn were some stretches that many women became hysterical, it is said, and a few fainted. A large tent served both as office and auditorium, in which guests received lectures twice a day. Society leaders and titled personages of Europe were given choice sites to induce others to purchase lots near by. Golf, swimming, and tennis champions were brought in to demonstrate their prowess and act as instructors at new courses, pools, and courts. Men prominent in business, politics, and the arts were hired to stimulate sales, either by pep talks or personal contacts. Some became so enthusiastic, perhaps influenced by their own oratory, that they organized 'cities' of their own. Every salesman had his 'bird dogs,' who met trains and busses, talked to passing motorists at filling stations, restaurants, and hot-dog stands, or roamed at large, rounding up prospects.

Auctions were popular, both for the Grand Opening, and whenever sales lagged. Patrons were attracted by blaring bands, free banquets, vaudeville shows, and the drawing of lottery tickets. Doctors, dentists, merchants, barbers, and motormen abandoned professions, trades, and prosperous businesses to become real-estate salesmen. Anyone could obtain a license, either to set up on his own or to join a large sales organization. Today, as a result of past experience, applicants for a license must have been a resident of the State for 6 months, must furnish character references and credentials detailing their activities for the preceding 10 years, and must pass a rigid examination on real-estate law and finance.

At the beginning raw land could be bought at $100 to $1,000 an acre; the cost of grubbing ranged from $30 to $100; the surfacing of streets and the laying of sidewalks added $500 to $1,000 to the cost of an acre, which was usually divided into five 50-foot lots. Landscaping costs ran as high as the promoter's imagination and purse allowed him to go. Whole developments were planted with 2-foot Australian pines at 10¢ each; others, with 20-foot royal palms at $100 to $200 each. Spectacular publicity campaigns were launched locally and on a national scale. One promoter with a lavish development in south Florida spent $3,000,000 on advertising in less than a year.

On the ocean is the municipal BATHING CASINO, with three bathing pools, two for children, and one for adults. The MUNICIPAL GOLF COURSE (*green fees* $1) lies west of 36th Ave.

RIVERSIDE MILITARY ACADEMY, Hollywood Blvd., occupies a boom-time hotel; it holds winter terms here, and fall and spring terms in Gainesville, Ga.

At the MUNICIPAL BAND SHELL, in Center Park, concerts are given throughout the season by the Riverside Military Band and others. FIREMAN PARK, Polk and 19th Ave., is interesting for its rose gardens, rock garden, and pool containing rare lilies and tropical fish. Facilities for shuffleboard and horseshoe pitching are provided in TOURIST CLUB PARK, Taylor St. and 18th Ave.

On Hollywood Blvd. between 19th and 20th Aves., is a GROVE OF CAJEPUT TREES. This tree, also known as the punk tree, provides the green cajeput oil used in salves, ointments, and oils for treatment of coriza and other respiratory troubles; its thick, creamy, parchmentlike bark is sometimes used for polishing furniture and floors, and for mops. In late autumn the cajeput bears aromatic white flowers, shaped like a bottle brush. A quick-growing ornamental tree, it is in demand for landscaping purposes.

OJUS (Ind., plentiful), 109.8 *m.* (13 alt., 600 pop.), originally an Indian trading post, was so named because of the luxuriant vegetation in the vicinity. A large quarry and a concrete block manufacturing plant are in operation here.

GREYNOLDS PARK, on the western edge of town, was built by CCC labor. Above stone walls rises the castlelike turret of an OBSERVATION TOWER, patterned on an Aztec temple, with a ramp spiraling to the top. Sweeping green lawns surround a stone pavilion, a structure architecturally in keeping with the English stone cottage of the caretaker. To the west are picnic grounds in a hammock covered with large stands of glossy Caribbean pines.

NORTH MIAMI BEACH, 110.2 *m.* (522 pop.), formerly called Fulford for an early settler, changed its name in the hope of becoming the railway terminal for Miami Beach, which lacks such facilities.

The NORTH MIAMI ZOO (*open* 9–6:30 *daily; adm.* 25¢ *children* 15¢), NE. 2nd Ave. and 132nd St., was formerly known as the Opa Locka Zoo. It has more than 200 exhibits, including 3,000 tropical birds and animals, and a reptile collection of unusual variety. An animal show is conducted every afternoon at 4 o'clock and hourly on Sunday afternoons, when trained monkeys, ponies, dogs, and birds are exhibited. Giant Galapagos turtles were sent here by the New York Zoological Society in an effort to prevent the species from becoming extinct. Many of these mammoth land turtles, although still relatively young, weigh 200 pounds. When brought to the zoo, they weighed about 7 pounds and may eventually attain a weight of 800 pounds.

At 111 *m.* is the junction with Golden Glades Road, also called Sunny Isles Road.

Left on this road 2 *m.* across salt marshes to SUNNY ISLES CLUB (*private*); near by is a fishing pier (*nominal charge*).

Right from Sunny Isles Club on State 140 3.7 *m.* to BAKER'S HAULOVER (*boats, bait, fishing tackle*), a bridge crossing an outlet of upper Biscayne Bay, where a long stone jetty extends into the ocean. Before the outlet was dredged, fishermen hauled their boats on rollers across the narrow sand strip between the ocean and bay, both to escape storms and to avoid a long sail around the end of the spit.

At 112 *m.* is a junction with the old Dixie Highway, heavily traveled during the boom but seldom used today.

Right on this road to ARCH CREEK NATURAL BRIDGE, 0.5 *m.*, a geological formation carved in oölitic (Latin, egglike) rock. The bridge has been used since early Spanish days. A hundred years ago, it was part of the Capron Trail (*see above*), over which United States soldiers marched in their successful efforts to cut off the Seminole from their source of supply in Cuba, thus ending the long war. At the south end of the bridge is (R) the SITE OF LUIS THE BREED'S STONE HOUSE AND MILL, where Seminole and Federal troops engaged in one of many bitter battles during the war. Luis, part Indian and part Cuban, was a link in the line of communication between the Seminole and Cuba; within his stone walls he stored supplies for the Indians. Advised of the fact, General W.S.Harney and his men advanced to destroy the base. The Seminole took shelter behind the walls, in the near-by woods, and in canoes in the black shadows beneath the bridge, but General Harney succeeded in routing them and demolishing the house and mill. In the melee Luis was killed, and the demoralized Indians retreated into the Everglades. No plaque marks the spot.

The route crosses ARCH CREEK, 112.9 *m.*, as it courses through a pleasant valley.

MIAMI, 122.2 *m.* (10 alt., 110,637 pop.) (*see Greater Miami*).

Points of Interest: Old Fort Dallas, Miami Aquarium, International Airport, Hialeah Race Track, Ocean Beaches, Indian villages, and others.

In Miami is the junction with US 94 (*see Tour* 5).

Section e. MIAMI to KEY WEST; 174.8 *m. State* 4*A*

An extension of US 1, State 4A, known as the Overseas Highway, crosses the southeastern fringe of the Everglades to Card Sound, over which it passes to Key Largo, first and largest link in the long chain of islands terminating at Key West, more than 100 miles out in the Gulf. The highway almost literally 'puts to sea' to reach its destination, crossing great expanses of water on a ribbon of concrete laid on long causeways and bridges. The waters of the Atlantic (L) and the Gulf (R) are frequently in view, an opalescent sheen of lilac, aquamarine, and indigo, reflecting towering cloud formations of blue and rose at sunset.

The history of the Overseas Highway, formally opened on July 4, 1938, is closely linked with that of the overseas extension of the Florida East Coast Railway, completed by Henry M. Flagler to Key West in 1912, at a cost of $50,000,000 and the lives of 700 workers. As early as 1831 proposals and abortive attempts had been made to construct a railroad along the keys.

Flagler, an associate of John D. Rockefeller and a pioneer railroad builder (*see St.Augustine and Palm Beach*) began the project in 1905. Men of many nations were employed—Scandinavians; Spaniards and Cubans; Negroes from the Bahamas, Lesser Antilles and Grand Cayman; deep-sea divers from Greece; and a large number of Americans. Several hundred deaths and long delays in construction were caused by hurricanes in 1906, 1909, and 1910, leading many Floridians to name the project 'Flagler's Folly.' Every kind of construction, from the simplest piling and rock filling to the reinforced viaduct at Long Key, was used. The foundation for one pier required a mixture of sand, gravel, and cement, equal in bulk to the cargo of a five-masted schooner. The opening of the line was celebrated in January 1912, and in 1915 train service to Cuba was instituted by means of a large car ferry between Key West and Havana.

The real-estate boom of the 1920's stimulated a demand for the construction of a highway parallel to the railroad. In 1923 the Dixie Highway was extended southeast from Florida City to the coast, and by 1928 it had been extended to Key West, except for a 40-mile gap, across which ferry service was maintained. The State legislature created the Overseas Road and Toll Bridge District in 1933 to bridge the water gap. World War veterans were brought in by the FERA in 1934 to aid in the construction of the project. Hundreds of the veterans were drowned (*see below*) in the hurricane of September 2, 1935, which swept away 41 miles of Florida East Coast tracks and trestles. This led the company to abandon its extension; its bridges and right-of-way were purchased for $640,000.

Financed by a $3,600,000 loan from PWA, the work of converting railroad bridges into highway spans began in November 1936; the first section was opened on January 1, 1938, and the entire road six months later. As the nearest fresh-water supply was 100 miles distant, specifications allowed salt water to be used in mixing cement. Rock was quarried along the route; sand was brought in by barge.

In the 44-mile stretch between Lower Matecumbe and Big Pine keys are 13 miles of bridges. All rest on concrete piers anchored to bedrock, some in 30 feet of water.

If and when the proposed eastern branch of the Pan-American Highway is established, the Overseas Highway will form an important part of the route planned to link Labrador and Guatemala City. As projected, the highway will carry vehicles from the Florida mainland to Key West, whence they will be ferried 90 miles across the Gulf to Cuba. Crossing the island on the Cuban National Highway, they will be ferried 110 miles to the Yucatan Peninsula; and proceed 500 miles southwest to Guatemala City, where the highway will connect with the present Pan-American Highway, which enters Mexico at Laredo, Texas.

South of MIAMI, 0 *m.*, State 4A runs through the fertile Redlands section, producing citrus fruits and winter vegetables.

At 6.3 *m.* is CORAL GABLES (11 alt., 5,697 pop.), an elaborate development, its architecture predominantly Florida-Mediterranean, one of the few boom-time cities to survive (*see Greater Miami*).

SOUTH MIAMI, 9 *m.* (1,160 pop.), originally named Larkins for an early storekeeper, was given its present name the day after his death. Several plants here pack tomatoes, truck crops, and citrus for shipment to market. South of the town are abandoned limestone quarries (L), filled with clear water and used as swimming pools.

KENDAL, 11.5 *m.* (13 alt., 345 pop.), a citrus settlement, contains the DADE COUNTY HOME AND HOSPITAL.

PERRINE, 16 *m.* (13 alt., 1,054 pop.), was named for Dr.Henry Perrine, physician-botanist, who in 1835 equipped a plant laboratory on Indian Key (*see below*), on which to conduct experiments with tropical plants; he introduced the sisal (*Agave rigida*), popularly called the century plant, which now has spread over south Florida.

PETERS, 17 *m.* (13 alt., 175 pop.), was named for Tom Peters, an early tomato grower, who in pre-railroad days ran a mule tramline to Cutler, whence he shipped his produce north by boat. The hamlet remains a tomato-growing center.

At 20 *m.* is the junction with paved road.

Right on this road to the TROPICAL MONKEY JUNGLE (*adm.* 25¢), 0.8 *m.*, in which Java monkeys run wild in a gumbo limbo hammock.

GOULDS, 22 *m.* (12 alt., 490 pop.), is a packing-plant town. Neighboring citrus groves and truck gardens provide a steady stream of produce to be crated and packed for shipping. Irish potatoes are one of the principal crops.

PRINCETON, 24 *m.* (12 alt., 300 pop.), a citrus and winter vegetable center, was known as Modello until 1905 when several university graduates established a sawmill here and erected a large sign bearing the name of their alma mater, Princeton. The sign was repeatedly removed and as frequently reappeared, until the Florida East Coast Railway finally adopted the name.

1. Right from Princeton on Coconut Palm Road is the REDLAND FARM LIFE SCHOOL, 2.3 *m.*, attended by pupils from a large area.

2. Left from Princeton on Coconut Palm Road to the ALLAPATTAH GARDENS (Ind., alligator), 2 *m.*, where, in winter, acres of sweet peas bloom.

At 26 *m.* is the junction with Newton Road.

Right on this road 0.5 *m.* to the FENNEL ORCHID JUNGLE (*open daily during winter; adm.* 25¢), containing hundreds of varieties of orchids, both native and transplanted. Among the more brilliant are the large Cattelya hybrid, with splashes of deep purple about a vivid yellow center; the Phalaenopsis, mottled with white; the Calanthe, with wine-colored hearts in the center of its small white blossoms; and the Albino, yellow-throated, with long curving petals. New varieties are developed here by cross-pollination.

The seeds, about 1,000,000 to the pod, are so minute that a podful can be held in a teaspoon. The seeds are planted in a bell-shaped container on a layer of specially prepared jelly, which supplies food for their initial growth. Sterilized to exclude fungus growths that might destroy the seeds, the container is placed in a glass incubator. One year after planting, the tender shoots are but a fraction of an inch high. They are then transplanted to pots filled with fiber. By the fifth year, perhaps one in twenty will blossom. Some do not bloom until the tenth year, a few not until the fifteenth.

HOMESTEAD, 30 *m.* (9 alt., 2,319 pop.), the trading center of the Redlands fruit and winter-vegetable area, developed rapidly from a primitive backwoods town into a modern community with the coming of the railroad in 1904. In the rich muck soil here on the border of the Everglades flourish many fine groves of oranges, grapefruit, kumquats, limes, avocados, and papayas, and extensive fields of tomatoes and potatoes. The HOMESTEAD AVOCADO EXCHANGE ships several thousand carloads of the fruit each season.

The SUBTROPICAL EXPERIMENTAL STATION, Waldin Drive, conducted by the University of Florida and the Dade County Commission in conjunction with the U.S. Department of Agriculture, devotes itself to research on the problem of raising citrus, avocados, and winter vegetables under subtropical conditions. Its experiments in cross-pollination have produced such hybrids as the tangelo, a cross between the tangerine and the pomelo, or grapefruit; the tangor, sprung from the tangerine and orange; and the limequat, from the lime and kumquat.

The JOHNSTON PALM LODGE (*open*), Krome Ave. and Avocado Rd., is the estate of Colonel H.W.Johnston, formerly a hardware merchant of Lebanon, Kentucky, who came to Homestead in 1912 and adopted horticulture as a hobby. The estate has on its 20 acres more than 8,000 varieties of tropical plants and trees, including more than 1,500 varieties of palms. Here grows the sago palm, said by scientists to have been the first plant to appear on earth millions of years ago. From its seeds is made the finest starch. Almost 270 kinds of tropical fruits are grown here, from which almost 100 different jellies and preserves are made and offered for sale, including East Indian mango chutney, a potpourri of 40 fruits and spices. About the base of the Java Jak tree lies its tremendous fruit, piled up like wine kegs, for a single fruit often weighs 100 pounds. Around the trunks of many of the trees winds the thin stem of the tall climbing orchid that produces the bean from which vanilla is extracted.

FLORIDA CITY, 31 *m.*, (9 alt., 452 pop.), its main street lined with royal palms, was incorporated in 1913; it was called Detroit until the Post Office Department objected.

Right from Florida City on State 205 is ED'S PLACE (10¢), 1 *m.*, a house of oölitic rock equipped with huge rock furnishings; it has massive chairs weighing from 700 to 1,500 pounds, a 3,000-pound rock couch, tables, beds, and rocking chairs. A map of Florida has been hewn from a one-ton slab, in which a punch bowl filled with clear water represents Lake Okeechobee.

The road crosses the eastern boundary of ROYAL PALM STATE PARK, 14 *m.*, a 4,000-acre tract of dense hammock, set aside as a wild-life sanctuary. The State Federation of Women's Clubs acquired the initial 960 acres in 1915 through a grant from the Florida legislature, and added 960 acres donated by Mrs. Mary Lily Kenan Flagler in the same year. The legislature added 2,080 additional acres in 1921. Although under State jurisdiction, the Federation supervises and cares for the area, which will become part of the proposed Everglades National Park (*see Tour* 5). Wild turkey, quail, waterfowl, raccoon, opossum, skunk, otter, bear, wildcat, and deer abound in the park; more than 140 varieties of birds have been identified in the sanctuary. Alligators wallow in the swamps, poking their snouts out of water. Multicolored tree snails and strangely marked butterflies, including the rare sleeping Heliconiidae, add their brightness to the scene.

State 205 leads into PARADISE KEY, a 300-acre hammock on the eastern edge of the park, surrounded by glade water and covered with luxuriant growth. Much of the vegetation is West Indian in character, and may have been seeded here by migratory birds or hurricane winds. Giant royal palms rise from enlarged bases, their pale gray trunks, tinted with orange, stretching upward to full crowns of 10- and 12-foot leaves, high above the surrounding forest. Great oaks, more than 60 feet high, support orchids with stalks 3 feet thick and leaves 5 feet long. There are 31 varieties of ferns, some 27 feet high, with 15-foot fronds. Seeds of strangler figs, dropped by birds on the branches of trees, grow into small air plants that send threadlike roots to the ground. Gripping the host tree, the roots grow and thicken, squeezing it to death; then the roots grow up and around the dead tree, 'swallowing' it, forming a false outer trunk.

At 14.2 *m.*, in the interior of the hammock, is the ROYAL PALM LODGE (*open all year; free picnic grounds*). South of the Lodge the route is paved for 26 miles, and thereafter is an unimproved road, following the southernmost drainage canal of the Everglades. The banks (R) are flanked for nearly 35 miles with buttonwood trees, and gallberry and elderberry bushes. In the distance are cypress hammocks and islands formed and covered by mangroves. In places forests of dead mangrove trees, their trunks twisted grotesquely, reveal the devastating power of the hurricane that swept the region on September 2, 1935.

On the shore of FLORIDA BAY is the rebuilt hamlet of FLAMINGO, 48.5 *m.* (21 pop.), the southernmost settlement on the Florida mainland. In 1930 it contained 25 houses and shacks occupied by fishermen who seined the near-by waters. Destroyed by the 1935 hurricane, it now consists of 6 buildings raised on stilts for protection against high water. On weekdays fishermen spread their nets in shallow Florida Bay for channel bass, mullet, grouper, salt-water trout, and mackerel. The catch is carried back to the fish houses and iced to await the arrival of large refrigerator trucks from Miami.

Grouper, trout, and tarpon in Florida Bay provide excellent sport fishing (*equipment and guides available at Flamingo; no accommodations; camp sites*). Food and water should be carried, for the only drinking water is rainwater from the roofs of shacks, and is not always plentiful.

The flamingo, for which the settlement was named, was once a familiar sight in the region, although native to the West Indies. John J. Audubon, the naturalist, noted them along the coast here in 1832, but found no evidence of a nesting colony. 'Their lovely forms,' wrote Audubon, 'appeared to be arrayed in more brilliant apparel than I have seen before, and as they gamboled in happy playfulness among the bushes, or glided over the light green waters, we longed to form a more intimate acquaintance with them.' Between 1890 and 1902 flocks aggregating 1,000 birds were observed along the shallow bays to the west. The last recorded capture of a flamingo occurred at Lake Worth (*see above*) in 1905; small flocks have been seen recently (1938) near Cape Sable.

The flamingo has a small oddly shaped body, with a long neck, slender yellow legs, webbed feet, and a broad curved bill, colored black and orange. Fledglings are covered with fuzzy white feathers, which gradually change to rose red within a year. The flamingo lives on small shellfish dug up in shallow water and swallowed whole, and twists its neck in such a way when feeding that its head is upside down.

Southeast of Florida City the highway runs in a straight line across a yellow-green flat savanna, with scattered rises of darker hammock, the southern extremity of the Everglades prairie. Herons feed in the canal along the road; an occasional eagle or hawk sits on a near-by mangrove; red-winged blackbirds and boat-tailed grackles are numerous.

On CARD SOUND BRIDGE, 43.7 *m.*, the highway crosses from the mainland to KEY LARGO, some 30 miles long and less than 2 miles wide, the northernmost of the chain of limestone and coral islands that extend in a sweeping curve to Key West, more than 100 miles out in the Gulf. The northern half of the chain consists of an old coral reef on the edge of the peninsular plateau, along which runs the Gulf Stream. The southern half formerly consisted of a single large limestone island, raised above the sea during the first Pleistocene era and later partially submerged.

Key is an English modification of cayo (Sp., small island). The designation in French patois is similar (*aux cayes*), which is also the name of a city in Haiti, renowned in early days for its rum. Pronounced 'O. K.,' it is said by some to be the source of the American slang expression. Others contend that the expression gained currency because Andrew Jackson, when president, endorsed official documents with the two letters, signifying that the documents were 'Oll Korrect.' Competent authorities, however, derive the term from the Choctaw oke, or hoke, (yes, it is).

All Florida fruits grow on the keys—coconuts, bananas, oranges, grapefruit, lemons, limes, tangerines, pineapples, guavas, avocados, papayas, mangoes, pomegranates, breadfruit, coco plums, tangeloes (*see above*), and kumquats, the smallest of the citrus family. Rarer fruits include the spherical roseapple; the acid-flavored tamarind, slightly curved, with glossy seeds; red berrylike Chinese dates; sticky Chinese limes; orange-yellow eggfruit, sweet and pasty; the Natal plum, with firm red pulp; juicy green-skinned Spanish limes; refreshing yellow loquats, or Japanese plums; purple star apples; spicy red Surinam cherries; and sugar apples, sweet and custardlike.

Very little is known of the aboriginal inhabitants of the keys. The Arawak and Caribee tribes were probably the first in the region, as evidenced by the discovery of pottery with incised designs in the many mounds along the keys. These tribes were driven out by the Calusa, who were skilled seamen, fishermen, and fierce fighters. The Calusa are known to have had at least two villages on the keys, Cuchiyago and Guarugunve, in which they accumulated much gold from wrecked and pillaged vessels.

Just north of Key Largo lies BLACK CAESAR'S ROCK (*accessible only by boat*), a tiny island between Old Rhodes and Elliott Keys, once a pirate stronghold. Although many different and conflicting tales are told of his depredations, Black Caesar, it is generally agreed, was a Negro who escaped from a wrecked slave ship. For a time he engaged in wrecking ships single-handed, having captured his first prize in that way; pretending to be adrift in an open boat, he was picked up by a small sloop and soon disposed of its captain and those of the crew who refused to join him. On the Island, embedded in the rock, is a huge iron ring, reputedly used by Caesar to heel over his ship so that its masts could not be seen by passing vessels.

Black Caesar became a trusted lieutenant of the notorious Teach, better known as Blackbeard. Flying the skull and crossbones, their ship, the *Queen Ann's Revenge*, was captured by Lieutenant Robert Maynard in 1718. Teach was killed during the battle, sustaining 25 wounds before he fell dead. Caesar attempted to blow up the ship and all on board by dropping a match into the powder magazine, but one of the men prevented him. Taken to Virginia, Black Caesar was hanged.

Black Caesar's cruelty, his love of luxury, his passion for jewels, and his ambition to rule these waters have become legendary. More than 100 women, it is said, graced his harem. Some evidence exists for the story that in the vicinity of Elliott Key he maintained a prison camp, incarcerating his prisoners and enemies in stone huts. Later, he abandoned the camp, leaving the prisoners to starve. Almost all perished, but a few small children escaped to wander about the key, subsisting on berries and shellfish, and in time developing a primitive language of their own. These savage creatures may account for the Seminole legend that the region was haunted.

Southward, the aspect of the key changes as the highway enters rolling hammock country. Only a few scattered houses appear along the road, although sand trails lead through dense forests of hardwood to secluded farms and groves along the waterfront. In the spring the shoulders of the road are bright with wild flowers. Huge grapevines and other creepers all but conceal the trees that support them.

On the keys grow 27 varieties of hardwood, some so heavy they will not float in water—notably, the madeira, tamarind, mahogany, crabwood, sarilla, granadilla, and black ironwood, a cubic foot of which weighs 81 pounds. Among the toughest of woods is the gnarled, silver-barked lignum vitae, used in the manufacture of mallet heads and bowling balls. Button wood is used locally as fuel, for it burns with intense heat and little smoke.

South of the hammock, lime groves border the highway, with wild tamarind and other hardy trees as windbreaks. The groves, haphazardly planted, are not always recognized by those familiar with the straight rows of trees in citrus groves farther north. Limes, the chief fruit of the keys, are small and quite juicy. The tree flourishes in leaf mould, thin soil, or equally well in rock crevices. A good grove yields an annual profit of more than $100 an acre, but hurricanes are ever a menace.

ROCK HARBOR, 64.9 *m.* (12 alt., 131 pop.), a fishing village surrounded by lime groves, has (L) a 30-foot observation tower, a square stucco structure anchored by cables to bedrock. From the tower is a wide view of Florida Bay and the Atlantic, their shores lined with racks on which fishing nets hang drying in the sun.

TAVERNIER, 71.3 *m.* (10 alt., 91 pop.), was named for the creek that winds past the southern end of Key Largo, said to have been a favorite hiding place of Tavernier, associate of Jean La Fitte, the pirate. 'Tavern-ear,' as local people call their hamlet, was merely a railroad station until the boom of the 1920's, when an enterprising promotor purchased much land here, installed public utilities, built a lumber shed, a moving-picture theater, and other facilities.

At Tavernier are some of the 'hurricane-proof' houses built on the keys by the American Red Cross and the FERA. The average four-room house of reinforced concrete construction contains approximately 80,000 pounds of steel; steel rods anchor the house to solid rock. The roof, floors, and walls are of concrete, the walls a foot thick. All partitions extend from the roof through the house to bedrock. Window sashes are of steel, with double-strength glass and double shutters. Wood is used only in the triple-strength cypress doors. Drain pipes run from the roof to a cistern cut in the bedrock under the house, providing water in emergencies.

PLANTATION KEY, 72 *m.*, (9 alt., 53 pop.), named for the pineapple and banana plantations that once flourished here, was first settled by Conchs, who migrated here from Key Vaca and Indian Key in search of farm land. Settlers lived along the bay shore, off which they anchored their center-board sloops. A few Bahaman Negroes are employed seasonally as field hands and subsist the remainder of the year on shellfish and produce from small garden patches.

Here, as elsewhere on the keys, plantation owners were handicapped by the remoteness of markets. Pineapples grown here could not compete with those grown in Cuba, and their cultivation was found to deplete the soil rapidly. Hurricanes periodically devastated and depopulated the islands. The advent of the railroad, completed to Key West in 1916, stimulated production, but the destruction of the railroad by the hurricane of 1935 had a deflationary effect.

The highway crosses SNAKE CREEK, 77 *m.*, to WINDLEY ISLAND, 77.3 *m.* (18 alt.), highest of all the Florida Keys, and named for an old settler. On a broad expanse of low prairie (L) is the SITE OF WORLD WAR VETERANS' CAMP NUMBER 1, one of three destroyed by the 1935 hurricane (*see below*). Quarries here produce Key limestone, used extensively as exterior and interior trim in buildings throughout the State.

UPPER MATECUMBE KEY, 79 *m.*, popular with anglers seeking bonefish, obtained its name, according to some authorities, from an Indian corruption of the Spanish *mata hombre*, kill man, which was also the meaning of Cuchiyaga, the Indian name for the island. The lime and pineapple groves that once grew on the island have all been destroyed.

In ISLAMORADA (Sp., purple isle), 79.9 *m.* (10 alt., 180 pop.), the only settlement on Upper Matecumbe Key, stands (R) the HURRICANE

MEMORIAL, dedicated to the memory of the World War veterans who lost their lives on the keys during the hurricane that struck on Labor Day, 1935.

The veterans had been members of the Bonus Army which assembled in Washington in 1934 to demand immediate payment of their bonus certificates. Offered $30 a month wages, hundreds were transported to the keys to work on the Overseas Highway (*see above*). One camp was established on Windley Island (*see above*), and two on Lower Matecumbe.

Hurricane signals began to fly on September 1, 1935. The next day a relief train was dispatched from Miami to remove the men from the low-lying keys to the mainland. With the gale increasing, the train steamed into Homestead (*see above*), and the engineer backed his string of empty coaches into the danger zone. Here at Islamorada a tidal wave overwhelmed the train, leaving only the locomotive on the rails. Wind and waves crushed the frail wooden shacks of the veterans. Many tied themselves to boats at anchor in an effort to survive. Miles of railroad embankment were washed away. Entire towns were obliterated; more than 500 bodies were recovered immediately after the storm subsided, and for months unidentified corpses were found in the mangrove swamps. The number of victims was estimated at 800.

While its path was relatively narrow, the hurricane was one of the most violent on record; the wind reached a velocity of 200 miles an hour, driving a tidal wave more than 12 feet high far inland, sweeping over many of the keys. The barometer dropped to 26.35 inches, the lowest sea level reading in the history of the U.S. Weather Bureau.

The FLORIDA KEYS MEMORIAL, designed by the Florida division of the Federal Art Project and erected by the WPA of the State, rises from a broad stone and concrete base; up five steps is a quadrangular platform, with stone benches on three sides. In the center of the platform, extending deep into bedrock, is a large crypt in which are buried the remains of a few veterans whose bodies were found after the storm. The crypt is faced with ceramic tile, on which appears a map of the chain of islands from Key Largo to Key Vaca, with Matecumbe half way between them.

Directly behind the crypt rises an 18-foot shaft. At the base is a bronze plaque inscribed with an account of the storm and the toll of lives it exacted. Carved in the shaft is a symbolic representation of the hurricane, depicting the palms as they bent under the force of the wind and the waves that swept the islands.

At 83.3 *m.* is the CARIBEE YACHT BASIN (*gasoline, refreshments, and charter boats available*).

Off the southern tip of Upper Matecumbe is (L) TEATABLE KEY (*accessible only by boat*), 1 *m.*, used as one of several naval bases along the keys during the Seminole War.

Visible (L) from the highway bridge connecting Upper and Lower Matecumbe is *Alligator Light*, about four miles offshore. In the foreground is INDIAN KEY (*accessible only by boat*), used as an Indian trading post by the Spanish. Early mariners feared this and other islands for their many hidden reefs. Their terror was heightened by reports that the Calusa Indians tortured shipwrecked sailors to death. Here, it is said, 400 shipwrecked Frenchmen were slaughtered about 1755, as a result of which the key for a time bore the name of Matanza (Sp., slaughter).

In 1835, because of Indian troubles, Dr.Henry Perrine (*see above*) chose Indian Key, instead of south Florida land granted by Congress, to conduct experiments in tropical plants and trees. He set out lime trees, date palms, and sisal plants, a number of which survived. He planned also to experiment with sugar cane, oranges, grapefruit, bananas, pineapples, coconuts, avocados, and mangoes, but Perrine's work was cut short when Indians raided the island in 1840 and killed him and several neighbors. Perrine's wife, son, and daughter escaped by hiding in a turtle crawl under the burning house, standing in water up to their shoulders; in the end they fled from the key in a boat and were picked up by a passing schooner.

On LIGNUM VITAE KEY (*accessible only by boat*), 2 miles west (R) of Upper Matecumbe, are stone fences, wells, pieces of carved wood and wrought iron, the ruins of what is believed by some to have been a Spanish village. The island is bright with sea lavender (*Limonium braseliense*), with myriads of rose-colored flowers, and a native leadwort (*Plumbago scandens*), which sprawls over rocks and shrubs and bears clusters of large pale flowers.

LOWER MATECUMBE KEY, 85.6 *m.*, was the site of two of the three camps of the World War veterans destroyed by the 1935 hurricane (*see above*). In the days when the dangerous reefs along the keys were unchartered, wreckers had their headquarters in the Matecumbes because of their central position in the string of keys.

'Wreck a-s-h-o-r-e!' was a familiar cry here, a clarion call that instantly aroused all inhabitants, as the 'good news' was relayed from key to key by plaintive signals blown on conch horns.

At 89.8 *m.* is the OVERSEAS ROAD AND BRIDGE TOLL STATION, (*car and driver* $1; *two-wheel trailer* $1; *each passenger* 25¢; *trucks* $1 *to* $4.50; *motorcycle* 50¢; *pedestrians* 25¢). This section of the Overseas Highway (*see above*), built for the most part on the abandoned fills and bridges of the Florida East Coast Railway, was opened in July 1938.

CRAIG, 91.3 *m.*, consisting of a filling station and a group of fishermen's shacks strung along the causeway, appeared in Robert Ripley's 'Believe It or Not' cartoon series as a 'town built on a highway, instead of a highway built through the town.'

On several long bridges and causeways the highway crosses LONG KEY and tiny CONCH KEY to GRASSY KEY, 100.2 *m.*, named for an early settler and not for its vegetation. Rumors that pirates buried treasure here were substantiated in 1911 when 61 gold pieces in a goatskin bag were unearthed on the key.

On CRAWL KEYS, 107.2 *m.*, are many turtle crawls, large pens extending into shallow water, in which turtles are kept until shipped to market. All of the keys are breeding and nesting grounds for the green hawkbill, loggerhead, and trunk turtles; the first two are sought for soup and other dishes, and the hawkbill is valued also for its shell. The trunk turtle, with a pelicanlike pouch, often grows to an enormous size but is seldom eaten. Many are captured when they come ashore in the spring to lay their eggs, which are round and small, with a soft shell. Many persons gather the eggs and eat them. Occasionally turtles are harpooned for sport; larger turtles will tow a boat for miles before expiring. Most turtles are captured in seines. While cruising along the keys in 1832 on the sloop *Lady of the Green Mantle*, Audubon watched the seiners as they stretched their nets across the mouths of streams and from them bought turtles to feed herons which he was carrying back to friends in Charleston.

West (R) of Crawl Keys is BAMBOO KEY (*accessible only by boat*), 1 *m.*, a small irregularly shaped island said to have fewer mosquitoes than other keys because of a malodorous parasitic plant, *Cuscuta umbalata*, which thrives there; the scientific validity of this theory has not yet been proved. East (L) of Crawl Keys is FAT DEER KEY, formerly the range of a deer peculiar to the keys. Once numerous on all the islands from Key West to Key Largo, the deer have been hunted in and out of season until, in 1938, the Audubon Society estimated that but 50 remained, largely concentrated on Big Pine Key (*see below*). To save the Key deer from extinction, a 1939 legislative act prohibited hunters from shooting them.

At 110.8 *m.*, is the junction with an unimproved road.

Left on this road to an EMERGENCY LANDING FIELD, 1 *m.*, graded from smooth prairie land near the ocean shore.

KEY VACA (Sp., cow), 111.7 *m.*, named for the cattle that once roamed the island, early attracted settlers interested in its fertile farm lands and many fresh-water wells. This is the southernmost key on which fresh water can be obtained by drilling.

MARATHON, 119.3 *m.* (7 alt., 100 pop.), the trading center of Key Vaca, was a boisterous settlement during the construction of the railroad. Liquor boats enjoyed a prosperous trade with the labor camps here and elsewhere on the keys. Church leaders sent a 'gospel boat' from Key West to the camps; services were held nightly, and thousands of religious tracts distributed.

LONG BRIDGE, 121.3 *m.*, almost 7 miles long, consists of five sections. The guard rail is constructed of old railroad rails, cut and welded together. The bridge spans PIGEON KEY, inhabited by several families occupying old houses built by the railroad, and named for the white-crowned wild pigeon, native to the West Indies and fairly numerous along the keys. It has bluish-black plumage; the upper part of its head is white, edged with deep brown at the sides of the crown. Its presence on the keys was first noted by Audubon, who painted one sitting on a bough of the rough-leaved cordia, or geiger tree. On his visit to the keys Audubon also discovered and named the Key West pigeon, with plumage of brilliant and constantly changing metallic hues; he pronounced it 'the most beautiful of woodland cooers.'

A ramp leads from the bridge down to PIGEON KEY FISHING CAMP. Here are parking spaces for cars and trailers; facilities for shuffleboard and horseshoe pitching; picnic grounds; boats for outside fishing.

BAHIA HONDA KEY (Sp., deep bay), 129.6 *m.*, marks the point of geologic transition from the upper to the lower keys. From this point to the Dry Tortugas, all islands are of white oölitic limestone, known as Key

West limestone, with tangles of mangroves holding together the soil of old islands and gradually building up new ones. These lower keys have a scant covering of topsoil, but lime trees grow in crevices of the limestone, and some tomatoes, okra, and melons are grown. The waters of Bahia Honda offer exceptionally good tarpon fishing. Specimens weighing 190 pounds have been landed here.

On WEST SUMMERLAND KEY, 132.8 *m.*, listed on geodetic charts as Spanish Harbor Keys, the roseate spoonbill, a beautiful wading bird nearly extinct in Florida (*see Animal Life*), feeds in the shallows along the highway.

BIG PINE KEY, 134.9 *m.* (8 alt., 53 pop.), one of the largest of the keys, is covered with Caribbean pines, dense growths of palmetto and cacti, and a few scattered hammocks. The key has been characterized as 'the most remarkable natural cactus garden east of the American deserts.' Five genera grow here, including three arboreal species, one with a columnar trunk as large as a man's body. The fires that occasionally sweep the lower keys destroy the hammocks and leave only the Caribbean pine, native to the West Indies, which is highly fire-resistant. The Caribbean pine is of little economic value. Its resin is too thick and gummy to permit satisfactory tapping; as lumber, it splits easily and warps badly; to cut it, saws must be flooded with kerosene to prevent gumming.

Occasionally highway and bridges are covered with armies of land crabs, which flee from mangrove swamps during bad weather and high water. These migrations, it is said by some, portend a hurricane; in any case, the wandering crabs are a nuisance, for their spiny shells frequently puncture automobile tires.

At 137.5 *m.* is THE BIG PINE KEY TOLL STATION, for northbound traffic on the Overseas Highway.

BIG PINE INN, 139.5 *m.*, is a sportsmen's lodge (*boats, guides, fishing equipment*).

At 140.2 *m.* is a junction with a paved road.

Right on this road to NO NAME KEY, 3.0 *m.*, formerly a ferry terminus. NO NAME LODGE (*lodging, guides, boats, tackle, bait*) has a business card reading, 'No Name Lodge, No Name Key, Phone No Name No. 1.'

LITTLE TORCH KEY, 142.6 *m.*, and MIDDLE TORCH KEY, 144.5 *m.*, were named for the resinous torchwood tree. The soapberry tree, from the seed hulls of which comes a soaplike substance used as a cleaner, also flourishes here. Early settlers sprinkled the crushed seeds in small streams and inlets; the seeds stupefied the fish, which floated to the surface and were easily gathered, a practice since declared illegal.

Crossing RAMROD KEY, 144.9 *m.*, (25 pop.), and SUMMERLAND KEY, 147 *m.*, with many lime and other citrus groves, the highway reaches CUDJOE KEY, 149.2 *m.*, the name a contraction of 'Cousin Joe's.'

SUGARLOAF KEY, 152.1 *m.*, was named for the sugarloaf pineapples once cultivated here. Experiments in growing sponges (*see Tour 6b*) are carried on in the waters of Sugarloaf Sound.

PIRATE'S COVE FISHING CAMP, 152.9 *m.*, is one of the better-known camps on the lower keys (*boats, guides, equipment, Jan.–May*).

Fishing along the keys has world renown among sportsmen, for the tides here bring together the game fish of both the Atlantic and the Gulf. In the Gulf Stream, about 7 miles from shore, lives the blue and white sailfish, one of the most beautiful and spirited of sea creatures. When hooked, it provides a rare thrill: with its high dorsal fin gleaming in the sun, it races along the surface of the water like a torpedo. Somewhat less numerous, the swordfish is a large and able fighter. Amberjack, bonita, Spanish mackerel, tuna, and kingfish are also found in the Gulf Stream.

BARRIER REEF, an underwater coral wall paralleling the Atlantic shore of the keys, is the feeding ground of white groupers, 300-pound black groupers (Jewfish), hog fish, muttonfish, and many others, including the barracuda, known as the 'tiger of the sea.' Armed with powerful jaws and sharp teeth, the barracuda strikes viciously and is a rapid and powerful swimmer.

The tarpon, or silver king, the prize sought by every deep-sea angler, is caught in the swift-running passes between the islands. Hooked, it leaps repeatedly from the water, shaking its great body, and at times apparently walks along the surface on its tail, its large iridescent scales shining like burnished silver.

Shallower waters are frequented by bonefish. Weighing from 4 to 8 pounds, the 'steel spring of the deep,' as it is called, is regarded by many as the most cunning and tenacious fighter of its size.

Bottom fishermen drop hooks in sheltered inland channels and lagoons to catch snappers, grunts, porgies, and scores of other fishes. Anglers fish from the rails of the wooden bridges that connect the many small islands between this point and Key West. Some have the most complete and elaborate tackle; others do quite as well with a cheap bamboo pole or hand line; few go home empty-handed, for here, as one old fisherman observed, 'you can catch most anything you want to bait up for.'

The highway spans SUGARLOAF CREEK, 158.5 *m.*, and winds in a series of hairpin curves across SADDLEBUNCH KEY. Much of the road is cut through mangrove and buttonwood thickets. The burning of mangroves to produce charcoal, which is sacked and sold in Key West, is carried on in the vicinity. Spires of smoke by day and rosy beacons by night indicate the site of burners on the lonely keys.

Frequently in view, the opalescent waters of the Atlantic and the Gulf change hues with the shifting sun and passing clouds. Scattered green islands gleam like emeralds on an azure field. On the distant horizon (L) the Gulf Stream pencils a line of indigo, with here and there above it a smudge of gray smoke from the funnels of a passing steamer.

Rumrunning and smuggling of aliens were once thriving enterprises here. Men familiar with the reefs and channels piloted their small open boats across the dangerous 90-mile passage to Cuba, took on cargoes of liquors or aliens, recrossed the channel, and landed at Key West or on one of the more isolated keys. The boats were often so heavily laden that only a few inches of free board stood above the water line. Storms and rough water frequently forced them to cast part or all their cargoes overboard, but only as a last resort; overloading caused frequent capsizing of boats and drownings.

The smugglers led customs officers and the Coast Guard a busy life. They traveled at night without lights so that Federal officers could detect their presence only by the sound of their muffled engines. When discovered far from shore, the rumrunners attempted to outdistance pursuers; if capture seemed certain, they dropped their cargo overboard. When they were caught empty-handed, the only charge against them was running without lights. If they escaped, they ran for shore, slipped into secret channels dug into the heart of the mangrove thickets, and covered their boats with branches, making it almost impossible to see them, even from the air.

Highjackers were a constant menace to the smugglers. Some operated in gangs and would surprise smugglers in their hiding places, or at sea, and seize their cargo. The less venturesome were known as 'Pelicans,' because they would spy on rumrunners to discover where their contraband was dropped in shallow water so that they could fish it up when the owners disappeared.

Smuggling of aliens—Cubans, Mexicans, Spaniards, and Chinese, for the most part—was less popular and far more hazardous than rumrunning. Although few boatmen on the keys have read Ernest Hemingway's novel, *To Have and Have Not* (1937), some contend that the chief character is more or less a portrait of a smuggler of Chinese, who on occasions proceeded to Cuba, shipped a company of 'monks' (Chinese), collected passage money, put to sea, and returned to the keys—with no passengers. In those years Federal officers rounded up many aliens left stranded for days on deserted islands; others were found clinging to buoys. One group of Chinese was picked up at sea in a drifting boat bearing also the bodies of the white skipper and mate, who had been killed, perhaps not without extenuating circumstances.

Crossing PELOTA CREEK the route traverses BOCA CHICA KEY (Sp., little mouth), 165.6 *m.*, and runs within 100 feet of a dazzling white beach, bordered with coconut palms, Australian pines, and clumps of green seagrape. This is a popular spot for surf bathing and picnics. At the lower end of the beach are cottages and a fishing camp (*boats*). From the high bridge over Boca Chica channel the three radio towers of the U.S. Naval Station in Key West are visible (*see Key West*).

STOCK ISLAND, 169.5 *m.*, was so named because in early days Key Westers kept their cattle here. On the KEY WEST MUNICIPAL GOLF COURSE (*greens fee* $1), 171.2 *m.*, players tee off within sight of the Gulf and face the Atlantic at the 8th hole.

Adjoining the fairway (R) is the KEY WEST BOTANICAL GARDEN, established as part of the Key West rehabilitation program, planted with thousands of exotic trees and shrubs furnished by the U.S. Plant Introduction Station. Among them are the sausage tree, bearing hard sausagelike fruit on long slender stems; the Norfolk Island pine, a tall pyramidal tree with spreading up-curved branches; the white orchid tree, covered with pale white flowers delicately veined with green; the soap tree; and the woman's-tongue tree, with long slender pods in which the seeds rattle monotonously at the slightest breeze.

The highway forks right and left, 171.5 *m.*, providing two routes into Key West.

KEY WEST, 174.8 *m.* (6 alt., 12,831 pop.) (*see Key West*).

Points of Interest: Fort Taylor, Martello Towers, U.S. Naval Radio Station, Bahama houses, Home of Ernest Hemingway, southernmost house in the United States, sponge docks, turtle crawls, Aquarium, and others.

Tour 1*A*

Jacksonville—Jacksonville Beach—St.Augustine—Daytona Beach; 102.7 *m.* State 78 and State 140.

Hard-surfaced roadbed except for occasional short stretches of shell road; watch for cattle and sand drifts.
Good accommodations.

This route, an alternate between Jacksonville and Daytona Beach, follows the coast, passing a number of resorts. For the most part, it runs within sight or sound of the ocean, although occasionally it turns inland to thread its way among hammocks of oak, palm, bay, and cedar.

Construction of the highway between Jacksonville and the beach presented a novel problem. The county bond issue to finance the project stipulated the construction of two parallel one-way highways. Instead, a single broad road was decided on. To meet the stipulations of the bond issue, two narrow lanes of concrete were constructed and the intervening space was later paved with asphalt.

Two expeditions—one French and one Spanish—landed within 50 miles and two days of each other on this section of the Florida coast late in the summer of 1565. Captain Jean Ribaut commanded the French expedition, which consisted of 600 colonists sent out to reinforce the 300 Frenchmen who had settled at Fort Caroline the previous year. The expedition led by Menéndez consisted of 600 Spaniards, who had embarked, according to Menéndez, to Christianize the Indians.

Each force knew of the presence of the other, and both prepared for hostilities immediately upon landing. The French disembarked at Fort Caroline on the St.Johns River; Menéndez and his men established themselves farther south, founding St.Augustine. The French decided to attack and put to sea, only to be struck by a hurricane. Menéndez seized the opportunity and marched quickly overland to seize Fort Caroline and the few men left behind to guard it. Returning to St.Augustine, Menéndez was informed by Indians that the main body of the French had been shipwrecked not far away at Matanzas Inlet.

Menéndez advanced to meet Ribaut and his shipwrecked force. While history is not clear on the negotiations between them, Spanish accounts reveal that almost all the French were executed—not as Frenchmen, but as Lutherans—after they had surrendered unconditionally.

Philip II, the Spanish monarch, was so pleased with the turn of events that he wrote Menéndez: 'Of the great success that has attended your enterprise we have had the most entire satisfaction; and as to the retribution you have visited upon the Lutheran pirates . . . we believe that you did it with every justification and propriety. . . .' The story of the massacre at Matanzas Inlet (Sp., massacre) was told throughout Europe by the few who managed to escape, but the Huguenots were denied the retaliation they asked in a petition submitted to Charles IX, King of France.

JACKSONVILLE, 0 *m.* (25 alt., 129,549 pop.) (*see Jacksonville*).

Points of Interest: Naval Stores Yard, Cotton Compress, Hemming Park, Memorial Park, and others.

Jacksonville is at the junction with US 1 (*see Tour 1a and b*), US 17 (*see Tour 2a and b*), and US 90 (*see Tour 7a*). State 78 branches east from US 1 at Atlantic Boulevard.

Almost hidden among cedar trees (L), 3.3 *m.*, a gray stone marker indicates the SITE OF FORT SAN NICHOLAS, which was 1,500 feet north on the St.Johns River. Don Manuel de Monteano, Spanish Governor, built it about 1740 when threatened with attack by James Oglethorpe, leader of the English in Georgia.

At 10.8 *m.* is the junction with an asphalt road.

Left on this road to FULTON, 5 *m.* (4 alt.), a popular fishing resort. Right from Fulton 1.5 *m.* to ST.JOHNS BLUFF, at the approximate SITE OF FORT CAROLINE, built in 1564 by Laudonnière, French explorer, and captured in 1565 by Menéndez (*see above*). The site of the fort has been washed into the river. The English established a settlement near the bluff in 1782, naming it St.Johns Town. Many Tories took refuge here at the end of the Revolutionary War. The town declined when Florida again passed into the possession of Spain, and by 1817 most of its 300 buildings had disappeared. Today, no vestige remains of either the fort or the town.

State 78 crosses the Pablo Creek drawbridge over the Intracoastal Waterway (*see Intracoastal Waterway*), 16.1 *m.*, a sheltered inland route followed by yachts and smaller craft sailing to and from southern Florida waters. Between the bridge and Mayport Road (*see below*), dark spiny Spanish bayonets line both sides of the road; in early days they were planted about Spanish fortifications as defense entanglements, hence the name. In late spring they send up tall pyramids of white blossoms, often called 'Madonna candles.'

At 17.3 *m.* is the junction with a road, known locally as the Mayport Road.

Left on this road is EAST MAYPORT, 4.5 *m.* (10 alt.), a small settlement in a dense subtropical forest. In this dell-like section fig trees grow along the roadside.

WONDERWOOD (R), 5.1 *m.*, once a landscaped estate, now consists of a cluster of cottages, an inn, a fishing pier (*boats for rent*), and a riding academy. Huge oaks, magnolias, and oleanders shade many bridle paths. RIBAUT MONUMENT, 5.2 *m.*, erected on a small knoll, commemorates the arrival of Huguenot colonists here in 1562. Masonic sunrise services are held here each Easter.

MAYPORT, 6 *m.* (8 alt., 511 pop.), a fishing village near the mouth of the St. Johns River, has docks providing moorage for a shrimp fleet and a number of small craft chartered for fishing in the channel close by and on the snapper banks 18 miles out. On the shore are drying nets, and an abandoned red lighthouse.

ATLANTIC BEACH, 18.6 *m.* (13 alt., 164 pop.), is a summer resort patronized by Jacksonville residents. When the tide is low, it is possible to drive along the smooth wide beach three miles north to the St. Johns River mouth, and six miles south, as far as Ponte Vedra (*see below*).

Once a part of Jacksonville Beach, NEPTUNE BEACH, 19 *m.*, is now an incorporated town; the beach is flanked with a concrete bulkhead.

JACKSONVILLE BEACH, 21.5 *m.* (10 alt., 409 pop.), has a concrete, mile-long boardwalk along the ocean front. An amusement park, bathhouses, hotels, apartments, and cottages provide facilities for summer visitors. A Red Cross Volunteer Life Saving Corp and a U.S. COAST GUARD RADIO STATION (*open*) are quartered here.

The entire beach section from Atlantic Beach to Ponte Vedra is the largest resort area in northeast Florida. Some 40,000 vacationists relax and play here during the summer. The municipalities have grown together, presenting an unbroken stretch of cottages, apartment houses and hotels along the highway for over six miles. Jacksonville Beach, with its varied carnival enterprises, is the midsummer center of activity.

PONTE VEDRA, 24.9 *m.*, now a restricted seaside development, with bath club, hotel, cabanas, and golf course (*greens fee* $1), was originally the National Lead Company's 'Mineral City.' For a number of years minerals used in the manufacture of their products were obtained from the sands here. Operations halted when the State obtained an injunction on the ground that the beach, a public highway, was being destroyed.

In 1916 two young chemical engineers from Harvard University sailed along the Atlantic coast from Brunswick, Ga., to Cape Canaveral (*see Tour 1B*), landing at intervals of 10 miles to take samples of beach sand. When analysis of the samples revealed the presence of many valuable minerals, they built a plant at Ponte Vedra to extract the minerals by an electrical process. During the World War the Federal Government took over the plant and produced ilmenite and rutile, both used in the manufacture of munitions. Zircon, monasite, and a silicate of aluminum also were found in the sand. After the War the mill and other properties were purchased by the lead company. All traces of 'Mineral City' have vanished.

South of Ponte Vedra the road skirts PALM VALLEY, rich hammock land covered with oaks, magnolias, and palms. This fertile area was once known as Diego Plains, named for Don Diego de Espinosa, who built a small fort some distance west of the highway in the early 1700's to defend his cattle ranch. The fort was strengthened in 1740 against Oglethorpe's expected attack on St.Augustine, but on May 9 of that year the Georgia Governor seized it, capturing 57 men, 11 cannon, 70 small arms, and much ammunition. Oglethorpe reported that the timber and underbrush in the territory was so dense that his men were compelled to march single file. The area, practically uninhabited today, is penetrated by a few sand roads. Palm Valley was a moonshine distilling center during the prohibition era; Palm Valley ''shine' was flavored with palmetto berries and was much in demand in this section.

MICKLER'S PIER, (*adm.* 25¢), 30.9 *m.*, extending 300 feet into the ocean, is popular with fishermen (*bait and tackle for pier and surf fishing*).

Between Mickler's Pier and St.Augustine the route runs between the ocean and the Intracoastal Waterway. The hard white beach with its curling surf lies hidden (L) behind high rounded sand dunes, covered with palmettoes, scrub oaks, and pines. Slat fences are strung along at intervals to prevent the dunes from 'walking' across the road. Low dense scrub extends (R) from the highway to the Intracoastal Waterway. In summer the road shoulders are carpeted with yellow partridge peas and pink horsemint, through which the gilia thrusts its vivid scarlet spears.

VILANO BEACH (L), 48.7 *m.*, has a small group of cottages for summer visitors. A wooden drawbridge with fishing platforms spans the NORTH RIVER, 49.2 *m.*, to Kurth's Island, originally called Isle of Tolomato (*boats, bait, and fishing equipment*). The highway crosses the island and returns to the mainland on a short bridge and causeway.

ST.AUGUSTINE, 51.2 *m.* (7 alt., 12,111 pop.) (*see St.Augustine*).

Points of Interest: Fort Marion, Catholic Cathedral, Flagler Memorial Chapel, Trinity Episcopal Church, old residences, and others.

St.Augustine is at the junction with US 1 (*see Tour 1b*).

South of St.Augustine the route follows State 140, crossing Matanzas River to ANASTASIA ISLAND on the BRIDGE OF THE LIONS, named for the two marble lions at its western entrance. The island is some 3 miles wide and extends southward 14 miles to Matanzas Inlet.

Monkeys and alligators, live and mounted specimens of birds, reptiles, and fish are exhibited at the MUSEUM OF NATURAL HISTORY (*open* 8:30 *to* 6; *adm.* 25¢), 51.8 *m.*

On ST.AUGUSTINE BEACH (*bathhouses, cottages*), 52.9 *m.*, the ST.AUGUSTINE LIGHTHOUSE rises 165 feet in a clearing amid scrub oak, its light visible 20 miles at sea. In 1586 Drake saw here a Spanish signaltower; the present lighthouse dates from 1874. The ST.AUGUSTINE OSTRICH AND ALLIGATOR FARM (*open* 8 *to* 6; *adm.* 25¢), 53.1 *m.*, contains 6,000 alligators of all ages and sizes, as well as ostriches, live snakes and turtles, and a museum of marine curiosities.

All that remains of a barracks, used by the men who quarried coquina for St.Augustine houses as well as for the construction of Fort Matanzas (*see below*) and Fort Marion (*see St.Augustine*), is the SPANISH CHIMNEY (L), 54.4 *m.* This and the old well near by are probably two of the oldest Spanish relics in the St.Augustine section. CRESCENT BEACH,

61.3 *m.*, is marked by a scattering of old frame houses on the high dunes along the shore.

FORT MATANZAS NATIONAL MONUMENT (R), 65.1 *m.*, is a Government reservation established in 1915. A short distance south of the entrance a tablet (R) marks the SITE OF THE HUGUENOT MASSACRE (*see above*).

Right from the reservation entrance on a graveled road to a boat landing, 0.2 *m.*, where an outboard motorboat (*free*) is available at all times for transportation to RATTLESNAKE ISLAND, near the west bank of the Matanzas River. On the island stands old FORT MATANZAS, a coquina structure 40 feet square and 30 feet high, built by the Spaniards about 1736. The fort replaced a tower erected to prevent enemy ships from moving up the river.

The highway crosses MATANZAS INLET, 66.1 *m.*, popular with both bridge and surf fishermen. Here sea oats and seaside morning glories, with green ropelike stems spread over the sand on the sweeping beaches. An expanse of green marshes and lagoons, suggestive of water hazards on a golf course, spreads southward from the inlet.

MARINELAND, 68.6 *m.*, in a landscaped ocean-front setting, is centered about the MARINE STUDIOS (*open 9–6; adm.* $1), a cream-colored concrete aquarium, pitted with tempered glass portholes, and resembling a stranded Caribbean cruiser. Two great tanks, one round, the other rectangular, contain many varieties of deep-sea life. Through the portholes visitors see porpoises, sawfish, sharks, giant green turtles, shrimp, the manta (devilfish), and numerous common food fish. Brilliantly colored tropical fish swim in sea gardens of coral and algae, while penguins brought from Robbin Island off the African coast paddle on the surface.

At 11 a.m. and 4 p.m. daily guides lecture over a loud-speaker system as the fish are fed by a sailor who calls them with a dinner bell. Porpoises frequently leap 6 feet out of water to snatch fish from the sailor's hands. When the dinner bell was first used, the fish fled to the opposite side of the tank, but they soon learned that it meant food, and they now rush toward the keeper at its first peal.

When the tanks were first stocked (May 1938), experts were unable to predict which species would live amicably together. They found that porpoises, sharks, and sawfish can share the same tank. A black grouper, however, recently swallowed a shark. The menhadens are not attacked because of their odor.

The clarity of the water, affording distinct views of even the very small creatures, is maintained by stations that pump in more than 5,000,000 gallons of water every 24 hours, effecting 6 complete changes during that period. Men in diving helmets, carrying underwater vacuum cleaners and brushes, clean the tanks. The sawfish and manta stay away from the commotion, although it is said a porpoise is apt to steal the dust cloth.

The studios are managed by Ilia Tolstoy, Russian scientist and explorer, who is also vice-president of the organization. Arthur Francis McBride, formerly a staff member of the American Museum of Natural History and now curator of the aquarium, is studying the lives and life cycles of the fishes.

South of Marineland the highway plunges into the shade of cabbage palms, oaks, cedars, and bay trees for 6 miles before returning to the shore. The ocean is screened from view, but its presence is indicated by the roar of the surf and the flight of pelicans in single file. Palmetto flats stretch away (R) to the high sand banks of the Intracoastal Waterway; farther in the distance appear smoky-blue forests of pine.

FLAGLER BEACH, 83.8 *m.* (198 pop.), a resort frequented by Floridians of near-by inland towns, has many old stucco houses and a 600-foot municipal fishing pier (*bass, pompano, Spanish mackerel, sea trout, whiting, drum fish, and flounder*). Hand lines, bamboo poles with line attached, and rods with reels to cast plugs and other artificial bait are used in angling for all these.

ORMOND BEACH, 97.8 *m.*, (43 pop.), is a winter resort with many large estates along both the Halifax River and the ocean front. Its development began in 1875 when John Anderson built a large and rambling frame hotel on the wooded banks of the river. Purchased and enlarged by Henry M. Flagler, pioneer railroad and resort promoter (*see Palm Beach*), the HOTEL ORMOND still stands on the John Anderson Highway, a winding and shaded drive along the river, affording fine views of its blue waters and white beaches. The hotel, built, owned, and operated by the Florida East Coast Railway, is painted bright yellow, with green trim.

Adjoining the hotel are the ORMOND BEACH GOLF LINKS (*greens fee* $2.50), a favorite of the elder John D. Rockefeller (*see below*).

Opposite the hotel is THE CASEMENTS, winter home of John D. Rockefeller (1839–1937), a relatively small and notably unpretentious house, with gray shingled walls and many large windows. Tall and spreading hedges of Turk's-cap enclose its two acres of ground, beautifully landscaped in a series of terraces descending to the Halifax River. Guards stood watch at all gates up to Rockefeller's death, and many gardeners tended its lawns and flower beds.

Much of the latter part of Rockefeller's long life was identified with The Casements. The elderly vacationer known to Ormond Beach was a remarkable transformation of the vigorous and relentless businessman who in the earlier days of his career had been prosecuted by the Government and vehemently denounced by the press as a ruthless exponent of Big Business, the first and perhaps the greatest of the trust builders, creator of a vast and efficient economic empire that in time encircled the globe. In Ormond Beach he was happy to be known merely as 'Neighbor John,' interested in local enterprises and institutions.

For many years Rockefeller presided over the annual charity bazaar at the Hotel Ormond, attracting large crowds to bid generously on the odds and ends he auctioned for the benefit of the local poor. On Sunday mornings he attended the nondenominational Ormond Union Church, and after the service stood on the lawn distributing bright new dimes to eager children, advising thrift and savings if they would amass a fortune. Every year, on the day he ordered his private railroad car for his journey north after the winter season, Rockefeller placed in the hands of the local pastor an envelope with money to pay his salary and all church expenses for the ensuing year.

Until he was almost 90, Rockefeller continued to play golf here with a few cronies and an occasional guest. He was usually accompanied by a servant with an umbrella to protect him from the sun. When younger, he had bicycled from stroke to stroke, followed by two valets, one with milk and crackers, the other with his golf clubs and a blanket to be spread on the ground when he wished to rest. For golf, as for church and for ordinary wear, he wore a special wig. He usually wore a vest of Japanese paper, to keep out the wind, and a straw hat, held securely in place by a large shawl-like handkerchief tied under his chin.

Rockefeller's pride in his golf is reflected in his remark in 1928, when finally forced at the age of 89 to reduce his physical exertions, that it was better to play well for six holes than like a dub for eight. He liked to win; after a game on one occasion with Will Rogers, the humorist, the latter said, 'I'm glad you beat me, John. The last time you were beaten, I noticed that the price of gasoline went up two cents a gallon.' Rockefeller's trouser pockets were always filled with newly minted coins, nickels in one, dimes in the other, the stock of each being replenished by a valet promptly at 7:00 each morning. The nickels were 'to encourage the downcast'; the dimes were 'to reward the triumphant who beat him at golf.'

'Be deliberate! Be deliberate! Take lessons! Play better!' was his advice to defeated opponents on the links. Of his partner in a foursome he demanded both skill and concentrated attention, being outspoken equally in criticism and praise. 'If money wasn't so scarce,' he exclaimed to a partner just after the 1929 crash, 'I'd give you a nickel for that drive.' Lost balls were always a matter of serious concern to him. On seeing a foursome abandon their search after beating the brush for an hour, he commented with interest, 'Those fellows must have plenty of money.'

Guests at The Casements received not only a new dime but a card on which was printed a bit of inspirational verse. Some bore these lines, believed to be the one original stanza from his pen:

I was early taught to work as well as play;
My life has been one long, happy holiday—
Full of work, and full of play—
I dropped the worry on the way—
And God was good to me every day.

Rockefeller had his first airplane ride here in Ormond Beach in January 1930. The plane taxied up and down the beach, but did not leave the ground. His last years were devoted to a passionate but methodical struggle to live at least to the century mark. He limited his physical activities to sitting in the sun a few hours a day or to a half-hour ride in his maroon automobile, so designed that it could be converted almost instantly from an open into a closed and warmly heated car. On his infrequent walks male nurses stood at either elbow. For the most part, he used a wheel chair or was carried by attendants to preserve every ounce of strength and energy. His diet was largely vegetable; he ate small quantities of food, carefully measured for calories and vitamins, at frequent regular intervals. In The Casements, as in his other residences used at different seasons, were machines to test basal metabolism, fluoroscopes, and all the equipment of a small hospital. Even his automobiles and his private railroad car carried oxygen tanks. But Rockefeller was denied his greatest ambition; he died here at The Casements on May 23, 1937, little more than two years before his 100th birthday.

On Granada Avenue, main thoroughfare of Ormond Beach, is the HOTEL COQUINA, of modified Spanish style, built of local coquina rock, a soft whitish limestone formed of broken shells and coral cemented together by the processes of nature. At the end of the avenue a ramp leads down to the white firm beach, along which motorists can drive at low tide to Daytona Beach (*see below*).

Right 1 *m.* from Ormond Beach on a bridge across the Halifax River to ORMOND (*see Tour 1b*).

South of Ormond Beach the highway parallels a long ridge of sand dunes matted with palmetto; red and white oleanders border the highway. A number of rutted roads cut through the dunes (L) to ramps leading down to the beach.

DAYTONA BEACH, 102.7 *m.* (7 alt., 16,598 pop.) (*see Daytona Beach*).

Points of Interest: Ocean Beach, Broadwalk, open-air Auditorium, Bethune-Cookman College (Negro), alligator and ostrich farms, and others.

Daytona Beach is at the junction with US 1 (*see Tour 1b and c*) and US 92-State 21 (*see Tour 8a*).

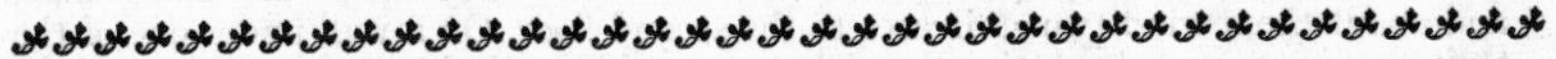

Tour 1B

Titusville—Merritt Island—Indiatlantic—Melbourne; 55 *m.* State 119 and State 219.

State 119, asphalt-paved; State 219, good sand or shell surface, two lanes wide. Accommodations at towns of Merritt Island and Cocoa Beach.

This route traverses part of Canaveral Peninsula and Merritt Island, a water-bound area with an unusual variety of temperate and tropical flora. The peninsula, a sand barrier from 200 yards to 4 miles wide, extends southward 100 miles from Ponce de Leon Inlet, opposite New Smyrna. Between the mainland and Cape Canaveral lies Merritt Island, approximately 40 miles long and 6 miles wide, with the Indian River on the west and Banana River on the east.

State 119 branches east from US 1 (*see Tour 1c*) at TITUSVILLE, 0 *m.*, crossing the Indian River on a wooden bridge to the CANAVERAL PENINSULA, 1.5 *m.* A thin blurred line of trees appears ahead as the highway enters grassy marshland. Presently the trees take shape as scattered clumps of cabbage palmettoes. Ferns and wild flowers grow abundantly along the edge of the marsh, and bright-colored butterflies zigzag across the highway.

At 2 *m.* is a junction with a sand road.

Left on this road to DUMMITT GROVE, 5 *m.*, one of the early orange groves in Florida. Planted between 1830 and 1835, the trees are still bearing; the largest is 4 feet in circumference and 30 feet high. Douglas D. Dummitt, planter of the grove, whose parents had settled in St.Augustine in 1807, later established other plantations in New Smyrna (*see Tour 1c*). Dummitt was commissioned a captain in 1845 as leader of the 'Mosquito Roarers' during the Seminole War. He was a familiar figure as he plied the river here in a dugout paddled by six sturdy Negroes or in a larger dugout rigged for sails.

Dummitt obtained budwood from a grove near Port Orange, which in turn had been budded from seedling stock brought to Florida by the Spanish. Dummitt's grove became widely known, and the Dummitt, Indian River, and seedless Enterprise oranges originated here. Among the RUINS OF THE DUMMITT HOUSE only the coquina chimney still stands; the old well near-by furnishes an ample supply of water.

Dummitt Grove passed in 1881 to an Italian nobleman, Eicole Tamajo, Duke of Castlellucia, who had married an American heiress, daughter of a St.Louis brewer. The duke completed the present house in the grove, known as DUKE'S CASTLE, a two-story octagonal structure built of timber from a ship that went aground near Daytona Beach. The vertical exterior planking consists of pieces more than 30 feet long and 10 inches wide; ship beams serve as corner uprights; with the exception of a rectangular reception hall and a billiard room upstairs, all rooms are octagonal in shape. The octagonal design of the house was adopted, it is said, as a streamlining measure against gales and hurricanes. Even gables were narrowed to lessen exposure to the winds. Inside the house, stout ship spars rise from two sides of the reception hall and lounge, and about them wind two staircases to the second floor. On a wall under one of the staircases is a penciled notation that J.J.Conwar of New York was the architect of the castle, and December 15, 1881, the date of its completion.

The duke entertained foreign and American friends at elaborate hunting parties here. Coffee was served to visitors at 11 in the morning and 4 in the afternoon at the COFFEE HOUSE, a small octagonal-shaped frame structure north of the castle. The duke supervised work in his well-kept victoria, driven by a liveried coachman. Failing health led him to sell the castle and leave Canaveral Peninsula in the early 1900's.

Continuing eastward, State 119 enters a palm savanna, carpeted with tall, dark, switch grass. Only an occasional cry of a water bird breaks the silence. Trees gradually thin out, and the road traverses a vast sandy wasteland of palmetto and wire grass. Here and there a lone group of Australian pines stands out against the sky, advance guard of the ornamental trees planted on Merritt Island (*see below*).

At 8.1 *m.* is (R) the junction with State 219, identified by a sign reading 'To Tower Farms.'

Left (straight ahead) on partly paved State 119 to TITUSVILLE BEACH, 9 *m.*, a small swimming resort on the ocean.

The route continues (R) on State 219, a smooth sand road that leads through a dense palmetto thicket. In this dry region are fields of bright wild flowers inhabited by many land birds.

At 10.5 *m.* the road forks; State 219 continues straight ahead. A short wooden bridge across BANANA CREEK, 12.5 *m.*, connects the peninsula with MERRITT ISLAND, 12.6 *m.*, named for an early settler to whom Spain granted the entire island about 1800. Its northern section is somewhat desolate and sandy, but stands of Caribbean pine and small farms appear as the road proceeds southward. Almost all the islanders are engaged in vegetable farming and citrus culture.

ORSINO, 17 *m.* (100 pop.), northernmost trading center on the island, has a store, post office, filling station, and church. Here the road forks; the route continues (R) on undesignated State 219, with alternate stretches of sand and shell. Beyond an outlying orange grove, 17.4 *m.*, appear a few banana plants, their vivid green leaves shining in the sun. In some places towering jungles of hardwoods, cedar, and pine crowd the road; in others, great gnarled Caribbean pines rise in the distance above cabbage palms. Abrupt swift changes of scenery follow; each turn of the road reveals small pine forests, sandy flats, shallow marshes, and tropical forests.

COURTENAY, 24.5 *m.* (61 pop.), a settlement that seems a part of the dark enveloping jungle, has old orange trees occupying almost all space between its weathered frame stores and houses.

South of Courtenay, State 219 is surfaced with asphalt. The many substantial dwellings along the highway have bright gardens of flowering hibiscus, bougainvillea, and allamandas. Bamboo, coco plumosa palms, and tall Australian pines border the road.

INDIANOLA, 29.3 *m.* (50 pop.), is another community with buildings dwarfed by the towering jungle about it.

MERRITT ISLAND, 32.3 *m.* (200 pop.), chief trading center of the island, has bright stucco houses set in well-kept lawns among ornamental shrubs.

1. Right from Merritt Island on paved State 206, which crosses Indian River to the mainland, to COCOA, 1.2 *m.* (26 alt., 2,164 pop.) (*see Tour 1c*).

2. Left from Merritt Island on an asphalt-paved road through a variety of roadside palms and a forest of Caribbean pines to NEWFOUND HARBOR, dividing the southern part of the island into two tongues of land. Here are many lagoons and grassy ponds, the feeding grounds of blue and white herons, bitterns, terns, and gallinules.

At 2.5 *m.* is the junction with a paved road; R. here along the Banana River, a shining arm of the sea separating Merritt Island and Canaveral Peninsula, to a wooden bridge, 6.3 *m.* Scattered groups of sun-browned fishermen are met along the way, angling in the shallow water, speckled blue and white. From the bridge the great bowl of the sky is impressive above the flat smooth horizon, broken only by thin green spires of Australian pines to the east. Crossing back to Canaveral Peninsula, 7.8 *m.*, the highway passes sparkling blue lagoons studded with tiny islands; the whole trackless wilderness resembles a landscaped park.

COCOA BEACH, 9.3 *m.* (31 pop.), is a small ocean resort built on a dune ridge along the shore. A large SEA SHELL COLLECTION (*free*), in Ocean Lodge (R), exhibits specimens of the rare pearly nautilus. Here, as elsewhere on the peninsula, sunsets are of exceptional beauty, particularly after thunderstorms in the late afternoon, when the western sky flushes rose behind the dark screen of Australian pines above the beach as the eastern heavens merge with a cobalt sea. A rainbow fragment is perhaps reflected momentarily in jade-green water; under the darkening sky the tumbling surf grows wine-dark, and a final touch of color is often added as a line of tropical birds rises, low and far away, and drops from view.

Left from Cocoa Beach on shell-surfaced State 140, through extensive thickets of myrtle, hickory, and scrubby live oak, interspersed with large saw palmetto, cactus, and wild lantana, to ARTESIA, 15.6 *m.*, a post office in a farmhouse set back from the road amid a tropical jungle, its white sand yard planted with blossoming shrubs. In summer, when land breezes now and again waft in great singing clouds of mosquitoes from the lagoons, residents spend much of their time indoors.

The SYLVAN TROPICAL NURSERY (*free*), 17.2 *m.*, lies in the jungle (L) a short distance from the road. The nursery contains some 500 plants collected over a period of 15 years, including century plants, night-blooming cereus, wild moonflower, terrestrial orchids, bignonias attaining heights of 20 feet, and 75 varieties of bougainvillea, one with yellow blossoms having been developed here. Among flowering shrubs of fantastic beauty is the flame o' the woods.

At 17.5 *m.* is the junction with State 273, a sand-and-shell road; R. on State 273 to CANAVERAL HARBOR FISHING PIER, 19.2 *m.*, with Cape Canaveral Lighthouse (*see below*) to the northwest.

A road at 20 *m.*, marked with a sign bearing the name of the company, leads (R) to the CAPE FISHING COMPANY PLANT, 21.5 *m.*, a group of weatherbeaten buildings surrounded by racks for drying nets. Fishermen here put to sea for shark with chain, rope, and shark hooks (*see Tour 1d*).

Left from the company plant (*inquire about road conditions*) to CAPE CANAVERAL (Sp., reedy point), first noted in 1513 by Ponce de Leon, who called it Cape of Currents. It appeared as Canaveral on LeMoyne's map of 1564. Shipwrecked here in July 1572, Menéndez walked to St.Augustine, arriving in late fall, having escaped death at the hands of Indians by telling them that a large Spanish force was following. CAPE CANAVERAL LIGHTHOUSE, banded white and black, rises 145 feet above sea level and has a 430,000 candlepower light visible 18 miles at sea.

South of the town of Merritt Island, State 219 (asphalt-paved) winds through a rich agricultural region. Passing through Caribbean pine woods and small orange groves, between border plantings of red and white oleanders, hibiscus, and wild flowers, the road climbs over a low hill from which is a view (R) of the Indian River. The orange groves on the rolling terrain contain trees so large that it is difficult to see beyond the first row. Several groves of mangoes and a great variety of shrubs appear; at intervals scarlet hibiscus grows along the road. In the background, between groves, are glimpses of pines hung with long strands of Spanish moss.

The highway is a densely shaded tropical drive. Palms, oaks, and cedars border the road. In this jungle, and elsewhere on southern Merritt Island where the land has not been cleared, are found trees growing more than 200 miles north of their native habitat on the Florida Keys. C.T.Simpson, naturalist, has noted 43 tropical and 25 warm temperate varieties; among others, ironwood, gumbo limbo, soapberry, torchwood, strangling fig, paradise tree, pond apple, and necklace bean. This varied flora is attributed to the narrowness of the island, washed on both sides by tides that carry warm water into the bays and sounds.

Emerging from the jungle, the highway skirts several unfenced orange groves and plunges into a stand of low trees with branches forming an arch over the road. As the island narrows, both the Indian and Banana rivers come in view; front yards of farmhouses run down to one river, their back yards to the other. Tapering to a width that a man can straddle, the tip of the island emerges from dense shrubbery as a wall of coquina 6 feet high.

The road crosses a narrow reach of the Banana River on a toll bridge (25¢), 48.6 *m.*, and traverses a marshy section of the peninsula.

At 50 *m.* is the junction with State 101, an asphalt-paved road.

Right on State 101, crossing the Indian River on a wooden bridge, to EAU GALLIE, 2.2 *m.* (19 alt., 871 pop.) (*see Tour 1c*).

South of the junction with State 101, the route cuts through level sandy pine flats.

INDIATLANTIC, 53.5 *m.*, has a beach frequented by residents of Melbourne.

Left (straight ahead) from Indiatlantic on a paved road to MELBOURNE BEACH, 1.5 *m.* (72 pop.), a swimming resort.

West (R) of Indiatlantic, the route follows Melbourne road.

MELBOURNE, 55 *m.* (22 alt., 2,677 pop.) (*see Tour 1c*), is at the junction with US 1 (*see Tour 1c*).

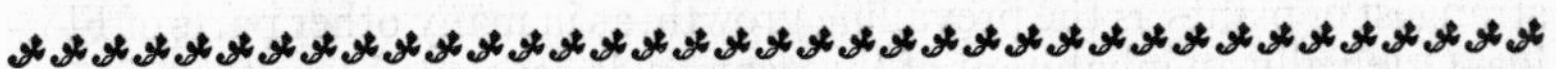

Tour 2

(Brunswick, Ga.)—Jacksonville—DeLand—Winter Park—Orlando—Winter Haven—Arcadia—Punta Gorda; 320.1 *m.* US 17.

Hard-surfaced roadbed throughout, mainly concrete- and asphalt-paved; watch for cattle.
Route paralleled by Seaboard Air Line Ry. between Georgia Line and Jacksonville, by Atlantic Coast Line R.R. between Jacksonville and Arcadia, by Atlantic Coast Line R.R. and Seaboard Air Line Ry. between Arcadia and Fort Ogden, and by Atlantic Coast Line R.R. between Fort Ogden and Punta Gorda.
Good accommodations.

US 17, main artery of passenger and truck travel between north and central Florida, serves thriving resort centers, large citrus- and vegetable-growing areas, cattle ranges, and phosphate-mining regions. Leaving the pine woods of north Florida, it parallels the western bank of the St. Johns River between Jacksonville and Palatka, and traverses the citrus belt of central Florida, a region of lakes and hills. Through the broad valley of Peace River it continues southwest to Charlotte Harbor, an arm of the Gulf of Mexico.

Section a. GEORGIA LINE to JACKSONVILLE; 30.6 *m.* *US* 17

Between the pine flatwoods of northern Florida and Jacksonville, this heavily traveled route is lined with billboards, filling stations, roadside eating places, fruit and pecan stands, and tourist cabin camps. The 'Free Garage' advertised by some is so attached that the cabin can be entered directly from a car. This type is said to be popular with patrons from near-by cities; others specify for 'Tourists Only.'

US 17 crosses St.Marys River, the Georgia Line, 0 *m.*, 44 miles south of Brunswick, Ga. (*see Ga. Guide, Tour* 1). On being expelled from the Georgia Territorial Assembly for seditious utterances in 1755, Edmund Grey fled to the banks of the St.Marys and founded a colony of outlaws and malcontents, later dispersed by British forces. When Spain ceded Florida to England in 1763, the boundary between Georgia and Florida was in part established along the river. Many Revolutionary War skirmishes were fought near by, and in 1783 when the American Colonies achieved independence, the St.Marys was confirmed as the southeastern boundary of the new Nation.

A railroad trestle (R) parallels the bridge over the St.Marys; sandy pine flats stretch back from the marshy banks. The broad thickly-turfed shoulders of the highway slope off into shallow ditches. Saw palmetto, one of the strangest of plants, is the prevailing growth, as in many other parts of Florida. Originally an inhabitant of the swamps, it developed a system of roots running down from its trunk to prevent its being washed away. Later, it invaded the woods and met a new enemy, fire, which it escaped by changing its direction of growth from the more or less vertical to the horizontal, learning to creep along the ground. As it advances, it sends down more roots and frequently branches. These branches in turn send down roots, and, as the old parent trunk and roots die, become independent new plants, and thus spread over wide areas by a process of parturition.

YULEE, 9 *m.* (39 alt., 155 pop.), a scattered settlement along the highway, was named for David L. Yulee, U.S. Senator from Florida (1845–51; 1855–61). After election he had his name changed by act of the State legislature from David Levy to David Yulee. Although he frequently denied that he favored secession, Yulee and his colleague, Senator Mallory, jointly requested from the War Department a statement of munitions and equipment in Florida forts on January 2, 1860, and he wrote to a friend in the State, 'the immediately important thing to be done is the occupation of the forts and arsenals in Florida.' *The New York Times* blamed 'the railroad class' of Florida for seeking secession and accused them of wishing to wipe out debts owed to the North. At this time the Florida Railroad, of which Yulee was president, owed one firm in New York $750,000. Later, when the Confederate army impressed some of the equipment of the road, Yulee instituted a civil action and obtained an injunction to prevent its removal.

At the end of the war, Yulee was arrested for aiding in the escape of Jefferson Davis, and was imprisoned at Fort Pulaski, Georgia. He was released several months later. During the Reconstruction the Republicans accused him of influencing the votes of employees of the railroad. He replied that the allegation was 'unfounded and untrue,' but added that, 'if the company had done what is alleged, it would have done only what it had a right to do.'

Agriculture

CITRUS GROVE, NEAR WINTER HAVEN

PICKING GRAPEFRUIT
Photograph by Dahlgren

Photograph by courtesy of Respess Engraving Company

DUSTING COTTON, NORTH FLORIDA

PLANTING CELERY, NEAR SANFORD

Photograph by courtesy of Farm Security Administration

STRAWBERRY PICKERS, STARKE

ANSPORTING SUGAR CANE FROM FIELDS, IN THE EVERGLADES

Photograph by courtesy of Florida Photographic Concern, Ft. Pierce

Photograph by courtesy of Farm Security Administra

BEAN PICKERS, HOMESTEAD

Photograph by Paul Diggs

STRAWBERRY PICKERS RETURNING FROM THE FIELD

Photograph by courtesy of Department of Agriculture

4-H CLUB BOYS MILKING GOAT

IN THE POTATO FIELD, DADE COUNTY

Photograph by Ted Ramsey

Photograph by courtesy of Department of Agriculture

FARM HOUSE

ARMER'S MARKET, MIAMI

Photograph by courtesy of Department of Agriculture

Photograph by courtesy of Department of Agricultu

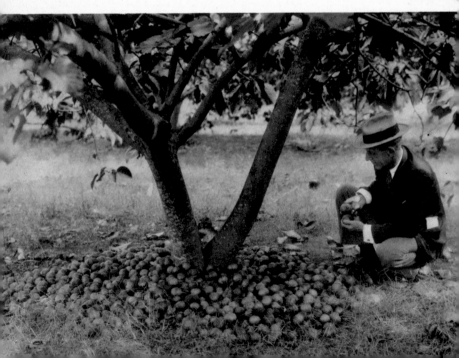

CUTTING PALMETTOS

TUNG TR

Yulee is at the junction with State 13 (*see Tour 3a*).

Saw palmetto and longleaf pine grow profusely along the curving highway, once part of the Kings Road, built by subscription in 1765 between New Smyrna and Colerain, Ga., running by way of St.Augustine and Cowford, as Jacksonville was then called. The highway crosses the NASSAU RIVER, 13.1 *m.*; during the American Revolution large plantations were developed along its banks by refugee Tories from the Colonies (*see History*). Salt marshes extend on both sides of the road for several miles, similar to those of Georgia described in Sidney Lanier's '*Marshes of Glynn*.'

The JACKSONVILLE MUNICIPAL AIRPORT (L), 23.9 *m.*, is the point of entry for Florida airline traffic. A white concrete station fronts a wide brick drive bordering the western edge of the runway; to the north stands a large hangar, repair shops, first aid and fire stations, and a power plant.

At 25.2 *m.* is the junction with Hecksher Drive.

Left on this road is the JACKSONVILLE CITY ZOO, 0.5 *m.*, an 11-acre tract on the Trout River, a tributary of the St.Johns. At the entrance (R) stands the small brick-and-stucco JACKSONVILLE AIRWAY RADIO STATION, which broadcasts weather information at half-hour intervals for aircraft approaching the Jacksonville Municipal Airport.

Right from the entrance is a drive lined on both sides with open-air cages, pools, and well-spaced animal houses. A circular pond (R) contains ducks, geese, and swans. Passing a pond for alligators (R), the driveway curves (L) along the river front. Here a smooth slope under oaks and pines provides a grassy breeze-swept picnic ground. Turning (L) from the river, the drive passes a group of white and orange frame buildings, including the elephant house (L), a small bird house (R) filled with chirping canaries and love birds, and (R) a row of cages. Among the caged animals are a mandril baboon from West Africa; a smaller chacma baboon from South Africa; a coati mundi, related to the raccoon, having brown and white fur, large piggish eyes, and a flexible snout; 'Snookums,' a lethargic sloth; ill-tempered wildcats; a honey bear; monkeys; and a Sphinx baboon from West Africa. There is a cage of bald eagles, and others for pheasants, peacocks, Florida's rare snowy egret, and a striking blue-black curassow from South America. Not far away are the cages (R) of the lions—Mike and Minnie, Leo, Mildred, and Tarzana.

At 0.6 *m.*, in the center of Hecksher Drive, is a toll house (*round trip to Fort George Island: passenger cars, 75¢; coupés, 50¢*). Beyond the toll house Hecksher Drive winds seaward through dense woodland; a salt-water marsh (R) lies between the highway and the St.Johns. Seagulls, fishhawks, and herons rise from the marshes, circling over the river. Bulky freighters and small ships are often within 500 feet of the road, plowing through the swift current. On both sides of the river are square and diamond-shaped wooden markers, range-finders used for navigation. Swinging their craft around a bend, pilots sight identical markers and by bringing them in line, maneuver their ships through the channel.

PILOT TOWN, 15 *m.*, with a dock and several weathered shacks, is a settlement of fishing guides, who live in small wooden houses and rent boats ($1) to anglers. A guide fishes with the incoming tide, making a daily check of the fishing grounds. Fall is his best season, and Sunday brings him the most customers. His regular patrons are year-round residents of Jacksonville. His income ranges from $12 to $15 per week.

East of Pilot Town the road follows a mile-long paved causeway across the marsh to FORT GEORGE ISLAND, 16 *m.*, near the mouth of the St.Johns River. In 1568 French soldiers crossed here to attack a blockhouse, built beside the river by the Spanish before 1567; in 1600 the mission of San Juan Del Puerto on Fort George Island had 500 Indian parishioners. James Oglethorpe, English general and Colonial leader of Georgia, invaded Florida, camped here in 1736, and in 1815 John McIntosh, President of the short-lived Republic of Florida (*see Tour 3a*), was a resident. Many of the buildings still standing were built by Zephaniah Kingsley, a prominent slave trader. He brought Negroes from Africa in his own ships. In 1817 he purchased land on the island and cultivated a large plantation which remained in the Kingsley family until 1868, when it was sold to John Rollins of Dover, N.H. On his arrival at Fort George, Rollins found many of the former Kingsley slaves still residing in cabins. He did much to develop the Mandarin orange and the shaddock, a forerunner of grapefruit. Later, when orange groves were not bearing and conditions for fruit and truck farming were poor, he built two large hotels, one on the present site of the Ribaut Club, the other fronting the St.Johns River; both were destroyed by fire. Today the entire plantation is owned by the Fort George Club, which uses the old plantation house (*see below*) as headquarters. Another tract on the island is owned by the Ribaut Club (*see below*).

At 16.6 *m.* the road forks; R. here to the RIBAUT CLUB (*private*), 20 *m.*, a Southern Colonial style house of white-washed brick.

The KINGSLEY PLANTATION HOUSE (*private*), 22 *m.*, is a two-story white frame building, with a porch extending around all four sides. The attic contains two small slave prisons; the doors are heavily studded with nails, and have large strap hinges and padlocks. The basement of the house was also used as a prison. A narrow staircase leads from the second floor to a mirador, said to have been used as a lookout to watch for approaching vessels. The old well, adjacent to the house, formerly equipped with sweep and bucket, was used by everyone in the neighborhood. Immediately to the rear is the whitewashed two-story brick MA'AM ANNA'S HOUSE, so designated by island residents in recollection of the name given Anna Madegigine Jai, wife of Kingsley. The front room is believed to have been Ma'am Anna's dining room, with a kitchen in the rear. Two rooms are on the second floor—one, her sleeping room; the other for children. Anna, daughter of a chief of Senegal, was married to Kingsley by native ritual when the latter was purchasing slaves in Africa. Tall, slender, and dignified, she insisted on following the native custom of serving her husband's guests, although she had many slaves.

Approximately 200 yards south of Ma'am Anna's House is the stable, consisting of a small white-washed brick structure and a tabby coquina-rock building, which many believe stands on the site of barracks built by James Oglethorpe about 1740. A few yards southeast of the stable are the foundations of a circular building known as the grist mill, the exact history of which is unknown. It was constructed of 'tabby' (*see St.Augustine*), a material made of lime and shells.

Approximately 2.5 miles south of the house are the slave quarters, a semi-circle of 34 roofless huts built of oyster shell. The two cabins nearest the road, each with two rooms, were used by 'drivers,' the Negro leaders of the slaves. A tabby house, believed to have been built on foundations of a mission, stands at the southern tip of the island.

JACKSONVILLE, 30.6 *m.* (25 alt., 129,549 pop.) (*see Jacksonville*).

Points of Interest: Naval Stores Yards, Cotton Compress, Hemming Park, Memorial Park, and others.

Jacksonville is at the junction with US 1 (*see Tour 1a and b*), US 90 (*see Tour 7a*), and State 78 (*see Tour 1A*).

Section b. JACKSONVILLE to DELAND; 110.1 *m.* *US* 17

South of JACKSONVILLE, 0 *m.*, the route offers frequent views of the broad St.Johns, a river of horizons; white bay, live oak, dogwood, and holly grow in the dense forests along its banks. Farther south, the highway crosses undulating sandy ridges covered with pine and gnarled blackjack oaks, with an occasional orange grove.

YUKON, 9.3 *m.* (400 pop.), was the site of an extensive plantation established by A.M.Reed. Many Negroes living here today are descendants of the slaves who remained loyal to their owner during the War between the States, and were given property by Reed.

Left from Yukon on a paved road to CAMP FOSTER (*fishing, crabbing*), 1 *m.*, on the shore of the St.Johns River. The camp was built during the World War and is now used by the National Guard. In 1939 the camp and adjoining properties were purchased by Duval County for the $15,000,000 Southeastern Air Base of the United States Navy.

At 12.5 *m.* is a junction with a brick-paved road.

Left on this road is the old residential section of Orange Park (*see below*), 1.5 *m.*, affording views of the wide reaches of the river.

MOOSEHAVEN (R), 1.7 *m.*, is the national home of the Loyal Order of Moose, a tract of 87 acres along the river. Its 39 buildings, ranging from five-room bungalows to large halls, house 200 old people, one-fifth of whom are women. Those who desire it are given light employment.

ORANGE PARK, 14.1 *m.* (24 alt., 661 pop.), occupies land granted by Spain in 1790 to Zephaniah Kingsley (*see above*), who was largely responsible for the early development of this area. Kingsley Avenue, with its double row of live oaks, traverses a part of Laurel Grove, the original Kingsley plantation.

The YALE ANTHROPOID EXPERIMENTAL STATION (*closed to public*), established in 1929 by the Yale University Laboratory of Primate Biology, houses about 30 chimpanzees used for the study of primate reproduction, genetics, behavioral adaptation, hygiene, and pathology.

Right from Orange Park on a paved highway is MIDDLEBURG, 16 *m.* (35 alt., 150 pop.), one of Florida's forgotten ports; during the 1840's cotton was brought here in ox carts. Black Creek here is narrow but deep enough for sea-going vessels. A wagon trail led from the settlement to roads connecting with Tampa, Tallahassee, and other points. The wooden METHODIST CHURCH is said to have been used for regular worship since its construction in 1847. The CLARK HOUSE (*private*), north of the post office, built in 1835, was occupied by officers under Generals Scott and Jesup during the Seminole Indian campaigns, and housed Union officers during the War between the States.

The highway crosses DOCTOR'S INLET, 15.1 *m.*, so named on Florida maps of the English period (1763–83). A fishing camp in an orange grove (L), 15.5 *m.*, marks the SITE OF AN OLD PLANTATION HOUSE built in the second Spanish period (1784–1821). During the Patriot's Rebellion against Spain (*see Tour 3a*), the owner was ordered to move across the river, but refused. The Spaniards burned the house.

At 20.9 *m.* is the junction with a macadam-paved road.

Left on this road to the HIBERNIA PLANTATION, 0.5 *m.*, remnant of a large Spanish grant of 1790 to the Fleming family, whose descendants live in the well-kept plantation house. The white structure along the river was one of the few to escape damage during the War between the States. Square columns, two stories high, support galleries along its north and east sides, and the high gabled roof is shaded by a patriarchal oak.

BLACK CREEK, its name corrupted from Río Blanco (Sp., white river), is spanned by a concrete bridge at 22.7 *m.* (*boats for fishing and crabbing, 50¢ to $1 a day*).

MAGNOLIA SPRINGS (*free mineral water*), 24.8 *m.*, was established before the War between the States. A large river-front hotel, which burned in 1920, was popular among tourists during the 1880's and 1890's, and numbered President Cleveland among its guests. The President, it is said, had the spring water sent regularly to the White House. Between the springs and the highway is a neglected MONUMENT TO UNION SOLDIERS who died in the Florida campaigns. The small stone shaft, surrounded by weeds and bushes, stands in an abandoned cemetery, said to have been used by whites before the war and as a burial place of Negro yellow-fever victims during the Reconstruction.

GREEN COVE SPRINGS, 27.6 *m.* (28 alt., 1,719 pop.), seat of Clay County, is a small resort centered around a spring that flows 3,000 gallons a minute, impounded to form a large swimming pool. Residents obtain fresh water from the spring every day, believing it loses its medicinal qualities and strength in 12 hours.

Green Cove Springs was a fashionable spa in the late 1870's and 80's. Steamers from Charleston and Savannah came up the St. Johns River and landed passengers at the resort piers. Band concerts were held daily during winter months. President Grover Cleveland (1885–89) and well-to-do northerners came annually. Gail Borden, condensed milk manufacturer, and J.C. Penney, chain-store magnate, bought property here and took an active part in the development of the town. Penney also established a farm colony 6 miles to the west (*see below*).

With the coming of railroads and the development of resorts farther south, the village lost most of its out-of-state patronage, but continues to attract visitors from various parts of Florida. Fishermen find black bass plentiful in the brackish waters of the St. Johns.

Augusta Savage, distinguished Negro sculptress, lived here in her childhood. When she was five years old, her father, a Methodist minister, chastised her for 'making graven images.' Now a resident of New York City, she has gained international recognition for her figures of whites and Negroes.

1. Left from Green Cove Springs on a sand road to the SITE OF FORT ST. FRANCIS DE PUPA, 3 *m.*, erected by the Spaniards in 1737. Destroyed by the British under Oglethorpe in 1740, the fort, originally of wood, was replaced with a stone structure. Although all traces of the building have been obliterated, the site is well defined by earthen embankments.

2. Right from Green Cove Springs on State 48 is the PENNEY FARMS MEMORIAL HOME COMMUNITY, 8 *m.* (366 pop.), a group of buildings of French Norman design containing 96 apartments and a chapel. It was built by J.C. Penney as a memorial to his father, the Reverend James Cash Penney, and his mother, Mary Frances Penney, and was dedicated in 1927 as a home for retired religious leaders of all denominations.

3. Left from Green Cove Springs on State 48 to SHANDS BRIDGE (*fishing boats*), 4 *m.*, spanning the St. Johns River. This bridge is 2.5 miles in length.

East of ORANGEDALE, 6.5 *m.* (29 alt., 50 pop.), State 48 continues to ST. AUGUSTINE, 26 *m.* (7 alt., 12,111 pop.) (*see Tour 1b*).

Between Green Cove Springs and Palatka the country is sparsely settled. The pine woods along the way abound in small game. Large tracts are owned by non-resident cattle and lumber interests, and for many years farmers who attempted to fence and cultivate land were warned to leave the county. Along the roadside are many varieties of wild flowers, notably the fly catcher, or pitcher plant; insects, attracted by a sweet fluid exuded by its veins, fall into its pitcherlike leaves and are unable to crawl out.

US 17 crosses the old BELLAMY ROAD, 33.4 *m.*, part of an early highway between Pensacola and St.Augustine. Initially proposed at the first Florida Territorial Convention in 1832 and approved by Congress two years later, the road was constructed by John Bellamy (*see Tour 7b*) from Deerfield, on Pensacola Bay, along an Indian trail to the Choctawhatchee River, thence to Ochesee Bluff on the Apalachicola River, and finally to St.Augustine. The length of the road was measured by counting the revolutions of an ox-cart wheel.

BOSTWICK, 43.1 *m.* (34 alt., 200 pop.), is a turpentine and truck-farming settlement, once the site of a large stock farm. Truck loads of cabbages roll out of this section in spring; signs posted along the highway direct truck drivers to farms when the crop is ready for market.

The cabbages are planted in straight furrows cut by mule-drawn plows, harrows, or discs. They are picked in the early spring by Negroes living in the vicinity of the farms, who bargain for wages ranging from $1 to $4 a day. The pickers cut the cabbage heads from the stalk with a knife and toss them into field crates which, when full, are carried to a packing shed in one corner of the field. Here the heads are trimmed, crated, and stacked to await the truckers. Truck drivers usually buy loads in bulk, paying the farmer by the ton.

PALATKA, 51.7 *m.* (25 alt., 6,500 pop.), seat of Putnam County, built at an elbow turn of the mile-wide St.Johns River, has been an important shipping center and port since the 1870's. Lumbering is the dominant industry; a cypress mill, one of the largest in the United States, cuts 40,000,-000 feet annually.

Some of the town's wide streets are paved with brick. In the shade of large oaks and magnolias are many old houses built in the period immediately following the War between the States, when Palatka was a popular tourist resort and river traffic reached its height. On the menu of one of the fashionable hotels of the day, patrons were offered 'adolescent chicken.'

The trading post established here on the river in 1821 took its name from the Indian word *pilaklikaha* (crossing over). On March 10, 1864, Palatka was occupied without resistance by Federal troops, supported by gunboats. After a number of skirmishes the Federals withdrew, but late in May landed another force 8 miles to the south from the steamer *Columbine*. While Confederate spies watched, the Federal troops set off overland for Volusia. As soon as they had disappeared, Confederates trained light artillery on the boat, which soon raised the white flag. Eighty-two Federals were killed and 65 taken prisoners; the Confederates suffered no losses. On August 3 Union troops abandoned the vicinity.

A dispatch in the Tallahassee *Floridian* of April 26, 1867, noted that a Union League had been formed in Palatka 'with a view of making a strict division in politics.' In December of that year a council of the Ku Klux

Klan was organized, according to its constitution to 'counteract the evil influences now being brought to bear on politics by the Union League.' The hand-written document, now in the State archives at Tallahassee, includes a diagram showing where each of the officers was to sit during conclaves.

From the late 1870's until the early 1900's, when railroads were extended into the territory, the St. Johns River carried quantities of timber, naval stores, and citrus fruit to market. Luxurious passenger steamers from as far as the Mississippi brought tourists up the river. As almost all vessels were wood burners, an extensive industry was founded on supplying them with fuel. Criblike piers were built out into the channel at intervals, and on them wood was stacked. During the day someone was on hand to check deliveries and receive tickets for the wood taken, but at night boat crews deposited tickets in a locked box or keg on the dock. Signed by the master or purser of the boat, these tickets passed for currency among river-town merchants and were redeemable in cash at Jacksonville.

In the AZALEA RAVINE GARDENS (*admission*, $1), Twigg St. between Division St. and Mosely Ave., 85 acres developed with the assistance of FERA and Civil Works Administration labor, more than 100,000 azaleas and thousands of palms, roses, flame vines, crape myrtles, magnolias, and other subtropical trees and shrubs are planted. Foot trails wind across the steep slopes and through the lush cool depths of the natural ravine, encircled by a 5-mile loop drive. Fed by springs and spanned by a number of suspension bridges, the creek widens frequently into quiet pools covered with lilies and other flowering plants.

ST. MARKS EPISCOPAL CHURCH, cor. Madison and 2nd Sts., erected about 1850, is a frame structure with a single steeple, vertical weatherboarding and battens, and small stained-glass windows. The building was designed by Richard Upjohn, designer of New York City's Trinity Church. Union troops used the structure during the War between the States.

The giant oak, on Rivers St., was formerly the scene of exciting political rallies. 'Governors were made and unmade beneath its branches,' it was said. At a big rally here in the 1870's orators first called Palatka the 'Gem of the St. Johns.' In later years the Gem City Guards and their band, part of the National Guard, were renowned throughout Florida.

The CONFEDERATE MONUMENT, in Courthouse Square, has at its base a 40-pound cannon ball fired during the Battle of Palatka in 1864 (*see above*).

The MESSMER HOUSE, 224 1st St., was erected by the Union army during the War between the States and periodically used as an officers' headquarters. The one-story structure, 90 feet long and 40 feet wide, is built of hand-hewn pine, and has pillars of coquina, said to have been hauled by oxen from St. Augustine.

The MULLHOLLAND PLACE (*open*), at the north end of 1st St., was the home and estate of Judge Isaac H. Bronson (1802–55). A Palatka social center in the 1850's, the square two-story house, with porch supported by tall square columns, sits back from the road amid old shade and fruit trees. Because of its strategic position on the river it was occupied in turn by Union and Confederate troops during the War between the States. Soldiers wrote fierce challenges to their enemies on the walls, it is said, but always made certain the house was unoccupied before venturing into it.

Palatka is at the junction with State 28 (*see Tour* 19), which unites with US 17 for 5.6 miles.

EAST PALATKA, 53.4 *m.* (17 alt., 1,000 pop.), on the east bank of the St. Johns River, is a shipping point for vegetables, fruit, and lumber. The road runs through a high hammock where dark green bay and magnolia trees predominate. The town was the northern terminal of the St. Johns & Halifax Railway, a primitive logging road that ran south to Garfield in 1886. In 1889, Utley J. White, owner of the road, disposed of it to Henry M. Flagler, who extended the line to Ormond and Daytona, and inaugurated passenger service (*see Transportation*).

Left from East Palatka on State 14 is HASTINGS, 8.5 *m.* (10 alt., 673 pop.), an unusually large early-potato market. During 1937 approximately 15,000 acres in the vicinity yielded 2,092 carloads of Spaulding Rose, Green Mountain, and Red Bliss varieties, valued at $1,882,800. In 1918 a scarcity of potatoes in northern markets boosted the price to $20 a barrel. Growers here harvested an unusually large crop, and buyers and commission men from all parts of the country rushed in and paid cash for their purchases. So heavy were deposits in the small local bank that the town officials called out the Home Guards to protect the building and its contents. Uniformed men patrolled the streets each night and remained on duty until armored trucks arrived to transfer the cash to Jacksonville banks. A field laboratory of the Agricultural Experiment Station of the University of Florida, under the direction of the State Board of Control in Tallahassee, is maintained here for experimental work in the study of potato diseases.

SAN MATEO, 56.8 *m.* (69 alt., 175 pop.), on a high bluff above the St. Johns River, contains fine orange groves, old frame houses, and many large oaks and magnolias. The fertile countryside has been cultivated for nearly two centuries; many orange groves have been bearing fruit for more than 50 years. Experiments were conducted here as early as 1912 in protecting citrus groves from frosts. Today some growers employ a skeleton structure of water pipes raised above the ground, with cross-pipes forming a roofing frame, which furnishes not only protection but irrigation. The method is not used extensively, however, because of its relatively high cost.

In 1760 the townsite was included in a land grant of 20,000 acres to Denys Rolle, a wealthy member of the British parliament. The village of Rollestown, called Charlotia by its visionary founder, was established in 1765 on the St. Johns River about a mile from San Mateo. Here Rolle brought a motley crew of men and women from the slums and streets of London, intending to rehabilitate these unfortunates, create a Utopia, and make Charlotia its capital. Disease, dissatisfaction, and desertion soon decreased the ranks of the colonists. Undaunted, Rolle purchased additional land until he controlled 80,000 acres; he worked his plantations with slave labor, and struggled along for several years, shipping rice, corn, beef, lumber, and naval stores. In one season he exported 1,000 gallons of orange wine. When Florida was returned to Spain in 1783, Rolle abandoned his plantation and removed with his slaves to the Bahamas.

San Mateo is at the junction with State 28 (*see Tour* 19).

SATSUMA, 63.1 *m.* (78 alt., 155 pop.), named for the orange grown throughout north Florida, is a small trading center in a citrus and truck-growing area. Rambling old two-story farmhouses sit back from the road, their driveways bordered with vine-draped oaks, their yards bright with flowering shrubs.

Right from Satsuma on State 308 is WELAKA, 7 *m.* (26 alt., 409 pop.); here is the FLORIDA STATE FISH HATCHERY AND GAME FARM (*open*), a 2,500-acre reservation developed by the Resettlement Administration with the State Board of Conservation. The shad hatchery on the river front annually releases millions of fingerlings into the St.Johns River. The aquarium contains various species of fresh-water fish native to Florida; 24 large outdoor brood ponds capable of holding 3,000 bass have been constructed. Adjoining the hatchery are the deer park, the quail farm, an aviary, and well-arranged exhibits of Florida bird life.

CRESCENT CITY, 76.4 *m.* (955 pop.), is built on a bluff overlooking Crescent Lake; orange groves crowd into the center of town. CRESCENT LAKE (L) and LAKE STELLA (R) offer good fishing and bathing.

SEVILLE, 84.8 *m.* (53 alt., 585 pop.), in the midst of the high pine and citrus belt, faces Lake Louise. On fertile hammocks of this section the small Seville orange grows wild; the trees are said to have been imported and planted by the Spaniards.

Between Seville and Barberville extensive orange groves border both sides of the highway. The Seville orange tree is unusually tall and wide spreading. While its fruit is smaller than other varieties, manufacturers of marmalade prefer it. Several small hamlets cluster around barnlike citrus-packing houses; occasionally a turpentine camp with a scattering of Negro shanties is passed. During winter when hickory trees are bare, large clumps of mistletoe among the boughs are gathered and sold by local people.

In the Florida scrub country east of the highway, tales are told of the dance of the whooping crane, a spectacle described by Marjorie Kinnan Rawlings in her novel *The Yearling* (1938). Assembling in marshlands, the cranes move in formations as if dancing a cotillion. Two of the birds stand apart, making strange not unmusical sounds. Others, silent, shuffle slowly in a circle about a group that moves counterclockwise. The dancers flap their wings and lift their feet, dropping and raising their heads from their white breasts. When the two 'musicians' finish and drop back into the outer circle, another pair takes their place, and the performance is repeated. After perhaps an hour the dance ends and the birds depart, whooping their strange harsh cries, forming a great circle that straightens into a long wavering line as they disappear beyond the horizon.

A large turpentine colony, 89.7 *m.*, consists of makeshift Negro cabins grouped about a smoke-blackened still. Barrels of turpentine and rosin line the roadside awaiting transportation to the nearest shipping point.

On Saturday nights many Negroes congregate in 'jooks' (*see Folklore*) to sing and dance. Some of the merrymakers prefer to gamble; others attend to meet women from other camps. Occasionally the music is broken by the crack of a pistol; at other times differences are settled with knives, notwithstanding signs reading, 'No Guns or Knives Aloud.' Patrons are also warned, 'You can DRINK in here, but go outside to get DRUNK!' Some jooks announce, 'No women allowed en hear; this don't mean Bob, it means you!'

BARBERVILLE, 95.2 *m.* (44 alt., 357 pop.), a trading community for farmers, was founded on the site of an old plantation. The settlement was at first without stores, and women are said to have driven ox teams over Indian trails to the Atlantic seaboard to obtain salt.

Barberville is at the junction (R) with State 19 (*see Tour* 21).

DE LEON SPRINGS, 102.6 *m.* (450 pop.), is a quiet village known chiefly for the PONCE DE LEON SPRINGS, on a short drive (R) through an arch and a dense growth of trees. The springs form a subterranean stream flowing approximately 94,000 gallons per minute, part of which is impounded in a large circular pool flanked by a concrete retaining wall. Excess water cascades over spillways into a lake and eventually flows to the St. Johns River, 7 miles to the west. A casino stands at the edge of the pool; a boathouse faces the lake below the springs. Near by are the RUINS OF A SUGAR MILL; according to local tradition, it was built by Spaniards previous to 1763, and additions to the mill were made by the British after Florida was ceded to them in 1763. Partly demolished by Indians during the Seminole War, the mill was rebuilt in 1854, only to be destroyed by Federal troops in 1864.

In 1819, when Florida became a Territory, this area, then known as Spring Garden, was exchanged for 50 Negro women, and the land planted to corn, sugar cane, and indigo. John James Audubon, the naturalist, visited here in 1832, traveling by horseback along sandy trails. He wrote of an old water wheel, a duplicate of which is in operation; he described a pair of ibises that he shot, the wild orange trees, and his wanderings along the creek and streams leading to the St. Johns River.

At 108 *m.* is a junction with US 92-State 21 (*see Tour* 8), which unites with US 17 for 2.1 miles.

DELAND, 110.1 *m.* (27 alt., 5,246 pop.), seat of Volusia County and center of a fertile citrus area, is also a college town. Many of its activities revolve about the campus of Stetson University.

DeLand was founded in 1876 by Henry A. DeLand, baking powder manufacturer, who planted water oaks 50 feet apart along prospective streets. So determined were early settlers to make their community notable for shade trees that in 1886 the city council ruled that property owners would be allowed a 50¢ tax rebate for each tree two inches or more in diameter, planted by them along the streets. The response threatened to bankrupt the town, and the ordinance was repealed less than two years later.

Lue Gim Gong, a Chinese known as the Luther Burbank of Florida, settled here in 1886 and soon gained recognition as a citrus culturist. In 1889 he introduced a new variety of orange, for which the U.S. Department of Agriculture awarded him the Wilder medal, and in 1892 perfected the Gim Gong grapefruit, which withstands 10 degrees greater cold than other varieties. He pollinated a currant with a grape to create the cherry currant, which attains the size of a cherry; perfected a peach for growth in greenhouses; and produced a salmon-colored raspberry.

Stetson University was established by DeLand in 1886, as DeLand University, with the financial assistance of John B. Stetson, hat manufacturer.

Co-educational and non-sectarian, it was incorporated as a university under its present name in 1889. The school is sponsored by a conference of Baptist churches. Many of its 1,000 students are from northern states.

The HULLEY MEMORIAL TOWER, a square red brick campanile 80 feet in height, rising from a dressed limestone base, stands on the campus as a memorial to Lincoln Hulley, a former president of the school, and his wife, Eloise. In the CARNEGIE-SAMPSON LIBRARY (*open* 7:30–10 *p.m.*), gift of Andrew Carnegie, are the library and the sorority and class rooms for women students. The Sampson Annex contains Government documents and spacious reading rooms.

ELIZABETH HALL, a two-story red brick structure with a square tower and an open arched and columned belfry, houses an ART MUSEUM (*open daily*, 9–5; *free*), established in 1910 by friends of Stetson. It contains several hundred paintings of American, French, and Italian Schools. The SCHOOL OF TECHNOLOGY AND HALL OF SCIENCE, opposite Elizabeth Hall, is a two-story gray stucco building set in landscaped grounds.

The DELAND PUBLIC LIBRARY, 449 E.New York Ave., founded in 1912, contains 13,000 volumes, and was given to the city by Seward W. Baker. The TOURIST COMMUNITY HOUSE AND RECREATION CENTER (*open Sept. to May*), City Hall Square, has assembly rooms, a checker pagoda, a bowling alley, shuffleboard and roque courts. In the attractively landscaped CITY PARK, Indiana Ave., is a municipal bandshell; in winter concerts are given (*free*) by the Stetson University Band on Sunday afternoons.

The ROYAL FRENCH MUSEUM (*open daily* 2–5; *adm.* 25¢), S.Spring Garden Ave. and Camphor Lake, was formerly the home of John B. Stetson. The paneling of its interior was once part of a French chateau. The museum contains documents and relics of medieval Europe, including the Shrine of the Bishops of Liège; the library of Louis XVIII of France and his cousin, Count d'Avaray; a will bearing the seal and signature of Louis XVIII; and rare books, furniture, tapestries, jeweled prayer books, crosses, prayer rings, and other objects.

DeLand is at the junction with US 92-State 21 (*see Tour* 8a).

Section c. DELAND to HAINES CITY, 79.9 *m.* *US* 17

Between DELAND, 0 *m.*, and Haines City the route penetrates the heart of Florida's winter-celery region and traverses a rolling lake-studded area covered with large citrus groves. Large cypress swamps and stretches of pine forests, worked by turpentine and lumber interests, are interspersed among the farms.

ORANGE CITY, 5.6 *m.* (35 alt., 572 pop.), founded in the 1870's by three families from Eau Claire, Wisconsin, attracted by the possibilities of citrus culture, was originally known as Wisconsin Settlement.

Left from Orange City 4 *m.* on a paved road to CAMP CASSADAGA, conducted by the Cassadaga Spiritualist Association, which was founded by George B. Colby in 1893. The first meeting of the association was held here in that year. Within a fenced area of 25 acres, deeded to the association by the founder, are a stucco auditorium seating 2,000, a frame two-story hotel, apartment houses, and many one- and two-story cottages on shaded lanes along the shores of small lakes. The post office, general store, and other residences lie outside the enclosed tract.

The camp is the second largest of its kind in the United States, ranking just below Lily Dale, New York, described in its literature as 'the fountain head of modern spiritualism.' To Cassadaga come mediums, who charge for seances in their own residences, and followers of spiritualism, eager for spiritual advice, messages from the other world, and the opportunity of public worship in the auditorium. During the November-to-April season the program includes lectures, public and private séances, and demonstrations in spiritual healing. Camp literature advertises, 'Lectures and message words by the Highest Talent Obtainable.' Typical also are: 'Following the Lily Dale Triumph! Moon Trail. Through the Trance Intermediaryship of Horace S. Hambling, on his second visit to the United States from London, England. Will be in Cassadaga the entire season.'—'P.L.O.A. Keeler, Noted Slate Writing Medium, will be in Cassadaga during February and March.'

The *Cassadagan*, published semi-monthly during January, February, and March, carries advertisements of mediums available for private appointments. 'Psychic power can be yours,' reads one, 'an amazing discovery enables anyone to develop psychic power . . . by means of the wonderful psychas . . . used with equal benefit by both ladies and gentlemen, singly or in groups.' An editorial declares that Cassadaga 'welcomes spiritualists, investigators, and all who are "thinkers" in the midst of a creed-bound world.'

The camp rules provide that 'all ordained spiritualist ministers may use the title of "reverend," and give spiritual advice and messages, and fulfill the duties and powers belonging to the pastorate of a recognized church. Certified mediums may exercise any and all phases of mediumship, trance, clairvoyance, clairaudience, trumpet, healing, etc., but not the duties of a pastor. The local board of directors shall specify the qualifications of their ministers, mediums, lecturers and healers, and shall duly certify the same when found satisfactory.'

At 7.4 *m.* on US 17 is the junction with a paved road.

Left on this road is ENTERPRISE, 3 *m.* (27 alt., 250 pop.), on Lake Monroe, formerly called Benson Springs, and once the southern terminus of St. Johns River shipping. The town was founded in 1841 by Cornelius Taylor, cousin of Zachary Taylor. Until 1888 it was the seat of Volusia County. Here is the FLORIDA METHODIST ORPHANAGE, in which approximately 400 children are cared for.

Right from Enterprise 1 *m.* on a paved road to GREEN SPRINGS, in a basin 50 feet wide and 100 feet deep. The near-by woodlands offer inviting spots for picnics. The rear yard of the old STARKE HOUSE, 1.8 *m.*, built in 1880 by Dr. James Starke, is the basin of a dried-up spring, the floor of which is carpeted with ferns. His gardener had been in the employ of Queen Victoria. An avenue of cedars leads from the house to a sink containing rare aquatic plants.

Along the St. Johns River the deer's tongue, a fragrant shrub, grows wild in the woods; its leaf is used in the preparation of smoking and chewing tobaccos.

The highway crosses the St. Johns River on a drawbridge, 13.6 *m.*; here the river is a narrow stream, its coffee-colored waters lined with thick woods. In spring and summer, water hyacinths become packed against the bridge underpinning, and often obstruct navigation, despite the efforts of government engineers to check its growth. The hyacinth, a native of Brazil, was introduced into America in 1884 when specimens were exhibited at the New Orleans' Cotton Exposition and carried from there to many parts of the lower South. A woman of San Mateo on the St. Johns River placed it in her garden pool where it multiplied so rapidly that she had to dump the excess into the river.

The highway swings (L) in a long sweeping curve along the shore of LAKE MONROE, which was lined with piers and warehouses in the 1880's. A large cypress swamp borders the road for nearly two miles—a gloomy, moss-draped mass of trees that seem dead in winter, but come to life again in the spring. Cypress, magnolias, gums, and occasional cabbage palms are unusually large here, and many of their trunks are swathed in ivy, woodbine, and wild grape vines. Clumps of willows, bright green in spring, and pools of water, covered with pale blue hyacinths and ivory white lilies, carpet the floor of the jungle swamp.

SANFORD, 17.9 *m.* (31 alt., 10,100 pop.), capital of the Florida celery belt, lies on a rich alluvial deposit 30 miles square. According to the report of the State Marketing Bureau for 1937, Florida shipped some 3,325,000 crates of celery to market, a large part of which were from this section. Land here is valued at $1,000 an acre. In the spring even the yards of city houses are planted to celery and lettuce.

Subirrigation systems utilize the abundant supply of water from flowing wells. Tile is laid with open joints about 18 inches below the surface of the fields, and water running through it is turned on and off as needed. Seed beds are planted during November and December, and the seedlings transferred to the fields a month later. The crop is planted, dug, trimmed, washed, tied in three-stalk bunches, and packed for shipment by Negro workers.

Sanford is an outgrowth of Mellonville, a trading post established in 1837 in the shadow of a frontier fort. The SITE OF FORT MELLON is marked by a stone monument, Mellonville Ave. and 2nd St. This outpost was the scene of many encounters with the Indians.

In 1871 General Henry R. Sanford, former U.S. Minister to Belgium, bought 12,000 acres here, including the townsite, and brought in 60 Negroes from central Florida to clear the land and plant citrus groves. Whites in the vicinity protested, and one night, armed with shotguns, attacked the camp, and drove the Negroes off, killing one and wounding several.

Unable to obtain other labor, Sanford sent an agent to Sweden who recruited 100 workers, offering them passage and all expenses in return for a year's work. This also aroused opposition, particularly in Jacksonville, where a campaign was begun against what was termed a disguised form of slavery. The Swedes were encouraged to run away; agents sent after them were arrested; lawsuits and other difficulties followed. But the majority of Swedes remained and fulfilled their contract, and Sanford gave each of them a 5-acre grove. In 1881 more Swedes arrived and soon prospered. The freeze of 1894–95 struck the community a hard blow, and it turned from citrus culture to truck gardening. Many of Florida's groves, however, benefited from the extensive and carefully conducted experiments that Sanford carried on here in the early years.

The MUNICIPAL PIER extends into Lake Monroe to a bandshell, 300 feet from shore; the approach to the pier is landscaped with coco plumosa palms and flowering shrubs. On Lake Shore Blvd. is a small Zoo with outdoor cages.

At 24.3 *m.* is the junction with two roads.

1. Right from this junction to a parking space, 2 *m.*, where a marker indicates a foot trail leading to the BIG TREE, a cypress estimated to be more than 3,000 years old, 47 feet in circumference at the base and 125 feet high. The tree was named 'The Senator' for M.O.Overstreet, State Senator (1920–24), who donated the tree and the land surrounding it to Seminole County as a park.

2. Left from the junction to the SEMINOLE DRIVING PARK, 2 *m.*, a club established by sportsmen as a training course for harness-racing horses. Every winter from 50 to 150 horses are trained here; Rosalind, the 1936 winner of the Hambletonian, a classic among harness races, was put through her paces here. In the park are stables, a training track, and a grandstand seating 2,000.

FERN PARK, 28.6 *m.* (120 pop.), is inhabited largely by employees of a large fernery which borders both sides of the road. Asparagus plumosus, Boston, and maidenhair ferns are grown in slat houses, cut, packed in dry ice, and shipped to northern florists. Many of the scattered dwellings are interesting because of their steep roofs, round shingled towers, and mullioned windows, very different from the pseudo-Spanish architecture of the boom period.

MAITLAND, 33.2 *m.* (91 alt., 511 pop.), was settled before the War between the States on the site of Fort Maitland, built in 1838, and named for Captain William S. Maitland of the U.S. army. A group of Union veterans, including Louis F. Lawrence, Captain Josiah Eaton, and E.C.Hungerford, settled here in the early 1880's. When they decided in 1884 to incorporate the settlement and found that the law required 30 registered voters, they induced Negroes employed in the groves to become residents. The Negroes soon outnumbered the whites, and some were elected to office. Lawrence asked the Negro leaders to start a community of their own, and offered them a tract at a low price. They accepted and moved to a new settlement, Eatonville (*see below*). In the latter part of the same decade Maitland, then the terminus of the South Florida Railroad, became a popular resort.

Maitland was the center of Florida's fruit-fly campaign in 1929–30, when intensive and successful efforts to rid the State of the pest were led by the U.S. Department of Agriculture. Infested fruit was first discovered on a grapefruit tree in Orlando (*see Orlando*), but the section about Maitland was hardest hit. All groves were inspected and sprayed, as were trucks leaving the area. Fruit stores and all freight cars and trucks passing through were screened. All fruit shipments were sterilized by steam. Crews of men cut, picked, or uprooted other plants harboring the destructive Mediterranean fruit fly, alias *ceratitis capitata*. This pest bores a hole in fruit and there lays its eggs in great numbers, for the fly is most prolific. The larvae consume the pulp, causing the fruit to drop. The larvae then burrow into the earth to emerge in time as flies and continue their life cycle. When the campaign closed, the pest had been eradicated.

Right from Maitland on a paved road to EATONVILLE, 1 *m.*, (136 pop.), dating back to 1886, one of the first towns incorporated by Negroes in the United States. It was named for Captain Josiah Eaton of Maitland (*see above*), a friend of H.W.Lawrence, who built an Odd Fellows Hall and a church, and gave them to the community. Among early buildings still in use is the HUNGERFORD NORMAL AND INDUSTRIAL SCHOOL FOR NEGROES, erected and supported by E.C.Hungerford, of Maitland, in memory of his nephew, a physician, who died of smallpox contracted while treating Negroes during an epidemic. Eatonville is the birthplace and home of Zora Neale Hurston (1903–), and the locale of her novel, *Their Eyes Were Watching God* (1937). This is Eatonville in her eyes:

'Maitland is Maitland until it gets to Hurst's corner, and then it is Eatonville. Right in front of Willie Sewell's yellow-painted house the hard road quits being the hard road for a generous mile and becomes the heart of Eatonville. Or from a stranger's point of view, you could say that the road just bursts through on its way from US 17 to US 441, scattering Eatonville right and left.

'On the right, after you leave the Sewell place, you don't meet a thing that people live in until you come to the Green Lantern on the main corner. That corner has always been the main corner, because that is where Joe Clarke, the founder and first mayor of Eatonville, built his store when he started the town nearly sixty years ago, so that people have gotten used to gathering there and talking. Only Joe Clarke sold groceries and general merchandise, while Lee Glenn sells drinks of all kinds and whatever goes with transient rooms. St.Lawrence Methodist church and parsonage are on that same side of the road between Sewell's and "the shop" and perhaps claim the soul of the place, but the shop is the heart of it. After the shop you come to the Widow Dash's orange grove, her screened porch, "double hips," and her new husband. Way on down at the end of the road to the right is Claude Mann's filling station and beyond that the last house in Eatonville, the big barn on the lake.

'Take the left side of the road and except for Macedonia Baptist Church, people just live along that side and play croquet in Armetta Jones' backyard behind the huge camphor tree. After the people quit living along that side of the road, the Hungerford Industrial School begins and runs along the road as far as the land goes. The inadequate buildings stop short in the cleared land on the fringe of Eatonville proper. And west of it all, beyond village and school, everybody knows that the sun makes his nest in some lonesome lake in the woods back there and gets his night's rest.

'But all of Eatonville is not on the hard road that becomes Apopka Avenue as it passes through town. There are back streets on both sides of the road. The two back streets on the right side are full of little houses squatting under hovering oaks. These houses are old and were made of the town's first dreams. There is loved Lake Sabelia, with its small colony of very modern houses, lived in by successful villagers. Away in the woody rises beyond Sabelia is Eatonville's Dogtown that looks as if it belonged on the African veldt. Off the road on the left is the brown-with-white-trim modern public school, with its well kept yards and playgrounds, which Howard Miller always looks after, though he can scarcely read and write. They call this part of town Mars Hill, as against Bones Valley to the right of the road. They call the tree-shaded land that runs past the schoolhouse West street, and it goes past several small groves until it passes Jim Steele's fine orange grove and dips itself in Lake Belle, which is the home of Eatonville's most celebrated resident, the world's largest alligator.'

This legendary alligator, it is said, is no other than a slave who escaped from a Georgia plantation and joined the Indians during the Seminole War. When the Indians retreated, he did not follow but instead made 'big medicine' on the lake shore, for he had been a celebrated conjuring man in Africa. He transformed himself into an alligator, the god of his tribe, and slipped into the water. Now and then he resumes human form, so people say, and roams the country about Eatonville. At such times all the alligators in the surrounding lakes bellow loudly all night long. 'The big one has gone back home,' whisper the villagers.

WINTER PARK, 36.5 *m.* (96 alt., 3,686 pop.), a suburb of Orlando, built around Lakes Maitland, Osceola, Virginia, and Killarney, has been called 'a town that has become a university,' because of the part Rollins College, a progressive co-educational school, played in the life of the community. The town was founded as Lakeview in 1858, its name being changed to Osceola in 1870 and to Winter Park in 1881, when New Englanders laid out a new 600-acre townsite according to a city plan which has since been followed.

ROLLINS COLLEGE, established in 1885 by the General Congregational Association, was named for Alonzo W. Rollins, a wealthy dry-goods merchant of Chicago, who with his family gave much money to the institution. Denominational affiliations have now been relinquished. The 600-acre campus, on the shore of Lake Virginia, is shaded by live oaks and pines. The newest buildings are of Spanish-Mediterranean style; the thick masonry and hollow-tile walls, window grilles, balconies, tile roofs, and walled gardens represent an adaptation of Spanish architecture of the Middle Ages.

The school's experiments in educational techniques include a conference plan of teaching, allowing the student during his two-hour class periods either to study, to confer with his instructor, or to join in group discussion; an achievement plan of graduation permits more time for specialization; the annual tuition fee is computed by dividing the actual cost of operating the school by the number of students. The enrollment is limited to 500 students. Dr.Hamilton Holt, former editor of the *Independent*, is president (1938).

The KNOWLES MEMORIAL CHAPEL, Interlachen Ave., of modified Spanish Renaissance design, was erected in 1932 by Mrs.Frances Knowles Warren in memory of her father, F.Bangs Knowles, one of the founders of Rollins College. The entrance is a deeply recessed doorway under a paneled arch, and above is a stone carving picturing a Franciscan friar planting a cross in the earth between two palms, with a group of *conquistadores* on one side and Florida Indians on the other; in the background are two Spanish caravels riding at anchor. The interior of the chapel reveals a wide lofty nave with narrow side aisles divided by massive piers with round arches. All interior structural stone is a warm-colored Florida travertine. The rear gallery, seating 110, is lighted by a large circular stained-glass window of Renaissance design.

The ANNIE RUSSELL THEATER, joined by a loggia to the chapel, harmonizes with the larger structure, both having been designed by Ralph A. Cram of Boston and Richard Kiehnel of Miami. Its façade is a triple-arched open loggia, above which is an arcaded porch reaching to the tile roof. Flanking loggias, polychromed rafters, and ornamental Florida travertine embellish the interior. The stage is flanked by a single box and crowned by a plain proscenium. Mrs.Edward W. Bok of Philadelphia gave the playhouse to Rollins.

The WALK OF FAME is constructed of more than 450 steppingstones taken from birthplaces or former homes of distinguished men and women, including Benjamin Franklin and Buffalo Bill.

During Founders' Week, celebrated annually in February, outstanding contemporaries talk on topics of the day in what is called the Animated Magazine. Among others who have contributed to these programs are former Attorney General Homer C. Cummings, Secretary of State Cordell Hull, Willa Cather, Rabbi Stephen S. Wise, and the late Jane Addams.

An INDIAN MOUND, cor. Interlachen and Knowles Aves., stands in a small park among many trees with Indian markings. This is said to have been a favorite camping ground of Osceola, Seminole leader (*see History*).

ORLANDO, 38.2 *m.* (111 alt., 27,330 pop.) (*see Orlando*).

Points of Interest: Zoo, Eola Park, Sunshine Park, old residences, and others.

Orlando is at the junction with State 22 (*see Tour 9*) and US 441 (*see Tour 21*).

At 42.6 *m.* is the junction with Gatlin Ave.

Left on Gatlin Ave. to the SITE OF FORT GATLIN, 1.5 *m.*, marked by a square granite column. The fort, established in 1837 and abandoned in 1848, was named for Dr. John S. Gatlin, Assistant Surgeon, U.S. Army, who lost his life in the Dade Massacre (*see Tour 22*).

PINECASTLE, 44.1 *m.* (421 pop.), on the shores of Lake Conway, was so named in the early 1870's when Will Wallace Harney, Orlando poet, built an octagonal house here and called it Pinecastle. Later settlers had their mail sent to Harney's, and when a post office was established it was named for his home.

At 46.3 *m.* is the junction with paved State 286.

Left on this highway to DAETWYLER'S NURSERY, 1.2 *m.*, a botanical park that contains more than 150,000 azaleas in 130 varieties, 75,000 palms, and many species of ornamental trees and plants, among them Australian tree ferns and Bird of Paradise plants.

TAFT, 47 *m.* (296 pop.), was called Smithville prior to 1909, when it was renamed in honor of President William Howard Taft, who was inaugurated that year. The land immediately south of the town is well adapted to cattle grazing, and during fall and winter stockmen burn over thousands of acres to furnish new pasturage for stock. Partridge peas and other vegetation bring quail and dove to the territory. The Florida Field Trial Association holds trials here annually for bird dogs.

KISSIMMEE, 57.7 *m.* (70 alt., 3,163 pop.), known colloquially as Cow Town, stands at the head of Lake Tohopekaliga in one of Florida's chief cattle areas. Its broad main street, lined with two- and three-story brick buildings, is divided by a parkway landscaped with cabbage palms. Many spacious old frame houses with galleries and wide porches, built and occupied by wealthy cattlemen more than half a century ago, still stand. Some are surrounded by large lawns as open as the range; others, far back from the road, are almost concealed by towering moss-hung oaks and clumps of bamboos and oleanders. High-booted cowhands invade the shopping district on Saturday nights; stores display saddles, spurs, 16-foot cow whips, and broad-brimmed felt hats. The first bars in America built to enable horsemen to take a drink without dismounting were popular in Kissimmee about 1870, a decade before they were introduced into the West.

During the second Spanish occupation of Florida, particularly between 1813 and 1821, many settlers, impressed with the success of the Indians in raising cattle, made requests for Spanish grants of land, which they stocked with cattle brought from the Old World, together with herds driven down from Georgia and the Carolinas. Gradually the pasturage of the Kissimmee Valley attracted stockmen, and as fast as the Indians retreated, cattlemen moved in.

Before 1825 there existed as a recognized type the Florida woods cow, descendant of the original Spanish stock. Unprepossessing in appearance, of outstanding value for neither beef nor milk, ridiculously small, weighing much less than 500 pounds, she could survive here where blooded cattle perished. She was content with 10 to 20 acres of pasturage; in dry weather she knew how to live in swamps, and in wet weather she could do well on higher ground; she required no feed other than what she could find for herself; snakes did not harm her; sand spurs she relished as dessert. On a visit to the region in 1895, Frederic Remington, writer and painter renowned for his Western scenes, described the cattle range here as 'flat and sandy, with mile on mile of straight pine timber, each tree an exact duplicate of its neighbor tree, and underneath the scrub palmettoes, the twisted brakes and hammocks, and the gnarled water oaks . . . the land gives only a tough wiregrass, and the poor little cattle, no bigger than a donkey, wander half starved and horribly emaciated in search of it.'

In sharp lines Remington etched the portrait of the Cracker cowboy of the time: 'Two emaciated Texas ponies pattered down the street,' he wrote, 'bearing wild looking individuals whose hanging hair, drooping hats, and generally bedraggled appearance would remind you at once of the Spanish moss which hangs so quietly and helplessly to the limbs of the oaks out in the swamps . . . They had about four dollars' worth of clothes between them, rode McClellan saddles with saddlebags, and guns tied on before.' The cowboys, he added, did not use ropes but worked their cattle into strong log corrals about a day's march apart, assisted by large fierce curs trained to pursue cattle and 'even take them by the nose.' Cattle stealing was common, and cowmen shot and stabbed each other for possession of 'scrawny creatures not fit for a pointer-dog to mess on.' Owners of ranches never ventured into the woods alone or to their doors at night, and seldom kept a light burning in their houses. The almost unexplored Everglades lay close by and with a half-hour's start a man who knew the country was safe from pursuit. As one man cheerfully confided to Remington, 'A boat don't leave no trail, stranger.'

The railroads that early penetrated the open ranges had their troubles with claims made against them for maiming or killing livestock. A long-haired Cracker would drop into the nearest station, with his rifle and pistol, and ask the telegraph operator to pay immediately an extravagant sum for a lean cow killed on the tracks. If the railroads raised objections, cowboys lined up in the brush on dark nights and pumped their Winchesters into the trains, and 'it took some considerable "potting" at the more conservative superintendents,' according to Remington, 'before the latter could bestir themselves and invent a "cow-attorney," as the company adjuster was called.'

The dialect of the Kissimmee cow country today resembles that of the southern Appalachians; one frequently hears the mispronunciation of 'it' as 'hit.' Feed for livestock is shipped here in cotton bags which farm wives bleach and convert into dresses, table covers, bed sheets, and even underwear. The women of the family still boil clothes in the back yard in blackened kettles. Grits are served regularly for breakfast, not as a cereal, but as a sponge for gravy. There are many double cabins with roofs over the passageway, known as 'dog trot' cabins in the Piedmont States, but local cowmen call them 'breezeways.'

Before the extension of the railroad from Orlando in 1881, Kissimmee had been a trading post for settlers farther south. Small sailing vessels plied Lake Tohopekaliga, but had difficulty navigating the tortuous river channel. Not until the Disston land purchase in 1881 (*see Tour* 10), when drainage and dredging projects made possible the establishment of sugar-cane plantations and sugar mills, did the new settlement begin to flourish. Foundries, machine shops, and shipyards were built along the river; freight and passenger boat lines ran on regular schedule south through the river and chain of lakes as far as Lake Okeechobee, the Caloosahatchee River, and the Gulf of Mexico.

Kissimmee is at the junction with US 192 (*see Tour* 10).

South of Kissimmee the route follows a stretch of old brick highway, often inundated during heavy summer rains. During the construction of the road through the swamp in 1916–17, workmen supplemented their wages by catching baby alligators and selling them to curio shops.

INTERCESSION CITY, 64.9 *m.*, was named Interocean City when platted in 1924, because it was midway between the Atlantic Ocean and the Gulf. Apartments, office buildings, and houses begun here during the boom were never completed; and the boom's puncture left only a silhouette of crumbling pink and tan stucco structures. In 1934, J.W.Wile of Indianapolis gave 5,000 acres of land, including the townsite, to the House of Faith, a nondenominational Christian sect with tenets based on the original teachings of John Wesley. The group has built a small orphanage and a vocational school for young men and women; a canning plant and garment factory are under construction (1938). Lots and small farms are sold on a penny-a-day plan. During the winter a 100-day camp meeting is held here with the assistance of visiting evangelists and ministers of many denominations.

Gophers, the Florida land tortoise, are often seen crawling along the road in this region. Many are crushed by passing cars and their carcasses attract squadrons of ever-vigilant buzzards. Made into stews, gopher meat is relished by local people. A Negro legend thus explains the origin of the gopher and accounts for its name:

One day God was sitting on Tampa Bay making sea-things and throwing them into the water. He made a shark, tossed it in, and it swam off. He made a mullet, then a stingray, finally a turtle, and they all swam off. The Devil, watching Him, said he could make a turtle. But God shook His head. 'That's somethin' ain't been done before and nobody can't do no creatin' but Me, not even a simple lookin' thing like a turtle. But if you thinks you can do it, go ahead an' try,' said God.

So the Devil went away and came back presently to show God what he had made. 'This ain't no turtle what you done,' God told him; 'but just to show I'm fairminded I'll blow the breath of life into it for you.' God blew on it and threw it into the sea, and it swam ashore. He tossed it in again, then again, and each time it quickly crawled upon land.

'I told you you couldn't make no turtle,' said God. 'A turtle is a sea-thing an' lives in the water, an' this thing you made won't even stay no longer than he can swim out.' The Devil, realizing he couldn't out-argue God, said: 'Well, if it ain't no turtle it'll go fer one sure enough, and folks'll eat him for a turtle.' From the 'go fer' came the animal's name.

DAVENPORT, 75.2 *m.* (650 pop.), center of a prosperous citrus region, has several fruit-packing and canning plants. A CITRUS CANDY FACTORY (*open*) makes crystallized fruit peel. Workers wash, size, and slice grapefruit and oranges, and then boil the peels in syrup, color them with vegetable dyes, and cut them with machines. The pulp is returned to the grower as fertilizer. From 5,000 to 8,000 pounds of this candy are made weekly during the winter season.

HAINES CITY, 79.9 *m.* (166 alt., 3,037 pop.), surrounded by hills covered with orange and grapefruit groves, is dominated by a 10-story hotel of gray stucco. Early settlers in the vicinity planted tomatoes and grapes, but by 1900 the majority were engaged in citrus culture. Most of the fruit is shipped through two co-operative marketing associations. Springing from an early settlement called Clay Cut, the city adopted its present name in 1887. The name was changed to Haines City, according to local story, in the hope that in being so honored Henry Haines, South Florida Railroad official, might use his influence in having trains stop here. The point was well taken, for the railroad erected a station soon after.

The FLORIDA MILITARY INSTITUTE, offering college preparatory work to 100 cadets, is built around a 6-acre campus on the shores of LAKE EVA, on which also is the MUNICIPAL BATHING BEACH.

Haines City is at the junction with US 92 (*see Tour* 20) and State 8 (*see Tour* 15).

Section d. HAINES CITY to PUNTA GORDA; 99.5 *m. US* 17

Known as the Scenic Highlands Route, this section of US 17 crosses the highlands near Winter Haven, proceeds south through the cattle ranges surrounding Arcadia, and turns southwestward to Punta Gorda on the Gulf of Mexico.

West of HAINES CITY, 0 *m.*, the highway is lined on both sides with citrus groves, planted in straight rows stretching away to the horizon.

FLORENCE VILLA, 9.8 *m.* (149 alt., 928 pop.), was founded by Dr.F.W.Inman, known as 'the father of Florida co-operative marketing.' On a knoll overlooking a small lake stands the rambling FLORENCE VILLA HOTEL, built by Inman in 1887, a notable winter hostelry since the turn of the century. The Florence Citrus Growers' Association packing plant employs 250 workers in season here and ships 700,000 boxes of fruit annually.

WINTER HAVEN, 11.5 *m.* (175 alt., 7,130 pop.), lies among extensive citrus groves in a cluster of lakes, 97 of them within a 5-mile radius. Several of the principal thoroughfares are bordered with mountain-ebony trees, and other streets are cut through the orange and grapefruit groves that completely surround the city. The Florida Orange Festival, held here every January, features a number of citrus, industrial, educational, and household exhibits. Permanent units are housed in two concrete buildings, and other exhibits extend for 5 blocks along NW.3rd St.

Winter Haven has 9 citrus packing houses and 3 fruit canneries, most of them owned and operated jointly by groups of 20 to 100 growers. Fruit is brought from the groves in field boxes. Packing house employees place the boxes in coloring rooms for 24 to 48 hours, where an appetizing hue is given the fruit by the use of ethylene gas. A series of sprays and longitudinal sets of roller brushes wash the fruit, which is then carried into the dryer, an oven about 100 feet long. When dried, it receives a coat of wax, passes through a series of polishing brushes, and is carried along a grading belt to be separated by hand into grades established by State law. Automatic 'sizers' drop the grades into their proper bins. Packers wrap the oranges by hand and place them in boxes containing 1.6 bushels; workers are paid 4¢ to 8¢ a box. Fast workers average $5 a day, but they must work long and irregular hours.

In the field headquarters and laboratory of the STATE CITRUS INSPECTION BUREAU, Postal Building, 3rd St. and Avenue D,NE., men are trained to test and grade samples of fruit from packing houses for acid and juice content; when trained, they are stationed in packing houses. FEDERAL CITRUS PRODUCTS STATION, 3rd St.SW. and Avenue E,SW., maintained by the Department of Agriculture, Bureau of Chemistry and Soils, and Food Research Division, conducts research in the utilization of surplus citrus fruits and in improving the methods of canning. Similar research is conducted on the most economical use of pineapples, papayas, tomatoes, strawberries, and other fruit.

Winter Haven has a municipal bathing beach on SILVER LAKE and a municipal pier on LAKE HOWARD (*bass, perch, and bream; boating*); at the pier motorboats are available for transportation to Cypress Gardens (*see below*).

ELOISE, 13.6 *m.* (144 alt., 200 pop.), is built around the Atlantic Coast Line station.

Left from Eloise on a concrete road to CYPRESS GARDENS (*adm.* 35¢), 4 *m.*, bordering Lake Eloise. Formerly a wild swamp, the gardens contain native and exotic plantings, shaded by huge cypress and oaks, and pierced by quiet log-spanned lagoons. Winding foot trails, paved with pecky-cypress blocks, are marked, as are the majority of plants. Massed banks of gardenias, azaleas, and camellias bloom during spring. A Gardenia Festival is held here annually during April. Flowers, photographs, and cypress novelties are displayed for sale at the clubhouse.

EAGLE LAKE, 15.3 *m.* (177 alt., 600 pop.), named for the body of water it borders, has a public bathing beach and pavilion (*picnic facilities*).

BARTOW, 23.8 *m.* (126 alt., 5,269 pop.), seat of Polk County, is a tranquil old town of oak-shaded streets and large white-columned frame houses clustered around a courthouse square. The surrounding level expanse of hammock land, site of Fort Blount, built during the Seminole Wars, was settled in 1851 by planters and their slaves. The town was named in 1867 for General Francis Bartow of the Confederate army. Jacob Summerlin, a pioneer, became one of Florida's wealthiest stockmen. Uneducated himself, he established SUMMERLIN INSTITUTE, on South Broadway, at one time an elementary and preparatory school, now the city's high school, which conducts its classes in the group of age-mellowed buildings.

The landscaped CIVIC CENTER, built with PWA funds, has a swimming pool, and courts for roque, shuffleboard, and tennis. The main building, built of rubble stone from local quarries, contains lounge and banquet rooms, and an auditorium. The 18-hole MUNICIPAL GOLF COURSE (*greens fee* $1) is on the eastern edge of the city.

Bartow is at the junction with State 79 (*see Tour* 11).

Right from Bartow on State 79 is MULBERRY, 7.5 *m.* (100 alt., 2,029 pop.), lying in the heart of the pebble phosphate-mining region (*see Tour* 20). The town received its name from a large mulberry tree growing beside the Seaboard Air Line tracks, at which freight was unloaded before a station was built. Shipments were frequently marked, 'Put off at the big mulberry tree.' The tree still stands, its top shattered by lightning, its thick trunk scarred by bullets. From its limbs several whites and Negroes were hanged during the turbulent 1880's, when the mines were first operated.

Throughout this period Mulberry resembled an early gold-mining town of the West, filled with gamblers, outlaws, and prostitutes. Saloons and dance halls were everywhere; almost everyone carried firearms; a coroner's inquest was held every Monday morning, it is said, over the victims of Saturday and Sunday festivities; brawls led to murders, and lynchings followed.

In 1919 miners here went out on strike, led by the Mineral Workers' Union. More than 1,000 men held a noonday parade in the town. Working 10 to 12 hours a day for $2.50, white and Negro miners demanded an 8-hour day, with a minimum of 37¢ an hour, as recommended by the National War Labor Board. The strike spread rapidly into adjoining Polk and Hillsborough counties and aroused State-wide comment. Counsel for the mine owners was quoted by the Tampa *Tribune* as saying: 'There are, of course, going to be no conferences nor any adjustment of matters between mine owners and the union because there is nothing to confer about, nor is there anything to discuss.' At a mass meeting in Tampa, Governor Sidney J. Catts stated: 'I know the strikers are right; if the other fellows had any right on their side they would be perfectly willing to arbitrate.' Clashes between miners and strikebreakers resulted in several casualties; Mulberry was 'shot up' by mine guards in a powerhouse at the edge of town. A train was stopped, fired on, and tank cars of oil emptied. Strikers asserted that this was done by strikebreakers to prejudice the public against them. The incident provoked a court injunction against the strikers, which in the end broke the strike. The men returned to work, but at an increased wage scale of $3 for an 8- to 10-hour day.

Fossils found during mining operations are on display in an open pavilion in the center of town.

Between Bartow and Fort Meade the country, dotted with gray and yellow spoil banks, somewhat resembles the Bad Lands of South Dakota. Abandoned phosphate pits have become small lakes, many stocked with bream and bass. Some, equipped with springboards and floats, are used as swimming pools by the inhabitants.

At 26.9 *m.* is the junction with an improved road.

Left on this road to KISSENGEN SPRINGS, 1 *m.*, a resort noted for mineral springs flowing at the rate of 135,000 gallons an hour.

FORT MEADE, 34.3 *m.* (130 alt., 1,981 pop.), is the trading center of an area growing winter vegetables, strawberries, and watermelons. The skeleton of an unfinished boom-time hotel rises above the scattered two-story brick business buildings and square frame dwellings. A military post was established here on the banks of the Peace River (L) during the Seminole War and named Fort Meade, for Lieutenant George Gordon Meade of the U.S. Army, who later won prominence at the battle of Gettysburg. Stonewall Jackson was stationed here in 1851. For many years the settlement was an important trading post; traffic in alligator hides was brisk; in 1881 a trapper contracted to supply 5,000 hides to a Paris leather firm. A large tobacco plantation was established here in 1895 and many Cuban workers imported, but the enterprise failed.

South of Fort Meade the highway passes several large phosphate-mining excavations with surrounding spoil banks, but the general background is one of hardwood hammocks and stretches of thick pine woods. Pinkish-white tar flowers color the clearings in spring and summer; roadside ditches are choked with ferns, cattails, and banks of blue iris.

BOWLING GREEN, 42.6 *m.* (116 alt., 1,025 pop.), was known as Utica until the late 1880's when farmers from Bowling Green, Ky., purchased large holdings and settled in the district. The town is surrounded with strawberry fields, and the Hardee County Strawberry Festival is held here each January.

WAUCHULA (Ind., sandhill crane), 49.1 *m.* (107 alt., 2,574 pop.), seat of Hardee County, like many other communities in the State, grew up around an early military post, Fort Hartsuff, built to protect settlers during the Seminole Wars. The frogs'-leg industry (*see Tour* 12) has prospered here. Frogs are caught at night in the surrounding swamps and creeks, and the 'saddles' shipped to northern markets.

ZOLFO SPRINGS (Ital., sulphur) 53.4 *m.* (61 alt., 272 pop.), lies immediately south of a large sulphur spring flowing into an outdoor swimming pool, the center of a municipal park. Italian laborers employed here during construction of the Atlantic Coast Line gave the village its name.

CHARLIE APOPKA CREEK, 61.7 *m.*, marked the northern boundary of a territory assigned to the Seminoles by an agreement made between the Indians and General Alexander Macomb in 1839. Between the creek and Arcadia, US 17 crosses cutover barrens, stretches of saw palmetto, and swamplands that provide grazing for range cattle. An occasional sawmill along the highway cuts logs brought from distant points by tractors. Drainage ditches crisscross the area, their yellow spoil banks contrasting sharply with the bright green willows that line their courses.

ARCADIA, 73.6 *m.* (56 alt., 4,082 pop.), an oasis in a vast Florida prairie, is built around the three-story red brick courthouse that occupies a landscaped square in the center of the city. For miles on every side stretch treeless flatlands used for grazing cattle. Cow camps are numerous in the vicinity and give the town a frontier atmosphere; cattlemen in ten-gallon hats walk the streets; rodeos, steak frys, and other range-hand activities impart color to social life in Arcadia; strings of colored lights festoon the main thoroughfare on festive occasions.

In the ARCADIA MUNICIPAL TOURIST CAMP, south of the business district, are 40 modern cabins. At Christmas every year the 'Tin Canners'

Homecoming' is celebrated here. The Tin Can Tourists of the World was organized in 1916 by tourists who live all or much of the year in trailers or house cars, many of them homemade. Although the ties binding them together are largely sentimental, the tourists maintain an organization, with regularly elected officers. This nomadic group begins its annual hegira to Florida with a 'home-coming' at Dade City (*see Tour* 22) in November. With ample leisure the tin-canners then wander about, either singly or in small groups, swimming and sun-bathing, attending church and the movies, enjoying long sessions of bridge, checkers, chess, horseshoes, and shuffleboard. At Yuletide they repair to Arcadia to celebrate the holidays. There are speeches of welcome by city officials, appropriate replies, and a long automobile parade by the tin-canners. Up to 1938 the tin-canners held their final celebration of the Florida season every spring at the Sarasota Municipal Tourist Camp (*see Sarasota*), but the organization has grown so large that the camp has been unable to accommodate them.

The FLORIDA BAPTIST CHILDREN'S HOME, established in 1907, cares for 150 children, operating its own farm, dairy, citrus grove, print shop, and canning factory.

Arcadia is at the junction with State 18 (*see Tour* 12).

NOCATEE (Ind., what is it?), 77.9 *m.* (38 alt., 900 pop.), has a crate factory and four citrus- and vegetable-packing plants with a seasonal shipment of 900 cars.

FORT OGDEN, 84.6 *m.* (37 alt., 250 pop.), trading center and shipping point for citrus fruit and livestock, occupies the site of an Indian fort of the same name, built in 1841. The site was selected because of its proximity to the source of materials used in the construction of canoes, militarily important because the Everglades, last stronghold of the Seminoles, could be invaded only in canoes. Fifty-five cypress canoes, each capable of carrying eight men, were built here and put into service during the Seminole War. Residents of near-by towns join in celebrating Fort Ogden's May Day Picnic, held annually for more than half a century. The picnic is a favorite with seekers of public office, who come to orate and distribute cards among their possible supporters.

Cowhands, both on horseback and in flivvers, are seen frequently along the road between Fort Ogden and Punta Gorda.

PUNTA GORDA, 99.5 *m.* (3 alt., 1,833 pop.) (*see Tour 4d*), is at the junction with US 41 (*see Tour 4d*).

Tour 3

Fernandina—Baldwin—Starke—Gainesville—Cedar Keys; 159.8 *m.* State 13.

Hard-surfaced roadbed throughout, except for short stretch between Callahan and Baldwin. Watch for cattle along highway.
Route followed by bus lines between Fernandina and Yulee, and between Baldwin and Gainesville; paralleled by Seaboard Air Line Ry. throughout.
Good accommodations.

State 13 crosses north Florida from the Atlantic to the Gulf, connecting old settlements dating back to the earliest Spanish occupation with the still primitive hammock country along the West Coast. Between them lies a fertile flatwood area, a dark green mass of slender slash pines, bled for the gum that supports the naval-stores industry of the State.

Section a. FERNANDINA *to* BALDWIN; 47.5 *m.*

West of Fernandina the highway traverses a thinly settled region of pine forests and small farms. Between Yulee and Callahan it is flanked with drooping willows, wild hibiscus in brilliant scarlet bloom, and elderberry bushes, white with blossom in spring, heavy with purple fruit in the late summer.

FERNANDINA, 0 *m.* (19 alt., 3,023 pop.), once an active port because of its natural harbor, is now an industrial city in which shrimp and menhaden fisheries and the manufacture of pulp paper are the leading industries. The tall white stacks and brick buildings of the Fernandina pulp mills rise abruptly from the low shores of the St.Marys River on the north and east sides of the town, overshadowing faded red brick buildings once occupied by ship chandlers. The sidewalks of Atlantic Avenue, the principal thoroughfare, are roofed over with metal awnings, providing shade for leisurely shoppers.

The town lies on the northwestern shore of Amelia Island, separated from the mainland by the St.Marys River estuary on the north, by the Amelia River on the west, and by Nassau Sound on the south. The city docks, 3 miles from the ocean, are reached by a 30-foot channel through Cumberland Sound and the Amelia River, a link in the Intracoastal Waterway (*see Intracoastal Waterway*). Three shrimp canneries along the waterfront rival the pulp mills in industrial importance. Other plants produce fertilizer, fish oil, and feed for livestock. Although the city does not depend on tourists for its livelihood, its exceptional beach attracts visitors from all the southeastern states.

North of the city on a hill above the marshes, a cluster of weathered dwellings occupied by fishermen and retired ship captains and pilots constitutes OLD TOWN, the first settlement. A Spanish post stood here as early as 1686, at which time the island was called Santa María. In 1699 the English King, in granting territory to Carolina, included in it the northern half of the Florida peninsula, and in September 1702 Governor James Moore of South Carolina led the English and their Indian allies to the island, captured the Spanish post, and destroyed its mission. Other attacks followed, forcing large groups of inhabitants to flee, and by 1730 the island was deserted. In 1735 General James Oglethorpe, founder of Georgia, established a post manned by 50 soldiers, finding the island so beautiful that he renamed it in honor of Princess Amelia, sister of George II. The War of Jenkins Ear, which began in 1739, brought renewed conflict between the Spanish and English. At its close the island was recognized as Spanish by the peace treaty of 1748, but retained a small English population, remnants of Oglethorpe's garrison.

At the outbreak of the American Revolution the Florida colonials were loyal to the crown, and a British fort was erected at the north end of the island, near the present site of Fort Clinch (*see below*). During a skirmish at the southern tip, the Americans burned a number of British houses and destroyed cattle. As the fortunes of the British in the Colonies waned, large numbers of Tories came south to the island and remained until forced to leave in 1783 when Florida was returned to Spain. Many disappointed Englishmen went to the Bahamas, West Indies, and Nova Scotia. Some went home, although a few transferred their allegiance to Spain and remained here. A large tract of land was granted by the Spanish government to Don Domingo Fernández; included in it was the village named Fernandina in his honor.

Fernandina, lying just across the American border, became a resort for pirates and smugglers in 1807 and 1808, when the Embargo Act and an act forbidding the importation of slaves were passed. A captain carrying a cargo of slaves not only had to run the gauntlet of government patrol boats, but also had to be on the lookout for hijackers, who usually lurked behind the marshy islands. Pierre and Jean LaFitte, it is said, were among the hijackers who preyed on the smugglers.

Meanwhile Spain, its attention distracted by an impending war with Napoleon, was losing its grip on Florida. France, England, and the United States all looked upon the peninsula as a key to the Caribbean and Gulf of Mexico, and at one time 26 English warships lay in Fernandina harbor. As war between the United States and England became imminent, President Madison attempted to forestall English seizure of Florida, and appointed a commissioner to carry out his plans. General George Matthews sought to accomplish this by organizing a Patriots' Rebellion on his arrival in Fernandina. In March 1812 an army of 200 occupied the Spanish fort without bloodshed and set up a 'Republic of Florida.' John McIntosh, its leader, had been promised protection and reimbursement by Matthews. Because of the objections of the Spanish and English ministers, McIntosh's followers finally withdrew, and Fernandina was again returned to Spain.

In the last few months of 1817, possession of Fernandina passed from one adventurer to another. Gregor MacGregor, a 31-year-old Scotch visionary and an advocate of South American independence, came into port with five vessels. The Spanish garrison surrendered, and MacGregor, with men recruited from Savannah and Charleston, formed a town government, appointed a mayor, and set up stores to sell merchandise landed from his ships. Soon Spaniards in East Florida joined forces and General MacGregor retreated.

Jared Irwin, a former U.S. Representative from Pennsylvania, took over MacGregor's command, recruited an additional force among the privateers operating in Fernandina, defeated the Spaniards after a short battle, and took undisputed possession. At this time Luis Aury, a pirate of French ancestry operating on the Gulf coast, put in with 13 ships carrying loot said to exceed $60,000. Aury claimed the island and appointed Irwin 'Adjutant-General.' Because he had been the first governor of Texas under Mexican rule and was still an official in that government, he raised the Mexican flag above the fort.

In December 1817, Captain J.E.Henry brought the U.S. Corvette *John Adams* into the harbor under secret orders from President Monroe. He landed troops, met no resistance, and hoisted the American flag. Presently Aury sailed away to resume his career as a pirate. The island became officially American in 1821, when Florida was ceded to the United States.

Because of Fernandina's importance as a port, the Government began to fortify the town in 1847, when work on Fort Clinch (*see below*) was started. Although there was a boom when the Florida Railroad made Fernandina its eastern terminus, the outbreak of the War between the States delayed the city's growth.

In 1888 Fernandina was hit by a longshoremen's strike and yellow-fever epidemic. The strike was attributed to the work of a Negro, a stranger, who arrived on a white horse, raised a flag, and addressed large crowds of longshoremen, most of whom were Negro. Race feeling ran high, and the State militia was called in. A sudden outbreak of yellow fever, bringing death to 52, put an end to the strike. During the early 1900's new railroads diverted shipping to Jacksonville and Savannah, and finally the 14 foreign consuls stationed here closed their offices and removed to busier ports.

The pulp mills were built in 1936–37, at a time when plants were being constructed in many other parts of the southeast. Introduction of the industry to the southern slash-pine regions was accomplished under the leadership of Charles H. Herty, a chemist of Savannah, Georgia. During the two years of the construction of the mills, prospects of employment brought many for whom there were no jobs. A housing shortage forced the mayor to make an appeal through the newspapers asking people not to come until new structures were completed. Lots were filled with tents and trailers. In 1938, after the mills had been completed, life returned to normal.

On the SHRIMP DOCKS, foot of Atlantic Ave., are trim white buildings in which shrimp is iced and packed for shipment. The trawlers in the shrimping fleet often leave before sunrise, and return irregularly, depending upon their luck. The first man to fish for shrimp here, Captain Billy Corkum, a New England fisherman, came to Florida in 1913 in search of bluefish. When he saw the netfuls of shrimp taken from the inland waterways, he decided to make trial of the ocean. His first catch filled his hold. Many improvements have since been made in shrimp fishing; better nets have been designed; high-powered Diesel craft from 50 to 75 feet long have replaced gas-driven launches.

Don Domingo Fernández, plantation owner, astronomer, and early settler, is buried in VILLALONGA PARK, N.4th Ave. and Broome St.

The FAIRBANKS HOME (*private*), 227 S.7th St., a two-story white frame building surmounted with a tower room, was the home of Major George R. Fairbanks, editor of the local Florida *Mirror* (1879–85), author of a *History of Florida*.

ST.PETER'S EPISCOPAL CHURCH, cor. 8th St. and Atlantic Ave., established as a mission in 1858, has survived several disasters, including two fires and confiscation by Federal forces during the War between the States. The present gray stucco structure contains a Tiffany glass window, dedicated to the memory of two young doctors who died of yellow fever while combating the epidemic that swept Fernandina in 1878.

BOSQUEBELLO CEMETERY (Sp., beautiful woods), N.14th St. and Bosquebello Entrance Drive, in a moss-hung grove of oaks and cedars on a high sandy knoll near the Amelia River, was given to the city about 1800 by Domingo Fernández. Many of the original markers in older sections of the cemetery have rotted and fallen; a number of graves are hidden by a dense growth of bamboos, cedars, and underbrush. The oldest marked grave is that of Peter Bouesson de Micon, who died in 1813. A cedar, 2 feet in diameter, has grown through the marker on the grave of Ant. Diz, a native of the Canary Islands, who was buried here in 1841. Another grave holds the body of a sea captain whose widow placed flowers on his grave daily, only to have them removed by another woman who, in turn, would place her flowers upon the grave. The widow finally went to law to stop her rival.

In Old Town, foot of Estrada St., are the RUINS OF FORT SAN CARLOS, built after 1784. A footpath from the site of the old plaza, once the parade grounds of the garrison, leads down to the Amelia River and the crumbling walls, all that remain of the fort. Many of the old buildings still standing in Old Town were built with hand-hewn cedar. A short street on the south side of Old Town is called 'Ladies Street,' a translation of *Pasco de las Damas*, the name given it by Spaniards because it was occupied by female camp followers of the garrison.

1. Right from Fernandina on N.14th St. to FORT CLINCH STATE PARK, 2 *m.*, covering 980 acres of the northern end of Amelia Island overlooking Cumberland Sound. Fort Clinch, named for General D.L.Clinch, Federal officer during the Seminole War, was begun in 1847 and completed in 1861. At the beginning of the War between the States, Confederate forces seized the fort to protect supply boats entering the harbor. In March 1862, on receiving word of the approach of the Union fleet, the Confederates at Fort Clinch were ordered to abandon the fort and dynamite the railroad bridge over the Inland Waterway. The town was almost evacuated when Federal gunboats arrived, and shells struck the last of two trains of refugees as they

crossed the bridge, killing several passengers. The steamer *Darlington* carrying refugees was captured at the drawbridge. Federal troops occupied the town for the duration of the war. It was garrisoned for six years after the war and again in 1898, when troops encamped here during the Spanish-American War.

Notable for fine brickwork, the inner wall is pierced with tunnels, while the outer wall, 8 feet thick, has large loopholes through which Cumberland Island is visible. Behind the fort are high sand dunes covered with dwarfed live oaks and cedars, their tops flattened by the prevailing east winds.

2. Right from Fernandina on Atlantic Ave. to FERNANDINA BEACH (*bathhouses, 25¢; cottages available*), 1 *m.*, a 14-mile stretch of hard sand, suitable at low tide for driving (*inquire about tides and condition of beach*).

An old wooden bridge, 3.1 *m.*, connects Amelia Island with the mainland. Reedy stretches along the highway shelter quail, doves, and rabbits.

YULEE, 13 *m.*, (39 alt., 155 pop.) (*see Tour 2a*), is at the junction with US 17 (*see Tour 2a*).

Between Yulee and Callahan are forests of young pines, alternating with smaller, denser stands of hardwood. For the most part, this is an uncultivated region, useful only to turpentiners and free-range cattlemen.

CALLAHAN, 26.9 *m.*, (26 alt., 637 pop.) (*see Tour 1a*), is at the junction with US 1 (*see Tour 1a*).

Southwest of Callahan the hard surface of the highway ends. Once Florida roads were of just two kinds, the narrow rut road and the semi-graded road, with the former preferred. A car, particularly if it were a pine-loving Model T, followed the ruts with the confidence of a train on a railroad track, swinging in animated fashion between stumps and around bends. The semi-graded road, on the other hand, was wide enough for winds to heap up sand. This meant much wear and tear on the motorist, who often found it easier to stop than to go. The highway between Callahan and Baldwin is similar to a semi-graded road.

BRYCEVILLE, 42.5 *m.* (69 alt., 300 pop.), is a livestock and dairying center. Cattle and razorback hogs roam the near-by woods. In the annual roundup of hogs here, as in other pine-woods grazing areas, range riders notch the ears of their stock instead of branding the animals. Boars are butchered, salted, and smoked for winter meat. Among the choice byproducts are 'cracklin's,' bits of meat left over after trying out hog fat to make lard. Mixed with coarse meal and water, salted to taste, shaped into pones, and baked until crusty brown, they are, to quote native epicures, 'the sort of stuff that sticks to the ribs after having tickled the gullet all the way down.' Another delectable dish is a mixture of corn meal and stewed pumpkin, cooked in similar fashion, and known as 'punkin bread.' A favorite breakfast consists of grits and chitlins, with a slab of sow-belly on the side, the whole washed down with 'pot likker.'

BALDWIN, 47.5 *m.* (86 alt., 749 pop.) (*see Tour 7a*), is at the junction with US 90 (*see Tour 7a*).

Section b. BALDWIN to GAINESVILLE 54.3 *m.*

This section of the route crosses the low sand hills of Trail Ridge and the rolling farm country stretches to the fertile lands about Gainesville.

South of BALDWIN, 0 *m.*, is HIGHLAND, 13.7 *m.* (201 alt., 100 pop.), on the crest of the Trail Ridge; it is marked by two concrete gateposts and the occasional whine of a sawmill in the woods.

LAWTEY, 19.5 *m.* (164 alt., 554 pop.), is a shipping point for Bradford County strawberry growers, whose well-groomed acres encircle the village. Farmers sell boxes of ripe berries at roadside stands. Large groves of Mahan pecan trees and vineyards specializing in scuppernong grapes grow in and about the town.

Dr.H.W.Abraham, a Negro voodoo doctor, lived and practiced his healing powers here among both whites and Negroes until his death in 1937. While in the employ of a turpentine company, according to one story, he was sent into Georgia to recruit Negro laborers. When likely workers proved reluctant to sign on, he rubbed two small pebbles together in his hand, glared at the men, and shouted: 'Niggers, see these here stones in my hand? If you don't git into that truck, I'll rub 'em together and put the worst spell on you you ever heard about.' The frightened Negroes immediately climbed into the waiting truck, and Abraham began his career.

In his treatments Abraham mumbled incantations and called on various Biblical prophets. Often he sold his patients, at $5 to $25, depending on the patient's financial status, a muslin packet known as a 'Jesus Letter,' to be worn at all times to ward off evil. In addition to his voodoo practice, Abraham owned and profitably operated a 200-acre farm near Lawtey.

STARKE, 27.3 *m.* (167 alt., 1,339 pop.), seat of Bradford County, was named for Starke Perry, Florida's last *ante-bellum* governor (1857–61). The community obtains its income from naval stores, a barrel-stave plant, strawberry cultivation, and truck farming. Strawberries are shipped in February and March, often among the first on the market. A large turpentine distillery is in the east section of town; other distilleries are scattered throughout the county.

The term 'naval stores' dates back to the early seventeenth century when wooden sailing vessels used large quantities of gummy substances for calking. Although the importance of rosin and turpentine in the maritime trade has greatly diminished, they are still known as naval stores. These products are manufactured by distilling the crude gum obtained by repeated scarring and chipping of pine trees. A small quantity is obtained by steam and destructive distilling, and extraction by solvents from stumps, knots, and mill refuse.

The first recorded observation of the potentialities of Florida as a source of supply was made by Sir John Hawkins, English admiral, in 1565. Considerable production of naval stores in Florida during the eighteenth century is evidenced by the discovery of trees containing within them 'chipped faces' buried beneath rings which date the scars as made about 1780.

Distribution of naval stores is in the hands of large corporations through which agents arrange financing, assembling, and marketing. Actual field work is conducted by individual operators, each connected with an agent. The operator advances cash to his white and Negro workers throughout the season, deducting these loans at the end of the year. A representative turpentine camp comprises a fire still, spirit shed and glue pot, rosin yard, blacksmith and cooperage shed, cup-cleaning vat, barn and wagon shed, and living quarters for the manager and workers. A typical camp harvests about 10 'crops'; a crop is a tract of approximately 250 acres of timber, comprising about 5,000 trees. The part of the tree to be cut is called the 'face.' Trees less than 9 inches in diameter are not used by progressive operators. For the most part, operators lease their lands.

A 'woods rider' makes the preliminary survey, marking those trees in a given area that are suitable for chipping by smoothing off the bark on the face with a broad ax. Cups, usually of clay or galvanized iron, are properly seated, and a metal gutter set above them to convey the sap to the containers. The 'chipper' then makes 3 to 5 slashes approximately three-quarters of an inch deep and 3 or 4 feet above the ground. When filled, cups are 'dipped' or emptied into metal buckets; these are emptied in turn into 50-gallon barrels, which are transported to the still on low-slung mule-drawn wagons.

The still, a huge copper kettle with a removable lid, is built into a brick firebox. From 8 to 10 50-gallon barrels of 'dip' are emptied into the kettle, water added, and the cooking begins. At 212° Fahrenheit turpentine rises in the form of vapor, and steam from an 'arm' attached to the lid is conducted through a copper worm submerged in a tank of cold water and is discharged into a separator barrel, which collects the condensed spirits of turpentine. This, poured into steel drums, becomes the marketable product. The substance remaining in the kettle is rosin. A tail-gate in the kettle is opened and the rosin drawn off through a series of strainers into a vat. The rosin is then poured into wooden barrels, usually made on the premises, for shipment to metropolitan naval-stores markets (*see Jacksonville*). The market price fluctuates according to demand and quality, and quotations are given daily in the newspapers.

Naval stores are in demand by manufacturers of paint, varnish, soap, paper, ink, plastics, pharmaceutical preparations, and leather dressings. In 1850 Florida ranked fourth in national production, rose to first place in 1910, and dropped to second place in 1938, supplying 31 per cent of national and 20 per cent of world production. Approximately 14,000 men, the majority being Negroes, are employed in the industry in Florida. The number of workers employed by a still depends not so much on the acreage of the turpentine lands as on the density of trees. In an area of sparse growth it is possible for one worker to care for 10 acres.

Starke is at the junction with State 28 (*see Tour* 19).

1. Left from Starke on State 48 to KINGSLEY LAKE (*cottages, bathhouses*), 6 *m.* (210 alt.), the northernmost lake in the Florida ridge section, a sandy area running southward along the axis of the peninsula for 200 miles. The lake marks the summit and terminus of the Trail Ridge, a gently-sloping elevation 105 miles long. Clear springs feed the circular lake, 2.5 miles in diameter, named for Zephaniah Kingsley, a wealthy plantation owner who traded in slaves from 1800 to 1839 (*see Tour 1a*). Small rough-barked blackjack or turkey oak, smooth-barked water oak, white-barked sweet bay, scarlet-leaved loblolly oak, and the white-blossoming magnolia spread their foliage over the sandhills and ravines along the shore.

2. Right from Starke on State 48 to the FLORIDA STATE PRISON, 15 *m.*, the State penitentiary, commonly called Raiford, name of a small settlement a few miles dis-

tant. Approximately one-tenth of its 1,750 inmates are women. On entering its walls, each male prisoner serves 90 days at hard labor in a field squad during which time he is not allowed to speak to anyone in working hours. After this probationary period the prisoner is assigned to a regular job by the labor director. Guiseppi Zangara, who fatally wounded Mayor Anton J. Cermak of Chicago in attempting to assassinate President Franklin D. Roosevelt at Miami in February 1933, was imprisoned here before his execution.

Prisoners here are employed in a factory manufacturing automobile license tags, or in the sawmill, carpentry shop, mattress factory, garage, canteen, kitchen, bakery, cannery, warehouse, or library. A factory processes all cigarette, pipe, and chewing tobacco used in State institutions. The prison maintains its own dairy, poultry, and vegetable farms, which supply a large part of its needs. All State institutions are supplied with syrup produced on its 200-acre cane plantation at Belle Glade. The large tannery supplies leather for prisoners' shoes. Alligator, deer, bear, goat, fox, cat, and 'possum skins are also tanned.

White women work in the sewing rooms, making sheets, pillowcases, prison uniforms, and other articles. Negro men and women are employed in the shirt factory; a New York wholesale house provides the machinery, raw materials, and supervision, while the prison supplies the building, power, and labor. Under the terms of the contract most of the output is shipped to the wholesale house.

The provisions established by law for the maintenance of the State farm and convict camps read: 'For refusal to work, or refusing to do his work in a proper and workmanlike manner, a convict shall be confined in solitary confinement for such a period of time as may be necessary . . . and at the same time placed upon a restricted diet, which may be reduced to one-half a pound of bread a day, and as much water as the prisoner may require. . . . To carry out these provisions, each convict camp . . . shall be provided with a building in which to enforce solitary confinement . . . the cells shall be three feet wide, six feet six inches long, and seven feet from the floor to the grating over the top . . . the cell shall be so constructed that it may be divided across in two equal parts, and a convict may be confined in one-half of the space in the day time . . .'

Daddy Mention (*see Tour* 20), Florida counterpart of John Henry and Paul Bunyan, was sentenced to Raiford, so the tale goes, and came to know Jinny. When Daddy 'finally got it through his head he had got two years, he began tellin' he wouldn't stay no two years. "You can't beat the Cap'n's Jinny," they tried to tell him, but Daddy laughed. Daddy wouldn't have it no other way but to try to escape and make it to Okeenokee [Okefenokee] Swamp, up the other side of Olustee.

'So one mornin', soon's they lets us out the yard, Daddy up and runs. He was in good shape, too. He beat them shotguns a mile. When he got a chance to look back over his shoulder, he saw one of the guards put his finger in his mouth and whistle. But didn't no dog come; out come trottin' a little, short, jackass-lookin' mule, and backed right into a little drop-bottom cart without nobody touchin' her. By the time the harness was on her, all the dogs was in the bottom of the cart, and it was flyin' down the field after Daddy Mention.

'Daddy had stole one of the other prisoner's shoes and when he got to the woods good, he put 'em on and threw his shoes in a ditch to fool the dogs. Daddy had time to find himself a good big oak tree and cover himself in it before the dogs come up and lost his trail, and went barkin' off the wrong way. The cart that Jinny was pullin' was standin' a little ways from his tree, too. Daddy was figurin' to himself when he'd come down, when he felt something grab at his pants. Before he could figure out what it was, it had tore the whole seat out of them. Then he saw it was Jinny. With two feet planted at the bottom of the tree, she was reachin' for another piece of Daddy's pants. He tried to hurry up higher, when his foot slipped. That's when Jinny showed she e't leather, too.

'Daddy slid round to the other side of the tree, jumped down and run. Jinny come right behind him. When Daddy knew anything, Jinny had chased him right back to the prison fence. But he calculated even gettin' inside would be better'n bein' e't up by that wild mule, so he lit out for the top of the fence. Just as he 'most got over,

Jinny nipped again. This time there wasn't no pants for her to bite, so she grabbed a mouthful of Daddy Mention. And that's where he was when the Cap'n come—right there with a good part of him in Jinny's mouth. It was a long time 'fore he could sit down to eat, but that didn't worry him so much, 'cause in the sweat box where he was, you don't eat much, noways.'

WALDO, 40.3 *m.* (157 alt., 703 pop.), knew an era of prosperity in the 1920's when the Seaboard Air Line shops were here. Today it is a trading point for farmers of the surrounding territory. In 1870 a canal was cut to near-by Lake Santa Fe, and the steamer *S.F.Lewis* brought passengers, fruits, and vegetables from points on the lake for transshipment by railroad. The canal is still used by motorboats and other small craft.

Waldo is at the junction with State 31 (*see Tour 22*).

The AUSTIN CARY MEMORIAL FOREST (L), 44 *m.*, was planted by the Society of American Foresters in memory of Dr.Austin Cary, U.S. Department of Agriculture forester. In a cabin near by is a display of Cary's field instruments.

TUNG ACRES (R), 51.3 *m.*, is one of several large groves of tung trees in this region. A native of China, the tung tree has been cultivated there by primitive methods for 5,000 years. Similar in climate and soil to the tree's native habitat, the surrounding region has been planted with 16,000 acres of tung trees since 1925. The tung tree is relatively immune to disease and requires no expensive spraying. The nuts drop at maturity and can be gathered at any time, for they do not deteriorate. They are delivered to a crushing plant to produce a water-proof oil essential in the manufacture of paints, lacquers, and varnishes.

A hospital, farm, and dairy are maintained at the FLORIDA FARM COLONY (*open*, 9–11, 1–4, *daily*), 52.1 *m.*, a State institution for feeble-minded children and epileptics.

GAINESVILLE, 54.3 *m.* (185 alt., 10,465 pop.), home of the University of Florida, lies on the northern fringe of the ridge section, midway between the Atlantic Ocean and the Gulf of Mexico. For nine months of the year it is a typical college town, with business, sports, and social activities centering around the pine-shaded campus. The business district clusters about a red brick courthouse of the 1850's; in the residential areas many of the large frame houses, set back in spacious lawns, date from Reconstruction days. Gainesville's existence and development are linked with Florida's pioneer railroad history, and trains are still routed along the center of Main St.

The Negro settlement northwest and south of the business section has its own mercantile establishments, schools, and churches. Many religious meetings are held in tents, barns, and abandoned houses, and sometimes continue for days, during which worshipers stroll in and out while the congregation and preachers shout and sing above the din of an improvised orchestra. Most of the Negroes are employed in domestic service, or in near-by lumber and turpentine camps.

Naval stores and sawmills are the major support of the Gainesville area, although it ranks high in truck farming, with early Irish potatoes and watermelons as its leading products. Light-wrapper and cigarette tobaccos are cultivated, and several large nurseries propagate subtropical plants for State and northern markets.

Two plants for the extraction of tung oil (*see above*) in the vicinity of Gainesville serve growers of Florida and parts of southern Georgia and eastern Alabama. Florida had an estimated crop of 800,000 pounds in 1938.

The Gainesville area was known as Potano Province when De Soto marched through it in 1539; the name was changed to Alachua (Ind., jug) when the Creek Indians took possession upon the English acquisition of Florida in 1763. A white settlement known as Hog Town grew up around a trading post established here in 1830, and was named Gainesville in 1853 for General Edmund P. Gaines, a Seminole War leader. Families from Georgia, Alabama, and the Carolinas came to lay out large cotton plantations. Completion of the Yulee railroad (*see Tour 2a*) across the State in the early 1860's stimulated development. A post office, abolished during the War between the States, was re-established in 1866; stagecoach service was opened with Ocala. As transportation facilities improved, truck farming and citrus culture grew in importance.

Gainesville became an educational center with the establishment in 1867 of an academy, the nucleus of the State Seminary for the region east of the Suwannee. Not until 1905, however, were State-supported schools for white males merged and consolidated as the University of Florida. The gala event of the university year is Homecoming Day, when graduates of all ages return to their Alma Mater for the season's important football game.

The UNIVERSITY OF FLORIDA, W. on University Ave., has a 200-acre-campus, shaded by a natural growth of pines and traversed by paved driveways and winding footpaths. Among the trees stand a score of three-story vine-covered red brick buildings, Tudor Gothic in style, the majority erected since 1910. Dividing the campus is the PLAZA OF THE AMERICAS, a landscaped parkway dedicated in 1925 to the 21 American Republics; a holly tree was planted for each Republic. The grounds include 1,500 acres, in addition to 1,519-acre Austin Cary Memorial Forest (*see above*) for use of the School of Forestry.

Although its beginnings preceded Florida's admission to the Union, the first college—the College of Arts and Sciences—did not open until 1853. During the War between the States the Federal Government, by the Merrill Act, provided lands for institutions in those States that would promote agriculture, the mechanical arts, and military training. An agricultural college was opened at Lake City in 1884, and the Experiment Station was established there later. In 1905 the Florida legislature consolidated all State-maintained colleges into three, of which the University of Florida was one. Until the World War its annual enrollment did not exceed 500, but during the next 20 years it reached 3,000, with 2,000 attending summer sessions, at which time the university is coeducational.

The FLORIDA UNION BUILDING, student community center, was begun under the Civil Works Administration and FERA and completed by WPA.

It contains lounges; offices for student government, alumni, religious organizations, and publications; banquet rooms and ballrooms; a small auditorium; and game and club rooms. The campaign to provide such a building was sponsored by the late William Jennings Bryan and his friend, the late Dr.A.A.Murphree, president of the university.

In the UNIVERSITY OF FLORIDA LIBRARY is the FLORIDA ROOM, containing volumes, pamphlets, diaries, church histories, and original old deeds and records pertaining to the State's history. This library, together with those in the P.K.Yonge School and other departmental buildings, contains more than 125,000 volumes.

The CHEMISTRY-PHARMACY BUILDING houses the EDMUND KIRBY-SMITH HERBARIUM, a collection of 6,000 specimens of flora from almost all States in the Union and many foreign countries.

Among other structures are SCIENCE HALL; ENGINEERING BUILDING; PEABODY HALL, with an art gallery displaying work of students and traveling exhibitions; AGRICULTURE BUILDING and EXPERIMENTAL STATION; the AUDITORIUM, seating 2,000; and two GYMNASIUMS, one used as a dressing room for an outdoor SWIMMING POOL.

FLORIDA FIELD, seating 23,000, was dedicated in 1930. Adjoining are the GRAHAM FIELD, an oval with a cinder track and facilities for field sports; and the MILITARY FIELD, used for drills, dress parades, and polo. The State-owned radio station WRUF, broadcasting farm reports, market news, frost and hurricane warnings between non-commercial programs, stands immediately south of the campus.

The P.K.YONGE SCHOOL, SE. corner 9th and Margaret Sts., a three-story red brick building of Tudor Gothic, named for the late P.K.Yonge of Pensacola, is a model or laboratory school. It includes a kindergarten, grade school, and high school; classrooms are equipped with radios. Results of the program and methods of the school have attracted national attention (*see Education*). The first floor auditorium is used for Little Theater plays and by the Florida Players, a university organization.

The JOHN F. SEAGLE BUILDING, 522 W.University Ave., a relic of the boom era, was originally intended as a hotel. Miss Georgia Seagle, pioneer resident of the city, later donated the building to the University for administration offices, and the city council and Alachua County commission provided funds to complete the structure, named in memory of the late John F. Seagle. The FLORIDA STATE MUSEUM occupies the first three floors. Exhibits include Indian relics, mounted Florida birds, a large collection of birds' eggs, and relics of early Florida history.

Gainesville is at the junction with US 441 (*see Tour 21*).

Section c. GAINESVILLE to CEDAR KEYS, 58 *m.*

Although the highway is level and well paved for the most part, west of GAINESVILLE, 0 *m.*, it is narrow, rough, and hilly. Gas and oil should be checked carefully as there are few filling stations. The countryside is beautiful in spring and fall, although many of the farm houses between the small settlements are dilapidated.

At 2.8 *m.* is the junction with State 65.

Left on this road to WACAHOOTA (Ind., cow pen), 5.2 *m.* (15 pop.), and the SITE OF THE MISSION FRANCISCO DE POTANO, established in the first years of the seventeenth century and visited by Fray Luis Ore in 1616. Bloody attacks on Francisco were made by heathen Indians who swooped down from the Carolinas in the latter half of the century. In 1704 ex-Governor James Moore of Carolina raided the region, burning and looting; he put to fire and sword those who resisted, and sold into captivity all who surrendered. Fort Wacahoota was built in this vicinity and garrisoned during the Seminole Wars. No traces remain of the fort or the older mission.

ARREDONDO, 5.5 *m.* (91 alt., 100 pop.), a small group of frame buildings providing stores and markets for near-by farmers, was named for Don Fernando de la Maza Arredondo, who in 1817 was given land in this region. The grant consisted of 'four leagues of land to each wind . . . to lie in a rectilinear figure,' and was settled by some 200 Spanish families.

ARCHER, 15 *m.* (88 alt., 576 pop.), founded in 1859 and originally called Deer Hammock, was renamed for Brigadier General James J. Archer of the Confederate army. Early settlers were attracted by its citrus-growing possibilities; a colony of Quakers from Ohio planted oaks as windbreaks for their new groves. Although the town depends for trade chiefly on surrounding farms, it draws additional income from a grist mill and a foundry for casting mining machinery.

BRONSON, 25 *m.* (75 alt., 694 pop.) (*see Tour 6a*), is at the junction with US 19 (*see Tour 6a*).

Between Bronson and Otter Creek, State 13 penetrates an area that serves as a range for isolated herds of semi-wild cattle and hogs; the region is drained by the Wacassassa River (Ind., cow range). In the back country are scattered sawmills cutting timber from hardwood hammocks.

OTTER CREEK, 37 *m.* (39 alt., 989 pop.), obtained its name from the abundance of otter in the vicinity; otter were hunted here by Indians until the early 1850's, and later by trappers. Surrounded by stands of pine, cypress, ash, and magnolia, the town manufactures hardwood slats for fruit crates. Logs brought in by trucks are cut by circular saws into lengths called 'flitches,' which are placed on a rolling carriage and sliced into slats. After being allowed to season, the slats are wired in bundles and shipped to crate mills in central and south Florida.

The route traverses a densely forested section known as the Gulf Hammock, a country of sluggish streams, cypress ponds, and bogs, never more than 75 feet above sea level (*good hunting in season; deer, small game*). Occasionally, in the course of a deer hunt, the small Florida black bear is encountered (*see Tour 14a*).

The mainland ends and the highway runs along a causeway, 54 *m.* In February 1865, two regiments of Federal troops at Cedar Keys made an attempt to advance inland against the Southern armies, but a Confederate force under Captain J.J.Dickison turned them back here after a four-hour battle.

CEDAR KEYS, 58 *m.* (13 alt., 1,066 pop.), a fishing village on a white sand island in the Gulf of Mexico, 3 miles from the mainland, was at one time a lively port and railroad terminal. Hotels were built to accommodate railroad and steamship passengers who transferred here to reach all parts of south Florida. A U.S. customs house and weather bureau were established. The Yulee railroad, officially named the Atlantic, Gulf and West Indies Transit Company, was extended from Fernandina in 1860, but service was suspended during the War between the States. In the early 1880's, because of the extensive tracts of cedar on the adjoining mainland, pencil companies erected large sawmills in the territory and shipped cedar slabs to their factories in the North. The completion of a railroad into Tampa in 1884 brought an end to Cedar Keys' prosperity. No longer an important port, with its railroad later abandoned, it dwindled rapidly in population. Commercial fishing, the gathering of oysters and sponges, and a factory manufacturing brushes from palmetto fiber are now the principal support of the inhabitants.

The site of the first settlement has not been determined, but it is known that the Spaniards early threw up fortifications and built boats near the present townsite. Spanish pirates knew the area; Gasparilla is said to have buried treasure near the mouth of the Suwannee River, 10 miles up the coast (*see Tour 6a*).

The islands in the vicinity were inhabited by pre-Columbian Timucuan Indians; burial mounds revealing well-preserved skeletons and pottery have been found on Way Key and West Key. Near the Way Key mound is a hill, open toward the east, presumably used by the Indians in their worship of the sun. Many of the islands are Government bird refuges. The muddy tidal shores of the islands and lagoons constitute the northern limit of the buttonwood, a tall narrow-boled tree with rounded top and dark green foliage.

SEA HORSE ISLAND, 3 *m.* to the southwest (*by chartered boats only*), approximately 1 mile wide and long, rises 47 feet above sea level; it is now uninhabited, covered with live and blackjack oaks and mangrove thickets. Sea horses are often caught here in the nets of shrimp and sponge fishermen. The male of these tiny crustacea carry the infant sea horses in a pouch. In January 1861, marines from the Federal gunboat *Hatteras* came ashore, spiked three cannons, and burned property on Way Key. On the southern shore is an abandoned LIGHTHOUSE, used as a Federal prison during the War between the States. Its walls are of brick, and solid wooden shutters protect the windows.

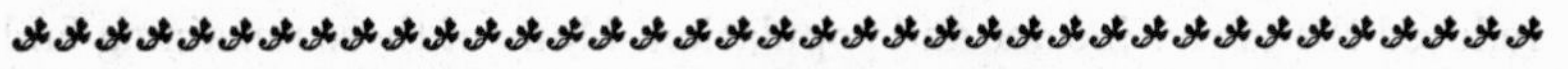

Tour 4

(Valdosta, Ga.)—Lake City—Williston—Brooksville—Tampa—Bradenton—Sarasota—Fort Myers—Naples; US 41.
Georgia Line to Naples, 381.9 *m.*

Hard-surfaced roadbed throughout; watch for cattle along the highway.
Route paralleled by Southern Ry. between Georgia Line and Lake City; by Atlantic Coast Line R.R. between High Springs and Inverness, Bradenton and Sarasota, Fort Myers and Naples; by Seaboard Air Line Ry. between Archer and Tampa, Parrish and Venice, Fort Myers and Naples.
Accommodations of all types.

US 41 crosses the State line in a thinly settled section of north Florida, near the Suwannee River. Proceeding down the peninsula, it crosses a gently rolling area of good-sized farms, and through the sandy pine woods of west central Florida to industrial Tampa. Curving around Tampa Bay, the highway passes fertile farm lands in the vicinity of Bradenton and reaches the Gulf at Sarasota, a town of art activities, circus quarters, and game fishing. Turning inland to tropical Fort Myers, on the Caloosahatchee River, it traverses a region of flatwoods, palms, and occasional marshland on the western edge of the Everglades. The route returns to the Gulf at Naples, where it joins US 94, a section of the Tamiami Trail leading across the Everglades.

Section a. GEORGIA LINE to WILLISTON; 104.5 *m. US* 41

Small farms lie in the foreground against stands of hardwood and pine on the rolling hills in this fertile section; and rich green vegetation blankets both sides of the road. Oxen drawing high-wheeled carts driven by Negroes plod along the highway, as in early Colonial days. Oxen are still used in lumber camps for snaking logs out of deeper swamps impenetrable by tractor.

US 41 crosses the Georgia Line, 0 *m.*, 19 miles south of Valdosta, Ga. (*see Ga. Guide*). The SMITH MONUMENT (R) was erected by the State of Florida to Michael McKenzie Smith, who in 1915–20 laid plans for the present Florida highway network. Georgia marked the boundary with a marble tablet (L) bearing the State seal.

JENNINGS, 1.8 *m.* (150 alt., 561 pop.), was named for George Jennings, a northerner who is said to have come into this section on a raft by way of the Alapaha River in 1844. Before the World War, when much sea-island cotton was grown here, the community prospered as a shipping point; but since the War the boll weevil and the low price of cotton have reduced the town's income and population. Many of those remaining find employment in naval-stores plants, lumber and grist mills.

The ALAPAHA RIVER is crossed on a long concrete bridge, 8.1 *m.*; along the river are many tobacco farms.

JASPER, 13.9 *m.* (152 alt., 1,748 pop.), was established as a trading post in 1830 by families from South Carolina and Georgia, and named for Sergeant William Jasper, who had served with distinction in a South Carolina regiment during the Revolutionary War. Red brick stores border the few paved streets; most of the houses are built along sand and clay roads. Farmers in the vicinity once produced the best variety of sea-island cotton, and were among the first in the State to produce flue-cured tobacco. Small factories in the town utilize the near-by lumber supply to manufacture plywood boxes and similar articles.

In the white limestone COMMUNITY CENTER, constructed in 1936 with WPA funds, is a large auditorium. The HAMILTON COUNTY COURTHOUSE, a dark red brick structure, was built in 1932 to replace an older building destroyed by fire a few years previously.

WHITE SPRINGS, 31.5 *m.* (126 alt., 618 pop.), is a quiet shady village built around medicinal springs. Founded in 1826 on the north bank of the Suwannee River, it has long been known as a health resort. In times of flood the river rises nearly 40 feet, and the springs, issuing from a rock hollow, are inundated, which accounts for the unusual three-story bathhouse (25¢), the third floor of which is level with the street. The springs were considered sacred by the Indians, who marked trees in a 5-mile circle around them. Warriors wounded in battle were not subject to attack when they came here to recuperate. During the War between the States the area was known as 'Rebels' Refuge.' Many plantation owners moved here with their families and slaves, living in safety throughout the war, out of the path of Union invasion.

A steel and concrete bridge spans the SUWANNEE RIVER (*see Tour 6a*), 32.8 *m.*, shadowed by oaks and pines, bordered with shrubs and wild flowers.

LAKE CITY, 44.4 *m.* (201 alt., 4,416 pop.) (*see Tour 7a*), is at the junction with US 90 (*see Tour 7a and b*) and State 28 (*see Tour 19*).

The SANTA FE RIVER, 68.1 *m.*, a branch of the Suwannee, was named for Santa Fé de Toloca, an early Spanish mission. At this point there is an extensive view of the river, its banks covered with oaks and drooping willows.

HIGH SPRINGS, 70.5 *m.* (75 alt., 1,864 pop.), named for a hilltop spring, was established as a trading post in 1885 and is today a shopping center for farmers of the back country who raise and ship bright-leaf tobacco, corn, and peanuts. A large number of the residents find employment in the repair shops of the Atlantic Coast Line Railroad here. Their houses and small neat gardens reflect the sense of order and the precision that often characterize the railroader.

High Springs is at the junction with US 441 (*see Tour 21*).

1. Left from High Springs on an unimproved road to NATURAL BRIDGE, 6 *m.*, on the Santa Fe River. The bridge is a limestone formation level with the surrounding

terrain. The river disappears at the bottom of a sink hole, follows its course underground, then returns to the surface 3.5 miles south of the bridge. The natural crossing was part of an old Spanish trail between St. Augustine and Pensacola (*see Tour 7a*). A half-century ago, trains of covered wagons often camped here for days until excess water drained off the bridge so that they could cross.

2. Right from High Springs on State 5A to FORT WHITE, 9 *m.* (63 alt., 272 pop.), named for a fort that stood here during the Seminole War. Today the village is the center of an agricultural area producing corn, peanuts, hogs, cattle, and turkeys. Approximately 5,000 turkeys are shipped each year.

Right from Fort White 0.3 *m.* on State 82 to a junction with an unimproved road; R. here 2.3 *m.* to ITCHETUCKNEE SPRINGS (Ind., cured tobacco) which flow at a rate of 300,000,000 gallons per day and create a swift stream, the Itchetucknee Run, which flows through a dense hardwood forest into the Suwannee River.

NEWBERRY, 83.3 *m.* (83 alt., 766 pop.), gains most of its income from the large crop of early watermelons grown on near-by farms and brought here for shipment; the production of rough pine lumber provides year-round employment.

ARCHER, 93.2 *m.* (88 alt., 576 pop.) (*see Tour 3c*), is at the junction with State 13 (*see Tour 3c*).

RALEIGH, 100.6 *m.* (78 alt., 147 pop.), is a cluster of weathered frame cabins around several limestone pits from which rock is quarried for road construction. Near by are abandoned sections of narrow paved roads of the type that brought Florida highways out of the sand in 1916–17. Dense growths of young pine about the village are tapped for turpentine.

South of Raleigh the route passes through a fertile agricultural region growing corn and tobacco; hog raising is profitable in the section.

WILLISTON, 104.5 *m.* (82 alt., 940 pop.), is headquarters for three large limestone companies, which quarry rock as white as chalk from strata formed ages ago from the skeletal remains of innumerable marine animals (*see Geology and Paleontology*).

Williston is at the junction with US 19 (*see Tour 6a*).

Section b. WILLISTON to TAMPA; 108.3 *m.* *US* 41

From highlands rich in phosphate deposits, the route passes through fertile valleys into a thinly settled region, dotted with ponds and stump-filled clearings, and on to Tampa, cigar capital of the United States, manifesting marked Latin influences.

South of WILLISTON, 0 *m.*, is ROMEO, 12.9 *m.* (42 alt., 100 pop.), a turpentine-producing settlement chiefly interesting to travelers for the link between its name and that of Juliette.

JULIETTE, 20.2 *m.* (56 alt.), was named, as was Romeo, for a local legend similar to that in the Shakespearean play; one of the lovers lived here and the other at what is now Romeo. The misspelling of the name was not intentional.

Left from Juliette on State 16 to RAINBOW SPRINGS (*glass-bottomed boats*, $1 *a passenger*), 1.3 *m.*, second in size to Silver Springs (*see Tour* 21). Rainbow Springs, with a flow of 421,000,000 gallons per day, carry off nearly 600 tons of solids in solution daily. At least 32 varieties of underwater plants grow on the rock bottom, and 18 varieties of turtles and 37 different kinds of fish inhabit the crystal-clear depths. The multicolored prisms sparkling in the waters when the sun is high have given them their name; the effect is caused by the deposit of minerals in solution on the sides of the pool. The springs have an attractive setting, with high banks, green slopes, and trees.

The large pine-covered mounds, 20.5 *m.*, were formed when limestone was mined here in the early 1890's.

DUNNELLON, 24 *m.* (50 alt., 1,194 pop.), on the north bank of the Withlacoochee River, is a compact little town of square-fronted business buildings, with arcades along the sidewalks of the main street; the shell-paved side streets of the residential section are arched over with huge oaks. The discovery of limestone deposits in the vicinity in 1889 brought prosperity to Dunnellon, and since that time the mining and shipping of phosphate and limestone rock have been a leading industry. Some of the larger mines are owned and operated by Belgian interests.

In the early 1860's the town was a lively trading center for planters and stockmen of the surrounding areas. Although some cattle are still raised, turpentine, lumber, truck, and dairy products, along with limestone, are the town's principal sources of revenue.

Along the banks of the Withlacoochee River, lined with primeval forests of cypress, magnolia, giant oaks, palms, wild cherry, and gum, fishing and hunting camps are numerous. In this district General Edmund P. Gaines, en route with 1,100 men from Fort King to Fort Brooke, attempted to cross the river in 1836. Refugee Negroes in this region, led by a Negro named Ino, joined forces with Osceola (*see Tour* 21) and his men, and made a sudden and vigorous attack on the Government troops. Stunned by the surprise assault, Gaines threw up a breastwork of logs and sent a messenger to General Duncan Clinch at Fort Drane, asking for reinforcements. Ten days later, when Gaines and his men had been forced to eat all their horses, John Caesar, one of the Negro leaders, approached the camp and asked for a parley. Osceola led the peace delegation to the army encampment, and, as the conference began, General Clinch arrived on the scene and immediately opened fire. Two Indians and one Negro were killed; the survivors broke and fled, charging bad faith.

Right from Dunnellon on State 16-A to DEAD LAKE (*excellent fishing*), 2 *m.*, a body of water nearly 8 miles long, created by the Florida Power Corporation dam on the Withlacoochee River. The lake is visible from the highway at intervals for 3 miles. The thousands of acres inundated when the dam was built present a forlorn spectacle of drowned oaks and pines.

INGLIS, 13.2 *m.* (136 pop.), consists of unpainted frame houses grouped about a general store.

YANKEETOWN, 15.6 *m.* (157 pop.), is a sportsmen's resort only a few miles from the Gulf of Mexico. Here the Withlacoochee River winds between islands studded with oyster bars, its shores covered with dense jungle growth. Yankeetown was founded during the boom days by Judge A.F.Knotts, who in 1905 had planned the city of Gary, Ind. The village has more than 200 lodges and cottages, a hotel, and community stores. Florida Chapter No.1 of the Izaak Walton League of America was organized here.

PORT INGLIS, 17.2 *m.* (16 pop.), a fishing camp near the mouth of the Withlacoochee River, will be the west terminus of the projected National Gulf-Atlantic Ship Canal (*see Tour* 21).

HERNANDO, 33.1 *m.* (50 alt., 365 pop.), lies on the west shore of LAKE TSALA APOPKA (Ind., lake where trout are eaten), an island-dotted lake that extends 20 miles south, center of a large hunting and fishing area (*see Tour 6a*). Named for Hernando de Soto, the town was settled in 1881, more than three centuries after the Spanish explorer and his men had marched through this territory.

The CHURCH OF THE NAZARENE, built of native stone and almost hidden by moss-draped oaks, is one of 38 churches of this denomination in Florida. There are 2,500 in the United States, with a total of 160,000 members. The church subscribes to the fundamental beliefs of John Wesley.

INVERNESS, 41 *m.* (38 alt., 1,215 pop.), on Lake Tsala Apopka, was named by an early settler for his home town in Scotland. Its streets, bordered with oaks and cabbage palms, radiate from a yellow brick courthouse topped with a copper clock tower. The town is the marketing center of a large and populous rural area, in which citrus growing, truck farming, beekeeping, and dairying are the chief occupations.

Right from Inverness on State 22 to CRYSTAL RIVER, 19 *m.* (4 alt., 869 pop.), at the head of the stream of the same name. The town has had a steady growth as a fish, oyster, and lumber center. CRYSTAL SPRINGS, also known as Cedar Hill Springs, has a flow of 26,000 gallons a minute. There are seven other springs in the vicinity; some are crystal clear, coming from cavernous depths, and many are surrounded with dense foliage. Both salt- and fresh-water fish are plentiful in the springs and runs.

Three blocks south of the business district, fronting the river, is SYLVAN GLEN PARK (*rustic lodge and swimming pool*). A stone's throw from the city docks is BUZZARD'S ROOST, an island popular with fishing parties. The red cedar growing in this section is considered the finest in Florida, and for many years carloads of cedar slabs were shipped to northern pencil manufacturers. The wood is now used for cabinet work and furniture.

Crystal River is at the junction with State 15; L. on State 15 is YULEE PARK, 5.3 *m.*, owned by the Affiliated Women's Clubs of Citrus County, once the site of a large sugar plantation established by David Yulee, one of Florida's first U.S. Senators (*see Tour 2a*). It was Senator Yulee's rule never to buy or sell a slave if it meant breaking up a family. This policy once brought a remonstrance from a slave whose wife was a veritable shrew: 'Massa, please don't let yo'self be put out about *dat*!' In the park are the RUINS OF A SUGAR MILL, destroyed by Federal troops during the War between the States. The ruins of the chimney and the oven vat supports are of local stone. Although they have been exposed to the weather for a century, the old iron boilers, engine beds, and kettles are not rust-pitted.

At 6.8 *m.* on State 15 is HOMOSASSA SPRINGS (50 pop.), best known for the hunting lodge conducted here by Dazzy Vance, retired baseball pitcher. The lodge is a favorite rendezvous for baseball men, and in winter a baseball school is conducted for rookies and youngsters. HOMOSASSA SPRINGS has a flow of 70,000 gallons a minute. The waters of the springs form a natural aquarium, part of a Federal fish preserve. The overflow empties into the Gulf and attracts a variety of fresh- and salt-water fish. From early fall to late spring the channel is literally filled with fish coming to spawn in the numerous underground caverns. On cool days a dense vapor envelops the springs and river, which supports the contention of some that the name is derived from an Indian word meaning smoking creek.

FLORAL CITY, 47.3 *m.* (57 alt., 300 pop.), at the south end of Lake Tsala Apopka, is headquarters for sportsmen attracted to the near-by lakes and hunting grounds. The village lies (L) off the highway, under a canopy of giant oaks.

Floral City is at the junction with State 22 (*see Tour 9*).

For 15 miles south of Floral City the highway, in a succession of sweeping curves, traverses a region of low hills. Flocks of herons and red-winged blackbirds live in the occasional reedy swamps.

The entrance to CHINSEGUT HILL SANCTUARY (*open* 8–4), 57.8 *m.*, is marked by rustic lodges. Wide landscaped driveways wind through the 2,200-acre park, given to the U.S. Department of Agriculture by Colonel Raymond Robins in 1932 for use as a wild-life refuge and forest conservation and experimental station. Research work is also conducted here in the cultivation of forage grasses for livestock, citrus fruits, and Florida ferns.

Colonel Robins (1873–), lecturer and social economist, was a leader in the National Christian Evangelistic Social campaign of the Y.M.C.A. and Y.W.C.A. in American colleges in 1915–16. He won his military title with the Red Cross Mission to Russia in 1917–18. After the War, he made a transcontinental and European tour advocating the outlawry of war. In 1933 he traveled 8,000 miles in the Soviet Union, studying collective farming, industry, and education.

The former HOME OF COLONEL ROBINS (*open Thurs.*, 1–5) was built by ships' carpenters in 1849. The framing consists of hand-hewn 12-inch cypress beams, mortised with pine pegs. All the timber was hauled here by oxen. Upper and lower verandas, 12 feet wide, run the length of this typical plantation house.

The BROOKSVILLE GOLF AND COUNTRY CLUB (*greens fee* $1), 60.5 *m.*, is surrounded by rolling hills and dense woodland.

BROOKSVILLE, 62.5 *m.* (144 alt., 1,405 pop.), with wide oak-shaded streets leading to a white-columned red brick courthouse, was named for Preston Brooks, Congressman from South Carolina, who in 1859 struck Senator Charles Sumner on the floor of the Senate during a heated debate on secession. The business district overlooks a rolling country dotted with summer camps and suburban estates. Tangerines are grown extensively throughout this section, dairy products are shipped to State-wide markets, but the quarrying of limestone rock is the leading industry. During the Volstead era there were many moonshine stills in the secluded palmetto scrub about the town.

During the late 1870's a stage line ran from the railhead at Gainesville to Tampa, with a stopover at Brooksville. Swampy stretches of the trail were paved with logs, constituting a 'corduroy' roadbed to keep the stage from bogging down. The coach was a lumbering, sturdily built four-horse vehicle, constructed in Cincinnati especially for such roads; a complicated system of springs was designed to compensate for the jolts and side-swayings. One of the drivers, adept at handling lines and blacksnake whip, was noted for his ability to expectorate through the front wheel of the coach without touching a spoke. He also enlivened the trip by 'gopher (turtle) grabbing'; he would leap from his seat, pick up a turtle from the road, and toss it on the baggage rack without halting his team.

Brooksville is at a junction with US 19 (*see Tour 6b*).

Left from Brooksville on the Spring Hill Rd. to the DEVIL'S PUNCH BOWL, 3.5 *m.*, a dry sink an acre in extent and from 60 to 80 feet deep. The conformation is that of a mammoth punch bowl, with steep, almost unscalable sides.

In a large group of frame and log cabins clustered around a turpentine still (*open* 8:30–5:30; *adm.* 25¢), 64.9 *m.*, can be observed the various processes in the distillation of pine sap. Almost all workers are Negroes. One of the larger cabins is occupied by aged Negroes, billed as ex-slaves, who sing, plunk banjoes, and tell tall tales for the entertainment of their visitors and the profit of themselves.

MASARYKTOWN, 71.5 *m.* (50 pop.), named for Thomas G. Masaryk (1850–1937), first President of Czechoslovakia, was founded as an agricultural colony in 1924 by Joseph Joscak, editor of a Czech newspaper in New York City. Poultry-raising and the production of citrus fruits and truck have brought prosperity to the town. A general store, a two-story hotel, and a small public library in a square pink stucco building lend an urban touch to the agricultural village. Characteristic of the colony are the half-dozen windmills that stand against the horizon.

For several years Masaryktown was culturally isolated, for the settlers spoke only the mother tongue. Although the younger generation is quite Americanized, the farming methods of Europe are still employed, and Old World feast days are celebrated. On Czechoslovakian Independence Day, October 28, the man for whom the village was named is toasted and honored. Some phase of the republic's history is told in a pageant, and special services are held throughout the day at the church. Folk dances conclude the festivities. The women wear wide flaring skirts, with bustle effects, and handmade bonnets of intricate pattern. Enlivened by native wines, all Masaryktown dances to the strains of Bohemian music.

Half a block from US 41, on a dirt road (L), stands the red brick ROMAN CATHOLIC CHURCH, in a grove of second-growth pines. Its wooden bell tower, topped with a gilded cross and a lightning rod, rises above a checkerboard-patterned roof of tin shingles painted yellow, orange, and brown.

South of Masaryktown the route traverses a long stretch of cypress ponds and cut-over pine lands, passing only a few isolated settlements and scattered farms. Near Tampa are many citrus groves, heavy with fruit and blooms in the spring.

SULPHUR SPRINGS, 102.7 *m.*, a suburb of Tampa, conducts most of its business in one building. An apartment hotel occupies the upper floor; on the ground floor are a post office, a café, a barber shop, a beauty parlor, a bank, and several stores. A GREYHOUND TRACK near by is open from December to April. The SULPHUR SPRINGS POOL (*open all year; adm. 25¢*) has an average temperature of 70° and a flow of 20,000 gallons a minute.

TAMPA, 108.3 *m.* (15 alt., 101,161 pop.) (*see Tampa*).

Points of Interest: Ybor City Latin Quarter, Estuary Docks, Plant Park, Tampa Bay Hotel, Davis Islands, cigar factories, and others.

Tampa is at the junction with US 541 (*see Tour 4A*) and US 92 (*see Tour 20*).

Section c. TAMPA to FORT MYERS; 134.3 *m.* US 41

Between Tampa and Naples, US 41 roughly parallels Florida's west coast, though for the most part it runs inland, out of sight of the Gulf of

Mexico. Touching the Gulf at Palmetto, the route enters a highly productive truck-garden section, passes through Sarasota with its art museum and winter headquarters of the world's largest circus, and reaches Venice, one-time boom city. US 41 crosses Charlotte Harbor at a town of the same name, once the haunt of famous pirates, and continues southeast to Fort Myers, with its towering royal palms, on the left bank of the tidal Caloosahatchee River. Skirting alternate stretches of salt marshes and thick stands of pine, the highway reaches Naples and a section of the Tamiami Trail (US 94), connecting Miami with the west coast.

East of TAMPA, 0 *m.*, US 41 unites with US 92 (*see Tour* 20), branching south at 7.4 *m.*, where SIX MILE CREEK is crossed. This spot, with its numerous tourist cabins and refreshment stands, was once a popular camping ground for settlers.

At 8.1 *m.* is the junction with State 79.

Left on this road to a junction with Lithia Road, 3 *m.*; R. on Lithia Road 12 *m.* to the BELL SHOALS BRIDGE across the ALAFIA RIVER (Sp., oleander). The stream here is 30 feet deep, its high banks wooded with magnolia and bay. The magnolia tree has dark green leaves, 5 to 8 inches long and 2 to 3 inches wide. Its smooth brown trunk climbs to a height of 80 feet; large fragrant flowers with white petals and yellow centers appear during summer. The bloom of the common white bay resembles the magnolia, though its white sweet-smelling flowers are smaller.

Right from the bridge 200 yards to BELL SHOALS, a favorite spot for hunting and fishing parties. Louis Bell settled here in 1846 and operated a cattle ferry; for many years the spot was called Bell's Ford. Bell provided for himself and family by assisting the cattlemen in transporting their unruly charges across the river during the annual migration to Gulf ports. He was harassed by the Indians and often forced to take refuge in a small log fort he had built. His six-year-old son was captured by the Indians, and it was only after the savages had been given all the blankets in the Bell homestead that the child was returned.

Bell Shoals was the locale of Jules Verne's fantastic novel, *From the Earth to the Moon* (1865). Here the 900-foot cannon was supposed to have been cast and erected. In the first edition of the novel the man-bearing projectile was not properly aimed, and remained whirling in a vast orbit around the moon. Readers objected so strenuously to this tragic ending that in later editions Verne brought the adventurers back to earth unharmed. For 60 years a semi-buried piece of machinery on the banks of the river was believed by some to be a fragment of the gigantic cannon. On being unearthed, it was found to be a 10-foot steel shaft with vanes attached at the ends. Although the origin and use of the shaft is unknown, it probably was a part of an old water-driven grist mill that served pioneers in this region. The shaft is on exhibition at the Colson farm, a mile south of Turkey Creek School on Pleasant Grove Rd.

RIVERVIEW, 14.9 *m.* (150 pop.), on the bank of the Alafia River, lies in a section densely wooded with magnolia, sweet gum, and water oak. First named Peru, it was settled in 1856; supplies were brought from Tampa on the small steamboat *Josephine* and distributed to farmers by ox cart; in the 1870's a shell road was built from Tampa. The town remains a center for truck-garden and citrus products.

PARRISH, 36.5 *m.* (41 alt., 721 pop.), is a citrus-fruit and vegetable shipping center.

South of Parrish the highway angles toward the Gulf, following the broad, jungle-walled MANATEE RIVER (L) for several miles. The river was named for the manatee, a herbivorous mammal, once plentiful in the brackish waters along both Florida coasts and still occasionally seen. The animal has a flat semicircular tail and two oval fins. Its flesh has the taste of fishy pork, but pirates of the eighteenth century relished it. Esquemeling, whose adventures are related in *Buccaneers of America* (1928), wrote that ships often put in at river mouths 'to make provisions of flesh, especially of a certain animal which the Spaniards call manati, owing to the hand-like use of the fore-limbs, and the Dutch called sea cow, because the head, nose, and teeth of this beast are very like those of a cow. The skin on its back is the thickness of two fingers, which being dried is as hard as any whale bone, and may serve to make walking sticks.' The Timucuan Indians, according to several early accounts, used to lasso the beasts, jab sticks in their air vents, and ride them ashore.

ELLENTON, 45 *m.* (11 alt., 569 pop.), is the center of a productive area of citrus groves and truck gardens. In the center of extensive grounds shaded by live oaks, entered through a gateway (R) of tall coquina columns, stands the JUDAH P. BENJAMIN MEMORIAL, also known as the Gamble Mansion (*open* 9–5; *free*). The two-story mansion, with thick walls, shuttered windows, and wide double verandas on three sides, supported by 18 columns, was built between 1842 and 1845 by Robert Gamble, banker and soldier, on his 3,000-acre plantation here. Slaves made bricks of broken shell and mortar for the walls; plaster was a mixture of sand, lime, and sugar, for so much sugar was raised on the plantation that it was found to be the cheapest available binder. Cypress and oak were fashioned into immense beams, windows and doors, wide plank flooring, banisters, and paneling. The mansion and the estate are minutely described in Lilli B. McDuffee's *The Lures of Manatee* (1933).

Flags of the Confederacy, pictures of military heroes, and similar relics are on exhibit in the mansion, now a memorial to Judah Philip Benjamin, Secretary of State of the Confederacy, who took refuge here at the end of the War between the States when Jefferson Davis and his cabinet endeavored to make their way to the Florida coast in the hope of finding a ship to carry them to the West Indies. News of Benjamin's presence in the vicinity, together with a $50,000 reward offered for his capture, brought Federal gunboats to Tampa Bay. Disguised as a Negro cook, Benjamin slipped on board a small sloop, passed the scrutiny of Federal officers who searched the craft at the mouth of the Manatee River, and escaped to England, where he distinguished himself as a member of the bar.

On the grounds are RUINS OF THE GAMBLE SUGAR MILL, one of the largest mills in the South at the time of the War between the States. Vats and various pieces of machinery have been preserved. The old CHIMNEY HOUSE (R), built by Gamble in 1840 as a stack for his mill, towers above the oaks.

Approximately 16,000 trees stand in the 230-acre ATWOOD GRAPEFRUIT GROVE (*open*), 45.8 *m.*, from which as many as 50,000 boxes of fruit are shipped annually. When the grove was first planted, grapefruit was not as well known as it is today. Newspapers reported in 1897 that a cluster of 16 grapefruit sold as a curiosity for $8, and 25 boxes brought a bid of $156.25. A story is told of a New York grapefruit vendor who could not dispose of his wares; when a Floridian finally approached and asked the price of the fruit, the vendor told him to name his own price, since he was the only man who knew 'what this darn stuff is.'

PALMETTO, 47.9 *m.* (9 alt., 3,043 pop.), on the north bank of the Manatee River, has low frame-and-brick business buildings and numerous clapboard houses. The river front is alive with fishing and pleasure craft. Much of the town's income is derived from the packing and shipping of fruits and vegetables. The PALMETTO GOLF AND COUNTRY CLUB, north of the town, has an 18-hole golf course (*greens fee* $1).

Palmetto is at the junction with US 541 (*see Tour 4A*).

The route crosses the MANATEE RIVER, 48.5 *m.* During pioneer days the banks and islands of the river were carpeted with wild flowers and provided feeding grounds for many beautiful birds. In 1841 a settler and his wife, looking across the stream one morning, discovered that the field on the opposite bank apparently had blossomed overnight with pink lilies. Determined to gather an armful, the two started to row across the mile-wide stream. As they neared the far bank, the 'field of lilies' suddenly rose in the air and revealed themselves as great pink birds. What the man and his wife had mistaken for flowers had been thousands of flamingoes.

BRADENTON, 49.2 *m.* (21 alt., 5,986 pop.), lies opposite Palmetto on the south bank of the Manatee River. The two towns are connected by a mile-long bridge. Boom-time hotels dominate the skyline and do a thriving business in winter, when the population almost doubles. In the residential sections comfortable houses are surrounded with aged trees. The neighboring area of rich muck land normally produces two or three crops each season, making Bradenton the principal shipping center for winter vegetables on the west coast. Celery, citrus fruits, tomatoes, cabbages, eggplants, green peppers, and squash are the main products.

Bradenton was named for Dr. Joseph Braden, who in 1854 built Braden Castle (*see Tour 12*). When the post office was established in 1878, the town was called Braidentown; the spelling was afterward changed to Bradentown, and in 1924 to Bradenton.

WATERFRONT PARK, planted with royal and coconut palms, has an auditorium, municipal pier, and yacht basin; the BRADENTON COUNTRY CLUB has an 18-hole golf course (*greens fee* $1). The BRADENTON RECREATION PARK contains shuffleboard, roque, and tennis courts.

Right from Bradenton on Cortez Road (State 18A) is CORTEZ, 6.5 *m.* (4 alt., 263 pop.), a fishing village with several small hotels and many cottages, filled from May to July when tarpon are running in the passes leading into bays and inlets, feeding on small fish as they come down with the tide. At 7.1 *m.* is ANNA MARIA KEY, lying to the south of Tampa Bay and separated from the mainland by Sarasota Pass, one of the many sand and shell islands bordering the west coast. It rises but a few feet above sea level, and is covered with mangrove swamps, palm savannas, salt flats, cacti thickets, and buttonwood trees.

ANNA MARIA, 12.3 *m.* (77 pop.), a resort at the northern extremity of Anna Maria Key, consists of many cottages in a jungle setting.

On the WHITFIELD ESTATES, 55.2 *m.*, a boom-time development on a bluff overlooking the Gulf, stand scattered stucco houses of Florida-Mediterranean style; many of the sidewalks run through vacant lots. Above the flatwoods along the highway rises blue smoke from isolated charcoal pits. Charcoal is made by setting fire to stacks of small pine and hardwood logs, which have been covered with a 6-inch layer of earth. The fire is left to smolder for days; then the mound is broken open, and the charcoal taken out. Backwoodsmen and Negroes use it as fuel, and large bags of the product are sold for a dime in general stores.

POINT WELCOME, 61.5 *m.*, is an information bureau maintained jointly by Sarasota County and the American Legion. Prospective visitors to Sarasota are given information, road maps, and orange juice.

SARASOTA, 61.7 *m.* (18 alt., 8,398 pop.) (*see Sarasota*).

Points of Interest: Ringling Museum, Municipal Pier, Caples Park, Gillespie Park, Sarasota trailer-car camp, reptile farm, Ringling Bros.-Barnum and Bailey circus winter quarters, and others.

At 65 *m.* is the junction with State 220.

Left on this road into MYAKKA RIVER STATE FOREST AND PARK, 12 *m.* (*cabins, pavilion, picnic grounds, outdoor fireplaces*). This 25,000-acre park is a forest of palm trees and widespreading live oaks bearing long heavy streamers of Spanish moss and vines. Through it flows the MYAKKA RIVER, bordered with thousands of tall palms. UPPER MYAKKA LAKE is adjacent to smaller LOWER MYAKKA LAKE, which during very dry seasons disappears into large limestone fissures leading to subterranean caverns.

At 68.8 *m.* is a junction with a paved road.

Right on this road to SIESTA KEY OUTDOOR SCHOOL, 2 *m.*; here classes are conducted on a broad expanse of lawn surrounding a group of cabins in which pupils study, work, and sleep. The 135 resident students, aged 3 to 16, receive instruction in grade and high-school subjects; among the correlated activities are music, dramatics, sport, and the arts and crafts. Each separate school group has its cabin with screened sides, surrounded by tropical ferns and flowers. The dining hall overlooks the Gulf of Mexico. Adjoining a sun-flooded infirmary is a sheltered patio which serves as a solarium. There is a bathing beach of fine white sand, and a protected swimming area with a diving platform. The school library, with puncheon floors and a huge open fireplace of rock, was built, furnished, and decorated entirely by the pupils; the Carnegie Foundation donated $2,000 worth of books. The school emphasizes health, social development, and progressive teaching methods; through a student government the children share in the duties and responsibilities of the school. Winter and spring terms are held here, and the fall term at Manchester, Vt.

OSPREY, 73.1 *m.* (17 alt., 100 pop.), a fishing settlement on the Gulf, was named for the osprey, or fish hawk, a bird almost as large as an eagle, whose strong wings often carry it many miles to sea.

NOKOMIS (Ind., my grandmother), 79.4 *m.* (12 alt., 79 pop.), a suburb of Venice, is separated from that town by Shackett Creek (*good fishing*).

VENICE, 79.5 *m.* (13 alt., 309 pop.), is a well-planned village built during the Florida boom by the Brotherhood of Locomotive Engineers. Although practically abandoned after the boom collapsed, it is being repopulated. During 1924–25 corporations organized by the Brotherhood spent about $14,000,000 in developing this 30,000-acre city-and-farm community. Most of the land was laid out in small farms and drained; roads were built, and a demonstration farm and dairy set up. Two thousand acres were reserved for a townsite, and John M. Nolen, eminent town planner, laid out a city of broad boulevards and parks, with zoned residential, business, and industrial districts. By 1926, when 2,000 workmen were employed, 3 large hotels, many apartment buildings, 4 blocks of shops, and 300 residences had been built. Building stopped abruptly when the boom collapsed. By 1930 the workmen and all but a handful of residents had departed and the town's financial resources were exhausted. To protect stockholders' interests and permit orderly liquidation, the Brotherhood levied assessments on its members, although few had purchased land here. To meet fixed charges, almost $300,000 was spent annually for several years before recovery began.

The FLORIDA MEDICAL CENTER, a 200-room hospital founded in 1935 by Dr.Fred H. Albee, specializes in heliotherapy in the treatment of disease and bone ailments. The orthopedic department, employing the newest methods of bone surgery, attracts patients from many States and even from Latin America. Dr.Albee (1876–), an internationally known figure in his field, is a founding fellow and governor of the American College of Surgeons, and the founder of the International Society of Orthopedic Surgery. He has been consultant on orthopedics for the Byrd Antarctic Expedition, and consulting surgeon of 20 hospitals. The author of several recognized medical works, he is editor-in-chief of the *Rehabilitation Review*.

The KENTUCKY MILITARY INSTITUTE holds its winter sessions in a hotel and adjoining building near the hospital grounds. An 18-hole golf course (*greens fee*, $1) is close by.

At 84.9 *m.* is the junction with State 311.

Right on State 311 is WOODMERE, 2 *m.*, a small settlement of fishermen and truck farmers, and ENGLEWOOD, 6.9 *m.* (280 pop.), a favorite headquarters for tarpon fishermen.

At 9.9 *m.* is the junction with State 173; R. (straight ahead) on State 173 to PLACIDA, 18 *m.* (*fishing boats and guides; inquire at post office*). On the open Gulf, Placida is a small fishing village built around an Indian mound. Visitors interested in archeology here find numerous mounds to explore.

A ferry ($5 *car and driver; passengers* 50¢) is operated between Placida and BOCA GRANDE (Sp., large mouth) (6 alt., 350 pop.), on the south end of Gasparilla Island. Named for the wide pass south of the island leading into the Gulf, the natural harbor with its 600-foot channel is one of the deepest in Florida. For many years the village has been a phosphate shipping point, and a noted tarpon-fishing resort.

USEPPA ISLAND (*reached by boat from Boca Grande*) has a large hotel, headquarters of the Tarpon Club of America, the first of the Florida developments of Barron Collier (*see Tour* 5).

Right 4 *m.* from Boca Grande on an unimproved road is GASPARILLA (6 alt., 110 pop.), a fishing village with a small deep harbor at the north end of Gasparilla Island. José Gaspar, who later changed his name to Gasparilla (Sp., little Gaspar), made this harbor his headquarters between forays on the Gulf and along the Spanish Main. A Spaniard who had stood in high favor at court until he stole a ship of the Spanish navy, he gathered a band of cutthroats and established a base on Gasparilla Island. Countless stories, many of them authenticated, have been told about this colorful pirate, described as a man of polished manners and faultless attire, and well read in the classics. He was known to offer places in his band to captives who preferred piracy to death. Victims were not killed by walking the plank, but were shot and tossed overboard. The chief trouble maker in his crew was Roderigo López, a brute with hawklike face and bushy eyebrows.

Records of Gasparilla's exploits were acquired from his brother-in-law, Juan Gómez, who lived the latter part of his life on Panther Key, one of the Ten Thousand Islands off the southwest coast of the State, and who died there in 1900 at the reputed age of 119. Gómez told of a Spanish princess, Maria Louise, who in 1801 sailed for Mexico. On her return she was accompanied by eleven beautiful Mexican girls, who were to be educated in Spain. Aboard the ship were their dowry chests filled with gold. When it was 40 miles off Boca Grande, Gasparilla captured the vessel, killed the crew, took the gold, and carried the girls to Captiva Island, where they were handed over to his men. Gasparilla took the princess, and when she spurned his advances, had her beheaded.

From 1784 to 1795 Gasparilla kept a diary, in which he recorded in a neat hand his captures and the amount of plunder. In 11 years he captured and sank 36 ships. One entry was a census of the pirate band as follows: 'eight officers, 43 ablebodied seamen, 23 wives, 12 manservants, eight maidservants, 16 probationary prisoners, who include seven men, six women, and two small boys.' The only official notice of a raid by Gasparilla in the American state papers states that the ship *Orleans*, a large heavily armed vessel with a $40,000 cargo, bound from New York to the West Indies, 'was robbed off Cape Antonio in September 1821, by an equally large piratical corvette mounting at least 14 guns . . . commanded by one Gasparilla, a noted desperado of blackest dye.' After plundering the ship, Gasparilla wrote the following note (translated from the French) to a U.S. Naval officer, a passenger on the *Orleans:*

At Sea, and in Good Luck

Sir:

Between buccaneers, no ceremony; I take your dry goods, and in return I send you pimento; therefore we are now even. I entertain no resentment. Bid good day to the officer of the United States, and tell him that I appreciate the energy with which he has spoke of me and my companions-in-arms. Nothing can intimidate us; we run the same fortune, and our maxim is that the goods of this world belong to the strong and valiant. The occupation of the Floridas is a pledge that the course I follow is conformable to the policy pursued by the United States.

RICHARD COEUR DE LION

The band was broken up in 1822 when Gasparilla gave chase to what appeared to be a large British merchantman; upon being overtaken, the vessel lowered the English Flag, ran up the Stars and Stripes, and uncovered a masked battery. With his ship riddled, Gasparilla wrapped an anchor chain about his waist and leaped into the sea. Ten of his crew were caught and hanged, but the few pirates ashore on the island escaped.

At 92.3 *m.* US 41 crosses the MYAKKA RIVER; on early Florida maps the name was that of an Indian mission on the St. Johns River, and is a possible variant of the Timucuan word *mayaca* (large).

CHARLOTTE HARBOR, 108.3 *m.* (225 pop.), is a fishing village near the mouth of Peace River, at the head of Charlotte Harbor Bay. The name Charlotte is probably a corruption of Carlos, one of the names used by the Spanish and French to denote the Calusa tribe which inhabited this section. These Indians, according to early records, occupied a province of over 90 villages. In February 1566 Menéndez, the Spanish conqueror, accepted an offer to dine with the chief of the Calusa. As they were eating, Menéndez' soldiers stood guard at the entrance, ready for any treachery. Instead, the Indian women began to sing for their distinguished guest, and the Spanish soldiers in turn responded with a tune. So delighted was the chief that he insisted on giving his sister to Menéndez as a wife. The Spaniard was obliged to accept her, and as a result of this diplomacy, a temporary alliance was made with the Indians.

PUNTA GORDA (Sp., flat point), 110.5 *m.* (3 alt., 1,833 pop.), on the southern shore of Charlotte Harbor, derives its name from its position on the peninsula extending into the harbor. The town has a large hotel and a pleasure pier; its streets are planted with royal palms. Punta Gorda is an important shipping point for salt-water fish. Hundreds of carloads are iced and packed at the municipal docks (*open*) and shipped to northern markets.

Early settlers here had no post office or general store. All mail and supplies were brought from Cedar Keys on Captain Tom Hodgeson's schooner, the *Mallory*. On its return trip the boat carried oranges, furs, and alligator hides. In 1880 Isaac Trabue, of Louisville, Ky., purchased 30 acres of land, platted it, and named the proposed townsite for himself. When it became the southern terminus of the Plant System, now part of the Atlantic Coast Line, Trabue constructed a hotel and pleasure pier.

Punta Gorda is at the junction with US 17 (*see Tour 2d*).

At 131.5 *m.* is the junction with State 183.

Right on State 183 across MATLACHA PASS (Ind., warrior's assistant), 12.4 *m.*, a shallow strip of water, to LITTLE PINE ISLAND, 13 *m.*, with a fishing camp at the head of the drawbridge.

At 16 *m.* is the junction with an island road.

1. Right on this road 4 *m.* to PINELAND (25 pop.) in an agricultural district. BOKEELIA (Sp., little mouth), 7 *m.* (55 pop.), on Bokeelia Island, is connected with Pine Island by bridge. Many cottages have been built along the beach.

2. Left from the junction 9 *m.* to ST. JAMES CITY (90 pop.), settled in 1887 by a group of wealthy New Englanders who constructed buildings of spruce and white pine shipped from Maine. Later the San Carlos Hotel was built and for a period before the extension of the railroad to Palm Beach, St. James City was one of the most popular resorts in south Florida. After the death of the principal owner, the resort deteriorated and was almost in ruins when purchased by a sisal hemp company. The new owners rebuilt the town, erected a large factory for the manufacture of rope, and planted hundreds of acres in sisal, but the project was not a success and was eventually abandoned. The settlement has a post office, school, general store, nursery, and several fish houses. Steamers from Fort Myers stop here twice daily on their way to other coastal resorts.

FORT MYERS, 134.3 *m.* (9 alt., 9,082 pop.), has a leisurely air but actually is a busy commercial center, shipping citrus fruit, winter vegetables, fish, and cattle. Seminole of the Cow Creek and Big Cypress tribes occasionally come from the Everglades to shop here, camping in the background of the home of their adopted counselor, W. Stanley Hanson.

The streets of the city are shaded by more than 60 varieties of palms. Among them are the graceful coconut palms, the fan-shaped traveler palm, the fish-tail palm, and, notably, the royal palm, often rising to a height of 100 feet, its straight gray bole topped with a green crown of feathery fronds. These royal palms, which distinguish the city, were transplanted in the early 1900's from the Royal Palm Park Hammock (*see Tour 5*) in the Everglades.

After a raid by the Seminole in 1839, Federal troops built a fort here, later named Fort Myers in honor of Colonel Abraham C. Myers, then chief quartermaster in Florida. The garrison protected settlers in the surrounding area, and a small community grew up around the fort. After the War between the States the frontier settlement developed into a thriving agricultural center and a rendezvous for sportsmen interested in angling for big fish, particularly tarpon. Novices ordinarily take tarpon on a 30-thread line, using heavy rod and tackle, but as they develop skill, they reduce the weight of rod and line. Tarpon of more than 200 pounds have been caught in Fort Myers waters.

Fort Myers is the western terminus of the Cross-State Canal (*see Tour* 13), connecting the Florida east and west coasts by way of the St.Lucie Canal, Lake Okeechobee, and the Caloosahatchee River; a large yacht basin accommodates pleasure craft using the canal. An annual New Year's Regatta held here on the river attracts enthusiasts interested in outboard and inboard motorboat racing.

The mile-long concrete EDISON MEMORIAL BRIDGE across the Caloosahatchee River, named for Thomas Alva Edison (1847–1931), who wintered here for nearly half a century, was dedicated, with the inventor present, in 1931. In a 'Believe It or Not' cartoon in 1935, Robert Ripley pointed out that the Edison Bridge was not illuminated, a condition remedied in 1937.

Edison came to Fort Myers in 1886, in search of a suitable filament for the incandescent lamp he was later to perfect. Thinking that the fiber of the bamboo plant that grew abundantly throughout the town would answer his purpose, he established the EDISON ESTATE, 2130 McGregor Blvd., where he spent many months in experimentation, but the bamboo was not used in the perfected electric bulb. On the estate is the inventor's modest frame house, surrounded by luxuriant tropical foliage and citrus trees. A high picket fence around the grounds gave him the privacy he needed for his work. The house is now occupied by his widow (now Mrs. Mina Jane Hughes) in the winter season.

As Edison extended his activities, the Edison Botanical Research Corporation was established here. The Federal Government, in conjunction with Henry Ford and Harvey Firestone, sponsored the research work. Edison spent long hours making tests of flora that might be used to provide an emergency rubber supply if tropical markets should suddenly be closed to the United States. More than 500,000 tests were made on various plants and trees, and the common goldenrod was found to have great possibilities. In the course of his experiments Edison cross-pollinated the small goldenrod and a giant variety, 14 feet tall, native to the Everglades. Using this hybrid, he eventually evolved a rubber-making process that could be adopted commercially. The Research Corporation has discontinued operations in Fort Myers, but rubber-bearing goldenrod is grown on a plantation opposite the Edison home, for use in the Edison Laboratories at East Orange, N.J. Here work is conducted on a chemical extraction process to produce a liquid latex and valuable by-products from goldenrod leaves. The U.S. Department of Agriculture is also conducting experiments with the goldenrod at its Savannah, Charleston, and Miami laboratories.

Many stories are told about Edison and his work in Fort Myers. When the electric lamp had been perfected, he is said to have offered to install free lights in the town, provided the residents would supply the poles and wires. But the town council rejected the proposal, because the lights might keep the cattle awake. On another occasion, when the Edison Light Golden Jubilee was being celebrated, a severe storm damaged the local power plant and the celebrants dined by candlelight. Edison Memorial Day is celebrated annually in Fort Myers on February 11, the inventor's birthday.

Shortly after Edison had established his Fort Myers home, Henry Ford bought an estate adjoining that of his friend. The FORD ESTATE, 2200 McGregor Blvd., is enclosed, like its neighbor, with a high picket fence; the unpretentious house is hidden from view. Ford soon joined Firestone and Edison in forwarding the experiments of the Edison Botanical Research Corporation (*see above*), and spent a great deal of time at the old Hendry home, near LaBelle (*see Tour* 13), where he liked to take long walks, accompanied by his secretary. One of Edison's most treasured gifts was an early Model T car given him by Henry Ford. In his later years Edison could often be seen driving through the streets of Fort Myers in this museum piece, with its great shiny brass headlights and high buggy top.

On First St. are the MUNICIPAL AUDITORIUM, seating 600, and EVANS PARK (*shuffleboard, roque, and tennis courts; swimming pool; chess pavilion*). The POST OFFICE, W.First St., a two-story reinforced concrete building of modified Spanish style, was built in 1932. Across the front runs an open loggia with 8 massive stone columns; at each end are enclosed lobbies finished in polychrome. Mangrove seeds occasionally sprout from fissures in the porous limestone of columns and facings.

In TERRY PARK, E.First St. and Tarpon Ave., products of the surrounding counties are exhibited at the Southwest Florida Fair, held here annually in February.

Fort Myers is at the junction with State 25 (*see Tour* 13).

Section d. FORT MYERS to NAPLES; 34.8 *m. US* 41

South of FORT MYERS, 0 *m.*, is the FORT MYERS GROVES (L), 5.2 *m.*, extending 2 miles along the highway and bordered with red hibiscus; it is a co-operative enterprise in the cultivation of oranges and grapefruit.

ESTERO (Sp., estuary), 14 *m.* (300 pop.), is the capital of KORESHAN UNITY, a religious co-operative community established here in 1894 by Cyrus R. Teed. At the general store (L) members of the cult obtain food by presenting requisitions from the colony's secretary. In the large yellow frame building (R) is the printing plant; a weekly paper, a monthly magazine, and a score of tracts and books on Koreshanity are published. That the universe is within the earth, the flesh is immortal through reincarnation, and perfection will be reached when the sexes blend into one everlasting human entity are tenets of this faith.

When the community was founded, Teed told his followers that within a few years 10,000,000 true believers would come here; accordingly, streets were cut through the pine woods, and business and residential sections were plotted. Evidence of this early planning can still be seen in the surrounding woods.

Because Teed had convinced his followers that he was immortal, on his death his body was placed on a cypress plank and laid on the banks of the Estero River. For several weeks his disciples awaited a triumphal reincarnation. It finally became necessary to place the remains in a bathtub. Soon a hurricane swept the bathtub away, and no trace of it or the body was ever found. The plank, however, was found unmoved on the spot where it had served as a bier, and this was enough to restore the faith of the sect. Koreshans practice celibacy; men and women occupy separate living quarters. Growth of the sect depends on obtaining new recruits, who are required to turn over to the community all their worldly possessions, which are not returned if they withdraw.

The Unity produces some of the finest citrus fruit and truck vegetables in the State, and has an excellent nursery; bamboo 80 feet tall is grown here. In the KORESHAN UNITY ART HALL (*open*) are paintings by various artists, including some by Douglass Teed, son of the founder of the colony.

BONITA SPRINGS, (Sp., good little springs), 20.9 *m.* (315 pop.), occupies high ground well adapted to fruit culture. There is good fishing in the deep IMPERIAL RIVER; on the Gulf beach near by are many varieties of shells.

NAPLES, 34.8 *m.* (390 pop.), was named for the Italian city and planned as a winter resort as early as 1887, when this part of the State was isolated and all mail and supplies had to be brought from Fort Myers by boat. A frame hotel and a few cottages were built, but the resort's growth was retarded by lack of transportation. The construction of the railroad and the Tamiami Trail led to the building of a large tourist hotel and numerous cottages along the 7-mile stretch of white beach. General W.N.Haldeman, former publisher of the Louisville *Courier-Journal*, and 'Marse' Henry Watterson, Kentucky journalist, were among the first settlers in Naples and aided in its development.

The FISHING PIER (*free*) extends more than 1,000 feet into the Gulf; almost every kind of salt-water fish is caught in these waters. A large shell mound at the south end of town, near GORDON'S PASS, has been partly excavated. The KEEWAYDEN OUTDOOR SCHOOL, for boys and girls, is on KEEWAYDEN KEY (*boats at Naples*), an island approximately a mile long and separated from the mainland by a 50-yard channel.

Naples is at the junction with US 94 (*see Tour* 5).

Tour 4A

Tampa—Ruskin—Palmetto; 39.3 *m.* US 541.

Concrete- and asphalt-paved roadbed.
Route paralleled by Atlantic Coast Line R.R.
Good accommodations.

US 541, popular short route to south Gulf coast cities, is known as the Bayshore Route, although it offers only brief glimpses of Hillsborough and Tampa Bays. The highway traverses long stretches of salt marsh and mangroves. Sand trails lead off to numerous fishing camps, Indian mounds, and sites periodically excavated in search of buried treasure. The route emerges from the flatwoods and sawgrass swamps into a section of citrus and truck farms. Acres of tomatoes are passed, with plants held upright on stakes. Three crops of vegetables are grown annually on much of the land, and packing houses operate 24 hours a day during harvest. At Palmetto US 541 joins US 41, a section of the Tamiami Trail.

TAMPA, 0 *m.* (15 alt., 101,161 pop.) (*see Tampa*).

Points of Interest: Ybor City Latin Quarter, cigar factories, docks, Plant Park, Tampa Bay Hotel, Davis Islands, and others.

Tampa is at the junction with US 92 (*see Tour* 20) and US 41 (*see Tour 4b and c*).

East on Lafayette St. to 13th St.; L. on 13th St. to 4th Ave.

Right on 4th Ave., along US 541-Alt., a short route over McKay bay, to 22nd St.; R. here across the 22nd St. Causeway to the junction with US 541, 5.5 *m.*

North (straight ahead) on 13th St. to E.Broadway; R. here to Bayshore Road; R. along Bayshore Road.

PALM RIVER, 7 *m.*, is a small fishing community (*boats, bait*) on MCKAY BAY. Speckled trout, sheepshead, mangrove snappers, mackerel, cobia, and robalo are caught in the bay.

EAST TAMPA CITY, 10.2 *m.*, is a residential suburb on the banks of the Alafia River (Sp., dog bane).

Right from East Tampa City on a concrete road to a large phosphoric mill (*open*), 0.1 *m.*, manufacturing a concentrated form of phosphate, as well as gypsum blocks and sulphuric acid. A channel leads from the main ship channel in Hillsborough Bay to the company dock.

The route crosses the Alafia River, 10.4 *m.*, a mangrove-bordered stream popular with local fishermen and canoeists. The bridge offers a view of a wide stretch of the river and Tampa Bay.

GIBSONTON, 11.2 *m.* (250 pop.), a small trailer camp and filling station town on the southern bank of the Alafia River, was named for the pioneer Gibson family. Residents have often searched for buried pirate gold in the vicinity. One group, in possession of an old chart, unearthed a skeleton sitting upright, and below it a metal disk with the points of the compass and a needle marked on its face; in the excitement one of the party snatched up the compass without noting the direction indicated by the needle. Although many days were spent in excavating the premises, no treasure was found.

Left from Gibsonton on a dirt road to the GIBSON FARM, 0.2 *m.*, on which stands a large olive tree, one of the few growing in Florida. The tree blooms in June and bears fruit during July and August.

RUSKIN, 23.2 *m.*, (600 pop.), a co-operative tomato-growing settlement at the mouth of the Little Manatee River, was founded in 1910 as a socialist colony by George M. Miller, Chicago lawyer and educator, and named for John Ruskin, English author and critic. Of the 6,000 acres purchased, 600 were set aside for a proposed Ruskin College, its curriculum to be modeled somewhat on that of Oxford University. Students were to have four hours of schooling and, quite unlike Oxford, four hours of farm work a day. The plans were abandoned at the outbreak of the World War.

The soil here is especially adapted to growing tomatoes, for the muck land, underlaid with marl, permits irrigation without loss of fertilizer. Numerous artesian wells provide ample water supply. The town has a co-operative canning plant employing 65 workers during harvest, and a community hall. An annual Tomato Festival is held here in spring when prize vegetables are displayed, a pageant staged, and the town's most popular girl selected as queen to preside over festivities.

At 24 *m.* is the junction with Gulf City Road.

Right on this dirt road to an INDIAN MOUND, 1.2 *m.*, the first in Florida in which archeologists found partially cremated bodies, 32 in all. The mound, 63 by 65 feet, contained the lower portion of the walls of what was evidently a burial temple. The posts supporting it were from 5 to 10 inches in diameter; as they had been charred before being implanted, they were partially preserved. The temple was shaped like a trapezium, the longest sides more than 25 feet in length. Within was a thick deposit of charcoal, ashes, and burnt human bone. Articles found in the mound are on exhibition at the University of Tampa Museum (*see Tampa*).

At 24.9 *m.* is the junction with a tarred road.

Right on this road to COCKROACH KEY, 2.3 *m.*, separated from the mainland by 50 yards of water (*boats at road terminus on permission from fishing camp*). On the 7-acre key are two large Indian mounds, 32 feet above low tide, and a number of shell mounds, convolutions, and courts. The entire key is a huge kitchen midden, containing shells, scraps, and utensils.

Excavations in 1936 by the Florida State Archeological Survey and WPA workers resulted in unusual discoveries. In the center of a court a burial mound was found to contain, in the upper part, a large number of infant burials, indicating a severe epidemic among children or ceremonial sacrifices on the death of a chief. A shark-tooth harpoon was found embedded in the arm bone of an adult. More than 5,000 small shell hammerheads were discovered, as well as a number of bone artifacts. Fragments recovered here indicate that the inhabitants had a well-balanced diet. Almost every edible variety of shellfish in west coast waters was found, as well as remains of shark, ray, sheepshead, and drum. That the Indians did not confine themselves to seafood is evidenced by the remains of turtles, terrapins, alligators, bears, deer, panthers, and rabbits. Crude undecorated pottery found here is similar to shell-mound pottery recovered from other sites.

SUN CITY, 25.9 *m.* (85 pop.), a ghost town in the flatwoods, was founded at the height of the boom in 1924 by promoters with confident hopes of luring the motion-picture industry to Florida. The large studio built at that time is now occupied by the Sun City School. When Sun City was yet a glowing dream, there hung in the studio an oil painting of the metropolis as it would appear when it had supplanted Hollywood. A number of weathered gray shacks in a state of disrepair are occupied by Negroes. The little railroad station with a still-bright sign reading 'Sun City,' a large gray powerhouse, and a long warehouse are falling to ruin; nothing else remains. The flatlands on every side are overgrown with palmetto and scrubby grass.

At 31 *m.* is the junction with an asphalt road.

Right on this road to PINEY POINT terminus of the TAMPA BAY FERRY, 1.2 *m.* (*toll 10¢ per foot-length of car, driver free; additional passengers 25¢*). The ferry crosses lower Tampa Bay and the main ship channel, a 45-minute trip to St.Petersburg. There are small fishing camps at both terminals (*boats, bait, and equipment*).

At 34.7 *m.* is the junction with a paved road.

Right on this road 0.8 *m.*, across a causeway and bridge, to TERRA CEIA ISLAND (Sp., heavenly land). Six miles square, almost all the island is under cultivation. At one time citrus was the principal crop, but today the rich muck land is used almost entirely for truck farming. Four crops are raised each year; in the early spring peppers, tomatoes, cauliflower, and squash are shipped in such quantities that two large packing houses operate 24 hours a day. Farms have from one to six flowing artesian wells, and much of the land is subirrigated (*see Tour 2c*).

In the southern part of the island are large Indian mounds not yet explored. Peculiar geological formations found in the vicinity are smooth round stones that shatter easily and appear to have been once subjected to intense heat. They are believed to be of meteoric or volcanic origin, acquired in trade by the Indians. Various excavations are evidence of treasure seekers' efforts. Papaya, mango, and avocado trees, some 50 feet high, line the roadways. Sea trout, snapper, sheepshead, and flounder are plentiful (*boats and equipment at camp on southern end of island*).

On May 25, 1539, Hernando de Soto, seeking conquest, wealth, and territory for the establishment of Spanish colonies in North America, came ashore at the deserted Indian village of Ucita on Terra Ceia Island, according to John R. Swanton, ethnologist, appointed as head of the De Soto Commission to study the route of De Soto in the Gulf Coast region. On Trinity Sunday, June 1, when the fleet of 5 large ships, 2 light caravels, and 2 pinnaces had moved nearer the coast, his army landed some distance below the island at a place later named Shaw's Point. In honor of the day De Soto named both village and bay Espiritu Santo.

This expedition, probably the largest and best equipped of any that reached American shores during the days of Spanish conquest, consisted of 600 foot soldiers and 213 cavalrymen, with cannon, livestock, and an immense store of supplies. Once on land, the guides lost their bearings and the army floundered through swamps and jungles, arriving at the beach opposite Ucita, with the harbor between them and their objective. Here the exhausted men spent the night without regard to military order or possible danger. At dawn they were attacked by Indians. Reinforcements from the fleet and Ucita put the natives to rout, and the army reached Terra Ceia Island after a long detour.

De Soto occupied the chief's house on a high fortified hill near the beach; other dwellings were taken over as barracks or warehouses. The unoccupied buildings, including a native temple, were burned. De Soto ordered the surrounding forests cleared for the distance of a crossbow shot, and posted sentinels around the village. While encamped here, De Soto learned that Juan Ortiz, a young Spaniard, had been captured by the natives while on an expedition seeking news of Narváez (*see St.Petersburg*). The youth was soon found and became a valuable guide and interpreter for the army. Meanwhile, De Soto had listened to tales of wealth to be found in the province of Ocali, north of the island. Sending all but three of his ships back to Havana, leaving a small garrison at Ucita, he began his march into the interior. His circuitous route passed near the sites of Manatee, Ruskin, Dade City, and Inverness, and across the Withlacoochee River to Ocala, where he found a large town of 600 houses in the center of a fertile agricultural region. Corn was plentiful, but there was neither gold nor silver, and the explorer pushed on, crossing the Suwannee River and reaching the village of Anhayea, near the present city of Tallahassee, where he established winter quarters.

The army, burdened with artillery, provisions, and livestock, struggled through seemingly interminable bogs and hacked their way through dense forests, under constant attack by hostile Indians who had not forgotten their brutal treatment at the hands of Narváez. Few native chiefs would treat with De Soto; straggling members of his band were killed, quartered, and left hanging from trees. As he proceeded northward, De Soto came to realize the truth of reports about the ferocity of the Apalache warriors through whose lands he passed. Incessant attacks, a constant deluge of arrows, a bitter implacable determination to halt or bar their progress met the invaders.

While in Anhayea, De Soto sent a detachment back to Terra Ceia, with orders to abandon the island and bring his three ships up the coast to the Bay of Aute. The small fleet then explored the Gulf coast as far west as the Bay of Anchusi (Pensacola), and in February 1540 sailed for Havana to obtain reinforcements and supplies. The fleet was to return to the Bay of Anchusi the following October, where De Soto planned to meet it. During the winter, however, De Soto heard such glowing accounts of the rich provinces to the north and east, where gold, silver, and precious stones abounded, that he broke camp in March and started on the long perilous journey that ended in his death near the Mississippi River in 1542.

RUBONIA, 35.1 *m.*, has only a railway depot and a filling station but is important as a shipping point for the tomatoes, green peppers, sweet potatoes, citrus fruit, sweet corn, beans, kale, cabbage, mustard, strawberries, and other truck grown on small fertile farm plots in the surrounding area.

PALMETTO, 39.3 *m.* (9 alt., 3,043 pop.) (*see Tour 4c*), is at the junction with US 41 (*see Tour 4c*).

Tour 5

Miami—Naples; 113 *m.* US 94.

Hard-surfaced roadbed throughout.
Route followed by Tamiami Trail Tours bus line.
Limited accommodations; camp sites.

This route is a section of the Tamiami Trail, a name compounded of the syllables from the names of its terminal cities, Tampa and Miami. The highway connects the Atlantic with the Gulf, proceeding in long straight stretches across the Everglades, a primeval swampland.

The Tamiami Trail was conceived by Captain J.F. Jaudon of Ochopee, who in 1916 completed surveys of the route. Dade County soon issued bonds for building a highway across the Everglades to the Lee County line. Construction began in 1917, but proceeded slowly because of labor shortage during the World War, and the success of the project was still in doubt in 1923. At that time Lee County citizens organized and dispatched a motorcade over the proposed route to arouse public interest and show the feasibility of the undertaking. The trail-blazing expedition, of 10 cars, 23 men, and 2 Indian guides, left Fort Myers on April 4, 1923. After a perilous 3-week trip, during which they were reported lost several times, 7 cars reached Miami, and the trail became the most discussed highway project in America.

The State Road Department took over construction, which proved a Herculean task. Surveyors and men clearing the right-of-way worked breast-deep in the swamps. After them came drillers, attacking the hard rock under the muck; more than 90 miles were drilled and blasted. Ox carts were used to haul dynamite; when these bogged down, men shouldered the explosives and floundered through the water. Giant dredges followed, throwing up the loose rock to provide a base for the road. Smoothed and surfaced, the road was opened to traffic on April 25, 1928, at a cost of $13,000,000. An immediate success, the highway helped to unite the lower east and west coasts of Florida. What once involved a 2-day roundabout journey by motor is now accomplished in little more than 2 hours.

Along the north side of the road runs the Tamiami Canal, a long ditch from which rock and muck were taken to build the elevated roadbed. Long stretches of straight road, with a mirage ahead, are often hypnotic to the driver, and care must be taken not to leave the road on the canal side. Rough stones are placed along the bank of the canal for many miles, recalling the tragic accident in 1937 when a bus carrying 12 passengers plunged into the canal and all were drowned.

The canal side of the road is alive with birds, reptiles, and fishes. The surface of the water is constantly broken by fish snapping at insects; sometimes a minnow bobs up; turtles bask in the sun; occasionally a poisonous cottonmouth moccasin twists across the surface; alligators are rarely seen although they inhabit the waters of the 'Glades. Dark-bodied, white-banded teal and more sober brown mallard ducks swim, dive, and preen in the canal; small white and blue herons stand in graceful attitudes; kingfishers poise on bare cypress limbs; crows flap across the road, and buzzards are not uncommon.

Photography of wild life here presents difficulties. Birds and reptiles, habituated to swift-moving motorcars, betray no alarm until a car slows down or stops, when the 'subjects' take alarm and vanish beyond camera range. The occasional Seminole seen poling his dugout along the canals is not a show-window sight.

On the highway, especially in the early morning after night traffic has taken its toll, lie the mangled corpses of snakes, which in large numbers crawl out of the swamps to sleep on the warm road, and the bodies of raccoons and other small animals crushed when blinded by headlights. These provide breakfasts for flocks of yellow-headed red-cheeked buzzards which look like turkeys from a distance and remain on the road until a car is almost on them. The 'Glades are thickly overgrown with marsh sawgrass, tough as bamboo, its edges razor-sharp. Out of this drowned plain thrust rounded hammocks, overgrown with scrub oak, willow, cypress, cabbage palm, and palmetto. No visible life stirs across these broad reaches of marsh except that on the road and canal.

A dozen Seminole villages, changing location from year to year, are scattered along the trail between Miami and Naples, hidden from view behind palisaded walls, above which rise the sun-bleached palmetto-thatched roofs of the native houses. Now and again promoters or enterprising owners of filling stations and other establishments assemble the Indians, transport them to sites along the highway, and direct the construction of a village to attract sight-seers. Paid a small weekly wage by the management, the Indians are free to come and go at will; they build their huts and choose a 'head man' to preside over the village and take charge of business affairs.

In front of each village is a shop in which Seminole jackets and dresses, dolls, miniature boats, metal pins and buttons, air plants, postcard photographs, and other native products are sold, including the large Seminole spoon, known as *cotaseechobee*, made of custard apple or cypress; it is light and cool to handle when stirring *sofkee*, a mush of cornmeal, meat, and vegetables. Men tend shop, for women are not permitted to speak to whites. Women sit quietly in the houses or sew on hand-operated machines.

Cleanliness is a part of the Seminole's creed and the sunrise bath is a requisite of the new day. Failure to bathe is punishable by scratching the leg or arm with an eagle or alligator claw. Clothes are usually washed at the same time and frequently donned wet so that body and garments dry together. Cooking utensils are washed before instead of after meals.

MIAMI, 0 *m.* (10 alt., 110,637 pop.) (*see Greater Miami*).

Points of Interest: Bayfront Park, Aquarium, Pan American Airport, Indian Village, Curb Market, Hialeah Park, Tropical Park, and others.

Miami is at the junction with US 1-State 4A (*see Tour 1d and e*).

CORAL GABLES, 5.5 *m.* (11 alt., 5,697 pop.), is one of the few boom-time cities to survive the crash. Its business district is restricted to buildings of Florida-Mediterranean style, and its streets bear Spanish names (*see Greater Miami*).

At 6.7 *m.* is the junction with Red Road.

Left on this road to junction with Bird Road, 2 *m.*; R. on Bird Road, 3.8 *m.*, to Lost Lake Road; L. to LOST LAKE AND CAVERNS (*open 2–6 daily; adm. 40¢, guides*), 4 *m.*, built around an abandoned rock pit. A wild duck show, given 5 times daily on the hour, features trained mallards. Ducks attracted from the Everglades include the hell-diver, a small black bird with a white bill, which gives it a parrotlike appearance. In the gardens are trees imported from Europe and South and Central America through co-operation with their respective governments. Included are bo trees, the sycamore fig, mangosteen, teakwood, banyan, rubber tree, fishtail palm, bauhinia tree, fountain tree, litchi, African oil palm, sealing-wax palm, and cajeput. A number of caverns have been excavated in the sides of a sink hole. Known as Fort Lonesome, the sink hole gave its name to the surrounding area, once the hiding place of soldiers during the Seminole War. In the caves are a museum and a small aquarium, with several varieties of gar pike, native to the Everglades.

A fishing camp (*tackle, boats*), 19.3 *m.*, stands (L) at the junction of two Everglades drainage canals. The fishing boats are propelled by long poles, with vestigial paddles attached at the end for steering.

At 37.3 *m.* is the unmarked eastern entrance to the proposed EVERGLADES NATIONAL PARK, an unimproved area of 2,000 square miles, embracing part of the Florida Keys (*see Tour 1e*), the Ten Thousand Islands (*see below*), and the Big Cypress Swamp (*see Tour 13*). In 1929 the Florida legislature provided for the acquisition and conveyance to the United States of lands in Dade, Collier, and Monroe counties for park purposes; Congress accepted in 1934. The Royal Palm State Park (*see Tour 1e*) will be the nucleus of the proposed park.

Gradually the low oak and willow hammocks give way to an unbroken cypress forest. Most of the growth is young, but around dark ponds are hoary old trees hung with Spanish moss. Cypress is one of the few coniferous or evergreen trees that sheds its leaves. From early winter to early spring the gray trunks and branches are bare, and it is an eerie experience to drive for miles through ghostly ranks of young and old cypress woods, the smoky skyline sweeping up from the younger growth to the tall tops of old cypresses around the pools.

Air plants grow in great profusion in these woods; these small spiny growths attach themselves firmly to trees and derive their sustenance from the air. The clusters of leaves bearing brilliant parched red blossoms grow in such a manner as to gather and retain quantities of water. Some air plants grow low enough to be picked, but persons leaving the highway should beat the grass ahead of them to drive off snakes.

A strange sylvan inhabitant of the 'Glades is the maple tree, seen now and then mingled with cypress in dense hammocks. Far south of its normal range, geologists surmise that it retreated before the glaciers during the Ice Age and became acclimated as conditions gradually changed.

OCHOPEE (Ind., big field), 75 *m.* (242 pop.), is the center of 2,000 acres of tomato farms in the heart of the swamp country. The soil is extremely rich, but only one crop of truck is grown each year because of high water during the rainy season. Prospecting for oil is carried on in the vicinity with the help of a specialized machine called the 'marsh-buggy,' a motor-driven vehicle with wheels 8 and 10 feet high, which carries prospectors far back into the swamp to make preliminary borings for oil. It operates both on land and water; the machine floats and is propelled by its huge cleated tires which carry only four pounds of air.

Ochopee is the home of Captain J.F.Jaudon, who made the first survey of the Tamiami Trail and operates a sugar-cane mill here. The town also has a small sawmill and several packing and canning plants.

On windless days stretches of milky water along the highway resemble sheets of opaque glass, and intervening patches of clear water reflect the clouds and the hard blue of the sky. Occasionally the heavens are alive with rustling wings as squadrons of birds wheel overhead. Rusting skeletons of abandoned dredges stand here and there along the highway, lone monuments to its builders. In dry periods fires are frequent. Draining the land has brought an unexpected hazard (*see Conservation*), for the peat soil, baked under a tropical sun, catches fire easily and burns for weeks. At times the highway is obscured; a pall of smoke hangs over the entire area. Driving becomes dangerous, and officials are prepared to close the trail to travel without notice.

At 78.4 *m.* is the junction with State 164.

1. Right on State 164 to DEEP LAKE, 10 *m.* (40 pop.), a small tomato and citrus growing settlement with packing houses and a canning plant. Grapefruit from this region is exceptionally fine.

2. Left on State 164 is EVERGLADES, 4.5 *m.* (172 pop.), a surprisingly complete town on the Barron River, 8 miles inland from the western boundary of the Everglades; its tall aluminum-painted water tower is visible for miles. It has a post office, a bank, a public library, a courthouse as the seat of Collier County, a rod and gun club, and fishing piers for departure to the Gulf. The town is landscaped with coconut and royal palms, Australian pine, century plants, and other subtropical growth. Here grows a great ROYAL POINCIANA TREE, one of the largest in Florida, with a spread of 68 feet. The tree blooms in summer and has clusters of brilliant scarlet blossoms several feet in diameter. There is a yacht anchorage, dock, and a shipyard for vessels up to 100 tons. The town is the southern terminus of the Atlantic Coast Line Railway.

ROYAL PALM HAMMOCK (R), 95.7 *m.*, offers the rare sight of white-boled royal palms growing wild, thrusting their straight trunks above the cabbage palms. It is commonly believed that the seeds were blown into the section more than a century ago by tropical storms, for the tree is a native of Cuba. Hundreds of these palms have been transplanted from the hammock to Fort Myers.

At 96.5 *m.* is the junction with State 27A.

Left on this road to MARCO ISLAND, 6.5 *m.*, the northernmost of the Ten Thousand Islands that fringe the lower Florida west coast. The route parallels a wide deep canal, dredged both for drainage purposes and to supply material for the roadbed, and runs between low bulwarks of dark green mangroves, above which tower isolated cabbage palms and buttonwood trees. Spindly piers, jutting into the canal at intervals, provide landings for fishing boats. Mullet splash on the surface of the slow-moving root-stained water; herons stalk gravely among the shallows, and innumerable other marsh birds, disturbed by passing motorists, rise from their feeding grounds and wheel above the mangroves. Colonies of white bee hives appear in the occasional clearings (L), but until the island is reached no human habitation is visible. Leaving the mainland, the highway crosses Marco Pass on a concrete bridge and enters a rolling area covered with palmettoes and a sparse growth of pines.

At 10.5 *m.* is a junction with an unnumbered shell road that bisects Marco Island and links its two settlements.

1. Right on this shell road is COLLIER CITY, 2.8 *m.* (250 pop.), formerly called Marco and renamed for Barron G. Collier (1873–1939), best known for his street-car advertising enterprises, who, with his associates, purchased large tracts of land here in the early 1920's. At the time of his death, Collier was the largest landowner in the State. Starting with the purchase of property on Useppa Island (*see Tour 4c*), he later acquired a large part of Collier County, which was renamed when it divided from Lee County in 1923. At the time of his death Collier's enterprises included a chain of hotels, bus lines, several banks and newspapers, a telephone company, and a steamship line. The settlement, lying at the northern extremity of Marco Island, consists of scattered groups of weatherbeaten dwellings occupied by fishermen and workers in the clam-canning plant, a general store and post office, and a rambling white clubhouse, formerly an inn, now headquarters of the Marco Island Club. The landscaped grounds surrounding the club run down to private boathouses and piers at the head of Marco Pass. The store displays everything from dress patterns to outboard motors, and among souvenirs to be purchased are fish scales so large that, addressed and stamped, they can be mailed as postcards. Live oaks, coconut palms, and royal poincianas shade the single shell street that wanders among the houses. Clumps of tall, pale green bamboo rise above the rooftops, and high above them are soaring birds, their snowy wings glistening in the sunlight. Old citrus and mango groves, many enclosed with wire fences covered with golden-flowered bignonia and coral vines, seem to flourish untended.

This lone outpost on the keys has long been a trading center for fishermen and wealthy sportsmen cruising the opalescent waters in quest of tarpon. A line of net-draped piers, fish houses, and the clam-canning plant occupies the major part of the waterfront. Beyond, in the shallow Gulf beds, giant dredges scoop up tons of round, hardshell Florida clams, some 6 inches in diameter and weighing more than 5 pounds. Brought to the plant on scows, they are cooked and canned as chowder and broth, and shipped to northern markets. Everywhere are gleaming mounds of clam shells, bleached white by the sun. The wide strip of dazzling white sand beach, one of the few on the Ten Thousand Islands, is reached from the settlement by a short woods trail; it has a tropical background of coconut palms, sea grapes, cocoplums, and sea lavender. The beach, noteworthy for its shells, attracts many collectors, and practically all varieties peculiar to the west coast (*see Tour 13*) are found here.

The country around Collier City is one of the richest points archeologically on the Florida west coast. It first came into prominence through the explorations of Frank H. Cushing, associated with the Bureau of American Ethnology, during 1895–97. Among his important discoveries, at what is known locally as Cushing's Point, were artifacts so radically different from any found elsewhere in Florida shell heaps that he regarded them as typical of an aboriginal culture theretofore unrecorded. These wooden slabs, carved from pine and cypress, probably used in worship, are incised on the surface with a circle and cross as if to represent the sun and a cosmic symbol. Artificial harbors, basins, and canals created by aborigines are still to be seen here as well as on other islands in the vicinity.

2. Left from the junction with the main road is CAXAMBAS, 2.6 *m.*, a small fishing village at the southern tip of the island, a cluster of sun-bleached houses and an abandoned clam-canning plant. A shell road winds among live oaks, royal poincianas, coconut palms, and gnarled copper-colored gumbo limbo trees, beheaded by passing

Along the Highway I

Photograph by courtesy of Farm Security Administration

FISHERMAN

SPONGE BOATS, TARPON SPRINGS

A DAY'S CATCH OF SHARKS, KEY WEST

URTLE HUNTING ON THE KEYS

Photograph by G. W. Romer

Photograph by courtesy of Farm Security Administratio

MIGRATORY WORKERS' CAMP, NEAR BELLE GLADE

Photograph by courtesy of Farm Security Administration
MIGRATORY WORKER'S FAMILY

STREET SCENE, BELLE GLADE

Photograph by courtesy of Burgert Brother[s]

GANDY BRIDGE, CONNECTING ST. PETERSBURG AND TAMPA

OVERSEAS HIGHWAY TO KEY WEST

Photograph by G. W. Romer

Photograph by courtesy of Farm Security Administration

MEMORIAL TO 1935 HURRICANE VICTIMS, MATECUMBE KEY

Photograph by courtesy of United States Forest Servi

SKIDDING LOGS WITH HIGH WHEELS AND OXEN, CHOCTAWHATCHEE NATIONAL FORE:

JACKSONVILLE, ST. AUGUSTINE & HALIFAX RIVER RAILWAY IN THE 1880'S

Photograph by courtesy of Florida East Coast Railway

hurricanes, and climbs a steep hill surmounted with a spacious white house. Battered dinghys are tied to the few sagging piers; nets on drying racks flap in the sun. Tanned bare-foot fishermen, who make a living from mullet and mackerel catches, and occasionally act as guides for visiting sportsmen, squat on their heels in the shade of the fish houses. Navigation of the labyrinth of unmarked channels separating the thousands of keys requires experienced helmsmen. Along these channels 'coon' oysters cling to the mangrove roots, high out of water at low tide, which gave rise to the story that in Florida oysters grow on trees. These bivalves, relished by raccoons, are seldom eaten by humans.

Caxambas was the site of an Indian village, and many shell mounds remain here. Several trough-like depressions extending around the mounds and leading to the water are believed to have been canals dug by early inhabitants. A number of conch shells show the characteristic hole made by aborigines, and some show a double hole for hefting. Fragments of undecorated pottery are common, but no burial remains have been found.

Few of the mangrove-forested keys south of Marco Island are inhabited. Chokoloskee, at the mouth of the river of the same name, 30 miles distant, is the only important trading center. The majority of commercial fishermen live here on the upper keys—squatters who have taken what land pleased them and are ready to fight to hold it. Some subsistence farming is done; cane grown for syrup; a few citrus groves have been planted; but all milk is from cans, and most wearing apparel comes from mail-order houses, as did a 'knocked-down' school house once shipped to Porpoise Point.

Groups of settlers live together and work co-operatively. Whole families, from mother to children, run trap lines, handle nets, and pilot boats through the maze of tortuous channels. The houses are mostly unpainted frame shacks, thatched with palm fronds, but a few are sided and roofed with sheets of corrugated iron. The majority are without sash, although all are screened with the best bronze wire against myriads of flying and crawling insects. Heavy wooden shutters are put up during stormy weather. Hurricanes are a menace from August to October, and the flimsy shelters offer little protection against the blows that sweep the islands.

Feuds between groups are not uncommon; nets are destroyed, houses and boats burned, and many killings occur in disputes over claims to fishing grounds. Channel markers placed by the Government have been repeatedly destroyed by natives who fear poachers. Mullet and mackerel constitute the most important catch, and are delivered to large fish houses and there iced; later, they are loaded on boats that regularly operate from Key West and Fort Myers. Fishermen are paid according to the season and the supply, receiving from 2¢ to 4¢ a pound.

Mango and avocado groves on keys near Chokoloskee were planted in the 1880's by early settlers, and spacious frame houses built by them still stand. Indian mounds are scattered throughout the territory, and archeologists with picks and shovels, dubbed 'bone-diggers' by the natives, are frequently encountered; both the Smithsonian Institution and the New York Museum of Natural History send expeditions into this region annually.

Many fishermen act as guides for wealthy sportsmen during winter at $10 to $15 a day. The Shark and Lostman Rivers are navigable for some distance into the interior, depending on the height of the water in the Everglades, which they drain. Here bear, deer, wild turkey, and an occasional panther are found. Signs of bear appear in the mutilated heads of cabbage palms, for the animal is fond of the tender white bud from which the new fronds sprout. Tarpon remain in these warm waters throughout the year, along with various waterfowl. Shark are plentiful; they are caught in the passes on huge hooks baited with a mullet, hauled to the surface, and shot.

Despite vigilant Audubon game wardens, small egret rookeries are occasionally 'shot out.' The birds will not desert their nests when eggs are hatched, so they are easily slaughtered. The contraband plumes are smuggled into Cuba and disposed of in European markets. Once a brisk and profitable trade existed in alligator hides, but hunters complain that the Dupont Corporation has succeeded in making such good imitations that the genuine article cannot be marketed at a profit.

Dental students gain experience and earn a summer livelihood by setting up makeshift offices in the fishing settlements and attending to the needs of the inhabitants who travel miles for treatment. The student's equipment consists of a borrowed rocking chair, a portable foot-power drill, and a supply of gold, since many patients insist on having front teeth filled with the metal, whether a cavity exists or not.

For years the Ten Thousand Islands region was a haven for outlaws and fugitives. Among those of the early 1890's was red-bearded 200-pound Ed Watson, accused of slaying three men in Georgia, who fled here with his wife and son. He established himself near Chokoloskee and engaged in growing cane and the manufacture of syrup. His plantation soon became a rendezvous for white and Negro fugitives, who were put to work in the cane fields and paid off at the end of the season with a bullet. There was none to object to these proceedings, for the arm of the law did not reach here. As his fame spread, he became known as Emperor Watson. A heavy drinker and expert with a knife, he was involved in several killings in Key West; bail posted by friends was always forfeited. Those attempting to collect from him usually disappeared, and for a long time no officer dared to venture into the Emperor's territory to investigate. A new sheriff, who had boasted that he would go in and bring out the killer, was captured by Watson and made to work a month in the fields before being shipped back to Key West. Finally in 1910, after a reign of 30 years, he forced a companion to murder a man and woman who lived on a near-by key. Chokoloskee residents organized a posse, cornered Watson, and shot him down. Witnesses declare that he was buried in a shallow trench, with an end of rope running from the grave and tied to a tree, signifying that shooting was too good for him. When Watson's wife heard the news and was informed that she might claim the body if she found the rope, her only comment was, 'Give me his watch.'

Between the junction and Naples are hammocks of cabbage palm and palmetto, with patches of pine and cypress. Water hyacinths grow in the canal along the highway; occasionally clumps of willows and cattails appear. Thistles, yellow buttercups, and white and yellow daisies add notes of color to the roadside in early spring.

NAPLES, 113 *m.* (390 pop.), is at the junction with US 41 (*see Tour 4d*).

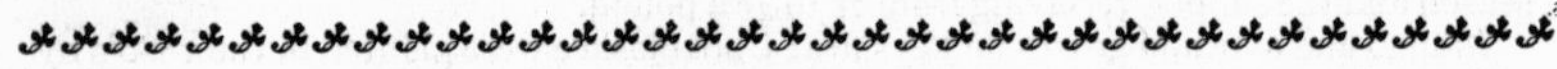

Tour 6

(Thomasville, Ga.)—Capps—Perry—Bronson—Williston—Brooksville—Tarpon Springs—Clearwater—St.Petersburg; US 19.
Georgia Line to St.Petersburg, 286.3 *m.*

Hard-surfaced roadbed throughout; watch for cattle.
Route used by Florida Motor Lines; paralleled by Atlantic Coast Line R.R. between Georgia Line and Monticello, Lamont and Chiefland, Williston and Inverness, Tarpon Springs and St.Petersburg; by Seaboard Air Line Ry. between Williston and Brooksville, New Port Richey and Tarpon Springs, Clearwater and St.Petersburg.
Good accommodations.

From red clay hills covered with oaks and magnolias, this route descends into a region of flatwoods and runs straight as an arrow for many miles, passing numerous turpentine and sawmill settlements, and then ascends to limestone hills, with lakes between. Green citrus groves, cypress hammocks, and scattered clumps of cabbage palms relieve the somber vista of cut-over pine land and scrub palmetto. Little of this sparsely settled territory is under fence, and free range cattle are a constant menace to motorists. Upon reaching the west coast the highway is within sight of the Gulf of Mexico, with its palm-fringed bayous and ribbon of low-lying keys, on which are miles of glittering white sand beaches.

Section a. GEORGIA LINE to WILLISTON, 144.2 *m.*

On this section of US 19 are many old towns in which little of importance has happened since the 1860's. Off the highway are long-abandoned plantations, once worked by hundreds of slaves. Former cotton and sugar plantations now grow tobacco, peanuts, and watermelons. The route crosses the storied Suwannee River and skirts dense hardwood hammocks offering excellent hunting.

US 19 crosses the Georgia Line, 0 *m.*, 14.8 miles south of Thomasville, Ga. (*see Georgia Guide, Tour* 6).

MONTICELLO, 8.5 *m.* (210 alt., 1,901 pop.), is at the junction with US 90 (*see Tour 7b*).

South of Monticello the route, bordered with trimmed cedar hedges, passes large nurseries raising subtropical shrubs and trees for landscaping purposes, and pecan and citrus stock.

DRIFTON, 12 *m.* (133 alt., 45 pop.), a small settlement glimpsed from a long overpass, is near the SITE OF IBITACHUCO, an Indian village with a recorded existence of 165 years, the home of Vitachuco, proud and stubborn chief of the province, who defied De Soto and his men in 1539. During a feast at De Soto's camp the chief and his tribesmen fell upon the Spaniards, using pots, clubs, stones, and blazing brands from the campfires as weapons. Vitachuco attacked De Soto and would have beaten him to death, had not soldiers interfered. The assault left De Soto with a disfigured face and a number of broken teeth, so that for nearly a month the leader was unable to eat solid food. So deadly and persistent were the encounters between the Indians and the Spaniards that before De Soto departed more than 1,300 of Vitachuco's warriors had been slain.

In 1633 the Franciscan mission of SAN LORENZO IBITACHUCO was established in the village. Raiding Florida in 1704, ex-Governor James Moore of South Carolina reported that he had spared this community when it offered tribute in the form of 10 horses loaded with provisions and its church plate.

CAPPS, 18.3 *m.*, is a center for growers of Satsuma oranges, pecans, and pecan nursery stock. The time-honored fish fry, a social 'get-together' enjoyed during pioneer days, is still popular throughout this section. Fish for the occasion are caught by the men and boys first on the scene. The best of the catch has been prepared and fires started by the time the women and children arrive. Tables under the trees are spread with great helpings of fried fish, vegetables, grits, and small game shot in the surrounding woods. The afternoon is spent in exchanging news, gossiping, and prolonged arguments among the menfolk.

Right from Capps on State 19 to a junction with a clay road, 8.1 *m.*; R. here 2 *m.* to the SITE OF EL DESTINO PLANTATION, whose owner at one time possessed 101 slaves. Roads converging at the entrance to the grounds form an avenue lined on each side for more than a mile with spreading live oaks. The plantation house, destroyed by fire in 1925, stood on an elevation between a shallow lake and a small stream. The gardens are still filled with old shrubs and flowers. Many slaves who cleared and plowed the thousands of acres are buried in the neglected graveyard. El Destino was obtained from the Federal Government in 1828 by John Nuttall, a Virginia planter, and his two sons, James and William B. In 1832 William Nuttall married Mary Wallace Savage, a Savannah heiress; her Negro slaves and fortune were used in developing the plantation. Cotton was the chief product, but corn, oats, sugar cane, potatoes, and rice were also raised. Household articles were handmade; baskets for carrying cotton to the gins were woven with white oak splints; sewed corn shucks were used to make the mule collars; plow lines were of homemade twisted cotton rope. Even the cloth, both wool and cotton, used for slaves' clothes and plantation sacks, was manufactured on the plantation until 1856, when a company opened a textile mill at Monticello near by. All food produced on the plantation was rationed. In good years large quantities of cowpeas, corn, hay, and fodder were harvested, but usually meat was not plentiful and the overseers had to purchase bacon and beef. Each week the hands received their allowances: a peck of corn and three and one-half pounds of meat. Other foodstuffs were frequently substituted and sometimes a half pound of meat was exchanged for a pint of syrup. Some of the slaves cultivated a variety of vegetables on small plots of ground when they could get the seed. Farm supplies, tools, and some food had to be brought from Tallahassee.

Relations between master and slaves were friendly. Very few changes occurred in the slave personnel; the same names appear again and again in the tabulations and reports for more than 20 years. Even the War between the States brought but few changes among the hands, for this part of Florida was never occupied by Federal troops. After emancipation many of the ex-slaves remained to work the fields on a crop-sharing basis. Births and deaths are shown in records of plantations, because they meant the gain or loss of valuable property, but little mention is made of marriages. It was customary to ask the overseer to grant a divorce. Religious teaching was not neglected, and slaves were given permission to hold revivals.

At 9.9 *m.* is a Resettlement Project, established by the Farm Security Administration in December 1936. Ten white families live here, cultivating 400 acres of the 565-acre tract; in the fields are corn, cotton, peanuts, tobacco, and vegetables. Neat frame farmhouses are on both sides of the highway. Produce is marketed at the project. At 14.9 *m.* is TALLAHASSEE (216 alt., 10,700 pop.) (*see Tallahassee*).

LAMONT, 24.8 *m.* (250 pop.), was originally called Lick Skillet, but in 1890 the villagers decided a more dignified name was needed. As Cornelius Lamont, Vice-president of the United States, had been a recent visitor, he was honored.

ERIDU, 31.4 *m.* (50 pop.), is a trading center for turpentine distillers. A wag with a classical bent gave this hamlet a name derived from Eridanus, mythological name of the River Po. In 1863 many Confederate soldiers and men opposed to conscription fled to the wilder portions of this region, forming themselves into bands, and defying both military and civil authorities. A detachment of Confederate cavalry invaded the country; unable to capture the deserters, they drove off the livestock, looted and burned houses, and took into custody the families of the men they sought.

Deer, wild geese, ducks, and turkeys are plentiful here, but employment of native guides and hounds is advisable.

The highway crosses the ECONFINA RIVER (Ind., earth bridge), 36 *m.* The roadbed stretches straight ahead for almost 10 miles, shimmering in the distance like a ribbon of dancing black water. Stump-filled flatwoods, dotted with cypress ponds, extend to the horizon in all directions.

PERRY, 48.5 *m.* (54 alt., 2,744 pop.), seat of Taylor County, is an industrial town built around a courthouse square. Towering stacks of freshly milled pine and cypress surround the large sawmills along the railroad sidings. In addition to softwood lumber, the mills produce barrel staves, flooring, and hardwood dimension stock for northern manufacturers. The town was known as Rosehead when the first post office was established in 1869.

Right from Perry on State 66 to HAMPTON SPRINGS, 4.5 *m.* (150 pop.). Old residents claim the springs were named by Joe Hampton, an early settler, who was directed here by an Indian medicine man before the War between the States. Because the waters were so beneficial in the treatment of rheumatism and kindred ills, Hampton bought the springs and much of the adjoining land for $10, and established a health resort. A hotel and cottages surround the swimming pool. The South Georgia Railroad, which has its southern terminus here, owns the resort.

South from Perry the highway winds through hardwood hammocks and piney flatwoods, a region noted for its fresh-water fishing and its hunting. A few sand trails lead off among the trees to emerge at small beach resorts on the Gulf. On the highway here, as elsewhere in the State, convict road gangs labor under the watchful eye of armed guards, and passing motorists catch snatches of their work chants, sung with a characteristic 'Ugh!' on the down-swing of a sledge or ax, or the heave of a shovel. A popular song of many stanzas is 'Louise.'

Lou-u-ise—UGH!—sweetest gal I know—UGH!
She made me walk from Chi—ca-go—UGH!
To the Gulf—UGH!—of Mexico—UGH!

Another of their songs has much the same theme:

Dat old black gal, she keeps on grumblin'
New pair shoes, Lawd, new pair shoes.
I'se goin' to buy her shoes an' stockings—
Slippers too, Lawd, slippers too.
I'se goin' to give her all my money—
Kisses too, Lawd, kisses too.

Or for variety this may be sung to the ring of hammers:

The hobo told the bum,
If you get any cornbread, save me some.

Cap'n got a burner I'd like to have,
A 32:20, with a shiny barrel.

The rooster chew tobacco, the hen dips her snuff,
The biddy can't do it but he struts his stuff.

At 76.8 *m.* is the junction with State 69.

Right on this road to DEADMAN'S BAY, 10 *m.*, which appeared under its present name on an eighteenth-century English map. During the War between the States a Federal gunboat put into the harbor and was destroyed by a detachment of Confederates. The crew waded ashore, sought refuge in the home of James Stephens, a fisherman, and was captured. Today Deadman's Bay is used by sponge fishermen as a shelter from Gulf storms. Some sponges are brought here, cured, and shipped to the exchange at Tarpon Springs. Shoals and oyster bars partly obstruct the approach to the bay.

A narrow bridge crosses the STEINHATCHEE RIVER (Ind., man's river), 78 *m.*, once a retreat for pirates in near-by Gulf waters; according to legend, treasure is buried along the palm-crowned banks, but no success has attended the frequent attempts to unearth it. The route skirts the eastern edge of Gulf Hammock (*hunting*). The roadside is resplendent in fall with yellow partridge peas and scarlet wallflowers. White and blue violets, dogwood, and Cherokee roses add to the spring colors of the landscape.

SHAMROCK, 94.5 *m.* (1,200 pop.), built around several large sawmills, has a hotel and rows of neat cottages, the latter all but hidden by stacks of cypress and pine. Cypress contains a large amount of oil, and must be stacked and seasoned for a year after being milled and dressed. As it is easily worked and does not split when nailed, it is the preferred wood for interior trim and outdoor furniture.

Cypress grows in swamps difficult to penetrate. Sawmill operators must build railroads into the areas, using sand or sawdust for roadbeds; sometimes canals are dug; in other places, caterpillar trucks are employed to snake out heavy logs. Huge two-wheel carts drawn by oxen are still used by smaller operators. 'Pecky' cypress, once used only for fencing, celery boards, and temporary structures, became popular and expensive during the boom era. The wood, charred and brushed, treated with acids or a sand blast, produces a desired antique effect for interior beams, paneling, and outer doors. Although pecky cypress appears to be rotten and worm-eaten, it is strong. The appearance is the result of a fungus disease which attacks the larger trees and seldom exists in those less than 100 years old.

Florida cypress is a member of a family 1,000,000 years old, which has spread all over North America, from Mexico to the polar regions. Stumps 8 feet in diameter have been found 30 feet underground; buried cypress forests, neither petrified nor decayed, have been discovered during excavations in northern cities. The tree grows slowly, increasing an inch in diameter every 30 years. Known in the trade as the 'wood eternal,' it is not affected by liquids, nor does it add color, taste, or odor to liquids.

CROSS CITY, 95.4 *m.* (53 alt., 1,071 pop.), seat of Dixie County, is a timber, turpentine, and fishing center. Pine and cypress are milled and dressed here; a cold-storage plant ships to northern markets fresh- and salt-water fish, including the Florida catfish, in demand in the North but not popular within the State.

Alternate stretches of hardwood and pine extend south of Cross City. Cattle stand knee-deep in shaded grassy ponds, and white herons feed undisturbed among them. During dry periods woodfires are frequent, creating great desolate areas. Some cleared land is planted to corn, green beans, and watermelons.

OLDTOWN, 104.9 *m.* (31 alt., 300 pop.), a scattering of frame, log, and small brick buildings, once called Suwannee Oldtown, occupies the site of one of the largest Indian villages in Florida. In 1818, General Andrew Jackson attacked the village, and captured a British army officer, Robert Ambrister. The young officer had come to Florida early in the same year and made the acquaintance of Hadjo, a Creek chief, who had been an ally of the British in the War of 1812. Confessing that he had counseled and aided the Indians here, Ambrister was court-martialed and executed (*see Tour 14a*). The incident created great tension with Great Britain and President John Quincy Adams was hard pressed to explain and justify Jackson's action.

A MOSS FACTORY here in a building of the *ante bellum* period prepares Spanish moss for mattresses and general upholstering purposes. The moss is stripped from trees and delivered to the drying yards; entire families, both white and Negro, are engaged in this industry. At the factory the moss is suspended on racks in the sun, sprinkled occasionally, and allowed to cure for 6 months. Sometimes it is dampened and packed into pits or trenches, where the moist heat hastens the process. When cured, the moss is put through a gin to remove the outer rotted husk. The finished product, resembling black horsehair, is highly resilient, stronger than hair, and does not attract vermin. Although the supply is great, the loss in curing and ginning is considerable, and the finished product represents less than 12 per cent of the weight of the raw material. As early as 1773, William Bartram, writer-naturalist from Philadelphia, described the process used in Florida to cure the moss, the use of which he recommended for stuffing cushions and padding horsecollars.

Spanish moss, native to America, was so named because it grows in regions first settled by the Spaniards. Biologically, the moss is not a parasite, but feeds from the air. Tiny yellow-green flowers, slightly fragrant at night, appear at the base of the awl-shaped leaves during May and June, but the seeds do not mature until the following March. Moss-bearing forests cover a large section of Florida. Long bamboo poles tipped with wire barbs are used to pull the moss.

The highway swerves south and crosses the SUWANNEE RIVER, 108.3 *m.*, the stream with which the beloved folk melody, *Old Folks At Home,* is associated. On both ends of the steel bridge an overhead inscription reads: 'Way Down upon the Suwannee River.' Although it is generally accepted that Stephen Foster chose the name without having seen the river, old residents insist that he visited Ellaville and Columbus, an old town in Suwannee County, during the 1850's, a year before the song was published.

Rising 215 miles to the north in the Okefenokee Swamp, Ga., the narrow Suwannee follows a serpentine course to the Gulf. All but 35 miles of its 250-mile course lie in Florida. In north Florida it tumbles swiftly over shoals and boulders between high limestone banks, topped for miles with thickets of second-growth cedar; in the past thousands of cedar logs were cut along the stream and floated down to market. Trees of other kinds and masses of underbrush in the valley change color with the seasons, shading from pale greens through yellows and reds to dusky brown. Bass, perch, catfish, and bream abound in the river; small game is plentiful along its banks, and an occasional alligator is seen.

Here the Suwannee flows serenely through wild hammock land toward the Gulf, its dark waters mirroring high, densely wooded banks. In dry seasons the stream shrinks to a narrow channel, revealing limestone strata sculptured into fantastic formations by erosion. At such times the water, subdued and hushed, is clear as a mountain brook for long stretches; in other places, where red clay predominates, it is wine-colored.

The Suwannee marked the boundary between the territories of two Indian confederations, the Timucua and the Apalachee; by them the Suwannee was first called Guasaca Esqui, or River of Reeds. Narváez crossed it in 1528, and De Soto in 1539; the latter christened it the River of the Deer. Indian guides led early Spanish explorers to believe its waters flowed over beds of gold. Its present name, as familiar as that of any river on the continent, is a Negro corruption of *San Juanee*, meaning 'little St.Johns.' Thus it was distinguished from the larger St.Johns River of east Florida.

In the early 1780's pirate craft made their rendezvous among the secluded inlets and bays of Suwannee Sound; tales of murder and buried treasure persist to this day. Expeditions have been outfitted, stock companies organized, and countless excavations made to recover hidden stores of gold, the whereabouts of which have been learned, as convention requires, from old maps, or the lips of dying sailors; no successful quests have been recorded, however.

Before and during the War between the States, cotton and tobacco plantations spread across the Suwannee Valley. Social and cultural life centered in the great manor houses built on the bluffs; below them, huddled among the oaks and magnolias along the banks, were the cabins of the Negro slaves. Small wood-burning sternwheelers of the Mississippi type plied the lower stretches of the Suwannee, carrying cotton, tobacco, peanuts, naval stores, and lumber from the interior to the high-masted schooners anchored at the river mouth. The *Belle of the Suwannee*, Captain Robert Bartlett commanding, was the queen of the fleet. During the war blockade runners traveled up and down the stream; several were burned and sunk, but many succeeded in eluding the Federal gunboats.

On a high bluff east of the river, 150 yards north of the bridge, is FANNIN SPRINGS, a resort occupying the SITE OF FORT FANNIN, built in 1838; ruins of old stone ovens are all that remain. The springs have a flow of 48,000 gallons a minute and an even temperature of 70° throughout the year. Numerous arrowheads and sharktooth fishhooks have been discovered on the near-by bluff, the probable site of an Indian village. Fannin Springs acquired importance as a shipping point in the latter part of the nineteenth century when river steamers en route from Cedar Keys and Branford landed freight at its docks. River transportation ended in

1900 as a result of railroad competition. Today the resort is the scene of picnics and political rallies.

Southeast of Fannin Springs the route enters a region known as the Gulf Hammock country, notable for its fishing and hunting (*see Tour 3c and Tour 4b*). Deer, quail, wild turkey, ducks, geese, panther, bear, and wildcats live in the wild hammock country, some 75 miles long and 30 miles wide, bounded by the Suwannee River on the northwest, the Withlacoochee River on the east, the Weekiwachee River on the south, and the Gulf on the west. Black bass, bream, speckled perch, warmouth, catfish, crappie, and pickerel are plentiful in the streams. Off the Gulf coast are caught salt-water trout, red bass, flounder, whiting, sheepshead, drum, bluefish, croaker, yellowtail, amberjack, kingfish, snook, Spanish mackerel, and the famed 'Silver King,' or tarpon. In deep water are dolphin, bonita, red snapper, and barracuda.

CHIEFLAND, 118.2 *m.* (43 alt., 421 pop.), a town of old frame buildings with tin roofs, shaded by water oaks and Chinaberry trees, lies a mile west of Old Chiefland, a settlement dating back to Territorial days. Here a Creek chief and his tribesmen lived peaceably beside their white neighbors and engaged in farming. Braves, laying aside guns and knives, demonstrated that they were as proficient in raising corn and potatoes as they had been in lifting scalps. An early white settler relates that the chief himself awarded blue and red feathers for the best agricultural exhibits at Indian fairs. In time, however, these peaceful natives were forced southward.

Chiefland is a shipping center for turpentine, rosin, livestock, and peanuts. The peanut or goober, a squat potato-like plant, grows in many climates. It is planted about 2 inches deep and lightly covered. When ready for harvest, it is dug up by workers, usually Negroes, who use a 3-pronged potato hoe. On larger plantations a digging machine, a plowlike contraption drawn by mules, is used. When peanuts are fed to hogs, the animals are given the chore of rooting them up for themselves.

After the vines have been stacked until thoroughly dry, the peanuts are threshed or stripped off by hand, and then roasted, shelled, and packed by machines in 50-pound drums. Raw peanuts are sold to wholesalers in 150-pound sacks, ultimately to be ground up in great hoppers and in time to appear in glass jars as peanut butter. Dried vines, or 'peanut hay,' are often fed to livestock.

BRONSON, 132.1 *m.* (75 alt., 694 pop.), seat of Levy County, depends largely on lumber and naval stores for its existence. The town was once called Chunky Pond, from the Indian word meaning dance. When incorporated in 1884, the town took its present name from an early settler. The former county seat was 7 miles west at Levyville, now practically abandoned. The shifting of population resulted from the construction of a railroad through present-day Bronson in 1860 by David Yulee (*see Tour 3a*), United States Senator at the outbreak of the War between the States.

Bronson is at the junction with State 13 (*see Tour 3c*).

WILLISTON, 144.2 *m.* (82 alt., 940 pop.) (*see Tour 4a*), is at the junction with US 41 (*see Tour 4a and b*), which unites with US 19 as far as Brooksville (*see Tour 4b*).

Section b. BROOKSVILLE to ST. PETERSBURG, 79.6 m.

In this section US 19 climbs and dips over a series of round hills. As far as the Gulf, the country is open and sparsely settled, matted with palmetto thickets, which give way to occasional burned-over areas and stretches of second-growth pines. Along the Gulf are shining beaches, large citrus groves, truck farms, and prosperous resort towns.

South of BROOKSVILLE, 0. *m.*, WEEKIWACHEE SPRINGS (Ind., little spring), 12 *m.* (42 pop.), which has a flow of 100,000 gallons a minute, the fifth largest in Florida (*bathing, fishing, glass-bottomed boats*). It is difficult to anchor a boat in the violently boiling spring, the source of the river of the same name which flows 12 miles west into the Gulf. Underwater growth is gathered here and shipped to aquaria to be used as fish food and for oxygenation of tank water. On the grounds is a log clubhouse built in the style of a Russian hunting lodge. In and around these springs Rex Beach obtained color and data for his novel, *The Mating Call.*

Southwest of Weekiwachee the highway follows the Gulf of Mexico, its waters glittering like blue diamonds in the sun. Between the road and lacy surf the sand dunes and clusters of palms resemble scenes from the West Indies. Here and there narrow lanes, surfaced with oyster shell, lead off to whitewashed houses, around which nets are laid out to dry on upturned boats or on racks built on spindly piers.

NEW PORT RICHEY, 34 *m.* (758 pop.), on the PITHLACHASCOTEE RIVER (Ind., river where canoes are made), is a resort town. Along the high banks of the river, commonly known as the 'Cootee,' are many small cottages, most of them built of brown and white stone from the bed of the stream; petunias, snapdragons, sweet peas, and calendulas bloom profusely in the gardens; the roads are shaded by large oaks and magnolias. In the 1880's the old town of Port Richey, the original settlement a mile west on the Gulf, was an important port of call for schooners plying between Cedar Keys and Key West.

Left from New Port Richey on State 293 to MOON LAKE GARDENS AND DUDE RANCH (*hunting, fishing, horseback riding; adm.* $1), 12 *m.*, a private game preserve of 7,000 acres enclosed with a wire fence. The tract has been stocked with wild turkeys, deer, otter, beaver, and numerous game birds. Trails wind through the woods and along the shores of Moon Lake; the gardens are planted with azaleas and roses. Various buildings and cottages have been erected for the accommodation of visitors.

Between New Port Richey and Tarpon Springs the highway traverses an area of woodlands, chiefly second-growth pine and small scrub oak. The fields are swampy in the wet season and matted with palmetto, through which forage lean range cattle.

The ANCLOTE RIVER, 42 *m.*, is spanned by a concrete bridge, from which can be seen (R) the docks and shipyards of the Greek sponge fishing fleet (*see below*).

TARPON SPRINGS, 43 *m.* (14 alt., 3,414 pop.), sponge capital of America, lies at a point where the Anclote River widens into palm-fringed bayous on its way to the Gulf. The streets of the town are paved with brick; its restricted business section is characterized by brick and stucco buildings with permanent awnings. Tarpon Avenue, the town's main thoroughfare, begins at the Municipal Pier on the Gulf, encircles SPRING BAYOU, passes close to the tourist center, becomes a two-block shopping district, and wanders on through scrub palmetto and truck gardens to the steep banks of Lake Butler on the east.

The town was founded in 1876 and named, it is said, because of a mistaken belief that tarpon spawned in Spring Bayou; but the fish seen splashing in the water here, as well as in the river and numerous lagoons, are mullet, for the most part. Early settlers built their homes around the spring; almost hidden by trees and bright subtropical foliage, many still stand, contrasting sharply with more modern houses. The shell paths that once followed the marshy banks of the bayou have been replaced with wide cement promenades and a sea wall.

Hamilton Disston, saw manufacturer of Philadelphia, whose purchase of 4,000,000 acres in the early 1880's (*see Tour* 10) included much of the territory in and around Tarpon Springs, persuaded influential friends to join his settlement here on the high wooded shores of Lake Butler. To accommodate them, he built a hotel that for a decade was the lone fashionable resort on the Gulf coast. On 30 pine-studded acres overlooking the lake, the Duke of Sutherland, having deserted his family in England, built a clapboard manor house in 1889, and for two years lived the life of a Florida planter with the woman of his choice, a commoner, whom he later married (*see below*). For this he incurred the displeasure of his cousin, Queen Victoria, and won headlines in the press of two nations.

With the perfection of deep-sea diving equipment in 1905, a colony of Greek sponge fishermen abandoned the waters of Key West and the method of 'hooking' sponges with long poles in shallow water, and came here to fish far out to sea, using divers to gather the sponges. Because of their willingness to remain at sea for long periods, their courage in overcoming the hazards of their craft, and their sound marketing methods, they have made Tarpon Springs one of the largest sponge markets in the world. As in other fishing communities, the life of the Greek colony centers around the docks, on the Anclote River, to which the 70 or more boats in the fleet bring their catches (*sponge fishing demonstration trips, depending on season and weather; fare* 50¢).

When the fleet departs, a bearded priest of the Greek Orthodox Church blesses each boat, and the air is filled with the calls and farewells of friends and families of the fishermen. While it is away, the houses clustered around the docks look like a discarded stage set. The only stir is in the stores, restaurants, and a few curio shops. But four times a year, barring storms, the fleet turns homeward with its cargo of sponges—always for Epiphany services, always at Easter, and then the whole community assembles to greet it. The gaily-painted boats come slowly up the Anclote channel, their decks heaped high with sponges; soft rubber diving suits dangle grotesquely from the stays. Blue and white pennants fly at the mastheads, and the Stars and Stripes at the sternposts, and lettered high on the bows are such names as *Venus*, *Apollo*, *Venizelos*, or *Bozzaris*, the last for the doughty Greek patriot who 'slew a thousand Turks before breakfast.' As the boats are warped in and tied up, the docks and narrow lanes about them ring with music, laughter, and the rhythm of folk dances.

The olive-skinned spongers debark immediately to celebrate in churches and in other places less sacred, leaving their haul behind to be sold at the COOPERATIVE WAREHOUSE, a rambling jail-like structure with iron-grilled storage cells that segregate the catches. In an open court sponges are sold at auction each Tuesday and Friday. Members have the right to reject bids which they do not consider high enough. Annual sales approximate $1,000,000.

Many who come to visit Tarpon Springs wonder at the size of the fishery, not realizing the innumerable uses of sponge. In addition to its conventional bathroom uses, sponge is in demand by surgeons and by manufacturers of linoleum and soundproofing materials, and is utilized for padding clothes, for fertilizers, and for cleaning garments. In glass factories it is indispensable, since it is fireproof and can be used for wiping off hot glass.

In the course of their operations the sponge fishermen occasionally make rare and valuable finds on the ocean floor. In 1938 a local deep-sea diver, Sozon Vatikiosis, brought in two seashells of hitherto unknown varieties, described by the Smithsonian Institution at Washington, to which they were sent, as 'tea-rose blossoms turned to stone in the full flush of their blooming.' In honor of the diver, one was named *Conus sozoni B.*, and the other was named for his wife, *Fusinus helenae B.*; in accordance with scientific practice, the 'B.' is for Dr. Paul Bartsch, Curator of Mollusks at the Smithsonian, to show that he named them. The value of these shells, the only ones of their kind yet discovered, can be judged from the fact that collectors pay from $600 to $800 for a specimen of another beautiful variety, of which there are 22 known examples.

On January 6, the twelfth night after Christmas, the orthodox Greeks celebrate not only the coming of the Wise Men but the baptism of Jesus by John the Baptist. According to their calendar, it is Christmas Eve, a time both for prayer and revelry. Candles gleam through the windows of the church to greet the dawn. Priests bedecked in white stole and cope and crimson mitre intone their chants, the very chants and responses that Emperor Justinian and his court heard as they knelt 14 centuries ago under the golden dome of St. Sophia in Constantinople.

At noon on Greek Cross Day the priests and their resplendent acolytes, with crosses and swinging censers, wind in a ceremonial march to Spring Bayou through streets gay with bunting and flags, and under banners depicting holy scenes. On a barge in the bayou a priest releases a white dove and flings a small gold cross into the waters. A score of young divers plunge after the emblem, and the one who retrieves it receives a blessing for the coming year. After the ceremony, worldly pursuits are in order; merry-making festivities last throughout the afternoon and night. Along the waterfront are heard the piping of flutes, the twanging of guitar and mandolin, and riotous songs. Dancing begins on the sanded floor of the houses, and during festivities a prodigious quantity of black syrupy coffee, honey cakes, salty Greek cheese, potent *masticha*, and native wines is consumed.

The inevitable foretoken of Easter is the arrival of a carload of sheep, to be killed and stuffed with rice, olive oil, and pecans, and seasoned with thyme and sweet origanum—but not before the gay and sauntering butcher has made his rounds, demanding a glass of wine from housewives for his labor.

On Easter night the men gather in the churchyard bearing long unlit tapers, as the women crowd the pews within. After chanters have told the story of the Resurrection, the lights are extinguished, and the priest steps down from the altar and holds forth candelabra with three small flames of sacred fire. The light passes from candle to candle until the church is aglow. The men bring their candles inside, and the churchyard is lighted. The priest leaves the church, followed by altar boys bearing a waxen figure of Christ. They halt three times, symbolizing Christ's three falls on His journey to Calvary.

On a slope overlooking Spring Bayou, George Inness, famous nineteenth-century American landscape painter, built a house and studio in 1877. Noted for his harmonious and placid representation of nature, he found the landscape of this section inspiring. His son, George Jr., is known principally for religious paintings, a number of which hang in the CHURCH OF THE GOOD SHEPHERD (*open* 3–5 *daily*), Grand Blvd. and Read St. The larger paintings include a trilogy; *The Promise*, *The Realization*, and *The Fulfillment*; a triptych: *Beside Still Water*, *He Leadeth Me*, and *In Green Pastures*; also *The Only Hope*, *The Shadow of the Cross*, and *The Crucifixion*.

The TARPON SPRINGS MUNICIPAL GOLF COURSE (*greens fee* $1), 44 *m.*, lies on both sides of the highway.

WALL SPRINGS (*bathing, boating, fishing*), 46 *m.* (250 pop.), is marked by a clump of three large oaks peculiarly bent and twisted; the Indians twisted the trees a century ago, so legend has it, to identify the spot. The lithia waters here have a temperature of 74° the year round; a natural formation at the base of the springs resembles the outline of a woman's head.

PALM HARBOR, 48.2 *m*, is surrounded by orange and grapefruit groves, with windbreaks of Australian pines. Roadside stands sell orange and wildflower honey taken from rows of white beehives in the groves. Remnants of boom-time boulevards and palm plantings can still be seen. The town was founded as Sutherland by real-estate promoters during the later 1880's in anticipation that the Duke of Sutherland (*see above*), then living on Lake Butler, would lend financial support, but the noble exile failed to respond. Sutherland was the original site of Sutherland College, later Southern College, since removed to Lakeland (*see Tour* 20).

With the Gulf frequently in view, the route passes numerous small groves and winter truck gardens. Intervening are stretches of pine, largely second-growth. Here, as elsewhere in Florida, early spring flowers are often found blooming with those that blossom in the late summer. Among them is Osceola's plume, also known as 'crow-poison,' identified by its slender leafless stem. It bears a conical cluster of small white flowers which change to pink and purple before seeding. A paste made from its roots is scattered over fields to rid them of crows, and used indoors to poison flies and mosquitoes.

DUNEDIN, 53 *m.* (13 alt., 1,435 pop.), a residential town that merges with Clearwater, extends more than three miles along St.Joseph's Sound, locally called Dunedin Bay. Numerous public and private piers along the waterfront offer facilities for boating and fishing. Originally called Jonesboro, the town was settled in the late 1850's. In 1878, with the establishment of a post office, it was given its present name by J.L.Douglas and James Somerville of Dunedin, Scotland. The little Episcopal church here was the scene of the wedding of the Duke of Sutherland and Mrs. Mary Carolina Blair, of London, in 1888 (*see above*).

Before a railroad penetrated this area, Dunedin was one of the chief Gulf ports between Cedar Keys and Key West. Early fruits and vegetables were shipped in barrels by schooners; at that time oranges brought 1¢ each, f.o.b. the dock. Citrus raising and packing, grapefruit-canning plants, a plant manufacturing canning and packing-house machinery, as well as equipment for overhead irrigation systems, provide the income of the town.

The DUNEDIN YACHT CLUB has a clubhouse, dock, and boat slips. Sailboat races are held during the year on the sheltered bay. DUNEDIN ISLES, a boom-time development along the waterfront north of the town, contains several fine estates, extensive flower nurseries, and an 18-hole golf course (*greens fee* $1).

CLEARWATER, 58 *m.* (29 alt., 7,607 pop.), seat of Pinellas County, occupies a high coastal elevation extending along the narrow part of Pinellas Peninsula. A tall white hotel, dominating the skyline, dwarfs the buff brick courthouse nearby. Proximity to the Belleview Hotel (*see below*) has brought to the city wealthy winter residents, whose Elizabethan manors, Florentine villas, and Spanish casas crowd the landscaped bluffs southward along the bay.

After Fort Harrison was established here in 1841, several families purchased land in and near the present site of the city. English and Scotch families followed and set out citrus groves. Clearwater today has 11 packing houses, in addition to several fruit and fruit-juice canning plants. Strings of red and yellow refrigerator cars line the tracks in the freight yards on the east side of town.

The town was incorporated as Clearwater in 1891, three years after the narrow-gauge Orange Belt Railroad reached the city, en route to St.Petersburg. After the freeze of 1894–95, having lost revenue from decreasing fruit shipments, the railroad was taken over by Henry Plant as part of his system. In 1896 Plant built on the Gulf coast the first of his large tourist hotels, the Belleview (*see below*).

Pinellas County was severed from Hillsborough in 1912, and in a wrangle over the position of the county seat, Clearwater stole the march on St.Petersburg by building a makeshift courthouse 'over Sunday,' conforming to a legislative act providing that once a courthouse was built, the county seat could not be moved for 20 years. A second railroad, the Tampa and Gulf Coast, now a part of the Seaboard Air Line, was routed through the city in 1914.

Landscaped with petunias, marigolds, and date, cabbage, and Washingtonian palms, the SOLDIERS' AND SAILORS' MEMORIAL CAUSEWAY extends from the mainland to CLEARWATER ISLAND, with miles of white sand beaches. Here, screened by Australian pines, is a large MUNICIPAL TRAILER-CAR CAMP (*water, lights, sanitary conveniences and police protection; weekly rates from* $1). The CLEARWATER YACHT CLUB, with clubhouse and boat slips on the bay, conducts a number of races during the winter. Numerous cabañas, cottages, and hotels are scattered along the shore. Salt-water fishing in the passes and Gulf waters is excellent (*boats, guides, and necessary equipment at docks on both sides of the bay*).

The PEACE MEMORIAL CHURCH, Fort Harrison Ave. and Pierce St., a pink stucco edifice of Spanish-mission style, was built in 1923 as a memorial to the World War dead. Above the educational wing and recreational hall-gymnasium is a roof garden. The memorial motif appears throughout the church. The cloisters are known as the 'Cloister of the Allies'; the domes as the 'Domes of Death'; surmounting the domes is the 'Tower of Thanksgiving.' Large Tiffany windows illustrate verses from the Psalms and are dedicated to the War dead of various states.

The ROEBLING HOUSE, Orange Ave. and Clearwater Bay, residence of Donald Roebling, is surrounded with a high brick wall and occupies a series of landscaped terraces sloping to the water. The house is of half-timbered Tudor style, built in 1929.

The ROBERT L. BROWN ESTATE, directly south of the Roebling property, has extensive landscaped gardens, terraces, and pools about a large mansion on the pattern of an Italian villa. A tower near the water is fitted with chimes that play at half-hour intervals. A bronze memorial tablet, framed in a semi-circular niche in the wall facing the street, marks the SITE OF OLD FORT HARRISON, established here in 1841, and named in honor of President William Henry Harrison.

The FRANCIS WILSON MEMORIAL THEATER, foot of Seminole St., a rustic theater in a small park, was endowed by Mrs. Edward Bok (*see Tour* 15) as a memorial to Francis Wilson (1854–1935), actor, author, and playwright, long a resident of the city.

The CLEARWATER PUBLIC LIBRARY, Osceola Ave., contains more than 18,000 volumes and a museum of old books and relics pertaining to the city's early history. At the approach of the Municipal Causeway is (R) the MUNICIPAL AUDITORIUM, with fully equipped stage, loud-speaker system, and a dance floor. The CLEARWATER COUNTRY CLUB, a mile east of the business district, has an 18-hole golf course (*greens fee* $1).

Clearwater is at the junction with State 17 (*see Tour* 20).

BELLEAIR, 59 *m.* (42 alt., 212 pop.), a residential suburb overlooking Clearwater Bay, was incorporated in 1925 to eliminate 'foreign' jurisdiction over the BELLEVIEW-BILTMORE CASINO, an institution comparable to Bradley's Beach Club at Palm Beach (*see Palm Beach*).

Construction of the Belleview Hotel, a rambling frame structure of 600 rooms, was begun by the late Henry Plant in 1896. Its grounds of 275 acres are fenced, and portions are protected by a moat. Here are two 18-hole golf courses (*open Jan. to Apr.; greens fee* $2.50), an indoor swimming pool, the casino, riding stables, and tennis courts. A spur of the Atlantic Coast Line runs to the hotel entrance, and a siding accommodates private cars. The Belleview has long been known as a leading social and fashionable winter resort of the Gulf coast.

On the southern outskirts of Belleair are the JAPANESE GARDENS (*open 9–5, Dec. to May; adm. 25¢*), containing rare Japanese plants, a Buddhist temple, pagodas, cascades, and bridges, a creation of F.Hayakawa, of Tokyo. Tropical lilies and lotus abound in numerous pools; Japanese girls serve tea in a Japanese tea house.

LARGO, 61.8 *m.* (56 alt., 1,429 pop.), is a shipping point for citrus and winter-truck growers. Several large fruit-packing and fruit-juice-canning factories (*open*) operate during the winter. The annual Pinellas County Fair (*adm. 25¢*) is held here in January.

Between Largo and St.Petersburg are almost continuous stretches of orange and grapefruit groves and small truck farms, which practically cover Pinellas Peninsula from Tampa Bay to the Gulf. Numerous roadside stands are bright with displays of fruit, marmalades, and jellies. Much of this region was settled shortly after the War between the States, and many of the large citrus groves were planted during the early 1880's.

The PINELLAS COUNTY HOME, 63.4 *m.*, an institution for aged indigents, consists of a two-story stucco building in the center of a large farm, formerly the site of a convict camp.

At 64.4 *m.* is the junction with a paved county road.

Right on this road on a short bridge across the northern tip of Boca Ciega Bay (Sp., blind mouth) to INDIAN ROCKS, 4.2 *m.* (6 alt., 80 pop.); the site was marked on maps as early as 1792 as St.Clements Point. Before 1914, Indian Rocks was popular as a resort for Tampa residents, being the nearest and most accessible beach. Cottages, bathhouses, a casino, and hotel overlook the Gulf.

Indian Rocks is at the junction with State 233.

Left on State 233, which connects Sand Key, Madeira Island, Treasure Island, and Long Key, a string of low islands lying between Boca Ciega Bay and the Gulf; the highway is bordered much of its distance with palms and Australian pines and is never out of sight of water. The communities along the shore, known as the Greater Gulf Beaches, maintain a joint water system. Bathing is permitted at almost any point (*exercise caution when turning off pavement*). The beaches are wide and shelving, and free from undertow, except near the passes. The BATH CLUB (*private*), 8.9 *m.*, a rambling tan stucco building, has an outdoor salt-water pool, restaurant, beach and recreational facilities. The route traverses a restricted residential section occupied by many large estates. Much of the land has been built up on the bayside and landscaped with palms, oleanders, hibiscus, and other winter flowering shrubs.

MADEIRA BEACH, 10.6 *m.*, has a stucco bath house, a casino, and a variety of beach concessions. The near-by one-story frame building with a wire enclosure belongs to the U.S. Veterans' Hospital (*see below*) and contains facilities for hydrotherapic and heliotherapic treatments. The building and enclosed beach are reserved for veterans.

The route crosses JOHNS PASS BRIDGE, 12.3 *m.*, over a deep channel of the same name to TREASURE ISLAND. Somewhere off this point the Narváez fleet is said to have anchored in 1528, and the Spanish explorer, having navigated the pass in small boats, marched to an Indian village on the mainland (*see St.Petersburg*). The bridge, its approaches, and the pass are popular fishing grounds (*boats, bait, and equipment at fish houses and piers at both ends of span*). Before the highway was built, the long narrow key was known as Coney Island; today it is occupied by shacks, garage apartments, tourist camps, night clubs, and substantial beach cottages. Many Indian mounds have been found and excavated on the smaller mangrove-covered islands in the bay.

LONG KEY, 14.9 *m.*, reached over BLIND PASS BRIDGE, is the largest of the islands fringing the Pinellas shore and the first to be developed. The greater portion of the island is covered with a dense growth of palmetto and scattered stands of cabbage palms. Blind Pass and adjacent waters offer excellent fishing (*equipment at piers along shore*). Several years before the bridge was built, a smuggler arrived from Cuba one night with a boatload of Chinese; having already collected their passage money, he decided to put his human contraband ashore on Long Key instead of landing them at their destination farther north. 'Keep under cover until dawn,' he warned them, 'then head north, and you'll be in New York.' But shortly after the smuggler had shoved off, his boat caught fire and he was forced to go overboard and swim back to the island. There he remained in hiding most of the next day. He saw his marooned passengers wandering about, hungry, without water, and aware by this time that they had been duped. Toward evening, sighting a fishing smack, the smuggler broke cover and hailed it. Discovering him, the Chinese pursued him from one end of the island to the other with clubs and knives. Finally he took to the water and reached the fishing smack, only to discover that it contained a United States marshal. The latter arrested the smuggler, and with the aid of county officials rounded up the Chinese, who were given a square meal and passage back to Cuba; the smuggler got ten years.

LIDO BEACH, 17.9 *m.*, facing a sea wall and driveway landscaped with Australian pines, consists of a group of white frame cottages and apartment buildings with Italian names. A general store, filling station, and administrative offices are housed in a building that resembles a ship.

The DON CE-SAR HOTEL, 18.7 *m.*, a 12-story concrete structure, overlooks the Gulf; the adjoining residential development extending to the bay is planted with a variety of palms, Australian pines, and flowering subtropical shrubs; yacht basins provide safe anchorage for small craft.

PASS-A-GRILLE BEACH, 20.5 *m.* (216 pop.), the first incorporated city on the Pinellas keys, occupies the southern end of Long Key. Approximately 2 miles long and 2 blocks wide, the town has several small hotels, apartment houses, furnished cottages, and a large hotel-casino-bathhouse, having long been headquarters for deep-sea fishing boats and tarpon-fishing guides. Two municipal piers provide shelters and platforms for bay fishing. The main thoroughfares are planted with Washingtonian palms and Australian pines. Voters in Pass-A-Grille Beach must be property owners and must have resided in the city 24 hours prior to elections. Captain Zephaniah Phillips of Martin's Ferry, Ohio, a Union veteran, was the first settler; he homesteaded the lower end of the island in 1886; the town was platted in 1892 and incorporated in 1911. The name is believed to have been coined by early smugglers, fishermen, or spongers, who landed to grill fish and beef on the shores of the pass at the southern end of the key. The PASS-A-GRILLE YACHT CLUB, on the bayfront, sponsors annual regattas for yacht-club entries from neighboring communities. In the city is the SUNSHINE SCHOOL, a unit of the Pinellas County public school system; the classes of the school are held on the beach.

SHELL KEY is a small island south of the city (*reached by boat during winter season from Municipal Pier No.* 1). The shores of the key are favorite hunting grounds of shell collectors.

UNITED STATES VETERAN'S ADMINISTRATION FACILITY, 70 *m.*, a group of tan stucco buildings of Florida-Mediterranean style, occupies a 600-acre reservation on a subpeninsula in Boca Ciega Bay. Here hospital and domiciliary care is given to honorably discharged veterans of all wars; the capacity of the hospital is 197 and of the dormitory 400. Recreational facilities comprise a bathing beach on the Gulf, ball fields, lawns for bowling, a library, pool and billiard tables, and an assembly hall, where motion pictures and stage performances are presented.

The SEMINOLE BRIDGE, 71.2 *m.*, crosses Long Bayou, an arm of Boca Ciega Bay.

Between Seminole Bridge and St.Petersburg are (R) a number of Indian mounds covered with dense jungle growth; only a few have been explored. A footbridge (R) across a small stream in the rear of Lighthouse Inn, 71.7 *m.*, leads to the top of the largest mound.

ST.PETERSBURG, 79.6 *m.* (41 alt., 40,425 pop.) (*see St.Petersburg*).

Points of Interest: Municipal Pier and Casino, Municipal Spa and Solarium, Historical Museum, Mirror Lake Park, Williams Park, Municipal Airport, Coast Guard base, Indian mounds, and others.

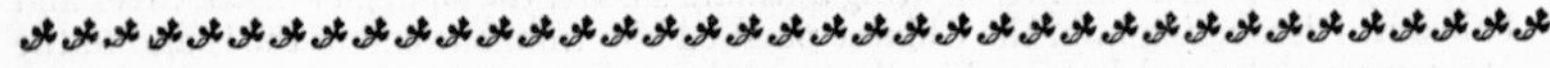

Tour 7

Jacksonville—Lake City—Tallahassee—Marianna—Pensacola—(Mobile, Ala.); US 90.

Jacksonville to Alabama Line, 406.2 *m.*

Hard-surfaced, except for short stretches of improved clay road; watch for cattle along highway.

Route paralleled by Seaboard Air Line Ry. between Jacksonville and River Junction, and by Louisville and Nashville R.R. between River Junction and Pensacola. Good accommodations.

US 90, Florida's longest and most heavily traveled east and west highway, roughly parallels the northern boundary of the State. It traverses pine lands, where lumbering and the production of naval stores are important industries, penetrates the State's principal cotton and tobacco areas, and passes through many plantation towns of *ante-bellum* days, and a few large cities. The people, architecture, and economic conditions of this region, first in the State to be settled and the first to have a railroad, remain largely untouched by the seasonal tourist influence, standing in sharp contrast to the Florida pictured in resort literature.

Part of the route follows or parallels an early trail that linked many Spanish mission settlements of the 1600's. Sections of the present highway were laid out in territorial days to facilitate travel and commerce between the capitals of East and West Florida; it later became a stagecoach route and grew in importance with the development of Tallahassee as a cultural and political center of the State.

Section a. JACKSONVILLE to LAKE CITY; 61.2 *m.* *US* 90

This section of the route, which becomes the main street of many small communities, is bordered with roadside refreshment stands, filling stations, tourist camps, and a multitude of signboards. For nearly 50 miles the highway runs in an almost straight line on fills across numerous swamps, and cuts through extensive pine flatwoods, dotted with turpentine camps. Between Jacksonville and Baldwin the road is used by trucks and trailers transporting citrus fruit and garden truck from central Florida to Jacksonville terminals and warehouses, returning with general merchandise.

JACKSONVILLE, 0 *m.* (25 alt., 129,549 pop.) (*see Jacksonville*).

Points of Interest: Naval-stores yards, cotton compress, Hemming Park, Memorial Park, cigar factory, and others.

Jacksonville is at the junction with US 1 (*see Tour 1a and b*) and US 17 (*see Tour 2a and b*).

Strung along the highway west of Jacksonville are many 'jooks' of the type found on the outskirts of almost all large Florida cities (*see Folklore*). These establishments, variously defined as roadhouses or suburban saloons, are gathering places for urban and rural patrons who drink and dance to the music of a 'jook organ,' a nickel-in-the-slot, heavy-toned, electric phonograph. The reputation of jooks depends on their record for fights and disorders, and they also differ in the kind of music played. Those featuring old-time or mountain music are known as 'beer joints,' and their walls often bear placards requesting customers to conduct themselves as 'ladies and gentlemen.' In others, groups of youngsters congregate to huddle about a booming loud speaker and stamp their appreciation of the latest swing pieces. Both Negro and white jooks are numerous.

WHITEHOUSE, 12 *m.* (84 alt., 135 pop.), is a naval-stores settlement, with US 90 as its main street. A steel LOOKOUT TOWER (*open*) of the Forestry Fire Prevention Service looms above a turpentine still and the pine shacks of Negro workers.

Forest Service units, jointly supported by counties and the Florida State Board of Forestry, protect landowners from fire and theft, and prevent turpentine and logging operations on tax delinquent lands. Each unit is directed by a chief ranger, four assistants, a dispatcher, and an assistant. Assistant rangers, in charge of specified areas, direct the work of wardens and deputy wardens of the WPA Forestry Project. The wardens are employed principally as towermen, in patrol work, and on fire fighting crews. Observation towers, manned day and night except in extremely wet weather, are connected by telephone, and some by radio also. The control towers, from which all messages to stations and individual rangers are sent, effectively cover protected areas. Each ranger has a half-ton truck equipped with water tank, high-pressure pump, and other fire fighting apparatus; in some counties a radio is included in the equipment. The CCC has constructed many miles of graded roads, fire breaks, and telephone lines in forested areas, and renders valuable service in fighting fires. In 1937 the Board of Forestry had more than 5,000,000 acres under contract for organized fire prevention and control.

West of Whitehouse the highway crosses extensive lowlands. In this vicinity, after the Battle of Olustee (*see below*), Confederate troops found several sidetracked box cars deserted by the Federals, one containing more than 400 cases of hard biscuit or crackers. The Confederates pushed the cars 3 miles to their camp, and thereafter the district was known as Cracker Swamp.

BALDWIN, 20.1 *m.* (86 alt., 749 pop.), is a junction point for several railroads. Formerly called Thigpen, the town was renamed for Dr.A.S. Baldwin, through whose leadership a railroad was built between Jacksonville and Lake City in 1860. Here are the freight yards of the Seaboard Air Line. Among the miles of cars on the sidings are 'pulpwood flats,' used to carry pine logs from north and west Florida to Fernandina and Jacksonville paper mills. These cars have ends of heavy iron bars and channel irons, securely braced to prevent logs from shifting. The logs, from 6 to 12 inches in diameter, are sawed into 5-foot sections, the width of the car, and stacked crosswise.

Baldwin is at the junction with State 13 (*see Tour 3a and b*).

MacCLENNY, 29.1 *m.* (134 alt., 519 pop.), is north Florida's 'Gretna Green,' and its squat red brick courthouse has been the scene of many weddings. When the judge is absent, his accommodating wife performs the ceremony. Local mercantile establishments furnish supplies for near-by naval-stores plants and lumber mills. The town has a small cigar factory and a grist mill.

In the back country around MacClenny and near-by towns the widely scattered families are frequently interrelated, forming a rather clannish group, and are apt to look on outsiders with suspicion. Among themselves, however, there is little restraint. Their social affairs are strenuous, not to say violent. Their dances bring together old and young from miles around; on the appointed night merrymakers arrive in battered flivvers, in wagons, on mules and horses, or on foot, at the country dance hall, usually of frame, hidden among the pines along a meandering sand road. Gasoline lanterns throw a dazzling bluish light on the dancers as the frail hall shakes under the thud of feet in a vigorous square dance to the accompaniment of fiddles, guitar, and piano.

Men leave the dance hall frequently to refresh themselves from bottles or jugs. There is often as much fighting as dancing. A muttered word—a curse—a flashing blow—and chaos! All dash from the hall, for propriety demands that a man must extend his enemy an invitation to 'step outside' to settle their differences. Now and again a gun or a knife is used, and another blood feud is started. Rarely are such proceedings reported to the authorities; retribution for anything less than murder is a personal matter, affording no cause for 'the law to mess in.'

GLEN ST.MARY, 31 *m.* (134 alt., 215 pop.), is known for the GLEN ST.MARY NURSERIES (*open*), one of the largest in the State. Acres of citrus stock, shrubbery, and vegetables border both sides of the highway. A short distance from the road are large fields of azaleas, lilies, and rose stock.

Right from Glen St.Mary on unimproved State 154 is TAYLOR, 12 *m.* (669 pop.). The BURNSED BLOCKHOUSE, built on a hill by a settler of that name as protection against Indians in 1837, is well preserved. From the hill is a wide view of the surrounding territory.

At 13 *m.* the route enters OKEFENOKEE SWAMP, a vast inundated region of cypress, bay, and pine forests, covering 660 square miles, one-tenth of which is in Florida.

EDDY, 21 *m.* (130 alt.), is a farming community in the midst of cleared patches of land planted with staple crops. For miles to the north stretches the swamp, dotted with islands, forested and thickly matted with palmetto and blueberry and gallberry bushes. Rattlesnakes and water moccasins are numerous; deer, wild turkey, wildcats, and an occasional bear are found in the hammocks. In open pools of stagnant water grow pickerel weed, maiden cane, and white and golden water lilies, known locally as bonnets. Men travel on horseback, by mule-drawn wagons, and even by ox carts in this remote and soggy region.

A large turpentine still, 32 *m.*, is surrounded by cabins of Negro workers. Many are painted and neatly kept, their gardens bright with flowers. Turpentine crews working deep in the woods have their typical songs and chants, and their singing is pitched to carry long distances. A favorite song runs:

Boss man's ridin' by;
Boss man's ridin' by;
Boss man's ridin' by;
Look out, Boy, look out!

Negroes have their mythical cities and countries which are discussed and referred to in everyday conversation as if they actually existed. Among them are Diddy-Wah-Diddy, Beluthahatchie, Heaven, and West Hell.

Diddy-Wah-Diddy, the largest and best known, is a place of no work and no worry for man or beast. The road to it is so crooked that a mule pulling a load of fodder can eat off the back of the wagon as he plods along. All curbstones are chairs, and all food is already cooked. Baked chickens and sweet potato pies, with convenient knives and forks, drift along crying, 'Eat me! Eat me!' The more one eats, the more remains. Everything is on a gigantic scale, and the biggest man of all is known as the Moon Regulator, because he starts and stops it at will. When nights are dark, it is because the Regulator was just too tired to hang out the moon. Everybody would live in Diddy-Wah-Diddy if it were not so hard to find and so difficult to get to, even if one knew the way.

Beluthahatchee is a country where all unpleasant doings and sayings are forgotten, a land of forgiveness and forgetfulness. When a woman accusingly reminds her man of something in the past, he replies, 'I thought that was in Beluthahatchee.' Or a person may say to another, to dismiss some matter, 'Oh, that's in Beluthahatchee,' signifying that the subject has long since been forgotten.

Heaven has a Sea of Glass on which angels go sliding every afternoon. There are many golden streets, but the principal thoroughfares are Amen Street and Hallelujah Avenue, which intersect in front of the Throne. These streets play tunes when walked on, and all shoes have songs in them. Few Negroes are permitted to wear wings these days, so rumor has it, because a recent arrival just couldn't wait until old Gabriel showed him how to fly, with the result that he tore down a lot of God's big gold and jeweled hangings. God was mighty upset, and Gabriel ripped off the flier's wings, shouting that it would be a long, long time before any Negro got himself a pair of wings again.

West Hell, said to be the hottest and toughest part of that notorious resort, was once the home of Big John de Conqueror, who eloped with the Devil's daughter. The pair fled on her father's favorite steeds, Hallowed-Be-Thy-Name and Thy-Kingdom-Come. The Devil pursued them on his famous jumping bull, and when they met, Big John tore off one of the Devil's arms and almost beat him to death with it. Before Big John left Hell, he passed out ice water to everybody, and even turned down the dampers, remarking that he expected to return to visit his wife's folks pretty soon, and he didn't like the house kept so hot.

SANDERSON, 38.4 *m.* (158 alt., 100 pop.), named in 1859 for an early settler, has a general store and a few straggling houses along the highway. Community life centers around a high school and several unpainted churches in the back country. The traveler venturing into the pine woods often comes upon huge-wheeled, ox-drawn carts carrying cypress logs to the lumber mill just outside of town. The workers carry lunch buckets filled usually with corn bread, blackeyed peas boiled with white bacon (salt pork), and a jar of cane syrup. After the peas and bacon are eaten, the cornbread is dipped in syrup held in the bucket lid. Greens and bacon, 'poke' chops and beans, biscuits, boiled sweet potatoes, rice, and cowpeas provide variety.

The FLORIDA FOREST SERVICE NURSERY (*open*), 39 *m.*, established with the slogan 'Plant Idle Acres,' was founded at Raiford in 1920 and removed here in 1933. This nursery represents one step taken by the State to protect and renew its forests. Plantings are scattered over an area of 175 acres. Approximately 5,000,000 slash pine seedlings, and 50,000 seedlings of longleaf pine, black locust, cypress, and cajeput were distributed at cost to landowners, turpentine, and sawmill operators throughout the State during the last quarter of 1937. Trees are sold for reforestation at $2 per thousand.

The southern boundary (R) of the OSCEOLA NATIONAL FOREST (*see below*), 41 *m.*, is paralleled by the highway for 17.5 miles.

OLUSTEE BATTLEFIELD, 45.9 *m.*, was the scene of the most sanguinary conflict fought in Florida during the War between the States. The highway traverses the battlefield, and a part (R) is maintained jointly by the United Daughters of the Confederacy and the State. Here on February 20, 1864, twelve regiments of Federal troops led by General Truman Seymour engaged 5,000 Confederates under General Joseph Finnegan and were repulsed with heavy losses. Toward evening, with the arrival of a fresh battalion of the 2nd Florida Cavalry, the Union forces retreated and delayed pursuit by chopping down trees. Two monuments on the site indicate a division of opinion on the name of the battle. One calls it the 'Battle of Olustee'; near by is a smaller monument erected by the United Daughters of the Confederacy as a memorial to the 'Battle of Ocean Pond.'

Right from Olustee Battlefield on a sand road into the OSCEOLA NATIONAL FOREST, 0.5 *m.*, consisting of 155,993 acres acquired by the Federal Government in 1931. Sand roads lead to three steel and seven wooden fire towers at strategic observation points. There are no facilities for camping or recreation, as the forest is maintained solely as an experimental ground for research and demonstration work of the

U.S. Naval Stores Station and the Southern Forest Experimental Station. Personnel, equipment, and records of the stations are housed in an attractive group of rustic buildings. A plot of 3,000 acres, of which more than 600 acres are planted in untapped trees, provides excellent facilities for the study of naval-stores problems. Experiments are conducted to determine the smallest tree that can be profitably worked for turpentine under a given set of conditions, to study the proportionate increase in yield as the tree matures, to find the best age for maximum yields, and to develop 'chipping' specifications that will result in high yields and long working life. The effects of fire and methods of caring for young stands of slash and longleaf pine are also studied.

OCEAN POND, 4.5 *m.*, was so named because it has a distinct current, the waves and whitecaps often resembling ocean waves. The water is of an even temperature (*no bathhouse facilities*).

OLUSTEE (Ind., black), 48.5 *m.* (165 alt., 452 pop.), is a naval-stores shipping point.

The OLUSTEE EXPERIMENT STATION (*open*), 49.6 *m.*, on the edge of the Osceola National Forest, occupies buildings of English half-timbered design; adjacent are the plain brick structures of the NAVAL-STORES STATION of the Bureau of Chemistry and Soils, established by the U.S. Department of Agriculture in 1932.

WATERTOWN, 58.5 *m.* (194 alt., 796 pop.), is headquarters for large lumber interests; railroad spur lines penetrate the woods in all directions to facilitate the transportation of logs to the sawmills.

Watertown is at the junction with State 28 (*see Tour* 19).

LAKE CITY, 61.2 *m.* (201 alt., 4,416 pop.), known as Alligator before 1859 because of its proximity to an Indian village ruled by a Seminole chief of that name, is a town of narrow brick-paved streets radiating from a central square. A post office of Spanish design and the old courthouse with a clock tower overlook the square. In the residential districts old houses shaded by large oaks and set in spacious lawns stand beside trim modern dwellings on formal landscaped terraces.

Chief Halpatter Tustenuggee (Alligator), one of the craftiest of the Seminole, was one of the leaders in the Dade Massacre in 1835 (*see Tour 22*). Induced by General Jesup to leave Florida for Indian territory in 1841, Alligator was later employed by military officers to persuade his tribesmen to capitulate and submit to removal from the State.

Lake City, center of good farming country, was one of the important towns of early Florida. From 1883 to 1905 it was the seat of the State Agricultural College, later removed to Gainesville. Lumber, naval stores, and tobacco are its chief sources of income.

The UNITED STATES VETERANS' HOME AND HOSPITAL (*open* 2–5), on US 41 in the southern section of the town, established in 1920 for white and Negro veterans of all wars, comprises a group of 9 brick buildings on landscaped grounds; the main unit is a hospital with 300 beds.

Lake City is at the junction with US 41 (*see Tour* 4*a*).

Section b. LAKE CITY to TALLAHASSEE; 112.1 *m.* *US* 90

US 90 follows an east-west watershed, the terrain gradually changing from the characteristic pine flatwoods of the coastal region to rolling red clay hills covered with hardwoods.

West of LAKE CITY, 0 *m.*, the route traverses rolling country dotted with small farms, open and fenced pastures, and occasional swamps. Tobacco and cotton are the chief crops.

LIVE OAK, 25.2 *m.* (108 alt., 2,734 pop.), which seems to drowse away more than 11 months of the year, suddenly becomes a hurly-burly city, crowded with thousands of visitors, during the first two weeks of August. The oldest and largest bright-leaf tobacco market in Florida, it has 6 auction warehouses at which were sold 11,000,000 pounds of tobacco in 1938, approximately four-fifths of the State's crop.

On opening day the warehouse district resembles a street carnival. Fakirs and vendors ballyhoo their wares through the streets; sound trucks move through the crowds blaring forth screechy music and thundering announcements of special events. Stores are decorated with bunting and their windows are filled with alluring signs; long counters heaped with merchandise are placed along the curbs; clothing is displayed on racks outside many shops.

For a fortnight before the auction all roads leading to the warehouses are congested with shiny new trucks, battered flivvers, and even mule-drawn farm wagons, all piled high with tobacco leaf. Day and night, officers direct the stream of traffic; tired drivers wait in line for hours to discharge their cargoes at the warehouses; temporary stands offer hot dogs, hamburgers, and drinks; portable shooting galleries and games of pitch help to while away the long hours of waiting.

The tobacco is delivered to the warehouses in burlap bags, which are weighed and placed on the floor in long rows. A ticket on each gives the weight and owner's name. Buyers and auctioneers pass along the rows and carry on rapid-fire bidding in a singsong jargon wholly unintelligible to the outsider. If a grower is not satisfied with a bid, he declines it and awaits the next auction. Buyers have their purchases carried quickly to waiting trucks and freight cars. Warehouse crews work as systematically as stage hands, and long before the last row has been auctioned off, the floor is set for the next day's sale.

Tobacco growing in Florida began a century ago but did not reach the million-pound mark until about 1850, when a light leaf suitable for wrappers found a ready market in Europe. The War between the States stopped these shipments. In the 1890's, with the introduction of shade-grown tobacco, plantings in this district covered 4,000 acres. As no local warehouses were available to growers, they were compelled to haul their crops to South Carolina markets. Later, when the boll weevil devastated cotton fields, tobacco acreage in Florida increased rapidly, and in 1926 one of the first marketing warehouses in the State was established here in Live Oak. By 1933 annual production had mounted to 1,500,000 pounds, and by 1935 to 3,000,000 pounds.

That tobacco was grown and smoked by Indians long before the appearance of white men in Florida is established by an entry in the log of the *Jesus of Lubeck*, the first English ship to visit Florida waters (1564), under the command of Captain John Hawkins, pirate and slave trader, who wrote: 'The Floridians when they travaile have a kind of herbe dried, who with a cane and an earthern cup on the end, with fyre and dried herbes put together, doe suck through the cane the smoke thereof, which smoke satisfieth hunger, and therewith do live four or five days without food or drinke.'

The naming of Live Oak preceded its founding. The old wagon road from the military post at Suwannee Springs to the Gulf passed a clear deep pond here under a huge live oak. Offering shade and an attractive camping ground, the spot became known as Live Oak. With the coming of the railroad the name was given to the local station.

The live oak, with thick trunk and long horizontal branches, is one of the handsomest of Southern evergreens. Great forests of live oak throughout northwest Florida were long held in reserve by the Federal Government for naval purposes in the days of wooden ships. When these lands were thrown open to homesteading in 1885, the forests were ruthlessly destroyed in the process of clearing fields.

The cutting and shipping of live-oak timber were important occupations here in the early 1830's. John James Audubon, in his *Delineations of American Scenery and Character* (1831–39), spoke of the woodcutters as Live-Oakers, saying, 'They are mostly hale, strong, and active men from the eastern part of the Union and receive excellent wages according to their different abilities. . . . They build shanties of small logs to which they retire at night. . . . The best time for cutting live oak is considered to be from the first of December to the beginning of March, or while the sap is completely down.'

The FLORIDA MEMORIAL COLLEGE, a coeducational junior college for Negroes, on the south side of town, was founded in 1873 by the Bethlehem Baptist Association. The first president was Dr.J.L.A.Fish of Boston, who was succeeded by the Reverend C.P.McKinney, a Negro. On the campus are 6 brick buildings; the enrollment in 1938 was 160.

West of Live Oak the route crosses a region of pine woods unusually free of underbrush; most of the drainage in this limestone area is subterranean; surface water is rare.

FALMOUTH, 35.2 *m.* (94 alt., 150 pop.), once known as Peacock, was renamed, according to tradition, by Colonel Duval, a leading citizen and dog fancier, for his favorite pointer, Falmouth, killed on a hunting trip. The hamlet centers on FALMOUTH SPRINGS, part of an underground stream exposed for 500 feet by the fall of the roof of the cavern through which it flows. The stream is apparently a tributary of the Suwannee River, for at times of highwater in the river, the direction of the springs' flow is reversed, and the normally clear water becomes muddy. The 40-foot ravine walls vary from yellow granular marl to hard cream-colored limestone.

At 36 *m.* is the junction with an unimproved road.

Left on this road is DOWLING PARK, 13 *m.* (500 pop.), a summer meeting place of Seventh Day Adventists. An orphanage supported by the church cares for 50 children. The park was named for the Dowling family, owners of a large sawmill, who in 1906 gave 120 acres of land to the church.

The highway crosses the SUWANNEE RIVER (*see Tour 6a*), 38.5 *m.*, which here flows swiftly between high limestone banks. Between the Suwannee and the Aucilla River, in what was known as the old Timucua region, 5 Spanish Missions were established by Franciscan friars in the early 1600's, part of a chain of 24 between St.Augustine and Pensacola. Those in this vicinity were San Francisco de Chuayain, San Pedro de Potohiriba, Santa Helena de Machaba, San Miguel de Asyle, and La Concepcion de Ayabali, or Concepcion de Apalache; the sites of the majority have not been identified. Many of the names were formed by combining the name of a saint with that of an Indian tribe or locale. They remained until 1703–04 when Colonel James Moore of Carolina, seeking to increase his fortune by acquiring Indian slaves, organized an expedition to raid the missions and Indian settlements of northern Florida.

These missions were among those visited in 1674 by Gabriel Diaz Vera Calderon, Bishop of Cuba, who traveled with a company of Spanish infantry and Indian escorts from St.Augustine to the Apalachicola River. While in St.Augustine, the bishop ordained seven young priests, the first known ceremony of the kind within the present territory of the United States. During his 10-month journey he personally spent more than $11,000 for the relief of natives and whites, and confirmed 13,152 Indians.

In a letter written to Queen Marianna of Spain in 1675, the bishop described the villages, life, and customs of the Indians. The natives, he wrote, were excellent carpenters and built large wooden churches; their principal diet was lye hominy, pumpkins, beans, and deer meat; they burned the grass and weeds in January, both to prepare fields for planting and to obtain game, among which the bishop noted buffalo.

The importance of these early missions varied, but the routine of community life in them was of uniform pattern. Fields were worked and herds tended in common. The priests supervised everything, although they did not interfere with the Indian council and managed the workers through their own leaders. Every hour of the day was planned; twice a day the Indians attended church and then departed to appointed tasks in the fields, forests, or elsewhere. Children attended a school taught by priests. Occasional evenings were spent in playing games and dancing.

A number of old customs persisted among the Christianized Indians. Each community had its ball team, and games were played regularly. The game, resembling lacrosse, was a rough and exhausting one that continued throughout the day. On the eve of a match the players worked up spirit by celebrations and appeared on the field the next morning, their bodies daubed with white clay from head to foot. This custom and the frenzy of the players displeased the priests, and the games were banned in 1681.

ELLAVILLE, 39.7 *m.* (64 alt., 100 pop.), the site of a large sawmill built by Governor George F. Drew in 1868, was named for Ella, an old Negro in the governor's employ. At the head of navigation on the Suwannee River, the town shipped much lumber before the coming of the railroads. Trappers and lumbermen in homespun jeans, and women in cotton dresses thronged the sandy streets on Saturdays to do their weekly shopping. Captain Bartlett of the steamer *Belle of the Suwannee*, in blue uniform with brass buttons and cap with gold braid, was regarded as the dandy of the town.

MADISON, 54.8 *m.* (133 alt., 2,189 pop.), an old town with wide oak-shaded streets and many white-columned houses, is the commercial center of a prosperous agricultural region. First called Newton, it was settled in 1838 by planters from South Carolina, who grew sea-island cotton which then commanded three times the price of the ordinary upland variety.

Early Colonials preferred long staple or sea-island cotton because of its strength, but before the invention of the cotton gin the difficulty of seeding it was such that a planter could prepare only enough for his own use. The entire family and slaves picked seeds in the evenings, and a shoeful of lint was considered a good night's work for one person. After washing and drying, the lint was beaten with willow switches, a process called 'willowing.'

More than 200,000 acres in the State were growing sea-island cotton by the early 1870's, and 263,000 acres by 1910, but the boll weevil and the effect of the World War on export trade reduced the total to less than 100 acres in 1935. Rehabilitation of sea-island cotton plantations was begun by the WPA in Madison County in 1935, with such good results that the project was made State-wide. The boll weevil was controlled by the 'afternoon method,' so called because poisoned syrup was applied to the tops of plants with a mop during the hottest part of the day when plants were driest and the weevils thirsty.

During the War between the States, Madison was a Confederate stronghold. An old resident has described the town's reception of the news of Secession: 'The streets were lighted up with bonfires, bells were rung and cannon fired; stirring speeches were made and Southern songs were sung, making it an event remembered to this day.'

In the central park, known as CONFEDERATE SQUARE, is the site of an old blockhouse, used as a refuge during the Seminole Indian War. OAK RIDGE CEMETERY, a pioneer burial ground, contains tombstones bearing photographs of the deceased, a curious custom still common in rural communities among both Negroes and whites who cannot afford to have the likeness of the departed preserved on stone.

Right from Madison on State 9 to CHERRY LAKE FARMS, 8 *m.*, a tract of 12,000 acres developed by the Resettlement Administration of the U.S. Department of Agriculture, and now operated by a nonprofit holding corporation. In the community are 170 four- and five-room cottages, with electric lights and running water, provided for families of moderate but assured means. The houses have been erected on plots ranging from a few to as many as 40 acres. Expert advice in home gardening, poultry raising, fruit and berry growing, and home economics is available at nominal cost. A community center building contains club rooms, library, post office, and an auditorium seating 600. There are two churches, a 9-grade community school, and a health clinic offering services of physician and nurses at cost. Food and clothing are sold through a co-operative store. A community plant for canning garden truck markets about 100,000 cans a year. All utilities are owned by the corporation, and services are distributed at cost. Cherry Lake provides good fishing and water sports.

Between Madison and Monticello the route crosses the middle Florida hammock area, a country of hills and flatwoods, with many coffee-colored streams and a few caves, sink holes, and springs.

The SITE OF HICKSTOWN, 65.1 *m.*, was the favorite camping place in the early 1800's of John Hicks (*Tokse Emathla*), a Mikasuki chief. In 1824,

Governor William Duval of Florida, in an effort to promote harmony between the white settlers and Indians, appointed Hicks chief of all tribes in the State. Two years later Hicks visited President Adams in Washington to adjust relations between his people and the whites. He was present at Payne's Landing (*see Tour* 18) in 1832 and signed the treaty by which the Indians agreed to leave Florida, but died before the removal took place.

GREENVILLE, 69 *m.* (106 alt., 904 pop.), is built around several lumber mills. Founded about 1850, the town was known as Sandy Ford, and later as Station Five, because it was the fifth railroad station east of Tallahassee. During the War between the States a women's society was organized here to sew for the soldiers, and the first box of supplies sent to the Confederate commissary in Richmond was marked, 'From Station Five.' The quartermaster receiving the articles wrote the society that in the future all donations would have to be sent from some designated station. As the majority of the early settlers had migrated from the vicinity of Greenville, South Carolina, that name was selected.

West of Greenville black-gum and cypress trees border the highway. The road shoulders are planted with Bermuda grass to prevent erosion, and the wide right-of-way is cleared of underbrush.

The route crosses the AUCILLA RIVER, 75.3 *m.*, on the west bank of which is the roadside stand of Charlie Hamilton, a half-breed Creek Indian chief, vendor of maple and white-oak baskets since 1928. The baskets, intended for utilitarian rather than decorative purposes, are made by members of his tribe living in a secluded camp several miles down the river.

At 77.2 *m.* is the junction with State 42.

Left on this road is AUCILLA, 1.4 *m.* (86 alt., 300 pop.). The Aucilla Academy was granted a charter in 1840. Previously, wealthy plantation owners in the vicinity had provided their children with private tutors; free schools were looked upon as charitable institutions. After the War between the States a new school building was erected, and 5 teachers were employed; no trace of the academy remains. A royal Spanish plantation was established here in 1640, and from it consignments of honey, dried venison, salted wild turkeys, corn, and deer hides were sent to St.Augustine for use in the city and as supplies for Spanish ships.

MONTICELLO, 85.6 *m.* (210 alt., 1,901 pop.), has a courthouse modeled on Thomas Jefferson's home at Monticello, for which the town was named. Its wide shady streets and old houses have the dignity and charm of the story-book South. Waxy camellias and Cherokee roses have been planted throughout the residential district. Monticello was founded in the early 1800's by planters from Georgia and the Carolinas, who took up land around a blockhouse standing on the site of the present courthouse. For several years the only business establishment was the log cabin of John G. Robinson, whose home was the post office, court room, and social center of the pioneer community.

In Monticello are the headquarters of Florida State Farms, an agency of the Farm Security Administration of the U.S. Department of Agriculture. Its purpose is to rehabilitate farmers on local farms rather than resettle them elsewhere. Farmers select their own tracts of ground, and if the agency approves the choice, loans are arranged for purchase or for long-term tenure lease. In Madison, Jefferson, and Leon counties some 70 farms of this type have been established, aggregating 8,500 acres, planted in various suitable crops.

The METHODIST EPISCOPAL CHURCH SOUTH, Walnut and Olive Sts., is a clapboard structure with a steep pitched roof, a square bell tower, and mullioned windows with pointed wooden arches notable for their carved ornamentation. These carvings and those on the altar, credence table, and prayer desk were done in native woods by a German-born cabinet maker.

MAHAN'S NURSERY, on US 90, has developed a large variety of pecan known as the Mahan, averaging 32 nuts to the pound, and the Dorothy Perkins rose, which has won national recognition.

Monticello is at the junction with US 19 (*see Tour 6a*).

Right from Monticello on State 133 is the BELLAMY PLANTATION, 5.5 *m.*, today a livestock farm and pecan grove. John Bellamy of South Carolina came to Florida and was one of the three settlers who laid out and named Jacksonville in 1821. In 1824, Bellamy was given a contract by the first Florida Territorial Council to build a portion of the road from Pensacola to St.Augustine, his section extending from the St.Johns River to the Ochlockónee River. Slave labor was used in the work. A Congressional appropriation of $20,000 specified a road width of 24 feet. Critics later complained that the road was only 15 to 21 feet wide, that stumps had been left standing to a height impeding the passage of wheeled vehicles, that bridges were flimsy, and causeways over swampy areas, inadequate and unstable. Friends of the contractor argued that stumps in the road did not bar the passage of carriages and wagons, and declared it impractical to cut a wide roadway, as the entrance of too much sunshine and air would promote a growth of underbrush and scrub oak would soon choke the highway. As State funds were lacking to complete the work, Bellamy accepted land for the money due him. The Bellamy Road, as it was called, was used until the beginning of the War between the States.

An industrious planter, Bellamy became one of the wealthiest men in the State. His home, built in a grove of hickory and live oaks, was burned in later years, and no houses remain on the property. The old family cemetery, enclosed with a brick wall, contains the graves of four generations of the Bellamys and three of the Baileys, the latter related to the Bellamys by marriage (*see below*).

At 7.1 *m.*, adjoining the Bellamy tract, is the 4,000-acre SILVER LAKE PLANTATION. The first house here was built by T.S.Johnson, who came from Virginia in the late 1840's. The present house, overlooking Silver Lake, was built in 1853 by Wilkins Cook Smith, son-in-law of Johnson.

The CEDARS, 12.1 *m.*, a 25,000-acre tract, known locally as the Georgia-Florida Farms, was once the property of General William Bailey. Although the plantation house is not standing, many slave cabins remain, as well as the old bell tower, well, and scale house. Bailey, a veteran of the War of 1812, came here from Georgia in 1822, married the daughter of John Bellamy (*see above*), and amassed a fortune. He served as a general in the Seminole War, later moved to Tallahassee, and in 1856 founded the Phifer State Bank of Florida at Gainesville, still in existence. He died in 1867, aged 77. The present owner, Gerald M. Livingston, one-time president of the New York Stock Exchange, has built a 37-room house on the site of the old manor, and uses the estate as a game preserve. A 9-hole golf course serves as a private landing field.

The FINLAYSON PLANTATION, 14 *m.*, is still owned by the Finlayson family, whose progenitors came to America from Scotland in 1800, and to Florida in 1839. They have been successful planters for 100 years. The driveway leading to the rebuilt plantation house is a long avenue lined with old oaks which form a moss-draped archway.

On the LYNHURST PLANTATION, 16 *m.*, stands the only *ante-bellum* plantation house of any size in the region. Built in 1850 by William J. Bailey, nephew of General William Bailey (*see above*), it is still occupied by his descendants. The lower story is of brick made on the plantation; much of the finished lumber was shipped from the north by schooner to St.Marks and hauled to the site. A wide hallway leads into the drawing and dining rooms. All rooms have lofty ceilings, large windows, and folding doors. The house stands at the end of a long drive, surrounded by spacious lawns and gardens. When guests were formally entertained at the early plantations, there was great revelry and much feasting, with toasts, songs, and an abundance of venison, salads, whips, sillabubs (a sweetened curd of wine and milk), jellies, cakes, fruits, and nuts. In the main hall or ballroom of the mansion, Negro fiddlers and banjo players twanged music for a breakdown, such as 'Polly Put the Kettle On,' or 'Leather Breeches.' The rooms were brightly lighted with hundreds of candles.

A swampy area (R), 93.1 *m.*, forms the southern shores of LAKE MICCOSUKEE, which was forded by General Andrew Jackson and his men in 1818. While crossing the lake, they beat off an Indian attack and later reached a village on the west shore. Here they found a large number of cattle stolen from Georgia settlers, together with 50 white scalps hanging from war poles. Jackson burned the town, sent a detachment under the half-breed leader, McIntosh, to pursue the Indians, and marched on to St.Marks (*see Tour 14a*).

At 95.1 *m.* is the junction with State 43.

Left on this road is LLOYD, 3 *m.* (82 alt., 250 pop.), a trading center surrounded by farms. Several sawmills, a grist mill, and a cotton gin are near by. Lloyd's Creek normally flows north, but when Lake Miccosukee, into which it empties, fills with water during the rainy season, the stream flows south to disappear in a sink. The old mill on its bank was once used by General William Bailey (*see above*) for grinding corn. The creek and town were named for W.F.Lloyd of New York, who moved here from Tallahassee in the early 1860's, to establish a large cotton plantation and open a general store.

The highway winds among low hills for many miles; springs are numerous along the road. Near Tallahassee the route is bordered with crape myrtles, laden with pink blossoms in spring and summer.

TALLAHASSEE, 112.1 *m.* (216 alt., 10,700 pop.) (*see Tallahassee*).

Points of Interest: State Capitol, Florida State College for Women, Florida Agricultural and Mechanical College for Negroes, old houses, and churches.

Tallahassee is at the junction with US 319 (*see Tour 14a*).

Right from Tallahassee on State 76 is the SITE OF FORT SAN LUIS, 2.1 *m.*, erected by the Spanish in 1640 and abandoned after the invasion of the English in 1704. Portions of the foundations were still intact as late as 1824, and a cannon, part of the armament of the fort, was fired in Tallahassee on January 8, 1825, to celebrate the 10th anniversary of Andrew Jackson's victory at New Orleans. In a deep wooded ravine a short distance to the east is a spring which, according to early records, was connected with the fort by a 'covered way.'

Here also is the site of the MISSION OF SAN LUIS DE TALIMALI, founded by Franciscans in 1633. In 1656, the friars accused Governor Diego de Roboledo of causing an Indian uprising by paying them for only 25 of the 96 days of labor they had spent in building the presidio at San Luis. The friars were further irritated when the governor stationed an armed guard at the presidio, saying that it served only to alienate the Indians.

OCHLOCKONEE, 8 *m.* (133 alt.), is a small community on so-called LAKE TALQUIN (*fishing, boats*), a widening in the Ochlockonee River.

Section c. TALLAHASSEE to MARIANNA; 71.9 *m.* *US* 90

West of TALLAHASSEE, 0 *m.*, US 90 crosses red clay hills and passes innumerable small lakes covered with water lilies and other water plants.

Throughout the section are numerous farms on which both 'sun' and 'shade' tobacco is grown and cured. 'Sun' tobacco is grown in open fields; 'shade' tobacco, protected from the sun by slat roofs or cheesecloth shelters, has tender leaves of lighter color. Tobacco seed is grown here, for the plants mature rapidly, owing to being subjected to long periods of sunshine. Truck farms are also numerous; field hands on farms and tobacco plantations work from sunup to sundown—or, as they express it, 'from kin see to can't see.'

LAKE JACKSON, 8.2 *m.*, is a small community on the western shore of a lake of that name (*fishing, hunting*). In his march through this district in 1818, Andrew Jackson burned 300 Indian houses, confiscated 3,000 bushels of corn, and drove off 1,000 head of cattle.

At 15.4 *m.* is the junction with State 58.

Right on this road is HAVANA, 5 *m.* (247 alt., 1,169 pop.), named for the Cuban capital. Surrounded by tobacco farms, it has several large cypress lumber and shingle mills.

The route winds over densely wooded hills past tobacco farms worked by Negro hands, whose cabins and small garden patches border the highway.

QUINCY, 26.6 *m.* (251 alt., 3,788 pop.), another tobacco center, has streets lined with sago palms and crape myrtles. On the outskirts lie tobacco fields, curing barns, and warehouses, the scene of great activity during the annual August auction (*see above*). Several small factories here produce 1,000,000 cigars a week.

Settled about 1824, Quincy was the home of wealthy planters and politicians during the Territorial period. In a letter written here in 1840 the physician-botanist, Dr. Alvan Wentworth Chapman (*see Tour 14a*), wrote: 'I am on the frontier and the Indians hold undisturbed possession of the country between me and the Gulf. The Andromeda rhomboidialis and rhododendron punctatu grow there, but it is as much as my neck is worth to venture down . . . No white person to my knowledge has ever traversed that unknown region, and you can imagine my anxiety to plant the standard of flora in the midst of these wilds.'

At the beginning of the War between the States, Quincy citizens were among the most belligerent in Florida; a few days before the State seceded, Quincy Guards seized a large supply of arms and ammunition in a U.S. arsenal on the Apalachicola River. The Quincy *Republican* reported in November 1860 that the town was flying a flag inscribed: 'Secession, Florida, Sovereignty, Independence.'

A deposit of fuller's earth, also known as Florida earth, was discovered near Quincy in 1893; previously, all supplies had been imported from England. Fuller's earth, a clay with the property of absorbing basic colors and removing them from solution in animal, vegetable, and mineral oils, is also used in clarifying oils, as an ingredient in talcum powders, and medicinally as a poultice. Ranging in color from brown to pale blue, the clay occurs in thick strata along river banks and is mined by the open-pit method. In near-by plants it is crushed, dried in oil-heated cylinders, and ground to various degrees of fineness by revolving stones. The mines within a 25-mile radius of Quincy produce more than half the fuller's earth used in the United States.

In Quincy are many descendants of the Swedes who settled the vicinity during the Reconstruction and became field laborers, servants, stock raisers, and merchants.

The Gadsden County Courthouse, in the center of town, stands on the site occupied by the original courthouse, a log cabin. The first trial here was held in the open, it is said, with a log as the jury box and a raw stump as the bench.

MOUNT PLEASANT, 35.4 *m.* (301 alt., 200 pop.), occupies one of the highest ridges in the State.

> Right from Mount Pleasant on an improved road to GLEN JULIA, 1.3 *m.*, a popular camping spot, with a crystal clear spring and stream in the depths of the glen. Here, far from anything approaching the size of mountains, grows the mountain laurel, found along the Appalachians and eastern highlands as far north as Nova Scotia.

West of Mount Pleasant are extensive fields of tobacco, corn, and general farm crops. Many of the large white farmhouses, far back from the road, are surrounded by flower gardens.

CHATTAHOOCHEE (Ind., marked rock), 46.8 *m.* (68 alt., 450 pop.), is the seat of the Florida State Hospital for the Insane (*ward visitors, 9–11 a.m. and 2–4 p.m.; hospital, 10–12 a.m.*). In the white green-roofed buildings scattered about the landscaped grounds, approximately 4,000 white and Negro patients are cared for. In the large enclosed yard adjoining the wards, inmates are allowed at liberty; groups are often taken on picnics. The institution has its own police and fire departments, as well as funeral home, barber shop, and beauty parlor, the last established when it was found that it alleviated the chronic rage of many women patients.

The highway crosses the APALACHICOLA RIVER, 47.9 *m.*, a muddy meandering stream.

At 68.6 *m.* is the junction with State 6 (*see Tour* 18), which unites with US 90 for 4.9 miles.

MARIANNA, 71.9 *m.* (117 alt., 3,372 pop.), on the Chipola River, was founded in 1829 and named for Mary and Anna, daughters of a pioneer merchant. Seat of Jackson County, the town is the center of a prosperous agricultural region, growing peanuts, corn, cotton, pecans, and fruit. A landscaped plaza, with a Confederate monument and bandstand, occupies the center of the business district; facing it is a 5-story hotel built as a community enterprise.

Marianna was the home of John Milton, Governor of Florida during the War between the States. A New England miss engaged to tutor his children kept a journal of her experience as a member of his amiable but happy-go-lucky household. It was a matter of great concern to her that holidays were declared on the slightest pretext. When she suggested that the boys tend the garden and the girls keep their rooms in order, the children protested that such duties were proper only for slaves.

After the War between the States an office of the Freedmen's Bureau was established in Marianna. The primary purpose of the bureau was to supervise contracts drawn up between the Negroes and their employers. The contracts specified the amount of work to be performed and the amount of food to be advanced to each worker, but officials permitted employer and employee to fix the wage or share of the crop to be paid. The weekly food allowance consisted of four pounds of bacon, one peck of meal, and one pint of syrup. For the most part, planters paid wages ranging from $15 to $40 a month, and from a third to two-fifths of the crop.

The Bureau permitted regular courts to handle penal and civil suits of freed slaves; it furnished transportation to freedmen and issued rations to the needy. In 1866 a fourth of Florida's Negro population, the majority in cities and noncotton producing counties, depended on the Bureau for food and clothing. With the aid of other agencies, it provided education facilities for the new citizens; by 1866 there were 38 Negro schools, 20 of them State institutions, with a combined enrollment of more than 2,600. Banks were established in Jacksonville and Tallahassee, and by 1870 the deposits had reached $75,000.

During the Reconstruction violence flared in Marianna and Jackson County, where a number of killings occurred. Trouble originated, it has been charged, in the activities of unscrupulous Bureau officials and politicians. Bishop Pearce of Massachusetts, who had first-hand knowledge of the situation, placed the guilt on the shoulders of the planters of Jackson County, saying that they could have stopped the conflict if they had desired; Judge Bush, an aristocrat of Marianna, claimed that 'ruffians' from the border States were responsible. Robert Meachan, preacher and legislator, pointed out that disputes over farm land caused much of the disorder, as poor whites objected to Negro ownership of choice farms. C.B. Wilder, a wealthy Bostonian living in Jacksonville, declared the lawlessness was caused by carpetbaggers.

NICHOLS INN, Market St. between Jefferson and Green Sts., a two-story rectangular clapboard structure, is one of the few houses of Southern Colonial style remaining in this section; four round fluted columns support a pediment and railed balcony. Built in 1835, it was popular with travelers for many years. During the War between the States the inn was robbed, and the silver and other valuables were found long afterwards in the Chipola River near by. The abandoned building stands in unkept oak-shaded grounds notable for their huge century plants.

The ST.LUKE'S EPISCOPAL CHURCH, Wynn St., is a simple white frame building with a steep pitched roof and long narrow stained-glass windows. A battle was fought around the church in September 1864, when Union forces attacked a regiment of Marianna Home Guards, 60 of whom were killed or wounded and 100 taken prisoners. Many of those killed are buried in the churchyard cemetery. Among the old graves is that of Governor John Milton (*see above*).

Marianna is at the junction with State 6 (*see Tour* 18).

1. Right from Marianna on a dirt road to the FLORIDA CAVERNS STATE PARK, 1.5 *m.*, 623 acres under development by the CCC and the State. The caverns are lighted with electricity; steps have been cut and paths cleared to the several

formations of stalactites and stalagmites. Tradition handed down from slave days has it that the caves extend in series to a point under the courthouse in Marianna.

In the park is a Natural Bridge, under which the Chipola River runs to reappear farther south. Marching westward in his Indian campaign of 1818, General Andrew Jackson crossed the river by this bridge, unaware that many Indians had taken refuge in the caverns below. One division of his troops moving westward by a parallel trail encountered the river and were delayed by the necessity of constructing rafts for a crossing. Jackson was incensed by the belated arrival of this division at the rendezvous and was further enraged by their tale of being forced to cross a river. Not until guides explained the disappearance of the stream under the natural bridge was Jackson appeased.

2. Right from Marianna on an unimproved road is the Florida Industrial School for Boys, 1 *m.*, a State reformatory. Upon arrival here each boy is given a thorough physical examination, followed by an intelligence test, and assigned to one of three large cottages. It is made clear to the newcomer that he is serving no sentence and will receive no punishment for what he has done. As a 'rookie,' he is given academic instruction, vocational and physical training, and a normal social life. The boy is graded each week; upon receiving a passing grade from every officer for a given period of time, he is promoted to the rank of 'polliwog' and enjoys additional privileges, such as the use of library books and taking supervised hikes in restricted areas. When he meets additional requirements for a given number of weeks, he becomes a 'pioneer.' Continued promotion is possible to the ranks of 'pilot' and 'ace.' The latter are permitted to visit town in groups of two or three once a week; they have the freedom of the campus and are granted leaves of absence from the school for reasonable lengths of time.

Section d. MARIANNA to ALABAMA LINE; 161 *m. US* 90

West of MARIANNA, 0 *m.*, US 90 traverses a fertile hilly area producing Satsuma oranges, pecans, sugar cane, and peanuts, and proceeds through forests of hardwood to tidewater at Pensacola.

COTTONDALE, 9.3 *m.* (135 alt., 550 pop.), is a farming, fishing, and hunting center. The fish in neighboring streams and lakes are so voracious, it is said, that fishermen have to stand out of sight behind trees while baiting their hooks. Unlike visitors, old residents refuse to fish on Sundays, for, as one explained, 'I ain't got nothing' else to do weekdays.'

Cottondale is at the junction with US 231 (*see Tour* 17).

West of Cottondale the route crosses the center of the undulating west Florida limestone region, embracing about 1,600 square miles, dotted with ponds and springs, and cut by numerous creeks and streams.

The Florida National Egg Laying Experiment Station (*open*), 16.2 *m.*, is conducted by the Agricultural Extension Service, Department of Agriculture, University of Florida. Poultrymen from many States enter fowl in the annual egg-laying contest, which opens in October and continues for 51 weeks. A single entry consists of 13 purebred pullets of any standard breed. Birds are fed identical food, and are watched and checked by experts. Scores are based on number, quality, and weight of eggs. Silver cups and ribbons are awarded to owners of hens laying from 250 to 300 eggs; a grand prize is awarded for the highest pen total; poultrymen from 22 States were represented at the contest in 1938.

CHIPLEY, 19.1 *m.*, (114 alt., 1,878 pop.), was founded in 1882 with the building of the Pensacola & Atlantic Railroad, later acquired by the Louisville & Nashville. The town was originally known as Orange, but was renamed in honor of Colonel William D. Chipley, a railroad official. Extensive stands of hardwoods in the vicinity supply raw material for several lumber and stave mills.

Among other social events of west Florida is the 'All-day Sing,' enjoyed in church or school yards and attended by neighboring farm families. Hymns are preferred, and the success of the performance is judged by its volume and enthusiasm. A dinner cooked at home is spread on the ground at noon when quantities of fried chicken, rabbit, squirrel, vegetables, coffee, and mounds of cornbread are consumed. More singing, perhaps not so enthusiastic, follows the meal. The party breaks up in the late afternoon, and the husky-voiced singers arrive home before dark.

Left from Chipley on State 52 to FALLING WATER HILL, 4 *m.*; approximately 250 feet high, it affords a view of several miles in all directions. Below the summit, on the southeast slope, emerges a spring of sufficient flow to create a waterfall from a ledge into a large round hole, or sink, 50 feet deep, with almost vertical walls. Surface water seepage and the weathering of the limestone have colored the walls various shades of green, beautiful in the slanting rays of the sun.

West of Chipley are large corn and cotton fields, between stands of pine and extensive pecan groves. Short fills over bay and cypress swamps are crossed; occasional stretches of road are bordered with crape myrtles planted by the State Highway Department.

BONIFAY, 27.9 *m.* (120 alt., 1,292 pop.), on Holmes Creek, has a business district a short distance (R) of the highway. The surrounding area provides good pasture for cattle, sheep, and hogs; livestock sales are held throughout the winter. Lonnie Weeks, leader of the Populist Party in Florida from 1892 to 1912, lived here; his 14,000 votes placed him second in the gubernatorial race of 1892.

CAREYVILLE, 36.1 *m.* (60 alt., 1,022 pop.), on the Choctawhatchee River, is a farming and lumber center, with a mill cutting 1,000,000 feet of pine and hardwood lumber a week.

PONCE DE LEON, 45.2 *m.* (64 alt., 382 pop.), is the SITE OF PONCE DE LEON SPRINGS, one of many 'fountains of youth' named for the Spanish explorer. In adjacent back country live 'Dominickers,' part Negro and part white, whose history goes back to the early 1860's. Just before the War between the States, Thomas, a white, lived on a plantation here, with his wife, two children, and several Negro slaves. After his death his wife married one of the slaves, by whom she had five children. As slaves often took the name of their masters, her Negro husband was also known as Thomas. Of the five children, three married whites, two married Negroes. Today their numerous descendants live in the backwoods, for the most part in poverty.

The men are of good physique, but the women are often thin and worn in early life. All have large families, and the fairest daughter may have a brother distinctly Negroid in appearance. The name originated, it is said, when a white in suing for a divorce described his wife as 'black and white, like an old Dominicker chicken.' Dominicker children are not permitted to attend white schools, nor do they associate with Negroes. About 20 children attend a one-room school. As no rural bus is provided, the pupils often walk several miles to attend classes. An old cemetery, containing a large number of Dominicker graves, adjoins the school.

Numerous curves and steep hills make driving west of Ponce de Leon somewhat dangerous; care and caution are advised.

DEFUNIAK SPRINGS, 58.9 *m.* (265 alt., 2,636 pop.), was named for Colonel Fred DeFuniak, an official of the Louisville & Nashville Railroad. Around the attractive spring (*swimming*), a mile in circumference and 80 feet deep, known in early days as Open Pond, are grouped the Walton County Courthouse, the railroad station, the business district, and many attractive houses.

The renovated CHAUTAUQUA BUILDING, in the municipal park on the west bank, is used as a civic center. When established in 1885, the second of its kind in the United States, the local institution was referred to as the 'Chautauqua that began under a tree,' because the organizers met under a large oak to discuss plans for a building.

On the courthouse grounds, overlooking the springs, stands Florida's first CONFEDERATE MONUMENT, erected in 1871, a white marble shaft, its apex a hand with index finger pointing skyward.

Left from DeFuniak Springs on an unimproved road to EUCHEE VALLEY, 6 *m.*, approximately 25 miles long and 12 wide, first settled about 1822 when Neil McLendon, a native of Scotland, brought his family here. Followers of McLendon dealt as fairly with the Indians as William Penn in Pennsylvania, and the native Euchee remained on friendly terms for many years, helping the settlers to repel raids of hostile Indians from Alabama.

The Euchee, of the same race and language as the Yamasee, employed a curious art in catching fish, making use of the plant *Galega officinalis*, or *Gracca virginia*, known to Floridians as devil's-shoestring and to those living farther north as catgut or goat's-rue. Roots of this plant thrown into the streams stupefied the fish, which floated to the surface. The Euchee chose the best of them and allowed the others to float downstream, where, according to early writers, they revived as the poisoned water became diluted. The Euchee settled in the valley after their migration from the North because they found that fish and this plant were both plentiful here.

The 'good old cracker eatin'' of this section is based on plain substantial dishes—grits, chitlins, sowbelly, side meat, corn bread, cane syrup, turnip greens, hog jowls, washed down with pot likker.

The curving road traverses a region of low hills; sheep graze in rich pastures along the route, and occasionally an ox team hauling a two-wheeled cart loaded with fat pine is passed.

CRESTVIEW, 87.5 *m.* (233 alt., 930 pop.), has several furniture and cabinet factories, a garment factory, and packing plants for pecans and blueberries. Blueberry bushes often grow 12 feet high here, and stepladders are necessary to harvest the crop.

FLORIDALE, 105.3 *m.*, ghost of a boom-time real-estate development, was intended as a model community of small farms; a stucco hotel was erected to accommodate workmen. Today, the deserted hotel keeps vigil with an abandoned railroad station and a watertower.

MILTON, 117.5 *m.* (9 alt., 1,466 pop.), seat of Santa Rosa County, was founded on the Blackwater River as a trading post in 1825. Like other north Florida communities of Territorial days, the town was built around a courthouse square. For many years the village could be reached only by river schooner or by stagecoach along the Geneva-Pensacola road. A correspondent of the Baltimore *Sun* wrote in 1851, 'Milton has three sawmills running 99 saws, and three confectionaries, one known as "Shades," where homefolk are wont to retire at 11 a.m. to partake of ice juleps . . . We have a moral society which bids a hearty welcome to the good and virtuous that come among us, but woe to evildoers . . . Our young ladies are beautiful, our wives lovely.'

Before the War between the States thousands of bales of cotton and much wool from near-by plantations were brought here by mule teams, shipped down the river to Pensacola, and across the Gulf to northern points. Milton remains an important cotton-ginning center, and also has lumber mills, barrel-stave factories, and naval-stores plants. A block south of the bridge spanning the river is the site of an old ferry crossing, and near by are small shipbuilding yards and stores supplying fishermen.

At 121.1 *m.* is the junction with State 187.

Left on this road is BAGDAD, 1 *m.* (500 pop.), a lumbertown, with a scattering of old frame houses along oak-shaded dirt roads. It received its name from the Bagdad Lumber Company, whose mills cut and shipped millions of feet of pine and cypress to New Orleans in the early 1850's. Among the pioneer settlers in the vicinity was John Hunt, who in 1828 purchased a tract of land along Blackwater River, built a large kiln, and established a brick-making business. Hunt planted lotus, cedar, and pecan trees on his plantation. He introduced the 'Turkey Egg' pecan from Mexico—an unusually large nut with a thin shell, speckled like a turkey egg—and won a prize with it at the Paris Exposition in 1873. Although no trees of this variety remain today, there is a large pecan grove on the property, and some of the bearing trees are 90 years old. After Hunt's death the land passed to others, among them a German baron, who used it as a hunting preserve. In the 1890's new owners destroyed the lotus gardens, cut down the large stand of cedars, and disposed of them to pencil manufacturers.

The route crosses a broad marshy area on a long causeway at the mouth of the ESCAMBIA RIVER, 130.9 *m.*; along both sides are scattered lagoons and innumberable waterways winding among reedy islands. On some of the islands, reached by footbridges, are small fishing camps (*boats, tackle*).

South of the causeway the highway follows red and brown cliffs overlooking the sparkling blue waters of Pensacola Bay. The heavily wooded shore is lined with cottages and piers; in fair weather the bay is dotted with sailboats. The wide bay was fortified by the Spanish in 1698 against French ambitions on the Gulf coast, and in 1693 was described by one of their survey parties as 'able to harbor all the armadas of the known world.'

PENSACOLA, 143.4 *m.* (13 alt., 31,579 pop.) (*see Pensacola*).

Points of Interest: Corry Field, Plaza Ferdinand VII, Seville Square, old Christ Church, old houses, and others.

Pensacola is at the junction with State 53 (*see Tour* 14*b*) and US 29 (*see Tour* 16).

Left from Pensacola on State 93 (Barrancas Road) to PENSACOLA NAVAL AIR STATION, 5.9 *m.*, established in 1914 with a complement of nine officers and 23 men, who were given four Curtis and two Wright airplanes of the 'pusher' type. Courses in aerial bombing, gunnery, and navigation are offered in the school here to students from the Navy, Naval Reserve Corps, Marine Corps, and Coast Guard.

The Air Station grounds, traversed by a winding road, were formerly part of the Pensacola Navy Yard, built in 1825 and almost entirely destroyed by Federal gunboats in 1862. The high brick wall and most of the old brick buildings date from their reconstruction in 1870. Along the landscaped drives and waterfront are hangars and huge barnlike repair and maintenance shops. The library, theater, post office, recreational hall, and administration buildings border the road just beyond the old brick walls. The landing field (L) occupies the filled-in site of Commodore Pond. During the War between the States the immense live oaks growing abundantly in this vicinity were so valuable for ship construction that Confederates cut large quantities of logs and rolled them into the pond to keep them from Federal hands. Here they remained, becoming hard as iron, until 1926 when some 240 logs, the largest weighing 5 tons, were recovered from the pond and shipped to the Boston Navy Yard to restore the *U.S.S. Constitution.*

FORT BARRANCAS BARRACKS, between the Naval Air Station and Old Fort Barrancas (*see below*), are quarters of the 13th Coast Artillery, the only garrisoned defense of Pensacola Harbor. The barracks serve as a training camp for the ROTC and the CMTC, and as regional headquarters of the CCC.

On a height commanding the harbor are (R) the RUINS OF FORT SAN CARLOS (*parking space from which visitors proceed on foot*). The massive semicircular brick fort was built between 1781 and 1790 on the approximate site of an earlier wooden fort, built in 1698 by d'Arriola, who came from Mexico with orders to occupy Pensacola Harbor for Spain. Captain Juan Jordon arrived from Havana almost simultaneously. This first fort, named San Carlos de Austria, was burned by the French in 1718. A British fort built here about 1771 was destroyed by the Spanish when they regained West Florida. The ruins are those of the fort that replaced the British redoubt. Cannon were mounted behind the low parapet facing the sea; the iron pintles and track for the guns are still in place. A wide staircase leads to an elevated vantage point for riflemen at the rear. Much of the exterior of the old fort is covered with ornamental plaster; surmounting the doors are plaster cornices lined with hand-hewn woodwork. The thin handmade bricks of the structure have stood up well under the elements for a century and a half.

Old FORT BARRANCAS (Sp. broken), with a dry moat on the north and west sides, rises abruptly behind Fort San Carlos and is connected with it by a bricked tunnel. The drawbridge that originally spanned the moat at the main entrance still has its iron operating mechanism and chains. This U-shaped fort, built by the United States between 1839 and 1844, was held by Confederates from early 1861 to 1862. Large soft-burned brick was used in its construction, but some granite was employed for stair treads, gun mounts, and at the main entrance. The interior is galleried with brick barrel-arches. All openings are of unusual workmanship, mortar joints are exceptionally thin, and the long straight joints show painstaking care; open joints were left to allow for expansion and settling, consequently few cracks have appeared in the brickwork after almost a century. Above the galleries and between the parapets is a sand fill.

FORT PICKENS (*not open*) occupies the western tip of Santa Rosa Island commanding the eastern entrance to Pensacola Harbor. Completed in 1834, the fort is pentagonal in shape, with a bastion at each of the 5 corners. A curved granite stairway has a rail of wrought iron. In the fort are cells in which Geronimo, the Apache chief, and his followers were imprisoned in 1886. At one time the second largest fort in the United States, Pickens was built under the supervision of Captain William H. Chase, U.S. army engineer, who later, as a Confederate general, was ordered to capture the fort, but failed.

The RUINS OF FORT MCRAE, built shortly after Fort Pickens, occupy a peninsula on the opposite side of the channel. Sweeping tides and pounding surf destroyed the fort; portions of the old brick foundations are visible only at low tide. The center of the parade grounds, where in 1852 the fort flagpole stood, is now covered by 30 feet of water in the present ship channel.

At 146.7 *m.* is the junction with a paved road.

Left on this road to CORRY FIELD, 1.9 *m.*, a base for Navy land planes. The grounds are fenced, but visitors are permitted to enter a parking area at the edge of the field.

The road skirts an EMERGENCY LANDING FIELD, 152.8 *m.*, its boundaries marked by red and white posts. West of the landing field the route crosses several narrow, one-lane bridges and traverses open rolling country growing pears and Satsuma oranges. A TUNG TREE NURSERY (*see Tour 3b*), 155.4 *m.*, borders both sides of the highway for more than a mile.

On the PERDIDO RIVER (Sp., lost), 161 *m.*, a ferry was established in 1818 as part of the stagecoach route between Pensacola and Mobile, and was continuously operated until 1919. It was acquired in 1849 by Henry Allen Nunez. Rumors circulated that Nunez had large sums of gold buried here, and he was seized in 1861 by raiders who demanded to know its whereabouts. When he refused, a rope was put around his neck; he was hauled up and only cut down when his terrified wife betrayed his secret.

US 90 crosses the Alabama Line on a bridge here over the Perdido River, 51.4 miles east of Mobile (*see Alabama Guide*).

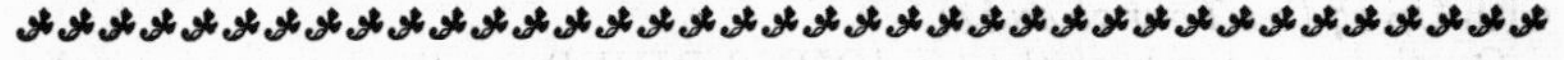

Tour 8

Daytona Beach—Deland—Eustis—Leesburg—Groveland—Lakeland; 129.9 *m.* State 21, State 2.

Hard-surfaced roadbed throughout; watch for cattle along highway.
Route paralleled by Atlantic Coast Line R.R. between Eustis and Okahumpka.
Good accommodations.

This route links Daytona Beach, one of Florida's popular winter and summer playgrounds, with several prosperous agricultural towns in the ridge section. From marshlands and tangled cypress hammocks the highway rises into a rolling prosperous countryside of citrus groves, truck gardens, poultry farms, and large vineyards. Between Leesburg and Lakeland the highway runs for many miles along the divide between Florida's east and west watersheds, a region of cypress swamps and cut-over pine land, in which a few isolated sawmills still operate. Mounds of sawdust and ruins of shacks that once housed hundreds of workers mark the sites of forgotten lumber camps. Farther south, citrus groves blanket low round hills and crowd down to shores of innumerable lakes.

Section a. DAYTONA BEACH to LEESBURG; 68.5 *m. State* 21

This section of the highway cuts through a fastness of swamp and forest, and occasional stretches of cut-over pine lands, the northern section of a low area known as the South Florida flatwoods, which extends as far as the Everglades, into which it merges. Farms and signs of human life are few. Numerous waterfowl feed in roadside ditches, choked with ferns, bright in spring with blue iris and lavender hyacinth. Gray and white herons frequent the marshes, and flocks of red-winged blackbirds nest in the tall sawgrass. West of the St. Johns River are sparkling lakes fringed with orange and grapefruit trees, or with dark stands of pine, the foliage blending with the brilliant blue of the water.

DAYTONA BEACH, 0 *m.* (7 alt., 16,598 pop.) (*see Daytona Beach*).

Points of Interest: Ocean beach, Broadwalk, Pier, open-air Auditorium, Bethune-Cookman College (Negro), alligator and ostrich farms, and others.

State 21 follows Bellevue Ave. out of Daytona Beach and passes (R) the MUNICIPAL AIRPORT, 3.4 *m.*, a regular stop on the U.S. Mail and Eastern Air Lines.

At 20.1 *m.* is the junction with US 17 (*see Tour 2b*), which unites with State 21 for 3 miles (*see Tour 2b*).

DELAND, 23.1 *m.* (27 alt., 5,246 pop.) (*see Tour 2b*), is at the junction with US 17 (*see Tour 2b and c*).

On the east bank of the ST. JOHNS RIVER, at the approach to the CROWS BLUFF BRIDGE, 28.6 *m.*, are (R) the docks and warehouses of the St. Johns River Line, which operates a fleet of small Diesel-powered boats for the transportation of fruit and other produce from this section to Jacksonville. Long before the advent of the railroads, settlements along the river were bustling ports. River craft stopped here regularly to discharge supplies brought from Jacksonville and to pick up on their return trip large cargoes of cotton, corn, peanuts, turpentine, rosin, and lumber.

Near by, along the river, there stood in 1600 the village and mission of Antonico, capital of the 'Fresh Water Province.' The village was ruled by an Indian chief named Antonio de Rio Dulce, who bowed only to the authority of Fray Pedro de Vermejo, one of many Spanish priests who braved the wilderness to convert the natives. Bishop Altamirano arrived by canoe in 1606 and confirmed 225 persons, and the mission was visited about 10 years later by Father Ore, who later wrote *The Story of the Martyrs of Florida*. Antonio persisted as the name of this locality for more than a century, the 'Island of San Antonio' appearing on the Puente map of 1765.

West of the St. Johns River the soil is sandy. Small lakes multiply as the highway rises and reaches the heart of Lake County, a region of excellent fresh water fishing (*black bass, speckled and warmouth perch, bream*). Its 1,400 lakes, surrounded with woods sheltering small and large game, have induced many retired army men to build their homes here.

The highway enters a 1,400-acre vineyard, 44.2 *m.*, in which are grown many varieties of grapes, chiefly the Carmen and the Beacon, the latter known as the Florida Concord; the cultivation of grapes is a minor element in Florida's economy.

Large drainage canals crisscross the countryside. Negro families often fish from the high banks for bream and perch. These diminutive fish, rolled in corn meal and fried crisp, are toothsome delicacies. At refreshment stands fried-fish sandwiches are more popular with the Negroes than hamburgers or hot dogs.

Along the highway, at times extremely rough and narrow, run rows of towering moss-draped oaks, planted shortly after the War between the States to shelter what was then a rutted sand trail. Extensive citrus groves are flanked with hedges of white Cherokee roses and unusually tall clumps of fragrant yellow jasmine. In many of the older groves are seedling orange trees, identified by their double and sometimes triple trunks. These grew from roots of trees cut down after the destructive freezes in the middle 1890's.

EUSTIS, 52.8 *m.* (71 alt., 2,835 pop.), on the east shore of Lake Eustis, a tourist town with pleasing houses and well-kept streets, lies at the apex of the 'Golden Triangle' (*see Tour* 21), and reflects the prosperity of a rich agricultural section, with citrus and watermelons as the chief crops. Sand pumped from Lake Eustis is used throughout the State for construction purposes.

Known successively as Highlands and Pendryville, the town was later named for Lake Eustis, itself named about 1828 for General Abram Eustis, prominent in the Seminole War, whose forces had a skirmish with the Indians on the south shore of the lake. In 1876, A.S.Pendry homesteaded land here and set out a citrus grove. In the fall of 1877 he opened the Oklawaha Hotel; the post office established in the hotel carried the sign 'Pendryville.' Before the advent of the railroads, the town was a busy port for steamers plying Lakes Eustis, Dora, Griffin, and Harris.

The Lake County Country Club's 18-hole golf course (*greens fee* $1) is the scene of many winter tournaments. Social activities and amusements for winter visitors center at the TOURIST CLUB and park on the lake front.

An annual trapshooters meet, the Winter Vandalia, is sponsored each February by the Eustis Gun Club under the supervision of the Amateur Trapshooting Association. Adopting the name of a shoot held for many years at Vandalia, Ohio, the Eustis meet competes for popularity with many oddly named rivals; among them the Daytona Beach Baby Grand, and the Jacksonville Gun Club's Great Southern. Amateur trapshooters from all parts of the United States enter the Eustis tournament to compete for the trophies offered: the Orange Blossom Handicap, the Orange Blossom Championship, and the Orange Blossom Consolation.

West of Eustis the route continues on State 2.

FORT MASON, 54.5 *m.* (75 alt., 25 pop.), a village settled in the early 1880's, was named for the stockade built in the vicinity by Major Richard Barnes Mason during the Seminole War of 1837.

Right from Fort Mason on State 55 is UMATILLA, (Ind., water rippling over sand), 5 *m.* (103 alt., 907 pop.), a citrus-growing center, settled in 1862 by Nathan J. Trowell. The HARRYANNA CRIPPLED CHILDREN'S HOME (*open*), established by and named for Harry and Anna Miller, is a charitable institution supervised by the Florida State Elks Ass'n. Here also is a factory producing brushes from saw palmetto. Bee culture is extensively followed; orange, grapefruit, gallberry, and palmetto blossoms impart a distinct flavor to the honey. During winter, when citrus trees are in bloom, many apiarists from northern states bring their bee colonies into this section, and are welcomed by grove owners as an aid in pollinating the trees.

GRAND ISLAND, 56.5 *m.* (108 alt., 198 pop.), settled in the late 1880's, was so named because it is almost encircled by Lakes Yale, Griffin, and Eustis. In this vicinity natal grass, a pink-topped flowering forage grass native to South Africa, grows abundantly in the fields.

At 66 *m.* is the junction with US 441 (*see Tour* 21), which unites with State 2 for 2.5 miles.

LEESBURG, 68.5 *m.* (97 alt., 4,113 pop.) (*see Tour* 21), is at the junction with US 441 (*see Tour* 21).

Section b. LEESBURG to LAKELAND; 61.4 *m. State* 2

South of LEESBURG, 0 *m.*, the route crosses grassy prairies broken at intervals by thickets of scrub oak and cypress. When inundated during wet seasons, the prairies are the feeding and nesting grounds of myriads of waterfowl. Heron—white, green, and slate-blue—are common; an occasional white-faced, glossy ibis, strikingly colorful at close range but dull gray at a distance, stands motionless as a statue until it darts its head forward with lightninglike rapidity to capture a frog or crayfish.

OKAHUMPKA (Ind., lonely or bitter waters), 4.2 *m.* (95 alt., 100 pop.), a lumber and turpentine community, with frame houses and stores scattered along the highway, was founded in 1885 by the Reverend Edmund Snyder of Germantown, Pa., on the site of an Indian village ruled until 1835 by Chief Micanope, leader of the attack on Major Francis L. Dade and his command (*see Tour* 18). Through the townsite ran the military road laid out by General Abram Eustis to link a chain of blockhouses from St.Augustine to Fort Brooke (Tampa).

Backwoodsmen of the turpentine country about Okahumpka, as in similar sections of Florida, tend and gash trees, empty spill cups, keep records of barrels of gum loaded for the stills, and depart at dusk for their homes hidden in swamps and pine forests (*see Tour 3b*). Their families are often large, and their wives and children shy of strangers. They care for their own sick, disabled, and aged, having a dread of institutions. 'Healing' is often practised with herbs, charms, and Negro voodoo ritual. In early days, before churches were built, families met by turn in one another's cabins when the neighborhood was visited by a circuit rider, who preached, led the prayers and singing, and gave advice on business, medicine, and legal problems.

Left from Okahumpka on State 214 is HOWEY-IN-THE-HILLS, 10 *m.* (338 pop.), founded by W.J.Howey in 1916, center of a vast citrus development embracing 60,000 acres, 10,000 of which have been planted in orange and grapefruit groves. Valencia oranges and Marsh seedless grapefruit are grown for spring markets; pineapple oranges and Duncan grapefruit for the mid-season markets. New plantings have been confined to the pink-meated grapefruit; the Hamlin orange, an early fruit of high quality; and the golden lime, or limequat, a cross between the lime and kumquat.

Individual owners of groves, which range from 5 to 100 acres, are offered the facilities of the Howey-in-the-Hills Service, Inc., which contracts to provide modern machinery and equipment, a corps of inspectors, and a personnel trained in citrus cultivation. In the case of absentee owners the service company assumes complete responsibility for the care of the grove and the picking of fruit. The Howey organization has an independent shipping and marketing agency.

South of Okahumpka the route crosses an area dotted with small grassy lakes, offering good fishing (*black bass, warmouth, copperhead, catfish, crappie, pickerel, speckled perch, and bream*). Citrus groves between the lakes are bordered with vine-clad fences and tall feathery plumosa palms. Red clay roads lead through scrub oaks and pines to small farms. Purple lupines, white flycatchers, and sparkleberry bloom in the fields and along the drainage ditches. The highway mounts an overpass, 85.1 *m.*, from which is an unusually fine view of lakes and rolling pine land.

At 17.4 *m.* is the junction with State 22 (*see Tour* 9), which unites with State 2 for 2.2 miles (*see Tour* 9).

GROVELAND, 18.5 *m.* (129 alt., 470 pop.), so named because of the extensive citrus farming in its region, was founded in the early 1900's as a naval-stores center and was first known as Taylorville. Later, lumbering was the chief industry until a fire destroyed the largest sawmills and millions of feet of timber. Many of the early settlers in this section were Swedes, who came to grow citrus, watermelons, and green beans. The town, renamed Groveland in 1911 and incorporated in 1922, has a municipal water system and an auditorium.

Passing through the 10-mile citrus belt south of Groveland, the highway traverses cut-over lands and vast swamps, some open and clotted with reeds and lilies, others dark with moss-draped cypress. Here and there on higher patches of ground are small fields and sun-warped shacks, abandoned by farmers who came during the boom and attempted to raise winter truck.

The road crosses the WITHLACOOCHEE RIVER (Ind., little great water), 101.5 *m.*, which rises in the swamplands of upper Polk County, being one of the few rivers in the State flowing northwest. Downstream, the river deepens and is used by shallow draft vessels. Between the river and Auburndale are a few isolated citrus groves and several large tracts of rolling land planted with tung-nut trees (*see Tour 3b*). The cultivated areas alternate with cypress swamps and pine thickets. Here on the watershed, a region of lakes and swamps, are the sources of the Withlacoochee, Hillsborough, Alafia, Peace, and Kissimmee rivers, all lying within a radius of 50 miles.

POLK CITY, 45 *m.* (135 alt., 222 pop.), founded in 1922 by Isaac Van Horn, lies on the northern shore of LAKE AGNES, one of many small lakes in the vicinity. The town is the trading center for timbermen of the surrounding district.

Left from Polk City on State 61, which winds for miles through unfenced orange and grapefruit groves. Low spreading trees, white with waxy blossoms or golden with fruit, reach out and all but touch passing cars; in season fallen fruit litters the road shoulders. Graveled roads lead into many groves with signs inviting the traveler to 'Come in and Pick an Orange.' Plumosa and cabbage palms border stretches of the route; tall clumps of oleander and trailing bignonia vines flaunt their orange-yellow blossoms in spring. Now and again the road follows the irregular shores of one of the numerous blue lakes, with rows of glossy-green citrus trees sloping toward them. Hillcrests offer vistas of groves extending far into the distance, of shining lakes, white farmhouses with tilled fields about them, and formal landscaped estates. On lower land thickets of scrub oak and pine are webbed with creepers and wild grapevines.

At 11 *m.* is AUBURNDALE, (167 alt., 1,849 pop.) (*see Tour* 20) at the junction with US 92 (*see Tour* 20).

LAKELAND, 61.4 *m.* (206 alt., 18,554 pop.) (*see Tour* 20), is at the junction with US 92 (*see Tour* 20).

Tour 9

Indian River City—Orlando—Winter Garden—Groveland—Floral City; 107.5 *m.* State 22.

Hard-surfaced roadbed throughout; watch for cattle along highway.
Route followed by Florida Motor Lines between Indian River City and Clermont; paralleled by Atlantic Coast Line R.R. between Winter Garden and Mascotte.
Good accommodations.

Known as the Cheney Highway between Indian River City and Orlando, State 22 connects the east coast and west-central Florida. Until 1925 much of the country traversed was accessible only by sand trails. The flora of the region varies from flat pine forests to marshland and scrub palmetto thickets. Skirting numerous lakes, the highway traverses a country of vineyards and citrus groves, and reaches its highest elevation near Oakland.

From the junction with US 1 (*see Tour* 1c) at INDIAN RIVER CITY, 0 *m.* (19 alt., 120 pop.) (*see Tour* 1c), State 22 proceeds west to the St. Johns River valley, a broad expanse of marsh and swamp, dotted with clusters of tall cabbage palms. Red-winged blackbirds and diminutive rice birds feed among the marsh grasses; flocks of ducks winter here, and ibis and herons remain the year round.

Crossing the St. Johns River (*fishing*), 10 *m.*, its many quiet lagoons blanketed with hyacinths, the highway passes through dense growths of palms into hammock country where, in spring, scarlet foliage of sweet gums contrasts vividly with the somber green of live oaks.

CHRISTMAS, 15 *m.* (250 pop.), is a little town which receives much mail during yuletide holidays, when more than 50,000 letters are run through the cancellation machines and relayed to all parts of the globe. People throughout the world mail gifts 'via Christmas' to have them bear the Christmas postmark. Hughlette Wheeler (1900–), the 'cowboy sculptor,' was born here and worked as a cowhand on a near-by ranch. Now a resident of Arizona, he enrolled in the Cleveland School of Art in 1925 and soon won recognition for his animal figures.

West of Christmas the grasslands support only an occasional crossroads settlement. Streams are lined with dense stands of oaks, bays, and gums. The highway crosses the ECONLOCKHATCHEE RIVER (Ind., earth-mound), 23 *m.*, here little more than a shallow creek meandering through a swamp. Scarlet cardinals, painted buntings, and various tiny warblers—'messengers of the sun,' the Indians called them—provide occasional bright flashes of color.

ORLANDO, 37 *m.* (111 alt., 27,330 pop.) (*see Orlando*).

Points of Interest: Zoo, Eola Park, Sunshine Park, Gaston Edwards Park, World War Memorial, old Courthouse, Albertson Public Library, and others.

Orlando is at the junctions with US 17 (*see Tour 2c*) and US 441 (*see Tour 21*).

Winding through suburban Orlando, State 22 enters a region of well-developed citrus groves and truck farms.

ORLOVISTA, 42.3 *m.* (300 pop.), an unincorporated community, is a relic of the real-estate boom of 1925. Signs along the main street advertise the prowess of rival astrologists in predicting, at varying prices, one's future from the stars.

On Deer Island (R), a misnomered promontory jutting into Lake San Susan, is the DEER ISLAND PIT, a barnlike structure with a seating capacity of more than 1,000, the scene of great activity and excitement during the cock-fighting season. The season extends from Thanksgiving to the Fourth of July, and reaches its climax here in January during the annual International Tournament, sponsored by the Orlando Game Club, one of the largest of its kind in the country. Held regularly since 1920, the tournament has become in its field what the Kentucky Derby is to followers of the turf.

For the occasion gamecocks are brought from Canada, Cuba, Mexico, Central and South America, and all parts of the United States. Some arrive by plane, others in private railroad cars. The fee for entering a string of birds is \$500; they fight for a top purse of \$4,000; during the boom fees ran as high as \$2,000, and purses occasionally reached \$25,000. Known as 'mains,' 'hacks,' or 'meetings,' the fights are not advertised by press or radio, but for several months before the tournament trade papers carry half-page announcements of the event, together with records of past performances of the contestants, and the advertisements of gamecock breeders and others connected with the sport.

The jargon of the cockers is apt to mystify the uninitiated. The metal spurs with which the cocks fight are known as gaffs, or 'heels,' which are fitted over the bird's spur (after it has been cut down) and held in place by a soft leather strap secured to the leg by waxed thread. Made of tool steel and costing $7.50 a pair, heels are limited in length to two and a half inches and must be conical in form; no sharp-bladed 'slasher' types are allowed. To heel a bird properly is an art demanding knowledge and experience; the build of the bird, its stance, its fighting technique, the curve of its natural spur, must all be taken into consideration.

Birds are matched by weight. The minimum is 4.12 pounds; those weighing more than 6.02 pounds are known as 'shakes' and fall into the heavyweight class, in which there are no limitations on poundage, as in prizefighting. A 'blinker' is a bird blinded in one eye and is usually given a four-ounce handicap. Rookies yet to pass their first moult are called 'stags,' and any mongrel is a 'dunghill.' Among blooded birds are many celebrated fighting strains, but the champions are usually Shufflers, Warhorses, Roundheads, or Mugwumps.

All battlers are put through a strenuous training period. For road work, they are 'walked' on an open range to harden their muscles. They are tossed and 'flirted' to develop wing power, balance, style, and punch. Miniature boxing gloves, or 'muffs,' are used in sparring matches. At times a stuffed cock on the end of a stick is the sparring partner.

The regulation pit is circular in form, 16 feet in diameter. As in the squared ring, fights are divided into rounds and usually last from 20 to 30 minutes. Prolonged bouts are transferred to a 'drag' pit, where the birds battle to a finish under another referee.

To the International Tournament here admission is $5, but the matinee and night contests attract capacity crowds. Roars of applause greet the referee as he steps into the pit, raises his arm, and announces: 'First fight . . . this afternoon . . . between Blue Falcon . . . weight, four-ten . . . and Irish Gray . . . weight, four-eleven and a half!'

The feathered warriors, their eyes gleaming wickedly, their curved gaffs shining, are brought in by their 'pitters,' or 'setters,' who are their seconds during the fight. Placed on measured lines at opposite sides of the pit, they are released at the referee's shout of 'Fight!' Advancing warily, necks outstretched, feathers ruffled, the birds crouch, shuffle, feint, like boxers sparring for an opening. Suddenly, they leap into the air in a confused tangle of beaks, wings, and gaffs. They drop and rise to attack again with fury. Blue Falcon strikes quickly and both fall, locked together. 'Handle!' calls the referee, noting that Blue Falcon has sunk his steel deep into Irish Gray.

The setters expertly separate the birds, stroke them, flex and rub their legs and thighs. At the end of 10 seconds the fight is resumed. As Blue Falcon rushes in, Irish Gray rises awkwardly on his spiked wing. They fly at each other and go down in a bounding ball. They pull apart; their long necks move in and out, and weave from side to side, like a rattlesnake's; powerful beaks tear wattles and combs. In a fierce encounter Irish Gray falls; Blue Falcon strikes at his prostrate foe, struts, and flaps his burnished wings. Watch in hand, the referee counts twenty. Irish Gray is still on the floor, bleeding in several places. Up goes the referee's hand as he shouts

'Fight won . . . by Blue Falcon!' The crowd roars, and as much as $1,000 is won in a single side bet.

At 43.4 *m.* is the junction with an unnumbered road, paved.

Right on this road to STATE TUBERCULOSIS SANITARIUM, 3.5 *m.*, a three-story brick building opened in 1938, the first institution of its kind in Florida. The hospital, serving white and Negro patients, has 400 beds.

The highway is flanked by citrus groves sloping down to Lake Hiawassa; straight rows of orange, grapefruit, and tangerine trees extend to the horizon in all directions. Blue lobelia, coreopsis, and yellow daisies carpet the shoulders of the road in late summer. The highway passes WOODLAWN MEMORIAL PARK, 45.5 *m.*, a cemetery on the brow of a hill landscaped with palms, cedars, and subtropical shrubs.

OCOEE (Ind., apricot vine place), 48.6 *m.* (156 alt., 794 pop.), its main street shaded by large oaks, grew up around a camp established by an early settler, Dr. J.S. Starke, who insisted on having his slumbers undisturbed. In 1859, with a company of slaves, he settled on the shores of Lake Apopka (*see below*), but mosquitoes from the canebrakes made sleep impossible. He soon moved a few miles eastward and settled here on the shores of Lake Starke, as it came to be called. The settlement that developed about the camp bore the same name until 1886, when the town was platted. Many old two-story frame houses, built before the turn of the century, sit back from the highway in seedling groves.

On election day, November 3, 1920, a race riot broke out at Ocoee, following a disturbance at the polls. One of several conflicting stories attributed the trouble to the fact that July Perry, Negro foreman of a large orange grove, appeared at the polls intoxicated, brandishing a shotgun, and killed two officers sent to arrest him at his home. According to another report substantiated by many eye-witnesses and published widely, the conflict arose when Mose Norman, prosperous grove owner and the town's most prominent Negro, ignored the threats of the local Ku Klux Klan and came to the polls to cast his ballot. Badly beaten, he retired to the home of his friend, July Perry. All versions of the conflict agree on what ensued. In an attack on the house two whites were killed, Perry was wounded. During a lull in the fighting Perry crawled away into the fields, but he was found and locked up in the Orlando jail. At sunrise the jail was stormed; Perry was dragged forth, tied to the back of an automobile, and finally hanged from a telephone pole along the highway. Meantime, mobs had surrounded the Negro section of the town and fired it, burning 30 houses and two churches, forcing men, women, and children back into the flames. In all, some 35 Negroes perished. The conflict spread to Orlando, Apopka, and Winter Garden, and for a week Negro districts in these towns were patroled by armed squads of whites. Since that time Negroes have not been permitted to live in the town of Ocoee.

Between Ocoee and Winter Garden lies one of the richest truck farming districts in Florida; many of the farms are equipped with subirrigation facilities (*see Tour 2c*).

WINTER GARDEN, 51.4 *m.* (123 alt., 2,023 pop.), with a railroad running down its main street, has large packing plants handling citrus fruit and winter vegetables grown in the vicinity. In the MUNICIPAL WATERFRONT PARK is a trailer camp, a swimming pool, and a yacht basin on Lake Apopka.

LAKE APOPKA (Ind., potato-eating place), 12 miles long and approximately 10 miles wide, one of the State's most popular fresh-water fishing grounds, is fed by springs and connected by subterranean streams with other lakes in the highland section. Four towns face the lake: Winter Garden and Oakland on the south, Ferndale and Montverde on the west.

The brick highway, bordered with groves, traverses rolling country; side roads lead to fishing camps on the lake, and numerous signs proclaim their virtues.

OAKLAND, 54.6 *m.* (140 alt., 879 pop.), occupies a wooded slope overlooking Lake Apopka. Giant oaks, for which the town was named, shade its quiet streets and shelter many large weatherbeaten frame houses erected in the early 1880's.

This rustic simplicity did not always prevail. Founded in 1854 by settlers from South Carolina, noisy sawmills, sugar mills, and cotton gins made Oakland a busy industrial center by 1860. In 1889 it became a junction on the Orange Belt and the Florida Midland railroads. Hotels, stores, and blocks of workmen's shanties were built around large railroad shops; when the Florida Midland became bankrupt, the shops were removed; a fire swept the business district and leveled the flimsy buildings. Today the town depends for its livelihood on the cultivation and packing of citrus fruit and winter vegetables.

At 58.7 *m.* is a junction with State 256.

Right on this road is MONTVERDE (Sp., green mountain), 2.5 *m.* (297 pop.), a village in the heart of an extensive grape-growing region. The MONTVERDE INDUSTRIAL SCHOOL, a coeducational preparatory institution established in 1912 by the D.A.R., specializes in vocational training, and students are given courses in agriculture, mechanics, and commerce, as well as general scholastic instruction through the 12th grade. In addition to its 50-acre campus, the school owns a 200-acre farm on which agricultural students help cultivate fruits and vegetables. The institution is supported through donations and the fees paid by its students.

Along the wooded irregular shores of Lake Minneola, which State 22 follows, are many summer cabins, picnic grounds, and fishing camps.

CLERMONT, 65 *m.* (105 alt., 1,086 pop.), with wide shady streets, is set among the steep rolling hills that encircle Lake Minneola. It was named for Clermont, France, the birthplace of A.F. Wrotnoski, one of its founders. From diatomite mined near by (*see below*), a local plant manufactures moisture-proof tops for salt shakers and cleaning cream. KEHLOR PARK serves as a community center.

Left from Clermont on State 55 to the marshes of LAKE LOUISA, 5 *m.*, where strata of diatomite were discovered in 1917 by Charles Lindly-Wood, agent for the British Admiralty. Diatomite consists of the fossilized skeletons of minute sea animals. An effective insulating material against heat, cold, and sound, it is used in the manufacture of rubber, explosives, fireproof felt, glass, porcelain, safety matches, calico, dental cream, and other articles. Diatomite sells at $250 a ton.

POSTAL COLONY, 7 *m.*, embracing 1,000 acres of citrus groves, was established by and for retired postal clerks in 1922, when Edward Denslow organized the Postal Colony Company, the group's operating organization. More than 100 families spend their winters here, and 25 remain the year round. The families own and cultivate their individual groves; but the company maintains a fleet of trucks and tractors, and provides sprayers and other modern equipment used jointly by the farmer-clerks, most of whom saw 30 to 40 years of service in the Post Office Department before reaching the retirement age of 62.

West of Clermont the route winds through extensive marshlands ribbed with small creeks; magnolias and moss-draped oaks line the shores of numerous lakes. On the higher sandy areas grow blackjack oaks and fields of ruddy-topped Natal grass.

GROVELAND, 71.7 *m.* (129 alt., 470 pop.) (*see Tour 8b*), is at a junction with State 2 (*see Tour 8b*), which unites with State 22 for 2.9 miles.

In MASCOTTE, 74.6 *m.* (135 alt., 260 pop.), a trading center for citrus growers built around a railroad station, State 22 branches (L) from State 2 (*see Tour 8b*).

West of Mascotte the route winds over hills to the crest of the central Florida ridge section. Here citrus groves give way to alternate stretches of pine woods, scrub palmetto, tilled fields, and pastures, on which graze sleek Jersey cattle.

CENTER HILL, 84.6 *m.* (91 alt., 726 pop.), settled in 1883, is a shipping point for growers of strawberries, watermelons, and winter vegetables, particularly green beans. Many farms are equipped with overhead irrigation systems (*see Tour* 20). In season truckloads of watermelons roll out daily for northern points; early melons are usually sold by the pound, and the larger may weigh as much as 40 pounds. People here sometimes prepare for festive occasions by plugging a melon, scooping out the center, and filling it with corn liquor. Kept on ice for 24 hours, the melon is then tapped with a bamboo spigot; 'watermelon 'shine' is a potent refreshment.

The pines thin out rapidly as the highway enters flat sparsely settled country, dotted with a few seedling groves and an occasional ghostlike stand of dead oaks, killed when 'ringed' by early settlers in preparing fields for cultivation. Soaring buzzards and isolated herds of cattle are almost the sole signs of life for many miles.

The BUSHNELL AIRPORT, 88.4 *m.*, is a well-marked emergency landing field surrounded by extensive fields producing vegetables in winter and planted to corn, cowpeas, and some tobacco in spring.

BUSHNELL, 92.8 *m.* (74 alt., 591 pop.) (*see Tour* 22), is at the junction with State 2 (*see Tour* 22).

Dense hardwood hammocks alternate with vast swamps along the highway west of Bushnell. There are no settlements, no filling stations, and few signs of human habitation. Small garden patches cleared in the wilderness support isolated settlers; now and again an old seedling grove is passed, hemmed in by towering oaks, gums, and a matted tangle of jungle creepers which threaten to smother the scraggy trees. This primitive region is much as it was in 1539 when De Soto and his army, 'sore vexed with hunger and evill waies,' floundered northward through a land 'barren of maize, low and full of water, bogs, and thicke woods.'

The highway crosses the WITHLACOOCHEE RIVER (Ind., little great river), 103.3 *m.*, its channel leading through a cypress swamp past a fishing camp (*cabins, boats, bait, tackle*) at the west end of the bridge. This swift-flowing rock-bottomed stream was named by Creek Indians for a river of the same name in the vicinity of their home in Georgia. Somewhere close by, De Soto and his men came upon 'a river with a great current, and upon a tree, which was in the midst of it, was made a bridge, whereon the men passed; the horses swam over by a hawser that they were pulled by from the other side; for one, which they drove in at the first without it, was drowned.'

FLORAL CITY, 107.5 *m.* (57 alt., 300 pop.) (*see Tour 4b*), is at a junction with US 41 (*see Tour 4b*).

Tour 10

Melbourne—Holopaw—St.Cloud—Kissimmee; 55 *m.* US 192.

Hard-surfaced throughout; watch for cattle along highway.
Limited accommodations.

US 192 crosses a sparsely settled region, parts of which, often under water, are still unexplored. Much of the territory near the coast, once covered with magnificent stands of pine, has been despoiled by naval-stores operators and loggers. Cypress and palm hammocks rise at intervals to relieve the monotony of the vast flat ranges on which cattle graze. Hump-shouldered Brahma cattle, the predominant strain, were brought from India to improve breeds on the local swampy range. A few lonely settlements with Indian names are strung along the branch line of a railroad, originally built to transport lumber.

US 192 branches west from US 1 (*see Tour 1c*) at MELBOURNE, 0 *m.* (22 alt., 2,677 pop.) (*see Tour 1c*).

At 1.5 *m.* is the MELBOURNE GOLF CLUB (*greens fee* $1).

Suburban cottages, small groves, and farms flank the route, planted on both sides with Australian pines, bamboos, and a variety of palms. Soon the highway is on the open prairie; low areas are a mat of sawgrass, tall cattails, and pond lilies, bright with white and pale yellow blossoms. The highway crosses the ST.JOHNS RIVER, 9.3 *m.*, whose source lies 7 miles south in unsurveyed swamps about Lakes Helen Blazes and Saw Grass. Here the sluggish stream winds through an extensive marsh filled with lilies, flags, and hyacinths, the feeding grounds of white and blue herons, blackbirds, and occasional egrets. At the western end of the bridge is a fishing camp (*boats, bait, tackle*), with a refreshment stand and gas station.

Before completion of US 192, automobiles and passengers were carried on the flat cars of a logging railroad to a point here 15 miles west of Melbourne, and proceeded hence along a treacherous sand trail, passable only in dry weather, which meandered across the prairie to a narrow brick road leading into St.Cloud.

Between stout fences the highway crosses a swamp over a long fill. Signs here and at intervals for some distance warn hunters and others that this region is a bird sanctuary, under the protection of the Audubon Society. Leaving the lowlands, the road runs straight as a line across a prairie dotted with lone cabbage palms. Distant cypress hammocks resemble misty blue hills. Along the road are piped wells, some spouting like miniature geysers, providing drink and shower baths for cattle, hard-riding cowhands, and their ponies.

Cow-camp frolics are gala occasions in this remote region, part of a vast range extending 200 miles to the south. Invitations to these parties are unnecessary; everyone for miles around attends—girls in mail-order finery; mothers with children in arms; cowhands in polished boots, bright bandanas, and new sombreros, which are not removed at any time, even during dances. At sunset all converge on the appointed ranchhouse in wagons, flivver trucks, and on horseback, and seat themselves on upturned boxes about the fires burning at the open end of the three-sided bunk house. From the ranchhouse, lighted with lanterns swung from the rafters, comes the music of fiddles, harmonicas, and 'gittars,' mixed with the clattering of bones and the stomp of booted feet accenting the beat of an old-time square dance. On occasion a wheezy phonograph emits a wail of rhythmic blues. Cane syrup bubbles in a great three-legged pot until thick enough to be scooped out, cooled, and seized in lard-smeared fingers for a taffy pull. Taffy is served throughout the evening, and usually more stimulating refreshments as well.

Red and white boundary stripes and a yellow 'sock' bellying in the wind mark the HOLOPAW EMERGENCY LANDING FIELD, 27.7 *m.*

HOLOPAW (Ind., place where something is hauled), 30.3 *m.* (79 alt., 500 pop.), built around a lumber mill, has a general store, hotel, and community church built by owners of the mill. To the northwest are large stands of cypress and pine; the timber is snaked out of the swamps and hauled to the mill by tractors. Negroes constitute a majority of workers and have their separate settlement. Many wrap a strip of red flannel around their arms, or an eelskin about their legs, to ward off 'rheumatiz.'

West of Holopaw, the route enters a rolling sandy section carpeted with saw palmetto and stands of blackjack oak. Far back from the highway cypress hammocks rise cloudlike against the sky. Citrus groves alternate with small truck farms producing winter vegetables. In April, after crops of green beans, peppers, and squash have been harvested, the fields are planted to corn. At 40.1 *m.* is (R) ALLIGATOR LAKE (*bathing, fishing, camping facilities*), 4 miles long and 1 mile wide, near the divide between the Kissimmee and St.Johns River basins; deer are found in the swamps east of the lake.

A small tourist camp (L), 41.1 *m.*, occupies the SITE OF SHAKER VILLAGE, founded in 1905 by Shakers from New York State. This religious group set up a commune, cultivated land, and for a few years prospered, but the venture eventually failed.

ST.CLOUD, 46.1 *m.* (63 alt., 1,863 pop.), on the eastern shore of EAST TOHOPEKALIGA LAKE, is sometimes called G.A.R. town because of the numerous veterans of the Grand Army of the Republic who settled here in 1909. In architecture, business, and mode of living, St.Cloud is typical of a northern village. May 30, Memorial Day, is not generally observed in Florida, but at St.Cloud it is celebrated with parades, services, and speeches. The town has an attractive park and a recreational center. Negroes have always been excluded from St.Cloud.

Founded in the early 1880's, St.Cloud prospered for almost a decade from its cattle shipments; later it became headquarters for lumber and naval-stores operators when Hamilton Disston of the Philadelphia Saw Works bought and began to develop millions of acres in the surrounding region, previously a wilderness of prairie, swamp, and hammock. At that time the State Internal Improvement Fund controlled 13,000,000 acres, described as overflow and swamp land, and was authorized to use this to stimulate railroad construction. But Florida railroads were bankrupt, and the Internal Improvement Fund was involved from having guaranteed payment of interest and principal on the railroads' bonds. To extricate itself, the State attempted to sell the lands, but under the circumstances it proved impossible to attract buyers.

Learning that Disston and friends were fishing and hunting above Tarpon Springs, Governor William D. Bloxham joined their party, described the financial plight of the State, and in 1881 succeeded in selling Disston and his associates 4,000,000 acres of land at 25¢ an acre. The purchase included scattered tracts extending from above Tarpon Springs on the Gulf, more than half way across central Florida, and as far south as Lake Okeechobee and the Caloosahatchee River. This transaction replenished the State treasury, attracted attention to Florida's resources, and opened the way for other entrepreneurs, notably Henry Plant and Henry Flagler (*see Transportation*).

A system of canals was laid out to drain Lake Okeechobee. Before work was halted by Disston's death, about 200,000 acres had been reclaimed as fields and pastures. In 1886 a large sugar-cane plantation was established in the vicinity of St.Cloud, and in the following year a sugar mill was built on the outskirts of the town. Numerous sawmills were erected to exploit the vast timber resources of the region.

In the late 1880's an English group settled near by on and above the shores of East Tohopekaliga Lake, to grow citrus. Many were of wealthy families and came with cricket bats and polo ponies. Several golf courses were laid out, among the first in the State, and a large frame hotel was built for the comfort of fashionable winter vacationists. The freeze of 1894–95 destroyed the citrus groves, and many of the planters drifted away. Set in attractive English gardens, a number of old houses still stand, occupied by descendants of the English pioneers.

West of St.Cloud are pine flatwoods and occasional stretches of oaks. An old Disston drainage canal, 48.7 *m.*, lined with willows and all but choked by hyacinths, was dug between Lake Tohopekaliga (Ind., fort site) and East Tohopekaliga in 1884. For several years small steamers plied the canals between these lakes and Lake Okeechobee. Deer and wild turkey are plentiful in the surrounding hardwood and cypress hammocks.

Gray streamers of moss festoon trees and telephone wires. Gathered by white and Negro workers, heaped high on large trucks until they resemble hay wagons, and carried to neighboring gins, the moss is dried and processed for upholstering purposes (*see Tour 6a*). Seedling groves, many dating back to the early years of the century, form attractive settings for large two-story frame houses, with wide porches and galleries.

KISSIMMEE, 55 *m.* (70 alt., 3,163 pop.) (*see Tour 2c*), is at the junction with US 17 (*see Tour 2c*).

Tour 11

Vero Beach—Lake Wales—Bartow; 97.8 *m.* State 30, State 79.

Hard-surfaced roadbed throughout; watch for cattle along highway.
Route paralleled by Seaboard Air Line Ry. between Hesperides and Bartow.
Good accommodations at Vero Beach, Lake Wales, and Bartow.

Before this coast-to-highlands route was built, travel through the dense hammock undergrowth of this region necessitated the use of axes; the inundated lowlands proved especially formidable. Between the wet and dry areas are thickly wooded sections called 'scrubs,' into which the Indians retreated and escaped capture when pursued by U.S. troops during the Seminole War. Today, penetrated by good roads, the region contains many lumber mills, citrus groves, and cattle ranches, but is still sparsely settled between Vero Beach and Lake Wales.

State 30 branches west from US 1 (*see Tour 1c*) at VERO BEACH, 0 *m.* (19 alt., 2,268 pop.) (*see Tour 1c*).

West of Vero Beach the narrow rough asphalt road is bordered with tall clumps of bamboo, brilliant scarlet hibiscus, graceful cocos plumosa palms, and symmetrical Australian pines, rows of which run on both sides of the highway, serving at once as windbreaks and boundaries of small citrus groves.

Thick tangled carpets of St.Augustine creeper grass, the seeds of which are said to have been introduced into America by the Spanish in the fodder brought for their horses, form bright green lawns about suburban houses, their gardens bright with bougainvillea, bignonia, and honeysuckle.

The elevated roadbed is paralleled by deep canals, choked with reeds, willows, cattails, and pond lilies. Fishermen cast their lines from the road embankment and from boats drifting among the lily pads. Narrow footbridges lead to cabins built on higher ground and almost concealed by cabbage palms and a tangle of jungle growth; some are used on holidays and weekends by fishing parties from Vero Beach; others are permanently occupied and surrounded by truck gardens. Bird life is protected here, and scarlet cardinals, meadowlarks, mockingbirds, doves, and herons are numerous. Dense woods give way to patches of second-growth pine and stretches of cut-over land, dotted with fire-blackened stumps and hillocks of rotting yellow sawdust, the only remains of long abandoned sawmills.

YEEHAW (Ind., wolf), 29.8 *m.* (8 pop.), a trading center for cattlemen and naval-stores workers, consists of a few scattered frame houses, a filling station, and a general store, being typical of a dozen other small settlements which sprang up along the Florida East Coast Railway during 1915–16 when sawmills were cutting pine and cypress in this region.

West of Yeehaw are 40 miles of grassy prairie, a vast pasture for herds of cattle. Occasional cowboys are met, either on horseback or in automobiles, wearing high laced boots, overalls, and Stetsons, but with no chaps, bandanas, or six-shooters.

To this region Coacoochee (Wild Cat) led his tribe during the Seminole Wars when striving vainly to prevent the expulsion of his people from Florida. Captured when he came under a flag of truce to visit his father, imprisoned in St.Augustine, Coacoochee was placed in Fort Marion (*see St.Augustine*) in October 1837, but later escaped through a narrow embrasure at the top of his cell and rejoined his band. In March 1841, Colonel William J. Worth persuaded the chief to visit a military camp on the Kissimmee River. Coacoochee and several of his band arrived in colorful garb, taken from the wardrobe of an American theatrical troupe they had attacked and killed the previous year. He promised to urge his people to depart in peace but when submission was delayed, the chief was arrested at Fort Pierce in May and started on his journey westward. Brought back to Tampa at Colonel Worth's insistence, Coacoochee was informed that he would be hanged if he did not immediately bring about the submission of his entire band. Realizing that defeat was inevitable, he succeeded through emissaries in bringing to the military post the remainder of his people. The chief and 211 of his tribesmen were removed to the Indian Territory in October 1841. Several years later they emigrated to Mexico, and while living there in the Santa Rosa Mountains, Coacoochee died of smallpox in 1856.

The highway crosses the KISSIMMEE RIVER, 52.8 *m.*, which here emerges from LAKE KISSIMMEE, one of the largest fresh-water lakes in the State. Both lake and river offer excellent fishing (*black bass, perch, pick-*

erel, bream, catfish). At the west end of the drawbridge are a gas station, a refreshment stand, and a fishing camp (*boats, bait, and tackle*). The Kissimmee River, fringed with hammock growth of oak, hickory, and magnolia, empties into Lake Okeechobee 100 miles to the south. The valley is rich and productive; well adapted to the growing of citrus fruit and garden truck and for use as pasture, it has attracted cattlemen, farmers, trappers, naturalists, sportsmen, and adventurers since the close of the Seminole Wars.

Attempts to make the river navigable began in 1883, when canals were dug and channels cleared, but not until the 1890's was a channel dredged to permit passage of small side-wheel and stern-wheel steamers. Many were built in Kissimmee (*see Tour 2c*), but the majority came from northern Atlantic ports or were brought down the Ohio and Mississippi Rivers, across the Gulf of Mexico, and up the Caloosahatchee River. All were light draft—so light, in fact, that some skippers boasted that they could navigate anywhere in the valley after a heavy dew. Landings with such names as Grape Hammock, Rattlesnake Hammock, Alligator Bluff, and Mary Belle, were built to accommodate passengers and freight, which included hides, furs, bird plumes, citrus fruit, and naval stores. With the construction of railroads and improved highways after 1920, commercial traffic on the river ceased. By 1930 the neglected waterways had become so filled with sandbars that they were navigable only by rowboats and canoes.

Although it has been a century since the first white settlers in the valley built their cabins, cleared patches for corn and sugar cane, and set out small groves, this region is still primitive, an isolated haven for deer, wild turkey, quail, rabbits, raccoons, and opossums. For miles along the river the only signs of human habitation are occasional crude piers and landing platforms.

Fur trappers have long plied their trade along the river and its branches; thousands of muskrat and other pelts are shipped annually. The Florida muskrat, a singular animal found only on the peninsula and in the swamps of lower Georgia, is about half the size of his northern cousins, and differs from them also in other respects. His tail is flat and not round, and his hind feet are not webbed for swimming. In trapping muskrats no bait is used; the trapper relies on his skill and cunning to place the trap so that prey will walk into it. Traps of the latest type have one jaw to catch the foot of the muskrat and another that whips over his body, crushing it, preventing prolonged suffering, and removing all possibility of escape. So far no method has been devised to avoid the capture and death of young muskrats, known as 'kits,' whose small pelts are of no value. Skins of full-grown muskrats bring an average price of $1.

West of the Kissimmee River are treeless prairies and occasional stretches of pine flatwoods, the habitat of the burrowing owl, a rather small white bird with brown spots, known locally as the Billy owl. Unlike most owls, he prefers daylight to dark; while small, he is aggressive and formidable, and will attack and kill nighthawks and other larger predatory birds. His presence in south Florida presents a mystery, for his nearest kin live on the western plains. These owls nest in abandoned burrows of foxes, salamanders, and other tunnelers, and are often seen standing guard at the mouth of their burrows. When approached, they make a series of rapid and profound bows, at once disconcerting and deferential, and with a final flip of the tail, whirl and disappear underground.

At 60.1 *m.* is the junction with State 79, which the route now follows.

As the highway ascends the eastern slope of the central Florida ridge section, forests of longleaf pine and of blackjack, live, and turkey oak, supplant saw palmetto and wiregrass, which in turn give way to large citrus groves as the narrow road mounts to higher levels.

HESPERIDES, 72.1 *m.* (118 alt., 50 pop.), a small village surrounded by orange groves, was well named for the mythological Greek garden in which grew the precious 'golden apples' sought by Hercules as one of his twelve labors.

At 73.3 *m.* is the junction with a county road.

Right 1 *m.* on this road to the SHRINE OF STE.ANNE DES LACS (*open*), built in 1920 by a group of French-Canadians of the Roman Catholic faith who settled on the near-by shores of Lake Anne. Pilgrimages are made here annually as to the shrine of Our Lady of Lourdes in France and the shrine of Ste.Anne de Beaupré in Canada. High dignitaries and priests of the Roman Catholic church in the United States and Canada assist the local priest in conducting the ceremonies. Tableaux and scenes from the Holy Land in murals, sculpture, and paintings decorate the little church. Relics of special interest include a particle of bone from the finger of Ste.Anne, and two pieces reputedly from the True Cross. The latter repose in a specially designed sanctuary (R); near the shrine is (L) a Biblical MUSEUM (*open*), containing 18 tableaux and 28 scenes from the Holy Land, executed by the French artist, François Morsollier.

LAKE WALES, 79.3 *m.* (152 alt., 3,401 pop.) (*see Tour* 15), is at the junction with State 8 (*see Tour* 15).

West of Lake Wales the narrow rough asphalt road, unmarked for miles and little traveled, winds around numerous small lakes and through large well-tended citrus groves, many screened from the road by rows of palms and bright subtropical shrubbery. Purple and red bougainvillea and golden flame vines cover gateways to the groves; driveways are landscaped with gay-colored petunias, phlox, and zinnias.

During the unprecedented drought in the spring of 1938, grove owners piped water from near-by lakes and streams to save their trees. Thousands of feet of old fire hose and carloads of galvanized pipe were laid between the rows; pumps operated day and night. Owners remote from lakes or creeks hauled in drums of water. Groves were harrowed and raked free of grass to eliminate danger from the fire sweeping the surrounding woods. Dense smoke from smoldering peat bogs in the Everglades blanketed the region and obscured the sun, darkening the sky as far north as Tampa.

The highway crosses PEACE CREEK, 96 *m.*, here narrow and shallow as it winds through a large cypress swamp. Rising in Lake Hancock, it flows into Charlotte Harbor at Punta Gorda, some 75 miles to the south. As early as 1544 the stream appeared on maps of Spanish explorers as Rio de la Paz (river of peace). The Seminole called it Talako Chapko (cow peas), for the abundance of such peas along its banks. Thus, curiously, translations of both the Spanish and Indian names have an almost identical sound in English.

The highway passes large excavations dug to obtain pebble phosphate, deposits of which were discovered along the Peace River in 1884. Many of the abandoned pits are filled with water and blanketed with hyacinths, but this relatively small area continues to produce more than half the world's supply of pebble phosphate, so called because it consists of granules and pebbles of various sizes. It is found embedded in a matrix of sand and orange-red clay, which is also rich in fossils of land and sea animals (*see Tour 20*).

BARTOW, 97.8 *m.* (126 alt., 5,269 pop.) (*see Tour 2d*), is at the junction with US 17 (*see Tour 2d*).

Tour 12

Fort Pierce—Okeechobee—Childs—Arcadia—Manatee—Bradenton; 156.2 *m.* State 8, State 18, State 161.

Hard-surfaced roadbed throughout; watch for cattle along highway.
Route paralleled by Seaboard Air Line Ry. between Arcadia and Bradenton.
Good accommodations.

This route from ocean to Gulf penetrates long stretches of flatlands and occasional cypress and hardwood hammocks and skirts the northern edge of the Everglades into an area of extensive citrus groves and truck farms. Signboards are conspicuously absent along the highway. Mosquito control units have done much since 1935 to eliminate insect pests, formerly an annoyance to travelers between Fort Pierce and Okeechobee.

State 8 branches west from US 1 (*see Tour 1c and d*) at FORT PIERCE, 0 *m.*, (24 alt., 4,803 pop.) (*see Tour 1c*).

West of Fort Pierce and outlying citrus groves the route winds through HALPATIOKEE SWAMP (Ind., alligator water), the hideout until recent times of cattle rustlers. Familiar with the trails, quick on the trigger, the thieves were for a time unmolested. As the swamp offered poor pasture, they promptly butchered the stolen stock, dressed the meat, and sold it to east-coast markets. At this time and for long after the region was known as 'Hungry Land.'

A large farm (R), 11.7 *m.*, has 800 acres growing tomatoes, peppers, Irish potatoes, and squash. More than 50 white and 600 Negro men are regularly employed here, and during harvesting season 150 additional whites are brought in to grade and pack the produce for shipment to northern markets.

For 25 miles is barren cut-over land, devoid of settlements. Once heavily timbered, the section was stripped of marketable lumber before 1900. Here and there mounds of rotting sawdust and abandoned shacks indicate where large sawmills and logging camps once stood. Cattle gather at numerous waterholes, or stand knee deep amid the lily pads in roadside ditches. An occasional cowhand rides his pony slowly across the woods' range. Some of these ponies, known as marshtackies (*see Tour 1b*), are descended from early Spanish stock. As a rule, they are smaller than the cow ponies of the western ranges, and exhibit great nimbleness and sureness of foot in penetrating treacherous palmetto land, filled with swamps, stumps, and fallen trees, but for 50 years most Florida cowboys have been riding mounts brought from Texas and Georgia.

OKEECHOBEE (Ind., *oki*, water, and *chobi*, big), 35.7 *m.* (38 alt., 1,795 pop.), seat of Okeechobee County, more than a mile north of LAKE OKEECHOBEE, has its business section built along a 5-block mall, planted with hibiscus and oleanders. Commercial center for the surrounding territory, the town ships hundreds of cars of winter vegetables annually; numerous poultry farms in the vicinity, a catfish shipping plant, and the breeding of giant bullfrogs provide additional sources of income.

Frog legs, or 'saddles,' bring high prices in the winter when frogs usually hibernate and are difficult to capture. Frog farmers enclose bottom lands, ponds, or swamps; as frogs live on insects, breeders strew the runs with rotting meat to attract blowflies. Some plant flowers and shrubs to lure bugs, and occasionally install electric lights to attract moths, beetles, and other nocturnal insects. A female frog lays from 10 to 30 thousand eggs a year; tadpoles appear from 60 to 90 days later, but frogs are seldom marketed before they are two years old.

One of the fiercest engagements of the Seminole Wars was fought in this vicinity on Christmas Day 1837, when Colonel Zachary Taylor led a force of 1,000 men through the swamps to attack less than half that number of Indians under Billy Bowlegs (*see Tour 13*). The Seminole retreated after three hours of hand-to-hand encounter, leaving few dead and wounded; American casualties totaled 138. Years later Billy Bowlegs visited Washington and on being escorted through the buildings of the Capitol and viewing many statues and paintings with lackluster eye, he suddenly halted before a portrait of Zachary Taylor, grinned, and exclaimed: 'Me whip!'

The highway crosses the WARREN HARDING MEMORIAL BRIDGE, 46.3 *m.*, over the broad and shallow KISSIMMEE RIVER (*see Tour 10*).

BRIGHTON, 53.6 *m.* (50 pop.), an incorporated community, was founded in 1924 by enterprising property owners who built (R) BRIGHTON LODGE, center of a Florida dude ranch, on which roam several small herds of cattle, and some real and many pseudo cowboys.

Left from Brighton on improved State 145 to SEMINOLE VILLAGE, 7.6 *m.*, on a 35,660-acre reservation. Here approximately 100 Indians are employed on CCC projects in road building, fencing, water development, and revegetation. All this group are

Cow Creek, or Muskogee, differing in language from the Big Cypress Indians of the west coast, who are Mikasuki. Reservation Indians farm the center of cleared hammocks and herd some 800 head of Hereford and Angus cattle on a subsistence basis. Families live in groups of palm-thatched *chuckoos*, 10 feet by 12 feet, containing raised sleeping platforms covered with mosquito netting. One *chuckoo* serves as the family dining room, another as the kitchen. Both children and adults receive instruction in the village school, which is equipped with modern facilities, including a community workroom and shop, men's and women's showers, and a laundry.

The route traverses flat open country dotted with sawgrass swamps and cabbage palm oases. Herds of cattle graze on the fenced range; salt licks under small covered shelters appear at intervals; the high banks of roadside ditches are cut through here and there to allow livestock to reach water.

CHILDS, 69.7 *m.* (132 alt., 30 pop.), on Lake Placid, is at the junction with State 67 (*see Tour* 15).

West of Childs the route follows State 18, crossing an area of white sand covered with blackjack oak, scrawny shortleaf pine, and clumps of sparkleberry bushes. Low saw palmettoes carpet the slightly rolling terrain. Creeping along the ground, the scaly trunk of the palmetto divides, sending out root stems which crawl over and under one another like writhing serpents. This strange growth is more clearly revealed after fire has swept away other vegetation. In moist regions the palmetto grows more erect; in and around swamps it often becomes a tree (*see Tour 2a*).

The 2,000-acre DORR FIELD (L), 89.8 *m.*, was established by the Government during the World War as an aviation training camp. Buildings and equipment were later sold at auction, and nothing remains but crumbling concrete roads, runways, and massive foundations, all but concealed by rank palmetto growth. West of the field the road passes (L) a large boom-time subdivision that did not progress beyond the blueprint stage, the entrances to its boulevards-to-be still marked by large stucco gate posts. Such subdivisions are typical of many so-called 'bus' developments, to which people were brought in busses from all parts of the State to be fed, entertained, and 'high-pressured' into buying small tracts of raw prairie land, represented as ideal for truck farms.

ARCADIA, 102 *m.* (29 alt., 4,082 pop.) (*see Tour 2d*), is at the junction with US 17 (*see Tour 2d*).

HORSE CREEK, 109 *m.*, a tributary of Peace River, is crossed on a long plank bridge. Stucco cottages built during the boom of the 1920's stand (L) on the high wooded bank. Before 1880 this and neighboring streams were favorite haunts of 'Alligator' Platt, renowned hunter, whose exploits are preserved in the lore of south Florida. He would hide along a bank until a 'gator floated to the surface, and then dive in and tackle the creature, it is said. Man and beast would vanish in a tremendous swirl of muddy water. Platt would shortly reappear, astride his victim, and ride it triumphantly ashore, his thumbs hooked in the 'gator's eyes. It was easy to capture the biggest saurian that way, with no expense for gunpowder and shell, said Platt, recommending the method to his contemporaries.

PINE LEVEL, 110.9 *m.* (30 pop.), a scattered settlement of small frame houses, owes its existence to the construction of the highway, which attracted farmers and sawmill workers from the original town of Pine Level two miles to the southwest. The early town, seat of De Soto County from 1866 to 1887, prospered for a time as a logging and sawmill center.

An abandoned branch of the Seaboard Air Line, constructed in the early 1890's to haul timber, parallels the highway for several miles. Reckless lumbering almost deforested this area, now used for grazing purposes; signs along the highway proclaim the district an open range. Rutted dirt roads lead to distant ranches, their names and brands displayed at turn-offs, but no houses are visible. 'The prairies furnish sustenance for lowing herds which are as wild as deer,' wrote a visitor in 1879. 'They are captured by a song the cowboys sing resembling nothing else in the world. Where it originated none can tell: but the cattle gather from afar whenever it is sung, and are then driven at will by those long, rawhide lashes that pop like pistols, many times cutting out pieces of quivering flesh, at which sight humanity would shrink.'

MYAKKA CITY, 123.7 *m.* (125 pop.), is a roadside settlement and trading center for near-by truck farmers and citrus growers along the MIAKKA RIVER (Ind., very large). In this section live many old-time Floridians, who settled here shortly after the War between the States. Almost all are landowners; their sun-bleached one-story frame houses, with center hall or 'breezeway,' sit well back from sandy roads. They are raised high above the ground on posts to prevent dry rot and to escape attacks of termites; all have vine-shaded verandas, occupied on Sunday by a rocking-chair brigade; even the poorest houses have well-tended vegetable and flower gardens about them, and in many cases a few citrus trees. These people live on their own garden produce, slaughter and cure their own meats, and depend on the market for little.

At 130.9 *m.* is the junction (R) with State 161, which the route now follows.

The narrow road traverses a region of cut-over land, palmetto swamps, and hardwood hammocks, the nesting place of scarlet cardinals, painted buntings, and yellow-throated warblers; herons and other waterfowl feed in the marshes. As the route approaches the Gulf, citrus groves become more numerous, many protected by windbreaks of Australian pines. Bee culture has long been profitable in this section; white hives dot the groves and open fields. Before the introduction of patented hives, a hollow log of the gum tree, known as a bee-gum, was set flat on the ground and used as a hive.

The highway crosses the BRADEN RIVER, 153 *m.*, which was named for Dr. Joseph Braden (*see below*), a pioneer settler in this district.

MANATEE, 155 *m.* (17 alt., 3,219 pop.), founded in 1842 on the south bank of the Manatee River, the oldest community in the county, has wide quiet streets bordered with old brick and frame dwellings, many erected when dormers, cupolas, and jigsaw cornices were in fashion. Ornamental iron fences enclose spacious lawns; large oaks lock arms over principal thoroughfares.

Extensive sugar plantations were laid out along the river here as early as 1846; mills were erected; raw sugar was shipped by schooners to New

Orleans and other Gulf ports. This prosperous trade ended in 1862 when Federal gunboats blockaded the mouth of the river, and armed forces advanced upstream, burning mills and plantation houses. Many orange and lemon groves were planted, but want of rapid transportation and primitive packing methods retarded development until the railroad was extended to Tampa in 1884. Today, the city depends on lumbering and the growing and packing of fruits and vegetables.

Manatee became a popular winter resort in the 1870's, at which time tourists and health seekers, as well as mail and supplies, were transported on sailing vessels from Cedar Keys, the nearest railroad station. Boarding houses stimulated appetites by offering wild turkey, venison, a variety of fresh- and salt-water fish, and lemon pie; one hostelry advertised its 'well-tended croquet grounds.' Grapes flourished, but no use was made of them, which led a visiting woman writer to remark that if the manufacture of wine were encouraged, 'this beastly drunkenness from strychnine whiskey would very soon be abandoned.'

The RUINS OF BRADEN CASTLE, near the confluence of the Manatee and Braden rivers, consist of the roofless remains of a two-story concrete house, with four chimneys, built about 1850 by Dr. Joseph Braden on his sugar plantation here. For several years the Indians were troublesome, and the dwelling often became a refuge for neighboring families when alarms were sounded. The last outbreak occurred in 1856, when Indians attacked the house while the Braden family was at supper. Although driven off, the raiders took with them Negro slaves, mules, and booty. The property was swept by a woods fire in 1903, and nothing remains but the crumbling outer walls of the house and the large ruins of a near-by sugar mill. The grounds, heavily wooded with oaks, palms, and pines, are used as a camp site by the Camping Tourists of America, Inc.

OLD MANATEE CEMETERY, Manatee Ave. and 15th St., sheltered by moss-draped cedars, contains the blackened vaults and weathered gravestones of many pioneer settlers, the oldest one bearing the name of Henry S. Clark, dated 1850.

Left from Manatee on the Old Sarasota Road, paved, is ONECO, 4.2 *m.* (30 alt., 200 pop.). Here, in 1883, Robert Reasoner established the ROYAL PALM NURSERIES (*open* 7:30–5:30 *weekdays;* 9.30–5:30 *Sundays*), in which grow mangoes, rare palms, ferns, vines, and other ornamental tropical plants. Citrus culture on the African Gold Coast was started with trees from this nursery. South American countries, China, and the Soviet Union buy citrus and avocado stock here. In the nursery's collection are the rose-pink bougainvillea, now in its 13th year, and the salmon-pink bougainvillea, nearly 40 years old.

BRADENTON, 156.2 *m.* (21 alt., 5,986 pop.) (*see Tour* 4*c*), is at the junction with US 41 (*see Tour* 4*c*).

Tour 13

West Palm Beach—Belle Glade—Clewiston—Fort Myers—Punta Rassa; 139 *m.* State 25.

Hard-surfaced roadbed throughout; long stretches with no service stations; watch for cattle.
Route paralleled by Atlantic Coast Line Ry. between South Bay and Clewiston; by Seaboard Air Line Ry. between LaBelle and Fort Myers.
Good accommodations.

State 25, the direct route from Palm Beach on the Atlantic to Fort Myers and the Gulf coast, crosses the northern section of the Everglades, America's largest swamp, its 4,000 square miles far exceeding the extent of the Dismal Swamp in Virginia and Okefenokee Swamp in Georgia and North Florida. The route follows the shore of Lake Okeechobee, encircled with fertile black fields growing great quantities of winter vegetables and sugar cane. Passing through the open range country of central Florida, reminiscent of the Old West with its cowboys and herds of range cattle, the highway follows the Caloosahatchee River to Fort Myers and the Gulf Coast at Punta Rassa, fringed with sand flats and low-lying keys overgrown with mangroves.

State 25 branches west from US 1 (*see Tour 1d*) in WEST PALM BEACH, 0 *m.* (14 alt., 26,610 pop.) (*see Tour 1d*).

The highway follows a straight course along the north bank of the West Palm Beach Canal (*bream, perch*), one of 5 channels cut from Lake Okeechobee to the Atlantic, part of an extensive project to drain the Everglades, still a vast wilderness. The territory first became known to Americans when troops were sent in pursuit of the Seminole. By 1839 numerous expeditions had penetrated the 'Glades. Buckingham Smith, a Federal reclamation inspector, visited the swamp in 1848 and described its wild beauty:

'Lilies and other aquatic flowers of every variety and hue are to be seen . . . and as you draw near an island, the beauty of the scene is increased by the rich foliage and blooming flowers of the wild myrtle, the honeysuckle, and other shrubs and vines that generally adorn its shores . . . The profound and wild solitude of the place, the solemn silence that pervades it, unless broken by the splashing of a paddle of the canoe or light bateau, with which only can you traverse the Pahayokee [Ind., *pay-hai-okee*, water grass] or by the voices of your *Compagnons du voyage*, add to awakened and excited curiosity, feelings bordering on awe . . . Except for the occasional flight of an eagle or a bittern, startled by the strange invaders of their privacy, or for a view of the fishes in the shallow waters

Along the Highway II

Photograph by courtesy of Van Natta Studio

SINGING TOWER, MOUNTAIN LAKE SANCTUARY

Photograph by courtesy of Jacksonville Journc

AFTER THE BEAR HUNT

ALLIGATOR FARM, ST. AUGUSTINE

Photograph by J. Carver Harris

PELICANS AND GULLS

Photograph by G. W. Romer

WHITE EGRET, A NATIVE OF THE EVERGLADES

Photograph by courtesy of Farm Security Administration

SEMINOLES

Photograph by The Everglades Federal Art Project
SEMINOLE INDIAN IN DUGOUT CANOE, THE EVERGLADES

SEMINOLE INDIAN HOME, NEAR LAKE OKEECHOBEE
Photograph by courtesy of Farm Security Administration

Photograph by Darel McConkey

TYPICAL PIONEER DWELLING

JUDAH P. BENJAMIN MEMORIAL (GAMBLE MANSION), BRADENTON

Photograph by courtesy of Farm Security Administration

THE SOUTHERNMOST HOUSE IN THE UNITED STATES, KEY WEST

Photograph by R. H. Le Sesne

HOME OF THE LATE JOHN D. ROCKEFELLER, ORMOND BEACH

STREET SCENE, BARTOW

Photograph by courtesy of Burgert Brothers

sliding swiftly from your boat as it goes near to them, your eye would not rest on a living thing abiding in this wilderness of grass, waters, shrubbery and flowers.'

The true Everglades, according to Smith, lie within a rock rim south of Lake Okeechobee, although any large marshy territory south and east of Lake Kissimmee is commonly regarded as part of the 'Glades, whether it lies within the rim or not. The 'Glades rest on a foundation of oölite limestone which dips slightly toward the south. The basin is scarred with potholes, fissures, jagged ridges, and seams, and was once an open sea, according to geologists. Wind and waves carried in sand until the water was sufficiently shallow for plant life to exist. By constant accretions through a long period the basin has been filled to the level of the marginal rock rim with deposits of sand and muck. The black muck soil of the 'Glades, the residue of centuries of rotted vegetation, is extremely fertile, and large areas have been cleared and planted to sugar cane, string beans, cabbages, lettuce, and other garden truck for northern winter markets.

Intensive efforts to reclaim the swamp began in 1903, when Florida obtained title to the 'Glades under one of the largest single patents ever granted by the Federal Government. In 1905 the Florida legislature established the Everglades drainage district, and in 1906 drainage operations started. The major problem was to control the overflow from Lake Okeechobee which inundated the territory to the south. To that end, the southern half of the lake was rimmed with dikes, and a series of canals was constructed, radiating from the lake to both the Atlantic and the Gulf. The main arteries are the West Palm Beach, Hillsborough, North New River, and Miami canals, which are joined by many smaller channels and ditches to canalize the flow. The Cross-State Canal, navigable by ships of 6-foot draft, has been established by joining the St.Lucie Canal, which extends from Stuart (*see Tour 1d*) to Lake Okeechobee, with a well-marked channel across the lake to Moore Haven (*see Tour 15*). Here a channel, with a lock, leads to Lake Hicpochee, the source of the Caloosahatchee River, down which the waterway proceeds to the Gulf.

At 2.1 *m.* is the PALM BEACH AIRPORT.

The LOXAHATCHEE PACKING PLANT, 13.7 *m.*, is surrounded by citrus groves. Long rows of feathery Australian pines serve as boundaries between individual groves and also as windbreaks.

Traversing a swampy area dotted with small pine and cypress hammocks, scattered stands of hardwood, and isolated clumps of cabbage palms, the highway crosses the West Palm Beach Canal at a point known as Twenty Mile Bend. Here, as far as the eye can see, the flatlands are carpeted with waving sawgrass, of the sedge or bullrush family, with long folded leaves edged with sharp teeth. Pale green in summer, brown in the dry season, the grass thrusts up a tall stalk, topped with panicles of brownish flowers. Mixed with it is gama grass, with long silken leaves, and the giant foxtail, occasionally 15 feet high, with flowering heads 2 inches in diameter. Less common is the spectacular *Agave Neglecta*, known as blue century plant, which grows in the pine lands along the borders of the 'Glades. Its huge rosette of basal leaves is frequently 14 feet in diameter, representing a growth of 6 or 7 years. From this base it shoots up at the rate of 2 feet a day a flowering stem, occasionally a foot in diameter, to a height of 40 feet.

In marshy spots wild rice flourishes; vegetable plots occupy higher bits of ground. Small animals find refuge in the undergrowth along the roadside; rabbits vanish at the approach of automobiles, but bolder field rats stand still and cock their heads at passers-by, scurrying for cover only when a car stops. In winter months mallards, blue bills, canvas backs, and other migratory waterfowl flock to the Everglades, a vast film of water dotted with miragelike hammocks of cypress and palmetto. During the summer rainy season the water often rises as much as 6 feet, but at other times its depth is from 3 inches to 3 feet.

The EVERGLADES EXPERIMENT STATION (*open*), 40.9 *m.*, is maintained by the University of Florida and the State Agricultural Experiment Station at Gainesville. Washingtonian palms line an entrance driveway bordered with lawns and flower beds. On 160 acres of black muck, characteristic of the greater part of the Everglades, 750 tropical and subtropical shrubs and trees have been planted, of which about 500 have thrived; a large greenhouse contains experimental plants. A 50-acre plot is used for the study of truck crops, and a 12-acre section for the study of general agricultural problems. Pure-bred Devons, native range cows, and cross-breeds graze on 48 acres, known as the 'cow cafeteria,' where the cattle are offered their choice of 14 different grasses, and studies are made to determine their value as fodder. In a laboratory building of hurricane-proof construction, with walls approximately 2 feet thick, are laboratories for research in plant pathology, agronomy, entomology, and soil.

BELLE GLADE, 42 *m.* (1,646 pop.), was hastily built in 1925 and virtually wiped out by the hurricane three years later in which hundreds of its citizens perished. The town has been rebuilt with more substantial structures; it has a municipal water plant, and for a short distance its main thoroughfare is brilliantly lighted at night. Belle Glade is a trading center for the fertile truck-growing area around Lake Okeechobee; from December to April tomatoes, green beans, peppers, and other winter vegetables are harvested, packed, and shipped, for the most part by Negro labor. A municipal ordinance requires that all Negroes, except those employed within the town, be off the streets by 10:30 p.m. On Saturdays they are permitted to remain in the business district until midnight. The fertility of the soil in this region is reflected in the Negro story of two boys who were planting corn one morning and discovered that it was sprouting immediately behind them. One boy shouted to the other to sit down on some of the seeds so that all of the corn would not grow to fodder before they finished planting. Next day the sitter dropped down a note, 'Passed through Heaven yesterday at 12 o'clock, sellin' roastin' ears to angels.'

Right from Belle Glade on State 143 to STATE PRISON FARM NO. 2 (*open Sat. and Sun. p.m.*), established in 1932 as a branch of the central institution at Raiford (*see Tour 3b*). On its 300 acres are 15 buildings, including cell houses, equipment sheds, and a sugar mill. Cane syrup, black-eyed peas, and navy and lima beans are shipped from the farm to other State institutions.

The highway roughly follows the eastern shore of Lake Okeechobee, but its waters are hidden behind the massive dike, or levee, which rims the entire southern half of the lake. After the 1928 hurricane President Hoover visited the Everglades to view the devastated scene and promised aid to prevent such widespread destruction in the future. In 1930 money was appropriated by Congress for the building of the levee. Built of earth, rock, and marl, 200 feet wide at the base and from 10 to 30 feet wide at the top, the levee rises 34 feet above mean low water and is 66 miles long. While its primary purpose is to protect life and property in the Everglades, it also makes possible the Cross-State Ship Canal (*see above*) from St.Lucie Inlet on the Atlantic to the mouth of the Caloosahatchee on the Gulf. Between the dike and the road are rich muck lands growing large crops of winter vegetables.

Tall royal palms and Australian pines border the route (R), and beyond extend vast fields of sugar cane. At intervals along the railroad tracks parallel to the highway are loading platforms and warehouses, practically deserted 8 months of the year. Garages, filling stations, general stores; jooks advertising food, drink, and entertainment; and long rows of Negro shacks are scattered along both sides of the road under clumps of bright green banana trees, royal palms, and castor-bean plants. The castor-bean plant, which often attains the size of a small tree, was introduced in this section at the beginning of the World War when experiments were made on the use of castor oil as a lubricant for airplane motors. The cultivation of the bean was abandoned after the development of other lubricating oils, but the plant continues to thrive here.

PAHOKEE (Ind., *pahi-oki*, grass water), 10.8 *m.* (2,256 pop.), a town built along the highway below the Okeechobee dike, is a shipping point for winter vegetables. Large warehouses, acres of loading platforms, and offices of produce brokers are crowded between one- and two-story frame business buildings and rooming houses. General stores offer everything from tractors to silk stockings. From Christmas until April, Pahokee is a 24-hour town; long trains of refrigerated cars roll out for northern markets day and night; the streets are noisy and crowded; bars, restaurants, and gambling places are seldom closed. As a rule, buyers of larger commission houses go into the vegetable fields, purchase an entire crop, and arrange for picking, packing, and shipping. When they desire only a limited number of barrels or hampers, cash is paid at the loading platforms. Few of the 12,000 acres under cultivation here are for sale. Farms are rented at $10 to $12 an acre a season. Frequently three crops are grown a year. Beans mature in 45 days; tomatoes in 90. A large packing plant (*open*) chills vegetables to a temperature of 45° and ships 20 refrigerator carloads a day. Itinerant pickers, both white and Negro, known as 'traveling hands,' swarm into this region at harvest time, as into other fruit- and vegetable-growing districts of the State, occupying tents, rows of tumble-down cottages, and ramshackle boarding houses. In her novel *Their Eyes Were Watching God* (1937), Zora Neale Hurston vividly describes the scene:

'Day by day now the hordes of workers poured in. Some came limping in with their shoes and sore feet from walking. It's hard trying to follow your shoe instead of your shoe following you. They came in wagons from way up in Georgia and they came in truck loads from east, west, north, and south. Permanent transients with no attachments and tired-looking men with their families and dogs in flivvers. All night, all day, hurrying in to pick beans. Skillets, beds, patched-up spare inner tubes, all hanging and dangling from the ancient cars on the outside, and hopeful humanity, herded and hovering on the inside, chugging on to the muck. People ugly from ignorance and broken from being poor.

'All night now the jooks clanged and clamored. Pianos living three lifetimes in one. Blues made and used on the spot. Dancing, fighting, singing, crying, laughing, winning and losing love every hour. Work all day for money, fight all night for love. The rich black earth clinging to bodies and biting the skin like ants.

'Finally no more sleeping places. Men made big fires and fifty or sixty men slept around each fire. But they had to pay the man whose land they slept on. He ran the fire just like his boarding house—for pay.'

Between Pahokee and Canal Point the route, still bordered with an unbroken hedge of thick-standing Australian pines, follows almost in the shadow of the Okeechobee dike, a tantalizing barrier that screens the lake from passers-by. At each turn the motorist hopes for a rise in the road or a gap in the interminable embankment; but the road continues as level as a table top, and the dike marches on like the great wall of China. Little breeze stirs between the high pine hedge and the dike; mosquitoes and gnats fill the air; clouds of white and sulphur-colored butterflies dance in the sunlight along the road, and myriads perish on windshields and radiators. This narrow ribbon of muck land along the highway, with its lush growth of bananas, palms, and bright-flowering subtropical shrubs, was once the eastern shore line of the lake. Negro shacks, singly and in groups; stores; and ramshackle jooks bearing such names as 'Wildcat's Hole,' 'Joyland,' and 'Shuffle-Inn,' appear at frequent intervals.

Many Negroes remain at Pahokee throughout the summer, tending small gardens, fishing, and doing such odd jobs as mowing grass. The clack and rattle of hand- and motor-driven mowers might be mistaken for the whir of locusts. Some pickers save enough money to tide them over the slack months; others are content to fish a little, loaf a lot, and trust to their luck in the gambling houses that know no season.

CANAL POINT, 14.4 *m.* (926 pop.), another scattered community in the Everglades sugar-cane and winter-vegetable section, is built below the dike and along both banks of the West Palm Beach Canal. Close to the massive hurricane gates at the mouth of the canal is one of the few points where a public road leads to the top of the 63-mile dike.

The sugar industry in the Everglades was founded on development work done here in 1923 by F.E.Bryan, E.T.Anderson, and associates. Before any roads were built, a second-hand 6-roll sugar mill was transported on barges through the canal from West Palm Beach and set up here, grinding about 750 tons of cane a day during the season. The plant was dismantled a few years later when the mill at Clewiston (*see below*) was built.

A large refuse mound, 43 *m.*, marks the site of a Calusa Indian village. Excavations here by the Smithsonian Institution in 1927–28 brought to light arrow and spear points, awls, long pins, and pipes. In an adjoining mound were found carved wooden plaques evidently used in religious ceremonies.

West of Belle Glade the route parallels the grass-covered dike along the southern shore of Lake Okeechobee. Much of the land between the dike and road is cultivated by small truck farmers whose houses and barns rise on stilts amid a scattering of royal palms, banana trees, and matted clumps of castor-bean plants. The wide drainage ditch (L), choked with white lilies and cattails, borders vast fields of sugar cane. In summer freshly plowed fields are black as ink, against which stand out sharply white herons and egrets, which alight to feed on grubs. Rats do great damage, destroying fields by gnawing roots and stalks; at times they move like a gray carpet over canal banks and across the highway; poisoned mash is used to exterminate them, and millions of dead rodents attract hosts of buzzards.

The harvesting of sugar cane begins in November and continues through April. Cane in the Everglades averages 15 feet and often attains 20 feet. Viewed from the air, the waving green fields resemble a gigantic checkerboard, divided by regularly spaced canals and by broad open lanes used by 'crawler' tractors, field wagons, and railroad tracks. Where the lanes intersect the highway, planks are embedded in the road to enable tractors and other heavy machines to cross without damage to the pavement.

The first step in the preparation of sugar-cane fields is provision for adequate drainage and water control. Ditches, laterals, and subsidiary canals are dug; pumps are installed to force the flow into the main arterial canals;

'mole-drains,' 3 feet deep, are connected with the field ditches to control the height of the water table.

The soil is aerated by rotary plowing, and after lying fallow for a time is again plowed and then planted. Seed is not used; long segments of cane are planted, and out of each node, or eye, a 'stool' sprouts. In 12 months the crop is ready for harvest. Cut by hand, topped, and stripped, the cane is loaded in wagons and conveyed to railroad cars for transportation to the mills. In the Everglades a single planting will produce 7 or 8 crops, for as soon as the matured cane is cut, new cane sprouts from the underground rhizomes, or 'rattons.'

SOUTH BAY, 46.2 *m.* (235 pop.), an unincorporated community on Lake Okeechobee at the entrance to the North New River drainage canal, is the terminus of the Atlantic Coast Line from the west and the Florida East Coast Railway from the northeast. South Bay was practically destroyed by the hurricane of September 1928. Many residents fled to West Palm Beach and other cities; those remaining found little shelter, although a canal boat in the locks near by gave refuge to 150. The storm, it is estimated, brought death to 1,810 persons, most of them Negroes. The loss of life, the highest recorded for any Florida storm, was caused not by the direct force of the wind, but by waters blown inland from Lake Okeechobee, flooding settlements and farms along the shore. For weeks after the waters had subsided, crews searched the fields and gathered up unidentified bodies; these were stacked like cordwood, drenched with kerosene, and burned as a health measure.

Indians of the Everglades can predict hurricanes by noting 'when the sawgrass blooms.' When the pollen of the sawgrass is seen floating in the air, the Seminole seek higher ground. During the 1926 and 1928 storms no Indian was reported drowned. It is not the providential blooming of the sawgrass that foretells the storm, but an atmospheric condition that makes the pollen visible for several days before the terrifying phenomenon.

A Negro field worker who passed unscathed through several hurricanes has graphically described the velocity of a tropical gale: 'One day the wind blowed so hard, it blowed a well up out of the ground; blowed so hard, it blowed a crooked road straight. Another time it blowed an' blowed, an' scattered the days of the week so bad that Sunday didn't come till late Tuesday mo'nin'.'

An observation point, 48.8 *m.*, reached by a foot trail (R), offers an excellent view of Lake Okeechobee, the second largest fresh-water lake lying wholly within the United States, covering 700 square miles. Viewed from this point it is a huge brimming saucer of water. The islands close to shore, the majority under cultivation, are edged with tall Australian pines, which at a distance resemble green-plumed headdresses. Flocks of herons wade far out from shore to feed in the shallows. On windless days the water mirrors the intense cobalt blue of the sky and white puff-ball clouds. When lashed by tropical storms, the lake becomes as turbulent as a gale-swept sea. The lake and canals offer good fishing (*black bass, speckled perch, pickerel, and catfish*). Commercial fishing is a large industry (*see Tour* 15), and to circumvent fresh-water fishing regulations and allow fishing at all seasons, Lake Okeechobee has been declared salt water by State law.

LAKE HARBOR, 53 *m.* (260 pop.), is on the east bank of the Miami drainage canal at its emergence from Lake Okeechobee. The locks here permit passage of small craft from lake to canal. North of the locks are immense steel and concrete flood gates through the Okeechobee levee.

The OSCEOLA GROVES (L), (56.2 *m.*), consist of several hundred acres of citrus trees; a landscaped section flanks the highway. Between the rows of trees beans are planted to provide an additional crop and as coverage to keep out weeds.

CLEWISTON, 62.5 *m.* (949 pop.), founded in 1921 as a construction camp during the building of the Moore Haven-Clewiston Railroad, has substantial white stucco buildings, wide paved streets, a landscaped residential district, and several parks, with tennis courts, a nine-hole golf course (*greens fee* 50¢), and an emergency landing field. The community's water and light plants, telephone company, and hotel are owned by the Clewiston Company, a subsidiary of the United States Sugar Corporation. Sugar-cane fields surrounding the town are worked principally by Negroes, whose settlement is named Harlem. Several fishing camps on the lake offer accommodations for sportsmen. At the first traffic light a road leads (R) to the top of the dike (*parking space*), affording one of the few views of Lake Okeechobee in this section.

Left from Clewiston on an improved road to the CLEWISTON COMPANY SUGAR MILL (*open Nov.–Apr.*, 9–12 *a.m.*, 1–4 *p.m.; guides*), 1.4 *m.*; surrounding the mill are 10 camps, with a total of 750 buildings, including apartments, barracks for white workers, mess halls, a commissary, medical stations, and a grade school for Negro children.

The plant has a crushing machine with a daily capacity of 5,500 tons. Cars of cane are brought to the mill by the company's railroad and emptied by hydraulically-operated tilting tables into a receiving pit. From the pit the cane is conveyed to a battery of slashing knives, then to a crusher, where most of the juice is extracted, and on through a 'train' of 6 sets of rollers, which extract the remaining juice. From the rollers the juice passes through a liming treatment, is brought to boiling point in heaters, clarified, and conveyed to evaporators where excess water is removed; the remaining heavy syrup is sent to the crystallizer pans. After crystallization, the molasses is removed by centrifugals, and the raw sugar delivered to storage bins to await packing in 325-pound bags for shipment to the refinery. The refuse fiber, or 'bagasse,' is burned as fuel under the boilers. Use of this waste product is so efficient that it is necessary to use other fuel only on the first day of operation. In 1937–38 approximately 25,000 acres here produced 582,834 tons of sugar cane, from which were made some 53,000 tons of raw sugar and more than 4,000,000 gallons of syrup, or blackstrap molasses. The molasses, used principally in making alcohol, is shipped in tank cars. At the peak of the season 4,000 workers are employed here in the fields and mill. An annual harvest festival is held in April at the close of the season.

West of Clewiston and the sugar-cane area is a region of pine land, swamps, and flat green prairies, studded with low cypress hammocks and clumps of cabbage palms. Isolated farmhouses and scattered herds of cattle appear, for this is the eastern boundary of central Florida's open range. Shallow drainage ditches flank the highway, their banks matted with willows and ferns, the dark water brightened by patches of white and yellow lilies and purple hyacinths.

At 71.4 *m.* is the junction with State 67 (*see Tour* 15).

The highway skirts many palm hammocks and thick stands of second-growth pines. At intervals clumps of cypress appear, and from their dense green growth rivulets of amber-colored water trickle into roadside ditches. Ferns grow in profusion, and the sunlight traces lacy patterns on the black spongy earth. The wooded area gives way to low stretches of grassy pastures, some under water in summer, crisscrossed by barbed wire fences. Some fields are being cleared of palmetto growth; once cleared, an occasional clipping is all that is required to grow carpet grass, ideal forage for stock. Although some range lands are individually owned, most are leased at an annual rent of 5¢ an acre. Almost all cattle are herded by their owners, with the assistance of members of their family. Hired riders are paid an average of $1 a day, in addition to board and room; foremen occasionally receive as much as $10 a week. The yellow-gray spoil banks (R) mark the route of the Caloosahatchee Canal, a link of the Cross-State Canal (*see above*).

GOODNO, 86 *m.* (27 alt., 20 pop.), a scattered community with cattle pens and chutes along the railroad tracks, was named for E.E.Goodno, cattleman from Kansas, who did much to improve Florida beef stock by importing Brahma bulls from India in the 1860's.

The Brahma bulls are better foragers in many respects than the Florida woods cows. They have increased the weight of local breeds and enjoy a degree of immunity to tick fever; cattlemen attribute this to their profuse sweating, which presumably drowns the ticks. Accustomed to heat, the Brahmas graze under the torrid midday sun when other cattle seek shade.

Captain Francis Asbury Hendry, a cattleman who drove his herds into this section from Fort Meade about 1870, took up 30,000 acres hereabouts and became a cattle king; the county was later named for him. In association with Hamilton Disston (*see Tour* 10), who had purchased immense tracts in the territory, Hendry sponsored the building of the canal to link the Caloosahatchee River with Lake Okeechobee. Operations began in 1884 and continued until 1888, when a channel, 40 feet wide and 5 feet deep, was completed at the cost of $500,000. The canal was used principally by mail boats and by supply launches transporting furs and alligator hides. For years, hides were the chief products of this remote swampy region, and as many as 50,000 were shipped north annually. Prime uncured hides brought hunters $1 a linear foot.

Opposite Goodno, in the Caloosahatchee River, is the massive ORTONA LOCK, which has replaced a small lock built in 1912. This toll-free lock, Government-maintained, is 300 feet long and 50 feet wide; with a lift of 11.5 feet, it can accommodate ships of 8-foot draft.

A new industry in this section is the cutting of 'swamp cabbage,' which is shipped to factories on the east coast to be cooked and canned. The swamp cabbage is the bud of the cabbage palm, a delicacy long relished in Florida but only recently known elsewhere. Uncooked, it appears on hotel menus as hearts of palms, often at $1 a portion. Equipped with knife and ladder, cutters climb the palms and snip out the sheathed top buds, for which they receive 3¢ apiece. This ruthless beheading kills the trees, but continues without restriction. Palm fronds are also shipped to northern markets for use on religious occasions, particularly on Palm Sunday.

For long stretches west of Goodno the highway crosses the grassy prairies on which graze herds of sleek cattle. Slaughterhouses in Tampa employ large trucks and trailers to transport their beef cattle from this range to stockyard pens.

LA BELLE, 94 *m.* (12 alt., 397 pop.), seat of Hendry County, is one of the last strongholds of the native Floridian. The coming of the improved highway linking the backwoods town with gay resorts on both coasts inspired the erection of a theater, a hotel, several modern business buildings, and a tan stucco courthouse, four stories high. But rough unpainted pine houses of two and three rooms flank the many unpaved roads within the town; on the outskirts are primitive one-story cabins with palm thatched roofs; these cabins are perched high on stilts to provide dry quarters in the rainy season, and on hot days hogs, dogs, and children retire under them to keep cool. Kerosene lamps light these houses, and home-cured hides are sometimes used as bed 'kivers.' Often ragged tow-headed children are seen following a stoop-shouldered mother riding her youngest on her hip; 'grannies' sit in the shade smoking pipes or 'dipping' snuff, watching the road from under their sun bonnets.

La Belle was named by Captain Francis Asbury Hendry (*see above*) for his two daughters, Laura and Belle. Sawmilling, cattle shipping, and the hewing of ties are the principal occupations. The town has no police force; county officials maintain law and order. During the boom several real-estate developments were started in the flatwoods, but nothing remains today but half-obliterated signs and a few crumbling pillars.

Cowboys ride into town from the surrounding ranches, wearing broad-brimmed hats, high boots, and other conventional trappings. La Belle's big event is the Fourth of July rodeo, at which range hands compete in riding Florida broncos and 'bull-dogging' steers. Roping and whip-cracking contests follow spirited horse races, on which wagering is heavy. A barbecue supper concludes the day, and in the evening square dances are enjoyed in jooks and homes to the music of guitars and fiddles, accented by the thumps of heavy boots.

This cattle country was the scene of many feuds in early days. A ranchman, according to one story, was hunting wildcats one day when he met an enemy of long standing, stalked him, shot him dead, and pitched the body into his wagon along with the game he had bagged. On reaching La Belle he narrowly escaped being lynched, not because of the killing but for his disrespect in throwing a human corpse on his load of dead wildcats.

The first cool winter month, when fog rolls across the prairies and hound dogs begin baying at the moon, marks the beginning of the Florida hunting season. Many men in this area earn a living by trapping and remain in the woods for months at a time. Early in November old trucks, piled high with bedding, grub, cooking utensils, and traps, rattle off into the 'Glades and the Big Cypress country. Hounds balance precariously on the loads or are penned on runningboards. On high ground a makeshift shelter of cypress and palmetto logs, chinked with moss, is erected. Clean swamp water serves cooking and drinking purposes. Following dim but familiar trails and carefully covering their tracks, the men set steel traps at strategic points, stringing their 'lines' for miles. The traps, few of which are baited, are visited regularly; the catch is collected and brought to camp. The pelts are pinned on boards, or stretched on frames made from stalks of palmetto, and left to dry in the open until the underside of the skins crackle when touched; some are left damp and salted down.

At the end of the season trappers return home to bargain with local buyers or agents of northern furriers who travel from town to town in the Everglades' district. Many Seminoles bring in their furs. Business is transacted along the sidewalks, and payments are always in cash. Muskrat, opossum, raccoon, wildcat, and bay-lynx pelts are most common, but that of the otter is the most valuable. The Florida otter is larger than its northern brothers, and its fur of finer texture; an uncured otter pelt frequently brings $25 on the sidewalk market.

Left from La Belle on State 164 is IMMOKALEE (Ind., tumbling water), 26 *m.*, (44 alt., 448 pop.), known in 1869 as Gopher Ridge. The surrounding region is practically uninhabited and offers one of the best hunting grounds in the State. In 1884, on the recommendation of the Women's National Indian Association, the Federal Government purchased 80 acres here, built a sawmill, supplied mules, oxen, logging carts, and farming implements, and induced Indians to come in from their camps. Curiosity sufficiently overcame their fears to permit them to saw a few boards and pull the whistle cord on the mill boiler. That done, they slipped back to the swamps, refusing to accept the benefits offered by the Episcopal Indian Mission Church and School. Hope that the Indians might be drawn permanently to the settlement was abandoned; the mission was destroyed by a hurricane in 1926.

At 38.1 *m.* the landscape changes abruptly from flatwoods and prairie lands to shallow ponds and hammocks on the northern edge of BIG CYPRESS SWAMP. Unlike the muck lands of the Everglades to the east and south, this area of approximately 2,000,000 acres is not adaptable to agriculture. Subject to inundation, undrained, and practically inaccessible, the Big Cypress is little more than a vast morass. Seen from the air, it resembles a green carpet drenched with a hose. Wild game is plentiful, and occasional hunting parties, led by Seminole guides, penetrate the region.

In the final years of the Seminole War several bands of Indians, under the leadership of Billy Bowlegs (*see Tour* 12) and Hospertacke, took refuge in the Big Cypress Swamp and waged a bitter fight against their removal to western reservations. By decree of these leaders, any Indian discovered communicating with white men was put to death.

Along the highway southwest of La Belle the prairie is spotted with huckleberry bushes loaded with fruit in June; later, the ranges are mottled with scarlet and yellow tiger lilies. Willow sloughs are white with fuzzy blossoms, fragrant in the spring; bunches of tall sawgrass encircle the shallow sloughs, choked with gold and purple flags. Wading birds roost and build their nests among the thick willows. During mating season the white ibis flies high over the sloughs, wheeling and circling in the sunlight, then drops as swiftly as a falling plane. Just above the tree tops the birds miraculously recover themselves and soar upward again to repeat the performance.

ALVA, 106.3 *m.* (11 alt., 540 pop.), occupies one of the highest elevations along the Caloosahatchee River. The town, a trading center for neighboring farmers, many of whom raise turkeys, has a fruit-packing plant.

Between Alva and Olga large cypress hammocks are scattered along the route, but much of the country is low open pasture. Orange and grapefruit groves occupy higher drained ground. Artesian wells provide a plentiful supply of water for irrigation of truck farms.

OLGA, 112.8 *m.* (100 pop.), overlooking the broad Caloosahatchee River, was a popular overnight stop on the trail used by cattlemen in the 1870's when driving their herds from the ranges to ports at the mouth of the river. Before the establishment of regular boat service, the settlement was a station on the overland mail route between the upper reaches of the river and Fort Myers.

BUCKINGHAM, 116.7 *m.* (100 pop.), surrounded by citrus groves, was formerly called Twelve Mile Creek, because it lies approximately 12 miles northeast of Fort Myers. Cattle are still raised in this region, but beeves from surrounding ranches are no longer delivered on the hoof, and roistering cowboys with their 12-foot whips are seldom encountered. The Orange River (*boating, bathing, fishing*), links the town with Fort Myers.

Approaching Fort Myers, the route traverses a section of cut-over flatwoods from which came immense supplies of timber in the 1890's. Here and there small palm hammocks and isolated stands of oaks remain.

FORT MYERS, 125.6 *m.* (9 alt., 9,082 pop.) (*see Tour 4c*), is at the junction with US 41 (*see Tour 4c and d*).

The FORT MYERS COUNTRY CLUB, 128.6 *m.*, has an 18-hole golf course (*greens fee* $1).

The EVERGLADES NURSERY, 131.8 *m.*, on the WYOMEHATCHEE RIVER (Ind., whiskey creek), covers 50 acres and contains nearly a million plants; carloads of young palms are shipped to many parts of the United States. The bougainvillea exhibit is an annual February event.

At 136.2 *m.* is the junction with a paved road.

Left on this road to FORT MYERS BEACH, 7 *m.*, an 8-mile stretch of white sand on crescent-shaped ESTERO ISLAND. The beach, used as a motor highway, is bordered with cottages, small hotels, apartment houses, and a tourist camp. Boats, guides, and all equipment for surf and deep-sea fishing are available at the casino and many fish houses. On the island is a plant canning coquina and turtle soup. Turtles are brought from interior points. The coquina, also known as the donax or pompano clam, a tiny mollusk seldom longer than half an inch, is found in great quantities at the surf line on Florida beaches. Standing on end, they burrow into the sand as each wave recedes. Their shells of infinite color and variety of markings are used in the preparation of shell flowers, butterflies, portières, and other novelties sold in curio shops. The broth, served hot or chilled, is a great delicacy and one of Florida's popular native dishes. At special Christmas celebrations held on the beach, a barefoot Santa Claus steps from a speedboat and distributes gifts to island children under the coconut palms.

For five miles the highway is built high above tidal flats covered with stunted mangroves and tall salt grass. Armies of brown fiddler crabs scuttle across the road; these diminutive crabs are scavengers and live in holes in the mud at tide line. The male has one large claw, often the size of its body, which it carries aloft and waves much like a violinist using his bow.

The crab is a favorite food of the blue heron and is excellent bait for sheepshead.

PUNTA RASSA (Sp., flat point), 141.4 *m.* (7 alt., 55 pop.), a fishing village, occupies the site of a military outpose established in 1837. Later abandoned, it was temporarily re-established in 1841 at the close of the Seminole War. During the War between the States it was again used as a military post. In 1866 the townsite was surveyed by the International Ocean Telegraph Company, which established cable service between the United States and Cuba. For a time the old wooden blockhouse was used as an office; the official news of the sinking of the *U.S.S. MAINE* on February 15, 1898, was first received here. Storms later destroyed the blockhouse; the station was rebuilt but was abandoned in 1936 when the cable was extended to Fort Myers.

Punta Rassa was a cattle-shipping point from the late 1830's until the outbreak of the Spanish-American War. As there were no railroads in the region until the 1880's, cattle were driven overland by easy stages to the town and shipped to Cuba by schooner. In 1870 Jacob Summerlin built a 300-foot pier of hewn timbers, fastened with wooden pins, from which he shipped thousands of steers brought from the Kissimmee River ranges. At that time a 3-year old steer brought an average price of $6 at the pier, cost approximately $3 to ship, and sold for $15 or $20 in Cuban and Nassau ports. Frequently Spanish Government agents made their purchases on the hoof in Punta Rassa and arranged for their transportation. Payments for cattle were made in Spanish doubloons, worth approximately $16, and the gold pieces became the principal medium of exchange in the surrounding territory.

SANIBEL ISLAND, 3 *m.* (100 pop.), opposite the mouth of the Caloosahatchee River, is reached by ferry from Punta Rassa (*8 and 10 a.m., 2 and 4 p.m.; $1 for car and driver, additional passengers 35¢*). The island, 2 miles wide and approximately 12 miles long, is a State game preserve; native and migratory birds are plentiful and can be studied at close range; wild flowers grow profusely in spring and summer; the Gulf and bay offer excellent fishing at all seasons. A large combination dredge and factory here gathers, cracks, cooks, and cans clams.

Sanibel Island is notable for the number and variety of sea shells on its beaches. Every tide and storm wash ashore thousands of specimens of some 300 varieties. Among them are the multicolored calico shells, of which the pale lemon-yellow is the rarest; the lion's paw, a dark orange-red; the white, bowl-shaped, yellow-lined buttercup, which comes from deep water and is seldom found in pairs; the delicately scalloped rose cockle, its interior shading from pale salmon pink to deep rose, and often tinged with orange and purple; the large red-brown cockle, used for souvenirs and in the manufacture of trays, lamps, and other objects; the fragile white angel's wing; the Chinese alphabet, a smooth white shell with curious markings; and the slender polished olive, tapering at both ends and shading from dark brown to light tan, also called the Panama shell. Perhaps rarest of all is the junonia, a deep-sea mollusk, its creamy white exterior marked with spiral rows of square brown or orange spots. Perfect junonia specimens have sold for $200. Florida shore life is described in *Florida Sea Shells* (1936), by B.D.E.Aldrich and E.Snyder. The Sanibel Sea Shell Fair is held annually in February.

From the 90-foot SANIBEL LIGHTHOUSE (*open; fishing from pier and Bailey's dock*), on Point Ybel, east end of the island, is a broad view of the Gulf, mainland, adjacent islands, and San Carlos Bay.

WULFERT, 13 *m.* (10 pop.), at Blind Pass on the northern tip of the island, is surrounded by a dense tropical jungle in which towering coconut palms predominate.

On CAPTIVA ISLAND (Sp., captive), 16 *m.* (45 pop.), reached by a bridge, are a Government lighthouse and quarantine station. According to legend, the pirate Gasparilla imprisoned captured girls here, hence its name. Captiva Island, however, was listed on maps before the pirate is credited with coming to Florida. President Theodore Roosevelt came here often for deep-sea fishing. A giant devilfish, or manta, measuring 30 feet across and weighing more than 2 tons, was landed by him after an all-day battle. Nearly 50 steel-jacketed .30 caliber bullets were fired into the creature before it was beached on a small island in Blind Pass, which was afterwards called Devilfish Key; Roosevelt Beach here was named for the President.

Tour 14

(Thomasville, Ga.)—Tallahassee—Apalachicola—Port St. Joe—Panama City—Pensacola; US 319, US 98, State 53.
Georgia Line to Pensacola, 272.7 *m.*

Hard-surfaced roadbed, except for occasional short stretches of improved clay road; watch for cattle along highway.
Route paralleled by Seaboard Air Line Ry. between Tallahassee and St. Marks, and Sopchoppy and Carrabelle, by Apalachicola Northern R.R. between Apalachicola and Port St. Joe.
Good accommodations.

This route passes through a section heavily wooded with live oak, hickory, and pine, and winds southward into sandy lowlands where, during *ante-bellum* days, prosperous plantation owners established summer homes. Paralleling the Gulf coast, the road runs westward through a region that played a prominent part in the early days of Florida. Here are one-street towns, quiet in the sunlight, their weathered century-old houses still in use. In Apalachicola Bay, more than 400 years ago, a handful of despairing Spaniards, survivors of the disastrous Narváez expedition, launched makeshift boats in an attempt to sail to Mexico, which a few ultimately succeeded in reaching after almost incredible adventures. This region heard the ring of Spanish hammers when forts were built in the 1600's; it saw buccaneer ships and yardarm hangings; it quartered French, Spanish, and British garrisons in quick succession.

Section a. GEORGIA LINE to APALACHICOLA; 101.1 *m. US* 319

US 319 crosses the Georgia Line, 0 *m.*, 15.7 miles south of Thomasville, Ga. (*see Georgia Guide Tour* 6.)

In the Tallahassee Red Hills. an area of rich red clay, the wide sloping shoulders of the road are planted with Bermuda grass; groups of crape myrtle trees, bright with pink blossoms during spring and summer, are spaced at regular intervals. The State Highway Department has sunk wells along the route to provide motorists with cool water from an artesian flow.

Stretches of hardwood forest on both sides of the wide road, all fenced and posted against trespassing, stand on former plantations, now the private estates and playgrounds of wealthy vacationers. Caretakers' lodges appear occasionally along the highway, but owners' mansions are remote from the road, at the end of narrow wooded lanes. Signboards, filling stations, and roadside stands are conspicuously absent.

A small marble MONUMENT TO ROBERT E. LEE (R), 8.9 *m.*, reached by a flight of concrete steps, was erected by the United Daughters of the Confederacy.

LAKE HALL (*swimming, picnic facilities*), 12.9 *m.*, is a small summer resort shaded by large oaks and magnolias.

TALLAHASSEE, 18.8 *m.* (216 alt., 10,700 pop.) (*see Tallahassee*).

Points of Interest: State Capitol, Florida State College for Women, Florida A. & M. College, State Geological Survey Museum, old houses, and others.

Tallahassee is at the junction with US 90 (*see Tour 7b and c*).

Right from Tallahassee on the Old Ochlockonee Road to the MURAT HOUSE, 2 *m.*, a story-and-a-half frame structure with twin brick chimneys, built in the early 1800's for Prince Achilles Murat and his wife. Sheltered by a group of old live oaks and a single large magnolia, it stands on a plantation named Belle Vue by Princess Murat. Former slaves who remained on the plantation after the war are buried on the slope of the hill. Murat never occupied the house, but the princess spent her last years here on an annuity granted by Louis Napoleon (*see Tallahassee*).

When white men first came to Florida, the region of red clay hills south of Tallahassee was occupied by Apalachee Indians, whose culture was more advanced than that of most Florida tribes. Other southeastern Indians believed that the Apalachee lived in a country rich in gold and held them in high repute as warriors. Many stories of their bravery, pride, and stoicism appear in early Spanish chronicles. Braves suffered their hands and noses to be cut off for their defiance of Spanish authority. On one occasion, when a village was about to fall, all the inhabitants hanged themselves rather than submit to capture.

The red clay hills merge into a region of dry buff-colored sand; limestone crops out occasionally in small boulderlike patches a few feet square. The open forest of longleaf pine and scrubby blackjack oak is spangled with numerous cypress ponds and shallow lakes.

WOODVILLE, 28.8 *m.* (42 alt., 200 pop.), is a farming community; naval-stores operations and the cutting of cross ties provide additional employment.

Left from Woodville on State 354, graded, to RHODES SPRINGS (*bathhouses, dance pavilion*), 4.6 *m.*, four springs shaded by large water oaks, the largest being 85 feet deep.

At 5 *m.* is (L) the NATURAL BRIDGE STATE MONUMENT; here the St.Marks River disappears underground, rising to the surface a short distance to the south. A monument in the 6-acre park marks the site of a battle fought here on March 6, 1865, when a group of boys from the West Florida Seminary in Tallahassee joined Confederate soldiers and on this natural bridge halted a Federal march on Tallahassee, the only Confederate capital east of the Mississippi never captured by Union troops. In the park are the remains of a plank road built in 1840 from St.Marks.

WAKULLA, 34.5 *m.* (17 alt., 497 pop.), bears in corrupted form the name of an early Indian tribe of Florida, the Guacara.

1. Left fom Wakulla on an unimproved road is NEWPORT, 4.2 *m.*, on the St.Marks River. Founded in 1843 after a hurricane had destroyed Port Leon, farther down the river, Newport prospered as a resort for many years.

2. Left from Wakulla on a graded sand road is ST.MARKS, 6 *m.* (8 alt., 217 pop.), a fishing village with a quarter-mile waterfront. On the apex of a peninsula formed by the junction of the St.Marks and Wakulla Rivers are the RUINS OF ST.MARKS FORT, a stone structure built in 1739. The island was fortified by Spain in 1677, and the bastions remaining are those of the fourth fort built on the site. Earlier structures were of wood, and the first was burned by pirates in 1682. The fort was strengthened and manned by an English garrison during the British occupancy of Florida from 1763–83 and was reoccupied by Spaniards in 1787. In 1800 it was captured by a party of Creek led by a white man, William Bowles (*see below*), but a Spanish force from Pensacola recaptured it a few weeks later. An American force under General Andrew Jackson seized the fort in 1818, and court-martialed and executed two Englishmen, Ambrister and Arbuthnot (*see Tour* 6*a*), for assisting the Indians. The fort was finally abandoned in 1824, and four years later the St.Marks lighthouse was built of stone from the fort. During the War between the States the fort was occupied by Confederate forces and was the objective of several unsuccessful Union forays.

West of Wakulla the highway skirts (R) TIGER HAMMOCK so named for the number of wildcats and panthers (cougars), which roamed the swamp in the 1860's. Although rarely seen, a few of these fierce cats still inhabit the hammock.

At 38.7 *m.* is the junction with an unimproved road.

Right on this road to WAKULLA SPRINGS, 2.3 *m.*, in a forested park covering approximately four acres. A bathhouse and hotel occupy landscaped grounds at the entrance to the park. The waters of the spring are so clear that objects can be seen on the bottom, more than 100 feet down. Through glass-bottomed boats (*fare* 50¢) it is possible to view fishes of many kinds, the petrified head and tusks of a giant mastodon, and limestone ledges of fantastic colors, ranging from jade green to flashing aquamarine. A mastodon found here is on exhibit at the State Geological Survey Museum (*see Tallahassee*). An Indian legend has it that small 'water people,' four inches tall, with long hair, once held dances in the depths of the springs on moonlit nights, and that at a certain hour a warrior appeared in a stone canoe, frightening them away. Wild life in the park is protected by the State. Blue herons and white egrets stalk the shore, capturing minnows within a few feet of bathers.

CRAWFORDVILLE, 44.2 *m.* (398 pop.), seat of Wakulla County, has a frame courthouse, one of the few remaining in the State.

South of Crawfordville the route traverses an agricultural area; neat farmhouses contrast sharply with the Negro workers' rickety log cabins, many with chimneys built of sticks and plastered with clay. Wooden and granite markers rise starkly amid weeds and sand in the occasional country graveyards passed along the way.

At 47.6 *m.* is the junction with an unimproved road.

Left on this road to Shell Point, 11 *m.*, a favorite fishing spot for more than 100 years. While digging shells in 1935 for road construction, workers uncovered a number of Indian skeletons, one of which is exhibited in the State Geological Survey Museum (*see Tallahassee*).

At 51 *m.* is the junction with State 110.

Left on this road is PANACEA, 4 *m.* (192 pop.), on King's Bay, known as Smith Springs until 1893 when some Bostonians purchased the land about the five springs here and renamed the town Panacea because of the curative properties of the waters. During the War between the States a large plant here supplied salt for much of western Florida. Redfish, snappers, trout, and groupers are caught in the bay and Gulf (*boats, guides, equipment at piers*).

SOPCHOPPY (Ind., red oak), 57.6 *m.* (400 pop.), gains its livelihood from lumber mills and the production of naval stores.

Crossing SOPCHOPPY RIVER, 60.4 *m.*, the highway passes through thick stands of second-growth pine worked by turpentiners. Negro cabins and cultivated fields enclosed with split rail fences flank the road. Huge fire-blackened stumps in the clearings indicate that the region was once heavily timbered. Blue iris and cattails flourish in roadside ditches, and along the streams grow black willows, which are burned to produce a fine charcoal used in the manufacture of gunpowder.

The OCHLOCKONEE RIVER (Ind., yellow water), 62.8 *m.*, navigable at this point by small boats, offers excellent fishing (*bass, bream, perch*); many trails lead through the flatwoods to fishing camps on the river. Along its heavily wooded banks grows the sycamore, America's tallest hardwood, which reaches a height of 160 feet; here also is the swamp or water ash, found as far north as Virginia and as far west as Texas.

The steel St. James Fire Tower, 65.6 *m.*, rises high above a small clearing landscaped with flower gardens and crape myrtles. On the drive into the grounds is a parking space for those desiring to climb to the lookout for a view of the surrounding countryside.

The route turns southwest along the Gulf, its sparkling blue waters glimpsed at intervals through towering pines festooned with moss and vines.

CARRABELLE, 78.6 *m.* (920 pop.), a resort and fishing village with a U.S. Weather Signal Tower, ships large quantities of shrimp, oysters, and fish, particularly mullet, throughout the year. The influence of the sea is evident even in the cemeteries, where coral of many colors, sponges, clam and conch shells are used as markers and monuments on both white and Negro graves.

Florida fishermen are of two types: the net fishermen and the sportsman's guide. The former are always vitally interested in whether mullet, Florida's staple fish, will bring 3¢ or 4¢ a pound on a particular day. In every fishing village stand great racks on which nets hang drying in the sun. While the menfolk concern themselves with the catching, icing, and marketing of fish, the women keep the nets in repair, constantly mending and reweaving gaps torn by sharp fins. Long before daylight, fishermen and their families are up preparing for the day's toil. Dawn finds their small string of boats, the majority provided with 'kickers' (small engines), heading for the tidal lagoons and the narrow channels between the reefs. Just before the tide changes, nets are set in wide semi-circles to catch the fish as they come down with the tide. When the fish strike the net, their gills become enmeshed. Hauled in, the fish are dumped into bins partially filled with cracked ice for delivery at the market before sundown.

As early as 1775, during the British occupation, the fishing resources of the Florida Gulf coast had attracted attention. In that year Bernard Romans, a member of DeBraham's party sent by the English Government to survey the coast, wrote in a report: 'I have Yearly Seen about One Thousand Tons Weight of dry'd Salted Fish go from the Western Shore of the Province of East Florida, to the Havannah, Besides what goes from the Eastern Shore. In this Trade they Employ about Thirty Vessels from fifteen to forty Tons, and none are Navigated with less than Twelve Men, the Largest Sometimes Twenty or Twenty Eight, and most Come and go twice every Season, . . . with this Fish the West Indian Markets, but more Particularly Jamaica, may be Supplied at a Season when all their Northward Fish is bad, and begins to decay . . . and I will be bold to say that the Coast will Admit of Six times that Number of Vessells to Load Annually.'

The sportsman's guide, usually a lone wolf, owns a sturdy motor launch, kept spotlessly clean, in which he carries from two to a half dozen anglers into the Gulf for deep-sea fishing. He knows the best fishing grounds and the hours that bring the grouper, mackerel, king fish, snapper, or tarpon to the banks and passes. On board are flies, plugs, hand lines, spoons, rods, reels, gaffs, sinkers, leaders, and bait: shrimp, shiners, crabs, and cut bait. The guide is less interested in the quantity of the catch than in the sport afforded his patrons. A number of good strikes and a few big fish landed make a successful day for him. Chartered boats for deep-sea fishing are available at a number of Carrabelle piers.

Swamp lands north of Carrabelle remain one of the few habitats of the Florida black or hog bear. Eating roots, climbing to the tops of cabbage palms to feast on the tender white buds, this bear is classified as a vegetarian but on occasion relishes fat porkers and tupelo honey. Hunters usually trail the animal with hounds (*guides, dogs, camping equipment available at Carrabelle*).

Left from Carrabelle 0.5 *m.* on a paved road to KITCHEN MIDDENS, heaped up by the Muskogean Indians, who here threw away their broken pottery and general refuse. Although the Muskogean grew maize and beans, their diet included shellfish. Noteworthy features of mounds on the northwest coast of Florida are the large caches of pottery found in them, the comparative absence of shell tools and ornaments, and the abundance of stone implements.

At 81.8 *m.* the CARRABELLE LIGHTHOUSE looms (R) above trees.

Between Carrabelle and Apalachicola the route follows the winding shore line of ST.GEORGE SOUND. Visible across the sound, through a fringe of slender pines are ST.GEORGE ISLAND and DOG ISLAND, narrow ribbons of sand providing sheltered water for small craft. The road cuts through high sand dunes covered with scrubby pines, sea oats, and trailing goat's-foot vines, which trace a green filigree over the glistening white sand. Within a few yards of the water are pine and cypress stumps, bleached gray by sun and surf. Wide stretches of salt meadows are feeding grounds of herons and other wading birds. Long piers jut out from shore, and mounds of oystershells surround the weathered frame shacks of the fishermen. Rising above the shifting sands, Indian mounds, once the sites of villages, provide substantial foundations for numerous beach cottages.

At 90.2 *m.* is the junction with an unimproved road.

Right on this road to the SITE OF FORT BLOUNT, 15 *m.*, where in 1814 the British helped runaway Negroes and Indians to build a fort, mount guns, and store ammunition. The post was known as Negro Fort, and around it the Negroes developed many plantations. The fields, one historian wrote, extended for more than 50 miles along the river. On July 24, 1816, Federal forces under Colonel Clinch and Captain Loomis attacked the fort by land and water. General Andrew Jackson's instructions were: 'Blow it up! Return the Negroes to their rightful owners.' The attack continued for four days, ending when a red hot cannon ball dropped into the powder magazine. All but 60 of the 334 occupants of the fort were instantly killed, including many women and children; only three escaped injury; two of the three, an Indian and a Negro, were executed at Jackson's orders.

GORRIE BRIDGE, 96 *m.*, 6 miles long, was named for Dr. John Gorrie, who discovered the process of making ice artificially (*see below*).

APALACHICOLA (Ind., *apalahchi okli*, people on the other side), 101.1 *m.* (5 alt., 3,150 pop.), noted for its oysters, lies at the mouth of the Apalachicola River. Almost destitute of trees, the business district has wide paved streets lined with rows of one- and two-story brick buildings, many built in the early 1830's, which face the barnlike corrugated-iron fish and oyster houses strung along the waterfront. In the residential district, shaded by sycamore and magnolia trees, are weatherbeaten frame houses, erected by pioneers who shared in the town's prosperity during the years it flourished as a cotton shipping port.

In 1528, Narváez and his followers, after a disastrous overland march from Tampa Bay, encamped on the shore of Apalachicola Bay to build boats in an attempt to reach Mexico (*see St. Petersburg*). In ships of native yellow pine, caulked with palmetto fiber and pitch, the explorer and his men set sail. A storm at the mouth of the Perdido River drove Narváez's ship out to sea and nothing more was heard of it. Only four survivors ultimately reached Mexico City, one being Cabeza de Vaca, who in his *Naufragio*, published in 1542, set down the fantastic and all but incredible adventures of this small band.

In the last quarter of the eighteenth century the Apalachicola region suffered from the depredations of William Augustus Bowles, English adventurer and pirate. Dismissed from the British Navy for insubordination, Bowles came to Georgia, married a Creek woman, and became influential in the tribe, leading a band of Creek against the Spanish in the siege of Pensacola by the English in 1781, for which he was reinstated in British favor. Spain offered a reward of $6,000 for his capture, and in February 1792 he was taken prisoner and sent to Madrid. In 1799 he escaped from his captors and rejoined the Creek near Apalachicola Bay, where he established headquarters, looted surrounding Spanish towns, and preyed on shipping. Again taken prisoner in 1804, he was carried to Havana and confined in Morro Castle until his death the following year.

Founded about 1821, the town was incorporated as West Point in 1827 and renamed Apalachicola in 1831; a post office was established the following year. Between 1834 and 1836 business lots sold for as much as $3,000, and 60 brick buildings were erected. After the channel and harbor had been dredged in 1837, the town became the third largest cotton-shipping port on the Gulf. In 1843, when the town of St. Joseph (*see below*) was virtually abandoned as the result of a yellow-fever epidemic, many of its inhabitants removed here, even bringing their houses, several of which are still standing.

Cotton shipping suffered a decline when Federal gunboats blockaded the port during the War between the States. Since that time, the town's chief income has been derived from its fisheries. In the protected waters of St. George Sound are more than 10,000 acres of oyster beds producing 90 per cent of the State's yield. The beds are diligently 'farmed'; oyster shells, or shucks, are dropped on the beds to provide young oysters with anchorage; to destroy starfish and the boring mollusk, enemies of the oyster, the beds are raked periodically with cotton mops attached to long drags or lengths of chain. Starfish clamp their tentacles around an oyster and gradually force the shell open; mollusks drill minute holes in the shells through which they suck the oyster.

In GORRIE SQUARE, Ave. D and 6th St., stands the GORRIE MONUMENT, erected by the Southern Ice Exchange in memory of Dr. John Gorrie, who patented the process of making ice artificially. Long a resident of Apalachicola, he built an ice-making machine in 1845 and used it to cool the rooms of patients stricken with fever. He patented the device in 1851 but was unable to raise capital to commercialize his invention. Gorrie died here in 1855 without having gained recognition for his work, and was buried in Magnolia Cemetery. Gorrie is one of two Florida men who have been honored with a niche in Statuary Hall in the Capitol at Washington. In the old Chestnut Street Cemetery is the GRAVE OF DR. ALVAN WENTWORTH CHAPMAN, physician-botanist, whose volume on the *Flora of the Southern United States* is a standard work on the subject.

The TRINITY CHURCH, on Gorrie Square, has two Ionic columns framing the narrow door, tall windows with green shutters, and a square belfry, topped with a metal cross. The third oldest Episcopal church in Florida, it was built in 1839 with lumber brought by schooner from New York. During the War between the States its bell was melted down to make cannon, and its carpets and cushions were donated to Confederate soldiers, presumably to keep them warm.

The ORMAN HOUSE (*private*), 5th St., a two-story frame structure on an elevation overlooking the Apalachicola River, was built in 1837. During the War between the States, Mrs. Sarah Orman, an ardent secessionist, placed a large keg on the roof of the house as a signal to warn Confederate soldiers returning on furlough that Federal troops were in the city.

The Raney House (*private*) Market St. and Ave. F, a two-story white frame structure with fluted Doric columns rising to a second-story pediment, was built in St.Joseph (*see below*) about 1838 and removed to its present site in the early 1840's. It housed Federal troops during the Reconstruction period.

1. ST.VINCENT ISLAND (*reached only by chartered boat from waterfront*), 8 *m.*, named by Franciscan friars during the Spanish occupation, is 9 miles long and 4 miles wide, with 5 fresh-water lakes, numerous springs, and a creek. Covered with a dense forest of magnolias, live oaks, and palms, it has been converted into a game preserve by Dr.R.V.Pierce, manufacturer of patent medicines, who has stocked it with deer, wild boars, turkeys, ducks, geese, quail, and squirrels.

2. Right from Apalachicola on an unimproved road to WIMICO LAKE, 8 *m.*, a part of the Gulf Intracoastal Waterway. In the surrounding territory many immense cypress trees have been cut for the mills at Apalachicola.

Section b. APALACHICOLA to PENSACOLA; 171.6 *m.* *US* 98, *State* 53

West of APALACHICOLA, 0 *m.*, the route follows US 98 through cut-over flatwoods and palmetto, broken by stands of young cypress and scattered cabbage palms. For a few miles the highway parallels broad St.Vincent Sound, with heavily wooded St.Vincent Island (*see above*) in the distance. The rolling white sand dunes are set off sharply against the opalescent blues and greens of the Gulf. Short groins running into the surf prevent erosion of the beaches. Fishermen draw seines through the shallows, hauling in trout, mullet, pompano, and many strange sea creatures. Fishing camps and groups of beach cottages appear occasionally in this sparsely settled region. The glare of the sun on sand and water is so intense that it is advisable to wear dark glasses and to protect the skin against severe burning. As the shoulders of the road are soft and treacherous for long stretches, motorists should not drive off the highway except on hard-surfaced lanes and parking areas.

MONEY BAYOU, 19.2 *m.*, a scattering of summer cottages along the sand dunes, has paved roads leading down to the beach, on which driving is possible at low tide.

The route swings abruptly north, with dense stands of pine and cypress (R); across St.Josephs Bay (L) are low-lying keys covered with cabbage palms.

The Site of St.Joseph (R), 25 *m.*, notable among Florida's ghost towns, had an estimated population of 6,000 in 1838, being at the time the largest town in the State. It owed its existence to a bitter dispute over homestead claims. Between 1804 and 1811 the Spanish granted a company of Indian traders a large tract of land on the Apalachicola River and St.Georges Sound which included the settlement of Apalachicola. With the cession of Florida to the United States in 1822 a legal battle over the validity of the title developed; the U.S. Supreme Court upheld the trading company's claims, making squatters of those who held property in Apalachicola. Many refused to come to terms with the company and selected a new townsite here on St.Josephs Bay.

A land company was organized; the Legislative Council was persuaded to name St. Joseph as county seat in place of Apalachicola, an act later invalidated. On February 1, 1838, the first constitutional convention of Florida was summoned to meet here, 'to adopt a bill of rights and a constitution and all needful measures preparatory to admission of Florida into the national confederacy.' The convention met on December 3 and remained in session until January 11, drawing up a liberal constitution, finding fault with the powers granted certain banking and railroad companies under their charters, and asking Congress to remedy 'the evils of the improvident and injudicious acts of the Territorial Legislature.' The Legislative Council, being the Territorial legislature, was displeased, charging the convention with exceeding its authority, and the issue of statehood was deferred, not being settled until 1845 (*see History*).

Meantime, St. Joseph boomed; town lots sold at fabulous prices; two railroads were built, one from Lake Wimico, the other from Iola. Palatial mansions, brick office buildings and warehouses, long wharves and piers were constructed. The harbor became a forest of spars and masts as vessels crowded the port to take on cargoes of cotton, carrying away from 100,000 to 150,000 bales annually. St. Joseph became known as the richest and wickedest city in the southeast.

In 1841 a ship from South America brought in yellow fever, and within a few weeks three-fourths of the town had succumbed. Panic-stricken survivors abandoned their homes and fled; ships avoided the port; hotels and business houses closed. For three years the town remained deserted. Fear of the plague was so great that only a few venturesome fishermen dared approach the spot. In 1844 a hurricane and tidal wave swept in from the Gulf, leveling empty buildings and floating many out to sea. Devastating storms followed at intervals, and bit by bit all remains of the town were effaced. Today the site is covered with a jungle growth of pines, matted creepers, and palmettoes.

At 28.5 *m.* is the junction with an unimproved road.

Right on this road to ST. JOSEPHS CEMETERY, 1.5 *m.*, sole memorial to the tragic fate of the town of St. Joseph. The story is told that many headstones disappeared without a clue, only to be found later, in shops of neighboring communities serving as counter tops.

At 29.1 *m.* is the junction with an unimproved road.

Right on this road to CONSTITUTION MONUMENT, 1.4 *m.*, a granite pergola in a small park enclosed with an iron fence, was built in 1922 to commemorate the first Florida constitutional convention, which met at St. Joseph (*see above*) in 1838.

PORT ST. JOE, 30.5 *m.* (851 pop.), on the shore of St. Josephs Bay, has plants manufacturing fish oil and fertilizers, and a large paper mill. The rapidly growing business district of one- and two-story frame and brick buildings is surrounded by the makeshift homes of mill workers. With Government and county funds the harbor and channel have been dredged to a depth of 30 feet. Canals dug north of the town permit transportation of pulpwood by barge.

The PORT ST. JOE PAPER MILL, a $7,000,000 structure opened in 1938, dominates the skyline of the town. Owned by Du Pont interests, it is one of the largest in the State manufacturing heavy brown paper for bags and other purposes by the 'kraft' process (*see Tour 3a*).

Port St. Joe is at the junction with State 6 (*see Tour 18*).

BEACON HILL, 39.6 *m.*, consists of a group of weathered fishermen's shacks and a few beach cottages under a wooded hill (R), on which stands the ST. JOSEPH POINT LIGHTHOUSE, its gray shaft barely visible above the trees.

Northwest of Beacon Hill the route traverses a long stretch of palmetto and stump-filled flatwoods; side roads give access to fishing camps and small beach resorts. Pelicans, gulls, herons, and other water fowl feed in the shallow inlets; armies of brown fiddler crabs march across the salt flats and scuttle into their burrows at the approach of an intruder. Wind ripples the powdered sand on the rounded dunes into fantastic ever-changing patterns. Clumps of dark-green sea grapes, acres of sandspurs, and waving fields of sea oats flourish here. In spring the dunes are carpeted with silver-leaved lupines, their blossoms weaving a blue tapestry on the blinding white sand. Years ago the fine sand along this coast was shipped north in quantities to be sprinkled on barroom floors. The route crosses a high concrete bridge, 59 *m.*, over EAST ST. ANDREWS BAY.

PANAMA CITY, 67.1 *m.* (5,402 pop.), seat of Bay County, lies on St. Andrews Bay, 7 miles from the Gulf of Mexico. The extreme western portion of the town, known as St. Andrews, now a residential section, was a flourishing community in the early 1800's. St. Andrews and Millville, adjoining communities, were merged with Panama City in 1909, and the three incorporated as a single municipality. During the Revolutionary War the surrounding territory was settled by homesteaders, many of them Tories, who established indigo plantations and engaged in lumbering and naval-stores industries. Large catches of mackerel, pompano, redfish, and mullet were salted and shipped until the War between the States, during which Federal troops destroyed the fisheries as well as the salt works.

Panama City has grown rapidly since the establishment of paper mills here in 1931. Within a short time a large hotel, office and public buildings, and municipal docks were erected; miles of paved streets were extended to numerous subdivisions in the environs to accommodate paper mill workers; wharves and fish packing and shipping plants along the waterfront were enlarged.

The harbor, from 30 to 60 feet deep, is protected by white marble jetties. Here the tide rises but once each 24 hours, because of the landlocked bay and flow of Gulf waters. Six transoceanic ship lines make the city a port of call, and the average annual tonnage exceeds 140,000 gross tons.

Fort Harrison Avenue, the main thoroughfare, terminates at the bay in a semicircular park, landscaped with tall cabbage palms. A long wooden pier in the park is used by the deep-sea fishing fleet which makes daily voyages into the Gulf and brings back large catches of snapper, redfish, and grouper. Fishing, yachting, and water sports are popular.

Panama City is at the junction with US 231 (*see Tour 17*).

The SITE OF A SALT WORKS (R), 72.5 *m.*, established by the Confederates in 1862, covers an area half a mile square. The works included 26 sheet-iron boilers and 19 kettles, each of 200-gallon capacity. With others in the region it was destroyed by Federal forces in 1862. The making of salt was an important business during the war, and Florida laws granted exemption from conscription and military service to those engaged in it, bringing large numbers of men to all Florida seacoasts. Salt was in great demand and often brought $1 a pound. Federal officers sent into St.Andrews Bay to destroy the works reported that at night 'the sky was lit up for miles to the east and west, away inland for great distances, the glare being reflected light from fires of countless salt works along the shores.'

The narrow strip of Gulf shore between Panama City and Pensacola is the popular weekend and summer vacation ground for many Alabamans who travel less than 100 miles to achieve a salt-water tan. Along the highways to the shore automobiles loaded with bathing, fishing, and golf paraphernalia are numerous from Friday to Sunday. Cottages, hotels, and rooming houses are filled; Saturday night dances are gala affairs at Panama City and Pensacola hotels, and at the many beach casinos between the cities. Fishermen in the villages along the waterfront get their boats and tackle ready and prepare for all-day trips to deep-sea fishing grounds. The summer season on the north shore of the Gulf resembles that on the north Atlantic seaboard, lacking the tropical background and professional glamour of Florida's more publicized resorts on the lower east and west coasts.

PANAMA CITY BEACH, 77.2 *m.*, is a bathing and fishing resort. Gay-colored summer cottages line the dunes west of Panama Beach; hard-surfaced parking places enable motorists to stop at intervals for a swim or picnic along the smooth beach. Salt marshes, with clusters of cabbage palms, border quiet bayous; sand dunes are cloaked with wild myrtle, dwarf magnolia, and rosemary. Tradition has it that the rosemary was brought here by the English during their occupation of the region in 1763–83. English soldiers were given grants of land in the St.Andrews Bay territory; the open fields along the shore, sites of old plantations, are now overgrown with rosemary.

DESTIN, 124.3 *m.* (25 pop.), an old and well-known fishing resort, occupies a narrow strip of land between the Gulf and CHOCTAWHATCHEE BAY.

FORT WALTON, 130.9 *m.* (150 pop.), a large summer resort on the site of a fort of the same name built during the Seminole War, is headquarters for yachts participating in the summer regattas held in near-by waters.

This section of the State contains numerous Indian mounds, some covered with large trees believed to have grown since the mounds were used. John L. McKinnon, in his *History of Walton County*, describes the excavation of the large mound in Fort Walton in 1861. At a depth of about 18 inches, McKinnon found 'great skeletons of men in perfect state of preservation, lying on their backs with hands crossed in front of their bodies and heads toward the west and north. They crossed each other and were filled in with a four-inch layer of preserving matter, a mixture of lime and some other mineral substance.' Many of the skeletons were removed, wired together by Confederate soldiers, and displayed in one of the wooden buildings of the fort. A few months later, during an attack by Federal troops, shells from a gunboat struck the building, burning it to the ground and destroying the collection.

Right from Fort Walton on State 10 is the SHALIMAR BONDED WINERY, 3.2 *m.*, surrounded by experimental vineyards; here a tangy wine is distilled from the juice of the Satsuma orange.

State 10 crosses the southern boundary of the CHOCTAWHATCHEE NATIONAL FOREST, 5.2 *m.*, an area of 368,048 acres set aside in 1908 for experimentation in the growing of pine trees and the production of naval stores. The forest is named for a tribe of Choctaw Indians, some of whom migrated to Florida in Spanish times. Elevations in the forest vary from sea level to almost 300 feet. The longleaf pine is abundant; its rate of growth is very slow, but it produces a high grade of timber. Hardwoods are found in the creek bottoms and the swamps, the latter often dense impenetrable thickets.

At 8 *m.* is an ARMY GUNNERY BASE, a camp and training station, and an airport (R), operated as an adjunct to Maxwell Field in Montgomery, Ala.

VALPARAISO, 10 *m.* (99 pop.), is a popular resort throughout the year. A local inn has an 18-hole golf course.

Left from Valparaiso 2.3 *m.* on State 54 into the CHOCTAWHATCHEE NATIONAL FOREST (*hunting in accordance with State laws, except where posted as a preserve; fresh-water fishing*), past feeding grounds of deer and wild turkey. Various trees, in addition to pines, are experimented with in this part of the forest. Flowers, both cultivated and wild, grow abundantly. On the banks of ROCKY CREEK, in the eastern section of the forest, grows the mountain laurel, an Appalachian Mountain shrub.

Between Fort Walton and Pensacola the highway cuts through high sand dunes; the titi, or ironwood tree, flourishes here, and in February and March is a mass of fragrant snowy bloom, set off by the delicate pastel shades of the flowering lupine and the plumelike Mexican firebush.

At 146.9 *m.* is the junction with State 53, which the route now follows.

Signs warn motorists to beware of oiled road shoulders which look safe but are almost as liquid as quicksilver. Tourist and summer camps, beach cottages, and substantial houses overlook the placid waters of Santa Rosa Sound, across the mouth of which lies tree-crowned Santa Rosa Island, a barrier against Gulf storms.

At 165.3 *m.* is the junction with a paved road.

Left on this road to PENSACOLA BEACH, 2 *m.*, a resort popular with Pensacola residents. The beach is lighted for night bathing; a casino provides dining and dancing facilities; and a long fishing pier is an attraction for anglers.

PENSACOLA BAY, 168.2 *m.*, is crossed on a long concrete bridge (*75¢ for car and driver; extra passenger 10¢; round trip 85¢*).

PENSACOLA, 171.6 *m.* (13 alt., 31,579 pop.) (*see Pensacola*).

Points of Interest: Naval Air Station, Seville Square, old Christ Church, old houses, and others.

Pensacola is at the junction with US 90 (*see Tour 7d*) and US 29 (*see Tour 16*).

Tour 15

Haines City—Lake Wales—Sebring—Moore Haven—Junction with State 25; 126.6 *m.* State 8, State 67.

Hard-surfaced throughout.
Route paralleled by Seaboard Air Line Ry. between Avon Park and Sebring; and by the Atlantic Coast Line R.R. between Haines City and Moore Haven.
Good accommodations.

This route climbs the rolling hills of the ridge section, circles sparkling blue lakes, and for miles winds through large citrus groves. From the hilltops the land is a changing checkerboard of green trees, sapphire and silver water, and brown tilled fields. On summer afternoons towering cloud formations pile up in the eastern heavens to frame the landscape, frequently blurred by a distant rainstorm. The road sweeps past sawmills and turpentine camps to the outskirts of the Everglades, where flat fields of cabbages, beans, and sugar cane flourish without regard to the calendar.

HAINES CITY, 0 *m.* (166 alt., 3,037 pop.) (*see Tour 2c*), is at the junctions with US 17 (*see Tour 2c and d*) and US 92 (*see Tour 20*).

LAKE HAMILTON, 4.7 *m.* (152 alt., 399 pop.), on the eastern shore of the lake for which it was named, contains many modern homes of citrus growers and a large fruit-packing plant.

DUNDEE, 8.2 *m.* (156 alt., 615 pop.), occupying the crest of one of many hills in the region, is a community of citrus growers. Here, as in many parts of southern Florida, grove owners live together some distance from their properties, a fact which accounts for the many groves along the highway with no farmhouses near them. Adjoining the town on the south is a branch of the GLEN ST. MARY NURSERIES (*see Tour 7a*).

Between Dundee and Iron Mountain are distant views of hillside orange groves, their straight green rows sloping to small valleys and lakes. Rows of palm and bamboo trees border the highway.

On the slope of IRON MOUNTAIN (324 alt.), 14.5 *m.*, is the entrance to the MOUNTAIN LAKE SANCTUARY (*open* 8–5; *picnicking prohibited; no dogs allowed; men requested to wear coats; parking* 25¢). Embracing 58 acres overlooking some 30 lakes, the sanctuary was established as a retreat for man, a refuge for birds, and a sylvan setting for the Singing Tower (*see below*), by Edward William Bok (1863–1930), journalist, editor of the *Ladies' Home Journal* (1889–1919), and winner of the Pulitzer Prize (1920). Here on Iron Mountain, according to tradition, the Indians of central Florida held their ceremony of the Rising Sun each spring. Near the crest of the mountain has been found a large stone circled by 13 smaller stones, representing the sun and the 13 moons of the Indian year.

More than 300 varieties of plants, vines, shrubs, and trees flourish in the sanctuary. In the GARDEN OF THE RESURRECTION are iris, callas, and hybrid amaryllis. Thirty-seven varieties of azaleas flower here from late summer until May, and are at their loveliest during February and March. More than 100 varieties of birds, native and migrant, have been identified since 1926. European nightingales introduced here compete in song with native mockingbirds (*see Animal Life*).

Rising 230 feet from the crest of Iron Mountain is the SINGING TOWER, a memorial to Edward Bok (*see above*), who is buried in a crypt at the base. Dedicated by President Calvin Coolidge on February 1, 1929, the tower consists of a steel frame enclosed in brick walls 4 feet thick, faced with coquina rock, and gray Creole and pink Etowah marble from Georgia. A lagoon bordered with lilies mirrors the tall hexagonal shaft.

Encircling the lower part of the tower is a frieze picturing pelicans, herons, and the fable of the fox and goose, and the hare and tortoise. The six days of creation as described in Genesis are represented on the north door, which is made of brass. The gates of the moat, the stairway with many fine architectural details, and the hanging lamps have been fashioned in wrought iron and hammered brass. The sundial carved in the south wall indicates the latitude and longitude of Iron Mountain, and the tablet at its base reveals the difference between sun and clock time for each day in this latitude. Around the dial runs a relief of the figures of the Zodiac and its ancient mythological symbols. Over the windows are grilles of marble, delicately and intricately carved, one representing a man planting a garden, the other a youth feeding cranes and flamingoes from a basket.

Above the massive fireplace in the room occupying the entire ground floor is a map showing the course of the winds. The painted ceiling depicts the Goddess of Plenty with a cornucopia overflowing with fruits and flowers, while the floor is patterned in colored ceramics. High up on the tower, at the seventh level, are 8 Gothic windows, each 35 feet high, from which the chimes issue.

The carillon of 71 bells has a range of four-and-a-half octaves, tuned in chromatic scale to the largest bell, which is E flat. The Bourbon bell, known as the tenor bell, weighs approximately 11 tons; the smallest bell, 12 pounds. Inscribed on the Bourbon bell are the names of those who helped Bok create the Mountain Lake Sanctuary and Singing Tower.

Carillon recitals are given at sunrise on Easter, at midnight on Christmas Eve and New Year's Eve, at 3 p.m. on Sundays and at noon on Tuesdays, Thursdays, and Saturdays, from December 15 to April 15. Also, recitals are given at the time of the full moon in January, February, and March each year.

The MOUNTAIN LAKE DEVELOPMENT, centering on the tower, comprises thousands of acres laid out as a residential and citrus-growing settlement by Frederick S. Ruth of Baltimore. Construction of hotels, apartment houses, and business buildings is prohibited. More than 2,000 acres have been planted with citrus groves. The development company maintains a clubhouse for the entertainment of residents and guests. On the western shore of Mountain Lake is an 18-hole golf course.

LAKE WALES, 16.9 *m.* (152 alt., 3,401 pop.), is one of the State's better-known small resorts because of its proximity to the Singing Tower and its setting amid numerous lakes. The modern shopping center is dominated by a tall white hotel built by public subscription. A hospital, golf course, and flying field are municipally owned. August Heckscher, New York financier, donated $25,000 toward the creation of CRYSTAL LAKE PARK, which contains a tourist club building, a bathing beach, and an open-air theater.

The name of the lake and town was originally spelled Waels, for the Waels family who settled on the shore of the lake in the early 1900's; the spelling was changed when the town was platted in 1911. Its industrial life revolves about several lumber mills, and fruit-packing and canning establishments.

Lake Wales is at the junction with State 79 (*see Tour* 11).

BABSON PARK, 23.9 *m.* (147 alt., 250 pop.), once called Crooked Lake for the body of water on which it lies, was renamed by Roger Babson, business prognosticator, who in 1923 purchased most of the land within the town. Webber College of Wellesley, Mass., founded by Mrs.Babson to train young women for executive and secretarial positions, maintains a branch here. Recreational facilities are provided on Crooked Lake (*bathing, boating, fishing*).

On the eastern edge of town is the 320-acre BREEZY POINT GROVE, where Perrine lemons and Persian limes are grown. Dr.Henry E. Perrine, naturalist, brought limes from Yucatan, Mexico, and transplanted them on the Florida Keys. To evolve the Perrine lemon, named in his honor, he crossed this small Key lime with an ordinary lemon. The resultant hybrid is larger and juicier than a lemon. Perrine was killed in a Seminole raid on Indian Key in 1840 (*see Tour 1e*).

FROSTPROOF, 31.2 *m.* (107 alt., 1,406 pop.), occupies an isthmus between LAKE REEDY and LAKE CLINCH, the latter named for General Duncan Clinch, who during the Seminole War built a fort here on the shore of the lake, which was then known as Lake Locha-Popka (Ind., place for eating turtles). Frostproof is a citrus center, with 7 packing and 2 canning plants. Its wide streets are lined with hibiscus and palms. Frostproof has not lived up to its name, disappointing the optimistic hopes of early settlers that the district would never know frost.

Between Frostproof and Avon Park is an area of uncultivated land, covered with scrubby sand pines and blackjack oaks. At the LAKE BYRD LODGE (R), 42 *m.*, a private clubhouse, is held the annual summer encampment of the Episcopal Diocese of South Florida.

AVON PARK, 44.2 *m.* (156 alt., 3,355 pop.), another attractive town in the ridge section, has a mile-long mall, 120 feet wide, extending the length of the business section. Along its many broad parkways grow more than 1,000 varieties of native and exotic plants. Jacaranda predominates, its clusters of dark blue and pale lavender trumpet-shaped blossoms flowering throughout the spring months. Within and surrounding the town are numerous deep lakes; along their curving shores are landscaped drives and wide sandy beaches.

In 1886, O.M.Crosby, of Danbury, Conn., president of the Florida Development Company, chose the site for settlement because of its 'open pine forests studded with clear water lakes, an abundance of fish and game, freedom from malaria, mosquitoes, and Negroes.' Crosby visited England, returned with many settlers, and named the town for Stratford-on-Avon. Large citrus groves were planted and the community grew rapidly, although mail and provisions had to be hauled many miles over sand trails from Fort Meade. Later, a stage line was established to provide free transportation to landowners and prospective lot buyers, anticipating the later boom-time practice of taking customers for a ride.

To advertise his development, Crosby established a newspaper, the *Florida Home Seeker*, widely distributed here and abroad. Land was offered at $25 an acre. 'An ideal proposition for a quiet man with a yearly income of about $500,' an early editorial stated. 'But do not come expecting an easy berth or that oranges grow without work. Mischief makers are not welcome; and above all, do not come to Avon Park if you must have strong drink or questionable entertainment. Do not come to sober up, or reform!'

The freeze of 1894–95 destroyed the groves and truck gardens, and the majority of the inhabitants abandoned their lands. Avon Park remained almost deserted until 1912 when construction of the Atlantic Coast Line Railroad brought a new influx of settlers. The town was incorporated in 1913; improved transportation facilities, the replanting of citrus groves, and establishment of three large fruit-packing plants have stimulated growth. The WARD NURSERIES (*open*) specialize in raising citrus and avocado stock, its 26-acre avocado grove being one of the largest in Florida. The REX BEACH FARM (*open*), owned by the novelist, occupies the bed of a drained lake and produces both gladioli flowers and bulbs for northern markets. On Lake Verona is DONALDSON PARK (*bathing beach, children's playground*).

South of Avon Park the route runs through extensive citrus groves which blanket the slopes and hilltops and reach down to the shores of numerous lakes; several are enclosed with wire fences covered with golden bignonia and purple bougainvillea. In spring the orange and grapefruit blossoms are starry white against the glossy green foliage, and their heavy fragrance persists long after the groves have been passed.

SEBRING, 54.6 *m.* (141 alt., 2,912 pop.), seat of Highlands County, is a 'tailor-made' city, built according to plan. The townsite, on the eastern shore of LAKE JACKSON, was purchased by George Eugene Sebring (1859–1927), a pottery manufacturer of Sebring, Ohio, who planned a city on the pattern of the mythological Grecian city of Heliopolis (city of the sun), with streets radiating from a central park representing the sun. Surveys were made and construction was begun in 1912, a few months before the coming of the Atlantic Coast Line Railroad. The freeze of 1917 killed and damaged many groves. These were replanted, and community life continued at a leisurely pace until the real-estate flurry of 1924–25, when the town hired an official greeter who spent his days in the streets and parks shaking hands with visitors. He never greeted the same tourist twice, it is said.

The SEBRING HOUSE, Lakeview Drive and Center St., occupied by the widow of George Eugene Sebring, the city's founder, is the scene of the annual Founder's Day pageant. The REX BEACH HOUSE, N.Lakeview Drive at Lake Jackson, is encircled by a high wall covered with flowering vines. Adjoining it on N.Lakeview Drive is the COURTNEY RYLEY COOPER HOUSE, a large white stucco mansion, the winter home of the popular writer, its grounds enclosed with a low picket fence through which hibiscus thrust their scarlet blossoms.

The SEBRING FRUIT GROWERS ASSOCIATION PACKING PLANT (*open*), Pear St. and Ridgewood Drive, controls hundreds of acres of citrus groves and serves many growers.

Right from Sebring on State 162, locally known as Lakeview Drive, to the BOTANICAL GARDEN AND ARBORETUM (*open 9–5; free, including guide*), 6 *m.*; in the greenhouses are many rare and exotic plants. Well-kept roads of bright orange-red clay wind through green lawns and forests.

At 7 *m.* the road crosses the eastern boundary of HIGHLANDS HAMMOCK STATE PARK (*open 9–5; car and driver 35¢, additional passengers 15¢; visitors may pick wild oranges, limes, and lemons*). Mrs.John A. Roebling of New Jersey, who first glimpsed the beauties of this area from a plane, envisioned it as a wild-life sanctuary, and negotiated its purchase. In 1934 the property was deeded to the State. Cypress, fern, wild sour orange, oak, swamp maple, and gum intermingle with needle palm, magnolia, bay, wild lemon, wild coffee, and wild avocado. Cabbage palms reach a height of 100 feet. Native wild animals have found these forests a natural haven; deer are so tame that they can be seen at close range. There are thousands of gray squirrels, foxes, opossums, raccoons, alligators, and turtles. The bird life, both native and migratory, includes more than 100 different varieties. Almost every section of the park is accessible, and improvements have been made carefully to preserve Highlands Hammock as a part of primeval Florida. A footbridge leads into a cypress swamp, through which flows Little Charlie Bowlegs Creek, its clear waters mirroring the dense swamp foliage. The stream was named for an Englishman, William Rogers, who married an Indian woman and became known as Charlie Bowlegs. A former associate of the notorious pirate, Jean Lafitte, Bowlegs buried his blood-stained gold in the Florida sands, settled on the near-by Gulf coast to guard his treasure, and lived to a ripe old age. So far as known, he never spent his ill-gotten wealth, nor has it ever been recovered. Near the center of the forest is a natural amphitheater (*vespers: Jan., Feb., Mar.; Sundays at 3 p.m.*). The entire park contains 2,385 acres.

South of Sebring the highway traverses a highly developed citrus area; intervening stretches of poor sandy soil are covered with scrub pine and blackjack oak. Small white mounds thrown up by salamanders dot the landscape, but the shy ratlike animal is rarely seen. To see a salamander in the morning, according to a Negro superstition, means good luck for the remainder of the day. Diminutive lakes, flashing like silver coins, are in view as the road circles among the hills. Now and then a few stunted palms along an overgrown road, with a once imposing Spanish gateway, now a skeleton of timber and chicken-wire, mark the entrance to a boom-time subdivision. Occasional bougainvillea or clumps of oleanders, nipped by woodsfires but still bravely flowering among the palmettoes, are the sole remaining evidence of a realtor's rosy dreams.

DE SOTO CITY, 62 *m.* (231 pop.), founded in 1916, lies on RED BEACH LAKE, with many little piers and boathouses. Its business buildings and brightly-colored dwellings, the majority of Florida-Mediterranean style, stand between the lake and the road. The slope of the ground and the curving highway form a natural amphitheater ringed with citrus groves and pines.

South of De Soto City the highway rises and dips over low hills. Rutted roads branching on either side are used chiefly by backwoods 'crackers.' These trails wind among trees and stumps, sometimes through sand too deep for anything but a wagon, and eventually reach an unpainted one-room frame shack, perched several feet off the ground. Children and 'houn' dawgs' scamper about the yard and front stoop. Small square holes, screenless and without glass, serve as windows. A chimney of twigs and stones, plastered with clay, rises above the warped mossy shingles on the roof. At the rear of the shack is a lean-to. Not far away is a pigsty, and a crude shelter for the mule. In a small garden grow cow peas, black-eyed peas, turnip greens, sugar cane, and yams. The pigs and the vegetables, supplemented by fish caught in a near-by lake, supply the family with food. Tobacco is a luxury; snuff is as popular with women as with men.

Within the shack is a bed or two, mattresses on the floor providing sleeping quarters for the 'young 'uns.' On nails in the walls hang overalls, frayed and faded dresses, and an assortment of garments made of meal sacks. Battered chairs, a table, and a few dishes complete the furnishings. Most of the cooking is done in the yard where an iron pot, also used for the family wash, hangs from a tripod or rests on a heap of stones.

Saturday is the day for a trek by wagon to the nearest town, to gossip with others assembled for the same purpose. Occasionally a family, not so fortunate as to own a mule, straggles into town barefoot, or carrying their shoes, for shoes, as a rule, are too valuable to be worn on long walks.

LAKE PLACID, 72.3 *m.* (582 pop.), on the slope of a hill in rolling terrain dotted with lakes and groves, was named Lake Stearns when founded in 1924 as part of a land and citrus development. Its name and that of a lake to the south were changed when the southern branch of Lake Placid Club of New York was established in the town.

Left from Lake Placid on an unimproved road to LAKE ISTOKPOGA (Ind., lake where a person was killed in the water), 4 *m.* Arbuckle Creek empties into it on the north and Istokpoga Creek flows east from it into the Kissimmee River; the creeks and lake afford excellent fishing.

The route follows a ridge between Lakes Placid and Huntley, passing (R) Lake June-in-Winter. Here the highway is a 'rollercoaster road,' dipping and rising so frequently and abruptly that fast driving is dangerous. Citrus groves alternate with dense forests of virgin pine.

CHILDS, 79.2 *m.* (132 alt., 30 pop.), is at the junction with State 18 (*see Tour* 12).

South of Childs the route follows State 67, which for a distance of 2 miles passes through the 10,000-acre JOSEPH ROEBLING ESTATE. The grassed road shoulders are kept rolled and mowed; allamanda hedges, bright with yellow trumpet-shaped blossoms throughout the summer, border the highway.

HICORIA, 83.7 *m.* (153 alt., 587 pop.), was founded in 1908 when a sawmill was built here. In the vicinity are several groves and poultry farms.

South of Hicoria the groves gradually thin out; stands of pines, dense palmetto thickets, and stretches of cut-over land appear. In some wooded portions are parallel rows of young pines, spaced 5 or 6 feet apart, marking the route of a long obliterated wagon road. Heavy wheels killed off vegetation in the ruts, and they became protected seed beds for falling pine cones. Here and there are tall trees, their trunks splintered and twisted by hurricanes, their tops gone.

VENUS, 92.9 *m.* (118 alt., 250 pop.), a scattering of weather-beaten houses in a pine clearing, was named for the Roman goddess of bloom and beauty, protectress of gardens. The post office occupies a diminutive one-room frame building beside the highway. A number of inhabitants find employment in near-by turpentine camps, surrounded by crude shacks occupied by Negro workers. Distant cypress hammocks and rounded clumps of oaks and bays loom against the western horizon like misty blue hills.

The route crosses FISHEATING CREEK, 104.1 *m.*, as it winds through prairies and marshlands on its way to Lake Okeechobee. A military map of 1839 gives the name of the creek as *Thlothlopopka-Hatchee* (Ind., stream where fish are eaten), and it is frequently mentioned in Seminole War histories. During the Indian campaigns American troops traversing this region found opportunity to make the first authentic charts of the territory. Sailors accompanying the expeditions became adept in handling the awkward flat-bottomed boats used at the time.

Fisheating Creek was the favorite haunt of 'Alligator' Ferguson, who, according to tradition, killed more alligators than any other man of his time (*see Tour* 12). Ferguson is said to have 'made his bed among them, eaten among them, and spent so many months in their company that it is probable he hardly ever thought or talked of anything but alligators.' He did not bother to sell the hides, although they were valuable, but only the teeth, for which he received about $5 a pound, often selling 5 pounds a week. In decoying 'gators within range of his gun, he would bark like a dog, or he would carry a little pig in his arms and twist its tail to make it squeal. Ferguson claimed that a squealing pig would excite the interest of even the most indolent alligator.

Except for distant clumps of mop-headed cabbage palms, which resemble islands floating on a green sea, trees disappear south of Fisheating Creek. The road, elevated for the most part, parallels a canal in which cattails, ferns, and water lilies flourish. Herons and red-winged blackbirds are numerous. Widely separated houses of truck farmers on the far bank of the canal are reached by short bridges; many of the houses are sheltered by towering bamboos and giant banana plants. Level green prairies covered with sawgrass and saltbush stretch southward to the Everglades.

MOORE HAVEN, 120.8 *m.* (9 alt., 612 pop.), seat of Glades County, lies on the southwestern shore of Lake Okeechobee, largest body of water in the State. The canal between Moore Haven and Lake Hicpochee is a link in the Cross-State Canal (*see Tour* 13), which extends from Stuart, on the Atlantic Ocean, through Lakes Okeechobee and Hicpochee and along the Caloosahatchee River to the Gulf of Mexico. Moore Haven is a trading and shipping point for tomatoes, beans, cabbages, and catfish. Two and sometimes three crops are grown during the year; approximately 500,000 pounds of catfish are shipped annually. Settled in 1915, the town was almost destroyed by a flood in 1926, but was quickly rebuilt. In 1917, Mrs. J. J. O'Brien was elected mayor, one of the first women in the United States to serve in that capacity.

Muck fires sometimes cast a heavy pall of smoke over Moore Haven and the surrounding territory during dry seasons. Ignited by grass fires, the peatlike soil burns like smoldering sawdust, eating into the earth, and once beyond control is extinguished only by rains. Fires are sometimes started by white and Indian hunters, when they burn off vegetation in their search for swales inhabited by alligators. A menace to inhabitants of the Everglades, the fires rob the soil of humus, and the smoke renders automobile driving hazardous. Although a State fire-control unit has a record of extinguishing more than 600 fires annually, the 'Glades are of such an extent that no thoroughly effective control has been achieved.

At 126.6 *m.* is a junction with State 25 (*see Tour* 13), 8.9 miles west of Clewiston (*see Tour* 13).

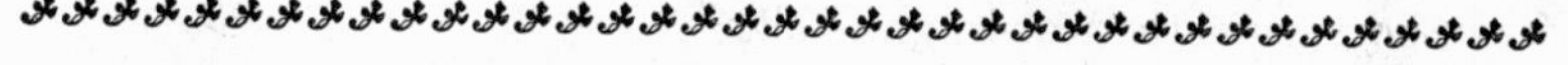

Tour 16

(Brewton, Ala.)—Century—Gonzalez—Pensacola; US 29.
Alabama Line to Pensacola, 44.6 *m.*

Concrete-paved roadbed; watch for cattle along highway.
Route paralleled by Louisville & Nashville R.R. between Alabama Line and Pensacola; by St. Louis-San Francisco R.R. between Cantonment and Pensacola. Good accommodations.

US 29 follows the route of an old trail over which General Andrew Jackson marched from Pensacola to Fort Montgomery in 1818. Roughly paralleling the Escambia River through a swampy country, it traverses a prosperous agricultural section producing pecans, grapes, Satsuma oranges, and small fruits. In many of the small towns are dilapidated red-roofed clapboard railroad stations, abandoned with the advent of the modern highway and motor busses.

US 29 crosses the Alabama Line at FLOMATON, 0 *m.* (69 alt., 915 pop.), 15 miles southwest of Brewton, Ala. (*see Alabama Guide*).

Flomaton, known as Pensacola Junction before 1884, straddles the State Line, with its post office in Alabama. The village is a business and recreational center for planters, turpentiners, and lumbermen in the surrounding area.

CENTURY, 2.2 *m.* (75 alt., 1,250 pop.), a mill town along the highway, commemorates in its name the establishment in January 1900 of the large sawmill around which the settlement grew. Most of the lumber produced here is purchased by exporting firms.

BLUFF SPRINGS, 5.8 *m.* (54 alt., 150 pop.), is a shipping point for carload lots of Irish and sweet potatoes, corn, and cabbage. A pottery (R) has utilized the excellent clay deposits in the vicinity for many years; samples of its products are displayed for sale. A spring (L) made the spot a favorite camp site for early travelers; Scottish settlers from North Carolina rested here for a time in 1820 on their way southeast along an Indian trail to Euchee Valley (*see Tour 7d*).

The hilly terrain typical of the northwest corner of Florida extends south to Bluff Springs. The winding highway dips and rises, occasionally cutting through red clay hills; herds of cattle and goats graze in the clearings.

McDAVID, 10.5 *m.* (36 alt., 450 pop.), owes its existence largely to naval-stores operations in the surrounding territory. In spring, dogwood trees in snowy bloom stand out sharply against the town's unpainted frame houses and the near-by green hills.

At 16.9 *m.* is a junction with a paved road.

Left on this road is PINE BARREN, 1 *m.* (21 alt., 100 pop.), founded by Luke and Rebecca Townley in 1821. The foundations of their log cabin, which stood in a group of giant oaks, are still visible. Memorials to these pioneers are in Pine Barren Cemetery.

At 21.4 *m.* is the junction with a graded road.

Left on this road is MOLINO (Sp. mill), 2 *m.* (27 alt., 438 pop.), in the center of a farming region; settled about 1820, the village was probably named for the sawmills that operated in this vicinity as early as 1812. The village has several brick plants which utilize local clay deposits; it is also a shipping point for farmers growing large crops of corn and potatoes.

The region to the south was once traversed by an Indian trail. Sometimes in early days travel over such trails resembled a game of leap-frog. Two men, having but one horse, would begin a journey, with one man walking, the other riding. The first rider, leaving the pedestrian far behind, would proceed to a designated point, dismount, tie the horse, and start walking. The man on foot, reaching the waiting horse, would then mount, pass the first rider, and ride on to a second designated point. Thus alternately riding and walking, they made steady progress, and both travelers and the horse had opportunities to rest.

COTTAGE HILL, 27.9 *m.* (130 alt., 300 pop.), built on gently rolling terrain, has many white cottages surrounded by rose gardens and pear orchards. A number of the residents are retired farmers from the North, with G.A.R. veterans among them.

CANTONMENT, 29.4 *m.* (142 alt., 100 pop.), in a prosperous naval-stores and lumbering section, has several mills manufacturing cypress and cedar shingles.

Left from Cantonment on an unnumbered sand road to the SITE OF FIFTEEN MILE HOUSE, 0.2 *m.*, in a grove of magnificent oaks. The house, approximately 15 miles north of Pensacola, was owned by Don Manuel González, an interpreter and Indian agent, who settled here on an extensive grant of land about 1800. General Andrew Jackson made his headquarters here in 1814 while preparing his attack on Pensacola (*see Pensacola*). González refused to act as a guide in spite of Jackson's threatening commands, and aroused the general's ire, although he later won his friendship. Jackson again occupied the house in 1821 when the transfer of Florida from Spain to the United States was being arranged. In July 1822, while holding its first meeting at Pensacola, the Florida Territorial Council was forced by a yellow-fever epidemic to adjourn to Fifteen Mile House, where it transacted the remainder of its business.

GONZALEZ, 31.8 *m.* (135 alt., 500 pop.), a trading center for farmers, dates from a settlement established here in the early 1800's. It was named for Don Manuel González (*see above*) and was so recorded on a Florida map of 1828.

South of Gonzalez are small farms, poultry ranches, pecan groves, and orchards, which sell most of their produce to the Army Post and Naval Air Station at Pensacola. Oaks, bays, and magnolias cover the rolling hills between cultivated fields, and stretches of cut-over timber lands afford pasturage for cattle, sheep, and goats.

GOULDING, 43 *m.* (82 alt., 300 pop.), is an industrial community with fertilizer factories, furniture and Venetian-blind factories, cooperage plants, and a chemical plant manufacturing rosin sizing used by paper-makers.

PENSACOLA, 44.6 *m.* (13 alt., 31,579 pop.) (*see Pensacola*).

Points of Interest: Naval Air Station; Forts Barrancas, San Carlos, and Pickens; Corry Field; Plaza Ferdinand VII; Seville Square; old Christ Church; old houses; and others.

Pensacola is at the junction with US 90 (*see Tour 7d*) and State 53 (*see Tour 14b*).

Tour 17

(Dothan, Ala.)—Cottondale—Panama City; US 231.
Alabama Line to Panama City, 67.9 *m.*

Hard-surfaced roadbed, with occasional stretches of improved clay; watch for cattle along highway.
Route paralleled by Atlanta & St. Andrews Bay R.R.
Good accommodations.

US 231, a direct route south to the Gulf, traverses fertile rolling country occupied before the 1860's by large plantation owners. The land still produces crops of cotton, peanuts, corn, and bright-leaf tobacco, and during late summer several drowsy little towns stir into life when auction sales of these products are held.

Dense forests of shortleaf pine, hickory, sweet gum, and cypress grow in the rich red loam of this territory; the streams flowing through limestone beds are unusually clear and blue, except during spring freshets. Deposits of limestone are often exposed in the uplands; the rock is used locally for chimneys and underpinning, and occasionally for buildings. Many farms in the northern section are owned and cultivated by Negroes.

US 231 crosses the Alabama Line 0 *m.*, 21 miles south of Dothan, Ala. (*see Alabama Guide*). A filling station (R) straddles the line; the owner operates a dance hall on the Alabama side to escape payment of the Florida tax on such establishments, and sells cigars, cigarettes, and soft drinks on the Florida side to avoid the Alabama sales tax.

CAMPBELLTON, 3.5 *m.* (314 pop.), a town dating from the English occupation (1763–83), has a grain elevator, lumber mill, and a grist mill handling 350,000 bushels of corn and 2,000 tons of peanuts annually. Large cornfields surround the town.

South of Campbellton are the Marianna Redlands, a hilly region with many sink holes and caves, the hiding places of runaway slaves before the War between the States.

At 11.8 *m.* is the junction with State 6 (*see Tour* 18).

COTTONDALE, 16 *m.* (135 alt., 550 pop.) (*see Tour 7d*), is at the junction with US 90 (*see Tour 7d*).

Corn, beans, peanuts, and cotton are grown in this section; arable land is often broken by small cypress swamps.

ALFORD, 23.1 *m.* (221 pop.), is a rural settlement among oak-crowned hills. Along the highway, which follows the main street of the village, are large pecan groves, and during summer and fall the nuts are for sale at roadside stands.

The route winds southward through hardwood forests in which grow fragrant wild jessamine, Cherokee rose, and clematis. In spring patches of white dogwood beautify the landscape; in fall the reds and browns of frost-touched oaks and hickories contrast sharply with the green of pines and magnolias.

ROUND LAKE, 26 *m.* (322 alt., 310 pop.), on a lake of the same name, has a co-operative Satsuma orange packing house. The Satsuma, native to China and a member of the mandarin family, is a small thin-skinned orange; because it is capable of withstanding 10° lower temperature than other varieties, it is profitably grown throughout northern Florida.

On both sides of the highway are fields of sorrel dock, known as sour grass, a stubby red plant adding color to the scene but regarded as a nuisance by farmers.

COMPASS LAKE, 31 *m.* (200 pop.), occupies a bluff overlooking a pine-fringed lake of the same name (*fishing, bathing*). A local packing house handles the Satsuma oranges of the region.

FOUNTAIN FIELD, 34.5 *m.*, is one of the many emergency landing fields in this vicinity used by fliers from the Naval Air Station at Pensacola.

FOUNTAIN, 39.3 *m.* (250 pop.), a flag station on the railroad, lies in rolling and thickly wooded country.

South of Fountain the highway penetrates deeper into the Apalachicola flatwoods, a level region with towering stands of longleaf pine. Here also grow the black gum, a weedy tree with olive-green leaves and blue berries, and the swamp maple, with gray bark and bluish leaves which turn orange-red and yellow in the fall; in January it blooms in large clusters of scarlet flowers.

Off the highway live many backwoodsmen, the so-called Florida crackers. Few of their one-room shacks have window sashes; board shutters are used to keep out cold and stormy weather. Chimneys built of sticks, clay, and moss lean at crazy angles and are often propped up with poles; roofs of pine slabs or crude hand-split shingles are chinked with mud and moss. Bedsteads are made of pine saplings, and the 'springs' consist of ropes interlaced between the posts. Fertilizer bags or gunny sacks are stuffed with corn shucks and transformed into mattresses and pillows; quilts made of odd pieces of cloth and discarded clothing serve as covers.

As a rule, cooking is done in open fireplaces, but an old gasoline and oil drum is sometimes used as a stove. One side of it is flattened as a stove top; a hole cut in one end serves as a fire door, and a length of pipe is inserted in a hole at the other end to provide a chimney.

Remote from towns of any size, the people of this section retain many strange beliefs and superstitions handed down from generation to generation. Many 'cure-alls' and 'conjures' are still in use. To drag a rake through the house or to stand a broom on its grass end brings bad luck; to hear a screech owl at midnight is a certain sign of death—unless the hearer immediately turns his right shoe upside down; a stiff dose of asafetida is a popular remedy for malaria (*see Folklore*).

YOUNGSTOWN, 47.4 *m.* (300 pop.), is a settlement of unpainted shacks tenanted by workers employed in a local turpentine still or in cutting cross ties and pulpwood in the neighboring woods. On cut-over lands to the south are patches of second-growth pine; a few herds of cattle graze in the clearings.

PANAMA CITY, 67.9 *m.* (5,402 pop.) (*see Tour 14b*), is at the junction with US 98 (*see Tour 14b*).

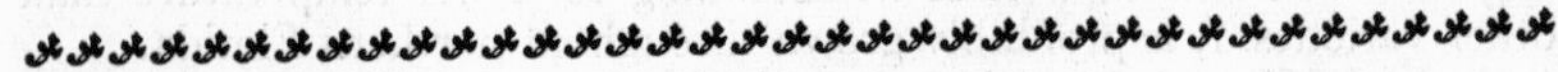

Tour 18

Junction with US 231—Marianna—Blountstown—Port St. Joe; 88.9 *m.* State 6.

Hard-surfaced roadbed, with a few short stretches of improved clay; watch for cattle along highway.
Route paralleled by Marianna & Blountstown R.R. between Marianna and Blountstown.
Good accommodations.

Along this route, which provides one of the short cuts across northwest Florida to the Gulf coast, towns are few and the countryside is sparsely settled. The highway runs through wooded areas, abounding in small game, where 'coon and fox hunts are customary sports and few inhabitants are without their favorite hounds. In the northern part of the State the route traverses a rolling agricultural section, with scattered stands of hardwood trees. Fields of corn, cotton, beans, and peanuts border the highway, and red clay roads lead to isolated farmhouses and cabins occupied by Negroes.

State 6 branches southeast from US 231 (*see Tour 17*), 0 *m.*, 8.3 miles south of Campbellton (*see Tour 17*).

MARIANNA, 8 *m.* (117 alt., 3,372 pop.) (*see Tour 7c*), is at the junction with US 90 (*see Tour 7c and d*), with which State 6 unites for 4 miles.

ALTHA, 25.3 *m.* (217 pop.), a farming community, has a cotton gin and a grist mill that grinds corn and polishes rice for near-by planters. Pecan and Satsuma orange groves provide income for many of the inhabitants.

South of Altha are pine flatwoods carpeted with coarse grass, a grazing area for free-range cattle. All larger trees have been logged off; younger timber suitable for paper manufacture is also being cut. Five-foot logs are stacked beside loading platforms at railroad sidings, awaiting transportation to Port St. Joe mills. A narrow red clay road used by ox- and horse-drawn carts parallels the highway at intervals.

BLOUNTSTOWN, 36.8 *m.* (51 alt., 1,270 pop.), seat of Calhoun County, a lumber and naval-stores center on a bluff above the Apalachicola River, has a large plant for the distillation of pine tar and oils, a hardwood mill manufacturing rotary-cut veneers and turpentine barrels, and a large brick kiln. Although not incorporated until 1925, the settlement was founded in 1823 and named for John Blount, Seminole Chief, a bitter opponent of the warring faction of the Creek, who for years kept settlers along the Georgia-Florida border in a state of constant alarm. When General Andrew Jackson marched through northern Florida in 1818 to end the Creek depredations, Blount acted as his guide, and Jackson attributed much of the success of his campaign to the chief's loyalty and knowledge of the country. Blount was one of six Indian leaders to whom the Federal Government granted a small reservation in this vicinity in 1824. Many of the fields surrounding Blountstown were cleared by these Indians. After the treaty of Payne's Landing in 1832, the reservation was ceded to the Government, and Blount accompanied his tribesmen to Indian Territory.

Left from Blountstown on State 19 to the APALACHICOLA RIVER, 0.2 *m.*, which is crossed on a small barge ferried by a motor launch (*free*), maintained by the State Road Department. Among the oaks and magnolias along the banks grows the pumpkin ash, rising from a buttressed base to a height of 90 feet or more. Somewhere on the river bottom between this point and the Gulf lies the wreck of the steamer *Alice*, 156 feet long, which struck a snag and went down in October 1865. Repeated but unsuccessful attempts have been made to find the vessel and salvage its cargo of 15,000 gallons of rum in oak casks.

BRISTOL, 2 *m.* (800 pop.), seat of Liberty County, founded as Riddeysville about 1850 and renamed in 1858, produces pine and hardwood lumber, cypress and cedar poles.

Left from Bristol on State 12, paved, to a junction with a dirt road, 6.5 *m.*; L. here to ROCK BLUFF (75 pop.), 10.5 *m.*, a farming community.

Left from Rock Bluff on a dirt road to TORREYA STATE PARK, 15.5 *m.* on the Apalachicola River. This 520-acre park was named for the evergreen *Torreya taxifola*, rarest species of the genus Torreya, found here and for 10 miles south along the eastern bank of the river. Because of its unpleasant odor when bruised, the tree is known as 'stinking cedar.' Two other varieties grow in Japan and California, but both differ in size, leaves, and color of fruit from the Florida tree, which rises in pyramidal form to a height of 40 feet. Its bark is orange-brown; its leaves are dark yellow-green on the upper side, marked with white lines underneath. The obovate purple fruit resembles an olive but is not edible.

The road from the park's entrance leads 0.5 *m.* to BATTERY POINT, fortified by Confederates guarding the river during the War between the States. On the point are the remains of old entrenchments, pits, gun emplacements, and an ammunition warehouse. The view from the point includes a broad sweep of the yellow river and surrounding country. A steel track is still embedded in the clay; on these rails donkey carts hauled freight from the landing; one of the carts is preserved at the CCC camp in the park, where is also shown a well-preserved dug-out canoe excavated from the river bank. Twenty-three feet long, two feet wide, and barely a foot deep, the canoe has a flat end on which the steersman stood.

South of Blountstown the highway runs through one of the most thinly populated areas in Florida. No town is passed, and there are few signs of human habitation. The highway crosses the CHIPOLA RIVER, 50 *m.*, on a one-way wooden bridge. For several miles the rolling hills are covered with scrub oak and second-growth pines. Occasional low areas are forested with dense hardwood hammocks.

CHIPOLA PARK (Ind., dance place), 56.5 *m.*, is the center of the Dead Lakes region, approximately 12 miles long and 2 miles wide, one of the best fishing grounds in northwest Florida (*black bass, pickerel, pike, perch*). Large signs advertise near-by fishing camps, each heralding the 'best fishing.' Dead Lakes were named for the countless dead cypress, oak, and pine trees drowned by the overflow of the Chipola River, which connects the chain of lakes. The maze of forested islands and winding channels makes navigation of the lakes difficult (*guides available at Chipola Park*).

WEWAHITCHKA (Ind., water eyes), 64.5 *m.* (584 pop.), seat of Gulf County, is said to have been named for near-by twin lakes which, in the imagination of the Indians, resembled eyes. The town ships 1,000 barrels of tupelo honey annually. The tupelo, or cotton-gum tree, grows in the swamps along the rivers and coasts of northern Florida; its large plumlike fruit distinguishes it from the common black gum. When it blooms in March and April, its white flowers are alive with bees. Tupelo honey does not granulate or become rancid, and is used largely for pharmaceutical purposes. Apiarists from adjoining States bring their swarms to this section each spring by motor trucks and on rafts floated down the streams. Tupelo, a hard wood, is used as flooring and in making bowling-alley equipment.

Skirting numerous cypress swamps, the road traverses open grassy plains. Drainage ditches border the highway, which at intervals crosses the roadbed of one of the first railroads in America, built in 1839 from St.Josephs Bay to the Apalachicola River, to transport cotton raised in southern Georgia and Alabama to Port St.Joe (*see Transportation*).

A one-way floating bridge, 81.9 *m.*, crosses the Inland Waterway Canal, which connects Lake Wimico with St.Andrews Bay.

Approaching the Gulf, the route runs through a swampy area matted with palmetto and dotted with scraggy pines. Along the road are small, corrugated-iron sheds, housing the pumps that supply much of the great volume of water used by the paper mills of Port St.Joe.

PORT ST.JOE, 88.9 *m.* (851 pop.) (*see Tour 14b*), is at the junction with US 98 (*see Tour 14b*).

Tour 19

Watertown—Starke—Palatka—Bunnell; 104.7 *m.* State 28.

Hard-surfaced roadbed throughout; watch for cattle along highway.
Route paralleled by Southern Ry. between Lake City and Lake Butler, Keystone Heights and Palatka; by Florida East Coast R.R. between Palatka and Bunnell.
Good accommodations.

This route runs southeastward through the center of north Florida, passing turpentine and lumber camps and small farms. Pine flats are succeeded by forests of oak, bay, and cedar. Numerous lakes and hills are in view in the vicinity of Keystone Heights. East of the St.Johns River, the highway traverses a sparsely settled region before reaching the fertile farming section around Bunnell.

State 28 branches southeast from US 90 (*see Tour 7a*) at WATERTOWN, 0 *m.* (194 alt., 796 pop.) (*see Tour 7a*), 1.6 miles east of Lake City (*see Tour 7a*).

CLIFTONVILLE, 15.9 *m.*, a typical turpentine camp, consists of orderly rows of shacks in the rear of a turpentine still. Here reside the families of Negroes whose job is to slash the trees and collect gum in the surrounding forest.

LAKE BUTLER, 20 *m.* (141 alt., 886 pop.), strung out for a mile along the highway, consists of one- and two-story brick and frame buildings. The town was named for Colonel Robert Butler, who in behalf of the United States accepted East Florida from Spain at the time of its cession on July 10, 1821. On Saturday nights farmers, white and Negro turpentine workers, and employees of the State prison at Raiford (*see Tour 3b*) crowd the shopping district. Occasionally the eerie prison siren warns town and countryside that a prisoner has escaped. Two plants here manufacture plows and farming implements, but the principal industry is the production of naval stores, which average 3,000 barrels of turpentine and 10,000 barrels of resin annually.

In the approximate center of town is (L) the flat-topped red brick UNION COUNTY COURTHOUSE, at the rear of which is the brick county jail. Many homes here adjoin pecan groves and vegetable gardens. At intervals along the highway are smooth-bark camphor trees, evergreens native to China; from the wood and leaves the Chinese distill a product used as a substitute for turpentine. The leaves, sometimes chewed by children, have the pungent antiseptic taste of camphor oil.

Between Lake Butler and Starke are stretches of slash pine worked by turpentiners. Frequently wagons loaded with barrels of sap can be seen winding along a sand trail. Lumbermen follow at the heels of naval-stores operators, leasing the land for timber. Gradually the forests become open pastures, or are grubbed, fertilized, and cultivated by small truck farmers.

When a farmer hauls his produce to the nearest town each week, he is often accompanied by his wife and children. The womenfolk of the region usually know one another, though they are not near neighbors. At dusk the family reassembles, is loaded in a truck or wagon, and jounces back to its isolated home in time for supper by lamplight.

STARKE, 34.9 *m.* (167 alt., 1,339 pop.) (*see Tour 3b*), is at the junction with State 13 (*see Tour 3b*).

South of Starke the route traverses the uplands of the lake region. Throughout this area scrubby blackjack oaks, identified by rough gray bark and deeply divided leaves, flourish in the deep sand of rounded hills.

KEYSTONE HEIGHTS, 47.9 *m.* (150 alt., 107 pop.), is the northernmost resort town of the lake region. Originally known as Brooklyn, the town was renamed in 1922 by J.J.Lawrence of Pennsylvania for the Keystone State. The town is fenced on all sides to keep out free-range livestock. At the central gateway in the fence (R), a broad paved street leads to LAKE GENEVA (*hotel, swimming, and picnic facilities*), on the southern edge of town. Cottages are scattered along the shaded slopes of the lake.

1. Left from Keystone Heights on State 68 to GOLD HEAD BRANCH STATE PARK, 9 *m.*, at the head of a ravine from which emerges GOLD HEAD BRANCH, a crystal-clear stream rising from a group of springs and flowing over a bed of white sand. A footpath descends the steep slopes to the bottom of the ravine, 65 feet below the highway. The gorge is a natural garden, overspread with wild flowers, shrubs, palms, and other subtropical growth. There is a motor road along the edge of the ravine to the site of a mill dam. In the park are Lake Sheeler and Pebble Lake, both well stocked with fish (*black bass, bream, shellcracker, jack, perch*). The park contains 1,080 acres.

2. Right from Keystone Heights on State 80 is MELROSE, 5 *m.* (161 alt., 300 pop.), one of the many resorts in the State popular with elderly visitors. Weather-beaten houses are almost hidden by vines and rambler roses; old-fashioned gardens, bright with blossoms, are shaded by large moss-shrouded oaks, tall pines, and palms. Settled in 1879 by Scottish pioneers, who planted large citrus groves here on the shores of Santa Fe Lake, the town was named for Melrose, Scotland. The lake was named for the Spanish mission of Santa Fé de Toloca, built along an old Spanish Trail which circled the southern shores of the lake. In 1718 Governor Benairdes wrote to the king of Spain, 'The nine settlements of Timuquan Indians located on the Royal Road which goes from la Florida [at St.Augustine] to the limits of the before mentioned province [Apalache] are distant from each other 28, 8, 2, 6, 1, and 5 leagues. They are La Florida, Santa Fé, San Franco, Santa Catalina, Ajuica, San Juan del Río, San Pedrio, Machaba, and Asile.'

East of Keystone Heights there are few villages along the route. Most of the small settlements and post offices in this section lie along the railroad that parallels the highway on the north. From the summit of a hill, 62.3 *m.*, is a fine view of the oak-covered terrain. Near Palatka are stands of hardwood, interspersed with widening tracts of slash pine.

PALATKA, 76 *m.* (25 alt., 6,500 pop.) (*see Tour 2b*), is at the junction with US 17 (*see Tour 2b*), with which State 28 unites as far as SAN MATEO, 83.2 *m.* (69 alt., 175 pop.) (*see Tour 2b*).

Southeast of San Mateo the highway traverses a dairying and potato-growing region; farms border both sides of the road. Despite comparative isolation in the thinly settled flatwoods, farmers in this area have built concrete silos, comfortable houses, and large barns. Signs of human habitation diminish as the route traverses a sparsely settled area of slash and longleaf pine forests, occasionally broken by stump-filled clearings and hardwood swamps. Along sluggish streams tree trunks are often solidly encased in vines to heights of 40 feet. This section is almost as primitive as it was in the 1830's, when stockades were built by settlers in an effort to confine the Seminole to central and southwest Florida. Near Bunnell are fertile farmlands.

BUNNELL, 104.7 *m.* (23 alt., 671 pop.) (*see Tour 1b*), is at the junction with US 1 (*see Tour 1b*).

Tour 20

Haines City—Auburndale—Lakeland—Plant City—Tampa—Clearwater; 87.5 *m.* US 92, State 17.

Concrete-paved roadbed for the most part, with occasional short stretches of asphalt and brick; watch for cattle along highway.
Route paralleled by Atlantic Coast Line R.R.
Good accommodations.

This section of US 92 runs almost due west through mammoth citrus groves, many of them on terraced slopes overlooking diminutive lakes. In February and March both ripe yellow fruit and waxy blossoms cover the orange and grapefruit trees lining the road for miles. The fragrance is especially noticeable during a season of 'bouquet bloom,' or unusually heavy blossoming. Roadside stands offer orange juice and blossoms for sale. The route reaches elevations of more than 200 feet, and the hilltops offer good views of well-tended groves, blue lakes, and modern houses.

US 92 branches west from US 17 (*see Tour 2c and d*) at HAINES CITY, 0 *m.* (166 alt., 3,037 pop.) (*see Tour 2c*).

LAKE ALFRED, 6.5 *m.* (175 alt., 629 pop.), a residential community, owes its prosperity to the surrounding groves. The town has been known successively as Barton Junction, Chubb, and Fargo; the present name, also that of the near-by lake, was selected in honor of Alfred Parslow, who acquired a franchise for an early local railroad and built a house on the townsite. The MUNICIPAL BEACH on the lake provides bathing and boating.

A CITRUS EXPERIMENT STATION, established in 1921 by the State Agricultural Experiment Station at Gainesville, conducts research and study of fertilizers, citrus soils, insect and disease control, and packing house problems. The ridge section here is the approximate center of the most productive citrus area of Florida, which, all in all, produced more than 50,000,000 boxes of fruit in 1937–38.

After clearing their land, grove owners purchase budded nursery stock and plant it in rows from 16 to 20 feet apart; an acre on the average has 70 trees, and 10 acres are considered the smallest profitable unit. Cultivation is highly specialized, involving the use of expensive fertilizers, the planting of cover crops to retain moisture and reduce weed growth, pruning, and frequent spraying to reduce insect life. Trees bear by the sixth year. Most of the citrus trees in western and central Florida are budded to a rough lemon root stalk that matures quickly in the ridge soil and withstands low temperatures; along the east coast sour or wild orange stock is preferred. The early maturing varieties of orange are Satsuma, Parson Brown, and Hamlin; those picked during midseason are Pineapple, Enterprise, and Jaffa; late maturing fruits include the Valencia and Lue Gim Gong, often seen on trees as late as June.

The earliest marketable grapefruit is the Duncan, followed by Florida common, and the Walker; the only late variety is the Marsh seedless. The Foster, a pink-meat grapefruit, is becoming popular. The original pink-meat fruit, the pomelo or shaddock, from which grapefruit was developed, is a rough-skinned, coarse, and bitter fruit, frequently 8 inches in diameter but of no commercial value. Grapefruit is said to have received its name because the fruit usually grows in clusters. The trees are long-lived and often grow to enormous size. The tangerine, of several varieties, ripens in midwinter. The tangelo, a relatively new fruit, is a cross between the tangerine and grapefruit.

Oranges are not actually picked, but cut with medium-sized curved clippers. The stem must be cut a short distance from the orange, or the fruit will rot. The oranges fall into bags strapped around the cutter's shoulders. When the bags are filled, they are dumped into field boxes of two bushels' capacity and loaded on trucks. Cutters are generally hired by the co-operative packing houses and transported by truck from grove to grove. In the field Negroes and whites, usually working in separate groups, receive about 6¢ a box for picking fruit. At other seasons cutters are employed in the care and cultivation of the groves and receive an average wage of $1.50 a day. Most of the citrus workers are native Floridians; it is not unusual to find entire families working together in the groves.

AUBURNDALE, 11.5 *m.* (167 alt., 1,849 pop.), originally named Sanitaria by the group of health seekers who founded it, was later renamed by settlers from Auburndale, Mass. Large frame residences, orderly groves, and two-story boxlike buildings line the principal thoroughfare. The houses and estates of fruit growers and packers border the shore of LAKE ARIANA (*good fishing*).

Groves become less numerous, replaced by stretches of pine woods and lowlands dotted with small lakes. Small farms off the main highway are on paved county roads kept in condition by white and Negro prisoners from near-by county jails. Many Negro workers are skilled woodsmen, expert with axes, crosscut saws, and grubbing hoes. In one of these gangs Daddy Mention (*see Tour 3b*) once worked, while serving time in a local jail.

'Daddy Mention liked the Polk County jails all right,' one of his associates relates, 'except for the little "jug" outside of Lakeland. He told them when they put him there, he didn't think he could stay with them too long. They'd locked him up for vagrancy, you see, and Daddy didn't think so much of that, for just like he'd told them, he'd been picking oranges and just had too much money to work for a week or two. So they locked Daddy up. He fussed a little, made up his mind to go to Tampa. He knew he couldn't just run away, though. You can't do that down here.

'We didn't know nothin' about his plan, 'cause he didn't talk much, but we begin seein' him do more work than anybody else in his gang. He'd chop down a tree by himself and wouldn't take more'n one man to help him lift it. And one day, when he was sure the cap'n seen him, he lifted a log all by himself and carried it a long ways. It wasn't long before the cap'n and his friends was pickin' up a little side money, bettin' people Daddy could walk off with any tree they could cut. It got to be a regular sight to see Daddy walkin' around the jail yard, luggin' a tree-butt in his arms.

'One afternoon we come in from the woods and Daddy brings in a big tree-butt with him. After dinner he picks up the butt and starts clownin' around, with the cap'n watchin' him and laughin'. When he started for the gate with the butt on his shoulder, none of the guards bothered him, 'cause who ever seen a man tryin' to escape with a pine-butt on his shoulders? The guards figured somebody was makin' a bet or somethin'. Right out of the gate Daddy went, onto the road goin' to Hillsborough County, and he still had the log on his shoulder. I never seen him again till a long time after in Tampa.

'"I didn't have no trouble," he told me later. "I jus' kep' that log on my shoulder an' everybody I passed thought it'd fallen off'n a truck an' I was carryin' it back. Soon's I got to Plant City, I sold the log for enough to *ride* to Tampa, and they ain't goin' to catch me again in Polk County."'

LAKELAND, 22 *m.* (206 alt., 18,554 pop.), the State's second largest inland city, is in the highland region of central Florida, with 14 natural lakes within or near its limits. Between business buildings and throughout the residential districts, modern houses intermingle with older frame dwellings of Colonial style. Almost all are surrounded by flowering subtropical gardens. On the northern limits of the city are the Negro sections, Teaspoon Hill and Morehead, most of whose residents work in local citrus groves, fruit-packing plants and truck gardens. They have their own schools, hospitals, churches, and theater; such unofficial names as Voodoo Corner, Jonk Street, and Careless Avenue add color to the neighborhoods.

The metropolis of a region growing one-third of Florida's citrus fruit, Lakeland is executive headquarters of large producing and shipping companies, and of the Florida Citrus Commission, instituted to enforce green fruit regulations, govern marketing, and control advertising. The region ranks second in the State as a strawberry-growing area, and stands high in the production of winter vegetables. Many of the larger farms employ overhead irrigation, a system of elevated pipes equipped with sprinklers which produce a man-made rain at the turn of a valve.

For berry and truck growers, the city operates an auction platform where these products are sold to local and northern buyers. Cold storage facilities and carload refrigeration are provided by a plant capable of icing 500 cars every 24 hours. A Federal Frost Warning Service is maintained for the benefit of growers throughout the State; it broadcasts bulletins daily on climatic conditions at principal markets.

Lakeland's history began with the coming of the South Florida Railroad in 1884; the town was incorporated the following year. At the same time a group of Englishmen established the town of Acton, two miles to the east, named for Lord Acton, British historian. During this settlement's brief existence it became in atmosphere, dress, and custom, a transplanted bit of England, with polo, fox hunting, and cricket as part of its daily life. When the founders scattered to other parts of the State after the 'freeze' of 1894, the town was absorbed by Lakeland.

The mid-State position of the city early made it an important railroad center. Many railroad employees bought houses and settled here. The large pay roll helped stabilize the development of the town, and discovery of near-by phosphate deposits in the early 1890's gave further impetus to its growth. Its relatively high altitude and plentiful supply of pure water induced the Federal Government to select Lakeland as an encampment ground for troops during the Spanish-American War, and these natural advantages later brought to the city the National Home of the United Carpenters and Joiners of America (*see below*). The removal of large railroad shops in 1926–27 struck the city an economic blow, but road building and the rapid development of citrus culture have sustained the city's growth.

LAKE MIRROR, in the heart of the city, encircled by a decorative retaining wall with lofty colonnades, forms a CIVIC CENTER, which includes a chain of parks with many recreational facilities. Vine-covered municipal buildings and churches, and several tall stucco hotels occupy terraced lawns sloping to the water. MUNN PARK, with bandstand, benches, and horseshoe pitching lanes, occupies a square block in the center of the shopping district.

LAKE WIRE, also in the city, is encircled by a landscaped drive; originally known as Israel's Dish, the lake received its present name when a telegraph line to the Havana-Punta Rassa cable was built along the shore. When encamped here in 1898, the Tenth U.S. Cavalry had as its quartermaster John L. Pershing, then a lieutenant, who was here dubbed 'Black Jack,' because the Tenth Cavalry was a Negro unit.

LAKE HOLLINGSWORTH, on Lake Hollingsworth Drive, is bordered with oaks, magnolias, orange groves, and many large estates. On the western shore is the pink stucco CLEVELAND HEIGHTS YACHT AND COUNTRY CLUB (*open*), with mooring floats and piers.

On the eastern shore of Lake Hollingsworth, in the center of a 63-acre orange grove, stands the two- and three-story buildings of FLORIDA SOUTHERN COLLEGE, a coeducational institution established at Leesburg by the Florida Methodist Conference in 1885, removed to Sutherland in 1902, reestablished at Clearwater Beach after a disastrous fire in 1921, and finally removed to its present location where permanent buildings were erected and formally dedicated in September, 1922. The college has an average enrollment of 800 students, representing 20 states and 12 denominations.

In striking contrast to the college buildings, of red brick with limestone trim, is a white HINDU TEMPLE, its 239 stones brought from Benares, holy city of the Hindus, by Frederick B. Fisher, Methodist bishop. As the Hindu worship singly and not in groups, the temple is small, being 5 feet wide, 9 feet long, and 25 feet high, topped with a Christian cross. On the small altar within stands a brass cross and two brass candelabra. Candles burn through the night in memory of Dr.Fisher.

In front of the temple is a reflecting pool, known as the WISHING POOL to students, who toss in pennies with a prayer that their wishes may come true. The superintendent of grounds retrieves the pennies, which are used to buy more candles for the altar. Around the pool and temple is the GARDEN OF MEDITATION, with marble benches and the statues of a sacred cow and two elephants, also from India and reputedly 500 years old. An extensive building program has been laid out by the college, and designs for twelve units, connected by gardens and courts, have been made by Frank Lloyd Wright, one of the most individual of American architects.

The ROSE KELLAR HOME, corner Riggins St. and Pennsylvania Ave., a two-story brown frame house with large screened porches, formerly a private sanatarium, was bequeathed by Dr. and Mrs.F.B.Kellar to the Children's Home Society of Florida. It serves as the Polk County branch of the Society and as a receiving home for the parent institution.

LAKE MORTON, encircled by Lake Morton Drive, is a feeding place for waterfowl during winter and is open for fishing at stated periods each year. The LAKELAND PUBLIC LIBRARY (*open* 9–9), on Lake Morton Drive between Iowa and Massachusetts Aves., a one-story cream stucco building with red tile roof, occupies terraced grounds landscaped with date, cabbage, and Washingtonian palms, and a profusion of pink and white oleanders. The library contains 11,000 volumes and is one of the 5 State depositories for Government publications.

CITY PARK, on 19th St. in the northern part of the city, is for the most part unimproved, but contains the municipal tennis courts, swimming pool, Adair Athletic Field, Morell Memorial Hospital, and the Armory.

Lakeland is at the junction with State 2 (*see Tour 8b*).

Right from Lakeland on Florida Ave. to the NATIONAL HOME OF THE UNITED CARPENTERS AND JOINERS OF AMERICA (*open* 2–5), 3.6 *m.*, established for aged and disabled members over 65 years old and of 30 or more years' standing in the union. More than half of the 1,950 acres in the grounds have been planted with orange groves. The cream-colored stucco buildings with red tile roofs are of Spanish Mission style; the main structure has three large wings containing a lounge, a dining room with a capacity of 800, an auditorium seating 900, an infirmary, the administration offices, and guest rooms. Scattered through the landscaped grounds bordering Lake

Gibson are tables and benches, roque and shuffleboard courts, lawns for bowling, and horseshoe pitching lanes. On the lake are docks and bathing pavilions; an 18-hole golf course (*open; greens fee* 75¢) lies on both sides of the main drive leading to the administration building. The institution has its own light, power, and water plants, and maintains a farm and dairy herd. The home represents an investment of $3,000,000.

A STATE WEIGHING DIVISION STATION (L), 28 *m.*, halts and checks occasional trucks to see that their weight conforms to State laws governing commercial vehicles.

Long stretches of second-growth pine, most of it large enough to be tapped for turpentine, border the highway. Occasional stump-filled clearings, many with small unpainted frame dwellings and sheds, are planted to garden truck; strawberries are cultivated in patches of muck land.

PLANT CITY, 33.1 *m.* (137 alt., 6,800 pop.), is a busy commercial center, with large warehouses, cold-storage plants, and long loading platforms on a web of railroad tracks for the shipment of agricultural produce. In the residential sections, landscaped with oaks and a variety of palms, subtropical vines, and shrubs, are comfortable old frame houses and many stucco dwellings of Florida-Mediterranean style, built during the boom.

The town occupies the site of the Indian village of Ichepucksassa (Ind., tobacco blossoms or fields), a name retained for several years. So much confusion arose over the spelling and pronunciation of the name that an Irish postmaster rechristened it Cork, for his home city. At the time of its incorporation in 1885 it was renamed for Henry B. Plant (*see Transportation*), who in 1884 had extended his South Florida Railroad into this section. In 1887 a yellow fever epidemic brought death to many citizens, and the entire southern half of the town was destroyed by fire in 1908.

Once a cotton center, Plant City now ships almost three-fourths of the Nation's midwinter strawberries. Modern refrigeration and express transportation bring the berries to northern markets within 48 hours of picking. The season lasts from early December to late in March, and during this period Plant City warehouses are scenes of excitement and great activity. Sample pints of berries are auctioned to clamoring Northern buyers, and consignments are immediately loaded into refrigerator cars. With high priced early berries, the 'pony express' method is used: berries are packed in small iced units and shipped with other express not requiring refrigeration. The climax comes with the Strawberry Festival in February. The crop brings an average annual return of $1,000,000.

Many families in Plant City have a strawberry patch, varying in size from a backyard bed to several acres. Boxes of the berries and strawberry shortcake are sold at roadside stands. Public schools are in session all year, so that children who help the harvesters during the winter can attend summer classes.

Strawberry culture has been termed a 'thirteen-months-in-the-year job.' In January and February farmers order nursery plants and set out runner beds for the next season. Runners are pulled from parent plants from July to September; those set out last are the first to bear, but develop into smaller plants. On small plots pine needles and meadow hay are often heaped up between the rows and raked over the plants to protect them from weeds and freezes.

In the KRUSE STRAWBERRY CANNING PLANT, 302 Reynolds St., berries are frozen and shipped to firms making preserves and syrups. GILCHRIST PARK, in the eastern part of the city, offers recreational facilities.

Left from Plant City on a paved road is CORONET, 3 *m.* (120 alt., 400 pop.), an industrial village built by a phosphate-mining company, which has erected attractive modern cottages for its employees. Known as the 'Spotless Town' because of its cleanliness, the community has a country club, library, and park system.

The Florida pebble-phosphate area lies within a 20-mile radius of Coronet. Small operators have practically disappeared; large corporations continue operations and produce 2,000,000 tons annually (*see Industry and Commerce*). The phosphate basin, or 'matrix,' varies in thickness from 1 foot to 40 feet, but nothing under 6 feet can be profitably worked. In early operations the overburden, ranging from 15 to 25 feet, was removed by Negroes with wheelbarrows and mule-drawn scrapers; later, steam shovels were used; today, electrically operated draglines are employed. The matrix is mined with hydraulic 'giants,' or 'guns,' which throw streams of water with a pressure strong enough to break up and wash the 'slurry' into basins, from which it is pumped to the washer or recovery plant. The limit of efficient pumping is about one mile, after which the pumps are moved forward along the mining cut. Approximately 85 per cent of raw phosphate is acidulated with sulfuric acid to make 'super-phosphate,' a necessary plant food in commercial fertilizers. Some 10 per cent is manufactured into disodium and trisodium phosphates for silk weighting and baking powder; the remainder goes into other phosphate compounds used in industrial chemistry, photography, and medicine.

The CORONET GOLF COURSE (*greens fee* $1) and RECREATIONAL GROUNDS (L), 34.5 *m.*, are patronized by Plant City residents.

Between Plant City and Tampa the route by-passes all towns, providing an express highway through fertile, rolling, truck-farming country. Small patches of bright green sugar cane appear frequently, and many farmers offer cane juice at 5¢ a glass; the grayish beverage is a refreshing drink. Along low stretches State highway signs have been erected to warn motorists that fog and smoke hang low over the roads, particularly at night and in the early morning, necessitating caution in driving. In many places tall elderberry bushes flank the highway. Near Tampa citrus groves again predominate. Colonies of bees in the groves and open fields produce a clear fragrant orange-blossom honey during spring months when citrus trees are in bloom. A dark heavy-bodied variety is obtained from palmetto blossoms and wild flowers. Honey in glasses and 5-pound tins is for sale at roadside stands.

At 47.8 *m.* is the junction (L) with US 41 (*see Tour 4c*), which unites with US 92 into Tampa.

At 50.9 *m.* is the junction with a paved road.

Right on this road to HILLSBOROUGH COUNTY HOME AND HOSPITAL (*open* 2–3 *and* 7–8 *p.m.*), 0.5 *m.*, a one-story brick building, with 14 lateral wings, built in 1936. The institution has 242 beds for the care of the aged and indigent sick.

The TAMPA WHOLESALE PRODUCE MARKET, 51.4 *m.*, a U-shaped frame building with an open court, contains 290 stalls for the display and sale of fruits, vegetables, poultry, and other local produce. Traders from northern states bring in apples, grapes, peaches, pecans, and cheese, and return with truckloads of Florida fruit, watermelons, and winter vegetables. The busiest hours are from 2 to 4 a.m., when Tampa merchants arrive to purchase their day's supply of farm products. The clamor and tumult of buyers and sellers blend with the music and sound of revelry from near-by jooks, patronized by truck drivers and growers. The highway here is a popular gathering place for hitch-hikers seeking rides on northbound trucks.

TAMPA, 56.9 *m.* (15 alt., 101,161 pop.) (*see Tampa*).

Points of Interest: Ybor City Latin Quarter, Cigar Factories, Docks, Plant Park, Tampa Bay Hotel, Davis Islands.

Tampa is at the junction with US 41 (*see Tour 4b and c*) and US 541 (*see Tour 4A*).

Right from Tampa on Bayshore Blvd. to BALLAST POINT PARK, 5.4 *m.*, with playgrounds, tables for picnickers, a pavilion with a refreshment stand, and a fishing pier (*boats, bait, and tackle*). This point has long been associated with the maritime history of Tampa. As early as 1853 it was an important cattle-shipping point, and received its name because inbound sailing vessels here dumped overboard their rock ballast before loading cattle and other freight. The accumulated ballast is said to include rock from almost every sea coast in the world. In the park is a huge BANYAN TREE, native to India. Shoots from its long branches drop to the ground and become rooted, acting as trunklike supports of the limbs, thus enabling them to spread until a single banyan resembles a miniature forest. Near the silex beds along the shore are found geodes, which are nodules of stone having a cavity lined with crystal and mineral matter. They were prized by the Indians for their beauty and rarity, and many have been found in both shell and sand burial mounds.

The TAMPA YACHT AND COUNTRY CLUB (*private*), 5.5 *m.*, adjoining Ballast Point Park on the south, occupies fenced waterfront grounds, landscaped with palms and oaks. Southwest of the Tampa Yacht and Country Club the route follows Interbay Blvd.

PORT TAMPA CITY, 9.4 *m.* (6 alt., 1,242 pop.), lies a mile inland from a deep-water harbor on Tampa Bay. Henry Plant (*see above*) extended his South Florida Railroad here from Tampa in 1887, constructed huge piers and warehouses, and dreamed of making the port the greatest in the South. The Port Tampa Inn was built on the waterfront and for a time attracted many winter visitors. Although the piers and warehouses remain, the hotel is not standing. The maritime trade of the town and port, usually designated as Port Tampa, has diminished since the dredging of a deep-water channel through Hillsborough Bay into Tampa. Huge phosphate elevators and oil tanks, surrounded by a network of tracks, tower above weather-beaten houses. Freighters flying flags of many nations line the piers, for approximately 1,500,000 tons of phosphate are shipped from here annually. Oil tankers from South America and Gulf ports discharge their cargoes into strings of tank cars for shipment inland.

In 1893, after the Louisiana State Lottery in New Orleans had been closed, its officials came to Port Tampa, erected a fortlike brick building, and opened the Honduras National Lottery. Puerto Cortéz, an island off the Honduras coast, was purchased and the operators proposed to make it an American Monte Carlo. The brick building was surrounded by a stockade and patrolled night and day by armed guards. The steamship *Breakwater*, equipped with printing machinery, made regular trips between Puerto Cortéz and Port Tampa. The lottery drawings were made at Puerto Cortéz, and printers set up lists of winning numbers en route to Florida. The company also organized the Central American Express Company, so that tickets and money could be transmitted without conflict with U.S. postal authorities. Employees of the lottery company had no associations outside their own circles; no tickets could be purchased locally, and no outsider had specific knowledge of what took place within the armed fortress. This secrecy gave rise to grim tales, and townfolk shunned the premises. The Federal Government closed the lottery in 1895 and the building was torn down. The Port Tampa Public School stands on the site today.

During the Spanish-American War, U.S. troops embarked here for Cuba, and many battleships lay in the harbor. The P. & O. Steamship Line operates between Port Tampa, Key West, and Havana.

North of Port Tampa City the route follows West Shore Boulevard to the junction with Gandy Boulevard, 11.1 *m.*, which the route now follows.

END'S RATTLESNAKE CANNERY AND REPTILORIUM (*open*), 11.3 *m.*, occupies a former filling station building, on which is a neon sign picturing a coiled rattlesnake. The cannery was established in Arcadia in 1931 and removed here in 1937. The novelty of the product has brought it wide publicity, and reptile meat is shipped to domestic and foreign markets. In addition, the plant markets 'Snake Snaks,' thin slices of rattlers, salted and smoked, to be served as hors-d'oeuvres. Visitors are given samples, which if consumed, entitle them to a card with a patch of rattlesnake skin as a seal to signify that they belong to the Ancient and Epicurean Order of Reptile Revelers. Before being butchered, snakes are milked of their venom, which is sold to concerns manufacturing anti-venom preparations (*see Tour* 21). Other by-products are skins, fats for medicinal purposes, and refuse that is made into fertilizer. The snakes on exhibition are obtained from Floridians who make a business of catching live rattlers, which bring from $1 upward, depending on size, and supply and demand.

At 11.5 *m.* is GANDY BRIDGE (*toll 55¢ car and driver; additional passengers* 10¢), spanning Tampa Bay. At both ends of the bridge are fishing camps (*boats, baits, and equipment*).

At 19 *m.* is the junction with State 230; L. on this road 6.5 *m.* to ST.PETERSBURG (41 alt., 40,425 pop.) (*see St.Petersburg*).

West of Tampa the route follows State 17, known here as the MEMORIAL HIGHWAY, dedicated to the memory of the World War dead. The boulevard is lined with water oaks, and pink and white oleanders. Once the widest highway in the Tampa Bay region, it has survived to become one of the narrowest, for there is no way of widening the roadbed without destroying the trees.

At 63.1 *m.* is the junction with Columbus Drive.

Left on Columbus Drive 1.5 *m.* to the DAVIS CAUSEWAY, (*toll 25¢ car and driver; additional passengers* 5¢), spanning the northern reach of Old Tampa Bay. The causeway, 9.5 miles long, offers a panorama of the bay with its irregular shoreline. The western terminus of DAVIS CAUSEWAY, 11 *m.*, is at the junction with Gulf-to-Bay Blvd., which the route now follows.

At 13.2 *m.* is the junction with State 73, paved.

Left on State 73 to the SEVILLE PEACOCK FARM (*open; adm.* 25¢), 2.2 *m.*, where a variety of peafowls, including many rare species, roam at large in an orange grove. Photographs and peacock feathers are for sale.

PINELLAS PARK, 13.2 *m.* (465 pop.), was incorporated in 1913 as part of an extensive agricultural project; the area was drained and the land divided up into small farms. Poultry and squab farms here supply the St.Petersburg dealers, and several large nurseries (*open*) specialize in bulbs and flowers shipped to northern markets.

At 20 *m.* on State 73 is ST.PETERSBURG (41 alt., 40,425 pop.) (*see St.Petersburg*).

On the Gulf-to-Bay Blvd. is CLEARWATER, 16.2 *m.* (29 alt., 7,607 pop.) (*see Tour 6b*).

TAMPA SHORES, 72.9 *m.* (10 alt., 231 pop.), was known as Oldsmar at its founding in 1916, when R.E.Olds, automobile manufacturer, purchased 27,500 acres of land here and laid out the settlement in connection with the sale of his holdings as farm tracts. The undertaking did not turn out as planned, and Olds disposed of much of the property to a syndicate, which endeavored to convert Oldsmar into a resort town. The group adopted the name Tampashores, installed many public improvements, and incorporated the town in 1926. At the collapse of the boom it was the only municipality in Pinellas County without bonded debt.

SAFETY HARBOR, 78.5 *m.* (17 alt., 765 pop.), at the head of Old Tampa Bay, is built around a group of mineral springs known to the Indians, early Spanish explorers, and pirates. Narváez marched into the territory after his landing at Boca Ciega Bay in 1529 (*see St.Petersburg*).

The first known white man to take up residence in the vicinity was Odet Philippe, a surgeon in Napoleon's navy, who had been captured at the battle of Trafalgar in 1805 and transported to the Bahama Islands, where he was held prisoner for two years. Upon his release he joined the French Huguenot colony in Charleston, S.C. There he married and resumed the practice of medicine. Leaving in 1819, he settled on the Indian River in Florida and began cultivating fruit. When sailing to the West Indies to secure citrus stock, according to papers in the possession of his descendants, he was halted and boarded by pirates who, disgruntled at finding no booty, threatened to scuttle his ship. Disclosure that Philippe was a doctor brought a welcome reaction, and he was taken on board the pirate vessel, 'a dirty craft manned by a similar crew, where lay a sick, offensive old Spaniard.' Later, both ships anchored in a near-by cove, and within a week the doctor had cured the sick man. So pleased was the old pirate that he presented Philippe with an iron chest filled with money, told him to be on his way, and assured him that in the future he would be 'as free as a fish in these waters.'

Four years later Philippe abandoned his Indian River plantation because of a threatened Indian uprising. With his household goods, family, and slaves, he embarked on his schooner and sailed southward along the Florida Keys, where he again encountered the old pirate. When the doctor explained what had befallen him and expressed a desire to find a new home, the pirate displayed a chart and pointed out Espiritu Santo Bay, as De Soto had named Tampa Bay in 1539. 'There is but one other to compare to it—Naples,' declared the pirate, who lyrically described the beauties of the place and the mineral springs at the head of the bay.

Philippe sailed around the keys and up to the bluffs at the head of the bay. Here, in 1823, the doctor and his slaves cleared the land and established a new plantation. During the succeeding years he made many trips to Cuba and the Bahamas, bringing back citrus stock, guavas, and avocados. Some tobacco was grown, and the doctor taught his nurse to make cigars, a trade he had learned in France and the Bahamas. In 1839 he established a fishery to supply the garrison at Fort Brooke in Tampa. Settlers from many parts of the State came to obtain citrus plantings and to learn how to graft buds of the sweet orange on the sour orange tree that grew wild in the hammocks. In 1848 a hurricane swept away Philippe's home and slave quarters, and damaged his groves; most of his papers and records, including the pirate chest, were lost. Philippe died in 1869 at the age of 100, and was buried in the dense hammock that bears his name.

Many Indian mounds at Safety Harbor were excavated by the Smithsonian Institution in 1930; the principal one in the group is a large mound with flat top and precipitous sides; 50 yards west is a small shell mound, 7 feet high; beyond is a low circular mound, 40 feet in diameter. The mounds contain both pre- and post-Columbian objects; shell and bone artifacts have been found deep in the mounds, and such articles as an iron axe and a silver tubular bead on the higher levels.

CLEARWATER, 87.5 *m.* (29 alt., 7,607 pop.) (*see Tour 6b*), is at the junction with US 19 (*see Tour 6b*).

Tour 21

High Springs—Gainesville—Ocala—Leesburg—Orlando; 136.9 *m.* US 441.

Hard-surfaced roadbed throughout; watch for cattle along highway.
Route paralleled by Atlantic Coast Line R.R. between High Springs and Mount Dora, and by Seaboard Air Line Ry. between Zellwood and Orlando.
Good accommodations.

This route traverses the western slope of the heavily timbered ridge section of north central Florida, winds around and between numerous lakes offering fine fresh-water fishing, and crosses a prosperous citrus-raising area. Side roads lead to several popular springs. Nearly four centuries ago Hernando de Soto and his army marched through this territory in search of fabulously rich cities which did not exist.

US 441 branches southeast from US 41 (*see Tour 4d*) at HIGH SPRINGS, 0 *m.* (75 alt., 1,864 pop.) (*see Tour 4d*).

Flatwoods along the route are broken by occasional rolling fields planted with tobacco, corn, and squash, and large pecan groves; many poultry farms specialize in white leghorns; a large hilltop farm, 4.5 *m.*, is planted with tung-nut trees (*see Tour 3b*), set out in 1932, as a large sign announces.

ALACHUA (Ind., jug: pronounced Ah-lah-chuay), 6.6 *m.* (81 alt., 865 pop.), is a hillside town with old frame houses scattered along quiet oak-shaded streets. Municipally-owned light and power, water, and refrigeration plants provide revenue for payment of all public expenses. Founded in 1884 when the Plant System, now the Atlantic Coast Line Railroad, was built through this section, the town developed rapidly as a shipping point for tobacco, sea-island cotton, and winter vegetables; today, it ships watermelons chiefly, dispatching as many as 700 carloads northward every June. An old map indicates that the Creek Indian settlement of Alachua occupied the approximate site of the present village in 1715.

Southeast of Alachua the route crosses rolling country with heavy stands of slash pine and a sprinkling of well-tended farms growing bright-leaf tobacco and corn. Parts of the rolling highway are bordered with oaks and cedars. The mission village of Santa Fé de Toloca, established in this vicinity early in the seventeenth century, was the scene of an Indian revolt in 1656. In the spring of 1702 marauding Creek from Georgia attacked the village; the inhabitants fled, saving the church vestments, but the church and village were burned.

PARADISE, 17.8 *m.*, (192 alt., 75 pop.), is a turpentine settlement surrounded by pine forests. Ramshackle unpainted cabins, occupied by Negro workers, are grouped about a new brick and frame still.

GAINESVILLE, 21.6 *m.* (185 alt., 10,465 pop.) (*see Tour 3b*) is at the junction with State 13 (*see Tour 3b and c*).

Right from Gainesville on State 14 to the junction with a paved county road, 3.5 *m.*; R. on this road to the junction with a woods road, 6.5 *m.*; R. here to DEVIL'S MILL HOPPER, 7 *m.* This 'sinkhole,' like others in the vicinity, was created by the action of an underground stream that weakened the limestone substructure and caused a cave-in. The sink forms a funnel-shaped depression sloping to a depth of approximately 100 feet. Fourteen small springs cascade down the sides, filling a pool and draining through an underground outlet. Violets, ferns, dogwood, and magnolias grow in profusion; the rim of the sink is surrounded with dense stands of hardwood.

PAYNE'S PRAIRIE, 26.1 *m.*, spanned by a two-mile causeway, is an extensive marsh blanketed with grasses, pontilana, beds of purple hyacinths, and yellow and white water lilies. This is one of the few spots where yellow lotus grows wild, blooming during the spring. The seeds of this flower were called *hatchee chinquapin* (water chinquapin) by the Timucuan Indians. The area has been under water several times; a small steamer plying the lake that existed in 1892 was marooned when the water disappeared through underground passages, a phenomenon that had previously occured in 1823 and 1870.

The prairie, dotted with ponds, drained by winding creeks, and crisscrossed by fences, is used to pasture cattle. Flocks of heron and other marsh birds are numerous. Hunters claim that the ducks killed on this and other north Florida prairies have a celerylike flavor, attributed to the arrowhead and other water grasses in their diet.

King Payne, nephew of Chief Secoffee, who in 1750 led the Seminoles into Florida from Georgia, became chief of this region after his uncle's death in 1785. During the early 1800's he and his tribe became so troublesome to American settlers along the Georgia border that, although Florida was a Spanish possession, Colonel Daniel Newnan and his force of volunteers were dispatched to the area. They clashed with the Indians here in October 1812, and King Payne was among the first to fall. When expected reinforcements failed to appear, Newnan's men were compelled to retreat. For several weeks the ragged soldiers, many of them barefoot, were forced to slaughter and eat the few horses they possessed. After subsisting on palmetto buds, gophers, and alligators, they finally reached a camp on the St. Johns River. In February of the following year, American troops routed the Indians, burning almost 400 villages and confiscating 300 horses, 400 head of cattle, and thousands of deerskins.

MICANOPY (Ind., head chief; pronounced Mik-an-opy), 33.2 *m.* (100 alt., 725 pop.), a village of old brick and frame buildings, is surrounded by large oaks, lofty cabbage palms, and pecan groves. The first citrus trees on the route appear here, and the landscape assumes a more tropical aspect. The town site was once occupied by Timucuan Indians, a tribe antedating the Seminole in Florida. In later years powerful Seminole chiefs ruled this territory, among them Micanope, for whom the settlement was named. White settlers arrived in 1817, following the grant of 290,000 acres of land to Don Fernando de la Maza Arredondo of Cuba (*see Tour 3c*). For several miles US 441 parallels (L) the shores of ORANGE LAKE.

McINTOSH, 38.9 *m.* (73 alt., 272 pop.), built on a rich hardwood hammock, is surrounded by large citrus and pecan groves.

ORANGE LAKE, 39.4 *m.* (88 alt., 200 pop.), is near the southern shore of the lake.

Left from Orange Lake on a paved road to a boat landing, 0.6 *m.*, where boats and guides are obtainable for a visit to BIRD ISLAND, a natural rookery and bird sanctuary owned and maintained by the American Audubon Society. The naturally formed 'floating islands' in this group vary in diameter from a few feet to several hundred, and in depth from 3 to 10 feet. They are formed from small clumps of roots, or matted grass, which have sunk to the bed of the lake, and during high water or hot weather have been forced to the surface by the formation of gas. Grass, aquatic plants, and weeds have grown on the islands; there are many elder, myrtle, and maple trees 25 feet high. This vegetation acts as sails, causing the islands to move when a breeze springs up. The birds of this region never lose track of their nests, although their home island may float to a different part of the lake at any time. Among the birds are American and snowy egrets, heron, ibis, anhinga or American snakebird, and gallinules. Early Indians believed that souls of the dead buried on these islands reached the 'Land of the Sure' when the islands sank.

At 51.1 *m.* is (R) the arched entrance to the grounds of the FESSENDEN ACADEMY, a training school for Negroes, sponsored by the American Missionary Association.

ZUBER, 52 *m.*, is a community built around a large rock-crushing plant, where limestone from adjacent pits is crushed, washed, and shipped for use in road construction.

South of Zuber the highway winds through a highly developed area of small farms, skirting the shores of many small lakes and passing occasional cypress hammocks and stands of slash pine. This region marks the approximate northern boundary of the State's citrus belt. Fields of black-eyed Susans, white and purple asters, and clumps of delicate white-and-lavender spiked lupines border the highway in spring.

OCALA, 58.2 *m.* (99 alt., 7,281 pop.), seat of Marion County, is a busy trading and shipping center for truck growers and phosphate- and limestone-mining companies. The town has the vigorous bustle of a modern northern city, although the square in the center of the business and shipping district, with its courthouse, huge oaks, and subtropical foliage, is typical of nineteenth-century Florida. The town's name is a corruption of Ocali (Ind., water's edge), the name of a near-by Indian village through which De Soto passed in 1539 on his march northward through Florida.

In 1825 an Indian trading post was established about two miles east of the townsite; in 1827 the post was manned with troops and named Fort

King; during the Seminole War the fort was headquarters for central Florida. Here, on April 3, 1835, Wiley Thompson, an Indian agent, called a council of chiefs to explain the Government's intentions of enforcing the 1833 treaty in which Indian leaders had agreed to emigrate to the Indian Territory. When an Indian named Jumper, speaking for Chief Micanope, declared his people would never sign the treaty, Thompson immediately prohibited the sale of arms and ammunition to the Indians. Thereupon the colorful Indian leader, Osceola, declared: 'Am I a Negro—a slave? My skin is dark, but not black. I am an Indian—a Seminole. The white man shall not make me black. I will make the white man red with blood, and then blacken him in the sun and rain, where the wolf shall smell of his bones, and the buzzard live upon his flesh.'

The following October Osceola and his followers executed Charley Emathla, a Mikasuki chief who had favored emigration, and scattered to the four winds the money Charley had received from the sale of his cattle to the hated white men. Thompson then threatened the Indian chiefs with withdrawal of annuities unless the emigration treaty was signed. Osceola rose dramatically and pinned the treaty to the desk with his dagger, crying, 'This is the only treaty I will ever make with the whites!' The treaty, still preserved in the National Archives Building in Washington, plainly shows the cut through three leaves made by Osceola's dagger. On December 28, 1835, Osceola appeared at Fort King and killed Thompson and Lieutenant Constantine Smith, and on the same day Major Dade and his entire command were annihilated by an Indian band on near-by Withlacoochee River (*see Tour 22*). Thus began the Seminole War (*see History and Archaeology and Indians*), which continued until August 1842.

When the first white settlers came into this section, acres of wild orange groves studded the rich hammock lands. After the Seminole War standard varieties of citrus fruits were introduced. During the subtropical expositions held in Jacksonville between 1888 and 1891, displays of fruits and winter vegetables caused much favorable comment, and are said to have aroused northern interest in Florida citrus.

By legislative act Ocala became in 1852 the seat of the East Florida Seminary, the first institution of learning established by the State; the school was later removed to Gainesville (*see Education*).

Ocala boomed in 1935 when work started on the Gulf-Atlantic Ship Canal. Tents and shacks were hurriedly put up in the environs to shelter newcomers and provide temporary quarters for new business enterprises. Camp Roosevelt (*see below*), constructed near by to house an army of workers, became a city in itself. Festivals, bands, sound trucks, and a flood of oratory enlivened elections on the question of whether or not the right-of-way should be provided at county expense; a bond issue of $1,500,000 was finally voted for the purpose. Although WPA supplied most of the labor, the unemployed in Florida and surrounding states, together with tradesmen, promoters, gamblers, and others attracted by visions of quick money, converged upon the town in large numbers.

Designed to aid national defense and facilitate shipping between the Gulf States and the Atlantic seaboard, the canal will provide a sea-level, toll-free waterway 195 miles long. As laid out by army engineers, the route of the canal follows the channel of the St. Johns River from its mouth through Jacksonville to Palatka, thence southwest along the Oklawaha River to a point 8 miles south of Ocala; continuing southwest, it cuts through the high ground of the Trail Ridge to join the Withlacoochee River near Dunnellon, which it follows to the Gulf at Port Inglis.

The building of such a waterway as a barge canal had been studied by Government engineers for a century; as a ship canal, it has been discussed since 1926. On August 30, 1935, President Roosevelt authorized the building of the canal and allocated $5,000,000 from emergency relief funds toward its construction; two additional allotments of $200,000 followed. On September 19, 1935, a charge of dynamite set off by wire from the White House officially inaugurated operations. By the summer of 1936, when work was suspended, 13,000,000 cubic yards of earth had been excavated, and 4,700 acres of right-of-way cleared.

After further studies had been made in the fall of 1936 and spring of 1937 by army engineers, a report was transmitted to Congress by Secretary of War Woodring in April 1937, recommending the completion of a canal 33 feet deep at a minimum and 400 feet wide, at a cost of $197,921,000. On June 8, 1937, the Committee on Rivers and Harbors of the House of Representatives recommended the passage of a bill authorizing the completion of the canal, but Congress adjourned before a vote was taken; the committee, it is anticipated, will submit a new bill at the next session of Congress (1939).

Ocala is at the junction with State 31 (*see Tour 22*), which unites with US 441 for 10.8 *m.*

Left from Ocala on State 19 to SILVER SPRINGS, 5.5 *m.* (47 alt.). South of the village is a group of 150 natural springs issuing from the porous Ocala limestone and flowing into a common basin. The combined flow, constituting the source of the Silver River, a tributary of the Oklawaha, varies from 500 to 800 million gallons a day. The abundant rainfall in this section rapidly passes through the surface soil and is absorbed in the underlying limestone; as this stratum is very thick, it stores immense quantities of water. This moisture is constantly seeping seaward through subterranean channels, but when the water finds a convenient opening at the surface, it bursts forth in a spring.

Silver Springs, estimated to be 100,000 years old, has one large aperture through which water gushes to the surface from a visible cavern 65 feet long and 12 feet high. The discovery of fossilized remains of mastodons and manatees indicate that this was a watering place for prehistoric mammals. The springhead is circular in shape and partly surrounded by a sand bathing beach (*diving towers, floats; swimming suits for rent*). The water, with a temperature of 72° throughout the year, has a magnesium and sulphate content. Filtered through limestone, it is so clear that light rays are broken into prismatic colors, giving the river an iridescent luster. Electrically-driven glass-bottomed boats (*short trips*, $1; *longer trips*, $2) enable visitors to view the formations and animal and plant life in the depths of the pools. At 80 feet objects at the bottom are clearly visible. Grapelike clusters of coral fern blossom and bear fruit in the depths; on the surface the 'bridal wreath' blooms with an orangelike fragrance. The many fishes in this natural aquarium include garfish, catfish, bass, eel, and such salt-water habitants as the mullet, flounder, and menhaden, which swim up the St. Johns and Oklawaha rivers to destroy scale parasites which cannot live in fresh water. There are 11 kinds of turtles, 7 varieties of shellfish, and 4 of crustacea, including the giant fresh-water shrimp.

Guides point out in the spring the Devil's Kitchen, Catfish Hotel, Blue Grotto,

Ladies' Parlor, and the legendary Indian Cave, in which, according to tradition, two Indian lovers, Chulcotah and Winonah, drowned themselves when their romance was opposed by their respective tribes.

FLORIDA REPTILE INSTITUTE (*open* 7:30–6 *daily; adm.* 25¢; *guides*), has on exhibition a large variety of snakes, lizards, turtles, alligators, and crocodiles, and maintains a 100-acre farm for the breeding and raising of reptiles and amphibians for sale to zoos, scientific institutions, clinics, and individuals. Diamondback rattlers cost from $1 to $5, depending on size; coral snakes bring from $3 to $5. A box of 8 assorted snakes, all more than 4 feet long, can be purchased for $10, and a collection of 10 small, highly colored snakes for $2.50. The Institute's catalog advises that it does 'not send poisonous snakes to minors.'

The price of a 2-foot baby crocodile is $3; that of a 10-foot monster, $300. Alligators are to be had at prices ranging from 25¢ for a baby, to $1,000 for a 12-foot specimen. Turtles and lizards bring from 50¢ to $15, and a choice black widow can be purchased for 50¢. Live food for reptiles varies in price; frogs cost 50¢ a dozen; mice, 10¢ a pair; earthworms, 25¢ a dozen; meal worms, 50¢ a hundred; and small snakes, $6 a dozen. Rattlesnake or alligator oil costs $1 an ounce. Here can be bought such necessary supplies and equipment as large and small snake hooks at 50¢ each, first-aid kits for snake bite at $2.50, and Sphagnum moss for cages at $1 a bushel.

Rattlesnake and moccasins are milked of their venom every Sunday at 3 p.m. The head of the reptile is held over a glass and an experienced operator presses his fingers against the sacks behind the fangs, from which the venom drains. This is centrifuged, crystallized by chemical dehydration, and sealed in bottles. The venom of diamondback rattlesnakes and cottonmouth water moccasins sells for $2 a gram; that of timber and Texas diamondback rattlers for $3; copperhead venom brings $5. The sale is largely to medical institutions, which use the venom in the preparation of anti-venom and as a substitute for morphine in the treatment of hemorrhagic conditions of the blood.

The OKLAWAHA RIVER (Ind., bad crossing; dark crooked river), 9.8 *m.*, crossed on a red iron drawbridge, forms part of Florida's extensive system of inland waterways, stretching from the St. Johns River at Jacksonville, by way of the Oklawaha River and lakes, with portage to the Kissimmee River and Lake Okeechobee.

At 19.1 *m.* the road enters the OCALA NATIONAL FOREST, a 286,000-acre preserve and game refuge, known locally as the 'Big Scrub' because of the predominance of scrub or sand pine. This tree, similar to the Virginia pine of the Middle Atlantic States, the jack pine of the Lake States, and the lodgepole pine of the Rockies, grows in dense stands amid thick undergrowth of saw palmetto, rosemary, and scrub oak. It is relatively short-lived and easily killed by fire. Sand pine, a light and brittle wood, is largely used in Florida as fuel, although it is potentially adaptable to paper manufacture. The porous sandy soil required by the scrub pine is characteristic of this area.

JUNIPER SPRINGS, 26.2 *m.* (*swimming free; bathhouse* 25¢; *picnic shelters; open fireplaces*), has a daily flow of 7,250,000 gallons of water with a year-round temperature of 72°. A mill wheel, turned by the overflow of the spring, operates a generator which furnishes electric light for the building and grounds. (*Canoe trips down Juniper Creek to Fern Hammock can be arranged here.*) State 19 continues eastward to BARBERVILLE, 47 *m.* (44 alt., 357 pop.) (*see Tour 2b*).

South of Ocala the route winds through dense thickets of oak, shortleaf pine, and hickory, and traverses open stretches of matted green palmetto. Throughout this area lives the scrub jay (*see Animal Life*), peculiar to Florida, lacking the crest of the blue jay. Early in February great flocks of robins descend in the fields, making a stopover on their long flight north. For a day or two they gather on telegraph wires and the bare limbs of cypresses and oaks. The air is filled with their twittering and then suddenly they are gone. Weeks later the press in some northern community announces that spring is just around the corner, for a robin has been seen on the courthouse lawn.

At 60.1 *m.* is the junction with paved State 239.

Right on this highway to the CANAL EXCAVATION, 6.8 *m.*, the first excavation of the National Gulf-Atlantic Ship Canal (*see above*), dug with mule-drawn scrapers. Right along the canal on a graded road 2 *m.* to the beginning of the MACHINE EXCAVATION, dug with steam shovels; high spoil banks rise on each side.

CAMP ROOSEVELT, 61.4 *m.*, engineering and administration headquarters for the National Gulf-Atlantic Ship Canal project (*see above*), has 75 modern cottages, an auditorium and community house, dormitories, and a cafeteria, serving as an NYA resident project. One hundred and twenty girls attend vocational classes in home making and beauty culture, and are employed in sewing for public agencies. On the landscaped grounds are broad winding drives.

The highway winds through rolling country of white sand, covered with blackjack oaks. Intervening fertile areas are planted to corn, green beans, and squash.

BELLEVIEW, 69 *m.* (83 alt., 400 pop.), a village of old frame houses surrounded by truck farms and citrus and pecan groves, has a fruit packing plant and several lumber mills.

Belleview is at the junction with State 2 (*see Tour 22*).

East of Belleview the road climbs several hills from which are good views of the surrounding open country. Thick stands of blackjack oak and numerous limestone sinks are passed.

OCKLAWAHA, 76.9 *m.* (66 alt., 220 pop.), is on the northern shore of Lake Weir. Like other towns in this section, its prosperity is dependent on the growing and packing of citrus fruit.

Right from Ocklawaha on a sand road to the BARKER HOUSE, 0.2 *m.*, a white, two-story residence in which Fred and 'Ma' Barker, leaders of the Karpis-Barker gang, were killed on January 16, 1935, by Federal agents. These criminals had been the principals in the Bremer kidnapping in Milwaukee, Wis., the previous fall. Ma ('Machine-Gun Kate') Barker, a woman well in her 50's, was an experienced criminal and the mother of three criminal sons. The trail of the fugitives was picked up in Chicago when the Department of Justice men raided an apartment used by the Barkers and found a map of Florida, with the name Ocala circled in pencil. The house on Lake Weir, in which Ma and her son, Fred, were hiding, was discovered, and one day the former was seen standing beside a rowboat, framed against a background of Spanish moss. All roads in the vicinity were blocked, the officers surrounded the house, and the Barkers were given a shouted warning that it would be best to surrender peaceably. The rattle of a machine gun was the answer, precipitating a fight that lasted several hours. When G-men entered the house, Ma lay dead beside her machine gun, the drum of which was empty, and Fred lay dead a few feet away.

LAKE WEIR, 78.7 *m.* (125 pop.), founded in 1874, is a popular resort for fishermen and campers. Orange and grapefruit trees cover the surrounding hills, and the crop is handled in a large packing house here. A superior quality of white sand, used in building operations, is pumped from the lake bottom and shipped throughout Florida.

WEIRSDALE, 81.7 *m.* (303 pop.), is another resort on the high slopes of the lake. Along the shore are many cottages, a community club, and bathing facilities. Four large citrus-packing plants are operated here during the season. (*Excursions up the picturesque Oklawaha River can be arranged here*).

LADY LAKE, 86.7 *m.* (72 alt., 233 pop.), a roadside settlement with several natural parks and a number of fishing camps, has the usual fruit-packing plant beside the railroad. In the vicinity are several large vineyards and extensive fields of watermelons, which are harvested early in May.

FRUITLAND PARK, 90.7 *m.* (113 alt., 270 pop.), is the home of many owners of citrus groves in the vicinity. The grove owners' big houses are near the lake; workers' cottages are scattered through the adjoining timberlands, convenient to the groves and packing houses. The families of grove owners, managers of fruit packing and shipping concerns, and gentlemen farmers lead an active social life. Their wives are smartly-dressed club women. Club meetings, church affairs, and sports occupy the leisure hours of the community.

Fruitland Park was founded in 1876 by Major O.P.Rooks, and named for the Fruitland Nurseries of Augusta, Ga. Here Rooks established a large nursery specializing in rare fruits and flowers. In 1883 a group of Englishmen settled here under the leadership of Granville Chetwynd Stapleton. The young men lived at 'The Hall,' a large boarding house, and organized the 'Bucket and Dipper Club.' The only refreshment at meetings was water, ladled from a bucket with a large dipper. Many stories of these settlers have been related by Marjorie Kinnan Rawlings in her novel, *Golden Apples* (1937).

Several nurseries and private homes are show places for plants and flowers. The palms at the FRIEDRICH HOME, on Mirror Lake, are considered among the finest in Lake County. The palms, roses, and cacti growing on the grounds and in the nursery of the CHARLES FOX ESTATE, attract many visitors. On the BOSANQUET ESTATE are Banksian roses and Clementine tangerines. About 30 varieties of hibiscus from Hawaii were sent here by the U.S. Department of Agriculture for cultivation.

The HOLY TRINITY EPISCOPAL CHURCH was erected in 1888 with funds raised principally in England. Under its lich gate, one of the oldest in America, biers are rested while the introductory part of funeral services is read.

LEESBURG, 95 *m.* (97 alt., 4,113 pop.), largest and oldest town in Lake County, founded in 1856 by the Lee family of New York, occupies an elevation between Lakes Griffin and Harris. The compact business district has two- and three-story brick and frame buildings facing several wide thoroughfares. Residential sections are landscaped with large oaks, a variety of palms, and flowering subtropical trees and shrubs. Particularly attractive are the scarlet poinsettias in full bloom throughout the Christmas holidays.

The surrounding area produces large quantities of citrus fruit, berries, grapes, and watermelons. The vineyards here are among the oldest in the State; a local factory manufactures jelly, jam, grape juice, and wine. Several kaolin mines in the vicinity supply clay for the manufacture of fine chinaware.

The VENETIAN GARDENS, bordering Lake Harris, are a civic development. More than 100 acres of soil pumped from the lake bottom have transformed a marsh into a park, with a yacht basin and several miniature islands; docks accommodate lake boats, gondolas, and other small craft. Varicolored lights play on a fountain on one of the islands. Thousands of hemerocallis bulbs, set out annually, present a strip of golden color from March to July.

The annual National Fresh Water Bass Tournament, held from January 10 to March 10, is a major sports event. Inboard and outboard motorboating and mothboat sailing are favored pastimes during the summer.

Leesburg is at the junction with State 2 (*see Tour* 8*a*), which unites with US 441 for 2.5 miles.

East of Leesburg, US 441 winds through large citrus groves, with lakes always in view. Tall oleander hedges, in white and red bloom during spring, and clumps of bignonia, bright with orange-gold blossoms, border the highway at intervals. The route crosses DEAD RIVER, 103 *m.* a waterway dug in 1878 to link Lake Harris and Lake Eustis, and so named because of its slow current. There is good fishing along its banks, which are lined with moss-draped cypress and willow thickets.

TAVARES, 105.5 *m.* (74 alt., 1,090 pop.), seat of Lake County, was named in 1875 by its founder, Alexander St.Clair Abrams, for a Spanish ancestor. The town is built around a four-story, gray brick courthouse of classic design, which looms above the business district. In the square, planted with cedars, oaks, and palms, stands a flagpole with a novel base, constructed of stones contributed by residents from other states and countries; the stones include pink granite from Georgia, black marble from Japan, amethyst quartz from Nova Scotia, petrified wood from Arizona, a brick from Virginia, and a lump of coal from West Virginia.

Abrams originally planned the town as a tourist community, but later decided that it was destined to become 'a great industrial and railroad center, the seat of a new county, and ultimately the capital of Florida.' He spent more than $500,000 in building a large hotel, lumber mills, stores, a cigar factory, and in financing railroads. Streets and avenues were named for his relatives and friends. At his hotel, The Peninsular, were entertained the Duke of Sutherland and other British noblemen. A large part of the town was destroyed by fire in 1888, and after a destructive freeze the site was practically abandoned for a few years. The first courthouse of yellow brick, a churchlike structure minus a steeple, was built by Abrams in 1888 and now houses the fire department.

Tavares is the western apex of the 'Golden Triangle,' a prosperous citrus-growing region, with Mount Dora and Eustis as the other points. SEMINOLE PARK, on the southern edge of the town, was dedicated to General Charles Summerall (1867–), Chief of Staff of the U.S. Army, born in this section.

US 441 follows the north shore of Lake Dora for several miles. A Government party surveying Orange County boundaries in 1882 included John Weeks, Secretary of War (1921–25), as one of the engineers. Invited to stay at the home of Dora Ann Drawdy, the party bestowed the name of Lake Dora on the body of water bordering her farm.

MOUNT DORA, 110.4 *m.* (107 alt., 1,613 pop.), founded in 1882, rises in successive terraces from the shores of the lake. The broad streets overlooking the water are shaded by oaks, magnolias, and a variety of palms. The neat white frame houses, set back in ample lawns, give the town the appearance of a quiet New England village. Mount Dora has long been a rendezvous for yachting and outboard motorboat enthusiasts. Lake Dora and other lakes are connected by canals, and it is possible to reach the Atlantic Ocean by inland waterways via the Oklawaha and St. Johns Rivers. The yacht club, one of the oldest in Florida, holds annual regattas here during February.

The South Florida Chautauqua at Mount Dora, established in 1885, was one of the first in the South. The assembly grounds and auditorium were in a tract of virgin forest between Lakes Dora and Gertrude, a site now known as Sylvan Shores, a residential development. The chautauqua was abandoned shortly after 1905 when the auditorium was destroyed by fire.

In DONNELLY PARK, adjoining the business district, are a large municipal auditorium and recreational grounds.

Between Mount Dora and Zellwood the highway penetrates a thickly forested area and makes many turns before again entering a citrus area.

ZELLWOOD, 116.5 *m.* (90 alt., 700 pop.), settled and named by Elwood Zell, prominent Philadelphia publisher, is the winter home of many northern visitors as well as local citrus growers. A large packing house handles fruit from neighboring groves.

Right from Zellwood on a graded sand road to the FLORIDA PEAT HUMUS AND EXPERIMENT GARDENS, 3.4 *m.*, where muck from the Lake Apopka region is processed for use as fertilizer. In its natural state this humus is used to fertilize poor soil; dried and ground, it serves poultry raisers as litter for chicken houses. The peat, cut into bricks and dried in the sun, is often used for fuel.

PLYMOUTH, 120.5 *m.* (120 alt., 150 pop.), a citrus-growing center, is the site of the PLYMOUTH CITRUS GROWERS PACKING HOUSE (*open*), which has an average annual output of 500,000 boxes. Apiaries yield an annual average of 25,000 pounds of orange-blossom honey.

APOPKA (Ind., potato eating place), 123.6 *m.* (145 alt., 1,134 pop.), was settled in 1856 and until 1887 was called The Lodge, for a Masonic lodge building erected here by slaves shortly before the War between the States. The LODGE (*members only*) is still used for meetings. Apopka, known as 'the Fern City,' is a trading and shipping point for growers of the surrounding area. Many slat houses for growing ferns are in the town and vicinity. Fern cultivation is not a seasonal industry, and cut sprays are shipped throughout the year. A fernlike herb, *asparagus plumosus*, is supplied to florists in all parts of the United States and Canada.

Left from Apopka on State 24 to ROCK SPRINGS, 6.5 *m.*, flowing from a 15-foot limestone bluff. HOWARD KELLY MEMORIAL PARK, donated by Dr. Howard Kelly of Johns Hopkins University, contains many native trees, birds, and animals, and a public swimming pool (*free*).

At 126.6 *m.* is the junction with an unimproved road.

Left on this road 4.5 *m.* to WEKIWA SPRINGS (*adm. 25¢; swimming, fishing, and scenic boat trip*), with a daily flow of 42,000,000 gallons.

FAIRVILLA, 133.1 *m.* (100 alt.), a small suburban settlement, has a large packing plant housed in three concrete buildings.

ORLANDO, 136.9 *m.* (111 alt., 27,330 pop.) (*see Orlando*).

Points of Interest: Orlando Zoo, Eola Park, Sunshine Park, Gaston Edwards Park, World War Memorial, Overstreet Residence, Old Courthouse, New Courthouse, Albertson Public Library, and others.

Orlando is at the junction with US 17 (*see Tour 2c*) and State 22 (*see Tour 9*).

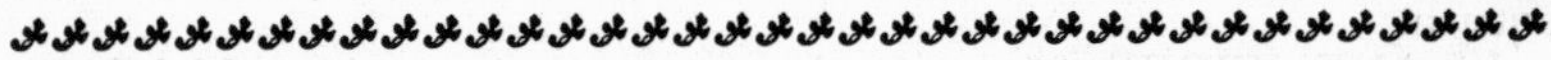

Tour 22

Waldo—Ocala—Belleview—Bushnell—Dade City—Plant City; 134.3 *m.*
State 31, US 441, State 23.

Hard-surfaced roadbed throughout; watch for cattle along highway.
Route paralleled by Seaboard Air Line Ry.
Good accommodations.

This direct route south through central Florida traverses rich truck-farming lands growing green beans, peppers, squash, and corn. Along the highway large pecan groves and extensive young citrus groves alternate with stretches of pines, scarred by turpentiners.

State 31 branches south from State 13 (*see Tour 3b*) at WALDO, 0 *m.* (157 alt., 703 pop.) (*see Tour 3b*).

Between Waldo and Campville, State 31 runs through pine woods for several miles. The trees stand bronze-green in the sun, their shadows long and black against the slopes. In the timber portable sawmills are noisily at work. Piles of freshly hewn cross-ties appear along sandy trails, awaiting transportation to railroad sidings. Negro women and children, with crude poles, fish for perch and bream in small ponds and in trickling roadside streams so narrow that they can be stepped across. In clearings are pine-slab cabins surrounded by beds of collards, cabbages, and corn, all tightly fenced to keep out wandering hogs and the family mule. Many of these primitive houses are covered with the delicate pink coral vine. Farther south, farmhouses and tilled fields appear; large oaks, magnolias, and chinaberry trees dot the landscape; acres of pecan trees, herds of cattle, and many corrals appear along the road.

CAMPVILLE, 9.7 *m.* (144 alt., 250 pop.), is a turpentine community. In contrast with its smoky still and rough unpainted shacks are fields of varicolored gladioli.

South of Campville the road traverses open country planted to corn, green beans, tobacco, and pecans.

HAWTHORN, 14.9 *m.* (146 alt., 600 pop.), is a quiet oak-shaded village in the midst of extensive bean fields. Incorporated in 1890, it was named for James M. Hawthorn, owner of the site. Between its few low brick business buildings stand several two-story frame houses with ornate jig-saw galleries.

Throughout this area trucks cruise day and night during spring months, picking up loads of vegetables, which are bought direct from growers and sold to wholesale markets in the larger cities. Farmers post signs along the highway instructing drivers at what fields to call for cabbages, beans, and squash.

ISLAND GROVE, 25 *m.* (69 alt., 275 pop.), occupying a high hammock, is encircled with citrus groves, in some of which unusually tall cabbage palms tower above orange and grapefruit trees. Island Grove is the home of Marjorie Kinnan Rawlings, whose novels *South Moon Under* (1933) and *The Yearling* (1938) deal with the inhabitants of the surrounding scrubland (*see Literature*).

Between Island Grove and Citra the route crosses an extensive swampland carpeted with small white lilies, locally known as Easter lilies, and penetrates an area of flourishing citrus groves, many flanked with beds of pink, lavender, and crimson petunias. Occasional stretches of lowlands are matted with blueberry and huckleberry bushes; in midsummer Negro families appear in the fields picking berries for their own use and for sale.

CITRA, 27.7 *m.* (69 alt., 485 pop.), founded in the early 1880's, is a village of large rambling houses and ample gardens shaded by giant oaks. The pineapple orange, an oblate variety maturing in midseason, was developed in a neighboring grove.

The highway, fenced on both sides, rises gradually to sandy ridges covered with blackjack oak, an indication of 'sorry' soil, as local farmers phrase it, and passes into rolling open country, dotted with symmetrical oaks and fields of corn, okra, squash, and beans.

ANTHONY, 36.8 *m.* (76 alt., 337 pop.), has a vegetable-canning plant and supplements its income by gathering, drying, and ginning Spanish moss, which is used in stuffing mattresses and for upholstering purposes (*see Tour 6a*).

On the rich lands between Anthony and Ocala, winter vegetables are planted in late February and harvested in April. Corn stands head-high by May, when roasting ears are shipped to market.

OCALA, 44.3 *m.* (99 alt., 7,281 pop.) (*see Tour 21*), is at the junction with US 441 (*see Tour 21*) which the route follows for 11 miles (*see Tour 21*).

BELLEVIEW, 55.3 *m.* (83 alt., 400 pop.) (*see Tour 21*) is at the junction with State 23 (R), which the route now follows.

SUMMERFIELD, 59.3 *m.* (92 alt., 400 pop.), lies in an area of rich muck soil, once the bed of ancient lakes. Many garden walls, fences, and chimneys in Summerfield have been built of rock removed from dry lake bottoms and sinks.

Between Summerfield and Wildwood the terrain changes from rolling, densely forested lands to open flat pine woods. Although the soil in low areas is sour, wild flowers grow profusely in all but the coldest months, notably gallberry, an evergreen with tiny white blossoms. In early spring the swamps are filled with blue iris. Later, red and yellow deergrass appears, and scarlet-striped tiger lilies. In places the highway is bordered with wide-spreading, moss-draped oaks planted before 1880, and in others with stone fences covered with wild blackberry vines. Most of the land is under cultivation; fields of tomatoes and corn are harvested throughout April; by late May watermelons are sent to market.

In WILDWOOD, 70.3 *m.* (57 alt., 1,409 pop.), a railroad center, are the freight classification yards of the Seaboard Air Line, together with repair shops and icing stations for refrigerator cars. The town was named in 1878, when the telegraph operator at the station here in the forest at the end of the wire, headed his dispatches 'Wildwood.'

COLEMAN, 75.2 *m.* (58 alt., 786 pop.), a railroad shipping point for agricultural products, has a crate factory and several hardwood lumber mills. Naval-stores operations and the cutting of ties furnish additional employment.

SUMTERVILLE, 79.1 *m.* (76 alt., 125 pop.), consisting of a few scattered houses, a filling station and general store, was named in the 1880's for General Thomas Sumter, a Revolutionary War officer. In 1885, when the population totaled a mere 200, the town had two newspapers. A mail stage from Orlando made four trips a week, with passengers constantly complaining of the fare, which was 10¢ a mile.

Right from Sumterville on State 225 is PANASOFFKEE (Ind., deep valley), 4.1 *m* (46 alt., 91 pop.), at the head of a lake of the same name. The valley was the hiding place of Halleck-Tustenugee, one of the most feared of Seminole chiefs, who led many attacks against settlers and American troops. He agreed several times to surrender, but on every occasion, after obtaining supplies, fled to the wilderness. On December 20, 1841, his men raided the town of Mandarin (*see Tour 1b*), near Jacksonville, killed several inhabitants, fired the town, and escaped. Not all of his men approved of Halleck-Tustenugee's obstinate resistance to the whites; some deserted. In April 1842 the chief came voluntarily to the camp at Warm Springs, near Lake Panasoffkee, and was induced to go to Fort King (Ocala), where he was held captive. Meanwhile, his band had been enticed to the camp, captured, and taken to Fort King. They were surprised to find their leader in captivity, and some accused him of having betrayed them. Aroused to fury by this insinuation, Halleck-Tustenugee raged like a madman, prostrated two of his followers, and bit off the ear of a third.

The town of Panasoffkee, founded in 1882, was laid out three years later with streets 80 feet wide; it soon had a 40-room tourist hotel, private and public schools, and a weekly newspaper. Citrus culture was the principal occupation, and the 737-acre Monarch grove in the hammock south of the lake is one of the oldest bearing groves in the State.

Between Sumterville and Bushnell long stretches of blackjack oak alternate with fertile farmlands. Many fields of tomatoes and beans in this area have overhead irrigation systems, consisting of elevated, perforated iron pipes carrying water from deep artesian wells. Drainage canals have reclaimed much swampland in this section. During the boom, enterprising promoters began real-estate developments along the highway, and sold town lots in the flatwoods. Occasional stone pillars, marking entrances to the prospective communities, represent the sole improvements.

Rutted sand trails lead into little country graveyards almost concealed by vines and underbrush among pines and blackjack oaks; few are fenced. Some markers are of concrete, one or two perhaps are of marble, but the majority are merely headboards, leaning at crazy angles, their inscriptions obliterated. On newer graves, weeded and swept clean of pine needles, appear flower offerings in mason jars and tin cans.

The annual 'cemetery cleaning' is a popular holiday in many parts of rural Florida. On a specified day, usually in the fall, residents gather to clean graves, plant flowers, and enjoy an all-day picnic; food is brought by all families attending. Chicken, fried, baked, and stewed; salads of endless variety; biscuits; sweet milk, coffee, and tea; watermelon and orange preserves; pies; chocolate, banana, and pineapple cakes—all are spread out on long tables under the trees. To eat from one's own basket would show lack of appreciation for a neighbor's cooking. The picnickers wander along the tables, sampling the dishes, and praising the contributions of friends. After all are well stuffed, work in the cemetery proceeds in a somewhat desultory manner. One first cleans one's own family lot, then helps those with larger plots, and finally works on the graves of those who have no surviving relatives.

BUSHNELL, 86.2 *m.* (74 alt., 591 pop.), seat of Sumter County, has a buff brick courthouse and a city hall, the latter occupying the lower portion of the municipal bandstand. The town, named for the engineer who surveyed the railroad right-of-way through this section, is a shipping point for winter vegetables, citrus fruit, dairy and poultry products.

Bushnell is at the junction with State 22 (*see Tour* 9).

At 88 *m.* is the junction with State 214, paved.

Right on a paved county road to DADE MEMORIAL PARK, 0.7 *m.*, on the site of old Fort Dade. This 80-acre reservation was dedicated as a State park in 1935 as a memorial to Major Francis L. Dade, who, with his men, was slain here by Indians on December 28, 1835. Setting out from Fort Brooke (Tampa) for Fort King, Dade and his company of 109 men were attacked in an open pine barren by Seminole under Chiefs Micanope and Jumper, and all but one killed. Private Ransom Clarke, left for dead, crawled from the field after dark, and though severely wounded, made his way back to Fort Brooke to report the tragedy. In February 1836, soldiers from the fort reached the scene and buried Dade and his men in two trenches; the officers in one, the men in the other. In 1842 their bodies were removed to the Federal cemetery in St.Augustine, where three pyramids mark their graves (*see St.Augustine*). The entrance arch and several foot bridges in the park are built of local rock. A low picket fence and gate mark the old Fort King and Fort Brooke trails. The crude log breastworks, which survivors of the first attack threw up, have been reproduced in concrete. A lifesize bronze figure of a soldier in the uniform of the period, mounted on a rock base, bears a bronze plaque with the names of the slain.

The WITHLACOOCHEE RIVER, 93.1 *m.*, is a deep narrow stream here where it flows through a cypress swamp. In this vicinity the Spanish explorer, Narváez, and his 300 followers crossed the river on their journey northward in May 1528 (*see St.Petersburg*). More than 200 Indians were encountered on the north bank, and in the battle that followed many of them were taken prisoner.

The highway traverses fairly level country, crisscrossed by drainage ditches choked with willows. Numerous small lakes offer good fishing; many swamps, filled with growths of cattails and arrowheads, are passed. The soil is an orange clay, used in surfacing road shoulders.

DADE CITY, 108 *m.* (98 alt., 1,811 pop.), seat of Pasco County and formerly an Indian trading post, is the commercial center of a prosperous truck-farming and citrus-fruit district. The town, typical of old Florida communities, clusters around a two-story courthouse of red brick, with Corinthian columns of white stucco, its roof pyramiding to a domed clock tower. The principal thoroughfare, with its low brick and frame buildings, is divided by a parkway landscaped with palms, oaks, and flowering shrubs. Here in November occurs the annual homecoming of the Tin Can Tourists (*see Tour 2d*).

Right from Dade City on State 210 is ST.LEO, 5 *m.* (140 alt., 158 pop.), an abbey of the Benedictine monks, established in 1889 and named for Pope Leo I. A Catholic school and summer camp, with an enrollment of 65 boys, is maintained here. Opposite the monastery is OUR LADY OF LOURDES GROTTO, built by Father Charles, whose grave is at the foot of the altar. Many pilgrimages are made to this shrine by health-seekers.

SAN ANTONIO, 8 *m.* (165 alt., 411 pop.), was founded in the early 1880's by Judge Edmund F. Dunne, former Chief Justice of Arizona, who later donated a 40-acre tract on which the HOLY NAME ACADEMY, a Catholic girls' school, was built in 1890. The school has 80 pupils. According to family tradition, Dunne once lost his way in the Arizona desert while prospecting for silver. Being a devout man, he prayed to his patron saint for rescue, vowing in return to give the name of San Antonio to the settlement he contemplated founding in Florida. Several years later, traveling through Florida, Dunne visited Clear Lake, as this spot was then called. Impressed by its beauty and in fulfillment of his promise, Dunne founded a settlement on the lake shore and named it San Antonio. The lake he renamed Jovita in honor of another Spanish saint; a village of that name lies a few miles west of San Antonio.

South of Dade City State 23 runs in a straight line over low hills offering vistas of citrus groves and cultivated farm lands. In the lower areas are hardwood sloughs and stretches of cypress swamps.

ZEPHYRHILLS, 117.3 *m.* (88 alt., 748 pop.), formerly known as Abbott's Station, has a broad main street lined with oaks. The town site was selected by Captain H.B.Jefferies, a Union army officer, as a home for G.A.R. veterans. A number of old soldiers established residences here in 1915, at which time the name of the town was changed. A crate mill and naval-stores plant are in operation here.

At 120 *m.* is the junction with State 156, a heavily traveled short cut to the outskirts of Tampa.

Right on State 156 to GLENNELL, 4.3 *m.*, a division camp of the Florida State Road Department; at 5.3 *m.* is a bridge over the Hillsborough River. Left from the bridge 200 yards to the SITE OF BURNT BRIDGE and of FORT ALABAMA. The bridge, crossed by Major Francis L. Dade and his men on their last march, was burned by the Seminole after the Dade Massacre (*see above*). It was twice rebuilt and as many times burned by raiding Indians.

HILLSBOROUGH RIVER STATE PARK (*25¢ a car*), 5.6 *m.*, a 720-acre tract bordering the road (L), was created to provide camping facilities (*tables, outdoor fireplaces, running water, furnished cabins*). Along the banks of the river, which flows the length of the park, a trail winds among towering cypress and cabbage palms. Other trails wander off to hammocks densely wooded with palms, oaks, magnolias, hickories, cedars, and sweet gums. More than 70 varieties of trees and shrubs have been marked with tags of identification for the benefit of visitors.

At 8.8 *m.* is the junction with the Temple Terrace-Thonotosassa Road; L. here to THONOTOSASSA (Ind., place of many flints), 1.2 *m.* (49 alt., 896 pop.), on an oval lake of the same name, loved by the Indians, who held here during the full moon in June their annual Green Corn Dance (*see Archeology and Indians*). At the ceremony marriages were celebrated, disputes settled, and punishments meted out to those transgressing the tribal laws during the time of feasting and rejoicing.

When Major Dade was marching with his men toward Fort King in 1835, they stopped to rest 3 miles southwest of the lake. In their supplies were Cuban oranges, which they ate, dropping the seeds, some of which sprouted. In 1846 William Miley laid out a homestead here and transplanted to his farm some of the seedlings, one of which still stands. Many old groves in this section have sprung from the seeds dropped by military expeditions. HARNEY, 13.8 *m.* (25 pop.), on the west bank of Hillsborough River, consists of a small group of houses, the remains of a cypress sawmill, and a fishing camp (*boats, fishing tackle*).

At 15.8 *m.* is the junction with US 92 (*see Tour 20*).

CRYSTAL SPRINGS, 121.2 *m.* (72 alt., 200 pop.), is built around springs with an average flow of 25,389 gallons a minute, emptying into the Hillsborough River. Below the spring, in the river, is a SWIMMING POOL, shaded by the forest; the water in the pool and for miles down the river is crystal clear.

PLANT CITY, 134.3 *m.* (137 alt., 6,800 pop.) (*see Tour 20*), is at the junction with US 92 (*see Tour 20*).

PART IV

Appendices

Chronology

1513 April 3. Juan Ponce de Leon lands on coast in vicinity of St. Augustine site and names land *Florida*, claiming it for Spain.

1516 Diego Miruelo, pilot from Cuba, obtains some pieces of gold from Florida natives.

1517 Spaniards, led by Francis Hernández de Cordova, land in Florida, but are driven off by natives.

1521 Returning to Florida, as *adelantado* (governor), Ponce de Leon attempts to establish colony; within 5 months, De Leon, fatally wounded in Indian encounter, returns with colonists to Cuba.

1528 Panfilo de Narváez leads Spanish expedition to Florida, landing on Pinellas peninsula and marching north as far as site of St. Marks. Setting sail in crude boats, De Narváez and majority of expedition lose their lives along coast. Four survivors reach western Mexico in 1536, led overland by Cabeza de Vaca.

1539 May. Hernando de Soto lands at Tampa Bay with large expedition and marches north through Florida; 4 years later remnant of expedition reaches Mexico with news of his death and burial in Mississippi River in 1542.

1540 Captain Maldonado, commander of De Soto's fleet, enters Pensacola Bay and christens it Puerto d'Anchusi.

1549 Fray Luis Cancer meets death leading expedition of missionaries to Florida.

1559 Don Tristan de Luna brings colonists to Pensacola Bay—naming it Santa Maria—starving survivors of colony later taken to Mexico.

1562 May 1. Captain Jean Ribaut, leader of French Huguenots, lands at mouth of St. Johns River, and christens it *Rivière de Mai*.

1564 Huguenot colonists, led by René Laudonnière, build Fort Caroline on a flat knoll a furlong or more above St. Johns Bluff on St. Johns River.

1565 John Hawkins, English slave trader, with 4 ships, anchors near Fort Caroline. Offers to take settlers back to France. Laudonnière refuses, but buys one of Hawkins' ships.

Ribaut brings reinforcements to Fort Caroline.

September 8. Don Pedro Menéndez de Aviles lands on shores of Matanzas River and founds St. Augustine.

September 20. Menéndez captures Fort Caroline.

September 29. Two hundred French Huguenot castaways from Ribaut's wrecked fleet are captured and killed by Menéndez near Matanzas Inlet.

October 12. Another group of castaways are captured and massacred by Menéndez at Matanzas Inlet.

1566 King Philip of Spain sends additional Jesuit priests to convert Florida Indians.

1567 Dominic de Gourges, a Frenchman, leads attack upon Fort San Mateo (Fort Caroline) and avenges deaths of his compatriots.

1568 Father Sedeno and Brother Baez begin missions in South Carolina. Baez translates Catholic catechism into Indian tongue.

1586 Sir Francis Drake, British admiral, burns St.Augustine.

1603 South Carolina missions destroyed in Indian uprising of 1597, restored by Governor Canzo of Florida.

1606 Bishop Altamirano of Cuba travels through north Florida, inspecting missions and confirming natives.

1638 Apalachee Indians are defeated by Spaniards and set to work on St.Augustine fortifications.

1639 Fort San Luis (in Tallahassee area) is completed.

1668 John Davis, English buccaneer, sacks St.Augustine.

1672 Construction begins on San Marcos, stone fort at St.Augustine.

1674 Bishop Calderon of Cuba confirms 7 young priests in north Florida, first ceremony of this kind in present territory of United States.

1675 Don Juan Rita de Salacar made captain general of Florida.

1677 Spaniards erect fortifications at St.Marks.

1680 Don Juan Marquez de Cabrera becomes captain general.

1686 Spaniards from St.Augustine disperse colony of Scots on Port Royal Island, S.C.
Fort San Fernando is constructed by Spaniards on Amelia Island.

1693 Don Laureano de Torres, governor of Florida.

1698 Don Andres d'Arriola arrives at Pensacola Bay and erects Fort San Carlos near by. First governor of Spanish colony at Pensacola.

1701 Don Joseph Cuniga, governor of Florida.

1702 English, under Governor Moore of South Carolina, invade Florida. Moore unsuccessfully besieges fort at St.Augustine, but captures Spanish fort at Amelia Island, destroys missions, and enslaves Spanish Indians.

1704 Governor Moore again raids Florida; besieges Fort San Luis near present Tallahassee, burns missions, and carries off Indians.

1718 Fort San Marcos de Apalache erected by Spaniards.

1719 French invaders capture and destroy Fort San Carlos at Pensacola.

1723 By terms of peace treaty of 1721, Pensacola area is restored to Spain.

1725 North Florida is invaded by English under Colonel John Palmer who unsuccessfully besieges St.Augustine.

1736 Spaniards begin construction of Fort Matanzas.

1740 General James Oglethorpe devastates northern Florida, captures number of Spanish outposts, but is unable to take St.Augustine.

1750 Party of Creek Indians under Secoffee migrate from Georgia into Florida and become known as the Seminole.

1763 Spain cedes Florida to England, in exchange for Cuba.
English king divides Florida into two provinces, east and west of Apalachicola River.
General James Grant becomes first English governor of East Florida. Pensacola is laid out as city.

1765 Denys Rolle founds settlement on St.Johns River after plan of Oglethorpe's Georgia colony.

Public subscription of funds to build Kings Road extending from New Smyrna to Colerain, Ga.

1768 Dr. Andrew Turnbull, Scottish physician, establishes New Smyrna colony of Minorcans, Italians, and Greeks.

1776 New Smyrna colonists remove to St. Augustine.

1777 British launch attack from St. Augustine against Savannah during Revolutionary War.

1778 General Robert Howe invades Florida with 3,000 Americans, but is repulsed by British.

1781 Pensacola is invested by Spanish force; Forts St. Michæl and St. Bernard surrender.

1782 English Tories, refugees from Georgia and South Carolina, build St. Johns Town on St. Johns River.

1783 *East Florida Gazette*, Florida's first newspaper, is published at St. Augustine.

Britain cedes Floridas, East and West, back to Spain.

St. Marys River is made part of southeast boundary of United States.

1795 All of West Florida west of Perdido River is retroceded to France by Spain.

1804 William Augustus Bowles, renegade and buccaneer, is captured by Spaniards and sent to Havana prison.

1811 January 15. Congress authorizes President 'to seize West Florida if a foreign power tries to take it.'

1812 Republic of Florida is organized by American 'patriots' with aid of American troops who occupy Spanish fort at Fernandina.

1814 August. British naval force enters Pensacola Harbor, and garrisons Forts Michael and San Carlos.

Runaway Negro slaves and Seminole Indians, aided by British, build fort, afterwards known as Negro Fort, on Apalachicola River.

November. American volunteers, under General Andrew Jackson, capture Pensacola and Fort Michael; British blow up Fort San Carlos.

1816 July. American forces under Colonel Clinch enter Florida and destroy Negro Fort on Apalachicola River.

1817 Gregor MacGregor, soldier of fortune, captures Amelia Island. During year successive adventurers, including Jared Irwin and Luis Aury, take command of island. Captain Henly, by order of President of United States, occupies island, and destroys depot of buccaneers.

Zephaniah Kingsley establishes slave training school on Fort George Island.

1818 General Andrew Jackson again invades Florida, seizes two Spanish forts, hangs two British subjects, and leaves American officials in charge of Pensacola.

1819 Treaty is prepared in Washington for transference of Florida from Spain to United States.

1820 Spain ratifies treaty with United States whereby latter purchases Florida for $5,000,000 and relinquishes all claims to Texas. No money is paid to Spain, however, as American indemnities equal the purchase price.

1821 July 10. United States formally receives East Florida from Spain.

July 14. *Florida Gazette*, Florida's second newspaper, is published in St.Augustine.

July 17. West Florida is formally transferred by Spain to United States.

1822 March 30. Act of Congress creates Territory of Florida, to govern lands ceded by Spain to United States. President appoints William P. Duval first governor of Territory.

July. First legislative council of Territory meets at Pensacola.

1823 Legislative council meets at St.Augustine.

Fort Brooke is erected at Tampa.

January 3. Joseph M. Hernández, of St.Augustine, takes his seat as delegate from Florida to Congress.

Key West is made United States naval depot and station, under Commodore Porter.

1824 U.S. Congress approves construction of Bellamy Road from Pensacola Bay to St.Augustine.

Tallahassee is selected as site of Florida capital.

1825 United States navy yard is established at Pensacola.

1829 Chipola Canal Co. is authorized to raise $50,000 by lottery to dig canal or build railroad from Chipola River to St.Andrews Bay.

1830 First Federal census gives Florida's population as 34,730.

1831 Cigar industry is established in Florida when W.H.Wall chooses factory site at Key West.

Florida Educational Society is formed at Tallahassee.

1832 Treaty of Payne's Landing whereby United States claims lands of Seminole Indians and subsequently demands removal of Indians to Arkansas.

1834 President Jackson appoints his former Secretary of War, John H. Eaton, as governor of Florida.

1835 February. Thermometer registers 7° above zero; St.Johns River is frozen several rods from shore. Frost destroys orange groves.

December 28. Osceola and Seminole band kill and scalp Indian agent, General Thompson, and five others, near Indian agency. Major Francis L. Dade and his command are massacred by Indians. These acts mark opening of seven years' warfare with Seminoles that cost United States lives of 1,500 soldiers and settlers, and $40,000,000.

1837 Decline in cotton prices, destructive frost ruinous to citrus crops, and losses suffered through Seminole War make nation-wide financial panic especially acute in Florida.

February 8. Coacoochee makes futile attack on Fort Mellon.

October 21. Osceola is captured under flag of truce and sent to Fort Moultrie, S.C.

December 25. Battle of Okeechobee occurs between Seminoles and U.S. troops under Colonel Zachary Taylor.

1838 December. First Constitutional Convention is held in St.Joseph.

1839 May 18. Seminoles are assigned territory below Charlie Apopka Creek after agreement between them and General Alexander Macomb.

1840 Population (Federal census), 54,477.

Oscilla (Aucilla) Academy, near Monticello, is given charter by legislative council.

August 7. Doctor Henry Perrine and associates murdered by Indians on Indian Key.

1841 Yellow-fever epidemic wipes out three-fourths of St.Joseph's population.
October. Coacoochee and 211 of his tribesmen are removed to Arkansas.
December 20. Indians under Halleck-Tustenugee raid Mandarin, murder several inhabitants, and fire town.

1842 Seminoles under Arpeika massacre number of whites in Colee hammock.
This year marks virtual end of Seminole War, but skirmishes continue.
August 15. Monument to soldiers who died in Seminole War is unveiled at St.Augustine.

1845 Doctor John Gorrie of Apalachicola builds first successful ice-making machine.
March 3. Congress admits Florida as a state into the Union, and grants public lands for school purposes.
May 26. William D. Moseley is elected first governor of State.

1846 Steam locomotives are introduced in State.
United States begins construction of Fort Jefferson on Garden Key.

1847 Construction begins upon Fort Clinch at Fernandina.

1849 July 17. Indians massacre D.Whidden and Captain George Payne, trading-post operators.

1850 Population 87,445.

1851 Legislature authorizes building of plank toll road between Jacksonville and Lake City (then known as Alligator).

1852 Jacob Brock starts Brock Steamship Line on St.Johns River.
Public Seminary is established at Ocala.

1856 Florida Historical Society is organized.
Indians attack Braden plantation, taking Negro slaves, livestock, and other booty; last outbreak of Seminoles against whites.

1857 Public Seminary is established at Tallahassee.

1858 Most of Florida Indians are moved to Indian Territory; state troops mustered out.

1860 Florida Railroad, first cross-State line, connects Fernandina and Cedar Keys.
Population 140,424.

1861 January 10. Ordinance of secession is passed, Florida being third State to secede from Union.

1864 February 20. Battle of Olustee, most serious conflict in Florida during War between States, results in victory for Confederacy.
September 27. Battle of Marianna, brief but fiercely contested conflict.

1865 February. Federal troops holding Cedar Keys attempt to advance inland, but are turned back by Captain J.J.Dickison and his men.
March 6. Battle of Natural Bridge, in which group of schoolboys join Confederate troops to repel invasion of Federal soldiers.
July 13. President Johnson appoints William Marvin as provisional governor.
October 25. Constitutional convention is called by Governor Marvin.
October 28. Ordinance of secession is annulled.
November. New State constitution is adopted.

1866 Florida Land and Lumber Co., composed of former Union army officers, makes futile attempt to establish large colony of freed Negroes on Florida east coast.

April 2. President Johnson proclaims 'that the insurrection which heretofore existed in the State of Florida is at an end and is henceforth to be so regarded.'

1867 December 22. Council of Ku Klux Klan is organized in Palatka.

1868 State Bureau of Immigration is established in effort to promote settlement of State.

Office of State superintendent of public instruction is created.

May. Fourth State constitution is ratified by voters.

June. Legislature meets and adopts 14th amendment; year later adopts 15th amendment.

1869 Harvey S. Harmon, first Negro lawyer, is admitted to practice in Florida.

Sporadic outbreaks occur this and following year in clashes at various points between friends and foes of Freedman's Bureau.

1870 Population 187,748.

1873 Florida Memorial College is founded at Live Oak.

Bonded debt of State, $1,430,223.48, is refunded.

1876 Florida State hospital for insane is established at Chattahoochee.

1877 Leasing of convicts is authorized by legislature.

1878 State-wide yellow-fever epidemic.

1880 Fire destroys business district of Pensacola.

Population 269,493.

Under Act of Congress relating to swamp and overflowed lands, 1,800,000 acres of public lands are conveyed to State.

1881 State sells 4,000,000 acres of State land south of Ocala and east of Kissimmee River for $1,000,000 to Hamilton Disston and other Philadelphia capitalists.

1882 Florida Coast Line Canal and Transportation Co. provides inland water communication between Matanzas and Halifax rivers.

Reclamation project, in region of Lake Okeechobee, is begun by Disston contractors.

1883 State Agricultural College at Eau Gallie is removed to Lake City and later (1903) is officially named University of Florida.

A Negro high school which later becomes Edward Waters College (Negro) is founded at Jacksonville.

DeLand Academy (now Stetson University) opens at DeLand.

Florida State School for Deaf and Blind is established at St.Augustine.

First electric lights in State are installed on premises of St.James Hotel in Jacksonville.

Major A.P.Williams heads New Orleans *Times Democrat* expedition through Everglades.

1884 Pebble phosphate deposits are first discovered along Peace River by J.Francis Le Baron.

1885 New State constitution is framed, and ratified following year.

Henry M. Flagler gains control of Jacksonville & St.Augustine Railroad, nucleus of Florida East Coast Railway system.

Florida Southern College is established at Leesburg, later moving to Lakeland.

Rollins College is established at Winter Park by General Congregational Association.

1886 Fire destroys approximately half of Key West, including Ybor factory.

Cigar industry, experiencing labor trouble in Key West, moves to Tampa.

Clyde Steamship Line inaugurates regular ship travel between Jacksonville and New York.

Stetson University is established at DeLand.

Eatonville, all-Negro town, is incorporated by State.

1887 Commercial exploitation of phosphate deposits is begun.

Normal School for Negroes is established at Tallahassee, later renamed Florida Agricultural and Mechanical College for Negroes.

January. Present State constitution becomes effective.

1888 Caloosahatchee Canal completed, linking Gulf of Mexico with Lake Okeechobee.

Statewide yellow-fever epidemic.

Fernandina has a longshoremen's strike.

1889 Pioneer line of river steamers is established on Indian River.

State Board of Health is created to combat yellow-fever epidemic.

Lue Gim Gong, great Chinese horticulturist, introduces new variety of orange.

Deposits of hard rock phosphate are discovered near Dunnellon.

1890 Population 391,422.

1891 June 17. Monument to Confederate dead is unveiled at Pensacola.

1892 Populist Party active in State politics.

Florida Normal and Industrial Institute is founded at St.Augustine.

Everglades are explored by expedition under J.E.Ingraham.

Lue Gim Gong perfects Gim Gong grapefruit.

1893 Deposits of fuller's earth are discovered at Quincy.

1894–95 Destructive frost ruins many citrus groves. Temperature at Tallahassee falls to 10°.

1896 Continuous railway facilities are completed between Jacksonville and Miami.

1898 Thousands of American soldiers encamp at various points in Florida and embark from Florida ports for Spanish-American War duty.

June 17. Monument to Confederate dead of Florida is unveiled at Jacksonville.

1899 February 13. Lowest temperature ever recorded in Florida: falls to 2° below zero at Tallahassee.

1900 March. Florida Audubon Society is founded.

Population 528,542.

1901 Jacksonville suffers disastrous fire; flames destroy almost entire city.

1902 May 21. St.Augustine experiences slight earthquake shock.

1903 Alexander Winton drives automobile at 68 miles per hour on Daytona Beach. R.E.Olds pilots racing car over measured mile in one minute, six seconds.

State of Florida obtains title to Everglades, largest area conveyed in single patent issued by Land Department of United States Government.

1904 Daytona Normal and Industrial Institute (now known as Bethune-Cookman College) is founded at Daytona Beach by Mary McLeod Bethune.

1905 Buckman Act consolidates State-subsidized institutions of higher learning into three State colleges: University of Florida, Florida State College for Women, and Florida Agricultural and Mechanical College for Negroes.

Greeks move from Key West, establish colony at Tarpon Springs, and begin sponge industry there.

1906 State begins drainage operations in Everglades.

Experimentation with growing of tung nut trees and production of tung nut oil begins.

1908 Choctawhatchee National Forest is established.

1909 Hurricane destroys construction work of overseas railroad.

1910 During 9-months strike of cigar makers in Tampa, three strikers are killed by vigilantes.

Population 752,619.

1912 Overseas railroad to Key West is completed after 8 years of construction work.

Montverde Industrial School is established under sponsorship of D.A.R.

1913 State child labor law is enacted.

1914 State prison farm at Raiford is completed.

United States establishes naval air station at Pensacola.

January 1. Initial flight of first American commercial air line operating on regular schedule (Tampa to St.Petersburg); is soon discontinued.

Tampa nursery introduces Temple orange.

1915 State road department is created.

School for delinquent boys is established at Marianna.

1917 School for delinquent girls is established at Ocala.

Construction of Tamiami Trail begins.

Many training camps and shipyards are active during World War.

Valuable deposits of diatomite are discovered near Lake Louisa.

1917–18 Floridians go into armed forces of Nation during World War.

1919 State penal labor lease system is abolished.

Tin Can Tourists of the World is organized at Tampa.

1920 Population 968,470.

U.S. Veterans' Hospital is established at Lake City.

November 21. Race riots start at Ocoee during election, spread to near-by cities, and result in burning of 30 Negro houses and two churches, and death of several Negroes.

1921 Seven new counties are formed.

Station WQAM (Miami), Florida's oldest radio station, begins broadcasting.

Colony for feebleminded children is opened near Gainesville.

1923 State abolishes lash and sweat box of prison system.

April 4. Expedition leaves Fort Myers for 3-weeks' journey through swamps and jungles of Everglades, arousing Nation-wide interest in Tamiami Trail.

1924 Clyde Steamship Line inaugurates passenger ship service between Miami and New York.

Gandy Bridge, spanning Old Tampa Bay, is completed.

November. Notorious Ashley gang is broken up after 14 years of bank robbing, hijacking, and rum running on Florida east coast.

1925 Peak of real-estate boom is reached.

1926 Real-estate boom collapses.

Number of deaths and much property loss during hurricane which sweeps east coast from Miami to Daytona Beach.

1927 St.Petersburg Junior College is established.

First large-scale operation of Everglades sugar cane industry begins at Clewiston.

1928 April 25. Tamiami Trail is opened to public.

September. Hurricane and resultant flood waters from Lake Okeechobee bring death to approximately 2,000 persons.

1929 Florida tourist trade and intra-State business are retarded by national depression.

State legislature provides for acquisition and conveyance of lands to United States to be included in the proposed Everglades National Park.

State-wide quarantine is established for citrus fruit infested with Mediterranean fruit-fly.

Yale Anthropoid Experimental Station for study of primates is established near Orange Park.

John Ringling selects Sarasota as winter quarters for his circus.

February 1. Bok Singing Tower at Mountain Lake Sanctuary is dedicated by President Calvin Coolidge.

1930 Population 1,468,211.

Congress appropriates funds for building Lake Okeechobee levees.

November 15. Mediterranean fruit-fly quarantine is lifted.

1931 Osceola National Forest, 230,000 acres, is acquired by Federal Government for use as forestry experimental ground.

Ringling Junior College is founded at Sarasota.

1932 Chinsegut Park, 2,200 acres, is donated to U.S. Department of Agriculture by Colonel Raymond Robins for wild life refuge and forest conservation and experiment station.

1933 February 15. In attempt to assassinate President Roosevelt at Miami, Guiseppe Zangara fatally wounds Mayor Anton Cermak of Chicago. Zangara is tried and electrocuted by State.

1934 Mrs. John Roebling deeds land to Florida for Highlands Hammock State Park.

1935 Workman's Compensation Law is enacted.

Florida industrial commission is created.

Homestead exemption law is enacted whereby homesteads with valuation up to $5,000 are exempt from taxes, except special assessments for benefits.

State welfare board is created.

State game and fresh-water fish commission is created (sale of black bass prohibited).

Products manufactured in State are valued at $162,359,000; citrus crops are valued at $53,189,000.

January 16. Fred and 'Ma' Barker of Karpis-Barker gang are slain by Federal agents near town of Ocklawaha.

March 7. Sir Malcolm Campbell pilots racing car, *Bluebird,* at speed of 276 miles per hour over sands of Daytona Beach.

September 2. Devastating hurricane sweeps Florida Keys, bringing death to more than 400 persons and large property losses including destruction of railway between Florida City and Key West.

September 19. Work is started near Ocala on projected Gulf-Atlantic Ship Canal, but is suspended following summer.

November 30. Joseph Shoemaker, Tampa labor leader, and two companions are abducted and flogged, resulting in death of Shoemaker.

1936 Earl Browder, Communist candidate for President, is prevented from making speech at Tampa.

Total of 2,920,000 tons of phosphate are mined in State.

Miami completes building program twice as large as that of 1926.

Excavation of Indian mounds by Florida State Archeological Survey and WPA results in many finds.

State board of conservation plants 500,000 bass fingerlings in lakes of State.

1937 Legislature abolishes $2 poll tax; and, empowered by amendment, appropriates $3,800,000 for old-age assistance, aid to blind, and other welfare services.

John and Mable Ringling Museum of Art at Sarasota is willed to State.

Labor strikes, involving dock workers, building trades workers, taxi cab drivers, and typographical workers, occur in various sections of State.

1938 Co-operative farming groups become important factor in State's agriculture.

Public parades of Ku Klux Klan are held at Jacksonville, Lakeland, Miami, St.Petersburg, and Starke.

New Dealer Claude Pepper is re-elected to United States Senate by large majority.

Marine studios are constructed on beach south of Summer Haven, providing unusual opportunities for study of marine life.

Paper-pulp mills at Port St.Joe, Fernandina, and Jacksonville begin operations.

July. Overseas highway to Key West is opened to public.

1939 Congress appropriates $25,000,000 for construction of Southeastern Naval Air Base near Jacksonville, Southeastern Army Air Base at Tampa, auxiliary seaplane base on the Banana River, and for additions to the Pensacola Naval Air Base.

General legislative appropriation, $19,284,416 for 1939–41 biennium, is largest in State's history. Governor Cone vetoes nearly $5,000,000 in special appropriations for education, State parks, agriculture, and general welfare as legislators fail to provide increased revenue funds.

State ships record citrus crop of 41,000,000 boxes.
WPA relief rolls are cut from 1938 peak of 55,000 persons to 37,000 on September 1.

1940 January freeze is most disastrous since that of 1894–95; loss to citrus and truck farmers is estimated at $20,000,000. Federal agencies rush aid to farmers and unemployed agricultural workers. Resort areas have their most profitable tourist season in Florida history, as the second World War prevents travel to Europe.

Bibliography

GENERAL INFORMATION

American Automobile Association. *Southeastern Tour Book*. Washington, D.C., 1938. 408p.,illus.,maps. See pp.26–67. Issued annually.

Barbour, Ralph Henry. *Let's Go to Florida!* New York, Dodd, Mead & Co., 1926. 288p.,front.,plates.

Dunbaugh, Frank M.,Jr. *Going to Florida? A Complete Guide to the State with Excursions to Havana and Nassau*. New York, Brentano's, 1925. 220p.,front., illus.,fold.map.

Florida. Hotel Commission. *Florida, Empire of the Sun . . .* Tallahassee, Florida State Hotel Commission, 1930. 160p.,illus. Text by Carita Doggett Corse; compiled and edited by Bernal E. Clark. Pub. as Vol.40, no.4, Quarterly Bulletin of Florida Dept. of Agriculture.

Rhodes, Harrison G., and Dumont, Mary Wolfe. *A Guide to Florida for Tourists, Sportsmen and Settlers*. With a chapter, 'The Inland Waterways from New York to Key West.' New York, Dodd, Mead & Co., 1912. 456p.,maps,illus., bibl.

Who's Who and What to See in Florida. Ed. by Homer E. Moyer. St.Petersburg, Current Historical Co., Inc., 1935. 379p.,illus.(incl.port.).

Works Progress Administration. Federal Writers' Project. *The Intracoastal Waterway:Norfolk to Key West*. Washington, Govt. Print. Off., 1937. 135p., illus.,map. (American Guide Series.)

DESCRIPTION AND TRAVEL

Aero-graphic Corporation. *Florida from the Air*. Pub. through the courtesy of and in conjunction with Eastern Air Lines, Aviation Div. of Florida State Road Dept., Florida State Chamber of Commerce. Louisville, 1936. 128p., illus.(incl.map). Compiled, edited, and photographed by Welman A. Shrader.

Bartram, William. *Travels through North and South Carolina, Georgia, East and West Florida . . .* Philadelphia, James & Johnson, 1791. 520p.,front., plates,map. New edition pub. by Macy-Masius, New York, 1928. (American Bookshelf.)

Brinton, Daniel G. *Notes on the Floridian Peninsula, Its Literary History, Indian Tribes and Antiquities*. Philadelphia, J.Savin, 1859. 202p.

Chambers, Henry E. *West Florida and Its Relation to the Historical Cartography of the United States*. Baltimore, 1898. 59p.,front.(map),bibl. (Johns Hopkins Univ. Studies in History and Political Science. Ser.16, no.5.)

Deland, Margaret. *Florida Days.* Ill. by Louis K. Harlow. Boston, Little, Brown & Co., 1889. 200p.

Easley, Philip S. *The 'Low-down' on Florida,* by Joshuay Whipple (pseud.). Statesville, N.C., Brady Print. Co., 1926. 48p.

Fox, Charles Donald. *The Truth about Florida.* New York, Charles Renard Corp., 1925. 260p.,plates,maps.

Harper, Roland M. 'Geography and Vegetation of Northern Florida.' In *Sixth Annual Report of Florida State Geological Survey.* Tallahassee, 1914; pp.163–451. Illus.,map.

Hearn, Lafcadio. 'Floridian Reveries.' (In his *Leaves from the Diary of an Impressionist.* Boston and New York, Houghton Mifflin, 1911. See pp.34–94.)

Jennings, John E.,Jr. *Our American Tropics.* New York, Crowell, 1938. 265p., plates.

Johnson, Clifton. *Highways and Byways of Florida; Human Interest Information for Travellers* . . . New York, Macmillan, 1918. 264p.,front.,plates. (American Highways and Byways series, no.8.)

La Gorce, John Oliver. 'Florida, the Fountain of Youth.' *National Geographic Magazine,* Jan.1930, v.57:1–93.

Lanier, Sidney. *Florida: Its Scenery, Climate, and History.* With . . . a chapter for consumptives; various papers on fruit-culture; and a complete handbook and guide. Philadelphia, Lippincott, 1876. 336p.,illus.,plates.

Muir, John. *A Thousand-Mile Walk to the Gulf.* Boston and New York, Houghton Mifflin, 1916, 219p.,col.front.,plates,port.,map,facsims.

Packard, Winthrop. *Florida Trails as Seen from Jacksonville to Key West and from November to April Inclusive.* Boston, Small, Maynard & Co., 1910. 300p.,illus.

Read, William A. *Florida Place-names of Indian Origin and Seminole Personal Names.* Baton Rouge, 1934. 83p. Louisiana State Univ. Studies, no.11.

Roberts, Kenneth L. *Florida.* New York and London, Harper, 1926. 324p.,front., plates.

Romans, Capt. Bernard. *A Concise Natural History of East and West Florida* . . . New York, Printed for the Author, 1775. 342p.,plates,maps.

Simpson, Charles Torrey. *In Lower Florida Wilds; a Naturalist's Observations on the Life, Physical Geography, and Geology of the More Tropical Part of the State.* New York and London, Putnam, 1920. 404p.,col.front.,illus.,plates, fold.maps.

——— *Out of Doors in Florida; the Adventures of a Naturalist; together with Essays on the Wild Life and the Geology of the State.* Miami, E.B.Douglas Co., 1923. 412p.,illus.

Stillman, Clara G. 'Florida, the Desert and the Rose.' In Gruening, Ernest, ed. *These United States.* 2d series. New York, Boni & Liveright, 1924; pp.48–63.

Stockbridge, Frank Parker, and Perry, John Holliday. *So This Is Florida.* Jacksonville, John H. Perry Pub.Co.,1938. 300p.,front.(port.),plates.

Stowe, Mrs. Harriet Beecher. *Palmetto-leaves.* Boston, Osgood, 1873 (later ed. 1901). 321p.,illus.,map.

Torrey, Bradford. *A Florida Sketch-book.* Boston and New York, Houghton Mifflin, 1894 (later ed. 1924). 242p.,front.,plates.

Verrill, A.Hyatt. *Romantic and Historic Florida.* New York, Dodd, Mead & Co., 1935. 291p.,front.,illus.,plates,port.,maps.

Winter, Nevin O. *Florida, the Land of Enchantment* . . . Boston, Page, 1918. 380p.,map,col.plates,bibl. (See America First series.)

CLIMATE

U.S. Dept. of Agriculture. Weather Bureau. *Florida Hurricanes.* By Richard W. Gray; rev. by Grady Norton. Washington, Govt.Print.Off., 1936. 3p., diagrs.

GEOLOGY AND PALEONTOLOGY

Florida Geological Survey. Publications and Reports. Tallahassee, from 1887 to date.

Matsen, George Charlton, and Sanford, Samuel. *Geology and Ground Waters of Florida.* Prepared in co-operation with U.S. Geological Survey and Florida Geological Survey, under direction of Thomas Wayland Vaughan. Washington, Govt.Print.Offi., 1913. 445p.,plates,fold.maps,fold.tables,diagrs. (U.S. Geological Survey. Water-supply Paper 319.)

Vaughan, Thomas Wayland. 'A Contribution to the Geological History of the Floridian Plateau.' In Carnegie Institution of Washington. Dept. of Marine Biology. *Papers.* Washington, D.C., 1910. Vol.4, pp.99–185. Illus.,plates, maps.

PLANT AND ANIMAL LIFE

Audubon, John James. *Ornithological Biography, or, An Account of the Birds of the United States of America.* Edinburgh, A.Black, 1831–39. 5 vols., illus. Numerous later editions.

Baker, Mary Francis. *Florida Wild Flowers.* With photographs by the author. New ed. New York, Macmillan, 1926 (later ed. 1938). 245p.,illus.,plates.

Blatchley, Willis S. *In Days Agone; Notes on the Fauna and Flora of Subtropical Florida in the Days When Most of Its Area Was a Primeval Wilderness.* Indianapolis, Nature Pub.Co., 1932. 338p.,plates. A diary of six trips made between 1911 and 1922.

'First Autochromes from the Ocean Bottom: Marine Life in Its Natural Habitat along the Florida Keys Is Successfully Photographed in Colors.' *National Geographic Magazine*, Jan.1927, v.51:56–60.

Howell, Arthur H. *Florida Bird Life.* Pub. by Florida Dept. of Game and Fresh Water Fish in co-operation with Bureau of Biological Survey, U.S. Dept. of Agriculture. New York, Pub. Agents, Coward-McCann, Inc., 1932. 579p., col.front.,plates,maps,bibl.

Longley, W.H. 'Life on a Coral Reef: the Fertility and Mystery of the Sea Studied beneath the Waters Surrounding the Dry Tortugas.' *National Geographic Magazine*, Jan.1927, v.51:61–83.

Longstreet, R.J. *Bird Study in Florida.* Daytona Beach, Halifax River Bird Club, 1930. 183p.,illus.

Mattoon, Wilbur R. *Common Forest Trees of Florida.* Tallahassee, Florida Forestry Association, 1930. 89p.,illus. (Rep. by Florida Forest Service, 1930.)

Millspaugh, Charles Frederick. 'Flora of the Sand Keys of Florida.' In Field Columbian Museum. *Publication 118*. Chicago, 1907; pp.191–245.

Shiras, George,3d. 'Wild Life of the Atlantic and Gulf Coasts: a Field Naturalist's Photographic Record of Nearly Half a Century of Fruitful Exploration.' *National Geographic Magazine*, Sept.1932, v.62:261–309.

Simpson, Charles Torrey. *Florida Wild Life; Observations on the Flora and Fauna of the State and the Influence of Climate and Environment on Their Development*. New York, Macmillan, 1932. 199p.,front.,illus.,plates.

Small, John Kunkel. *Ferns of Tropical Florida* . . . New York, The Author, 1918. 80p.,front.,illus.,plates,bibl.

——— *Florida Trees* . . . New York, The Author, 1913. 107p.

——— *Manual of the Southeastern Flora* . . . New York, The Author, 1933. 1,554p.,illus.

Stork, William. *A Description of East-Florida, with a Journal, Kept by John Bartram of Philadelphia, Botanist to His Majesty for the Floridas* . . . With explanatory botanical notes. 3d ed. London. Sold by W.Nicoll, 1769. 40p., maps,plan. First pub. 1766.

RESOURCES AND THEIR CONSERVATION

Florida. State Board of Conservation. Bulletins. Tallahassee, from 1908 to date.

Gifford, John Clayton. *The Reclamation of the Everglades with Trees*. New York, Boston, Books,Inc.; Coral Gables, Univ. of Miami, 1935. 92p.

——— *The Rehabilitation of the Floridan Keys*. New York, Boston, Books, Inc.; Coral Gables, Florida, Univ. of Miami, 1934. 79p.

Goulden,J.J. *Florida's Forest Land Problems* . . . Tallahassee, 1931. 31p. (Forest Service. Bulletin no.6.)

Lloyd, Edward R. *Agricultural Possibilities of the Florida Everglades*. Letter from the Secretary of War transmitting a report made to the division engineer at New Orleans by Mr.E.R.Lloyd. Washington, Govt.Print.Off., 1930. 21p. (U.S. 71st Cong., 2d sess. Senate. Doc.85.)

ARCHEOLOGY AND INDIANS

Bushnell, David L. *Mounds and Other Ancient Earthwork of the United States*. Washington, 1929. (Smithsonian Institution Publication 3004.)

Fewkes, Jesse Walter. *Aboriginal Wooden Objects from Southern Florida*. Washington, 1928. 2p.,plates. (Smithsonian Miscellaneous Collections. Vol.80, no.9.)

——— *Preliminary Archeological Explorations at Weeden Island, Florida*. Washington, 1924. 26p.,map,plates. (Smithsonian Miscellaneous Collections. Vol. 76, no.13.)

Hrdlicka, Ales. *The Anthropology of Florida*. DeLand, The Society, 1922. 140p., illus.,maps,tables. (Publications of Florida State Historical Society, no.1.)

Kunz, George F. *Gold and Silver Ornaments from Mounds of Florida*. Chicago, 1887. 9p.,illus. (Repr. from *American Antiquarian*.)

MacCauley, Clay. '. . . The Seminole Indians of Florida.' In U.S. Bureau of Am. Ethnology. *Fifth Annual Report*, 1883–84. Washington, 1887; pp.469–531,illus.(incl. map).

MacCurdy, George Grant. *Archaeological Evidences of Man's Antiquity at Vero, Florida.* Chicago, 1917. 62p., illus. (Repr. from *Journal of Geology.*)

Moore, Clarence B. *Certain Aboriginal Mounds of the Florida Central West-Coast.* Philadelphia, P.C.Stockhausen, 1903. [363]–494p., illus.(incl.maps). (Repr. from *Journal of the Academy of Natural Sciences.*)

——— *Certain Aboriginal Remains of the Northwest Florida Coast* . . . Philadelphia, P.C.Stockhausen, 1901–02. 2 vols.,illus.,maps. (Repr. from *Journal of the Academy of Natural Sciences.*)

——— *Moundville Revisited. Crystal River Revisited. Mounds of the Lower Chattahoochee and Lower Flint Rivers. Notes on the Ten Thousand Islands, Florida.* Philadelphia, P.C.Stockhausen, 1907. 476p.,illus.(incl.maps). (Repr. from *Journal of the Academy of Natural Sciences.*)

Schoolcraft, Henry Rowe. *Notices of Some Antique Earthen Vessels, Found in the Low Tumuli of Florida* . . . New York, W.Van Norden, printer, 1847. 15p., plates.

Swanton, John R. *Early History of the Creek Indians and Their Neighbors.* Washington, Govt.Print.Off.,1922. 492p.,maps. (Smithsonian Institution. Bureau of American Ethnology. Bulletin 73.)

U.S.Office of Indian Affairs . . . *Survey of the Seminole Indians of Florida* . . . Washington, Govt.Print.Off., 1931. 88p.,incl.tables,fold.map. (71st Cong., 3d sess. Senate. Doc.314) Signed: Roy Nash, Special Commissioner to Negotiate with Indians.

HISTORY

General

Brevard, Caroline Mays. *A History of Florida from the Treaty of* 1763 *to Our Own Times.* Ed. by James A. Robertson. DeLand, 1924–25. 2 vols.,fronts. (ports.),maps. (Publications of Florida State Historical Society, no.4.)

Chapin, George M. *Florida,* 1513–1913, *Past, Present and Future.* . . . Chicago, S.J.Clarke Pub.Co., 1914. 2 vols.

Cutler, Harry Gardner. . . . *Florida, Past and Present, Historical and Biographical.* Chicago and New York, Lewis Pub.Co., 1923. 3 vols.,illus.,ports., maps.

Dickison, Col.J.J. *Military History of Florida.* Atlanta, Confederate Pub.Co., 1899. 212p.,front.,port.,maps. In Evans, C.A.,ed. *Confederate Military History.* Atlanta, 1899; Vol.11.

Florida Historical Society. Publications and Reports. Jacksonville, from 1908 to date.

Florida State Historical Society. Publications and Reports. DeLand, from 1922 to date.

French, Benjamin F.,ed. *Historical Collections of Louisiana and Florida.* 1st series: New York, J.Sabin & Sons, 1869. 362p. 2d series: New York, A.Mason, 1875. 300p.

Ranson, Robert. *Chronology of the Most Important Events Connected with Florida History during Four Hundred and Seventeen Years,* 1513 *to* 1930 . . . 2d ed. St.Augustine, R.Ranson, 1930. 40p.

Rerick, Rowland H. *Memoirs of Florida; Embracing a General History of the*

Province, Territory and State . . . Atlanta, Southern Historical Assn., 1902. 2 vols.,port.

Early Period

Barrs, Burton. East Florida in the American Revolution. Jacksonville, Guild Press, 1932. 42p.,bibl.

Bolton, Herbert Eugene. *The Spanish Borderlands; a Chronicle of Old Florida and the Southwest.* New Haven, Yale Univ. Press, 1921. 320p.,col.front.(port.), fold.map. (Chronicles of America series. Allen Johnson, ed. Vol.23.)

Bourne, Edward G., ed. *Narratives of the Career of Hernando de Soto in the Conquest of Florida as Told by a Knight of Elvas* . . . tr. by Buckingham Smith. New York, A.S.Barnes & Co., 1904. 2 vols.,fronts.

Campbell, Richard L. *Historical Sketches of Colonial Florida* . . . Cleveland, Williams Pub.Co., 1892. 284p.,double plates. Treats at length the history of Pensacola.

Connor, Mrs. Jeannette Thurber, ed. and tr. *Colonial Records of Spanish Florida; Letters and Reports of Governors and Secular Persons.* DeLand, 1925–30. 2 vols.,front.,facsim. (Publications of Florida State Historical Society, no.5.)

Davis, Thomas Frederick. *MacGregor's Invasion of Florida,* 1817; *together with an Account of His Successors, Irwin, Hubbard, and Aury on Amelia Island, East Florida.* Jacksonville, Florida Historical Society, 1928. 73p.,front. (port.),maps.

Dickinson, Jonathan. *God's Protecting Providence . . . Evidenced in the Remarkable Deliverance of Robert Barrow, with Divers Other Persons, from the Devouring Waves of the Sea; amongst Which They Suffered Shipwreck; and also from the . . . Canibals of Florida.* Philadelphia, printed; London, reprinted, T.Sowle, 1699.

Fairbanks, George R. *History of Florida from Its Discovery by Ponce de Leon, in* 1512, *to the Close of the Florida War in* 1842. Philadelphia, Lippincott; Jacksonville, C.Drew, 1871. 350p.

Fuller, Hubert B. *The Purchase of Florida; Its History and Diplomacy.* Cleveland, Burrows Bros.Co., 1906. 399p.,maps.

Garcilaso de la Vega. 'History of the Conquest of Florida; or, A Narrative of What Occurred in the Exploration of This Country by Hernando de Soto.' Tr. from the French version of Pierre Richelet, from the original Spanish. In Shipp, Barnard. *The History of Hernando de Soto and Florida.* Philadelphia, 1881; pp.229–487.

Giddings, Joshua R. *The Exiles of Florida: or, The Crimes Committed by Our Government against the Maroons, Who Fled from South Carolina and Other Slave States, Seeking Protection under Spanish Laws.* Columbus, Ohio, Follett, Foster & Co., 1858. 338p.,front.,port.

Hakluyt, R.,comp. *Divers Voyages Touching the Discovery of America and the Islands Adjacent.* Collected and published by Richard Hakluyt . . in the year 1582. Edited, with notes and an introduction, by John Winter Jones. London, Printed for the Hakluyt Society, 1850. 171p., 3 fold.facsims.(incl. 2 maps). (Works issued by the Hakluyt Society. 1st series, no.7.)

Irving, Theodore. *The Conquest of Florida under Hernando de Soto.* London, E.Churton, 1835. 2 vols.

Jones, George Noble. *Florida Plantation Records* . . . ed. by Ulrich Bonnell

Phillips and James David Glunt. St.Louis, Missouri Historical Society, 1927. 596p.,front.(fold.map),plates. Covers years 1847 to 1857.

King, Grace. *De Soto and His Men in the Land of Florida*. New York and London, Macmillan, 1898. 326p.

Laudonnière, René Goulaine de. 'The First Voyage of Jean Ribault to Florida, 1562.' In Shipp, Barnard. *The History of Hernando de Soto and Florida*. Philadelphia, 1881; pp.495–509.

——— 'History of the First Attempt of the French to Colonize the Newly Discovered Country of Florida.' In French, Benjamin Franklin, ed. *Historical Collections of Louisiana and Florida*. New York, 1869; pp.165–362.

Lowery, Woodbury. *The Spanish Settlements within the Present Limits of the United States*. New York and London, Putnam. 2 vols. Vol.1 (1901) covers years 1513–61; Vol.2, with subtitle 'Florida' (1905) covers years 1562–74. Fronts.,maps.

Núñez Cabeza de Vaca, Alvar. *Relation That Alvar Núñez Cabeza de Vaca Gave of What Befel the Armament in the Indias Whither Pánphilo de Narváez Went for Governor (from the Years* 1527 *to* 1537) . . . Printed from the Buckingham Smith translation of 1871. San Francisco, Grabhorn Press, 1929. 122p., illus.(map,facsim.,col.coat of arms). First Spanish ed. pub. at Zamora, 1542.

——— *The Journey of Alvar Núñez Cabeza de Vaca and His Companions from Florida to the Pacific*, 1528–1536. Tr. by Fanny Bandelier; with an introduction by Ad.F.Bandelier. New York, A.S.Barnes & Co., 1905. 231p.,front. (fold.map),facsims.

Parkman, Francis. 'Huguenots in Florida.' In his *Pioneers of France in the New World*. Boston, Little, Brown & Co., 1907; pp.3–181.

Ribaut, Jean. *The Whole and True Discouerye of Terra Florida*. A facsimile reprint of the London ed. of 1563, together with a transcript of an English version in the British Museum with notes by H.M.Biggar and a biography by Jeannette Thurber Connor. DeLand, 1927. 139p. (Publications of Florida State Historical Society, no.7.)

Shea, John Gilmary. 'Ancient Florida.' In Winsor, Justin, ed. *Narrative and Critical History of America*. Boston and New York, 1884–89. Vol.2 [1886], pp.283–98. A critical essay on the sources of information.

Shipp, Barnard. *The History of Hernando de Soto and Florida; or, Record of the Events of Fifty-six Years, from* 1512 *to* 1568. Philadelphia, Collins, printer, 1881. 689p.,maps.

Siebert, Wilbur H. *Loyalists in East Florida*, 1774 *to* 1785 . . . DeLand, 1929. 2 vols.,bibl. (Florida State Historical Society. Publications, no.9.)

——— 'Slavery and White Servitude in East Florida.' In *Quarterly* periodical of the Florida State Historical Society. Jacksonville, 1931; Vol.10, no.1, pp.1–23.

Solís de Merás, Gonzalo. . . . *Pedro Menéndez de Avilés, Adelantado, Governor and Captain-General of Florida*. Tr. from the Spanish, with notes, by Jeannette Thurber Connor. DeLand, 1923. 286p.,front.(port.),plates,map, facsims. (Publications of Florida State Historical Society., no.3)

Sprague, Capt. John T. *The Origin, Progress, and Conclusion of the Florida War* . . . New York and Philadelphia, Appleton, 1848. 557p.,map. Deals with the Seminole War.

Williams, John Lee. *The Territory of Florida . . . from the First Discovery to the Present Time . . .* New York, A.T.Goodrich, 1837. 304p.,front.(port.), plates,fold.map.

Later Period

Couch, W.T., ed. *Culture in the South.* Chapel Hill, Univ. of North Carolina Press, 1935. 711p. Contains 31 essays (by Broadus Mitchell, George Fort Milton, Donald Davidson, Bruce Crawford, B.A.Botkin, Charles W. Pipkin, etc.).

Davis, William W. *The Civil War and Reconstruction in Florida . . .* New York, 1913. 771p. (Theses [Ph.D.] Columbia Univ.)

Johnson, James Weldon. *Negro Americans, What Now?* New York, Viking, 1934. 103p.

Odum, Howard W. *Southern Regions of the United States.* Prepared for the Southern Regional Committee of the Social Science Research Council. Chapel Hill, Univ. of North Carolina Press, 1936. 664p.,maps,charts,tables.

Reese, Joseph H. *Florida's Great Hurricane.* Miami, L.E.Fesler, 1926. 93p.

Vannest, Charles G., and Smith, Henry L. *Socialized History of the United States.* New York, Chicago, Scribner, 1931. 694p. 'Supplementary History of Florida,' by Carita Doggett Corse, has special title page and separate pagination. 94p.

Wallace, John. *Carpetbag Rule in Florida. The Inside Workings of the Reconstruction of Civil Government in Florida after the Civil War.* Jacksonville, Da Costa Print. and Pub. House, 1888. 444p.,front.,ports.

GOVERNMENT

Florida. Constitution. *Constitution of State of Florida.* Adopted by the Convention of 1885 (as amended). R.A.Gray, Secretary of State. Tallahassee, 1937. 77p.

Florida. Laws, Statutes, etc. *The Compiled General Laws of Florida, 1927 . . .* Comp. and ed. by Harry B. Skillman. Atlanta, Harrison Co., 1928. 6 vols.

King, Clyde L., Barnard, J.Lynn, and Gray, R.A. *Our Community Life, with the Civil Government of Florida.* Philadelphia, Chicago, John C. Winston Co., 1930. 632p.

Legislative Blue Book, 1917. 'Through Green Glasses,' being a historical sketch of legislatures of Florida for thirty years by Pat Murphy. Tallahassee, T.J. Appleyard, 1917. 130p.

AGRICULTURE

Brooker, Marvin A., and Hamilton, H.G. *Farmers' Cooperative Associations in Florida.* 1. Status and Legal Phases. Gainesville, 1932. 47p. (Agricultural Experiment Station. Bulletin no.245.)

Davis, George W. *A Treatise on the Culture of the Orange . . .* Jacksonville, C.W.Dacosta, 1881. 60p.

Florida. Dept. of Agriculture. Bulletins and Reports. Tallahassee, from 1889 to date.

——— *Florida Citrus Fruit Marketing, Its Volume, Distribution and Sale.* Prepared by Neill Rhodes, assistant marketing comm. Nathan Mayo, comm. of agriculture. Tallahassee, 1934. 79p.,tables,diagrs.

Hume, Harold H. *The Cultivation of Citrus Fruits*. New York, Macmillan, 1926. 561p.,illus.

McKinley, Bruce. *An Economic Study of 249 Dairy Farms in Florida*. Gainesville, 1932. 119p. (Agricultural Experiment Station. Bulletin no.246.)

Vosbury, E.D., and Winston, J.R. *Pineapple Culture in Florida*. Washington, Govt.Print.Off., 1931. 36p. (U.S. Dept. of Agriculture. Farmers' Bulletin, 1237.)

INDUSTRY, COMMERCE, AND LABOR

Campbell, Archer Stuart. *The Foreign Trade of Florida . . .* Gainesville, 1935. 89p.,bibl. (Univ. of Florida Publication. Economic Series, Vol.1, no.7.) Photolithographed.

Economic Survey of Florida. New York, Joseph W. Young Properties (535 Fifth Ave.), 1927. 23p.

Florida. Dept. of Agriculture. *Florida, an Advancing State*. An industrial survey authorized by the Legislature of 1927 and carried through under direction of Nathan Mayo, comm. of agriculture. St.Petersburg, Lansing Pub.Co., 1920, 342p.

Read, Henry H. *The Industries of Florida Illustrated*. New York, Savannah, Read Press, 1921. 58p.

Seldes, George. *You Can't Do That. A Survey of the Forces Attempting, in the Name of Patriotism, to Make a Desert of the Bill of Rights*. New York, Modern Age Books, 1938. 307p. With 46-page bibliography on civil liberties in the United States (including 6-page section on the rights of labor). See pp.56–58 for account of the Joseph Shoemaker case in Tampa.

Trust Company of Florida, Miami. *Business Survey of Florida, a Record of Florida's Permanent Development*. Miami, 1926. 70p.

U.S.Women's Bureau. *Women in Florida Industries*. Washington, Govt.Print. Off., 1930. 115p. (Bulletin of the Women's Bureau, no.80.)

Vanderblue, Homer B. *The Florida Land Boom . . . A Research Study Made under the Auspices of . . . Northwestern University*. [Chicago? 1927.] 37p., diagrs.

Weigall, Theyre H. *Boom in Paradise*. New York, A.H.King, 1932. 255p.,front., plates,port. London edition (John Lane) has title: *Boom in Florida*.

TRANSPORTATION

Buckman, Henry Holland, comp. *Documentary History of the Florida Canal. Ten-Year Period January 1927 to June 1936*. Washington, Govt.Print.Off. 1936. 513p.,tables,plates,maps. (U.S. 74th Cong., 2d sess. Senate. Doc.275.)

Cricher, Aaron L., and Edwin Bates. *Florida Transportation Field Survey*. Washington, Govt.Print.Off., 1927. 111p. (U.S. Bureau of Foreign and Domestic Commerce [Dept. of Commerce]. Domestic Commerce series, no.17.)

Florida East Coast Railway Company. *Official Industrial and Development Directory of the Florida East Coast Railway Company, Flagler System . . .* 1926–

27. Oak Park, Ill., Printed by the Delmont Railroad Advertising Agency, 1927. 452p.,illus. Compiler: D.N.Felthousen.

Florida Inland and Coastal Waterways Association. *Inland and Coastal Waterways of Florida.* Report . . . presented by Mr.Fletcher. Washington, Govt.Print.Off., 1929. 96p.,fold.map. (U.S. 71st Cong., 1st sess. Senate. Doc. 14.)

Florida. State Road Dept. *Florida Highways.* Tallahassee, from 1923 to date.

Read, Henry H. *The Waterways of Florida Illustrated* . . . New York, Savannah, Read Press, 1921. 256p.

FOLKLORE

Boggs, Ralph S. 'Spanish Folklore from Tampa, Florida.' *Southern Folklore Quarterly,* September 1937, v.1:1–12; Dec.1937, v.1: 9–13; June 1938, v.2: 87–106.

Hauptmann, O.H. 'Spanish Folklore from Tampa, Florida.' *Southern Folklore Quarterly,* September 1938: v.2:11–30.

Hurston, Zora Neale. *Mules and Men.* With intro. by Franz Boas; illus. by Miguel Covarrubias. Philadelphia, London, Lippincott, 1935. 343p.,front., illus.,plates. Contains a collection of Negro folk tales and describes voodoo practices in Florida, Louisiana, etc.

Smiley, Portia. 'Folk-Lore from Virginia, South Carolina, Georgia, Alabama, and Florida.' *Journal of American Folklore.* 1919, v.32: 357–83.

EDUCATION

Bush, George G. *History of Education in Florida.* Washington, Govt.Print.Off., 1889. 54p.,plates. (U.S. Bureau of Education. Circulars of Information, 1888, no.7.)

Cochran, Thomas E. *History of Public-School Education in Florida.* Lancaster, Pa., Press of New Era Print.Co., 1921. 270p. (Thesis Ph.D.) Univ. of Pennsylvania.

Ezell, Boyce F. *The Development of Secondary Education in Florida, with Special Reference to the Public White High School.* DeLand, 1932. 144p.

Florida. Dept. of Public Instruction. *Progress and Status of Negro Education in Florida.* . . . Tallahassee, Art-craft Printers, 1926. 11p. (Florida School Bulletin. Vol.3, no.1.)

——— Reports and bulletins. Tallahassee, from 1868 to date.

RELIGION

Díaz Vara Calderón, Gabriel. . . . *A 17th Century Letter of Gabriel Díaz Vara Calderón, Bishop of Cuba, Describing the Indians and Indian Missions of Florida.* Transcribed and translated by Lucy L. Wenhold. Intro. by John R. Swanton. Washington, 1936. 14p.plates. (Smithsonian Miscellaneous Collections, Vol.95, no.16.)

Ley, John Cole. *Fifty-two Years in Florida.* Nashville,Tenn.,Dallas,Tex., Publishing House of M.E.Church, South, Barbee & Smith, agents, 1899. 156p.

O'Daniel, Victor F. *Dominicans in Early Florida.* New York, 1930. 230p.,bibl. (U.S. Catholic Historical Society. Monograph series, no.12.)

Oré, Luis Gerónimo. *The Martyrs of Florida* (1513–1616). Translated with biographical introduction and notes, by Maynard Geiger . . . New York, J.F.Wagner,Inc., 1937. 145p. (Franciscan Studies, no.18.)

LITERATURE AND PRINTING

Florida Poets, 1930. Newport, Ky., International Writers' League, 1930. 116p. Editors: Ethel B. Koger, H.A.L.DeAryan.

Florida Poets, an Anthology of Contemporary Verse and *Second Florida Poets, an Anthology of 42 Contemporaries.* Forewords by Vivian Yeiser Laramore. New York, Henry Harrison, 1931 and 1932. Each vol. 144p.

Johnson, James Weldon. *Along This Way; the Autobiography of James Weldon Johnson.* New York, Viking, 1933. 418p.,front.,plates,ports.,facsims.

Kern, John Dwight. *Constance Fenimore Woolson, Literary Pioneer.* Philadelphia, Univ. of Pennsylvania Press; London, H.Milford, Oxford Univ.Press, 1934. 198p.,front.(port.).

Knauss, J. O. *Territorial Florida Journalism.* DeLand, 1926. 250p.,ports.,facsims. (Publications of Florida State Historical Society, no.6.)

McMurtrie, Douglas C. *The First Printing in Florida.* Atlanta, Priv. print.. 1931. 18p. (Repr. from *Southern Printer.*)

ART AND ARCHITECTURE

Le Moyne de Morgues, Jacques. *Narrative of Le Moyne, an Artist Who Accompanied the French Expedition to Florida under Laudonnière*, 1564. Tr. from the Latin of De Bry, with heliotypes of the engravings taken from the artist's original drawings. Boston, J.R.Osgood & Co., 1875. 42p.,map.

Newcomb, Rexford. *Spanish-Colonial Architecture in the United States.* New York, J.J.Augustin, 1937. 39p.,front.,130 plates (incl.plans).

MUSIC

Delius, Clare. *Frederick Delius: Memories of My Brother.* London, I. Nicholson & Watson, 1935. 276p.,front.,plates,ports.

Johnson, James Weldon, ed. *The Book of American Negro Spirituals.* Musical arrangements by J.Rosamond Johnson, additional numbers by Lawrence Brown. New York, Viking Press, 1925. 187p.

——— *The Second Book of Negro Spirituals.* New York, Viking Press, 1926. 189p.

SPORTS AND RECREATION

Aflalo, Frederick G. *Sunshine and Sport in Florida and the West Indies.* Philadelphia, G.W.Jacobs & Co., 1907. 272p.

Cory, Charles B. *Hunting and Fishing in Florida, Including a Key to the Water Birds Known to Occur in the State.* 2d ed. Boston, Estes & Lauriat, 1896. 304p.,illus.,plates.

Dimock, A.W. *The Book of the Tarpon.* Ill. with photographs by Julian Dimock. New York, Outing Pub.Co., 1911. 256p.,front.,plates.

Florida. Dept. of Game and Fish. Publications. Tallahassee, from 1913 to date.

Gregg, William H. *Where, When, and How to Catch Fish on the East Coast of Florida.* Buffalo and New York, Matthews-Northup Works, 1902. 267p.

Kaplan, Moise N. *Big Game Fishermen's Paradise; a Complete Treatise . . . on Angling Philosophy, Sidelights and Scenes in Florida Salt-Water Fishing Ventures.* Tallahassee, Rose Print.Co., 1936. 324p.,illus.,maps,tables.

La Gorce, John Oliver. 'Devil-fishing in the Gulf Stream.' *National Geographic Magazine*, June 1919, v.35:476–88.

Miller, Stewart. *Florida Fishing.* New York, G.H.Watt, 1931. 320p.,front.,illus., plates.

Schroeder, William C. *Fisheries of Key West and the Clam Industry of Southern Florida.* Washington, Govt.Print.Off., 1924. 74p.,illus.,plates. (U.S. Bureau of Fisheries. Doc.962.)

COUNTIES, CITIES, ETC.

Ballinger, Kenneth. *Miami Millions; the Dance of the Dollars in the Great Florida Land Boom of* 1925. Miami, Franklin Press, Inc., 1936. 160p.,illus.(incl. ports.). 'Originally published under the title of *Boomerang.*'—The Author.

Brooks, A.M. *The Unwritten History of Old St.Augustine.* Copied from the Spanish archives in Seville, Spain, by Miss A.M.Brooks and translated by Mrs. Annie Averette. St.Augustine, Record Co., 1909. 233p.

Browne, Jefferson B. *Key West, the Old and New.* St.Augustine, The Record Co., 1912. 226p.,plates.

Clarke, J.O.D. *Ocala, Fla. A Sketch of Its History: Residences: Business Interests: etc.* New York, Republic Press, 1891. 154p.,front.,illus.,plates,port.

Davis, Thomas Frederick. *History of Jacksonville, Florida, and Vicinity,* 1513 *to* 1924. Jacksonville, Florida Historical Society. 1925. 513p.,illus.,plates, maps,plans.

Fairbanks, George R. *The History and Antiquities of the City of St.Augustine, Florida, Founded A.D.* 1565 . . . New York, C.B.Norton, 1858. 200p., front.,plates,port.,maps,coat of arms.

Florida. Works Progress Administration. Federal Writers' Project. *Seeing St.Augustine.* St.Augustine, Record Co., 1937. 73p.,illus.,maps,bibl. Sponsored by City Commission of St.Augustine.

Gold, Pleasant Daniel. *History of Duval County, Florida* . . . St.Augustine, Record Co., 1928. 693p.,front.,illus.,ports.

Gonzalez, Thomas A., comp. *The Caloosahatchee; Miscellaneous Writings concerning the History of the Caloosahatchee River and the City of Fort Myers, Florida.* Estero, Fla., Koreshan Unity Press, 1932. 124p.

Rinaldi's Official Guide Book of Tampa and South Florida. Comp. & ed. by Charles Vincent Van Horn. Tampa, Rinaldi Print.Co., 1920. 512p.

St.Augustine Institute of Science and Historical Society. *Fort Marion and City Gates, St.Augustine, Florida* . . . St.Augustine, 1915. 12p.

Sweett, Mrs. Zelia W., and Marsden, John C. *New Smyrna, Florida, Its History and Antiquities.* DeLand, E.O.Painter Print.Co., 1925, 55p.,front.,illus.

Willson, Mrs. Minnie Moore. *History of Osceola County; Florida Frontier Life.* Orlando, Inland Press, 1935. 59p.,front.,plates,ports.

POINTS OF INTEREST

Beach, Rex E. *The Miracle of Coral Gables.* Nashville, Baird-Ward, 1926. 48p.

Corse, Mrs. Carita Doggett. *The Key to the Golden Islands.* With foreword by Percy MacKaye; ill. by Louise Turck. Chapel Hill, Univ. of N.C. Press, 1931. Bibl. An account of Fort George Island, here interpreted as the key not only to a chain of islands known to the Spaniards as the Golden Islands, but also to Florida itself.

——— *Shrine of the Water Gods.* Gainesville, Pepper Print.Co., 1935. 48p.,illus. maps,bibl. Describes Silver Springs.

List of Consultants

Abbey, Dr.Kathryn. Professor of History, Florida State College for Women. Tallahassee.

Adams, Franklin G. Member, American Institute of Architects. Tampa.

Alsop, John T. Jacksonville.

Becker, Henry Floyd. Associate Professor of Geography, Florida State College for Women. Tallahassee.

Bellamy, Dr.Raymond. Professor of Sociology, Florida State College for Women. Tallahassee.

Berg, Mrs. Greta Challen. Jacksonville.

Black, James R. State Director, Federal Music Project, Jacksonville.

Bohnenberger, Mrs. Elizabeth. Librarian, State Board of Health. Jacksonville.

Briggs, Dr.Harold E. Professor of History, University of Miami. Coral Gables.

Bristol, L.M. Professor of Sociology, University of Florida. Gainesville.

Brooks, T.J. Assistant State Commissioner of Agriculture. Tallahassee.

Buswell, Walter A. Department of Botany, University of Miami. Coral Gables.

Byrnes, Joseph E. Director of Recreation, City of Jacksonville. Jacksonville.

Campbell, A.Stuart. Professor of Economics, University of Florida. Gainesville.

Cash, W.T. State Librarian. Tallahassee.

Close, Bernard. Director, American Sites Survey. Jacksonville.

Cody, M.D. Professor of Botany and Bacteriology, University of Florida. Gainesville.

Colee, Harold. President, State Chamber of Commerce. Jacksonville.

Cone, Dr.D.N. State Board of Health. Jacksonville.

Conradi, Dr.Edward. President, Florida State College for Women. Tallahassee.

Curtis, A.E. Public Relations Representative, Pan-American Airways, Inc. Miami.

Diettrich, Sigismond de Rudesheim. Professor of Economic Geography, University of Florida. Gainesville.

Drane, Col.Herbert J. Lakeland.

Eliason, Dr.M.E. Professor of English, University of Florida. Gainesville.

Elliot, Mrs. Fred C. Tallahassee.

Fifield, Stephen. Vice President, Barnett National Bank. Jacksonville.

Foster, Mrs.Bertha. Dean, School of Music, University of Miami. Coral Gables.

Fuller, Mrs.Eve Alsman. State Director, Federal Art Project, Jacksonville.

Gadsby, J.H. Regional Director, National Park Service. Atlanta, Ga.

Glynn, James L. Superintendent of Indian Tribes in Reservations in Florida. Dania.

Gunter, Herman. State Geologist. Tallahassee.

Halstead, Jackson. Architect. Tallahassee.

Hamilton, H.G. Professor of Agricultural Economics, University of Florida. Gainesville.

Hanson, W.S. Seminole authority. Fort Myers.

Hawkins, William. Architect, National Park Service. St.Augustine.

Henry, Mrs.A.J. Tallahassee.

Hochberger, Simon. Professor of Journalism, University of Miami. Coral Gables.

Holloway, Mrs.Rose B. President, Tampa Civic Art Commission. Tampa.

Hubbell, Henry Salem. Portrait painter. Miami.

Irish, Miss Marian Doris. Associate Professor of Political Science, Florida State College for Women. Tallahassee.

Jacobs, William F. Assistant State Forester. Jacksonville.

Jeffreys, Mrs.Lynwood. Secretary, State Board of Forestry. Jacksonville.

Jelks, Dr.Edward. Riverside Hospital. Jacksonville.

Kennedy, I.N. Secretary, State Department of Conservation. Tallahassee.

Lewis, Lester. Livestock Statistician, State Marketing Bureau. Jacksonville.

Longstreet, Rupert James. President, Florida Audubon Society. Daytona Beach.

Lynch, Dorothea. Former State Director, Federal Theater Project. Jacksonville.

Marron, Joseph. Librarian, Public Library. Jacksonville.

McCracken,Dr.E.M. Professor of Economics, University of Miami. Coral Gables.

McGuire, Will. Editor, *The Florida Review*. University of Florida. Gainesville.

Morris, Alton C. Editor, *Southern Folklore Quarterly*. Chapel Hill, N.C.

Myer, D.F. Planning Chief of Soil Conservation Service, U.S. Department of Agriculture, Washington, D.C.

Norton, Pete. Sports Editor, Tampa *Morning Tribune*. Tampa.

Partridge, Miss Sara. Former Editor, *Outdoor Sport*. Tallahassee.

Phillips, L.Z. General Passenger Agent, Seaboard Airline Ry. Jacksonville.

Phillips, Walter S. Assistant Professor of Botany, University of Miami. Coral Gables.

Phinney, J.B. President, St.Augustine Arts Club. St.Augustine.

Porter, Mrs. Emma. Assistant Editor, *Florida Historical Society Quarterly*. Jacksonville.

Powell, Maj.Garland. Director, Radio Station WRUF. Gainesville.

Putnam, Nina Wilcox. Delray Beach.

Rogers, Dr.John Speed. Professor of Biology, University of Florida. Gainesville.

Scott, F.J. Superintendent, Indian Agency. Dania.

Simmons, Glen Ballard. Assistant Dean, College of Education, University of Florida. Gainesville.

Southworth, Mrs.Rolla A. Director, Professional and Service Division, Florida Works Progress Administration.

Spencer, R.C. Gainesville.

Stoney, Samuel Gaillard. Curator of South Carolina Culture, Charleston Museum. Charleston, S.C.

Strum, Louie. Federal Judge, U.S. District Court. Jacksonville.

Sutton, George A.K. Attorney. Jacksonville.

Tietjens, Eunice. Miami.

Wand, Ben. Editor, *Southern Lumber Journal*. Jacksonville.

Weaver, Rudolph. Dean, School of Architecture and Allied Arts, University of Florida. Gainesville.

Webb, R.F. Assistant Professor of Geology, University of Tampa. Tampa.

West, Henry S. Dean, School of Liberal Arts, University of Miami. Coral Gables.

Whitfield, J.B. Justice, Supreme Court of State. Tallahassee.

Wilkes, John. President, Jacksonville Terminal Co. Jacksonville.

Woods, Dexter. Key West.

Yerkes, Damon. Assistant U.S. District Attorney. Jacksonville.

Yonge, Julien C. Editor, *Florida Historical Society Quarterly*. Pensacola.

Youngberg, Col.Gilbert A. Consulting Engineer. U.S. Army (retired). Jacksonville.

Index